Fodor's 5th Edition

D0104949

Greece

Fodor's Travel Publications • New York, Toronto, London, Sydney, Auckland
www.fodors.com

CONTENTS

MAPS

Circled letters in text correspond to letters on the photographs. For more information on the sights pictured, turn to the indicated page number Ⓐ⟩ on each photograph.

DESTINATION
GREECE

On Santorini, while gazing at the whitewashed houses perched on a cliff 1,000 feet above a wine-colored sea, you may decide you've found the sort of spectacle that drew you to Greece. This shock of recognition will occur again and again during your visit. You may experience it looking down the 55 rows of seats from atop the perfectly preserved theater at Epidauros; glancing up from a bustling street in Athens to see the silhouette of the Acropolis against a bright blue sky; or even tucking into a platter of fresh fish at a simple taverna in the port of Pylos. The truth is, just about anywhere else your wanderings take you, you'll come upon sights that fulfill long-held expectations by being quintessentially, delightfully, Greek.

ATHENS

In Greece, all roads lead to Athens, a fascinating city that is both the birthplace of Western civilization and a bustling boomtown. The Athenians seem to take the resulting juxtaposition of ancient splendor and cacophonous modernity with good-natured appreciation, and you would be wise to do likewise. Raise your eyes nearly anywhere and you're likely to be stopped in your tracks by the sight of the Ⓑ**Acropolis,** where Pericles rose to the heights of power, and creative achieve-

Ⓑ 41

Ⓒ 60

ment, with the construction of the Parthenon and Propylaea. After enjoying this time-trip back to the golden age of Greece, join Athenians for some contemporary delights. Take in a twilight view from their favorite "violet-crowned" aerie, Ⓓ**Mt. Lycabettus,** and drink in the twinkling lights of the metropolis that is home to 4.5 million souls, still growing and still counting. To leave the whirl of cars behind, stroll through the 19th-century Ⓕ**Plaka** district, where pastel-hued houses and vestiges of an earlier, simpler life keep beloved traditions intact, and then explore the port of Ⓐ**Piraeus,** the lusty setting for the film *Never on Sunday.* Stock up on essentials for a picnic at the Ⓒ**Central Market.** Pay a call on the Ⓔ**Tomb of the Unknown Soldier** on Syntagma Square—if you catch the changing of the Evzone Guard here, the sight of a soldier in 19th-century ceremonial garb parading in front of a funeral oration by Pericles will put the many layers of Athens perfectly in perspective.

Ⓔ▷ 70

Ⓕ▷ 47

ATHENS

G 54

H 43

You don't have to look far in Athens to encounter perfection. Towering above all—both physically and spiritually—is the ⓙ**Acropolis,** the ancient city of upper Athens and the stony remains of one of the greatest civilizations the West has ever produced. Sooner or later, you will climb the hill to witness, close-up, monuments of beauty and grace that have not been surpassed in two millennia. Nowhere, in fact, has ancient allure been more elegantly expressed than in the six caryatids that support the porch of the ⓗ**Erechtheion.** No matter that these maidens are copies (the originals are in the adjacent Acropolis Museum)—when the setting sun bathes them in rosy hues, these great sculptures of the 5th century BC fire the imagination. The few friezes that remain in

situ at the ⓚ**Parthenon,** the loftiest point of the Acropolis, are enough to evoke the splendor with which this masterpiece of Doric architecture was once adorned. And at the ⓘ**National Archaeological Museum,** a 3,500-year-old funeral mask is but one of the treasures reflecting centuries of artistic achievement. Lest so

I 62

many noble ruins and museums create the impression
the ancients were one-track
aesthetes, pay a visit to the
Ⓖ**Hephaistion**—this well-
preserved Doric temple graces
not hallowed ground but the
Agora, the marketplace and
hub of everyday life in ancient
Athens.

EXCURSIONS FROM ATHENS

Ⓐ▷ 143

Ⓑ▷ 151

When Athenians want a break, they often make a quick crossing to the islands in the Saronic Gulf. You're well advised to follow suit, and all the better if your island of choice is Ⓐ**Hydra,** where what's here (stone houses set above a welcoming harbor) and what's not (cars) provide a relaxing retreat. Back on the mainland, legendary sights will lure you to the classical landscape of Attica. Here, the ruins at Ⓑ**Delphi** bear eloquent testimony to the power of its ancient oracle, while at Sounion the Ⓒ**Temple of Poseidon** still summons strong emotions in this land of seafarers.

Ⓒ▷ 126

NORTHERN SPORADES

Ⓐ 196

Ⓑ 176

Ⓒ 184

The sight of a white village tumbling down a hillside—and that is exactly what will greet your eyes as you approach Ⓐ**Skyros Town**—is just one of the visual delights that make the Northern Sporades a favorite port of call. Discovered, yes, but these pine-covered islands remain an idyllic getaway. Plot a course for any one of them, and you'll soon be dining alongside a tranquil harbor, such as the one at Ⓒ**Skopelos,** or basking in the crystal blue waters—the clearest in the Aegean—that surround Ⓑ**Skiathos.** If you crave yet more, set sail for Alonissos, fertile with oak and fruit trees, to discover an uninhabited islet that, at least for a spell, can serve as your private paradise.

EPIRUS AND THESSALY

Ⓐ 229

Here in the most remote corner of Greece, landscape and legend conspire to twist reality into fantasy. It's not by accident that the stark mountains and dense forests of Epirus were once the "lair of the lion"—the domain of Ali Pasha, a larger-than-life despot who, from 1788 until he was mortally shot in 1821, carved his fiefdom from much of what is now western Greece. Get a grasp on his cunning exploits in lakeside Ioannina, with its minarets, mosques, and impressive pentagonal citadel. Then

Ⓑ 232

move on to exotic ⒠**Dodona,** where the oldest oracle in Greece once made pronouncements from Zeus (by reading leaves from a sacred oak) and where 17,000 spectators still gather for festivals held in one of the largest theaters on the mainland. Next, visit the spectacularly remote mountain village of Metsovo (it's not Greek you hear in the streets but the ancient language of Vlach). Here you can try some of Greece's best smoked cheeses before continuing through dramatic Katara Pass. Just when you think you've had your fill of breathtaking sights, you descend into the realm of Thessaly, where you enter the ⒶⒹ**Meteora,** with its extraordinary eroded pinnacles of rock. The name means "to hang in midair," and the region's celebrated monasteries—including thickly frescoed ©**Ayia Barbara** and 800-year-old ⒝**Ayios Stephanos** —seem to do just that, giving anyone fortunate enough to come upon them the impression that heaven may indeed be within easy reach.

⒝⟩**229**

⒠⟩**221**

13

Ⓐ▷246

At the crossroads of East and West, Northern Greece bears the traces of many civilizations. Roman, Byzantine, and Ottoman rulers left their mark on Thessaloniki, where churches and medieval monuments like the Ⓐ**White Tower** provide a dramatic backdrop for crowded markets and lively cafés. The home of the gods, Ⓑ**Mt. Olympus,** is a solid, if ethereal, Greek realm, often shrouded in clouds and lightning as if to prove Zeus still holds sway. Ⓒ**Mt. Athos,** pinpointed with monasteries, is Greece's most solemn precinct; off limits to women, it is an exclusive bastion as well.

NORTHERN
GREECE

Ⓑ▷267

Ⓒ▷272

NORTHERN ISLANDS

Despite their proximity to Asia Minor, the islands of the northern Aegean are quintessential Greek. Here, off the beaten tourist track, are the arbored hillsides of Ⓐ**Samos,** home to some of the best grapes in Greece (Lord Byron loved the wines here); Ⓑ**Mytilini Harbor** in Lesbos, scene of one of the most drama-filled moments of the Peloponnesian War; and plenty of local color, especially in places like Ⓒ**Chios Town.** Most of all, you'll find islanders who go about their business as they have for centuries, and greet visitors—fairly new arrivals in these parts—with a warm welcome.

CORFU

Ⓐ▷327

There must be something special about a coastal island that is said to have been the inspiration for Prospero's island home in Shakespeare's *The Tempest*; moved Homer to call it a "beautiful and rich land"; possibly sheltered Odysseus on his journey homeward; and today seduces more than a million visitors a year. As soon as you set foot in ⒶⒺ**Corfu Town** you begin to get a sense of just how considerable this island's charms are. This little beauty of a city retains evocative traces of its Venetian, French, and British occupiers, and is such a pleasant stage setting as to turn a simple stroll along the Esplanade, or selecting produce in an outdoor market, into a special outing. Across this

Ⓑ▷338

Ⓒ▷337

island—and many admirers claim it's the greenest and perhaps prettiest in all Greece—popularity may take its toll with summertime crowds, but no matter how clogged the roadways or how sophisticated the pleasures, nature still dominates the scene with a profusion of emerald mountains and bougainvillea-clad hillsides. Quiet, uncrowded beaches like those near Ⓑ**Paleokastritsa** are never far away, while Ⓓ**Pontikonisi** —according to legend, Odysseus's ship turned to stone—is an easy swim offshore. Even the gaudiness of the Ⓒ**Achilleion,** a villa built for Empress Elizabeth of Austria in Gastouri, is more than redeemed by its enchanting seaside gardens. Back in town, explore the quaint Corfu Reading Society library, discover the medieval Campiello district, tour the grand salons of the Palace of St. Michael and St. George, cheer on a town cricket match, and then get Corfu-comfortable at a seaside café to enjoy an ouzo sundowner.

Ⓓ 337

(A) 383

(B) 372

The ®**Corinth Canal** provides tight but easy passage between the Aegean Sea and the Gulf of Corinth, and for the overland traveler serves as the entrance to a beautifully rugged terrain containing numerous remnants of great kingdoms and empires of past eras. Practically a stone's throw from the canal spread the vestiges of the ancient city of Corinth, and just south of that is the Ⓓ**Theater at Epidauros**—the best-preserved Greek theater anywhere, with acoustics so perfect you can hear every syllable from the top tier. (You can run your own test during the annual summer drama festival.) While it's been a very long time since Ⓐ**Olympia** hosted the

NORTHERN
PELOPONNESE

Ⓒ 357

games that originated here in 776 BC, this ancient sanctuary of Zeus and once-thriving city has lost none of its appeal, especially for art lovers who flock to the museum to marvel at the *Hermes* of Praxiteles and metope sculptures depicting Herakles' Twelve Labors. Even more ancient is the city of ⒠**Mycenae**—the fabled realm of Agamemnon—where you can explore the Lion Gate and other archaeological discoveries of Heinrich Schliemann. Mycenae's satellite, ⒡**Tiryns,** was also a center of wealth and power as early as the 17th century BC. Later empire-builders—Byzantines, Venetians, and Turks—created the city of ⒢**Nafplion,** considered by Greeks their most beautiful for its historic, stunning assemblage of medieval churches, Turkish mansions, stone stairs, fountains, tree-shaded plazas, and mighty offshore fortress.

E⟩ 368

F⟩ 366

It's not that the southern realms of the Peloponnesian peninsula aren't endowed with their fair share of ancient splendors. The scant remains of Sparta—

Ⓐ 403

the powerful city-state that made war and austerity its motto—are here, as are the remote, hilltop Temple of Apollo at Bassae, the perfectly intact walls of ancient Messene, and the even

SOUTHERN PELOPONNESE

older Mycenaean ruins of Nestor's Palace. But medieval monuments of mellow stone seem to make the most striking statements in this sun-drenched landscape of olive groves and mighty mountain ranges. ©**Mystras,** whose golden-hued palaces and monasteries adorn an herb-scented mountainside, saw the last hurrah of the Byzantine emperors in the 14th century. ⒹⒺ**Monemvassia,** another Byzantine stronghold, is even more dramatic, clinging to a rock that seems to erupt from the sea; facing inland, the town's enchanting cluster of narrow streets tempt you to linger in an outdoor taverna or, better yet, rest for a night or two in a restored, centuries-old house. Much of the region's charm has nothing to do with past civilizations, though. The pretty ports of Ⓐ**Pylos** and

Ⓑ 409

Ⓒ 413

Methoni dispense a Greek tonic of blue sea, cloudless sky, and sandy beach (the entire coast here was once the haunt of pirates). Ⓑ**Gythion** is the gateway to another world altogether—the mysterious Mani, a wild region that plunges south across barren mountains to land's end and the entrance to the mythical Underworld.

THE CYCLADES

Homer is allegedly buried in these islands, and there couldn't be a more fitting resting place for the peerless poet. Neither can there be a better recipe for the living than this heady mix of vineyards, olive trees, whitewashed houses and churches, bright skies, and sapphire seas. As memorably picturesque as they are, though, the six major Cyclades—Andros, Paros, Mykonos, Naxos, Tinos, and Santorini—along with dozens of smaller islands, provide much more than hedonistic pleasures. On ⒷMykonos, for instance, backpackers and jet-setters alike share the beautiful beaches and the Dionysian nightlife (this island is not called the St. Tropez of the Aegean without reason), but the old ways of life continue undisturbed in fishing ports and along mazelike town streets. In fact, uninhabited and ruin-strewn Delos, just a short boat trip away, is proudly *other*-worldly, a sacred island that was once the religious center of the ancient world. On ⒹSantorini—Atlantis refound, according to some wishful historians—the striking combination of natural beauty, stunning architecture, and ancient ruins is a perennial winner. Here you'll find villages so artfully designed they seem to be posing for your cameras. There's no shortage of sophisticated pleasures on this island, from shopping to yachting, but pastimes need be no more fancy than climbing up a snakelike staircase to the top of the 1,000-foot-cliffs encircling

⑧▷438

©▷431

Santorini's flooded caldera—always rewarding, all the more so at sunset—or simply gazing out to sea across the cubes of Ⓐ**Fira**'s Cycladic architecture (blindingly white except for colorful doors and shutters). The too-fierce winds and too-few good beaches of ©**Tinos** are no deterrent to the hardy souls who come on pilgrimages to the Church of the Evangelistria—the Greek Lourdes—and the island's 799 other churches, and then stay on to taste the charms of the fancifully ornamented villages, truly lovely spots in an archipelago with no shortage of beauty.

Ⓓ▷464

CRETE

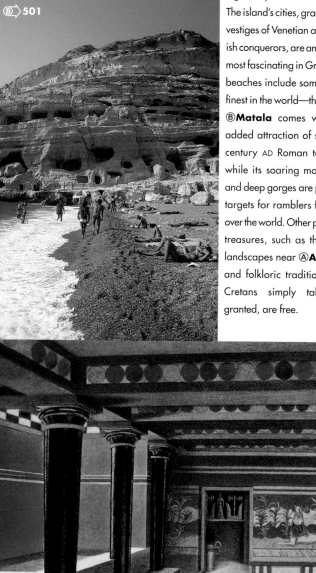

Ⓐ 473

The largest and southernmost of the Greek islands, Crete seems to have a continent's worth of extraordinary sites and mysterious landscapes. Evidence of the brilliant Minoan civilization lies thick on the ground, most splendidly at the Palace of Ⓒ**Knossos**—it is a spectacular sight to see the oldest throne in Europe still standing in the original throne room, adorned with legendary frescoes of griffins. The island's cities, graced with vestiges of Venetian and Turkish conquerors, are among the most fascinating in Greece. Its beaches include some of the finest in the world—the one at Ⓑ**Matala** comes with the added attraction of second-century AD Roman tombs—while its soaring mountains and deep gorges are popular targets for ramblers from all over the world. Other priceless treasures, such as the rural landscapes near Ⓐ**Akrotiri** and folkloric traditions that Cretans simply take for granted, are free.

Ⓑ 501

Ⓒ 492

RHODES AND
THE DODECANESE

Ⓐ 515

Ⓑ 531

A succession of remarkable visitors has left its mark on the twelve islands that wrap around the coast of Asia Minor. St. John the Divine received the Revelations in a cave on Ⓑ**Patmos,** still a place of pilgrimage. For those with less spiritual goals, however, the island of Symi beckons with its unsullied villages and topaz coves. Everyone begins on the big island of Rhodes—including the medieval Knights of St. John, who, back in the 11th and 12th centuries, fled from Palestine to ⒶⒸ**Rhodes,** where they lavished their wealth on building palaces, churches, and loggias. An ancient cult settled the island of Kos and established the Asklepieion, the once-great healing center and medical school that produced the most famous physician of all time, Hippocrates. No less a force are today's visitors, who not only enjoy the landmarks left by their predecessors but also delight in the verdant landscapes and glitzy resort life of Rhodes, the tempting beaches of Kos, the easygoing ways of Symi and—despite centuries of invasion and visitation—all the other pleasures in which these Greek islands abound.

Ⓒ 515

GREAT ITINERARIES

Highlights of Greece
16 days

Even those who have "little Latin and less Greek" never fail to respond to the pleasures of Greece, whether this means scrambling over time-burnished ruins, discovering an island you never want to leave, or simply enjoying a glass of ouzo on a taverna's terrace. The following grand tour explores many scenic cornucopias of this ancient land. To shorten the itinerary, visit the Meteora and Delphi as a long day trip or bypass Corfu. To do so, however, means foregoing the experience of randomly rambling through achingly beautiful mountain villages and island ports. The grand overture, of course, will be your two-day tour of Athens. From the majestic Parthenon to the hip Thission quarter, the city remains a dazzling paradox —the word is Greek—of old and new, ancient and modern, Zeus and Zorba.

HYDRA
1 day. After your two days in Athens, hop the Flying Dolphin hydrofoil from Piraeus harbor for the 45-minute trip to this traffic-free island of stunning 19th-century stone mansions and idyllic seaside walks.
☞ *The Saronic Gulf Islands in Chapter 2.*

NAFPLION
2 days. The charm continues in Nafplion, whose wide waterfront promenades, hilltop Venetian fortress, and maze of neoclassical houses make it the prettiest town in the Peloponnese. Classical ruins are abundant here, so explore Bronze-Age Mycenae, the acropolis of Tiryns, or the great theater at Epidauros. If a beach beckons, head to nearby Tolo or Porto Heli.
☞ *Argolid and Corinthiad in Chapter 8.*

ARCADIA
1 day. The Arcadian mountains have many picturesque villages, but if you stay in Andritsena, you will be well poised to visit the Temple of Apollo at Bassae in the clear light of early morning.
☞ *Arcadia in Chapter 9.*

OLYMPIA
1 day. Explore the site where Olympic games were held since time immemorial in honor of Zeus. The god's Doric temple still dominates the sacred sanctuary as it has since the 5th century BC, though many of its broken columns now lie scattered under the noble pine trees.
☞ *Achaea and Elis in Chapter 8.*

PATRAS–CORFU
3 days. A travel day takes you north to the transportation hub of Patras, from where you can book a ferry ride for the ten-hour trip over Homer's "wine-dark" sea to the Ionian islands, the realm of Odysessus. On Corfu, stroll up Venetian arcaded streets and down the Esplanade, then ride a donkey through the gorgeous country-side—no wonder Shakespeare set *The Tempest* here.
☞ *Corfu in Chapter 7 and Achaea and Elis in Chapter 8.*

THE METEORA
2 days. After taking the Igoumenítsa ferry back to the mainland, begin the scenic drive through the Pindos mountains to the slate-roofed village of Metsovo. Then drop onto the ⒶMeteora Plain, where Byzantine monasteries appear to float in midair atop their rocky pinnacles.
☞ *Epirus and Thessaly in Chapter 4.*

Ⓐ **229**

THESSALONIKI
2 days. Head north to the city of Thessaloniki, which, like the mythical god Janus, is two-faced: a charming old town of churches, gardens, and monasteries backs into a vibrant modern town set along the bay. Don't forget the treasures on view at the Archaeological Museum.
☞ *Thessaloniki in Chapter 5.*

MT. OLYMPUS
1 day. An easy excursion takes you to the village of Litochoro on Mt. Olympus. It's easy to see why the gods chose to inhabit these airy heights.
☞ *Central Macedonia in Chapter 5.*

DELPHI
1 day. Next morning travel to Delphi, the "navel of the earth," to feast your eyes on the Temple of Apollo and the museum's celebrated *Charioteer* bronze. At sunset, when this spur of Mt. Parnassus is bathed in warm, deep purple light, ponder the Delphic Oracle's most famous pronouncement—"Know thyself." Overnight here, then head back to Athens.
☞ *Delphi in Chapter 2.*

By Public Transportation
In peak season, more than 10 hydrofoils leave Piraeus's Marina Zea daily for Hydra;

Map showing routes through Greece with locations: Thessaloniki, Mount Olympus, Litochoro, Metsovo, Kalithea, Larissa, Kaditsa, Arta, Lamia, Nafpaktos, Delphi, Thebes, Patras, Diakofto, Corinth, Olympia, Mycenae, Tiryns, Epidauros, Piraeus, Athens, Tripolis, Andritsena, Nafplion, Tolo, Bassae, Porto Heli, Hydra. Distances shown: 119 km, 155 km, 251 km, 85 km, 90 km, 128 km, 82 km, 25 km, 45 km, 32 km, 63 km, 79 km, 25 km. Road markers: E92, E75, E65, E55, E94, E962, 48, 3.

they also sail (but never on Sunday) for Nafplion, and at least a dozen buses a day make the run from Athens. Buses link Nafplion to Mycenae and Epidauros; the Nafplion–Argos bus goes to Tiryns. Take the bus to Tripolis to change for Andritsena in Arcadia. Express buses link Tripolis to Olympia and Patras, with its daily ferry—more frequent in high season—to Corfu. From Igoumenitsa, bus east to Ioannina; continue to Metsovo and on to Kalambaka to tour the Meteora; from Larissa—the hub of Thessaly—train north to Thessaloniki. Heading back south, buses and trains stop at Litochoro for Mt. Olympus, and continue on to Thebes, where you can make a bus connection for Delphi, from which there are frequent buses back to Athens.

The Glory That Was Greece: The Classical Sites
9 days

Lovers of art, antiquity, and mythology journey to Greece to make a pilgrimage to its great archaeological sites. Here, at Delphi, Olympia, and Epidauros, the gods of Olympus were revered, Euripides' plays were first presented, and some of the greatest temples ever built still evoke the genial atmosphere of Greece's golden age (in spite of 2,500 years of wear and tear). Take this grand tour and you'll learn it is not necessary to be a scholar of history to feel the proximity of ancient Greece.

ATHENS
2 days. Begin at the beginning—the Acropolis plateau, where you can explore the greatest temple of Periclean Greece, the ⓑParthenon, while drinking in heart-stopping views over the modern metropolis. After touring the ancient Agora, the Monument to Lysikrates, and the Odeon of Herod Atticus, finish up at the fabled National Archaeological Museum.
☞ Chapter 1.

SOUNION
1 day. Sun and sand, art, and antiquity lie 44 miles southeast of Athens in Sounion. Here, the spectacular Temple of Poseidon sits atop a cliff 195 feet over the Saronic Gulf. Pay your own respects to the god of the sea at the beach directly below or enjoy the coves of the Apollo Coast as you head back west 30 miles to the seaside resort of Vouliagmeni for an overnight.
☞ Attica in Chapter 2.

Lamia
EVIA
Skyros
Kymi
Messolongi
Anitrion
Delphi
115 km
E65
48
90 km
Rion
Galaxidi
3
Thebes
Patras
Gulf of Corinth
E962
Diakofto
Eleusis
Athens
128 km
Corinth
82 km
E94
E55
E65
25 km
Aegina
Vouliagmeni
Olympia
74
135 km
45 km
Mycenae
74
Tiryns
Epidauros
Kea
34 km
E65
Argos
Sounion
Tripolis
Nafplion
Poros
Bessae
Kythnos
Hydra
Seritos
Hania
CRETE
Miles

ELEUSIS, CORINTH

1 day. Heading 12 miles west of Athens, make a stop at Eleusis, home of the Sanctuary of Demeter and the haunted grotto of Hades, god of the Underworld. Past the Isthmus of Corinth—gateway to the Peloponnese—ⓒAncient Corinth and its sublime Temple of Apollo beckon. Head 40 miles south to the coast and Nafplion—en route, stop at a roadside stand for some tasty Nemean wine.
☞ *Attica in Chapter 2 and Argolid and Corinthiad in Chapter 8.*

ⓒ➪ 372

TIRYNS, MYCENAE, EPIDAUROS

2 days. Set up base in Nafplion—a stage set of Venetian fortresses, Greek churches, and neoclassical mansions—then set out to explore the mysteries of forgotten civilizations in nearby Tiryns, Mycenae, and Epidauros. Five miles north is Tiryns, where Bronze Age ramparts bear witness to Homer's "well-girt city." Fifteen miles farther north is Agamemnon's blood-soaked realm, the royal citadel of Mycenae, destroyed in 468

Ⓓ➪ 354

BC. Then take a day trip 25 miles east to the famous ancient theater at Epidauros, where Ⓓdrama festivals still present the great tragedies of Euripides.
☞ *Argolid and Corinthiad in Chapter 8.*

OLYMPIA, BASSAE

2 days. After your third overnight in Nafplion, head west via either Argos (with helpful train connections) or Tripolis (by car on the E65) 85 miles west to Olympia—holiest site of the ancient Greek religion, home to the Sanctuary of Zeus, and birthplace of the Olympics. Walk through the olive groves of the sacred precinct, then get acquainted with Praxiteles' *Hermes* in the museum. Overnight here and then make a trip 20 miles south to the remote Temple of Apollo at Bassae, the second best-preserved temple in Greece.
☞ *Achaea and Elis in Chapter 8 and Arcadia in Chapter 9.*

DELPHI

1 day. Head up through verdant forests of the Elis region 50 miles north to Patras or nearby Rion for the ferry across the Corinthian Gulf; 40 miles east along the coast overnight in chic Galaxidi, with its elegant stone seafarers' mansions. The final day, set off to discover Delphi, whose noble dust and ancient ruins are theatrically set amid cliffs. Despite the tour buses, it is still possible to imagine the power of the most famous oracle of antiquity. From here, head back to Athens.
☞ *Delphi in Chapter 2.*

By Public Transportation

KTEL buses leave from the Platia Aigyptou, Liossion, and Odós Kifissoú terminals in downtown Athens and connect to most of the major sites—east to Sounion along the coast, west to Delphi and the Peloponnese—although in some cases you will need to take the bus to the provincial capital (Corinth, Argos, Tripolis), then change to a local bus. Ten trains daily connect Athens's Peloponnísou Station to Corinth and Argos, with bus connections to Nafplion and Olympia. Buses travel from Napflion to Olympia via Argos and Tripolis.

Island-Hopping
12 days

Fair warning: the danger of sailing through the Greek islands is that you will refuse to ever leave them. From these landfalls, some of the most justly famous, you can set off to find other idyllic retreats on your own.

(E) ⇨ 515

RHODES
2 days. In one of the first Aegean playgrounds to be discovered by tourists, luxurious resorts are one draw; the magnificently preserved old town is another, with its 12th-century palaces and legendary (E)harbor.
☞ *Rhodes in Chapter 12.*

SYMI, PATMOS
3 days. Only a short cruise from busy Rhodes, Symi is a world apart—quiet, undeveloped, and a perfect retreat. Its main town, Chorio, is a treasury of neoclassical architecture. End your journey on a high note—a day excursion to Patmos to visit its venerable monasteries and the site where St. John allegedly wrote the Revelations. ☞ *Symi and Patmos in Chapter 12.*

By Public Transportation
High-speed catamarans began crossing the Aegean in 2000 and have halved travel time between Piraeus and Santorini. In summer, when ferries and boats run frequently, you should have little trouble moving from any of these islands to another. Except for Patmos and Symi, all are served by air as well.

MYKONOS
2 days. Jewel of the Cyclades, this very discovered island manages to retain its seductive charm. The main town is fascinating, despite the crowds in its narrow alleys. The beaches are world-renowned, and the spectacular temple ruins of Delos are only a short sail away.
☞ *Mykonos and Delos in Chapter 10.*

SANTORINI
2 days. With its astonishing caldera ringed by cliffs topped by the gorgeous white towns of Fira and Ia, Santorini is irresistible. As if the natural setting wasn't enough, add in ancient ruins, whitewashed chapels, and cliff villas.
☞ *Santorini in Chapter 10.*

CRETE
3 days. Despite the attractions of sea and mountains, it is still the mystery surrounding Europe's first civilization and empire that draws the great majority of travelers to Crete. Like them, you'll discover stunning testimony to the island's mysterious Minoan civilization, particularly at the legendary (F)Palace of Knossos. Along these shores are blissful beaches as well as the enchanting Venetian-Turkish city of Hania.
☞ *Crete in Chapter 11.*

(F) 492

FODOR'S
CHOICE

Even with so many special places in Greece, Fodor's writers and editors have their favorites. Here are a few that stand out.

ANCIENT SPLENDORS

ⓔ **Delphi, Central Greece.** One of the most venerated of ancient sites in Greece, dramatic Delphi is where the priestesses of antiquity uttered their enigmatic prophecies. Follow the sacred way taken by ancient pilgrims and contemplate the remnants of their offerings to the god Apollo. ☞ p. 151

ⓓ **Goulandris Cycladic and Greek Ancient Art Museum, Athens.** Few places still bear witness to the mysterious Cycladic civilization (3000–2000 BC), so pay a call on this collection, dominated by the slender marble figurines that millennia later inspired artists like Picasso. ☞ p. 67

ⓐ **Parthenon on the Acropolis, Athens.** Shimmering golden-white on the city's horizon, this architectural monument is a testament to the golden age of Greece. ☞ p. 42

ⓖ **Temple of Poseidon, Sounion.** Sitting on a cliff hundreds of feet over a sun-dazzled sea, this temple honors the deity of ancient mariners. In spite of Poseidon's perpetual bad temper, the Aegean coastline here remains idyllic and tranquil. ☞ p. 126

ⓒ **Theater at Epidauros.** The best-preserved ancient Greek theater in the world is still in use. Whether you're here during the day or for a summer show, you're sure to sense how seriously the Greeks took drama. ☞ p. 354

MAGICAL PLACES

Anafiotika quarter of Plaka, Athens. Nestled below the Acropolis on land the Delphic Oracle once declared sacred, this serene "island village," with its tiny churches and bougainvillea-framed houses, is a blissful contrast to the cacophony of the modern city. ☞ p. 49

Corfu, Ionian Islands. No wonder Empress Elizabeth of Austria built her 19th-century summer palace here—Corfu is a memorable tapestry woven of Venetian arcaded streets, neoclassical esplanades, and romantic vistas. ☞ p. 322

ⓗ **Mystras, Laconia.** At the sunset of the dying Byzantine Empire a brief renaissance lit up the Eastern Mediterranean. Today the ruins of the sprawling city it left behind engage you as thoroughly as the intellectuals of Mystras enraptured the Greeks. ☞ p. 413

ⓕ **Monemvassia, Laconia.** Part ancient site, part living Byzantine town, Monemvassia has been called the Greek Gibraltar. Built on a rock jutting out from the southern Peloponnese, its jumble of ruins next to shops and old churches disorients in a delightful way. ☞ p. 415

Ia, Santorini. What may be the most beautiful settlement in the Aegean islands straddles the wondrous caldera: a crescent of cliffs, striated in black, pink, brown, white, and pale green, rising 1,100 ft. Here you will find the cubical white houses you've dreamed of, and a sunset that is unsurpassed. ☞ p. 469

Symi, the Dodecanese. The cognoscenti's new favorite, the picturesque island of Symi is just a yacht trip away from Turkey's Turquoise Coast. Both the shoreline and the houses here are in quintessential island colors—blue and white. ☞ p. 525

DINING

La Maison de Catherine, Mykonos. You will savor exquisite French cuisine amid a mélange of Cycladic and château artifacts. Just one tantalizing *amuse-gueule* is baby squid stuffed with rice and Greek mountain spices. $$$$ ☞ p. 440

To Varoulko, Athens. Melina Mercouri, who filmed *Never on Sunday* near this Piraeus place, would have loved acclaimed chef Lefteris Lazarou's lobster with wild rice, celery, and champagne sauce—it's nearly aphrodisiacal. $$$–$$$$ ☞ p. 81

1800. This magnificent old captain's house is a delicious setting in which to enjoy such delights as Missolonghi caviar atop olive mousse. For dessert, drink in the caldera view from the roof garden. $$$ ☞ p.470

Aristera-Dexia, Athens. Superstar chef Chris Karalomengos creates fusion fireworks such as his signature Greek sushi. Part art gallery, part wine cellar, this place (the name means "Left-Right") has been an instant success on the city's dining scene. $$–$$$ ☞ p. 79

Es Aei, Ioannina. Rare specialties are the lure of this restaurants in a meticulously renovated 200-year-old house near the town castle. Anyone for Cretan snails fattened on uncooked pasta? $$ ☞ p. 218

LODGING

ⓙ **Elounda Mare, near Elounda, Crete.** This Relais & Château hotel on the Mirabello Gulf rivals the best in the world. Stunning design, superlative service, private villas and pools, and extensive wine lists are among the enticements. $$$$ ☞ p.496

ⓘ **Atlantis Villas, Santorini.** Each "villa" is actually built inside a cave in Ia's cliff face in this hostelry, one of the most unusual and dramatic places to stay in the world. Balconies have an epic view, 600 ft up, across the magnificent caldera. $$$–$$$$ ☞ p. 470

ⓑ **Epaminondas, Andros.** Cool, handsome interiors, ensconced in marble, promote relaxing. A favorite pastime: a midnight dip in the freshwater pool. $$$–$$$$ ☞ p. 428

Milia-Bay, Alonissos. Small, private, and infinitely luxurious, these family-run villa-apartments come complete with verandas set over green gardens and blue waters. On a clear day you can see all the way to Skyros. $$–$$$ ☞ p. 194

1 ATHENS

Arriving in a taxi (sorry, no chariots), you
may be surprised to find Athenians garbed
by Armani and driving motorcycles.
Shouldn't they look like truncated statues
in the British Museum and have brows
habitually crowned with wild olive?
Incongruous as it may seem, most natives
have two arms attached to the torso in the
normal place—and today, many residents
are busy dressing up Athens for the 2004
Olympic Games. Long a city of Olympic
proportions, Athens offers treasures like the
Parthenon and myriad other pleasures—the
purple glow of sundown on Mt. Hymettus,
the candlelight of a Byzantine church, and
Zorbaesque nights in timeless tavernas.

By
B. Samantha
Stenzel
and Toula
Bogdanos

Updated by
Toula
Bogdanos

WOULD URGE THAT YOU FIX YOUR EYES on the greatness of Athens as she really is and fall in love with her. . . ." These are the words (as reported by Thucydides) of Pericles, the mastermind of Greece's golden age, in his oration for the dead of the Peloponnesian war. In 1185, Michael Akominatos, archbishop of the city, wrote otherwise: "You cannot look upon Athens without tears. . . . She has lost the very form, appearance, and character of a city." Today, after another 800 years, the truth falls somewhere in between. Raise your eyes 200 ft above the city to the Parthenon, its honey-color columns of Pendelic marble rising from a massive limestone base, and you behold architectural perfection that has not been surpassed in two and a half thousand years. But this perpetual shrine of classical architecture, symbol of western civilization and political thought, dominates a 21st-century boomtown. Athens is now home to 4.4 million souls, many of whom spend the day discussing the city's faults: the murky pollution cloud known as the *nefos,* the overcrowding, the traffic jams with their hellish din, and the characterless cement apartment blocks. Romantic travelers, nurtured on the truth and beauty of Keats's Grecian Urn, are aghast to find that much of Athens has succumbed to that red tubular glare that owes only its name, neon, to the Greeks.

Still, it's no wonder this fascinating and maddening metropolis is the point to which all roads lead and from which most tours take off. To experience Athens fully is to understand the essence of Greece: ancient monuments surviving in a sea of cement, startling beauty amid the squalor, tradition juxtaposed with modernity—a smartly dressed lawyer chatting on her mobile phone as she maneuvers around a priest in flowing robes waiting for the trolley. Locals depend upon humor and flexibility to deal with the chaos; visitors should do the same. The rewards are immense for those who take the time to catch the purple glow of sundown on Mt. Hymettus, light a candle in a Byzantine church amid heavy incense and black-shrouded grandmas while teens outside arguevociferously about soccer, or breathe in the tangy sea air while enjoying a Greek coffee after a night at the coastal clubs.

Although Athens may seem like one huge city, it is really a series of small villages strung together. Most of the major historic sites are within the central area; it is possible to see them on foot. When you (inevitably) wander off your planned route into less touristy areas, take the opportunity to explore. You will often discover pockets of incomparable charm, in refreshing contrast to the dreary repetition of the modern facades. For instance, a visit (if possible by moonlight) to the Plaka, the historic district set on the northern slope of the Acropolis, takes you back to the 19th-century city once beloved by Lord Byron. In this maze of narrow, winding streets and steps, vestiges of the older city are everywhere: small, color-washed houses with wooden upper stories; miniature Byzantine chapels; dank cellars filled with wine vats; occasionally a court or tiny garden, enclosed within high walls and filled with magnolia trees and the flaming trumpet-shape flowers of hibiscus bushes; and narrow crumbling stairways lined with festive tavernas.

Here, in this lovely Athenian neighborhood, you can still delight in the pleasures of strolling. *Peripato,* the Athenians call it, and it's older than Aristotle, whose students learned as they roamed about in his peripatetic school. Today, be sure your wanderings take you to a taverna to observe modern Athens and the Athenians in their element. They are lively and expressive, their hands fiddling with worry beads or gesturing excitedly. While often expansively friendly, they are aggressive and stubborn when feeling threatened, and they're also insatiably curious.

As you take in the city from its ancient treasures—the Acropolis, the Agora, and the Roman theater of Herod Atticus—to the more recent 19th-century pleasures of Anafiotika and Plaka, you'll see that the pickax, pneumatic drill, and cement mixer have done their work: there are countless office buildings, modern apartments, and streets choked with vehicles (an official report once stated that 75% of females had lost their sexual ardor as a result of air pollution in the capital—but failed to tell how it arrived at this depressing conclusion, or why males apparently had been spared). It's true: there is hardly a monument of importance to attest to the city's history between the completion of the temple of Olympian Zeus 19 centuries ago and the present day. That is the tragedy of Athens: the long vacuum in its history, the centuries of decay, neglect, and even oblivion. But if a tragedy, why not also a symptom of the vitality and amazing powers of recovery of the Greeks? Is it not fair to remember that within the last 150 years they have created a modern capital of more than 4 million inhabitants out of a village of 5,000 souls centered on a group of ruined marble columns?

New and Noteworthy

Work has finally begun on **Athens's Archaeological Park,** a 25-year-old dream to link the capital's ancient sites in a street network closed to all vehicles except public transportation. Pedestrianization is underway below the Acropolis in front of the construction site for the new museum, where Greece hopes someday to display the British Museum's collection of Parthenon marbles removed by Lord Elgin 200 years ago. The park will allow walkers to stroll through the center undisturbed by traffic all the way from the ancient stadium, home of the first modern Olympics, past the Acropolis, to Kerameikos cemetery and Plato's Academy. By summer 2001, about a mile (1.7 kilometers) of asphalt road from Hadrian's Arch to the Dipylon Gate will be paved over in Cycladic marble and stone. Most walkways will be done in time for the 2004 Olympics, thus joining the Temple of Olympian Zeus, the Acropolis, Filopappou hill, the Greek and Roman agoras, Hadrian's Library and the cemetery. Eventually, the pedestrian zone will stretch as far as ancient Eleusis, 22 kilometers (13.6 miles) to the west. As part of the ten-year project, the ancient sites will be somewhat restored somewhat, and Athens's four modern squares—Omonia, Syntagma, Monastiraki and Koumoundourou—will undergo a facelift, which includes the dismantling of billboards that obscure the city's architectural lines.

In preparation for the **2004 Olympic Games** in Athens, the city is in a whirlwind of renovation projects. Throughout the metropolis, there is an intensified focus on remodeling city squares, revamping neoclassical mansions, and reasphalting grand boulevards. As part of the campaign to make Athens more livable and environmentally friendly, cars were banned from several streets in the historical center, a popular move that has led to the creation of even more pedestrian zones downtown. Several natural gas buses, free to passengers, will now begin circulating in the historical center, as well as electric cars, some equipped for individuals with special needs. The city will set up information booths detailing local bus lines, taxi drivers will post mandatory fare scales in three languages (complete with suggested prices to landmarks), new signs at Piraeus harbor will indicate ferries' locations and sailing times, and more tourist police will be hired.

Located in Spata, 23 kilometers (14.2 miles) east of Athens in a rural, vineyard-clad region, **Greece's new international airport** is scheduled to begin operating flights on March 1, 2001. One of Europe's largest construction projects, the airport will serve 16 million passengers during its first year, making Athens an important air transport hub. Construction has also begun on a five-star hotel in the area. Besides the better airport service, tourists will also benefit from the upgrading of nearby Rafina and Lavrion ports, which means easier travel to the Aegean islands and less congestion at Piraeus. Heartened by the sleek efficiency of Athens's new Metro, Greeks are hoping the new airport will reinforce the country's emergence as a regional leader in southeastern Europe.

Pleasures and Pastimes

Cafés and Kafenias

On any street corner, at any time of day, you will see Athenians practicing the fine art of "hanging out," sipping their coffees, debating the latest political fiasco, or just watching the world go by. Walking in the city may seem difficult at times because of cars parked on the sidewalk and uneven pavements, but there is no shortage of squares, *kafenia* (traditional Greek coffeehouses), trendy cafés, or makeshift arrangements—two tables set up outside a dairy store—where you can sit for hours with an ouzo or the ubiquitous summer refreshment called frappé: instant Nescafé shaken with ice water, milk, and sugar. The *kafenion*, in fact, is a cross between a living room, an office, a reading room, a club, and a gambling casino (backgammon is the favorite game of chance, played for very low stakes but with a passion that makes the Monte Carlo Casino seem like a bingo game in a church basement). The social life of the average Athenian takes place in the kafenion—this is where the heart is; home is often just a place to sleep.

Dining

Recently, awards were handed out to the city's top 10 restaurants by the weekly entertainment guide *Athinorama*; not one winner offered traditional Greek cuisine. Instead, the spotlight went to places offering the food of France, Thailand, Italy, Polynesia, and Japan. As it turns out, some honorees blended those cuisines with that of Greece, making nouvelle Greek a leading contender in the city's oven-hot dining scene. Today, chic spots like Aristera-Dexia are turning Athens into a place gourmands are traveling to just for the sake of food. Remember, however, that Greece is the land where lunch can be bread and olives. The simple, traditional dishes are still to be had at many restaurants, some featuring the pots du jour on view back in the kitchen. And in a land where the prices are still gentle, Athens has many options for bargain "dining." After all, nothing beats a souvlaki—charcoal-grilled shish kebabs swathed in warmed pita bread—as a take-out snack to enjoy on your stroll through Plaka.

Nightlife

Athens is a sociable, late-night town where people love to see and be seen, and the action goes on until morning: even at 3 AM central *platias* (squares) and streets are often crowded with revelers. Options range from *rembetika* (Asia Minor blues from the 1920s) clubs to *bouzoukia* joints where popular singers belt out contemporary hits to the gyrating crowd to seaside bars blasting rave or rock. First-time visitors might want to check out a musical taverna, an institution as old as Greece itself. The entertainment, often featuring those extraordinary dances, the *zeimbekiko,* usually performed by men, is sure to be vigorous, colorful, spontaneous, and Zorbaesque. Neither the increasingly European work hours, frozen wage scales, nor changing bar curfews seems to slow the social pace—clubs and restaurants are usually packed.

EXPLORING ATHENS

Although Athens covers a huge area, the major landmarks of the ancient Greek, Roman, and Byzantine periods are conveniently close to the modern city center. You can easily stroll from the Acropolis to the other sites, taking time to browse in shops and relax in cafés and tavernas along the way. The center of modern Athens is small, stretching from the Acropolis to Mt. Lycabettus, crowned by the small white chapel of Ayios Georgios. The layout is simple: three parallel streets—Stadiou, Eleftheriou Venizelou (familiarly known as Panepistimiou), and Akadimias—link two main squares, Syntagma (Constitution) and Omonia (Concord). Try to wander off this beaten tourist track: seeing the Athenian butchers in the Central Market sleeping on their cold marble slabs during the heat of the afternoon siesta may give you more of a feel for the city than seeing scores of toppled columns.

From many quarters of the city one can glimpse "the glory that was Greece" in the form of the Acropolis looming above the horizon, but only by actually climbing that rocky precipice can you feel the impact of the ancient settlement. The Acropolis and Filopappou, two craggy hills sitting side by side; the ancient Agora (marketplace); and Kerameikos, the first cemetery, form the core of ancient and Roman Athens. In the National Archaeological Museum is a vast array of artifacts illustrating the many millennia of Greek civilization; smaller museums such as the Cycladic and the Byzantine illuminate the history of particular regions or periods.

The city's Eastern character after the 400-year rule under the Ottoman Empire is still evident in Monastiraki, the bazaar area near the foot of the Acropolis. Strolling through Plaka, a delightful area of tranquil streets lined with renovated mansions, you will get the flavor of the 19th century's gracious lifestyle. The narrow lanes with tiny churches and the whitewashed, bougainvillea-framed houses of Anafiotika, a section of Plaka, are reminiscent of an island village. Formerly run-down old quarters, such as Thission and Psirri, popular nightlife area with a string of bars and *mezedopolia* (like tapas bars), are now in the process of gentrification, although they still retain much of their original charm, as does the colorful produce and meat market on Athinas. The area around Syntagma Square, the tourist hub, and Omonia Square, the commercial heart of the city about 1 km (½ mi) northwest, is distinctly European, having been designed by the court architects of King Otho, a Bavarian. The most modern neighborhood downtown, ritzy, chic Kolonaki with its smart shops and bistros, is nestled at the foot of Mt. Lycabettus, Athens's highest hill (909 ft). Each of Athens's outlying suburbs has a distinctive character: in the north is wealthy, tree-lined Kifissia, once a summer resort for aristocratic Athenians, and in the south is down-to-earth Piraeus, with its bustling harbors and Saronic Gulf views.

Except for August and major holidays, when Athenians migrate to their ancestral villages outside the city, the streets are crowded. The best times to visit Athens are late fall and spring, when you can avoid the oppressive heat and the hordes of package tourists at major archaeological sites; you can also enjoy the bustling "winter" nightlife in the center, because after June many restaurants and clubs shut down or relocate to the seaside. Holy Week of the Orthodox Easter, usually in April or May, affords visitors the chance to observe Greece's most sacred holiday, including mournful Good Friday processions accompanying Christ's bier, and the candlelit Easter midnight service, complete with fireworks. If you must come in summer, visit the sights in the early morning; then—as the Greeks do—take a nap or eat a leisurely lunch before continuing your explorations after 5 PM, when several museums and sites are still open.

Admission to almost all museums and archaeological sites is free on Sundays from mid-November through March. Entrance is usually free every day for EU students, half off for students from other countries, and about a third off for senior citizens. Sights are open in winter (November through April), usually 8:30–3, though in summer, opening hours are extended, sometimes to 7 PM, depending on available personnel. Most museums close one day a week, usually Monday. Throughout the year, arrive at least 45 minutes before closing times to ensure a ticket. Archaeological sites and museums stay closed on January 1, March 25, the morning of Orthodox Good Friday, Orthodox Easter, May 1, and December 25–26. Sunday visiting hours apply to museums on the following holidays: Epiphany; Ash Monday, Good Saturday, Easter Monday, and Whitsunday (on the Orthodox dates, which change annually); August 15; and October 28. Museums close early (around 12:30) on January 2, the last Saturday of Carnival, Orthodox Good Thursday, Christmas Eve, and New Year's Eve. The Hellenic Ministry of Culture's Web site provides a good description of museums and archaeological sites, although the listed opening hours are often out-of-date (www.culture.gr).

The best time to visit churches is during a service, especially on Sundays (dress conservatively). Otherwise, hours are not set in stone; try from about 8 AM to noon and 5:30 PM to 7:30 PM on any day, unless otherwise noted. For walking in Athens, city streets are considerably less crowded Saturday afternoon through Sunday. And when you try to decipher certain street signs, keep in mind that Vas. is an abbreviation for King (Vassileos) or Queen (Vasilissis), while Ay. is an abbreviation for Saint.

Great Itineraries

IF YOU HAVE 1 DAY

Early in the morning, pay homage to Athens's most impressive legacy, the **Acropolis.** Then descend through **Anafiotika,** the closest thing you'll find to an island village. Explore the 19th-century quarter of **Plaka,** with its neoclassical houses, and stop for lunch at one of its many tavernas. Do a little bargaining with the merchants in the old Turkish bazaar around **Monastiraki Square.** Spend a couple of hours in the afternoon marveling at the stunning collection of antiquities in the **National Archaeological Museum**; then pass by **Syntagma Square** to watch the changing of the costumed Evzone guards in front of the Tomb of the Unknown Soldier. You can then window-shop or people-watch in the tony neighborhood of **Kolonaki.** Nearby, take the funicular up to **Mt. Lycabettus** for the sunset before enjoying a show at the **Odeon of Herod Atticus,** followed by dinner in the newly revived district of **Psirri.**

IF YOU HAVE 3 DAYS

After a morning tour of the **Acropolis,** with a stop at the **Acropolis Museum** to view sculptures found on the site, pause on your descent at **Areopagus,** the site of the ancient supreme court; the view is excellent. Continue through **Anafiotika** and **Plaka,** making sure to stop at the **Greek Folk Art Museum**; the **Roman Agora,** with its Tower of the Winds, an enchanting water clock from the 1st century BC; and the **Little Mitropolis church** on the outskirts of the quarter. After a late lunch, detour to **Hadrian's Arch** and the **Temple of Olympian Zeus,** Athens's most important Roman monuments. In **Syntagma Square,** watch the changing of the Evzone guards, and then head to **Kolonaki,** followed by an ouzo on the slopes of **Mt. Lycabettus** at I Prasini Tenta, with its splendid panorama of the Acropolis and the sea. Dine in a local taverna, perhaps in a neighborhood near the **Panathenaic Stadium,** which is lighted at night. This Roman arena was reconstructed for the first modern Olympics in 1896. On day two, visit the cradle of democracy, the **ancient Agora,** with Greece's best-preserved temple, the Hephaistion. Explore the **Monastiraki area,** including the tiny Byzantine chapel of **Kapnikarea,** which stands in the middle of the street. In Monastiraki you can snack on the city's best souvlaki, then hop the metro to **Piraeus** to explore its neighborhoods and feast on fish in Mikrolimano Harbor. On the third day, start early for the **National Archaeological Museum,** breaking for lunch in one of the city's mezedopolia. Swing through the city center, past the **Old University complex,** a vestige of King Otho's reign, to the **Cycladic Museum** in Kolonaki, with the curious figurines that inspired artists such as Modigliani and Picasso, or the newly reopened **Benaki Museum** down the street, which moves chronologically from classic vases to recreations of Macedonian mansions to the gold medal awarded to Nobel Laureate Odysseus Elytis. Stroll through the **National Garden,** and have a coffee in the romantic setting of To Kafenedaki café. Complete the evening with a ballet performance or pop music show at **Herod Atticus,** a movie at a *therina* (open-air cinema), or, in winter, a concert at the Megaron Symphony Hall.

IF YOU HAVE 5 DAYS

Spend your first three days as detailed above. On the fourth, see the **Byzantine museum,** which houses Christian art from the 4th to the 19th century, including masterful icons and rooms that are arranged like Greek Orthodox churches; then take a taxi (or Bus 224 followed by a 30-minute walk) to the peaceful Byzantine monastery of **Kaisariani** in the foothills of Mt. Hymettus. Here you can enjoy a picnic lunch with your Acropolis view. In the evening, splurge at Aristera-Dexia, Athens's best haute-cuisine restaurant, and then dance the *tsifteteli* (the Greek version of a belly dance) to Asia Minor blues in a rembetika club, or, if it's summer, visit the coastal stretch toward the airport, where the irrepressible bars stay open until dawn. On the last day, elbow your way through the boisterous **Central Market,** then visit some of the many new galleries that dot the area. Cut over to **Kerameikos,** Athens's ancient cemetery. After lunch in **Thission,** for a complete change from the urban pace take the metro to the lovely suburb of **Kifissia** and view the grand homes from a horse-drawn carriage, shop, or relax in one of the many cafés. As an alternative, you may want to catch a bus near the Zappion hall entrance of the National Garden to one of the government-run beaches in Varkiza, Vouliagmeni, or Voula.

The Acropolis, Filopappou, and Environs

Described by the French poet Lamartine as "the most perfect poem in stone," the Acropolis, or "High City," is a true testament to the golden age of Greece. From 461 to 429 BC was the magical period when the intellectual and artistic life of Athens flowered at the height of the Athenian statesman Pericles' influence. Archaeological evidence has shown that the flat-top limestone outcrop, 512 ft high, attracted settlers as early as Neolithic times because of its defensible position and its natural springs. It is believed to have been continuously inhabited throughout the Bronze Age and since.

Over the years the Acropolis buildings have borne the damages of war as well as unscrupulous transformations into, at various times, a Florentine palace, an Islamic mosque, and a Turkish harem. The hazards of war continued up to 1944, when British paratroopers sited their bazookas between the Parthenon's columns. Since then, a more insidious enemy has arrived—pollution. The site is now undergoing conservation as part of an ambitious 20-year rescue plan launched in 1983 by Greek architects with international support. Despite the restoration works under way, a visit to the Acropolis can evoke the spirit of the ancient heroes and gods who were once worshiped there. See the buildings first and save the museum for last; familiarity with the overall setting will give the statues and friezes more meaning. The "Acropolis" neighborhood includes fine neoclassical buildings lining its main street, Dionyssiou Areopagitou; the centuries-old Odeon of Herod Atticus; the Dionyssos theater; and one of the newest museums in Greece, the Ilias LALAoUNIS Jewelry Museum. Nearby is Filopappou, a pine-clad summit that offers the city's best view of the Acropolis and the tiny, rustic church of Ayios Dimitrios Loumbardiaris.

Numbers in the text correspond to numbers in the margin and on the Exploring Ancient Athens, Exploring Athens, and Exploring Piraeus maps.

A Good Walk

If you see nothing else in Athens, you must visit the **Acropolis** ①. Even jaded Athenians, when overwhelmed by the city, need only lift their eyes to this great monument to feel renewed. Wear a hat for protection from the sun and low-heel, rubber-sole shoes, as the marble on the Acropolis steps and near the other monuments is quite slippery. Take a taxi or Bus 230 to Dionyssiou Areopagitou (a metro stop will open here as well), which winds around the Acropolis to its entrance at the Beulé Gate. Buildings include the architecturally complex Erechtheion temple, most sacred of the shrines of the Acropolis, and the Parthenon, which dominates the Acropolis and, indeed, the city skyline: it is the most architecturally sophisticated temple of its period. Time and neglect have given its marble pillars their golden-white shine, and the beauty of the building is made all the more stark and striking. Even with summer's hordes wandering around the ruins, you will still feel a sense of wonder.

While on the outcrop, pause at the edge of the southern fortifications, where, on a clear day, you can see the coastline toward Sounion and the Saronic Gulf Islands of Aegina and Salamina. Be sure to leave enough time for the **Acropolis Museum** ②, which houses some superb sculptures from the Acropolis, including most of the caryatids and a large collection of colored *korai* (statues of women dedicated to the goddess Athena). As you exit the gate, detour right to the rock of **Areopagus** ③, the ancient supreme court, from which St. Paul later preached to the Athenians.

Cross Dionyssiou Areopagitou to **Filopappou** ⑤, but before climbing the summit, via the footpaths crisscrossing the hill, stop at tiny **Ayios Dimitrios Loumbardiaris** ④ church, and then for a coffee at the tourist pavilion. Descend Dionyssiou Areopagitou, past the **Odeon of Herod Atticus** ⑥ and the Hellenistic **theater of Dionyssos** ⑦. Nearby is the **Ilias LALAoUNIS Jewelry Museum** ⑧, with more than 3,000 pieces and a workshop where visitors can observe ancient techniques still used today.

TIMING

Normally, the earlier you start out the better, but a summertime alternative is to visit the Acropolis after 5 PM, when the light is best for taking photographs. Depending on the crowds waiting to get in, the walk takes about four hours, including one actually spent in the Acropolis Museum. The Ilias LALAoUNIS Jewelry Museum is closed Tuesdays, so you may want to take this tour another day.

Sights to See

★ ❶ **Acropolis.** Today's traveler to the Acropolis is, almost perforce, a pilgrim returning to the very source of the highest civilization that the West has produced. Even in its bleached and silent state, the Parthenon—the great Panathenaic temple that crowns the Akropolis (to use the Greek spelling), the tablelike hill that represented the "upper city" of ancient Athens—has the power to stir the heart as few other ancient relics can. Seeing it bathed in the sunlight of the south, or sublimely swathed in moonlight, to which has been added the incandescent glow of the spirit that seems to emanate from Greek art itself, one marvels at the continuing vitality of this monument of ageless intellect. Well, not completely ageless. Foundations for a grand new temple honoring the city's patron, goddess Athena, were, in fact, laid after the victory at Marathon in 490 BC but were destroyed by Persians in 480–79 BC. After a 30-year building moratorium, ended by the peace treaty at Susa in 448 BC, Pericles undertook the ambitious project of reconstructing it on a monumental scale. This extraordinary Athenian general is an enigmatic figure, considered by some scholars to be the brilliant architect of the destiny of Greece at its height and by others a megalomaniac who bankrupted the coffers of an empire and an elitist who catered to the privileged few at the expense of the masses.

The appearance of the buildings that composed the major portion of the Acropolis remained largely unaltered until AD 52, when the Roman Claudius embellished its entrance with a typically flamboyant staircase. In the 2nd century Hadrian had his turn at decorating many of the shrines, and in 529 Justinian closed the philosophical schools in the city, emphasizing the defensive character of the citadel and changing the temples into Christian churches.

Visitors enter through the **Beulé Gate,** a late Roman structure named for the French archaeologist Ernest Beulé, who discovered it in 1852. Made of marble fragments from the destroyed choregic monument of Nikias on the south slope of the Acropolis, it has an inscription above the lintel dated 320 BC, dedicated by "Nikias son of Nikodemos of Xypete," who had apparently won a musical competition. Before Roman times, the entrance to the Acropolis was a steep processional ramp below the Temple of Athena Nike. This Sacred Way was used every fourth year for the Panathenaic Procession, a spectacle that ended the festival celebrating Athena's remarkable birth (she sprang from the head of her father, Zeus), which included chariot races, athletic and musical competitions, and poetry recitals. Toward the end of July, all strata of Athenian society gathered at the Dipylon Gate of Kerameikos and followed a sacred ship wheeled up to the summit. The ship was anchored at the rocky outcrop below Areopagus, just northwest of the Acropolis.

The **Propylaea** is a typical ancient gate, an imposing structure designed to instill proper reverence in worshipers as they crossed from the temporal world into the spiritual world of the sanctuary, for this was to be the main function of the Acropolis. Conceived by Pericles, it was the masterwork of the architect Mnesicles. It was to have been the grandest secular building in Greece, the same size as the Parthenon. Construction was suspended during the Peloponnesian War, and it was never finished. The Propylaea was used as a garrison during the Turkish period; in 1656, a powder magazine there was struck by lightning, causing much damage; and the Propylaea was again damaged during the Venetian siege under Morosini in 1687.

The Propylaea shows the first use of both Doric and Ionic columns together, a style that can be called Attic. Six of the sturdier fluted Doric columns, made from Pendelic marble, correspond with the gateways of the portal. Processions with priests, chariots, and sacrificial animals entered via a marble ramp in the center (now protected by a wooden stairway), while ordinary visitors on foot entered via the side doors.

The slender Ionic columns (two-thirds the diameter of the Doric) had elegant capitals, some of which have been restored, along with a section of the famed paneled ceiling, originally decorated with gold eight-pointed stars on a blue background. The well-preserved north wing housed the Pinakotheke, or art gallery, specializing in paintings of scenes from Homer's epics and mythological tableaux on wooden plaques. Connected to it was a lounge with 17 couches arranged around the walls so that weary visitors could enjoy a siesta. The south wing was a decorative portico (row of columns). The view from the inner porch of the Propylaea is stunning: the Parthenon is suddenly revealed in its full glory, framed by the columns.

The 2nd-century traveler Pausanias referred to the **Temple of Athena Nike** as the Temple of Nike Apteros, or Wingless Victory, for "in Athens they believe Victory will stay forever because she has no wings." Designed by Kallikrates, the mini-temple was built in 427–24 BC to celebrate peace with Persia, with four Ionic columns at each portico end. It was from this temple's platform that, according to Pausanias, the distraught King Aegeus flung himself into the sea—no mean achievement considering the 10-km (6-mi) distance—which was then named after him. His son, Theseus, had forgotten to hoist the white sails proclaiming his slaying of the Minotaur, and on seeing the black sails, the aggrieved father committed suicide. The bas-reliefs on the surrounding parapet depicting the Victories leading heifers to be sacrificed must have been of exceptional quality, judging from the portion called "Nike Unfastening Her Sandal" in the Acropolis Museum. The best sections of the temple's frieze, which includes the Battle of Plataia with Greeks fighting the Persians, were whisked away to the British Museum two centuries ago and replaced with cement copies. In 1998 Greek archaeologists began the arduous task of dismantling the last original but badly weathered sections for conservation. They will laser or microblast the sculpted reliefs to clean them of soot before installing them in the new Acropolis museum to be built nearby.

At the loftiest point of the Acropolis is the **Parthenon,** the architectural masterpiece conceived by Pericles and executed between 447 and 438 BC by the brilliant sculptor Pheidias, who supervised the architects Iktinos and Kallikrates in its construction. Although dedicated to the goddess Athena (the name Parthenon comes from the Athena Parthenos, or the virgin Athena) and inaugurated at the Panathenaia Festival of 438 BC, the Parthenon was primarily the treasury of theDelian League. For the populace, the Erechtheion—*not* the Parthenon—remained Athena's sanctified holy place.

One of the Parthenon's features, or "refinements," is the way it uses *meiosis* (tapering of columns) and *entasis* (a slight swelling so that the column can hold the weight of the entablature), thus deviating from strict mathematics and breathing movement into the rigid marble. Architects knew that a straight line looks curved and vice versa, so they built the temple with all the horizontal lines somewhat curved. The columns, it has been calculated, lean toward the center of the temple; if they were to continue into space, they would eventually converge to create a huge pyramid.

Though the structure of the Parthenon is of marble, the inner ceilings and doors were made of wood. The original building was ornate, covered with a tile roof, decorated with statuary and marble friezes, and so brightly painted that the people protested, "We are gilding and adorning our city like a wanton woman" (Plutarch). Pheidias himself may have sculpted some of the exquisite, brightly painted metopes, but most were done by other artists under his guidance. The only ones remaining in situ show scenes of battle: Athenians versus Amazons, and gods and goddesses against giants. One of the most evocative friezes, depicting the procession of the Panathenaia, was 524 ft long, an extraordinary parade of 400 people, including maidens, magistrates, horsemen, and musicians, and 200 animals. To show ordinary mortals, at a time when almost all sculpture was of mythological or battle scenes, was lively and daring. About 50 of the best-preserved pieces, called the "Parthenon marbles" by Greeks but known as the Elgin Marbles by almost everyone else, are in the British Museum; a few others can be seen in the Acropolis Museum. In the first decade of the 19th century, during the time of the Ottoman Empire, Lord Elgin, British ambassador in Constantinople, was given permission by the Sultan Selim III to remove stones with inscriptions from the Acropolis; he took this as license to dismantle shiploads of sculptures. It remains a highly controversial issue to this day: on one side, many argue that the marbles would have been destroyed if left on site; on the other side, a spirited campaign spearheaded by the late Melina Mercouri, the actor turned politician, aims to have them returned to Greece, to be appreciated in their original context.

Pheidias's most awesome contribution to the Parthenon was the 39-ft-high statue of Athena that stood in the inner chamber of the sanctuary. It was made on a wooden frame, with ivory for the flesh and more than a ton of gold for the ankle-length tunic, helmet, spear, and shield. The alleged theft of some of this gold (some say the ivory) was the basis of charges against Pheidias, who is said to have cleared his name by removing it from the statue and having the statue weighed to prove it all was there. After the Christian emperor Thesodosius II closed all pagan sanctuaries in AD 435, the statue seems to have disappeared. The Parthenon was later converted into a church, but the basic structure remained intact until the Venetian siege of Athens in the 17th century, when Morosini's artillery hit a powder magazine, causing a fire that burned for two days. Many of the 46 columns were destroyed, along with the roof and most of the interior.

If the Parthenon is the masterpiece of Doric architecture, the **Erechtheion** is undoubtedly that of the more graceful and feminine Ionic order. A considerably smaller structure than the Parthenon, for sheer elegance and refinement of design and execution, it cannot be matched by any other building of the Greco-Roman world. More than any other ancient monument, this temple has its roots in the legendary origins of Athens. Here it was that the contest between Poseidon and Athena took place for the possession of the city. On this spot, the sea god dramatically plunged his trident into the rock next to the Erechtheion and produced a spring of water; Athena more prudently created an olive tree, the main staple of Greek society. The panel of judges declared her the winner, and the city was named Athena. A gnarled olive tree outside the west wall was planted where Athena's once grew, and marks said to be from Poseidon's trident can be seen on a rock wedged in a hole near the north porch. His gift should not be slighted, for the continual springs of the Acropolis have made habitation possible from earliest times, as well as the watering of the olive trees. Completed in 406 BC, the Erechtheion was actually divided into two Ionic sanctuaries. The eastern one contained an olive-wood statue of Athena Polias, protectress of the city, as well as the gold lamp which burned always, so large it was filled with fuel just once a year. The western part of the Erechtheion was dedicated to Poseidon-Erechtheus.

The most endearing feature of the Erechtheion, which has undergone extensive repair, is the south portico, facing the Parthenon, known as the **Caryatid Porch.** It is supported on the heads of six strapping but shapely maidens (Caryatids) wearing delicately draped Ionian garments, their folds perfectly aligned to resemble flutes on columns (what you see today are copies; except for the caryatid dismantled by Lord Elgin, now in the British Museum, the originals were removed in 1977 to the Acropolis Museum to protect them from erosion caused by air pollution). Wherefore the significance of the name Caryatid? One version claims that the Athenians, to punish the people of Caryae in Laconia for collaborating with the Persians, seized the women of Caryae, or Caryatids, and made them Athenian slaves. Because they were stunningly beautiful, the name came to be used for any attractive woman, including the maidens on the temple.

If asked what is the best time to see the Acropolis, one might be hard put to find an answer. Such is the beauty of the monument and the grandeur of the setting that a visit in all weathers and at all hours is rewarding. A moonlight visit—sometimes scheduled by the authorities during the full moon period in summer—is generally the most romantic. But in winter if there are clouds trailing across the mountains, and shafts of sun lighting up the marble columns, which glisten with added brilliance after a shower of rain or a thunderstorm, the setting takes on an even more dramatic quality. In summer the heat is blistering at noontime, and the reflection of the light thrown back by the rock and the marble ruins almost blinding, so morning and early afternoon are preferable. But the ideal—indeed, Platonic—time might be the two hours before sunset; it is then that the famous violet light can occasionally be seen spreading from the crest of Mt. Hymettus, gradually embracing the Acropolis in all its radiance, and reminding us that Athens was once called "the violet-crowned" by the ancients. After dark, of course, the Acropolis is spectacularly floodlighted, visible from many parts of the capital. ⊠ *Dionyssiou Areopagitou,* ☏ *01/321–4172 and 01/321–0219.* ▣ *2,000 dr./€5.88, joint ticket for Acropolis and Acropolis Museum.* ⊙ *May–Oct., daily 8–6:30; Nov.–Apr., daily 8–4:30.*

★ ❷ **Acropolis Museum.** Full of fabled objects of Attic art found on the Acropolis, this museum is unobtrusively snuggled in the southeast corner of the Acropolis site. Among the exhibits are legendary sculptures, plus the votive offerings to Athena. The displays are well executed, but their labeling in English is sketchy. In Room I, the anguished expression of a calf being devoured by a lioness in a porous-stone pediment of the 6th century BC brings to mind Picasso's *Guernica.* Room II contains the charismatic *Calf-Bearer,* or *Moschophoros,* an early Archaic work showing a man named Rhombos carrying on his shoulders a calf intended to be sacrificed. A porous-stone pediment of the Archaic temple of Athena shows Heracles fighting against Triton—on its right side, note the rather scholarly looking "three-headed demon," bearing traces of the original red-and-black embellishment. The most notable displays of the museum are sculptures from the Archaic and classical periods, pieces of unique appeal, including, in Room IV, the *Rampin Horseman* and the compelling *Hound,* both by the sculptor Phaidimos. In Rooms IV and V, take a good look at the exquisite korai, with fascinating details of hair, clothing, and jewelry of the Archaic period. Room V also has striking pedimental figures from the Old Temple of Athena (525 BC), depicting the battle between Athena and the Giants. In Room VI is the 5th-century BC relief *Mourning Athena,* a fine ex-

WHEN GREECE WORSHIPED BEAUTY

GREEK ART DID NOT SPRING IN a blinding flash like Athena fully modeled from the brain of Zeus. The earliest ceramic cup in a Greek museum, said by legend to have been molded after the breast of Helen of Troy, is a libel on that siren's reputation: it is coarse, clumsy, and rough. But fast-forward a millennium or so and you arrive at the golden age, when Greek art forevermore set the standard for ideals of beauty, grace, and realism in Western art, when the Parthenon gave proof of an architectural genius unique in history. The time was the 5th century bc, about 2,000 years before the Italian Renaissance. Just as that glorious age flourished, thanks to Italian city-states, so did ancient Greece reach its apogee in its cities. And it was in Athens that Greek citizens realized they could reveal the free blossoming of the human being and respect the individualistic character of men and women through art and architecture. This affirmation was largely the work of one man, Pericles.

To understand this celebrated Athenian general you must understand that amazing conundrum called Athenian democracy. This democracy was really an aristocracy, the watchdog of private property and public order. It financed athletic games and drama festivals; it constructed the Parthenon. Its model was not only *live,* but *live well.* Surrounded by barbarians, the age of Pericles was the more striking for its high level of civilization, its qualities of proportion, reason, clarity, and harmony. This is nowhere more apparent than in Greek art and architecture. Greek artistic genius fed on a physical ideal—spectacularly represented in the culture with its hero worship of athletes—as it did on religion, and religion itself, far from being an abstraction, was an anthropomorphic reflection of a passion for physical beauty.

The inspiration, however, would not have sufficed to ensure the grandeur of Greek art had it not been served by a perfection of technique. Whoever created any object had to know to perfection every element of his model, whether it was a man or woman or god or goddess. Witness the marvels of the sculpture of the age, such as the *Delphi Charioteer,* the Parthenon frieze figures, or the *Venus de Milo.* Basically the cult of the god was the cult of beauty. The women of Sparta, desirous of having handsome children, adorned their bedchambers with statues of male and female beauties. Beauty contests are not an invention of modern times. The Greeks organized them as early as the 7th century BC, until Christianity came to frown on such practices.

In like form, architecture was also the reflection of the personality of this Greek world. Thus, when we note the buildings of the Acropolis, we note the Doric order is all mathematics; the Ionian, all poetry. The first expresses proud reserve, massive strength, and severe simplicity; the second, suppleness, sensitivity, and elegance. No matter what the order, the column was the binding force—the absolute incarnation of reason in form. Study the columns of the Parthenon and you quickly realize that the Greeks did not propose to represent reality with its clutter of details; their aim was to seize the essence of things and let its light shine forth.

But it would be false to conclude, as certain romantic spirits have done, that the Greeks were mere aesthetes, lost in ecstasy before abstract beauty and subordinating their lives to it. Quite the reverse: it was the art of living which, for the Greeks, was the supreme art. A healthy utilitarian inclination combined with their worship of beauty to such an extent that art within their homes was not an idle ornament, but had a functional quality related to everyday life.

ample of the severe style favored in the classical period. In Room VIII, a superbly rendered slab by Pheidias from the eastern side of the Acropolis represents the seated Poseidon, Artemis, and Apollo. Incomparably graceful movement is suggested in *Nike Unfastening Her Sandal*, taken from the parapet of the Temple of Athena Nike. In a dimly lighted, air-conditioned glass case in Room IX are the badly damaged original Caryatids, salvaged from the Erechtheion. ⊠ *Acropolis,* ☎ *01/ 323–6665.* 🎫 *2,000 dr./€5.88, joint ticket for Acropolis and Acropolis Museum.* ⊙ *May–Oct., Mon. 11–6, Tues.–Fri. 8–6, weekends 8:30–2:30; Nov.–Apr., Mon. 10–2:30, Tues.–Fri. 8:30–3; weekends 8:30–2:30.*

❸ Areopagus. From this limestone rock, named after either Ares, the god of war, or the Arae, goddesses of vengeance, surefooted visitors have a good view of the Propylaea, the ancient Agora below, and the surrounding modern metropolis. This was once Athens's supreme judicial court, and legend says that Orestes was tried here for the murder of his mother, Clytemnestra. According to Pausanius, the accused stood at the Stone of Injury while the prosecutor pleaded his case at the Stone of Ruthlessness. From the outcrop, St. Paul delivered such a moving sermon on the "Unknown God" that he converted the senator Dionysius, who became the first bishop of Athens. Some of St. Paul's words (Acts 17:22–34) are written in Greek on a bronze plaque at the foot of the hill. ⊠ *Outside the Acropolis's entrance.* 🎫 *Free.* ⊙ *Always open.*

❹ Ayios Dimitrios Loumbardiaris. A delightful grove borders this church, which derives its name from *loumbarda* (cannon). Here in 1656 on St. Dimitrios's Day, as is told in a text posted on the church, the congregation was gathered, while on the Acropolis a Turkish garrison commander readied the cannons of the Propylaea to open fire during the final Te Deum. The moment it started, a bolt of lightning struck the cannons, blowing up the Propylaea and killing the commander and many of his men. The stone church contains many icons and has an old-fashioned wood ceiling and roof. ⊠ *At the base of walkway to Filopappou hill.* ⊙ *Daily 7–7.*

NEED A
BREAK?

The little **Tourist Pavilion** (⊠ Filopappou hill, ☎ 01/923–1665) is a blissful hideaway far from the bustle of the archaeological sites and the streets. It is beautifully landscaped and shaded by overhanging pines, and the background music is provided by chirping birds. It serves drinks, snacks, and a few hot plates.

---

❺ Filopappou. This summit includes **Lofos Mouseion** (Hill of the Muses), whose peak offers the city's best view of the Parthenon, which appears almost at eye level, and the **Monument of Filopappus**, a Syrian prince who was such a generous benefactor, the people accepted him as a distinguished Athenian. The marble monument is a tomb decorated by a frieze showing Filopappus driving his chariot. In 294 BC a fort strategic to Athens's defense was built here, overlooking the road to the sea. On the hill of the **Pnyx** (meaning "crowded"), the general assembly (Ecclesia) met during the time of Pericles. Gathering the quorum of 5,000 citizens necessary to take a vote was not always easy. Archers armed with red paint were sent out to dab it on vote dodgers; the offenders were then fined. Originally, citizens faced the Acropolis, but they tended to lose their concentration as they gazed upon the monuments, so the positions of the speaker and the audience were reversed. The speaker's platform is still visible on the semicircular terrace; from here, Themistocles persuaded Athenians to fortify the city and Pericles argued for the construction of the Parthenon. Farther north is the **Hill**

of the Nymphs, with a 19th-century observatory, designed by Theophilos Hansen, responsible for many of the capital's grander edifices. He was so satisfied with his work, he had *servare intaminatum* (to remain intact) inscribed over the entrance.

⑧ Ilias LALAoUNIS Jewelry Museum. Housing the creations of the internationally renowned artist Ilias Lalaounis, this private foundation also operates as a study center. The 45 collections include 3,000 pieces inspired by subjects as diverse as the Treasure of Priam to the wildflowers of Greece; many of the works are eye-catching, especially the massive necklaces evoking the Minoan and Byzantine periods. Besides well-made videos that explain jewelry making (order up No. 11 on goldsmithery through the intercom), craftspeople in the workshop demonstrate ancient and modern techniques, such as chain weaving and hammering, for visitors. During the academic year the museum can arrange educational programs in English for groups of children. The founder also has several stores in Athens (☞ Shopping, *below*). ⊠ *Kallisperi 12, at Karyatidon, Acropolis,* ☎ *01/922–1044.* ⌨ *800 dr./€2.35, free on Wed. after 3 PM and Sat. 9–11.* ◷ *Mon. and Thurs.–Sat. 9–4, Wed. 9–9, Sun. 11–4. Closed 1st 2 wks of Aug.*

⑥ Odeon of Herodes Atticus. This hauntingly beautiful ancient theater was built in AD 160 by the affluent benefactor Herodes Atticus in memory of his wife, Regilla. Known as the Irodion by Athenians, it is nestled Greek-style into the hillside, but with typically Roman arches in its three-story stage building and barrel-vaulted entrances. The circular orchestra has now become a semicircle, and the long-vanished cedar roof probably covered only the stage and dressing rooms, not the 34 rows of seats. The theater, which holds 5,000, was restored and reopened in 1955 for the Elliniko Festival, or Hellenic Festival (formerly known as the Athens Festival) and is now open only to ticket holders who are attending the scheduled summer performances, which range from the Royal Ballet to ancient tragedies and Attic comedies usually performed in modern Greek. Contact the Elliniko Festival box office for ticket information (☞ Nightlife and the Arts, *below*). ⊠ *Dionyssiou Areopagitou near intersection with Propylaion St.,* ☎ *01/ 323-2771.* ◷ *Open only during performances.*

⑦ Theater of Dionyssos. It was on this spot in the 6th century BC that the Dionyssia festivals took place; a century later, dramas such as Sophocles' *Oedipus Rex* and Euripides' *Medea* were performed for the entire population of the city. Foundations are visible of a stage dating from about 330 BC, when it was built for 15,000 spectators as well as the assemblies formerly held on Pnyx. In the middle of the orchestra stood the altar to Dionyssos. Most of the upper rows of seats have been destroyed, but the lower levels, with labeled chairs for priests and dignitaries, remain. The fantastic throne in the center was reserved for the priest of Dionyssos: it is adorned by regal lions' paws, and the back is carved with reliefs of satyrs and griffins. On the hillside above the theater stand two columns, vestiges of the little temple erected in the 4th century BC by Thrasyllus the Choragus (the ancient counterpart of a modern impresario). ⊠ *Dionyssiou Areopagitou, across from Mitsaion St.,* ☎ *01/322–4625.* ⌨ *500 dr./€1.47.* ◷ *May–Oct., daily 8–6; Nov.– Apr., daily 8:30–2:30.*

Plaka and Anafiotika

One of Athens's prettiest neighborhoods, Plaka remains the last corner of 19th-century Athens, with Byzantine accents provided by churches. During the 1950s and '60s, the area became garish with neon as nightclubs moved in and residents moved out, but locals, architects, and academicians joined forces in the early 1980s to transform a decaying neighborhood. Noisy discos and tacky pensions were closed, streets were changed into pedestrian zones, and old buildings were well restored. At night the area is still crowded with merrymakers visiting the old tavernas, which feature traditional music and dancing, many with rooftops facing the Acropolis. If you keep off the main tourist shopping streets of Kidathineon and Adrianou, you will be amazed at how peaceful the area can be, even in the height of the summer. Above Plaka is Anafiotika, built on winding lanes that climb up the slopes of the Acropolis, its upper reaches resembling a tranquil village. In classical times it was abandoned because the Delphic Oracle claimed it as sacred ground. The buildings here were constructed by masons from Anafi island, who came to find work in the rapidly expanding Athens of the 1830s and 1840s. They took over this area, whose rocky terrain was similar to Anafi's, hastily erecting homes overnight, taking advantage of an Ottoman law that decreed if you could put up a structure between sunset and sunrise, the property was yours. Ethiopians, imported as slaves by the Turks during the Ottoman period, stayed on after independence and lived higher up, in caves, on the northern slopes of the Acropolis.

A Good Walk

After the Acropolis, the historical quarter of Plaka is the next must-see. Take time to explore the side streets graced by old mansions under renovation by the Ministry of Culture. Begin your stroll at the **Monument of Lysikrates** ⑨, one of the few remaining supports (334 BC) for tripods awarded to the producer of the best play in the ancient Dionysia festival; off the square on Galanou and Goura is the pretty church of **Ayia Aikaterini** ⑩. Take Herefondos to Plaka's central square, Filomoussou Eterias (or Platia Kidathineon), a great place to people-watch.

Up Kidathineon is the **Greek Folk Art Museum** ⑪, with a rich collection ranging from 1650 to the present, including works by the beloved naive artist Theophilos. Across from the museum is the 11th- to 12th-century church of **Sotira Tou Kottaki,** set in a tidy garden with a fountain that was the main source of water for the neighborhood until sometime after Turkish rule. Around the corner on Hatzimichali Aggelou is the **Center of Folk Art and Tradition** ⑫. Continue west to the end of that street, crossing Adrianou to Hill, then right on Epimarchou and the striking **Church House** ⑬ (on the corner of Scholeiou), once a Turkish police post and home to Richard Church, who led Greek forces in the War of Independence.

At the top of Epimarchou is **Ayios Nikolaos Rangavas** ⑭, an 11th-century church built with fragments of ancient columns. The church marks the edge of the **Anafiotika** ⑮ quarter, a village smack dab in the middle of the metropolis: its main street, Stratonos, is lined with cottages, occasional murals painted on the stones, and a few little shops. Wind your way through the narrow lanes off Stratonos, visiting the churches **Ayios Georgios tou Vrachou, Ayios Simeon,** and **Metamorphosis Sotiros.** Another interesting church is **Ayii Anargyroi** ⑯, at the top of Erechtheos, an 8th-century chapel that according to legend was built by Empress Irene. From the church, make your way to Theorias, which parallels the ancient *peripatos* (public roadway) that ran around the Acropolis. The collection at the **Kanellopoulos Museum** ⑰ spans Athens's history; nearby on Panos you'll pass the **Athens University Museum (Old University),** the city's first higher-learning institution.

Walk down Panos to the **Roman Agora** ⑲, which includes the **Tower of the Winds** and the **Fethiye Mosque.** Nearby visit the engaging **Museum of Greek Popular Musical Instruments** ⑱, where recordings will take you back to the age of rembetika. On your way back to Syntagma Square, cut across Mitropolis (Cathedral) Square to the 12th-century Byzantine church known as **Little Mitropolis** ⑳, whose outer walls are covered with reliefs. Closer to Syntagma Square, on the corner of Pendelis and Mitropoleos, is the curious sight of **Ayia Dynamis** ㉑, a chapel peering out from between the cement columns of a Ministry building.

TIMING

Plaka is a delight any time of day, liveliest in the early evening, or Sunday afternoons, when locals congregate at its outdoor cafés. Perhaps the best time to explore Anafiotika is just before sunset, when the haze is reduced and you can catch great views of the city. If you want to visit the museums (usually open until 3 PM) or the churches (open from 8 AM to noon and sometimes from 5 to 7 PM), begin your excursion as early as possible. For planning ahead, note that some of the museums are closed Mondays (Center of Folk Art and Tradition, the Greek Folk Art Museum, the Roman Agora, Museum of Greek Popular Musical Instruments, and the Kanellopoulos Museum). The walk, with leisurely stops at one or two museums, and time for a coffee break, takes about three hours. During Carnivali in February, costumed Athenians gather evenings in Plaka for a stroll through the quarter, bopping each other with plastic clubs, showering confetti, and spraying foam at passersby: beware!

Sights to See

★ ☙ ⑮ **Anafiotika.** Set in the shadow of the Acropolis, this is the closest thing to a Cycladic village one will find in Athens. Still populated by many descendants of the Anafi stonemasons who arrived in the 19th century to expand the capital, Anafiotika is an enchanting area of simple stone houses, many nestled right into the bedrock, most little changed over the years, others stunningly restored. Cascades of bougainvillea and pots of geraniums and marigolds enliven the balconies and rooftops, and the prevailing serenity is in blissful contrast to the cacophony of modern Athens. You seldom see the residents—only a line of washing hung out to dry, the lace curtains on the tiny houses, or the curl of smoke from a wood-burning fireplace indicate human presence. Perched on the bedrock of the Acropolis is **Ayios Georgios tou Vrachou** (St. George of the Rock), which marks the southeast edge of the district. One of the most beautiful churches of Athens, it is still in use today. **Ayios Simeon,** a neoclassical church built in 1847 by the settlers, marks the western boundary and contains a copy of a famous miracle-working icon from Anafi, Our Lady of the Reeds. The **Church of the Metamorphosis Sotiros** (Transfiguration), a high-dome 14th-century stone chapel, has a rear grotto carved right into the Acropolis. For those with children, there is a small playground at Stratonos and Vironos. ⊠ *On northeast slope of Acropolis rock.*

⑩ **Ayia Aikaterini.** Built in the late 11th to early 12th centuries and enlarged in 1927, the church took its name in the 1760s when it was acquired by the Monastery of Saint Catherine in the Sinai. Of the original structure, only the octagonal dome and central apse survive. The church is cruciform, its dome resting on a drum supported by four interior columns. The large sunken courtyard with royal palms and olive trees makes Ayia Aikaterini popular for baptisms and weddings; its choir is one of the city's best. ⊠ *Off square on Galanou and Goura,* ☎ *01/ 322–8974.* ☉ *Weekdays 7 AM–12:30 PM and 5:30–7 (in winter 7:30– 12:30 and 5–6:30), weekends 7 AM–12:30 PM and 5–10.*

㉑ **Ayia Dynamis.** The "Divine Power" chapel, named for the Virgin Mary's supposed ability to help childless women conceive and topped by a dainty arch and bell, peeks out between the cement columns of the modern Ministry of Education and Religion. Its romantic history makes it worth mentioning. A Greek named Mastropavlis made cartridges here for the Turkish garrison, which had turned the church into a munitions works. At the same time, he secretly made ammunition for the Greek revolutionaries, which was smuggled to them by a courageous washerwoman. These were the first bullets fired at the Turks on the Acropolis when the War of Independence broke out. ⊠ *On corner of Pendelis and Mitropoleos.*

⑯ Ayii Anargyroi. According to legend, the church, also known as Metochion Panagiou Tafou, was built in the late 8th century by the Empress Irene, once an Athenian orphan, and sole ruler of Byzantium, after the death of her husband. The Church of the Holy Sepulchre at Jerusalem, needing an outpost in Athens, acquired it in the 1700s and continues to occupy it today. The church has a gingerbread-like exterior, a delightful little garden containing fragments of ancient ruins, and a well that was used as a hiding place in troubled times. ⊠ *Top of stairs where Erechtheos meets Pritaniou.*

⑭ Ayios Nikolaos Rangavas. On the southeast side of this 11th-century Byzantine church rebuilt in the 18th century, you can see fragments of ancient columns and capitals incorporated into its walls, an example of the pragmatic recycling of the time. The church was the first to have a bell tower after the Greek revolution (bells were forbidden on Ottoman land. It is located above the stairs off Prytaniou, a street named after the center of the ancient city where a sacred flame was kept burning. The best approach to the church is to walk up Epimenidou, down Thespidos, and left onto the Rangava path. ⊠ *Prytaniou 1, at top of Epimarchou,* ☎ *01/322–8193.*

⑬ Center of Folk Art and Tradition. Exhibits in this comfortable family mansion of folklorist Angeliki Hatzimichali include detailed costumes, ceramic plates from Skyros, handwoven fabrics and embroideries, and family portraits. ⊠ *Hatzimichali Aggelou 6,* ☎ *01/324–3972.* 💲 *Free.* 🕑 *Sept.–July, Tues.–Fri. 9–1 and 5–9, weekends 9–1.*

NEED A BREAK?   **Vyzantino** (⊠ Kidathineon 18, ☎ 01/322–7368) is directly on Plaka's main square—great for people-watching and a good, reasonably priced bite to eat (try the fish soup, roast potatoes, or baked chicken). Go around the corner to **Glikis** (⊠ Aggelou Geronta 2, ☎ 01/322–3925) and its shady courtyard for a Greek coffee or ouzo and a *mikri pikilia* (a small plate of appetizers, including cheese, sausage, olives, and dips).

☝ ㊼ Children's Museum. In the courtyard, you may see children pressing melted chocolate into molds; upstairs in the neoclassical building, groups are concocting toys out of recycled materials, or learning to blow gigantic soap bubbles. The museum allows visitors up to the age of 12 to play freely and experiment; experienced staff encourage them to interact. New exhibits include the "family," where children take on the role of their parents, the kitchen, where they tackle food preparation, and the *horo katastrophis* (catastrophe space), where they are allowed to wreak havoc. Throughout the year, parents can sign children up for events such as "a night at the museum," where they play, cook, and overnight in the room of their choice. The museum also runs a shop with toys and books. ⊠ *Kidathineon 14,* ☎ *01/331–2995.* 💲 *Free.* 🕑 *Sept.–July, Tues.–Sun. 10–2.*

⑬ Church House. The striking, abandoned tower house with tiny windows, thick stone walls, and a tall chimney still bears traces of its past glory but is in danger of collapse after the September 1999 earthquake. Dating from the mid-18th century and used as a Turkish police post (it appears in several engravings of Turkish-occupied Athens), the tower was bought after liberation by historian George Finlay. He and his wife lived here for half a century, while he wrote on Greek history, including what is considered the definitive work on the War of Independence. Finlay repaired the complex of buildings, renting one of them to General Richard Church, commander-in-chief of the Greek forces during the War of Independence. For many years, Church House served as a reference point among Athens's one-story buildings, a rare vestige of pre-revolutionary Athens. Today the roof is in shambles, the Byzantine-style cornice has come loose, and cracks split the walls; officials are still discussing its preservation. ⊠ *Corner of Epimarchou, Hill, and Scholeiou.*

⑪ **Greek Folk Art Museum.** Run by the Ministry of Culture, the collection includes examples of folk art from 1650 to the present, with especially interesting embroideries, stone and wood carvings, carnival costumes, and *Karaghiozis* (shadow player figures). Everyday tools—stamps for communion bread, spinning shuttles, raki flasks—attest to the imagination with which Greeks embellished the most utilitarian objects. Don't miss the room of uniquely fanciful landscapes and historical portraits by naive painter Theophilos Hatzimichalis, from Mytilini, one of the most beloved Greek artists. ⊠ *Kidathineon 17,* ☎ *01/322–9031.* 💷 *500 dr./€1.47.* ☉ *Tues.–Sun. 10–2.*

⑰ **Kanellopoulos Museum.** The stately Michaleas Mansion built in 1884 now showcases the Kanellopoulos family collection, spanning Athens's history from the 3rd century BC to the 19th century, with especially fine Byzantine icons, jewelry, and Mycenaean and Geometric vases and bronzes. Note the painted ceiling gracing the first floor. ⊠ *Theorias and Panos,* ☎ *01/321–2313.* 💷 *500 dr./€1.47.* ☉ *Tues.–Sun. 8:30–3.*

NEED A BREAK?   Pause for a cool drink at the **Nefeli Café** (⊠ Panos 24, ☎ 01/321–2475), a large complex with an idyllic outdoor café shaded by smart awnings and draped with grapevines. It's perched just below the Acropolis cliffs, looking down on Ayia Anna church. Or go around the corner to less upscale **Cafe Dioscouri** (⊠ Dioscouron and Mitroou, ☎ 01/321–9607), which lines the pedestrian zone by the same name and has a view of the Hephaistion temple.

★ ⑳ **Little Mitropolis.** This church snuggles up to the pompous **Mitropolis** (⊠ On the northern edge of Plaka), the ornate Cathedral of Athens. Also called Panayia Gorgoepikoos (the Virgin Who Answers Prayers Quickly), the chapel dates to the 12th century, and its most interesting features are its outer walls, covered with reliefs of animals and allegorical figures dating from the classical to the Byzantine period. Look for the ancient frieze with zodiac signs and a calendar of festivals in Attica. Most of the paintings inside were destroyed, but the famous 13th- to 14th-century Virgin, said to perform miracles, remains. If you would like to follow Greek custom and light an amber beeswax candle for yourself and someone you love, drop the price of the candle in the slot. ⊠ *Mitropolis Sq.* 💷 *Free.* ☉ *Hrs depend on services, but usually open daily 8–1.*

★ ⑨ **Monument of Lysikrates.** This monument was built by a *choregos* (producer) as the support for the tripod he won for sponsoring the best play at the Theater of Dionyssos. It dates to 335–34 BC. Six of the earliest Corinthian columns are arranged in a circle on a square base, topped by a marble dome from which rise acanthus leaves. In the 17th century the monument was incorporated into a Capuchin monastery where Byron stayed while writing part of *Childe Harold*. The monument was once known as the Lantern of Demosthenes because it was incorrectly believed to be where the famous orator practiced speaking with pebbles in his mouth in an effort to overcome his stutter. ⊠ *Lysikratous and Herefondos.*

⑱ Museum of Greek Popular Musical Instruments. An amusing crash course in the development of Greek music, especially rembetika, this museum has three floors of instruments. Headphones are available so visitors can appreciate the sounds made by such unusual delights as goatskin bagpipes and the Cretan lyra. The museum is also the Fivos Anoyiannakis Center of Ethnomusicology. ⊠ *Diogenous 1–3,* ☎ *01/ 325–0198 or 01/325–4129.* 🎟 *Free.* ☉ *Tues. and Thurs.–Sun. 10–2, Wed. noon–6.*

★ **⑲ Roman Agora.** The Roman market served as the city's commercial center from the 1st century BC to the 4th century AD. The large rectangular courtyard had a peristyle that provided shade for the arcades of shops. Its most notable feature is the west entrance's Bazaar Gate or **Gate of Athena Archegetis,** completed around AD 2; the inscription records that it was erected with funds from Julius Caesar and Augustus. Halfway up one solitary square pillar behind the gate's north side an edict inscribed by Hadrian regulates the sale of oil, a reminder this was the site of the annual bazaar where wheat, salt, and oil were sold. On the north side of the Roman Agora stands one of the few remains of the Turkish occupation, the **Fethiye (Victory) Mosque.** The eerily beautiful mosque was built in the late 15th century on the site of a Christian church to celebrate the Turkish conquest of Athens and to honor Mehmet II (the Conqueror). During the few months of Venetian rule in the 17th century, the mosque was converted to a Roman Catholic church and is now used as a storehouse. It's closed to the public. Three steps in the right-hand corner of the porch lead to the base of the minaret, the rest of which no longer exists. The octagonal **Tower of the Winds (Aerides)** is the most appealing and well preserved of the Roman monuments of Athens, keeping time since the 1st century BC. It was originally a sundial, water clock, and weather vane topped by a bronze Triton with a metal rod in his hand, which followed the direction of the wind. Expressive reliefs around the octagonal tower personify the eight winds, called *I Aerides* (the Windy Ones) by Athenians. Note the north wind, Boreas, blowing on a conch and the beneficent west wind, Zephyros, scattering blossoms. ⊠ *Pelopidas and Aiolou,* ☎ *01/324– 5220.* 🎟 *500 dr./€1.47.* ☉ *Tues.–Sun. 8:30–3.*

Ancient Agora, Monastiraki, and Thission

The Agora was once the focal point of community life in ancient Athens. It was the place where Socrates met with his students and where merchants squabbled over the price of olive oil. It was here that the Assembly first met, before it moved to the Pnyx, and where locals gathered to talk about current events. The Agora became important under Solon (6th century BC), founder of Athenian democracy; construction continued for almost a millennium. Today, the site's sprawling confusion of stones, slabs, and foundations is dominated by the best-preserved Doric temple in Greece, the Hephaistion, built during the 5th century BC, and the impressive reconstructed Stoa of Attalos II, which houses the Museum of the Agora Excavations. You can still experience the sights and sounds of the marketplace in Monastiraki, the former Turkish bazaar area, which retains vestiges of Orientalism from the 400-year period when Greece was subject to the Ottoman Empire. On the opposite side of the Agora is another meeting place of sorts:

Thission, a former red-light district complete with a hat factory, has in the last decade become one of the most sought-after residential neighborhoods while still being a popular nightspot draw.

A Good Walk

Approach Monastiraki from the pedestrian street of Ermou, jammed from Syntagma Square to Aiolou street with shops, cafés, sidewalk vendors, and wandering performers, including fire eaters, digiridoo musicians, and hurdy-gurdy players. In the middle of the Kapnikareas intersection is striking **Kapnikarea Church** ㉒. Make your way to Pandrossou, an older shopping street that leads to **Monastiraki Square** ㉓, graced by the **Tzistarakis Mosque** and **Panayia Pantassa church**, exemplifying the East-West paradox that characterizes Athens. Unfortunately, as in many other parts of the city, the square is marred by metro construction. Walk up Areos, which during the Ottoman Empire was the Lower Bazaar, roofed and covered with vines. On the corner of Aiolou, you'll pass a nicely restored Othonian building, the former Aeolos Hotel, built in 1837 just after Athens was made capital of Greece. Advertisements boasted that it offered all European conveniences, including beds, at a time when guests in public lodging usually brought their blankets and slept on the floor. This area was the edge of the Upper Bazaar. You will arrive at what remains of **Hadrian's Library** ㉔, built in AD 132 and the intellectual center of its time. Return to the square and head west on Ifestou to **Abyssinia Square** ㉕, where junk dealers and antiques merchants gather; it's the perfect place to see a side of the city that is vanishing. It is also the heart of a rambunctious Sunday **flea market** ㉖.

After browsing through the stalls, enter the **ancient Agora** ㉗ at the corner of Kinetou and Adrianou (the latter runs parallel to Ifestou). Be sure to visit the site's **Museum of Agora Excavations,** which offers a fascinating glimpse of everyday life in the ancient city. Exit at the site's opposite end onto Dionyssiou Areopagitou, crossing the boulevard to the **Thission** ㉘ quarter, a lively area with neoclassical homes overlooking trendy cafés. At the **Melina Mercouri Cultural Center** ㉙, exhibits re-create the streets of Athens during different epochs.

Those who want to escape Athens for a while should board the metro at the Thission station (at the end of Dionyssiou Areopagitou) or the Monastiraki station to the northern suburb of **Kifissia,** once a summer resort for wealthy Athenians, evident in its tree-lined boulevards and grand villas.

TIMING

Monastiraki is at its best on Sunday mornings, when the flea market is in full swing; Ermou street, on the other hand, is most interesting (and compared by Athenians to Covent Garden) Saturday mornings. The ancient Agora is closed Mondays; it offers little shade, so in summer it's better to visit the site in early morning or late afternoon. Late-afternoon visits are strongly encouraged, as you can stay to ease into Thission's café scene. Assuming you visit the Agora for about two hours, including a visit to the Museum of Agora Excavations, allow about four hours for the walk. You can spend an entire afternoon or evening in Kifissia. The trip takes about 40 minutes each way; the last train leaves Kifissia for Athens around midnight.

Sights to See

㉕ **Abyssinia Square.** Operating as a second-hand market since the early 20th century, the square hustles with activity all day long, with shop owners refinishing furniture and rearranging the bric-a-brac in their stalls. Weekend mornings, dealers flock from all over Greece to peddle an incredible array of goods, from old toasters to exquisite icons, while street musicians stroll amid the café tables, jostling their accordions and singing ballads of love and loss. ⊠ *Entrance off Ermou, between Normanou and Kinetou.*

★ **㉗** **Ancient Agora.** This marketplace was the hub of ancient Athenian life. Besides administrative buildings, it was surrounded by the schools, theaters, workshops, houses, stores, and market stalls of a thriving town. Look for markers indicating the circular Tholos, the seat of Athenian government; the Mitroon, shrine to Rhea, the mother of gods, and the state archives and registry office ("mitroon" is still used today to mean registry); the Bouleterion, where the Council met; the Monument of Eponymous Heroes, the Agora's information center where announcements such as the list of military recruits were hung; and the Sanctuary of the Twelve Gods, a shelter for refugees and the point from which all distances were measured.

Prominent on the grounds is the **Stoa of Attalos II,** a two-story building, now a museum, designed as a retail complex and erected in the 2nd century BC by Attalos, a king of Pergamum. The reconstruction in 1953–56 (funded by private American donors) used Pendelic marble and creamy limestonefrom the original structure. The colonnade, designed for promenades, is protected from the blistering sun and cooled by breezes. The most notable sculptures, of historical and mythological figures from the 3rd and 4th centuries BC, are at ground level outside the museum. In the exhibition hall, chronological displays of pottery and objects from everyday life (note the child's terra-cotta potty) demonstrate the continual settlement of the area from Neolithic times. There are such toys as knucklebones, and miniature theatrical masks carved from bone (Case 50); a *klepsydra* (a terra-cotta water clock designed to measure the time allowed for pleadings in court), and bronze voting discs (Cases 26–28); and, in Case 38, bits of *ostraka* (pottery shards used in secret ballots to recommend banishment), from which the word "ostracism" comes. Among the famous candidates for a 10-year banishment—considered a fate worse than death—were Themistocles, Kimon, and even Pericles, who had his fair share of enemies.

Take a walk around the site and speculate on the location of Simon the Cobbler's house and shop, which was a meeting place for Socrates and his pupils. The carefully landscaped grounds display a number of plants known in antiquity, such as almond, myrtle, and pomegranate. By standing in the center, you have a glorious view up to the Acropolis, which on a clear day is given a mellow glow by the famous Attic light. **Ayii Apostoloi** is the only one of the Agora's nine churches to survive, saved because of its location and beauty. Inside, the dome and the altar sit on ancient capitals. You can get an idea of the church's thousand-year-old history from the plans displayed in the narthex.

On the low hill called Kolonos Agoraios in the Agora's northwest corner stands the best-preserved extant Doric temple, the **Hephaistion,** sometimes called the Thission because of its friezes showing the exploits of Theseus. Like the other monuments, it is roped off, but you can walk around it to admire its 34 columns. It was originally dedicated to Hephaistos, god of metalworkers; metal workshops still exist in this area near Ifestou. The temple was converted to Christian use in the 7th century; the last services held here were a Te Deum in 1834, to celebrate King Otho's arrival, and a centenary Te Deum in 1934. Behind the temple, paths cross the northwest slope past archaeological ruins half hidden in deep undergrowth. Here you can sit on a bench and contemplate the same scene that Englishman Edward Dodwell saw in the early 19th century, when he came to sketch antiquities. ⊠ *Three en-*

trances: from Monastiraki on Adrianou; from Thission on Apostolou Pavlou; and descending from Acropolis on Ay. Apostoloi, ☎ 01/321–0185. 🎫 1,200 dr./€3.52. ⊘ Tues.–Sun. 8:30–3.

26 Flea market. For Athenians, all the world's a stage. Just watching the social interplay between Greeks, complete with wildly gesturing hands and dramatic facial expressions, can provide hours of entertainment. The Sunday morning market is a fitting setting in which to see lively haggling, and a fine destination in itself. Music blares from the carts pushing bootleg cassettes, mingling with the twang of a bouzouki a prospective buyer is strumming. Peddlers shout their wares: everything's for sale here, from gramophone needles to old matchboxes, from nose rings sold by young nomads to lacquered eggs and cool white linens by the Pontian Greeks from the former USSR. Haggle, no matter how low the price. ⊠ Along Ifestou, Kynetou, and Adrianou.

24 Hadrian's Library. Built in AD 132, it is closed to the public, but you can easily see the remains of this public building (400 ft by 270 ft). The east wall is supported by six attached Corinthian columns, and Pausanias mentions "one hundred splendid columns of Phrygian marble," which apparently enclosed a cloistered court with a garden and pool. On the east side was the library itself, the intellectual center of its age, decorated with statues and murals under an alabaster and gold ceiling. Other areas were used for lectures and classes. On the west wall are traces of a fresco showing the outline of the Byzantine Ayii Assomatoi, which stood next to it. ⊠ Areos and Dexippou.

22 Kapnikarea Church. It's said that the chapel was named for the kapnikarious (tax collectors who during the Byzantine period assessed residents for smoke coming from their chimneys); emanating smoke meant wealth enough to burn possessions. All pointy eaves and curvy arches, the church is really two adjoining chapels, one a cruciform structure of the 11th century, and the other a 12th-century heavier building of typical Byzantine raised brickwork, with a dome supported by four Roman columns. The latter was carefully restored by the University of Athens, of which it is now the official church. A prominent modern mosaic of the Virgin and Child adorns the west entrance, and the interior includes sentimental Western-style paintings installed before a 1930s decision that only traditional Byzantine icons and frescoes should appear in Greek churches. ⊠ In middle of intersection at Kapnikareas and Ermou, ☎ 01/322–4462. ⊘ Mon., Wed., and Sat. 8–2, Tues. and Thurs.–Fri. 8–12:30 and 5–7:30, Sun. 8–11:30.

29 Melina Mercouri Cultural Center. Installed in the former Poulopoulos hat factory built in 1886, the center offers a rare glimpse of Athens during the 19th century. Visitors can walk through a reconstructed Athens street whose facades of neoclassical homes evoke the civilized elegance of the past (note the sign on the mayor's house, which warns he's only available at the town hall), a pharmacy, printing press, dry goods store, kafenion, and dress shop, all painstakingly fitted out with authentic objects collected by the Greek Literary and Historical Archives. The center plans eventually to exhibit re-created elements of ancient and Byzantine Athens. Throughout the year it showcases temporary exhibitions, usually featuring contemporary Greek art. ⊠ Iraklidon 66 at Thessalonikis, ☎ 01/345–2150. 🎫 Free. ⊘ Tues.–Sat. 9–1 and 5–9, Sun. 9–1.

23 Monastiraki Square. The square takes its name from the **Panayia Pantanassa Church,** commonly called Monastiraki (Little Monastery) because of its smallness. It once flourished as an extensive convent, perhaps dating to the 10th century, which stretched from Athinas to

Aiolou streets. The nuns took in poor people, who earned their keep weaving the thick textiles known as *abas*. The buildings were destroyed during excavations and the start in 1896 of the metro line. The convent's basic basilica form, now recessed a few steps below street level, has been altered through a poor restoration in 1911, when the bell tower was added. The square's focal point, the **Tzistarakis Mosque** (1759) houses a **ceramics collection** that is beautifully designed, with the exhibits handsomely lighted and labeled. The mosque's creator, a newly appointed Turkish civil governor, knocked down a column from the Temple of Olympian Zeus to make lime for the mosque. Punished by the Sultan for his audacity, he was also blamed by Athenians for an ensuing plague; it was believed the toppling of a column released epidemics and disasters from below the earth. ⊠ *Square: south of Ermou and Athinas junction; museum: Areos 1,* ☎ *01/324–2066.* 🖾 *500 dr./€1.47.* ☉ *Wed.–Mon. 9–2:30.*

NEED A BREAK? On Mitropoleos just off Monastiraki Square you'll find a handful of counter-front places selling souvlaki, grilled meat rolled in a pita with onions, *tzatziki* (yogurt-garlic dip), and tomatoes—the best bargain in Athens. Your choices include **Thanassis** (⊠ Mitropoleos 69, ☎ 01/324–4705)—which is always crowded with Greeks—for its juicy meat and crunchy pitas, and **Savvas** (⊠ Mitropoleos 86, ☎ 01/321–3201), which also serves gyros—sandwiches of spicy spit-roasted meat—to patrons who can carry them across the road to a small umbrella-shaded square. Make sure you specify either a souvlaki sandwich, or a "souvlaki plate," an entire meal.

㉘ Thission. Whether you want to enjoy a snack in a turn-of-the-20th-century *ouzeri* (pub-like eatery), listen to hard rock in a bar that was once the Royal Stables, or sit down to a late supper after a show at the Herodion, you will enjoy this vibrant neighborhood, which, in the last few years, has become one of Athens's popular gathering places, rivaling upscale Kolonaki Square and the Psirri district. The main strip is the Nileos pedestrian zone across from the ancient Agora entrance, lined with cafés that are cozy in winter and have outdoor tables in summer. The rest of the neighborhood is quiet, an odd mix of mom-and-pop stores and dilapidated houses that are now slowly being renovated; take a brief stroll along Akamantos (which becomes Galatias) around the intersections of Dimofontos or Aginoros to get a feel for the quarter's past. ⊠ *West of ancient Agora, Apostolou Pavlou, and Akamantos.*

NEED A BREAK? It's a great concept: an old-style kafenion complete with ouzo, Greek coffee, and *tavli* (backgammon games) for customers, but with mod decor, designer lighting, foreign music, and delicious iced cappuccino *freddo*. No wonder most people rolling the dice at **Kafenion Thission** (⊠ Akamantos 2, ☎ 01/347–3133) are not elderly gents but the under-40 set, who, when the weather warms up, spill out onto the sidewalk. At night, the Thission becomes a bar.

OFF THE BEATEN PATH **KIFISSIA –** For a peaceful afternoon, hop on the metro heading to this northern suburb, a summer resort for aristocratic Athenians at the turn of the century. The cooler temperatures also persuaded Herodes Atticus to build his summer villa here. The streets north of the Kifissia station, with their verdant landscaping and ostentatious villas, evoke another, gentler era. Especially rewarding are Dragoumi, Diligianni, Tatoi, Rangavi, Pan, Tsaldari, Amalias, and Strofiliou streets. After exploring the area, return to the 21st century and Kifissia's main street, Kassaveti, where young people flock to the cafés and shopaholics cluster to the boutiques and upscale malls, which also line Levidou, Kiriazi, and Kolokotroni streets. In Kifissia Park, across from the metro station, the **annual May flower show** displays a dazzling array of plants, with experts standing by to give tips on proper plant care, competitions, and children's activities (✉ between Kifissia metro station and Platia Platanos). Be sure to stop for a pastry or a *rizogalo* (rice pudding) at **Varsos** (✉ Kassaveti 5, ☎ 01/801–2472), a Kifissia institution. If you have children, you may want to stop at **Goulandris Natural History Museum** (✉ Levidou 13, ☎ 01/808–6405 or 01/801–5870, ☉ Sat.–Thurs. 9–2), admission 1,000 dr./€2.94, for its displays of animal and plant life, fossils, and reconstructed prehistoric animals; it's closed the last week of July through mid-August. Intersecting Levidi is Kolokotroni, which ends at shady Kefalari Square, where decorated horse-drawn carriages await to take you on a ride through the cool, quiet roads.

Central Athens, Kerameikos, and Psirri

Downtown Athens—an unlikely combination of the squalid and the grand—is not for the fainthearted. The cavernous, chaotic Central Market, which replaced the Bazaar when it burned down in 1885, is just 10 minutes from the elegant, neoclassical Old University complex. But to central Athens all must journey to see one of the must-dos of Greece: the stately National Archaeological Museum, home to one of the most exciting collections of Greek antiquities in the world. Here are the sensational finds made by Heinrich Schliemann, discoverer of Troy and father of modern archeology, in the course of his excavations of the royal tombs on the Homeric site of Mycenae in the 1870s; here, too, are the world-famous bronzes of the Jockey of Artemision and of Poseidon throwing a trident (or is it Zeus hurling a thunderbolt?).

Archaeology buffs will also want to visit Kerameikos, the main cemetery in ancient Athens until Sulla destroyed the city in 86 BC. The name is associated with the modern word "ceramic": in the 12th century BC the district was populated by potters who used the abundant clay from the languid Iridanos River to make funerary urns and grave decorations. It contains the foundations of two ancient monuments: the Dipylon Gate where visitors entered the city, and the Sacred Gate used for both the pilgrimage to the Eleusinian rites and for the Panathenaic procession in which the tunic for the statue of Athena was carted to the Acropolis. The area outside Kerameikos was settled by Turkish gypsies before the War of Independence, and then by Athens's Jewish community. The shops of the leading families ran along Ermou; on Melidoni stands the Synagogue Beth Shalom, where congregants still worship. Nearby Psirri, one of the city's oldest neighborhoods, though still rather ramshackle, is now being renovated, with new bars and restaurants opening monthly.

A Good Walk

Those interested in archaeology should begin at **Kerameikos Cemetery** ㉚, where ancient Athens's famous citizens were buried. Continue east on Ermou to the intersection with Ayion Assomaton, where the 11th-century church of **Ayii Assomatoi** ㉛ stands. The quirky, run-down neighborhood of **Psirri** ㉜, which affords visitors a different view of the city, starts here. After taking some time to explore its narrow streets, make your way to Evripidou and the oddest church in Athens, **Ayios Ioannis Kolonastis** ㉝, at the intersection with Menandrou.

Continue east on Evripidou, lined with aromatic shops selling herbs, nuts, olive oil soap, and household items, until you reach the **Central Market** ㉞ on the corner of Athinas. Hectic, crowded Athinas stretches from Omonia Square to Monastiraki and is replete with everything from

58

Exploring Athens

canaries to garlic braids, but it is the 19th-century meat and fish market that is the most entertaining. Evripidou ends at **Klafthmonos Square** ㉟ and what is perhaps the oldest church in Athens, **Ayii Theodoroi.** Cross Stadiou, walking up the Korai pedestrian zone to the **Old University complex** ㊱ on Panepistimiou. Those who are saving the National Archaeological Museum for another day can detour a few blocks back along Panepistimiou to the **Numismatic Museum** ㊲, ensconced in Schliemann's neoclassical house, the "Palace of Troy."

Cut through the student neighborhood of Exarchia or take Trolley 2, 4, or 11 from Panepistimiou to the **Politechnio** ㊳, a national symbol of student resistance, and the **National Archaeological Museum** ㊴, one of the most important museums in Greece. Athens's other main square, Omonia, is to the west, but it serves more as a traffic hub than a tourist sight. Most of the neoclassical buildings still standing in the area were designed by architect Ernst Ziller. Two blocks up from the museum at the intersection of 28 Oktovriou (Patission) and Leoforos Alexandras is Athens's largest park, **Pedion Areos** ㊵, which provides visual relief from the urban sprawl.

TIMING

Weekday mornings are the best time to take this approximately five-hour walk, including a visit to one or two of the museums. The Central Market, which is closed Saturday afternoon and Sunday, bustles with pensioners picking over the produce and Athenians exchanging news with the fishmonger. Those coming from Omonia should walk down Aiolou Street, a pedestrian zone with cafés and old shops as well as an interesting view of the Acropolis. You'll get a good sense of Psirri as a neighborhood then, but the area is liveliest during Sunday afternoons and evenings, when Athenians congregate in its new bars and mezedopolia and the churches are illuminated. Try to visit the National Archaeological Museum after lunch, when most tour groups have departed. Look at a floor plan to organize your visit; the collection is too huge to cover comfortably in one stretch. If you hang on to your admission ticket, you can take a break at the pleasant although pricey garden café in front of the museum. The National Archaeological Museum, Numismatic Museum, and Kerameikos Cemetery are closed on Mondays; the Vouros-Eftaxias Athens City Museum is closed Saturday through Tuesday—plan accordingly.

Sights to See

㉛ **Ayii Assomatoi.** Named after the Bodiless Angels, the church dates to the 11th century. It was poorly rebuilt in 1880 but properly restored in 1959. It is in the form of a Greek cross, with a hexagonal dome and impressive exterior stonework. Some fragments of frescoes inside are probably from the 17th century, but art historians dispute the claim that an oil painting to the left of the entrance is by El Greco. ✉ *At intersection of Ermou and Ayion Assomaton.*

㉝ **Ayios Ioannis Kolonastis.** St. John of the Column is undoubtedly the most peculiar church in Athens. A Corinthian column, probably from a gymnasium dedicated to Apollo, protrudes from the tiled rooftop of the little basilica built around it in AD 565, and people with a high fever still come here to perform "curative" rituals that include tying a colored thread to the column and saying a special prayer. Mosaic floors that were unearthed here were probably part of an ancient temple to Asklepeios. ✉ 72 *Evripidou, at intersection with Menandrou, behind square.*

㉞ **Central Market.** The market runs along Athinas: On one side are open-air stalls selling fruit and vegetables at the best prices in town, although wily merchants may slip overripe items into your bag. At the corner of Armodiou, shops stock live poultry and rabbits. Across the street, in the huge covered market built in 1870, the surrealistic composition of suspended carcasses and shimmering fish on marble counters emits a pungent odor that is overwhelming on hot days. The shops at the north end of the market, to the right on Sofokleous, offer the best cheese, olives, halvah, bread, and cold cuts, including *pastourma* (Mediterranean pastrami), available in Athens. ⊠ *Athinas.* ⊙ *Closed Sat. afternoon and Sun.*

NEED A BREAK?	"If you don't behave, I won't take you to **Krinos**" (⊠ Aiolou 87, ☎ 01/ 321–6852), mothers in the Central Market used to warn unruly offspring. The lure: *loukoumades* (an irresistible, doughnutlike fritter sprinkled with cinnamon and drizzled with a honeyed syrup based on a Smyrna recipe), which the shop has been serving since it opened its doors in the 1920s. The shop is closed Sunday.

㉚ Kerameikos Cemetery. From the entrance of ancient Athens's cemetery, you can still see remains of the **Makra Teixoi** (Long Walls of Themistocles), which ran to Piraeus, and the largest gate in the ancient world, the **Dipylon Gate,** where visitors entered Athens. The walls rise to 10 ft, just a fraction of their original height (up to 45 ft). Here was also the **Sacred Gate,** used by pilgrims headed to the mysterious rites in Eleusis and those who participated in the Panathenaic procession, which followed the Sacred Way. Between the two gates are the foundations of the **Pompeion,** from where the Panathenaic procession began. It is said the courtyard was large enough to fit the ship on which the huge peplum banner dedicated to Athena was hung. On the **Street of Tombs,** which branches off the Sacred Way, plots were reserved for affluent Athenians. A number of the distinctive *stelae* (funerary monuments) remain, including a replica of the marble relief of Dexilios, a knight who died in the war against Corinth (394 BC), who is shown on horseback preparing to spear a fallen foe. By law, Athenians had to care for their parents and arrange their burial; otherwise, they would pay a hefty fine and lose their civil rights and their personal honor. As part of the elaborate ritual, a coin was often placed in the deceased's mouth, so he could pay the ferryman who transported him across the river Styx, separating the world of the living from the world of the dead. From the terrace near the tombs, Pericles gave his celebrated speech honoring those who died in the early years of the Peloponnesian War, thus persuading many to sign up for a campaign that ultimately wiped out thousands of Athenians. To the left of the site's entrance is the **Oberlaender Museum,** whose four rooms contain sculpture, terra-cotta figures, and some striking red-and-black-figured pottery. The extensive grounds are marshy in some spots; in spring, frogs exuberantly croak their mating songs near magnificent stands of lilies. ⊠ *Ermou 148,* ☎ *01/346–3552.* ⊠ *Site and museum 500 dr./€1.47.* ⊙ *Tues.–Sun. 8– 2:30 (8:30–3 in winter).*

㉟ Klafthmonos Square. Public servants from the surrounding ministries lamented loudly here after being dismissed; hence, its name, the Square of Wailing. Behind the square at the corner of Evripidou and Aristidou is **Ayii Theodorii,** a lovely mid-11th-century cruciform church, probably the oldest in Athens. The **Vouros-Eftaxias Athens City Museum,** across from the square, was home to the teenage King Otho and his bride Amalia for seven years, while the royal palace was being built. The museum displays personal objects of the royal couple, as well as King Otho's throne. In a subbasement you can see a segment of the ancient city walls, and on the ground floor a model of Athens in 1842 shows how sparsely populated the new capital was. The first floor displays paintings by European artists who came to Athens, such as Edward Lear, Gasparini, and Dodwell. ✉ *Off Stadiou, between Paparigoupoulou and Dragatsaniou; museum: Paparigoupoulou 7*, ☎ *01/324–6164.* 🎫 *500 dr./€1.47.* 🕐 *Mon. and Wed.–Sun. 9–1:30; closed Sun. July–Sept..*

NEED A
BREAK?

> As you sit gazing at the vast, silent courtyard stretched before you at **Polis** (✉ Pesmazoglou 5, between Panepistimiou and Stadiou, upstairs in Stoa tou Vivliou (Arcade of Books), ☎ 01/324–9588), you won't believe you're smack dab in the downtown madness. Located on the roof of an elegant arcade, the café-bar, which serves light refreshments such as chicken salad pita and leek pie, cappuccino, and alcohol drinks until late at night, is surrounded by buildings that cut off the city's sights and sounds, a secret enclave of shimmering white marble contrasted with shiny blue sky. Inside the café, you can peer through the windows below to the crowd milling in the arcade.

★ ㉟ **National Archaeological Museum.** By far the most important museum in Athens, this collection contains artistic highlights from every period of ancient Greek civilization, from Neolithic to Roman times. Sculpture is on the ground floor, ceramics on the first floor, and ceramics and **frescoes from Santorini** on the upper level of the first floor. These outstanding frescoes, delightful recreations of daily life in Minoan Santorini, should not be missed. They are scheduled to be returned to Santorini upon completion of its long-awaited museum. In fact, new discoveries are constantly added to the collection, though on occasion they remain only until the construction of a local museum.

By far, the most celebrated finds are in the central **Hall of Mycenaean Antiquities,** Room 4. Here are the stunning gold treasures from Schliemann's excavations of Mycenae in 1876: the funeral mask of a bearded king, once thought to be the image of Agamemnon but now believed to be much older, from about the 15th century BC; a splendid silver bull's-head libation cup; and the 15th-century BC Vaphio Goblets, masterworks in embossed gold. Mycenaeans were famed for their carving in miniature, and an exquisite example is the ivory statuette of two curvaceous mother goddesses with a child nestled on their laps.

Rooms 7–14 contain Geometric and Archaic art (10th–6th centuries BC), and Rooms 11–14 have kouroi and funerary stelae (8th–5th centuries BC), among them the stelae of the warrior Aristion signed by Aristokles, and the unusual *Running Hoplite.* Rooms 15–21 focus on classical art (5th–3rd centuries BC) and contain some of the most celebrated ancient statues extant: the bareback *Jockey of Artemision,* a 2nd-century BC Hellenistic bronze salvaged from the sea; from the same excavation, the bronze *Artemision Poseidon* (some say Zeus), poised and ready to fling a trident (or thunderbolt?); and the *Varvakion Athena,* a marble version of the goddess half the size of Pheidias's gigantic gold-and-ivory cult statue that stood in the Parthenon.

Room 28 displays funerary architecture: the spirited 2nd-century relief of a rearing stallion held by a black groom, which exemplifies the transition from classical to Hellenistic style. Room 30 holds the famous humorous marble group of a nude *Aphrodite* getting ready to slap an advancing Pan with a sandal, while Eros floats overhead and grasps one of Pan's horns. ✉ *28 Oktovriou (Patission) 44,* ☎ *01/821–7717.* 🎫 *2,000 dr./€5.88.* 🕐 *May–Oct., Mon. 12:30–7, Tues.–Fri. 8–7, weekends 8:30–3; Nov.–Apr., Mon. 10:30–5, Tues.–Sun 8:30–3.*

㊲ **Numismatic Museum.** Even those uninterested in coins might want to visit this museum, just for a glimpse of the former home of Heinrich

Schliemann, who excavated Troy and Mycenae. More than 600,000 coins are set to advantage in this magnificent neoclassical building designed by Ernst Ziller for Schliemann and his young Greek wife Sophie. Note the Pompeiian aesthetic in the ocher, terra-cotta, and blue touches, the mosaic floors inspired by Mycenae, and the dining room ceiling painted with food scenes, under which Schliemann would recite the *Iliad* to guests. The displays range from the archaeologist's own coin collection to 4th-century BC measures employed against forgers to coins grouped according to what they depict—animals, plants, myths, famous buildings like the Lighthouse of Alexandria. Instead of trying to absorb everything, concentrate on a few cases for what catches your eye—a pile of coins dug up on a Greek road, believed to be used by Alexander the Great to pay off local mercenaries; a superb 4th-century BC decadrachm with a lithesome water goddess frolicking among dolphins (the designer signed the deity's headband); or a silver didrachm issued after Philip II's death by the powerful Amphictyonic League, with Demeter on one side, and on the other, a thoughtful Apollo sitting on the navel of the world. ⊠ *Panepistimiou 12,* ☎ *01/364–3774.* ☷ *1,200 dr./€3.52.* ☉ *Tues.–Sun. 8–2:30.*

㊱ Old University complex. In the sea of concrete that is central Athens, this imposing group of marble buildings conjures up an illusion of classical antiquity. These three dramatic buildings belonging to the University of Athens were designed by the Hansen brothers in the period after independence, and are built of white Pendelic marble, with tall columns and decorative friezes. In the center is the **Senate House** of the university. To the right is the **Academy,** flanked by two slim columns topped by statues of Athena and Apollo (this structure was paid for by the Austro-Greek Baron Sina and is a copy of the Parliament in Vienna). Frescoes in the reception hall depict the myth of Prometheus. At the left end of the complex is a griffin-flanked staircase leading to the **National Library,** containing more than 2 million Greek and foreign-language volumes and now facing the daunting task of modernization. ⊠ *Panepistimiou between Ippokratous and Sina,* ☎ *01/361–4301 Senate; 01/360–0209 Academy; 01/361–4413 Library.* ☉ *Senate and Academy weekdays 9–2; library Mon.–Thurs. 9–8, Fri. 9–2. Library closed Aug.*

NEED A BREAK? The spacious **Athinaiko Kafenio** (⊠ Akadimias 50, entrance on Solonos in the rear of the Municipal Cultural Center, ☎ 01/361–9265) beckons, offering good coffees, drinks, and tempting sweets, with both indoor and shady outdoor seating.

☾ ㊵ Pedion Areos. Athens's largest park is open 24 hours a day. Statues of war heroes from the 1821 revolution dot the many walkways and hidden corners, and during the summer a small theater and cultural center stage performances. The park, once a firing range, was appropriately named for Ares, the god of war. It extends all the way to a section near the **Courts** where at night several ouzeris are packed with Athenians taking advantage of the cool forest air. There are three **playgrounds:** two near the central entrance and one off Evelpidon. A small train for youngsters traverses the park, though its proprietor doesn't keep fixed hours. ⊠ *Main entrance at 28 Oktovriou (Patission) and Leoforos Alexandras,* ☎ *01/821–2239.*

㊳ Politechnio. In late 1973 students occupied this University of Athens building to protest the junta. In response to their calls for resistance, many Greeks disobeyed military orders and showed their support by smuggling in supplies. On the night of November 16, snipers were ordered to fire into the courtyards while tanks rammed the gates: no one

knows how many students were killed because they were secretly
buried in mass graves. The public was outraged, and less than a year
later, the junta was toppled. Every year on November 17, students still
march from the Politechnio to the embassy of the United States, which
supported the dictatorship. It is still the site for frequent student
demonstrations, especially since police are legally barred from entering its gates. ⊠ *28 Oktovriou (Patission) 42,* ☏ *01/772–4000.* ☉ *Offices weekdays 8–2; grounds always open. Closed 1st 3 wks in Aug.*

❸❷ **Psirri.** The district has many buildings older than those in picturesque
Plaka, though until lately it has been less fashionable. Similar to New
York City's TriBeCa, it has been targeted by developers eager to ren-
ovate, resulting in a flurry of building, with new restaurants and bars
opening rapidly. Defined by Ermou, Kerameikou, Athinas, Evripidou,
Epikourou, and Pireos streets, the area was the setting for a number
of popular Greek novels around the turn of the 20th century, a marginal
mercantile area that had a slight underground appeal, home to the dis-
possessed, workers, and *manges,* or "tough guys." This was a place
where a murder could take place over a misunderstood song request
in a taverna. Peek over the wrought-iron gates of the old houses on
the narrow side streets between Ermou and Kerameikou to see the charming courtyards bordered by long, low buildings, whose many small rooms
were rented out to different families. Little indicates that at night the
quiet quarter becomes a whirl of theaters, clubs, and restaurants, dotted with dramatically lighted churches and lively squares, including Platia Iroon, or Square of the Heroes, where revolutionary fighters once
met to plot against the Ottoman occupation. Whether you want to dance
on tabletops to live Greek music, sing along with a soulful accordion
player, salsa in a Cuban club, or just watch the hoi polloi go by as you
snack on trendy or traditional *mezedes* (appetizers), this is the place.
⊠ *Off Ermou street, centered on Iroon and Ay. Anargiron squares.*

NEED A   Late on weekend afternoons, Athenians, be it couples from Kolonaki or
BREAK?   elderly women from Patissia, head for Psirri and **Taki 13** (⊠ Taki 13, ☏
              01/325–4707) for its unusual mezedes and live Greek music, which
              often sets the crowd to dancing, or at least clapping and shouting enthu-
              siastically as young gypsies shimmy between the tables.

Syntagma Square, National Garden, and Kolonaki

Sooner or later, everyone passes through spacious Syntagma Square, the
center of an area with several sights spanning Athens's history, from Emperor Hadrian (Temple of Olympian Zeus) to King Otho's reign after
the War of Independence in 1821 (the National Garden and Parliament).
Neighboring Kolonaki—the chic shopping district and one of the most
fashionable residential areas—occupies the lower slopes of Mt. Lycabettus.
Besides visiting its several museums, you will enjoy window-shopping and
people-watching, since cafés are busy from early morning to dawn.

A Good Walk

Begin at the site of the first modern Olympics (1896), the **Panathenaic
Stadium** ㊶ on Vasileos Konstantinou. You may want to detour right
onto Irodou Attikou, which leads to the **Presidential Palace,** used by
Greece's kings after the restoration of 1935 and now by the head of
state. Across the street from the stadium is the **National Garden** ㊷, a
pet project of Queen Amalia. Bear right, past the neoclassical **Zappion
hall,** where you exit onto Vasilissis Olgas, dominated by the **Temple of
Olympian Zeus** ㊸, built by Emperor Hadrian in AD 132, and around
the corner on Amalias, **Hadrian's Arch** ㊹, which marks the spot where
the ancient city ended and Hadrian's Athens began.

Off Amalias is the large Russian Orthodox church of **Ayios Nikodimos** ㊺ and, nearby, the **Jewish Museum of Greece** ㊻, which details the history of one of Greece's decimated communities. Amalias also passes above **Syntagma Square** ㊽ in front of the **Parliament** and the **Tomb of the Unknown Soldier,** guarded by massive Evzones. Proceed up Vasilissis Sofias (often indicated as Eleftheriou Venizelou on maps) to the **Benaki Museum** ㊾ and the delightful **Goulandris Cycladic and Greek Ancient Art Museum** ㊿, with nearly 100 exhibits of the Cycladic civilization (3000–2000 BC). A few blocks up Vasilissis Sofias, the **Byzantine Museum** �, housed in an 1848 mansion built by an eccentric French aristocrat, features a unique collection of icons.

Five minutes east of the museum is the **National Gallery of Art** ㊼, worth a visit more for its special exhibits, which have improved tremendously in the last five years. Turn off Vasilissis Sofias onto Gennadiou, passing the 12th-century **Moni Petraki** ㊾, to **Gennadius Library** ㊿, containing one of the greatest collections on Greek subjects. Go left on Souidias (which becomes Spefsipou); at Ploutarchou, steps ascend to the funicular to the top of **Mt. Lycabettus** ㊿, which reaches to three times the height of the Acropolis. The view from the top—pollution permitting—is one of the finest in Athens. You can see all the Attica basin, the harbor, and the islands of Aegina and Poros laid out before you. Minibus 060 from Kolonaki Square also drops you at the funicular station. Walk or ride back to **Kolonaki Square** ㊿, which, especially on Saturdays at noon, is crammed with chattering crowds that relax on the café-lined pedestrian zones or shop in the designer boutiques.

TIMING

Because most of the museums close around 3 PM—as do shops on Monday, Wednesday, and Saturday—plan your walk for mid-morning. The walk takes about four hours, but you may want to extend this to visit Mt. Lycabettus in the late afternoon, when the light produces the best view. Kaisariani monastery stays open until about 2:30, but you can hike through its wooded grounds until sunset. Most of the sites are closed one day a week, though all are open Wednesday through Friday; choose your route accordingly.

Sights to See

㊺ **Ayios Nikodimos.** In 1780 the notoriously brutal Hadji Ali Haseki pulled down this 11th-century chapel of a convent and used the stone to build a defensive wall around Athens. The church was sold to the Russian government, who in 1852–56 modified it into a larger, cruciform building with a distinctive terra-cotta frieze; the separate tower was built to hold a massive bell donated by Tsar Alexander II. Note the displays of ornate Russian embroidery and the bright blues of the Pantocrator (Godhead) overhead. The female chanters of this Russian Orthodox church are renowned. ⊠ *Fillelinon 21,* ☎ *01/323–1090.*

★ ㊾ **Benaki Museum.** Greece's oldest private museum, established in 1926 by an illustrious Athenian family, the Benaki was one of the first to place emphasis on Greece's later heritage at a time when many archaeologists were destroying Byzantine artifacts to access ancient objects. The museum finally reopened in summer 2000 after a renovation program that cost $20 million and lasted a decade. The collection (more than 20,000 items are on display in 36 rooms and that's only a sample of the holdings) now moves chronologically from the ground floor upward, from prehistory to the formation of the modern Greek state. You might see anything from a 5,000-year-old hammered gold bowl to an austere Byzantine icon of the Virgin Mary to Lord Byron's pistols to the Nobel medals awarded to poets George Seferis and Odysseus Elytis. Some exhibits are just plain fun—the re-creation of a Kozani living room; a tableau of costumed mannequins; a Karaghiozi shadow puppet piloting a toy plane—all contrasted against the marble-and-crystal-chandelier grandeur of the Benaki home. The mansion was designed by Anastassios Metaxas, the architect who helped restore the Panathenaic Stadium. Other parts of the collection—Islamic art, Chinese porcelain, 18th- to 20th-century toys—will be displayed in branches throughout the city. The second-floor café serves coffee and snacks, with a few daily specials, on a veranda overlooking the National Garden. ⊠ *Koumbari 1,* ☎ *01/367–1000.* ⊑ *2,000 dr./€5.88, free Thurs.* ☉ *Mon., Wed., and Fri.–Sat. 9–5, Thurs. 9 AM–midnight, Sun. 9–3.* ⊛

★ ⑤ **Byzantine Museum.** One of the few museums in Europe concentrating exclusively on Byzantine art, this is housed in the porticoed winter villa of the Duchess of Plaisance, built from 1840 to 1848 by Stamatis Kleanthis. Rooms are arranged to look like Greek churches of different eras—an early Christian basilica, a medieval cross-in-square domed church, a post-Byzantine chapel—and the upper floor contains mostly icons, many quite valuable. Much of the museum is still closed due to construction work being done on the new wings. ⊠ *Vasilissis Sofias 22,* ☎ *01/721–1027, 01/723–2178, or 01/723–1570.* ⊑ *500 dr./€1.47 during restoration.* ☉ *Tues.–Sun. 8:30–3.*

OFF THE
BEATEN PATH

MONASTERY OF KAISARIANI – For an exceptional trek outside central Athens, head to the slopes of Mt. Hymettus, where you'll find one of the city's most evocative Byzantine remains. The well-restored 11th-century church, built on the site of a sanctuary of Aphrodite, is surrounded by cells, a bathhouse, and refectory. Most of the frescoes date back to the 17th century—note the embroidered cloth worn by prophets and angels in the dome's drum, reproductions of Turkish fabrics of the period. The oldest mural is in the side chapel of St. Anthony, a praying Virgin Mary depicted in the provincial style of the 14th century. On the hill above the monastery is a fountain whose waters were prescribed for curing sterility; according to local legend, a dove flew over the waters on Ascension Day. The now-destroyed, adjacent Aphrodite temple was the backdrop for the jealous lovers in Ovid's *Ars Amatoria* (*Art of Love*). Nearby is a ruined basilica and a picnic site with a superb view of the Acropolis and Piraeus. It's forbidden to pick the flowers, but you can buy plants from the nursery located just below the monastery; proceeds go the area's reforestation. Take a taxi or Bus 224 from in front of the Byzantine Museum for 6 km (4 mi) east of central Athens to the end of the line in the suburb of Kaisariani. The monastery is an additional 35-minute walk along the paved road that climbs Mt. Hymettus. ⊠ *Mountain road starting at Ethniki Antistaseos,* ☎ *01/723–6619.* ⊑ *800 dr./€2.30.* ☉ *Tues.–Sun. 8:30–3; grounds daily sunrise–sunset.*

⑤ **Gennadius Library.** Book lovers who ascend the grand staircase into the hallowed aura of the Reading Room may have difficulty tearing themselves away from this superb collection of material on Greek subjects, from first editions of Greek classics to the papers of Nobel Laureate poets George Seferis and Odysseus Elytis. The heart of the collection consists of thousands of books donated in the 1920s by Greek diplomat John Gennadius, who haunted London's rare book shops for volumes connected to Greece, thus amassing the most comprehensive collection of Greek books by one man. He died bankrupt, leaving his wife to pay off his debts, mostly to booksellers. The library's collection includes Lord Byron's memorabilia (including a lock of his hair); Schliemann's diaries, notebooks, and letters; and impressionistic watercolors of Greece by Edward Lear. Pride of place is given to the first edition printed in Greek of Homer (the *Iliad* and the *Odyssey*). Needless to say, this is not a lending library. Renovated in 1999, the library is in the custody of the American School of Classical Studies. ⊠ *Souidias 61,* ☎ *01/721–0536.* ☉ *Mid-Sept.–mid-Aug., Mon.–Tues. and Fri. 9:30–5, Wed.–Thurs. 9:30–8, Sat. 9:30–2.*

★ ⑤⓪ **Goulandris Cycladic and Greek Ancient Art Museum.** Funded by one of Greece's richest families, this museum has an outstanding collection dating from the Bronze Age, including many of the enigmatic Cycladic marble figurines, whose slender shapes so fascinated such artists as Picasso, Modigliani, and Brancusi. A glass corridor connects the main building to the gorgeous adjacent Stathatos Mansion, where temporary exhibits are held. ⊠ *Neofitou Douka 4 or Irodotou 1,* ☎ *01/722– 8321 through 01/722–8323.* ☞ *800 dr./€2.35.* ☉ *Mon. and Wed.–Fri. 10–4, Sat. 10–3.* ☜

④④ **Hadrian's Arch.** This marble gateway was built in AD 131 with Corinthian details. It was intended both to honor the Hellenophile emperor Hadrian and to separate the ancient and imperial sections of Athens. On the side facing the Acropolis an inscription reads THIS IS ATHENS, THE ANCIENT CITY OF THESEUS, but the side facing the Temple of Olympian Zeus proclaims THIS IS THE CITY OF HADRIAN AND NOT OF THESEUS. ⊠ *Vas. Amalias at Dionyssiou Areopagitou.* ☞ *Free.* ☉ *Always open.*

④⑥ **Jewish Museum of Greece.** The museum's vivid memorabilia, relocated in 1998 to an elegantly renovated neoclassical building near Plaka, tells the story of the Jews in Greece, from the 6th century BC to the Holocaust, when 87% of the Greek Jews were killed; only about 5,000 remain today. The museum pays tribute to the diversity of the various Jewish communities with a collection organized according to periods and themes. These include the early history of the Romaniotes (Jews who espoused Greek culture and wrote Greek in the Hebrew script), many of whom lived in Halkida, one of Europe's oldest Jewish communities; the arrival of the Ladino-speaking Sephardic Jews after they were expelled from Spain during the Holy Inquisition in the late 15th century; the Jewish calendar and holidays; and religious items used in synagogues as well as in everyday domestic life. One room contains the reconstruction of the interior of the old Romaniote Synagogue of Patras, a community established by Jews from Syria in 323–281 BC. ⊠ *Nikis 39,* ☎ *01/322–5582.* ☞ *500 dr./€1.47 (ring bell).* ☉ *Weekdays 9–2:30, Sun. 10–2.*

☝ ⑤⑥ **Kolonaki Square.** Athenians don't actually gather on the square, officially called Filikis Eterias, but along the Tsakalof and Milioni pedestrian-zone cafés, to see and be seen. Glittery models, middle-aged executives, elegant pensioners—all congregate here for a quick coffee before work, after a hard day of shopping, or for foreign newspapers at the all-night kiosk. On the lower side of the square is the **British Council Library** (⊠ Kolonaki Sq. 17, ☎ 01/364–5768), which has some children's videos and a screening facility. ⊠ *Where Patriarchou Ioakeim and Kanari meet.* ☉ *Library Mon. and Thurs. 3–8, Tues.–Wed. and Fri. 9:30–2:30 (weekdays 9:30–1:30 in June–July). Closed 3 wks in Aug.*

| NEED A BREAK? | Enjoy a cappuccino and an Italian sweet standing at **Da Capo** (⊠ Tsakalof 1, ☎ 01/360–2497), frequented by young trendsetters, especially on Saturday afternoons. Or you can walk to **Ouzeri Dexameni** (⊠ Deinokratous and Xanthippou, Dexameni Sq., ☎ 01/729–2578), a favorite whose tables line either side of a tree-shaded lane, making it an ideal spot for people-watching over a frappé or Greek salad and marinated octopus. |

53 **Moni Petraki.** Tucked into a sweet little park at Iassou, this church was built in the 12th century and decorated with paintings by Yiorgios Markos in the 18th century. ✉ *Off Moni Petraki,* ☎ *01/721–2402.* ☉ *Mon.–Sat. 6–noon, Sun. 6–noon and 6:30–9:30 PM (opens 5:30 PM in winter).*

★ **55** **Mt. Lycabettus.** Myth claims that Athens's highest hill came into existence when Athena removed a piece of Mt. Pendeli, intending to boost the height of her temple on the Acropolis. While she was en route, a crone brought her bad tidings, and the flustered goddess dropped the rock in the middle of the city. A steeply inclined *teleferique* (funicular) takes visitors to the summit, crowned by whitewashed **Ayios Georgios** chapel with a bell tower donated by Queen Olga. On the side of the hill, near the I Prasini Tenta café, there is a small shrine to **Ayios Isidoros** built into a cave. It was here that in 1859 students prayed for those fighting against the Austrians, French, and Sardinians with whom King Otho had allied. From Mt. Lycabettus you can watch the sun set and then turn about to watch the moon rise over "violet-crowned" Hymettus as the lights of Athens blink on all over the city. ✉ *Base: 15-min walk northeast of Syntagma; funicular every 10 mins from Ploutarchou 1, at Aristippou (take Minibus 060 from Kanaris St. or Kolonaki Sq., except Sun.),* ☎ *01/722–7065.* 🎫 *1,000 dr./€2.94 round-trip, 500 dr./€1.47 one-way.* ☉ *May–Oct., daily 9:15 AM–12:45 AM; Dec.–Apr., 9:15 AM–11:45 PM. Closed Nov.*

NEED A BREAK?   The pricey café at the top of Lycabettus may be the most convenient place to stop, but persevere and you'll get a better deal and a more romantic, pine-scented setting at **I Prasini Tenta** (✉ 5 mins down path that leaves from Ayios Giorgios or, if driving, turn left at fork when descending, ☎ 01/361–9447), an outdoor café where you can savor an ouzo and appetizers such as mushrooms stuffed with four cheeses along with your Acropolis view.

52 **National Gallery of Art.** The permanent collections of Greek painting and sculpture of the 19th and 20th centuries, including the work of naive artist Theophilos, have made way for long-running exhibitions, making the gallery a livelier place popular with the public. The exhibitions are usually major loan shows from around the world, such as "Theotokopoulos to Cézanne," an El Greco retrospective, Dutch 17th-century art, and an exhibit tracing the influence of Greece on works of the Italian Renaissance. ✉ *Vasileos Konstandinou 50,* ☎ *01/723–5857 or 01/723–5937.* 🎫 *2,000 dr./€5.88.* ☉ *Mon. and Wed. 9–3 and 6–9, Thurs.–Sat. 9–3, Sun. 10–2.*

OFF THE BEATEN PATH   **DESTE FOUNDATION, CENTRE FOR CONTEMPORARY ART –** Art collector Dakis Joannou, who owns one of the world's largest collections of modern art, opened this lively complex in 1998 in a renovated paper warehouse. His private holdings range from Duchamp to Warhol to Koons, but the exhibition space is more often devoted to progressive exhibits designed to develop audiences for contemporary art in Greece and to offer opportunities for up-and-coming artists. The complex eschews the usual formality of museums and instead casually mixes art, entertainment, new media, and shopping. Included are the ground-floor Cosmos bar-restaurant, a video projection room, an art shop, and a Cybercafé. ✉ Omirou 8, Neo Psychiko, ☎ 01/672–9460. 🎫 Free. ☉ Weekdays 11 AM–midnight, Sat. noon–4. Closed Sun. and middle 2 wks in Aug.

42 **National Garden.** When you can't take the city noise anymore, step into this oasis completed in 1860 as part of Otho and Amalia's royal holdings. Here old men on the benches argue politics, policemen take their coffee breaks, and animal lovers feed the stray cats that roam among the more than 500 species of trees and plants, many labeled. At the east end is the neoclassical **Zappion hall,** built in 1888 and used for major political and cultural events: it was here that Greece signed its entrance into what was the EC. Children will enjoy the **playgrounds, duck pond, and small zoo** (⊠ East end of park). The Hellenic Ornithological Society runs an **information kiosk** on birds with an activity program for children, including games to recognize the park's visitors, drawing contests, and the making of swallow's nests to ensure sanctuary for homeless birds (⊠ Irodou Attikou entrance, near playground, ☎ FAX 01/381–1271 or 01/330–1167); it's open all year (though August depends on the volunteers) weekends 11–2:30. Youngsters age 5–15 may settle into a good book at the **Children's Library** (☎ 01/323–6503), a rustic, vine-covered stone cottage in a tranquil corner of the garden; it is open September–July, Tuesday–Saturday 8:30–2:30. Of its 4,000 books, only 60 are in English and French. It also has games and puzzles (some in English), a chess set, dominoes, crayons, and coloring books. Albums, including a large selection of classical music, can be played on the turntable. ⊠ *East of Vasilissis Amalias, between Vasilissis Olgas and Vasilissis Sofias,* ☎ *01/721–5019.* ☉ *Daily 7 AM–sunset.*

NEED A BREAK? Visit the romantic café **Kafenedaki** (⊠ In the National Garden), sometimes called Kipos, a cool spot with wrought-iron chairs and tables nestled under a bower of flowering vines. The café is next to a stone cottage just inside the park's Irodou Attikou entrance (near Lykeiou). The menu is limited to a *poikilia* (variety) of mezes, grilled "toast" (with ham and cheese), ice cream, apple cake, and drinks.

④ Panathenaic Stadium. Constructed by Lykourgus from 330 to 329 BC and used intermittently for Roman spectacles, the stadium was reseated for the Panathenaic Games of AD 144 by Roman citizen Herodes Atticus of Marathon, a magistrate, senator, and wealthy patron of Athens. It later fell into ruin, and its marble was quarried for other buildings. By the mid-18th century, when it was painted by French artist Le Roy, it had become little more than a wheat field with scant remains and was later the midnight site of the secret rites of the witches of Athens. A blinding-white marble reconstruction of the ancient Roman stadium was rebuilt for the first modern Olympics, in April of 1896, and is now used mainly for an occasional concert and the finish of the annual marathon; it seats 80,000 spectators. ⊠ *Near junction of Vas. Olgas and Vas. Konstantinou, across from National Garden.* ☜ *Free.* ☉ *Daily 9–2 but can be viewed in its entirety without entering.*

OFF THE BEATEN PATH **FIRST CEMETERY OF ATHENS –** This is Athens's equivalent of Paris's Père-Lachaise, but it is whitewashed and cheerful rather than gloomy and Gothic. The graves of the rich and famous are surrounded by well-tended gardens and decorated with small photographs of the departed, and birds chirp perpetually in the stately cypress and mandarin trees. The main entrance off Anapafseos, which means "eternal rest," leads to an open-air museum of mind-boggling funerary architecture, including the imposing temple dedicated to Heinrich Schliemann, which is adorned with scenes from the Trojan War, and the touching marble *Sleeping Maiden* sculpture by Yiannoulis Halepas on the grave of Sophia Afendaki. It was commissioned by her parents in the hope that some day their young daughter would be awakened by a prince's kiss. Perhaps the most visited grave is that of actress and national sweetheart Aliki Vouyiouklaki, bedecked with lighted candles, flowers, and fan letters left daily. The film star and politician Melina Mercouri is also buried here, as is the popular, controversial former prime minister Andreas Papandreou, who died in 1996. ⊠ *Anapafseos and Trivonianou, near Panathenaic Stadium,* ☎ *01/923–6118 or 01/923–6720.* ⊙ *May–Sept., daily 7:30 AM–8 PM; Oct.–Apr., daily 8–5.*

★ ④ **Syntagma (Constitution) Square.** At the top of the city's main square stands **Parliament,** formerly the royal palace, completed in 1838 for the new monarchy. It seems a bit austere and heavy for a southern landscape, but it was proof of progress, the symbol of the new ruling power. Its saving grace is the stone's magical change of color from off white to gold to rosy mauve as the day progresses. Here you can watch the **changing of the Evzone guard** at the **Tomb of the Unknown Soldier**—located in front of Parliament on a lower level—which takes place at intervals throughout the day. On Sunday the honor guard of tall young men don dress costume—a short white *foustanella* (kilt) with 400 neat pleats, one for each year of the Ottoman occupation, and red shoes with pompons—and still manage to look brawny rather than silly. A band accompanies a large troop of them in a memorable ceremony that leaves from the nearby barracks, arriving in front of Parliament by 11:15 AM. On a wall behind the Tomb of the Unknown Soldier, the bas-relief of a dying soldier is modeled after a sculpture on the Temple of Aphaia in Aegina; the text is from the funeral oration said to have been given by Pericles. Pop into the gleaming **Syntagma Metro Station** (⊠ Upper end of Syntagma Sq., ⊙ daily 5 AM–midnight), opened in 2000, to examine artfully displayed artifacts uncovered during subway excavations and a floor-to-ceiling cross-section of earth behind glass with the finds in chronological layers, ranging from a skeleton in its ancient grave to traces of the 4th-century BC road to Mesogeia to an Ottoman cistern. ⊠ *At intersection of Vas. Amalias and Vas. Sofias.*

NEED A
BREAK?

Since 1910, **Ariston** (⊠ Voulis 10, ☎ 01/322–7626) has been turning out arguably the city's best *tiropites* (cheese pies) since 1910; these are a little more piquant than usual and have a thicker phyllo. Avoid the tasteless variety often sold on the street and make a pit stop here for the real thing, or try the equally good potato pies; the establishment is open during shopping hours. Another place to break near Syntagma is a tiny, no-name *galaktopolio,* or milk shop, with marble-top tables and rickety chairs, where you will eat the best, creamiest Greek rice pudding, nothing like the heavy American version (⊠ Nikis 26, ☎ 01/323–8248). Ask for it on a plate (not in takeaway plastic) and sprinkled with cinnamon. The kindly owners also will assemble a simple breakfast of fried eggs, toast, and coffee, for those who woke up too late for the hotel buffet.

④ **Temple of Olympian Zeus.** Begun in the 6th century BC, it was completed in AD 132 by Hadrian, who had also built one huge gold-and-ivory statue of Zeus for the inner chamber and another, only slightly smaller, of himself. Only 15 of the original Corinthian columns remain, but standing next to them inspires a sense of awe at their bulk, which is softened by the graceful carving on the acanthus-leaf capitals. The clearly defined segments of a column blown down in 1852 give you an idea of the method used in its construction. The site is floodlighted in summer, a majestic scene when you round the bend from Syngrou. On the outskirts of the site to the north are remains of houses, the city walls, and a Roman bath. ⊠ *Vasilissis Olgas 1,* ☎ *01/922–6330.* 🗺 *500 dr./€1.47.* ⊙ *Tues.–Sun. 8:30–3.*

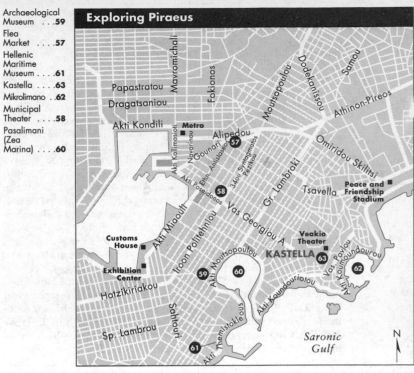

Exploring Piraeus

Piraeus

To those who remember the film *Never on Sunday,* the name Piraeus evokes images of earthy waterfront cafés frequented by free-spirited sailors and hookers, though many Athenians regard Piraeus (except for Mikrolimano or Kastella) as merely low class. Neither image is correct: the restoration of older buildings and the addition of shopping centers and cafés have brought about a rejuvenation, both of place and community pride. Piraeus caters more to Greek families and young singles than to the rough-and-tumble crowd, and living in some parts of it carries a certain cachet these days. Also in its favor: the air pollution, noise level, and temperatures are considerably lower than they are in inner Athens.

Today, Piraeus remains the port of Athens, 11 km (7 mi) southwest of the center, and a city in its own right (third-largest after Athens and Thessaloniki), with a population of about 500,000. In 1834, after gaining independence from the Turks, the government offered land in Piraeus (at that point a mere wilderness) on favorable terms, and it was resettled by islanders from other parts of Greece. The first factory was founded by Hydriots in 1847, and by the turn of the 20th century there were 76 steam-powered factories. After the 1920s Piraeus developed as an economic center, while Athens maintained the cultural sphere. In the years following 1922, refugees from Asia Minor swelled the population, bringing with them rembetika music.

A Good Walk

The fastest and cheapest way to get to Piraeus from central Athens is to take the electric train (about 20–30 minutes, depending on whether you leave from Syntagma, Omonia, Monastiraki, or Thission station). The metro station is just off Akti Kallimasioti on the main harbor. For those who don't have much time, take Bus 904, 905, or 909 opposite the Piraeus station directly to the Archaeological Museum rather than walking there; get off at the Fillelinon stop. If it's Sunday, detour a few blocks from the metro to the **flea market** ⑤, along Omiridou Skilitsi, and then stop for a coffee in one of the popular spots at the intersection with 34ou (which translates as 34th) Syntagmatos Pezikou where Athenians come Sunday afternoons. If walking, turn left when exiting the metro, following Akti Kallimasioti to Akti Poseidonos. South of here is the Customs House and Port Authority—through which one passes to board boats going to other countries—and a modern exhibition center, where the Poseidonia Shipping Exhibition is held in June in connection with a biannual Nautical Week. Continuing on Akti Poseidonos, turn onto Vasileos Georgiou A' (A' translates as 1st), which passes the imposing 800-seat **Municipal Theater** ⑧ near Korai Square. Head south on Iroon Polytechneiou, cutting through Terpsithea Square, and then go east on Harilaou Trikoupi to the remodeled **Archaeological Museum** ⑨, containing such rare finds as the Piraeus Kouros, a cult statue of Apollo from the 6th century BC. The street ends at the harbor of **Pasalimani** ⑥ (Zea Marina). To the west is the coastal road Akti Themistokleous, whose lantern-lined stretch offers good views and reasonably priced seafood restaurants. Incorporated into the foundation of the **Hellenic Maritime Museum** ⑥, also on the road, are the original Long Walls. To the east is the pretty, crescent-shape harbor of **Mikrolimano** ⑥, lined with seafood restaurants (a 10-minute walk from the Neo Faliro station for those who want to save their strength). Mikrolimano had lost favor with some Athenians because the harbor suffers from pollution, but the delightful atmosphere remains intact, the harbor is still crowded with yachts, and young people flock to its cafés on Sundays.

Above Mikrolimano is charming **Kastella** ⑥, terraces of 19th-century houses tucked up against the sloping hillside—an ideal spot for a walk before dinner on the harbor or a show at its **Veakio Theater.**

TIMING

On a day trip to Piraeus you can see the main sights, explore the neighborhoods around its three harbors, and have a seafood meal before returning to Athens. If you are taking an early morning ferry or seeing a performance at the Veakio Theater, it makes good sense to stay in one of the seaside hotels. Note that the flea market is held only on Sunday, the Archaeological Museum is closed Monday, the Maritime Museum is closed on Sunday and Monday, and the Municipal Theater is closed weekends.

Sights to See

★ ⑨ **Archaeological Museum.** Despite a 1998 refurbishing and new impressive finds now on display, the museum does not get many visitors— perhaps because of its drab exterior and its distance from the center. That's too bad, because the museum's prize exhibits include four of the world's very few surviving classical bronze statues: the exquisitely made life-sized **Piraeus Kouros** (probably a cult statue of Apollo from the late 6th century or early 5th century BC, and therefore the oldest known hollow-cast bronze statue); a 4th-century bronze of a pensive Athena, in a helmet decorated with griffins and owls; and two bronze versions of Artemis. Discovered in 1959, the works had been hidden in a warehouse during the 1st century BC, probably in anticipation of the 86 BC siege by Roman general Sulla, and were overlooked in the havoc that followed the sacking of Athens and Piraeus. Unfortunately, the statues lose a bit of their impact as they are displayed in glass cases filled with nitrogen to prevent corrosion. Another older exhibit is a bro-

BLUE GLAMOUR: YACHTING IN GREEK WATERS

BY FAR THE MOST UNIQUE WAY to see the Greek islands is a yachting vacation. Discovering these 1,425 geological jewels—thickly scattered over the Aegean Sea like stepping stones between East and West—by yacht, boat, or caïque is a once-in-a-lifetime experience. Many yachting expeditions set out or pass through Piraeus harbor—offering the most modern mooring and wintering facilities in the country—to discover magic in the Aegean. Greece's jagged coasts let you explore a world of secluded hamlets, white chapels, and little villages reflected in blue water, as you ride out the sunny breeze that blows over the hills. Not that Zeus should set your schedule (during the idyllic days in mid-winter he forbade the winds to blow), but keep in mind the Aegean can be a great deal rougher than most people think during August, when the *meltemi*, the north wind, is a regular visitor to these waters.

The array of seaside destinations in Greece is spectacular. If you are sailing directly from Italy or along the Dalmation Coast, Corfu is the first destination, a lush Ionian resort once the favorite of yachtsman King Paul of Greece. From here, yachters sometimes work their way down to Messolonghi, in the Gulf of Patras, where Byron died and where the sunsets can be unbelievable. You would be wise to land at Patras, at the entrance of the Gulf of Corinth, for this is one of the main crossroads of travel in Greece. It is here that yacht crews decide to take a short cut through the Corinth Canal to Piraeus or the long way around the Peloponnese. If you choose the short cut, a short bus ride from the harbor of Itea takes you to Delphi, the most venerated sanctuary of ancient Greece. Southward, few people fail to put in at Crete—the island where civilization is counted by the millennium. Sailing in a counterclockwise direction—old sea dogs maintain that this is the best way of covering the Aegean—you can enter the waters of the Dodecanese from the southwest, but this trip across the open sea lacks the surprises you discover traveling from harbor to harbor.

Another Mediterranean delight is Rhodes, with its ancient temples and medieval fortresses *and* wide range of discos. If you are looking for dreaminess, head west across waters of the Dodecanese to the Cyclades. The island of Milos does not mass-produce Venuses and the volcano on Santorini, or Thira, is not in constant eruption, of course, but, even so, the islands here are all winners: Delos, for its archaeological wealth; Mykonos, where the Greek nobs go to outsnob the snobs; Paros, whence the fabled marble came; Tinos, the Greek counterpart of Lourdes; Naxos, whose new wine is harvested in September. Next port of call could be the Northern Islands, including Chios, Lesbos, Sappho, and, on the far, far horizon, Samothrace, famed as the home of the Louvre's *Winged Victory*. Crossing the Gulf of Salonika to reach the Sporades requires good skill, but once you round Cape Sounion—give thanks to Poseidon at his incredible cliff-top temple here—you enter the hospitable waters of the Saronic Gulf. If you head back to anchor in Piraeus, you return to Attic soil, your odyssey now having taken you to the heart of Greek civilization—ancient Athens, Mycenae, and Epidaurus. For practical details about yachting and an extensive list of outfitters, *see* Cruise Travel and Yachting *in* Smart Travel Tips A to Z.

You can "do" Greece in your own yacht according to your taste, pausing at will for scenery, swimming, or sightseeing, setting your own schedule and your own itinerary. However, to *enjoy* yachting, remember to "shift gears" mentally from the smooth speed of straight paved highways to the far more leisurely route of bay-indented coasts, lovely isthmuses, and beckoning bays.

ken bronze ram, probably from an ancient trireme, next to the sculpted marble eye that adorned the vessel's bow. A new room contains unusual Mycenaean chariot figurines from a sanctuary near Methana, early Geometric vases, and musical instruments and writing tools from a 4th-century BC poet's grave. Those who can read ancient Greek should look for the stele inscribed with price regulations for tripe and other goodies like feet and lungs served at meat tavernas, then called *epthopoleia*. The collection of 5th and 4th century BC funerary steles and statues include the urn of Lysis, about whom Mary Renault wrote *The Last of the Wine*. The ground floor has been revamped to fit the newly reassembled 7-meter-high Kallithea funerary monument made in the late 4th century BC. It includes statues of a rich Black Sea immigrant, his son, and a young slave inside in a mini-temple atop a high base embellished with reliefs. It was showy grave monuments like this that sparked a stern backlash represented by a 317 BC ruling that banned funerary architecture. ⊠ *Harilaou Trikoupi 31, at Fillelinon,* ☎ *01/452–1598.* ⊠ *500 dr./€1.47.* ⊙ *Tues.–Sun. 8:30–3.*

㊼ Flea market. In the "Monastiraki" of Piraeus, outdoor stalls overflow on Sunday with household items, electronic goods, and offbeat videocassettes, but there are also several interesting shops and stalls throughout the week selling everything from antique Mytilini mirrors ("antique" at the flea market means from about 1850 on) to Thracian wedding gowns to '50s furniture. The most rewarding stretch is along Omiridou Skilitsi between Ippodamias Square and Pilis Street. On Navarinou, parallel to Akti Kallimasioti, there's another market selling cheese, cold cuts, dried fruit, bread, and nuts. It's good to buy provisions before taking a ferry because the snack bars on board have just a few items, and at high prices. ⊠ *Omiridou Skilitsi, parallel to metro tracks.* ⊙ *Sun. 8–2.*

� ㊅ Hellenic Maritime Museum. The 13,000 items on display include scale models and actual sections of triremes and famous boats, Byzantine flags, figureheads, documents, and uniforms. A section of the **Long Walls** is incorporated into the museum's foundation, and other well-preserved segments run along Akti Themistokleous, south of Zea Marina. ⊠ *Akti Themistokleous, Freattida Sq.,* ☎ *01/451–6264 or 01/428–6959.* ⊠ *500 dr./€1.47.* ⊙ *Sept.–July, Tues.–Fri. 9–2, Sat. 9–1:30.*

㊳ Kastella. This neighborhood behind Mikrolimano retains the charm of a bygone era, its neoclassical houses skillfully restored. In antiquity the hill was known as Mounichia and served as the acropolis of Piraeus. On the hill the **Veakio Theater** (⊠ Idis on Lofos Prof. Ilias, ☎ 01/419–4520) has a cultural festival late June through September, featuring visiting dance troupes, plays, and concerts. ⊠ *Behind Mikrolimano.*

★ ㊒ Mikrolimano. The most touristy part of Piraeus, this graceful, small harbor is known to old-timers as **Turkolimano.** Sitting under the awnings by the sea and watching the water and the gaily painted fishing boats is the next best thing to hopping on a ferry boat and going to an island. During high season, it is a good idea to have lunch here, as in the evening most of the many restaurants lining the harbor are packed. The hawkers in front of the restaurants are entertaining but can be aggressive. Don't be afraid to ask to see the prices on the menu or go to look at the fish stored in iced compartments. Be sure to specify how large a portion you want, and ask its price in advance. ⊠ *Akti Koumoudourou.*

㊸ Municipal Theater. The 800-seat theater was modeled after the Opéra Comique in Paris and finished in 1895. In the same building is the **Panos Aravantinos Decor Museum,** which displays sketches and models of the artist's theatrical sets. ✉ *Theater: Iroon Polytechniou,* ☏ *01/419–4584 for information; 01/419–4550 box office.* ☉ *Only open during performances.* ✉ *Museum: Ayios Konstantinou 2,* ☏ *01/419–4578.* 🎫 *Free.* ☉ *Sept.–July, Mon. 3–8, Tues.–Fri. 8–2.*

60 **Pasalimani (Zea Marina).** Once Athens's main naval base, lined with 196 boathouses, each big enough to hold one trireme, this small harbor is now a yachting marina with berths for more than 400 boats. The surrounding area has been rejuvenated, with the addition of many enticing cafés and pubs. There's a Greek National Tourist Organization (GNTO or EOT) office with maps, brochures, and timetables on the west side of the harbor close to the departure point for Saronic Gulf Islands hydrofoils.

DINING

Whether you sample octopus and ouzo near the sea, roasted goat in a turn-of-the-20th-century taverna, or cutting-edge cuisine in Athens's latest restaurants, dining in the city is just as relaxing as it is elsewhere in Greece: waiters never rush you, reservations are often unnecessary, and no matter how crowded, the establishment can always make room for another table. The best of Athens's restaurants have recently made enormous strides in quality and style, thanks to the new influence on native dishes by foreign cuisines, particularly French, Italian, and Japanese. Indeed, you may have a hard time finding a traditional *taramosalata* (roe dip), as many chefs are eager to take Aegean-inspired cuisine and tweak it a notch higher: boar with watermelon chutney, anyone? So forgo the ubiquitous moussaka and opt instead for the newer-than-now nouvelle house specialties—for a while, at least. After all, native Greek food can be sensational, as you'll find out if you taste *Iman Bayildi* ("the cleric fainted"—presumably because the eggplant with garlic and tomato was so delicious). Don't hesitate to try the barrel wine, inexpensive and often quite good. If you can't understand the menu, just go to the kitchen and point at what looks most appealing. This is a good idea especially in tavernas, where not everything on the menu may be available at the time you order. In most cases, you don't need to ask—just walk to the kitchen (some places have food displayed in a glass case right at the kitchen's doorway), or point to your eye and then the kitchen; the truly ambitious can say "Bo-*ro* na dtho tee *eh*-he-teh steen koo-*zee*-na?" or "May I see what's in the kitchen?" When ordering fish, which is priced by the kilo, you will often go the kitchen to pick out your individual fish, which is then weighed and billed accordingly. At some rustic places, like Margaro in the port of Piraeus, you may wind up in the kitchen for another reason: when it's crowded, the staff asks you to prepare your own salad. Most places serve lunch from about noon to 4 and dinner from about 8:30 to at least midnight.

CATEGORY	COST*
$$$$	over 16,000 dr. (€47.05)
$$$	10,000 dr.–16,000 dr. (€29.41–€47.05)
$$	5,500 dr.–10,000 dr. (€14.70–€29.41)
$	under 5,500 dr. (€14.70)

per person for a three-course meal, including service and tax but excluding drinks and tip

In the last three weeks of August, when the city empties out and most residents head for the seaside, more than 75% of the restaurants and tavernas popular among the locals close, though hotel restaurants, seafood restaurants in Mikrolimano, and tavernas in Plaka usually remain open.

Eating Places

A few years ago the category of "haute cuisine" would not have existed, but Athens now has restaurants of international standard, in both preparation and presentation. The category of **international restaurants** includes those serving foreign cuisine, whether classic Italian, French, or Japanese, and the truly international, i.e. hard to place in any category. **Greek/Mediterranean (Contemporary)** establishments are a fairly recent arrival in Athens, the playground for innovative chefs offering a sophisticated mélange of dishes that pay vague homage to Greek cooking but borrow heavily from other cuisines ("fusion"). The less trendy **Greek/Mediterranean (Traditional)** restaurants serve Greek cuisine a little closer to what a Greek grandmother would make, but in a more formal setting and with a wider selection than the **tavernas** to be found in every neighborhood. Truly authentic tavernas have wicker chairs that inevitably pinch your bottom, checkered tablecloths covered with butcher paper, wobbly tables that need coins under one leg, and wine drawn from the barrel and served in small metal carafes. If a place looks inviting and is filled with Greeks, give it a try. **Mezedopolia,** sometimes called **ouzeri,** serve plates of appetizers—basically Levantine tapas—to feast on while sipping ouzo, though many now serve barrel and bottled wine as well. **Greek fast-food** and **seafood** spots offer a change of pace.

What to Wear

As in most other cosmopolitan cities, dress varies from casual to fancy, according to the establishment. Although Athens is informal and none of the restaurants listed here require a jacket or tie, you'll feel more comfortable dressing up a bit in the most expensive places. Conservative casual attire (not shorts) is acceptable at most establishments.

Greek/Mediterranean (Contemporary)

$$$　✕ **Azul.** In this jewel of a restaurant, the room may be cramped but the food is heavenly. Start with mushrooms stuffed with nuts and *anthotiro* (soft, mild white cheese made from goat and sheep milk), or salmon and trout wrapped in pastry with champagne sauce. The spaghetti à la *nona* (godmother) with chamomile, Gorgonzola, and bacon is an unparalleled combination. Other memorable main dishes are beef fillet with raisins and cedar needles, and chicken prepared with lemon leaves. In summer, Azul sets up tables outside in the pedestrian walkway, the location for several popular bars. ⊠ *Haritos 43, Kolonaki,* ☎ *01/725–3817. Reservations essential. AE, DC, MC, V. Closed last 2 wks. in Aug. and Sun. in winter. No lunch..*

$$–$$$　✕ **Kouzina Cine-Psirri.** Once a dilapidated wood factory, this chic dining space features lots of stone, golden wood, cement touches, and a partial glass floor revealing the wine cellar. The best place to be is the roof terrace with its view of the illuminated Acropolis and the nearby observatory. The talented chef comes up with creative, even, at times, provocative, Greek cuisine. Try the appetizer of crab with smoked eggplant puree and fennel root, or fish soup accompanied by grilled skate, then move on to such entrées as boar with watermelon chutney or grilled rooster breast with kumquats. There isn't a large selection of noted wines, but the restaurant bottles many vintages from local producers; thus, prices are quite reasonable. After dinner, catch a summer movie at the outdoor Cine Psirri or a winter play at Apothiki theater next door. ⊠ *Sarri 40, Psirri,* ☎ *01/321–5534 or 01/321–2476. Reservations essential. MC, V. Closed Mon.*

$$　✕ **Stous 7 Anemous.** A peculiar ridged ceiling, tiled wooden tables, and seven antique fans for which the restaurant is named ("anemous" means wind): the decor is beautiful but not exactly unified, a bit of

postmodern pastiche in Monastiraki. Never mind—the playful food with intense flavors is what's impressive here. Appetizers not to be missed are the fried Dodoni feta wrapped in a sesame-enhanced crust and served with fleshy marinated tomatoes and walnut sauce, and the tortillas filled with octopus. Main dishes might include lamb ribs with a refreshing kiwi chutney spiked with mint; moist pork fillet with a dense coffee–black currant sauce; grilled tuna with tomato, thyme, and chamomile; and salmon, monkfish, and shrimp poached in lettuce leaves and topped with lemon-chive sauce. End your meal with the almond pastry (*amigdaloto*) and a shot of *tsipouro*, a fiery ouzo-like liqueur. ⊠ *Astiggos 17 (from Ermou 121), Monastiraki,* ☎ *01/324–0386. Reservations essential. AE, DC, MC, V. Closed Aug.*

Greek/Mediterranean (Traditional)

Also *see* reviews under Mezedopolia and Tavernas, *below.*

$$ ✕ **Ideal.** The original Ideal burned down after almost 70 years, and its art deco protégé is in bright contrast, with comfy booths and tasteful decor. The oldest restaurant in the city center, it has a following for its large gamut of traditional Greek dishes cooked with unremitting reliability and its interesting daily specials, depending on what's good at the market. Best bets on the regular menu are the egg-lemon soup, leek croquettes, pork with celery, grilled Aivaliotika minced beef with sweet peppers and mustard sauce (from Anatolia), and the Smyrnaika *tsoutsoukakia* (spicy meat patties made with ouzo and cumin). Sweet wines, such as mavrodaphne, are available by the glass, making a smooth partner for the strawberry coupe. The service is fast but fastidious. ⊠ *Panepistimiou 46, Omonia,* ☎ *01/330–3000. Reservations essential. AE, DC, MC, V. Closed Sun.*

$$ ✕ **Tade Efi Anna.** Near the end of the Ermou pedestrian zone, this relaxed yet trendy restaurant, complete with a "chill-out" room for waiting diners, serves Greek regional cuisine with a modern touch. Look for the narrow doorway—easy to miss—and proceed upstairs. Try what is perhaps the best *pita Kaisarias* in Athens, spicy, cured meat called pastourmas with tomato and Kasseri cheese in a crisp phyllo, or *melitzanes amigdalou,* thinly sliced eggplant layered with tomatoes and cheese with a thick topping of crushed almonds. The rabbit is cooked with cinnamony prunes, nicely contrasted with fresh spinach, and the chicken fillet is first wrapped around Gruyère, then baked in a crust of Aigina pistachios. ⊠ *Ermou 72, Monastiraki,* ☎ *01/321–3652. V. Closed Mon. and June–Aug.*

International

$$$$ ✕ **Vardis.** Compared to Taillevent in Paris, this grand restaurant is worth
★ the ride to the northern elegant suburb of Kifissia. The award-winning chef, perfectionist Jean de Grylleau, executes both classic and modern French dishes with finesse. He demands quality ingredients, transporting sweetwater crayfish from Orhomenos and rare large shrimp from Thassos island. Many of the dishes on the four seasonal menus have a Mediterranean touch, for example eschewing cream for olive oil. Starters might include pigeon cassoulet with foie gras in fig juice, octopus (boiled in milk) with hazelnut sauce, or langoustines en croute. Especially good are the superb crayfish linguine, caramelized lamb cutlets with morel and porcini mushrooms, rock perch à l'étouffée, and salt-crusted duck filled with foie gras and served with a fragrant sherry sauce. Few can say *"non"* to the desserts, which include an irresistible Grand Marnier-and-forest-berries soufflé. In summer, diners eat outside in the hotel garden. ⊠ *Diligianni 66 in Pentelikon Hotel, Kefalari,*

Kifissia, ☎ *01/623–0650 through 01/623–0656. Reservations essential. AE, DC, MC, V. Closed Sun. and Aug. No lunch.*

$$$–$$$$ ✕ **Kiku.** For those in need of a sushi fix, this has become an Athenian favorite despite hefty prices. Besides flawless sushi and sashimi, which often utilize local catch like bonito, dorado, sea bass, and cuttlefish, the restaurant offers classics like perfectly fried vegetable and seafood tempura, dainty dumplings, *yaki soba* (shrimp with noodles), beef sukiyaki, and chicken teriyaki. For Japanese clients there is a separate menu written in Japanese that includes gems such as melt-in-your-mouth eggplant with miso flavored with sake and poppy seeds, pork fried in bread crumbs, and a memorable *oden moriawase* (fish-cake soup); ask the server for recommendations. ✉ *Dimokritou 12, Kolonaki,* ☎ *01/ 364–7033. Reservations essential in winter. AE, DC, MC, V. Closed Sun. and Aug. No lunch.*

$$$ ✕ **Boschetto.** Set in Evangelismos park, Boschetto pampers diners with
★   a soothing view, an expert maître d', and creative Italian nouvelle cuisine: you may even forget you're in the center of Athens. The specialty here is fresh pasta, such as shrimp cannelloni, green gnocchi with Gorgonzola sauce, or ravioli with duck livers and truffle zabaglione. Favorite entrées include sea bass with a potato crust, succulent rooster in Riesling, sweetbreads with al dente artichokes, and grilled wild buffalo steak with a sauce of coffee, figs, and mavrodaphne wine. End your meal with the *crema cotta,* a baked vanilla custard with caramelized sauce, followed by the finest espresso in Athens (cigars available). The tables tend to be close together; reserve near the window or in the courtyard during summer. ✉ *Alsos Evangelismos, near the Hilton,* ☎ *01/ 721–0893 or 01/722–7324. Reservations essential. AE, V. Closed Sun. and 2 wks in Aug. No lunch Oct.–Aug.*

$$$ ✕ **Edodi.** For years Bajazzo restaurant reigned as the best restaurant in Athens, and when legendary chef Klaus Feuerbach died in 1999, the city mourned, for it was he who introduced Athenians to haute cuisine. Now, two of his closest associates (the maître d' and the sous-chef for 15 years) have opened a tiny dining room with fewer than 10 tables in a neoclassical house that evokes the gastronomic grandeur that was Bajazzo (with the bonus of lower prices). Ingredients are still brought theatrically to the table on the same plate service, and some dishes remain true to the original Feuerbach creations. The tart with feta, tomato, eggplant, and prosciutto and the swordfish in a crust of potatoes in mustard sauce are as good as ever. Other noteworthy dishes include lobster with spinach and spicy Parmesan sauce, Chinese noodles with smoked fish in an aromatic saffron-mastic sauce, and leg of lamb stuffed with herbs and raki (similar to ouzo) sauce. Marinated fruit dominates the dessert list: plums stewed in wine and cinnamon, mangos steeped in rum and served with caramel ice cream. ✉ *Veikou 80, Koukakki,* ☎ *01/921–3013. Reservations essential. AE, DC, MC, V. Closed Sun. and 2 wks in Aug. No lunch.*

$$$ ✕ **Royal Thai.** Silk-clad waitresses will settle you comfortably amid the Thai antiques, gilded dishes, and soothing decor of the restaurant that successfully brought the tantalizing flavors of a relatively unknown cuisine to Athens. The knowledgeable staff can explain dishes to the uninitiated, but you won't go wrong if you concentrate on appetizers, the restaurant's forte. Near flawless tidbits include the blue dumplings stuffed with aromatic minced chicken and topped with toasted garlic; *yawalat* pork spare ribs slow-cooked in a sour plum, chili, and soy sauce; fish cooked in banana leaf and served with coriander sauce;and *tom kha gai* soup, a delicate chicken broth with nuances of coconut milk. If you're ordering a main dish, opt for thinly sliced beef with green curry, first deceptively mild, then deliciously hot. ✉ *Zirini 12, Kifissia,* ☎

01/623–2322 or 01/623–2323. Reservations essential Fri.–Sat. AE, DC, MC, V. No lunch except Sun. in winter.

$$$ ✕ **Spondi.** This vaulted stone-interior restaurant used to suggest a me-
★ dieval wine cellar, but now after its renovation, the ambience is as cool and contemporary as the cuisine. Perfectly balanced are the artichoke terrine with duck confit or black ravioli with honeyed leek and shrimp. Savor such entrées as grilled John Dory with a spirited orange and mus-tard sauce; lamb tail so tender it falls from the bone, with couscous, raisins, and cumin; lobster *pappardelle* (butterfly-shaped pasta); and chicken with foie gras, truffles, and asparagus in porcini sauce. For dessert: bitter chocolate soufflé or mille-feuille with fresh figs and sauce made of Visanto sweet wine. After dinner, there is a choice of cigars to accompany your cognac, port, or whiskey. When weather per-mits, diners sit in the bougainvillea-draped courtyard. ✉ *Pirronos 5, Varnava Sq., Pangrati,* ☎ *01/752–0658,* ☎ ℻ *01/756–4021. Reser-vations essential. AE, DC, MC, V. No lunch.*

$$$ ✕ **White Elephant.** Except for the leopard-print chairs, there's nothing exotic about the discreet decor at this restaurant, but it serves the best Pan-Asian cuisine in the city, mostly Polynesian with some continen-tal Asian dishes. This is the one place to embrace that old standby, spring rolls, because here they are perfectly crunchy and perfumed with five spices; the more adventurous might try Thai ribs or delectable quail salad. Appealing entrées include the marinated salmon framed by sautéed spinach and cream shot with ginger; crispy duck served with wafer-thin pancakes; and—the hands-down winner—juicy sweet-and-sour chicken with macadamia nuts and plum sauce. ✉ *Timoleondos Vassou 22 in Andromeda Athens hotel, near U.S. Embassy,* ☎ *01/643–7302 through 01/643–7304. Reservations essential. AE, DC, MC, V. Closed Sun.*

$$–$$$ ✕ **Aristera-Dexia.** Chef Chrisanthos Karalomengos enjoyed such a
★ stellar reputation with the now-defunct Vitrina that his latest creation was an instant success. His "fusion" cuisine combines Japanese with Italian cuisine, French with Thai. Though located in an unglamorous neighborhood, the restaurant conveys an authoritarian sense of style. Two large partitions suspended from the ceiling divide the 900-square-meter dining room (hence the name, "Left-Right"). A glass runway af-fords a peek at the cellar beneath, housing one of the city's most extensive wine collections, and diners exit through an art gallery. They can also sit at the counter running along the open kitchen. Dishes change all the time. Popular selections are the pheasant sausage with parsnips in madera sauce; a tower of *haloumi* (Cypriot cheese) and feta croquettes in a melon-mirin-chili sauce; sardine tempura with black sesame seeds and a vinaigrette with port and dried figs; pork tenderloin with apri-cot, Gewürztraminer, ginger, and *bukova* (red pepper); smoked quail in a nest of wild black mushrooms with whisky-lime vinaigrette; and the Greek version of sushi, raw squid on a puree of eggplant with hints of anchovy and trout roe. For the insatiable, dessert includes an airy mille-feuille of mascarpone and Ricard-lemon sauce or champagne mousse with strawberries and green peppers. In summer, diners feast in the courtyard. Ah, bliss! ✉ *Andronikou 3, Rouf,* ☎ *01/342–2380. Reservations essential. AE, MC, V. Closed Sun. No lunch.*

$$ ✕ **Il Tinello.** Walking into this Italian trattoria is like dropping in on a dinner party: a boisterous atmosphere, convivial guests, and a host who tells jokes as he strolls from table to table, taking orders, humming along to the canzione, and occasionally asking a guest to dance. Scrumptious dishes include roasted goat cheese with anchovy sauce and parsley; in-tense risotto with garlic, Parmesan, and porcini mushrooms; and plate-brimming servings of rustic pastas such as ravioli with chamomile or fettuccine with almonds and chicken. Top it all off with homemade tiramisu. ⊠ *Knossou 54, Alimos,* ☎ *01/982–8462. Reservations essential. No credit cards. Closed Sun.–Mon. and mid-July through Aug. No lunch.*

Mezedopolia

$$–$$$ ✕ **Kaldera.** Dedicated to specialties not found at most tavernas, this restaurant brings back fond memories to those who love the Greek islands. Amid the blue-and-white Cycladic decor, diners can indulge in such delights as *soupies krasates* from Smyrna—cuttlefish with pine nuts and raisins; *gavros* (fresh anchovy) marinated in vinegar as it's done in Salamina; a salad of sun-dried mackerel from Chios; and steaming hot mussels in mustard sauce from Skopelos. Non-seafood appetizers include a tangy, bright orange cheese dip from Mykonos, *skordalia* (but here the garlic-mashed potatoes are made with walnuts), squash croquettes sparked with mint from Ermioni, and *saganaki* (fried cheese pastries), in this case with pastourmas and phyllo. If you can manage an entrée, try the *makaronada thalassina* (al dente pasta with crab, shrimp, and mussels) or any of the fresh catch, such as sargus, sole, sea bream, orKaldera's specialty, monkfish. ⊠ *Leoforos Poseidonos 54, Palio Faliro,* ☎ *01/982–9647 or 01/983–9636. Reservations essential weekends. AE, DC, MC, V. Closed a few days around Christmas, New Year's, and Greek Easter.*

$$ ✕ **Athinaikon.** This renowned establishment moved here after almost 60 years near the law courts, and it is still a favorite of attorneys and local office workers. The decor is no-nonsense ouzeri, with marble tables, dark wood, and framed memorabilia. Abide by the classic specialties: grilled octopus, shrimp croquettes, giant beans in a decadent tomato sauce, swordfish souvlaki with bay leaves and a light mustard sauce, and *ameletita* (sautéed lamb testicles). A favorite dish is *patsanga* (pastourmas wrapped in phyllo with cheese and tomato). All go well with the light barrel red. ⊠ *Themistokleous 2, Omonia,* ☎ *01/383–8485. No credit cards. Closed Sun. and Aug.*

$$ ✕ **Kafenio.** A Kolonaki institution, this ouzeri reminiscent of a French bistro is slightly fancier than the norm, with cloth napkins, candles on the tables, and a handsome dark wood interior. The menu is enormous, with many unusual creations. The tender marinated octopus, fried eggplant, stuffed squash in egg-lemon sauce, and the onion pie with fragrant dill are good choices. ⊠ *Loukianou 26, Kolonaki,* ☎ *01/722–9056. No credit cards. Closed Sun. and 3 wks in Aug.*

$$ ✕ **Ta Tria Tetarta.** There's something dollhouse-like about this tri-level stone-and-wood interior with nooks and crannies, decorated with eye-catching objects such as an old narghile. The mezedes served here include spicy feta sprinkled with red pepper and roasted in foil, cheese bread, skewered *seftalies* (a tasty mix of lamb liver bits and onions wrapped in suet), seafood pie, and spinach crepes with tomato, basil, and yogurt. ⊠ *Oikonomou 25, Exarchia,* ☎ *01/823–0560. Reservations essential. No credit cards. Closed mid-June–Aug. No lunch Mon.–Sat.*

$ ✕ **Monopolio Athinon.** Formerly a state-run monopoly that sold such goods as matches and petroleum, this has the feeling of a '50s *oinomageirio,* or "eating house." The emphasis is on regional Greek cuisine, with a few dishes from Asia Minor, Sicily, and Morocco. It is run by an actor and his mother, who turns out some of the best *pites* (pies) in the city. Try the traditional Cypriot *eliota,* its crisp, sesame-sprinkled pastry a deft contrast to the olive-onion filling, or the Cretan *souhli,* stuffed with meat, tomato, and kefalograviera cheese. Skip the osso buco and opt for the tsoutsoukakia Smyrnaikia, spicy patties with a dash of cumin and filled with olives, or "Aggeliki's tigania," bites of pork with mustard and *throubi,* a Sifnos herb resembling oregano. ✉ *Ippothontidon 10 at Keiriadon, Kato Petralona,* ☎ *01/345–9172. No credit cards. Closed Mon. and July–Aug.*

$ ✕ **Zeidoron.** This usually crowded Psirri hangout has decent mezedes, but the real draw is its strategic location, with metal tables lining the main pedestrian walkway, great for watching all the world go by or for enjoying the neighborhood's illuminated churches and alleys. Appetizers include hot feta sprinkled with red pepper, grilled green peppers stuffed with cheese, crisp meatballs, pork in mustard and wine, eggplant baked with tomato and pearl onions, and shrimp with ouzo. The wines are overpriced; opt for ouzo instead. ✉ *Taki 10 at Ayion Anargiron, Psirri Sq.,* ☎ *01/321–5368. No credit cards. Closed Aug.*

Seafood

$$$–$$$$ ✕ **To Varoulko.** Acclaimed chef Lefteris Lazarou is constantly trying
★ to outdo himself, with magnificent results. Rather than sticking to the menu, it's often best to give him a general idea of what you like and let him select your dish, depending on what he found that day at the market. Customers reserve days in advance, hoping to sample such appetizers as crab salad studded with mango and grapes, with bits of leek to cut the sweetness; fresh mullet roe from Messolonghi laced with honey and accompanied by cinnamony cauliflower puree; sea urchin risotto; and carpaccio made from *petrobarbouno* (a kind of rockfish). Although the restaurant is famous for its creative presentations of monkfish, there is a mind-boggling array of other seafood dishes: red mullet marinated in lemon and swirled with fuchsia-colored beet cream; cockles steamed in Limnos sweet wine; and lobster with wild rice, celery, and champagne sauce. For dessert, try the carrot-filled *kaïdaifi* (a pastry with shredded wheat). In summer, the chef moves to a seaside location. ✉ *Deligeorgi 14, Piraeus,* ☎ *01/411–2043 or 01/411–1283. Reservations essential. AE, DC, V. Closed Sun. No lunch.*

$$–$$$ ✕ **Kollias.** This restaurant's terrace, with pots of geranium and jasmine,
★ evokes the Athens of the '60s. Friendly owner Tassos Kollias creates his own dishes that range from the humble to the aristocratic, from fried whole squid in its ink or cuttlefish stew with broccoli and cream to sea urchin salad and lobster with lemon, balsamic vinegar, and a shot of honey. He is also known for bringing in the best quality catch, whether oysters culled by sponge divers from Kalymnos or mullet from Messolonghi, and his prices are usually 25% lower than most fish tavernas. Order the grilled scorpion fish flavored with mastic; the flambéed mackerel; or mussels stuffed with rice, grapes, and pine nuts. Besides piping-hot tomato and other vegetable croquettes, there are large mixed salads with white beets, arugula, lettuce, parsley, caper leaves, endive, and radishes. A fitting end to such a meal: fresh loukoumades or *bougatsa* (custard in phyllo). Ask for directions when you call—even locals get lost trying to find this obscure street in a working-class quarter of Piraeus. ✉ *Stratigou Plastira 3, near junction of Dramas and Kalokairinou, Tabouria,* ☎ *01/462–9620 or 01/461–9150. Reservations essential weekends. AE, DC, MC, V. Closed Sun. nights and Aug. No lunch Mon.–Sat.*

$$ ✕ **Trata O Stelios.** Hidden at the back of the lively main square in Kaisariani, a suburb 10 minutes' drive from the city center, this casual fish taverna consistently offers masterfully grilled fish. The owner works directly with fishermen, so you're guaranteed the freshest catch (if he has to resort to fish farms, he'll let you know). The only time to avoid Stelios (as the locals know it) is Sunday lunch, when it's dauntingly packed with Athenian families after 2 PM. Even those who scrunch up their nose at fish soup will be converted by the dense yet delicate

82

kakkavia. Other good appetizers include the homemade taramosalata, grilled octopus, and marinated beet salad. As for the fish, just point to your preference (prices, as always, are by weight), and it will arrive soon after in the way Greeks hope for and insist upon: grilled with exactitude, coated in the thinnest layer of olive oil to seal in juices, and accompanied by lots of lemon. ⊠ *Anagenniseos Sq. 7–9, off Ethnikis Antistaseos st., Kaisariani,* ☎ *01/729–1533. No credit cards. Closed 10 days at Greek Easter.*

$ ✕ **Margaro.** If you are in Piraeus and want to forego the tourists and undeservedly expensive fish places on Mikrolimano, consider this popular, no-nonsense fish taverna in the nearby neighborhood of Hatzyikyriakeio. Opened in the 1930s by a Mykonos islander hoping to improve her luck in Athens, it is still run by her two grandsons. There is no menu, since the establishment serves just five items, along with excellent barrel wine: fried crayfish, fried red mullet, fried pandora, fried *marida* (a small white fish), and huge Greek salads—which you may be asked to prepare yourself when the staff is overwhelmed by a hungry rush-hour crowd. Tables on the terrace offer a view of the busy port. Try to arrive before 8:30 PM. ⊠ *Hatzikyriakou 126, Piraeus,* ☎ *01/451–4226. Reservations are not accepted. No credit cards. Closed 15 days at Greek Easter. No Sun. dinner.*

Tavernas

$$ ✕ **Kostoyiannis.** If you're looking for authenticity, this is the place to go, liveliest late at night after the theatergoers arrive. One of the oldest and most popular tavernas in the area, it has an impressively wide range of Greek dishes—including shrimp salads, stuffed mussels, rabbit *stifado* (a stew of meat, white wine, garlic, cinnamon, and spices), and sautéed sweetbreads. ⊠ *Zaimi 37, Pedion Areos, behind the Archaeological Museum,* ☎ *01/821–2496 or 01/822–0624. No credit cards. Closed Sun. and last wk of July through 3rd wk of Aug. No lunch.*

$$ ✕ **Strofi.** Just a few blocks from the Odeon of Herodes Atticus, this taverna draws theatergoers for its congenial service and dramatic roof garden views of the illuminated Acropolis. Inside the old two-story house, signed glossy photos indicate the many performers who have dined here after a show at the ancient theater. Despite the many tourists, Strofi continues to attract locals who have been coming here for decades. The tzatziki, with its ground cucumber, abundant garlic, and velvety yogurt, goes well with the perfectly fried, thinly sliced zucchini, or the village bread. Another good appetizer is *fava*, a puree of yellow split peas. Reliable entrées include roast lamb with homemade noodles called *hilopites*, rabbit stifado, veal with eggplant, kid prepared with oil and oregano, and rooster stewed in red wine. ⊠ *Rovertou Galli 25, Makriyianni,* ☎ *01/921–4130 or 01/922–3787. DC, MC, V. Closed Sun. No lunch.*

$$ ✕ **Taverna Xynos.** Stepping into the courtyard of this Plaka taverna is like entering a time warp: Athens in the '50s. According to loyal customers, nothing has changed much since then, including the consistently good *magirefta*, stove-top or oven-cooked dishes, usually made earlier. Start with the classic appetizer of stuffed grape leaves, and then move on to the taverna's strong suit—cooked dishes such as lamb *youvetsi* (meat baked in ceramic dishes with tomato sauce and barley-shaped pasta), livers with sweetbreads in vinegar and oregano, and piquant tsoutsoukakia laced with cinnamon. This is one place where you could actually order the moussaka and not be disappointed. In summer, tables move outside; nightly, a guitar duo drops by to charm the crowd with ballads of yesteryear. ⊠ *Aggelou Geronda 4, Plaka (entrance down the walkway next to Glikis kafenion),* ☎ *01/322–1065. No credit cards. Closed weekends and July. No lunch.*

$$ ✕ **Vlassis.** Relying on traditional recipes from Thrace, Roumeli, Thes-
★ saly, and the islands, the cooks here whip up Greek home cooking in
generous portions. The best way to sample as much as possible is to
order several appetizers for a meal (there are more than 20, all rea-
sonably priced). Essentials include the peppery cheese dip called *tirokaf-
teri*, *lahanodolmades* (cabbage rolls), *pastitsio* (baked minced meat and
pasta made here with tiny bits of lamb liver), and the octopus stifado,
tender and sweet with lots of onions. Also good are the kebabs, sef-
talies, oven-baked lamb, and *katsiki ladorigani* (goat with oil and
oregano). Fresh fish is also available and sensibly priced. For dessert,
order the *halva*, a semolina pudding, or the huge slice of delicious *galak-
tobouriko* (custard in phyllo). ⊠ *Paster 8, Mavili Sq. (near U.S. Em-
bassy)*, ☎ *01/646–3060. Reservations essential. No credit cards. Closed
Aug.–mid-Sept. No Sun. dinner.*

$–$$ ✕ **I Palia Taverna tou Psarra.** Founded in 1898, this Plaka favorite reopened after a brief hiatus, with new decor but the same satisfying food
and ideal setting on a mulberry-shaded staircase (bonus: the new waiters are much friendlier than the last batch). The owners claim to have
served such luminaries as Brigitte Bardot and Laurence Olivier, but it's
the number of Greeks who continue to come here that testifies to
Psarra's appeal. The numerous appetizers range from seafood such as
oil-oregano octopus or marinated gavros to heartier inland fare. Entrées include magirefta, such as rooster in wine and *arnaki pilino* (lamb
baked in clay pots), and grilled meats such as pepper fillet and pork
chops with ouzo. If you're hankering after fish, this is probably the
best place in Plaka to get the catch of the day, as well as grilled swordfish, salmon, and shrimp. For those who just can't choose, there's always the *ouzo katastasi* (or, "ouzo situation"), a plate of tidbits to tide
you over until you make up your mind. ⊠ *Erechtheos 16 at Erotokritou
12, Plaka*, ☎ *01/321–8733. AE, MC, V.*

$ ✕ **Karavitis.** In this neighborhood favorite near the Panathenaic Sta-
★ dium, the winter dining room is insulated with huge wine casks, and
in summer there is garden seating in a courtyard across the street (get
there early so you don't end up at the noisy sidewalk tables). The classic Greek cuisine is well prepared, including pungent tzatziki, excellent with lightly fried zucchini slices; *bekri meze* (lamb chunks in zesty
red sauce); lamb ribs (when in season); and *stamnaki* (beef baked in a
clay pot). ⊠ *Arktinou 35 at Pausaniou 4, Pangrati*, ☎ *01/721–5155.
No credit cards. Closed a few days around Aug. 15. No lunch.*

$ ✕ **O Platanos.** Set on a picturesque corner, this is one of the oldest tav-
★ ernas in Plaka, a welcome sight compared with the many overpriced
tourist traps in the area. Tourism hasn't seemed to affect this place at
all, other than the now-multilingual menus rife with amusing spelling.
The waiters are fast but far from ingratiating, and the place is packed
with Greeks. The shady courtyard is fine for outdoor dining. Don't miss
the oven-baked potatoes, roasted lamb, fresh green beans in savory olive
oil, and the exceptionally cheap but delicious barrel retsina. To get here,
from Adrianou heading toward Ermou, turn left on Mnissikleous and
right on Diogenous, or enter Diogenous from the Tower of the Winds.
⊠ *Diogenous 4, Plaka*. ☎ *01/322–0666. No credit cards. Closed Sun.*

$ ✕ **Sigalas–Bairaktaris.** Run by the same family for more than a cen-
tury, this is one of the best places to eat in Monastiraki Square. After
admiring the painted wine barrels and black-and-white stills of Greek
film stars, go to the window case to view the day's magirefta—beef
kokkinisto (stew with red sauce), tsoutsoukakia spiked with cloves—
or sample the gyro platter. Appetizers include small cheese pies with
sesame seeds, tender mountain greens, and fried zucchini with a gar-
licky dip. ⊠ *Platia Monastiraki 2*, ☎ *01/321–3036. AE, MC, V.*

$ ✕ **Skoufias.** Bare stone, white oil paint, and rustic touches such as a mirror framed with bits of wood belie the ultramodern approach of this taverna, located in the increasingly popular neighborhood Ano Petralona, north of the Acropolis. Exceptional entrées to try are the *makaronada tis magirissas* (cook's pasta), enhanced with cream, bacon, cauliflower, broccoli, pomegranate, and dried fruits; the baked honeyed pig tails served with sauerkraut; and a lively *hungiar begendi*, kebab balanced with mint-spiked tzatziki and smoky eggplant puree with just a hint of vinegar (good with the Katogi Averof red from the small wine list). At press time, the owners were opening a seafood restaurant by the same name in the Rouf area. ✉ *Troon 63, Ano Petralona,* ☎ *01/ 341–1488. No credit cards. No lunch. Closed Sun. and 1 wk in Aug.*

$ ✕ **Vassilenas.** Longtime residents and frequent visitors rejoice in this precious vestige of the good old days, a family-run taverna that is probably as good a bargain now as it was 70 years ago, when it operated as a grocery store during the day and a diner at night. The decor is minimal; in warm weather the operation moves to the upper terrace. Come here ravenously hungry with friends, so you can do justice to the set menu of 16 dishes (5,500 dr./€16.17 per person), brought in a steady stream to your table. Zesty shrimp saganaki and fried monkfish or red mullet are two standouts, as is the dessert called *diples* (a deep-fried pastry served with walnuts and honey syrup). ✉ *Etolikou 72 and Vitolion, Ayia Sofia, Piraeus,* ☎ *01/461–2457. No credit cards. Closed Sun. and 3 wks in Aug. No lunch.*

Fast Food

The souvlaki joints in Monastiraki (☞ Exploring Athens, *above*) provide a satisfying and cheap snack. The souvlaki chain **Loxandra** (✉ Ermou 2, Syntagma Sq., ☎ 01/331–2212) has branches throughout the city, including one near the National Archaeological Museum (✉ 28 Oktovriou [Patission] 43, ☎ 01/522–4296). Especially good are the chicken Loxandra, a roasted breast served in a homemade pita, and the pita Loxandra with spicy seftalies. Night owls looking for a snack will probably find something to their liking at **Everest** (✉ Syntagma Sq. between Ermou and Karageorgi Servias, ☎ 01/331–2100; ✉ Tsakalof 14, Kolonaki, ☎ 01/361–3477; ✉ Omonia Sq. 18, ☎ 01/ 324–2329), with a wide menu, including various pites with meat, spinach, and cheese fillings; pastries; and *tost,* grilled sandwiches you stuff with as many ingredients as you can handle. Order first, and then pay, bringing your receipt to pick up the food.

More upscale though still self-service is the **Flocafe Espresso Bar** chain, which has baguette and croissant sandwiches for the health-conscious, salads, sinful pastries, and a variety of coffees; branches are scattered around the city, including one across the street from the National Archaeological Museum (✉ 28 Oktovriou [Patission] 39, ☎ 01/522–6818) and another off Syntagma (✉ Stadiou 5, ☎ 01/324–3028).

Neon (✉ Omonia Sq. and Dorou, ☎ 01/522–3201), a remodeled cafeteria in a landmark 1920s building that's open until at least 2 AM, was so popular that other branches immediately appeared at Tsakalof 6, Kolonaki; Mitropoleos 3, Syntagma Square; and G. Lambrakis 156, Zea Marina. The vast selection ranges from salad-bar fare, pasta, and meat dishes to sandwiches, ice cream, and other desserts, and prices are moderate.

If you *must* placate the children in American terms, there are local **McDonald's, Wendy's, Kentucky Fried Chicken,** and **Pizza Huts,** as well as **Goody's,** a Greek chain that serves good, inexpensive burgers.

LODGING

Athens has true luxury hotels and many in the budget range, but a shortage of middle-rank family-style hotels. The Greek word for hotel is *xenodochion,* meaning container for strangers, and occasionally, this is all they are: adequate for a rest and a wash, but not to spend a great deal of time in. The Greeks are an outdoor people and they rarely spend much time at home, let alone in an hotel. Staying in the northern suburb of Kifissia or along the coast is a good way to beat the heat and smog of the city center in summer, although the extra traveling time may be a deterrent.

Greek hotels are classified as De Luxe (L) and A–E, though the government, which awards the ratings (and therefore determines the official price), has announced it will switch to a star system to encourage hotels to upgrade. Within each category quality varies greatly, but prices usually don't. Still, you may come across an A-class hotel that charges less than a B-class, depending on facilities. Paradoxically, you may get up to a 20% discount if you book the hotel through a local travel agent; it's also a good idea to bargain over the rack rates in person at smaller hotels, especially off-season. Some of the older hotels in Plaka and near Omonia are comfortable and clean, their charm inherent in their age. But along with charm may come leaking plumbing and sagging mattresses—take a good look at the room. The thick stone walls of neoclassical buildings keep them cool in the summer, but few of the budget hotels have central heating, and it can be devilishly cold in the winter, especially in the $$ and $$$ categories; also, don't assume all rooms have TVs. All hotels in the $$$ and $$$$ categories have air-conditioning; those in the lower-price categories that have air-conditioning are indicated. A buffet breakfast is often served, which includes cold cuts and cheese, even poached eggs and other meat, but nothing cooked to order. The cost is not included unless noted.

CATEGORY	COST*
$$$$	over 55,000 dr. (€161.76)
$$$	35,000 dr.–55,000 dr. (€102.94–€161.76)
$$	19,000 dr.–35,000 dr. (€55.88–€102.94)
$	under 19,000 dr. (€55.88)

All prices are the official rates for a standard double room, including tax and service, in high season.

☜ following the text of a review is your signal that the property has a Web site, where you will find details and, usually, images; for a link, visit www.fodors.com/urls.

Athens

$$$$ 🏠 **Andromeda Athens Hotel.** Set on a quiet street near the U.S. Embassy and the city's concert hall, this small luxury hotel caters to business travelers, but all guests will relish the meticulous service and sumptuous decor of Persian carpets, Italian pastels, and designer furniture. The spacious rooms have a salmon color scheme with quilted headboards, wall-to-wall carpeting, double-glazed windows, and an ISDN digital connection, for those who need to be plugged in. The hotel also operates a property across the street with security system and 12 executive suites (one- and two-room apartments), which include fully equipped kitchenettes. The White Elephant restaurant features excellent Polynesian cuisine. ✉ *Timoleondos Vassou 22, Platia Mavili, 11521,* ☎ *01/643–7302 through 01/643–7304,* 🖷 *01/646–6361. 30 rooms, 5 suites, 4 penthouses. Restaurant. AE, DC, MC, V.* ☜

$$$$ 🏨 **Athenaeum Inter-Continental.** With its marble atrium lobby, central fountain, and private art collection, this hotel is a cool oasis on busy Syngrou Avenue, the main road from the center to the sea, ideal for those who insist on comfort over setting. The rooms are spacious, with sitting areas, marble bathrooms, and thick carpeting; ask for one with an Acropolis view. The hotel has long been in the process of renovating all its floors; at press time, only the fourth and fifth floor still needed work, and the hotel could almost pass for new. The Club section, on the eighth and ninth floors, includes private check-in, lounge with Acropolis view, and library; complimentary breakfast, coffee, and evening cocktails; and rooms with video, stereo, and CD players, trouser press, and safe. Twice each morning a shuttle takes guests to the airport, and then throughout the day to Syntagma Square, about 15 minutes away. ⊠ *89–93 Syngrou Ave., near Neos Kosmos, 11745,* ☎ *01/920–6000,* FAX *01/920–6500. 548 rooms, 59 suites. 2 restaurants, pool, health club. AE, DC, MC, V.* ✆

$$$$ 🏨 **Athens Hilton.** A 200-year-old olive tree with a Turkish cannonball lodged in its branches adds an earthy touch to the glamorous entrance, with its multilevel lobby of variegated marble and eye-catching collection of works by Greek artists. Opened in 1963, this is still one of the top hotels in the city, giving an impression of calm confidence amid the comings and goings of various conventions, banquets, and meetings. The rooms have a subdued color scheme and carpeting, double-glazed windows and thick curtains buffer the street noise, and the balconies face either the Acropolis or Mt. Hymettus. On the top floor, the Galaxy bar with its long terrace and Athens panorama is a wonderful place to recoup from a hard day of sightseeing; for livelier nightlife, there is a strip of popular bars behind the Hilton. Syntagma Square is about a 20-minute walk away with many museums en route, but a shuttle transports less energetic guests during the day. ⊠ *Vasilissis Sofias 46, 11528,* ☎ *01/728–1000; 01/728–1100 for reservations;* FAX *01/728–1111; 01/725–1919 for reservations. 454 rooms, 19 suites. 4 restaurants, pool, wading pool. AE, DC, MC, V.* ✆

$$$$ 🏨 **Grande Bretagne.** Built in 1842, the G. B. is an Athens landmark, and its guest list testifies to its colorful history, with such visitors as Edith Piaf, Jackie Kennedy, various royals, and rock stars. During World War II, the G. B. served, in turn, as the headquarters for the Greek, German, and British forces; when Churchill was visiting on Christmas Eve 1944, a plot to blow up the hotel from the sewers was foiled. Renovated in 1992, the hotel's marble lobby is graced with Oriental rugs, tapestries, and ornate chandeliers. The most coveted rooms are the Syntagma rooms, with Acropolis views and huge balconies. There are also "Smart" rooms, with desk, printer, fax, photocopier, and direct phone line with voice mail, and the third floor is no-smoking. ⊠ *Vasileos Georgiou A' 1, Syntagma Sq., 10564,* ☎ *01/333–0000; 01/331–5555 through 01/331–5559 for reservations;* FAX *01/322–8034; 01/322–2261 or 01/333–0910 for reservations. 364 rooms, 23 suites. Restaurant. AE, DC, MC, V.* ✆

$$$$ 🏨 **Holiday Inn.** Despite its location—about a 10-minute drive from Syntagma—this has become a favorite with businesspeople, especially after the hotel completed a two-year renovation in 1998, earning it several awards. The light, modern rooms now have voice mail, satellite TV, video, hair dryer, trouser press, fireproof doors, computer hookups dubbed "PC points," and express check-out. The Executive Rooms on the fifth and sixth floors also provide complimentary juice, coffee, and newspaper, private balcony, and twice-daily maid service. The rooftop health studio includes weight machines, a sauna, and various cardiovascular contraptions such as treadmill and stepper; massage is available. The rooftop pool sits alongside a snack bar, which operates as a full-fledged restaurant on summer evenings. ✉ *Mihalakopoulou 50, Ilisia, 11528,* ☎ *01/727–0000,* FAX *01/727–8600. 189 rooms, 3 suites. Restaurant, pool, massage, exercise room. AE, DC, MC, V.* ✎

$$$$ 🏨 **Ledra Marriott.** Just down the street from the Athenaeum Inter-Continental, the Ledra's main calling cards are its high-performance staff and its attractive decor. The lobby piano bar sits below a spectacular 1,000-crystal chandelier; Kona Kai, the Polynesian restaurant, is excellent; and the Zephyros Café has a bountiful Sunday brunch. The pastel rooms have vast closet space and armchairs, and some have views of the Acropolis. The fourth floor was renovated in 2000 to create executive lodgings with such amenities as separate check-in/out and an exclusive lounge. The health club now has all new Cybex machines, as well as sauna, and massage is available on request. Guests will have difficulty tearing themselves away from the pool, which boasts a view of the Acropolis that is breathtaking at sunset. Shuttles run daily to and from Syntagma Square. ✉ *Syngrou 115, near Neos Kosmos, 11745,* ☎ *01/930–0000,* FAX *01/935–8603. 259 rooms, 8 suites. 3 restaurants, 2 bars, pool. AE, DC, MC, V.* ✎

$$$$ 🏨 **N. J. V. Athens Plaza.** At an exclusive Syntagma Square address, this is a good alternative if the more historic Grande Bretagne next door is full. In 1998 the hotel was completely renovated by Grecotel, and now its "1913" lobby, named after the year Crete (the proprietors' island) united with Greece, is a cool mixture of light wood floors, white marble, spiky light fixtures, and burgundy and gray-green upholstery. The spacious rooms, again in gray and burgundy, come equipped with minibar, direct-dial phones with voice mail, satellite and pay TV, and large marble bathrooms with phone extensions and a dual voltage (220/110V) plug. Under the family plan, one child under 12 may stay with parents at no extra cost. Named after designers, the individually decorated suites on the sixth and ninth floors have sitting areas, inspiring Acropolis views, and interiors decked out with designer fabrics and furnishings. The Parliament restaurant specializes in Mediterranean cuisine, and the Explorers Bar is soothing, with dark wood and leather chairs. ✉ *Vasileos Georgiou A' 2, Syntagma Sq., 10564,* ☎ *01/335–2400,* FAX *01/323–5856. 182 rooms, 25 suites. Restaurant, bar. AE, DC, MC, V.* ✎

$$$$ 🏨 **St. George Lycabettus.** This hotel, in a great location on the wooded slopes of Mt. Lycabettus in upscale Kolonaki, has a splendid view. Getting there, however, involves a steep, short walk or a ride up (remember: taxis are inexpensive), though the hotel offers minibus service regularly until early afternoon. The modern, stylish rooms (those facing outward have balconies) and suites include the sumptuous Marie Christina presidential suite, inaugurated by Princess Michael of Kent. Business guests become members (no fee) of the Privilege Club, with such benefits as children up to 12 years staying free with parents, in-room voice-mail and fax service, guaranteed rooms, upgrades, and extended check-out to 3 PM. The hotel has a rooftop pool with a summer bar; the soothing Tony's Bar; and its trump card, Le Grand Balcon, a fine Mediterranean restaurant with an unbeatable panoramic view. Buffet breakfast is included in the price. ✉ *Kleomenous 2, Kolonaki, 10675,* ☎ *01/729–0711 through 01/729–0719,* FAX *01/729–0439 or 01/724–7610. 162 rooms, 5 suites. 2 restaurants, bar, pool. AE, DC, MC, V.* ✎

$$$ 🏨 **Electra Palace.** At the Plaka's edge, this hotel has cozy rooms done in warm hues, complete with cable TV and pay-per-view movies, plenty of storage space, and hair dryers—for comparatively low prices. Keep in mind that rooms from the fifth floor up are smaller but have larger balconies and Acropolis views. The staff is helpful, though a bit slow to answer the phone, the included buffet breakfast is one of the

city's best (sausage, pancakes, home fries), and best of all, you can spend hours by the rooftop pool, sipping a cool drink and gazing at the Parthenon. ⊠ *Nikodimou 18, Plaka, 10557,* ☎ *01/337–0000,* 𝖥𝖠𝖷 *01/ 324–1875. 106 rooms, 5 suites. Restaurant, pool. AE, DC, MC, V.*

$$$ ▥ **Herodion Hotel.** A good compromise between the area's budget venues and the one deluxe chain, this hospitable hotel is just down the street from the Odeon of Herodes Atticus, where Athens Festival performances are held, and just a few minutes from the Acropolis and Plaka. Renovated in 1999, the rooms have such amenities as mini-refrigerators and hair dryers, and the hotel has a roof terrace with a Parthenon panorama where guests can relax on deck chairs, a coffee shop serving light snacks, and a peaceful, tree-shaded courtyard. American buffet breakfast is included in the price. ⊠ *Rovertou Galli 4, Makriyiannis, 11742,* ☎ *01/923–6832 through 01/923–6836,* 𝖥𝖠𝖷 *01/923–5851. 86 rooms, 4 suites. Restaurant, bar, coffee shop. DC, MC, V.* ✧

$$ ▥ **Acropolis View.** Major sights are just a stone's throw away from this hotel tucked into a quiet neighborhood below the Acropolis. About half of the agreeable, air-conditioned rooms with balconies have Parthenon views. There is a roof garden, staff members in the homey lobby are efficient, and buffet breakfast is included in the price. ⊠ *Webster 10, Acropolis, 11742,* ☎ *01/921–7303 through 01/921–7305,* 𝖥𝖠𝖷 *01/923–0705. 32 rooms. Air-conditioning. DC, MC, V.*

$$ ▥ **Athens Cypria Hotel.** A little-known gem in the city center, this hotel, which opened in summer 1999, is a few minutes from Syntagma square, offering a reasonably priced alternative for those who want convenience and comfort. Enter the faintly art deco–style lobby from the quiet street, and the staff will take care of you from there. The air-conditioned rooms are simple and clean, done in shades of blue, and furnished with satellite TV and standard amenities such as hair dryer, minibar, and safe box. Some on the upper floors open out onto a balcony; those on the sixth floor have Acropolis views. American buffet breakfast is included in the price. ⊠ *Diomias 5, Syntagma, 10557,* ☎ *01/323–8034 through 01/323–8038,* 𝖥𝖠𝖷 *01/324–8792. 71 rooms. Bar, air-conditioning, minibars. AE, V.*

$$ ▥ **Austria.** This small, unpretentious hotel is at the foot of Filopappou Hill, ideal as a base for wandering around the heart of ancient Athens (the owners say it is 462 steps, or seven minutes, to the Acropolis). The peaceful neighborhood is home to such artists as composer Mikis Theodorakis and filmmaker Michael Cacoyiannis, and there is a lovely Parthenon view from the hotel's roof terrace. All rooms have air-conditioning, TV, balcony, and a jack for computer hookup. Continental breakfast is included in the price. ⊠ *Mouson 7, Filopappou, 11742,* ☎ *01/923–5151 or 01/922–0777,* 𝖥𝖠𝖷 *01/924–7350. 37 rooms. Air-conditioning. AE, DC, MC, V.*

$$ ▥ **Hotel Achilleas.** This modern, family-owned hotel is just a few minutes from the central Syntagma district but priced at the low end of its category. It has plain but spacious rooms with TV, direct-dial phone, minibar, safe, and air-conditioning. On the top floor, two rooms share a bath, convenient for larger parties. Breakfast, including fruit and corn flakes, is served in an interior courtyard filled with jungly plants and cheerful marble-topped blue tables. ⊠ *Lekka 21, Syntagma, 10562,* ☎ *01/322–5826, 01/322–8531, or 01/323–3197,* 𝖥𝖠𝖷 *01/322–2412. 36 rooms. Air-conditioning, minibars. AE, DC, MC, V.* ✧

$$ ▥ **Lycabette.** At the low end of its price category, especially if you don't take breakfast, this convenient hotel near Syntagma has a gregarious atmosphere and pleasant service, with the advantage of a location on one of Kolonaki's most popular pedestrian walkways lined with cafés. About 12 of the comfortable rooms have TV and all have air-conditioning; try to get a room (quieter and with balconies) overlooking the walkway rather than busy Akadimias street. The lobby is cheerful, and the optional Continental breakfast is served in a pretty breakfast room. ⊠ *Valaoritou 6, Syntagma, 10671,* ☎ *01/363–3514 through 01/363– 3517,* 𝖥𝖠𝖷 *01/363–3518. 39 rooms. Breakfast room, air-conditioning. AE, DC, MC, V.*

$$ ⛨ **Plaka Hotel.** Close to the ancient sights and the Monastiraki Square metro, this hotel has a roof garden overlooking the Plaka's neoclassical houses to the Parthenon. Double-glazed windows cut down on the noise; the highest floors are the quietest. All rooms, done in blue and white, have TV and are simply furnished; those in back from the fifth floor up have the best Acropolis views. ⊠ *Kapnikareas 7, Plaka, 10556,* ☎ *01/322–2096 through 01/322–2098,* 𝖥𝖠𝖷 *01/322–2412. 67 rooms. Air-conditioning. AE, DC, MC, V.*🏵

$–$$ ⛨ **Adams Hotel.** Favored by young people for its clean rooms and good value, this quiet hotel sits across from Ayia Aikaterini church in Plaka. Most of the rooms have balconies, and many, including all on the top floor, enjoy views of the Acropolis. The three rooms that don't have air-conditioning are cooled by ceiling fans. Travelers on a very tight budget might consider the four rooms that have their private bath outsidethe room (about 5,000 dr./€14.70 less). The owners, who also run the Meltemi Hotel in Paros, are helpful to first-time visitors to Athens. ⊠ *Herefondos 6, at Thalou, Plaka, 10558,* ☎ *01/322–5381 or 01/324– 6582,* 𝖥𝖠𝖷 *01/323–8553. 14 rooms. Air-conditioning (some). MC, V.*

$ ⛨ **Acropolis House.** Ensconced in a 19th-century Plaka residence, this landmark pension is frequented by artists and academics, who appreciate its large rooms, original frescoes, and genteel owners, the Choudalakis family. All rooms have private bathrooms, though about 10 have their bath immediately outside in the hallway. Most rooms have air-conditioning, and a full breakfast is included in the price. ⊠ *Kodrou 6–8, Plaka, 10558,* ☎ *01/322–2344 or 01/322–6241,* 𝖥𝖠𝖷 *01/ 324–4143. 20 rooms. V.*

$ ⛨ **Art Gallery Pension.** On a residential side street not far from the Acropolis, this handsome house has an old-fashioned look, with family paintings on the muted white walls, comfortable beds, hardwood floors, and ceiling fans. Many rooms have balconies with views of Filopappou hill or the Acropolis. A friendly place, much prized by visiting students and single travelers, the pension draws a congenial crowd. ⊠ *Erechthiou 5, Koukaki, 11742,* ☎ *01/923–8376 or 01/ 923–1933,* 𝖥𝖠𝖷 *01/923–3025. 21 rooms, 2 suites. No credit cards. Closed Nov.–Feb.*

$ ⛨ **Attalos Hotel.** Gentlemanly owner Kostas Zissis's personality is reflected in the friendly, helpful atmosphere of this central hotel, just a few minutes from the trendy Psirri district. It has a rooftop garden, and 12 rooms offer an exceptionally fine view of the Acropolis and Mt. Lycabettus; 37 rooms include balconies. All have direct-dial phone, satellite TV, hair dryers, and a safe. Try to get accommodations in the rear, where the street noise is less, though it's also reduced by double-glazed windows. ⊠ *Athinas 29, Monastiraki, 10554,* ☎ *01/321–2801 through 01/321–2803,* 𝖥𝖠𝖷 *01/324–3124. 80 rooms. Air-conditioning. AE, V.*🏵

$ ⛨ **Marble House.** This popular pension, on a cul-de-sac about a 15-minute walk from the Acropolis, has a steady, satisfied clientele—even in winter, when it offers low monthly and weekly rates. Rooms are clean and quiet, with ceiling fan, minibar, and wooden furniture; eight rooms have air-conditioning (2,000 dr./€5.88 more). The international staff is always willing to help out, there is a breakfast room, and the courtyard is a lovely place to relax. Take Trolley 1, 5, or 9 from Syntagma and get off at the Zinni stop. ⊠ *A. Zinni 35, Koukaki, 11741,* ☎ *01/ 923–4058 or 01/922–6461. 16 rooms, 11 with bath. Breakfast room, air-conditioning (some). No credit cards.*

$ ☷ **Orion and Dryades.** These two hotels in a residential area across from the park on craggy Lofos Strefis are often booked by local fashion agencies, who house their models here. Orion is the humbler and cheaper, with smaller rooms and shared baths for every two rooms; its third-floor roof garden serves as the breakfast area for both hotels (Continental breakfast is available for 1,500 dr./€4.41). Each hotel has a kitchen guests may use, and most rooms have balconies. For those who don't want to go far for dinner, the park has inexpensive ouzeris open in summer. ⊠ *Emmanuel Benaki 105, Lofos Strefi, 11473,* ☎ *01/382–7362, 01/330–2387, or 01/382–0191,* FAX *01/380–5193. Orion: 23 rooms share bath; Dryades: 15 rooms. V.*

$ ☷ **XEN (YWCA).** This centrally located budget choice for women (from 4,000 dr./€11.76 for a bed in a triple room with shared bath to 9,500 dr./€27.94 for a double with private bath) has rooms mostly with shared bathrooms. The marble floors have rugs in winter; sheets and blankets are provided. The rooms are not air-conditioned, but those at the back are cooler and quieter; all have fans. There is a TV lounge on the fourth floor, but it would be a shame to stay indoors evenings, when the neighborhood is full of cafés, theaters, and student hangouts. Overnight guests pay an additional membership fee of 600 dr./€1.76, good for a year. ⊠ *Amerikis 11, Syntagma, 10672,* ☎ *01/362–4291 through 01/362–4293,* FAX *01/362–2400. 26 rooms share bath, 4 with private bath. No credit cards.*

Athens Environs: Piraeus, Kifissia, Vougliagmeni

$$$$ ☷ **Astir Palace Vouliagmeni.** Sprawling across a pine-studded promontory 25 km (16 mi) south of downtown Athens, with a view of nearby islands, this 80-acre resort offers a haven from the city's heat and commotion—which is yours soon enough to enjoy, thanks to the hotel's shuttle bus which transports guests to the center in the mornings. From the moment you pass the guard gate on the cobblestone road, the soothing, seaside setting makes it difficult to think about going into town. Less expensive than the center's luxury-category establishments, the complex is actually made up of three hotels. Linger at the Arion's '60s-style bar or sip coffee in its huge lobby overlooking the sea. Take a dip at the Nausika's seaside pool and you might bump into a visiting dignitary outside your cabana. Or settle for the Aphrodite, the only building still to be renovated (scheduled for 2001), knowing that you'll have the best view for the lowest rate, because of its location at the end of the peninsula. A hefty buffet breakfast is included in the price (croissants, raisin rolls, hot plates such as eggs and roast tomatoes). ⊠ *Apollonos 40, Vouliagmeni 16671,* ☎ *01/890–2000,* FAX *01/896–2582 for reservations. 476 rooms, 73 bungalows, 32 suites. 5 restaurants, 4 pools, beach, water sports. AE, DC, MC, V.* ✆

$$$$ ☷ **Divani Apollon Palace.** Towering above the posh, residential area
★ of Kavouri, this seaside resort (which opened in summer 1999) offers a casual ambience but sophisticated service and sparkling facilities. Take a few laps in the indoor pool, dip into the Aegean across the street (idyllically lined with shady lawn and seafood tavernas here), or rent wind surf and water-ski equipment. You can also arrange to play a round of golf at the Glyfada links 3 km (2 mi) away, or take the hotel shuttle to Glyfada for some serious shopping (the shuttle continues to downtown Athens). The airy white-and-yellow rooms all have balconies with sea view, satellite/pay TV, direct dial phones with voice mail, hair dryer, and minibar. The suites even include fireplaces. Best though are the hotel's large, gleaming public spaces, from the Anemos dining room (where the breakfast buffet comes with a Saronic Gulf view) to the outdoor pool with hydromassage where you can enjoy cocktails.

Other amenities include shops, a beauty parlor, sauna, and business center. At press time, the hotel was planning to open a *thalasso* (water-based) therapy center. The hotel is 3 km (2 mi) from the airport's international terminal (which means you will notice the planes overhead when suntanning), and limo service is available. ⊠ *Ay. Nikolaou 10 at Iliou, Vouliagmeni, 16671,* ☎ *01/891–1100,* FAX *01/965–8010. 286 rooms, 7 suites. 2 restaurants, bar, 2 pools, wading pool, tennis court. AE, DC, MC, V.* ⊛

$$$–$$$$ ★ 🏨 **Kefalari Suites.** Escape Athens's commotion among the neoclassical mansions and tree-lined boulevards of Kifissia at this hotel with imaginatively themed rooms. Installed in a turn-of-the-20th-century building, the hotel offers suites at a range of prices lower than downtown deluxe lodging—for example, the Deck House (no need to go to sea), the chateau-inspired Malmaison, exotic Aqaba, and the romantic Daphnis and Chloe. Although the neighborhood is known for several fine restaurants, the suites include kitchenettes with utensils and refrigerators. Other amenities include minibars, satellite TV, queen-size beds, modem connection, and verandas or balconies; guests share the sundeck with whirlpool tub. Continental deluxe breakfast (cheese, cold cuts, cereal, yogurt, and cake) is included in the price. ⊠ *Pentelis 1 at Kolokotroni, Kefalari, Kifissia, 14562,* ☎ *01/623–3333,* FAX *01/623–3330. 13 suites. Kitchenettes, outdoor hot tub. AE, DC, MC, V.* ⊛

$$ 🏨 **Castella Hotel.** Perched on the hill above Piraeus's picturesque small harbor of Mikrolimano, just east of the main port, this is a fine choice if you have an early boat to catch. Rooms are fairly large; some have a sea view, as does the flower-filled roof garden that overlooks the small harbor and the yacht club. ⊠ *Vasileos Pavlos 75, Piraeus, 18533,* ☎ *01/411–4735,* FAX *01/417–5716. 32 rooms. Restaurant, air-conditioning. AE, DC, MC, V.*

NIGHTLIFE AND THE ARTS

The weekly magazines *DownTown* and *Athinorama* (both in Greek) cover current performances, gallery openings, and films, as do the English-language newspapers, *Athens News* (athensnews.dolnet.gr), published Tuesday through Sunday, and *Kathemerini,* inserted in the *International Herald Tribune,* available Monday through Saturday. The free magazine *Now in Athens* (www.monopoli.gr/english), distributed at various hotels and EOT (or Greek Tourism Organization, the main tourist board), offers extensive information on culture and entertainment in the capital.

Nightlife

Bars

Bars are the staple of Greek nightlife, with new establishments opening every week. In summer, many of the most popular spots, especially dance clubs, move to temporary venues along the coast (check with your hotel concierge on seasonal whereabouts of clubs). Frequented by the under-30 crowd, these clubs are usually huge, lively, and packed, featuring either Greek or foreign dance hits, but getting to them can be a nightmare, especially on weekends, when the coastal road, Poseidonos, becomes a kilometers-long traffic jam. Parking requires creative maneuvers, and given the penchant for drinking and driving, pedestrians should be extremely cautious when crossing the freeway-like road. Most bars stay open at least until 3 AM. Drinks are rather steep (around 2,000 dr./€5.88) but generous, and often there is a surcharge on weekend nights at the most popular clubs, which also usually have bouncers, aptly called "face-control" by Greeks. Foreigners usually will get in automatically; large groups of single men may have some trouble on a busy night. Most clubs and bars do not take credit cards for drinks.

Balthazar (⊠ Tsoha 27, Ambelokipi, ☎ 01/644–1215 or 01/645–2278) is a bar-restaurant in a neoclassical house, with a lush garden courtyard and subdued music, where Athenians of all ages come to escape the summer heat.

Banana Moon (⊠ Vas. Olgas 1, Zappio, ☎ 01/321–5414) offers both a lively bar with loud music and a glamour crowd and quieter surrounding tables set among the trees of the National Garden. In winter the bar moves across the street.

Movie stars, romancing couples, girlfriends, the local Lotto vendor—all show up at **En Delfois** (⊠ Skoufa 75, on Delfon pedestrian zone, Kolonaki, ☎ 01/360–8269) for its see-and-be-seen atmosphere in a friendly setting with good snacks, eclectic music played at conversational level, and generous drinks. It's a cross between the *poza* (posing) of chi-chi Kolonaki and the casualness of Exarchia. During the day, it's also a good place to stop for a coffee.

Folie (⊠ Eslin 4, Ambelokipi, ☎ 01/646–9852) has a congenial crowd of all ages dancing to reggae, Latin, funk, and ethnic music.

A relaxed café during the day, **Horostasion** (⊠ Skouleniou 2, Klathmonos Sq., ☎ 01/331–4330) morphs into a packed club with rock music and special nights dedicated to everything from hip-hop to alternative. The upstairs-downstairs space is comfortable with dark wood, handmade candlesticks, and ceiling-high windows for those who want to check who's walking by on the pedestrian zone outside or gaze upon illuminated Ayii Theodoroi church. Afterward, just step outside to enjoy a souvlaki from one of the several joints nearby—Greek youngsters have dubbed this evening duo "beat and eat."

Gregarious **Memphis** (⊠ Ventiri 5, Ilisia, behind the Hilton, ☎ 01/722–4104) is an Athens classic, where the good-natured crowds listen to predominantly '80s music, as well as Gothic-theme nights and occasional live music. In summer, the courtyard is open.

You'll find an artsy, happy crowd enjoying the playlist that runs from cabaret to ethnic to freestyle, along with eclectic snacks, at the bar-restaurant **Multi-Culti** (⊠ Ayia Theklas 8, Psirri, ☎ 01/324–4643).

With low-key music and a romantic park setting, **Parko** (⊠ Eleftherias Park, Ilisia, ☎ 01/722–3784) is another summer favorite.

All ages will feel comfortable at **Stavlos** (⊠ Iraklidon 10, Thission, ☎ 01/345–2502 or 01/346–7206), in what used to be the Royal Stables. Sit in the courtyard or the brick-walled restaurant for a snack like Cretan *kaltsounia* (similar to a calzone) or dance in the long bar. Stavlos often hosts art exhibits, film screenings, miniconcerts, and other "happenings," as the Greeks call them, throughout the week.

Glitzy **Wild Rose** (⊠ Panepistimiou 10, in the arcade, Syntagma, ☎ 01/364–2160) attracts an older crowd studded with Beautiful People, even though it's been around for more than a decade. It now features predominantly house music and some rock.

Bouzoukia

Many tourists think Greek social life centers on large clubs where live bouzouki music is played and patrons get their kicks by smashing up the plates. This practice, called *spasta,* is now prohibited. Instead, plates of flowers are sold for scattering over the performer or your companions when they take to the dance floor. An upscale form of bouzoukia is found from the lower end of Syngrou all the way south to the airport, where top entertainers command top prices. Be aware that the food is overpriced and often second-rate. There is a per-person minimum (5,000 dr./€14,70–9,000 dr./€16.47) or a prix-fixe menu; a bottle of whiskey costs from 32,000 dr./94.11 to 49,000 dr./€144.11. For those who choose to stand at the bar, a drink runs 3,000 dr./€8.82 to 5,000 dr./€14.70

Apollon Palace (⌂ Syngrou 259, Nea Smyrni, ☎ 01/942–7580 through 01/942–7583) is the most popular place with Athenians who want to hear Greece's singing stars, such as Antonis Remos and Stelios Dionyssiou; it's closed Monday and Tuesday. Decadence reigns at the slightly more casual **Iera Odos** (⌂ Iera Odos 18–20, Kerameikos, ☎ 01/342–8272 through 01/342–8275) as diners dance the seductive tsifteteli to big names such as Notis Sfakianakis; it's closed Sunday and Monday.

Dance Clubs

Dance clubs come and go every year, and most move around the town, especially in summer when they go seaside. Currently popular among young Athenians, who swarm the dance floors for everything from house to Greek pop tunes, are the following (more permanent winter addresses listed):

Of the bars for the under-40 crowd, mainstream, ritzy **Privilege** (⌂ Pireos 130 and Alkioneos, Gazi, ☎ 01/347–7388) is especially popular, though tough to get into, as is **Plus Soda** (⌂ Ermou 161, Thissio, ☎ 01/345–6187), the dance temple of Athens. Both usually move to the seaside in summer.

Jazz and Blues Clubs

The jazz scene has built up momentum in Greece, and there are now several venues from which to choose. Tickets to shows can be purchased at the clubs or major record stores.

The original and best venue in town, sophisticated **Half Note Jazz Club** (⌂ Trivonianou 17, Mets, ☎ 01/921–3310 or 01/923–2460) is the place for serious jazz fans. It's a good idea to reserve a table, especially one near the stage, but latecomers can always stand at the bar in back. Cozy **Parafono** (⌂ Asklippiou 130a, Exarchia, ☎ 01/644–6512) leaves the big names to other clubs and instead taps into the homegrown jazz circuit. The laid-back **House of Art** (⌂ Santouri 4 and Sarri, Psirri, ☎ 01/321–7678) hosts small, mostly blues, groups. At lively **Hi-Hat Cafe** (⌂ Dragoumi 28 and Krousovou 1, Hilton, ☎ 01/721–8171), even the blues are scorching, perhaps a vestige of the club's Latin days—often, several groups are invited to improvise together. The best seats are on the higher level in the back for a good view.

Live-Music Bars

Many venues close during August, if not for the entire summer. A small bar with few tables, **Asánte** (⌂ Damareos 78, Pangrati, ☎ 01/756–0102) hosts ethnic music groups (Afro-Cuban, Indian, Peruvian); be sure to order potent *rakomelo* (raki with honey). Named after an important Maya city, **Palenque Club** (⌂ Farantaton 41, Goudi, ☎ 01/748–7548 or 01/771–8090) also features musicians from around the world (Peru, Brazil), as well as happenings such as salsa parties, live flamenco acts, and weekly tango lessons for the public. Rock fans should check the big-name listings for **Rodon** (⌂ Marni 24, Vathis Sq., ☎ 01/524–7427); blue jeans and anything black are the usual attire. In summer, the popular music acts usually appear at the outdoor Lycabettus amphitheater (☞ Elliniko Festival *in* The Arts, *below*).

Every July Athens hosts the three-day outdoor **Rockwave Festival,** a dense lineup including such mega-acts as Sonic Youth, Garbage, Radiohead,

Lou Reed, Patti Smith, Prodigy, and Sisters of Mercy in the past. A member of YOUROPE (Union of European Festivals), it has become a major musical event that now includes bungee jumping, in-line skating, tattooing, and any other youthful trend; in 2000 it was held at an ecopark in a western Athens suburb. Tickets, which run around 12,000 dr./€35.29 for each day (festival passes are available) are more expensive if bought at the door (⊠ Ticket House box office: Panepistimiou 42, in arcade, ☎ 01/360–8366 or check with downtown record stores).

Plaka Tavernas with Music

Klimataria (⊠ Klepsidras 5, ☎ 01/324–1809 or 01/321–1215), a century-old taverna with music, is in an old house without a roof. It features a guitarist and an accordion player in winter and various combos in summer that play sing-along favorites much appreciated by the largely Greek audience. This slice of old-style Greek entertainment is surprisingly reasonable.

Stamatopoulou Palia Plakiotiki Taverna (⊠ Lysiou 26, ☎ 01/322–8722 or 01/321–8549) is in a converted 1822 Plaka house. Here you'll find good food and an acoustic band of three guitars and bouzouki playing old Athenian songs. In summer the show moves to a cool garden. Greeks will often get up and dance, beckoning you to join them, so don't be shy.

Rembetika Clubs

The Greek equivalent of the urban blues, rembetika is rooted in the traditions of Asia Minor and was brought to Greece by refugees from Smyrna in the 1920s. It filtered up from the lowest economic levels to become one of the most enduring genres of Greek popular music, still enthralling clubgoers today. At these thriving clubs, you can catch a glimpse of Greek social life and even join the dances (but remember, it is considered extremely rude to interrupt a solo dance). The two most common dances are the zeimbekikos, in which the man improvises in circular movements that become ever more complicated, and the belly dance–like tsifteteli. Most of the clubs are closed in the summer, so call in advance. They have reasonable prices for an evening of live entertainment (drinks range from 1,500 dr./€4.41 to 2,500 dr./€7.35, a bottle of whiskey from 17,000 dr./€50 to 23,000 dr./€67.64), but the food is often expensive and unexceptional; it's wisest to order a fruit platter or a bottle of wine.

Anifori (⊠ Vasileos Georgiou A' 47, Pasalimani, Piraeus, ☎ 01/411–5819) is a friendly club popular with young people that plays both rembetika and *dimotika* (Greek folk music). It is closed Monday through Thursday.

An ambience underscored by old posters and photographs and a dedication to authenticity make **Stathmos** (⊠ Mavromateon 22, Pedion Areos park, ☎ 01/883–2393 or 01/822–0883) a good choice for newcomers to the music. It's closed Monday through Wednesday.

Deka Entoles (⊠ Aharnon 257, Ayios Nikolaos, ☎ 01/832–5523), or "10 Commandments," is dark and smoky in the best rembetika tradition, featuring such classic groups as Athinaiki Compania. The club is closed Tuesday.

At **Mnisikleous** (⊠ Mnisikleous 22 and Lyceiou, Plaka, ☎ 01/322–5558 or 01/322–5337), the authentic music of popular *rembetis*, gravel-voiced Bobbis Goles, draws audience participation. Closed Monday through Wednesday.

Usually crowded and pleasantly raucous **Boemissia** (⊠ Solomou 19, Exarchia, ☎ 01/384–3836 or 01/330–0865) attracts many young people, who quickly start gyrating in various forms of the tsifteteli. Doors are shut on Monday.

Stoa ton Athanaton (⊠ Sofokleous 19, Central Market, ☎ 01/321–4362 or 01/321–0342), or Arcade of the Immortals, has been around since 1930 in a renovated warehouse in the meat market. Not much has changed since then. The music is enhanced by an infectious, devil-may-care mood and the enthusiastic participation of the audience, which comes especially for the "best-of-rembetika" afternoons (3:30–7:30). The small dance floor is jammed; the food is delicious and reasonably priced, but liquor is expensive. Reservations are essential for evenings, when the orchestra is led by old-time rembetes Takis Binis, Dimitris Tsaousakis, and Koulis Skarpelis, who is in his eighties. The club is closed Sunday.

The Arts

Concerts and Operas

Concerts and operas are given September through June at the Megaron by world-class Greek and international artists. Information and tickets are available from the **Megaron Athens Concert Hall** (⊠ Vasilissis Sofias and Kokkali, ☎ 01/728–2333, FAX 01/728–2300), open weekdays 10–6 and Saturday 10–4, next to the U.S. Embassy. Prices range from 1,500 dr./€4.41 to 22,000 dr./€64.70. There is a substantial discount for students and those aged 8–18. Tickets go on sale a few weeks in advance, but many events sell out within hours. On the first day of sales, tickets can be purchased by cash or credit card only in person at the Megaron. From the second day on, remaining tickets may be purchased by phone or in person from the **Megaron's downtown box office** (⊠ In the arcade at Stadiou 4, ☎ 01/322–1459). You can also check ticket availability and buy tickets on-line at www.megaron.gr.

Inexpensive and often free classical concerts are held November through May at the **Philippos Nakas Conservatory** (⊠ Ippokratous 41, ☎ 01/363–4000, FAX 01/360–2827). Tickets cost 2,000 dr./€5.88 to 3,000 dr./€8.82

Every March the Goethe Institute hosts a **piano festival,** featuring high-caliber soloists such as Claudius Tanksi, Heidrun Holtmann, Frierich Horicke, and Konstanze Eickhorst (⊠ Omirou 14–16, Kolonaki, ☎ 01/360–8111). Tickets, which run about 3,500 dr./€10.29 (a season ticket is available), may be purchased weekday mornings at the institute or a few hours before the performance.

Elliniko Festival and Other Shows

The city's primary artistic event, the **Elliniko Festival,** or Hellenic Festival (formerly known as the Athens Festival) in the Odeon of Herodes Atticus from June through September, has showcased performers such as Dame Kiri Te Kanawa, Luciano Pavarotti, and Diana Ross; such dance troupes as the Royal London Ballet, the Joaquin Cortes Ballet, and Maurice Béjart; symphony orchestras; and local groups performing ancient Greek drama. The festival usually commissions a world premiere, such as the recent musical theater production of *Casanova,* coproduced by Milan's Piccolo Teatro and the Modena Opera House, choreographed by Carol Armitage and accompanied by Mikis Theodorakis's Orchestra of Colors. The theater is a delightful setting, with the floodlighted Acropolis looming behind the audience and the Roman arches below making a stunning backdrop for the performers. The upper-level seats have no cushions, so come prepared with something to sit on, a light wrap, and low shoes, since the marble steps are steep. For most performances the Gamma zone is the best. Tickets sell out quickly for popular shows; they are available from the **Festival box office** (✉ In the arcade at Stadiou 4, ☎ 01/322–1459) or before the show at the **Odeon of Herodes Atticus (Irodion)** (☎ 01/323–2771 or 01/323–5582 box office). Prices range from 4,000 dr./€11.76 to as high as 20,000 dr./€58.82 for the big names.

Other festival events are held at the more intimate **Lycabettus Theater** (✉ At the top of Mt. Lycabettus, ☎ 01/322–1459, Elliniko Festival, formerly known as Athens Festival; 01/727–2233 or 01/722–7209 theater box office), set on a pinnacle of Mt. Lycabettus. The specialty here is popular concerts, with such performers as B. B. King, Bob Dylan, Smashing Pumpkins, and Paco de Lucia. Since buses travel only as far as the bottom of the hill, and taxi drivers often won't drive to the top, buy a one-way ticket on the funicular and walk about 10 minutes to the theater.

The **Krystalleia Festival** stages local and international musical and dance groups from June through July and September in the stately Plakendias mansion (✉ 16 km [10 mi] northeast of Athens on Mt. Pendeli). The concurrent **Pendelis Festival** (end July and September) focuses on classical music, often importing international orchestras to take advantage of the acoustics of the mansion. For information on both festivals, contact EOT (☞ Visitor Information *in* Athens A to Z, *below*). Tickets run from 2,000 dr./€5.88 to 5,000 dr./€14.70 and are usually sold at major record stores in downtown Athens.

Emerging as a main summer concert venue, the **Vyronas Festival** held mid-June through July (✉ Theatro Vrahon, Vyrona where Trolley 11 ends, ☎ 01/762–6438 ✆) offers performances in an old quarry, ranging from well-known Greek musician Dimitris Mitropanos to international acts such as Goran Bregovic or the Beijing Opera to ancient theater classics, such as Aristophanes' *The Frogs*. Performances begin around 9:30 PM. Buy tickets, about 3,000 dr./€8.82–4,000 dr./€11.76, at the theater before the show, major record stores, the Vyronas Cultural Center (✉ Kiprou and Evaggelikis Scholis, ☎ 01/766–2066), or the Vyronas Town Hall (✉ Karaoli Dimitriou 32–36, ☎ 01/765–5748).

Every evening from April through October, **Sound and Light Spectacles** casts dramatic lighting upon the Acropolis along with a brief recorded history. The English-language narration is at 9 PM. Seating is on the **Pnyx hill** opposite the Acropolis, a great place to view the sunset before the show. Tickets are sold at the box office of the **Pnyx** (✉ Off Dionyssiou Areopagitou, ☎ 01/922–6210 or 01/928–2907) before shows; tickets cost 1,500 dr./€4.41 and the box office opens at 8:20 PM.

The **Dora Stratou Troupe,** the country's leading, spirited folk dance company, performs a fine selection of **Greek folk dances** from all regions, as well as from Cyprus, in eye-catching authentic costumes. The programs change every fortnight. Performances are held Tuesday through Sunday from the end of May through September at 10:15 PM; Wednesday and Sunday there are additional shows at 8:15 PM at the **Dora Stratou Theater** (✉ Arakinthou and Voutie, near Filopappou, ☎ 01/921–4650 theater; 01/324–4395 troupe's office; ℻ 01/324–6921 ✆). Tickets cost 4,000 dr./€11.76 and can be purchased at the box office before the show.

Film

Films are shown in original-language versions with subtitles (except for major animated films), a definite boon for foreigners. Tickets run about 1,800 dr./€5.29–2,000 dr./€5.88. Check the *Athens News* or *Kathemerini* in the *International Herald Tribune* for programs, schedules, and addresses and phone numbers of theaters (including the outdoor theaters, and the Hellenic-American Union and the British Council, both of which screen films free).

Best bets are the **downtown theaters,** which have the most advanced equipment and most comfortable seats (tickets are about 2,000 dr./€5.88). Near Syntagma, try **Apollon Renault** (✉ Stadiou 19, ☎ 01/323–6811) or **Attikon Renault** (✉ Stadiou 19, ☎ 01/322–8821); close to Omonia Square is **Ideal Ericsson** (✉ Panepistimiou 46, ☎ 01/362–6720), which has the plushest seats in Athens and cheaper (1,500 dr./€4.41) seats on Monday. The spacious **Danaos 1 Ericsson** (✉ Kifissias 109, 100 yards from Panormou metro, Ambelokipi, ☎ 01/692–2655) is a bit farther out but worth it for its comfortable seats and great sound system.

Unless theaters have air-conditioning, as do all the aforementioned, most close June–September, giving way to **therina,** an enchanting, uniquely Greek entertainment that offers instant escapism under a starry sky. A feature of postwar Mediterranean countries that has survived only in Greece, open-air cinemas saw their popularity decline after the arrival of television. Recently, there has been a resurgence in their appeal, and about 75 now operate in the greater Athens area. They are usually set up in vine-covered empty lots and on rooftops with customers sitting on lawn chairs at small tables, where they enjoy snacks and drinks ordered from the bar. A disadvantage is the mandatory low sound level at the second screening, so audiences have to resort to lip reading, especially a drag at comedies, when the laughter drowns out the lines. Ticket prices range from 1,800 dr./€5.29 to 2,000 dr./€5.88. Some of the most popular theaters include the following: **Cine Paris** (✉ Kidathineon 22, Plaka, ☎ 01/322–2071 or 01/324–8057), which, although it only has stereo rather than Dolby digital sound, is convenient for most tourists since it sits on Plaka's main walkway; **Thission** (✉ Apostolou Pavlou 7, ☎ 01/342–0864 or 01/347–0980), where films compete with a view of the Acropolis, often dramatically lighted during the sound-and-light shows; **Dexameni** (✉ Dexameni Sq., Kolonaki, ☎ 01/361–3942 or 01/360–2363), which screens only new films; and **Cine Psirri Refresh** (✉ Sarri 40–44, Psirri, ☎ 01/321–2476 or 01/324–7234), close to Psirri's mezedopolia but far away enough from apartment buildings so the sound isn't lowered during the second show.

Galleries

Galleries that hang some of the more interesting contemporary work include **Kappatos** (✉ Ayia Irinis 6, Psirri, ☎ 01/321–7931); **Bernier/Eliades** (✉ Eptahalkou, Thissio, ☎ 01/341–3935); **Ileana Tounda** (✉ Armatolon kai Klefton 48, Ambelokipi, ☎ 01/643–9466); **Nees Morphes** (✉ Valaoritou 9, Syntagma, ☎ 01/361–6165); **Rebecca Camhi** (✉ Sofokleous 23, Central Market area, ☎ 01/321–0448); **Sigma** (✉ Ayion Anargiron 20–22, Psirri, ☎ 01/322–1675); and three galleries in the same building (✉ Armodiou 10, Varvakeio Sq.) near the fruit-and-vegetable market, **Epikentro** (☎ 01/331–2187), **Diana Yiulia Gallery** (☎ 01/324–9626), and **Artower Agora** (☎ 01/324–9606).

OUTDOOR ACTIVITIES AND SPORTS

Beaches and Beach Volleyball

Volleyball games open to the public begin in July at Palio Faliro, Schinias, and Palaia Fokaia beaches.

The beaches at **Palio Faliro** and **Piraeus** have signs warning you of the high levels of pollution. Believe them. The **Greek National Tourist Organization** (GNTO or EOT; ☞ Visitor Information *in* Athens A to Z, *below*) can give you a list of their beaches, which have snack bars and beach umbrellas, chairs, dressing rooms, various courts for basketball, tennis, and volleyball, water slides, banana rides or other children's activities, sports equipment for rent, and occasionally windsurfing and waterskiing lessons. Most are open from 8 AM to 8 PM in summer; tickets run about 600 dr./€1.76–700 dr./€2.05, with reduced rates for children.

The main beaches close to Athens are found at the shoreline in the regions by the same name: **Alimos** (☎ 01/982–7064); **Avlaki** (☎ 0299/72826), which is actually organized by the municipality Markopoulos; **Voula** (☎ 01/895–3248 1st beach; 01/895–9587 2nd beach); **Vouliagmeni** (☎ 01/896–0906); and **Varkiza** (☎ 01/897–2434 or 01/897–2436). **Vouliagmeni Lake** (☎ 01/896–2237), whose spring-fed waters are reputed to have curative powers, is popular with older Greeks. You can swim year-round since the water remains a steady 20°C (68°F). The lake opens at 6:30 AM; tickets are 1,100 dr./€3.23. A number of pleasant tavernas line the sandy shoreline.

Bird-Watching

The **Hellenic Ornithological Society** arranges two- and three-day trips to important bird habitats, like the Dounavi Delta, the Vikos Gorge, and the Messolonghi wetlands (⊠ Em. Benaki 53, Athens, ☎ FAX 01/381–1271 or 01/330–1167).

Golf

Glyfada Golf Course (⊠ Konstantinos Karamanlis behind Ellinikon airport, Glyfada, ☎ 01/894–6820) has 18 holes, locker rooms, a restaurant, and a bar, all open to the public. Rates are 14,000 dr./€51.17 for the day, 18,000 dr./€52.94 for the weekend (for the latter, call to reserve one week in advance, in case of tournaments).

Health Clubs

Health clubs abound these days, and you'll have little problem finding one near your hotel. The Athens Hilton, Holiday Inn, and Athenaeum Inter-Continental have excellent facilities with saunas and pools that can be used by the general public for a fee.

Hiking and Mountain Biking

Both the E4 (Florina to Githio, about 1,600 km [1,000 mi]) and the E6 (Igoumentisa to Samothraki, about 1,000 km [600 mi]) pass through Greece. The **Hellenic Federation of Mountaineering and Climbing** (⊠ Milioni 5, Kolonaki, ☎ 01/364–5904, FAX 01/364–2687) supplies details on mountain paths and refuges and has contact numbers for local hiking groups. Trips in and around Athens are often offered by specialist travel agencies. One local hiking group to try is **Alpine Club of Aharnon** (⊠ Filadelfias 126, Aharnes, ☎ 01/246–1528, FAX 01/246–9777), which runs the Flambouri refuge on nearby Parnitha (☎ 01/246–4666). The **Alpine Club of Athens** (⊠ Ermou 64 and Aiolou, 5th floor, Monastiraki, ☎ 01/321–2355, FAX 01/324–4789) runs the Bafi refuge on Parnitha (☎ 01/246–9050) and arranges hikes to such places as Evritania and Arcadia, ski trips, rock climbing and bouldering seminars, and adventure camps for children in summer.

Try **Trekking Hellas** (⊠ Fillelinon 7, 3rd floor, Syntagma, 10557, ☎ 01/331–0323 through 01/331–0326, FAX 01/323–4548) for trips. **F-Zein** (⊠ Syngrou 132, 5th floor, near Olympic Airways office, 11741, ☎ 01/921–6285, FAX 01/922–9995) offers trips and also organizes kayaking, rafting, mountain biking, and camping expeditions for youngsters.

Sailing and Windsurfing

The **Hellenic Yachting Federation** (⊠ Leoforos Posidonios 51, Moschato, ☎ 01/940–4825, FAX 01/940–4829) can provide lists of local yachting clubs where visitors can windsurf, sail, and take lessons. The Attica peninsula's best windsurfing beaches are Schinias, Varkiza, Vouliagmeni, Rafini, Loutsa, and Anavyssos.

Many sailing clubs in the area give lessons and information. **Vouliagmeni Nautical Club** (✉ Laimos Vouliagmenis, ☎ 01/896–2142, FAX 01/896–4022) sails out of Vouliagmenis Bay, 20 km (12 mi) south of Athens, and offers lessons to children only. **Piraeus Sailing Club** (✉ Mikrolimano, ☎ 01/417–7636, FAX 01/411–0287) also gives sailing courses. For children's sailing lessons only, contact **Alimos Nautical Club** (✉ Loutra Alimou, off Leoforos Poseidonos, ☎ 01/983–8358, FAX 01/988–5566). Sailing and windsurfing lessons are available at the **Varkiza Nautical Club** (✉ Varkiza beach, ☎ 01/897–4305, FAX 01/965–3593).

Those who have a diploma for sailing on the open sea can legally rent a sailboat (without a captain, if two people on board are licensed); rentals range from about 30,000 dr./€88.23 to 210,000 dr./€618 a day, depending on the size and age of the boat and whether a skipper is included. Charter companies usually will provide a list of suggested sailing routes. Most have branch offices at designated marinas along each of these routes, and sometimes you can avoid the capital altogether by picking up your boat at these stations. Contact **Ghiolman Yachts** (✉ Fillelinon 7, Syntagma, ☎ 01/322–8530 or 01/323–0330, FAX 01/322–3251 ✍), **Kyriacoulis Mediterranean Cruises** ✉ Leoforos Poseidonos 51, Palio Faliro, ☎ 01/988–6187 through 01/988–6191, FAX 01/984–7296 ✍), **Sun Yachting** (✉ Leoforos Poseidonos 21, Kalamaki, ☎ 01/983–7312, FAX 01/983–7528 ✍), or **Vernicos Yachts** (✉ Leoforos Poseidonos 11, Alimos, ☎ 01/985–0122 through 01/985–0128, FAX 01/985–0130 ✍).

Scuba Diving

Scuba diving is heavily restricted, to protect underwater artifacts, although there are about seven designated diving areas near Athens and another 15 within a radius of 100 km (60 mi). It is forbidden to dive at night and to remove anything from the sea floor. A travel agent can direct you to a supervised diving trip or a less-populated diving base, or you can call the **Greek Diving Center** (✉ Vasileos Pavlou 26, Kastella, ☎ 01/412–1708, FAX 01/411–9207), which offers lessons up to the instructor's level, rents equipment, and organizes one- to two-day diving excursions on weekends. The **Aegean Dive Center** (✉ Pandoras 42 and Zamanou 53, Glyfada, ☎ 01/894–5409, FAX 01/898–1120) provides equipment rental and service, diver training including first-aid courses, dive trips, and an air center. For those who want an introduction to the sport, **Scuba Diving Club of Vouliagmeni** (✉ Leoforos Poseidonos below the Agnadi café-bar, Ormos Vouliagmeni, ☎ 01/896–4609, FAX 01/896–1914) runs a one-hour orientation for about 15,000 dr./€54.11 called Discover Scuba, where total beginners can dive with an instructor; visitors just show up with towel and bathing suit). The 23-year-old center, which is one of the few run on a private bit of seaside, also offers regular diving courses, equipment, boat rentals with guides for expeditions, and water sports. A 12-day course, leading to the 1* diploma, costs 70,000 dr./€205. Call a day ahead for reservations. Remember that any school dispensing diplomas must be recognized by the Greek state.

Tennis

The **Hellenic Tennis Federation** (✉ Ymittou 267, Pangrati, ☎ 01/756–3170 through 01/756–3172, FAX 01/756–3173) can give you information on the nearest tennis clubs and where rental courts are available by the hour; several are near the EOT beaches.

SHOPPING

The main shopping districts are in the area bounded by Syntagma, Monastiraki, Omonia, and Kolonaki. For serious retail therapy, most natives head to the shopping streets that branch off central Syntagma and Kolonaki squares. Syntagma is the starting point for popular Ermou—now a pedestrian zone lined with hundreds of stores and adorned with the occasional street performer—which leads down to Monastiraki. Streets parallel and perpendicular to Ermou make up this shopping area: Mitropoleos, Voulis, Nikis, Perikleous, and Praxitelous among them. Much ritzier is the Kolonaki quarter, with boutiques and designer shops on fashionable streets near the square like Anagnostopoulou, Tsakalof, Skoufa, Solonos, and Kanari. One of the main hurdles is figuring out when shops in Athens are open—there always seems to be some bill in parliament to change the hours. Shops may stay open from 9 AM to 9 PM in summer, though most stores close Monday, Wednesday, and Saturday afternoons around 3 or 4. On Tuesday, Thursday, and Friday, many shops close between about 3 and 5. In winter (October–mid-April) hours are slightly reduced.

The **souvenir shops** in Plaka are usually open from early morning until the last tourist leaves. Originally set up by the government to provide employment for veterans, the sidewalk kiosks called *periptera* are the Greek version of a convenience store. Many of them have public phones, some metered for long-distance calls. Those in central squares are often open until very late and occasionally are open around the clock.

The **flea market** centered on Pandrossou and Ifestou in Monastiraki operates on Sunday mornings and has practically everything, from secondhand guitars to Russian vodka (☞ Ancient Agora, Monastiraki, and Thission *in* Exploring Athens, *above*). No matter how low the price, always bargain. **Ifestou,** where coppersmiths have their shops, is more interesting on a weekday—and you can pick up copper wine jugs, candlesticks, cookware, and more for next to nothing.

Antiques and Icons

Antiques and older wares are in vogue now, so the prices of these items have naturally soared in price. Shops on Pandrossou sell small antiques and icons, but keep in mind that many of these are fakes, and you must have government permission to export genuine objects from the Greek, Roman, or Byzantine periods.

The **Benaki Museum gift shop** (✉ Koumbari 1 and Vasilissis Sofias, Kolonaki, ☎ 01/362–7367) has excellent copies of Greek icons at fair prices.

Martinos (✉ Pandrossou 50, Monastiraki, ☎ 01/321–2414) should be the destination for serious antiques collectors, including such items as exquisite dowry chests, old swords, and Venetian glass.

Motakis (✉ Abyssinia Sq. 3, in the basement, Monastiraki, ☎ 01/321–9005), run by the same family for more than 90 years, is a *palaiopolio* (junk dealer), and it sells antiques, beautiful old objects, or that fabulous old trident you simply cannot live without.

At **Nasiotis** (✉ Ifestou 24, Monastiraki, ☎ 01/321–2369), with a little perseverance, you can make some interesting finds in this huge basement stacked with books, engravings, old magazines, and first editions.

Clothing

Greece is known for its well-made shoes (most shops are clustered around the Ermou pedestrian zone and in Kolonaki), its furs (Mitropoleos near

Syntagma), and its durable leather items (Pandrossou in Monastiraki). Fishermen's caps—always a good present—have now surfaced at high prices across the United States (triple the Athens price), as have the natural wool undershirts and hand-knit sweaters worn by fishermen; all can be found in many Plaka shops.

Stavros Melissinos (✉ Pandrossou 89, Monastiraki, ☎ 01/321–9247), a legendary poet and gentle soul, sends many tourists packing with his handmade sandals. The Beatles once visited his shop.

Despite the anti-fur campaign, Mitropoleos is lined with shops selling everything from pieced-together stoles to full-length minks, often from the northern city of Kastoria. Try **Kaplan Furs** (✉ Mitropoleos 22–24, ☎ 01/322–2226) or **Eleni Samaras Furs** (✉ Mitropoleos 13a, ☎ 01/322–3506).

Coins and Stamps

Check out **Kiritisis** (✉ Areos 1 and Pandrossou, Monastiraki, ☎ 01/324–0544), a small shop with old coins from Greece and around the world, stamps, and medals.

Gold Coin Jewelry (✉ Stadiou 10, Syntagma, ☎ 01/322–0600) is known for its decorative copies of ancient Greek coins.

Gifts

Athens has great gifts, particularly handmade crafts. Better tourist shops sell copies of traditional Greek jewelry, silver filigree, Skyrian pottery, onyx ashtrays and dishes, woven bags, attractive rugs (including *flokati,* or shaggy goat wool rugs), and little blue-and-white pendants designed as amulets to ward off the *mati* (evil eye).

An inexpensive but unusual gift is a string of *koboloi* (worry beads) in plastic, wood, or stone. You can pick them up very cheaply in Monastiraki or look in antiques shops for more expensive versions, with amber, silver, or black onyx beads. Reasonably priced natural sponges from Kalymnos also make good presents. Look for those that are unbleached, since the lighter ones tend to fall apart quickly. They're usually sold in front of the National Bank on Syntagma and in Plaka souvenir shops. The price is set by the government, so don't bother to bargain.

Greeks can spend hours heatedly playing tavli. To take home a game set of your own, look closely for the hole-in-the-wall, no-name shop affectionately called **Baba** (✉ Ifestou 30, Monastiraki, ☎ 01/321–9994), which sells boards and pieces in all sizes and designs.

Goutis (✉ Dimokritou 40, Kolonaki, ☎ 01/361–3557) is one of the more interesting stores on Pandrossou; it has an eclectic jumble of jewelry, costumes, embroidery, and old, handcrafted silver objects.

At **Riza** (✉ Voukourestiou 35 and Skoufa, Kolonaki, ☎ 01/361–1157) you can pick up wonderful lace in romantic designs, often handmade. The shop also carries fabric at good prices, and decorative items such as handblown glass bowls and brass candlesticks.

Mati (✉ Voukourestiou 20, Syntagma, ☎ 01/362–6238) has finely designed amulets, for protection against the evil eye and an unusual collection of monastery lamps and candlesticks that make excellent gifts.

Mazarakis (✉ Voulis 31–33, Syntagma, ☎ 01/323–9428 or 01/322–4932) offers a large selection of luxurious flokatis in a variety of colors and will ship your purchases to your home so you don't have to carry them with you.

Karoukis (⊠ Skoufa 25, Kolonaki, ☎ 01/361–1012) carries all kinds of miniatures, and if you browse long enough, the proprietor is likely to brew you a Greek coffee.

"Mediterranean design" comes and goes on magazine pages, but you can always pick up a few pieces that offer form and function from **The Shop** (⊠ Lysicratous 3, Plaka, ☎ 01/323–0350), which stocks items that embody Greek village life, mostly of handmade aluminum, like *fanaria*—birdcage contraptions in which to store fresh food—plain or brightly colored olive oil pourers, and traditional kafenion trays.

The best thing at **Fresh Line** (⊠ Skoufa 10, Kolonaki, ☎ 01/364–4015), among all the solid shampoo cakes, body oils, and face packs, is the tremendous range of Greek-made soaps that are sliced from big blocks or wheels as though they were cheese; you pay by weight. The strawberries-and-cream soap Rea contains real berries; the Orpheus and Eurydices soap for sensitive skin is made with vanilla, milk, and rice, just like Greek rizogalo.

Century-old **Ilias Kokkonis** (⊠ Stoa Arsakeiou 8, Omonia [enter from Panepistimiou or Stadiou St.], ☎ 01/322–1189 or 01/322–6355; ⊠ Kifissias 264, Halandri, ☎ 01/689–1491 or 01/683–4708) most certainly stocks any flag you've always wanted—large or small, from any country.

Handicrafts

The **National Welfare Organization** (⊠ Ipatias 6 and Apollonos, Plaka, ☎ 01/321–8272), relying on craftspeople throughout Greece, carries fine examples of folk crafts: stunning handwoven carpets, flat-weave kilims, and tapestries from original designs, as well as hand-embroidered tablecloths and wall decorations. Napkins and place mats, ceramics, and embroidered pillowcases make handsome presents, and the shaggy woolen flokati rugs can be found here, too.

The **Center of Hellenic Tradition** (⊠ Entrance on Mitropoleos 59 or Pandrossou 36, Monastiraki, ☎ 01/321–3023; 01/321–3842 café) is an outlet for quality handicrafts—ceramics, weavings, sheep bells, and old paintings. Afterward, you can take a break from shopping in its wonderful Oraia Ellada café, in clear view of the Parthenon.

At **Amorgos** (⊠ Kodrou 3, Plaka, ☎ 01/324–3836) the owners make hand-carved and hand-painted wood furniture using motifs from regional Greek designs. They also sell needlework, hanging ceiling lamps, shadow puppets, and other decorative accessories.

EOMMEX (⊠ Mitropoleos 9, Syntagma, ☎ 01/323–0408), the Greek cooperative, operates a showroom with folk and designer rugs made by more than 30 weavers from around the country.

At the gracious **P. Serafetinidis** (⊠ Haritos 29, Kolonaki, ☎ 01/721–4186; ⊠ Parnassou 7, Karitsi Sq., ☎ 01/322–5207), enjoy the stunning colors and patterns of rare rugs and kilims from Persia, the Caucasus, and Turkey.

Jewelry

Prices are much lower for gold and silver in Greece than in many Western countries, and jewelry is of high quality. Many shops in Plaka carry original pieces available at a good price if you bargain hard enough (a prerequisite).

Great values in gold, often designed by the owners, can be purchased at **Byzantino** (⊠ Adrianou 120, Plaka, ☎ 01/324–6605).

For those with more expensive tastes, the Voukourestiou pedestrian mall off Syntagma Square has a number of the city's leading jewelry shops: **Pentheroudakis** (⊠ Voukourestiou 19, ☎ 01/361–3187) has classic designs and even some cheaper trinkets like silver worry beads that can be personalized with cubed letters in Greek or Latin with the stone of your choice. **Xanthopoulos** (⊠ Voukourestiou 4, ☎ 01/322–6856) has traditional gold, silver, and jewels. The baubles at **J. Vourakis & Fils** (⊠ Voukourestiou 8, ☎ 01/331–1087), both unique modern designs and older, collector's items, will put a twinkle in your eye.

Some of the most original work in gold can be had at **Fanourakis** (⊠ Patriarchou Ioakeim 23, Kolonaki, ☎ 01/721–1762; ⊠ Evangelistrias 2, Mitropoleos, ☎ 01/324–6642; ⊠ Panagitsas 6, Kifissia, ☎ 01/623-2334), where Athenian artists use gold almost like a fabric—creasing, scoring, and fluting it.

LALAoUNIS (⊠ Panepistimiou 6, Syntagma, ☎ 01/361–1371; ⊠ Athens Tower, Sinopis 2, ☎ 01/770–0000; ⊠ Athens Hilton, Vasilissis Sofias 46, ☎ 01/725–0201), the world-famous Greek jeweler, is always experimenting with designs, taking ideas from nature, biology, and ancient Greek pieces, the latter so close to the original, that they're mistaken for museum pieces.

Zolotas (⊠ Pandrossou 8, Plaka, ☎ 01/323–2413; ⊠ Stadiou 9, Syntagma, ☎ 01/322–1212), LALAoUNIS's main competitor, is noted for its superb museum copies.

Other finely rendered copies of classical jewelry are available at the **Benaki Museum gift shop** (⊠ Koumbari 1 and Vasilissis Sofias, Kolonaki, ☎ 01/362–7367). The **Goulandris Cycladic Museum** (⊠ Neofitou Douka 4, Kolonaki, ☎ 01/724–9706) sells exceptional modern versions of ancient jewelry designs as well.

Local Delicacies

Try the central market on Athinas for tasty local foods to bring home: packaged dried figs, packaged pistachios, *pastelli* (sesame seed and honey candy), and olives other than those from Kalamata, which are widely available outside of Greece.

Brothers (Afoi.) Hatzigeorgiou (⊠ Evripidou 37, Central Market area, ☎ 01/325–0434), founded in 1935, is an assault on the senses, with bags of Greek herbs and spices from around the world.

Bachar (⊠ Evripidou 31 and Athinas, Central Market area, ☎ 01/321–7225), one of the numerous spice shops lining Evripidou, carries aromatic and pharmaceutical herbs, many of which grow in this part of the Mediterranean.

At **Papalexandris** (⊠ Sokratous 9, Central Market, ☎ 01/321–1461), the gentlemanly owner will walk you through the array of multihued olives, gathered from throughout Greece and sold by the kilo, along with grapevine leaves, pickled vegetables, and other deli items.

For an inexpensive but unique gift, pick up some freshly ground Greek coffee and the traditional pot called *briki* at **Miseyiannis** (⊠ Levendis 7, Kolonaki, ☎ 01/721–0136).

Music

CDs of Greek music are much cheaper before they've been exported. One of the biggest selections, along with knowledgeable English-speaking staff, is at the **Virgin Megastore** (⊠ Stadiou 7–9, Syntagma, ☎ 01/331–4788 through 01/331–4796), where you can listen before you purchase.

ATHENS A TO Z

Arriving and Departing

By Bus

Travel by bus is inexpensive, usually comfortable, and relatively fast. The journey from Athens to Thessaloniki takes roughly the same time as the train, though the IC express covers the distance 1¼ hours faster. To reach the Peloponnese, however, buses are speedier than trains. Information and timetables are available at tourist information offices. Make reservations at least one day before your planned trip, earlier for holiday weekends.

Terminal A (⊠ at Kifissou 100, ☎ 01/512–4910) is the arrival and departure point for bus lines that serve parts of northern Greece, including Thessaloniki, and the Peloponnese destinations of Epidaurus, Mycenae, Nafplion, Olympia, and Corinth. Each has its own phone number; EOT offices distribute a list. **Terminal B** (⊠ Liossion 260, ☎ you must call each region's ticket counter for information: Delphi 01/831–7096; Livadia [Ossios Loukas via Distomo] 01/831–7173; Trikala [Meteora] 01/831–1431) serves Evia, most of Thrace, and central Greece, including Delphi. EOT provides a phone list (☞ Visitor Information, *below*). Tickets for these buses are sold only at this terminal, so you should call to book seats well in advance during high season or holidays.

From Terminal A, take Bus 051 to Omonia Square; from Terminal B, take Bus 024 downtown. To get to the stations, catch Bus 051 at Zinonos and Menandrou off Omonia Square (for Terminal A) and Bus 024 on Amalias in front of the National Garden (for Terminal B). International buses drop their passengers off on the street, usually in the Omonia or Syntagma Square areas or at Stathmos Peloponnisos (train station).

By Car

The main highways going north and south link up in Athens and both are called *Ethniki Odos* (the National Road). At the city limits, signs in English clearly mark the way to both Syntagma Square and Omonia Square in the town center. Leaving Athens, routes to the National Road are well marked; signs usually name Lamia for points north and Corinth or Patras for points southwest. On the road map distributed by the EOT (☞ Visitor Information, *below*), the National Roads are yellow and are marked by European road numbers, although these are not used on the roads themselves. Beware: the highways are very slick when wet, and there are many fatal accidents. Avoid driving in rain and on days preceding or following major holidays; Greece's car-accident rate, one of the highest in the European Union, escalates wildly during the mass migrations to and from the city. The speed limit is 120 kph (74 mph) on the National Road (but watch for temporary speed signs where the highway is under repair), 90 kph (54 mph) outside urban areas, and 50 kph (31 mph) in town. From Athens to Thessaloniki, the distance is 515 km (309 mi); to Kalamata, 257 km (154 mi); to Corinth, 84 km (50 mi); to Lamia, 214 km (128 mi); to Patras, 218 km (131 mi); to Igoumenitsa, 472 km (283 mi).

By Plane

Athens's **Ellinikon Airport** (⊠ Vasileos Georgiou B' 1, ☎ 01/936–3363 West Terminal; 01/969–4466 East Terminal) is between Alimos and Glyfada on the southwest coast of Attica, about 10 km (6 mi) from the city center. **Air Greece** (⊠ Fillelinon 22, Syntagma, Athens, ☎ 01/324–4457 for reservations) flies from Athens to Rhodes, Mytilini, Corfu, Kavala, and Heraklion and Hania in Crete. **Cronus Airlines** (⊠

Othonos 10, Syntagma, Athens, ☏ 01/994–4444 for reservations) flies regularly from Athens to Thessaloniki, as well as to Heraklion and Hania. **Olympic Airways** (✉ Fillelinon 15, near Syntagma, Athens, ☏ 01/966–6666 for reservations) has service between Athens and most large cities and islands in Greece.

All domestic and international Olympic Airways flights depart from the **West Terminal** (☏ 01/936–3363 through 01/936–3366 for arrival and departure information). Other airlines use the **East Terminal** (☏ 01/969–4466 for arrivals and departures, 01/969–4531 to make announcements in the waiting areas). For information on flights using the **New Charter Terminal** (Terminal B), just before the East Terminal on the former U.S. military base, call ☏ 01/997–2686 and 01/997–2581; the terminal operates May through October.

For travel to and from the airport, **express buses** connect the three airport terminals, Syntagma Square, Omonia Square, and Piraeus. Express bus (No. E93) runs between the three terminals every 40 minutes around the clock. Between the terminals and Athens, the express bus (No. E91) runs about every half hour around the clock. You can catch the bus to the airport at the bottom of Syntagma Square between Ermou and Mitropoleos or off Omonia Square at the intersection of Stadiou and Aiolou. From the airport terminals to Karaiskaki Square in Piraeus, the express bus (No. E19) leaves about every hour from 5 AM to midnight. The fare is 250 dr./€.73, 500 dr./€1.47 from 11:30 PM until 5:30 AM (check with EOT, ☞ Visitor Information, *below,* for schedules). You can also take the regular city line (No. B2) from Syntagma Square to the West Terminal (Olympic Airway flights) from about 4:30 AM to 11:50 PM, every 15 minutes for most of the day; cost is 120 dr.

It's easier to take a **taxi** from the airport stands: about 2,300 dr./€6.76 to Piraeus; 1,200 dr./€3.52 between terminals; 2,400 dr./€7.05 to the center, more if there's traffic. The price goes up by about two-thirds between midnight and 5 AM. If you want to arrive at your hotel in style, **Royal Prestige Limousine Service** (☏ 01/988–3221; 0944/305–000 mobile phone, ☏ 𝖥𝖠𝖷 01/983–0378) will pick you up at the airport and drop you at your hotel or vice versa. The owner says he has Greece's only Silver Spur Rolls (1997). Prices start at 16,000 dr./€47.05 one-way for transfer from the airport to a central hotel; call in advance.

By Ship

Cruise ships and ferries to and from the Aegean islands dock at **Piraeus** (✉ Port Authority, Akti Miaouli, ☏ 01/451–1311 through 01/451–1319), the main port, 10 km (6 mi) southwest of Athens. Ships for the Ionian islands sail from ports nearer to them, such as **Patras** and **Igoumenitsa.** Connections from Piraeus to the main island groups are good, connections from main islands to smaller ones within a group less so, and services between islands of different groups or areas—such as Rhodes and Crete—are less frequent. Travel agents (☞ *below*) and ship offices in Athens and Piraeus have details. EOT (☞ Visitor Information, *below*) distributes boat schedules updated every Wednesday; you can also call a daily Greek recording (☏ 143) for departure times. Timetables change very frequently, and boats may be delayed by weather conditions, so your plans should be flexible. Buy your tickets two or three days in advance, especially if you are traveling in summer or taking a car. Reserve your return journey or continuation soon after you arrive.

From Piraeus, the quickest way to get into town center, if you are traveling light, is to walk to the metro station and take an electric train to Omonia Square (150 dr./€.44) or Syntagma Square (250 dr./€.73, change at Omonia to the line going to Ethniki Aminas), a trip of about 25–

30 minutes. Those arriving by hydrofoil at the smaller **Zea Marina Harbor** should take Bus 905 or Trolley 20 (120 dr./€.35) to the Piraeus metro station. Alternatively, you can take a taxi (if you find one), which may take longer owing to traffic and will cost around 2,000 dr./€5.88. Often, drivers will wait until they fill their taxi with people debarking and headed in the same direction. It's faster to walk to the main street and hail a passing cab.

The other main port is **Rafina** (✉ Port, Port Authority, ☎ 0294/ 22300), on the eastern coast of Attica, where boats to and from Evia and some of the closer Cyclades dock. KTEL buses (☎ 01/821–0872) make the trip to Athens every half hour from about 5:30 AM to 9:30 PM; they leave from the station slightly up the hill from the port, and the fare is 500 dr./€1.47. The trip takes about one hour.

By Train

Greek trains have a well-earned reputation for being slow and for having a limited network. The main line runs north from Athens, dividing into three lines at Thessaloniki. The main line continues on to Skopje and Belgrade, a second line goes east to the Turkish border and Istanbul, and a third line heads northeast to Sofia, Bucharest, and Budapest. The Peloponnese in the south is served by a narrow-gauge line dividing at Corinth into the Tripolis–Kalamata route and Patras–Kalamata.

The **Greek Railway Organization (OSE)** has two stations in Athens, side by side off Diliyianni street not far from Omonia. Trains from the north and international trains arrive at, and depart from, **Stathmos Larissis** (☎ 01/529–8837). Take Trolley 1 from the terminal to Omonia Square, or the metro to Omonia and Syntagma squares. Trains from the Peloponnese use the ornate **Stathmos Peloponnisou** (☎ 01/529–8735) next door (ornate is right—the café continues the station's striking art-nouveau motif, from its burgundy ceiling with ornate moldings and antique crystal–teardrop chandelier to its original bronze gas lamps). To Omonia and Syntagma squares take Bus 057 or the metro. Both stations have left-luggage service and snack bar. Since the phones at the stations are inevitably busy and the clerks harried, it's best to call the general information switchboard for timetables and prices (☎ 01/ 529–7777); it's open daily 7 AM–9 PM. You may also call 145 for a recorded departure timetable, in Greek, of trains within Greece, or 147 for information on trains to Europe.

OSE buses (☎ 01/513–5768 or 01/513–5769) for Albania, Bulgaria, and Turkey also leave from Stathmos Peloponnisou station. To Omonia and Syntagma squares, take Bus 057.

The **IC express service** from the north is fast and reliable (Thessaloniki–Athens takes six hours). Express service has also begun on the Athens–Patras line (about four hours). On any train, it is best to travel first class, with a reserved seat, as the difference between the first-class and tourist coaches can be vast: without a seat reservation you could end up standing or crouched among the baggage.

For those already in the center who want to buy tickets ahead of time, it's easier to visit a **railway office** downtown (✉ Karolou 1, near Omonia Sq., ☎ 01/529–7006 or 01/529–7007; ✉ Sina 6, ☎ 01/529–8910; ✉ Filellinon 17, near Syntagma Sq., ☎ 01/323–6747, ☉ Mon.–Sat. 8–2).

Getting Around

Many of the sights you'll want to see, and most of the hotels, cafés, and restaurants, are within a fairly small central area. It's easy to walk everywhere, though sidewalks are sometimes obstructed by parked cars.

The price of public transportation has risen steeply in the last couple of years, but it is still less than that in Western European capitals. Riding during rush hours is definitely not recommended. Upon boarding, validate your ticket in the orange canceling machines at the front and back of buses and trolleys and in the stations of the electric trains. Keep your tickets until you reach your destination, as inspectors occasionally pop up to check that they have been canceled and validated. They are strict about fining offenders, including tourists.

The **Organization for Urban Public Transportation** (⊠ Metsovou 15, ☎ 185 from 7:30–3 and 7 PM–9 PM) answers questions about routes (usually only in Greek). The office, open weekdays 7:30–3, distributes maps with street names in Greek. EOT (☞ Visitor Information, *below*) also distributes information about bus lines.

By Bus and Trolley

Main bus stations are at Akadimias and Sina and at Kaningos Square. Bus and trolley tickets cost 120 dr./€.35. No transfers are issued; you validate a new ticket every time you change vehicles. Monthly passes for 5,000 dr./€14.70 are sold at the beginning of each month at special booths at the main terminals. Purchase individual tickets at terminal booths or at selected periptera. Buses run from the center to all suburbs and nearby beaches from 5 AM to about midnight, and very few routes have infrequent owl service. For suburbs north of Kifissia, change at Kifissia's main square, Platia Platanou.

KTEL buses provide efficient bus service throughout the Attica basin. Most buses to the east Attica coast—including those for **Sounion** (☎ 01/821-3203), fare 1,150 dr./€3.38 for inland route or 1,200 dr./€3.52 for coastal road, and **Marathon** (☎ 01/821–0872), fare 750 dr./€2.20—leave from the **KTEL terminal** (⊠ Platia Aigyptou at corner of Mavromateon and Leoforos Alexandras near Pedion Areos park).

By Car

Driving in Athens is not recommended unless you have nerves of steel. Red traffic lights are frequently ignored, and it is not unusual to see motorists passing other vehicles on hills and while rounding corners. Driving is on the right, and, although the vehicle on the right has the right-of-way, don't expect this or any other driving rule to be obeyed. The speed limit is 50 kph (31 mph) in town. Seat belts are compulsory, as are helmets for motorcyclists, though many natives ignore the laws. In downtown Athens do not drive in the bus lanes marked by a yellow divider; if caught, you may be fined.

Unless you are a citizen of an EU country, you must have an international driver's license. The **Automobile Touring Club of Greece** (ELPA; ⊠ Messoghion 395, Agia Paraskevi 15343, ☎ 01/606–8800; 104 in an emergency, FAX 01/606–8981) no longer issues these, so non-EU members should arrange for a license through their local automobile association. ELPA can help with tourist information for drivers (☎ 174), and they assist tourists with breakdowns free of charge if they belong to AAA or to ELPA (35,500 dr./€102.94 a year); otherwise, there is a charge.

Downtown **parking spaces** are hard to find—you can pay to use one of the few temporary parking areas set up in vacant lots, but you're better off leaving your car in the hotel garage and walking or taking a cab. Gas pumps and service stations are everywhere, and lead-free gas is widely available. Be aware that all-night stations are few and far between.

By Subway

In 2000, Athens opened two new metro lines, significantly extending Line 1, which runs through the city from the plush suburb of Kifissia in the north to Piraeus harbor in the south. Downtown stations on Line 1 most frequented by tourists include Platia Victorias, which is within walking distance of the National Archaeological Museum; Omonia Square; Monastiraki, located in the old Turkish bazaar; and Thission, near the ancient Agora and the nightlife districts of Psirri and Thission. The new Line 2 presently cuts northwest across the city, starting from Syntagma Square station (located in front of the Parliament), and passing through such useful stops as Panepistimiou (near the Old University complex and the Numismatic Museum); Omonia Square; and the Stathmos Larissis stop next to Athens's train stations. Scheduled to open in early 2001 was a station at the foot of the Acropolis (Acropolis). Line 3 runs from Syntagma Square northeast to the Greek "Pentagon" (Ethnikis Aminas). The stops of most interest for tourists are Evanglismos, which is near the Byzantine Museum, Hilton Hotel, and National Gallery, and Megaro Mousikis, next to the U.S. Embassy and Athens's concert hall. The subway fare is 150 dr./€.44 if you stay only on Line 1; otherwise, it's 250 dr./€.73. You can buy a monthly pass covering the subway, buses, and trolleys for 10,000 dr./€29.41 at the beginning of each month. Remember to validate your ticket by stamping it in the orange machines at the entrance to the platforms, or you will be fined.

By Taxi

Taxi rates are still affordable compared to fares in other European capitals, mainly because taxis operate unofficially on the jitney system, indicating willingness to pick up others by blinking their headlights or simply slowing down. Would-be passengers shout their destination as the driver cruises past.

Radio taxis can be booked by your hotel (a good idea when taking an early morning flight) with a surcharge of 400 dr./€1.17 for immediate response and 600 dr./€1.76–700 dr./€2.05 for an appointment to come later. Some radio-taxi companies are **Athina 1** (☎ 01/921–7942); **Hellas** (☎ 01/645–7000 or 01/801–4000); **Kosmos** (☎ 01/1300); and **Parthenon** (☎ 01/532–3300).

Most taxi drivers are honest and hardworking, but a few con artists infiltrate the ranks at the airports and near popular restaurants and clubs frequented by foreigners. Get an idea from your hotel how much the fare should be, and if there's trouble, ask to go to a police station, although most disagreements don't ever get that far. Most drivers speak basic English. Make sure the driver turns on the meter and that the rate listed in the lower corner is 1, the normal rate before midnight. Don't be alarmed if your driver picks up other passengers (although protocol indicates he should ask your permission first and will never pick up anyone if you are a woman traveling alone at night). Each passenger pays full fare for the distance he or she has traveled.

The fare begins at 200 dr./€.58, and even if you join other passengers, you must add this charge to the final amount: note the fare on the meter when you get in an occupied taxi. The minimum fare is 500 dr./€1.47. The rate is 71 dr. per 1 km (⅔ mi), 130 dr. between midnight and 5 AM and outside city limits. Surcharges are made for holidays (120 dr./€.35); fares to and from the airport (300 dr./€.88); fares to, but not from, ports, railway stations, and bus terminals (150 dr./€.44); and for each bag weighing more than 10 kilograms (55 dr./€.16), though drivers expect more (100 dr./€.29). Waiting time is 2,300 dr./€6.76 per hour.

Taxi drivers know the major central hotels, but if your hotel is less well known, show the driver the address written in Greek and make note of the phone number and, if possible, a nearby landmark. If all else fails, the driver can call the hotel from his mobile phone or a kiosk.

Athens has thousands of short side streets, and few taxi drivers have maps. If your driver gets lost despite all precautions, use the time to practice answering personal questions graciously.

Contacts and Resources

Doctors and Dentists

Most hotels will call a **doctor** for you. You can also call your embassy. For a doctor on call 2 PM–7 AM on Sundays and holidays, call ☎ 105 (in Greek). For a **dentist,** check with your hotel or embassy.

Embassies

U.S. Embassy (✉ Vasilissis Sofias 91, ☎ 01/721–2951 through 01/721–2959); **Canadian Embassy** (✉ Gennadiou 4, ☎ 01/727–3400); **U.K. Embassy** (✉ Ploutarchou 1, ☎ 01/723–6211 through 01/723–6219 or 01/727–2600); **Australian Embassy** (✉ D. Soutsou 37, ☎ 01/645–0404); **Irish Embassy** (✉ Vasileos Konstantinou 7, ☎ 01/723–2771); **New Zealand (consulate)** (✉ Kifissias 268, Halandri, ☎ 01/687–4700 or 01/687–4701).

Emergencies and Hospitals

For auto accidents call the **city police** (☎ 100). **Tourist police** (✉ Dimitrakopoulou 77, Koukaki, ☎ 171). **Fire** (☎ 199). **Ambulance** (☎ 166), though a taxi is often faster. **Coast Guard** (☎ 108).

Not all hospitals are open nightly. Call ☎ 106 (in Greek), check the *Athens News* or the English-language *Kathemerini,* or ask your hotel to check the Greek papers to find out which emergency hospitals are open.

Asklepion Hospital (✉ Vasileos Pavlou 1, Voula, ☎ 01/895–8301 through 01/895–8306); **KAT Hospital** (✉ Nikis 2, Kifissia, ☎ 01/801–4411; 166 for accidents); **Ygeia** (✉ Er. Stavrou 4 and Kifissias, Maroussi, ☎ 01/682–7940 through 01/682–7949). One maternity hospital is **Mitera** (✉ Er. Stavrou 6 and Kifissias, Maroussi, ☎ 01/686–9000). Children go to **Aglaia Kyriakou Hospital** (✉ Levadias 3 and Thivon, Goudi, ☎ 01/777–5611 through 01/777–5619) or **Ayia Sofia Hospital** (✉ Mikras Asias and Thivon, Goudi, ☎ 01/777–1811 through 01/777–1816). Note that children's hospitals answer the phone with "Pedon" and not the specific name of the institution.

English-Language Bookstores and Libraries

I Folia tou Vivliou or Booknest (✉ Panepistimiou 25–29, in arcade on mezzanine, near Syntagma, ☎ 01/322–9560) has an ample selection of American and British authors, including secondhand volumes. **Compendium** (✉ Nikis 28, upstairs, near Syntagma, ☎ 01/322–1248) has travel books, books on Greece, one of Athens's few women's-studies sections, and used books. Go to **Eleftheroudakis** (✉ Nikis 4, Syntagma Sq., ☎ 01/322–9388) for fiction, language guides, and coffee-table editions and its newer six-floor store with a great café that provides reading material and serves fresh salads, pastas, and luscious desserts (✉ Panepistimiou 17, ☎ 01/331–4180 through 01/331–4183). There's also **Kauffman** (✉ Stadiou 28, Center, ☎ 01/322–2160), for a limited selection of American fiction. Try **Pantelides** (✉ Amerikis 11, Syntagma Sq., ☎ 01/362–3673). Worth a visit is **Reymondos** (✉ Voukourestiou 18, Center, ☎ 01/364–8188 or 01/364–8189).

At the **Hellenic-American Union** (✉ Massalias 22, Kolonaki, ☎ 01/368–0000, ⊙ Mon.–Thurs. 10–8, Fri. 10–4; closed Aug.), the **library** includes both American fiction and nonfiction books in English on Greek topics. Also try the **British Council Library** (✉ Kolonaki Sq. 17, ☎ 01/364–5768, ⊙ Sept.–May, Mon. and Thurs. 3–8, Tues.–Wed. and Fri. 9:30–2:30; June and July, weekdays 9:30–1:30; closed 3 wks in Aug.).

The **Gennadius Library, American School of Classical Studies** (⊠ Soudias 61, Kolonaki, ☎ 01/721–0536, ☾ Mon.–Tues., Fri. 9:30–5, Wed.–Thurs. 9:30–8, Sat. 9:30–2; closed Aug.) is also interesting, though it is not a lending library. Call first; hours change frequently.

Guided Tours

EXCURSIONS

Most agencies offer excursions at about the same prices, but **CHAT** (☞ *below*) is reputed to have the best service and guides. Taking a half-day trip to the breathtaking Temple of Poseidon at Sounion avoids the hassle of dealing with the crowded public buses or paying a great deal more for a taxi. The 8,200 dr./€24,11 cost is well spent. A new half-day tour to the Isthmus and ancient Corinth is now available (13,500 dr./€39.70). A one-day tour to Delphi with lunch costs 21,500 dr./€63.23 (18,500 dr./€54.41 without lunch), but the two-day tour (34,000 dr./€100 including half-board in first-class hotels, 29,500 dr./€86.76 for tourist-class) is far preferable. There's also a one-day tour to Nafplion, Mycenae, and Epidauros (21,500 dr./€63.23 with lunch), and a two-day tour to Mycenae, Nafplion, and Epidaurus (34,000 dr./€100 first-class, 29,500 dr./€86.76 tourist-class). A three-day tour takes in both Delphi and the stunning monasteries of Meteora with half-board in first-class hotels (79,000 dr./€232.35, 69,000 dr./€202.94 tourist-class). For those who have more time, the four-day tour covers Nafplion, Mycenae, Epidauros, Olympia, and Delphi for 107,000 dr./€314.70 (first-class) and 93,500 dr./€275 (tourist-class). The five-day "classical tour" (144,000 dr./€423 first-class, 126,000 dr./€370 tourist-class) covers all major sights in the Peloponnese, as well as Delphi and Meteora. A full-day cruise from Piraeus, visiting three nearby islands—Aegina, Poros, and Hydra—costs around 20,500 dr./€60.29 (including buffet lunch on the ship). Athens travel agencies can also arrange a six-day **northern Greece** tour including Delphi, Meteora, Thessaloniki, and outlying archaeological sites for 210,000 dr./€617.

ORIENTATION TOURS

Most travel agencies offer four-hour morning bus tours of Athens (10,500 dr./€30.80), including a guided tour of the Acropolis and its museum. Reservations can be made through most hotels or any travel agency; many are clustered around Filellinon and Nikis streets off Syntagma Square (☞ *below*).

PERSONAL GUIDES

Major travel agencies can provide English-speaking guides. The **Union of Official Guides** (⊠ Apollonas 9A, ☎ 01/322–9705, ℻ 01/323–9200) provides licensed guides for individual or group tours, starting at about 28,000 dr./€82.35 including taxes for a four-hour tour of the Acropolis and its museum. Only hire guides licensed by the EOT, which means they have successfully completed a two-year state program.

SPECIAL-INTEREST TOURS

Athens by Night tours, offered by all agencies, are a convenient way to see some of the touristy evening entertainment, especially for single travelers who may not want to venture out alone. For those interested in **folk dancing**, there is a four-hour evening tour (10,000 dr./€29.41) from April to October, which includes the Sound and Light Spectacle and a performance of Dora Stratou folk dances. Another evening tour follows the Sound and Light Spectacle with a **dinner show at a Plaka taverna** (14,000 dr./€41). Any travel agency can arrange these tours, but go first to CHAT Tours (☞ *below*) for reliable and efficient service. For organized adventure travel, contact **Trekking Hellas** and **F-Zein** (☞ Travel Agencies, *below*).

The **Amphitrion Holidays,** part of the Amphitrion Travel group (☞ *below*), specializes in educational and offbeat tours for individuals in Athens and elsewhere, including island-hopping tours and treks in the Pindos mountains.

Cruises to the four most popular islands—Mykonos, Rhodes, Crete, and Santorini—usually operate from mid-March through October. Try **Golden Sun Cruises** (✉ Akti Miaouli 85, Piraeus, ☎ 01/429–0650 through 01/429–0660, FAX 01/420–0660 for reservations ✆) and **Royal Olympic Cruises** (✉ Akti Miaouli 87, Piraeus, ☎ 01/429–0700 for reservations, FAX 01/429–0636 for reservations ✆). Most also have downtown Athens representatives.

For hiking tours, the **Hellenic Federation of Mountaineering and Climbing** (✉ Milioni 5, Kolonaki, ☎ 01/364–5904, FAX 01/364–2687) supplies details on mountain paths, refuges, and contact numbers for local clubs.

For horseback riding tours, the helpful **Hellenic Equestrian Federation** (✉ Messinias 55, Goudi, ☎ 01/748–6875 or 01/748–6876, FAX 01/778–1572) provides a list of Athens's riding clubs.

Late-Night Pharmacies

Call ☎ 107 for a Greek-language recording of pharmacies open on holidays and late at night or check the *Athens News*. Each pharmacy posts in its window a list of establishments close by that are open during the afternoon break or late at night. Many pharmacies in the center have someone who speaks English, or try **Thomas** (✉ Papadiamantopoulou 6, near the Hilton Hotel and Holiday Inn, Ilissia, ☎ 01/721–6101) for convenience and spoken English.

Travel Agencies

American Express (✉ Ermou 2, ☎ 01/324–4975, FAX 01/322–7893); **Amphitrion Travel LTD** (✉ Syngrou 7, ☎ 01/924–9701, FAX 01/924–9671; ✉ Deuteras Merachias 3, Piraeus, ☎ 01/411–2045 through 01/411–2049, FAX 01/417–0742); **CHAT** (✉ Stadiou 4, ☎ 01/322–2886, FAX 01/323–5270); **Key Tours** (✉ Kallirois 4, ☎ 01/923–3166, FAX 01/923–2008); **Magic Travel Service (Magic Bus)** (✉ Filellinon 20, ☎ 01/323–7471, FAX 01/322–0219); and **Travel Plan** (✉ Christou Lada 9, ☎ 01/323–8801 through 01/323–8804, FAX 01/322–2152).

Closer to Omonia, try **Condor Travel** (✉ Stadiou 43, ☎ 01/321–2453 or 01/321–6986, FAX 01/321–4296), the ubiquitous **Manos** (✉ Panepistimiou 39, ☎ 01/323–9003 through 01/323–9007, FAX 01/322–9908), and **Pharos Travel and Tourism** (✉ 18 Triti Septemvriou, ☎ 01/523–3403 or 01/523–6142, FAX 01/523–3726). In the U.S., **Pharos Travel and Tourism** (✉ 25–36 31st St., Astoria, New York, 11102, ☎ 718/932–3960, FAX 718/932–7759) can help you put together an independent tour at competitive prices.

Visitor Information

Greek National Tourist Organization (EOT) offices (✉ Amerikis 2, near Syntagma Sq., ☎ 01/331–0565 or 01/331–0692; ✉ East Terminal [Arrivals] of Ellinikon Airport, ☎ 01/961–2722 or 01/969–4500; ✉ EOT Building, 1st floor, near where the hydrofoils dock, Zea Marina, ☎ 01/452–2591 or 01/452–2586).

The **tourist police** (✉ Dimitrakopoulou 77, ☎ 171) can answer questions in English about transportation, steer you to an open pharmacy or doctor, and locate phone numbers of hotels and restaurants.

2 EXCURSIONS FROM ATHENS

ATTICA, THE SARONIC GULF ISLANDS, AND DELPHI

Want to escape from the cacophony of Athens? Head for the interior of Attica, the heartline of the surrounding region, set with rustic inns, local wineries, small towns, and rolling hills covered with citrus orchards and olive groves. It is inevitable that the fame of Marathon, or the rich iconography of Daphni monastery, will inspire an excursion over the forbidding mountains guarding the passes into Athens. All who land in Athens are destined sooner or later to make a pilgrimage to Delphi, where the priestesses of antiquity uttered their enigmatic prophecies. Then steal away to the Saronic Gulf islands and discover the crumbling 19th-century merchants' mansions of Aegina and Hydra, the ghosts of Spetsiot pirates, the white and periwinkle homes in the labyrinthine streets of Poros, and, of course, the immutable sea.

By Catherine
Vanderpool

Updated by
B. Samantha
Stenzel

I F ANYTHING WAS EVER TRULY "CLASSICAL," it is the landscape of
Attica. Atikí is, like most of Greece, a mountainous region, bounded
on three sides by sea and an indented coastline fringed with innu-
merable sandy beaches and rocky coves. On the stony foothills, only
a few pungently aromatic shrubs grow in the poor soil: thyme, myrtle, and *lentisk*. Higher up, the feathery Aleppo pine of Attica (from
which the resin is tapped to make retsina) is supplanted by dramatically tall, pyramidal-shaped fir trees. But it is the *mesogeion,* or "inland," that comes to mind when we think of Attica: gently undulating
hills and fields laced with vineyards and citrus orchards and dotted with
olive trees. It is still blanketed in part by sweet-smelling thyme, food
for the bees, whose hives in blue boxes were once a familiar sight along
any country road and are still seen on many of them. Here, too, are
the quarries of Mt. Penteli, the inexhaustible source for a special quality of marble that weathers to a warm golden tint. Over all hangs that
famed "Attic light," the purest of rays sharply delineating the exquisite
configuration of mountains, sea, and plain that is Attica.

It is the proper setting for a region immensely rich in mythological and
historical allusions. In fact, it is believed that recorded history began
here, in the towns of the Boetian plain, although where legend leaves
off and fact begins is often a matter of conjecture (witness Thebes, home
to the luckless Oedipus). Historians can be sure that since the first millennium BC, the story of Attica has been almost inextricably bound to
that of Athens, the most powerful of the villages that lay scattered over
the peninsula. By force and persuasion Athens brought these towns together, creating a unit that by the 5th century BC had become the center of an empire. The heart of the region was the sacred precinct of
Delphi. For the ancient Greeks, this site was the center of the universe,
home to Apollo and the most sacred oracle, and today it remains a principal place of pilgrimage for visitors to Greece, as well as Greeks. Delphi is also the most evocative of the ancient sites, one in which a
visitor can truly feel the presence of the pagan deities.

Northeast of Pendeli, between the slopes and the sea, lies the fabled
plain of Marathon, its flat expanse now dotted with small agricultural
communities and seaside resorts, second home to many Athenians. Attica includes such sites as the Temple of Poseidon, spectacularly perched
on Cape Sounion, and, up the coast and around the northern flank of
Pendeli, the enchantingly rural archaeological site at the Amphiareion.
It takes in the Fortress of Phyle, on the slopes of Parnitha; the Sanctuary of Demeter and Kore at Eleusis; and the Monastery of Daphni.

It is in the small towns of the interior of Attica—bucolic retreats such
as Markopoulo (home of Kourtaki, the most popular bottled retsina,
also famed for its barrel wine and country-style bread) and the wooded
towns of Paenia and Pikermi—that the soul of Attica lies. This undulating landscape has been slow to be developed since most Athenians
have gravitated to the coastal areas for vacations and to build second
homes. However, and unfortunately, vast changes will no doubt occur
in this region due to the construction of the nearby Spata airport, directly west of Athens, and now slated to be completed by 2002—it will
immediately assume the mantle of the main airport of Athens.

So, for true escape, you may need to head to the sun-gilt sea and the
Saronic Gulf Islands, which straddle the gulf between Athens and the
Peloponnese. Aegina, Poros, Hydra, and Spetses are especially popular with Athenians, owing to their proximity and, especially in the case
of the latter two, their natural beauty. Yet they all retain their distinct

cultural traditions, best appreciated out of high season, when the isles are not inundated with mainlanders and tourists. Aegina, the closest Saronic island to Piraeus, in ancient times was renowned for its bronze work; it eventually succumbed to the power of Athens and two millenniums later played a pivotal role in the War of Independence. Tiny Poros, almost grazing the shores of the Peloponnese, was once the site of an imposing 6th century BC Temple of Poseidon, now nothing more than a few columns and a pile of fragments. Extant proof of Hydra's and Spetses' prosperity in the 18th and 19th centuries are the stately, forbidding mansions built by the fleet-owning shipping magnates; they are now the playground of carefree European vacationers. All in all, many of the region's sights enjoy singularly memorable settings and make for enchanting destinations.

Pleasures and Pastimes

Dining

The cuisine of Attica resembles that of Athens, central Greece, and the Peloponnese. Local ingredients predominate, with fresh fish becoming scarcer and more expensive. Since much of Attica's vegetation is used to support herds of grazing sheep and the omnivorous goat, the meat of both animals is also a staple in many country tavernas. Although not as common as they were a decade ago, a fair number of traditional Greek tavernas can be found in the market towns and villages of Attica, as well as along the back streets of the Saronic Gulf islands. These family-run, rustic haunts still entice with their large stew pots full of the day's special, or big *tapsi* (pans) of *pastitsio* (layers of pasta, meat, and cheese laced with cinnamon) or *papoutsakia* (eggplant slices filled with minced meat)—all tasty, inexpensive meals. Always ask to see the *kouzina* (kitchen) to look at the day's offerings, or even peer inside the pots. Regional cuisine in Delphi and Arachova relies heavily on meats, including game, and game is also a specialty of the smaller Attica villages such as Paenia and Pikermi. On the Saronic islands and in the coastal town of Galaxidi, fresh fish and seafood courses dominate. Informal but discreet and neat dress is appropriate at all but the very fanciest of restaurants, and, unless noted, reservations are not necessary.

CATEGORY	COST*
$$$$	over 15,000 dr. (€44.24)
$$$	9,000 dr.–15,000 dr. (€26.54–€44.24)
$$	5,000 dr.–9,000 dr. (€14.74–€26.54)
$	under 5,000 dr. (€14.74)

for three-course meal, including VAT and service charge but excluding drinks and tip

Lodging

Many of the hotels in Attica are resorts catering to package tourists or to Athenian families who move to the coast for the summer. In the last two decades, many have been built of reinforced concrete slabs, with spindly metal balconies and diverse facilities, but the decor, which varies little from one to the next, tends to be a modern "Greek island" look: simple pine furnishings, tile floors, and, at most, a colorful bedspread. Be forewarned: some of the large hotels ask you to take halfboard, particularly in high season. If you know your plans ahead of time, you should book through a travel agent, who can negotiate a good price and eliminate the half-board requirement, if you wish. Delphi and Arachova, which have had recent minibooms in hotel construction, have a number of appealing small establishments, with fresh, cheerful rooms and public spaces, but elsewhere, these picturesque, cozy, family-owned country inns and pensions are rare. Note also that many hotels close in late fall and reopen usually around Easter week, except in Delphi and Arachova, where high season (with top prices) is during ski season, though even then weekdays are about half the price of weekends. Accommodations on the islands range from elegant 19th-century mansions, usually labeled as traditional settlements, to spare rental rooms overlooking a noisy waterfront. Note that many of these small hotels—even those at the upper end—use solar energy exclusively in the summer. If this is the case, find out when it is best to bathe, so you can get to a shower or tub before the hot water runs out—otherwise you may be forced to take a freezing cold shower, or not bathe at all! In the listings, all $$$ and $$$$ hotels have air-conditioning unless otherwise noted.

CATEGORY	COST*
$$$$	over 60,000 dr. (€176)
$$$	35,000 dr.–60,000 dr. (€103.24–€176)
$$	20,000 dr.–35,000 dr. (€58.99–€103.23)
$	under 20,000 dr. (€58.99)

All prices are the official rate for a standard double room, including taxes but excluding breakfast unless so noted, during the summer high season (Arachova and Delphi's high season is winter).

✇ *following the text of a review is your signal that the property has a Web site, where you will find details and, usually, images; for a link, visit www.fodors.com/urls.*

Nightlife

Perhaps it is the daytime heat through so many months of the year; perhaps it is an excess of energy; perhaps it is their intense sociability, unrequited during the workday; but whatever the reason, Greeks love going out at night. Traffic can be as bad at 3 AM as in the morning rush hour. Some nightspots emphasize the show over the cuisine, others do the opposite, and they range from the simplest taverna with a bouzouki trio to fancy nightclubs where Greek youths party beachside until dawn.

For dancing, the discos at most large resort hotels are usually open to outsiders as well as guests, but more popular are the Athens dancing clubs that move to rented space on the coastal road, especially south of the capital from Glyfada to Vouliagmeni, and at eastern beach towns like Porto Rafti and Nea Makri. Clubs and addresses change annually, so ask around or, if you can read Greek, check the weekly entertainment guide *Athinorama,* available at kiosks, or pick up a copy of the English language guide, *Athenscope,* at a tourist office. Of the islands, Hydra and Spetses offer the most sophisticated bars and discos. Many discos feature Greek music and dancing at about midnight; a few clubs and restaurants feature it during the summer season.

Exploring Attica, the Saronic Gulf Islands, and Delphi

Athens lies in a basin defined by three mountain masses: Mt. Hymettus to the east, Mt. Aigaleos and Mt. Parnis (called Parnitha in Greek) to the west, and Mt. Pendeli to the north. Set out from this region and first head south along the coast down to Cape Sounion and the breathtaking Temple of Poseidon, then back up along the water to storied Marathon and the sylvan glades of Amphiareion. As you travel back to Athens, the tour takes in the great Byzantine monastery of Daphni and the famous sanctuary of Demeter. The second tour explores the lovely Saronic Gulf islands, beloved by Athenians for their pleasure and proximity. The third tour is a pilgrimage to Delphi, seat of the most important oracle in ancient Greece and of the then known world; it enjoys a classic setting straight out of a picture book.

Numbers in the text correspond to numbers in the margin and on the Attica and the Saronic Gulf Islands and Delphi maps.

Great Itineraries

If you only have a few days to explore the areas around Athens, you'll probably want to stick to the most important site, which is Delphi. In a five- or six-day itinerary you'll be able to see Delphi, some of the major sites around Athens such as Daphni and Sounion, and maybe an island (Aegina is the closest). A 9- or 10-day trip will enable you to see all of the above, a few more sites in Attica, and the farther Saronic Gulf islands, such as Hydra and Spetses.

IF YOU HAVE 3 DAYS

A three-day trip means concentrating on the essentials so you get the most out of your time. Exploring ⛫ **Delphi** ㉓–㉖ requires at least one full day, so be sure to go early in the morning (it's a three-hour drive or bus ride) or better yet, the night before. A second day could be spent visiting the principal sites of Attica, starting with ⛫ **Sounion** ④, up to ⛫ **Marathon** ⑧, and **Amphiareion** ⑪. A third day offers the chance to visit ⛫ **Aegina** ⑯, the Saronic Gulf island closest to Athens.

IF YOU HAVE 6 DAYS

Attica makes the most reasonable start of a six-day tour; begin by going to Poseidon's temple at ⛫ **Sounion** ④, followed by a foray north to **Brauron** ⑦, ⛫ **Marathon** ⑧, and either **Rhamnous** ⑨ or the **Amphiareion** ⑪. A morning seeing the Sanctuary of Demeter at ancient **Eleusis** ⑭ is best succeeded by an afternoon at the Byzantine **Monastery of Daphni** ⑬. Spend your third and fourth days in and around ⛫ **Delphi** ㉓–㉖, where nearby **Osios Loukas** ㉑, with its early Byzantine monastic complex, and ⛫ **Arachova** ㉒, with its juxtaposition of colorful tavernas and sophisticated cafés and bars, or **Galaxidi** ㉗, a pretty port with fine fish and seafood, offer pleasant digressions from the ancient sites. Finally, a couple of days among the Saronic Gulf islands will round out your trip. Two days could pass very quickly on ⛫ **Aegina** ⑯, but you could also see the principal sites (the **Sanctuary of Aphaia** ⑰ being the foremost) in one day, and spend a second on ⛫ **Hydra** ⑱, an island blissfully free of vehicles, whose shops, nightlife, and pace appeal to an international clientele.

IF YOU HAVE 9 DAYS

A thorough exploration of Attica, the Saronic Gulf islands, and Delphi requires nine days. Step into ancient Greece on your first day with visits to ⛫ **Sounion** ④, **Brauron** ⑦, ⛫ **Marathon** ⑧, and the **Amphiareion** ⑪, or perhaps the ancient fortress of **Phyle** ⑫ on Mt. Parnitha. On day two, take a break from ancient Greece and visit the Byzantine **Monastery of Kaisariani** ①, and the Vorres museum at **Paiania** ⑥. Next day, go west from Athens to the **Monastery of Daphni** ⑬ and ancient and vast **Eleusis** ⑭. After three days of Attica start your journey to ⛫ **Delphi** ㉓–㉖, deep in the mountains northwest of Attica. Delphi is one of Greece's most impressive sites, with an excellent museum, a world-famous archaeological site, and stunning scenery; the region can be seen in a day or two. The nearby mountain village of ⛫ **Arachova** ㉒ and the charming harbor town of ⛫ **Galaxidi** ㉗ make fabulous alternative bases for Delphi, especially for those eager for a taste of modern as well as ancient Greece. While in the vicinity don't forget to visit **Osios Loukas** ㉑, a monastery with priceless frescoes, nestled in a secret valley. Your last three or four days will find you relishing the surprisingly varied Saronic Gulf islands, each with its own

Attica and the Saronic Gulf Islands

Skala Oropou

Thebes

Assopia

BOETIA

TO DELPHI, LEVADIA (see inset)

Amphiareion
11 Kalamos

Pili

Erithres

Kapandriti

Rhamnous Archaeological Site
9

Inoi

Lake Marathon
10

Mt. Parnitha
Varibombi

Mt. Pendeli

8 **Marathon**

Nea Makri

Fortress of Phyle ■

Ayia Triada ■
12 **Phyle**

ATTICA

Ano Liosia

Aspropirgos

Monastery of Daou Pendeli ■

Mandra

Mt. Aigaleos

Peristeri

Pallini

Rafina

14 **Eleusis**

Straits of Salamis

13
Monastery of Daphni

★

Pikermi

Loutsa

Megara

Perama

Athens

1

6 **Paiania**

7 **Brauron**

Salamis

Piraeus

Monastery of Kaisariani

Salamina **15**

Voula

Hymettos

Koropi

Porto Rafti

2

Markopoulos

Glyfada

3 **Vouliagmeni**

Keratea

Theater of Thorikos ■

Sanctuary of Aphaia
17

Palaia Fokaia

Lavrion **5**

Aegina town **16**

Ayia Marina

4 **Sounion**

Legrena

Patroklou

Aegina

Gulf of Epidauros

Methana

TO ALL AEGEAN ISLANDS

Poros

18

TO CRETE

Troezen

Galatas

KEY
- - - Ferry

Ermioni

19

Hydra

Dokos

Hydra

N

Spetses **20**

Spetses

0   50 miles

0   75 km

MT. PARNASSUS

Delphi
23 — **26**

Amfissa

22 **Arachova**

Itea   48

Dhistomo

Levadia

Desfina

27

Galaxidi

21

Osios Loukas

TO ATHENS, THEBES

N

Gulf of Corinth

flavor, but all sharing in the common credo that the leisurely life is better than the fast track. Your island tour can begin at ☷ **Aegina** ⑯, where you can snack on the island's famous pistachios and visit the **Sanctuary of Aphaia** ⑰. A day on Aegina can only be outdone by a day on ☷ **Hydra** ⑲, to which the European jet set escapes when struck by an urge to lounge in beautiful mansion-hotels and putter about the island's shops, cafés, and nightclubs. Once you've wandered around the car-free streets of Hydra you may not want to go anywhere else, but ☷ **Spetses** ⑳ also doesn't allow cars (motorcycles are permitted), and it has about an equal number of sites scattered along its extensive shoreline and pine-forested hills.

When to Tour

As with elsewhere in Greece, services in these areas are greatly reduced during the winter, except in Delphi and Arachova, which are refuges for skiers who usually flock to Mt. Parnassus up north. The islands explode into activity during July and August, so be prepared to go head to head with the crowds and the heat; a better time to visit is May or September through October. In spring an extraordinary variety of wild flowers carpets the arid hillsides of Attica and the Marathonian plain and hills leading to Rhamnous.

ATTICA

Glyfada, Vouliagmeni, Sounion, Lavrion, Paiania, Brauron, Marathon, Phyle, Daphni, Eleusis

The bulk of Attica, which stretches southeast into the Aegean, lies east and north of Athens. Separated from Central Greece by mountains—Pateras, Kithairon, Pastra, and Parnitha—and bordered by the sea, Attica was easily defensible. It also had several fertile plains, well watered with rivers and seasonal streams, and its coves and natural harbors encouraged the development of seafaring and trade.

Kaisariani

6 km (4 mi) east of Athens center.

❶ The **Monastery of Kaisariani** lies on the slopes of Hymettos, the eastern "wall" of Athens, which yields the sun each morning and catches its last purple shadows at night. Denuded of its pine forests in the destructive years during World War II, the mountain has since been successfully reforested by the Athenian Friends of the Trees Society, and is fragrant with the scent of pine, olive, and eucalyptus trees.

An ascent on natural stone steps brings you to a glen of pine, cypress, and plane trees, fed by a copious flow of water (the source of the famed Illissos River): the cradle for the beautiful walled complex of the Monastery of Kaisariani. Its setting, serene with the babble of streams and rustling of leaves punctuated mainly by the hum of the bees feeding on nearby thyme, provides a sharp contrast to modern Athens set far below (take advantage of the picnic benches placed here for a relaxing rest stop before or after a visit inside the monastery). An ancient temple of Aphrodite stood on the hill just above the present-day monastery, which dates to the 11th century. The exquisite, medieval buildings, surrounding a central court, include the *katholikon* (or church, built in the traditional cross-in-a-square), a refectory, cells, and a bathhouse, all restored in 1956–57. Most of the frescoes (except for those in the narthex, which have been credited to Ioannis Ipatos, a 17th-century Peloponnesian artist) are from the 17th and 18th centuries and are in the Cretan style. The oldest, dating from the 14th century, are in the side chapel of St. Anthony and show the Virgin Mary at prayer. The grounds of the monastery are worth a walk; an herbal garden is thriving and, along with honey and wine, is a source of income for the few monks who remain in residence.

A spring feeds the ram's head fountain to the left of the monastery's entrance; the original is in the Acropolis Museum, and was part of a Roman sarcophagus. To the right just after the courtyard, a path leads to the *aghiasmos,* or sacred fountain, coming from the sacred spring that is the source of the famed Illissos River. It has also been identified as the site of the ancient temple dedicated to Aphrodite (the backdrop for the jealous lovers in Ovid's *Ars Amatoria,* or The Art of Love), although no traces remain. Amazingly, this spring supplied the water for all of Athens until the Marathon Dam was built (1925–31). Greeks often come to fill bottles with water from the fountains, reputed to aide conception of healthy children, and mothers often bathe sick children in its waters. A mystical ancient cult ritual is still celebrated here on August 15—the feast day of the Assumption of the Virgin Mary. After the service in the catholikon, the clergy has a procession up to the fountain, where they wait to sight a dove that is believed to have descended from heaven to hover over the spring to renew its powers. Everyone then drinks from its waters and a feast follows.

From the aghiasmos, you get a spectacular view of Athens, including the Acropolis, the ships in Piraeus harbor, and the Saronic islands with the Peloponnese in the background. Painter Edward Dodwell spent some days here in the beginning of the 19th century and commented, "But no view could equal that from Hymettos, in rich magnificence or attractive charms." ⊠ *Mountain road starting at Ethnikis Antistaseos, 6 km (4 mi) east of Athens center,* ☎ *01/723–6619.* ⌨ *800 dr./€2.35.* ⊙ *Tues.–Sun. 8:30–2:45; grounds daily sunrise–sunset.*

The **Moni Asteriou** (⊠ 9 km [5½ mi] up the hill from Kaisariani Monastery) also dates to the 11th century. A nearby path descends 1½ km (about 1 mi) to the chapel of Byzantine **Ayios Ioannis Theologou** above the suburb of Goudi. On this pleasant detour, you will enjoy another view of Athens, the mesogheion of Attica, the Marathon plain, and a closer look at—and scent of—the tiny aromatic shrubs (sage, mostly) that still lure the bees of Mt. Hymettos, giving that special flavor to its famous honey.

Festivals

From June through July and again in September, the **Krystalleia Festival** offers outdoor evening concerts of pop and classical music in the Megaron Plakentias, the former Rododafni Palace that served as the Duchess de Plaisance's home in Pendeli (⊠ 16 km [10 mi] northeast of Athens on Mount Pendeli, near the Athenian suburb of Ayia Paraskevi). It was built for this eccentric lady in 19th-century neo-Gothic style by the architect Stamatis Kleanthis, who also designed the Villa Ilissia, now Athens's Byzantine Museum, for her. Alongside the Krystalleia Festival is the **Pendelis Festival** (end of July and September), which focuses on classical music, often importing international orchestras to take advantage of the Megaron's excellent acoustics. For information on the festivals, contact the Greek National Tourist Organization (GNTO or EOT) in Athens or the Megaron (☎ 01/804–2575). Tickets run from 2,000 dr./€5.89 to 4,000 dr./€11.79 and are usually sold at major record stores in downtown Athens.

Glyfada

❷ *17 km (10½ mi) southeast of Athens, 21 km (13 mi) south of Kaisariani.*

This prosperous seaside resort town is best used as a base from which to explore Attica. Glyfada has a few beautiful villas, a fine golf course, several large marinas, and the dubious distinction of offering the highest concentration of shopping centers found in Greece. Its proximity to the airport should please those with early morning flights but distress all others.

Beaches

Attica's southwestern coast is mainly rock, with some short sandy stretches in **Glyfada** and **Voula,** which have been made into public pay beaches by EOT, with snack bars, changing rooms, beach umbrellas, rental water-sports equipment, and sometimes windsurfing and waterskiing lessons. Most are open from 8 AM to 8 PM in summer, unless there is a heat wave, when the government has kept them open to the public, free, until midnight. Tickets are 600 dr./€1.76, with reduced rates for children. In recent years, western Attica's beaches have become cleaner, though those on the east side are preferable in this respect. The pay beaches close to Glyfada are those at **Alimos** (☎ 01/982–7064) and **Voula** (☎ 01/895–3296 1st beach; 01/895–9587 2nd beach), which all received Blue Flags for cleanliness from the European Union despite their proximity to Athens.

Dining and Lodging

$$$ ✕ **Sphinx.** Successful in Santorini, the owners opened this second Sphinx in 1998, and it has received raves from diners ever since. Who can resist dining in this elegant garden or the cozy dining room, complete with glass roof, while listening to light jazz. The house features "fusion" cuisine, with a sampling of various Mediterranean cultures and an emphatic Italian influence, as you'll see in the wide variety of pastas, including pesto Genovese, spaghetti with lobster, and black risotto with cuttlefish. House specialities include the sliced veal fillet with foie gras and a sauce made from Santorini Vizanto and pork loin stuffed with pesto. Diners can also choose from a selection of fresh fish, such as baked grouper with lemon, capers, and thyme sauce, and daily specials. Hats off to the chef for the sweets—one of the restaurant's strong suits—particularly the chocolate soufflé, crème brûlée and mille-feuille with chocolate sauce. ✉ *Kyprou 65A, behind the Glyfada public pool,* ☎ *01/894–0050. Reservations essential. AE, DC, MC, V. Closed Sun. and four days around Aug. 15. No lunch.*

$$ ✕ **Loxandra.** Known for home-style Greek cuisine, Loxandra also provides bouzouki-guitar accompaniment with your meal winter weekends, October through Easter. Enjoy *magirefta* (stove-top or oven-cooked dishes, usually made earlier) in winter such as *yiouvetsi Loxandra* (pork with miniature macaroni), and in summer the many tis ores, such as beef stuffed with *graviera* cheese and served with mushroom sauce. No matter the season, order the well-made appetizers such as *bourekakia* (cheese fingers in flaky pastry) and the zucchini pie. Sweets lovers will get their fix from *karidopita,* a syrupy walnut cake. ✉ *Eleftherios Venizelou 15, near golf course,* ☎ *01/963–1731. DC, V. Closed Mon. and Aug. No lunch July–mid-Sept.*

$$ ✕ **Palai Pote.** This *mezedopolio* (casual café specializing in appetizers) evokes bygone years with its old-fashioned courtyard and popular music companies, who usually play evenings October through April. Try the *yiaourtada,* lamb baked in the oven with yogurt and grapes; fat sardines wrapped in vine leaves and cooked with onion; and the shrimp lavished with poppy and sesame seeds. Other popular dishes include the spicy lobster claws, and mussels with a fragrant sauce of orange and saffron; a few fresh pastas are also on the menu. ⊠ *Gr. Lambraki 75,* ☎ *01/963–2739. Reservations essential Fri.–Sat. V. Closed Mon. No lunch except Sun. Oct.–Apr. (with music).*

$$$ 🖬 **Hotel Best Western Fenix.** This professionally maintained and well-run hotel offers comfortable rooms decorated in earth tones, modern facilities, and proximity to the airport and the Glyfada golf course; yet prices are at the low end of its category. Renovated in 1995, all rooms have new furniture and redone bathrooms, satellite TV with a pay-movie system, direct-dial phones, and balconies. In summer, guests can lounge at the poolside bar or in the gregarious cocktail bar. Double-glazed windows eliminate any noise from the main road and nearby airport. A bountiful buffet breakfast is included in the price. ⊠ *Artemisiou 1, Box 70183, Fleming Sq., 16610,* ☎ *01/898–1255 to 01/898–1259,* ℻ *01/894–9122. 129 rooms, 3 suites. Restaurant, bar, pool, airport shuttle. AE, DC, MC, V.* ✆

$$ 🖬 **Zina Hotel.** If you have children or are traveling with a group of friends or family, Zina is a fine selection, offering a good alternative to staying in the center of Athens. It is set in a quiet area with lots of trees and flowers, just a short walk from the large Lambrakis playground and park. All spacious apartments can sleep at least four, are fully appointed and air-conditioned, and have double-glazed windows and balconies. The Astir Beach Glyfada is five minutes away by taxi or car and the airport 10 minutes. The large penthouse has a view over all of Glyfada. ⊠ *Evangelistrias 6, close to Lambrakis playground, 16674,* ☎ *01/960–3872,* ℻ *01/960–4004. 19 apartments. Air-conditioning, kitchens, laundry. V.*

Festival

Glyfada hosts a **summer concert festival** featuring ethnic and Greek music at the carved marble open-air theater Aixoni (⊠ Hydras 11, Glyfada) in July. Tickets are available from the box office (☎ 01/898–2506) or the **Glyfada town hall** (⊠ Saki Karagiorga 2, Glyfada, ☎ 01/898–2182) and cost 3,000 dr./€8.84–5,000 dr./€14.74.

Nightlife

CLUBS

Glyfada is renowned as a summer party spot, since some of Athens's most popular discos and clubs close up shop downtown and move here in the summer. For example, in 1998 the popular rock-oriented club **Camel Club (Tube)** (⊠ Vouliagmenis 268, ☎ 01/971–6145) operated near the town golf course; **Tango** (⊠ Alkyonidon 4, ☎ 01/895–6577) moved to EOT Voula's second beach; the super disco **Plus Soda** (⊠ Evrialis 2) relocated from Thission, where the Nea Deilina bouzoukia operates in winter. **Bio-Bio** features current superstars of Greek popular music where it sets up shop in Glyfada (⊠ 5th bus station past the airport in Glyfada, ☎ 01/894–1300). **Yahoo** (☎ 01/894–4166) is a new complex next to Bio-Bio and has a large disco, Asian restaurant, and computer terminals in the lobby for young and restless clients who get bored with the live action. Last but certainly not least, **Posidonio** (⊠ Posidonios 18, ☎ 01/894–1033), near the international airport, is the classic bouzouki club: huge, featuring the biggest stars, and filled with hedonistic Athenians who all seem to be celebrating something while decked out in their glitziest garb, making this *the* place to see and be seen. It's best to ask your hotel for the latest information concerning any other current hot spots, locations, and telephone numbers, many of which change season to season.

Outdoor Activities and Sports

GOLF

The **Glyfada Golf Course** (⊠ End of Pronois, at the southeast side of Athens International Airport, ☎ 01/894–6820, FAX 01/894–3721) has on its roster many distinguished politicians, businessmen, and members of the diplomatic community. Visitors need to make reservations for the weekends by Wednesday. The greens are open Tuesday through Sunday from 7:30 AM to sunset and on Monday 1 PM (noon in winter) until sunset; the greens fee is 14,000 dr./€41.29 during the week, 18,000 dr./€53.09 on weekends.

SAILING

Yachts can be rented year-round, but spring and fall are less expensive than the summer and, even better, the northerly *meltemi* winds are not blowing then. Many yacht brokers charter boats and organize underwater "safaris," scuba tours, and "flotilla" cruises in small, rented sailboats around the islands. **Viking Star Cruises** (⊠ Artemidos 1, Glyfada 16674, ☎ 01/898–0729 or 01/898–0829, FAX 01/894–0952) arranges weeklong cruises from April through October, leaving every Friday for Mykonos, Santorini, Delos, Paros, Naxos, Ios, and Tinos on a 14-cabin yacht. Tourists who have a diploma for the open sea can legally rent a sailboat (without a captain if two people on board are licensed); rentals range from about 45,000 dr./€132 to 200,000 dr./€389 a day, depending on the size and age of the boat and whether a skipper is included. Located in a nearby seaside suburb is **Vernicos Yachts** (⊠ Leoforos Poseidonos 11, Alimos, Athens 17455, ☎ 01/985–0122 through 01/985–0128, FAX 01/985–0130).

Vouliagmeni

❸ *25 km (15½ mi) south of Athens, 8 km (5 mi) southwest of Glyfada.*

Vouliagmeni is now a classy seaside residential suburb and the most prestigious address for an Athenian's summer home or business. It is coveted for its large yacht harbor and its most scenic corner, the Laimos (Neck) Vouliagmenisa promontory, which is lined with umbrella pines and includes an area called Kavouri, with several seaside fish tavernas. Much like Glyfada, Vouliagmeni can serve the tourist as a convenient base from which to explore Attica, but it is far less crowded than Glyfada.

Beaches

Cleaner than the pay beaches farther north are the EOT-run **beaches** in this area, including **Vouliagmeni** (☎ 01/896–0906) and **Varkiza** (☎ 01/897–2402), which are always popular. They're open 7:30 AM to 9 PM; tickets are 800 dr./€2.35, with lower rates for youngsters. Varkiza's bay is popular with windsurfers. The more upscale **Asteras Beach** (☎ 01/890–1774) on the promontory belongs to the Astir Palace Vouliagmenis hotel but is open to the public from 8 AM to 9 PM for a hefty fee (2,000 dr./€5.89 weekdays, 2,500 dr./€7.37 weekends), which means its green lawns and sandy stretch are usually less crowded. **Vouliagmeni Lake** (☎ 01/896–2237), whose part salt, part spring-fed waters are reputed to have curative powers, is popular with older Greeks; the lake opens at 7 AM to 7 PM, and tickets are 1,300 dr./€3.83. Facilities include lockers and showers and there's a pleasant snack bar. The lake has a gradual slope and sandy bottom, both good features for kids.

En Route   Beyond Vouliagmeni the road threads along a rocky coastline dotted with inlets, where intrepid bathers swim off the rocks, after leaving their cars in the roadside parking areas and scrambling down to the inviting coves below. If you join them, take along your snorkels, fins, and masks so you can enjoy the underwater scenery, but avoid the sea urchins (you won't have to be reminded the second time) clustered on rocks. The coastal road south of Vouliagmeni is one of the most heavily developed seacoasts in Greece; only the many tavernas, especially in Palaia Fokaia, proclaiming *psaria freska* (fresh fish) remind us of the former fishing villages here. Two of them are reviewed here.

Dining and Lodging

$$-$$$ ✗ **Apaggio.** A top spot in the countryside outside Vouliagmeni (☞ *above*), this is run by the owner of the well-known Apaggio in Athens. Newly opened, this multilevel seafood restaurant (it holds 500) offers the same high quality and traditional Greek recipes, now with a view of the Saronic Gulf. The menu is always changing, but if you're lucky you can find among the seafood and magirefta dishes such as *sinagrida* (snapper) made Rhodes-style (with white sauce and mushrooms); codfish croquettes from Andros; a saganaki crammed with mussels, shrimp, and crayfish; or a fried mix of squid, mussels, and other shellfish. More than 70 Greek labels are featured on the wine list, and you can stop here just for an ouzo, a cocktail, or a coffee from noon until late at night. ✉ *On coastal road to Sounion, about 17 km (10½ mi) after Vouliagmeni, at 41-km (25½-mi) mark, Lagonissi,* ☎ *0291/26441 or 0291/ 26261. AE, DC, V. Closed weekdays Oct.–Apr.*

$$ ✗ **I Remvi.** The last of the fish tavernas lining the coastal road in Palaia Fokaia (☞ *above*), this is the smallest, the cheapest, and the most romantic. "Remvi" means daydreaming, easy to do as you sit seaside at the little tables with checkered tablecloths and contemplate the small beach and Mediterranean while waiting for your fish soup, made with the freshest bream, sweet onions, carrots, and potatoes (it takes a little time, but it's worth it). The superfresh fish, even the red mullet, runs about 1,000 dr./€2.94 a kilo less than at the other tavernas, but you can also order seafood appetizers like crab salad and fried squid (throughout Greece fresh only in spring, otherwise fresh frozen), grilled bread called *lagana* brushed with olive oil and oregano, and potent wine from the barrel (about 1,300 dr./€3.83 for a kilo). ✉ *On Leoforos Sounio coastal road 16 km (10 mi) before Sounion, Palaia Fokaia,* ☎ *0291/36236. No credit cards.*

$$ ✗ **Panorama.** For the best food in Vouliagmeni, head to the seaside
★ stretch called Kavouri. Panorama is almost impossible to get into for Sunday lunch because of the crowds of Athenians who come to feast on the large selection of fish and relax on the cool seaside terrace. Besides the fresh catch, especially good are the squid and the *garides yiouvetsi* (shrimp baked in a red sauce with tiny noodles). You can also stuff yourself on a sampling of appetizers, such as seafood salad and *mides gemistes,* mussels stuffed with rice. ✉ *Iliou 4, Kavouri,* ☎ *01/895–1298 or 01/965–8401. Reservations essential. V.*

$$$$ 🏨 **Astir Palace Vouliagmeni.** The most exclusive and secluded resort in the Athens area, this 80-acre compound—complete with helicopter pad—is spread across a pine-studded promontory. It is actually made up of three hotels: the **Nafsika,** which is built into the hillside and has the loveliest view; the **Aphrodite,** with balconies on the sea, is the newest; and the **Arion,** the oldest, which has chic secluded bungalows with very large rooms. All have been freshly decorated in the last few years. The compound is often used for international summits, because of its expansive and prestigious location, and amenities include a private beach, sports, lovely landscaping, pools, several restaurants with superb Greek and international specialties, and sea views. Staying here carries quite a cachet, and you'll be in the midst of the Greek jet set, including tycoons and celebrities. A twice-daily shuttle transports guests to and from

downtown Athens, some 25 km (16 mi) away, in the mornings. Buffet breakfast is included in the price. ⊠ *Apollonos 40, 16671,* ☎ *01/890–2000; 212/682–9191 in the U.S.,* FAX *01/896–2582; 212/682–9254 in the U.S. 456 rooms, 73 bungalows, 30 suites. 5 restaurants, bar, 4 pools, beach. AE, DC, MC, V.*

$$$ 🏨 **Armonia.** Just 300 ft from the sea, the Armonia hotel (part of a complex that includes the smaller Paradise hotel) has a sterile modern facade but impeccable rooms, decorated with wood furniture and light brown appointments, all with private terraces, and one-third with sea views. Each room has satellite TV and a refrigerator, but no hair dryers (ask at the desk to borrow one). If the sea is unswimmable during your stay, the pool offers an alternative, one that features a snack bar with refreshments and a section for children. Buffet breakfast is included in the price. ⊠ *Armonias 1, 16671,* ☎ *01/896–0030, 01/896–0105, 01/896–2656, or 01/896–3184,* FAX *01/896–3698. 160 rooms, 22 suites. 2 restaurants, snack bar, pool. AE, DC, MC, V.*

$ 🏨 **Stefanakis Hotel and Apartments.** The modern Stefanakis is nicely located within walking distance of the Varkiza waterfront and beach, yet is quieter than seafront hotels in neighboring Glyfada. You'll get good value for your money here, much more than the price-range would indicate. All rooms and apartments are very clean and have a tub and shower, air-conditioning, radio, telephone, and balcony. Cabanas shade lounge chairs and the pool bar. Staff is friendly and helpful, and the breakfast buffet has lots of tasty treats and real drip coffee to get you energized for your day's activities. ⊠ *Aphroditis 17, Varkiza 16672,* ☎ *01/897–0528–30,* FAX *01/897–0249. 40 rooms, 16 apartments. Pool, bar, air-conditioning. No credit cards. Closed Nov.–mid-Apr.*

Sounion

❹ *70 km (43½ mi) southeast of Athens, 50 km (31 mi) southeast of Vouliagmeni.*

Here at the southernmost tip of Attica, the ancients chose to honor the
★ god of the sea by building their enormous **Temple of Poseidon.** No wonder: the site is magnificent—a rugged cliff rises 195 ft high, overlooking an expanse of azure water at the entrance to the Saronic Gulf. Arrange your visit so that you enjoy the panorama of sea and islands from this airy platform either early in the morning, before the tour groups arrive, or at dusk, when the Sounion promontory offers one of the most spectacular sunset vantage points in Attica. The view from the cliff was matched emotion for emotion in antiquity by the sight of the cape (called the "sacred headland" by Homer) and its mighty temple when viewed from the sea—a sight which brought joy to sailors, knowing upon spotting the massive temple that they were close to home. Today, Athenians returning from a sea journey exhibit the same gratitude, rushing to the side of the ferry to point out Sounion to their children. Although the columns appear to be gleaming white from a distance in the full sun, when you get closer you can see that they are made of gray-veined marble, quarried from nearby Agrilesa, and have 16 flutings rather than the usual 20. Today, the site is one of the most photographed in Greece. Beyond, a seaport with a well-protected harbor, a beach, a hotel, and a few tavernas accommodate visitors and those paying homage to the gods.

Beyond the scanty remains of an ancient *propylon* (gateway), you enter the temple compound. On your left are the **Temenos** (precinct) **of Poseidon,** on your right a **stoa** and **rooms.** The temple itself (now off-limits to tourists) was commissioned by Pericles, the famous leader of Greece's Golden Age. It was probably designed by Ictinus, the same architect who designed the Temple of Hephaistos in the ancient Agora of Athens, and was built between 444 and 440 BC. The people here were considered Athenian citizens, the sanctuary was Athenian, and Poseidon occupied a position second only to Athena herself. Situated on the highest point of the acropolis, the temple was built on the site of an earlier cult to Poseidon, and two colossal statues of youths, perhaps votives to the god, carved well over a century before the temple's construction, were discovered in early excavations (both are now in the National Archaeological Museum in Athens). The remaining 16 Doric columns, some of which have recently been re-erected, now stand sentinel over the Aegean, visible from miles away. Lord Byron had a penchant for carving his name on ancient monuments and you can see it and other graffiti on the right corner pillar of the portico. The view from the summit is breathtaking. In the slanting light of the late afternoon sun, the land masses to the west stand out in sharp profile: the bulk of Aegina backed by the mountains of the Peloponnese. To the east, on a clear day, one can spot the Cycladic islands of Kea, Kythnos, and Serifos. On the land side, the slopes of the acropolis retain traces of the fortification walls. ✉ *From promontory, pass through gate and climb rocky path that follows, roughly, the ancient approach,* ☎ *0292/39363.* 🎫 *800 dr./€2.35.* ☉ *Daily 10 AM–sunset.*

Beach

If you spend the morning at Sounion and have lunch on the beach below, you may also want to take a swim, although the sandy strip becomes uncomfortably crowded in summer. On your approach to the temple (4 km [2½ mi] north of Sounion) there is a decent beach at Legrena, and sometimes a small boat ferries across to the uninhabited isle of Patroklou—look for the sign shortly before the turnoff for Haraka (6 km [4 mi] north of Sounion).

Dining and Lodging

$$ ✕ **Akroyiali.** Run by the Trikaliotis family, including Barba (Uncle) Giorgos—well past 80 and keeping an eagle eye on proceedings—this place is full on weekends, when locals stop in for the fresh white and saddled bream, pandora, and red mullet, caught by fishing caïques in Lavrion. There are just a few appetizers—*taramosalata* (fish roe salad), octopus, shrimp salad—and a small selection of wine. ✉ *On beach below Temple of Poseidon,* ☎ *0292/39107. No credit cards. Closed for dinner weekdays Nov.–Feb.*

$–$$ ✕ **Assimakis.** On the road between Sounion and Lavrion, just a few yards from the sea, this simple restaurant overseen by Vangelis Assimakis will keep everyone happy with its large selection of reasonably priced fish—pandora, sole, red mullet, white and common bream— and its magirefta, including *tas kebab* (slow oven-baked beef in fresh tomato sauce), pastitsio, and moussaka. Regulars savor the tender boiled octopus marinated in vinegar and lemon and the crispy rings of fried squid. You can also order grilled chops, souvlaki, and chicken. The large, flower-filled veranda has a soothing view overlooking the coast, and for those too weary to continue, the friendly Assimakis family, who lives here, also rents a few apartments. ✉ *4 km (2½ mi) from Sounion at 60-km (37-mi) mark on Sounion–Lavrion coastal road,* ☎ *0292/39442 or 0291/39270. No credit cards.*

$$$ 🏨 **Cape Sounion Beach.** The rooms at this self-contained complex of little bungalows are tasteful, with solid furniture, refrigerator, fan, and attractive Greek-island colors. All have balconies and many have a view over the garden and southeast toward the Temple of Poseidon. The hotel's cove-embraced beach would be idyllic without the din of the nearby road. The obligatory half-board includes American breakfast and à la carte lunch or buffet dinner; nevertheless, room rates re-

main at the low end of its price category. ⊠ *Poseidonios at 67-km (37-mi) mark, Plakes 19500,* ☎ *0292/39391 or 0292/39821; 01/861–7837 winter in Athens,* Ⅸ *0292/39038; 01/861–6473 winter in Athens. 188 bungalows. 2 restaurants, 3 bars, pool, 5 tennis courts, exercise room, beach, dance club. AE, DC, MC, V. Closed Nov.–Mar.*

$$ 🏨 **Aegeon Hotel.** This hotel has seen better days but is starting to renovate on a piecemeal basis, and nothing can beat its location—much objected to by environmentalists and archaeologists—on *the* beach below the Temple of Poseidon, at the very harbor where ancient ships once navigated. Even the rooms in back (all have balconies), which look up the slopes flanking the acropolis, have a good view. All rooms now have TVs and air-conditioning. The restaurant, from where you can enjoy the sunset, serves Continental and Greek cuisine and fresh fish. Be warned: the beach will be crowded in high season, and the heating system may or may not be effective in the winter. ⊠ *Sounion Beach 19500,* ☎ *0292/39200,* Ⅸ *0292/39234. 44 rooms, 1 suite. Restaurant, air-conditioning, beach. MC, V.*

Lavrion

⑤ *80 km (50 mi) southeast of Athens, 10 km (6 mi) north of Sounion.*

After Sounion, roads enter a dreary stretch of country—curiously metallic in color and completely un-Attic in contour and quality. There is a reason for this: Lavrion, a postindustrial town with a few remnants of belle epoque architecture, was celebrated in antiquity for its silver mines. Several thousand ancient shafts have been discovered in the area, and, without the riches they yielded, Themistocles could not have built the fleet that saved Greece from the Persians, nor Pericles the monuments on the Acropolis. There is a one-room **mineralogical museum,** housed in the remains of an 1875 building, displaying an eclectic collection of jewel-color minerals from the surrounding hillsides, as well as mining tools used by the slaves. ⊠ *Leoforos Kordela next to the school (Lykeiou), Lavrion,* ☎ *0292/26270.* 🎫 *500 dr./€1.47.* ☉ *Wed. and weekends 10–noon.*

Dining and Lodging

$ ✕ **Archontiko.** Set in a captivating, restored mansion, Archontiko has charmed even jaded Athenians, motivating them to drive out to little-known Lavrion to enjoy an old-fashioned taverna meal at old-fashioned prices. Food is basic country fare, with emphasis on red meats, best washed down with local wines. Appetizers include *spetsofai* (Pelion-style sausage stew with peppers) and *pittas* (small cheese and spinach pies). Moist and aromatic lamb cooked in a clay pot and rooster in a red sauce are highlights of the main dishes; in winter, game—especially hare—is featured. Semolina-style halvah and buttery walnut cake are choice desserts. Live Greek music, played on Saturday night (Friday night and Sunday afternoon in winter), inspires spontaneous dancing. ⊠ *Athinon 1,* ☎ *0292/25863 or 0292/28188. No credit cards.*

$ 🏨 **Belle Epoque Hotel.** Not even the inhabitants of Lavrion know about this small, quite inexpensive in-town hotel set in a renovated belle epoque house, a welcome alternative to the area's high-priced resorts. The outside is much more inviting than the inside, whose cell-like rooms are now air-conditioned, but the public areas have been lovingly decorated with the owners' collections of minerals, shells, and bric-a-brac. The hotel includes a small cafeteria serving refreshments, and the owner can whip up a breakfast of fresh orange juice, eggs and sausage, and bread with homemade marmalade for those too lazy to try their luck on the waterfront. ⊠ *Pleion 33, 19500,* ☎ *0292/27130* or 0291/26564, FAX 0292/26059. 20 rooms. Cafeteria, air-conditioning. No credit cards.

En Route   The road winds inland, through bare hilly country spoiled by some cement-box dwellings, but also by some bucolic country homes, running past **Keratea, Koropi,** and **Markopoulos;** the latter two are market centers of the mesogeion, known for its wine and good-quality bread. You can follow the lead of oenophiles from Athens, who drive here with large wicker-covered bottles that are filled with the local retsina and musty reds. Empty soda or water bottles will serve the same purpose. Stop at a roadside bakery to get the coarse-grained bread, and in October look for *mustolevria,* a jelly-like candy made from the grape must from the wine harvest—a Greek delicacy since ancient times. Continuing through stands of olive trees and vineyards, the road now runs almost due west, with Mt. Hymettos hovering straight ahead.

Paiania

❻ *18 km (11 mi) east of Athens, 34 km (21 mi) northwest of Lavrion.*

Paiania was the birthplace of the famous orator Demosthenes, and although there's not much to see of the ancient town now, most people come to visit the unique **Vorres Museum,** which displays folk art and an intriguing collection of contemporary Greek works in buildings restored in traditional style. Ion Vorres owns, operates, and even lives in the museum. He has salvaged many treasures and incorporated them beautifully: a stack of millstones transformed into sculptures when embedded in a wall; polished marble well-heads emerging from a flower bed; oak tables fashioned from monastery doors; commemorative plates bestowed by returning sea captains on their loved ones; paintings of historic moments such as the opening of the Corinth canal. The modern gallery and sculpture courtyard are dedicated to postwar art, including work by Moralis, Tsarouchis, Ghika, Pavlos, and Vassiliou. When he's not busy in his museum, Mr. Vorres wears the hat of mayor. Those without cars can take Bus A5 from Akadimias in Athens; in Ayia Paraskevi transfer to Bus 308 or 310 and get off in Paiania's main square. The museum is about 328 ft farther. ⊠ *Diadochou Konstantinou 1,* ☎ *01/664–2520 or 01/664–4771.* ⊡ *1,000 dr./€2.94.* ☉ *Aug. 26–July, weekends 10–2.*

☾ The **Koutouki cave,** discovered in 1926 by a shepherd who had lost his goat, is just the right depth and darkness to awe young children into silence without frightening them. High on the eastern slopes of Hymettos, connected to Paiania village by a good paved road, the cave has been rigged with paths, lights, and sound to highlight the stalagmites and stalactites—one is named "Statue of Liberty"—the cavernous vaults and narrow corridors, and rainbow-color walls formed at the rate of half an inch a year. There are regularly scheduled 20-minute tours; guides can speak English. There is no public transportation here. ⊠ *Above village of Paiania on road to cemetery,* ☎ *01/664–2108.* ⊡ *1,500 dr./€4.42.* ☉ *Daily 9–4.*

Dining

$ ✕ **Kyra Elli Paradisos.** A touch of the old days in the mesoghia, Kyra Elli serves up hearty taverna favorites, along with heady barrel wine, all to the accompaniment of live popular Greek and *rembetika* music. Juicy grilled chicken, tender lamb chops, and bonfilet are perennial favorites; in winter, hare and partridge are often also on the menu. Try *ravani,* a rich semolina cake laced with brandy and cinnamon and topped with almonds or the special ice creams. ⊠ *Lavriou 76,* ☎ *01/664–5024. No credit cards. Closed Mon. No lunch except Sun.*

Brauron

➐ *40 km (25 mi) east of Athens, 40 km (25 mi) southeast of Paiania, via Markopoulo.*

Brauron, where the **Sanctuary of Artemis** rises on the site of an earlier shrine, lies in a waterlogged depression at the foot of a small hill. Found here are a **5th-century** BC **temple** and a horseshoe-shape **stoa.** Here, the virgin huntress was worshiped as the protector of childbirth. Every four years, the Athenians celebrated the Brauronia, an event in which girls between ages 5 and 10 took part in arcane ceremonies, including a dance in which they were dressed as bears. The **museum** next to the site contains statues of these little girls, as well as many votive offerings. The carless should take Bus A5 from Akadimias to its terminus in Ayia Paraskevi, switch to Bus 304, 305, or 316, and ride to the end; the site is 1 km (½ mi) from there. ⊠ *At foot of hill near fork in road to northern Loutsa,* ☎ *0299/27020.* 🎟 *500 dr./€1.47.* ☉ *Museum and site Tues.–Sun. 8–2:30 (in winter, museum Tues.–Fri. 8:30–3, site Thurs.–Sun. 8:30–3).*

Beach
The coast road north from Brauron, which skirts an extensively (and poorly) developed coastline, leads to a pleasant **beach** at Loutsa (⊠ 8 km [5 mi] north of Brauron), framed by a backdrop of umbrella pines and with shallow waters—perfect for small children, though crowded in the summer.

Dining and Lodging
$$ ✕🏨 **Mare Nostrum Hotel Club.** Visit the antiquities in the morning, go for a swim on the beach midday, and then spend the afternoon getting facials or seaweed treatments. It all makes for an ideal day, here made possible thanks to the addition in 1996 of a thalassotherapy (sea-therapy treatment) spa. Visit the Olympiades section, which includes sauna, *hamam* (Turkish steam bath), and a fitness room; Nereides, devoted to hydrotherapy with seaweed and mud remedies for ailments such as arthritis and varicose veins; or the Aphrodite, with beauty treatments such as Swedish massage, reflexology, shiatsu, and facials. You can also regenerate at the hotel proper, which features myriad sports facilities—from volleyball to minigolf to waterskiing—several eateries, including a taverna and sea-view bar, and rooms with balcony or terrace and air-conditioning. If all this isn't enough, the restless can zip over to the beach town of Loutsa, about 5 km (3 mi) away, for some taverna-and-bar-hopping; KTEL buses pass regularly near the hotel. Buffet breakfast is included in the price, and both half- and full board are available. Room rates don't include spa services, but guests may sign up for various packages, just as tourists passing by may simply use the spa. ⊠ *Above Brauron (Vravrona) Bay, 19003,* ☎ *0294/48412 or 0294/47712; 01/362–0619 Athens,* 🖷 *0294/47790; 01/364–1391 Athens. 237 rooms, 125 bungalows, 3 suites. 3 restaurants, bar, air-conditioning, pool, miniature golf, 3 tennis courts, exercise room, volleyball, waterskiing. AE, DC, MC, V.* ✇

Marathon

➑ *42 km (26 mi) northeast of Athens, 33 km (20½ mi) north of Brauron.*

Today, Athenians enter the fabled plain of Marathon only to enjoy a break from the capital, visiting the freshwater lake created by the dam or sunning at the area's beaches. But when the Athenians' hoplites, assisted by the Plataians, entered the plain in 490 BC, it was to crush a numerically superior Persian force. Some 6,400 invaders were killed fleeing to their ships, while the Athenians lost just 192 warriors. This, their proudest victory, became the stuff of Athenian legends; the hero Theseus was said to have appeared himself in aid of the Greeks, along with the god Pan. The Athenian commander Miltiades sent a messenger, Pheidippides, to Athens with glad tidings of the victory; it's said he ran the 42 km (26 mi) without hardly taking a breath, shouted *Enikisame!* ("We won!"), then dropped dead of fatigue (more probably of a heart attack), the inspiration for the marathon race in today's Olympics.

At the foot of the 30-ft-high **Marathon Tomb,** built over the graves of the 192 Athenian dead, is a reproduction of the original gravestone, the Soldier of Marathon, which depicts a hoplite; the original is in the National Archaeological Museum in Athens. Usually those who died in war were returned to their homes, but this collective tomb, which contains the cremated remains of the national heroes, was built to honor them. About 1½ km (1 mi) north is the smaller burial mound of the Plataians and the **Museum of Marathon,** consisting of five rooms labelled in English and Greek, which contain objects from excavations in the area, ranging from Neolithic pottery from the cave of Pan to Hellenistic and Roman inscriptions and statues. One of the most touching exhibits is a funerary urn for a child, shaped like a cocoon. In the center of the small courtyard, among bitter-orange trees, is a tall Ionic capital which is believed to have supported a large trophy honoring the soldiers at Marathon. Excavations continue around a nearby prehistoric cemetery, which will eventually be open to the public. ✉ *Plataion 114, approximately 6 km (4 mi) south of modern village of Marathon, 2 km (1 mi) from Leoforos Marathonas,* ☎ *0294/55155.* ✆ *500 dr./€1.47 for both the tomb and museum.* ☉ *Tues.–Sun. 8:30–3:00.*

⑨ Fifteen kilometers (9 miles) north of Marathon, the archaeological site at **Rhamnous,** an isolated, romantic spot on a small promontory, overlooks the sea between continental Greece and the island of Euboia. From at least the Archaic period, Rhamnous was known for the worship of Nemesis, the great leveler, who brought down the proud and punished the arrogant. The site, excavated over many years, preserves traces of temples from the 6th and 5th centuries BC. The smaller temple from the 6th century BC was dedicated to Themis, goddess of Justice; the later temple housed the cult statue of Nemesis, envisioned as a woman, the only cult statue (even fragmentary) left from the high classical period. Many fragments have turned up, including the head, now in the British Museum. The acropolis stood on the headland, where ruins are visible from a fortress (5th and 4th centuries BC). Recently, excavations helped archaeologists locate the garrison headquarters and determine exactly where the permanent guard was housed. As you wander over this usually serene, and always evocative, site you'll discover at its edge little coves where you can enjoy a swim. For those going by public transportation, take a KTEL bus from Athens toward the Ayia Marina port, get off at the Ayia Marina and Rhamnous crossroads, and follow the signs on the flat road, about 3 km (2 mi). Or take a taxi from Marathon village (1,700 dr./€5). ✉ *10 km (6 mi) northeast of Marathon,* ☎ *0294/63477.* ✆ *500 dr./€1.47.* ☉ *Daily 7–6.*

⑩ **Lake Marathon** (✉ 8 km [5 mi] west of Marathon, 9 km [5½ mi] west down a side road from the village of Ayios Stefanos), a huge man-made reservoir formed by the **Marathon Dam** (built by an American company in 1925–31), was the sole source of water for Athens but since World War II is supplemented with water from Parnitha and Boetia. It is claimed to be the only dam faced with marble. You may be astonished by the sight of all that landlocked water in Greece and want to contemplate it over a drink or snack at the café on the east side. At the downstream side is a marble replica of the Athenian Treasury of Delphi.

The port of **Rafina,** midway between Marathon and Vravrona, has now become more developed and congested with traffic as the ferry boat and catamaran routes to the Cyclades (which cut the travel time in half using ferry boats) have become more popular. Rafina still has a pleasant fishing harbor and some seafood tavernas (such as Ta Kavouria, Tis Asimakis, and Kala Krassia) with bird's-eye sea views. If you spend the night here before catching a morning ferry or catamaran, the Aello outdoor cinema and *luna park* (carnival with rides) can provide you with amusement in the evening.

Beaches

Near Marathon, the best beach is the long, sandy, pine-backed stretch called **Skinies,** until recently little known but now crowded with Athenians on the weekend. Other, less populated beaches (pebble), usually lined with a taverna or two, include **Paralia Varnavas,** reached from Varnavas village, and **Sessi** near Grammatikon village, both accessible only by car. The coves at **Rhamnous** are delightful (about 2,000 ft from the site), but beware of spiny sea urchins when swimming off the rocks.

Dining and Lodging

$$ ✕ **O Hondros.** Opened in 1999 on the busy main harbor road of the resort community of Nea Makri (south of Marathon), O Hondros ("The Fat One") is a breath of fresh air for those seeking a change from the standard meat or seafood tavernas, as it specializes in more than 80 *mezedes* (appetizers) from all of the regions of Greece. Try the leek and vegetable pies, grilled stuffed green peppers with herbs, and curried chicken accented with parsley—or ask your waiter for his recommendations. ⊠ *Leoforos Posidonios and Masaioi St., harbor of Nea Makri,* ☎ *0294/50430. No credit cards.*

$–$$ ✕ **Argentina.** While living in South America, owner Nikos Milonas learned how to carve beef, how high to fire up the grill, and exactly how to time a perfect medium-rare steak, and the meat-loving population of Greece has been benefiting from his expertise ever since. At his taverna, which on a clear day offers a peek of the sea from its large veranda, young beef brought from Holland is priced by the kilo, grilled, and then served for you to slice off as much as you can handle. The rest of the fare is simple but solid: dense tzatziki that's light on the garlic; well-fried eggplant, pepper, and zucchini slices; mountain greens; and the classic Greek tomato, cucumber and feta cheese salads, *horiatiki,* in summer and grated cabbage-carrot in winter. The service is polite and the prices are low. ⊠ *Bitakou 3, Kaletzi about 1½ km (1 mi) after the dam crossing,* ☎ *0294/66476 or 0294/67814. Reservations essential. AE, V. Closed 3 wks in Aug. No lunch weekdays.*

$$ 🏨 **Golden Coast Hotel and Bungalows.** Right on the beach, the Golden
☼   Coast has the kind of simple, functional, air-conditioned rooms and facilities that are perfect for families; you don't have to go anywhere else during your stay since it has a disco, three bars, a restaurant, grill, and evening programs with skits, games, and Greek dancing. Guests can stay either in the main building or in the bungalows set in a verdant garden. Half-board is available for another 4,500 dr./€13.27 per person. Although the beach is narrow and rocky—as on most of this coast—children have a choice of two pools, and the adults can take a dip in three others. There's a wide variety of sports available. The restaurant's food is unusually good, and buffet breakfast is included in the price. Golden Coast is joined by a seaside promenade to the nearest beach town, Nea Makri, 2 km (1 mi) on foot, or 4 km (2½ mi) by

car, which in summer is jumping with clubs and tavernas. A hotel shuttle takes guests to Nea Makri three times daily, and the closest bus stop is 1,500 ft from the hotel. ⊠ *Marathon Beach, 19005,* ☎ *0294/57100; 01/362–0662 Athens,* FAX *0294/57300; 01/364–1391 Athens. 240 rooms, 256 bungalows, 45 apartments. Restaurant, 3 bars, air-conditioning, 5 pools, 3 tennis courts, volleyball, minigolf, Ping-Pong, basketball, waterskiing, windsurfing, dance club. AE, DC, MC, V. Closed Nov.–Mar.*

$$ 🏨 **Hotel Avra.** The Avra, operating for 30 years, has begun a renovation of the rooms and public areas. Almost 25 rooms have been redecorated and upgraded so far (and command a slightly higher price), and owner Kaiti Pandeleon plans to continue until all 96 have been modernized, complete with safes and refrigerators. Rooms now have typical pine furniture and matching spreads and curtains; about 75% have sea views from the balconies, so be sure to request a room that does. Breakfast is included. ⊠ *South of square on seaside, 19009,* ☎ *0294/22780,* FAX *0294/23320. 96 rooms. Restaurant, bar. No credit cards. Closed Nov.-Apr.*

Outdoor Activities and Sports

RUNNING

Every year on November 1 the **International Athens Peace Marathon** is run over the same course taken in 490 BC by the courier Pheidippides, when he carried to Athens the news of victory over the Persians. The 42-km (26-mi) race, open to men and women of all ages, starts in Marathon and finishes at the Olympic Stadium in Athens. There is a $50 entry fee. Apply by mail. Even if you don't have the stamina for the race, cheer on the runners at the end of the route in Athens—there is an amazing variety of runners, representing all ages, nationalities, and physiques, who finish the course and triumphantly sprint into the city stadium. ⊠ *SEGAS, Race Organizers, Syngrou 137, Athens 17121,* ☎ *01/935–9302, 01/934–4126, or 01/934–1603,* FAX *01/934–2980 or 01/935–8594.*

Amphiareion

⑪ *49 km (30½ mi) northeast of Athens; 18 km (11 mi) north of Lake Marathon.*

Cradled in a hidden valley at a bend in the road, the **Sanctuary of Amphiareos** is a quiet, well-watered haven, blessed with dense pines and other foliage. It is startlingly different from the surrounding countryside, where overgrazing, fires, and development have destroyed most of the trees. Amphiareos was the Bronze Age king of Argos, a mortal transformed after death into a healing divinity. In the sanctuary dedicated to his cult are the remains of a miniature **theater**; a 4th-century BC **Doric temple**; the long **stoa**; and **Enkimiterion** (literally, "dormitory"), where patients stayed awaiting their cure. They would sacrifice a ram, then lie down wrapped in its skin, waiting for a dream, which resident priests would interpret for the prescribed cure, usually involving baths in the miraculous waters. It was customary for patients to thank the gods by throwing coins into the water, which priests retrieved to melt into votives they could sell. At the sanctuary's entrance to the left stand many statueless pedestals. Look for the pedestal in the middle (with the date 240 BC) that once supported a likeness of Brutus, whose murder of Julius Caesar scored big points in Greece. The easiest way to get to the site, after driving, is to take a KTEL bus to Skala Oropos and then a taxi (about 800 dr./€2.35). The guards can help you call a taxi for a pickup. ⊠ *Site,* ☎ *0295/62144.* 🎟 *500 dr./€1.47.* 🕐 *Weekdays 8–2:30, weekends 8:30–3.*

Mt. Parnitha

33 km (20½ mi) northwest of Athens but accessible from sites in east Attica, such as Amphiareion, Marathon, and Rhamnous.

The summit of Mt. Parnitha offers a splendid view of the plain of Athens cradled by Mt. Pendeli and Mt. Hymettos. In spring the forest blooms with wildflowers, red poppies, white crocuses, purple irises, and numerous species of orchids. Once the heavily wooded habitat of wolves and bears, the mountain provided fuel for the charcoal burners of Acharnes in the days before oil. There are many lovely nature walks through the Mt. Parnitha massif, reachable from the chapel of Ayia Triada, including two-hour walks to the Cave of Pan or the Skipiza spring. There is a map behind the church.

Phyle

⑫ *31 km (19¼ mi) northwest of Athens.*

Evidence of the modern village Fili's source of wealth, livestock, is everywhere: in the dozens of whole lambs, pigs, and goats strung up in front of butcher shops; in the numerous tavernas lining the main street; in the many window displays of fresh sheep yogurt. Beyond the village, known as Khasia by locals, the road climbs Mt. Parnitha; there is a turnoff for Moni Kleiston.

The Athenians built several fortresses on the ancient road between Mt. Parnitha and Thebes, including the untended 4th-century BC **Fortress of Phyle** (⊠ on a high bluff west of the road to Thebes, 9½ km [6 mi] north of Fili village). The road looping back and around the flank of Mt. Parnitha climbs slowly through rugged, deserted country along the ancient road northwest to Thebes. Here the fortress watched over the passes between Attica and Boetia, offering a dramatically beautiful vista, with the fortress's rugged rectangular masonry scattered about the site. Fragments of the wall still stand; it was made of blocks, each up to 9 ft high, and was reinforced with five towers (two are still visible).

Dining

$ ✕ **To Frourio.** If you visit the Fortress of Phyle on a weekend, be sure to stop at "The Fort" for great, inexpensive lamb and other grilled meats, potatoes, and salads. On cold days, you'll wish you had marshmallows for the fireplace; on warm days the outdoor terrace offers an unforgettable setting. *Note:* When it snows on Parnitha, the road up to the fortress may be closed, so check with your hotel about weather conditions on the mountain. The taverna closes early, around 9 or 10 PM. ⊠ *Several hundred ft beyond turnoff to ruins, Phyle.* ☎ *No phone. No credit cards. Closed weekdays.*

Monastery of Daphni

⑬ *11 km (7 mi) west of Athens.*

Due to the Fall 1999 earthquake, this famous monastery is closed for reconstruction; it is hoped that it will reopen in 2001 or 2002. In turn sacked by Crusaders, inhabited by Cistercian monks, and desecrated by Turks, Daphni remains one of the most splendid Byzantine monuments in Greece. Dating from the 11th century, the golden age of Byzantine art, the church contains a series of miraculously preserved mosaics without parallel in the legacy of Byzantium: powerful portraits of figures from the Old and New Testaments, images of Christ and his mother in the *Presentation of the Virgin,* and, in the golden dome, a stern Pantokrator, "ruler of all," surrounded by 16 Old Testament prophets who predicted his coming. Daphni means "laurel tree," sacred to Apollo, which reminds us that his sanctuary once occupied this site. It was destroyed in AD 395 after the antipagan edicts of the emperor Theodosius, and the Orthodox monastery was probably established in the 6th century, incorporating materials of Apollo's sanctuary in the church and walls. Reoccupied by Orthodox monks only in the 16th century, Daphni has since been a barracks and mental institution, and it has been restored extensively in several phases. ✉ *End of Iera Odos (also reached by taking the A16, B16, or G16 bus from Platia Koumoundourou in Athens), Haidari,* ☎ *01/581–1558. Closed for renovation until 2001 or 2002.*

Eleusis

⑭ *22 km (13½ mi) west of Athens, 11 km (7 mi) west of the Monastery of Daphni.*

The growing city of Athens co-opted the land around Eleusis, placing shipyards in the pristine gulf and steel mills and petrochemical plants along its shores. It is hard to imagine that there once stretched in every direction fields of corn and barley sacred to the goddess Demeter, whose realm was symbolized by the sheaf and sickle. The **sanctuary of Demeter** now lies in the new town, on the east slope and at the foot of the acropolis, which is hardly visible amid the modern buildings. The legend of Demeter and her daughter Persephone explained for the ancients the cause of the seasons and the origins of agriculture.

It was to Eleusis that Demeter traveled in search of Persephone after the girl had been kidnapped by Hades, god of the underworld. Zeus himself interceded to restore her to the distraught Demeter, but succeeded only partially, giving mother and daughter just half a year together. Nevertheless, in gratitude to King Keleos of Eleusis, who had given her refuge in her time of need, Demeter presented his son Triptolemos with wheat seeds, the knowledge of agriculture, and a winged chariot so he could spread them to mankind. Keleos built a *megaron* (large hall) in her honor, the first Eleusinian sanctuary.

The worship of Demeter took the form of mysterious rites, part purification and part drama, and both the Lesser and the Greater Eleusinian rituals closely linked Athens with the sanctuary. The procession for the Greater Eleusinia began and ended there, following the route of the Sacred Way. Much of what we see now in the sanctuary is of Roman construction or repair, although physical remains on the site date back to the Mycenaean period. One follows the old Sacred Way to the **Great Propylaea** (gates) and continues on to the **Precinct of Demeter,** which was strictly off-limits on pain of death to any but the initiated. The **Telesterion,** or Temple of Demeter, now a vast open space surrounded by battered tiers of seats, dates to 600 BC when it was the hall of initiation. It had a roof supported by six rows of seven columns, presumably so the mysteries would be obscured, and it could accommodate 3,000 people. The **museum,** just beyond, contains an array of pottery and sculpture, particularly of the Roman period. ✉ *Iera Odos 1,* ☎ *01/ 554–6019.* 💷 *500 dr./1.47.* ☉ *Tues.–Sun. 8:30–3.*

The Arts

FESTIVAL WITH GREEK DRAMA

From the end of August to mid-September, Eleusis hosts the **Aeschilia** festival, with ancient Greek drama presented on the archaeological site and at an old soap factory on the beach next to the Titanas plant. Performances start at 9 PM, and tickets, which cost 2,000 dr./€5.89 (5,000 dr./€14.74 for a festival pass), are available at the sites before the show, at major Athens record stores, and at the Elefsina Cultural Center (✉ Pangalou 52, ☎ 01/554–8997), which can supply more information.

Straits of Salamis/Salamina Island

45 km (23 mi) west of Athens, 20 km (12 mi) south of Eleusis.

It was in the Straits of Salamis that the desperate and wily Athenians aided by Sparta, Corinth, and Aegina destroyed the Persian fleet. In 480 BC, the Persians had returned to exact revenge for their defeat at Marathon in 490 BC, attacking and burning the Acropolis. The Athenians, told by the Delphic oracle to protect themselves with "wooden walls," interpreted this to mean their ships. Evacuating their women and children, they drew up their wooden boats and, by a ruse, lured the Persians into a trap. So sure were the Persians of a devastating victory that Xerxes, the king, had a fine silver throne placed on the hill overlooking the strait, to watch his troops thrash the Greeks. He witnessed instead a disaster that, even more than that at Marathon, put a definitive end to Persian ambitions in the western Aegean.

⑮ Ferries leave Perama (15 km [9⅓ mi] west of Athens) around the clock, crossing the straits (3 km [2 mi]) to the island of **Salamina,** which in 1998 suffered heavily from forest fires. The ferry boat goes to **Paloukia,** the main port, which is home to about 18,000 of the island's 23,000 population. It's not a particularly interesting town, but from here you can catch buses to **Faneromeni,** which has a 17th-century monastery with frescoes, perched high above the gulf. **Selinia** is a pretty resort town which has hotels and tavernas, but continue farther south to **Eandio** for a view of an idyllic village with a small pebble beach. To the southeast toward Kanakia is the laid-back resort of **Peristeria.** As for the ferry boat, from 5 AM to 6 AM and from 10 PM to 1 AM the boat leaves every half hour, from 6 AM to 10 PM every 15 minutes, and from 1 AM to 5 AM every hour; tickets cost 130 dr./€.38. For more information, call the Perama port authority (☎ 01/441–0441 or 01/441–4676).

Lodging

$ 🏨 **Hotel Gabriel.** The best hotel on Salamina island, in operation for 30 years now, is owned by gentle poet Giorgos Tzimas (who sometimes is inspired to recite some of his poems). Rooms are simple but comfortable, and the view from the 18 rooms facing the bay is entrancing. Breakfast can be taken in the seaside restaurant or in the garden. Prices drop after the summer season. Since the cleanliness of the straits has improved in recent years, you can take a swim at any time from the little pebble beach. Breakfast is 1,500 dr./€4.42 extra. ✉ *Angelos Sikelianos 8, Eandio, Salamina Island 18900,* ☎ 🖷 *01/466–2275. 23 rooms. Restaurant, bar, beach. No credit cards.*

THE SARONIC GULF ISLANDS

Aegina, Poros, Hydra, Spetses

The Saronic Gulf islands are a diverse group: Aegina's pine forests mix with groves of pistachio trees, a product for which Aegina is justly famous. Water taxis buzz to Poros, more like an islet, from the Peloponnese, carrying weary locals eager to relax on its beaches and linger in the island cafés. Hydra and Spetses are farther south and more rewarding: both ban automobiles, and though Hydra's restaurants and boutiques cater to the sophisticated European traveler, Spetses' broad forests and scattered resorts lure Greeks.

Aegina

30 km (18½ mi) south of Piraeus.

Aegina has become an inexpensive resort area frequented primarily by Athenians. It is remarkably unspoiled, although it is only 35 minutes by hydrofoil from Athens. Ayia Marina caters to package tour groups, primarily from Great Britain, leaving Aegina town as a haven for Greeks and independent foreign travelers. Aegina town still has a large population of fisherman, who add character to the waterfront cafés and *ouzeris* (casual bars). Although some unattractive modern buildings mar the waterfront, a number of well-preserved neoclassical buildings and village houses are found on the back streets and in the small towns.

Although it may seem hard to imagine, by the archaic period (7th–6th centuries BC), Aegina was a mighty maritime power. It introduced the first silver coinage (marked with a tortoise) and established colonies in the Mediterranean. By the 6th century BC, Aegina, the commercial entrepôt, had become a major art center, known in particular for its bronze foundries, worked by such sculptors as Kallon, Onatas, and Anaxagoras, and its ceramics, which were exported throughout the Mediterranean world. This powerful island, lying so close off the coast of Attica, could not fail to come into conflict with Athens. As Athens's imperial ambitions grew, Aegina became a thorn in its side. In 458 BC Athens laid siege to the city, eventually conquering the island. In 455 BC the islanders were humiliated by being forced to migrate from the island, and Aegina never again regained its former power.

In Byzantine times Aegina formed a bishopric with the island of Kea, off the coast of Lavrio. Saracen pirate raids caused the islanders to move the capital to Paliochora, where it remained until the 19th century. After 1204 the island was a personal fiefdom of both Venice and Spain; in 1451, it was claimed fully by Venice. After it was devastated and captured by Barbarossa the pirate in 1537, it was repopulated with Albanians. Morosini recaptured Aegina for Venice in 1654, and it was not ceded to Turkey until 1718. In the 19th century, it experienced a remarkable rebirth as an important base in the War of Independence, and it was briefly the capital of the new Greek state in 1826–28. The first modern coins were minted here. At this time many people from the Peloponnese, plus refugees from Chios and Psara, emigrated to Aegina, and many of the present-day inhabitants are descended from them.

⓰ Boats and hydrofoils dock at the main town, **Aegina town,** a busy little harbor city on the western side of the island, where a few surviving neoclassical buildings mingle with a modern cement-and-cinder-block sprawl. Idyllic seascapes, and a number of beautiful gardens in courtyards, make Aegina attractive; its numerous cafés and restaurants lining the harbor face a road along the water teeming with horse-and-carriage traffic, trucks, and taxis. It's best to make the town your base for exploration of the island. This side of the island is more fertile and less mountainous than the east side; its gardens and fields are blessed with grapes, olives, figs, almonds, and, above all, the treasured pistachio trees.

As you approach from the sea, your first view of the town of Aegina takes in the sweep of the harbor, punctuated by the tiny white chapel of **Ayios Nikolaos** (✉ Aegina town harbor). During the negotiations for Greece, Ioannis Kapodistrias, the first president of Greece, conducted meetings in the medieval **Markelon Tower** (✉ Aegina town center).

Much of the ancient city lies under the modern, with public buildings and sanctuaries built on the promontory just north of the modern town. Still visible on this hill (known as Kolonna, or "column") is a single column of a late-archaic Temple of Apollo. The small **archaeological museum** on the site has finds from the Temple of Aphaia and excavations throughout the island, including early and middle Bronze Age pottery found in the excavations; archaic and classical pottery, including the distinctive "Ram Jug" and reliefs; and a 5th-century BC sphinx. Also notable is a Hercules sculpture from the Temple of Apollo. ⊠ *Aegina town, 100 ft from where ferries dock on the harbor (follow signs),* ☎ *0297/22248 or 0297/22637.* ☜ *500 dr./€1.47.* ☉ *Tues.–Sun. 8–2:30 (8:30–3 in winter).*

NEED A
BREAK?

A must in Aegina is to have a bite to eat in the *psaragora* (fish market). On narrow Pan Irioti street behind the harbor you'll find ouzeries and tavernas—generally without an official name—try the grilled octopus, monkfish with garlic potatoes, or crisp fried shrimp from **Geladakis** (☎ 0297/27308), perfect with an afternoon ouzo. Inside you'll find fisherman gathered in midafternoon and early evening, creating an intensely Greek atmosphere, worrying their beads while seated beside glistening octopus hung up to dry—as close to similar scenes in the film *Zorba the Greek* as you are likely to see in modern Greece.

The haunting remains of the medieval "Old Town," or **Palaiochora** (⊠ 1 km [½ mi] east of the monastery), built in the 9th century by islanders whose seaside town was the constant prey of pirates, are set on the rocky barren hill above the monastery. Capital of the island until 1826, Palaiochora has the romantic aura of a mysterious ghost town, a miniature Mistras that still has more than 20 **churches.** They are mostly from the 13th century, and a number of them have been restored and are still in use. They sit amid the ruins of the community's houses abandoned by the inhabitants in the early 19th century. It's best to pick up a booklet on the island which will give you a history of the settlement and direct you to several of the most interesting churches. Episkopi (often closed), Ayios Giorgios, and Metamorphisi all have lovely but faded (by dampness) frescoes. The frescoes of the church of Agioi Anargyroi are especially fascinating because they are of pagan subjects, such as the mother goddess Gaia on horseback and Alexander the Great.

Beaches

Aegina's beaches near town are pleasant enough, though crowded. South of town toward scenic Perdika village there are some good swimming spots at **Aiginitissa** and around **Marathonas.**

Dining and Lodging

$–$$ ✕ **Taverna O Kyriakos.** Serving some of the freshest fish on the island, this inexpensive taverna looks out over the sea. Order the pandora, red mullet, or sargus, expertly grilled. Magirefta such as oven-roasted lamb and *kokkinisto* (chuck roast in tomato sauce) are even cheaper options, and, for meat lovers, there is the gamut from chops to souvlaki. Excellent appetizers include eggplant salad, zucchini pie, and bourekakia, all a heady mix with the sea air and potent barrel retsina. ⊠ *Marathona beach, 5 km (3 mi) from Aegina town,* ☎ *0297/24025. No credit cards. Closed Dec. and weekdays Oct.–Nov. and Feb.–Mar.*

$–$$ ✕ **To Maridaki.** The gracious owner will do his best to make you feel welcome at this crowded waterfront restaurant at the south end of the harbor near the National Bank. In addition to the large selection of fresh fish (try the fried *koutsomouries,* sweet baby red mullet), the restaurant also serves grilled octopus and grilled meats—souvlaki, beef patties heavy on the onions, pork chops—and of course, magirefta such as pastitsio, pepper stuffed with rice, delicious okra stewed with tomatoes, and moussaka. Be sure to have a nibble of the homemade *tiropites* (phyllo-crust cheese pies). ⊠ *Dimokratias St. between Town Hall and Panagitsa church, Paralia Aeginas (Aegina beach),* ☎ *0297/25869. AE, V.*

$-$$ ✕ **Vatsoulia.** Ask a local what is the best restaurant in Aegina and the response is invariably this island institution. A 10-minute walk from Aegina town gets you to this rustic 50-something-year-old building, in recent years upgraded from an older taverna. In summer, the garden is a pleasant oasis, scented with jasmine and honeysuckle; in winter, it's cozy to nestle in the little dining room. Start with eggplant in garlic sauce, beets, or zucchini croquettes. Continue with taverna classics such as veal in red sauce; thick, juicy grilled pork chops; moussaka enlivened with cinnamon and a wonderfully fluffy bechamel; and in winter, the hare stew. In summer you'll end your meal as the Greeks do with some deliciously sweet fresh fruit, while in winter candied quince and prunes are popular. The restaurant only serves dinner, from 7 PM to 1 AM. ⊠ *Ayii Assomati 75,* ☎ *0297/22711. Reservations essential on weekends. No credit cards. Closed Mon., Tues., Thurs., Fri.*

$ ✕ **En Aigini.** In a newly renovated neoclassical mansion, this is actually three spaces in one: a lovely tree-shaded courtyard that operates as a taverna in summer; the upper floor rec room with billiards, backgammon, TV, and fireplace, where guests can also dine in summer or winter weekends; and a cellar featuring live music in winter. The cook's specialties include the onion, cheese, or leek pies; an unusual dish called *manti tis Rozi,* consisting of minced lamb pies with yogurt and tomato; and *strapazada,* a scrambled-egg dish with tomatoes and paprika. Hungrier diners can order one of the magirefta, such as *lahanodolmades* (cabbage rolls), *tzoutzoukakia* (spicy meat patties), stuffed peppers and tomatoes, and beef kokkinisto, or the grilled meats such as turkey souvlaki (seldom seen on a Greek menu). ⊠ *Spiro Rodis 44, Aegina town,* ☎ *0297/2922; 094/596318 mobile. AE, DC, MC, V. Taverna closed Nov.–Apr. No dinner on upper floor weekdays Nov.–Apr. No lunch.*

$ ✕ **Karafaki.** A little ouzerie that is reminiscent of the best of these time-honored establishments, Karafaki is appropriately located in the fish and produce market. Plan on coming with friends, if possible, and order a number of little mezedes to share. Some outstanding plates are the black-eyed peas with dill and scallions, artichoke hearts with beans, carrots and peas in an egg-lemon sauce, slightly bitter boiled wild greens, *maridhes* (fried smelt), and *soupies* (cuttlefish) in red sauce. Ask for daily specials or go take a look at the pots in the kitchen. Make sure to order some barrel retsina or red or white wine in the namesake *karafaki* (copper-colored metallic carafe). ⊠ *Fish market on Irioti St.,* ☎ *no phone. No credit cards.*

$-$$ 🏠 **To Petrino Spiti (The Stone House).** Owner Elpida Thanopoulou lives adjacent to this delightful 18-year-old stone compound, built in the traditional style, and she keeps an eagle eye on the operation, making sure the rooms are spotlessly clean and well-maintained. Cozy studios, maisonettes, and a suite have all been beautifully appointed with traditional furniture, folk crafts, and paintings; all have fully equipped kitchens, ceiling fans, and spare beds to accommodate families or extra guests. It's in a quiet area of Aegina town, set a little back from the harbor and Ayios Nikolaos church. Studios (in the basement) and maisonettes (on the ground floor) are cooler in the summer, while the maisonettes on the second floor have excellent views of the sea and nearby Angistri. ⊠ *Stratigou Petriti 5, 18910,* ☎ *0297/23837,* FAX *01/ 331–1974 Athens. 4 studios, 4 maisonettes, 1 suite. Kitchens. No credit cards.*

$ ⛫ **Eginitiko Archontiko (Traditional Settlement).** This jewel of a pension was once the home of the wealthy Bitrou merchant family and their daughter, the legendary Zinovia, who garnered fame for her independent ways (she created a vivid image as she puffed on cigarettes and raced her motorcar around the island). Her literary salons attracted such luminaries as Kazantzakis and the island's own St. Nektarios. The great lady died in 1985, but her spirit lives on in the house. Care has been taken to preserve the original painted walls and ceilings in the salon and the suite, and every nook and cranny has been fitted out in period style; guests can even stay in Kazantzakis's room with its lovely balcony. The wonderful sunporch has colored glass windows, an ideal place to enjoy breakfast in winter or a drink from the small bar; in summer guests may eat breakfast in the roof garden. A small communal kitchen has a refrigerator and range. The pension's in-town location, 300 ft from the port and opposite the Markelos Tower, is most convenient, but ground-floor rooms may be noisy due to motorcycle traffic on the small road adjacent to the house. ⊠ *Ayiou Nikolaou and Thomaidou 1, 18010,* ☎ *0297/24968,* FAX *0297/26716. 12 rooms, 1 suite. Air-conditioning. AE, DC, MC, V.*

$ ⛫ **I Pansion tis Renas.** Gracious owner Kyria Rena Kappou has decorated the eight rooms of this pension with taste and loving care, creating a homey atmosphere reinforced by the handmade lace curtains, solid wood and marble furniture, and tasteful knickknacks. To make guests feel especially welcome, she places a rose from her garden in each newcomer's room. All rooms have a refrigerator, air-conditioning, balcony, TV, and telephone; those on the upper floor boast sea views. The pension, opened in 1990, is at the edge of Aegina town, about a 15-minute walk from the port. Breakfast (cake, homemade sweets, fresh juice and delicious jams), included in the price, is served family-style in the dining room or in the courtyard. If you request so in advance, she can also cook dinner for guests, including her specialties: *yiouvetsaki* (meat baked in ceramic dishes with tomato sauce and barley-shaped pasta), *kokoro kokkinisto* (rooster in red sauce), and *kasseropita* (a pie made from Kasseri cheese). ⊠ *Parodos Ayias Irinis, Faros, Aegina town 18010,* ☎ *0297/24760,* ☎ FAX *0297/24244. 8 rooms. AE, MC, V.* 🐢

Festivals

Local festivals, or *panagyria,* are a time when you can observe Greek rituals and liturgies at close hand, and they are often followed by a feast and dancing, to which outsiders are welcome. If you are in Aegina on such days, ask at your hotel or look for printed notices advertising the festivities. On St. George's Day, or April 23 (or the day after Easter if the 23rd falls during Lent), a *panagyri* (saints day festival) is celebrated at Ayios Giorgios (St. George) of Palaiochora, when feasting and dancing follow a liturgy at the church. Several festivals are held at Ayios Nektarios monastery throughout the year; three of the most important are Whitmonday, or the day after Pentecost (the seventh Sunday after Easter), September 3, and November 9, when the remains of the saint are brought down from the monastery and carried in a procession through the streets of town, which are covered in carpets and strewn with flowers. On the Assumption of the Virgin Mary on August 15—the biggest holiday of the summer—a celebration is held at the mountain monastery of Chrysoleontissa. On September 6 and 7, Ayios Sostis is celebrated at Perdika, and on December 6, the feast day of Ayios Nikolaos, the small chapel on the harbor and the large twin-towered church in town hold festive celebrations.

Nightlife

Some popular bars include the classic **Perdikiotika,** set in an 1860 building that was once a combination bank–produce store, with beat sounds, lots of wood, a painted ceiling depicting Hermes, and the original safe; **Tsitras,** which plays rock and occasionally jazz in a British pub atmosphere; **Avli** (⊠ Pan Irioti 17), a cozy courtyard that serves as a café-bistro days, and as a bar that plays taped Greek, retro rock, and Latin music at night; and **Taverna I Synantasis** (⊠ Aphias 40), with live Greek music on weekends. The **Bel Epoque** (⊠ Eandos and Pileos) attracts a crowd of varied ages, with its mostly Greek pop tapes and exotic cocktails. This is the place to shuck your inhibitions and learn some Greek dances to impress the folks back home. Two open-air cinemas, the **Akroyiali** (⊠ At south end of harbor on road leading to Perdhika) and the **Olympia** (⊠ Near football grounds at north end of harbor near Miranda Hotel), are a fun way to while away a balmy summer evening; they are very social affairs that will give you a glimpse of the local community. Greek cinemas have an intermission in the middle of the film; both theaters have snack bars and serve beer and wine.

Shopping

CERAMICS

Close to the Markelos Tower is **Ergastiri** (⊠ Pileos 7, ☎ 0297/23210), a small shop which carries an eye-catching selection of vividly colored and unusual ceramic plates, pitchers, and cups, along with outstanding examples of glass candle holders (which are suspended from the ceiling in imitation of Orthodox church candles), plus finely crafted *mati* (evil eye amulets)—cobalt blue beads that make excellent conversation pieces to bring home as gifts. If you don't see exactly what you want on the premises, owner Evangelos Linos can send for others from his workshop on Aegina. Shipping is not done in the shop (and it is expensive to send items home on your own), but items can be carefully wrapped in layers of bubble paper which should ensure their safety in your baggage.

LOCAL FOODSTUFFS

Aegina's famous pistachios, much coveted by Greeks, can be bought from stands along the harbor. They make welcome snacks and gifts. Another unusual treat found at some of the local bakeries behind the harbor is *amigdalota,* rich almond cookies sprinkled with orange flower water and powdered sugar. If you want to have a picnic lunch on the island or on the ferry boat while en route to another Saronic island, check out the lusciously displayed fruit on several boats in the center of the harbor.

Eastern Aegina

Area approximately 11 km (7 mi) east of Aegina town.

The eastern side of Aegina is rugged and sparsely inhabited, except for a former fishing hamlet now given over to mainly package tours. The small port of **Ayia Marina** (⊠ Below the Sanctuary of Aphaia [☞ *below*], via the small paved road) has many hotels, cafés, restaurants, and a beach to accommodate visitors.

⑰ Don't miss visiting the **Sanctuary of Aphaia,** which perches on a pine-clad promontory and offers superb views of Athens and Piraeus across the water—with binoculars you can see both the Parthenon and the Temple of Poseidon at Sounion. This site has been occupied by many sanctuaries to Aphaia; the ruins visible today are those of the temple built in the early 5th century BC. Aphaia was apparently a pre-Hellenic deity, whose worship eventually converged with that of Athena. The temple, one of the finest extant examples of archaic architecture, was adorned with an exquisite group of pedimental sculptures that are now in the Munich Glyptothek; 25 of the original 32 Doric columns were either left standing or have been reconstructed. The on-site museum now opens at 9, 11, noon, and 1 for 15 minutes (only) for no extra fee. The exhibit has many of the fragments from the once brilliantly colored interior of the temple and inscriptions of an older temple of the 6th and 5th centuries BC, as well as drawings that show a reconstruction of the original building. From Aegina, catch the bus for Ayia Marina on Platia Ethniyersias, just north of where the ferries dock; ask the driver to let you off at the temple. A gift and snack bar is a comfortable place to have a drink and wait for the return bus to Aegina town or for the bus bound for Ayia Marina. ✉ *13 km (8½ mi) east of Aegina town,* ☎ *0297/32398.* ☜ *800 dr./€2.35.* ☉ *Weekdays 8–8 (8–5 in winter), weekends 8–2:30 (8:30–3 in winter).*

Aegina is one of the best islands to hike on since the interior *messoghia* is gently undulating, older dirt trails are often still marked by white paint markings, and the terrain offers an incredible variety of landscapes that run the gamut of the Greek countryside. Those who are ambitious might want to hike from Aegina to the Temple of Aphaia or on the unspoiled eastern coast from Perdika to Ayia Marina, two routes described in detail in Gerald Thompson's *A Walking Guide to Aegina* (available at Kalezis gift shop at Dimokratias 35, right in the middle of the Aegina waterfront; they also sell other English language paperbacks and international newspapers).

OFF THE
BEATEN PATH

Follow the lead of the locals and visiting Athenians—take a bus from Platia Ethniyersias, the main bus station on the port in Aegina Town, about 20 minutes to pretty **Perdika** and unwind over a seaside taverna lunch. Tavernas and cafés in Perdika have multiplied over the years, but are still low-key and charmingly decorated, transporting you light years away from the bustle of much of modern Greece. Try **O Nondos**, the first fish taverna after the bus station, for a fine meal on the canopied terrace overlooking the little bay and the islet of Moni. Nondos serves traditional favorites, highlighted by various fresh fish and seafood dishes and is adorned with dozens of multi-colored olive oil tins—used as planters, they create a Nikon-worthy, joyful explosion of greenery and flowers. Other interesting cafés include the inviting **Remetzo**, the **Kioski**, set in a little stone building, and the **Skipper**, at the very end of the waterfront, which attracts a slightly bohemian crowd.

Perdika has a small beach and wildlife sanctuary sponsored by the Friends of the Strays of Aegina and Angistri, who also have several animal shelters and an office and gift shop in town. During the summer, caïques make frequent trips of 10 minutes to the little islet of **Moni**, inhabited only by birds and relocated *kri-kri* (Cretan goats). Trails are good for hiking, after which a swim off a little sand beach in the marvelously clear water is most welcome. If you want to stay for a few hours, it is best to make an appointment for your boatman to return for you (pay him when he does). A small snack bar operates during the summer, although you would be better off bringing a picnic lunch.

Beaches

Besides Ayia Marina, which can become very crowded, you can swim at sandy **Tourlo** and **Vayia**, on the northern coast of the island.

Lodging

$$ ⌂ **Hotel Apollo.** To take advantage of the fine location on the beach at Ayia Marina, all (except singles) of the air-conditioned, fairly quiet rooms at this hotel have balconies and sea views. TVs and refrigerators are available for rent. While its 1997 renovation didn't improve its cement-block exterior, the hotel has many amenities ideal for ac-

tive travelers who don't want to go far, including a large terrace with seawater pool. The hotel is surrounded by greenery, and steps lead down to a rocky beach with a sand floor. Buffet breakfast is included in the price, and the restaurants serve Greek and Continental cuisine. Buses pass regularly for the overdeveloped resort of Ayia Marina, a 10-minute walk from the hotel, and for Aegina; the stop is 750 ft from the hotel. ✉ *Ayia Marina beach, 18010,* ☎ *0297/32281 or 0297/32271 through 0297/32274; 01/323–4292 winter in Athens,* FAX *0297/32688; 01/322–4136 winter in Athens. 107 rooms. 2 restaurants, air-conditioning, saltwater pool, tennis court, minigolf, table tennis. AE, DC, MC, V. Closed Nov.–Mar.* 🐾

Poros

⑱ *21½ km (13½ mi) south of Aegina.*

The island of Poros sits due south of Aegina, separated from the Peloponnese by a narrow strait. **Poros town** (✉ Draped over the promontory guarding the strait) has a long, attractive waterfront skirting the base of the hill. In antiquity, Poros was the site of an important **Sanctuary of Poseidon,** whose scrappy ruins can be seen at the approximate center of the island. Many of the blocks from the temple were carried off in the 18th century to build the monastery on nearby Hydra, reachable by hydrofoil or ferry.

As you clear the narrow straits of Poros and head east, you will see on your left the 18th-century monastery of **Zoodochos Pighi,** or Life-giving Spring (✉ On a pine-clad hillside just east of the town of Poros).

Hydra

⑲ *28 km (17½ mi) south of Poros.*

Hydra has come a long way from the days of the early 1960s when an Italian starlet named Sophia Loren emerged from its harbor waters in the Hollywood flick *A Boy and A Dolphin.* Fortunately, its noble port and houses have since been rescued and placed on the Council of Europe's list of protected monuments, with strict ordinances regulating construction and renovation. Although there are many reasons that Hydra may become endeared to you, not the least of them is the fact that all motor traffic is banned from the island (except for several rather noisy garbage trucks). After the racket of inner Athens and ear-splitting assaults on the eardrums by motorbikes in Aegina, Poros, and Spetses, Hydra's blissful tranquility, especially off-season, is a cause for rejoicing.

Your initial reaction to Hydra, as its full length stretches before you as you round the easternmost finger of the Northern Peloponnese, might not, in fact, be a joyful one: the island seems so gray, mountainous, and barren. But this will no doubt be replaced with delight as you approach the island's curved harbor—one of the most picturesque in all of Greece (when you arrive by boat, mule tenders in the port will rent you one of their fleet to transport your baggage—or better yet you—to your hotel, for around 2,500 dr./€7.37–3,000 dr./€8.84). **Hydra town,** invisible at first, gradually reveals itself with gray and white houses climbing steep slopes surrounding a nearly round harbor, looking much as it did in 1821, when Hydra was crucial in the struggle for independence. Many of the waterfront houses, built between 1770 and 1821, consist of a rectangular basic unit two to three stories tall, with the upper floor set back to create a terrace, and most have courtyards with large subterranean cisterns. (People claim that the cisterns were also used to hide gold and other treasure in the 18th and 19th centuries, and that eels were introduced in them to keep the water clean and drinkable.)

Although there are traces of an ancient settlement, the island was sparsely inhabited until the Ottoman period. In the 16th century, its rugged slopes offered a haven for refugees from the Peloponnese during the constant wars between the Ottomans and the Venetians. The settlers turned to the sea and began building boats, and by the early 18th century, their trade routes stretched from the mainland to Asia Minor and even America. By its end, the fleet, profiting from the Napoleonic Wars, had captured much of the lucrative grain trade between the Ukraine and western Europe, earning great fortunes and much notoriety in blockade-running. After the Greek Revolution, Hydra sank into relative obscurity until well past the middle of the 20th century, when it was discovered by outsiders. It became a haven for artists and writers and discriminating travelers who wanted a tasteful, tranquil holiday. Most of the artists and early inhabitants have been priced off the island or were frightened away by the summer crowds, although you'll still find a core of this community remaining in the winter months.

In the early 19th century, the tremendous surge in disposable wealth enabled shipowners to build the characteristic *archontika* (or great houses), massive gray-stone mansions facing the harbor, with forbidding, fortresslike exteriors. Good examples include the **Tsamados House,** which now shelters the School of the Merchant Navy (⊠ On harbor opposite ferry landing); the **Tombazi House,** an annex of Athens's School of Fine Arts (⊠ Halfway up west side of harbor); the **Voulgaris (Merikles-Oikonomou) House** (⊠ On west harbor); and the **Koundouriotis House** (⊠ Looming on west headland). The **Monastery of the Panaghia** (⊠ Along central section of harbor) was built in the late 18th century partly of stone taken from the Sanctuary of Poseidon on Poros. The monastery's bell tower is a fine example of the early 19th-century marble carving done by a guild of traveling artisans (perhaps from the island of Tinos) who left their mark all over the Aegean in this period.

After exploring Hydra, pack a picnic and set out of town, looking back through the labyrinth of lanes for views of the red roofs set against turquoise waters, perhaps stopping at Kanoni Square, which overlooks the gulf. The convent of **Ayios Nikolaos Monastery** is located to the southeast of Hydra town, after you pass between the monasteries of Agios Triadas and Agias Matronis (the latter can be visited.) The two remaining nuns of Ayios Nikolaos monastery (the term is actually used for colonies of men or women in Greece) crochet curtains and embroider intricate folk patterns on tablecloths and aprons (some are for sale and make memorable gifts) when they are not outside hammering or painting or tending to their garden. Pelaghia, a serene nun beloved by the older residents of Hydra, has a radiant smile that transcends any language barrier. Stop here for a drink and a sweet (a donation is appropriate), and Pelaghia will be glad to show you the beautiful 16th-century icons and frescoes in the sanctuary. Although the hike is not overly strenuous if you stick to the mule paths, wear sturdy walking shoes, long pants, and carry a bottle of water. Because of the heat, start out very early in the morning if you make this hike in the summer. Your reward: stunning vistas over the island (resplendent with wildflowers and herbs in the spring), the western and eastern coasts, and nearby islets such as Dokos. You will no doubt encounter some mule traffic en route, as this is the time-honored and most practical mode of transport up to the crest since cars and trucks are not allowed. You'll see mules patiently hauling everything from armchairs and building materials to cases of beer. Agios Nikolaos Monastery is between an hour and a half and two hours from town.

Beaches

The only sandy beach near town lies east at Mandraki, the private domain of the Miramare, though the windsurfing center is open to everyone. West of town is **Vlichos bay,** a 30-minute walk past Kamini, a pretty hamlet with tavernas, a historic bridge, and a rocky beach, or a 45-minute water taxi ride from the port. You may also hire a water taxi to transport you to a more private beach, such as **Avlaki, Bisti,** or **Limnioniza,** or a nearby **islet,** such as Dokos, Kivotos, or Petasi.

Dining and Lodging

$$ ✕ **Iliovasilema.** At sunset, the breathtaking view from this place is unforgettable (yes, the translation of *iliovasilema*). No matter what time you dine here, however, you'll find owner Marina Lembessi to be both a consummate cook as well as an extremely gracious hostess. Try the terrific *tiropitakia* and *spanakopitakia* (crispy little cheese and spinach pies in phyllo dough), sardine salad, or *bekri mezze* (marinated lamb, called the "drunkard's appetizer"). Main dishes include terrific *klephtiko* (pork slices cooked in an enclosed packet with aromatic herbs). If it's not too hot and you're lucky, Marina will have cooked some halva or creamy brandy-spiked *galaktobouriko* (custard in phyllo). If it's a clear moonlit night, you're in luck again—it's very romantic to walk back to Hydra under the star-laden sky. ⊠ *Up above the pebble beach of Vlichos Harbor,* ☎ *0298/52496. No credit cards.*

$–$$ ✕ **Vigla.** This handsomely appointed restaurant is a cut above an ordinary taverna. Set in a stately old archontiko with a large balcony overlooking the port (*vigla* means "crows' nest" and it's a crows' nest view you get), this place is run by brothers Dimitris and George Vlachododimitris of Kondylenia's fame (☞ *below*) and has collected a legion of fans since it opened in 1997. International dishes, such as Italian salad and *coco vin krassato* (chicken cooked in red wine) take their place on the menu beside Greek classics such as *katsikaki sto fourno* (kid baked in the oven). Or try their popular specialty of beef filet and vegetables rolled in phyllo with Roquefort cheese and mushrooms, followed by the crunchy rich walnut cake. ⊠ *Up steps above Pirate bar at south end of harbor,* ☎ *0298/54154. V.*

$ ✕ **Kondylenia's.** Set on a promontory overlooking the charming little
★   harbor of Kaminia, Kondylenia's is irresistible. You'll join a gregarious group of Hydriots as well as scores of weekending Athenians, to whom a visit to this marvelous eatery is something of a spiritual pilgrimage—few other places serve the essence of Greek country cooking in such a serenely lovely setting. Look in the kitchen below the terrace to see what's cooking: it's likely to be anything from whole fish charcoal-grilled to plump strands of lobster-like octopus marinated in vinegar and oil. In spring the boiled greens and tender lamb stew are not to be missed. ⊠ *On the headland above Kaminia harbor,* ☎ *0298/52075 or 0298/54154. No credit cards. Closed Nov.–Lent.*

$ ✕ **To Geitoniko.** Great home-style cooking by Christina and her husband, Manolis, at fair prices is the hallmark of this restaurant, where you can dine on a starlit terrace on summer nights or in the cozy old Hydriot house with stone floors and wooden ceilings. Try the baby beet salad, complete with boiled greens and topped with a dollop of garlic potatoes; the magirefta-like octopus *stifado,* a kind of stew; and oven-baked pork stuffed with Parmesan and peppers. Eggplant Hydra—eggplant stuffed with beef, tomato, and feta and spiced with paprika—is a favorite with regulars. Grilled meats and fresh fish are available, and the cooks prepare scrumptious desserts: halvah, baklava, and some Hydriot delicacies such as an irresistible almond-honey square. Because there are only 20 tables and one can't make reservations, it's a good idea to go early to beat the crowd; the restaurant starts serving dinner around 9 PM. ⊠ *Spiliou Harami St. opposite Pension Antonis,* ☎ *0298/53615. No credit cards. Closed Nov.–Jan.*

$ ✕ To Krifo Limani. Called the "Secret Harbor," this spot still attracts groups of fishermen on their days off, even though Capt. Andreas Voulgaris has retired. He passed on this small taverna to his son Dimitris, who still has time to catch some of the fish, spear the octopus, and run this busy little place. Sit in the courtyard and order whole fresh fish such as sea bass, or for a cheaper seafood selection, sweet and crisply fried *maridakia* (smelts), which are eaten whole, bones and all. Plump snails, served in the shell with toothpicks to extract them, are also a delicacy much savored by locals. Known for its fish soup, the taverna also serves several magirefta, such as *kotopoulo lemonato* (chicken in lemon-oil sauce) and kokkinisto (lamb or beef), as well as appetizers— zucchini croquettes, homemade dolmades, *keftedakia* (fried meatballs), and dips like taramosalata. Do like the fishermen do and wash it all down with carafes of barrel white or rosé wine. ⊠ *On alley near Bratsera off main road, left side of harbor,* ☎ *0298/52585. No credit cards. Closed Jan.–mid-Feb.*

$ ✕ To Steki. Shuck your tourist inhibitions and skip the fixed-price menu at this classic hangout with gray shutters, a veranda, and folk murals of Hydriot life, located on a quiet cul-du-sac. Instead, order what the locals do, the delicious fish soup, and reliable magirefta, such as stuffed peppers, lamb in red sauce or roasted in the oven, and *briam* (a type of ratatouille). Run by the brothers Christos and Argyris (the latter sports what may be the bushiest mustache on the island), the taverna also serves grilled meats—*paidakia* (lamb ribs), beef patties, souvlaki—fresh local fish, and numerous appetizers, such as taramosalata, eggplant dip, and tender octopus *xidato,* marinated in oil and vinegar. Barrel white and rosé and some Greek bottled wines are available. ⊠ *Miaouli St., in "Droom" alley, across from Loulakis store, Hydra town,* ☎ *0298/53517. MC, V.*

$$$ ✕🛏 Bratsera. An 1860 sponge factory was transformed into this posh
★ hotel with doors made out of old packing crates still bearing the "Piraeus" stamp. Hints of the former factory are still visible in the Hydriot gray stonework and timber beams incorporated into the lounge and the restaurant, blending harmoniously with the modern furnishings. The service is excellent in the hotel, which is just minutes from the port. The rooms, located in two old buildings and one new one, are all decorated individually, some with four-poster beds, others with cozy lofts, and all with portraits and engravings. The restaurant operates in the oleander- and bougainvillea-graced courtyard, and its kitchen, which specializes in European cuisine, is considered one of the island's best. The courtyard pool makes up for Hydra's dearth of beaches and becomes part of the extended bar with quiet music at night. Buffet breakfast is included in the price. ⊠ *1st street to left as you leave ferry, near Hydra Tours office, 18040,* ☎ *0298/53971 through 0298/ 53975; 0298/52794 restaurant; 01/721–8102 winter in Athens,* 🖷 *0298/ 53626; 01/722–1619 winter in Athens. 19 rooms, 4 suites. Restaurant, bar, pool. AE, DC, MC, V. Closed Nov.–Clean Mon. weekend, usually mid-Feb.* 🍃

$$$ 🛏 Orloff. Built in 1798 by Catherine the Great for Count Orloff, who came to Greece with a Russian fleet to try to dislodge the Turks, this archontika still retains the splendor of the past with the added benefit of modern amenities. The heavy single shutters, which were used to defend against attack, have been preserved, and antiques—walnut furniture, paintings, and lithographs—grace the lace-curtained rooms. No two are alike; those categorized superior rooms have sitting areas and color TVs (about 8,000 dr./€23.59 more), and all have minibars and views of the town or the pretty courtyard, shaded by a mulberry tree. Included in the price, the breakfast is one of the best in town, with corn flakes, boiled eggs, yogurt bought from a local shepherd, pastries, orange juice, and fruit. ⊠ *Rafalia 9, 18040,* ☎ *0298/52564 or 0298/52495; 01/522–6125 winter in Athens,* 𝔽𝔸𝕏 *0298/53532; 01/522–7265 winter in Athens. 10 rooms. Minibars. AE, V. Closed Nov.–late Mar.*

$$ ★ **Miranda.** Artists and art collectors alike will feel at home in this aesthetically decorated traditional Hydriot home, built in 1821 by a Captain Danavasi and now classified by the Ministry of Culture as a national monument. It contains an interesting collection of 18th- and 19th-century furniture and art—Oriental rugs, wooden chests, nautical engravings—and the ground-floor art gallery hosts local exhibits and international artists in July and August. The suites on the top floor have huge balconies, air-conditioning, sea views, and graceful ceilings done by Venetian painters. The price includes full breakfast, served in the interior courtyard fragrant with lemon blossoms, jasmine, and bougainvillea. Highly informative owner Miranda speaks fluent English and will be glad to give you a crash course in Hydriot history, as well as helping you with details for walks and dining choices. ⊠ *Miaouli, 2 blocks inland from center of port, 18040,* ☎ *0298/52230 or 0298/53953; 01/684–9268 winter in Athens,* 𝔽𝔸𝕏 *0298/53510. 9 rooms, 3 suites. Air-conditioning. No credit cards. Closed Nov.–Feb.*

$ **Hotel Hydra.** One of the oldest hotels in Hydra, this beautifully preserved archontika (two-story stone mansion) has large stately rooms, some balconies with views over the harbor, and attractive lounge areas decorated with antiques. It's a long climb up the hill, but you'll be rewarded by a tranquil area undisturbed by any noise from the harbor. Owner Dimitris Davis, who has operated the hotel since 1982, takes pride in offering genteel hospitality to guests, who tend to keep flocking back each year. A complete breakfast, including country bread, marmalade, boiled egg, fresh juice, and cheese, is included in the price. Note that 5 of the 13 rooms only have bathrooms (private, albeit) in the hallway. To get to this hotel, turn left at Votsi street after the clock tower on the harbor; keep to the right on Sahini as you weave up high above the port. ⊠ *Voulgari 8,* ☎ 𝔽𝔸𝕏 *0298/52102. 13 rooms. AE, MC, V.*

Festivals

For three days in mid-July, the alleys of Hydra resemble Lilliputia, with colorful marionette troupes from all over the world performing for free during **International Puppet Theater Days.** A longtime collaboration between Greek puppeteers Lakis Christidis and Antigoni Paroussi and the founder of Sweden's Marionetteatern, Michael Meschke, the festival has attracted such diverse groups as Compagnie Danaye of Togo, El Khatib from Palestine, and the Brazilian group Amaglama Production. There are also puppet exhibitions and workshops for children. For more information, call the organizers (☎ 0298/53105). The island also celebrates its crucial role in the War of Independence with the **Miaoulia,** which takes place the third week of June; it includes military parades and dancing and culminates in a reenactment of the night Admiral Miaouls loaded a vessel with explosives and sent it upwind to the Turkish fleet. Naturally, the enemy's ship goes down in flames. On **Good Friday** of Orthodox Easter, a mournful procession of parishioners holding candles follows the funeral bier (*Epitaphio*) as it winds its way to Kaminia harbor, where the bier is set afloat, illuminated by several fishing boats; youth dive in to retrieve it. Greek Orthodox Holy Week ends in midnight **Anastasi** liturgies, with the joyful singing of hymns, exploding fireworks, and churches competing to see who can raise the Resurrection cross highest. Contact the Hydra tourist police for more information (☞ Visitor Information *in* Excursions from Athens A to Z, *below*).

Nightlife

CLUBS

Around forever, **Pirate** nevertheless remains popular for its location on the south end of the harbor and long list of celebrity visitors; note that it can get pretty raucous during the high season. Close by is **To Rolloi,** which attracts an older, more sedate crowd that enjoys classy cocktails in a homey setting, while listening to taped Greek music. Another die-hard club, **Cavos** near Kamini, goes wild after midnight, when revelers start to dance on the tables. Less boisterous spots include minuscule **Hydronetta,** which has an enchanting view from its perch above the harbor on the way to Kamini, on the coast just past Kanoni, and remains the place to enjoy an ouzo or fruity long drink at sunset. **Amalour,** up Tombazi Street behind the port, attracts a mature crowd who sip fresh juice as well as alcoholic drinks. Bars often change names, ownership, and music—if not location—so check with your hotel for what's in season.

Shopping

A number of elegant shops (some of them offshoots of Athens stores) sell fashionable and amusing clothing and jewelry, though you won't save anything by shopping here. Although the sponge-fishing trade is long gone, you can still find natural sponges (from other locales) sold here on the waterfront. In larger versions the sponges are perfect for gently stimulating the skin while bathing (or for artistically dabbing paint on your walls to achieve an artsy effect); in the petite variety, they are great for applying makeup.

Spetses

⓴ *24 km (15 mi) southwest of Hydra.*

In the years leading up to the revolution, Hydra's great rival and ally was the island of Spetses. Lying at the entrance to the Argolic Gulf, just off the mainland, Spetses was known even in antiquity for its hospitable soil and verdant, pine-clad slopes. The pine trees on the island today, however, were planted by a Spetsiot philanthropist dedicated to restoring the beauty stripped by the shipbuilding industry. There are far fewer trees than there were in antiquity, but the island is still well watered, and the many prosperous Athenians who have made Spetses their second home compete to have the prettiest gardens and terraces. The island shows evidence of continuous habitation through all of antiquity. From the 16th century, settlers came over from the mainland and, as on Hydra, they soon began to look to the sea, building their own boats. They became master sailors, successful merchants, and later, in the Napoleonic Wars, skilled blockade runners, earning fortunes that they poured into building larger boats and grander houses. With the outbreak of the War of Independence in 1821, the Spetsiots dedicated their best ships and brave men (and women) to the cause.

Ships meet Spetses at **Dapia,** the jetty protecting the modern harbor. Fortified with cannons dating from the War of Independence, it faces the attractive waterfront, full of outdoor cafés and restaurants. The harbormaster's offices, to the right as you face the sea, occupy a building designed in the simple two-story, center-hall architecture typical of the period and this place.

In front of a popular park is **Bouboulina's house,** where guided tours in English on this interesting heroine's life are given. Laskarina Bouboulina was the bravest of all Spetsiot revolutionaries, the daughter of a Hydriot sea captain, and the wife, then widow, of two more sea captains. Left with a considerable inheritance and nine children, she dedicated herself to increasing her already substantial fleet and fortune. On her flagship, the *Agamemnon,* the largest in the Greek fleet, she sailed into war against the Ottomans at the head of the Spetsiot ships. Her fiery temper led to her death in a family feud many years later. ⊠ *Behind Dapia, near the harbor,* ☏ *0298/72416.* ⌷ *1,000 dr./€2.94.* ⊙ *45-min tours in English daily 9:30–3:30 and 4:30–8:30 (last tour). Closed Nov.–mid-Mar.*

Spetses' **museum** found an unlikely home in a fine late-18th-century archontiko built in a style that might be termed Turko-Venetian. It contains articles from the period of Spetses' greatness, including Bouboulina's bones, in a room festooned with the revolutionary flag. ⊠ *Near town center in the Archontiko Hatziyianni-Mexi, 600 ft south of harbor,* ☏ *0298/72994.* ⌷ *500 dr./€1.47.* ⊙ *Tues.–Sun. 8–2:30 (8:30–1 in winter).*

The promontory is the site of the little 19th-century **Church of Ayios Mamas.** On the headland sits the **Monastery of Ayios Nikolaos** (⊠ On road heading southeast from Dapia), now the episcopal seat. Its lacy white-marble bell tower recalls that of Hydra's port monastery, and it was here that the islanders first raised their flag of independence.

Spetses has two harbors, with the **Old Harbor** slumbering in obscurity. It is dominated by the gray-stone mansion of the Botassis family, one of the earliest to settle on Spetses. The Old Harbor is perfect for an afternoon or evening stroll, while you might imagine it as it was in its heyday: the walls of the mansions resounding with the noise of shipbuilding and the streets humming with discreet whisperings of revolution and piracy.

Well-to-do Athenians would descend to the 1914 **Posidonion Hotel** (⊠ Immediately west of Dapia, near harbor), the scene of glamorous society parties and balls in the era between the two world wars. The hotel's public rooms have retained this marvelous, unusual elegance.

The **Anargyrios and Korgialenios School** (⊠ ½ km [¼ mi] west of Dapia), established as an English-style boarding school for the children of Greece's Anglophilic upper class, is known as the inspiration for the school in John Fowles's *The Magus.*

You may wish to walk up to **Kastelli,** the original settlement of Spetses, of which little remains but four churches: the **Panaghia** or *Koimisis tis Theotokou* (the Assumption of the Virgin Mary), from the 17th century; **Ayios Vassilis** (Saint Basil); the **Taxiarchoi** (Archangels), early 19th century; and **Ayia Triada** (Holy Trinity), late 18th century. The churches are kept locked, but ask for the property owner or the guardian, who has a key.

Beaches

Spetses' best beaches are on the southwest side of the island, in **Ayioi Anargyroi** and **Ayia Paraskevi**; on the east side of the island, head for **Ayia Marina,** which has the pleasant taverna **Paradisos.** In the northeast, just past Anargyrios and Korgialenios College, is **Ligioneri,** reachable by bus from town.

Biking

The lack of cars and the predominantly level roads make Spetses ideal for bicycling. One good trip is along the coastal road that circles the island, going from the main town to Ayia Paraskevi beach. You can also rent a mountain bike to use on the paths that zigzag through the island. Contact **Trek Mountain Bikes,** run by Nikolaos Kondaratos and his British wife, Elizabeth Allen, located on the main road about 750 ft left of the new harbor (☎ 0298/74505). They rent well-maintained bikes and equipment and can dispense advice about where to go, including crossing over to the Peloponnese for a few days.

Dining and Lodging

$–$$ ✕ **Exedra.** Called Sioras or Giorgos by locals (all three names are on the sign), this waterside taverna is in the old harbor where the yachts pull up. House specialties are fish Spetsiota, baked with tomato and wine; a dish called Argo, shrimp and lobster baked with feta; and mussels saganaki; fresh fish is always available. Magirefta include the hard-to-find *gouronopoulo kokkinisto,* (suckling pig in red sauce). One can also order grilled meats such as souvlaki and even schnitzel. ⊠ *At edge of Palio Limani (go left from new harbor, 10-min walk),* ☎ *0298/73497. MC. Closed Nov.–Feb.*

$ ✕ **Lazaros.** One of the last traditional tavernas in town, Lazaros draws a boisterous local crowd to its place, decorated with old family photos and barrels of retsina lining the walls. The small selection of well-cooked dishes includes some daily specials, such as goat in lemon sauce, chicken kokkinisto, grilled meats, and, occasionally, fresh fish at good prices. Tasty appetizers include homemade tzatziki and taramosalata, which is properly made with grayish roe instead of the bright pink color induced by food dye. Also good is the black-eyed bean salad called *mavromatika,* garlic potatoes, and tender, marinated beets. Order the barrel retsina (priced by the kilo). In summer, diners eat outside in a courtyard. ⊠ *Botassi St., 900 ft up from Dapia,* ☎ *0298/72600. No credit cards. Closed mid-Nov.–mid-Mar. No lunch.*

$ ✕ **Patralis.** The seaside veranda here is the best place in town to savor
★ seafood mezedes and fresh fish—fried, grilled, or baked. Especially good are the fish soup, the lobster with spaghetti, and a kind of paella stuffed with mussels, shrimp, and crayfish. Fish is a must here; try the house specialty of *psari a la Spetses,* which is a flaky swordfish or tuna steak baked with garlic-laced vegetables. Other fish are subject to availability and include the dorado, red mullet, pandora, common bream, and *skarptharia* (somewhat similar to bream). Magirefta include stuffed peppers and tomatoes, oven-baked lamb, and eggplant with minced meat (papoutsakia, or "little shoes") or with tomatoes and onion. They make a mean baked apple for dessert, and the service is especially friendly. ⊠ *2,500 ft right of new harbor, near Spetses Hotel,* ☎ *0298/72134. MC, V. Closed Nov.–Dec.*

$$$ ✕🏨 **Spetses Hotel.** This self-contained resort has the best of both worlds: privacy and proximity to the delightful town. The rooms are comfortable, with TVs, and some of them have a sea view. Moreover, the hotel has its own beach, and buffet breakfast is included in the price. ⊠ *Spetses beach, 18050,* ☎ *0298/72602 through 0298/72604; 01/821–3126 winter in Athens,* 🖷 *0298/72494; 01/821–0602 winter in Athens. 77 rooms. Restaurant, beach. MC, V. Closed Nov.–Mar.*

$$$ 🏨 **Nissia Traditional Residences.** The impressive entrance of this new,
★ deluxe waterfront hotel is like a movie set, its facade the carefully restored Daskalakis factory. Each suite is named after an island and there are rooms for all tastes—romantic, modern, aristocratic—with direct-dial phone, color satellite-TV, private veranda or balcony, and fully equipped kitchen. Even the smallest accommodations seem roomy, and two-thirds have spacious sitting areas with fireplace. Only the studios don't have a sea view, and overlook the garden instead. The splurge-worthy "presidential" suites are in two towers with exceptionally roomy layouts and top-view verandas. Buffet breakfast is bountiful and included in the rates. ⊠ *1,500 ft from Dapia, Kounoupitsa, 18050,* ☎ *0298/75000 through 00298/75011; 01/346–2879 or 01/342–1279*

Athens, FAX *0298/75012; 01/346–5313 Athens. 14 studios, 15 suites. Restaurant, pool. AE, DC, MC, V.*

$$
★ 🏨 **Hotel Posidonion.** This glorious fin-de-siècle waterfront hotel dating from 1911 has a remarkable vantage stretching from Spetses Harbor to the mainland opposite. The belle epoque public areas, replete with two grand pianos, have the grace of an earlier age and an air of grandeur atypical of Greece. The high-ceiling guest rooms are more modest than the public rooms, although the windows in the front rooms frame the wonderful view and huge bathtubs. Facilities include a bar and breakfast room. ⊠ *Dapia waterfront, 18050,* ☎ *0298/ 72308 or 0298/72006; 01/361–3751 winter in Athens,* FAX *0298/72208; 01/360–7964 winter in Athens. 50 rooms. Restaurant, bar, breakfast room. AE, DC, V. Closed mid-Oct.–Mar.*

Festival

BATTLE REENACTMENT
Spetses puts on an enormous reenactment of a War of Independence naval battle for one week in early September, complete with costumed fighters and burning ships. Book your hotel well in advance if you wish to see this popular event; check with the Spetses tourist police for more information (☞ Visitor Information *in* Excursions from Athens A to Z, *below*).

Nightlife

CLUBS
Surviving many years and with ever bigger dimensions, including a seaside patio, is **Figaro** (⊠ Palio Limani), which plays international rhythms earlier in the evening; late at night, it's packed with writhing bodies, and when the music switches to Greek at midnight, as the Greeks say, *ginete hamos*—chaos reigns. The **Fox** is a newer addition, which features live Greek music and dance lessons, great fun for all who join in. **Socrates** and **Anchor** are two of the most popular bars in the middle of Dapia. To the west of town at Kounoupitsa is **Veranda,** which plays tasteful Greek music for a more sedate crowd. For the newest "in" bars, ask your hotel or just stroll down to the old harbor, which has the highest concentration of clubs.

DELPHI

Arachova, Delphi, Galaxidi

The sublime ruins of Delphi will invigorate visitors who have little knowledge of ancient Greece, as well as those who have long awaited a chance to see where the Pythian priestesses uttered their cryptic prophecies. After the Acropolis of Athens, the site of Delphi is the one that is likely to make the most powerful and lasting impression on the traveler in Greece. Its history reaches back at least as far as the Mycenaean period, and in Homer's *Iliad* it is referred to as Pytho. Nearby is Mt. Parnassus, where the formerly quiet mountain village of Arachova is now a successful confluence of traditional Greek mountain village and Athenian-style cafés, thanks to the proximity of ski lifts. On the coast, picturesque Galaxidi now caters to wealthy Athenians who have restored many of the mansions once owned by shipbuilders.

The preferred route to Delphi follows the National Road to the Thebes turnoff, at 74 km (46 mi). Take the secondary road south past Thebes and continue west through the fertile plain—now planted with cotton, potatoes, and tobacco—to busy Levadia, capital of the province of Boetia. Almost halfway between Levadia and Delphi the traveler passes the famous junction of roads, the Triple Way, where the roads from

Delphi, Daulis, and Levadia meet. It was in Thebes, according to legend, and so described by Sophocles in *Oedipus Rex,* that the infant Oedipus was left by his father, Laios, on a mountainside to die after an oracle predicted he would murder his father and marry his mother. Some shepherds, ignorant of the curse, rescued him, and he was raised by the king of Corinth. The saga unfolded when, as a young man, Oedipus was walking from Delphi and met his father, Laius, King of Thebes, near the Triple Way. The latter, having struck Oedipus with his whip in order to make room for his chariot to pass, was in turn attacked and accidentally killed by the young man, who did not recognize his father, not having seen his parents since his birth. Journeying to Thebes, he solved the riddle of the terrible Sphinx and, as a reward, was offered the throne and the hand of Jocasta (who was, unbeknownst to him, his mother). When they discovered what had happened, Oedipus blinded himself and Jocasta hanged herself—one of the most defining and shattering denouements in all literature.

If you detour in Levadia by following the signs for the *piges,* you will come to the banks of the ancient springs of Lethe and Mnemosyne, or Oblivion and Remembrance (these springs are about a 10-minute walk from the main square); in antiquity the Erkinas (Hercyne) gorge was believed to be the entrance to the underworld. Today, the plane- and maple tree–shaded river is spanned by an old stone arch bridge built in Ottoman times.

Osios Loukas

★ ㉑ *150 km (93 mi) northwest of Athens, 24 km (15 mi) southeast of Arachova.*

The monastic complex Osios Loukas, still inhabited by a few monks, is notable for both its exquisite mosaics and its dramatic setting, looming on a prominent rise with a sweeping view of the Elekonas peaks and the sparsely inhabited but fertile valley. It is especially beautiful in February when the almond branches explode with a profusion of delicate oval pinkish-white blooms.

The katholikon was built in the 11th century over the tomb of Luke the Hermit and was used for pilgrimages. It remains one of the masterpieces of Byzantine architecture and the highlight of the complex, which includes the *theotokos,* a smaller communal church of the Virgin Mary, to the left. On the periphery is the monks' cells and a refectory. The monastery was named after a local hermit called Luke, not the Evangelist Luke who wrote a book of the New Testament. Luke the Hermit was probably born in Delphi after his family fled from Aegina during a raid of Saracen pirates. He was a medieval oracle and founded a church at this site and lived here until his death in 953 AD. This important monastery was founded by the emperor Romanos II in 961, in recognition of the accuracy of Loukas's prophecy that Crete would be liberated by an emperor named Romanos.

The outside of the buildings is typically Byzantine, with rough stonework interspersed with an arched brick pattern. The katholikon follows to perfection the Byzantine cross in a square plan, all under a central dome; it was, in fact, inspired by Ayia Sophia in Constantinople and, in turn, used as a model for both the Daphni monastery and Mystra churches. The katholikon can also be compared to the Church at Daphni in the quality of the mosaics in the narthex and in portions of the domed nave. They are set against a rich gold background and are done in the somber but expressive 11th-century hieratic style by artists from Thessaloniki and Constantinople. In the second niche of the entrance is a mosaic showing Loukas sporting a helmet and beard, with his arms raised. Particularly interesting are the reactions evident on the faces of the apostles, which range from passivity to surprise, as Christ washes their feet in the mosaic of *Niptir,* to the far left of the narthex. The engaging *Nativity, Presentation in the Temple,* and the *Baptism of Christ* mosaics are on the curved arches that support the dome. Two of the most treasured mosaics are facing each other in the little apse; Daniel in the lion's den and Shadrach, Meshach, and Abednego in the flames of the furnace. Unfortunately, the priceless icons from the late 16th century, by Damaskinos, a teacher of El Greco, were stolen a few years back from the white marble iconostasis, and have been replaced with copies. The tomb of Osios Loukas is set in the crypt of the katholikon; his relics, formerly in the Vatican, were moved here in 1987, making the monastery an official shrine. Note that visitors must wear either long pants or a skirt. Bring a small flashlight to help see some of the frescoes. ⊠ *On rise above valley,* ☎ *0267/22797.* ⌨ *800 dr./€2.35.* ☉ *May–mid-Sept., daily 8–2 and 4–7; mid-Sept.–Apr., daily 8–5.*

En Route From Dhistomo, 10 km (6 mi) west of Osios Loukas, an alternative, less-traveled route to Delphi climbs over the plain of Desfina and descends sharply to the sea just east of Itea. This route is slightly longer but more pleasant and lets you stop in Itea for a seaside lunch. (The conventional route ignores Dhistomo and continues west past the Schiste turnoff, climbing ever higher as it nears Mt. Parnassus.)

Arachova

㉒ *24 km (15½ mi) northwest of Osios Loukas, 157 km (97 mi) from Athens.*

Arachova's gray-stone houses with red-tiled roofs cling to the steep slopes. Mt. Parnassus, the highest mountain in Greece after Mt. Olympus, has been undergoing development for skiing since 1980 and is now a popular winter resort. The new energy and money the change has brought into the region have been put to good use: the sophisticated newcomers (mostly Athenians) have preserved and restored many otherwise doomed houses—eschewed by locals as too old to be any good—and several good tavernas and cozy hotels now line the cobbled alleyways.

If you're lucky enough to be in Arachova on **St. George's Day**— April 23, or the Monday after Easter (if April 23 falls during Lent)—you're in for the time of your life. St. George the dragon-slayer is the patron saint of Arachova, and the largest church on the top of the highest hill in town is dedicated to him. So, naturally, the festival here lasts three days and nights, starting with a procession behind the generations-old silver icon from the church, in which the villagers don the local costumes, most of them ornately embroidered silken and brocaded heirlooms that testify to the rich cultural heritage of the town. The festival is kicked off in fine form with the race of the *yeroi,* the old men of the town who are astonishingly agile as they clamber up the stone steps without so much as a gasp for air. The following days are filled with athletic contests, cooking competitions, and, at night, passionate dancing in the tavernas until long after the goats go home.

Dining and Lodging

$$ ✕ **Agnandio.** The Agnandio is set in a well-appointed older house warmed by a couple of fireplaces and graced by impressive views of the mountainous terrain. The kitchen has given a new spin to mountain-style classics. Start with tangy *tirokafteri,* a piquant cheese spread that is a perfect accompaniment to the country stone-ground bread. Try some of the large purplish Amphissa olives, *fava* (mashed yellow split peas, lemon, and raw onions), carrot and cabbage salad perked with pepper and lemon, and potent *skordalia* (potato-garlic spread). It's hard to choose from among the delectable main courses—but don't worry: you can't really lose no matter what you order. Have some of the marvelous potatoes stuffed with bacon, cheese, garlic and fresh cream—not really Greek, but perfect to warm the cockles of your heart on a brisk night. Ouzo, *tsipouro* (grape spirits), and the potent dark red local wine are all available to accompany the fine food. ⊠ *On Delphon St. right next to Town Hall,* ☎ *0267/32114. No credit cards. Closed June–Aug.*

$$ ✗ **Fterolakka.** Cozy up to the fireplace in winter and enjoy the mouth-watering game: local pheasant and quail, wild duck and goose baked in clay pots, *lago stifado* (hare with tiny sweet onions), and wild boar. The restaurant also prepares numerous magirefta, including rooster in wine sauce with fat spaghetti, and lamb or beef kokkinisto. Grilled meats cover everything from a simple souvlaki to the more exotic *kokkoretsi* (lamb innards on a spit, held together by intestines). A local tasty dessert is *strifto,* similar to baklava, with home-made phyllo. ⊠ *Delfon St. at bottom of stairs ascending to Ayios Giorgos church, near Platia Tomarovrissi,* ☎ *0267/32556. AE, MC, V. Closed June–Oct. (open only for tourist groups).*

$ ✗ **Taverna P. Dasargiris (Barba Yiannis).** The son of the late Barba Yiannis (Uncle John) now runs this busy taverna, the first in Arachova. The gargantuan summer and winter throngs can cause occasional surliness among the staff, but the food is worth your patience. In a town that counted its wealth by the size of its flocks, this taverna fittingly serves standard meat dishes and, above all, lamb. Excellent magirefta include the lamb with oregano and the beef in red sauce, both served with the noodles called *hilopites,* for which the area is known. Sample the fried *formaella* (a mild local sheep's milk cheese); the *hortopites* (pastries filled with mountain greens); grilled beef patties stuffed with formaella, gouda, or kefalograviera cheese; or splinandera (a tasty mix of various lamb organs), which Greek customers swear by. At Easter, the cook makes an unforgettable roast lamb and the famous egg-lemon soup called *magiritsa.* Don't forget to try the homemade *brusco* wine (a dark red), which seemingly cuts right through the cholesterol. ⊠ *Arachova–Delfon 56 Rd.,* ☎ *0267/31291. No credit cards. No lunch May–Oct.*

$$ ⊞ **Arachova Inn.** Opened in 1991 and run by friendly staff, about half of this inn's small, efficient, yellow-and-peach-tone guest rooms have a view of the lower town and valley. All have color TV and direct-dial phone. The sitting rooms and dining area have touches of local handicrafts and rustic wood furnishings. In winter the dining room and the lounge are warmed by fireplaces; buffet breakfast is included. ⊠ *Arachova–Delfon Rd., 32004,* ☎ *0267/31353, 0267/31497, or 0267/32195,* ⅏ *0267/31134. 42 rooms. Restaurant. AE, DC, MC, V.*

$$ ⊞ **Hotel Anemolia Best Western.** At this homey hotel on a bluff above
★   the Delphi road at the western edge of Arachova, most of the large guest rooms have a view of the plain of Amphissa from their balconies; on a clear day you may be able to see as far as the Peloponnese. All rooms have TV and some have bathtubs instead of showers; the eight new rooms have fireplaces but no balconies. Enjoy après-ski among the simple furnishings, large lobby fireplace, and country antiques. The only covered swimming pool in Arachova here is usable year-round. Buffet breakfast is included in the price, at the high end of its category. ⊠ *Arachova–Delfon Rd., 32004,* ☎ *0267/31640 through 0267/31643,* ☎ ⅏ *0267/31644. 63 rooms. Restaurant, bar, pool, sauna, exercise room. AE, DC, MC, V.*

$ ⊞ **Hotel Parnassos.** Offering a rock-bottom solution to the housing problem, this little family-run hotel is comfortable for the budget price.

The quiet bedrooms in the old two-story family home are of various sizes, mostly large, with high ceilings and neat, plain furniture. The six rooms in the front have a view of the illuminated clock tower, Mt. Xerovouni, and the valley below. There is a sitting area with fireplace and a loft where guests eat breakfast. ⊠ *Delfon 18, near the traffic bridge, 32004,* ☎ *0267/31307. 9 rooms with shared bath. DC, MC, V.*

Nightlife

On winter weekends Arachova streets are jammed with Athenians who come almost as much for the nightlife as for the skiing. Clubs change frequently; recent popular additions are **Petra,** located on Platia Lekka, with quiet foreign and Greek music, and small rooms with fireplaces and darts; the rowdier **Cinema Snow Me,** a split-level club with young things dancing on the bar and "face control" to keep out the unhip; and lovely **Emboriko** on Delfon Street, for the older crowd, where politicians, journalists, and artists mingle with the anonymous, either in the two quieter sections where you can order a bite or in the action-packed bar. Check with your hotel for the latest in the club scene, which can only get more hectic in the coming years.

Outdoor Activities and Sports

HIKING

The summit of Mt. Parnassus (8,061 ft) is now easily accessible, thanks to roads opened up for the ski areas. The less hardy can drive to within 45 minutes of the summit. You can also drive to the Hellenic Alpine Club's refuge at 6,201 ft to spend the night and then walk to the summit in time to catch the sunrise—the best way to climb Mt. Parnassus!

SKIING

If you hear that the snow is good on Parnassus, go for it. Ski with the muses, just 40 minutes from Arachova, at the **Ski Center Parnassos** (☎ 0234/22689 or 0234/22695). **Kelaria** has more challenging runs, but **Fterolakka** has better restaurants and beginners' slopes. Rental equipment is available at both and in Arachova. Contact the EOT for a brochure on skiing in Greece or the **Hellenic Skiing Federation** (⊠ Karageorgi Servias 7, 8th floor, Syntagma, Athens 10563, ☎ 01/323–0182 or 01/323–4412, FAX 01/323–0142). The **Alpine Club of Athens** (Kapnikareas Sq. 2, Athens 10563, ☎ 01/321–2355 or 01/321–4412, FAX 01/324–4789) organizes mountain-skiing classes for experienced skiers and snowboarding classes for children.

Shopping

Arachova's main street is lined with shops selling rugs and weavings; the town was known even in preski days as a place to shop for handicrafts, honey, and wine.

HANDICRAFTS

The modern mass-produced bedspreads, woolly *flokati* rugs (sometimes dyed vivid colors), and kilim-style carpets sold today in Arachova are reasonably priced. If you poke into dark corners in the stores, you still might turn up something made of local wool, though anything that claims to be antique bears a higher price.

LOCAL SPECIALTIES

Here you'll also find delicious Parnassus honey; formaella (local, rather sweet) cheese; and hilopites, or "thousand pies" (thin homemade noodles cut into thousands of tiny squares, often served with chicken and lamb). Be sure to try the fiery *rakomelo,* a combination of raki and honey, served in most of the bars and cafés.

Delphi

189 km (117½ mi) northwest of Athens, 10 km (6 mi) west of Arachova.

Home to Apollo and to the most famous oracle of antiquity, Delphi enjoys a site of the greatest possible grandeur, whether seen from the ruins of the sanctuary or from one of the town's hotels or terraced village houses. The road from Arachova to Delphi is guarded by great twin cliffs, the **Phaedriades** (the Bright Ones)—at sunset the sides of the cliffs glow red with the reflection of the sun's rays, and the whole ravine of the Pleistos and the steep terraced vineyards in the valley leading to the rocky pass of Arachova are bathed in a warm, deep purple light. These cliffs form the eastern gate, so to speak, of the site, whose ancient ruins lie cradled in a theatrical curve between the Phaedriades and Mt. Profitis Ilias to the west. In the gorge below Delphi, the bed of the Pleistos winds between a narrow strip of olive trees flanked by precipitous cliffs, opening out into the Sacred Plain, where the silvery-green sea of olives, possibly the largest grove in all Greece, ends in the calm aquamarine waters of the Bay of Itea. The modern city of Delphi is traversed by a main street, thick with restaurants and souvenir shops, with the entrance to the sanctuary reached easily from almost any point in the central town, at most a 5- to 10-minute walk.

When first seen from the road, it would appear that there is hardly anything left to attest to the existence of the religious city. Only the treasury of the Athenians and a few other columns are left standing, but once you are within the precincts, the plan becomes clearer and the layout is revealed in such detail that it is not impossible to conjure up a vision of what the scene must have once been when Delphi was the holiest place in all Greece.

At first the settlement probably was sacred to Gaia, the mother goddess; toward the end of the Greek Dark Ages (circa 1100–800 BC), the site incorporated the cult of Apollo. According to Plutarch, who was a priest of Apollo at Delphi, the oracle was discovered by chance, when a shepherd noticed that his flock went into a frenzy when it came near a certain chasm in the rock. When he approached, he also came under a spell and began to utter prophecies, as did his fellow villagers. They chose from among their number young girls to interpret the oracle's pronouncements. When one of the young girls was abducted, an older woman on a three-footed stool was placed over the chasm to interpret the prophecy.

Traditionally, the Pythia was a woman over 50, who, upon her anointment, gave up normal life and lived thereafter in seclusion. On oracle day, the seventh of the month, the Pythia prepared herself by washing in the Castalian Spring and undergoing a purification involving barley smoke and laurel leaves. If the male priests of Apollo determined the day was propitious for prophesying, she entered the Temple of Apollo to sit on the tripod, where she drank the Castalian water, chewed laurel leaves, and presumably sank into a trance. Questions presented to her received strange and garbled answers, which were then translated into verse by the priests. A number of the lead tablets on which questions were inscribed have been uncovered, but the official answers were inscribed only in the memories of questioners and priests. Those that have survived, from various sources, suggest the equivocal nature of these sibylline emanations: perhaps the most famous is the answer given to King Croesus of Lydia, who asked if he should attack the Persians. "Croesus, having crossed the Halys River, will destroy a great realm," said the Pythia. Thus encouraged, he crossed it, only to find his *own* empire destroyed.

Delphi

TO STADIUM

Dionysian Shrine

N

| 0 | 20 yards |
| 0 | 20 meters |

Stoa of Attalos

Altar of Apollo

25

Treasury of Corinth

24

Sacred Way

Sacred Way

23

Syracusan Treasury

Treasury of the Boeotians

Theban Treasury

TO THE MUSEUM

Base of Marathon Monument

ENTRANCE

Spartan Monument

TO SANCTUARY OF ATHENA

During the 8th and 7th centuries BC, the oracle's advice played a significant role in the colonization of southern Italy and Sicily (Magna Graecia) by Greece's Amphictyonic League. By 582 BC the Pythian Games had become a quadrennial festival similar to those held at Olympia. Increasingly an international center, Delphi attracted suppliants from beyond the Greek mainland, including such valued clients as King Midas and King Croesus, both hailing from wealthy kingdoms in Asia Minor. During this period of prosperity many cities built treasure houses at Delphi. The sanctuary was threatened during the Persian War but never attacked, and it continued to prosper, in spite of the fact that Athens and Sparta, two of its most powerful patrons, were locked in war.

Delphi came under the influence first of Macedonia and then of the Aetolian League (290–190 BC) before yielding to the Romans in 189 BC. Although the Roman general Sulla plundered Delphi in 86 BC, there were at least 500 bronze statues left to be collected by Nero in AD 66, and the site was still full of fine works of art when Pausanias visited and described it a century later. The emperor Hadrian restored many sanctuaries in Greece, including Delphi's, but within a century or two the oracle was silent. In AD 385, Theodosius abolished the oracle. Only in the late 19th century did French excavators begin to uncover the site of Apollo.

Start your tour of the site in the same way the ancients did; with a visit to the **Sanctuary of Athena** just below the Arachova road before you reach the Phaedriades. Pilgrims who arrived on the shores of the Bay of Itea had a procession up to the sanctuary, where they paused in order to purify themselves before going on to the upper region of the site. The most notable among the numerous remains on the terrace is the **Tholos,** or Round Building, a graceful 4th-century BC ruin of Pendelic marble, whose purpose and dedication are unknown, although round templelike buildings were almost always dedicated to a goddess. By the second millennium BC, the site was already a place of worship of the earth goddess Gaia and her daughter Themis, one of the Titans. They expressed themselves through the murmuring of water flooding from the fault, from the rustle of leaves and the booming of earth tremors. The Tholos remains one of the purest and most exquisite monuments of antiquity still to be seen at Delphi. Theodoros, its architect, wrote a treatise on his work: an indication in itself of the exceptional architectural quality of the monument. Beneath the Phaedriades, in the cleft between the rocks, a path leads to the **Castalian Fountain,** a spring where visitors bathed to purify themselves before approaching the sanctuary. Access to the fountain is presently restricted because of the danger of falling rocks.

On the main road, beyond the spring, is the modern entrance to the sanctuary. Passing through a **square** surrounded by late-Roman porticoes, the path leads through the main gate onto the **Sacred Way.** On its way up the hill the Sacred Way passes between building foundations and bases for votive dedications, stripped now of ornament and statue, mere scraps of what was one of the richest collections of art and treasures in antiquity. Thanks to the 2nd-century AD writings of Pausanias, archaeologists have identified treasuries built by the Thebans, the Corinthians, the Syracusans, and others—a roster of 6th- and 5th-century BC powers.

㉓ The **Treasury of the Athenians** was built with money from the victory over the Persians at Marathon. Northeast of the treasury are the re-
㉔ mains of the **Stoa of the Athenians,** which housed, among other objects, an immense cable with which the Persian king Xerxes roped together a pontoon bridge for his army to cross the Hellespont from Asia to Europe.

㉕ The **Temple of Apollo** visible today (there were three successive temples built on the site) is from the 4th century BC. Although ancient sources speak of a chasm within, there is no trace of that opening in the earth from which emanated trance-inducing vapors. Above the temple is the
㉖ well-preserved **Theater** (which seated 5,000); it was built in the 4th century BC, restored in about 160 BC, and later was restored again by the Romans. From a sun-warmed seat on the last tier, the visitor may obtain a panoramic bird's-eye view of the sanctuary and the convulsed landscape that encloses it. Also worth the climb is the view from the **Stadium**, still farther up the mountain, at the highest point of the ancient town. Built and restored in various periods and cut partially from the living rock, the stadium underwent a final transformation under Herodes Atticus, the Athenian benefactor of the 2nd century AD. It lies cradled in a grove of pine trees, a quiet refuge removed from the sanctuary below and backed by the sheer, majestic rise of the mountain. Markers for the starting line inspire many visitors to race the length of the stadium. ⊠ *Delphi site, immediately east of Delphi modern town along road to Arachova,* ☎ *0265/82312.* ⌘ *1,200 dr./€3.53.* ◎ *Weekdays 7:30–7:30 (9:30–3:30 in winter), weekends 8:30–3.*

Housed in an older building with a new facade, the **Delphi Museum** contains a wonderful collection of art and architectural sculpture, principally from the Sanctuaries of Apollo and Athena Pronoia. Here is one of the greatest ancient statues of all, the bronze *Charioteer,* a sculpture whose delicate size (said to be scaled to life) is surprising if you are seeing it in person for the first time. Created in about 470 BC to commemorate the victory of a Syracusan prince in the Pythian chariot races, the statue is believed to have stood on a terrace wall above the Temple of Apollo, near which it was found in 1896. It was part of a larger piece, which included a four-horse chariot. It is not established who executed the work, although Pythagoras of Samos is sometimes mentioned as a possibility. The donor is supposed to have been a well-known patron of chariot racing, Polyzalos, the Tyrant of Gela in Sicily. Historians now believe that a sculpted likeness of Polyzalos was originally standing next to the charioteer figure. The statue commemorates a victory in the Pythian Games at the beginning of the 5th century BC. Most striking is the severe classical simplicity of the execution, which does not detract from the intensely natural and lifelike aspect of the beautiful young man holding the reins. Note the eyes, inlaid with a white substance resembling enamel, the pupils consisting of two concentric onyx rings of different colors. The sculpture of the feet and of the hair clinging to the nape of the neck is perfect in detail. This is one of the few ancient bronzes to survive pillage and war, and its strength and quality remind us of what we have lost.

Other masterpieces on view are two Ionian chryselephantine (ivory heads with gold headdresses) heads from the archaic period, probably from statues of Apollo and his sister Artemis, who has a sly smirk on her face; sculpted scenes from the Siphnian Treasury, showing an assembly of the gods sitting and watching part of the Trojan War and also the Olympic gods in battle with the Giants; a lovely Imperial Age (2nd century BC) marble statue of Antinoos, Emperor Hadrian's favorite; and the twin statues of Kleobis and Biton, stylized representations of young brothers who were given the gift of eternal sleep by Hera, after collapsing after yoking themselves to a chariot to carry their mother a little more than 5 mi to Hera's temple, and of whom it was said, "those whom the gods love die young." Dating to the first half of the 6th century BC, these statues are related to the series of *kouroi* (stylized statues of young men) in the National Archaeological Museum in Athens.

There are also fragments of a silver-plated bull of the 6th century BC, the largest example surviving from antiquity of a statue in precious metal.

The imposing winged Sphinx of Naxos was crouched upon a tall Ionic column (560 BC). One of the most enigmatic and joyful pieces, which illustrates the change from the severe archaic form of sculpture to the flowing lines of the classical, is the column of the "dancing girls," three korai carved from Pendelic marble on an acanthus column, which was probably the base of a tripod from the 4th century BC. Finally, in Room 11, note the family monument of nine statues, which reproduces in marble a group originally sculpted in bronze, at least partially by Lysippos, one of the best artists of the 4th century BC. ⊠ *Immediately east of Delphi modern town along road to Arachova,* ☎ *0265/82312.* 🖾 *1,200 dr./€3.53, 2,000 dr./€5.89 for both the site and museum.* ☉ *Weekdays 6:45 AM–7:30 PM (9:30–3:30 in winter), weekends 8:30–3.*

As for modern-day Delphi, although it doesn't have many of the charming village-style houses of Arachova or any of the stone mansions of Galaxidi, the hospitable people of Delphi take great pride in their town. They keep up a tradition of maintaining comfortable, small hotels which are reasonable and clean. This combined with Delphi's outstanding position, nestled in the mountain cliffs and perched dramatically on the edge of the "mystical grove" which leads to the sea, can mean that a stay here will prove most memorable—especially if you come at *pasxa* (Easter).

Easter is the most important holiday in Greece, and Delphians celebrate it with true passion. The solemn Good Friday service in Ayios Nikolaos church and the candlelight procession following it, accompanied by the singing of haunting hymns, is one of the most moving rituals in all of Greece. By Saturday evening, the mood is one of eager anticipation, as the townspeople are decked out in their nicest finery and the earnest children are carrying *lambades,* beautifully decorated white Easter candles. At midnight, the lights of the cathedral are extinguished, and the priest rushes into the sanctuary shouting "Christos Anesti!" (Christ is arisen.) He lights one of the parishioner's candles with his own and the flame is passed on, one to the other, until the entire church is illuminated with candlelight which is reflected in the radiant faces of the congregation. Firecrackers are set off by the village schoolboys outside to punctuate the exuberance of the moment. After the liturgy is finished, each person tries to get her or his candle home while still lighted, a sign of good luck for the following year, whereupon the sign of the cross is burnt over the door. Then the Easter fast is broken, usually with magiritsa and brilliantly red hard boiled eggs. On Easter Sunday, the entire village works together to roast dozens of whole lambs on the spit. It is a joyous day, devoted to feasting with family and friends, but visitors are welcome; they will often be offered slices of the delicious roast lamb and glasses of the potent dark red local wine. In the early evening, a folk dance performance is held in front of the town hall square, followed by communal dancing and free food and drink.

Dining and Lodging

$$ ✕ **Iniochos.** This excellent restaurant serving local specialties offers some of Delphi's best eating, with an emphasis on appetizers: zucchini croquettes, roast feta, bekri mezze. In winter, warm yourself at the fireplace in the dining room; in summer eat on the enormous veranda overlooking the valley of Delphi. Try the hortopites, quail filled with cheese, pork with celery, or *kokkora krasato* (wine-stewed rooster), a regional favorite. Many residents stop by late at night for a nightcap and a snack, such as fried formaella cheese, *sfongato* (country vegetable omelet), or a sweet such as baklava, in order to sing along to pianist

Yiannis's amazing repertoire of old Greek songs; foreigners will rarely come up with a tune he doesn't know as well. ⊠ *Vas. Pavlou and Friderikis 19,* ☎ *0265/82710, 0265/82151, 0265/82316, or 0265/82480. Reservations essential. AE, DC, MC, V.*

$ ✕ **Gargantouas.** Although just down from the main road, this simple taverna gives you the impression that you are sitting in a small countryside inn far from the madding crowds. Seating is outside on a veranda; get a table with a bird's-eye view of the nearly mystical valley that leads to the Sea of Olives and the Bay of Itea. Start with a refreshing horiatiki, distinguished by creamy feta and sweet red tomatoes. Try charcoal-grilled chicken, lamb chops, spaghetti marinara (tomato and meat sauce), or pork souvlaki. Portions are generous and prices most reasonable. ⊠ *Terminus of Vas. Pavlou and Friderikis, near the bus stop,* ☎ *No phone. No credit cards.*

$ ✕ **Lekaria.** Peaceful Lekaria is a family-run operation on a side lane, perched high above the main street (which can be noisy during the busy season). It serves typical Greek taverna food in a covered courtyard with lots of plants. Try the *loukaniko* (spicy Greek sausage) served in a pan that is doused with brandy and flambéd at your table or the *soutzoukakia* (spicy meatballs Smyrna style). *Briam*—a casserole made with eggplant, carrots, and potatoes—and juicy grilled chicken fillet are two house specialties. For dessert you can follow the Greeks' lead and have sliced apples and oranges simply topped with cinnamon—or live it up with a real banana split. ⊠ *Apollonos 33,* ☎ *0265/82864. MC, V.*

$ ✕ **Taverna Vakchos.** A local favorite, Vakchos is an established taverna with a spacious inner dining room and a large flower-bedecked veranda, covered with a canopy when it is cool, but always offering a stunning view. Taverna favorites include moussaka, boiled wild greens, spinach and cheese pies, and tomatoes stuffed with rice and roast chicken. In winter, you can get game, such as hare and roast suckling pig. ⊠ *Apollonos 31,* ☎ *0265/83186. No credit cards.*

$$$ 🏨 **Hotel Vouzas.** The hotel crests the edge of a gorge and has won-
★ derful views from every room and an intimate living room with a fireplace. It is also the closest (about 1,600 ft) to the archaeological site. A fantastic new veranda, where breakfast is served half the year, overlooks the gorge, olive groves, and the Pleistos river. Rooms have TVs, minibars, and hair dryers. The hotel fills up on winter weekends with Athenians who come to challenge Mt. Parnassus, fortified by the buffet breakfast. Half-board is available. ⊠ *Vas. Pavlou and Friderikis 1, 33054,* ☎ *0265/82232 through 0265/82234,* FAX *0265/82033. 58 rooms, 1 suite. Restaurant, bar. MC, V.*

$$ 🏨 **Apollo.** Owned and operated by a husband-and-wife team ("She's
★ the decorator, I do the public relations," says he), this hotel is lovely. The *saloni* (living room) here has traditional wall hangings and old prints among its carefully selected furnishings. The cheerful rooms have lightwood furniture set off by blue quilts and striped curtains, with pretty bathroom tiles, hair dryers, TVs, and minibars. Many have wood balconies with black-iron railings, and a full breakfast is included. ⊠ *Vas. Pavlou and Friderikis 59B, 33054,* ☎ *0265/82580 or 0265/82244,* FAX *0265/82455. 21 rooms. Air-conditioning, minibars. MC, V. Closed weekdays Jan.–mid-Mar.*

$$ 🏨 **Villa Filoxenia-Apollo.** Rustic, charming, and tastefully decorated by the same people who own the Apollo hotel (☞ *above*), one of Delphi's newest additions has amenities such as electronic keys and air-conditioning, a game area, and a lounge with fireplace, despite its price at the low end of its category. Rooms include TV, minibar, and hair dryer; most have balconies and a view. Full breakfast is included. ⊠ *Vas. Pavlou and Friderikis 15, 33054,* ☎ *0265/83114,* FAX *0265/82455. 14 rooms. Air-conditioning. MC, V. Closed weekdays Jan.–mid-Mar.*

$ ⊞ **Acropole.** This friendly, family-run hotel has a garden and a spec-
★   tacular view—bare mountainside and a sea of olive groves—so that
guests feel as though they're completely secluded. The rooms are
freshly furnished with carved Skyrian furniture, traditional linens, and
paintings, strangely enough, of the islands. Ten rooms have air-conditioning; all have satellite TV, direct-dial phones, and hair dryers. ⊠
Filellinon 13, 33054, ☎ *0265/82675,* FAX *0265/83171. 42 rooms. Air-
conditioning (some). AE, DC, MC, V.*

$ ⊞ **Kastri.** Epitomizing the friendly family-style hotels of the region, the
Kastri has been run by the Avgeris family for 32 years. Just recently,
they did a complete renovation and welcomed their two daughters—
proficient in English and other foreign languages—to the staff. The entire family is gracious and helpful, takes great pride in Delphi, and runs
a tight ship: the small, simply furnished rooms are all spic and span
with public areas cheerfully decorated with folk crafts and flowers. A
bountiful breakfast with a boiled egg, bread, juice, and homemade marmalade is included in the price. If you are here for the Easter celebration, the Kastri is conveniently located right down the road from the
large cathedral, which has the main liturgies. All rooms now have air-
conditioning, TVs, radio, and balconies; those facing the sea have a
fantastic panoramic view. The location is a couple of streets above the
main drag, so it is very quiet at night. ⊠ *Sigrou 23, 33054,* ☎ *0265/
82322 or 0265/82238; 01/962–3816 or 01/962–4317 in Athens,* FAX
0265/82322. 24 rooms. Air-conditioning. No credit cards.

$ ⊞ **Pan.** This small hotel, at the quiet end of the main drag, is a delight.
Rooms are small and simply decorated, with pine beds and earth-tone
blankets as spreads—but it has amenities not usually found at such a
reasonable price: all rooms have been newly refurbished, with TVs, air-
conditioning, bathtubs, and large balconies, most of which come with
a superb view of the rose-tiled rooftops of Delphi and its huge olive grove,
the largest in Greece (which leads down to the Bay of Itea). Brothers
Yiannis, Andreas, and Kostas Lefas (who doubles as the mayor of Delphi) know English and, over the last two decades, have developed a solid
clientele which returns year after year. The cheerful breakfast room (breakfast is included in the room rate), on the lower level, is filled with
blooming geraniums and has a panoramic view of the valley. ⊠ *Vas.
Pavlou and Fredirikis 53, 33054,* ☎ *0265/82294,* FAX *0265/82320. 20
rooms. Breakfast room, air-conditioning. AE, DC, MC, V.*

Festival

Sit in the ancient stadium of Delphi under the stars and watch everything from the National Beijing Opera Theater doing *Bacchae* to *Pour
Antigone* danced by the Centre Choréographique National du Mont-
pellier Languedoc-Roussillion at the **summer arts festival,** organized
by the European Cultural Centre of Delphi in July. The festival is in
conjunction with an annual symposium. All performances, which
begin around 8:30 PM, are open to the public and require a token fee.
For program information, call the center in Athens (☎ 01/331–2781
through 01/331–2785), or the ancient stadium (☎ 0265/82731).

En Route   The road west from Delphi winds down into the Sacred Plain, passing the modern village of Chryssa and leading through olive groves to
the seaside port of Itea, which takes its name from the *ites* (willows)
that used to stretch down to the sea.

Galaxidi

㉗   *17½ km (11 mi) southwest of Itea.*

The harbor town of Galaxidi still has preserved traces of classical masonry but enjoyed its heyday in the 19th century, thanks to shipbuild-

ing and a thriving mercantile economy. After the invention of steamships, the town faded until its recent discovery by outsiders, who appreciated the sea captains' fine houses and the idyllic atmosphere, reminiscent of an island. Now classed as an historical monument, the old town of Galaxidi is undergoing renovation and restoration. If you are a shore person rather than a mountain person, Galaxidi is a good alternative to Delphi as a base. After a late-afternoon swim in one of the pebbly coves around the headland to the north, dine along the waterfront.

NEED A
BREAK?

For a frappé, cocktail or snack, head for the **Omilos** (✉ Old Yacht Club, ☎ 0265/42111), at the entrance to the main harbor, open from early morning until late at night. The chairs and tables set out on the little beach make a tranquil setting, and the excellent cook, Stamatis Banas, also doubles as an expert bartender. The view is unforgettable, especially at sunset: the Gulf of Itea stretches before you, and the peaks of Parnassus tower in the background, with the little gray stone houses of Delphi, accented by faded rose slate roofs, clustered on its slopes. If you want really fresh fish and have time to relax, watch as one of the staff casts a line offshore and hauls in a *sargos* or *tsipoura* (bream or panfish) just for you. Then have it grilled to a golden brown and lightly embellished with oil, lemon, and oregano. Or try the *midhia Massalias* (Marseille mussels), a delicious thick soup laden with plump mussels and redolent with garlic and lemon, a creation that exuberant Dimitris Marmarelis, Omilos's owner, claims is only made here. You can swim off the pebble beach (and midnight dips are encouraged).

Stroll Galaxidi's narrow streets with their elegant stone seafarers' mansions and squares with geraniums and palm trees, taking a peek into **Ayios Nikolaos**—the cathedral is named after the patron saint of sailors and possesses a beautiful carved 19th-century altar screen. The little **Nautical Museum** at Mousiou Street 4 has a collection of local artifacts from ships and the old ships captains' houses. If you walk to the far side of the sheltered harbor, Galaxidi will appear reflected in the still waters. ✉ *Mousiou St. 4.* ☞ *Free.* ☉ *9:30–1:30 weekdays; 9:30–2 weekends.*

Dining and Lodging

$-$$ ✗ **Porto.** This popular restaurant is one of many near the harbor that, unsurprisingly, specialize in fish: porgy, common bream, sea bass, dentex (when in season), and, of course, mussels, served several ways. You could buck the trend and order the equally good meat dishes such as *kotopoulo krasato* (chicken stewed in wine); oven-baked lamb; beef yiouvetsi, made with rice-shape noodles; or succulent lamb ribs. ✉ *Akti Ianthis 53, near start of harbor,* ☎ *0265/41182. No credit cards.*

$-$$ ✗ **Varko tis Maritsas.** This charming restaurant, located in a former captains' *kafenion* (coffeehouse) (1850) and decorated with a nautical theme, serves traditional Greek cuisine, including some local specialties. Interesting are the pies—zucchini pie with dill, and spinach pie—as well as the eggplant dip enhanced by grated walnut. There is a large selection of fresh fish and seafood appetizers, but mussels are what Galaxidi is known for—here they're served in a saganaki (fried in a small pan with cheese, tomato, and peppers), steamed, and in a pilaf. Another local dish is *kemelia*, minced meat and rice wrapped in onion. Homemade sweets include the regional *amigdalopasta,* made with almonds and topped with *kaimaki* (rich clotted cream) ice cream. On Clean Monday during Carnival, the restaurant hosts a rambunctious *glendi* (celebration), with live music, dancing, and an enthusiastic rendering of a unique Galaxidi custom of having a select group spray bystanders with water and then throw flour on them. It's great fun, but come only if you're prepared (and dressed) to be among the "victims"; anybody, even foreigners, are fair game. ✉ *Akti Ianthis 34, on the waterfront,* ☎ *0265/41059. Reservations essential. No credit cards.*

$ ✕ **O Dervenis.** Galaxidi's tiny main port is lined with restaurants, bars, and cafés, but some of the best food in town can be found a few blocks inland, at O Dervenis. The restaurant has a covered garden for outdoor dining and serves excellent taverna fare. It will be tough choosing an appetizer from the homemade tzatziki, the spinach pie made with feta and kefalograviera; marinated octopus or *gavros* (resembles a large anchovy); minced meat wrapped in fresh vine leaves (that are only tender enough to use for the first few weeks of the summer); and a local specialty, *avgopita* (egg pie). ✉ *N. Gourgouri St. next to old girls' school,* ☎ *0265/41177. No credit cards.*

$ ✕ **O Tassos.** Tassos, the first taverna you see on the waterfront road as you approach the harbor, is a favorite of townspeople and frequent visitors. It has a large terrace facing the waterfront, and in the summer and on weekends year-round, it is packed with happy hedonists who relish its fresh seafood, fish, and taverna specialties and pleasant view. Fresh seafood is the big draw, but Tassos also offers appetizers and vegetable and meat dishes. The *karavidhes* (crayfish), raised in nearby beds, are simply boiled and sprinkled with lemon—a true delicacy. Mussels are also farm-raised and served in a variety of ways, including delicious *axnisto,* in a broth with hot peppers and cheese. Crispy fried calamari and whole fish, such as charcoal-grilled snapper are fresh as can be. You can complete this feast with boiled greens and garlic-potato sauce, a large village salad, and a carafe of local wine. ✉ *Akti Ianthis 69, at far end of harbor as you approach waterfront,* ☎ *0265/41291. V.*

$$ ▥ **Galaxa Hotel.** Opened in 1988 in a 180-year-old blue-and-white captain's house by the nice, professional Emanuel Papilaris, the Galaxa has simple rooms decorated with reproductions of antique ship photos. All have color TV, phone, and air-conditioning; six have a coveted sea view, but if yours doesn't, you have an excuse to sidle up to the terrace garden, which also serves as a bar and breakfast area. A full breakfast is included in the price: juice, eggs, homemade marmalades, and local honey. The owner's wife, Maria, will cook for guests on request: *pites* (savory pies) with homemade phyllo, baked gavros, mussels, and other shellfish. Guests may also rent a boat that holds over 15 people with a licensed captain for excursions at reasonable prices. ✉ *Eleftherias 8, near John Kennedy Rd., 33052,* ☎ *0265/41620 or 0265/41625,* ☎ *0265/42053. 10 rooms. Bar, air-conditioning. AE, DC, MC, V.*

$ ▥ **Ganimede.** Owner Brunello Perocco has taken full advantage of the
★ elegant spaces provided by a typical 19th-century Galaxidi captain's house (1881). He combines Italian finesse with Roumeliot sensibility. Here and there stand furnishings from the former residents—a secretariat with white marble, trunks, old closets, and grand mirrors—interspersed with modern artifacts such as Arachova weavings and small sculptures and paintings. Each room is decorated differently; all have independent heating and air-conditioning. In winter the sitting room with a blazing fire beckons for breakfast, a space where the owner sometimes hosts art exhibits when the weather warms. In summer, breakfast moves to the lush courtyard and is a legendary feast: bread, cake, cheese scones, Bruno's concoctions such as olive cream and garbanzo bean pâté, and his famous marmalades—apricot chutney, plum-fig jam, tangerine with whiskey— all accompanied by the owner's gentle multilingual humor. Book ahead in high season; the few rooms go fast. ✉ *N. Gourgouris 20, 33052,* ☎ *0265/41328; 094/834354 (mobile phone),* ☎ *0265/42160. 8 rooms. Air-conditioning. No credit cards. Closed Nov.–Dec. 20.*

EXCURSIONS FROM ATHENS A TO Z

Arriving and Departing

See Athens A to Z in Chapter 1.

Getting Around

By Bus

Places close to Athens can be reached with the blue city bus lines (100 dr./€.29): Bus A16 from Platia Eleftherias for **Dafni** and **Elefsina**; Bus 224 from Akadimias station coupled with a 25-minute walk for **Kaisariani**; the A3 from Syntagma Square for **Glyfada, Vouliagmeni,** and **Varkiza**; Bus A2 from Syntagma for **Voula.** For the rest of the destinations, if you can't rent a car, the next most efficient mode of travel is the regional KTEL bus system in combination with taxis. The extensive network serves all points in **Attica** from Athens, and local buses connect the smaller towns and villages at least daily. The orange **KTEL** buses leave hourly from their main station in downtown Athens (⌂ Platia Aigyptou at the corner of Mavromateon and Leoforos Alexandras) for Sounion (☎ 01/821–0872 for departure times); fare is 1,250 dr./€3.68 inland route through Mesogeion, and 1,300 dr./€3.83 for coastal road. One can also catch this bus from Klathmonos Square or Fillelinon Street. They also leave regularly for Marathon (☎ 01/821–0872), with fare of 800 dr./€2.35, and every half hour to Lavrio (☎ 01/821–3203), with fare of 1,050 dr./€3 For more distant locales, see the individual site listings; the EOT distributes a list of bus schedules. For Delphi, there are six departures daily from Terminal B at Liossion 260 in Athens (☎ 01/831–7096), beginning at 7:30 AM. The journey takes about three hours and costs 3,150 dr./€9.29. From the same station, there are four buses daily making the four-hour trip to Galaxidi (☎ 01/831–7096), starting at 7:30 AM; the fare is 3,750 dr./€11.06. Buses depart hourly from 5:50 AM to 8:30 PM for Levadia near Osios Loukas (☎ 01/831–7173). The journey takes two hours and costs 2,500 dr/€7.37. To get to Terminal B from downtown Athens, catch Bus 024 on Amalias Street in front of the National Gardens. Tickets for these buses are sold only at this terminal, so you should call to book seats well in advance during high season or holidays.

By Car

Points in Attica can be reached from the main Thessaloniki–Athens and Athens–Patras highways, with the National Road (Ethniki Odos) the most popular route. From the Peloponnese, you can drive east via Corinth to Athens, or from Patras, take the Rion–Antirion ferry or the Egio–Ayios Nicholaos ferry (less crowded, especially in summer) across the Bay of Corinth and the coast road, visiting Delphi first. Most of the roads when you get off the highway are two-lane secondary arteries; a few of them (notably from Athens to Delphi and Itea and to Sounion) have been recently upgraded, are very good, and are often spectacularly scenic. Expect heavy traffic to Delphi in summer and ski season, and to and from Athens on weekends. Cars are not allowed on Hydra and Spetses.

The **Automobile Touring Club of Greece** (ELPA, ⌂ Athens Tower, Messoghion 2–4, 11525, ☎ 01/778–6642; 104 in an emergency, FAX 01/748–8800) can help with tourist information for drivers (☎ 174), and it assists tourists with breakdowns free of charge if they belong to AAA or to ELPA; otherwise, there is a charge.

By Ferry

The islands of Poros and Spetses are so close to the Peloponnese mainland that you can drive there, park, and ferry across the channel in any of a number of caïques (price negotiable), but to get to them from Athens or to visit the other Saronic Gulf islands, you must take to the sea in a ship.

The **Argosaronikos Lines** (☎ 01/412–6181 or 01/417–6792; or call Piraeus port authority, ☎ 01/422–6000 or 01/451–1311) will take you and your car from the main port in Piraeus to Aegina (1½ hours) and Poros (3 hours, 40 minutes), or you alone to Hydra (4 hours, 10 minutes) and Spetses (5 hours, 25 minutes). The **Consortium Poseidon** also travels to Aegina and Poros (☎ 01/417–5382 or 01/417–1395). You can get a weekly boat schedule from the EOT. There are approximately a half dozen departures per day, and fares range from about 1,800 dr./€5.30 per person for Aegina to about 3,600 dr./€10.61 for Spetses. Car rates are usually four times the passenger rate. These ferries are the leisurely—meaning *very* slow—and cheap way to travel. From downtown Athens take the metro station to the port, a trip of about 25 minutes (150 dr./€.44).

Most people now prefer the speedier **MInoan Flying Dolphins** (☎ 01/ 419–9000), hydrofoils (no cars carried) that depart from the Zea Marina, also in Piraeus. There are about a half dozen departures daily, and you should make reservations ahead of time—they fill quickly. The cost ranges from 2,000 dr./€5.89 for Aegina to 6,100 dr./€17.99 for Spetses. You can also reserve through a travel agent. From downtown Athens take the metro to the port, then Trolley 20 to Zea Marina. Or you can take a taxi, about 2,500 dr./€7.37.

Contacts and Resources

Car Rentals
Most international agencies have offices in Athens and desks at the airport.

Avis (⊠ Amalias 46–48, ☎ 01/322–4951 through 01/322–4957, FAX 01/322–0216; ⊠ West Terminal, ☎ 01/981–4404; ⊠ East Terminal, ☎ 01/995–3440; ⊠ Athens Hilton, ☎ 01/725–0200; ⊠ Akti Miaouli 7 [Piraeus], ☎ 01/428–0218). **Budget** (⊠ Syngrou 8, ☎ 01/921–4771 through 01/921–4773, FAX 01/924–1603; central reservations center ☎ 01/922–6666 or 01/342–8536; ⊠ West Terminal, ☎ 01/988–3792; ⊠ East Terminal, ☎ 01/961–3634). **Europcar** (⊠ Syngrou 4, ☎ 01/958– 8990 for reservations, FAX 01/959–5382 for reservations; ⊠ West Terminal, ☎ 01/982–9565; ⊠ East Terminal, ☎ 01/961–3424). **Hertz** (⊠ Syngrou 12, ☎ 01/922–0102 through 01/922–0104, FAX 01/922–7921; ⊠ Vas. Sofias 71, ☎ 01/724–7071, ☎ FAX 01/722–7391; ⊠ West Terminal, ☎ 01/981–3701; ⊠ East Terminal, ☎ 01/961–3625). A good local agency to call is **Swift Car Rental** (⊠ Nikis 21, near Syntagma Sq., ☎ 01/324–7875 or 01/324–7855, FAX 01/325–0671), where the manager, Elias Manoua, will take good care of you; he'll even arrange to drive clients awed by Athens traffic to the edge of the city.

Emergencies
Tourist Police: Aegina (☎ 0297/27777); Attica (☎ 171); Delphi (☎ 0265/ 82222); Hydra (☎ 0298/52205); Poros (☎ 0298/22462); Spetses (☎ 0298/73100).

Police (☎ 100). **Fire** (☎ 199). **Ambulance** (☎ 166, but hailing a cab may be faster). **Forest Service (fires)** (☎ 191). **Road Assistance** (☎ 104).

Guided Tours
Most agencies offer excursions at about the same prices, but **CHAT** (⊠ Stadiou 4, Syntagma, Athens 10564, ☎ 01/322–2886, FAX 01/323–5270) is reputed to have the best service and guides, plus comfortable ac-

commodations in the nicely appointed Amalia Hotels. Taking a half-day trip to the breathtaking Temple of Poseidon at Sounion avoids the hassle of dealing with the crowded public buses or paying a great deal more for a taxi. The 8,000 dr./€23.59 cost is well spent. A one-day tour to Delphi with lunch costs 21,500 dr./€61.94 (19,000 dr./€56 without lunch), but the two-day tour (34,000 dr./€100) is far preferable. A full-day cruise from Piraeus, visiting three nearby islands—Aegina, Poros, and Hydra—costs around 20,500 dr./€60.47 (including buffet lunch on the ship).

Moped Rentals

On the islands of Aegina and Spetses, many people rent scooters, mopeds, and bicycles from shops along the harbor, but extreme caution is advised: the equipment may not be in good condition, roads can be narrow and treacherous, and many drivers scorn your safety. Wear a helmet, and drive defensively.

Outdoor Activities and Sports

HIKING

Some Attica hiking groups include the **Alpine Club of Aharnon** (✉ Filadelfias 126, Aharnes, 13671, ☎ 01/246–1528 or 01/246–6666, ℻ 01/246–9777), which runs the **Flambouri** refuge on Parnitha (☎ 01/246–4666), and the **Alpine Club of Athens** (✉ Kapnikareas Sq. 2, top floor, Monastiraki, 10563, ☎ 01/321–2355 or 01/321–2429, ℻ 01/324–4789), which operates the **Bafi** refuge on Parnitha (☎ 01/246–9050). For a booklet on Greece's refuges and information on hiking paths, including the E4 and E6 trails, and local hiking groups, contact the **Greek Federation of Mountaineering Associations** in Athens (✉ Milioni 5, Kolonaki, 10673, ☎ 01/364–5904, ℻ 01/364–4687). Hiking trips are offered regularly by specialist travel agencies. Try **Trekking Hellas** (✉ Fillelinon 7, 3rd floor, Syntagma, Athens 10577, ☎ 01/331–0323 through 01/331–0326, ℻ 01/323–4548) or **F-Zein** (✉ Syngrou 132, 5th floor, Athens 17561, ☎ 01/921–6285, ℻ 01/922–9995), which, besides hiking expeditions, arranges all kinds of adventure travel, including rafting, mountain climbing and biking, and canyoning.

RUNNING

Athens Open International Peace Marathon (✉ SEGAS, Race Organizers, Syngrou 137, Athens 17121, ☎ 01/932–0636, ℻ 01/934–2980).

SCUBA DIVING

Aegean Diving Center (✉ Pandoras 42 and Zamanou 53, Glyfada, ☎ 01/894–5409, ℻ 01/898–1120✆). **Scuba Diving Club of Vouliagmeni** (✉ Leoforos Poseidonas at Vouliagmeni Bay, ☎ 01/896–4609).

TENNIS

Hellenic Tennis Federation (✉ Ymittou 267, Pangrati, Athens 11631, ☎ 01/726–3170, ℻ 01/726–3173).

WINDSURFING

Hellenic Windsurfing Association (✉ Fillelinon 7, 1st floor, Syntagma, Athens 10557, ☎ 01/323–3696 or 01/323–0068, ℻ 01/322–3251).

Visitor Information

Tourist office: Municipal tourist office **Aegina** (✉ Town Hall, ☎ 0297/22220); **Arachova** (winter only; ✉ Arachova–Delfon Rd., ☎ 0267/31692); **Delphi** (✉ Vas. Pavlou and Friderikis 12, ☎ 0265/82900).

Tourist Police: Aegina (✉ Leonardou Lada 11, ☎ 0297/22777); **Attica** headquarters (✉ Dimitrakopoulou 77, Koukaki, Athens, ☎ 171); **Delphi** (✉ Angelos Sikelianou 3, ☎ 0265/82220); **Hydra** (✉ Port,

0298/52205); **Poros** (✉ Dimosthenous St. off Platia Iroon, ☎ 0298/
22462); **Spetses** (✉ Near museum on Hatziyianni-Mexi St., ☎ 0298/
73744).

Greek National Tourist Organization (GNTO or EOT) Athens (✉ Amerikis
2, near Syntagma, ☎ 01/331–0561 through 01/331–0562; ✉ East Terminal of Ellinikon Airport, ☎ 01/961–2722 or 01/969–4500; ✉ Zea
Marina near the hydrofoils, EOT Building, 1st floor, Zea Marina, ☎
01/452–2591).

3 THE NORTHERN SPORADES

SKIATHOS, SKOPELOS, ALONNISOS, SKYROS, AND EVIA

Island-hopping the Northern Sporades, strung from Mt. Pelion to the center of the Aegean, delivers quintessential Greek-island pleasures: boat journeys, pretty harbors, villages spilling down hillsides like giant sugar cubes, Byzantine monasteries, screaming nightlife. Weekenders don't make it far beyond Skiathos, but the special charm of the Sporades is found on the quieter islands, where the tinkle of goat bells may be the only sound for miles and springtime brings scarlet poppies which line silent paths cobbled in the last millennium.

By Lea Lane

Updated by
Melia Tatakis

L IKE EMERALD BEADS SCATTERED ON SAPPHIRE velvet, the verdant Northern Sporades islands of Skiathos, Skopelos, and Alonnisos, and a nearby host of tiny, uninhabited islets—resplendent with pines, fruit trees, and olives and marked with sloping, slate roofs and wooden balconies—strongly resemble the Pelion peninsula to which they were once attached. Only on Skyros, farther out in the Aegean, will you see a windswept, treeless landscape, or the cubistlike architecture of the Cyclades. Sitting by itself east of Evia, Skyros is neither geographically nor historically related to the other Sporades, though in recent years air shuttles from Athens and hydrofoils skimming between the islands and Evia, and the mainland, have brought these aptly named Sporades ("scattered ones") closer together. Evia itself—Greece's second-largest island (after Crete)—presents a curious mix of mainland and island culture. A kind of Long Island or Cape Cod escape for harried Athenians, it remains a favorite for sun seekers of all nationalities.

The Sporades have changed hands constantly throughout history, and wars, plunder, and earthquakes have eliminated all but the strongest ancient walls. A few castles and monasteries remain, but these islands are now geared more for fun than for sightseeing. Skiathos, closest to the mainland and the first to be discovered, is the most touristy—to the point of overkill—with a diverse social scene, international restaurants, English pubs, and luxury hotels. Less-developed Skopelos has several lovely villages to explore by day—its main town is said to be the most beautiful of the Sporades—though far fewer beaches and much less nightlife.

Owing to natural disasters, the second half of the 20th century has been hard on Alonnisos, once called Evoinos (Goodwine). In 1950 its grapevines suffered a plague of phylloxera that destroyed most of them virtually overnight, and 15 years later, an earthquake ruined the lovely acropolis. Still, its scenery is so stunning that nature-lovers flock there in increasing numbers and visitors are reclaiming and reinventing the hilltop town. Skyros, late to attract tourists, is the least traveled of the Sporades. Yet those who discover its well-preserved traditions, its arcane rabbit warren of a town, and its expansive beaches are drawn to return year after year.

The once undiscovered Northern Sporades are no longer so—after all, they are so easily reached from Athens, Thessaloniki, and Volos. They may be close to each other yet they remain so different in nature they offer the visitor a widely diverse spectrum of Greek life—even so, some parts of all remain idyllic. Quintessential Greek-island delights beckon: sun, seabathing, and surf, with memorable dining under the stars. Almost all restaurants have outside seating, often under leafy trees, where you can watch the passing Greek dramas of daily life: dark-haired lovers arm-in-arm, stealing a kiss; animated conversations between shopkeeper and patron that may last for the entire meal; fishermen cleaning their bright yellow nets and debating and laughing as they work. All in all, the Northern Sporades offer wondrous places to relax and immerse yourself in the blue and green watercolor of it all.

Pleasures and Pastimes

Beaches

The Sporades boast a huge number of beaches, both pebbly and sandy, and with a bit of research and adventuresome spirit you will find one you like—from those crowded with people, water sports, and music to secluded coves accessible only by boat; and of course, nude beaches can be found on each island. Of all the islands, Skiathos is perhaps best for major beaches—the star location remains Koukounaries, whose golden sands are famous throughout Greece.

Dining

By the water or in the heart of a rural village, in a simple taverna or a fancier restaurant, dining in Evia and the Sporades is as much to savor the day as to consume the fresh island food. Greeks here, as on the mainland, love to eat and drink, share and talk. To facilitate these pleasures, tavernas are tucked throughout the islands, and pastry shops offer afternoon respite with refreshing frappés, tall glasses of cold, sweetened coffee and milk. If in doubt, eat where the locals do; few tourist hangouts are as good, and prices decrease the farther you get from views or water. Although you may not have many great meals in the Sporades, you'll have a hard time finding a bad one, and the service inevitably will be friendly and caring.

Ask your waiter for suggestions about local specialties–you won't go wrong with the catch of the day on any of the islands. Octopus and juicy prawns, grilled with oil and lemon or baked with cheese and fresh tomatoes, are traditional dishes. Alonnisos and Skyros especially are noted for spiny lobster, which is almost as sweet as the North Atlantic variety. Of course, ordering several *mezedes* (starters) rather than a first and second course is a tasty and popular option. Sadly, only on Skyros will you find barrel wine; the small amount produced elsewhere is savored at home. As in all of Greece, portions are large, and desserts simple—puddings, spoon sweets (such as preserved figs or cherries), and pastries.

CATEGORY	COST (ALL ISLANDS)*
$$$$	over 10,000 dr. (€29.49)
$$$	7,000 dr.–10,000 dr. (€20.64–€29.49)
$$	4,000 dr.–7,000 dr. (€11.79–€20.64)
$	under 4,000 dr. (€11.79)

per person for two appetizers, salad, and main course, including service and tax but excluding drinks

Festivals

The **Apokries, pre-Lenten Carnival** revelry, on Skyros relates to pre-Christian fertility rites and is famous throughout Greece. Young men dressed as old men, maidens, or "Europeans" roam the streets teasing and tormenting onlookers with ribald songs and clanging bells. The "old men" wear elaborate shepherd's outfits, with masks made of baby goat hides and belts dangling with as many as 40 sheep bells. Their costumes and antics are simply extraordinary.

Also on Skyros the August 15 **Panayia** (Festival of the Virgin) is celebrated on the beach at Magazia, where children race on the island's domesticated small ponies, similar to Shetland ponies. The Skopelos Municipality sponsors a Panayia on August 15 and a series of cultural events in late August, with the last day a celebration of the plum harvest (☞ Visitor Information *in* The Northern Sporades A to Z, *below*). The pre-Lenten Carnival traditions of Skopelos, although not as exotic as those of Skyros, parody the expulsion of the once-terrifying Barbary pirates. Skiathos hosts a series of cultural events in the summer, including a dance festival in July. Evia holds a Drama Festival all summer long, in Halkidha. Finally, the islands celebrate **feast days** in honor of their patron saints, with special banquets, carnivals, processions from the church, costumes, folk dancing, fireworks. and revelry late into the night. Skiathos's feast day is July 26, in honor of St. Paraskevi; on Skopelos it is February 25, in honor of St. Riginosi. And if you are lucky enough to happen by a wedding party on any of the islands, you may be invited to join in the fun—eating, dancing, and feeling part of the family in no time.

Hiking

All the islands are wonderful for walking, especially in spring, when Greece's wildflowers are unsurpassed. For those who like isolated beauty and smaller scale, Skyros and Alonnisos are special, with their acropoli and rural vistas, and once out of the main town you are in isolated environs. Alonnisos has made quite a name for itself among Greek hikers, with 17 clearly marked trails (and guided walks sponsored by Icos Tours several times a week which usually combine walking, swimming, and a picnic). Some of the islands' monasteries and more remote refuges are only accessible on foot and often are linked together by marked trails. Skopelos has old stone farmhouses set in plum orchards. Evia offers an exhilarating mountain climb up Mt. Ochi. You can buy walkers' maps in souvenir shops and tourist offices in the main towns.

Lodging

Accommodations reflect the pace of tourism and vary greatly in level and number from town to town and island to island. Skopelos has a fair number of hotels, Skiathos and Evia a huge number; there are not many hotels on Alonnisos, and Skyros has even fewer. Most hotels close for winter, as noted in their individual listings; reservations are a good idea, unless you are looking for a private room. The best bet, especially for those on a budget, is to rent a converted room in a private house— look for the Greek National Tourist Organization (GNTO or EOT) license displayed in windows. Owners meet incoming boats to offer rooms; negotiate over the price and ask about the island location. At the height of summer, island-hopping without reservations might be risky, especially on Evia, which fills with weekenders driving across the bridge from the Athens area.

In Skyros most people rent rooms in town or along the beach at Magazia and Molos. Accommodations are basic, and television sets are not standard. You must choose between being near the sea or the town's bars and eateries. The average room cost in August is about 10,000 dr./€29.49–12,000 dr./€35.39. In Skiathos, tourists are increasingly renting private apartments, villas, and minivillas with kitchen facilities. Contact the local island travel agents to discuss the range of possibilities.

The hotels recommended here vary from simple, clean, family-run pensions to large, impersonal, self-contained resorts. You can expect air-conditioning in $$$ and $$$$ hotels (we only mention air-conditioning in our reviews when it makes a rare appearance in the $ and $$ categories), and buffet breakfast is usually included in the rate everywhere. Rates fluctuate considerably from season to season; the August prices listed in the lodging chart below may drop by more than half between October and May. You should always negotiate off-season.

CATEGORY	COST (ALL ISLANDS)*
$$$$	over 35,000 dr. (€103.24)
$$$	25,000 dr.–35,000 dr. (€73.74–€100.29)
$$	15,000 dr.–25,000 dr. (€44.24–€73.74)
$	under 15,000 dr. (€44.24)

for a standard double room for two, including breakfast, service, and tax

✒ *following the text of a review is your signal that the property has a Web site, where you will find details and, usually, images; for a link, visit www.fodors.com/urls*

Nature Cruises

Alonnisos is the gateway to the National Marine Park, which comprises all the islands in the vicinity, some of which are off-limits to all visitors. Found here is one of the last preserves of the endangered monk seal, **Piperi Island.** Nature-lovers can enjoy excursions such as the caïque cruise on the *Oceanis* (run by **Madro travel**), from Skopelos to Psathoura and Kyra Panayia in the National Marine Park. On the other islands, you can hire a caïque and explore the natural beauty of the coastline and islets.

Sailing

With some of the clearest waters in the Aegean and hundreds of protected coves, the Northern Sporades (excluding Skyros) are ideal for yachting, especially the uninhabited islands. Mooring can be arranged at the ports at each island.

Shopping

Evia caters to short-term tourists, with lots of forgettable trinkets, but all the Sporades have some charming local handicrafts and also sell goods from other islands and the mainland, including attractive pottery, kilims, antiques, jewelry, and embroideries. Skopelos has galleries selling paintings and photographs; on Skiathos, boutiques display an array of modern jewelry and stylish items. Save money for shopping on Skyros. This isolated island's traditional handcrafted ceramics, carpentry work, rugs, and detailed embroidery are among the finest in Greece.

Exploring the Northern Sporades

Each of the Northern Sporades has a distinct character. Touristed, sophisticated Skiathos is closest to the mainland; it has the liveliest nightlife and a pretty harbor area. Due east is Skopelos, covered with dense, fragrant pines, where you can enjoy scenic villages, hundreds of churches, and lovely beaches. Farther east in the Aegean, and close by, is rugged and rural Alonnisos, the least progressive of the islands, but the most naturally beautiful, with an exceptional old hill town.

Mythic Skyros, southeast of the other islands, has quiet fishing villages and a stunning cubist town that seems to spill down a hill. It is the most remote and quirky of the Sporades, but as a current citadel of Greek defense it also has the bonus of an airport; it is often difficult to get to Skyros from the other Sporades without a mainland stop, but from Athens by air it is a quick daily connection.

Evia—not really part of the Sporades but so near them it seems to be—is even closer to the mainland; you could drive back and forth, as it is connected by a bridge. The island is a vast, elongated strip of coast with plenty of beaches, fishing villages, and touristy towns. Each of these islands is connected by ferry and/or hydrofoil, although some are infrequently scheduled, especially in the off-season. A number of uninhabited islands in the Sporades archipelago can also be visited by boat.

Numbers in the text correspond to numbers in the margin and on the Northern Sporades map.

Great Itineraries

If you are taking it easy, you can generally just jump on a caïque and island-hop as you choose. If time is limited and you want to do something in particular, it is best to plan your schedule in advance. Flying Dolphin hydrofoils and Olympic Airways timetables are available from travel agents; for regular boats, consult the EOT in Athens (☞ Visitor Information *in* The Northern Sporades A to Z, *below*).

You could get around Skiathos, Skopelos, and Alonnisos in three days, but to enjoy the relaxed nature of the islands, stay on one, and take a day trip or two to the others. The trip between these three and Skyros requires advance planning and more time; except for the summer, ferries and Flying Dolphin hydrofoils may run sporadically and can cause havoc with your schedule. Also, make sure that you are arriving and leaving from the correct harbor; some islands, such as Evia and Skopelos, have more than one area from which to leave. Five days can be just enough for touching each island in the summer; off-season you will need more days to adjust for the ferry schedule. Eight days would be more than enough to see all the islands and still enjoy a delightfully relaxed sojourn.

IF YOU HAVE 3 DAYS

Inveterate island-hoppers might spend one night on each of three islands. Otherwise, choose one and stay there, with day trips to a nearby island or two if you wish. On ⛴ **Skiathos** ①–⑩, by day take in the beautiful but crowded beaches and a museum or perhaps **Evangelistria monastery** ⑩, and at night join the night owls at a taverna or restaurant, and then a bustling nightclub. Day people should stay on ⛴ **Skopelos** ⑪–㉓ to explore the numerous monasteries and churches. If you want to escape civilization as much as possible, head for ⛴ **Alonnisos** ㉔–㉗. Or you could drive to Evia, spend some time there, and then take a ferry from its harbor at Kimi to ⛴ **Skyros** ㉙–㉞ with its slower pace and shopping opportunities. Or leave the car in Evia, ferry over to Skyros, and fly back to Athens from there.

IF YOU HAVE 5 DAYS

Pick and choose. You can rush through every island with a well-thought-out schedule, or be selective and come away with the essence of a few of these distinctive islands. Fly to ⛴ **Skyros** ㉙–㉞ from Athens. Spend a couple of relaxing days and take a day or so to explore Evia. Alternatively, base yourself in the main group of Skiathos, Skopelos, and Alonnisos. If you like it lively, spend a day and a couple of nights on **Skiathos** ①–⑩; then head for ⛴ **Skopelos** ⑪–㉓ and stay there for three nights. You can take a day cruise from Skopelos to see **Alonnisos** ㉔–㉘ and some of the uninhabited islands, with deserted beaches, ancient monasteries, and wildlife reserves. If natural beauty and peaceful surroundings are your thing, split the nights between the latter two islands.

IF YOU HAVE 8 DAYS

This is long enough for a truly relaxed exploration of the Sporades, and you can divide the time depending on your interests and scheduling. Start in Evia and visit **Halkidha** and **Eretria** before heading to **Kimi** for the boat to ⛴ **Skyros** ㉙–㉞. Alternatively, you can fly from Athens direct to Skyros, which, although it is undeveloped and small, has a military airport. Enjoy the handicrafts and dramatically set Skyros town, and plan ahead so that you can catch the sporadic Flying Dolphin to ⛴ **Alonnisos** ㉔–㉘. Spend a night or more there or at least visit it as part of a cruise from **Skopelos** ⑪–㉓. Its natural, unspoiled beauty captivates nature-lovers, and its part-destroyed hilltop village is haunting. Stay awhile on **Skopelos** and perhaps rent a car to explore the inland forests and out-of-the-way churches. If you seek a lively club and social scene, spend your last couple of nights on ⛴ **Skiathos** ①–⑩; from here you might leave time to go on to **Volos** and **Pelion** on the mainland.

When to Tour

Winter is least desirable, as the weather is iffy; most hotels, rooms, and restaurants are closed, and ferry service is minimal. If you do go from November through March, book everything in advance and leave

The Northern Sporades

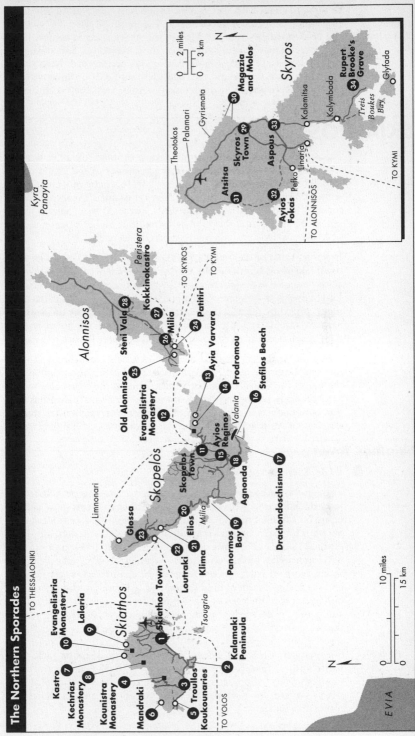

Skyros

2 miles / 3 km

Rupert Brooke's Grave 34

Glyfada

Magazia and Molos 30

Gyrismata

Palamari

Theotokos

Kalamitsa

Kolymbada

Treis Boukes Bay

Skyros Town 29

Aspous 33

Atsitsa 31

Ayios Fokas 32

Pefko

Linaria

TO KYMI

TO ALONNISOS

Kyra Panayia

Peristera

Alonnisos

Kokkinokastro

Steni Vala 28

27

Milia 26

24 Patitiri

Ayia Varvara

TO SKYROS

TO KYMI

Old Alonnisos 25

Evangelistria Monastery

12

13

14 Ayia Varvara Prodromou

16 Stafilos Beach

Valania

Ayios Reginas

11

15

18

17 Drachondoschisma

Agnonda

Skopelos Town

Skopelos

Limnonari

Glossa

23

Elios 20

Milia

Panormos Bay 19

22 21

Loutraki Klima

TO THESSALONIKI

Skiathos

Evangelistria Monastery

Lalaria

9

10

Kastro

Kechrias Monastery 7

Kounistra Monastery 8

Mandraki 4

Skiathos Town 1

Tsougria

Kalamaki Peninsula 2

TO VOLOS

Troullos 3

6

5 Koukounaries

EVIA

10 miles / 15 km

N

nothing to chance. The same advice applies to July and August, when everything is open but overcrowded, except on Skyros. The *meltemi,* the brisk northerly summer wind of the Aegean, keeps things clearer and cooler than the mainland even on the hottest days. Late spring and early summer are ideal, as most hotels are open, crowds have not arrived, the air is warm, and the roadsides and fields of flowers are incredible; September is also lusciously sensual, and the beach crowds have returned to work.

SKIATHOS

Part sacred, with scores of churches, part profane, the hilly, wooded island of Skiathos is the closest of the Sporades to the Pelion peninsula. It covers an area of only 42 square km (16 square mi), but it boasts some 70 beaches and sandy coves. A jet-set island 25 years ago, today it teems with tourists on package deals, attracted by promises of sun, sea, and parties—and these are delivered. But higher prices and a bit of Mykonos-style attitude can be delivered as well.

In winter most of the island's 5,000 or so inhabitants live in its main town, Skiathos, built after the War of Independence on the site of the colony founded in the 8th century BC by the Euboean city-state of Chalkis. Like Skopelos and Alonnisos, Skiathos was on good terms with the Athenians, prized by the Macedonians, and treated gently by the Romans. Saracen and Slav raids left it virtually deserted during the early Middle Ages, but it started to prosper during the later Byzantine years.

When the Crusaders deposed their fellow Christians from the throne of Constantinople in 1204, Skiathos and the other Sporades became the fief of the Ghisi, knights of Venice. One of their first acts was to fortify the hills behind the islet separating the two bays of Skiathos Harbor. Now connected to the shore, this former islet, the Bourtzi, still has a few stout walls and buttresses shaded by some graceful pine trees.

Skiathos Town

❶ *8 km (5 mi) east of Troullos.*

Though the harbor is picturesque from a distance—especially from a ferry docking at sunset when a purple light casts a soft glow and the lights on the hills behind the quay start twinkling like faint stars— Skiathos town close up has few buildings of any distinction. Many traditional houses were burned by the Germans in 1944, and postwar development has pushed up cement apartments between the pleasantly squat, red-roof older houses. Magenta bougainvillea, sweet jasmine, and the casual charm of brightly painted balconies and shutters camouflage most of the eyesores as you wander through the narrow lanes and climb up the steep steps that serve as streets. Activity centers on the waterfront or on Papadiamantis Street, the main drag: banks, travel agents, telephones, post office, and police and tourist police stations, plus myriad cafés, fast-food joints, postcard stands, tacky souvenir shops, tasteful jewelry stores, and rent-a-car and bike establishments. Shops, bars, and restaurants line the cobbled side streets, where you will also spot the occasional modest hotel and rooms-to-rent signs.

A **museum** devoted to Alexandros Papadiamantis (1851–1911), one of Greece's finest writers who wrote about Skiathos in his short stories, stands near the entrance to the street named after him. Three humble rooms with his bed, the low, narrow divan where he died, some photos, and a few personal belongings are all that is exhibited, but the case with his

Close-Up

AND THE PRETTIEST PLACE IN GREECE IS . . .

IF YOU WANT TO TAKE a quick survey of the leading contenders in Greece's geographical beauty contest, we suggest you read The Most Beautiful Villages in Greece (Thames & Hudson, 1998), a spectacular art book written by Mark Ottaway and with photography by Hugh Palmer. Here, in 224 sumptuous pages, are collected the most visually luscious destinations in Greece, from the Maniot towns of the Peloponnese to the flat-roofed white villages of the Cyclades. But to some travelers, one area will always stand out as the Platonic ideal of Greek country style—the Pelion peninsula, across the water from Skiathos town, on the mainland about 320 km (200 mi) northeast of Athens. Here, an incredibly charming landscape of stone churches, elegant houses adorned with rose arbors, and storybook town squares lies to seduce all.

While a realm small in size, Pelion looms large in myth and legend. Jason and the Argonauts are said to have embarked from the port of ancient Iolkos, once set opposite modern Volos, located on the northwestern tip of the peninsula, to make good a vague claim to the Golden Fleece. Mt. Pelion, still thickly wooded with pine, cypress, and fruit trees, was the home of the legendary Centaurs, those half-man-half-horse beings notorious for lasciviousness and drunkenness. Here, too, on a cypress-clad hill overlooking Volos, was the site of the wedding banquet of Peleus and Thetis, where the uninvited goddess of discord, Eris, flung a golden apple between Athena and Aphrodite, asking Prince Paris of Troy to decide who was the fairest (and thereby giving Homer one heck of a plot).

Today, the Pelion country is much more serenely peaceful, dotted with no fewer than 24 lovely villages. As you leave Volos (having explored its waterfront esplanade and splendid archaeological museum), you ascend along serpentine roads into the cooler mountains, enjoying great views over Volos Bay. Some roads wind down to beautiful white-sand or round-stone beaches, such as Horefto and Milopotamos. Nestled among the forests are delightful villages, such as Tsangarades, Milies (with the beautifully frescoed Ag Taxiarchis church), and Vyzitsa, while high above Volos is exquisite Portaria, whose *kokkineli* red wine has to be consumed on the spot, as it does not stand up well to transport. Neither visitors nor locals complain of this. Separated by a deep ravine is Makrynitsa, incredibly rich in *couleur locale*. Here, the village square would not be amiss in fairyland: a large, paved terrace, overhanging the town and gulf below, and keeping its intimacy by a backdrop of huge plane trees that shade a small Byzantine church and a lulling fountain.

On the numerous feast days in the Pelion, there is dancing till late at night, and in their natural surroundings, the national dances have none of the stiff artificiality they assume in town. Local custom prescribes that every *zembeikiko* dancer should perform for his friend, squatting at the edge of the dance floor and keeping time by clapping his hands. Each dancer rewards the partner with an occasional high kick over the head.

Most of the Pelion villages have archetypal Greek houses whose elegance, replete with bay windows, stained glass, and fine ornamentation, cannot be bettered. To get to Pelion from Skiathos by car, take the three-hour ferry down to Volos; you can also board the hydrofoil and rent a car in Pelion. There is daily train service to Volos from Athens's Stathmos Larissa station (this ride takes six hours). For information on the Pelion region and accommodations in the lovely government-renovated village inns, contact the **EOT** in Volos (✉ Riga Fereous Sq., ☎ 0421/23500), open weekdays, 7–2:30.

pen, inkwell, and pot of sand for blotting recall times past. For further understanding, try to find a translation of his most famous novel, *The Murderess*. ⊠ *In small platia to right of Papadiamantis at fork in road,* ☎ *0427/23843.* 🖼 *250 dr./€.73* ⊙ *Tues.–Sun. 9:30–1 and 5–8.*

The **Bourtzi** is a piney islet that was once a fortress. It divides the harbor and now is a cultural center with numerous activities in the summer. West of the waterfront is the fishing port and the dock where caïques depart for round-the-island trips and the beaches. The sidewalk is filled with cafés and *ouzeris* (casual bars) catering more to people-watchers than gourmets. At the far end of the port, beginning at the square around the 1846 church of Trion Hierarchon, fancier restaurants spread out under awnings, overlooking the sea. A few good restaurants are hidden on backstreets in this neighborhood, many of them serving foreign foods. The east side of the port, past the Bourtzi, where the larger boats and Flying Dolphins dock, is not as interesting. The little church and clock tower of Ayios Nikolaos watch over it from a hill reached by steps so steep they're almost perpendicular to the earth.

Beaches
Skiathos is known for its beaches, but as has happened so many times before, popularity has a way of spoiling special places. Since the arrival of English expatriates in the early 1960s, the beautiful, piney 14-km (9-mi) stretch of coast running south of town to famed, gold-sand Koukounaries has become almost one continuous ribbon of villas, hotels, and tavernas. This development is a real blight on the landscape. One beach succeeds another, and in summer the asphalted coast road carries a continual stream of cars, buses, motorbikes, and pedestrians buzzing beach to beach, like frenzied bees sampling pollen-laden flowers. To access most beaches, you must take a little, usually unpaved, lane down to the sea. Along this coast, the beaches, **Megali Ammos, Vassilias, Achladia, Tzaneria, Vromolimnos,** and **Platania,** all offer water sports, umbrellas, lounge chairs, and plenty of company.

Dining and Lodging
$$$$ ✕ **The Windmill.** Views from the outdoor platform of this old mill turned elegant restaurant are spectacular, but be prepared to climb up to— and descend from—the top of the hill above Ayios Nikolaos. Here a Scottish couple has created an eclectic, emphatically French menu, with traditional meat-with-sauce dishes, as well as offerings for vegetarians. Diners giddily dip fruit and sweets into the chocolate Cointreau fondue. Follow signs near the clock tower; the restaurant is at the top of the short but steep staircase. ⊠ *Skiathos town,* ☎ *0427/24550, 0427/ 21223, or 0427/21224. V. Closed mid-Oct.–mid-May. No lunch.*

$$$ ✕ **Asprolithos.** Despite the backstreet location, this fine taverna with
★   a stone fireplace is not a paper-tablecloth, set-your-own-cutlery establishment. The kitchen is surprisingly ambitious and it's easier to list what's *not* on the menu. Interesting dishes include artichokes and prawns with cheese and snapper with wild greens. The wine selection is also extensive. ⊠ *Skiathos town,* ☎ *0427/23110 or 0427/21016. AE, D, MC, V. No lunch.*

$$–$$$ ✕ **Family.** Not much is homey here, except for the owner's mother's baklava. The tables, on three levels under capacious white awnings, have a superb view of the harbor. Miniature cheese pie and cabbage roll appetizers, among others, are delightful, and the wine list is extensive. It's halfway up the steps to the Ayios Nikolaos clock tower, hidden in the back alleys. ⊠ *Ouranitsa St., Skiathos town,* ☎ *0427/21439. AE, MC, V. Closed Oct.–May. No lunch, but will usually serve on request anyway.*

$$–$$$ ✕ **Kastro.** This sweetly informal ouzeri-restaurant is a pleasant spot to enjoy an evening meal. The menu is substantially varied, and if you're

not in the mood for the full Greek fare try the French-flavored mussels with mustard sauce or one of the pasta dishes. If in season, order *kritama* (a succulent plant which grows on the rocks at the sea's edge) for a delicious and strange change of pace. The fresh octopus—hanging to dry on the railings of the awning—is, when grilled, delicious though chewy. ⊠ *Waterfront, Skiathos town,* ☎ *0427/23580. No credit cards.*

$$ ✕ **Ta Psarädika.** You can't get any closer to the fish market than this next-door neighbor taverna, and the fresh seafood dishes served in summer prove it. Locals love the tripe soup in winter, but you might want to sit at an outside table, sip the local wine, and stay with the mezedes and finny creatures. ⊠ *Skiathos town,* ☎ *0427/23412. AE, MC, V.*

$$$$ ⌷ **Skiathos Princess.** Covering virtually the whole of Platania Bay below Ayia Paraskevi, this luxury-class hotel has all the expected amenities, but not much in the way of charm. Air-conditioned rooms with patios or balconies are comfortable and private, built in three tiers around a lawn. The carpeted pink rooms have luxurious marble bathrooms. There's also a money-exchange service, a *kafenion* (traditional Greek coffeehouse), and a poolside bar. ⊠ *Ayia Paraskevi 37002 (Amalias 42, Athina 10558),* ☎ *0427/49226 or 0427/49369; 01/324–2152, 01/324–2153, or 01/324–5963 in Athens,* FAX *0427/49666; 01/323–3667 in Athens. 132 rooms, 27 suites. Restaurant, 2 bars, in-room safes, refrigerators, 2 pools, beauty salon, hot tub, sauna, waterskiing, shop, playground, laundry service, meeting rooms. AE, DC, V. Closed Nov.–Apr.*

$$$ ⌷ **Alkyon.** Don't be disappointed by the boxy exterior and the lack of architectural embellishments—this is a discreet, pleasant hotel which offers charming views of the old harbor and is ideally situated just off the motion and commotion of Skiathos's main artery, affording some tranquility for those who wish to unwind. The rooms are comfortable and sunny (all come with private terraces), and the lounge areas are spacious, flooded by sunlight, and inviting. ⊠ *Old harbor, Skiathos town 37002,* ☎ *0427/22981 through 0427/22985,* FAX *0427/21643. 90 rooms. Bar, minibars, pool, shop. AE, MC, V.*

$$ ⌷ **Bourtzi and Pothos.** To be near the action and have some peace and ★ quiet, too, choose either of these hotels (run by the same management, Kosta and Mary Agiotis). Both are no-frills and spotlessly clean, with rooms that look onto a pleasant green garden and courtyard untouched by the bustle on nearby Papadiamantis. The furniture is simple but functional; the staff, warm and conscientious. Bourtzi is two or three streets farther from the waterfront than Pothos. Both cater to groups but you should be able to find a room with advance booking. ⊠ *Skiathos town 37002,* ☎ *0427/22694 or 0427/21304,* FAX *0427/23243. Pothos: 22 rooms; Bourtzi: 23 rooms. Refrigerators. AE, DC, MC, V. Closed Nov.–Apr.*

$ ⌷ **Pension Danaos.** A first choice for budget travelers, this basic hotel is centrally located, and there is even a roof garden. Despite the meager facilities, these clean, airy rooms, most with small balconies, are among the cheapest in Skiathos (except during August). The owner often waits at the pier to find guests. ⊠ *Skiathos town 37002 (just off Odhos Papadhiandi, 2 blocks inland from the post office),* ☎ *0427/22834. 16 rooms. Refrigerators. No credit cards.*

Nightlife

Skiathos is filled with night owls, and for good reason. Bars for all tastes are on main and side streets, from pubs with draft beer run by Brits to quintessential Greek bouzouki joints in beach tavernas. You can sometimes spot a celeb making the summer scene—such as Jack Nicholson—among the throngs of tanned, hard-drinking northern Europeans on package tours.

MUSIC AND NIGHTCLUBS

For oldies-but-goodies, try the **Kentavros,** a small music bar. For mainstream dance music (after midnight, it usually turns into Greek), **Blue Chips** is the place. **Borzoi,** the oldest club in Skiathos, is decorated like a folk art museum and has a tiny dance floor, too. Popular **Remezzo** (⊠ Near the old shipyards) airs a blend of old and new music at the water's edge. And that's just scratching the surface.

Outdoor Activities and Sports

FISHING

The Aegean is a haven for fresh seafood, but overfishing and such scurrilous practices as dynamiting and bottom trawling have greatly diminished the once abundant resources of the Northern Sporades. It is now illegal to fish with scuba equipment. You can hire fishing boats to seek what remains, and what remains tastes wonderful; look for signs on the boats at the ports.

HIKING

Other islands in the Sporades have more expanses of unspoiled walking terrain. In Skiathos, a Dutch couple takes people on nature walks; check with **Mare Nostrum Travel.** In Alonnisos there are about five guided hikes a week (in English) along some of the 17 trails which have been carefully designed to lead you through forests, past monasteries, and onto secluded beaches. All the information you'll need is available at **Ikos Travel** (☞ Contacts and Resources *in* The Northern Sporades A to Z, *below*).

SAILING

Nine idyllic islets lush with pines and olive groves surround Skiathos, and two lie across the main harbor, with safe anchorage and a small marina. You can sail over, or hire a caïque, to swim and sun on the isolated beaches. The **Yachting Club** (⊠ Skiathos town, ☎ 094/505426) organizes daily and moonlight cruises, two-day trips to Planitis, and special charters.

SCUBA DIVING

Skiathos is the only island with a scuba diving school, the **Dolphin Diving Center** (⊠ Porto Nostos Beach, ☎ 0427/21599, FAX 0427/22525). Popular beaches often have diving equipment and instructors on hand.

Shopping

ANTIQUES AND CRAFTS

The **Archipelago** (⊠ Near Papadiamantis museum, ☎ 0427/22163) is the most stunning shop on the island. Browse here among the antiques, pottery, jewelry made from fossils, and embroideries. Opening May 2000, **Loupos and his Dolphins** (⊠ Adjacent to Papadiamantis museum, ☎ 0427/23777) is the first arrival of the millennium. The jewelry, in both gold and silver, is unique—hand-crafted pieces are sophisticated and eye-catching, while the selection of hand-painted ceramics is also gorgeous. **Galerie Varsakis** (⊠ Trion Hierarchon Sq., ☎ 0427/22255), another fabulous antiques store, has kilims, embroideries, jewelry, and hundreds of other objects, set off by the proprietor's unusual surrealistic paintings. The Blue House, or **To Galazio Spiti** (⊠ Waterfront near the fish markets, ☎ 0427/21681 or 0427/24466), is another interesting place to browse and hunt for the perfect present or souvenir.

JEWELRY

Seraïna (⊠ Near Papadiamantis museum, ☎ 0427/22039) has jewelry and unusually eclectic tourist junk. **Simos** (⊠ Waterfront, opposite the excursion caïques, ☎ 0427/22916) has unique silver and gold designs. **G&P Papapanagiotakis** (⊠ Waterfront, opposite the excursion caïques, ☎ 0427/21056) also has fine gold and silver.

Kalamaki Peninsula

2 *6 km (4 mi) south of Skiathos town.*

The less-developed area on the south coast is the Kalamaki peninsula, where the British built their first villas. Some are available for rent in summer, many above tiny, unfrequented coves. Access here is by boat only, and you can usually find your own private beach to get away from the crowds. Motor launches run at regular intervals to the most popular beaches, and you can always hire a boat at the harbor for a private journey.

Lodging

$$$–$$$$ ⊡ **Atrium.** Stone and ocher walls, terra-cotta tiles, and sloping roofs fulfill its claim to resemble "a Mt. Athos monastery." There's nothing monastic, however, about its squashy white leather sofas, mellow antiques, cozy nooks for conversation, TV room, backgammon, top-floor pool, and bar. Quiet, air-conditioned rooms with balconies have in-your-face green wood furniture and apricot fabrics. Ask for a room with a sea view, and prepare for the climb up from the beach at Ayia Paraskevi. ⊠ *7 km (4½ mi) west of Platanias town, 37002, ☎ 0427/49345 or 0427/49376, FAX 0427/49444. 75 rooms, 6 suites. Restaurant, bar, pool, exercise room, Ping-Pong, shop, billiards. AE, DC, MC, V. Closed mid-Oct.–Apr.* ✍

Troullos

3 *8 km (5 mi) west of Skiathos town, 4 km (2½ mi) west of Kalamaki peninsula.*

On the coast road west of Kalamaki peninsula are Troullos and Troullos Bay, a resort for visitors to Koukounaries seeking a relatively isolated beach. The curve of the sand and the islets beyond are appealing.

4 The dirt road north of Troullos leads to beaches and also branches off to the small and now deserted **Kounistra Monastery,** 4 km (2½ mi) north of Troullos. It was built in the late 17th century on the spot where an icon of the Virgin miraculously appeared, swinging from a pine tree. The icon spends most of the year in the church of Trion Hierarchon, in town, but on November 20 the townspeople parade it to its former home for the celebration of the Presentation of the Virgin the following day. The interior of the monastery church has been blackened by fire, and its 18th-century frescoes are hard to see.

Beaches

5 Though **Koukounaries** (⊠ 12 km [8 mi] west of Skiathos town and 4 km [2½ mi] northwest of Troullos) has been much touted as Greece's best beach, photos displaying it must either have been taken a long time ago or on a brilliant winter's day. All summer it is so packed with umbrellas, beach chairs, and blistering tourists that you can hardly see the sand. The beach can only be reached from its ends, as a lagoon separates it from the hinterland.

Around the island's western tip are more **beaches facing Pelion** (⊠ 13 km [8 mi] west of Skiathos town and 1 km [½ mi] west of Koukounaries beach), which looms close by. These are Ayia Eleni and **Krassas,** also known as Big and Little Banana, perhaps because sun worshipers—mainly gay guys on Little—peel their clothes off on these beaches. Toplessness is in vogue just about everywhere, but around here, rocky coves provide some privacy.

6 You'll find better privacy but less organization at some of the more remote beaches. **Mandraki** (⊠ 5 km [3 mi] west of Troullos Bay and 12 km [8 mi] west of Skiathos town), for example, is a 25-minute walk.

Sometimes called Xerxes' Harbor, this is where the Persian king stopped on his way to ultimate defeat at the battles of Artemisium and Salamis. The reefs opposite are the site of a monument he supposedly erected as a warning to ships, the first such marker known in history.

Megalos Aselinos and Mikros Aselinos beaches (⊠ about 8 km [5 mi] west of Skiathos town and 7 km [4½ mi] north of Troullos), north of Mandraki beach, can be reached by car or bike. Except for a ramshackle taverna, there is nothing here but broad sands and, at times, local women donning hair rollers.

Dining and Lodging

$$ ✕ **Trouillos.** Swordfish souvlaki is delicious, typical of the simple variety of fish dishes at this friendly taverna, with tables practically up to the water's edge. ⊠ *On the beach, Trouillos,* ☎ *0427/49255. MC, V. Closed Apr.–Oct.*

$$$$ 🏨 **Skiathos Palace.** On the famed beach at Koukounaries, this deluxe resort hotel set amid the pines offers views of, and easy access to, the action. The beautiful beach and all the available water sports (and then some) will lure you out of the modern, air-conditioned rooms, which have balconies. ⊠ *Koukounaries 37002,* ☎ *0427/22261,* 𝖥𝖠𝖷 *0427/49666. 246 rooms, 8 suites. Restaurant, 2 bars, minibars, pool, sauna, massage, tennis court, playground, meeting room, car rental. AE, D, MC, V. Closed Nov.–Apr.* ✎

$$–$$$ 🏨 **Troullos Bay.** This homey beachfront hotel invites reading, chatting, and relaxing in bamboo chairs around the lobby's usually unlighted fireplace. Bedrooms have wood furniture, striped duvets, tile floors, and colorful prints. Most rooms have balconies and views of the pretty beach. The restaurant, decorated with bamboo and chintz, serves good food and opens onto the lawn near the sand's edge. ⊠ *Troullos Bay 37002,* ☎ *0427/49390, 0427/49391, or 0427/21223,* 𝖥𝖠𝖷 *0427/49218. 43 rooms, 6 suites. Restaurant, bar, air-conditioning. V. Closed Nov.–Apr.*

Outdoor Activities and Sports

HORSEBACK RIDING

Skiathos's **Pinewood Riding Centre** (⊠ On road to Aselinos Beach) conducts lessons, mountain-trail outings, and all-day excursions for beginners and experienced riders.

Kastro

❼ *5 km (3 mi) north of Skiathos town.*

A caïque will bring you to Kastro, perched on a forbidding promontory high above the water and accessible only by steps; you can also take the three-hour walk from Skiathos town (☞ *below*). Skiathians founded this former capital in the 16th century when they fled from the pirates and the turmoil on the coast to the security of this remote cliff—staying until 1829. Its landward side was additionally protected by a moat and drawbridge, and inside the stout walls they erected 300 houses and 22 churches, of which only two remain. The little Church of the Nativity has some fine icons and must have been filled with prayers for deliverance from the sieges that left the Skiathians close to starvation.

❽ Four kilometers (2½ miles) southwest of Kastro is the deserted **Kechrias monastery.** Be warned: the road to Kechrias and the beach below is tough going; stick to a four-wheel-drive vehicle.

Outdoor Activities and Sports

HIKING

Birds, mountain springs, deserted monasteries, churches, wildflowers—if you'd like to find some of these remote pleasures on this active island, and if you like to hike, wear comfortable shoes, leave the boat at Kastro, and walk back to Skiathos. The walk takes about three hours through the orchards, fields, and forests of the interior; the paths are well marked and are downhill most of the way.

Lalaria

⑨ *7 km (4½ mi) north of Skiathos town.*

Roads are being carved out of the pine forests, but some key spots still can only be reached by caïque. Chief among them is the much-photographed, lovely Lalaria, on the north coast, flanked by a majestic, arched limestone promontory. The polished limestone and marble beach adds extra sparkle to the already shimmering Aegean. In the same area are **Skoteini (Dark) Cave, Galazia (Azure) Cave,** and **Halkini (Copper) Cave.** If caïque-hopping, you'll stop an hour or two here to swim and frolic. Bring along a flashlight to turn the water inside these grottoes an incandescent blue.

⑩ The island's best-known and most beautiful monastery, **Evangelistria,** was dedicated in the late 18th century to the Annunciation of the Virgin by monks from Mt. Athos. It encouraged education and gave a base to the revolutionaries, who pledged an oath to freedom and first hoisted the blue and white flag of Greece here in 1807. Looming above a gorge, and surrounded by pines and cypresses, the monastery's high wall once kept pirates out; today, it encloses a ruined refectory kitchen, the cells, a small museum library, and a magnificent church with three domes. It's about a 10-minute drive from town, or about an hour's walk. ⊠ *5 km (3 mi) north of Skiathos town, 2 km (1 mi) south of Lalaria.* ⊙ *Daily 9–5.*

NEED A BREAK? A couple of miles south of Evangelistria monastery, the dirt road veers off toward the north and northwest of the island. Follow this route for a quick repast; about 2 km (1 mi) farther on, an enterprising soul has set up a café and snack bar, **Platanos** (⊠ On route south of Evangelistria monastery), where you can stare at the astounding view of the harbor for as long as you like.

SKOPELOS

This triangular island's name means "a sharp rock" or "a reef"—a fitting description for the terrain on its northern shore. It's an hour away from Skiathos by hydrofoil and is the second largest of the Sporades. Most of its 122 square km (47 square mi), up to its highest peak on Mt. Delfi, are covered with dense pine forests, olive groves, and orchards. On the south coast, villages overlook the shores, and pines line the pebbly beaches, casting jade shadows on turquoise water. Although this is the most populated island of the Sporades, with two major towns, Skopelos retains a peaceful, quaint atmosphere and absorbs tourists into its life rather than giving itself up to their sun-and-fun needs. It's not surprising that ecologists claim it's the greenest island in the region.

Legend has it that Skopelos was settled by Peparethos and Staphylos, colonists from Minoan Crete, said to be the sons of Dionysos and Ariadne, King Minos's daughter. They brought with them the lore of the grape and the olive. The island was called Peparethos until Hellenistic times, and its most popular beach still bears the name Stafilos. Here, in the 1930s, a tomb believed to be Staphylos's was unearthed, filled with weapons and golden treasures (now in the Volos museum on the Pelion peninsula).

The Byzantines were exiled here, and the Venetians ruled for 300 years, until 1204. In times past, Skopelos was known for its wine, but today its plums and almonds are eaten rather than drunk, and incorporated into the simple cuisine. Many artists and photographers have settled on the island and throughout the summer are part of an extensive cultural program. Little by little, Skopelos is establishing an image as a green and artsy island, still unspoiled by success.

Skopelos Town

⑪ *11 km (7 mi) southeast of Loutraki.*

Pretty Skopelos town, the administrative center of the Sporades, overlooks a bay on the north coast, on a steep hill below scant vestiges of the ancient acropolis and medieval castle. It works hard to remain charming—building permits are difficult to obtain, signs must be in native style, pebbles are embedded into the stones of walkways. Three- and four-story houses rise virtually straight up the hillside, reached by flagstone steps, where women sit chatting and knitting by their doorways. The whitewashed houses look prosperous and well tended, their facades enlivened by brightly painted or brown timber balconies, doors, shutters, flamboyant vines, and potted plants. Interspersed among their red-tile roofs are several with traditional gray fish-scale slate—too heavy and expensive to be built much nowadays.

For a glimpse of the interior of a Skopelan house, visit the **Folk Art Museum,** a 19th-century mansion with period furniture, traditional tools, and an example of an elaborate festive women's costume: silk shirt embroidered with tiny flowers, velvet coat with wide embroidered sleeves, and silk head scarf. Even today, women in the villages will dress up in this way for special occasions. The museum is open July and August. ⌧ *Hatzistamati, Skopelos town.* 🖼 *500 dr./€1.47* ⊙ *Daily 7 AM–10 PM.*

NEED A BREAK?	Walking around the steep and twisted streets of Skopelos town you're bound to want to sit down, refresh, and fuel up. If so stop at **Mihalis** (turn left at the OTE and down the street, ☎ 0424/22014) for his delicious *Skopelitiki tiropita* (cheese pie), or indulge in a *rizogalo* (rice pudding). The setting here is picturesque—bougainvillea galore, the warble of canaries, and set opposite a barber's shop that is redolent of the charm of another era. The hand-painted sign is well worth a photograph.
	A Greek coffee—which by now is most certainly an acquired taste—should be drunk in the garden of **Café Ermionat** (⌧ At end of Giorgiou Rembaki St.). But before you make yourself comfortable in the shady oasis of the garden make sure to take a look inside and see what an original Greek kafenion was like—note the marble-top tables huddled around an old wooden stove—before the days of cappuccino.

Off the waterfront, gear your legs for a breath-snatching climb up the almost perpendicular steps in Skopelos town, at the sea wall. You will encounter many **churches** as you go. The uppermost, the 11th-century **Ayios Athanasios,** was built on a 9th-century foundation. At the top you'll be standing within the walls of the 13th-century castle, erected by the Venetian Ghisi lords who held all the Sporades as their fief. It in turn rests upon polygonal masonry of the 5th century BC, as this was the site of one of the island's three ancient acropoli. Once you've admired the view and the stamina of the old women negotiating the steps like mountain goats, wind your way back down the sea-wall steps by any route you choose. Wherever you turn, you'll probably spy a church; Skopelos claims some 360, of which 123 are in the town alone. Unfortunately, most of them seem to be curiously locked, though you'll nevertheless be taken with their exteriors—some incorporating ancient artifacts, Byzantine plates, or early Christian elements—and their slate-capped domes.

A few of Skopelos's 40 monasteries—dazzling white and topped with terra-cotta roofs—are perched on the mountainside opposite, circling in tiers to the shore. Most offer spectacular views of the town; some are deserted, but others are in operation and welcome visitors (dress appropriately: no bare legs or arms; women must wear skirts). You can drive or go by bike, but even with just a good walking guide, you can

⑫ visit them all in a few hours. One is **Evangelistria Monastery** (✉ On mountainside opposite Skopelos town, 1½ km [1 mi] northeast), founded in 1676 and completely rebuilt in 1712. It contains no frescoes, but it is justly proud of its intricately carved iconostasis and an 11th-century icon of the Virgin with Child, said to be miraculous.

⑬ Following the signs east of Skopelos town will bring you first to **Ayia Varvara**, empty behind fortresslike walls. The **Metamorphosis tou Sotera,** the oldest monastery on the island (circa 1600), is open only
⑭ on August 6 and is occupied by a sole monk. The **Prodromou** (Forerunner), dedicated to St. John the Baptist, now operates as a convent and is found 2½ km (1½ mi) east of Skopelos town. Besides being of an unusual design, its church contains some outstanding 14th-century triptychs, an enamel tile floor, and an iconostasis spanning four centuries (half carved in the 14th, half in the 18th). The nuns sell their elaborate woven and embroidered handiwork.

⑮ About 2 km (1 mi) south of Skopelos town, the **Ayios Reginos** monastery, the namesake of the island's patron saint, is disappointingly modern.

Beaches
Most beaches lie on the sheltered coast, south and west of the main town, and are reached from the road by footpath. The water in this area is calm, and pines grow down to the waterfront. Scattered farms and tavernas, houses with rooms for rent, and one or two pleasant ho-
⑯ tels line the road to **Stafilos Beach** (✉ 8 km [5 mi] southeast of Skopelos), the closest to town and the most crowded. Prehistoric walls, a watchtower, and particularly an unplundered grave suggest that this was the site of an important prehistoric settlement. **Velania** (✉ East of Stafilos Beach), reachable by footpath, takes its name from the *valanium* (Roman bath) that once stood here, which has since disintegrated under the waves. It is a nude beach today.

Dining and Lodging
$$ ✕ **Alexander.** When you've had enough of the waterfront, follow the signs up from the waterfront (then turn inland after the corner shop Armoloi) to this little garden restaurant. Here, none of the main dishes are prefab; your order is cooked for you. Especially recommended are *orektika* (appetizers) such as fried eggplant or zucchini, served with *tzatziki* (garlic and yogurt dip) or *tirosalata* (cheese dip). After these you might not have room for the main courses! ✉ *Odhos Manolaki,* ☎ *0424/22324. MC, V. Closed Nov.–Mar. No lunch.*

$$ ✕ **Perivoli.** Locals come to get away from the tourists and to enjoy a gourmand menu in this candlelighted garden. The menu is not only varied—Malaysian chicken is one option—but imaginative and delicious. If you want to stick to something safe, the pepper steak is exquisitely prepared. Make sure to leave room for dessert as the *amigdalopita* (almond cake) is a winner. With all these pluses, the secret is out—this place is usually crowded. Follow the signs up from Platanos (a.k.a. Souvlaki) Square. ✉ *Skopelos town,* ☎ *0424/23758. Reservations essential. No credit cards. Closed Oct. 1–May 31. No lunch.*

$–$$ ✕ **Tarsanas.** This unassuming taverna is at the far western end of the waterfront and you might easily miss it. Don't. The fish is fresh, the meat cooked outside on a spit, and the *Sti Souvla* (the typical Skopelos cheese and spinach pies) are a meal in themselves. Good food at good prices often makes up for the lack of atmosphere, so come to eat and not to gaze. Remember that fish is often expensive and can hike up your bill, but how often do you get to eat fish that's been caught just hours before it is served? ✉ *Waterfront,* ☎ *0424/23635. No credit cards.*

$ ✕ **Klimataria.** Next door to Molos, this restaurant is notable for its *magirefta* (pre-prepared dishes). The *papoutsakia* (aubergines, ground lamb, and bechamel sauce) is rich and so delicious you'll find yourself doing what the locals do: the quintessential Greek *papara*—sponging the plate clean with a piece of bread. ✉ *Waterfront,* ☎ *0424/22273. No credit cards.*

$ ✕ **Molos.** The best of the cluster of tavernas near the ferry dock, Molos serves excellent orektika and precooked dishes. Exceptional is the Melitzanes Imam, eggplant in a rich sauce, that might just make you swoon, as did the Turkish Sultan to whom it was first served. It's one of the few places in town open for lunch, especially delightful at an outdoor table. ✉ *Waterfront,* ☎ *0424/22551. No credit cards. Closed Nov. 1–May 25.*

$$$–$$$$ ⊞ **Skopelos Village.** Bungalows on the water each have a balcony or a patch of lawn, kitchen, large bedroom(s), and a living room, and sleep from two to six people. The decor is traditional northern Greek, with a large corner hearth. Children will enjoy the pool and playground, parents the congenial bar and taverna, and the housekeeping service. Don't confuse this place with Sunrise Village next door. It's about a 15-minute walk from the town center. ✉ *Skopelos town 37003,* ☎ *0424/ 23011–12 or 0424/22517,* ℻ *0424/22958. 36 bungalows. Bar, pool, playground. AE, V. Closed Nov.–Apr.*

$$–$$$ ⊞ **Dionysos.** Although it's in town, this hotel is well appointed: from
★ the umbrellas that shade the bamboo chairs on the terrace, to the lobby with embroidered curtains, to the air-conditioned rooms with balconies and a view of the hills, to the pool (with a bar, of course). The rooms, with brown woodwork, slate floors, and rustic-style furniture, are spotless. Intelligent design and traditional decor help it blend in with its neighbors. ✉ *Skopelos town 37003,* ☎ *0424/23210 through 0424/23215,* ℻ *0424/22954. 52 rooms. Restaurant, 2 bars, pool. DC, MC, V. Closed Nov.–mid-Apr.*

$–$$ ⊞ **Pension Andromache.** Situated in the heart of the web of Skopelos's crisscross alleys just behind the waterfront, this small treasure of a rooming house is a real find. A traditional house tastefully remodeled into a welcoming pension, it has large guest rooms, with wooden floors and paneled ceilings; the furniture is a delightful mix of old and new. The only problem is noise—we're in the nerve-center of town here, complete with motorcycles zipping back and forth. If you're on a budget *and* a light sleeper, this place could pose a bit of a problem, but if you enjoy a bit of mid-summer clamor, this is an ideal place to stay. ✉ *Skopelos town, opposite OTE, 37003,* ☎ *0424/22940 or 0424/22145,* ℻ *0424/22941. 7 rooms. No credit cards.*

$–$$ ⊞ **Pension Sotos.** This cozy, remodeled family house on the waterfront is near the action, inexpensive, and extremely casual. Tiny rooms look onto one of the hotel's two courtyard terraces, where guests can bring their own food and are welcome to use the kitchen and refrigerator. It's not very private, but it's fun. ✉ *Skopelos town 37003,* ☎ *0424/22549,* ℻ *0424/23668. 12 rooms. No credit cards. Closed Nov.–Mar 15.*

Outdoor Activities and Sports

NATURE CRUISES

A big caïque captained by a marine biologist makes two-day weekend cruises from Skopelos to Psathoura and Kyra Panayia in the National Marine Park. Videos, slides, binoculars, snorkeling equipment, underwater cameras, and hydrophones to record dolphin signals make the trip educational and fun. The overnight trip costs 50,000 dr./€147; make reservations at Madro Travel (☞ Contacts and Resources *in* The Northern Sporades A to Z, *below*).

Nightlife

BARS AND DISCOS

Nightlife on Skopelos is more sedate than it is on Skiathos. There is a smattering of cozy bars playing music of all kinds, and there is at least one disco, which changes each year (look for advertisements). Most of the bars are along the waterfront or just off it, so take an evening stroll and pick your bar of choice; most have tables outside so you really can't help but walk right into them. **Platanos Jazz Club,** on the eastern part of the harbor, is atmospheric and quietly popular. You could always venture into the back alleys and have a drink at **Ionos Blue Bar,** but the *"kefi"* (good mood) is to be found at the western end of the waterfront where a string of bar-nightclubs come to life after midnight. Start your evening at **Mercurios.** Others end the night at **Ntokos.** In between, the **La Costa Rock Café** is a lively option.

OUZERI

At **Anatoli** (⊠ In Old Kastro), tap into a true Greek vein, thanks to proprietor Giorgo Xithari, who strums up a storm on his bouzouki and sings *rembetika* blues (without the benefit of a microphone). Sometimes other musicians join in, sometimes his sons, and with enough ouzo, you might, too. This is one place where Greeks get down and really groove—the real thing!

Shopping

The town's tiny shops are tucked into a few streets behind the central part of the waterfront. Handicrafts include loom-woven textiles made by nuns. Local honey, prunes, almonds, and candy are especially delicious. Take home a box of *hamalia* or *rozethes,* which are the local sugar, almond paste, and plum specialties.

CLOTHING

There are numerous clothing stores found throughout the alleyways of Skopelos town. Most, however, don't just restrict themselves to selling clothes, but offer a hodgepodge of other accessories, so it's fun to browse. Try **Risko** (☎ 0424/23339) for children's clothing. Aside from clothing, **Teratakia** (☎ 0424/24149) offers some interesting furniture, lamp-shades, and other household furnishings.

LOCAL CRAFTS

Most of the shops line the waterfront or are just off it. One of the most alluring shops is **Archipelago** (☎ 0424/23127), the sister shop of Archipelagos on Skiathos; it has modern ceramics and crafts, great jewelry, handbags, and a wonderful selection of pricey antiques. **Armoloi** (☎ 0424/22707), one of the neatest shops, displays an array of ceramics made by local potters, kilims, tapestries, embroideries, and bags crafted from fragments of old Asian rugs and kilims. Also try **Ploumisti** (☎ 0424/22059) for kilims, bags, hand-painted T-shirts, and jewelry, **Yiousouri** (☎ 0424/23983) for decorative ceramics, and **Cactus** (☎ 0424/23665) for jewelry and handicrafts and some great fish patterned tea cups. **Photo Gallerie** has a large collection of cards and photographs from all over the island.

Drachondoschisma

⑰ *Peninsula about 5 km (3 mi) south of Skopelos town.*

The road from Stafilos Beach runs southwest through the rounded Drachondoschisma peninsula, where Reginos dispatched the dragon.

Agnonda

⑱ *5 km (3 mi) south of Skopelos town.*

The tiny port of Agnonda has many tavernas along its pebbled beach. It is named after a local boy, Agnonas, who returned here from Olympia in 546 BC wearing the victor's wreath.

Panormos Bay

⑲ *6 km (4 mi) west of Skopelos town, 4 km (2½ mi) northwest of Agnonda.*

Due northwest of Agnonda is Panormos Bay, the smallest of the ancient towns of Peparethos, founded in the 8th century BC by colonists from Chalkis. A few well-concealed walls are visible among the pine woods on the acropolis above the bay. With its long beach and its sheltered inner cove ideal for yachts, this is fast becoming a holiday village, although it retains its quiet charm. Inland, the interior of Skopelos is green and lush, as is much of the Sporades, but not far from Panormos Bay you'll find traditional farmhouses called *kalivia,* set in plum orchards. Some are occupied; others have been turned into overnight stops or are used only for feast-day celebrations. Look for the outdoor ovens, which baked the fresh plums when Skopelos was turning out prunes galore. This rural area is charming, but the lack of signposts makes it easy to get lost, so mark your route.

Beaches

Just north of Panormos Bay is pebbly **Milia,** Skopelos's longest beach, considered by many its best. Deserted beaches in the vicinity include Adrina. Dassia, the verdant islet across the bay, was named after a pirate who drowned there—a woman. Though still secluded, Milia Bay is up and coming—parasols and recliners are lined across the beach ready and waiting for the summer crowd. There's an enormous taverna, thankfully ensconced by pine trees; the food is only decent, but cold drinks and ice cream are a luxury in the noonday sun. No matter what, Milia is breathtaking, and if you want to minimize the distance between you and the deep blue sea, there are villas for rent right on the beach. They're well tended and just a few short strides from the water's edge.

Lodging

$$–$$$ ⊡ **Adrina Beach.** Atop a picture-book cove, this terraced hotel boasts uninterrupted views of Panormos Bay from every level. Outside there is multihued bougainvillea; indoors, the blue and white is carried throughout, complemented by terra-cotta floors. Plates adorn the walls, amphorae the corners. The comfy bedrooms have fans but no air-conditioning. The only fly on the baklava might be the stairs between the private beach, pool, taverna area, and your room, and the steep walk back from the little town. ⊠ *Adrina Beach 37003,* ☎ *0424/23373 through 0424/23375,* ℻ *0424/23372. 45 rooms, 10 suites. Restaurant, bar, snack bar, pool, beach, jet-skiing, parasailing, waterskiing, playground. AE, DC, MC, V. Closed Nov.–Apr.* ⊛

$$ ⊡ **Panormos Beach.** The owner's attention to detail shows in the beau-
★   tifully tended flower garden, the immaculate, air-conditioned rooms with pine furniture and handwoven linens, the country dining room,

and the entrance case displaying his grandmother's elaborate costume. Don't miss the Skopelan mezedes prepared by his mother-in-law. This traditional, exceptionally peaceful hotel is a five-minute walk from the beach. ⊠ *Panormos Beach 37003,* ☎ *0424/22711,* F̅A̅X̅ *0424/23366. 34 rooms. Bar, snack bar, air-conditioning, playground. No credit cards. Closed Nov.–Apr.*

Elios

㉑ *6 km (4 mi) west of Skopelos town, 4 km (2½ mi) north of Panormos Bay.*

Residents of Klima who were dislodged in 1965 by the same earthquake that devastated Alonnisos now live here in a new development. The origin of its name is more intriguing than the village: legend has it that when Reginos arrived to save the island from a dragon that demanded human nourishment, he demanded, "Well, where in *eleos* (God's mercy) is the beast?"

Lodging

$$ 🏨 **Zanétta.** If you want to feel as if you've really escaped from the rat race, stay awhile in these fully equipped, air-conditioned apartments surrounded by woods but close to the sea. The well-equipped kitchen means you can stay put and spend some time exploring the rural interior of this lush island. The hotel is about five minutes from the water. ⊠ *Elios 37005,* ☎ *0424/33140,* F̅A̅X̅ *0424/33717. 16 apartments. Restaurant, kitchenettes, air-conditioning, pool. MC, V. Closed Nov.–Apr.*

Klima

㉑ *10 km (6 mi) northwest of Skopelos town, 3 km (2 mi) north of Elios.*

Klima means "ladder," and Kato ("Lower") Klima leads to Ano ("Upper") Klima, clinging to the mountainside. The area is being slowly restored from the 1965 earthquake, but plenty of ruined houses are still for sale. If you crave an island retreat, this could be your chance.

Loutraki

㉒ *11 km (7 mi) northwest of Skopelos town, 1 km (½ mi) northwest of Klima.*

Loutraki is the tiny port village where the ferries and hydrofoils stop, and it is not very charming. Three hundred yards away are the remains of the **acropolis of Selinous,** the island's third ancient city. Unfortunately, everything lies buried except the walls.

Glossa

㉓ *19 km (11¾ mi) northwest of Skopelos town, 1 km (½ mi) north of Loutraki.*

Delightful Glossa is the island's second-largest settlement, where whitewashed, red-roof houses are clustered on the steep hillside above the harbor of Loutraki. Venetian towers and traces of Turkish influence remain; the center is closed to traffic. This is a place to relax, dine, and enjoy the quieter beaches. Just to the east, check out Ayios Ioannis monastery, dramatically perched above a pretty beach.

Dining

$$ ✕ **Taverna T'Agnanti.** Moussaka and the other classics are good and inexpensive at this popular taverna, which has been spruced up and decorated anew to herald in the new century. The food remains as delicious as before, staying true to the spirit which first gave this restaurant its renown. Ask the owners to recommend a room to rent in this charming town that doesn't cater to tourists. ✉ *Above the bus stop, on the left side of Agiou Riginou,* ☎ *0424/33606. No credit cards.*

ALONNISOS

Ah, Alonnisos. Set in the clearest waters of the Aegean, this is the unspoiled Greece tourists long for, and until recently, most of the rugged coast was accessible only by boat. Barter was still the usual method of trade until the late 1960s, when tourism finally catapulted this serene island into the 20th century, sort of. Nature has conspired to keep Alonnisos underpopulated and undeveloped. Although the island was famous for its wine in past centuries, the vines were ruined by disease in the 1950s, and many residents left. Another fiasco was the proposed airport. When rocks made it hard to complete a runway, the project was abandoned, and jets, and big-time package tourism, never got off the ground. As a relative backwater the island may lack chic beaches and groovy nightclubs, but the trade-offs are big-time: forest walks, boat trips to islands and nature preserves, caves and beaches where jet-skiing and parasailing are unknown. You'll find a few hotels, several rooms to rent, some nice tavernas, and a cheerful laid-back atmosphere. Europeans love it, but most of the tourists and day-trippers are nature-lovers rather than party people. Thank God.

Alonnisos hardly gets more than a line or two in the history books, and because of its different names—Ikos and Liadromia—researchers find it difficult to trace. Peleus, Achilles' father, once lived on the island; Philip of Macedon coveted it; the Venetians erected a fortress here. Its waters cover dozens of fascinating shipwrecks, not to mention a ruined city or two, but little else is known of its past. The center of the island submerged long ago, perhaps in a cataclysmic earthquake, leaving only islets and a rock called Psathoura.

While Skiathos and Skopelos were sending merchant fleets to the Black Sea and Egypt in the 18th and early 19th centuries, sailors from Alonnisos were probably plundering them. When the Sporades and Greece gained independence, the pirates turned to fishing. Today, their heirs are still fishing, farming, and herding sheep. Most of the 3,000 or so inhabitants (half that in winter) live in and around the port of Patitiri, hurriedly developed to house victims of the 1965 earthquake, which devastated the hilltop capital. Many fishing families live in Steni Vala, farther northeast. On a conical hill 600 ft above the port is haunting Old Alonnisos, or Chora. Its tiny houses, deserted after the earthquake, have been lovingly restored by Athenians and Europeans who bought them for next to nothing and thus are somewhat resented by the re-settled villagers in the port areas below. Chora comes to life in summer, but for much of the time it seems almost a ghost town, aside from an occasional cat and a few stalwart year-rounders.

Lush with pine, oak, fruit trees, and mastic and arbutus bushes, hilly Alonnisos has small, fertile plains, a steep northwestern coastline, and an east coast with pebbled beaches. To explore beyond Patitiri and Old Alonnisos, you can either rent a motorbike or car, or take a caïque, which can also take you to the neighboring islets. The roads to the various beaches along the way have fairly decent dirt surfaces. The road from Patitiri to Steni Vala is now paved; north of Steni Vala are virtually no signs of habitation. The interior of the island is dirt tracks, where hikers, bikers, and shepherds sporadically wend their ways.

Patitiri

㉔ *7 km (4½ mi) southwest of Steni Vala.*

Patitiri ("Winepress") was once a wine-making center, but today it's the island's main port, set in a pretty cove flanked by white, pine-clad cliffs. Along the diminutive waterfront are tavernas and cafés, a couple of hotels, the boat agency, and a gas station. Most of the buildings are modern and drab, built to house and serve the refugees from Old Alonnisos, the half-destroyed old capital up the hill. But the backstreet houses have flower-filled boxes, and the sun twinkling on the blue Aegean keeps things cheery. Nearby, 4 km (2½ mi) north of Patitiri, is Votsi, a tiny harbor set among cliffs—a perfect spot to sit in a taverna, watch the fishing boats come in, and sip ouzo. Swimming off the rocks here is excellent.

Beaches

Find one and claim it. Rocks and coves throughout the coast are quiet havens tucked among cliffs, and you can easily clamber from rocky ledges to the calm and sparkling turquoise water. Most beaches are on the east coast. Going north from Patitiri, unpaved roads will get you to swimming areas with some facilities, including **Hrysi Milia, Kokkinokastro, Tzórtzi, Steni Vala, Kalamakia,** and, farther north, **Aglos Dimitrios,** a nudist beach. At the tip of Alonnisos, the deserted beach at **Gerakas** is good for snorkeling.

OFF THE
BEATEN PATH

The islets surrounding Alonnisos, reachable by caïque from Patitiri, are special for many reasons; excursions can be arranged on Skiathos or Skopelos. **Peristera** ("pigeon") is the closest. It has a tiny shepherd population, the ruins of a castle, and a few delightful sandy beaches that the caïques buzz along. Take a chartered caïque ride southeast to **Skantzoura,** which has marble beaches, a monastery, and the submerged ruins of the ancient town of Skandyle. Bring binoculars, and if you're lucky you'll spot an Eleanora falcon, or a rare Aegean seagull with white wings and a black hood. The biggest in the island group is **Kyra Panayia** (Pelagos), which has sometimes been identified as ancient Alonnisos. Here, too, there is a monastery (16th century) and traces of a Neolithic settlement. Its two bays, Planitis and Ayios Petros, are often filled with flotillas—groups of yachts usually chartered by visitors. **Yioura,** to the northeast, was once used as place of exile for undesirable politicos. Unusual flora and a rare species of wild goat thrive here, and the most impressive of its caves, crammed with colorful stalactites and stalagmites, is said to be where Homer's Cyclops lived. Recent excavations show remains from 3000 BC, including pottery and hooks made of bone (but not a giant monocle). This local civilization is not found in any other part of Greece. Excavations were going on at press time—check if the cave is open. **Psathoura,** the most northerly of the Sporades, has a big, old lighthouse said to have the brightest beacon in the Aegean, and for good reason. The islet is so low in the water it can hardly be seen until you're on top of it. Near its harbor are the ruins of yet another sunken city—perhaps ancient Ikos?

Dining and Lodging

$$–$$$ ✕ **Argo.** A great place for brunch, this quiet restaurant on a cliff overlooking the rocky east coast has a garden setting and serves good fresh fish, crayfish, and lobster. For dinner it's romantic: enveloped in flowers, tiles, breezes, and, on some nights, moonlight, sparkling silver on the Aegean. ⊠ *Next door to Paradise Hotel,* ☎ *0424/65141. No credit cards. Closed Nov.–Apr.*

$$ ✕ **To Kamaki.** Locals love this basic ouzeri, renowned for its calamari, baked mussels, and large portions of assorted seafood appetizers. In summer, when the boats leave a daily haul, the fish and shellfish, grilled by owner Spiros, couldn't be fresher. Outdoor tables beckon. ⊠ *Ikion Dolopon,* ☎ *0424/65245. No credit cards. Closed Nov.–Mar.*

$ ✕ **Flisvos.** Outdoor tables are across the road under a shady awning, next to the water, and this is an excellent spot to await the boat. The specialty is *tiropita alonnisou* (a deep-fried cheese pie formed of swirls of pastry). Freshly made pizza and pasta add an Italian accent to the usual taverna food. Don't miss the salad with locally produced olive oil. It's open at 7 AM for breakfast and lunch—a rarity here. ⊠ *Patitiri (on corner of main street and seafront),* ☎ *0424/65307. No credit cards. Closed Oct. 16–May.*

$$ ⊞ **Haravgi.** Harbor comings and goings can be enjoyed from the balconies of this simple, clean, conveniently located hotel set in a garden and near swimming areas and tavernas. A renovation in 1999 has added on a new wing of spacious studios with kitchen facilities, ideal for families. All the rooms share the spectacular view of the sparkling waters below. ⊠ *On the waterfront, Patitiri 37005,* ☎ *0424/65090. 19 rooms. No credit cards. Closed Nov.–Apr.*

$$ ⊞ **Liadromia.** Most rooms in this three-story hotel overlook the port, but there's an even better view from the rooftop terrace bar and breakfast room. Traditional furnishings include dark wood, mustard-and-green striped fabrics, and built-in beds. The halls display family memorabilia and photos of Alonnisos before the quake. Some rooms have refrigerators, and some have double beds—ask. In fact, ask anything, as the owner Mary Athanassiou is probably better informed about the sights of Alonnisos than any travel book or tourist office anywhere. ⊠ *Patitiri 37005,* ☎ *0424/65521 or 0424/65095,* 🖷 *0424/65096. 20 rooms. Bar. MC, V.* ✎

$$ ⊞ **Paradise.** Although the rooms and balconies here are small and rudimentary, the hotel's flower garden is lovely, and just below, among the pines and rocks, guests can swim at any time in secluded coves. Some hang out all day talking to Kostas, the handsome owner, at the bar or shady terrace beside the pool, which doubles as a snack bar and breakfast area. ⊠ *Patitiri 37005,* ☎ *0424/65160 or 0424/65213,* 🖷 *0424/65161. 31 rooms. 2 bars, pool. MC, V. Closed Oct. 20–May 15.*

Nightlife

Surprisingly, the island has lots of little bars and cafés, some with live music. Ask the locals when you get here for whichever is best at the moment. Two clubs, **Hot Stuff** and **Club Enigma,** near the harbor, offer a combination of recorded music and live bouzouki. **Cafe Symbol,** next to the National Bank, is quite a favorite among the local youth of Alonnisos. It's open in the morning for breakfast and in the evening blares music and serves cocktails. The tiny and very quaint interior turns wild with dancing. If you need more music than this, bring a CD player.

Outdoor Sports and Activities

HIKING

If there's time to spare while in Patitiri (or, indeed, anytime during your stay in Alonnisos), be sure to pop into **Ikos Travel** (⊠ Patitiri) and corner Paki Athanassiou into pointing out a hiking trail that suits your mood. There are guided hikes four times a week that usually head to picturesque parts of the island and include a picnic lunch on a beach. You can also travel to the Marine Park on the twice-weekly cruise that departs Alonissos port. Beware of Paki's charm or you might never leave Alonissos, as his love for the island is infectious.

Old Alonnisos (Chora)

㉕ *1½ km (1 mi) west of Patitiri.*

Despite its still-ravaged state, in many ways this traditional village, which was once the island capital, is the most spectacular in all the Sporades. The destruction caused by the 1965 earthquake is still being repaired, but it has been repopulated by Europeans who cherish its beauty. The original town dates from the 10th century, when the population sought safety above the sea. Ruins of walls from the 15th-century Byzantine-Venetian fortress still crown the peak, and the little chapel called tou Christou, with a fish-scale roof, is especially charming (you'll need to find the man who keeps the key to let you in; ask a nearby shopkeeper where to find him).

The town seems frozen in time. Indeed, until the earthquake, all goods were hauled up by mule. The narrow cobbled paths of Old Alonnisos are lined with whitewashed stone buildings hung with ornate wooden balconies painted in varied hues and dripping with vines, wildflowers turning cracks into beauty spots, and old pots standing guard by ancient doorways. Each corner offers quirky angles, sharp shadows in the sunshine, and glimpses of blue sea beyond. The scale of the town is intimate and compelling, and if you peek inside the villas' windows as you navigate the mud and stone, you will most often see books and the household items of the contented new residents, mainly German and English, who took the place of the residents after they were moved by the government to safer quarters in the harbor area.

At the top is a 360° view of the Aegean, cove beaches set within cliffs, and medieval watchtowers, and on the clearest days you can see as far as Mt. Olympus in northern Greece, 177 km (110 mi) away. A few charming restaurants, a couple of transient boutiques, and a tiny museum, midway in the maze of buildings, make up the tourist attractions. In addition, in a small plaza is a memorial to 11 Greek patriots executed by Germans in World War II.

You might decide to stay in rooms here rather than in the port below, to contemplate it all. If you can't hack the steep 45-minute hike up the ecological trail from Patitiri to Old Alonnisos—through forest, fields of mustard and poppies, lemon orchards, and olive groves—you can forego exercise for ease and take the island's single bus.

Dining

$$–$$$ ✕ **Astrofengia.** In this restored family house you can enjoy a delightful garden and the stunning view (the name means "starlight"). dFrom the varied, innovative menu choose one of the many organic salads, some Cypriot hummus, three-cheese pie, or tagliatelli with a choice of sauces, and tiramisu. It's just before the entrance to Old Alonnisos; take the path to the left as soon as you get off the bus. ⊠ *Old Alonnisos,* ☎ *0424/65182. No credit cards. Closed Oct.–May. No lunch.*

$$ ✕ **Paraport.** With views of the sea and nearby islands on both sides of Alonnisos, the setting is as good as the food. Tables spill out in both directions on the narrow, winding main street just underneath the picturesque ruins of the Kastro. Taverna fare is spicier here on this island than in most of Greece, but for a mild old standby, try the potatoes au gratin. ⊠ *Old Alonnisos,* ☎ *0424/65608. No credit cards. Closed Oct. 1–May 19. No lunch.*

$$ ✕⊞ **Fantasia House.** If you don't mind residing over a busy restaurant, this is an option to consider. It's central, near the bus and taxi stops, which means you don't have to hike all the way up steep alleys to get a good night's sleep. The studio rooms are clean and comfortable, and all have views of the sea that shimmers far below. Even if you choose to stay elsewhere the food in the restaurant—a cozy little place, sheltered under the shade of an enormous vine—is simple and delicious. You must sample the very large *hortopita* (vegetable pie wrapped in phyllo pastry), as the phyllo here is made the old fashioned way—with a rolling pin in Mother's hands. ⊠ *Main street of Old Alonnisos,* ☎ *0424/65186. 10 rooms. No credit cards. Nov.–Apr.*

Shopping
There are a growing number of small shops that have recently mushroomed throughout the old town of Alonnisos, particularly in the Kastro area. The most interesting perhaps is **Argo,** where the silver jewelry is actually made on the premises.

Milia

㉖ *2 km (1 mi) northeast of Patitiri.*

This is a charming, secluded area to come to for a swim and to be the ultimate recluse. There are a number of little coves to choose from, some more private than others.

Lodging
$$–$$$ 🏨 **Milia-Bay.** Let's give thanks that hotels of this class still exist. Small,
★ private, infinitely luxurious, family-run, and built in 1998, these villa-apartments make you feel as if you're living in a private, tasteful home. Rooms are adorned with select antiques while the grounds have been sculpted into gardens which you can view from large verandas. Beyond lies the beckoning Big Blue—on a clear day you can see all the way to Skyros. A pool bar, where a homemade snack or dish of the day is always available, only adds to the sensation of luxury and relaxation. The Menayas family are obviously lovers of antiques, with testimony provided by the old tiles that have been transformed into poolside tabletops, or the weather vane remodeled into a signpost depicting the islands of the marine park which stretches out before the hotel. This is a place to fall in love in or with. ⊠ *Milia 37005,* ☎ *0424/66032; 01/895–0794 or 01/895–6911 Athens.* 🅵🅰🆇 *0424/66037; 01/895–3591 Athens. 12 apartments. Bar, kitchenettes, pool. MC, V. Closed Oct. 15–Mar.* ✎

Kokkinokastro

㉗ *4 km (2½ mi) northeast of Patitiri.*

At Kokkinokastro, where the red cliffs and pebble beach contrast with the surrounding pines and water, you can find traces of an acropolis—shards, tombs, walls—as well as a Ghisi fortress. Some experts think Kokkinokastro was also the site of the ancient city of Ikos.

Steni Vala

㉘ *3 km (2 mi) northeast of Kokkinokastro.*

Steni Vala, a tiny fishing village, has little to offer except that it's the headquarters of the International Centre for Research on the Mediterranean Monk Seal, providing useful displays and a video. The islands around Alonnisos are some of the last preserves of this endangered mammal; only about 500 exist throughout the world, about 10% of them here. Scientists are always on the lookout for orphans, and they track the mature seals, too. This is the gateway to the National Marine Park, founded in 1992, which comprises the waters and all the islands in the vicinity, some of which are off-limits to visitors.

A day trip by boat to the National Marine Park is a must for nature-lovers. You'll need to be on a guided tour unless you get a special permit. While watching for the winsome but elusive monk seals, you will also discover a wide variety of rare wildlife, flora, and fauna. Gulls, terns, warblers, falcons, herons, kingfishers, and migrant birds all fill the air throughout different times of the year. Elaborate jellyfish colonies look like iridescent balloons bobbing with the waves, and groups of playful dolphins love to dive in wakes of boats.

Dining

$$ ✕ **Steni Vala.** Whether overlooking the fjordlike harbor from the terrace or in the large dining room, you'll enjoy seafood caught in the waters near here, as well as freshly made Greek specialties, such as cheese pie. This is a great place to eat after a day on the water, or to start, with breakfast. ✉ *Steni Vala,* ☎ *0424/65545. No credit cards.*

OFF THE
BEATEN PATH

Make a detour to **Lefto Yialo**—a small bay midway between Steni Vala and Hrisi Milia—where you'll find one of the most gorgeous pebble beaches on the island. After a swim, why not stop at the restaurant Eleona, just off the beach, and sample the traditional *boureki* (meat pie in phyllo pastry)?

SKYROS

Even among these unique isles, Skyros stands out. Its rugged terrain looks like a Dodecanese island, and its main town, occupied on and off for the last 3,300 years and filled with mythic ghosts, looks Cycladic. It has military bases, and an airport with connections to Athens, yet it remains the most difficult ferry connection in the Sporades. With nothing between it and Lesbos, off the coast of Turkey, its nearest neighbor is the town of Kimi, on the east coast of Evia.

Strangely enough, although the island is adrift in the Aegean, the Skyrians have not had a seafaring tradition, and they have looked to the land for their living. Their isolation has brought about notable cultural differences from the other Greek islands, such as pre-Christian Carnival rituals and a renowned style in home decoration. Here you'll find an almost extinct breed of pony, and exceptional crafts—carpentry, pottery, embroidery—practiced by dedicated artisans. You will not find luxury accommodations or swank restaurants: this idiosyncratic island makes no provisions for mass tourism, but if you've a taste for the offbeat, you'll feel right at home.

Surprisingly beguiling, this southernmost and largest (209 square km [81 square mi]) island of the Northern Sporades divides into two almost equal parts, whose names reflect their characters—*Meri* or *Imero* (tame) for the north, and *Vouno* (literally, mountain) for the south, with Mt. Kochilas its highest peak (2,598 ft). The southern half of Skyros (meaning tough, stony) is forbidding, barren, and mountainous, its western coast outlined with coves and deep bays dotted with a series of islets. The heavily populated north, attached by a narrow, flat isthmus, is virtually all farmland and forests.

Until Greece won independence in 1831, the island's population squeezed sardine-fashion into the area under the castle on the inland face of the rock. Not a single house was visible from the sea. Though the islanders could survey any movement in the Aegean for miles, they kept a low profile, living in dread of the pirates based at Treis Boukes bay on Vouno.

In the *Iliad,* legends interweave about Skyros: before the Trojan War, Theseus, the deposed hero-king of Athens, sought refuge in his ancestral estate on Skyros. King Lykomedes, afraid of the power and prestige of Theseus, took him up to the acropolis one evening, pretending to show him the island, and pushed him over the cliff—an ignominious end. In historical times, Timon of Athens unearthed what he said were Theseus's bones and sword, and placed them in the Theseion—more commonly called the Temple of Hephaistion—in Athens (☞ The Ancient Agora *in* Exploring Athens *in* Chapter 1), in what must be one of the earliest recorded archaeological investigations.

Linaria

40 km (25 mi) northeast of Kimi on Evia.

All boats and hydrofoils dock at the tiny port of Linaria because the northeast coast is either straight, sandy beach or steep cliffs. A bus to Skyros town meets arrivals. To get to the otherwise inaccessible sea caves of Pentekáli and Diatryptí, you can take a caïque from here. This dusty area offers scenes of fishermen tending their bright yellow nets, and not much more.

Skyros Town

㉙ *10 km (6 mi) north of Linaria.*

As you drive south from the airport, past brown, desolate outcroppings with only an occasional goat as a sign of movable life, Skyros town suddenly looms around a bend, looking for all appearances like a breathtaking amalgam of an imaginary painting by Monet, Cézanne, or El Greco: blazing white, cubist, dense and otherworldly, clinging, precariously it seems, to the precipitous rock beneath it, and topped gloriously by a fortress-monastery.

Called *Horio, Hora,* and *Chora* (town) by the locals, Skyros town is home to 90% of the island's 3,000 inhabitants. The impression as you get closer is of stark, simple buildings creeping up the hillside, with a tangle of labyrinthine lanes winding up, down, and around the tiny houses, Byzantine churches, and big squares.

Most commercial activity takes place in or near Agora (Market) Street (familiarly known as Sisifos, as in the myth, because of its frustrating steepness). Found here are the town's pharmacies, travel agencies, shops with wonderful Skyrian pottery, and an extraordinary number of tiny bars and tavernas, but few boutiques and even less kitsch.

The best way to get an idea of the town and its history is to follow the sinuous cobbled lanes past the mansions of the old town to the **Kastro**, the highest point, and the 10th-century fortified **Monastery of St. George,** which stands on the site of the ancient acropolis and Bronze Age settlement. Little remains of the legendary fortress of King Lykomedes, portrayed in Skyros's two most colorful myths (☞ *above*), though lower down on the north and southwest face of the rock are the so-called Pelasgian bastions of immense rectangular fitted blocks, dated to the classical period or later.

A white marble lion, once thought to be left over from the Venetian occupation, is in the wall above the entrance to the monastery. This classical symbol is a reminder of when Skyros was under Athenian dominion and heavily populated with Athenian settlers to keep it that way. This part of the castle was built on ancient foundations (look right) during the early Byzantine era and reinforced in the 14th century by the Venetians. The monastery itself was founded in 962 and radically rebuilt in 1600. Today it is inhabited by a sole monk.

Unfortunately, the once splendid frescoes of the Monastery of St. George are now mostly covered by layers of whitewash, but look for the charming St. George and startled dragon outside to the left of the church door. Within, its ornate iconostasis is considered a masterpiece. The icon of St. George on the right is said to have been brought by the waves of settlers from Constantinople traveling to Skyros during the Iconoclast Controversy of the 9th century. The icon has a black face and is familiarly known as Ayios Georgis o Arapis (the Negro); the Skyrians view him as the patron saint not only of their island but of lovers as well.

Take the vaulted passageway from the monastery courtyard to the ruined church of **Episkopi,** the former seat of the bishop of Skyros, built in 895 on the ruins of a temple of Athena. This was the center of Skyros's religious life from 1453 to 1837. Farther up, the summit is crowned with three tiny cubelike churches with blue and pink interiors, and the ruined Venetian cistern, once used as a dungeon. From here, you have a spectacular view of the town and surrounding hills. The roofs are flat, the older ones covered with a dark gray shale that has splendid insulating properties. The house walls and roofs are interconnected, forming a pattern that from above looks like a magnified form of cuneiform writing. Here and there, the shieldlike roof of a church stands out from the cubist composition of white houses that fills the hillside—with not an inch to spare.

As you stroll down from the ruins and churches of the Kastro, or explore the alleyways off the main drag, try to peek discreetly into the houses. Skyrians are house-proud and often leave their windows and doors open to show off. You'll find walls and conical mantelpieces richly decorated with European- and Asian-style porcelain, copper cooking utensils, wood carvings, and embroideries. Wealthy families originally obtained much of the porcelain from the pirates in exchange for grain and food, and its possession was a measure of social standing. Then enterprising potters started making exact copies, along with the traditional local ware, leading to the unique Skyrian style of pottery. The furniture is equally beautiful. Typical is the miniature carved Skyrian chairs, which can just about accommodate adult posteriors. If peeking into windows isn't your thing, a traditional house with local furnishings is re-created at the **Municipal Museum.** ⊠ *Megálou Stratoú,* ☎ *0222/91256.* ⊑ *500 dr./€1.47 (free Sun.).* ⊙ *Daily 8–2:30. Closed winter.*

The tiny **archaeological museum** contains finds, mostly from graves, from Neolithic to Roman times. Weapons, pottery, and jewelry are represented. ⊠ *Eternal Poetry Sq. (at far end of Sisifos),* ☎ *0222/91327.* ⊑ *500 dr./€1.47* ⊙ *Tues.–Sun. 8:30–3.*

The **Faltaits Historical and Folklore Museum** has a rich collection of Skyrian decorative arts. This house, built after independence by a wealthy family who later gave it to the town, is far larger than the usual Skyros dwelling, and it is almost overflowing with rare books, costumes, photographs, paintings, local embroideries, and other heirlooms. The embroideries are noted for their flamboyant colors and vivacious renderings of mermaids, hoopoes (the Skyrians' favorite bird), and human figures whose clothes and limbs sprout flowers. ⊠ *Eternal Poetry Sq.,* ☎ *0222/91232.* ⊑ *500 dr./€1.47* ⊙ *Daily 10–1 and 5:30–8.*

You can't miss the **statue dedicated to Rupert Brooke** (⊠ Eternal Poetry Sq.), the English poet we all read about in high school. The Skyrians call this well-known landmark *To Brook,* and every street seems to lead either to it or to the Kastro. He was 28, on his way to the Dardanelles in 1915 to fight in the first world war, but died of septicemia on a French hospital ship just off Skyros. You can visit his grave in the southern part of the island, near where he died (☞ *below*). Brooke was a socialist, but he became something of a paragon for war leaders such as Churchill. The imposing statue, a classical bronze symbolizing poetry, provokes strong emotions among islanders who object to the nudity and have defaced it accordingly.

Beaches

Around the northern tip of the island is a dirt road to **Theotokos** beach. The large Greek air base near the northern tip is off-limits.

Dining and Lodging

$$ ✕ **Margetis Taverna.** A vest-pocket taverna wedged in among shops on the main drag, it is known locally as the best place for meat and fish on the island. It's popular, so get there early (8–8:30). Though fish and lobster are always pricey, they are worth it here, as is the lamb. Try the good barrel wine, and sit outside under the big tree and watch the folks walk by. ⊠ *Market St.,* ☎ *0222/91311. Reservations not accepted. No credit cards. No lunch.*

$ ✕ **To Glaros.** Stuffed tomatoes, moussaka, vegetable dishes—if simple, good, precooked classics with no frills are your choice, this small taverna is the place for you. It's a fine place for lunch, if you're not relaxing on the beach. ⊠ *Market St., near the central square,* ☎ *0222/92363. No credit cards.*

$$ ✕🖼 **Pegasos.** Longtime chatelaine of Christina's restaurant, the charming Australian owner and chef, Christina, has now moved her pots and pans to this new location. Happily, the food remains as savory and imaginative as ever and includes her classic warm herb bread and light cheesecake. Also recommended are the chicken fricassee and the barrel wine. To find the restaurant, stop at the tourist police and ask for directions—it's only two blocks away. By the way, friendly Christina knows everybody and everything about Skyros (and also rents rooms at her nearby Pension Nicholas. ⊠ *Skyros town,* ☎ *0222/91778. No credit cards. Closed Sun. Oct. 1–May 31.*

$$ 🖼 **Nefeli.** You'll feel like you're living in a traditional Skyrian house. This unassuming but superb little hotel has special duplexes that show off the artful nature of these islanders, with a loft king-size bed overlooking a charming main room decorated with handcrafted artifacts and embroidery, a working fireplace, kitchen, and a balcony with view of the town. Everything sparkles, including the new pool. The hotel is located five minutes from town center and the beach. ⊠ *Plageiá area, Skyros 37007,* ☎ *0222/91964,* 🅵🅰🆇 *0222/92061. 12 rooms, 9 cottages. Bar, breakfast room, pool. AE, MC, V.*

$$ 🖼 **Paliopirgos Hotel.** Five minutes between both the beach at Magazia and the town center, rooms at this intimate hotel are air-conditioned and pristinely decorated, each with a small, well-equipped kitchen area, a single and double bed, and a balcony with a sea view. The rental mopeds are fun for tooling around the island. Maria Makris is the perfect host at breakfast in the roof garden; in the evening, sip a cocktail in the same spot, and watch the sun set and the moon rise. A second hotel, **Makris Studios**, run by the family nearby offers the same particular brand of gracious hospitality and accommodates the ever-growing number of visitors. ⊠ *Skyros town 37007,* ☎ *0222/91014 or 0222/92964,* 🅵🅰🆇 *0222/92185. 9 rooms. 2 bars, air-conditioning, breakfast room. MC, V. Open winter with advance booking.*

Nightlife

BARS

Local bars with loud music are the extent of Skyros nightlife. **Calypso** (⊠ Market St.) is the oldest, opened in 1982. **Rodon** (⊠ Market St.)

is popular and open late. **Renaissance** (✉ Market St.) is another hot spot that blares on until the wee hours.

Shopping

Want to buy something really unusual for a shoe lover? Check out the multithonged *trohadia,* worn along with pantaloons by Skyrian men as part of their traditional costume. You can find these conversation stoppers at the **Argo Shop** (✉ Near Plateia Rupert Brooke).

FURNITURE

Skyrian furniture can be shipped anywhere. **Lefteris Avgoklouris** is a carpenter with flair; you may visit his workshop (✉ About 100 yards from square on right of road heading down the hill, ☎ 0222/91106). Ask around to find other master carpenters and craftspersons for original furniture and other artistic handicrafts.

POTTERY

Skyrian pottery is both utilitarian and decorative. Although you will see it all over town, the best places to shop are all on Market Street. First on the right near the square is **Emmanouil Andreou's** (✉ Market St., ☎ 0222/91631), with both local and imported ceramics. Also on the right is **Stamatis Ftoulis's** (✉ Market St., ☎ 0222/91559 or 0222/91887), with a big selection of plates, bowls, cups, and vases. You can watch him and his assistants painting the pottery at his workshop in Magazia. Perhaps the most interesting for reproductions is **Kallio,** G. Nittis's tiny atelier (✉ On left behind pale blue kiosk, just before turn for *To Brook,* ☎ 0222/92213). He specializes in meticulously exact copies of historic pieces of Anatolian origin and enjoys talking about his research over a glass of ouzo. It is hard to find pottery of this kind and quality outside Turkey.

Magazia and Molos

30 *1 km (½ mi) northeast of Skyros town.*

Coastal expansions of the main town, these two resort areas are the place to stay if you love to swim. **Magazia,** where the residents of Horio used to have their storehouses and wine presses, and **Molos,** a bit farther north, where the small fishing fleet anchors, are both growing fast. You can hire a boat, explore the isolated coastline, and stop at sea caves for a swim. Nearby are rooms to rent and tavernas serving the day's catch and local wine. From here, Skyros town is only 15 minutes away, along the steps that lead to Eternal Poetry Square past the archaeological museum.

Beaches

Just north of Molos, past low hills, fertile fields, and the odd farmhouse, a dirt road leads to the beach at **Palamari.** Between Molos and Magazia is a long, sandy beach. A short walk south of Magazia, **Pouria** offers good snorkeling, and nearby on the cape is a small treasure: a sea cave turned into a chapel.

Lodging

$$$ 🏨 **Skyros Palace.** With a big fresh-water pool and an isolated, adjacent beach, this is a water baby's idea of paradise. Separate low-rise buildings with arched windows and comfortable, traditionally furnished rooms and verandas are evocative of cubist Skyros town. ✉ *Girismata, just north of Molos, 34007,* ☎ *0222/91994, 0222/91310, or 0222/92212,* ℻ *0222/92070. 83 rooms. Restaurant, bar, cafeteria, pool. AE, MC, V. Closed Oct.–June.* ✎

$$ 🏨 **Skyron Studios.** Recently renovated and looking fresh and sparkling, these traditional white Skyrian bungalows with verandas are set among the pines overlooking the Aegean. They are fully equipped with kitchens, and can easily accommodate up to four people. ✉ *Molos, on Vina Beach, 34007,* ☎ *0222/91376,* ☎ 🖷 *01/7230957; 01/7226806 in Athens. 3 cottages, 12 rooms. No credit cards. Closed Oct.–May.*

Nightlife
DANCE CLUB

For late-night dancing, the best club is **Skiropoulo** (✉ On beach just before Magazia). Music is Western and (later on) Greek, and its laser lighting system illuminates the rocks of the acropolis after the sun has gone down. It can be reached from Eternal Poetry Square by descending the steps past the archaeological museum.

Atsitsa

③ *13 km (8 mi) west of Skyros town.*

The beaches along the way from Skyros town, Kalogriá and Kyrá Panagriá, are sheltered from the strong northern winds called the meltemi. Atsitsa, farther along on the northwest coast, has pine forests growing down the rocky coast. It is home to the chapel of **Ayios Panteleimon** (✉ On dirt road south).

Skyros Centre was founded in 1978 in this remote area. It was the first and remains the foremost center for holistic vacations. Participants come for a two-week session and can take part in activities as diverse as windsurfing, creative writing with well-known authors, art, tai chi, yoga, massage, dance, drama, and psychotherapy. Courses also take place in Skyros town, where participants live in rooms in villagers' houses. Skyros's courses are highly reputed and have been well reviewed by hardened journalists. For more information, contact the London office well in advance of leaving for Greece. ✉ *Skyros, 92 Prince of Wales Rd., London NW5 3NE, England,* ☎ *0171/267–4424; 0171/284–3065; 0222/92279 on Skyros,* 🖷 *0171/284–3063.*

Outdoor Activities and Sports
HIKING

Experienced hikers can take the 6-km (4-mi) walk around the headland from Atsitsa to Ayios Fokas, but the trek takes skill to negotiate at times and can be hazardous in bad weather.

Ayios Fokas

㉜ *12 km (7½ mi) west of Skyros town, 5 km (3 mi) south of Atsitsa.*

At Ayios Fokas, you will find three lovely white-pebbled beaches and the fabulous cooking of Kyria Kali, who serves her husband's just-caught fish with her own vegetables, homemade cheese, and bread at her small taverna. This is a real end-of-the-road atmosphere in more ways than one, because if you're coming from Atsitsa, the road south deteriorates into a rutted track, nerve-wracking even for experienced motorbike riders. If you want to stay overnight, Kyria has a couple of rooms, but without electricity or plumbing. We're talking basic.

Beaches
The **beaches** at Aherounes and Pefko (✉ 7½ km [5 mi] southeast of Ayios Fokas, near Linaria) are most accessible from the Linaria–Horio main road. At Pefko, the dirt road south from Atsitsa becomes smooth and paved again.

Vouno

Access to southern territory starts at Ahilli, 4 km (2½ mi) south of Sky-
ros town. Points south: Kalamitsa 4 km (2½ mi) south of Ahilli; Kolym-
bada 5 km (3 mi) south of Kalamitsa.

㉝ This is the mountainous southern half of Skyros, though a passable
dirt road heads south at the eastern end of the isthmus, from **Aspous**
to **Ahilli.** The little **bay of Ahilli** (from where legendary Achilles set sail
with Odysseus) is a yacht marina. Some beautiful, practically un-
touched beaches and sea caves are well worth the trip for hard-core
explorers.

Thorny bushes warped into weird shapes, oleander, and rivulets running between sharp rocks are the predominant features here; only
goats and rare Skyrian ponies can survive this desolate environment.
Many scholars consider the beautifully proportioned, diminutive horses
to be the same breed as the horses sculpted on the Parthenon frieze.
They are, alas, an endangered species, and only about 100 survive.

㉞ Pilgrims to **Rupert Brooke's grave** should continue along the wide dirt
road through this wilderness down toward the shore. As you reach the
valley, you'll catch sight of the grave, set in an olive grove, on your
left. He was buried the same night he died on Skyros, and his marble
grave was immortalized with his prescient words, "If I should die
think only this of me: /That there's some corner of a foreign field/ That
is forever England." Restored by the British Royal Navy in 1961, a
stout wrought-iron and cement railing surrounds the grave site. You
can arrange for a visit by taxi or caïque in the town.

Beaches

The beach of **Kalamitsa** (⊠ Western coast) is 4 km (2½ mi) along the
road south from Ahilli. Three tavernas are at this old harbor.

The inviting, deserted **Kolymbada** beach is 5 km (3 mi) south of
Kalamitsa.

EVIA

In any other country, an island as large and beautiful as Evia would
be a prime tourist attraction. Yet it is often ignored by travelers to Greece,
who tend to think of it not as an island but a suburb, as it is only 80
km (50 mi) north of Athens. Athenian day-trippers and weekenders
do crowd in, ironically, to get away from it all. Lying to the south and
west of the Sporades, and connected to the almost contiguous mainland by bridge and frequent ferry service, Evia is the second-largest island in the country, after Crete. It has sandy beaches, fertile valleys,
wooded mountains, and some pretty villages—just what tourists think
of as pleasantly Greek.

Long and narrow, with mountains running north to south, the island
has good roads and varied terrain, with steep cliffs in the east and beach
resorts in the west. Some towns along the main route are touristed and
commercialized while others, off the beaten track, remain peaceful and
basically unchanged. A tour of the highlights of Evia could be done in
a couple of days, as an easy island getaway from Athens, by ferry or
car. This tour begins in Karystos in the south, one of the ferry and hydrofoil ports, and ends in the north coast, characterized by fishing villages and miniresorts; you may also start where the boats port (in
Marmari, Eretria, Kimi, Aedipsos) or you can cross the bridge at
Halkidha.

Karystos

90 km (56 mi) southeast of Halkidha.

Set in a valley below Mt. Ochi on the Karystian Bay, Karystos is one of the most popular southeastern resorts in Evia, a one-hour boat ride from the mainland port of Rafina. This neoclassical town was designed in a grid pattern by a Bavarian architect named Bierbach, commissioned by King Otho. Ancient ruins are scattered through the area, and a Byzantine church is worth visiting. Near the harbor are the remains of a 14th-century Venetian castle called the **Bourtzi,** its walls filled with marble quarried near here, confiscated from an earlier temple to Apollo. Four kilometers (2½ miles) away, near the village of Myli, are the russet ruins of a 14th-century Franco-Turkish fortress, built with the colorful stone that gave the town its earlier name, Castel Rosso. An aqueduct behind it once carried spring water by tunnel to the Bourtzi.

To climb the 4,610-ft Mt. Ochi, take the path from Myli in the lush slopes above the town to the bizarre half-hewn marble columns lying like felled logs among the rocks; near the summit is a structure called the Dragon's House, thought to be a temple of Hera. The mountain was a quarry site in the Roman era, and the Dragon's House, which is unlike anything Greek, may have been erected by workers from Asia Minor. On the coast below Karystos are beaches; tucked among them is the lighthouse that marks the Cava d'Oro, the strait between Evia and Andros.

Dining and Lodging

$$ ✕ **Kavo d'Oro.** This gold-star taverna has outdoor dining and local wine to go along with the hearty home-style Greek meals, which feature meat stews, vegetables cooked in olive oil, great stuffed grape leaves, and freshly cooked eggplant. ⊠ *Parados Sachtouri,* ☎ *0224/22326. No credit cards. Closed Oct.–Dec.*

$$$ ▥ **Apollon Suite Hotel.** Shining white, and modern throughout, this all-suites hotel's accommodations have separate living areas overlooking palm-studded lawns, a terraced pool, and the beach beyond. For families or friends traveling together, it is an especially good value. ⊠ *Beachside, Karystos 34001,* ☎ FAX *0224/22045 through 0224/22049. 36 suites. Restaurant, pool, meeting rooms. MC, V. Closed Nov.–Mar.*

Marmari

80 km (49½ mi) southeast of Halkidha, 10 km (6 mi) northwest of Karystos.

The port of Marmari, rapidly sprouting with hotels and summer homes, is served by Rafina on the mainland. The road north goes inland along the middle of the island, flaunting glimpses of Frankish watchtowers and bisecting tiny villages inhabited by Greeks of Albanian origin. Their ancestors were brought by the Venetians during the 14th century, and later by the Turks, to supplement the declining local population. Many still speak Albanian at home, and their own Greek dialect.

En Route On the drive from Marmari to Eretria you'll pass several interesting towns and sights. **Stira,** set amid streams and forests, has an ancient citadel. **Nea Stira,** on a bay, has beaches with changing facilities and mysterious, huge blocks of stone. In this wooded area, fossils of prehistoric animals have been discovered. **Aliveri,** along with Byzantine churches and an old tower, also has a major power plant belching smoke.

Eretria

15 km (9 mi) southeast of Halkidha, 65 km (40 mi) northwest of Marmari.

In ancient times, this was Evia's second city, after Halkidha—a major maritime power, with a school of philosophy, founded in the 3rd century BC, by one of Plato's pupils. Today, drab, dusty Eretria is regarded just as a place where people board the 30-minute ferry to the mainland. Neither its interesting ruins nor its jewel of a museum is even signposted, but do persevere.

West of the acropolis are the ruins of a temple, a palace, and Eretria's **ancient theater** (⊠ North of the museum). It has two vaulted passageways—one leading to, the other under, the orchestra—no doubt used for deus ex machina solutions and spectral apparitions. You can tour the ruins at any time.

The **museum** (⊠ Odhos Archaio Theatrou), set amid cypress trees, opened in 1991 in collaboration with the Swiss School of Archaeology, which is responsible for digging at Eretria. It has beautifully exhibited finds from the area—including magnificent Black Figure vases, ex-votos galore, and children's toys and jewelry. ⊠ *Odos Archaio Theatrou,* ☎ *0229/62206.* 🎫 *500 dr./€1.47* ⊙ *Tues.–Sun. 8:30–3.*

Ask the guard to take you to the **House of the Mosaics,** five minutes away, to view the 4th-century BC treasures. (Hours are the same as for the museum; ☞ *above.*)

Kimi

50 km (31 mi) northeast of Halkidha, 40 km (29 mi) northeast of Eretria.

Kimi, the port for Skyros, is a fishing village that sits high on a plateau, overlooking its harbor. It has stone houses; a busy main square; pine, fir, and mulberry trees everywhere; and good beaches (follow the secondary roads).

In a traditional house is a charming little **folk museum,** which has displays of memorabilia, costumes, and historical facts. Probably the dried-fig capital of Greece, Kimi was an important port in the late 19th century and has a good deal of Victoriana and some diaphanous silk garments; it was once known for its silk production. It is also the birthplace of George Papanicolaou, who developed the Pap test technique to detect uterine cancer. ⊠ *On road to the port,* ☎ *0222/22011.* 🎫 *400 dr./€1.17* ⊙ *Daily 10–1 and 6–8:30.*

NEED A
BREAK?
Stop to rest your feet at **To Balkoni** (⊠ Above port), with its splendid view of the extravagant hillside vegetation and the sleepy, one-street port below.

Dining

$$ ✕ **Lalari.** Set on the waterfront, this taverna is one you can count on for succulent seafood, dressed simply with lemon. Locals recommend the grilled shrimp and octopus, washed down with local wine. Service is caring, outside tables are appealing, and live music adds to the experience. ⊠ *At the harborside, Kimi,* ☎ *0424/22624. No credit cards. Closed Nov.–Apr.*

Halkidha

90 km (56 mi) northeast of Athens.

Halkidha (Chalkis), Evia's largest town, has been linked by a bridge to the mainland since the 5th century BC. It was a major producer of weaponry, and its metalwork can be seen at Olympia, Delphi, and other ancient sites. The current rushing through the 50-yard channel changes direction several times a day, confounding travel plans in past generations and perplexing scientists. Halkidha is still a major commercial center; cement factories blight its southern suburbs. It is a big market town, with a population mix of Orthodox Greeks, Muslims, and Jews working together, reflecting the trade routes of Evia over the centuries. Though the town may have more urban problems than blessings, you can dine royally in its fish tavernas for a pittance.

OFF THE
BEATEN PATH

STENI – If you head 30 km (18½ mi) north from Halkidha's extended suburbs, you'll see signs for Steni, a pretty village with clear mountain springs, halfway up Mt. Dirfis, Evia's highest mountain. At 5,725 ft, it's a challenge to hikers, a boon to botanists because of its many unique species, and to ordinary mortals a place of glorious views. You can drive a good way up it.

Dining and Lodging

$$ ✕ **Tsaf.** The most traditional ouzeri in Halkidha, this is a wonderful place to try all types of seafood (especially shellfish). The *poikilia* (assorted mezedes) is grandiose, while the *kidonia* is heartily recommended. Don't be put off by the fact that these clams are raw: with a drizzle of lemon juice and accompanied by an ice-cold ouzo, you'll find they are the perfect summer meal. There is no phone. ⊠ *Papanastasiou 3, Agora Sq. No credit cards.*

$$–$$$ ⊞ **Lucy.** Right on the beachfront of Halkidha and in the midst of all the merriment, this 1950s hotel was built with style and high standards in mind. Time has certainly taken its toll—yet the hotel's singular design imbues it with a charm that some would call "retro chic." Better, the Lucy always offers impeccable and eminent service. Guest rooms are spacious and feature double-glazed windows (which keep out the noise of the busy strip below); most of them offer a panoramic view of the gulf, the fortress, and Evia's old bridge. Try to book rooms on the forth and fifth floors, as they have been recently refurbished. ⊠ *Leof. Voudouri 10, Halkidha, 34100,* ☎ *0221/23831 through 0221/ 23835,* FAX *0221/22051. 93 rooms. Restaurant, bar, minibars, meeting rooms. MC, V.* ✎

En Route On the coast going north from Halkidha, the road runs parallel to a river shaded by enormous plane trees. One of them is so huge it takes 27 men to encircle its trunk.

Aedipsos

80 km (50 mi) northwest of Halkidha, 30 km (18½ mi) northwest of Limni.

For a therapeutic spa with state-of-the-art facilities, head to the fishing village of Aedipsos, via the corniche road full of spectacular views. Here hot springs have been soothing aches and pains since antiquity, and the likes of Aristotle and Plutarch have sung its praises. Take a whiff of the sulfurous vapors and a peek at the yellow rocks, and if you're stiff from all that driving, take a dip. Hotels here have the bubbling waters piped right into their private rooms. The ferry here goes to Arkitsa, the National Road, and to Athens.

Lodging

$$$$ ⊞ **Thermae Sylla Grand Hotel.** This is the lap of luxury—literally. If you want to take to the waters, this place combines the advantages of a health spa (with an emphasis on thalassotherapy) and an island holiday. Set a mere 50 yards from the beach, this spectacular hotel comes complete with health food and lean cuisine. The 1998 renovation added a spacious and stylish new wing, in relaxing earthy tones and with enormous rooms to regale guests. Ultimately, what makes this hotel so special is that Aedipsos's noted sulfur springs are set right on the grounds. ✉ *Aedipsos,* ☎ *0226/60100; 01/211–0601 or 01/211–0602 in Athens,* FAX *0266/22055; 01/211–0603 in Athens. 230 rooms. Restaurant, pool, wading pool, beauty salon, sauna, spa, tennis court, exercise room, waterskiing, parasailing, windsurfing. AE, MC, V.* 🐾

THE NORTHERN SPORADES A TO Z

Arriving and Departing

By Bus and Ferry

For information, it is always best first to contact the EOT (☞ Visitor Information, *below*), where someone will be able to give you the information you need in English. Car ferries vary, but most provide clean and comfortable service and private overnight quarters between destinations.

ALONNISOS, SKIATHOS, AND SKOPELOS

Leaving from Athens's Terminal B, buses for Lamia stop in Ayios Konstandinos (usually just called Ayios), the main port for the Sporades. The bus fare is about 3,000 dr./€8.84, and the trip takes about 2½ hours. There are at least two or three ferries per day during the summer, fewer in winter: check with the EOT's Athens office (☞ Visitor Information, *below*). Tickets are available from several travel agents on the dock. From Ayios Konstandinos, the trip costs 3,300 dr./9.73 to Skiathos and about 1,000 dr./€2.94 extra to Skopelos or Alonnisos; the trip takes about 3½ hours to Skiathos, and about an hour between each island. Tickets for the islands can be bought at the **travel agencies** (☞ *below*). (Hydrofoils are twice as expensive but also twice as fast.)

SKYROS AND EVIA

You can buy boat tickets on the dock when you get off the bus. The boat trip from Kimi takes two hours and costs 1,700 dr./€5. The return boat from Skyros leaves at 8 AM except Sunday (3 PM).

Buses (☎ 01/831–7147 Athens–Ayios Konstandinos; 01/831–7163 Athens–Skyros).

Port Authorities (☎ 0424/65595 Alonnisos; 0235/31759 Ayios Konstandinos; 0222/22606 Kimi; 0427/22017 Skiathos; 0424/22180 Skopelos; 0222/96475 Skyros).

By Car

SKIATHOS, SKOPELOS, AND ALONNISOS

You must drive to the port of Ayios Konstandinos (Ayios) and from there take the ferry. The drive to Ayios from Athens takes about two hours. Visitors with cars might have to reserve a place on the car ferry a day ahead.

SKYROS AND EVIA

You must drive to the port of Kimi on Evia. From Athens, take the Athens–Lamia National Road to Skala Oropou and make the 30-minute ferry crossing to Eretria on Evia (every half hour in the daytime). No reservations are needed.

Because it is so close to the mainland, you can skip the ferry system and drive directly to Evia over a short land bridge connecting Ayios Minas on the mainland with Halkidha. From Athens, about 80 km (50 mi) away, take the National Road 1 to the Schimatari exit, and then follow the signs to Halkidha.

By Hydrofoil

The **Flying Dolphins** are about twice as fast as ferries and cost twice as much. They call at ports more frequently, and with careful planning in summer it is possible to use them to travel the entire distance from Evia to Skyros and the other Sporades, continuing on to either Volos or Ayios Konstandinos. Ask any travel agent for a timetable.

From Athens, a **Ceres Lines** bus (Pireas: ☎ 01/428–0001 or 01/428–3555) leaves Syntagma (Constitution) Square to meet Flying Dolphins at Ayios Konstandinos. Ask for information when you book. Fares are as follows: bus from Athens to Ayios Konstandinos, 3,000 dr./€8.84; Ayios Konstandinos to Skiathos, Skopelos, and Alonnisos, at least three times per day, 6,000 dr./17.69–9,000 dr./€2:26.54; Kimi to Skyros, the other Sporades, and Volos, Tuesday only, 4,600 dr./€13.56–19,000 dr./€56.

By Plane

Alonnisos, Skopelos, and Evia have no air service. **Skiathos airport** (✉ 5 minutes northeast of Skiathos town, ☎ 0427/22049) handles direct charter flights from many European cities and **Olympic Airways** (☎ 01/936–9111 Athens; 0427/22220 Skiathos) flights (at least daily, more often in summer) from Athens's **Ellinikon Airport West Terminal** (☎ 01/969–9466). The trip takes 40 minutes; the fare is 12,200 dr./€35.98. In summer there are daily **Olympic Airways** (Skyros: ☎ 0222/91600) flights from Athens to **Skyros airport** (✉ 11 km [8 mi] northwest of Skyros town, ☎ 0222/91625). The flight takes 50 minutes; the fare is 13,300 dr./€39.23

Getting Around

By Boat

SKIATHOS

Small motorboats can be rented at the **Marine Center** (✉ Near the airport runway, ☎ 0427/22888 or 0427/21178, 𝐅𝐀𝐗 0427/23262).

ALONNISOS

Boats can also be rented at the **Marine Center** (✉ Near the Elinoil gas station on the waterfront, ☎ 0424/65206).

By Bus

SKIATHOS

Buses on Skiathos leave Skiathos town to make the beach-run as far as Koukounaries every 30 minutes from early morning till 11:30 PM.

SKOPELOS

Buses on Skopelos run six times a day from Skopelos town to Glossa and Loutraki, stopping at the beaches.

ALONNISOS

Alonnisos has one bus that makes the trip from Patitiri to Alonnisos town (Chora) and back from 9 AM to 2 PM only.

SKYROS

Skyros buses carry ferry passengers between Linaria and Horio, stopping in Molos in summer.

EVIA

All cities are serviced with frequent bus service. For information contact the **KTEL bus station** (☎ 0221/22026).

By Caïque

On all islands, caïques leave from the main port for the most popular beaches, and inter-island excursions are made between Skiathos, Skopelos, and Alonnisos. You can also hire a caïque (haggle over the price) to tour around the islands; they are generally the preferred way to get around by day. For popular routes, captains have signs posted showing their destinations and departure times. On Skyros, check with Skyros Travel (☞ Travel Agencies, *below*) for caïque tours. In Alonnisos, day trips are organized to the many smaller islands in the vicinity.

By Ferry or Hydrofoil

Journeys between islands are usually made by ferry or hydrofoil. There are usually several boats per day between Skiathos and Skopelos, and they almost always serve Alonnisos as well. Hydrofoils usually ply between these islands at least three times per day. Between Skyros and the other Sporades there is no regular boat service, but there is a hydrofoil on Tuesdays, and sometimes on other days.

Because schedules are likely to change, check the times listed outside travel agencies.

By Motorbike and Car

The road networks on all four islands are so rudimentary that cars are not really needed, but it's not a bad idea to rent one for a day to get a feel for the island, then use the bus or a motorbike thereafter. Four-wheel drives and other cars can be rented everywhere. If you rent a motorbike, however, be extra cautious: many of those for hire are in poor condition. The locals are not used to the heavy summer traffic on their narrow roads, and accidents provide the island clinics with 80% of their summer business. Check with the travel agencies (☞ *below*) for information.

By Taxi

All the islands have taxis waiting at the ferry landings. Even Alonnisos has three. They are unmetered, so negotiate your fare in advance.

Contacts and Resources

Emergencies

SKIATHOS
Police (☎ 0427/21111). **Medical center** (☎ 0427/22222).

SKOPELOS
Police (☎ 0424/22235 Skopelos town; 0424/33333 Glossa). **Medical center** (☎ 0424/22222).

ALONNISOS
Police (✉ Patitiri, ☎ 0424/65205). **Medical center** (☎ 0424/65208).

SKYROS
Police (☎ 0222/91274). **Medical center** (☎ 0222/92222).

EVIA
Police (✉ Karystos, ☎ 0224/22262; ✉ Marmari, ☎ 0224/31333; ✉ Eretria, ☎ 0229/61111; ✉ Kimi, ☎ 0222/22555; ✉ Halkidha, ☎ 0221/87000 or 0221/83333; ✉ Prokopi, ☎ 0227/41203; ✉ Limni, ☎ 0227/31209; ✉ Aedipsos, ☎ 0226/22456). **Medical center** (✉ Karystos, ☎ 0224/22207; ✉ Marmari, ☎ 0224/31300; ✉ Eretria, ☎ 0229/62222; ✉ Kimi, Oxylithos, ☎ 0222/46202; ✉ Halkidha, ☎ 0221/21901; ✉ Prokopi, ☎ 0227/41212; ✉ Limni, ☎ 0227/32222; ✉ Aedipsos, ☎ 0226/55311).

Travel Agencies

SKIATHOS

Mare Nostrum Travel (✉ Papadiamantis 21, 37002, ☎ 0427/21463 or 0427/21464, FAX 0427/21793), aside from handling all your inquiries and issuing boat and plane tickets, is the only American Express representative in the Sporades.

SKOPELOS

Madro Travel (✉ On waterfront, ☎ 0424/22145, 0424/22300, 0424/22767, 0424/23060, or 0424/23061, FAX 0424/22941).

ALONNISOS

Alonnisis Travel & Tourism Agency (✉ Near waterfront, ☎ 0424/61588 or 0424/65619, FAX 0424/65511). Anything and everything on the island can be arranged here.

SKYROS

Skyros Travel (✉ Market St., Skyros town 34007, ☎ 0222/91123 or 0222/91600, FAX 0222/92123) has a virtual monopoly on hydrofoil tickets, rooms, excursions, and car rentals.

Visitor Information

Greek National Tourist Organization (GNTO or EOT) office (✉ Karageorgi Servias 2, in the National Bank Bldg., Athens, ☎ 01/322–2545). **Travel agents** can be helpful on Alonnisos and Skyros.

SKIATHOS

Tourist police (✉ At inland end of Odhos Papadhiamndiou, ☎ 0427/23172).

SKOPELOS

Tourist offices and facilities (✉ On waterfront under a row of mulberry trees or on first street parallel to it). **Skopelos Municipality** (✉ Chora, ☎ 0424/22205).

4 EPIRUS AND THESSALY

IOANNINA, METSOVO, AND THE METEORA MONASTERIES

Monasteries-in-air, the seraglio of Ali Pasha, and the Dodona oracle all beckon the inquisitive traveler to remote Epirus and Thessaly. At Meteora, a spiritual center of Orthodox Greece, the quiet contemplation of generations of monks is preserved in wondrously frescoed monasteries hovering on rocky pedestals above the plain. Nearby, spectacular mountain passes reveal shepherd villages with richly costumed women whispering the strange, secret Vlach vernacular. Over in Epirus, discover Ioannina and track the exotic shadows of that larger-than-life Byronic figure Ali Pasha.

By Toula
Bogdanos

Updated by B.
Samantha
Stenzel

BORDERED BY ALBANIA AND THE IONIAN SEA, the province of Epirus is a land of stark mountains, lush forests, swift rivers, and remote villages marked with unique customs, language, and architecture. Epirus means "the mainland," standing in contrast to the neighboring islands of Corfu, Paxi, and Lefkas, strung along the littoral. The abrupt changes from the delicately shaded green of the idyllic olive and orange groves on the coast to the tremendous solidity of the bare mountains have been faithfully depicted by that intrepid Victorian author and artist Edward Lear (of limerick fame). This was the splendid massive landscape that came to cast its spell over Lord Byron, who traveled here to meet the most extraordinary figure in modern Greek history, Ali Pasha. The tour described below begins in the Epirote capital of Ioannina, which still bears many vestiges of this larger-than-life figure who seems to have stepped from the pages of the *Arabian Nights*.

Sinan Ali Pasha was just the latest tyrant in this region, for millennia a stormy backwater of tribal warfare. Mountainous provinces may often be spared a surfeit of history, but in Greece the last 4,000 years have been so crammed with momentous events that Epirus received its fair share. Going back in time, and an easy trip southwest of Ioannina, you can visit Dodona, the site of the oldest oracle in Greece. The itinerary continues on to the thriving traditional village of Metsovo in the Pindos Mountains and over the Katara Pass on one of the most dramatic roads in Greece. It ends in the fertile province of Thessaly where, on the edge of the plain, the Byzantine-era monasteries of Meteora seem to float in midair, built atop bizarrely shaped pinnacles that tower over the town of Kalambaka.

Viewing these extraordinary rock-pinnacle monasteries—today one of Greece's most famous attractions—it's easy to credit the story about the original ascent being achieved by way of a rope fastened to an eagle's leg, whose nest lay atop one of the rocks. The days of jointed ladders, pulled up in an emergency, are no more, and the nets are strictly limited to hauling up supplies, rather than terrified visitors. Today, a comfortable road winds ingeniously through the sandstone labyrinth close to the breathtaking cliff, making Meteora a destination for thousands of travelers eager to discover an extinct way of life, whose infinite pain and labor required a religious fervor incomprehensible to later generations.

For a literary treat, get ahold of Tim Salmon's book *Unwritten Places*, published by Lycabettus Press. It is a fascinating account of his decade-long wanderings over the ancient mule paths and summer pastures of the Pindos mountains in Epirus south of Albania and in Thessaly, focusing on his friendship with a family of Vlach shepherds. It gives an insight into the customs of this elusive group and an historical background starting with the battles and occupation of World War II through the turbulent Greek civil war, times in which many of the significant events took place in Epirus.

Pleasures and Pastimes

Dining
The curious diner will muse over Epirus's local specialties. In Ioannina's lakeside restaurants you can sample unusual dishes such as those using ingredients culled from lakes: frogs' legs, eel, crayfish, and turtles. But Epriote kitchens also have delicious tried-and-true recipes, such as *moschato kokinisto* (tomato-based veal stew with carrots, onions, and

peas), lamb in lemon sauce, and *ladhera* (stove-top vegetable stews made with artichoke hearts, beans, okra, and tomatoes). For Greeks, Metsovo brings to mind the costly but delectable smoked Metsovone cheese and Katogi wine pressed from French Bordeaux grapes grown locally. Other Metsovo specialties include boiled goat, *trahanas* soup (made from cracked wheat boiled in milk and dried), and sausages stuffed with leeks. Those with a penchant for sweets will savor *bougatsa,* a local custard served fresh at breakfast time at many places. For dessert, *galaktobouriko,* a creamy custard encased in phyllo dough and soaked with brandy-spiked citrus syrup, is a heavenly treat when served fresh from the oven; other treats include *kataifi Ioanniotiko* (shredded wheat pastry, Ioannina style) and baked apples. In all but the fanciest restaurants, check out what's cooking, because the menus change seasonally. Informal dress is usually appropriate.

CATEGORY	COST*
$$$$	over 9,000 dr. (€26.54)
$$$	5,000 dr.–9,000 dr. (€14.74–€26.54)
$$	3,000 dr.–5,000 dr. (€8.84–€14.74)
$	under 3,000 dr. (€8.84)

per person for appetizer, main course, and fruit or dessert, including taxes and service charge but no drinks

Lodging

Except for the best hotels, rooms in the region are simply decorated. Though prices don't vary much within each government classification category, quality does. Ask to see the room first, and don't assume anything; if you have special requests, such as a mountain view, a *diplo krevati* (double bed) rather than a *diklino* (twin bed), a balcony, or a bathtub, speak up. Rooms are usually easy to find in Ioannina. Reservations might be necessary for Kalambaka, which is packed with tour groups in late spring and summer, and in Metsovo during ski season or the town's July 26 festival. In these two towns, private rooms are likely to be far cheaper than comparable hotel rooms—look for advertisements as you arrive. Off-season, prices drop drastically from those listed here, and you should always try to negotiate. Hotels in the $$$–$$$$ range are assumed to have air-conditioning and televisions; listings indicate them only when they are present in hotels in the $–$$ range.

CATEGORY	COST*
$$$$	over 45,000 dr. (€132)
$$$	25,000 dr.–45,000 dr. (€73.74–€132)
$$	15,000 dr.–25,000 dr. (€44.24–€73.74)
$	under 15,000 dr. (€44.24)

for a standard double room in high season, including taxes but not breakfast, unless indicated

✍ *following the text of a review is your signal that the property has a Web site, where you will find details and, usually, images; for a link, visit www.fodors.com/urls.*

Exploring Epirus and Thessaly

The region consists of two areas: the mountainous province of Epirus, with villages such as Metsovo and its capital, Ioannina, to the west; and the Thessalian plain, an agricultural heartland with Meteora at its edge.

Numbers in the text correspond to numbers in the margin and on the Epirus and Thessaly map.

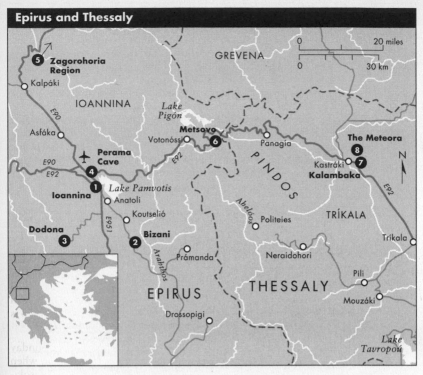

Epirus and Thessaly

Great Itineraries

The distance from Ioannina to Meteora is small, but the mountain road that connects the two cannot be negotiated swiftly; a tour of the region should take this into account. If you only have two days, visit the Meteora monasteries and head to Metsovo if you have time. In three days, you can spend a half day and night in Ioannina, visit Metsovo on the way to Meteora, and have a full-day tour of the monasteries. Five days will allow you to cover, at a fair pace, all the sites described in this chapter, or to concentrate on a smaller area. Eight days will allow a thorough exploration of the region, leaving the tourist trail to visit remote villages and sights.

IF YOU HAVE 3 DAYS

Take a morning flight from Athens to 🏨 **Ioannina** ① and spend the late morning in the citadel, visit the island in the afternoon, and stay overnight. The next day visit **Metsovo** ⑥ on your way to 🏨 **Kalambaka** ⑦ and spend the night there. Spend a full day at **Meteora** ⑧, returning to Ioannina for the night.

IF YOU HAVE 5 DAYS

Start with 🏨 **Ioannina** ① and visit **Dodona** ③ in the morning to see the ancient oracle of Zeus. See the citadel in the afternoon and the nearby island that night. The next morning head to the **Perama cave** ④, then on to 🏨 **Metsovo** ⑥; spend the day exploring Metsovo (and be sure to get a taste of the Metsovone cheese!). After staying overnight in Metsovo, move on to 🏨 **Kalambaka** ⑦ to make the trek along the monastery route of **Meteora** ⑧. After staying overnight in either Kalambaka or Kastraki, on your last day return to Ioannina and visit sights you may not have been able to fit in on your first day: the archaeological museum, Folk Museum, and old market.

With eight days you can explore the region at your leisure; if you prefer a speedy pace, you might find yourself with too much time on your hands. Base yourself in 🏛 **Ioannina** ① for three nights, taking two days to visit the island, citadel, and museums of the city. To get the most out of the experience, the third day rent a car or hire a taxi to visit the **Perama cave** ④ and explore mountain villages in the **Zagorochoria Region** ⑤ northwest of Ioannina and spend the third night there at one of the villages (like Megalo Papingo) or return to Ioannina. Continue the fourth day by driving to 🏛 **Kalambaka** ⑦ and stay there for a couple of nights while visiting the monasteries of **Meteora** ⑧. On your sixth day, head back west and stop at **Metsovo** ⑥ and spend the night there. Midday on the next day, return to Ioannina for your last night and fly from here to Athens or Thessaloniki the next morning.

When to Tour

As in all of Greece, places are more likely to be open in the mornings than in the afternoons, and museums and sites are often closed on Mondays. Metsovo might be blissfully cool even in high summer (especially at night), making the town *panagyri* (festival) for Agia Paraskevi, held July 26, quite pleasant, but the heat is oppressive elsewhere in this region at this time. The mountain roads to Metsovo are often blocked and impassable in winter; if you get there, however, the ski center will be open. The ancestral home of Baron Michalis Tositsa in Metsovo is closed on Thursday, so plan accordingly.

The Meteora monasteries are open Wednesday, Saturday, and Sunday year-round. They attract considerably fewer visitors in winter, when you might find an enhanced sense of spirituality in their windy isolation.

EPIRUS

Ioannina, Dodona, and Metsovo

Ancient Epirus was once a huge country that stretched from modern-day Albania (an area the Greeks still call "Northern Epirus" and where Greek is still spoken by large communities) to the Gulf of Arta and modern Preveza. The region is bordered by the Mediterranean Sea to the west, the islands of Lefkadha to the south, and Corfu to the north. Inland it is defined by a tangle of mountain peaks and upland plains, and the climate is markedly Balkan.

Despite the region's natural physical barriers, it has been invaded many times. Its hinterland character has made it the perfect hideout for rebels and has led it to be inhabited by disparate peoples. In ancient times the province was ruled by a king, the last being the famous Pyrrhus (319–272 BC), who united the tribes of Epirus and began an expansionist policy that mimicked that of Alexander the Great. But his territorial gains came through overwhelming loss of lives, giving rise to the expression "Pyrrhic victory."

The name "Ioannina" was first documented in 1020 and may have been taken from an older monastery of Saint John. Although invaded by Normans in 1080, Epirus gained in importance after the influx of refugees from Constantinople and the Morea beginning in 1205 and was made a despotate. Ioannina was subsequently made the capital of Epirus and fortified by Michalis Angelos, the first despot. In 1345 AD the Serbs captured Epirus and established a monarchy from 1348 to 1386 AD. In 1431, Ioannina surrendered to the Ottomans and and Epirus remained a part of its empire until it became part of Greece in 1913, almost 100 years after Greece's liberation from the Turks. The cultural influence from its Ottoman occupation is evident. Besides this influence, Metsovo and the surrounding area contain the largest concentration of the non-Greek population know as the Vlachs, nomadic shepherds said to be descendants of legionnaries from garrisons on the Via Egnatia, one of the Roman Empire's main east–west routes. The Vlachs speak a Romance language (related to Italian and Romanian).

In this section we describe—in geographical succession—the capital of the province, Ioannina, with its rich Ottoman heritage; nearby Dodona, most ancient of Greek oracles; and the traditional Vlach mountain village of Metsovo to the west, perhaps the most accessible of these villages and a good base for exploring.

Ioannina

❶ *305 km (189½ mi) northwest of Athens, 204 km (126¾ mi) west-southwest of Thessaloniki.*

On the rocky promontory of Lake Pamvotis lies Ioannina, its fortress punctuated by mosques and minarets whose reflections, along with those of the snowy peaks of the Pindos range, appear in the calm water. Although on first impression the city may seem noisy and undistinguished, its old quarter, encircled by the somber castle walls, and its peaceful islet, called Nissa, or "island," where nightingales still sing and fishermen mend their nets, make it an ideal retreat from the bustle of Athens. Today, Ioannina is the capital of Epirus, with a population of around 100,000. A lively provincial city, it not only preserves its rich heritage, but has also developed a thriving contemporary cultural scene, thanks to a resident branch of the Greek national university (and the subsequent proliferation of good restaurants and lively bars). Ioannina's history, however, is what draws the visitor, who can happily give the city a couple of days of exploration to fully discover its beautiful setting and outstanding folk architecture. With the best extant examples remaining within the Kastro walls (and in the neighborhoods surrounding them), Ioannina's historic mansions, folk houses, seraglios, and bazaars are a reminder of the city's illustrious past as a wealthy educational and intellectual center. Set at a crossroads of trading, the city's landscape is sculpted by Balkan, Ottoman, and Byzantine influences, all of which combine to create a unique—and uniquely seductive—atmosphere.

This is particularly the case during the first two weeks of July when the city's International Folk Festival is held. For those seeking the haunting *klarino* (clarinet) music and graceful circle dances of Epirus such as the *pogonisios* and *beratis,* this is a fascinating festival. Local groups also perform eerie polyphonic singing, another unique folk tradition rooted in Epirus. Another event, the Epirotika Festival, is held in late July and August and also includes performances of local music and dancing. In fact, throughout the summer months, the abundance of panagyria for saints' days means more live music, often performed by well-known groups such as the Halkias family, legendary clarinet players. During these celebrations, and often at the many weddings held during the summer, visitors are often invited to join in the fun (although keep in mind there are certain Epirote dances and rituals which are restricted by common consent to the locals).

Founded by Emperor Justinian in AD 527, Ioannina suffered under many rulers: it was invaded by the Normans in 1082, made a dependency of the Serbian kingdom in 1345, and conquered by the Turks in 1431. Above all, this was Ali Pasha's city, where, during its zenith from 1788 to 1821, the cunning despot carved a fiefdom from much of western Greece. Born in the 1740s in Tepeline, Albania, Ali rose to power by unscrupulous means. He was made pasha of Trikala in 1787 and a year later seized Ioannina, the largest town in Greece. For the next 33 years, Ali pursued his lifelong ambition: to break from the Ottoman Empire and create his own kingdom. He paid only token tribute to the Sultan and allied himself according to his needs with the French, the British, and the Turks. In 1797 he collaborated with Napoléon; the next year he seized Preveza from the French; and by 1817 he was wooing the British and Admiral Nelson, who gave him Parga. His territory extended from the Ionian sea to the Pindos range and from Vaona in the north to Arta in the south.

The most notorious ruler of Epirus, Ali Pasha had a guard of assassins to carry out his plots of murder and brigandage. Historic accounts always focused on the fact that he had an insatiable libido and combed the countryside looking for attractive concubines, eventually accumulating a harem numbering in the hundreds. He attacked the Turkish Porte (from "Sublime Porte" [or gate] of the Sultan's palace, where justice was administered; by extension, the Ottoman government), and he brutalized his Greek subjects.

Perhaps Ali's most infamous crime was the drowning of the beautiful Kyra Frosini, his son's mistress, and 16 other women, by tying them in stone-laden bags and dumping them in the lake. Apparently, he was in love with Frosini, who rejected him, and, spurred on by his jealous daughter-in-law, Ali had Frosini killed on charges of infidelity. He regretted his deed and ordered that 1,000 *kantaria* (250 pounds) of sugar be thrown into the lake to sweeten the water Frosini would drink. A local superstition persists that Frosini's ghost hovers over the lake on moonlit nights.

Start your city walk at the entrance to the citadel on Dionysiou Skylosofou Street and proceed to the Aslan Pasha Tzami to study its exterior and grounds before going inside to see theMunicipal Museum. Then walk over to the Fortress to look at the collection in the Byzantine Museum. Take a look inside the adjacent Fethiye Tzami, if possible. Stop for a drink or snack at the Fortress Café. Continue on Paleologou Street to the synagogue on Ioustinianou, just inside the Citadel's western wall—call before visiting if you want to arrange a tour of the synagogue. Continue to the Old Bazaar, near the gates at Ethnikis Antistasios and Averoff streets. Follow Mitropoleos Street to the Archaeological Museum and visit its impressive collection. Walk to nearby Platia Akadamias and from there take Dodonis Street south to Michail Angelou Street, turn right, and walk a short distance to the Folklore Museum. After you view its displays, go back to Dodonis Street and head northeast to Karamanli Street, which follows the west wall of the Citadel. On the northeast corner of Platia Mavili, board a boat to Nissi. When you leave the boat, go to the Ali Pasha Museum, then have lunch at one of the lakeside restaurants. Afterward go to see the monasteries, particularly Agios Nikolaos ton Filanthropon. You may want to browse for silver gifts in some of the small tourist shops and then head back to the dock for the return trip to Ioannina.

The spacious, well-arranged **archaeological museum** is the best in the area, with finds from several ancient sites. (Your children may prefer to stay in the nearby **playground**.) Of special interest are the artifacts from ancient Dodona, a 200,000-year-old Paleolithic stone axe found near Preveza, and two winsome bronze statuettes from the late 3rd century BC of two boys playing, one throwing a ball and the other holding a dove. The bronze warrior wearing nothing but a waist guard to protect his belly is of the archaic period (first half of the 6th century BC). Best of all is the collection of inscribed lead tablets (6th–3rd centuries BC) found at the oracle. The questions for the gods are translated for your amusement: "Shall I take another wife?" "Has Pistos stolen the wool from the mattress?" "Will it be all right to buy the small lake by the sanctuary of Demeter?" Read the evolution of the temple of Zeus, especially if you plan to visit the site (☞ Dodona, *below*). ⊠ *Platia 25 Martiou,* ☎ *0651/33357 or 0651/25490.* ☜ *500 dr./€1.47.* ☉ *Tues.–Sun. 8:30–3.*

Along with the archaeological museum, Ioannina's other main attraction is the **citadel,** at the lakeside end of Odhos Averoff. The citadel's massive stone walls, which once dropped into the lake on three sides, are more or less intact; Ali Pasha completely rebuilt them in 1815. The city's once-large Romaniote Jewish population, said to date from the time of Alexander the Great, lived within the walls, alongside Turks and Christians. The Jews were deported by the Nazis during World War II, never to return; of the 4,000-odd around the turn of the century, there are fewer than 100 remaining today. Outside the citadel walls, near the lake, a **monument** at Karamanli and Soutsou streets commemorates the slaughter of the Jewish community. The dignified **Synagogue of Ioannina,** active during the days of the Romaniote Jewish community but no longer in regular use, is a couple of blocks inside the citadel gate. Generally, it is only open for religious services on holidays, but a tour can be arranged by making a reservation with guides Sam Cohen and Avram Zivolis (phone numbers listed below). ⊠ *Ioasaf Eliyia 18-B and Ioustianou St.,* ☎ *0651/28541 or 0651/28801.* ☜ *Free.* ☉ *Tour by appointment, otherwise closed except for religious holidays.*

Tree-lined **Dionissiou Filosofou Street** (named for a defrocked Trikala bishop who led an ill-fated uprising against the Turks in 1611 and was flayed alive as a result), which circles the **castle** along the lake, is ideal for a late-afternoon stroll. A moat, now filled, ran around the southwest landward side, and today the walls divide the old town—with its rose-laden pastel-colored houses, overhanging balconies, cobblestone streets, and birdsong—from the new. ⊠ *At lakeside end of Odhos Averoff.*

At the north end of the citadel is the remarkably well-preserved **Aslan Mosque,** now the municipal museum, whose collection recalls the three communities (Greek, Turkish, Jewish) that lived together inside the fortress from 1400 to 1611. In Greece, it is rare to glimpse the interior of a mosque. The vestibule has recesses for shoes and, inscribed over the doorway, is the name of Aslan Pasha and THERE IS ONLY ONE GOD, ALLAH, AND MUHAMMED IS HIS PROPHET. The mosque retains its original decoration and *mehrab* (altar), which faces Mecca. Exhibited around the room are a walnut and mother-of-pearl table from Ali Pasha's period, ornate inlaid *hamam* (Turkish bath) shoes on tall wooden platforms, clothes chests, and a water pipe. ⊠ *North end of citadel,* ☎ *0651/26356.* ☜ *700 dr./€2.06.* ☉ *Winter: weekdays 8–3, weekends 9–3; summer: weekdays 8–8, weekends 9–7.*

The **fortress,** called *Its Kale* by the Turks, is where Ali Pasha built his palace. Full-scale excavation and renovation are under way in this area, revealing remains from the Byzantine period; in 1995 the **Byzantine Museum** opened in the fortress. Its small collection of artworks, curiously enough almost all post-Byzantine, includes intricate silver manuscript Bible covers, wall murals from mansions, and carved wooden benediction crosses covered in lacy silver, gathered from all over the countryside of Epirus. It is carefully arranged in the front half of the museum with good English translations. The second half of the museum houses an important collection of icons and remarkable iconostases, painted by local masters and salvaged from 16th- and 17th-century monasteries. The most interesting section is devoted to silver works from Ali Pasha's treasury from the seraglio. Nearby is the **Fethiye (Victory) mosque,** which purports to contain Ali Pasha's tomb. ⊠ *Palace grounds, eastern corner of citadel,* ☎ *0651/39692.* ☎ *500 dr./€1.47.* ⊙ *Tues.–Sun. 8:30–3; palace grounds daily 7 AM–10 PM.*

NEED A
BREAK?

In the summer, stop for a drink or snack in the **café** (⊠ Fortress grounds. ⊙ 7 AM–10 PM, no credit cards), and enjoy a panoramic view of Lake Pamvotis.

You'll immerse yourself in the vestiges of 19th-century Ioannina in the **old bazaar** (⊠ Clustered around the citadel's gates at Ethnikis Antistasios and Averoff streets). On Anexartisias Street, you may still see some Turkish-era structures, such as the Liabei arcade located across from the bustling municipal produce market and, on Filiti Street, a smattering of the copper-, tin-, and silversmiths who fueled the city's economy for centuries. Some of the workshops still offer their wares for sale.

The small **Folk Museum,** located in a restored Ottoman house, has a collection of richly embroidered local costumes, rare woven textiles made by the nomadic tent-dwelling Sarakatsanis, ceramics, and cooking and farm implements. ⊠ *Odhos Michail Angelou 42,* ☎ *0651/25015.* ☎ *200 dr./€.58.* ⊙ *Mon. 5:30–8 PM, Wed. 10–1.*

NEED A
BREAK?

Except during July and August, when it is closed, stop at **Filistrou** (⊠ Andronikou Paliologou 20, ☎ 0651/72429), an intimate café on a main street in the adjacent Citadel area. It is in a 200-year-old residence, now restored with a brilliantly colored folk interior featuring decorated ceilings. Why not pamper yourself with a nurturing breakfast of thick strained yogurt topped with chestnut-colored honey and chopped walnuts accompanied by sage herbal tea—or stop by in the late evening for a nightcap of Metaxa brandy and a *visino* (spoon sweet made from black cherries).

The square **Platia Mavili** (⊠ On the waterfront) is lined with smart cafés, which are full of tourists having breakfast or waiting for the next boat to the nearby island; in the evening this is *the* place to hang out—the youth of Ioannina while away the hours here over frappés or long drinks. At night, the area is especially gregarious, with vendors selling corn, halvah, and cassettes of Epirot clarinet music. At sunset, catch the *volta* (ritual promenade), when all and sundry take to the streets to check out the action and gossip. Sunday evening, this takes on the added aspect of the "bride's bazaar." Traditional Ioanniote families with eligible daughters parade by in attractive finery, providing an opportunity to let the girls be eyeballed by families with potential suitors.

As you chug from the shore toward the small islet, or **Nissi,** look back at the outline of the citadel and its mosques in a wash of green. The whitewashed lakeside island village, founded in the late 16th century by refugees from the Mani (in the Peloponnese) still allows no outside recreational vehicles—without the din of motorcycles and cars, the village seems centuries away from Ioannina. Ali Pasha once kept deer here for hunting. With its neat houses and flower-trimmed courtyards, pine-edged paths, runaway chickens, and reed-filled backwater, it's the perfect place to relax, have lunch, visit some of the monasteries (dress appropriately and carry a small flashlight to make it easier to see the magnificent frescoes), and enjoy a pleasant restaurant dinner. Frogs' legs, eel, and carp take center stage, although traditional taverna food can also be found.

Lake Pamvotis remains very picturesque but is now so seriously polluted and its water level so low (streams that feed it from Mt. Mitsikeli are drying up) that swimming is forbidden. Below the citadel near Platia Mavili you can catch a boat to the island. The boat leaves every half hour from 8:30 AM to 10:30 PM; the ride takes 10 minutes and costs 300 dr./€.88.

The main attraction on Ioannina's island is the 16th-century **Pandelimonos Monastery,** now the **Ali Pasha Museum.** The ticket taker often gives a tour of the museum in Greek (although there is some English translation); the tour is free, but it's customary to give her a good tip. It was in the monks' cells here on January 17, 1822, that Ali Pasha was killed, after holding out for almost two years. In the final battle, Ali ran into an upstairs cell, but the soldiers shot him through its floorboards from below. You'll hear more than one version of his last days, each more romantic than the last. Until recently you could see the original floorboards with the seven bullet holes, but the floor had to be replaced, and, now, newly drilled holes indicate the position of the deadly bullets. The museum has a famous portrait of Ali Pasha, seen in happier days asleep on his wife Vasiliki's lap. You'll also see the crypt where Vasiliki hid, some evocative etchings and paintings of that era, an edict signed by Ali Pasha with his ring seal (he couldn't write), and his magnificent *narghileh* (water pipe) standing on the fireplace. ⊠ *On island, take left from boat landing and follow signs,* ☎ *0651/81791.* 🎟 *150 dr./€.44.* ⊘ *Any time boats are running.*

Agios Nikolaos ton Filanthropinon has the best frescoes of Nissi island's several monasteries. The monastery was built in the 13th century by an important Byzantine family, the Filanthropinos, and a fresco in the northern exonarthex depicts five of them kneeling before St. Nikolaos (1542). Many of the frescoes are by the Kontaris brothers, who later decorated the mighty Varlaam in Meteora. You will note the similarities in the bold coloring, expressiveness, realism, and Italian influence—especially in the bloody scenes of martyrdom. Folk tradition says the corner crypts in the south chapel were the meeting places of the secret school of Hellenic culture during the Ottoman occupation. A most unusual fresco of seven sages of antiquity, including Solon, Aristotle, and Plutarch, is located there and gives credence to this story. It is not really feasible, however, that the school would be kept a secret from the Ottoman governors for long; it is more likely that the reigning Turkish pasha was one who allowed religious and cultural freedom (as long as the taxes were paid). Instead of returning to the landing when you head back to the main road, follow signs for the oldest monastery, the 11th-century **Stratigopoulos,** set on a grassy knoll at the other side of the village. Stunning 16th-century frescoes are highlighted by an Adoration of the Magi, a fantastic Apocalypse over the door, and a Nativity (note the angel reprimanding Joseph); the frescoes have been cleaned recently. The spry caretaker will let you in; if she doesn't see you immediately, hang around conspicuously for a few minutes. ⊠ *On island, follow signs.* 🎟 *Leave 300 dr./€.88 donation.* ⊘ *Daily 8–8.*

Dining and Lodging

$$ ✕ **Es Aei.** This new addition to the Ioannina dining scene, located in
★ a meticulously renovated 200-year-old house in the old Jewish neighborhood adjacent to the Kastro, has already attracted a legion of fans. Owners Manos Chronakis and Haris Stavrou pride themselves on creating authentic fare, mostly rare specialties which, in fact, change every 40 days as they focus on a different region of Greece. Various *poikilias* (variety plates) provide a convenient way to sample the marvelous *pittas*—small wedges of crisp phyllo stuffed with spinach,

greens, or chicken sausage. Raw artichoke salad, smoked river trout, Cretan snails fattened on uncooked pasta and served in an aromatic wine-onion sauce, and local cheeses (such as *galotyri,* a cream cheese in yogurt) are just a few of the treats that will warm your soul. For a festive touch, have a candlelight toast with the local version of champagne—a refreshing sparkling white wine bottled by the owners. A new exhibition space on the second floor will be devoted to handicraft exhibits by local artists. ⊠ *Koundouriotou 50,* ☎ *0651/34571. No credit cards. Closed July–Aug.*

$–$$ ✕ **To Mandeio.** Opposite the entrance to the citadel, this spot is open
★ all day and is particularly popular for late meals. The menu has all the usual taverna favorites: order appetizers to share such as *koloukithakia* (fried zucchini), *gigantes* (baked giant beans), saganaki, and *piperato* (spicy cheese dip). Mandeio is known for its juicy *souvla* (spit-roasted meats) such as *provio* (mutton) and chicken. Fruit is the traditional way to end a meal in summer when no desserts are served. The menu has entries printed in English and Greek; only the items with prices next to them are available, and they change with the seasons. ⊠ *Platia Yoryiou 15,* ☎ *0651/25452. No credit cards.*

$ ✕ **Ivi.** Homey Ivi (written HBH in Greek) is an old-fashioned no-nonsense Ioannina landmark that, for 35 years, has been serving excellent *magirefta,* or precooked dishes, in large portions for lunch; sometimes there's a line outside the door. You choose your dishes from the steam table, eliminating any language snafus. Especially good are the vegetable dishes, such as leeks sautéed and baked with celery or the green bean ragout. Meat dishes include boiled goat, *tas kebab* (cubed pork baked in red sauce), and beef *yiouvetsi* with *kritharakia* (goulash with rice-like pasta). There's usually a fish entrée such as grilled *kolios* (mackerel), *bakaliaros* (fried cod), or *galeos* (shark) with *skordalia* (garlic-potato sauce). Late at night, the cook serves pasta Ioannina style and a tripe soup with the cow's head and feet (said to be good for hangovers!). Whatever is left over from lunch is served at dinner, and though it may not look as inviting, remember that magirefta taste just as good after sitting for hours. ⊠ *Platia Yoryiou 4,* ☎ *0651/73155. No credit cards. Closed every other Sun.*

$$$ ✕⊡ **Du Lac.** Opened in 1998, the Du Lac fills the need for a fully appointed modern hotel and congress center in Ioannina. Built in traditional Ioannina style, its two ocher-color buildings sit on spacious landscaped grounds opposite the lake to the south of the old town. Although it's ideal for business travelers or those attending a conference (each room has a special phone jack for Internet access), the children's pool and quiet setting attract many families as well. Guest rooms are spacious, posh, carpeted, individually climate-controlled, and decorated in attractive sun tones, with prints or photographs of old Ioannina on the wall. Marble bathrooms all have tubs and hair dryers, and some rooms have balconies that either face the lake or the city. A buffet breakfast is included in the price. ⊠ *Akti Miaouli and Ikkou Sts., 45221,* ☎ *0651/59100,* ☒ *0651/59200. 129 rooms, 9 suites. Restaurant, cafeteria, bar, pool, wading pool, conference center. AE, D, MC, V.* ✎

$$$ ⊡ **Xenia.** One of the nicest hotels in Ioannina, Xenia is set back from
★ a central street behind huge oak trees and a rose-studded gazebo. The soothing lounge and eating areas, with mirrored columns and pastel upholstery, are pleasant retreats. The quiet guest rooms are done in the same gray-white-rose hues and have either mountain or garden views. The hotel has central heating, but no air-conditioning, which is rarely necessary. Buffet breakfast is included in the price. ⊠ *Dhodhonis 33, 45221,* ☎ *0651/47301, 0651/47187, or 0651/47188,* ☒ *0651/47189. 60 rooms. Restaurant, bar, refrigerators, meeting rooms. AE, DC, MC, V.*

$$-$$$ ⊡ **Kastro Hotel.** The Kastro Hotel—opened in 1998 and the only hotel
★   within the old town walls—is a brilliant new addition to Ioannina's lodg-
          ing scene. Set in a carefully restored neoclassical mansion, it only has
          seven rooms, so it may soon be difficult to make reservations, especially
          when word gets out about the well-appointed quarters, the gorgeous wood
          beams, the painted wooden ceiling of the second-floor lobby, and the
          two working fireplaces. Size keeps other services modest (and the break-
          fast room is on the dollhouse-small size), but the location, charm, and
          helpfulness of George and Vassiliki Zannis and their staff at this hotel
          make it a delight. Breakfast with homemade jams, ham, cheese, and local
          honey is included. ⊠ *In Old Town, just outside Inner Castro, 45332,*
          ☎ *0651/22866 or 0651/22780. 7 rooms. Breakfast room. V.* ⊛

$ ⊡ **Pension Dellas.** What makes this place so special is the hospitality
          of the owners (Titika and Sotirios Dellas), freshly picked flowers,
          maybe a homemade *koulouraki* (bread ring) made from their chick-
          ens' eggs, and hand-pressed linens. A delightful change from hotels in
          town, this lakeshore pension was originally built for the Dellas chil-
          dren. Rooms are immaculate, sunny, and quiet, with balconies or ac-
          cess to the courtyard, a congenial meeting place. Most visitors come
          March through October since the pension has no central heating, but
          you'll get a portable heater and plenty of blankets in winter. Call be-
          forehand and someone will meet you at the main dock, about five min-
          utes away. ⊠ *Island, 45444,* ☎ *0651/81494. 8 rooms, 1 with bath.*
          No credit cards.

Nightlife and the Arts

BARS

There are several excellent bars and clubs in Ioannina, including **Ky-
knos** on Platia Pirrhou, which has live foreign and Greek rock and is
very popular with students. **Iperokeanios** and the adjacent **Gallery** are
hip coffee shops on Platia Mavili (or Molos, as it is familiarly known)
serving ice cream and sweets. Karamanli, adjacent the citadel, is lined
with trendy *mezodopoleio* (Greek-style tapas bars) and smart pubs.

Right smack in the center of town near Platia Pirrhou is **Oasis** (☎ 0651/
92128) which serves as a restaurant-bar-café (it's open 24 hours) in
one. Seating is extensive: on one side, there's an outdoor patio overlooking the platia; on the other, a patio overlooking the lake and the
island. In between there's the restaurant proper, complete with steam-
ing dishes of food displayed in the front foyer.

FESTIVALS

Ioannina hosts the **Epirotika Festival** in July and August, with performances at the Frontzos Theater. An **International Folk Festival,** which
includes performances of local groups, also takes place in the Frontzos Theater. For information, contact the Ioannina Tourist Office (☞
Visitor Information *in* Epirus and Thessaly A to Z, *below*).

FILM

Several **cinemas,** including the **Granada** and **Beta** opposite the Lithar-
itsa Prison and clock tower and **Polytheama,** on Platia Pirrhou, feature an array of new releases and art-house movies. The closest open-air
cinema is 3 km (2 mi) away in Eastern Ioannina.

Shopping

CRAFTS

Ioannina has long been known throughout Greece for its silver crafts-
manship. There are many silver shops on Odhos Averoff, near Platia
Yoryious, and a careful eye can discern some prizes amid the tourist
dreck. In particular, avoid the shinier and brighter items in stores near
the entrance to the citadel.

Bizani

② *12 km (7½ mi) south of Ioannina.*

Pavlos Vrellis wax museum, in the village of Bizani, is where you'll see a collection of historical Epirote figures, among them a tableau of Ali Pasha's murder sculpted by a local man. ✉ *Mouseio Pavlos Vrellis, Bizani,* ☎ *0651/92128.* 🖅 *1,000 dr./€2.94.* ☉ *Daily 10–5.*

Dodona

③ *22 km (13½ mi) southwest of Ioannina, 20 km (12 mi) east of Bizani.*

Said to be the oldest in Greece, the **Dodona Oracle** flourished from at least the 8th century BC until the 4th century AD, when Christianity succeeded the cult of Zeus. Homer, in the *Iliad,* mentions "wintry Dodona," where Zeus's pronouncements, made known through the wind-rustled leaves of a sacred oak, were interpreted by priests "whose feet are unwashed and who sleep on the ground." The oak tree was central to the cult, and its image appears on the region's ancient coins. It was here that Odysseus sought forgiveness for slaughtering his wife's suitors, and it was from this oak that the Argonauts took the sacred branch to mount on their ship's prow. According to one story, Apollo ordered the oracle moved here from Thessaly; Herodotus writes that it was locally believed a dove from Thebes in Egypt landed in the oak and announced, in a human voice, that the oracle of Zeus should be built. The oracle had its ups and downs. Consulted in the heroic age by Heracles, Achilles, and all the best people, it went later into a gentle decline, because of its failure to equal the masterly ambiguity of Delphi. Enduring for a time as the poor man's Delphi, Dodona became again fashionable under the Macedonian dynasty.

As you enter the archaeological site of Dodona, you pass the **stadium** on your right, built for the Naïa games and completely overshadowed by the **theater** on your left. One of the largest and best preserved on the Greek mainland, the theater once seated 17,000, and it has been restored for the annual summer festival. Its building in the early 3rd century BC was overseen by King Pyrrhus of Epirus, from whose name comes the phrase "Pyrrhic victory": his armies habitually won battles with great losses. The theater was destroyed, rebuilt under Philip V of Macedon in the late 3rd century, and then converted by the Romans into an arena for gladiatorial games. Its retaining wall, reinforced by bastions, is still standing. East of the theater are the foundations of the **bouleuterion** (headquarters and council house) of the Epirote League, built by King Pyrrhus, and a small rectangular temple dedicated to Aphrodite. The remains of the **acropolis** behind the theater include house foundations and a cistern that supplied water in times of siege.

The remains of the **sanctuary to Zeus Naios** included the Sacred Oak and temples to Zeus, Dione, and Heracles; until the 4th century BC there was no temple. The Sacred Oak was surrounded by abutting cauldrons on bronze tripods. When struck, they reverberated for a long time, and the sound was interpreted by soothsayers. Fragments from as early as the 8th century have been recovered. In the 4th century BC, a small temple was built near the oak, and a century later the temple and oak were enclosed by a stone wall. By King Pyrrhus's time, the wall had acquired Ionic colonnades. After a 219 BC Aeolian attack, a larger Ionic temple was built, and the surrounding wall was enhanced by a monumental entrance. The oak tree currently on the site was planted by archaeologists; the original was probably cut down by Christians in the 4th century AD.

Two buses leave daily from Ioannina's Vyzantinou station. For about 5,000 dr./€14.74, you can hire a taxi, which will wait an hour at the site. Negotiate with one of the drivers near Ioannina's clock tower or call a radio taxi (☎ 0651/46777, 0651/45777, or 0651/25452). ⊠ *Archaeological site,* ☎ *0651/82287.* 🖃 *500 dr./€1.47.* ☉ *Apr.–Oct., daily 8–7; mid-Oct.–Mar., daily 8–5; museum closed Mon.*

The Arts

For information about the **ancient Greek drama at Dodona** contact the Ioannina Tourist Office (☞ Visitor Information *in* Epirus and Thessaly A to Z, *below*).

Perama Cave

❹ *4 km (2½ mi) northwest of Ioannina.*

Perama cave's passageways, discovered in the early 1940s by locals hiding from the Nazis, extend for more than 1 km (½ mi) under the hills. The high caverns and multihued limestone stalagmites and stalactites have names such as Statue of Liberty and Sphinx, which you'll learn during the 45-minute guided tour; one begins every 10 minutes; one of the guides will speak English. You can catch Bus 8 from Ioannina's clock tower. ⊠ *Along E 92 east from Ioannina,* ☎ *0651/81521.* 🖃 *1,500 dr./€4.42.* ☉ *Summer 8–8; winter 8–5.*

Zagorohoria Region

❺ *60 km (45 mi) north of Ioannina.*

If you want to see one of the most beguiling and untamed sections of Greece, take an exotic detour north to the Zagorohoria (pronounced zah-go-ro-*hor*-ee-ah), or Zagori, which comprises 46 villages to the north and northwest of Ioannina. If you only have a day to spare, you can rent a car or bargain with a taxi driver to transport you to the many villages connected by well-paved roads. In that time, you can see a fascinating array of the *archontika* (dignified stone mansions with walls and roofs made of gray slate from surrounding mountains), winding cobbled streets, graceful arched Turkish bridges, village churches with painted interiors, *kalderimi* (old mule trails), and forests of beech, chestnut, and pines. The lucky traveler will opt to spend the night in one of the villages, to truly soak up the local color, get a look at the interiors of some of the Ottoman-style living quarters, and partake of some of the tastiest food in all of modern Greece.

Due to lack of employment opportunities, some of the most significant depopulation in Greece took place in the Zagorohoria after World War II. The area's new-found popularity makes it possible for more inhabitants to make a living in their home towns—but it also means some of the more accessible villages, such as Megalo, Mikro Papingo, and Monodhendhri are likely to be packed with travelers in July and August (in fact, during weekends and major holidays all accommodations are quickly booked up). At these times, book ahead, or better yet, plan to stay in some of the (even) lesser known villages.

Here are some of the highlights of the Zagorohoria region. **Konitsa** is a pretty market town served by bus from Ioannina and a good base for exploration in the northern Zagorohoria. The best place to stay is **To Dendro Guesthouse** (☎ 🛆 0655/22055), which has a taverna as well; owner Ioannis can answer all your questions and help you plan your itinerary. A must-see village is **Monodhendhri**, at the start of a gorge trek—a handsome well-preserved settlement perched right on the rim of a gorge, with a stunning vista from an abandoned 15th-century monastery. For a scrumptious dining experience, have a fried *tiganopita* (skillet pie with feta cheese), a regional specialty best served at **Kyria Kykitsas Pie Cafe.** **Vikos Hotel** (☎ 0653/71232) has comfortable rooms. If Monodhendhri is booked up, stay in the nearby town of **Ano Pedina,** in which you can visit a restored convent. Lovely rooms are available in the newly opened **Hostel Koukouli** (☎ 0653/71267 or 0653/71070, FAX 0651/22866), run by the owners of the Kastro Hotel in Ioannina.

Megalo has delightful architecture, varied scenery, and friendly locals, although it was among the first villages here "discovered" by wealthy Greeks. **Megalo Papingo** is a picturesque choice—make it your home by staying at **Ta Spitia Tou Saxoni** (☎ 0653/4615), a gorgeously re-stored stone retreat run by Nikos and Poli. **Ouzerie Nikos Tsoumanis** has irresistible *mezedes* (appetizers) and a potent *tsipouro* (grape spir-its) that will help you leave all the cares of the real world behind. In **Mikro Papingo,** Xenon O Dhias (☎ 0653/41257, FAX 0653/41892) has excellent rooms and meals, and owner Kostas can help trekkers with transportation and supplies.

Tsepelovo in the central Zagori is one of the most authentic villages; the pension run by **Anthoula Gouris** (☎ 0653/81214) is charming and reasonable. **Kipi** is famous for its three-arched packhorse bridge, while the best-known kalderimi is between Kapesovo and Vradheto.

If you have three days or more and are a physically fit hiker, you can not only visit the Zagori villages, but also hike at least part of the **Vikos Gorge.** To get to the gorge, you follow a precipitous route from the upper limestone table lands of **Monodendri** down almost 3,300 feet to the clear, rushing waters of the Voidomatis trout stream (no swimming allowed) as it flows north into Albania. It's a strenuous, but exhila-rating eight-hour hike on which you are likely to see breathtaking vis-tas, birds of prey, waterfalls, a proliferation of flowers and herbs, and hooded shepherds tending their flocks. *Never* undertake this trip with-out proper footwear, hiking gear, food and water, and emergency sup-plies and provisions, and *never* in heavy rains or in groups of fewer than four. Your safest and most convenient way to hike the gorge is to have your trip arranged by **Robinson Expeditions,** an adventure-tour operator based in Ioannina and Kipi (☞ Travel Agencies *in* Epirus and Thessaly A to Z, *below*); Robinson also operates kayaking trips, moun-tain-biking, and white-water rafting. Another tour guide is Aris Talaris, based at the Hotel Egnatia (✉ Arvantinou 20) in Ioannina (☞ Guided Tours *in* Epirus and Thessaly A to Z, *below*).

Metsovo

⑥ *58 km (36 mi) east of Ioannina, 293 km (182 mi) northwest of Athens,*

The traditional village of Metsovo cascades down the mountain at about 3,300 ft above sea level, below the 6,069-ft Katara Pass, which is the highest in Greece and marks the border between Epirus and Thessaly. Early evening is a wonderful time to arrive. As you descend through the mist, dazzling lights twinkle in the ravine. Stone houses with gray slate roofs and sharply projecting wooden balconies line steep, serpentine alleys. In the square, especially after the Sunday service, old men—dressed in black flat caps, dark baggy pants, and wooden shoes with pom-poms—sit on a bench, like crows on a tree branch. Should you arrive on a re-ligious feast day, many villagers will be decked out in traditional costume. Older women often wear dark blue or black dresses with em-broidered trim every day, augmenting these with brightly colored aprons, jackets, and scarves with floral embroidery on holidays.

Although most villages are fading, Metsovo, designated a traditional settlement by the Greek National Tourist Organization (GNTO or EOT), has become a prosperous community with a growing population. In winter it draws skiers headed for Mt. Karakoli, and in summer it is a favorite destination for tourist groups. Despite the souvenir shops offering "traditional handicrafts" that may sell you imports, the slate roofs that have been replaced with easy-to-maintain tile, and the kitsch that occasionally mars the scene, for the most part Metsovo has preserved its character.

The natives are descendants of nomadic Vlach shepherds, once believed to have migrated from Romania but now thought to be Greeks trained by Romans to guard the Egnatia Highway connecting Constantinople and the Adriatic. The Vlach language is so influenced by Latin that it was used during World War II to communicate with occupying Italian forces, and villagers still speak it among themselves. During winter, while the village lies buried in snow, shepherds move their flocks from the mountains to the lowlands around Trikala, while their wives, aptly nicknamed the "white widows," tend to their hearths in isolation. The shepherds' numbers are dwindling, however (they herd about 15,000 sheep today), as many have turned to tourism for their livelihoods.

After Metsovo became an important center of finance, commerce, handicrafts, and sheepherding, the Vlachs began trading farther afield— in Constantinople, Vienna, and Venice. Ali Pasha abolished the privileges in 1795, and in 1854 the town was invaded by Ottoman troops led by Abdi Pasha. In 1912 Metsovo was freed by the Greek army. Many important families lived here, including the Averoffs and Tositsas, who made their fortunes in Egyptian cotton. They contributed to the new Greek state's development and bequeathed large sums to restore Metsovo and finance small industries. Testimony to their largesse is the **Foundation Baron Michalis Tositsa** (⊠ In square, ☎ 0656/41205), which helped the local weaving industry get a start (one year its stock was used in Yves Saint Laurent's Paris collection) and also financed the nearby **ski resort** (⊠ Just outside village, ☎ 0656/41206), which has one chairlift, nestled in the slopes of Mt. Karakoli.

For generations, the Tositsa family had been one of the most prominent of Metsovo, and to get a sense of how Metsovites lived (and endured the arduous winters in style), visit the restored late-Ottoman-period stone-and-timber **ancestral home of the Barons Tositsa.** Now a museum of popular art, it is devoted to local Epirote crafts. Built in 1661 and renovated in 1954, this typical Metsovo mansion has carved woodwork, sumptuous textiles in rich colors on a black background, and Vlach handcrafted furniture. In the stable you'll see the gold-embroidered saddle used for special holidays and, unique to this area, a fanlight in the fireplace, ensuring that the hearth would always be illuminated. The goatskin bag on the wall was used to store cheese. ⊠ *Up stone stairs to right off Tositsa (main road) as you descend to main square,* ☎ *0656/41024.* ▱ *300 dr./€.88.* ☉ *Fri.–Wed. 8:30–1 and 4–6 (3–5 in winter). Guided tours every ½ hr; wait for guard to open door.*

NEED A   Metsovo is famous throughout Greece for its expensive smoked cheeses.
BREAK?   Sample one or two of them, and some *metsovella* at the *tiropolio* **cheese shop** in the main square; the owner is happy to let you taste before you buy.

The 18th-century church of **Agia Paraskevi** (⊠ Main square) has a flamboyantly decorated altar screen that's worth a peek. Note that July 26 is its saint's day, entailing a big celebration in which the church's silver icon is carried around the town in a morning procession, followed by feasting and dancing.

At **Averoff Gallery** you may view Evangelos Averoff's outstanding personal art collection: 19th- and 20th-century paintings of historical scenes, local landscapes, and daily activities. Most of the major artists, such as Ghikas and Fassianos, are represented and their works displayed in a well-lighted and properly labeled setting. One painting known to all Greeks is Nikiforos Litras's *The Burning of the Turkish Flagship by Kanaris,* a scene from a decisive battle in Chios. Look on the second floor for Pantazis's *Street Urchin Eating Watermelon,* a captivating portrait of a young boy. Paris Prekas's *The Mosque of Aslan Pasha in Ioannina* depicts what contemporary Ioannina looked like in the Turkish period. ✉ *Main square,* ☎ *0656/41210.* ✎ *500 dr./€1.47.* ☺ *Wed.–Fri. 10–4, Sat. 10–7 (10–4:30 in winter). Closed Mon.*

Visit the **cooperative** (✉ Metsovo village, ☎ 0656/41235), open daily 6:30–1:30, to see how cheeses are made. The **winery** (✉ Outside village, in Upper Aoos Valley, ☎ 0656/41010) also welcomes visitors. It's open Tuesday through Saturday 8–2.

OFF THE BEATEN PATH

AYIOS NIKOLAOS MONASTERY – Not to be missed, unless you are pressed for time, is a visit to the restored 14th-century Ayios Nikolaos monastery, about 30 minutes into the valley (with the trip back up about an hour). The *katholikon* (main church) is topped by a barrel vault, and what may have once been the narthex was converted to a *ginaikonitis* (a women's gallery). Two images of the *Pantocrator* (Godhead), one in each dome—perhaps duplicated to give the segregated women their own view—stare down on the congregation. You can also see the monks' cells, with insulating walls of mud and straw; the abbot's quarters; and the school where Greek children were taught during the Turkish occupation. The keepers will give you a closely guided tour and explanation of the frescoes. ✉ *Down into valley via footpath (follow signs near National Bank of Greece; turn left where paving ends).* ✎ *Leave a 200 dr./€.58 donation in the box.* ☺ *Usually until 7 PM (1 PM in winter).*

Dining and Lodging

$$ ✕ **Taverna Metsovitiko Saloni.** The dining room seduces its patrons with a large fireplace, Metsovo costumes on the walls, charming old photos, and carved wooden furniture. Try the various vegetable pies especially the koloukithakia, made from *bobota* (corn flour), an unusual crust in Greece, although an Epirot favorite; in addition, the saganaki made with four Metsovo cheeses is a winner. Savor the large wine selection, fork-tender lamb yiouvetsi (baked in tomato-wine sauce and served with orzo), and a generous choice of desserts, including Metsovitiko baklava, thick sheep yogurt (with pastry, honey, and walnuts), and gliko. ✉ *Tositsa 10, above post office,* ☎ 0656/42142. V.

$$ ✕ **To Paradosiako.** The name means "traditional" and that's what this comfortable spot is, quaintly decorated with colorful weavings and folk crafts. Opened in 1997, Vasilis Bissas's place lives up to its name as the owner/chef has revived many of the more esoteric regional specialities. Try the *fileta tou dasous,* or fillet of the forest—a choice beef fillet stuffed with cheese, ham, tomato, mushrooms, and "woodcutters' potatoes" (spud slices baked with bacon and four kinds of cheese). The mouthwatering "grandmothers' bread" is toasted and stuffed with cheese, bacon, tomato, peppers, and onions, then baked in the oven. The heady red *katogi* wine, much coveted by locals, is sometimes in stock. ✉ *Tosista 44,* ☎ 0656/42773. V.

$ ✕ **To Koutouki Tou Nikola.** Koutouki ("little box"), aptly named for its diminutive interior, proves to be one of the best—it's popular among locals and is a good value. All the taverna favorites are here, but order something made with the local cheese, or be bold and try real country fare such as *kokoretsi* (skewered, grilled mixed innards). Don't miss the strong barrel wine, because, as owner Kostas Todis jokingly points out, high altitudes go hand in hand with *zali* (giddiness). It's open late, sometimes until 3 AM. ⊠ *On Aghiou Georgiou (under post office),* ☎ *0656/41732. No credit cards.*

$$$ ▣ **Apollon.** The Apollon's traditional lobby has a carved pine ceiling,
★   a fireplace, chandeliers, red-and-green woven upholstery, hammered-copper plates, and a pet bird, whose cheery song brings spring to mind, no matter what the season. Built in 1986 in typical Metsovo style with stone and wood, the hotel has cozy, carpeted rooms with pine furniture, televisions, and balconies overlooking the gorge. The best are those in the *sofrita* (attic), but they're approximately 8,000 dr./€23.59 extra; several have hot tubs. ⊠ *Near main square, behind Tositsa Foundation, 44200,* ☎ *0656/41844, 0656/42442, or 0656/41833,* FAX *0656/42110. 28 rooms, 2 suites, 10 attic-suites. Bar, breakfast room, refrigerators. AE, DC, MC, V.*

$$ ▣ **Victoria.** Views from the reception area here offer a panorama of Metsovo—one of the pluses of this pleasant hostelry owned by Tassos Vadivoilis. Opened in 1981 and set in a traditional building near the north entrance of the town, it was renovated in the mid-1990s; a sauna and swimming pool were just added. Rooms are simple but comfortable, enhanced with colorful bedspreads, natural wood beams, hand-carved beds, and balconies; all rooms have television and phones. Especially inviting is the public salon when its large stone fireplaces are blazing on a cold winter's eve. The bar and restaurant are enlivened with weavings, and a buffet breakfast is included in the price. ⊠ *Agiou Yiorgiou (just above winery at top of north end of village),* ☎ *0656/41771. 37 rooms. Restaurant, bar, breakfast room, pool, sauna. MC, V.*

$ ▣ **Athine Hotel.** For budget-level food and lodging, this hotel is a good choice. Built in 1925 it was the first hotel in the area, and owner Yiannis Bitounis named it after Athens to remind him of a sister who had gone to that faraway metropolis to marry. The hospitality is superb: the owners, who now sleep upstairs, gave up their private quarters to guests. The rooms have no views, but they're comfortable enough, with carpeting and central heating. At the taverna, the mother prepares traditional fare and her own specialties—pies, soups, and meats—and there's usually a roaring fire in winter. ⊠ *S. Klidi 2 (below National Bank off main square), 42200,* ☎ *0656/41332 or 0656/41725. 9 rooms. No credit cards.*

Shopping

Although Metsovo now imports a wide variety of low-quality imitations of traditional arts and crafts, with a little prowling and patience, you can still make some real "finds," especially if you are looking for textiles and weavings. **Vasilis Topis** (⊠ Tositsa, near post office, ☎ 0656/41235) is a shop crammed with the captivating weavings and embroideries of the area; many of them are genuine antiques that will naturally cost a good deal more than the newer versions, but, of course, are far superior in quality. **Aris Talaris** (⊠ Tositsa, in Hotel Egnatia, Arvantinou 20, ☎ 0656/41901) has two shops: one sells quality silver jewelry made in his own workshop, while the other offers fine gold pieces. Near the Hotel Egnatia is the shop of **Vangelis Balabekos,** which sells traditional clothing from Epirus and other areas of Greece (for local hand-carved wooden handicrafts, check out the stand across the street).

THESSALY
Kalambaka and the Meteora Monasteries

Though Thessaly is the home of the immortal gods, a Byzantine site holds pride of place: Meteora, the amazing medieval monasteries on top of inaccessible rock-needles. Their extraordinary geological setting stands in vivid contrast to the rest of Thessaly, a huge plain in central Greece, almost entirely surrounded by mountains: Pindos to the west, Pelion to the east, Othrys to the south, and the Kamvounian range to the north. It is one of the country's most fertile areas and has sizable population centers in Lamia, Larissa, Trikala, and Volos. Thessaly was not ceded to Greece until 1878, after almost five centuries of Ottoman rule; today, vestiges of this period remain. Archaeology enthusiasts will be intrigued by its Neolithic sites to the east, Dhimini and Sesklo near Volos. Kalambaka and Meteora are in the northwest corner of the plain, just before the Pindos Mountains. The best time to come here is the spring, especially at the Meteora monasteries, when the mountains are still snow-covered and blend harmoniously with the green fields, the red poppies, and the white and pink fruit trees.

Kalambaka

❼ *71 km (44 mi) east of Metsovo, 154 km (95½ mi) southwest of Thessaloniki.*

Kalambaka may be dismissed as one more drab modern town, useful only as a base to explore the fabled Meteora complex just north of town (☞ *below*). Yet an overnight stay in Kalambaka, complete with a taverna dinner and a stroll in the main squares, will give you a taste of everyday life in a provincial Thessalian town. Of course, this will prove quite a contrast to an afternoon spent at nearby Meteora, where you can get acquainted with the glorious history and architecture of the Greek Orthodox Church. Invariably, you'll then return to modern Kalambaka and wind up at a poolside bar to sip ouzo and contemplate the asceticism of the Meteora monks. If you'd rather stay in a more attractive setting closer to the monasteries, head right to nearby **Kastraki,** a charming hamlet with some attractive folk-style houses about 2½ km (1 mi) north of the border of Kalambaka.

Burned by the Germans during World War II, Kalambaka has only one building of interest, the cathedral church of the **Dormition of the Virgin.** Patriarchal documents in the outer narthex indicate that it was built in the first half of the 12th century by Emperor Manuel Comnenos, but some believe it was founded as early as the 7th century, on the site of a temple of Apollo (various classical drums and other fragments are incorporated into the walls, and mosaics can be glimpsed under the present floor). The latter theory explains the church's paleo-Christian features, including its center-aisle *ambo* (great marble pulpit), which is usually to the right of the sanctuary; its rare *synthronon* (four semicircular steps where the priest sat when not officiating) east of the altar; and its Roman-basilica style, originally adapted to Christian use and unusual for the 12th century. The church has vivid 16th-century frescoes, work of the Cretan monk Neophytos, son of the famous hagiographer Theophanes. The marble baldachin in the sanctuary, decorated with crosses and stylized grapes, probably predates the 11th century. The courtyard outside the church provides welcome respite under the cool shade of a eucalyptus tree. Behind the church you can stroll through a small necropolis: boxes upon boxes of bones that have been disinterred and washed in accordance with Orthodox tradition.

✉ *North end of town, follow signs from Platia Riga Fereou or from central square,* ☎ *0432/24297.* 🎫 *400 dr./€1.17.* ⊘ *Daily 8 AM–10 AM and 4–8.*

Dining and Lodging

$$ ✕ **Estiatorio Meteora.** At this spot, a local favorite since 1925, the Gert-
★ zos family serves food prepared by the family matriarch, Ketty. Mete-
ora is known for hearty main courses—try Ketty's special wine and
pepper chicken or veal *stifado* (stew)—and some specialties from Asia
Minor, including *tzoutzoukakia Smyrneika,* aromatic meatballs in a
red sauce laced with cumin. For a light lunch, try one of the salads and
a tasty bottled wine from Tiryns in the Peloponnese. No desserts are
served. ✉ *Ekonomou 4, main square (Platia Dimarchiou),* ☎ *0432/
22316. No credit cards.*

$$ ✕ **Kipos.** This taverna's traditional 140-dish menu—traditional Greek
with the addition of Mexican and even some children's dishes—might
make the journey outside town worthwhile. Elias Mavradhinis opened
Kipos in December 1993 and has succeeded in bringing flawless service and quality food to Kalambaka at reasonable prices—so much so
that Kipos has since played host to the rich and famous, including the
Queen of Spain. You'll enjoy the garden setting, complete with waterfalls,
and the antiques proudly pointed out by the owner. Unusual appetizers include spicy saganaki with peppers, fresh grilled mushrooms, and
fried feta. Main dishes include beef *stamna* (baked in a covered clay
pot with herbs, potatoes, and cheese), rabbit with onions, and vegetable
croquettes. Finish up with the sublime baked apples topped with
cream. ✉ *Trikalon Rd. at the terminus of Ayia Triada, before entrance
to Kalambaka,* ☎ *0432/23218. V.*

$ ✕ **Paradissos.** Paradissos is truly a slice of paradise. This traditional
taverna in Kastraki has a spacious flowering garden that is a delight
to sit in while having a relaxing meal of stellar standards, all rendered
with loving care by owner Kyriakoula Fassoula. All of the favorite *tis
ores* (cooked-to-order) entrées, such as pork and lamb chops, are
grilled to perfection. Vegetarians have much to choose from as well,
including delectable eggplant *papoutsakia* (little shoes), fried zucchini
with garlic sauce, and various boiled greens. Complimentary fruit is
served for the finale, but it would be a shame to pass up the flaky baklava
or creamy galaktobouriko. ✉ *On main road to Meteora across from
Spania Rooms in Kastraki,* ☎ *0432/22285. No credit cards.*

$$$ 🏨 **Amalia.** Built in 1991, Amalia's low-lying, clay-colored complex out-
side Kalambaka (on the road to Trikala) has spacious, handsome pub-
lic rooms that somehow avoided the generic stamp. Relax in the sitting
room, with a fireplace, striking antiques, and floral murals, or enjoy
the poolside bar, with glistening blue tiles and rustic rafters. Grounds
are beautifully landscaped and blissfully quiet. Rooms are done in sooth-
ing colors and have large beds and prints; some also have TVs and bal-
conies. Buffet breakfast is included in the price. Ask the receptionist
to arrange for a taxi to take you to Meteora (if you are going to Del-
phi from here, you can also arrange to go by taxi for about $120). ✉
Trikalon 14, Theopetra, 42200, ☎ *0432/81216,* 🖷 *0432/81457. 171
rooms, 2 suites. Restaurant, 2 bars, cafeteria, pool, shops, meeting rooms.
AE, DC, MC, V.*

$$$ 🏨 **Motel Divani.** A few minutes from the center of town, this A-class
hotel has optimal views of the Meteora rocks from the rooms' balconies
(an advantage over the Amalia; ☞ *above*). Its large open spaces, quiet
corners, and private garden encourage relaxation. The exterior is plain,
as are the rooms, but they're shielded from outside noise. However,
readers have written to note the frayed state of furniture throughout
the "past-its-prime" complex. The professional reception staff will ar-

range and negotiate a price for a leisurely taxi ride to the monasteries. Breakfast is included. ⊠ *Trikalon 1, 42200,* ☎ *0432/23330,* FAX *0432/ 23638. 165 rooms. Restaurant, 2 bars, pool, shop, meeting rooms. AE, DC, MC, V.*

$–$$ ⊞ **Hotel Edelweiss.** This hotel, built in 1990, has a bright and clean sparkle. Almost too much so: every room is spotless and white, but the walls are completely bare, and you feel a little like you're in a hospital. The rooms are comfortable enough, with TVs and air-conditioning. They look out over the pool and the towering Meteora rocks beyond. The bar has a lively local crowd, and the hotel runs a Western and Greek popular music club right next door. ⊠ *E. Venizelou 3, 42200,* ☎ *0432/23966, 0432/23884, or 0432/24918,* FAX *0432/24733. 60 rooms. Restaurant, 2 bars, air-conditioning, pool, dance club. MC, V.*

$ ⊞ **Doupiani House.** Located in the upper reaches of the idyllic village of Kastraki and signposted and set amid vineyards, Doupiani House is set back off the main road that heads to Meteora. Built in the mid-1990s, the hotel is designed in the traditional style. Each air-conditioned room has a balcony, and many of them have panoramic views of both Meteora and Kastraki. Vivacious owner Toula Naki serves breakfast around the quaint pergola in the large garden that is perfumed with the scent of roses, jasmine, and honeysuckle. If you have good walking shoes and enough stamina, you can walk to the monasteries from here (be sure to bring some water and food for a picnic along with you). ⊠ *To left off main road going to Meteora; look for hotel signposts near Cave Camping, Kastraki 42200,* ☎ FAX *0432/77555 or 0432/75326. 10 rooms. Air-conditioning. MC, V.*

Nightlife

BARS

Kalambaka doesn't have much in the way of nightlife, but several **Internet cafés** on the main drag have now been added to the mix of rousing rock bars, some of which are fun places to meet Greeks and foreigners. Some cafés and ice-cream parlors, such as Alpha Beta Gamma, set along the Trikala Road, stay open very late.

NIGHTCLUB

For dancing, try the **Hotel Edelweiss club,** right next to the hotel (☞ *above*).

En Route On the road to the Meteora monasteries, which begins just outside of Kalambaka in Kastraki, you'll pass the 12th-century **Chapel of the Virgin** (⊠ At Doupani), where the monks first gathered. About 8 km (5 mi) outside Kastraki on St. George's Day (celebrated on April 23 or on the Tuesday following Easter, whichever comes first) you will spot what looks like a clothesline hung with brightly colored fabrics set high up in a crevice. According to legend, a woodcutter who lost his leg promised to give St. George all his wife's clothing if he was healed—which he was. On St. George's Day, women offer scarves or other items of clothing and young men scale the rocks to hang them up for the saint.

The Meteora

❽ *3 km (2 mi) north of Kalambaka, 178 km (110½ mi) southwest of Thessaloniki.*

The name Meteora comes from the Greek word *meteorizome* ("to hang in midair"), and the monasteries, perched on a handful of strangely shaped pinnacles that rise 984 ft above the Peneus Valley, seem to do just that. Their lofty aeries imbue them with an otherworldly quality; the azure heavens seem close enough to touch while the valley of worldly distractions remains far below. Looming between the Pindos range and the Thessalian plain, the rocks remain an enigma. Some geologists say a lake that covered the area 30 million years ago swept away the soil and softer stone as it forced its way to the sea. Others believe the Peneus River slowly carved out the towering pillars, now eroded by wind and rain. Legend, of course, has a more colorful story—these rock needles were meteors hurled by an angry god.

By the 9th century ascetic hermits were inhabiting the rocks' crevices. On Sundays and holidays they gathered at Stagi (present-day Kalambaka) and Doupiani, and they eventually formed religious communities. With Byzantine power on the wane and an increase in religious persecution from invading foreigners, the monks retreated to the inaccessible rocks. In 1336 they were joined by two monks from Mt. Athos, Abbot Gregorios of Magoula and his companion St. Athanasios. The abbot returned to Athos, but he commanded St. Athanasios to build a monastery here. Notwithstanding the legend that says that the saint flew up to the rocks on the back of an eagle, St. Athanasios began the backbreaking task of building the Megalo Meteoro (1356–72) using pulleys and ropes to haul construction material. The monks themselves had to endure a harrowing ride in a swinging net to reach the top.

Despite St. Athanasios's strictness of rule, the monastery attracted many devotees, including, in 1371, John Urosh of Serbia, who relinquished accession to the throne to become a monk, using the name Ioasaph. His royal presence brought contributions to the monasteries, and the congregation grew quickly. By the 16th century, there were at least 20 smaller settlements and 13 monasteries, which were embellished with frescoes and icons by such great artists as Theophanis Strelitzas, a monk from Crete. The larger monasteries prospered on revenues from estates in Thessaly and eastern Europe; during the late-Byzantine period, they served as bastions of Christianity against Turkish domination.

The architecture of the monasteries is conditioned by the restricted space available, with buildings rising from different levels. Some are whitewashed, while others display the pretty Byzantine pattern of stone and brick, the multiple domes of the many churches dominating the wooden galleries and balconies that hang precariously over frightening abysses.

The monastic communities eventually disappeared for several reasons. Some of the wealthy monasteries were plagued by bitter power struggles. Monasticism as a vocation gradually lost its appeal, causing even grand communities to dwindle. Smaller, poorer monasteries could not afford to maintain the old buildings; many of their structures were neglected or abandoned. Today only six monasteries at Meteora are open to the public. After the Greco-Turkish War of 1919–22, the already diminished monastic lands and revenues were appropriated by the state on behalf of refugees from Asia Minor, another blow to the few remaining monasteries.

Visitors are expected to dress decorously: men must tuck up long hair and wear long pants, women's skirts should fall to the knee, and both sexes should cover their shoulders, if bare. Some monasteries provide appropriate coverings at their entrances. Opening hours vary depending on the season, but information is readily available in Kalambaka from your hotel receptionist. All monasteries can be visited in a single journey from Kalambaka—a 21-km (13-mi) round-trip by car. A bus leaves Kalambaka for Megalo Meteoro five times daily (once daily in winter). Megalo Meteoro and Varlaam are the two most rewarding monasteries to visit. You can hike along the footpaths between monasteries, but you'd better be in good shape, because there are many steps up to most monasteries. Once on the monastery circuit, you'll find just a few overpriced concession stands; if you plan to make a day of it, stock up on picnic goods in town.

The monastery of **Ayios Nikolaos Anapafsas** seems impossibly crammed atop its narrow rock. The katholikon was built in 1388 and was later expanded; the monastery itself dates from the end of the 15th century. Because of the rock's peculiar shape, the katholikon faces north rather than the usual east. Its superb 16th-century frescoes are the work of Theophanis Strelitzas. Though conservative, his frescoes are lively and expressive: mountains are stylized, and plants and animals are portrayed geometrically. Especially striking are the treatments of the Temptation, the scourging of Christ, and a scene of Adam naming the animals. The serpent is in the form of the legendary basilisk, which could kill with a mere look or a breath. The rock's small area precluded the construction of a cloister, so the monks studied in the larger-than-usual narthex. Visitors are admitted in small groups. ⊠ *Along monastery route, about 3 km (2 mi) outside Kalambaka,* ☎ *0432/22375.* ⊠ *500 dr./€1.47.* ☉ *Daily 9–3:30. Closed Fri.*

The inaccessible **Ayia Moni** monastery has been deserted since an 1858 earthquake. Locals believe the area is haunted owing to its ominous ambience. ⊠ *Along monastery route, across from Agios Nikolaos monastery.*

Because of its breathtaking location, the compact monastery of **Ayia Barbara,** also called Roussanou, is the favorite for picture-taking. Abandoned in the early 1900s, it stood empty until nuns moved in some years ago and began a restoration program. Its founding in 1288 by the monks Nicodemus and Benedict has yet to be confirmed, but it is known that 156 years later the monastery was restored for the first time. The main church, dedicated to the Transfiguration, has well-preserved frescoes dating from the mid-16th century. Most depict gory scenes of martyrdom, but one shows lions licking Daniel's feet during his imprisonment. ⊠ *Along monastery route, across vertiginous bridges from Ayia Moni area,* ☎ *0432/22649.* ⊠ *500 dr./€1.47.* ☉ *Daily 9–6.*

The highest and most powerful monastery is **Megalo Meteoro,** or the Church of the Metamorphosis (Transfiguration). Founded by St. Athanasios, the monk from Athos, it was built of massive stones on the highest rock, 1,361 ft above the valley. As you walk toward the entrance, you will see the chapel containing the cell where St. Athanasios once lived. This monastery had extensive privileges and held jurisdiction over the others for centuries; an 18th-century engraving in its museum depicts it towering above the other monasteries.

The sanctuary of the present church was the chapel first built by St. Athanasios, later added to by St. Ioasaph. The rest of the church was erected in 1552 with an unusual transept built on a cross-in-square plan with lateral apses topped by lofty domes, as in the Mt. Athos monasteries. To the right of the narthex are the tombs of Ioasaph and Athanasios; a fresco shows the austere saints holding a monastery in their hands. Also of interest are the gilded iconostasis, with plant and animal motifs of exceptionally fine workmanship; the bishop's throne (1617) inlaid with mother-of-pearl and ivory; and the 15th-century icons in the sanctuary. The expressiveness and attention to color and detail of these icons have led art historians to conclude they may also be the work of Theophanis Strelitzas. In the narthex are frescoes of the Martyrdom of the Saints, gruesome scenes of persecution under the Romans. A chamber stacked with skulls and bones of monks is opposite.

The refectory now houses the treasury, with fine miniatures, golden bulls, historic documents, and elaborately carved crucifixes, including one that the monk Daniel labored over for 10 years. The front shows 10 scenes with several figures each, and representations of 24 single figures. Portable icons include the Virgin, by Tzanes, another well-known artist. The adjacent kitchen is blackened by centuries of cooking. ⊠ *Along monastery route, past the intersection for Varlaam monastery,* ☎ *0432/22278.* ⌫ *500 dr./€1.47.* ⊙ *Wed.–Mon. 9–1 and 3:20–6 (winter hrs vary).*

The monks from **Varlaam,** which is situated atop a ravine and reached by a climb of 195 steps, were famous for their charity. Originally here were the Church of Three Hierarchs (14th century) and the cells of a hermitage started by St. Varlaam, who arrived shortly after St. Athanasios. Two brothers from the wealthy Aparas family of Ioannina rebuilt the church in 1518, incorporating it into a larger katholikon called Agii Pandes (All Saints). A church document relates how it was completed in 20 days, after the materials had been accumulated atop the rock over a period of 22 years. Its main attraction is the 16th-century frescoes—mostly of ascetic subjects, including scenes from the life of John the Baptist and a disturbing Apocalypse with a yawning hell's mouth—which completely cover the walls, beams, and pillars. The frescoes' realism, the sharp contrasts of light and dark, and the many-figured scenes show an Italian influence, though in the portrayal of single saints they follow the Orthodox tradition (the West had no models to offer). Note the Pantocrator peering down from the dome. These are the work of Frangos Katellanos of Thebes, one of the most important 16th-century hagiographers.

Other buildings include the infirmary, a chapel to Sts. Cosmas and Damien, and the refectory, now a sacristy, which displays the manuscript Gospel Book of the Byzantine emperor Constantine Porphyrogennetus, bearing his signature. There are storerooms with the monks' 2,640-gallon barrel and an ascent tower with a net and a winch. Until the 1920s the only way to reach most of the monasteries was by retractable ladder or net. A bishop of Trikala subsequently decreed that steps be cut to allow access to all the monasteries, and today the ropes are used only for hauling up supplies. ⊠ *Along monastery route, 328 ft southwest of intersection,* ☎ *0432/22277.* ⌫ *500 dr./€1.47.* ⊙ *Fri.–Wed. 9–2 and 3:20–5.*

The least-visited site, along the eastern route, is **Ayios Stephanos,** which is the oldest monastery. According to an inscription that was once on the lintel, the rock was inhabited before AD 1200 and was the hermitage of Jeremiah. By the beginning of the 14th century, the monks lived a cenobitic life. After the Byzantine emperor Andronicus Paleologos stayed here in 1333 on his way to conquer Thessaly, he made generous gifts to the monks, which funded the building of a church in 1350. A permanent bridge has replaced the movable one that once connected the monastery with the hill opposite. Today Ayios Stephanos is an airy convent, where the nuns spend their time painting Byzantine icons, writing, or studying music; some are involved in the community as doctors and professors. The katholikon has no murals but boasts a fine carved wooden baldachin and an iconostasis depicting the Last Supper. You can also visit the **old church of Ayios Stephanos,** with late-15th-century frescoes, as well as a **small icon museum.** ⊠ *Along eastern monastery route (from main road at intersection for Kalambaka, bear right at fork),* ☎ *0432/22279.* ⌫ *500 dr./€1.47.* ⊙ *Tues.–Sun. 9–1 and 3:20–6 (3–5 in winter).*

NEED A
BREAK?   Although you may stop anywhere on the circuit, the stretch approaching Ayia Triada from Ayios Stephanos has the best views for a midday **picnic.** Just hike a few yards off the road to a spot overlooking the valley and unpack.

James Bond fans will recognize **Ayia Triada** from the movie *For Your Eyes Only.* Of all the monasteries, it feels the most primitive and remote, and in fact, if pressed for time, you'll want to skip this one. According to local legend, the Monk Dometius was the first to arrive in 1438; the main church, dedicated to the Holy Trinity, was built in 1476, and the narthex and frescoes were added more than 200 years later. Look for the fresco with St. Sisois gazing upon the skeleton of Alexander the Great, meant to remind the viewer that power is fleeting. In the early 1980s thieves stole precious antique icons, which have never been recovered. The iconostasis has one icon (1662) that depicts Christ in local costume; another scene, of three angels, symbolizes the Holy Trinity. The apse's pseudo-trefoil window and the sawtooth decoration around it and beneath other windows lend a measure of grace to the structure. There are also a chapel dedicated to St. John the Baptist, a small folk museum, the monks' cells, a kitchen, a refectory, and cisterns. Ayia Triada is best known for its view, with Ayios Stephanos and Kalambaka in the south and Varlaam and Megalo Meteoro to the west. A footpath near the entrance (red arrows) descends to Kalambaka, about 3 km (2 mi). ⊠ *Along eastern monastery route, 656 ft north of Ayios Stefanos,* ☎ *0432/22220.* ⊠ *500 dr./€1.47.* ⊙ *Fri.– Wed. 9–12:30 and 3–5.*

EPIRUS AND THESSALY A TO Z

Arriving and Departing

By Bus

The **KTEL bus** system is preferable to the train. Eight or nine buses daily go from Athens's **Terminal A** (⊠ Kifissou 100, ☎ 01/512–5954) to **Ioannina station** (⊠ Between Sina and Zosimadou, ☎ 0651/26286); the trip takes about seven hours. Some buses take the longer route east through Kalambaka and Trikala rather than the usual southern route to the Rion–Antirion ferry and the Peloponnese. The 110-dr./€.32 ferry ride is not included in the bus ticket.

From Athens's dismal **Terminal B** (⊠ Near Liossion 260, ☎ 01/831–7153) seven buses leave daily for Trikala (six hours), where you then make the 25-minute connection to Kalambaka. On Sundays there is a reduced schedule for all towns.

For information in English on bus schedules, telephone the **EOT** in Athens (⊠ Syntagma [Constitution] Sq., ☎ 01/322–2545).

By Car

Driving to Kalambaka or Ioannina from Athens takes the greater part of a day. To reach Ioannina, take the National Road west past Corinth in the Peloponnese, to the Rion–Antirion ferry (9 km [5½ mi] before Patras), then continue north past Mesolonghi, Agrinion, Amfiloxia, and Arta (447 km [277 mi]). For Kalambaka, take the National Road north past Thebes and Lamia to North Monastirio (about 53 km [33 mi]) north of Lamia, where there is a turnoff for Trikala and Kalambaka (a total of 330 km [204 mi]). You may then drive on to Metsovo and Ioannina (another 126 km [78 mi]).

By Plane

Olympic Airways has two or three flights daily from Athens to Ioannina, and one flight daily from Thessaloniki. In Athens (⊠ Odos Othonos 6, Syntagma Sq., ☎ 01/966–6666); Ioannina (⊠ Katsadima 1, Platia Pirrou, ☎ 0651/28526; ⊠ Ioannina airport, 5 km [3 mi] outside town, ☎ 0651/27058); Thessaloniki (☎ 031/473212 or 031/473312).

By Train

The cheapest way to get to Kalambaka is by train, though it is not recommended. From Athens you must change trains at Palaiofarsalo, and the trip takes at least eight hours (the IC express cuts the time by an hour but costs 2,000 dr./€5.89 extra). For more information, contact the **Greek Railway Organization (OSE)**: Athens (✉ Karolou 1, ☎ 01/524–0601); Kalambaka (☎ 0432/22451).

Getting Around

By Bus

Four buses (KTEL) daily leave Ioannina for Metsovo (1½ hours) and two buses make the full journey to Kalambaka (three hours); frequencies are the same in the opposite direction. One bus daily leaves Ioannina for Dodona, returning in the afternoon. There is a bus to most villages once a day, but getting around is much easier in a rented car.

By Car

A rented car is by far the best way to explore the region, and one is essential to go beyond the main sights. The road from Ioannina to Metsovo to Kalambaka is one of the most scenic in northern Greece, but it traverses the famous Katara Pass, which is curvy and possibly hazardous, especially in winter (snow chains are necessary). If you have a few people, it might be more relaxing and almost as economical to hire a taxi to drive you around, at least for a day.

Contacts and Resources

Car Rentals

Ioannina: Avis (✉ Dodonis 96, ☎ 0651/46333). **Budget** (✉ Dodonis 109, ☎ 0651/43901; ✉ Airport, ☎ 0651/25102). **European** (✉ Koundourioti 2, ☎ 0651/70086). **Hertz** (✉ Dodonis 105, ☎ 0651/66900).

Emergencies

IOANNINA

Police (☎ (Tourist Police) 0651/25673 or 0651/26431). **Emergencies** (☎ 100). **Hospital** (☎ 0651/99111 or 0651/80111).

KALAMBAKA

Police (☎ 0432/76100). **Hospital** (☎ 0432/22222).

METSOVO

Police (☎ 0656/41233). **Health Center/First Aid** (☎ 0656/41111).

Guided Tours

In Athens, **CHAT** (✉ Stadiou 4, ☎ 01/322–2886) and **Key Tours** (✉ Kallirois 4, ☎ 01/923–3166) offer guided trips to Meteora and northern Greece. A three-day, two-night tour to Delphi and Meteora with lodging and half-board costs 79,000 dr./€233, with double-room accommodations, 95,000 dr./€280 for single.

In Ioannina, contact the **Greek Alpine Club** (✉ Despotatou Ipirou 2, ☎ 0651/22138) for walking-tour information; it's open from 7 PM to 9 PM. They organize a one-day trek in the Pindos Mountains every Sunday between June and October at a reasonable cost.

Aris Talaris (✉ Hotel Egnatia, Arvantinou 20, ☎ 0656/41263, FAX 0651/75060) can arrange excursions in the Metsovo area and hiking trips to the Zagorohoria and Vikos Gorge.

Metsovo Alpine Club (☎ 0656/41249) has information on hiking trails and the nearby ski center.

Travel Agencies

In Metsovo, **Kassaros Travel** (✉ Tsourmaka 3, ☎ 0656/41800, 0656/41346, 0656/41662, 094/4383131, 094/383131, or 094/397778, FAX 0656/41262) can issue plane tickets, arrange accommodations, and occasionally organize trips to the nearby lake or ski center.

In Ioannina, **Robinson Expeditions** (✉ 8 Merarhias 10, ☎ 0651/29402, FAX 0651/25071✉) specializes in outdoor tours and can make arrangements for single travelers or groups to trek in the Zagorohoria or hike the Vikos Gorge; other programs offer hang-gliding, rafting, kayaking, or nature study groups.

Visitor Information

IOANNINA

Greek National Tourist Organization (GNTO or EOT) (✉ N. Zerva 2, Platia Pirrou Dodonis 39, 45332, ☎ 0651/25086, 0651/41868, or 0651/46662, FAX 0651/72148 or 0651/49139) is open weekdays 7:30–2:30 and 4–8, weekends 9–2:30. **Ioannina Tourist Office** (☎ 0651/25086).

KALAMBAKA

Tourist Police (✉ Hatzipetrou 10–11, ☎ 0432/22109). In the summertime a tourist information booth is erected in the main square.

5 NORTHERN GREECE

THESSALONIKI, CHALKIDIKI, AND THE ALEXANDER THE GREAT SITES

From the frescoed tomb of Philip II of Macedon to Zeus's mythical throne atop Mt. Olympus, Northern Greece bestows surprising superlatives. You can observe (and sometimes join) a dig at Greece's most active archaeological site, stroll empty beaches, hike virgin trails through rampant wildflowers, or experience the solitary majesty of Mt. Athos monastery. Thessaloniki was once home to Alexander the Great and the crossroads of the ancient world; today, it is Greece's second city, as it was Byzantium's, brimming with antiquities, street markets, and the shadows of history.

By Lea Lane

Updated by
B. Samantha
Stenzel

THE REGION WE CALL NORTHERN GREECE, comprising Macedonia in the west and Thrace in the east, covers the Balkan frontier from Albania to Bulgaria and also touches Turkey. It is both a meeting point and a crossroads for Europe, the Mediterranean, and Asia, and is imbued with the sights, sounds, and colors of cultures that have, in some periods, blended harmoniously and in others clashed violently.

This mountainous fist of land with three fingerlike peninsulas jutting into the Aegean has vast, fertile plains overflowing with monuments and artifacts of the powerful and rich civilizations that fought and lived here: marble temples and fortifications built by Athens and Sparta, rough-hewn Macedonian tombs, the arches and rotundas of Imperial Rome, the domes of Byzantium, and the minarets and *hamams* (baths) of the Ottomans.

From archaeological remains, we know that settlements in the area that is now Thessaloniki were first inhabited some 6,000 years ago. Historians today tell us the region was established as the state of Macedonia in the 8th century BC by a wave of settlers from Thessaly. According to one tradition, the monarchy is believed to have been established by the 7th century BC and the region unified by Perdikkas I, the son of Temenos, who had fled from Argos in the Peloponnese. During the reign of Amyntas I (circa 540–05 BC), Macedonia was virtually a Persian province. His son Alexander I (died 454 BC) was a surreptitious Philhellene—despite the fact that he accompanied Xerxes as he crossed the Dardenelles and invaded Greece (480 BC), the prelude to the Second Persian War (described by Herodotus in his histories). The decisive battle took place at Thermopylae, north of Delphi; Greek forces numbered only about 8,000, while the Persians had (by some accounts) about 30,000 soldiers, and the Greeks went down in a great defeat. However, later that year, the Greeks turned the tide against the Persians at the Battle of Salamis and a second victory at Plataia in 479 BC, finally driving them out of Greece. Within a hundred years, Philip II (382–36 BC) and his son Alexander the Great had conquered all of Greece except Sparta, and all of Persia as well. After Alexander's death his brother-in-law Cassander established Thessaloniki as the capital (316 BC), naming it for his new bride, Alexander's half-sister. She was the daughter of the much-married Philip, who had named her after his famous *nike* (victory) in Thessaly, where her mother had been one of his prizes. Quite a saga.

Profiting from squabbles among Alexander's successors, the Romans took over Macedonia, and by 146 BC, the rest of Greece had become a Roman province. In 42 BC, after the assassination of Julius Caesar, Marc Anthony defeated Brutus and Cassius at the double battles of Philippi in Macedonia. Under the Pax Romana that followed, St. Paul twice traveled through on his way to Corinth, paving the way for the second great flowering of Greek and Macedonian culture—that of the Byzantine Empire.

Byzantium held sway for 1,100 years, the center of Greek civilization shifted from Athens to Constantinople, and Thessaloniki became the second most important city in the empire. It remained that way under the Ottoman Turks, who sacked Constantinople in 1453 and whose dominance over Northern Greece lasted until the 1912–13 Balkan Wars. Macedonia was then united with the rest of Greece, and the 1923 Peace of Lausanne established the present-day borders of Thrace—but two of the bloodiest battles were yet to come. In 1941, Mussolini's troops invaded Northern Greece and were pushed back into Albania, causing the German army to intervene and fight its way through the country from the north. Then, at the end of World War II, Epirus and Macedonia became the principal arena for the Greek Civil War (1946–49) between the Communists and Royalists.

Today, Northern Greece still feels a bit threatened, as the collapse of Yugoslavia has brought to life age-old ethnic and religious animosities. Because the Serbians are Orthodox Christians, they are natural allies in any confrontations against non-Christians. It was difficult, therefore, for the Greeks to understand (needless to say, particularly during the bombing of Serbia in 1999) why the rest of the Christian world seemed to be against their fellow believers. Northern Greeks are especially resentful of the southernmost former Yugoslavian state's insistence on calling itself "Macedonia," and its decision to have the star of Vergina, the representation of the ancient Macedonian dynasty, as a national symbol on its flag. Despite the fierce opposition of the Greeks to its existence, in 1993 it was officially recognized by the European Union and the United Nations as the former Yugoslav Republic of Macedonia (FYROM). In 1995, the Greeks lifted an embargo of Macedonia and opened up the borders for trade; in return, FYROM removed the star of Vergina from its flag and revised its constitution to remove sections that Greece claimed was threatening. Nevertheless, rumors remain of international plots to redraw the map of the Balkans. These things have happened so often through the ages, this generation sees no reason why they won't again. In spite of continuing tensions, Northern Greece, and especially Thessaloniki, is flourishing. The city is the site of Greece's annual Trade Fair and of the country's largest university; new hotels have been built and older ones upgraded; the highway connecting Macedonia with more remote regions of Thrace has been widened and extended; and Thessaloniki was the proud and successful 1997 Cultural Capital of Europe.

Pleasures and Pastimes

Dining

The cosmopolitan, multiracial character of Thessaloniki—building on its historic Byzantine and Ottoman influences—has created a multifaceted cuisine of sometimes subtle sophistication; in fact, many Greeks feel Thessaloniki has the best food in the country. It is distinguished by its liberal use of fragrant Levantine spices, including hot red peppers from Florina called *Florines* and sweet peppers known as *boukova*. Traditional Thracian and Macedonian cooks adapt to the seasons: in winter, rich game such as boar and venison is served, and in summer, mussels and other seafood from the Aegean, and fruits and vegetables from the fertile plains. Wheat, corn, rye, and barley grown in this breadbasket of Greece yield especially fine baked goods. The relatively cooler climate here is reflected in rich chicken soups, roast chicken, stuffed vegetables, and stewed lamb and pork.

Thessaloniki is especially known for its *mezedes* or small portions of food; every little *ouzerie* (casual bar) or taverna has at least one prized house recipe. The sensual joy of good food and the ritual of eating out, both so essential to Greek life, involve shared emotions, new friends, and treasured family. Leisurely lunches consisting of a multitude of little plates take place every weekday in tiny storefronts in little cul-de-sacs in or near Modiano Market or in the Upper City or on breezy terraces near the seaside, and are the focal point of a typical Thessaloniki day. Specialties include *medhia* (mussels) which come from farms outside the bay and are served in a variety of styles, including *saganaki* (fried in a pan with tomatoes, peppers, and feta) and *achnista* (steamed in broth with herbs); and *soutzoukakia* (Anatolian-style meatballs in tomato sauce, seasoned with cumin). *Amiletita* (the unmentionables or lambs' testicles) are tender and flavorful, a delicacy for those who have the nerve to give them a try. *Peinerli* (an open-faced boat of bread filled with cheese and ham) is a Black Sea specialty brought here by the *Pontii*, Greeks who emigrated from that area. Along the coast, informal restaurants specialize in barbecued chicken. Meals are complemented by generous amounts of wine, ouzo, and *tsipouro*, the local version of grappa. In most villages, pastry shops offering traditional sweets, and cafés pouring dark, strong coffee, are bustling at all hours.

Neighborhoods center on tavernas and casual bars. You are encouraged to go to the kitchen and choose your meals, generally from a dozen or so pots filled to the brim. Try the excellent barrel or bottled local wines, especially reds under labels such as Naoussa or Porto Carras or a little bottle of Mavromatina retsina, considered the best bottled version in all of Greece. Even at the best restaurants dress is usually casual (neat and dark colors are favored for evening). Although at higher-priced establishments reservations are theoretically possible, nothing is guaranteed. It is prudent to arrive around 8 PM, earlier than most Greeks like to eat (but note that many places do not open before then)—but it's much more fun to come at 9 PM or even later; after all, you're in Greece to mix with the Greeks and do as they do. If it's very crowded, the management will usually manage to squeeze you in somewhere or you can sit at the bar and people-watch while you have a drink and wait for a table.

CATEGORY	COST*
$$$$	over 9,000 dr. (€26.54)
$$$	6,000 dr.–9,000 dr. (€17.69–€26.54)
$$	3,500 dr.–6,000 dr. (€10.32–€17.69)
$	under 3,500 dr. (€10.32)

*for a three-course meal, including tax and service but excluding drinks

Lodging

Despite some recent improvements, Thessaloniki's hotels (much like Athens's) are nothing to write home about and are mostly geared to the needs of transient businesspeople, with little emphasis on capturing the spirit-of-place so appealing to tourists. Selection of hotels elsewhere in Northern Greece varies from exclusive seaside resorts in Chalkidiki to modest, family-managed hostel-like housing on the slopes of Mt. Olympus. Throughout the area, hotels are usually small, somewhat spartan affairs whose charm comes mainly from their surroundings. Some establishments, particularly in Chalkidiki, close for the winter (we've noted when it's otherwise); it is best to make arrangements ahead.

CATEGORY	COST*
$$$$	over 45,000 dr. (€132.74)
$$$	30,000 dr.–45,000 dr. (€88.49–€132.74)
$$	15,000 dr.–30,000 dr. (€44.24–€88.49)
$	under 15,000 dr. (€44.24)

*All prices are for a standard double room, including tax, service, and breakfast unless noted otherwise.

✍ *following the text of a review is your signal that the property has a Web site, where you will find details and, usually, images; for a link, visit www.fodors.com/urls.*

Monasteries

Monks got to Northern Greece long before tour groups, and the sites they chose for their monasteries are the most beautiful locations throughout the cities and countryside. In this region of extraordinary Byzantine architecture, one of the the the most impressive monastic complexes in the world is near the Ayion Oros (Holy Mountain) of Mt. Athos.

Exploring Northern Greece

A delightful geographic mix awaits you: in the mountains, from snow-covered Mt. Olympus to the mineral-rich eastern ranges, forests of pine, spruce, juniper, oak, and chestnut abound, and ski resorts and climbing opportunities beckon. Cosmopolitan Thessaloniki lies in the strategic center of Macedonia, nestled gracefully in the wide but protective arms of the Thermaic Gulf and buttressed on its inland side by a low-lying mountain range around which the Axios River flows south to the Aegean. This is a vast, fertile plain of grain, vegetables, and fruit. In the lowlands of Chalkidiki, parts of Thrace, and the island of Thasos, fruit and olive trees flourish with vineyards and tobacco plantations. In summer the air is redolent of thyme and oregano. White-sand beaches along miles of inleted coastline are lapped by a turquoise sea. You don't have to travel far from Thessaloniki to find these pleasures: The famed three-fingered peninsulas, with their vistas of mountain and sea, and tipped by famed Mt. Athos monastery, are only a few hours away by car on good highways.

Numbers in the text correspond to numbers in the margin and on the Exploring Thessaloniki and Northern Greece maps.

Great Itineraries

Thessaloniki's central location in Macedonia makes it a perfect base for the short itinerary; the ancient sites are within a couple of hours by car or bus. For the longer itineraries, a car rented in Thessaloniki will simplify drives and give you time for serendipitous pleasures. As Kavala has an airport with frequent flights back to Thessaloniki and Athens, and frequent ferry service to Aegean islands, you don't necessarily have to drive back to your western starting point. Make sure you have up-to-date ferry schedules, and take hydrofoils to cut time in half going to and from the island of Thasos.

IF YOU HAVE 3 DAYS

Starting in 🖼 **Thessaloniki** ①–⑳, explore both the old and the new city, not missing the **archaeological museum** ②, the Kastro, and the **White Tower** ①. Take a long promenade on the boardwalk to people-watch and join all the Thessalonians for coffee by the sea. Overnight in Thessaloniki. Spend your second day visiting the famous Alexander the Great sites: **Pella** ㉑ and **Vergina** ㉒, and then head back to Thessaloniki for nightlife. On the third day, relax, visit a museum or shop in the morning, then have lunch on Mt. Olympus and explore 🖼 **Dion** ㉓, or spend the entire day in the mountain area.

IF YOU HAVE 8 DAYS

Begin in your home base, 🖼 **Thessaloniki** ①–⑳, taking a day to explore the city. On the second day head northeast to 🖼 **Kavala** ㉚ and **Philippi** ㉛, enjoying the seaside and historic sites, and staying over in Kavala. Or take a late-evening ferry to the island of 🖼 **Thasos** ㉜ with its excellent beaches, ruins, traditional villages, and mountain hikes. Spend the third day there, and next morning, return to Thessaloniki by way of Alexander the Great territory, including **Pella** ㉑ and **Vergina** ㉒. After viewing those sights, backtrack to overnight in Thessaloniki for your fourth night. On the fifth day, hike or take a four-wheel drive through the terrain of ▦ **Dion** ㉓ and ▦ **Mt. Olympus** ㉔—overnight in the village of Litochoro on the slopes of the mountain. On the sixth day venture off the beaten path northwest to **Lake Prespas** and Kastoria; for your sixth overnight, head for the ▦ **peninsula adjacent to Mt. Athos,** or simply head back to the hub of Thessaloniki, which is only a couple of hours away from most of these sights. The next morning drive to **the Chalkidiki area,** and spend the seventh day outdoors, or (if you can) at Mt. Athos. Return that evening to Thessaloniki for further delving into museums, historic areas, and shops before departing.

When to Tour

Thessaloniki provides interesting events and cultural activities throughout the year, and all seasons have their special treats. Even winter—less crowded with tourists—offers the savory pleasures of hot coffee, fiery ouzo, and warm Thessalonian friendship. Note, however, that September and October are especially crowded due to festivals and trade fairs, when prices go up and accommodations are almost impossible to find.

Travel throughout the rest of Northern Greece is best from May through October, when all establishments are open. A profusion of red, yellow, and purple wildflowers edges most roads in spring, and the golden harvest season is a mellow time of wheat, wine, and olives. Summer months are most crowded but best for sunning, swimming, and schmoozing with northern Europeans and Greek families on holiday. Get an early start in warmer months, because the days heat up and siesta hours cut them short. Do as the Greeks: indulge in a rest in the afternoon, so you can enjoy the late hours!

THESSALONIKI

At the crossroads of East and West, where North blends into South, Thessaloniki (accent on the "ni") has seen the rise and fall of all manner of civilizations: Macedonian, Hellenic, Roman, Byzantine, Ottoman, and that of the Jews and of the modern Greeks. Each of its successive conquerors has plundered, razed, and buried much of what went before. Thus, little remains of the Macedonian-Hellenistic civilization that built the city's fortifications. The Romans took most of what was of portable value back to Italy and buried the rest. The Roman temples then became Byzantine churches, and structures were torn down to refortify the walls and build the towers, where both Hellenistic and Roman elements can still be seen. The Ottoman Turks, in turn, transformed the Byzantine churches into mosques and demolished many other buildings for their minarets, hamams, *imarets* (almshouses), fountains, and private mansions. When the Greeks regained the city, they had their churches reconsecrated and tore down most of the minarets. Then, in 1917, a great fire destroyed much of what was left of the colorful, teeming blend of cultures that the Ottoman reign had packed in: the bazaars, the elegant hotels and banks, the multistoried Turkish town houses, and the distinctive European Christian, Jewish, and Greek quarters.

Thessaloniki—usually called Salonika by Greeks—is today a vibrant city of close to 1 million people, and its spacious layout is partly a result of the orderly vision of the French architect Ernest Hébrard, who rebuilt the city after the fire. But its more distant past can still be seen and sensed, and a little walking will be well rewarded: parks, squares, old neighborhoods with narrow alleyways and gardens, courtyards draped with laundry, neoclassic mansions, more than 50 churches and 40 monasteries—the mix is exciting, charming, ever-changing, and ongoing. For example, Ladadika, the former warehouse district by the port was the home of hookers and toughs a decade ago. Today the warehouses have been recycled into a pedestrian zone of restaurants and clubs, and the scene is filled with young and old, strolling by fountains, snapping fingers to the music in the air, and enjoying mezedes and microbrewery beers at tables spilling onto the stone squares. Adjacent Ksiladika, or woodworkers district, has little cafés and terrific restaurants specializing in mezedes and is frequented by the craftspeople who run little shops in the area.

Unlike Athens, which sprawls among hills and is difficult to get a handle on, Thessaloniki is fairly centralized and easy to get used to; whether it's the upper old town or the modern city along the bay, its charm in part is its warmth and accessibility. Thessalonians resisted the implementation of continuous hours for shops and businesses, now in effect in Athens: the afternoon *mesimeri*, or siesta, is still sacrosanct (don't ever call a Thessalonian between 3 and 5 PM!), preceded by an abundant, leisurely lunch with friends and family. Salonika lends itself to lazy meandering, the exploring of in-town archaeological sites and Byzantine treasures, and café-style people-watching. Ask locals where a pastry shop is and chances are they will not only tell you (especially if you smile with a Greek "thank you," *efcharisto,* and invariably get answered with a delighted *parakalo,* or "you are welcome"), but will lead you there—and then *buy* you the pastry!

Exploring Thessaloniki

We suggest two routes for exploring some highlights. The best tour, however, is simply to wander through the streets responding to whatever you encounter. It is hard to get lost, since the entire city slopes downhill to the bay, where you can always align yourself with the White Tower and the city skyline.

The White Tower, Sintrivaniou Square, and Southern City Environs

Exploring the area from the White Tower west along the gulf to Aristotelous Square reveals icons of the city's history: grand monuments of Emperor Galerius, artifacts from the Neolithic period through the Roman occupation housed in the archaeological museum, prominent churches, as well as the city's most important landmark, the tower itself. The lively shopping streets, bustling markets, and cafés reward with the fascinating, unexpected encounters and sensual treats of a great city.

A GOOD WALK

Begin at the **White Tower** ①; after viewing the Byzantine works, take in the city's expanse from the rooftop. From the White Tower walk east on the seaside promenade Nikis until you see the dramatic bronze **statue of Alexander and his horse, Bucephalus.** Meander for five minutes through the lovely park to the north, with its inviting cafés and children's playground; across the wide promenade cutting through the park is the renowned **archaeological museum** ②, with finds dating from prehistoric Greece to Alexander's Macedonia. The **Byzantine Museum** ③ is just east of the museum, and farther east, at the intersection of Vasilis Olgas and 25 Martiou (25th of March Street), is the **Pinacothiki** (Municipal Gallery). Head across the street toward the city center to the beginning of the city's fanciest shopping street, **Tsimiski.** In the middle of the city block is the beautiful pedestrian **Dimitriou Gounari street** lined with delightful shops and cafés. It crosses Tsimiski and leads you north directly to the **Arch of Galerius** ④. Even if the **Rotunda** ⑤ is closed, try to explore the narrow streets surrounding the area, rich with cluttered junk and antiques shops; on Wednesday you'll see the eclectic Russian Market. Cross Egnatia again to the south side of the street and continue west to the lovely 14th-century **Church of the Metamorphosis** ⑥. Continuing west on Egnatia, turn right and walk a half block up Ayios Sofias to the oldest Byzantine church in the city, the 5th-century **Panagia Achiropiitos** ⑦. Next head south again on Ayias Ayios Sofias for a short downhill walk to reach the 8th-century church of **Ayia Sofia** ⑧.

To explore a more contemporary part of the city center, exit via Ayia Sofia's parklike entrance, cross the street, and walk due west on Ermou. Ermou will carry you directly into **Modiano Market** ⑨, the heart of the central marketplace, complete with myriad foods and faces to check out. Take a look at the evocative **Memorial to Grigoris Lambrakis** ⑩ just west of the market. Then continue on to the fascinating **Museum of Ancient Greek, Byzantine and Post-Byzantine Instruments** ⑪, which has more than 200 instruments of all sizes and shapes dating from the Bronze age until the beginning of this century. You can quit now or head south to Aristotelous Square, the *kafenia-* (traditional Greek coffeehouses) lined village square of the city center, for a drink and postcard-writing session before a well-deserved Greek siesta.

TIMING

Leave most of a day, depending upon your speed. Plan to spend at least an hour at the archaeological museum. The best time to explore smaller Byzantine churches is during a service, especially on Sundays, because they may be closed most of the time. But be sure to be conservatively dressed and respectful; talking or walking in front of people with a guidebook in hand interferes with the worshipful demeanor of the congregants. Otherwise, hours are not set in stone; try from about 8 AM to noon and 5:30 to 7:30 on any day, except where noted.

SIGHTS TO SEE

❹ **Arch of Galerius.** The imposing arch, or *kamára,* is one of a number of monuments built by Galerius around AD 305, during his reign as co-emperor of Diocletian's divided Roman Empire (☞ Rotunda *and* Platia Navarino, *below*). It was built to celebrate the victory over Persia in AD 297, and you can still see scenes of those battles on the badly eroded bas-reliefs. Originally, the arch had four pediments and a dome and was intended to span not only the Via Egnatia, the ancient road leading Rome to the rest of its territory, but also a passageway leading north to the Rotunda. Only the large arches remain. ⊠ *Egnatia Odos, Sintrivaniou Sq.*

★ ❷ **Archaeological Museum.** This unpretentious, single-story white structure gives no hint from the outside of the treasures within, including a superb collection of artifacts from Neolithic times, with sculptures from the archaic, classical, and Roman eras and remains from the archaic temple at Thermi. (However, its extraordinary Philip of Macedon finds from the tomb of Vergina have been transferred to the museum there.) Start off in Gallery 4, which traces the ancient city's history from archaeological finds. ⊠ *Hanth Sq., opposite the exhibition grounds,* ☎ *031/830538.* ☞ *1,500 dr./€4.42* ۞ *Mon. 12:30–7, Tues.–Fri. 8–7, weekends 8:30–3.*

★ ❽ **Ayia Sofia.** Although this is the focal point of the city's Easter and Christmas celebrations, its founding date has experts disagreeing over the centuries. From its architecture it is believed to be late 8th century, a time of transition from the domed basilica toward the cruciform plan. Ecclesiastics think it was built after the first Council of Nicea (325), when Christ was declared a manifestation of Divine Wisdom; other church historians say it was contemporaneous with the magnificent church of

Ayia Sofia in Constantinople, on which it was modeled. In any case, its rather drab interior contains two superb mosaics: one of the Ascension, and the other of the Virgin Mary holding Jesus in her arms. This latter mosaic is an interesting example of the conflict in the Orthodox Church (726–843) between the Iconoclasts (icon smashers, which they often literally were) and the Iconodules (icon venerators or "slaves"). At one point in this doctrinal struggle, the Virgin Mary in the mosaic was replaced by a large cross (still partly visible), and only later, after the victory of the Iconodules, was it again replaced with an image of Virgin Mary holding baby Jesus. ⊠ *Pavlou Mela, Ayias Sophias Sq.*, ☎ *031/270253.* ✆ *Free.* ◷ *Daily 8–9.*

Ayios Panteleimon. A prime example of Macedonian 14th-century church architecture, the facades of this church reveal the ornamental interplay of brick and stonework and a dome displaying typical, strong upward motion. ⊠ *Egnatia Odos.*

❸ Byzantine Museum. Inaugurated in 1994, this structure is the most modern museum in Greece and the repository of most of the country's finest Byzantine art: priceless icons, frescoes, sculpted reliefs, jewelry, glasswork, manuscripts, pottery, and coins. Eight rooms hold treasures such as a gold-embroidered epitaph and a silver relic case with engraved scenes from the Bible. Its 1997–98 exhibition in conjunction with the Cultural Capital of Europe celebration displayed the coveted Byzantine collection from Mt. Athos (you may, unfortunately, have to wait another millennium to see it again). Meanwhile, the Byzantine treasures that had been stored in the White Tower have been transferred to their new home here. ⊠ *2 Leoforos Stratou*, ☎ *031/868570.* ✆ *2,000 dr./€5.89* ◷ *Mon. 3–9, Tues.–Sat. 11–1 and 5–9, Sun. 11–3.*

❻ Church of the Metamorphosis. This sunken church is a fine example of 14th-century Macedonian church architecture, with a decorative mix of brick and stonework and the strong upward thrust of the dome. ⊠ *Egnatia Odos.*

Egnatia Odos. It was during the Byzantine period that Thessaloniki came into its own as a commercial crossroads, because the Via Egnatia, which already connected the city to Rome (with the help of a short boat trip across the Adriatic), was extended east to Constantinople. Today Egnatia Odos virtually begins along the same path; it is Thessaloniki's main commercial thoroughfare, although not as upscale as the parallel Tsimiski Street, two blocks to the south. ⊠ *City points southwest to northeast.*

❿ Memorial to Grigoris Lambrakis. This is especially moving if you have read the novel *Z* by Vassilis Vassilikos or seen the Costas-Gavras film about the murder of the leftist member of Parliament (played by Yves Montand) by rightists in 1963, which precipitated the events that resulted in the 1967 takeover of the colonels' junta. Marking the site of the murder is a dramatic bronze head and arm, above which flutters a sculpted dove. ⊠ *Just west of Modiano market, on corner of Ermou and Eleftherios Venezelou.*

★ ❾ Modiano Market. This old landmark was overhauled in 1922 by a Jewish architect who gave the covered market its name. It is especially popular with students and artists, and worth a visit—as is the generally cheaper **open-air market** (⊠ On the north side of Ermou)—even if you have no intention of buying anything. Both are rich not only with all manner of fish, meats, vegetables, fruits, breads, spices, wines, and household items but with true human characters as well: the whole spectrum of colorful hangers-on who congregate at markets the world over, even strolling gypsy musicians (best watched on Saturday afternoons after the stores close at 2 PM), while eating and drinking in the market's ouzeries and tavernas. ⊠ *Along city block on south side of Ermou.*

Municipal Gallery (Pinacothiki). Housed in the 1905 Villa Mordoh, amid lush gardens, the art gallery has a collection of more than 800 pieces, including etchings, engravings, sculpture, Byzantine icons, and modern Thessaloniki art from the turn of the 20th century to 1967. ⊠ *162 Vasilis Olgas,* ☎ *031/425531,* 𝔽𝔸𝕏 *031/411101.* 🎟 *Free.* ☉ *Tues.–Fri. 9–1 and 5–9, Sat. 5–9, Sun. 9–1.*

⑪ Museum of Ancient Greek, Byzantine, and Post-Byzantine Instruments. Located in a handsome renovated building in Ladadika, this new museum has more than 200 ancient to modern instruments which are stunningly displayed with dramatic lighting (and thorough labeling in Greek and English). Some are replicas modeled after those seen on ancient vase paintings, sculptures, and manuscripts (which are often reproduced and displayed, so that one can compare them to the instruments). The unique collection includes a variety of fantastically shaped instruments, works of art in their own merit. The oldest instrument on display is a triangular psaltery, copied from an exquisite sculpture of one of the Cycladic idols (dating to 2800 BC and on display in the National Archaeological Museum in Athens). A five-stringed lyre with a sound box made from a tortoise shell, Pan pipes, an ancient guitar, and wind instruments are some of the other exhibits. Stop for a drink in the chic café on the second floor; the museum's conference center often has talks and concerts. ⊠ *12 Katouni St., Ladadika.* 🎟 *1,500 dr./€4.42* ☉ *Tues.–Sun. 9–3 and 5–9.*

⑦ Panagia Achiropiitos. This 5th-century Byzantine church is an early example of the basilica form and marvels the eye with arcades, monolithic columns topped by elaborate capitals, and exquisite period mosaics of birds and flowers. It is the second oldest church in Thessaloniki and probably the oldest in continuous use in the Eastern Mediterranean. Its name means "made without hands," because in the 12th century an icon supposedly appeared there, miraculously. An inscription in Arabic on a column states "Sultan Murat captured Thessaloniki in the year 1430," which was the year it was converted into a mosque, much to the dismay of the Thessalonians. ⊠ *Ayios Sofias.*

Platia Navarino. This tree- and awning-shaded square proper, its fountain a marvelous bronze of a young boy peeing, is a favorite drinking, eating, and nightlife hub among students. The remaining structures in Galerius's city-center complex include a racetrack (hence the name of Platia Hippodromiou, which covers it today), a palace, and an octagonal structure that may have been his throne room. Parts of these buildings have been excavated and can be seen in sunken areas around the square and the pedestrian street bordering it. ⊠ *Directly south of Rotunda and Triumphal Arch.*

★ ⑤ Rotunda. Also known as Ayios Giorgios, this brickwork edifice has become a layered monument to the city's rich history. Built in AD 306, it was probably intended as Roman Emperor Galerius's mausoleum. However, when he died in Bulgaria, his successor refused to have the body brought back. Under Theodosius the Great, the Byzantines converted the Rotunda into a church dedicated to St. George (thus, the name), with minimal alterations, except for adding impressive 4th-century AD mosaics of early saints; the Ottomans made it a mosque (whose minaret still stands), and it was last restored after the damage suffered in a 1978 earthquake. Today, it occasionally houses art exhibits and concerts and remains a veritable museum of Christian art. If you have time, explore the narrow **surrounding streets**; on Wednesday they are flooded with the **Russian Market,** a novel commercial enterprise featuring tchotchkes and the occasional interesting heirloom, antique, or folk art piece hawked by Eastern European refugees, a good many of Greek descent. ⊠ *On D. Gounari St., just off Sintrivaniou Sq.,* ☎ *031/ 213627.* ☉ *Special events.*

★ ❶ **White Tower.** The formidable sea walls and intermittent towers encircling the medieval city were erected under Theodosius the Great, probably in the 15th century on the site of earlier walls. In 1866, with the threat of piracy diminishing and European commerce increasingly imperative, the Ottoman Turks began demolishing them. This tower is the only one along the seafront left standing (the other remaining is its twin, the Trigoniou, in the old city). During the 18th century the tower was an infamous prison and later a place of execution, and became known as the Bloody Tower. But the Turks literally whitewashed it, perhaps in deference to the foreign businessmen whom they hoped to attract, and it has become the city's most famous landmark. These days, the tower that looks like a big chess piece houses interesting artifacts from the history and cultural life of the city from AD 300 to 1400. ⊠ *Waterfront Promenade, Nikis and Pavlou Melas Sts.,* ☎ *031/ 267832.* 🎟 *Free* ☉ *Mon. 12:30–7, Tues.–Fri. 8–7, weekends 8:30–3.*

Upper City, Panagia Chalkeon, and Aristotelous Square

Upper City (*Ano Polis*) is called Ta Kastra ("the castles") because of the castle of Eptapyrghion and the many fortified towers that once bristled along the walls. This is the former Turkish quarter, comprising what is left of 19th-century Thessaloniki, and is filled with timber-framed houses with their upper stories overhanging the steep streets. The views of the modern city below and the Thermaic Gulf are stunning, but other than Byzantine churches, there are few specific places of historical interest. You'll find it an experience in itself to navigate the steps, past gossipy women, grandfathers playing backgammon in smoky cafés, and giggling children playing tag in tiny courtyards filled with sweet-smelling flowers, stray cats, and flapping laundry.

Unfortunately, getting there can be a chore, as taxi drivers often try to avoid the cramped, congested streets and fear missing a fare back down. Have your hotel find a willing driver, or take a local bus. Buses 22 and 23 leave from the terminal at Platia Eleftherios (⊠ 2 blocks west of Aristotelous Square) every 10 to 15 minutes and follow an interesting route through the narrow streets of the Upper City.

A GOOD WALK

Start this excursion with the superb aerial city view from the **Tower of Trigoniou** ⑫; then walk west along the inside of the seaward wall (the wall should be to your right). Walk a few yards past the second *portara* (large open gateway) and to your left you will see the entrance to the grounds of **Moni Vlatádon** ⑬ and its tiny chapel to Sts. Peter and Paul. The **castle of Eptapyrghion** ⑭ is north along Eptapyrghiou. Backtrack to the Tower of Trigoniou and continue west along Eptapyrghiou street to the first wide street on your left, Dimitriou Poliorkitou, and take the broad flight of stairs to the beginning of the **Old Turkish Quarter** toward the sea. Follow Dimitriou Poliorkitou west, bearing left, and take the winding descent to the left and then to the right until you come to the doors of the 5th-century **Osios David** ⑮.

Turn right and continue down the narrow cobblestone street to the first intersection. Below a strange tin "palace" of the self-proclaimed "King of the Greeks," follow Akropoleos to the small Platia Romfei; walk

Exploring Thessaloniki

along Eolou to see the beautiful frescoes in the small but exceptional 14th-century **Ayios Nikolaos Orfanos** ⑯.

Walk downhill on Apostolou Pavlou, the legendary path Apostle Paul took to the Upper City to address the Thessalonians, and cross busy Kassandrou. At Ataturk turn right onto Ayiou Dimitriou, which can be crowded, noisy, and not very attractive, so you may choose to walk along a smaller, more pleasant parallel street. Continue west about six blocks until you reach **Ayios Dimitrios** ⑰ church, named for Thessaloniki's patron saint and where he was martyred. Forge on downhill, one block south from the church, to the very active excavation of the ancient **Roman Forum** ⑱. Walk west on Olimbou and turn left at the second corner onto short, diagonal Tositsa Street, and you will enter the *paliatzidiko* (flea market), the city's primo junk, antiques, and roaming-peddler promenade. From **Panagia Chalkeon** ⑲, on the southwest corner of the immense Dikasterion Square, cross to the lower side of Egnatia Odos; a half block down, take a right on Aristotelous. Along Aristotelous, take a right on Vasiliou Irakleiou, the corner after Ermou, and walk half a block to the **Jewish Community Memorial Museum** ⑳, a moving tribute to the persecution during World War II.

TIMING

This tour should take a few hours, at least. You will want to spend some time at Ayios Dimitrios, possibly to observe a mass (☞ Timing *in* A Good Walk, *above*). Of course, finding yourself gazing endlessly at evocations of the city's rich past, both artistic and historic, plus enjoying attractions such as flea markets—especially if you get caught up in haggling over a Byzantine trinket—can easily mean an exploration of this district can take a whole day.

SIGHTS TO SEE

★ **Ano Polis (Upper City).** The Upper City is also called Ta Kastra ("the castles") because of the castle of Eptapyrghion (☞ *below*) and the many fortified towers that once bristled along the walls. The area within and just outside the remains of the walls is like a village unto itself, a charming jumble of the rich, the poor, and the renovated. Rustic one-story peasant houses, many still occupied by the families that built them, sit side by side with houses newly built or restored by the wealthier class. And as the area continues to be upgraded, new tavernas, café-bars, and restaurants spring up to serve the visitors, both Greek and foreign, who flock there for a cool evening out. ⊠ *Elevated northern area of city.*

Ataturk's House. The birthplace of Mustafa Kemal, which also houses the Turkish Consulate, is a high point for those interested in the history of the Turkish influence in Thessaloniki. The soldier and statesman who established the Turkish republic, and became its president, Ataturk was born here in 1881. He participated in the city's Young Turk movement, which eventually led to the collapse of the sultanate and the formation of the modern Turkish state. In this modest, wood-frame house, which was renovated in 1981 and is decorated in Ottoman style, you can also explore a museum with personal photos and clothing dating from his early life in Thessaloniki. To get in, ring the bell at the Turkish Consulate down the block and show your passport, and you'll be given an escorted tour. Ask to take a walk in the little sculptured rose garden. ⊠ *151 Ayiou Dimitriou,* ☎ *031/269964.* ☞ *Free.* ☉ *Mon.–Fri. 9–1, 2–5.*

NEED A
BREAK?

Throughout the city, little shops and cellars specialize in a Macedonian treat called a submarine, a spoonful of sweets such as *visino* (black) cherries in syrup, dipped in a glass of ice water. In nice weather, sit outside and enjoy the sweet street life as well.

★ **⑰ Ayios Dimitrios.** This magnificent five-aisle basilica, covered in mosaics, is Greece's largest church and a powerful tribute to the patron saint of Thessaloniki. It was rebuilt and restored from 1926 to 1949 with attention to preserving the details of the original; the marks left by a fire can still be seen throughout. In the time of the emperor Galerius, the young, scholarly Dimitrios was preaching Christianity in the coppersmith district, in contravention of a recent edict. He was arrested and jailed in a room in the old Roman baths, on the site of the present church. While he was incarcerated in AD 303, Dimitrios gave a Christian blessing to a gladiator friend named Nestor, who was about to fight Galerius's champion, Lyaios. When Nestor fought and killed Lyaios, after having made Dimitrios's blessing public, the enraged Galerius had Nestor executed on the spot and had Dimitrios speared to death in his cell. His Christian brethren were said to have buried him there. A church was built on the ruins of this bath in the 5th century AD but was then destroyed by an earthquake in the 7th century. The church was rebuilt, and gradually the story of Dimitrios and Nestor grew to be considered apocryphal until the great 1917 fire burned down most of the 7th-century church and brought to light its true past. The process of rebuilding uncovered rooms beneath the apse that appear to be those very baths, and the discovery there of a reliquary containing a vial of bloodstained earth leaves little doubt that this is indeed the spot where St. Dimitrios was martyred. You can enter through a small doorway to the right of the altar. The church had been plastered over by the Turks, who had turned it into a mosque, but eight original mosaics remain on either side of this altar. You may work your way through the crypt, containing sculpture from the 3rd to 5th centuries AD and Byzantine artifacts, or peruse the parish women's craft-works cooperative. ⊠ *Ayiou Dimitriou and Ayios Nikolaos at Egnatias St.,* ☎ *031/221–3627.* 🎫 *Free.* ☉ *Mon. 12:30–7; Tues., Thurs., and Sat. 8–10; Fri. 8–11; Sun. 10:30–8.*

⑯ Ayios Nikolaos Orfanos. This small 14th-century church became a dependency of the Vlatádon monastery in the 17th century, and is noted for marvelous frescoes, particularly the unusual *Ayion Mandilion* in the apse, which features Christ's head superimposed on a veil sent to an Anatolian king, and the *Niptir,* also in the apse, in which Christ is washing the disciples' feet. The artist is said to have depicted himself in the right hand corner wearing a turban and riding a horse. The church is also known for an intriguing mix of Byzantine architectural styles, and perhaps the most beautiful midnight Easter service in the city. ⊠ *Eolou and Apostolou Pavlou sts., Upper City.*

⑭ Castle of Eptapyrghion. This Byzantine bastion—its name means "the seven towers"—was in modern times a notoriously abysmal prison, closed only in 1988. Plans for its future entail a cultural center with a memorial dedicated to former prisoners, many of whom were incarcerated for political reasons. The walls and the area just inside the portara have been restored and made into a park—a pleasant place to sit and survey Thessaloniki below. The castle is next to a number of tavernas that accommodate throngs of locals in the evening. ⊠ *Eptapyrghiou, Upper City.*

⑳ Jewish Community Memorial Museum. The original Jewish population of Thessaloniki, with whom the Apostle Paul argued while proselytizing on his visit in AD 49, were called Romaniote. They could trace their origins to Alexander the Great's mission to Jerusalem in 333 BC. Thessaloniki was the center of culture for Sephardic Jews, who made up a huge percentage of the city from their arrival in 1492 until this century. Tragically, almost 95% of the Jewish community was exterminated during World War II, so this museum is of great interest to those who want to learn not only about Judaism but about this city's cultural loss. The tiny, but very active, Jewish community presents artifacts and a collection of photographs of the city's Jewish heritage and the Holocaust, in modest quarters in the heart of the Modiano Market. A simple, first-floor **synagogue** is also at the site, as moving as the museum by its mere existence. ⊠ *Vasileos Irakleou 26, 2nd floor,* ☎ *031/273767 or 031/223231.* ☞ *Free.* ☉ *Call ahead to check on sporadic hours. Closed Sat.*

⑬ **Moni Vlatádon** (Vlatades Monastery). Shaded with pine and cypress, this structure is cruciform and displays a mixture of architectural additions from Byzantine times to the present. It is known for its Ecumenical Foundation for Patriarchal Studies, the only one in the world. The small central church just right of the apse has a tiny **chapel dedicated to Sts. Peter and Paul**, though it is seldom open. It is believed to have been built on the spot where Paul first preached to the Thessalonians, in AD 49. ⊠ *Eptapyrghiou, Upper City.*

★ **Old Turkish Quarter.** During the Ottoman occupation, this area, probably the most picturesque in the city, was considered the best place to live. In addition to the superb views, in summer it catches whatever breeze there is. Until recently the home of some of the poorest families in Thessaloniki, the area is rapidly gentrifying, thanks to EU development funds (which repaired the cobblestones), strict new zoning and building codes, and the zeal of young couples with the money to restore the narrow, charming old houses.

If you really want to step back in time and partake of the atmosphere of the Upper Town as it was at the turn of the 20th century, go to the district of **Tsinari** in the Old Turkish Quarter. Its name comes from the Turkish word *jhinar* (meaning plane tree), and just such a tree graces Tsinari's main square, shading the terrace and Aegean blue multipaned storefront of the **Tsinari Café**, at Alexandras Papadopoulou 72 and Kleious, the last remaining Turkish-style coffeehouse (opened in 1850) and the only one to have survived the fire of 1917. During the 1920s, it became the social hub for the large community of Asia Minor refugees who were relocated in the old Ottoman houses in the area. It is now run as a café-ouzerie and is especially popular before siesta time (3:30–4 PM)—why not recharge your batteries here with a thick, black coffee? Or do as the Greeks do: have an ouzo and share a variety of delicious appetizers such as eggplant puree or charcoal-grilled sardines. After your rest, explore the historic neighborhood—the most notable houses are on Papadapoulou, Kleious, and Poliorkitou streets. ⊠ *Upper City, south of Dimitriou Poliorkitou.*

★ ⑮ **Osios David** (Blessed David). This entrancing little church was supposedly built about AD 500 in honor of Galerius's daughter, who was secretly baptized while her father was away fighting. It was later converted into a mosque, and somewhere along the line it lost its western side—the traditional place of entrance (in order to look east when facing the altar)—so you enter Osios David from the south. No matter; this entirely suits the rather battered magic of this tiny church, which has a kind of street-urchin feel to it. You can still see the radiantly beautiful mosaic in the dome of the apse, which shows a rare beardless, somewhat Orphic Christ, as he seems to have been described in the vision of Ezekiel: Christ is seen with a halo and is surrounded by the four symbols of the Evangelists—clockwise, from top left, is the angel, the eagle, the lion, and the calf. To the right is the prophet Ezekiel and, to the left, Habakuk. The special magic of this mosaic is that it was forgotten for centuries and then found through a vision, or so the local tale goes. To save it from destruction, the mosaic was hidden under a layer of calfskin during the Iconoclastic ravages of the 8th and 9th centuries. Plastered over by the Turks when the church was converted into a mosque, it seems to have been forgotten until 1921, when an Orthodox monk in Egypt had a vision telling him to go to the church. On the day he arrived, March 25 (the day of Greek Independence from the Turks), an earthquake shattered the plaster and revealed the mosaic to the monk—who promptly died. ⊠ *Dimitriou Poliorkitou, Upper City.*

⑲ **Panagia Chalkeon.** The beautiful "Virgin of the Copper Workers" stands in what is still the traditional copper-working area of Thessaloniki. Completed in 1028, it is one of the oldest churches in the city displaying the domed cruciform style and is filled with ceramic ornaments and glowing mosaics. You may encounter artisans and workers who frequently drop by during the day to light a candle to this patron of physical laborers. The area offers many shops featuring traditional copper crafts at low prices. ⊠ *Southwest corner of Dikasterion Sq.*

⑱ **Roman Forum.** This large open area is undergoing vigorous excavation. Its small amphitheater is often the site of romantic concerts on balmy summer evenings. **Tositsa Street,** one block west, is the best junk, antiques, and roaming-peddler street in the city, where good finds range from brass beds to antique jewelry. The area is flanked by coppersmith shops and the Church of the Panagia Chalkeon, the Virgin of the Coppersmiths, to the southeast. ⊠ *Between Olimbou and Filipou, just south of Ayios Dimitrios.*

⑫ **Tower of Trigoniou.** From here, you can see the city spread out below you in a graceful curve around the bay, from the suburbs in the east to the modern harbor in the west and, on a clear day, even Mt. Olympus, rising near the coastline at the southwest reaches of the bay. There is, however, little of historic interest to see within the walls. ⊠ *Upper City.*

Dining

$$$$ ✕ **Krikelas.** The grandmother of upscale tavernas, opened in 1940 and looking every bit its age, with murals in arches and diamond-pattern floors, Krikelas is a standby for old-fashioned cooking. It is famous for its local wines, variety of mezedes, and venison, boar, and other specialty game dishes. Try the homemade cheese and the mixed grill, and leave room for Asia Minor–influenced sweets such as *dandourma,* an ice cream concoction flavored with mastic from the island of Chios and mixed with milk and cherry syrup. ⊠ *32 Ethnikis Antistasis, about 1 km (½ mi) east of the amusement park,* ☏ *031/451690. Reservations not accepted. DC, MC, V.*

$$$$ ✕ **Porto Marina.** One of the best fish tavernas in the region, it offers simple surroundings and friendly service. Come here for fresh seafood, from grilled fish to lobsters, but be prepared for slightly elevated prices. You will find it in the noisy seafood restaurant strip in Nea Krini, slightly out of the city center but worth the trek. ⊠ *79 Plastiras, Kalamaria,* ☏ *031/451333. Reservations essential weekends. AE, DC, MC, V.*

$$$ ✕ **Aristotelous Ouzeri.** Behind an ornate wrought-iron gate, artists, ★ scholars, and businesspeople pack marble-topped tables at this convivial place which epitomizes the quality and *joie de vivre* of Thessaloniki dining; inevitably, you will have to wait for your table. But once you sample the cuttlefish stuffed with cheese, fried eggplant with garlic, or crispy fried smelts, you'll understand why no one is in a hurry to leave. ⊠ *8 Aristotelous, in a hidden alleyway just off the main street leading to Aristotelous Sq.,* ☏ *031/230762. Reservations not accepted. No credit cards.*

Thessaloniki Dining and Lodging

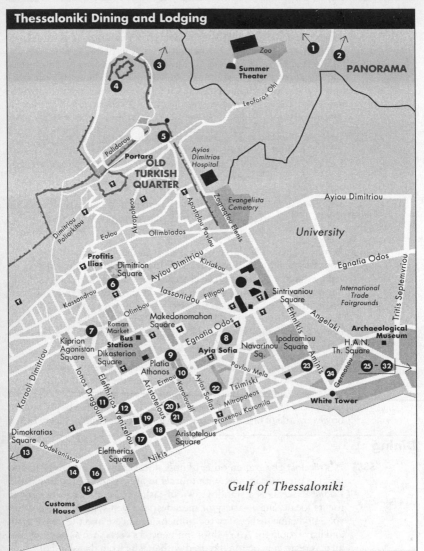

$$$ ✕ **Kioupia.** Family run, this former warehouse is filled with candle-light, brick, chandeliers, antiques, and charm. Especially good are casseroles such as chicken and mushrooms with fresh vegetables, whether served outdoors across from the splashing fountain or under the indoor Gothic arches. Service is tops—a waiter actually ran out to departing guests to return money left for a tip (don't expect this again!). ⊠ *Pl. Morichovou, in the revived district of Ladadika, ½ km (¼ mi) from the train station,* ☎ *031/553239. AE, DC, MC, V.*

$$$ ✕ **Aigli.** Set in a two-dome Turkish hamam (with a renovated outdoor
★ Greek cinema in the center courtyard), this is one of Thessaloniki's most authentically Greek restaurants, with lots to do besides eat. Delicately prepared and spiced dishes are evocative of old Levantine Thessaloniki and Constantinople. In the evening, Aigli presents entertainment, from Greek and French singers to instrumentalists from Turkey. ⊠ *Corner of Kassandrou and Ayios Nikolaos, just behind Ayios Dimitrios church,* ☎ *031/270715. Reservations not accepted. No credit cards.*

$$$ ✕ **Miami.** More reminiscent of a white-and-blue Cycladic beach house than South Florida, this seafood taverna, acquired by the owners of the institution Krikelas (☞ *above*), has been featuring mezedes and traditional seafood since 1945. The food is good, and the wine list has more than 100 choices, most of them regional. ⊠ *18 Thetidos, Nea Krini, about 15 mins from city center,* ☎ *031/447996. Reservations essential weekends after 9. AE, DC, MC, V.*

$$$ ✕ **Panselino** (Full Moon). In a renovated neoclassical mansion, this place has excellent food and great charm but will not break the fanny pack. The famous wine cellar alone makes this restaurant worthwhile—you can even sip fine vintages in the *cava* itself. ⊠ *133 Vasilis Olgas,* ☎ *031/860978. Reservations essential. AE, DC.*

$$ ✕ **Gondola.** This family seaside taverna in the nearby village of Ayia Triada is a good-quality, low-cost option. Grilled octopus is to die for, and fried everything—from smelts to zucchini—is light and delicious. Dress is informal, and the seaside view is nothing less than the Thessaloniki skyline. ⊠ *Seafront restaurant strip, Ayia Triada, 40 mins by bus or taxi from city center,* ☎ *0392/51311. Reservations not accepted. No credit cards.*

$$ ✕ **Gonia tis Soulis** (Souli's Corner). Converted from a family home into an intimate restaurant by Souli, who decorated it herself with personal bric-a-brac, this restaurant brims with charm. Live music is played nightly, but Souli provides the best entertainment, moving from table to table welcoming everyone while they savor traditional mezedes and Thessalonian specialties. ⊠ *12 Raidestou, just below large church at top of hill at 40 Ekklesias, Upper City,* ☎ *031/201113. Reservations not accepted. No credit cards.*

$$ ✕ **Klimataria.** This *psistaria* (grilled-meat taverna) dishes up typical good meals, supported by Greek salad, fresh bread, and other staples, in a simple atmosphere—at low prices. For an after-dinner treat head across the street to one of the best chocolate shops in Greece, Hadjifotiou (which now has a branch near the Makedonia Palace hotel). ⊠ *34 Pavlou Mela, just behind Ayia Sofia church,* ☎ *031/277854. Reservations not accepted. No credit cards.*

$$ ✕ **Loutros.** This Thessaloniki institution where you'll rub shoulders with lawyers, students, out-of-towners, and market workers was ousted from its previous location of 50 years due to renovation of the flower market hamam (the *loutros.*) It has lost much of its uniquely earthy ambience (your wine will no longer be served out of huge barrels in the corners of the room, for instance) in its new trendily traditional digs opposite the Bezesten gold market. *Dhen pirazi* (never mind), as the Greeks say; the great menu is pretty much the same and portions very ample. Try grilled *koutsomoura* (literally fatheads or baby red mul-

lets), grilled eggplant, mussels in pilaf, or smelt or shrimp sautéed in a casserole with cheese and peppers. Don't miss the exquisite *kazandibi,* a marvelous flan with a slightly burnt top, sweetened with a hint of rose water. ⊠ *M. Kountoura 5 (opposite the Bezesten),* ☎ *031/228895. No credit cards.*

$$ ✕ **Ta Louloudadika Fish Restaurant and Ouzerie.** Location is everything
★ here: set on a lively cul-du-sac across from the colorful *louloudadika* (flower market) and its hamam—being restored at time of writing— the street action at lunchtime is worth the price alone. But the food is not an afterthought—crisp calamari rings, sweet morsels of rosy *kara- vides* (crayfish), and tender stuffed *soupies* (cuttlefish) are only some of the delicacies that draw faithful diners day after day. If it's an inclement day, the gold interior with folk accents is also charming and a mellow setting for an ouzo and a variety of excellent mezedes. ⊠ *Komninon 20,* ☎ *031/225624. Reservations not accepted. No credit cards.*

$$ ✕ **Tiffany's.** Not as swank as its namesake, this downtown favorite among Thessalonians has paneled walls, sconces, long tables, outside dining on a pedestrian walk, and the feel of a Parisian bistro. Its grilled meats and stews are the essence of Northern Greece: simple, tasty, and traditional. ⊠ *3 Iktinou,* ☎ *031/274022. Reservations not accepted. No credit cards.*

$$ ✕ **To Spiti Tou Pasa.** The name, meaning the "House of the Pasha," is appropriate. It is set in a beautifully renovated Ottoman-style house— exotic murals, elegant tapestry wall-hangings, peacock feather clusters, and delectable food make this place quite fit for a pasha. Try the *meze tou Pasa,* a selection of different dishes including *pastourma bourek* (a flaky phyllo pie filled with cheese) and *pastourma* (similar to pas- trami), stuffed potatoes, *xtipiti* (a piquant cheese spread which is a Thes- saloniki specialty), and soutzoukakia politika (in tomato sauce à la Constantinople). Portions are very generous. Popular and *rembetika* music is played some afternoons and evenings. ⊠ *Taken only in win- ter. No credit cards.*

$$ ✕ **To Yenti.** In the Upper City, with tables under the trees, on the side- walk, and even spilling onto the street, this charming taverna-ouzeri serves delicious grilled and ready-made favorites. The *keftedes* (fried meatballs) and mezedes are especially good. Arrive early to avoid crowds. ⊠ *7 Ioan- nis Papareka, outside gates of castle of Eptapyrghion,* ☎ *031/246495. Reservations not accepted. No credit cards. Closed Sun.*

$$ ✕ **Tsambouro.** One of the favorites in Athonos Square—which is a less touristy version of Ladadika—this spot offers up a particularly lively lunchtime, when the nearby pedestrian walkway is clustered with ta- bles of gregarious—and ravenous—groups, attracted by the bohemian atmosphere, terrific food, and reasonable prices. Try the outstanding grilled octopus, as tender and flavorful as lobster, and delicious fried *marides* (smelt). ⊠ *Athonos Sq.,* ☎ *no phone. No credit cards. Closed Sun.*

$$ ✕ **Vrotos Ouzerie.** Some of the most delicious and innovative appe-
★ tizers in Thessaloniki are served at this little storefront run by the Vro- tos family in this *ksiladika* (woodworkers neighborhood). You can sit in the noisy interior, decorated with old movie posters, or at the tables out front, all jammed with the cognoscenti. A strong Anatolian influ- ence is evident in the absolutely terrific mezedes. Try the cheese spread made with Roquefort, eggplant, and walnuts, *pseftiko dolmades* (vine leaves stuffed with rice), and baked feta cheese. Other highlights among the outstanding selections include *bougiourdi* (feta and other cheeses, tomatoes, and peppers baked in a clay pot), *tsigerosarmas* (eggplant, liver, and raisins wrapped in innards), and *prassopita* (leek pie) or, for that matter, any of the other pies. ⊠ *Mitropolitou Gennadiou 6,* ☎ *031/223958. Reservations not accepted. No cards accepted.*

$$ ✗ **Wolves.** The name has nothing to do with the cuisine or staff attitude but comes from the original owner's allegiance to an English soccer club. (In Greek, it's called *Oi Lykoi*.) Comfortable, with high ceilings and well-spaced tables, it dispenses classics such as moussaka and *pastitsio* (a casserole of pasta, meat, and cheese with cinnamon). ✉ *6 Vasilis Olgas, near the Makedonia Palace hotel,* ☎ *031/812855. Reservations not accepted. No credit cards. No dinner Sun.*

$$ ✗ **Zythos Dore.** Named after, and on the same spot as, the legendary and now-vanished Café Dore, this spacious bistro has tile floors, towering columns, and the city's best buzz. Greek and international food and bottled or barrel beers and wine from around the world offer something for anyone, from a drink to a bite to a big-deal meal, late into the night. Noisy, crowded, and lots of fun, it also has a great view of the White Tower. ✉ *7 Tsiroyiannis, across a little park near White Tower,* ☎ *031/279010. Reservations not accepted. No credit cards.*

$ ✗ **Myrovolos Tis Smyrnis.** Going to this friendly and beloved hangout—
★ also called *tou Thanassi*, after its owner Thanassis—on a Saturday afternoon will introduce you to one of Thessaloniki's most colorful rituals. Set in the Modiano Market, you'll be surrounded by a cross-section of Salonika's society, from market workers to society matrons, while being entertained by roaming gypsy musicians. And the food is good as well! Try grilled octopus (sliced off specimens hanging nearby), stuffed squid, midhia saganaki, and soutzoukakia. If you hit this place on Saturday, try to make a reservation—it's the only day they are accepted. ✉ *Komninon 32 (in Modiano Arcade),* ☎ *031/274170. No credit cards. Closed Sun.*

Lodging

$$$$ ⊞ **Capsis.** An old standby that was recently overhauled, this big, full-facility hotel is now stylish and sophisticated, with inlaid marble halls and comfortable rooms done in soothing tones, providing king-size beds, 24-hour room service, and in-room movies. The view from the popular rooftop restaurant sweeps the city. Beware of long lines when conferences take over, but otherwise this is one of the best-managed venues in the city. ✉ *18 Monastiriou St., 54629,* ☎ *031521321,* FAX *031/510555. 415 rooms, 7 suites. 2 restaurants, 2 bars, minibars, pool, shops, meeting rooms. AE, DC, MC, V.* ✍

$$$$ ⊞ **Electra Palace.** On the most interesting seaside square, this curving, arcaded, and venerable hotel has a graceful facade and is centrally located, but it could use some more modernizing (double-glazed windows, for instance). Upper, front rooms are the largest, with the best views, but are more susceptible to noise from the streets and from the events—political and musical—that take place on the square. ✉ *9 Aristotelous Sq., 54624,* ☎ *031/232221 through 031/232229,* FAX *031/235947. 65 rooms, 5 suites. 2 restaurants, bar, refrigerators, convention center. AE, MC, V.*

$$$$ ⊞ **Makedonia Palace.** This modernized luxury hotel has a sterile fa-
★ cade, but within evokes a real sense of place, with marble mosaics, classical murals, and local artifacts. One of the only buildings rising on the coastline, it offers stunning views of the city sunset over the Aegean (and on a clear day, Mt. Olympus) from most rooms and its rooftop bar and restaurant (which serves excellent international food). The breakfast room is attractively decorated with lots of greenery, and the buffet is one of the best in the city. The adjacent boardwalk is great for early morning or late-night runs, walks, and people-watching. A state-of-the-art convention center lures business travelers, but you're almost as apt to see a rock star or the president of Albania. ✉ *2 Alexander the Great Ave., 54640,* ☎ *031861400,* FAX *031832291. 272 rooms, 16*

suites. 3 restaurants, 2 bars, 3 pools, beauty salon, spa, shop, meeting rooms. AE, DC, MC, V.

$$$$ ⌸ **Mediterranean Palace.** Built in 1997, this luxury addition to the hotel scene competes with the Makedonia Palace (☞ *above*) for upper-end and business travelers—but is only half its size, so you feel you're in a more personal atmosphere. High-tech from the get-go, it offers Internet service as well as amenities expected from international-level hostelries, such as soundproofed windows. Just opened, it is bright and shining, and the polish extends to exemplary service. ⌧ *3 Salaminos and Karatasou Sts., near the Astoria, 54626,* ☎ ℻ *031/552554. 118 rooms. 2 restaurants, bar, lobby lounge, meeting rooms, parking. AE, DC, MC, V.* ✎

$$$ ⌸ **Astoria.** This attractively renovated hotel is conveniently located near
★   the picturesque area of Ladadika, with its restaurants, clubs, and lively nightlife. A great bargain for the price, it is friendly and has a helpful, well-informed staff. Rooms are small, but all have balconies, TVs, air-conditioning, modems, double-glazed windows and mini-bars. The buffet breakfast, included in the price, is a real winner. The happy hour in the lobby bar, which has changing art exhibits, is a fun people-mixer. ⌧ *7 Salaminos, at western end of Tsimiski, 54626,* ☎ *031/554902,* ℻ *031/531564.. 84 rooms, 6 suites. Restaurant, bar, meeting rooms, parking. AE, MC, V.* ✎

$$$ ⌸ **Metropolitan.** Locals love this renovated hotel near the bayside, within walking distance of major museums and the White Tower. It has been around since the late 1960s, but its major overhaul in 1995 was a great success. The results are well-maintained, basic rooms, with traditional floral drapes and spreads. ⌧ *65 Vasilisis Olgas, at 2 Fleming St., 54629,* ☎ ℻ *031/824221. 111 rooms, 7 suites. Restaurant, bar, minibars, meeting rooms. AE, DC, MC, V.*

$$$ ⌸ **Nepheli.** Right near the bus stop in peaceful Panorama, this friendly hotel sits among the pine trees circling the summit. Rooms are simply but tastefully decorated, and public areas are spacious and gregarious. Breakfast is included in the room rate. ⌧ *Komninon 1, Panorama, 55236,* ☎ *031342024,* ℻ *031/342002. 65 rooms, 5 suites. Restaurant, bar, meeting rooms, parking. AE, MC, V.*

$$$ ⌸ **Olympia.** Near the flea market, copper market, Roman Forum, and Ayios Dimitrios, this well-maintained modern hotel on a corner is simple but professionally managed. And location counts. ⌧ *65 Olympou, 54631,* ☎ *031/235421,* ℻ *031/276133. 115 rooms. Restaurant, bar, cafeteria, meeting rooms, free parking. AE, DC, MC, V.*

$$$ ⌸ **Panorama.** This is one of the loveliest hotels and settings in Thessaloniki, truly a place to get away from the crowds and traffic. Set on a quiet side street in the posh suburb of Panorama, this hotel is a short bus or taxi ride away from the center of Thessaloniki (although rush hours are to be avoided). Each room has individual designer color schemes, rich patterned bedspreads and matching curtains, and a balcony with a view of either the pine forest and mountains or the bay; on a clear day the view extends all the way to sacred Mt. Olympus. Breakfast is included in the room rate. ⌧ *Analipseos 26, 55236,* ☎ *031/344871,* ℻ *031/344872. 45 rooms, 5 suites. AE, DC, MC, V.* ✎

$$$ ⌸ **Philippion.** For those who are driving around, or dislike staying in the city center, this modern and well-appointed hotel sits in a lovely location in the forest of Sheih-Sou on a hilltop overlooking Thessaloniki. The city center is 5 km (3 mi) away—a 15-30 minute ride (depending on traffic) on the hotel shuttle bus, which leaves by prearranged schedule (available at the desk) mornings intermittently until 3 PM. The airport, too, is an easy 15-minute drive away. ⌧ *Box 19002, 56610,* ☎ *031/203321,* ℻ *031/218528. 85 rooms, 4 suites. Restaurant, bar, coffee shop, pool, minibars, nightclub, business services, meeting rooms, parking. AE, DC, MC, V.* ✎

Paris, France.

Paris, Texas.

When it Comes to Getting Local Currency at an ATM,

Same Thing.

Whether you're in Yosemite or Yemen, using your Visa® card or ATM card with the PLUS symbol is the easiest and most convenient way to get local currency. For example, let's say you're in France. When you make a withdrawal, using your secured PIN, it's dispensed in francs, but is debited from your account in U.S. dollars. This makes it easy to take advantage of favorable exchange rates. And if you need help finding one of Visa's 627,000 ATMs in 127 countries worldwide, visit **visa.com/pd/atm**. We'll make finding an ATM as easy as finding the Eiffel Tower, the Pyramids or even the Grand Canyon.

It's Everywhere You Want To Be.®

SEE THE WORLD
IN FULL COLOR

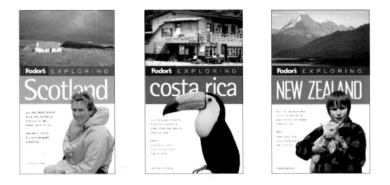

Fodor's Exploring Guides bring all the great sights vividly to life with hundreds of photographs, fascinating historical background, and colorful anecdotes. Detailed maps and practical information keep you headed in the right direction.

Pair a **Fodor's** Exploring Guide with your trusted Gold Guide for a complete planning package.

$$ ⊡ **Pallas.** Although set on one of the main thoroughfares, this art deco gem is a well-kept secret among savvy business travelers and Greek tourists. Completely remodeled in 1998, its atmospheric lounge, café, and restaurant are all popular with neighborhood people as well. Rooms have wooden floors, smartly designed bathrooms, and tasteful decor; a bountiful buffet breakfast is included in the price. ⊠ *Tsimiski 12 and Venizelou, 54624,* ☎ *031/257400,* 𝖥𝖠𝖷 *031/256589. 54 rooms. Restaurant, café. MC, V.*

$$ ⊡ **Tourist.** This modest family-run hotel in a quaint, high-ceilinged belle-
★ epoque building has recently been updated and, since it is at the low end of its price category, represents a good value for those on modest budgets (and breakfast is included in the room rate). Its location, one block off Aristotelous Square, is prime, and all rooms have air-conditioning, TVs, and en suite bathrooms and toilets (except for the three singles). ⊠ *Mitropoleos 21, in city center, 1 block west of Aristotelous Sq., 54624,* ☎ *031/276335. 37 rooms, 34 with shared bath. Air-conditioning. No credit cards.*

Nightlife and the Arts

Nightlife

Except for summertime, Thessaloniki's nightlife is one of its true assets. Bars, pubs, breweries, discos, and clubs within the city center—particularly in the area east of Aristotelous Square and in Ladadika, the former warehouse district near the port—fill the streets with an endless barrage of young people in search of fun. In summer, most clubs close, as their clients flock to the beaches of Chalkidiki. There are several discos on the road to the airport, but since they go in and out of fashion, ask at your hotel for the newest and best.

CASINO

The **Hyatt Regency Casino** (⊠ Just outside the airport, ☎ 031/491234, 𝖥𝖠𝖷 031/476129) is one of the largest and most elaborate in all of Europe. The entrance fee is 2,000 dr./€5.89, which includes markers for slot machines; it's open daily 1 PM–8 AM.

CLUBS

The road to the airport is the best area to hear bouzouki and other Greek music, while the city center is filled with cafés, clubs and discos. A premier coffee bar is the **Balkan** (⊠ Proxenou Koromila, close to Platia Aristotelous), reputed to have the best java, luscious chocolate cookies, and excellent taped music. A perennial favorite is the **Olympion** (⊠ Platia Aristotelous and Mitropoleos), with a subdued restaurant on the top floor and a jazzier lower establishment. To get to **It's Only,** a surrealistically decadent disco attracting a lively younger crowd, follow the red carpet down an alley from Venizelou Street below Egnatia. Open year-round, the extraordinary **Mylos** (⊠ 25 Andreadou Georgiou, on the southwest edge of the city just off October 28th St., ☎ 031/516945) is a complex of clubs, bars, discos, bars and ouzeristavernas, art galleries, and a concert stage. This former mill has become perhaps the best venue in all of Greece for jazz, folk, and pop groups, Greek and foreign. Visiting foreign and Greek pop, jazz, and folk artists occasionally appear at the **Palais de Sports** (⊠ International Trade Fairgrounds, ☎ 031/516945), and at Mylos.

JAZZ

Jazz gurus perform at local clubs such as **Malt and Jazz, Indrogeios,** the **Mill,** and **Radio City.**

The Arts

As the Cultural Capital of Europe in 1997-98, Thessaloniki established itself as a venue for world-class touring performances, as well as local artists. Check with your hotel or the Greek National Tourist Organization (GNTO or EOT) for current happenings.

FESTIVALS

Apokreas, or Carnival celebrations, mark the period preceding Lent and end on "Clean Monday," the day before the beginning of Lent. They often have roots in pre-Christian pagan celebrations and are particularly colorful (and often bawdy) in Northern Greece. Visitors are most welcome to join in the fun. Thirty-two kilometers (20 miles) to the northeast of Thessaloniki the town of **Sohos** hosts a festive event in which the Carnavali cavort about in animal hides with huge sheep bells tied around their waist and large multicolored phallic headdresses on top. In **Naoussa,** 112 km (70 mi) to the west of Thessaloniki, the *yianitsari* wear *fustanellas* (short, pleated white kilts), special masks, and chains of gold coins crossing their chests, which they shake to "awaken the earth." As they dance in public squares during day and night, the whole town dons costumes and takes to the streets behind the brass marching bands—the only ones in Greece who have a tradition of playing New Orleans–style jazz.

No chapter on Northern Greece would be complete without mention of the famous *anastanarides* (fire dancers). Every year on May 21, the feast day of Sts. Constantine and Eleni, groups of religious devotees in the villages of **Langadha** (25 km [15 mi] north of Thessaloniki) and **Ayia Eleni** (80 km [50 mi] northeast of Thessaloniki) take part in a three-day rite called the *pirovassia* (literally, "fire dancing") in which, unharmed, they dance barefoot over a bed of hot coals while holding the saints' icons. Although assumed to be of pre-Christian origin, the tradition adopted its Christian aspects about 1250 in the eastern Thracian village of Kosti. At this time the villagers are said to have rescued the original icons from a burning church, all unharmed by the blaze. For information, check with the EOT or American Educational Services(☞ Visitor Information *in* Northern Greece A to Z, *below*).

In mid-September the **International Trade Festival** is celebrated at the Fairgrounds just north of the archaeological museum, marked by the modern, pinnacled tower of the Greek Telecommunications Organization (OTE), called the Pirgos Oté.St. Dimitrios's feast is celebrated on October 26, but its secular adjunct has developed into a series of cultural events that brings an enormous amount of outside commerce. The October **Dimitria festival** exhibits works by artists and musicians from all over the country.

FILM

Thessaloniki has more than a 100 movie theaters, but most in the city center close in summer. The poshest and largest cinema (1,000 seats) is **Aristotelion** (☒ Ethnikis Aminis 1), close to the White Tower; it closes in May for the summer. Across the street from the Aristotelion cinema is the **Alexandros** (☒ Ethnikis Aminis 1). A popular option is the **Esperos** (☒ Svolou 22), an indoor cinema that offers quality programming and stays open in summer. The **Alex** (☒ Olympou 106,) is set in the two-domed hamam at the corner of Kassandrouand Ayios Nikolaos and is one of the few of the outdoor cinemas in the city and suburbs that shows movies in English with Greek subtitles. In November, there is an annual **International Film Festival**; the best of the season's Greek films, which vie for awards, are subtitled or simultaneously translated. Tickets can be purchased for individual screenings but are hard to come by.

MUSIC

Thessaloniki was known as the "City of Refugees" because it was one of the major destinations for the thousands of displaced Asia Minor refugees during the population exchange starting in 1923 after the signing of the Lausanne Treaty. They made Greeks a majority in Thessaloniki (surpassing the Turks and Jews) and brought along their form of *rembetika,* similar to the blues in lyrical content, but set to plaintive minor chord music highlighted by the bouzouki. You can still hear it in bouzoukia in and around the city, and the melodies fill the streets into the early hours outside little clubs such as **Modiano** (⊠ Irakliou 37, at Aristotelous, in Modiano Market, ☎ 031/237315). Other popular clubs are **Ta Tsilika** (⊠ Doxis 5, ☎ 031/551440) in Ladadika and **Maskes** (⊠ Platia Aristotelous at Mitropoleos), a spirited bouzouki club that attracts a colorful cross-section of various types and ages, all intent on partying until the wee morning hours. A fascinating and unique ethnic music style heard very rarely in Greece is Pontic, brought along with another group of refugees (after 1922) from the Black Sea Coast. Large communities of Pontii (Greeks from the Pontic area) live in Thessaloniki and outlying communities, and on weekends the dance halls are packed with fans who enjoy listening to the traditional instruments such as *kemence* (a form of lyra), bagpipe, and *diaouli* (large drum). Instruments accompany the exciting staccato rhythm and sometimes athletic dances such as the *tik* and *serra* performed by men clothed in dramatic black shirts, baggy britches, and headresses. Be warned that the music is usually quite loud, as it is now accompanied by heavily amped keyboards and guitars.

International orchestras perform classics throughout the year, and the **Municipal Orchestra of Thessaloniki** plays at its concert hall (⊠ In the university, just opposite northern entrance of International Trade Fairgrounds) from fall through spring.

THEATER
In winter, the State Theater of Northern Greece sponsors plays, ballets, and special performances of visiting artists at the **Kratiko Theatro** (State Theater; ⊠ just opposite the White Tower, ☎ 031/223785). In summer, performances are given at the **Theatro Kypou** (Garden Theater; ⊠ in Municipal Park off Germanou St. between State Theater and archaeological museum) and at **Theatro Dasous** (Forest Theater; ⊠ in the forest east of the Upper City, ☎ 031/218092). All performances are in Greek, although there are occasional visits by English-speaking groups.

Outdoor Activities and Sports

Beaches
Beaches in Thessaloniki and its suburbs are on water too polluted to be recommended, even though you may see locals swimming there.

The nearest safe beaches are in **Perea** and **Ayia Triada,** past the airport, about 15 and 25 km (10 and 15 mi, just over half an hour by bus) away, respectively, from the Thessaloniki city center. At Ayia Triada, on the headland of the bay, the EOT runs a bathing facility at **Akti Thermaikou** (⊠ Ayia Triada, ☎ 0392/51352), with changing cabins, snack bars, tennis courts, and a children's playground.

Participant Sports
HORSEBACK RIDING
Contact **ALMA,** the eco-adventure tourism office, which can help you arrange daily riding or weeklong riding excursions in recommended areas (☞ Contacts and Resources *in* Northern Greece A to Z, *below*). The **Thessaloniki Riding Club** (⊠ Panorama, near Anatolia College, ☎ 031/270676) has riding outside of the city. An alternative is **Cavalier** (⊠ 14th km Georgikis Scholis, ☎ 031/473537).

SAILING

The bay here offers a safe harbor for sailors, with a dramatic back-drop of mountains, the hilltop old city, and the more modern city sky-line. Try the **Sailing Club** (⊠ Megalou Alexandrou Ave., ☎ 031/830939) or **Thessaloniki Yacht Club** (⊠ 96 Themistokli Sofouli St., Mikro Emvolo, ☎ 031/414521). Like to row your boat, even in Thessaloniki? You can, from the **Kalamaria Yacht Club** (⊠ Mikro Emvolo, ☎ 031/412068).

SWIMMING

As most lodgings cater to business travelers in this business-oriented city, hotel pools are not a given. Check before booking if it's a prior-ity. An acceptable alternative, aside from Waterland (☞ *below*), is the **National Swimming Pool of Thessaloniki** (☎ 031/203126), where you can splash with the locals.

TENNIS

Courts can be rented at the **Tennis Club** (⊠ 16 Kiprou St., ☎ 031/411569) and **Poseidonio Athletic Center** (⊠ Nea Paralia and 25th of March St., at the eastern end of the seaside promenade, ☎ 031/427414). Outside the city try **Anatolia College** (⊠ On road to Panorama after Pylea vil-lage, ☎ 031/323711) and **Akti Thermaikou** (⊠ Ayia Triada, ☎ 0392/51352).

☾ **Waterland,** a water-activity amusement park (⊠ Off highway to Chalkidiki, just past airport exit, ☎ 0392/72025), has six well-kept courts available at inexpensive prices. It's especially nice for families, as there is something for everyone—wave pools, water slides, children's pools, restaurants, and basketball courts.

Spectator Sports

BASKETBALL

Basketball fans here are as rabid as those in NBA championship cities in the United States, since Thessaloniki has three of the best basket-ball teams in the country: **Aris, Iraklis,** and **PAOK,** all three with Americans and Eastern Europeans on the roster. Aris and PAOK play at the Palais de Sport, the domed athletic center within the Interna-tional Trade Fairgrounds; Iraklis has its own large sports complex north of the university.

SOCCER

Two of the best teams in Greece—again **Aris** and **PAOK**—play their seasons in the spring and fall. The **Aris stadium** is in the suburb of Har-ilaou (⊠ Papanastasiou St., about 1 km north of the seafront amuse-ment park, ☎ 031/305402). The **PAOK stadium** is several blocks northeast of the International Trade Fairgrounds (☎ 031/238560).

Shopping

Thessaloniki has a very cosmopolitan polish, and its women are noted for being tastefully and stylishly dressed. Although Thessaloniki may not have anywhere near the choice or variety of goods for tourists' tastes as those found in Athens, you will find a higher quality of clothing, and interesting items can be picked up in the shops of local craftspeople. Among the best buys are folk arts and crafts, leather, and jewelry. Com-plicated regulations control the opening and closing hours of shops. The afternoon siesta is still honored, which means that the shops are open from about 9 to 1:30 or 2, and most open again in the evenings, but only on Tuesday, Thursday, and Friday, and never in July. The best shopping streets are Tsimiski, Mitropoleos, and Proxenou Koromila, which run east–west, between Pavlou Mela (the diagonal street con-necting Ayios Sofias with the White Tower) and Eleftherios Venizelou.

Antiques

Antiques shops on Mitropoleos Street between Ayios Sofias and the White Tower are perfect for leisurely browsing. One of the best is **Relics** (✉ 6 Giorgio Lassani, east of Mitropoleos cathedral, ☎ 031/226506), which has an interesting selection of nonclassical, exportable antiques; look for quality, not bargains. The best places to shop for finds—besides prowling through the **street markets**—are in the narrow streets around the **Rotunda** and the **flea market** on Tositsa Street. The latter offers a marvelous jumble of fascinating, musty old shops, with the wares of itinerant junk collectors spread out on the sidewalks, intermingled with small upscale antiques shops.

Books

Newspapers and magazines are also sold at kiosks at the intersection of Tsimiski and Aristotelou streets, and at another kiosk near the White Tower. All of the following bookstores are rich with beautifully illustrated children's books on ancient Greek heroes and myths—a thoughtful gift to take home.

The oldest bookshop in the city is **Molchos** (✉ 10 Tsimiski, just west of Elefthirios Venizelou, ☎ 031/275271), which has a wide selection of newspapers and magazines in myriad languages, and specializes in English and French books. **Ianos** (✉ 7 Aristotelous St., just north of Electra Palace) is another well-stocked bookstore for foreign travelers. **Mariaris** (✉ Aristotelous 9, ☎ 031/277113) is another bookstore with a large stock of books in English and other foreign languages.

Greek Souvenirs

Just south of Egnatia Odos, the narrow streets between Aristotelous and Ayios Sofias around **Platia Athanos** in Ksiladika (the "woodsellers' neighborhood") are loaded with local color, and many small craft shops have been opened by the craftspeople themselves. A most unusual craft emporium, opened in 1992, is named after **Haido Deliali** (✉ Vagdamali 1, ☎ 031/269375), the stylish woman who creates delicately crafted necklaces and earrings from tin and clay and wonderful oil paintings and sculptures. Near the Haido Deliali shop is the **Ergastirio Kouklis,** or Doll Workshop (✉ Mitropolitou Gennadiou 2, ☎ 031/236890), displaying dolls artistically designed by Artemis Makridou. Nearby the Doll Workshop is the lively ceramics shop of **Alexandra Theodossiou** (✉ Dragoumi 16, ☎ 031/265039). When you have become sated with shopping, plop down at **Café Bazaar** (✉ Papamarkou 34, ☎ 031/241817), a charming café in a historic building which reflects the classiness of this area, a district which remains undiscovered by most tourists.

Sweets

It seems that every neighborhood in Thessaloniki can claim the city's best candy shop—and each has a delicious specialty, such as chocolate baklava. The truth is that as you walk through the city, you can usually find the best sweetshops by their seductive aroma. One of the best is **Agapitos** (✉ North side of Tsimiski between Ayios Sofias and Karolou Dil, ☎ 031/279107), which aptly means "loved one," owned by the oldest son of a venerable Thessaloniki family. A great sweet and pastry shop is **Terkenlis** (✉ Odos Tsimiski 30), which is proclaimed the best in the city by its loyal clientele.

Toys and Handicrafts

Greek toys are rare, but a wonderful and inexpensive locally produced gift is the playful **Kouvalias** pull toy. They are usually hidden away behind the more glamorous toys, but look for their bright paint and solid-wood construction.

One delightful store is **Skitso** (⊠ 11 Grigori Palama, a short diagonal street between Tsimiski and Platia Navarino, ☎ 031/269822), which sells a cornucopia of toys, ships, puppets, crosses, and other handmade objects. **Rotunda** (⊠ Just behind the Rotunda, off Sintrivaniou Sq.) offers some interesting Greek toys.

CENTRAL MACEDONIA
Pella, Vergina, Dion, Mt. Olympus

Few places in the world have greater ancient sites than Pella, Vergina, and Dion, the three major areas of Central Macedonia, which are connected to Alexander the Great and his father, Philip II, heroes of the ages. Even one would be worth a detour, but they are so close to Thessaloniki that it is easy to see all of them. You can rush and explore all three in a harried day trip from Thessaloniki. Better would be scheduling a relaxed day for each, allowing time for contemplation, or after seeing the first two, spending the night near Dion or Mt. Olympus and visiting both of these the next day.

In the 7th century BC the Dorian Makednoi tribe moved out of the Pindos mountains (between Epirus and Macedonia), settled in the fertile plains below, and established a religious center at the sacred springs of Dion at the foot of Mt. Olympus. Perdikkas, the first king of the Macedonians, held court at a place called Aigai, now known to have been at Vergina, and in the 5th century BC, the king of that time, Archelaos (413–399), moved his capital from Aigai to Pella, which was then on a rise above a lagoon leading to the Thermaic Gulf.

In 359 BC, after a succession of kings and assassinations and near anarchy exacerbated by the raids of barbarian tribes from the north, the 23-year-old Philip II was elected regent. Philip II pulled the kingdom together through diplomacy and by his seven marriages, and then began expanding it, taking in the all-important gold mines of the Pangeon mountains, and founding Philippi there. In 356 BC, on the day that Alexander the Great was born, Philip II was said to have simultaneously taken the strategic port of Potidea in Chalkidiki, received news of his horse's triumph in the Olympic Games, and learned of a general's victory against the Illyrians. That was also the day the temple of Artemis at Ephesus was destroyed by fire, which later prompted people to say that the goddess was away on that day, tending to Alexander's birth. In 336 BC, Philip II was assassinated in Vergina at a wedding party for one of his daughters. (It had been assumed that his tomb there had been looted and lost, until it was discovered in 1977 by the Greek archaeologist Manolis Andronikos.) Alexander, then 20, assumed power, and within two years he had gathered an army to be blessed at Dion, before setting off to conquer the Persians and most of the known world.

Pella

㉑ *40 km (25 mi) west of Thessaloniki.*

Alexander's birthplace, and the capital of the Macedonian state in the 4th century, Pella is farthest from the sea of these ancient sites. A sign on the right points to the modern-day village, but the archaeological site and its museum are on either side of the main road toward Edessa (its waterfalls invite a possible further trip for nature-lovers). It's best to visit the Pella museum first, to understand what you will see at the site.

Northern Greece

The **museum** stands just northwest of the old lagoon; it contains fascinating artifacts of Neolithic, Bronze, and Iron Age settlers, some as old as the 7th century BC, as well as a model of the 4th-century BC dwelling that stood across the road. Note also the unique statuette of a horned Athena, apparently influenced by Minoan Crete, and the statue of Alexander sprouting the horns of Pan. Both the museum and site are best known for their intricate, artful, beautifully preserved floor mosaics, mainly of mythological scenes. ⊠ *Pella, Archaeological Site and Museum,* ☎ *0383/31160 or 0383/31278.* 🎫 *1,000 dr./€2.94* ⊘ *Weekdays 8–7, weekends 8:30–3.*

In 1914, two years after the departure of the Turks, the people who lived on the land were moved to a village north of here, and excavations of the **ancient site** began. These include portions of the walls; the sanctuaries of Aphrodite, Demeter, and Cybele; the marketplace; cemetery; and several houses. In 1987, on a small rise to the north, the remains of the **palace** came to light, though at present they're of little interest to the general public. It's hoped that the **theater** where Euripides' *The Bacchae* was first performed may also be located here (he is known to have written while in exile at the court).

Four important 4th-century BC **Macedonian tombs** with magnificent frescoes can be seen (⊠ Along the main road, before the turnoff to Naoussa).

OFF THE
BEATEN PATH

KASTORIA AND LAKES OF PRESPA – Nestled in the Pindos mountains in Western Macedonia, 221 km (137 mi) west of Thessaloniki and 168 km (104 mi) west of Pella, is the beautiful town of Kastoria, filled with narrow lanes and stately homes. It sits on a promontory projecting into a lake garlanded in poplar and willow trees and mirroring the mountains, while ducks, swans, and flat-bottom skiffs glide across the surface. In the Byzantine era, the town was famous for its Macedonian school of religious painting; its many fine Byzantine churches, most notably Ayios Nicholaos Kasnitsi and the 9th-century Taxiarches tis Mitropoleos, are richly decorated with frescoes and icons. To enter interiors, you need to contact the key keeper at the small but worthwhile **Byzantine Museum** on Platia Dexamenis. The city prospered during the Turkish occupation, and the 18th- and 19th-century three-story mansions, best seen in the lakeside district of Karydis (also called Doltso), reflect those good times. Here you'll also find the **Folklore Museum,** at Kapetan Lazou 10, housed in a mansion. Ask the custodian to direct you to nearby *archontika* (old mansions). Today Kastoria is still known for its embroidery and fur trade. The place to stay is the Tsamis Hotel, which overlooks a mountain-rimmed lake in an enchanting setting and whose comfortable, traditionally styled lodgings provide a get-away-from-it-all atmosphere (⊠ 3 km [2 mi] along the National Road between Athens and Thessaloniki, ☎ 0467/85334). About an hour drive northeast of Kastoria, set near the village of Nymfaio, directly south of Florina, is the **Arcturos Environmental Center** (⊠ Aetos, Florinas 53075 ☎ FAX 0386/41500, 093/738615, ✉), which sponsors the Brown Bear Information Center and Bear Sanctuary—a loving home to Balkan bears snatched from their mothers at an early age by gypsy trainers, who used cruel methods to train them and keep them tamed. Now fed and loved, they offer a splendid sight for children and nature lovers alike. Two hours northwest of Kastoria are the serenely lovely lakes of Prespas along the border Greece shares with Albania and the former Yugoslavia. These peaceful waters are officially designated bird sanctuaries, home to more than 250 species of birds, with observation towers at Vromolimni and Ayios Anhilios.

Vergina

22 *135 km (84 mi) southwest of Thessaloniki.*

Some of antiquity's greatest treasures await you at the **Royal Tombs** of
Vergina, opened to the public only in 1993, 16 years after their discovery. Today, the complex has been made into a new museum, a fitting shrine to the original capital of the kingdom of Macedonia (then
known as Aigai). The entrance is appropriately stunning: you walk down
a white sandstone ramp into the partially underground structure,
roofed over by a large earth-covered dome approximately the size of
the original tumulus. Here on display are some of the legendary artifacts from the age of Philip of Macedonia.

For years, both archaeologists and grave robbers had suspected that
the large mound that stood on this site might contain something of value,
but try as they might, neither of these professional groups was successful
in penetrating its secret. In his fascinating book *The Royal Tombs of
Vergina,* Professor Andronikos theorizes that one of Alexander's successors, wanting to protect Philip's tomb from robbers, had it covered
with broken debris and tombstones to make it appear that the grave
had already been plundered, and then built the tumulus so that Philip's
tomb would be near the edge rather than the center. But this was speculation after the fact: when Andronikos discovered it, on the last day
of excavation in 1977 before closing the site for the winter, he had been
trying one of the last approaches, with little hope of finding anything—certainly not the tomb of Philip II, in as pristine condition as
the day it was closed.

This was the first intact Macedonian tomb ever found—breathtaking,
imposing, exquisite, with a huge frieze of a hunting scene, a masterpiece similar to those of the Italian Renaissance, but 1,000 years older.
It, along with a massive yet delicate fresco depicting Pluto's abduction
of Persephone (a copy of which is displayed along one wall of the museum), is the only original work of great painting surviving from antiquity. On the left are two tombs and one altar that had been looted
and destroyed in varying degrees by the time Andronikos discovered
them. Macedonian Tomb III, on the right, found intact in 1978, is believed to be that of the young Prince Alexander IV, Alexander the Great's
son, who was at first kept alive by his "protectors" after Alexander's
death and then poisoned (along with his mother) when he was 14. To
the left of Tomb III is that of Philip II. He was assassinated in the nearby
theater, a short drive away; his body was burned, his bones washed in
wine, wrapped in royal purple, and put into the magnificent, solid gold
casket with the 16-point sun, which is displayed in the museum. His
wife, Cleopatra—not the Egyptian queen—was later buried with him.

The tombs alone would be worth a special trip, but the treasure trove
of golden objects and unusual artifacts that were buried within them
is equally impressive. First housed in the archaeological museum in Thessaloniki, they have been artfully transferred here to their stunning, permanent home. Among them, in practically perfect condition and
displayed in dramatic dimmed light, are delicate ivory reliefs, elegantly
wrought gold laurel wreaths, and Philip's crown, armor, and shield.
Especially interesting are those items that seem most certainly Philip's:
a pair of greaves (shin guards), one shorter than the other—Philip was
known to have a limp. ⊠ *Archaeological site,* ☎ *031/830538.* ☜ *1,200
dr./€3.53* ☉ *Tues.–Sun. 8:30–3.*

The winding road to the **site of Philip's assassination** goes through rolling
countryside west of the village, much of it part of the vast royal **burial
grounds of ancient Aigai.** On the way, you pass three more Macedo-

nian tombs of little interest, being rough-hewn stone structures in typical Macedonian style. The palace itself is nothing more than a line of foundation stones that shows the outline of its walls. It was discovered by French archaeologists in 1861 but not thought to have any particular significance; ancient Aigai was then thought to be somewhere near Edessa. In the field just below are the remnants of the **theater,** located by Andronikos in 1982. It was on Philip's way here, for the wedding games that were to follow the marriage of his daughter to the king of Epirus, that he was murdered.

Dining

$$ X **Philippion.** Eat outside under the trees, where a colorful chicken may wander under your table (probably hiding). Inside, under an arched ceiling, you can choose from a tasty lineup of traditional foods, such as moussaka. Vegetables grown in this region are especially delicious, and fresh frozen yogurt is made from local fruits. The charismatic manager, Philippides Manolis, couldn't be friendlier—nor could the chicken. Reservations are not needed, but try to get in ahead of tour buses. ⊠ *Across from the tombs,* ☎ *031/92892. AE, MC, V.*

Dion

㉓ *87 km (54 mi) southwest of Thessaloniki.*

At the foothills of Mt. Olympus lies ancient Dion. Even before Zeus and the Olympian gods, Mt. Olympus was home to the Muses and Orpheus, who entranced the men of the area with his mystical music. The story says that the life-giving force of Dion came from the waters in which the murderers of Orpheus (the women of Mt. Olympus, jealous for attention from their men) washed their hands on the slopes of the sacred mountain to remove the stain of their own sin. The waters entered the earth to cleanse it, and rose again in the holy city of Dion. Today, underground streams from the sacred mountain emerge where ancient Dion was founded, consecrating the ground, as it were, with its bubbling, life-giving springs.

Although a lesser-known ancient site to the non-Greek visitor, Dion is especially exciting because of daily discoveries being made throughout the year. The superb **museum** contains the best finds from the area, which is still under intense excavation. (The friendly excavators may even let you dig around the edges a bit in mock labor and take a photo—if you are careful.) It's best to visit the museum first and view the videotape (in English) prepared by the site's renowned archaeologist, Dimitris Pandermalis, which describes the excavations, the finds, and their significance. (His efforts to keep the artifacts in the place where they were found have won him the unqualified admiration of the villagers and established a new trend for decentralization of archaeological finds throughout Greece.) On the second floor, there is an excellent topographical relief of the area, and in the basement you'll see a wooden model of the ancient city, together with interactive learning centers about the daily life of ancient Greece. ⊠ *Next to archaeological site,* ☎ *0351/53206.* ⊡ *800 dr./€2.35* ☉ *Mon. 12:30–7, Tues.–Sun. 8–7.*

The road from the museum divides the diggings at the **archaeological site** into two areas. On the left is the **ancient city** of Dion itself, with the juxtaposition of public toilets and several superb floor mosaics. On the right side is the **ancient theater** and, a bit farther on, the **Sanctuaries of Asklepios and Demeter** and the **Sanctuary of Isis.** In the latter, a vividly beautiful approximation of how it once looked, copies of the original statues, now in the museum, have been put in place.

Today a feeling of peace prevails at Dion, at the foot of the mountain of the gods. The grounds are beautifully maintained. Visitors are few at this vast, underrated site, and the silence is punctuated now and then by goats, their bells jangling, driven around the toppled columns and mosaic floors by shepherds and their busy dogs. Springs bubble up where excavators dig, and scarlet poppies bloom among the cracks. This is the essence of Greece. ⊠ *Archaeological site,* ☎ *0351/53206.* 🎫 *800 dr./€2.35* ☉ *Tues.–Sun. 8:30–3 (Mon. noon–7 in winter).*

Dining and Lodging

$$ ✕ **Dionysos.** A combination tourist shop, café, and restaurant in a setting of varnished modernity, Dionysos has excellent food and good, cheerful service. Try the specialty of the area, roast goat on a spit. Also recommended are the *loukaniko* (sausages); rolled, spiced, and spit-roasted meat; and the saganaki (fried feta or *kefaloteri* cheese). ⊠ *Village center, directly opposite museum,* ☎ *0351/53276. No credit cards.*

$ 🏨 **Dion Resort Hotel.** Proximity to the beach, Mt. Olympus, and the archaeological site is the selling point here. Every room has an excellent view of either the sea or the peaks. Direct-dial phones are available, and a small selection of water sports is offered. ⊠ *Paralia Dion 60100,* ☎ *0352/61222,* 📠 *0352/61220. 200 rooms. Restaurant, bar, snack bar, air-conditioning, minibars, 2 pools, tennis court. AE, DC, MC, V.*

Mt. Olympus

㉔ *100 km (62 mi) southwest of Thessaloniki, 17 km (10½ mi) southwest of Dion.*

As you drive from the sea to Mt. Olympus, this site appears as a conglomeration of thickly bunched summits and not as a majestic single peak. To understand how the mountain must have impressed the ancient Greeks and caused them to shift their allegiance from the earth-rooted deities of the Mycenaeans to those of the airy heights of Olympus, you need to see the mountain clearly from several different perspectives. From the south, if there is still snow on the range, it appears as a massive, flat-topped acropolis, much like the one in Athens, its vast, snowy crest hovering in the air, seemingly capable of supporting as many gods and temples as the ancients could have imagined. On its northern side, the Olympus range catches clouds in a turbulent, stormy bundle, letting fly about 12 times as many (surely Zeus-inspired) thunder-and-lightning storms as anywhere else in Greece. The third perspective comes from actually climbing the mountain, to the truly awe-inspiring summit at the throne of Zeus. **Litochoro** is the town nested at the foot of the mountain and is the modern address for Olympus these days.

If you hike up Mt. Olympus (☞ *below*), when you come from Prionia take time to visit the **monastery of Ayios Dionysus** (⊠ In forest at bottom of turnoff to right just below refuge). During World War II, the monastery, rightly suspected of harboring resistance fighters, was blown up by the Nazis. It is now slowly being restored by the single monk who lives there and in its unfinished state has a stark and impressive beauty.

Lodging

$$ 🏨 **Aphrodite Hotel.** On the village square, this lodging is acceptable but doesn't live up to its name and lacks Myrto's (☞ *below*) spiffier character. ⊠ *Plateia Kentriki, Litochoro 60200,* ☎ *0352/21868. 24 rooms, 10 with bath. No credit cards.*

$$ 🏨 **Hotel Myrto.** White walls and wood decor give this hotel a cheery Alpine flavor, and every room has a lovely view from a balcony. Near

the main square, this is the best hotel in Litochoro village, bright and clean, and with a paneled TV lounge and bar. ⊠ *Off main road, Litochoro 60200,* ☎ *0352/81498. 18 rooms. Bar. No credit cards.*

Outdoor Activities and Sports

HIKING

Mt. Olympus provides the traveler with some of the most beautiful nature trails in Europe. Hundreds of species of wildflowers and herbs bloom in the spring, more than 85 of which are found only on this mountain.

From **Litochoro** you can climb all the way on foot or take a car to the end of the road at Prionia and trek the rest of the way. The climb to Prionia takes about four hours; the ride, on a bumpy gravel road with no guardrails between you and breathtakingly precipitous drops, takes little less than an hour, depending on your nerves. If you can manage to take your eyes off the road, the scenery is magnificent. The hiking refuge **Spilios Agapitos** (Refuge A; ⊠ two-thirds of way to summit, ☎ 0352/81800) is run by Kostas Zolotas, the venerable English-speaking guru of climbers. In the morning, it is just another two hours— some of it a bit hair-raising—to the Throne of Zeus and the summit, at 9,751 ft. The trail is snow-free from about mid-May until late October. For further details, contact ALMA or the Hellenic Alpine Club (☞ Contacts and Resources *in* Northern Greece A to Z, *below*).

EASTERN MACEDONIA
Chalkidiki, Kavala, Philippi, Thasos

Eastern Macedonia, with its curving sand beaches, coves, and Mediterranean landscape, has had a considerably less violent history than the western end of the realm. The birthplace of Aristotle, it was colonized in the 5th century BC by settlers from Athens and Evia and later, in 1922, saw large numbers of Greek refugees from Asia Minor who were resettled in the exchange of populations.

Caves of Petralona

㉕ *50 km (31 mi) southeast of Thessaloniki.*

On the northern edge of the first peninsula of the three-fingered hand of Chalkidiki, past golden fields, pine forests, and rural towns, you can stop at the dramatic Paleolithic caves of Petralona, at the foot of Mt. Katsika, 750 ft high. With huge stalactites and stalagmites configured like a fantasy scene from a Disney animation, the caves are easily accessible for those in good shape and good shoes; walkways take you through dramatically lighted grottoes, some with life-size figures of cave dwellers squatting before their fires. Traces of fire, dating back more than a million years, are the earliest yet found on earth; the ancient human skeleton, one of the oldest in the world—and definitely the oldest in Europe—was found in the 11th level of the cave. An adjoining museum offers in-depth explanations of the cave and the findings but needs some TLC to improve lighting and displays, which at press time looked a bit like a 1965 high school science fair. Happily, Aris Poulianos, the anthropologist who found the ancient skeleton at Petralona and named him Archanthropus Europaeus Petraloniensis, is still hardy and loves to talk prehistory. He is charming and modest and will pull up a chair by the site's snack bar, share a soft drink, and practice (good) English with interested visitors. Ask for him after you visit the cave, and a couple of ready questions will make the most of the time. ⊠ *16 km (10 mi) before turnoff for Nea Moudania,* ☎ *0396/31300.* ▨ *800 dr./€2.35* ⊘ *Daily: winter 9–5, summer 9–8.*

Kassandra

26 *69 km (43 mi) southeast of Thessaloniki, 19 km (11¾ mi) southeast of the Caves of Petralona.*

The most westerly of the three peninsulas, Kassandra was named after Cassander, the man who founded Thessaloniki. He also named a city on the peninsula after himself, presently called **Potidaia,** which once was important but gradually faded into insignificance as Thessaloniki became the major port. Potidaia's medieval walls date from 600 BC, when it was founded by Corinth. The small canal that leads to the town was cut across the isthmus in 1937.

Kassandra's white-sand beaches, rocky coves, and hour-or-so proximity to Thessaloniki have made it the most popular—and populous—resort area in Chalkidiki. Pine-forested promontories isolate the resort areas from one another, so it feels less crowded than it actually is. Farming villages with stone houses, fishing hamlets, and Byzantine towers remain, alongside a plethora of fast-food joints, discos, shopping centers, good hotels, and resort complexes. Kallithea has the the ruins of the Temple of Ammon Zeus, an Egyptian-Libyan version of the Greek god, said to have inspired Alexander the Great to set off for the Nile area. Kalandra has a 7th-century church with gorgeous frescoes. For an interesting look at how the life-loving Greeks celebrate their vacations, dip into the energy generated at seaside villages such as **Hanioti** and **Paliouri** near the tip of the peninsula, particularly in the evenings.

Lodging

$$$$ ☲ **Alexander the Great Hotel.** Set on a pine-clad shoreline with white-sand beaches and crystal-clear waters, this cluster of modern buildings and bungalows incorporates traditional Macedonian architectural features, such as red slate roofs, and is surrounded by beautifully landscaped gardens. In fact, this hotel has been given numerous awards for its "green programs," the name for its environmental projects. Its Roxani Restaurant is exceptional and attracts Thessalonians who make the drive just to savor its extraordinary creations. This hotel is perfect for families with children, and its "Greek nights," in which dancing is taught, its calendar of barbecues and beach parties are all great for teenagers. People seeking a quiet retreat will be rewarded as well. Guest rooms are handsomely decorated in sun and sea colors; ask for one with a sea view from the balcony—you'll wind up being mesmerized for hours. A half-board plan is available. ✉ *Kryopigi Kassandra, 63077,* ☎ *0374/20210, or 0374/20220,* ℻ *0374/23588. 210 rooms. 2 restaurants, 3 bars, grocery, swimming pool, wading pool, 2 tennis courts, basketball court, playground, water sports, bicycles, car rental, business services. AE, MC, V. Closed late Oct.–mid-Apr.* ☜

$$$$ ☲ **Athos Palace.** Along with the Alexander the Great Hotel (☞ *above*), this is one of the best in the area. The modern building has well-landscaped grounds, excellent service, views of the sea or the hills from room balconies, lots of activities, and a wonderful beach. ✉ *Kallithea, Kassandra, Chalkidiki 63077,* ☎ *0374/22100 through 0374/22109,* ℻ *0374/23605. 465 rooms, 44 suites, 18 bungalows. 2 restaurants, 2 bars, 2 pools, horseback riding, nightclub, meeting room. AE, DC, MC, V.*

Sithonia

27 *76 km (47½ mi) southeast of Thessaloniki, 26 km (16 mi) east of Kassandra.*

Olive groves, red-roof and half-timbered houses, pine trees turning the blue of the Aegean green at its rugged shoreline—that is Sithonia, the middle peninsula, with perhaps the most beautiful scenery and coast-

line in all of Chalkidiki. Because it is farther from Thessaloniki than
Kassandra, it is far less developed and crowded. Narrow-laned villages
are inviting, and a tour around the entire peninsula with leisurely
stops for lunch and a swim, round-trip from Thessaloniki, is an easy
day trip. Keep in mind that most establishments on the peninsula are
open only during the tourist season (May–late October).

The area of **Ormos Panayias** and its adjoining bay of **Vourvourou,** midway on the eastern coast of the peninsula, provides an idyllic setting.
Tiny pine-blanketed islands dot the shoreline and harbor, and fishing
caïques bob at anchor in charming coves. Many feel that the look is
similar to that of the northern California coast. Boats leave at 9:30 AM
for a round-trip to Mt. Athos, on the adjoining peninsula, stopping
for lunch at Ouranopolis, and get back around 5. This is a convenient
way to see the third peninsula without having to drive there.

On the drive south, excellent views of the holy peninsula of Mt. Athos
rise across the bay. This is as close as most will come to seeing the great
monastery at Mt. Athos. **Sarti,** the next village down from Vourvourou, is the fishing port settled by refugees in the 1922 population
exchange with Turkey. Each family built its house according to its own
visions, resulting in a glorious lack of uniformity and, sometimes,
taste. The beach is long and wide, and it drifts right up to the little flower
gardens fronting the houses. Rooms for rent are plentiful; one hotel
sits on the southern outskirts of the village.

The secluded bay of **Porto Koufo,** on the southwestern end of the tip
of the peninsula, is almost completely encircled by rocky headlands,
and the sea is so still here the name translates as "deaf port." It has
several tavernas, their relaxing setting warranting an eye-opening
drink. North of Porto Koufo are a succession of small, not-yet-overly
commercialized beach communities, of which nearby **Toroni,** with a
few tavernas and cafés and an excellent beach, is probably the most
picturesque. Its ruins of Byzantine fortifications and early Christian basilicas offer a good opportunity to walk and stretch your limbs after a
long drive. In the bustling fishing village of **Neos Marmaras,** north of
Toroni, fishermen haul their catch in front of numerous cafés, tavernas, bars, and restaurants along the seafront. Nightlife is lively, and
big resort hotels are being developed to add to the plethora of rooming houses.

Dining and Lodging

$$ ✕ **Pergola.** Two friends from the area have painted this little house
purple and orange, and claim their cuisine is "Greek and exotic," but
you won't go wrong with traditional fried calamari or roast chicken,
accompanied by salad with feta, tomato, and cucumber. You're out of
luck if a tour bus has just unloaded, but otherwise it's fun to sit on the
porch and talk with the outgoing owners over wine poured from the
barrel. ✉ *Sarti, 2 blocks from the seaside on the main road into town,*
☎ *0375/94005. No credit cards.*

$$$$ 🏨 **Grecotel Meliton Beach.** The best in Chalkidiki, this huge new fam-
ily resort offers every activity and is within a few minutes' drive of 33
beaches, so getting away to a secluded stretch of sand is possible when
you tire of group fun. There's a huge array of water sports available.
Cheerful accommodations have plenty of space and built-ins. ✉ *Neos
Marmaras, near the Marina, part of the Porto Carras complex, 63081,*
☎ FAX *0375/7138. 428 rooms, 18 suites. 3 restaurants, 3 bars, grocery,
2 pools, nightclub, children's program, meeting rooms. AE, DC, MC,
V. Closed Nov.–Apr.*

En Route If you are bypassing the fingers that are the Kassandra and Sithonia peninsulas, the best route from Thessaloniki to Chalkidiki's eastern-most peninsula is not, as it would seem, directly across the palm to Ouranopolis. This route from west to east involves much uphill driving, particularly frustrating if you get behind a bus or truck. Therefore, leave Thessaloniki at Platia Vardaris, take the E79 north toward Serres, then turn east onto the E90 toward Kavala. Continue past the long and beautiful lakes of **Koronia** and **Volvi** until you come to the forested turnoff for the coast, signposted to **Stavros** and **Olympiada.**

Between these charming little fishing villages (as yet relatively unrav-aged), you'll see some of the most spectacular landscape—rivaling Big Sur in California—as the road travels high above the coast through pine-scented forests. After Olympiada, a popular family and tourist spot for locals with its recently excavated old walls, an optional turnoff of about 10 km (6 mi) leads to Stagira, Aristotle's birthplace. A statue of the great philosopher stands on a wooded knoll as you approach the modern town. The mining town of **Stratoni** appears irresistible from above but is most depressing up close. You'll pass **Nea Roda,** near the site of Xerxes' Canal, dug by the Persian king in 480 BC to avoid having his ship hit the rocks in the violent storms around Mt. Athos. Today the canal is barely visible in the grassy marsh.

Ouranopolis

㉘ *110 km (68½ mi) east of Thessaloniki.*

Meaning "Heaven's City" in Greek, Ouranopolis is a charming cul-de-sac on the final point of land that separates the secular world from the sacred walled-off sanctuaries of Mt. Athos. The village, noted for its rug and tapestry weaving, is particularly entrancing because of the bay's aquamarine waters. However, the narrow village beaches are over-crowded in high season, and the town overrun with package tours and day-trippers from Thessaloniki. It's probably best to stay at one of the hotels on an islet or slightly outside the main town.

Ouranopolis was settled by refugees from Asia Minor in 1922–23 and before that was occupied only by monks from Mt. Athos, who lived in the Byzantine **Tower of Proforion** (✉ On the point), built in the 12th century by Emperor Andronicus II. When the villagers arrived, the monks fled, and the tower subsequently became the abode of Joice and Sydney Loch, a couple who worked with Thessaloniki's noted American Farm School to help the refugees develop their rug-weaving industry. The tower has now been fully restored and is occasionally open for various exhibitions by local artists.

Floating on its turquoise waters are the **tiny emerald islands** and **atolls** of **Drenia** and **Amouliani,** which are reachable by a 15-minute caïque ride and by small outboard motorboats, which you can rent by the day. All have glorious white-sand beaches, and two—**Gaidoronisi** (part of the Drenia group) and the fishing hamlet of **Amouliani**—have places to eat.

Dining and Lodging

$$ ✕ **Kritikos.** The owner is a local fisherman, so everything is served catch-of-the-day at this simple restaurant. The family re-creates traditional village recipes—but never gives away the secrets. Their lobster with pasta is haute cuisine on paper tablecloths. ✉ *Town center, just north of village square (you may have to ask the way),* ☎ *0377/455760. No credit cards.*

$$
★ ✕ **Skites Restaurant.** On a terrace overlooking the sea, in the hotel of the same name, this restaurant serves home-style meals that change from

day to day, according to the season. ⊠ *Skites hotel, southeast of Oura-nopolis,* ☎ *0377/71140. No credit cards.*

$$$$　🏨 **Agionissi Resort.** This tastefully elegant and environmentally friendly
★　island resort is the perfect solution for couples or families whose men-
folk want to make the pilgrimage to Mt. Athos; those left behind will
be so pampered and catered to that they won't feel the slightest bit
cheated. The private boat *Megalexandros* will transport guests from
Ouranopolis to the secluded little island of Amouliani, which still has
a traditional village populated by 500 fishing families (set a mile from
this hotel). The hotel Sea Grill has marvelous seafood and fresh fish
and an impressive selection of delicious wines from Chalkidiki and Mt.
Athos (note that half-board is required), while the pool bar has a stunning view of Mt. Athos from its wooden terrace. Its three private
beaches have the Blue Flag designation for water cleanliness; one of
them, Glarotopos Beach, has private wooden kiosks on a rocky beach
and appeals to adventurous guests. ⊠ *Amouliani Island, 63075,* ☎
0377/51102–3, 𝔽𝔸𝕏 *0377/51180. 68 rooms. Restaurant, salt-water
pool, 2 tennis courts, playground, business services, spa, health club,
beach. AE, MC, V. Closed mid-Oct.–Apr. 30.* 🐢

$$$　🏨 **Xenia.** Tucked among tamarisk and olive groves on the beach near
the main entrance to Ouranopolis, this hotel is a tranquil retreat and
definitely the best buy for the money. Its low-lying design and white-
washed wood and natural stone facade by famed architect Konstan-
tinidis makes it almost invisible from the village, and its interior makes
the most of the natural setting: French windows open to balconies with
only the blue of the sea as a background. Each room and bungalow is
furnished with simple pine furniture with neutral tone bedspreads and
curtains, brightened by Greek blue accents. A private white-sand beach
beckons, and the sea is only yards away; a large pool will suit those
who prefer fresh water. The restaurant is noted for its seafood and local
specialties. Buffet breakfast is included; half- or full-board is preferred.
⊠ *Ouranopolis 63075,* ☎ *0377/71202 or 0377/71412,* 𝔽𝔸𝕏 *0377/
71362. 20 rooms, 20 bungalows. Restaurant, bar, pool, air-condi-
tioning, beach. AE, MC, V.* 🐢

$$　🏨 **Skites.** Set on a bluff 1 km (½ mi) outside Ouranopolis, this is one
of the peachiest hotels in the area. All bungalow-style rooms are small,
with separate entrances, flower gardens, and privacy. You'll enjoy
views from the restaurant's terrace and the comforts of home: nostalgic cooking and a personal atmosphere. ⊠ *Ouranopolis 63075,* ☎ *0377/
71140,* 𝔽𝔸𝕏 *0377/71322. 13 bungalows, 4 apartments, all with bath.
Restaurant, bar, air-conditioning, pool. MC. Closed mid-Oct.–Easter.*
🐢

Mt. Athos

㉙　*120 km (74½ mi) southeast of Thessaloniki.*

One of the last great bastions of exclusivity, Mt. Athos isn't easy to
enter, even for men (women must content themselves with shopping
and sunning far from the boundaries of the holy settlements). Reservations, especially for summer and Easter, must often be made months
in advance. With booking in hand (or to apply for one) you must go
in person to the Pilgrim's Office for Mt. Athos in Thessaloniki to obtain your visa (☞ Visitor Information *in* Northern Greece A to Z, *below*).
Visas are issued only to adult males, and boys if they are accompanied
by an adult. Stays for non-Greeks are limited to four days.

This third peninsula of Athos, an isolated landscape of virgin forest,
valleys, and gorges, is called Ayion Oros (Holy Mountain) by the
Greeks, although it does not become a mountain until its southernmost

point, and there are no monasteries actually on its slopes. Its 6,670-ft height once prompted Alexander the Great's architect to suggest carving it into a replica of Alexander, a proposal that did not come to fruition.

The Virgin Mary, it is said, was brought here by accident from Ephesus, having been blown off-course by a storm. She found the spot to be a holy one and asked that it be venerated as her own very special place. This story has since become the rationale for keeping it off-limits to all women but the Virgin herself!

In the 5th–6th centuries the peninsula was occupied by only a few cave-dwelling hermits, and in 885 the Byzantine emperor Basil I decreed the area to be exclusively the province of hermits and monks. It was not until the 11th century that another decree specifically prohibited "smooth-faced persons" from entering: women, young boys, children, and eunuchs. Today, men do not have to grow a beard to visit.

In 963, the first organized monastic community (*lavra*) was established at the foot of the mountain. Called Great Lavra, it is still functioning today. Nineteen other communities followed (including some Orthodox Russians), the last in the 14th century. Since then, a number of hermitages and the separate dependencies called *skites* have been built, some precariously clinging to the rocky slopes. In 1926, Athos was formally united with Greece, but it still remains theoretically autonomous in its administration, similar to that of the Vatican. Hence the need for visas and a *diamonitirion* (official residence permit).

EXPLORING MT. ATHOS

A small boat leaves from the Ouranopolis dock daily at 9:45 AM. Before boarding, you go to the office near the dock with your visa to obtain the diamonitirion, which permits you to stay for the night. The boat then leaves you off at the tiny, somewhat disreputable-looking port of **Daphni,** a loading point for goods. From here, caïques take you to the monasteries along the western coast; otherwise, a rickety bus takes you up the steep promontory to the administrative center at **Karyes,** and you are on your own to walk or find a ride to the monastery of your choice. Be aware that most monasteries close for the night at sunset, about 9 PM in summer, and dinner is served at about 7.

Men visiting Mt. Athos should remember that it is a place of religious pilgrimage and should maintain a subdued demeanor and low profile. Wear long pants and shirts with sleeves at least to mid-arm. Wearing hats inside the monasteries is forbidden, as is smoking. Swimming (always with suits) should be far from the monasteries. Singing, whistling, and loud laughter are also taboo. Video cameras are banned from the mountain, and some monasteries also forbid still photography.

An alternative excursion (women allowed here, thank you very much!) would be one of the **daily cruises** around the spectacular coast of the peninsula. Book either in Thessaloniki (☞ Contacts and Resources *in* Northern Greece A to Z, *below*) or Ouranopolis at any of various agencies. You can see many superb monasteries that are built at the water's edge or clinging to rocky outcroppings.

Applications for bookings and visas (men only) can be made by writing to or visiting the **Pilgrim's Office for Mount Athos** (⊠ Karamanli 14, ☏ 031/861611). First, apply over the phone to the above number between 9 and 4:30 weekdays and between 10 and noon on Saturday; then bring your confirmation of booking and your passport to the office between Monday and Saturday 8:30–1:30, or 6–8 PM weekdays, except Wednesday. Ten permits are issued daily to non-Orthodox and at least 100 to Orthodox visitors.

An easier way of traveling to Mt. Athos, particularly from abroad, is to contact Christos Sigoulis, manager of **Athos City Tours** (☞ Northern Greece A to Z, *below*; he can do all of the paperwork for your visa and bookings prior to your arrival.

Women (or men who do not want to stay overnight at Mt. Athos) who want to get a good view of many of the monasteries from the required distance of 500 yards from the shore can book in Thessaloniki at **Doucas Tours** (✉ Venizelou 8, Platia Eleftherias, ☎ 031/224100), which arranges day-long coach tours that go to Ormos Panayia on Sithonia and then transfer passengers to a boat which cruises to Ouranopolis and around the area; cost is around $60.

Kavala

🔞 *136 km (84½ mi) northeast of Thessaloniki.*

Exceptionally pretty for a commercial city, and blessed with natural riches, architectural treasures, and a thriving economy, Kavala is the main city of eastern Macedonia. When Philip II founded Philippi to protect the eastern route to the mineral riches of the Pangeon mountains, he made Kavala—in those days, Neapolis—its port. Today, besides being a major gateway for the islands in the northeast Aegean, it is the capital of Greece's tobacco industry. A combination of old and new, its buildings rise like tiers in an amphitheater up Mt. Simvolo. The aqueduct built around 1550, possibly by the Ottoman Süleyman the Magnificent, is the boundary between the modern, bustling town and the older section of town, known as **Panayia,** and worth a walk along its cobbled paths with fragrant gardens spilling over walls, steep and cobbled alleyways under jutting, enclosed balconies, and squares with domed, 18th-century Turkish houses.

The imposing eastern promontory is dominated by a **Byzantine castle** overlooking a harbor lined with brightly colored seafaring caïques and a number of fine seafood tavernas and clubs. Visiting the castle is free and can be done Tuesday to Sunday from 8:30 to 7. The Panayia district is just below it on the hill, and from here you can get a good view of the aqueduct. The friendliest and best tavernas, cafés, and ouzeris are in this area.

The most prominent building on the hill below the fortress on Poulidhou Street is the **Imaret,** built by **Mehmet Ali,** who was born in 1769, the son of a wealthy Albanian tobacco merchant who became an Egyptian pasha and founded the dynasty ending in King Farouk. The Imaret is a complex of exotic structures, built in Islamic style, topped by 18 domes and bearing Arabic inscriptions over the doorways. It was an almshouse run by dervishes who fed and housed 300 indigent students. Part of it has now been restored and opened as a popular café and restaurant (☞ Dining, *below*).

The **Birthplace of Mehmet Ali,** which still belongs to the family of Mehmet Ali, is maintained by the Egyptian government. Its wood-paneled rooms, harem, and ground-floor stables provide an interesting glimpse into Ottoman daily life in the 1800s and are well preserved. ✉ *Polidhou and Mehmet Ali Sts. (near the equestrian stature of Mehmet Ali).* 🎫 *Free (but tip the guide).* ⊙ *Tues.–Sun 10–2.*

It was at the site of the **Archaeological Museum,** on the west side of town near the harbor, that the apostle Paul disembarked on his first trip to Greece in AD 49, en route to Philippi. Today you can see sculpture, such as the bronze of a kneeling captive, graceful mosaics of dolphins and lilies, a reconstructed Macedonian tomb and gold jewelry, and painted terra-cotta figurines from Amphipolis. ⊠ *17 Erythrou Stavrou,* ☎ *051/222335.* ▣ *800 dr./€2.35* ⊙ *Tues.–Sun. 8:30–5.*

On Saturday mornings, a huge outdoor bazaar is held close to the Archaeological Museum. You'll see a vast array of trinkets, as well as some interesting folk-crafts and weavings from merchants coming from Xanthi and other parts of Thrace.

Three blocks from the Archaeological Museum is the small **Folk Art Museum.** It has a collection of folk costumes and household artifacts, plus some sculptures of Polygnotos Vayis, born in Thassos. ⊠ *Philipou 4,* ☎ *051/227820.* ▣ *Free.* ⊙ *Weekdays 8–2, Sat. 9–1.*

Dining and Lodging

$$ ✗ **Beautiful Mytilini.** This extraordinary seafood taverna under the fortress promontory specializes in mussel pilaf and other *fruits de mer* (shellfish). ⊠ *Eastern end of harbor,* ☎ *051/223034. MC, V.*

$$ ✗ **Imaret.** The exotic restored almshouse of Mehmet Ali makes for a very romantic setting for an evening drink or meal and is frequented by Kavala's younger set. Candlelit tables are set on multiple-levels, some with panoramic views of the sea, others in little nooks just made for a private téte-a-téte. The menu consists of tasty mezedes such as oven-baked potato salad or stuffed mushrooms, cheese pies, zucchini cro-quettes, or the house special *al halili*—a divine Anatolian bruschetta, in which toasted rounds of bread are laden with several cheeses, scal-lions, tomatoes, and hot peppers and heated in the oven. ⊠ *Poulid-hou 32,* ☎ *051/836286. No credit cards.*

$$ ✗ **O Faros.** This little taverna is on the road leading to the Byzantine castle and is the heartbeat of the picturesque Panayia neighborhood. It specializes in fresh fish and seafood, such as smelt and bream, as well as stuffed tomatoes, lamb stew, and veal stew with onions. Wash it all down with carafes of Limnos wine. You'll enjoy the passing multi gen-erational foot traffic, from wizened *yia-yiadhes* (grandmothers) in black dresses (with toddlers in tow—to show off to neighbors) to courting couples. ⊠ *Poulidhou 25,* ☎ *051/838986. No credit cards.*

$$ 🏨 **Filoxenia Hotel.** Set in a bucolic wooded area outside the town of Kavala about 10 minutes away by taxi, this hotel offers more value for the money than those right in the center. The staff is exceptionally helpful. A modern building in the traditional style, guest rooms have tile floors, arched wooden bed frames, neutral and earth-colored spreads and drapes, and balconies. The lounge areas have a rustic ski-lounge ambience, and in winter a fireplace is ablaze. The curved pool is set in landscaped gardens and has a canopied bar and restaurant that has live entertainment in the summer. Breakfast is included in basic rate; half- and full-board are available. ⊠ *A. Apostolakis in Ayios Silas, 65000,* ☎ *051/240001, 051/240070, or 051/240071,* ℻ *051/245368. 30 rooms. Restaurant, bar, air-conditioning, pool. MC, V.*

$$ 🏨 **Nepheli Hotel.** Across from the park near the Archaeological Museum, this hotel gets less street noise than neighboring hotels on the waterfront. Guest rooms are large and simply furnished but comfortable and clean; some have balconies with a sea view, while the view from the roof gar-den—which takes in the sweep of the harbor as well as the castle—is stunning. Breakfast is included in the price. ⊠ *Erythrou Stavrou 50, 65403,* ☎ *051/227441 through 051/227444,* ℻ *051/227440. 88 rooms, 6 suites. Restaurant, bar, air-conditioning (some rooms). MC, V.*

$ 🏨 **George Alvanos Rooms.** You can't beat the location, on a back street of Panayia near the Byzantine castle, for charm and peacefulness . . . or the price. Guest rooms are cheerful, large, and spic-and-span, but only two have en-suite bathrooms. Book early. ⊠ *Anthemiou 35, Panayia, 65403,* ☎ *051/221781. 6 rooms. No credit cards.*

Philippi

③① *150 km (93¼ mi) northeast of Thessaloniki, 14 km (8½ mi) west of Kavala.*

Philippi is most famous for two historic reasons: in AD 42, the armies of Antony and Octavian caught up here with Caesar's assassins, Brutus and Cassius, and defeated them; and it was here that the apostle Paul first preached the gospel in Europe, later writing his famed Epistle to the Philippians. Just outside the west wall of Philippi on the banks of the river Gangitis he also performed the first baptisms on European soil. Noteworthy are an expansive **theater,** where ancient Greek plays are performed in summer, and the **Roman crypt** from which Paul was miraculously freed by an earthquake. ✉ *Archaeological site:* ☎ *051/ 516470.* 🎫 *800 dr./€2.35* ☉ *Tues.–Sun. 8:30–3. Museum:* ☎ *051/ 516251.* 🎫 *800 dr./€2.35* ☉ *Tues.–Sun. 8:30–7. Closed in winter.*

Amphipolis, 60 km (42 mi) southwest of Philippi, once the most important Athenian colony in Northern Greece, and now a modern village, still offers up sections of its acropolis and tombs. Of special note is the **Lion of Amfipolis,** a 4th-century BC burial monument, beyond the bridge over the Strymon River. Ruins of early Christian basilicas with exceptional mosaic floors are also worth seeking out.

Thasos

③② *About a 75-minute ferry ride from Kavala, 45 min by hydrofoil.*

Land of the mythical Sirens, the ancient and lovely island of Thasos has a past whose significance far outweighs its relative obscurity to today's overseas travelers. Traces of life date back to 2000 BC. Hercules was considered a guardian of the island, and Hippocrates, father of medicine, studied botany here. Tribes fought in the Trojan War, and the first Greek colonists, who received an oracle from the Temple of Apollo in Delphi, arrived in 700 BC.

Only 8 km (5 mi) from the northern Greek mainland, Thasos is known as "The Green Island" because of its thick pine-and-cypress forests and tracts of olive and fruit trees. It could just as well be called "Gold Island," for the precious metal mined here in the Pangeos mountains since the time of the Phoenicians, or "White Island," for its fine sand and local marble. The circular coastline is etched out in coves and beaches, and the island has two distinct sections: the north and east region is mountainous, with rocky cliffs and sandy bays; the south and west region is strung with traditional villages, set among low hills and olive groves. Most people head to the island via the hydrofoil from Kavala which docks in Limenas, the main town; from there, a ferryboat goes to Skala Prinou, a small port. An alternative route is the ferryboat from Keramoti (take a bus from Kavala bus station to this shipping yard and dock).

Parts of its main harbor town of **Limenas** (also known as Thasos) are touristy, but wander off a bit and you will find ruins and sanctuaries scattered among the houses, and sections of old stone walls still intact. The small, excellent **museum** holds traces of Greek, Roman, and early Christian figurines and statues, including the *kouros* (young man) carrying a ram, which came from the Acropolis. Also notable is an ivory lion's head, a Hellenistic head of Dionysos, and some Roman bas-reliefs and statues. It's open daily 9–2; admission is 500 dr./€1.47. **Classical ruins,** including an acropolis; temples to Dionysos, Poseidon, and Athena; an agora; and an amphitheater nestled in the forest above the town, were built from local quarries.

The villages of Thasos are by and large rural and retain a quiet beauty. **Panagia,** east of the harbor of Limenas and overlooking Golden Beach, is named after the Virgin Mary and the village most Thassians consider the prettiest on the island. Founded by refugees from Constantinople in the 16th century, it was the island's capital under the Ottomans. Whitewashed houses contrast with green pines and russet mountains, and the charming square, with its fountain and 700-year-old platanos tree, is an ideal place to snack on traditional walnuts or figs in syrup. Check out the nearby church, which houses elaborate altar carvings and a crusader's banner. Skala Panagia, the beach resort below, still has archaic walls, classical ruins, and a round watchtower from the 5th century BC. Tavernas are built into the cliffside.

To the west of Limenas, **Kazaviti** is divided by a stream—each half claims to be the real village, but locals distinguish them by using the prefixes "big" and "small." The more diminutive side is perched on the mountainside, with narrow lanes and courtyards draped with scented vines. Houses are built of stone, with wood-supported balconies; try to peek in to see the painted ceilings. The bigger side of the village has some shops and tavernas that serve simple fare and local wine, made from black grapes.

The ancient fishing village of **Skala Prinos** is still home to shipbuilders, and wooden boats are crafted in the small shipyard on the waterfront. Ferries leave for Kavala from here as well as from Limenas. Hard to find, and high in the center of the island, **Kastro** is the oldest village on Thasos. Ruins of a 15th-century Genoese wall and ruined houses are all around, but locals are starting to rebuild in the traditional style. The church has pretty hand-painted walls, a carved pulpit, and a harem section. To enter you have to ask for the heavy, hand-forged key.

The fishing port of **Limenaria,** now a commercial fishing port, was a major wine exporter in ancient times. Here you can still find Amelia, a local liquor of walnuts and honey, and Pergoula, a wine distilled from Thassian Georgina grapes.

During the Byzantine period the village of **Theologos** was the mountain capital of Thasos and remained so during Turkish rule in the 19th century. It's the greenest part of the island, and the slate-roofed traditional houses are well preserved and surrounded by small gardens or high walls. An old-fashioned baker and sandal maker are among the shops on the main street. A folklore museum in a Thassian-style house displaying costumes, household items, rugs, old flour mills, and antique olive presses is interesting for a brief stop. For an unforgettable country repast, stop at Psistaria Lambiris on the edge of town or Kleoniki Tou Iatro, with a wonderful terrace in the center of town, two tavernas that are notable for *souvla* or spit-grilled suckling pig and goat. St. Dimitris church has wood carvings of religious themes that took a monk 18 years to complete. Small waterfalls are nearby.

Beaches

Thasos has dozens of good beaches, ranging from hidden coves to long sunny stretches. The largest have changing facilities and umbrellas; the most secluded, like **Paradise Beach** on the southeast coast down from Kinyra, are perfect for nude bathing; and all overlook a clear, turquoise sea. Ten minutes from the center of town is **Limenas Beach,** with views of the harbor, and a backdrop of the acropolis. Families might prefer **Makryammos Beach,** 10 minutes farther, with a children's playground. The traditional villages of **Panagia** and **Potamia** overlook Golden Beach, named after the color of its sand, a 20-minute drive away from the harbor. Brightly colored beehives dot the road, and indeed, the area is known for its delicate pine-blossom honey. **Alyki** in the south, is the only village to have forbidden any modern construction. It is a gorgeous little hamlet with sand and pebble beaches and excellent snorkeling off its marble headlands.

Hiking

A walkers' guide is available at the tourist office near the dock at the harbor. Trails connect villages throughout the island, each of which has a distinct identity. Terrain varies from mountainous to flat, affording options for just about any walker or hiker. Even day-trippers can have a fascinating walk to the ancient ruins above the harbor town. One of the most challenging hikes is from Potamia, at the foot of Ipsarion, up the highest peak on Thasos (3,500 ft) almost in the center of the island. In the village itself, you can stroll through the **Polygnotos Vargis Museum,** housing the expressionistic works of the local sculptor, who gained fame in New York City and bequeathed most of his art to the Greek state. It's at least a three and 1/2 hour ascent on steep, overgrown paths and almost as long for the descent. Other hikers, who want to be out among the island's famed pines, plane, and chestnut trees and study typical village life, will tackle the 6-mile walk from Potos to Theologos or the 4-mile walk from Prinos, on the coast, to Mikro and Megalo Kazaviti. A series of fires devestated the island's vegetation in the 1980s, but a vigorous reforestation program has restored affected areas. Along the way, small, homemade ouzo distilleries tempt you with glasses of potent *tsipouro* (grape spirits)—limit your intake to one large shot if you plan to continue hiking. Everywhere, everyday scenes reflect life unchanged here for millennia: outdoor clay ovens and the scent of freshly baked bread; women on doorsteps, creating needlework; bags set in trees, straining whey for feta cheese; wood fires with bubbling cauldrons of figs and walnuts for Thassian sweets; donkeys laden with olive branches led by wizened villagers; herds of goats scattered over the roadside, foraging for anything within range. A walk in Thasos offers photo-ops around every turn.

Dining and Lodging

$$–$$$ ✕ **Zorba's.** Zorba's, as the name implies, is the place to seize the moment and let loose. Live music is performed every night, and the floor is crowded with Greeks and foreigners who often punctuate their excitement by smashing a few plates—*real* ceramic ones, an almost extinct ritual in modern Greece (it's actually against the law in many areas). It's lots of fun, the music is good and not overbearingly loud, and the food is well-made and not expensive. Try cheese and eggplant croquettes, lamb-and-rice-filled dolmades, and chicken in spicy tomato sauce. ⊠ *Behind the harbor, near Aranopoulos Super Market, Limenas,* ☎ *0593/22704. No credit cards. Closed Nov.–Apr.; no lunch served.*

$$ ✕ **Simi.** If you ask locals where they go for the best taverna food in Limenas, they're most likely to say "Simi," which opened in 1952. The decor is quintessential island—whitewashed exteriors accented with Aegean blue trim and checkered tablecloths–and the location on the old harbor is perfect for nibbling on mezedes while sipping an ouzo at sunset. Most of the fare is traditional: whole fish grilled and simply brushed with lemon and oil and sprinkled with a crushed pinch of the aromatic Thasos oregano; mussels in tomato sauce, feta, and peppers; a rice pilaf and lamb chops, all accompanied by the barrel retsina. For an innovation, try the Simi Salad, a Greek salad with beans and olives topped with a dollop of thick homemade yogurt or, for dessert, the Thasos-style halva (semolina-type pastry laced with cinnamon). ⊠ *Old Harbor, Limenas,* ☎ *0593/22517. V.*

$ ✕ **Sirtaki.** Under tamarisk trees on the edge of a tiny beach at the far
★ end of the Limenas harbor, dig into the fried squid or "sun-fried fish"—

start with any salad. Vegetables are organically raised, and the loving care lavished on the food reflects the nature of the owners. Try the Thassian wine, dry, with a light aroma. (The area has been a major wine exporter since ancient times but today keeps most of it to itself.) Also good are Amelia, a brew made from local walnuts and honey, and fiery tsipouro, similar to ouzo and just as potent. ⊠ *East end of town, past the harbor, Limenas,* ☎ *0593/22651. No credit cards.*

$ ✕ **Taverna Vergina.** Time seems to stand still in the traditional village of Kazaviti. After enjoying its plane trees and old stone houses, why not stop for a break to sate your hunger and thirst at Yiannis's taverna—the favorite of locals (and foreigners, who have renovated some of the old houses). Settle in at one of the tables set under a gigantic plane tree on the main square. The day's fare will be made of whatever is freshest and readily available; options include hearty bean soup, lamb with potatoes, moussaka, stuffed tomatoes, or juicy pork chops and grilled chicken. Also enjoy a carafe of the local *tsipouro*, a firewater punctuated with some anise flavor. ⊠ *Megalo Kazaviti, Kazaviti.* ☎ *No phone. No credit cards.*

$$$$ 🏨 **Makryammos.** Surrounded by a lush game preserve with strolling
★ peacocks, this complex of private bungalows on a curving, white-sand beach is a relaxing venue, especially for families. Guest rooms, while adequate, are not up to the surroundings. ⊠ *Limenas 64004,* ☎ *0593/ 22101 or 0593/22102,* FAX *0593/22761. 196 bungalows, 10 suites. Restaurant, bar, pool, 2 tennis courts, waterskiing, boating, children's programs. AE, MC, V.*

$$$ 🏨 **Amfipolis.** Behind an imposing iron gate, this converted tobacco ware-
★ house, one block inland from the harbor, is the most elegant place to stay in Limenas. Guest rooms are immaculate, wood-trimmed with handsome, local furnishings. The pleasant pool bar is a social center for guests, who are often repeat visitors, and there is a lush garden to enjoy. A full breakfast buffet with fresh juice is included. Ben, the huge, rumply dog often slumbering by the reception desk, is a sweetheart who loves a nuzzle. ⊠ *Limenas 64004,* ☎ *0593/23101 through 0593/ 23104,* FAX *0593/22110. 42 rooms. Bar, dining room, outdoor café, pool. AE, MC, V.*

$$ 🏨 **Dionysos.** Set in the village of Panagia, and spilling down a hill among pine forests, with splendid views of the Aegean, this group of blindingly white buildings outside a quiet, traditional village has locally inspired decor, and verandas from which to gaze and relax. It hugs the rugged terrain as if it has been there for years, but it was built in 1994. ⊠ *Panagia 64004,* ☎ *0593/61822, 33 rooms. Restaurant, bar, pool, meeting rooms. MC, V. Closed Nov.–Mar.*

$$ 🏨 **Filoxenia Inn.** Filoxenia is the Greek word for hospitality and you'll find that offered here at a bargain price. Set back from the harbor behind the Archaeological Museum, smack dab in the center of town, the location is quiet but convenient. A recent upgrading has resulted in sparkling fresh rooms with minibars and radios, a pretty garden with a pool, and breakfast area. Ten rooms on the upper floor have air-conditioning. ⊠ *Pavlou Mela, behind the museum, Limenas 64004,* ☎ *0593/23331,* FAX *0593/22231. 24 rooms. Air-conditioning (some rooms), pool. No credit cards. Closed Nov.–Mar.*

$$ 🏨 **Garden.** Set in a quiet cul-du-sac away from the bustle of the harbor, this small studio hotel owned and run by Christos Archonditis has won favor with German and British tourists. Each studio is bright, fully equipped, and spotlessly clean. The small pool is a gathering point for guests, and the restaurant is remarkably good for a hotel, worth a visit on its own. Breakfast is included. ⊠ *On north end of Limenaria town in area set back from harbor (look for signs), Limenaria 64002,* ☎ *0593/*

52650, ⊠ 0593/52660. *14 studios. Restaurant, air-conditioning, pool.*
MC, V.

NORTHERN GREECE A TO Z

Arriving and Departing

By Bus

The trip from Athens takes about seven hours, with one rest stop. Buy tickets at least one day in advance (⊠ 100 Kifissou St., ☎ 01/514–8856) or in Thessaloniki (⊠ Monastiriou 67, ☎ 031/510834); one-way fare is 8,700 dr./€25.66.

By Car

Driving to Greece from Europe through the former Yugoslavia is possible but often time-consuming owing to many border problems. You may prefer to drive through Italy and take a car ferry from Bari, Ancona, or Brindisi to Igoumenitsa on the west coast of Greece. This more beautiful route takes seven to eight hours, either by the northern route via Ioannina and Kozani, or via Ioannina, Kalambaka (and the famous Meteora monasteries), and Larissa. Both drives are spectacular, but the one to the south, used by regional buses, is much less treacherous and marginally faster. The Athens–Thessaloniki part of the National Road (500 km [310 mi]), the best in Greece, takes five to seven hours.

By Plane

There are direct flights to Thessaloniki from London, Amsterdam, Brussels, Paris, Frankfurt, Stuttgart, Munich, Zurich, and Vienna, with good connections from the United States. You can also take an **Olympic Airways** flight to Thessaloniki from Athens. The airport is at Mikras (⊠ On the coast some 13 km [8 mi; 20 minutes] southeast of the city center). A municipal bus to the airport (30 minutes; 200 dr./€.56 exact change) leaves at irregular intervals from the train station and makes a stop at Aristotelous Square opposite Electra Palace. Kavala also has an airport, with daily flights to Athens, although the tickets should be booked in advance.

By Train

Three daily **express trains** connecting Athens and Thessaloniki take five to six hours; they are comfortable and air-conditioned. You can also take an **overnight train** with sleeping accommodations. Make reservations a few days in advance at the station or in Thessaloniki (⊠ 18 Leoforos Aristotelous, ☎ 031/517527 or 031/517517); express fare is 9,000 dr./€26.54; for other trains: first-class fare, 6,000 dr./€17.69; second-class, 4,100 dr./€12.09; sleeper surcharge, from 1,100 dr./€3.24 to 7,500 dr./€22.12. Tickets can also be purchased at **Zorpidis Travel** (⊠ Egnatia 76, corner of Egnatia and Aristotelous).

Getting Around

By Bus

Intercity **KTEL** buses connect Thessaloniki with locations throughout Greece. There are small ticket office terminals (*praktorio*) for each line, usually located on the side of the city toward their destination. **Ticket offices** for departure to Athens (⊠ 67 Monastiriou, opposite the Thessaloniki train station, ☎ 031/510834 or 031/516104); Chalkidiki (⊠ 68 Karakasi St., in the southeastern suburb of Harilaou, ☎ 031/924444); Kavala (⊠ 59 Langada St., on the northwest side of Thessaloniki, ☎ 031/525530). For information about other offices contact the EOT (☞ *below*) or check the listings in the daily newspaper of all buses, trains, and airlines.

By Car

The roads in general are well maintained and constantly being improved and widened throughout the region. A good **four-lane highway** that begins in Athens (E90) goes to the border with Turkey (E84); beware, posted speedlimits are exceedingly fast. Mobil gas stations sell excellent **road maps.** You can get information from the **Greek Automobile Touring Club** (ELPA; ✉ 228 Vasilis Olgas St., ☎ 031/426319 or 031/426320, ℻ 031/411155). You can reserve space for yourself and your car on ships and car ferries traveling between ports throughout Greece at the **Plaris Travel Agency** (✉ 22 Pavlou Mela, ☎ 031/278613 or 031/232078, ℻ 031/286825) and **Zorpidis Travel** (✉ 76 Egnatias St., ☎ 031/286812, ℻ 031/274422). In summer you should reserve a month in advance.

Car Rental. Driving in Thessaloniki is not recommended because of the congestion, frequent traffic jams, and scarcity of parking. Walking and taking a local bus or taxi are much easier on the nerves. For exploration within Macedonia or Thrace, you can rent cars at **AutoEurope** (✉ Komninou and Nikis, ☎ 031/242121); **Avis** (✉ Airport, ☎ 031/473858; ✉ Nikis 3, ☎ 031/227126); **Budget** (✉ Airport, ☎ 031/471491; ✉ Makedonia Palace hotel, ☎ 031/868394); **Hertz** (✉ Airport, ☎ 031/473952; Venizelou 4, ☎ 031/277787).. In Thasos, rent cars at **Potos Car Rental** (☎ 0593/23969; also **Rent-A-Car Thasos** (☎ 0593/23969).

By Plane

Domestic carriers connect Thessaloniki with a number of cities and Mykonos, Santorini, Crete, Rhodes, Corfu, Limnos, Chios, and Lesbos. There are usually at least five daily flights to and from Athens, which take 40–45 minutes.

By Ship

Nomicos Lines ships connect Thessaloniki to Chios, Heraklion (Crete), Lesbos, Limnos, Mykonos, Paros, Santorini, Skiathos, Skyros, and Tinos. Buy tickets at the **Karaharissis Agency** (✉ N. Kountouriotous 8, near Platia Eleftherios, ☎ 031/513005, ℻ 031/532289).

By Train

The regional train service is not recommended; travel by bus is usually faster and always more dependable.

Contacts and Resources

Emergencies

Tourist Police (☎ 031/554871). **American Consulate** (☎ 031/242905). **Honorary British Consulate** (☎ 031/286696). **Honorary Canadian Consulate** (☎ 031/230456).

Guided Tours

Athos City Tours: Thessaloniki (✉ 5 Ayios Sofias, ☎ 031/238521); Ouranopolis (☎ 0377/71150, ℻ 0377/71393, ✍); Kassandra (☎ 0374/916913); Athens (✉ Zalakosta 6, ☎ 01/362–8581, ℻ 01/362–8708). **Doucas Tours** (☎ 031/269984). **Zorpidis Travel** (☎ 031/244400).

Hiking and Climbing

ALMA eco-adventure tourism office (☎ 031/855629). **Chalkidiki Hotel Association** (✉ 33 G. Papandreou, Thessaloniki, ☎ 031/429020, ℻ 031/429021). **Hellenic Alpine Club** (✉ Thessaloniki, ☎ 031/278288 or 035/281944). **Trekking Hellas** (✉ Mitropoleos 60, Thessaloniki, ☎ 031/264082) arranges mountain trekking and other outdoor excursions.

Pharmacies

Lists of late-night pharmacies are published in newspapers and posted in the windows of all pharmacies.

Visitor Information

In Thessaloniki, the **Greek National Tourist Organization** (GNTO or EOT) central regional office on Aristotelous Square is open summer 8 AM–8 PM, but call first if you're not close to the office as unscheduled breaks are common (✉ 8 Aristotelous Sq. Thessaloniki, ☎ 031/222935, FAX 031/265504); Airport (☎ 031/269984, ext. 215); Kavala (✉ 5 Filellinon St., ☎ 051/228762 or 051/222425, FAX 051/223885).

6 THE NORTHERN ISLANDS

CHIOS, LESBOS, AND SAMOS

Flung like puzzle pieces into the Aegean, each of these green and gold islands is distinct: though ravaged by fire, Chios retains an eerie beauty and fortified villages, old mansions, Byzantine monasteries, and stenciled-wall houses; Lesbos, Greece's third-largest island and birthplace of legendary artists and writers, is dense with gnarled olive groves and dappled with mineral springs; and lush, mountainous Samos, land of wine and honey, whispers of the classical wonders of antiquity.

By Lea Lane
and Toula
Bogdanos

Updated by
Melia Tatakis

Q UIRKY, SEDUCTIVE, FERTILE, sensual, faded, sunny, worldly, ravishing, long-suffering, hedonistic, luscious, mysterious, legendary—these adjectives only begin to describe the northeastern Aegean islands of Lesbos, Chios, and Samos. Closer to Turkey's coast than to Greece's—and quite separate from one another—they zigzag from north to south, respectively. Other islands most often considered a part of this startling and rather arbitrary archipelago are Ikaria, Samothraki, and Thasos—and four islets: Fourni, southeast of Ikaria; Psara and Inousses, flanking Chios to the west and east; and Agios Efstratios, south of Limnos.

Despite the Northern Islands' proximity to Asia Minor, they are the essence of Greece, the result of 4,000 years of Hellenic influence that lasted until 1923. Although Lesbos, Chios, and Samos fell into obscurity in later centuries, especially under the Ottoman Empire, in the ancient world they prospered gloriously as important commercial and religious centers. They also were cultural hothouses, producing such geniuses as Pythagoras, Sappho, and probably Homer.

Whether or not they once again become centers of art and culture, these islands are becoming popular travel destinations for Europeans, despite a military presence, and the vestiges of bitterness about their mainland neighbors (and former conquerors) a few miles east. Despite the rhetoric—mostly instigated by the two governments—islanders don't hesitate to shuttle people back and forth to Turkey. And why not, when tourism has at last arrived?

Hilly, sometimes mountainous, with uncrowded beaches, natural attractions, noteworthy architecture, and historic sites, these are Greek islands to one-up your well-traveled friends with; they probably haven't even heard of most of them. They are not "party" islands, but towns and villages operating on a year-round schedule, much as the Cyclades may have been 50 years ago. People here go about their business as they have for centuries, with a gratifying Greek temperament of generosity, humor, open-mindedness, and optimism.

Pleasures and Pastimes

Beaches
From golden sand to black and red pebbles, from isolated turquoise coves to long sweeps of sunny coastline, beaches here are varied and often excellent. The relative lack of tourism often results in deserted stretches, rare in the more popular Greek islands. Many beaches allow topless sunbathing, unless they're part of the town's waterfront, but there is almost always a designated non-nude stretch where families congregate. Nude bathers should use discretion; in general, if you choose your spot carefully, you should have no problem with local people or the law.

Dining
Dine as the Greeks do on these islands, nursing an ouzo, observing the world, chatting with the service staff (even if you don't speak the same language, a smile and some hand motions will work wonders). Hospitality and good, fresh food abound. Although waterfront restaurants in the touristed areas can be mediocre, you will most often find delightful meals, especially in the villages. Unless noted, reservations are unnecessary, and casual dress is always acceptable. Go to the kitchen and point to what you want, or be adventurous and let the waiter choose for you (although you may wind up with enough food to feed a vil-

lage). Except for smaller catch, fish is relatively expensive (but much less so than on other islands) and usually sold by the kilo. Remember that Greek lobster is often not the same sweet, succulent crustacean Americans enjoy now and then. Most Greek restaurants feature "lobster"—*astakos*—but this is really a sort of saltwater crayfish (its smaller cousin is called *karavides*). Shrimp is usually frozen, but most fish is fresh, except for the dried cod used in *bakaliaro* (fried cod with garlic sauce). If you can find it, try *kakavia* (a fishermen's soup with small catch, stewed with onions and tomatoes).

Besides being recognized for its mastic products, Chios is known for tangerines, eaten fresh or preserved in *gliko koutaliou* (a thick sugar syrup). In Lesbos, try the *keskek* (a special meat mixed with wheat served most often at festivals), and Kalloni bay sardines, the fleshiest in the Mediterranean; eat them with lemon and oil. Octopus simmered in wine, another island dish, goes perfectly with the famous island ouzo, most of which is made in Plomari. Fresh figs, almonds, and raisins are delicious; a local dessert is *baleze* (almond pudding). Lesbos is renowned for it's unusually good food. Samos is known for its thyme-scented honey; its wines, both pale dry white and Samian *moskhato* (sweet dessert wine); *yiorti* (the local version of keskek); and *revithokeftedes* (garbanzo patties).

CATEGORY	COST*
$$$$	over 15,000 dr. (€44.24)
$$$	10,000 dr.–15,000 dr. (€29.49–€44.24)
$$	5,000 dr.–10,000 dr. (€14.74–€29.49)
$	under 5,000 dr. (€14.74)

per person, for a three-course meal, including appetizer, entrée, and dessert (usually fruit), service, and tax but excluding drinks

Hiking

Mountains and deep valleys, deserted towns, and craggy coasts provide for great walking or hiking. Be it while walking along flat coastal areas or trekking to summits, hikers can cover a variety of terrains and, through the seasons, a plethora of wildflowers, birds, and butterflies.

Lodging

Restored mansions, village houses, sophisticated resorts, and budget hotels are all in place, and with the exception of summer you'll have little trouble finding accommodations. Local tourist boards will help, and cooperatives have been established in some villages, such as Mesta and Pirgi in Chios, which offer private rooms for rent. So in off-season here you might want to take a chance and wait till you get to town, to seek the best match, in person. Also, bargaining a bit is easier that way. Most hotel rooms are basic, with simple pine furniture and sparse furnishings often created by local craftspeople. These islands are still less costly than most, but prices are starting to go up and deluxe resorts are expensive. You should assume that hotels of $$$$ and $$$ rating will have air-conditioning; air-conditioning is noted when available at less-expensive establishments.

Reserve early for better-category hotels, especially in Pythagorio on Samos and Molyvos on Lesbos. Off-season you can usually bargain over the official prices and avoid paying for a compulsory breakfast. Hotels are not air-conditioned unless noted, and, even in those that are, you must sometimes insist that it be turned on. Islanders are extremely friendly hosts, and although they may get a little irritable when the hordes descend in August, they still consider you a guest rather than a billfold. Unless noted otherwise, all hotels are open year-round.

CATEGORY	COST*
$$$$	over 40,000 dr. (€117)
$$$	25,000 dr.–40,000 dr. (€73.74–€117.99)
$$	15,000 dr.–20,000 dr. (€44.24–€58.99)
$	under 15,000 dr. (€44.24)

Prices are official rate for a standard double room with bath in high season, including tax and service and excluding breakfast. For those hotels in which half-board is compulsory, meals (one is breakfast) for two are included in price.

✒ *following the text of a review is your signal that the property has a Web site, where you will find details and, usually, images; for a link, visit www.fodors.com/urls.*

Monasteries

Aglow in jewel-toned marble and golden icons and fragrant with incense, some of Greece's best-preserved Byzantine monasteries are scattered throughout these islands, especially on Chios, Lesbos, and Samos. Sometimes they are in marvelous villages that are also filled with Byzantine treasures; often they are set high in the hills, so you can hike and enjoy the scenery and views as well. The bearded, ponytailed monks in their long black robes present dramatic visages and are often friendly and informative, happy to enlighten you on Greek Orthodox rituals and history. Be sure to cover your skin as much as possible, and show respect for the sanctity of the premises.

Nightlife and the Arts

Nightlife is expanding, especially in harbor towns such as Chios. Outdoor movie theaters are popular summer entertainment for islanders and tourists alike. They can be found in Mytilini, Molyvos, Eressos, Kokkari, and Karlovassi. Check the billboards in the town square for showings. Every summer brings a new wave of trendy bars and discos, usually clustered on the beach. They come and go, so ask what's new when you arrive.

Island municipalities often organize cultural events that range from philosophy conferences to evenings of folk music. Chios usually is host to the summer conference of the International Society of Homeric Studies. The best-known celebration is the **Molyvos Theater Festival** (☎ 0253/71323 tickets; 0253/71347 tourist office) held July–August in Lesbos.

Sailing

The islands' ragged coastlines, calm and uncrowded waters, strong winds, and deserted beaches make sailing a particular pleasure. Boat rentals are available on all the islands; repair services, fuel, and water are available at many of the larger ports on the islands, and moorings are available at some. Your charter agency can usually give basic details about where to find fuel and water.

Shopping

Unique products, hard to find in Athens—and on other Greek islands—make interesting and original gifts. Snatch up the Samian wine, honey, and ceramics. The wine comes in several varieties: Samena is a dry white with a tinge of green; Fokianos is a rosé; Nectar and Dux are two familiar names for the sweet dessert wines favored by locals. On Lesbos, olive oil, chestnuts, local liquors, and local fabrics and pottery are popular. On Chios look for the unique mastic products, preserved fruits, ceramics, handwoven fabrics, and ouzo.

Traditional Festivals

As is true throughout this ancient country, festivals offer the visitor a wonderful view into age-old traditions—and lots of fun. Samos is filled with celebrations year-round. A wine festival in late-summer to early fall pleases with Panhellenic dances. In the height of summer, a fisherman's festival centers on the harbor at Pythagorio. Swimming races in Pythagorio commemorate the battle of Cavo Fonias on August 6, a day of celebration for the entire island. On Samos, on September 7 and 8 at Vourliotes village and the nearby Vrondiani monastery, there's dancing in the square and a distribution to the faithful of yiorti to celebrate the birthday of the Virgin. On September 14, the Timiou Stavrou monastery on Samos celebrates its feast day with a service followed by a *paniyiri* (feast), with music, firecrackers, booths of coconut candy, plastic toys, and *loukoumades* (honey-soaked dumplings). In October, Platanos, on Samos, throws a big bash when the new batch of wine and raki is ready. The firewater flows freely, served with *mezedes* (appetizers) and fruit macerated in alcohol.

On August 15 the islanders of Lesbos flock to Agiassos to celebrate the Feast of the Assumption of the Virgin with dancing, drinking, and eating. On Clean Monday, at the end of Carnival in February, costumed islanders take part in a custom known as *vallia* (an improvised exchange of satirical verse). On Chios, festivities are held the last Sunday in Lent in Mostra Thymianon. In Thimiana, on Chios, on the last Sunday of Carnival (late February), islanders reenact the expulsion of the pirates in the Festival of Mostras; youths wave swords and dance the vigorous *talimi*. On Chios in Pirgi on August 15 and August 23 villagers perform local dances to commemorate the passing of the Virgin, the second most important religious holiday of the Greek Orthodox Church. On Chios on Easter Saturday night the effigy of Judas is burned in Mesta. Olympoi, southeast of Mesta, is host to festivities on the first Monday of Lent.

Turkish Jaunts
All within a few miles of the Turkish coast, the islands are good springboards for day trips (and longer) to ports such as Bodrum, Izmir, and Kuşadası in Turkey. Ferry schedules can be checked at individual ports on the islands and at travel agencies. Day-trippers must carry passports.

Exploring the Northern Islands

These unspoiled islands offer commodities that are valued in the ever-growing tourist business—a sense of discovery and a dose of reality. Here you'll get a chance to hang out with the locals and be treated more as a new friend than a tourist. Visitors to Lesbos, Chios, and Samos tend to be Greeks or Europeans who have previously traveled to other Greek islands. Charters are limited because of lack of major airports, and English is not spoken as frequently as it is in more touristed areas. Trendy nightlife-seekers should stick to Mykonosynos; here the pleasures are quiet charms and great people. Each of these islands is worth a visit, even if it only a quick one.

Numbers in the text correspond to numbers in the margin and on the Lesbos and Chios and Samos maps.

Great Itineraries
Seeing all four islands without having to rush—or hang around terminals—will take some preparation, as interisland transportation may not be as frequent as it is on the more touristed islands and boat journeys are often long and slow, even though—during the summer—you might be able to catch one of the newer, faster, high-speed boats which could cut your traveling time by half. Check ahead for transportation schedules. Lesbos has daily air service from Athens and Salonica and daily ferry service from Piraeus; it makes a good base from which to start exploring.

The packed four-day itinerary will give you a brief overview of each island; more relaxed travelers can pick and choose among the islands. The 7- and 10-day itineraries will allow you to explore each island in greater depth, pursuing what strikes your fancy. In general, it is best to arrive on Lesbos; take the ferry or hydrofoil to nearby Chios and then to Samos, the most southerly island of the four. You can go on from Samos to other Greek islands, the Turkish coast, or back to Athens or Piraeus, as connections are good by sea and sometimes by air.

IF YOU HAVE 4 DAYS

This is a real challenge, but you can at least manage an overview of each island. Start in ⊞ **Lesbos** ①–⑰. On day one explore the capital, **Mytilini** ①, then move out into the countryside on day two to northern villages such as **Petra** ⑨ and dreamy **Molyvos** ⑧, to Sappho's birthplace in Eressos, to Agiassos hill village and Plomari, a fishing hamlet that's also a resort. Day three begins on ⊞ **Chios** ⑱–㉙ in the Ottoman quarter of **Chios town** ⑱. It continues to **Nea Moni monastery** ㉓, with its fine mosaics and tragic history. From hilltop Avgonima, head west down to the coast road; then travel via Lithi and Vessa to the southern mastic villages of stenciled **Pirgi** ㉕ and labyrinthine **Mesta** ㉗. Day four circles ⊞ **Samos** ㉚–㊷, including **Pythagorio** ㉚ and the **Temple of Heraion** ㉛, one of the Seven Wonders of the Ancient World. Then travel through mountain villages such as **Pirgos** ㉝ to the tiny harbor of **Ormos Marathokambou** ㉟ and the fishing village of **Kokkari** ㊳, ending at **Samos town** ㊵, the capital.

IF YOU HAVE 7 DAYS

Enhance the four-day schedule, exploring your interests in greater depth. Depending on how you add the time, for the three extra nights you could remain in one favorite place to cut down on traveling. You might add another day on ⊞ **Chios** ⑱–㉙, traveling north from the capital to **Daskalopetra** ⑳ (Teacher's Rock), where Homer is said to have taught, visiting the Byzantine village there, and the isolated beaches of the north. You could spend more time in **Pirgi** ㉕ and **Mesta** ㉗, with time for shopping, and relaxing at the volcanic beach at **Emborio** ㉖, near the mastic villages. On ⊞ **Lesbos** ①–⑰, you could visit the hot springs around Eftelo, east of Mithymna. Or on ⊞ **Samos** ㉚–㊷, meander on the trails around the picturesque hill villages between **Kokkari** ㊳ and Kondeika.

IF YOU HAVE 10 DAYS

Stick to the seven-day schedule, adding three extra days wherever they fit best, on the islands of your choice, for relaxing and recreation—hiking, enjoying water sports, shopping, or just lazing on an Aegean beach. You might bird-watch on ⊞ **Samos** ㉚–㊷ or study ancient ruins on ⊞ **Lesbos** ①–⑰. You could visit the other nearby north-Aegean islands and islets, or take a ferry to ⊞ **Turkey** from Chios or Samos.

When to Tour

Ask locals and they'll usually say May. But also April, June, and September through October are especially lovely periods—the weather is ideal, wildflowers and shrubs are in bloom, and the crowds have thinned. Since these four islands are not yet overrun with tourists even in summer, you will find isolated nooks where you can enjoy the therapeutic sounds of the wind, the birds, and the lapping water.

When booking, keep in mind the enlightening cultural events and religious festivals called **paniyiri,** which usually take place on a saint's day or patriotic holiday. Easter, in April, comes later than the time celebrated at home. On Lesbos a cultural week of drama, dance, and music exhibitions occurs each May. On Chios, festivities take place during Lent and summer.

LESBOS

This third-largest island in Greece is filled with beauty, but its real treasures are the creative artists and thinkers it has produced and inspired though the ages. Lesbos was once a major cultural center, known for its Philosophical Academy, where Epicurus and Aristotle taught; it was the birthplace of the philosopher Theophrastus, who presided over the Academy in Athens; of the great lyric poet Sappho; of Terpander, the "father of Greek music"; and of Arion, who influenced the later playwrights Sophocles and Alcaeus, inventors of the dithyramb (a short poem with an erratic strain). Even in modernity, artists emerged from Lesbos: Theophilos, a poor villager who earned his ouzo by painting some of the finest naive art modern Greece has produced; novelists Stratis Myrivilis and Argyris Eftaliotis; and, more recently, the latest Greek Nobel Prize winner, poet Odysseus Elytis.

The island's history stretches back to the 6th century BC, when its two mightiest cities, Mytilini and Mithymna, settled their squabbles under the tyrant Pittahos, considered one of Greece's Seven Sages. Thus began the creative era, but later times brought forth the same pillaging and conquest that overturned other Greek islands. In 527 BC the Persians conquered Lesbos, and the Athenians, Romans, Byzantines, Venetians, Genoese, and Turks took their turns adding their influences. After the Turkish conquest, from 1462 to 1912, much of the population was sent to Turkey, and traces of past civilizations that weren't already destroyed by earthquakes were wiped out by the conquerors.

Lesbos has more inhabitants than either Corfu or Rhodes, with only a fraction of the tourists, so here you'll get a good idea of real island life in Greece. It looks like a giant jigsaw-puzzle piece, carved by two large sandy bays, the gulfs of Yera and Kalloni. The Turks called Lesbos the "garden of the empire" for its fertility: in the east and center of the island, about 12 million olive trees line the hills in seemingly endless undulating groves, reputedly producing Greek's finest oil. The western landscape is filled with oak trees, sheep pastures, rocky outcrops, and mountains. Wildflowers and grain cover the valleys, while the higher peaks are wreathed in dark green pines. Marshes, beaches, springs, desert, even a petrified forest—Lesbos terrain provides a little something for everyone.

Mytilini

❶ *42 km (26 mi) northeast of Plomari.*

This busy main town and port, with stretches of grand waterfront mansions and an interesting old bazaar area, was once the scene of a dramatic moment in Greek history. Early in the Peloponnesian War, it revolted against Athens, but surrendered in 428 BC. As punishment, the Athens assembly decided to kill all men in Lesbos and enslave all women and children, and a boat was dispatched to carry out the order. The next day a less vengeful mood prevailed and the assembly repealed its decision and sent a second ship after the first. The second ship pulled into the harbor just as the commander of the first finished reading the death sentence. Just in time, Mytilini was saved.

Mytilini (so important through history that many call Lesbos by the port's name alone) is set on the ruins of an ancient city and sprawls across two bays like an amphitheater. The intervening pine-covered headland—a nice spot for a picnic—supports a **Kastro** stone fortress, its intact walls seeming to protect the town even today. Built by the Byzantines on a 600 BC temple of Apollo, it was repaired with available material (note the ancient pillars crammed between the stones) by Francesco Gateluzzi of the famous Genoese family. Look above the gates for the two-headed eagle of the Palaiologos emperors, the horseshoe arms of the Gateluzzi family, and inscriptions made by Turks, who enlarged it; today it is a **military bastion.** Inside the castle there's only a crumbling **prison** and a **Roman cistern,** but you should make the visit for the fine view. ⊠ *On pine-covered hill,* ☎ *0251/27297.* ⊇ *500 dr./€1.47.* ⊙ *Daily sunrise–sunset.*

The only vestige of ancient Mytilini is a Hellenistic theater, the **Archaio Theatro** (⊠ in pine forest northeast of town), one of the largest in ancient Greece. Pompey admired it so much that he copied it for his theater in Rome; it is currently under excavation.

The bustling waterfront just south of the headland is where most of the town's sights are clustered. Stroll the main bazaar street **Ermou,** of the former Turkish quarter, preferably in the quieter, siesta hours as there are no pavements to walk on and traffic tends to be a little hectic during business hours. Walk past the fish market on the southern end, where men haul in their sardines, mullet, and octopi. Narrow lanes are filled with antiques shops and grand old mansions. The enormous post-baroque church of **Ayios Therapon** built in the 19th century, is reminiscent of some styles in Italy. It has an ornate interior, a frescoed dome, and, in its courtyard, a **Vizantino Mouseio,** or Byzantine Museum, filled with icons. ⊠ *Southern waterfront,* ☎ *0251/28916.* ⊇ *200 dr./€.58.* ⊙ *Mon–Sat. 10–1.*

In front of the cathedral of **Ayios Athanasios,** there is a **traditional Lesbos house,** restored and furnished in 19th-century style. Call owner

Marika Vlachou to arrange a visit. ⊠ *Mitropoleos 6,* ☎ *0251/28550.* ☞ *Free.* ⊙ *By appointment only.*

The **Archaiologiko Mouseio,** or Archaeological Museum, in a neoclassical mansion, will help you imagine Lesbos's past. Among its treasures are finds from prehistoric Thermi, mosaics from Hellenistic houses, and reliefs of comic scenes from the 3rd-century Roman House of Menander. A garden in the back holds an annex and some grave stelae. Note that a new wing of the museum is nearby at the corner of Noemvriou and Melinas Merkouri. ⊠ *Argiri Eftaliotis 7, behind the ferry dock.* ☎ *0251/28032.* ☞ *500 dr./€1.47.* ⊙ *Tues.–Sun. 8:30–3.*

Dining and Lodging

$$ ✕ **Dimitrakis.** As many as 10 types of decidedly fresh fish are available at this restaurant, which locals call the "little boat grill" because of its nautical decor. Start your meal with *bourekakia* (ham and *kasseri*-cheese pie); favorites are the simple grilled fish and the bakaliaro. This restaurant is hopping, but you can enjoy dinner outside, lulled by the sounds of rocking boats. ⊠ *Hristouyennon 1944, Fanari quay of Mytilini,* ☎ *0251/23818. No credit cards.*

$$ ✕ **O Stratos.** Here you'll feel quite at home among the Greeks—this is a local, no-nonsense, no-decoration restaurant, but it features the best fish in town. No surprise, then, that tables are hard to come by, so plan to come early if you want to sit outside. Ask for the catch of the day or go into the kitchen to take a look at the *sargoi* (sea bream), *tsipoures* (dorado), or *barbounia* (red mullet) before making your pick. If fish is not what you're in the mood for, take cheer; there is an abundance of other dishes to choose from. There is also an extensive selection of Greek wines—so be adventurous. ⊠ *Hristouyennon 1944 St.,* ☎ *0251/2173. No credit cards.*

$$ ✕ **To Zoubouli t'Aklidiou.** Not every taverna has been around for 90 years, so this one must be doing something right. In summer, its Mytilini town spot closes up and it relocates to the beautiful area of Aklidi, just a 2-km (1-mi) drive along the road to the airport from the center of town. Tables are strewn under the shade of pine trees and offer a clear vista over rooftops to the sea and beyond (that's Turkey on the horizon). The food here is sinful—rich and heavy with an oriental flare. Forget calories and try the *seftelia* (chicken or meat patties). Fish is fresh and plentiful; try the *ksifia* (swordfish) or the grilled octopus. Don't forget to quaff the delicious house wine, particularly the red—a semisweet Lymnian wine. ⊠ *Aklidi, near the church of Panagia Evangelistras.* ☎ *0251/44890. No credit cards.*

$ ✕ **To Kalderimi.** Remember the good old days when you could eat regally and still pay a pittance? Turn back the clock and head to this traditional *ouzo mezethopoleion* (ouzo and mezedes shop), wedged in the center of the bustling center around Ermou Street. The bakaliaro *skordalia* (with garlic sauce) sells like hotcakes here. For the health conscious, the seasonal vegetable dishes are plentiful and delicious; try the *mavromatika* (black-eyed beans) or the *horta* (boiled greens much like chard) and the *lahanodolmades* (cabbage leaves stuffed with meat and rice)—all as good as homemade, if not better. And remember, this is the ouzo island, so we're drinking ouzo here: the menu has about 30 different kinds to choose from. ⊠ *Thassou,* ☎ *0251/46577. No credit cards.*

$$$$ ⌂ **Pyrgos of Mytilene.** With a blue and white wedding-cake facade that attracts many a passing photographer, this small, luxury hotel in the Sourada area is a carefully restored 1916 mansion. It opened in August 1999 and promises its guests both modern-day amenities and 19th-century nostalgia. The guest rooms are lavish, with period furniture, chandeliers, and stucco moldings, and each of the 12 has its own unique style and color scheme, ranging from pistachio green to Venetian red. Particularly charming are the round rooms in the towers. Though slightly too ornate, the reception rooms are inviting, elegant, and spacious. ⊠ *El. Venizelou 49, Mytilini 81100,* ☎ *0251/27977 or 0251/25069,* FAX *0251/47319. 12 rooms. Bar, room service, minibars. AE, V.* ✈

$$$ 🏨 **Laureate Hotel.** Encompassing an 1880 stone mansion with friezes, cornices, pedestals, and other architectural delights, this hotel lets you live like well-off islanders have here for a century. Located on the beach, the modern complex has most of the rooms and facilities; the mansion building contains seven of the suites. All units have kitchenettes, balconies, and phones in the bathrooms, and rooms are available for disabled guests. Locals say this is the best in town. ⊠ *Varia, 2 km (1 mi) from Mytilini, 81100,* ☎ *0251/43111,* FAX *0251/41629. 6 rooms, 14 suites, 6 studios, 2 junior suites. 2 restaurants, 2 bars, kitchenettes, pool, meeting rooms. AE, MC, V.*

$$ 🏨 **Aklidi.** Here is a small, neat, and spotlessly clean pension, ideal for a family or for travelers who like peace and quiet. Less than 2 km (1 mi) outside of the center of Mytilini, you can enjoy all the bustle of the main town without actually being in its noisy heart. This pension operates much like a large house—every room has its own private bathroom, and many have kitchenettes, TV, air-conditioning, and private terraces. ⊠ *Evangelistrias 9, Akleidi,* ☎ *0251/46573 or 0251/44072,* FAX *0251/44074. 40 rooms. Breakfast room, air-conditioning (some). No credit cards.*

$$ 🏨 **Villa 1900.** This renovated neoclassical house, in a fairly quiet lo-
★ cation near the stadium, is a real treat, with stonework, a lush garden, and old-fashioned details such as iron beds, family photographs, and, in a few rooms, ceilings painted with women and flowers. The best rooms are the three in the converted garret. Guests sit in the garden for breakfast, which includes fresh juice from the hotel's own fruit trees. ⊠ *Vostani 24, Mytilini 81100,* ☎ *0251/23448 or 0251/43437,* FAX *0251/ 28034. 9 rooms. Breakfast room. No credit cards. Closed Nov.–Mar.*

Nightlife

BARS

Action is at both ends of the harbor, with lots of variety. Packed on summer nights is **To Mouseio** (The Museum; ⊠ Vournazi 21, Mytilini, ☎ 0251/42140), so called because it's ensconced in a neoclassical house with traditional furnishings.

The café-bar **Marush** (⊠ Koundourioti 59, ☎ 0251/26410) is one of the most popular waterfront spots. Open all day long for coffee, it doubles as a trendy bar after sundown. The theme here—of all things—is 1950s paraphernalia and Harley-Davidson motorcycles. Be sure to check out the original wooden football game machine in the back room.

If you feel the overwhelming urge to play pool during your vacation, pull into the **Cinema** (⊠ 9 Smyrnis, ☎ 0251/47584), which is a favored hangout for the young, thanks to its music, decoration, and lively atmosphere.

Outdoor Activities and Sports

WATER SPORTS

You can moor at most large coastal villages in Lesbos, including Mytilini, Molyvos, Skala Sikaminias, Sigri, Plomari, and Skala Eressou, for fuel and water. Paddleboats, canoes, and sailboarding equipment are available on Lesbos at Sigri, Molyvos, Petra, Vatera, and Skala Eressou.

Varia

➋ *4 km (2½ mi) southeast of Mytilini.*

This suburb is a cultural center, the home village of early 20th-century painter Theophilos. Crammed sometimes to the ceiling in the **Mouseio**

Theophilou, or Theophilos museum, are 80 of his imaginative works—great washes of color detailing the everyday life of local folk such as fishermen and farmers, and fantasies of another age. Theophilos lived in poverty but painted airplanes and exotic cities—which he had never seen. His work is also displayed in the folk museum in Athens. ☒ *Near the sea,* ☎ *0251/28179.* ☜ *500 dr./€1/47.* ☉ *Tues.–Sun. 10–1 and 4:30–8.*

The **Mouseio Modernas Technis,** or Museum of Modern Art, was the home of Stratis Eleftheriadis, better known by his French name, Thériade. This artist and critic helped publicize Theophilos and rose to fame as the foremost publisher of graphic art in Paris. The museum exhibit includes his publications—*Minotaure* and *Verve* magazines—and his colorful collection of works (mostly lithographs) done exclusively for the avant-garde publisher by Picasso, Matisse, Chagall, Roualt, Giacometti, and Miró. The display is surprisingly joyous and, combined with a visit to the Theophilos museum (☞ *above*), is a must for art lovers who enjoy originality, whimsy, and new works by favorites. ☒ *Next to Teriade Library,* ☎ *0251/23372.* ☜ *500 dr./€1.47.* ☉ *Tues.–Sun. 9–2 and 3–5.*

Moria

❸ *6 km (4 mi) northwest of Mytilini, 7 km (4½ mi) northwest of Varia.*

Moria's **To Romaiko Hdragogeio,** or Roman aqueduct, dates back to the 2nd century. It was in Lesbos that Julius Caesar first made his mark. Sent to Bythinia to drum up a fleet, he hung around so long at King Nicodemus's court that he was rumored to be having an affair with the king, but he finally distinguished himself by saving a soldier's life.

Pamfila

❹ *8 km (5 mi) north of Mytilini, 4 km (2½ mi) north of Moria.*

In the 19th century, Pamfila's traditional tower mansions were used by wealthy families as summer homes. The views across the straits to Turkey are wonderful. Equally beautiful are the old stone factories you'll encounter in this area, some of which are still in use.

Pirgi Thermis

❺ *8 km (5 mi) northwest of Mytilini, 2 km (1 mi) east of Pamfila.*

Pirgi Thermis is known for its tower mansions and for its 12th-century church, **Panayia Tourloti** (☒ Near the outskirts).

The village of **Loutropouli Thermis,** about 3 km (2 mi) northwest of Pirgi Thermis, is aptly named for its *loutra* (hot springs). These sulfur baths are dramatically enclosed with vaulted arches. A settlement existed here, centered on the spa's curative properties, from before 3000 BC until Mycenaean times. In all, remnants of five cities have been excavated at this site.

Lodging

$$$ ☷ **Lesbos Inn.** This small, well-managed hotel sits smack on a sandy beach, framed by a backdrop of green-dappled hills. Built in 1996 in sleek international style, each well-equipped, air-conditioned room offers a curving balcony from which to view the Aegean. A minibus shuttles you around if you care to have lunch at the town taverna, or you can just stay put and enjoy the alluring comforts of minibars, room service, and chaises by the pool. ☒ *Pirgi Thermis, 81100,* ☎ *0251/*

71781 through 0251/71784, ☒ *0251/71711. 38 rooms. 2 restaurants, bar, room service, pool, exercise room, meeting rooms. AE, MC, V.*

Mandamados

6 *36 km (22½ mi) northwest of Mytilini, 7 km (4½ mi) northwest of Pirgi Thermis.*

Mandamados is a pretty village of stone houses, wood carvings, and the ruins of a medieval castle. It is famous for its pottery, *koumari* urns (they keep water cool even in scorching heat), and for its black icon of Archangel Michael in the 17th-century monastery dedicated to the island's patron saint, **Taxiarchis Michail** (☒ Just north of village). Legend has it that the icon was carved by a monk who used mud and the blood of his comrades, slain in an Ottoman attack, to darken it. Visitors used to make a wish and press a coin to the archangel's forehead; if it stuck, the wish would be granted. Owing to wear and tear on the icon, the practice is now forbidden. In another ceremonial mode, on the third Sunday after Easter a bull is slaughtered here, and the celebrants dine on the stewed meat.

Skala Sikaminias

★ **7** *35 km (21¾ mi) northwest of Mytilini, 5 km (3 mi) north of Mandamados.*

At the northernmost point of Lesbos, past Pelopi (the ancestral village of 1988 presidential candidate Michael Dukakis), is the exceptionally lovely fishing port of Skala Sikaminias. If you crave picturesque harbor towns you'll flip over this miniature gem—serene, quaint, real, with several good fish tavernas on the edge of the dock where you can eat, relax, and soak up the atmosphere. The novelist Stratis Myrivilis used it as the setting for *The Mermaid Madonna*. If you've read the book, you'll recognize the tiny chapel at the base of the jetty. The author's birthplace and childhood home is in Sikaminia, a corkscrew road above, overlooking the Turkish coast.

En Route   To get to Molyvos, most people take the main road a bit inland from Sikaminia. But there is a little-trafficked coastal route rimming the water from Skala Sikaminias, unpaved for much of the way. To drive on this narrow path takes about 20 minutes, to walk about an hour, and there are hotels at which to refresh. You are amply rewarded along the way with close-up views of passing fishing boats and fresh sea breezes.

Dining

$$$ ✕ **Sikamia.** The scene: you at a table under a mulberry tree sipping a glass of ouzo from nearby Plomari, watching the boats bob and the fishermen hauling in sardines, anchovies, squid, and bigger catch, practically at your feet. Then squeezing lemon on your own grilled fish, perhaps with some squash blossoms, or cucumbers and tomatoes tossed with local olive oil. This oldest taverna on the tiny harbor can provide a memorable experience, so leave some time. ☒ *Skala Sykaminias, on the waterfront,* ☎ *0253/55319. No credit cards.*

Molyvos

★ **8** *61 km (38 mi) west of Mytilini, 17 km (10½ mi) southwest of Skala Sikaminias.*

Molyvos, also known as Mithimna, is a place people have been wanting to visit since antiquity. Legend says that Achilles besieged the town until the king's daughter fell for him and opened the gates; then, in a surprising act, or acting out of she-loves-me, she-loves-me-not, he killed her. Before 1923 the Turks made up about a third of the population, living in many of the best stone houses. Today these balconied buildings with center staircases are weighed down by roses and geraniums; the red-tile roofs are required by law, and the street cobbles are mandatory. As proof of the town's visual charms, many artists live here. Although new hotels have been banned in the old town, Molyvos swells with tour groups in summer and its edges are getting a bit touristy; you may want to stay overnight in nearby Petra.

Come before high season and ascend to the **Kastro,** or Byzantine-Genoese castle, for a hypnotic view down the tiers of red-tile roofs to the glittering sea. At dawn the sky begins to light up from behind the mountains of Asia Minor, casting silver streaks through the placid water as weary night fishermen come in. The grapevine-sheltered lane that descends from the castle passes numerous Turkish fountains, some still in use. ⊠ *Above town,* ☎ *0253/71803.* 🖭 *500 dr./€1.47.* ☉ *Tues.–Sun. 9–3.*

Dining and Lodging

$$ ✕ **Gatos.** Gaze at the island and the harbor from the veranda, or sit inside and watch the cooks chop and grind in the open kitchen. Fish plates are limited; a better bet is the kokkinisto with garlic and savory onion. The beef fillet is tender, the lamb chops nicely grilled. Breakfast is also served. ⊠ *Main pedestrian street, Molyvos,* ☎ *0253/71661. No credit cards. Closed Oct. 15–Mar. 15.*

$$ ✕ **Medusa.** In a traditional stone house on the wharf, this restaurant
★ offers some interesting specialties, including *pita thalassinon* (seafood pie), *mydia akhnista* (steamed mussels), and *kalamarakia yemista* (squid stuffed with rice). The owners provide flawless service and quality at low prices. ⊠ *Molyvos Harbor, across from Ayios Nikolaos chapel,* ☎ *0253/72080. MC, V. Closed Nov.–Apr.*

$–$$ ✕ **Vafeas.** Sitting in a stone-bordered yard, on a balcony hanging over Molyvos entire, you'll wonder if food has ever been this good. That may be the magic of the moment, but the culinary flair of the chefs here can't be denied. All made from regional meats and produce, dozens of local dishes and side dishes are perfect accompaniments with which to down your ouzo. Try the *giouzlemedes* (cheese pies with phyllo rolled by hand) or the delicious *sougania* (dolmades made from onions). If you're in the spirit for more robust fare there's roast lamb and *gemista* (stuffed tomatoes with rice and orange zest). Whatever your choice, you'll leave licking your fingers. ⊠ *Molyvos,* ☎ *0253/ 71752. No credit cards. Closed Nov.–Mar..*

$$ 🏨 **Aeolis.** This cluster of beach bungalows offers all the comforts of a resort complex. From the raised pool area with its eye-popping purple umbrellas (preferable to the mediocre beach), guests have a great view of the sea as well as of Molyvos castle. Most of the bungalows have two or three beds, thick armchairs that fold out, and French doors opening onto a veranda. Kick back in the lounge's deep-seated sofas near the fireplace and potted plants. A hotel shuttle service runs up to town, as does the local bus. ⊠ *Outside Molyvos on road to Eftalou, 81108,* ☎ *0253/71772,* 🖷 *0253/71773. 52 rooms. 2 restaurants, 2 bars, pool. MC, V. Closed Nov.–Mar.*

The Arts

FESTIVAL

The best-known celebration on the islands is the **Molyvos Theater Festival,** held July through August. With the castle as backdrop, artists from all over Europe stage entertainments that range from a Dario Fo play to contemporary music concerts. For tickets call ☎ 0253/71323; for information call the Molyvos tourist office (☞ Visitor Information *in* The Northern Islands A to Z, *below*).

Outdoor Activities and Sports

TENNIS

Hotels near Molyvos with courts to reserve include **Sun Rise Bungalows** (⊠ Efthalou, ☎ 0253/71713), **Alkeos** (⊠ Mithimna, ☎ 0253/71002), **Aphrodite** (⊠ Mithimna, ☎ 0253/71725), **Delfinia I Hotel and Bungalows** (⊠ Mithimna, ☎ 0253/71373), and **Olive Press** (⊠ Mithimna, ☎ 0253/71246).

Shopping

FINE ARTS

In Molyvos, the **Scholi Kalon Technon,** or Athens School of Fine Arts (⊠ in Krallis Mansion near town center, ☎ 01/361–6930 in Athens) occasionally holds sales of its paintings.

Petra

⑨ *55 km (34 mi) northwest of Mytilini, 5 km (3 mi) south of Molyvos.*

Petra stretches along the shore of a large sandy bay fringed by tamarisk trees. Tavernas line the harborside, tempting the tourists with Greek versions of fast-food. Its oldest section still retains traditional stone houses with overhanging balconies, which the government now protects. Atop a giant monolith (*petra* means "rock" in Greek) is the 18th-century church **Panayia Glikofiloussa** (Virgin of Tenderness), reached by climbing 114 steps. The less ambitious may want to stroll the **beach**, visit **Ayios Nikolaos** church (⊠ Off the square) with its 16th-century frescoes, or tour the intricate **Vareltzidaina mansion** (⊠ Near marketplace).

Lodging

$$$ 🏨 **Clara.** A superior hotel of its class, completed in 1991, the Clara ★   has a striking contemporary reception area done in cool whites, pastel pinks, and gray. The bungalows all have spacious verandas with simultaneous views of Petra, Molyvos, and the sea, and with their comfortable gray beds, steel-blue covers, and pink curtains, they are a cut above the usual. Guests (mostly German package groups) can hop the shuttle bus to explore Petra, float in the large L-shape pool, or play a few sets of tennis. A buffet breakfast is served out on the terrace. ⊠ *Avlaki, south of Petra, 81109, ☎ 0253/41532 through 0253/41534,* 📠 *0253/41535. 41 rooms. 2 restaurants, 2 bars, pool, wading pool, tennis court. AE, MC, V. Closed Nov.–Apr.*

Skalohori

⑩ *58 km (36 mi) west of Mytilini, 3 km (2 mi) south of Petra.*

Skalohori is set beautifully in a valley, with tiered houses facing west toward the Aegean sunsets. Until recently the volcanic northwestern part of Lesbos around Skalohori and Andissa was home to wild horses, believed to be the last link with the horse-breeding culture of the Troad, mentioned by Homer.

⑪ The **monastery of Ayios Ioannis Theologos,** or Moni Ipsilou, was founded in 800 and rebuilt in the 12th century. Of special note are the small collection of 12th-century manuscripts, icons, and textiles; the tiles embedded in the facade; and the outstanding wood-lattice ceiling. ⊠ *On summit of extinct volcano.*

Sigri

⑫ *93 km (57¾ mi) west of Mytilini, 4 km (2½ mi) south of Skalohori.*

Sigri is built around a lovely cove; at water's edge is a small but impressive **Tourkiko Kastro,** or Turkish castle (⊠ Waterfront) with the sultan's monogram over the gate. A much-touted **Apolithomeno Dassos petrified forest** (⊠ Between Sigri and Eressos, ☎ 500 dr./€1.47) consists of conifer trees fossilized by volcanic ash up to 20 million years ago. If you expect a thick woods resembling the redwoods of California, this seemingly barren site at first appears like a bunch of stumps leaning every which way among shrubs and rock and even sea. But a closer look reveals delicate colors and a stark, strange beauty. You can also study the specimens in **Sigri's Square,** or at **Ipsilou** (⊠ Below monastery), a large monastery on the highest peak in this wild, volcanic landscape, overlooking western Lesbos and Asia Minor across the Aegean.

Beaches

Throughout the island beach composition varies from pebble to sand. Some of the most spectacular sandy beaches and coves are in the southwest. Exceptional dark-sand beaches stretch from **Sigri** to **Skala Eressou.**

Skala Eressou

⑬ *89 km (55¼ mi) west of Mytilini, 15 km (9¼ mi) southeast of Sigri.*

On the acropolis of ancient Eressos (⊠ 1 km [½ mi] north of Skala Eressou) overlooking the coastal area and beach are **remains of pre-Hellenic walls, castle ruins,** and the 5th-century church, **Ayios Andreas.** The church has a mosaic floor (currently covered over) and a tiny adjacent **museum** housing local finds from tombs in the ancient cemetery.

The poet Sappho was born here in the 7th century BC. Dubbed the Tenth Muse by Plato because of her sensual lyric poetry and new poetic meter, she ran a school for young women. Though she was married and had a daughter, she is reputed to have been homosexual because her surviving poetry is dedicated to her students. Sappho's works were burned, and only fragments of her books survive. Despite its erotic reputation, Sapphic meter was in great favor in the medieval ages and used in hymns, especially by Gregory the Great. Today, besides European and Greek tourists, many lesbians come here to visit her birthplace. (The word "lesbian" derives from Lesbos.)

The modern town of **Eressos** (⊠ 11 km [7 mi] inland), separated from the coast by a large plain, developed to protect its inhabitants from pirate raids. Along the mulberry tree–lined road leading from the beach you might encounter a villager wearing a traditional head scarf (*mandila*), plodding by on his donkey. This charming village of two-story, 19th-century stone and shingle houses is filled with superb architectural details. Note the huge wooden doors decorated with nails and elaborate door knockers, loop-hole windows in thick stone walls, elegant pediments topping imposing mansions, and fountains spilling under Gothic arches.

Beaches

Some of the island's best beaches are in the vicinity of Skala Eressou. This area has been built up very rapidly—and not always tastefully—but its proximity to the water is one of its great advantages. There are many rooms to rent within walking distance from the beach. Especially popular is the **town's dark-sand beach,** long and wide and lined with tamarisk trees. A small island is within swimming distance, and northerly winds lure windsurfers as well as swimmers and sunbathers.

Dining

$$ ✕ **Bennett's.** Max and Jackie Bennett's place has seating on elevated wooden platforms, near the illuminated resort. This British-run es-

tablishment offers an unusually full menu of Greek and Western meat and vegetarian specialties. When listless from Greek food, you'll appreciate such novelties as lasagna, mushrooms in garlic sauce, and apple crumble smothered in cream. ⊠ *At east end of beach, Skala Eressou,* ☎ *0253/53624. No credit cards. Closed Nov.–Apr.*

$$ ✕ **Soulatso.** The enormous anchor outside means you're in for some seriously good seafood here. The look is fetching: tables are set on a wooden deck just a stone's throw from the break of the waves. The food is bona fide: there's a real Greek mama slaving in the kitchen, so the owner son can bask in the glory of all the happy diners. The stuffed calamari is delicious, so, splurge. ⊠ *At west end of beach,* ☎ *0253/ 52078. No credit cards. Closed Nov.–Apr.*

Kalloni

40 km (24¼ mi) west of Mytilini, 4 km (2½ mi) northeast of Skala Eressou.

Known for the anchovies in its gulf, this agricultural market town in the center of Lesbos is rather quiet, but 5 km (3 mi) northwest of ⑭ Kalloni is the sprawling **Moni Limonos,** a monastery filled with frescoes and patrolled by peacocks and the tenants of the sanitarium here. Three stories of cells ring the courtyard. A bishop has collected a jumble of plates and doodads in a sort of **folk-art museum** upstairs, but more interesting is the ground-floor **treasury** of 450 Byzantine manuscripts. Women are not allowed inside the main church. ⊠ *On northern outskirts of village.* ☑ *Museum/treasury 100 dr./€.29* ☉ *Daily 9–1 and 5–7:30.*

Agiassos

★ ⑮ *28 km (17½ mi) southwest of Mytilini, 10 km (6 mi) northeast of Kalloni.*

Agiassos village, the prettiest hill town on Lesbos, sits in an isolated wooded valley near the middle of the island at the foot of Mt. Olympus, the highest peak. (In case you're confused, there are 19 mountains in the Mediterranean named Olympus, almost all of them peaks sacred to the local sky god, who eventually became associated with Zeus.) Exempted from taxes by the Turks, the town thrived. Despite its recent discovery by tourists and the spread of tacky souvenir shops, Agiassos remains a special settlement with gray stone houses, cobblestone lanes, a medieval castle, and worthwhile local handicrafts, particularly pottery and wood crafts. The church of **Panayia Vrefokratousa** was founded in the 12th century to house an icon believed to be the work of St. Luke. Built into its foundation are shops whose revenues support the church, as they have through the ages. This has always been a pilgrimage site and even today celebrates festivals in an especially lively style.

NEED A BREAK?

Stop at one of several cafés in the winding streets of the old bazaar area past the church of Panayia Vrefokratousa. On weekend afternoons sip an ouzo and listen to a *santoúri* band, featuring hammered dulcimer, accompanied by clarinet, drum, and violin. As the locals dance, rather haphazardly, on the cobblestones, you might be tempted to join in the merriment.

Dining

$ ✕ **Dagieles.** If nothing else, you must stop here for a coffee made by ★ owner Stavritsa. And you might try the *kolokitholouloudo* (stuffed squash blossoms) and the dishes that entice the local police throughout the winter: *kritharaki* (barley-shape pasta), kokkinisto, and *varkoules* ("little boats" of eggplant slices with minced meat). For a few short weeks in spring the air is laden with the scent of overhanging wisteria. ⌧ *Agiassos near bus stop,* ☎ *0252/22241. No credit cards.*

Plomari

⑯ *42 km (26 mi) southwest of Mytilini, 20 km (12½ mi) south of Agiassos.*

Plomari, the second-largest town on Lesbos, is dramatically set in a cliff face overlooking a wide harbor and Aegean sunsets. This was once a major maritime area but today is a cheerful mix of package resort and quiet fishing village with narrow, cobbled lanes and houses spilling down to the sea. Known for its potent ouzo and its happy Scandinavian crowd, there's a lively night scene on the harbor, where tourists gather after a long day at the beach.

Lodging

$$ ⊞ **Aegean Sun.** Right on the beach of Agios Isidoros, centered on a small pool, this new hotel has the feel of a traditional seaside village, with two-story, tile-roof bungalow units; iron balconies; and flowers spilling over stairways. All rooms have Aegean views and TVs. Lots of charm and comfort are here indeed. ⌧ *Plomari, on the water, 81200,* ☎ *0252/31830 through 0252/31833,* ℻ *0252/31829. 43 rooms. Restaurant, bar, pool. MC, V. Closed Nov.–Mar.*

Vatera

⑰ *53 km (33 mi) east of Mytilini, 6 km (4 mi) west of Plomari.*

The village of Vatera is all about its 9-km-long (5½-mi-long) sandy strip of sparkling water, lined with tamarisk trees and framed by green hills. Local families favor the relaxed atmosphere and the mineral springs nearby. You can sit and enjoy the view of the cape of Ayios Fokas, with its newly excavated temple of Dionysus. As is often the case in succeeding cultures, the temple's marble fragments were recycled, built into the center aisle of a Christian basilica.

Beaches

The **town beach,** with its curving, southern exposure, is idyllic. In the southeast, there is a good sand-and-pebble beach at **Ayios Isidoros** (⌧ Near Plomari). A sandy beach southeast in **Gera Bay** (⌧ Just south of Skala Polihnitos) is another good choice.

Lodging

$$ ⊞ **Vatera Beach.** This low-key but well-designed hotel has all the makings of a higher-category lodging. Rooms in the four white-and-blue buildings have their own entrances, balconies, and a sea view. Small groups can visit in winter, when a fireplace and central heating make it a treat. Most of the food for the hotel's restaurant, served under tamarisk trees on a terrace with an Aegean view, is raised or grown organically: fruits, vegetables, rabbits, and even pigs. ⌧ *Vatera beach, 81300,* ☎ *0252/61212,* ℻ *0252/61164. 24 rooms, 16 with bath. Restaurant, bar. No credit cards. Closed Nov.–Apr.*

CHIOS

Chios could use better press. "Craggy Hios" is what local boy Homer, its first publicist so to speak, called this starkly beautiful island, which almost touches Turkey's coast and shares its topography. It may not seem to offer much charm when you first see its modernized capital, but consider its misfortunes: the bloody Turkish massacre of 1822 in its fight for Greek independence; major earthquakes, including one in 1881 that killed almost 6,000 Chiotes; severe fires, which in the 1980s burned two-thirds of its pine trees; and, through the ages, the steady stripping of forests to ax-wielding boatbuilders. But look a bit deeper and Chios will surprise you. Within are rare mosaics and villages so unique that even one of them would make this island worth a special stop.

The name Chios comes from the Phoenician word for mastic, the resin of the *Pistacia lentisca,* evergreen shrubs that with few exceptions thrive only here, in the southern part of the island. Every August incisions are made in the bark of the shrubs; the sap leaks out, permeating the air with a sweet fragrance, and in September it is harvested. This aromatic resin, which brought huge revenues until the introduction of petroleum products, was used in varnishes, waxes, cosmetics, and in the chewing gum used by odalisques in the Ottoman harems. Today we may not use the mastic, but you will be enchanted by the *mastikhohoria* (the villages where mastic is produced and processed) (☞ Pirgi and Mesta, *below*).

Until charter tourism began in the late 1980s, Chios prospered through the centuries from medicinal brews, turpentine, wine, silk production, and mainly from its mastic export. It is also home to the elite families that control Greece's private shipping empires: Livanos, Karas, Chandris; even Onassis came here from Smyrna. The island did not seem to need tourists, nor to draw them. Yet Chios intrigues, with its deep valleys, uncrowded sand and black-pebble beaches, fields of wild tulips, Byzantine monasteries, and haunting villages—remnants of a poignant history. It is both demanding and giving, memorable even among these special islands.

Chios Town

⑱ *24 km (15 mi) northeast of Pirgi.*

The main port and capital, Chios town, or Chora (which means "town"), is a busy commercial settlement on the east coast, across from Turkey. Since most of the buildings were constructed after the 1881 earthquake, and the modern waterfront is crowded with private yachts, its charm is limited. But in the evening when the lights twinkle on the water and the scene is softened by a mingling of blues, the many cafés begin to overflow with ouzo and good cheer, and locals proudly promenade along the bay side.

The capital is crowded with half the island's population, but its fascinating heart is the **bazaar district** (⊠ Sprawling south and east of Platia Vounakiou, main square). Merchants hawk everything from local gum and fresh dark bread to screeching monkeys.

The **old quarter** (⊠ On northern highlands) is found inside the **kastro** (castle), built in the 9th century by the Byzantines. Later, under Turkish rule, the Greeks lived outside the wall; the gate was closed daily at sundown. A deep dry moat remains on the western side. Note the old wood-and-plaster houses on the narrow backstreets, typically decorated with latticework and jutting balconies, on which you might find a woman in black smoking a thin cigar. This old Muslim and Jewish neighborhood, full of decaying monuments, fountains, baths, and mosques, wears an air of mystery.

The **Ktirio Ektheseon Giustiniani Giustiniani museum,** inside a 15th-century mansion, has religious art and has wood carvings, mosaics, and airy rooms hung with frescoes from Nea Moni and Panayia Krina church (☞ *below*). ⊠ *Just inside old quarter in Giustiniani mansion,* ☎ *0271/ 22819.* 🎫 *500 dr./€1.47.* ☉ *Tues.–Sun. 9–2.30.*

In **Platia Frouriou** (⊠ In the fort's small square), look for the **Turkish cemetery** and the large **marble tomb** (with the fringed hat) of Kara Ali, chief of the Turkish flagship in 1822. Along the **main street** are elegant **Ayios Georgios** church (closed most of the time), which has icons from Asia Minor; houses from the Genoese period; and the **remains of Turkish baths** (⊠ North corner of fort).

NEED A BREAK?	Try a Chiote snack of rice pudding or sheep's-milk yogurt and thick honey. The food is fresh and authentic at the unnamed **little dairy shop** (⊠ Corner of Roihou and Venizelou, behind Appolonio lodgings). And if you're very hot or just craving something sweet, two scoops of the infamous Kronos Praline ice-cream might hit the spot. **Kronos Ice Cream Parlor** (⊠ Philipos Argenti 2, ☎ 0271/22311) has been making this best-seller with the same recipe ever since 1930.

In 1822, in the tiny **prison** (⊠ Just inside main gate), 75 leading Chiotes were jailed as hostages before they were hanged by the Turks, part of the worst massacre committed during the War of Independence. The Turks, who drove out the Genoese in 1566, had been fond of the island for its mastic, which they chewed in the company of their harems to sweeten their breath in the days before packaged mints. But Chios, spurred by Samians who had fled to the island, joined the rest of Greece in rebellion. The revolt failed, and the Sultan retaliated: the Turks killed 30,000 Chiotes and enslaved 45,000, an event written about by Victor Hugo and depicted by Delacroix in *The Massacres of Chios*. The painting shocked Western Europe and led indirectly to support for Greek independence. Copies of the Delacroix hang in many places here, including the dusty **Vizantino Mouseio–Tzami post-Byzantine museum,** filled with odds and ends and housed in the only intact mosque, complete with a slender minaret, in this part of the Aegean. Note the *tugra* (the swirling monogram of the sultan that shows royal possession). Although the tugra is common in Istanbul, it is rarely seen elsewhere, and its presence indicated the favor Chios enjoyed under the sultan. But more poignant are the Jewish, Turkish, and Armenian gravestones leaning with age in the courtyard, a silent reminder of past suffering. ⊠ *Platia Vounakiou,* ☎ *0271/26866.* ⌧ *500 dr./€1.47.* ☉ *Tues.–Sat. 10–1, Sun. 10–3.*

The **Archaiologiko Mouseio,** or archaeological museum, has a collection that ranges from proto-Helladic pottery dug up in Emborio to a letter from Alexander the Great addressed to the Chiotes dated 332 BC. ⊠ *Michalon 5,* ☎ *0271/26664.* ⌧ *500 dr./€1.47.* ☉ *Tues.–Sun. 9–3.*

The **Ethnologiko kai Laografiko Mouseio Argenti,** or Philip Argenti Museum, is the most interesting collection in town, housed on the top floor of the **Korais Library,** one of Greece's largest. It holds self-serving portraits of the aristocratic family that endowed it, and more copies of the Delacroix painting, but also some fascinating costumes, embroideries, implements, and engravings evocative of earlier times. ⊠ *Koraii 2, near cathedral,* ☎ *0271/23462.* ⌧ *Free.* ☉ *Mon.–Thurs. 8–2, Fri. 8–2 and 5–7:30, Sat. 8–12:30.*

Beaches
Karfas beach (⊠ 8 km [5 mi] south of Chios town) fronts a shallow sandy bay. Tavernas are in the area, and in summer, there's transportation to town. Farther south, Komi has a fine, sandy beach.

Dining and Lodging
$$ ✕ **Karatzas.** At a table by the water, you'll savor the fresh grilled seafood at this informal taverna, where locals congregate to enjoy simple pleasures. Enjoy lots of fresh Chiote vegetables and local fruits

as well as classic Greek dishes such as moussaka, which are always a tasty backup. This is a place where you can sit nursing a coffee and you won't be disturbed. ⊠ *Karfas, on the waterfront,* ☎ *0271/3122. MC, V.*

$$ ✕ **O Hotzas.** This spacious taverna, reputed to be the capital's best, has a medieval interior with a beamed ceiling, brass implements, and family portraits. Most dishes are deep-fried, but you may also nosh on succulent lamb with lemon sauce, and many vegetable dishes. The squid is always reliable, and it's delicious with the homemade retsina or ouzo. For dessert, order yogurt with homemade cherry or quince preserves. ⊠ *Yioryiou Kondili 3, Chios,* ☎ *0271/23117 or 0271/ 42787. No credit cards. Closed Sun. No lunch.*

$$ ✕ **Oinomageirion tou Iakovou.** Not only is this the only place to eat in the charming Kastro district (the old Ottoman neighborhood), it's quite a delight. Sitting under the arches of a former wine warehouse, you drink in the stylish atmosphere and the even more stylish people, as the people-gazing here takes in the crème de la crème of Chios society. You'll know why the tables are always crowded, after you taste the prawns *saganaki* (fried with cheese), the marinated anchovies, or the deep-fried aubergines. ⊠ *Agiou Giorgiou 20, Kastro,* ☎ *0271/23858. No credit cards.*

$ ✕ **To Kentron.** This is one of the last surviving *kafeneion* (coffee shops) on the Chios waterfront—a perfect place to sip a rich Greek coffee or cool off with an ouzo, or that great thirst quencher, the fizzy local lemonade. There's not much to eat by way of a full meal, but the *pikilia* (assortment of mezedes) is generous and filling. ⊠ *Chios Harbor,* ☎ *0271/23024. No credit cards.*

$$$ ▥ **Chios Chandris.** On the water, midway between the port and the beach, this big, bustling, and boxy member of the Greek hotel and ship chain is considered one of the capital's best. The pool and stone terrace by the sea, lunch buffets, disco, and friendly social staff make for a resortlike atmosphere, but with in-town convenience. Rooms are basic but comfortable in shades of Aegean blue, but best are the balconies, with views of the mountains or of the caïques and fishing boats plying the harbor. ⊠ *Prokymea, between port and beach, 82100,* ☎ *0271/44401 or 0271/44402,* ᶠᴬˣ *0271/25768. 141 rooms, 16 suites. Restaurant, 2 bars, pool, meeting rooms. AE, MC, V.*

$$–$$$ ▥ **Fedra.** From the moment you enter this neoclassical former mansion, painted ocher and planted with jubilant flowers, you feel at home. A pension run by a playwright, it is an appealing, inexpensive choice. All the rooms have baths, air-conditioning, and heating. The summer outdoor bar generates some noise, so ask for a back room. Off-season, a piano bar warms up the place. ⊠ *M. Livanou 13, Chios 82100,* ☎ *0271/41129 or 0271/41130. 10 rooms. Bar, café, air-conditioning. MC.*

$$–$$$ ▥ **Kyma.** Begun in 1917 for a shipping magnate, this neoclassical villa was completed in 1922, when it served as General Plastiras's headquarters after the Greek defeat in Asia Minor. From here he ordered the deposition of the king and the court martial of six cabinet ministers. A modern cement addition only slightly mars the stone facade and grillwork. Some rooms have whirlpool baths. The only problem is noise from the street below. With the great breakfast, waking up won't be so bad once you taste the fresh Chios tangerine juice. ⊠ *Chandris 1, Chios 82100,* ☎ *0271/44500,* ᶠᴬˣ *0271/44600. 59 rooms. Air-conditioning, hot tubs. No credit cards.*

The Arts

Chios usually is host to a summer conference at the **International Society of Homeric Studies** (⊠ 5 Heroon Polytechneiou St., ☎ 0271/44391).

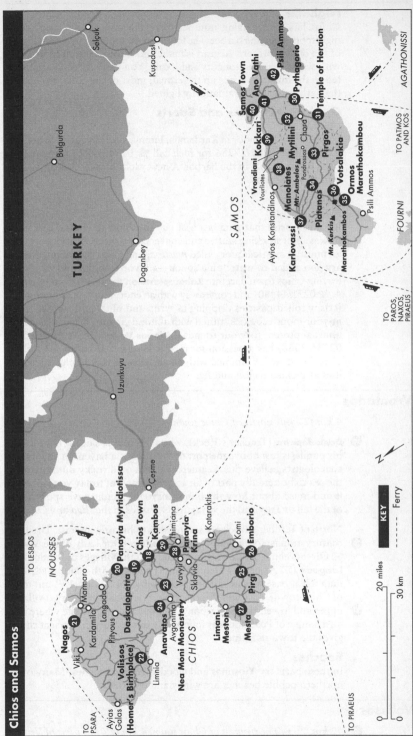

Chios and Samos

TURKEY

Selçuk

Kuşdasi

Bulgurda

Doganbey

Uzunkuyu

Çeşme

TO LESBOS

INOUSSES

TO PSARA

Viki
Kardamila
Marmaro
Langada
Pityous
Limnia
Ayios Galas

21 Nagos

22 Volissos (Homer's Birthplace)

20 Panayia Myriidiotissa

19 Daskalopetra

18 Chios Town

Kambos

29

28

23

24 Anavatos

Nea Moni Monastery

Avgonima

Vavyli

Sklavia

Thimiana

Panayia Krina

Kataraktis

Komi

25 Pirgi

26 Emborio

27 Mesta

Limani Meston

CHIOS

TO PIRAEUS

20 miles

30 km

N

SAMOS

Ayios Konstandinos

Vrondiani
Vourliotes

38

39

40 Samos Town / Ano Vathi

41

42

Psili Ammos

30 Pythagorio

31 Temple of Heraion

32 Myrtilini

Chara

Pandrosso

33 Pirgos

34 Platanos

37 Karlovassi

Manolates
Mt. Ambelos

35

36 Ormos Marathokambou

Mt. Kerkis

Marathokambos

Psili Ammos

AGATHONISSI

TO PATMOS AND KOS

FOURNI

TO PAROS, NAXOS, PIRAEUS

Votsalakia

KEY

- - - - - Ferry

Nightlife

Chios has a surprising number of restaurants, clubs, and stylish nightspots along the harbor. The look is more sophisticated than in most of the other northern Aegean islands, and most of the clubs are filled with well-off young tourists and locals. You can just walk along, listen to the music and size up the crowd; most of the clubs are open to the harborside and dramatically lighted.

Outdoor Activities and Sports

SAILING

In Chios you can moor in Kardamila, Limnia, and Chios town. In Chios town call ☎ 0271/27286 for fuel; call ☎ 0271/27377 for water; repairs are available in the harbor. A new yacht marina is near completion at Vrondados.

Shopping

LOCAL CRAFTS

It's no surprise that gum is a best buy in Chios; the brand is Elma. It makes a fun stocking stuffer and conversation piece. You can also find an unusual mastic liquor called *mastíha,* and gliko koutaliou, the sugary goo added to water on a spoon—a favorite with children. Before leaving Chios town dart into **Zaharoplasteion Avgoustakis** (✉ Psychari 4, ☎ 0271/44480) and come away with an enormous box of *masourakia* (crispy rolled pastries dripping in syrup and nuts) and *rodinia* (melt-in-your-mouth cookies stuffed with almond cream). Bring back a truly unusual present for your friends—**Yiogos Varias** (✉ Venizelou 2, ☎ 0271/22368) has a passion for pickles inherited from his forefathers. This tiny store is crammed with 36 varieties of pickle, plus such oddities as pickled melon and fig.

Vrontados

4 km (2½ mi) north of Chios town.

⑲   **Daskalopetra** (Teacher's Rock), where Homer is said to have taught his pupils, is just above the port of Vrontados, a haven for sailors. Archaeologists believe this weathered lectern on a rocky outcrop above the sea to be actually part of an ancient altar, but today you can sit on it and muse about how the blind storyteller might have spoken here of the fall of Troy and the voyage of Odysseus in the *Iliad* and *Odyssey.*

⑳   North of Teacher's Rock are several sites of historic interest. The 19th-century monastery of **Panayia Myrtidiotissa** (Our Lady of the Myrtle; ✉ On shoreline) overlooks the Aegean past the villages of Pandoukios. **Langada** (✉ At nearby Delphinion) is where a 5th-century BC Athenian naval base was unearthed. **Kardamila** (✉ 28 km [17½ mi] north of Chios town), a former shipowner enclave, actually has two villages, upper and lower. **Nagos** harbor, a swampy area, is the site where a ruined temple of Poseidon was found early this century. Its ancient church gives the town its name.

㉑

Beaches

In these parts try **Yiosonas** and wooded **Nagos** beaches. Many of the northern pebble beaches are windy and deserted.

Volissos

㉒   *42 km (26 mi) northwest of Chios town, 4 km (2½ mi) west of Vrontados.*

Homer's birthplace is thought to be here at Volissos, though Smyrna, Colophon, Salamis, Rhodes, Argos, and Athens also claim this honor. Once a bustling market town, this pretty, narrow-laned northern village is today half empty, with only a few hundred inhabitants. Solid stone houses march up the mountainside to the Genoese fort, where Byzantine nobles were once exiled. Atop the hill is the place for sunset lovers.

Beaches

Some of the best beaches on the island are in the vicinity, including **Limia** (⊠ 2 km [1 mi] south of Volissos).

Dining and Lodging

$$ ✕ **Epsilon.** On a magical roof terrace high above the village and the shimmering sea, this 10-table establishment is a Volissos landmark. Lively Niko Koungoulios produces a remarkable array of Mediterranean dishes—including summer pasta with feta and fresh basil, roast red pepper and yogurt dip, seafood risotto, and, for dessert, a sinfully rich chocolate crepe. ⊠ *Kastro area, Volissos Village,* ☏ *0274/21480. No credit cards.*

$$ ▦ **Village Houses.** Since 1987, energetic Stella Tsakiri has overseen the meticulous restoration of 11 medium-size houses, preserving where possible such vernacular touches as unworked tree trunks supporting a sleeping loft. Yet all modern conveniences are present, and each unit, designed for two to five people, has a fully equipped kitchen and a terrace with sweeping views—you're just under the half-ruined Byzantine castle. It's ideal for families on a get-away-from-it-all holiday. ⊠ *Volissos village, Chios 82100,* ☏ *0274/21421,* ☏ *0274/21521. 11 units. Kitchenettes, air-conditioning. No credit cards.*

The Arts

In summer, arts events are held in historic Vrontados, during the annual **"Homeria."**

Nea Moni

17 km (10½ mi) west of Chios town, 59 km (36½ mi) southeast of Volissos.

★ ㉓ Almost hidden among the olive groves, the island's most important monument—and one of the finest examples of mosaic art anywhere—is the **Nea Moni monastery** (⊠ high in mountains of Nea Moni). Emperor Constantine Monomachos VIII ordered it built where three monks found an icon of the Virgin in a myrtle bush. The octagonal *katholikon* (medieval church) created by architects and painters from Constantinople exemplifies the artistic ideas prevailing during the 11th century in that city. Its distinctive three-part vaulted sanctuary has two narthices, with no buttresses supporting the dome. This design, a single square space covered by a dome, is rarely seen in Greece. Aged, but still blazing with color, the church's interior gleams with marble slabs and mosaics of Christ's life, austere yet sumptuous, with azure blue, ruby red, velvet green, and skillful applications of gold. The saints' expressiveness comes from their vigorous poses and severe gazes, with heavy shadows under the eyes. On the iconostasis hangs the icon—a small Virgin and Child facing left. Also inside the grounds are an **ancient refectory, a vaulted cistern, a chapel** filled with bones of Turkish massacre victims, and a large **clock** still keeping Byzantine time, with the sunrise reckoned as 12 o'clock. ⊠ *In mountains.* ☉ *Daily 8–1 and 4–8.*

En Route Heading toward Anavatos via the Nea Moni side-road junction, the main road turns southwest to **Avgonima,** one of the many distinctive villages on the island and from which there is an expansive view of the west coast. Its name means "clutch of eggs," perhaps because its buildings seem to touch each other like eggs in a basket. Many Greek-Americans have bought ancestral homes here, lovingly restoring them to their original beauty and using them for vacation and retirement. To return here for their own wedding is a goal of many expatriates.

Anavatos

★ ㉔   *16 km (10 mi) west of Chios town, 5 km (3 mi) northwest of Nea Moni.*

The haunting, mud-color village of Anavatos blends into its hillside like a chameleon, built that way to hide from pirates. About 50 crumbling houses still stand. Climbing the steep paths and gazing into tumbled houses filled with rubble and wildflowers is a good half-hour workout each way, but it's a walk you won't forget. In this once heavily fortified town, where seven people—give or take a few—live year-round, the biggest sign of life is the farmers who come to gather pistachios that grow in the untended orchards below. In 1822, during the revolution, 400 women and children threw themselves over the cliff here rather than surrender to the Turks, and their presence can be felt if you stand at the summit and observe a minute of silence.

NEED A BREAK?   A tiny café is at the base of Anavatos, where you park your car. Try the fresh-made spoonsweets made of local figs or pistachios in syrup. Washed down with a cold bottle of water it seems a perfect ending to the climb.

Pirgi

★ ㉕   *24 km (15 mi) south of Chios town, 22 km (13½ mi) southeast of Anavatos.*

From the 14th century, the Genoese founded 20 or so inland, fortified villages in southern Chios, which got the name Pirgi from the lucrative gum product in the region. They shared a defensive design with double thick walls, a maze of narrow streets, and a square tower in the middle—a last resort to hold the residents in case of pirate attack. The villages prospered on the sales of mastic gum and were spared by the Turks because of it. Today they depend on tangerines, apricots, olives—and tourists.

Pirgi is the largest of these mastic villages, and in many ways the most wondrous. It could be a graphic designer's model or a set from a mad moviemaker, or a town from another planet. Many of the buildings along the tiny arched streets are adorned with *xysta* (like Italian sgraffito). They are coated with a mix of cement and volcanic sand from nearby beaches, then whitewashed and stenciled, often top to bottom, in traditional patterns of animals, flowers, and geometric designs. The effect is both delicate and dazzling. Especially lavish are xysta on buildings near the main square, including the **Kimisis tis Theotokou** church (Dormition of the Virgin; ⊠ Near main square), built in 1694.

This exuberant village has more than 50 churches (successful people afraid of attack tend to pray for a continuation of life). Check out the fresco-embellished 12th-century church **Ayii Apostoli,** a very small replica of the earlier Nea Moni katholikon. The 17th-century frescoes that completely mask the interior, the work of a Cretan artist, have a distinct folk-art leaning. To get in, ask at the main square for the current doorkeeper. ⊠ *In town, northwest of square.* ☉ *Tues.–Thurs. and Sat. 10–1.*

About 50 people named Kolomvos live in Pirgi, claiming kinship with Christopher Columbus, known to have been from Genoa, the power that built the mastikhohoria (some renegade historians claim Columbus, like Homer, was really born on Chios).

Lodging

$–$$ ⊞ **Women's Agricultural Tourist Cooperative of Chios.** This local agency can find you a room in the town or the area, perhaps even on a farm. These may be basic digs, some without private baths, but if in doubt, check out the lodgings first. If you choose to, you may get the added experience of harvesting mastic or cooking local dishes with inevitably congenial Greek hosts. This is an especially wonderful opportunity for families. ⊠ *Pirgi, near the center square, 82102,* ☎ *0271/72496.*

Beaches

From Pirgi it's 8 km (5 mi) southeast to the glittering **black volcanic**
㉖ **beach** near **Emborio.** Known by locals as Mavra Volia ("black pebbles"), the cove is backed by jutting volcanic cliffs, the calm water's dark-blue color created by the deeply tinted seabed. Here perhaps was an inspiration for the "wine-dark sea" that Homer writes about.

Shopping

CERAMICS

In the small mastic village of **Armolia,** 20 km (12½ mi) south of Chios town, pottery is a specialty. In fact, *armolousis* ("man from Armola") is synonymous with potter.

Mesta

★ ㉗   *28 km (17½ mi) southwest of Chios town, 11 km (7 mi) west of Pirgi.*

Pirgi is the most unusual of the mastic villages, but Mesta is the island's best preserved, a labyrinth of twisting vaulted streets linking two-story stone-and-mortar houses, which are supported by buttresses against earthquakes. The striking, somber village sits inside a system of 3-ft-thick walls, and the outer row of houses also doubles as protection. Most of the narrow streets lead to blind alleys; the rest lead to the six gates; the one in the northeast still has an iron grate.

One of the largest and wealthiest churches in Greece, the 18th-century **Megas Taxiarchis** commands the main square, its vernacular baroque and rococo features combined in the late-folk-art style of Chios. It was built on the ruins of the central refuge tower. Ask at the main square for Elias, the gentle old man in the village who is the keeper of the keys.

As you head out of town, on the way to Chios town, near Vavili, is the
㉘ 12th-century **Panayia Krina** (Our Lady of the Source; ⊠ On road to left marked TO SKLAVIA), where three layers of frescoes spanning six periods were discovered. The very earliest period is represented by portraits of the saints facing the entrance; most of the restored frescoes hang in the Giustiani mansion in Chios town (☞ *above*). The church is rarely open, but the finely worked exterior makes the trip worthwhile.

Beaches

Escape to the string of **secluded coves** (⊠ Between Elatas and Trahiliou bays) with good swimming; a **nudist beach** (⊠ About 2 km [1 mi] north of Lithi) with fine white pebbles is among them.

Dining and Lodging

$$ ✕ **O Moreas sta Mesta.** The proprietor spends winter and spring gath-
★   ering herbs and greens from nearby hills and seashores. Typical are *kritama,* to give salads a tang, and horta (greens such as Swiss chard and dandelion sautéed with lemon and oil) for his excellent *hortopita* (a pie made with horta). Unusual for a taverna, there's excellent brown bread and a potent, semisweet red wine made from raisins. The goat fricassee must be ordered in advance, and ksifias souvlaki (swordfish chunks on a spit), *domotokeftedes* (fried tomato patties), and *hirino*

krasato (pork simmered in wine) are usually available. ✉ *Mesta Sq., Mesta, Chios,* ☎ *0271/76400. No credit cards.*

$ ✕ **Limani Meston.** This taverna has something for every budget: mostly *magirefta* in summer, with a few inexpensive fish. Meats include home-made sausage, whole roasted piglets (order ahead), and lamb or beef on the spit. You can sit outside among the ivy and blossoms, where Mesta's working harbor unfolds before you; or on colder days, enjoy the fireplace with the locals. ✉ *Mesta Harbor, 3 km (2 mi) from Mesta village,* ☎ *0271/76367 or 0271/76265. No credit cards.*

$$–$$$ 🏠 **Anna Floradhi.** The charming Floradhi family have remodeled a medieval-era home into a miniature guest house. The four large rooms have rustic traditional furnishings and cooking facilities. Ask for one of the rooms upstairs—they open out onto an alfresco den built around an old wood oven. ✉ *Mesta, 82102,* ☎ *0271/28891,* 🖷 *0271/76455. 4 rooms. No credit cards.*

$$ 🏠 **Rooms to Let.** This group of houses with charming, authentic, and well-maintained rental properties in Mesta and the nearby harbor of Limenas is the largest cooperative here. Stone, wood, stucco, antiques, verandas filled with geraniums, and balconies overlooking labyrinthian lanes or the Aegean sea make these properties special indeed. Most have kitchens and two or more bedrooms. Each house has individual phones, but you can fax for general information or a brochure. ✉ *Mesta, built into maze; Limenas, by the harbor, 82102,* ☎ 🖷 *0271/76290. 19 houses, 6 with bath. No credit cards.*

Nightlife

Karnayio (✉ Leoforos Stenoseos, outside town on road to airport) is a popular spot for dancing.

Shopping

Artists hang out in this area. Ilias Likourinas, an icon painter who will paint to order, has a workshop on the main street in Mesta. Sergias Patentas, whose shop is on the road between Mesta and the harbor of Limenas (✉ 3 km [2 mi] north of Mesta), sculpts fantasies based on mythology and history. He is currently setting up a history museum in Mesta.

Kambos

★ ㉙   *4 km (2½ mi) south of Chios town, about 29 km (18 mi) northeast of Mesta.*

Mastodon bones were found here in the Kambos region, a fertile plain of tangerine, lemon, and orange groves, which is perfect for cycling. Since medieval times, wealthy Genoese and Greek merchants built ornate, earth-color, three-story mansions. Behind forbidding stone walls adorned with coats of arms, each is a world of its own, with multicolored sand-stone patterns, arched doorways, and pebble-mosaic courtyards. *Manganos* (waterwheels), a part of most mansion courtyards, were once powered by donkeys to draw water and irrigate the orchards; they are used now for decorations and pools filled with carp and waterlilies. Some houses are crumbled and some still stand, reminders of the wealth, power, and eventual downfall of an earlier time. These suburbs of Chios town are exceptional but the unmarked lanes can be confusing, so leave time to get lost and to peek behind the walls into another world.

Lodging

$$$ 🏠 **Pension Perivoli.** Behind an ornate pediment-topped gate and across from the (closed) Villa Argentiko, this grand yet informal two-story 18th-century mansion is set in an orange orchard (think fresh-squeezed at breakfast in the large garden). Fireplaces, a massive outdoor stair-

case of native stone, a mangonos, now usually just a showpiece), and local furnishings and antiques combine for an evocative ambience. The rooms are spare, but the grounds sing. ✉ *9–11 Argenti St., Kambos district, 82100,* ☎ *0271/31513,* ℻ *0271/32042. 15 rooms. Restaurant, bar. No credit cards.*

$$$ 🏨 **Perleas Mansion.** This is a sumptuous refuge tucked away in the orchards of the Kambos area. A grand old estate has been painstakingly restored by owners Vangelis and Chryssa Xydas. The discreet attention of the staff will make you feel like an aristocrat from a previous era. The special care the owners take with everything begins the moment you face the day and wake up to a breakfast featuring homemade lemonade and preserves from organically grown citrus fruit. ✉ *Vitiadou St., Kambos district, 82100,* ☎ *0271/32217 or 0271/32962,* ℻ *0271/32364. 5 rooms. Restaurant. MC, V.*

SAMOS

The southernmost of this group of four north Aegean islands, Samos is the closest to Turkey of any Greek island, separated by only 3 km (2 mi). It was, in fact, a part of Asia Minor until it split off during the Ice Age. Samos means "high" in Phoenician, and its abrupt volcanic mountains soaring dramatically like huge hunched shoulders from the rock surface of the island are among the tallest in the Aegean, geologically part of the great spur that runs across western Turkey. Approaching from the west, Mt. Kerkis seems to spin out of the sea, while in the distance Mt. Ambelos guards the terraced vineyards that produce the famous Samian wine. The felicitous landscape has surprising twists with lacy coasts and mountain villages perched on ravines carpeted in pink oleander, red poppy, and purple sage.

When Athens was young, in the 7th century BC, Samos was already a naval power. In the next century during Polycrates' reign, it was noted for its arts and sciences and the expanded site of the vast Temple of Hera, one of the wonders of the ancient world. Herotodus wrote extensively of Samos, and Plutarch wrote that in Roman times Anthony and Cleopatra took a long holiday here, "giving themselves over to the feasting," and that artists came from afar to entertain them, and kings vied to send the grandest gifts.

Small though it may be, Samos has a formidable list of great Samians stretching through the ages. It was home to fabled Aesop, to the philosopher Epicurus, and to Aristarchos (first in history to place the sun at the center of our solar system). The mathematician Pythagoras was born in Samos's ancient capital in 580 BC; it was renamed Pythagorio in AD 1955 (it only took a couple of millennia).

Pirates controlled this deserted island after the fall of the Byzantine empire, but in 1562 an Ottoman admiral repopulated Samos with expatriates and Orthodox believers. It languished under the sun for hundreds of years until tobacco and shipping revived the economy in the 19th century. Although in the last decade Samos has become packed with European charter tourists in July and August, its curving terrain allows you to escape the crowds easily and feel as if you are still in an undiscovered Eden.

Pythagorio

③⓪ *14 km (8¾ mi) southwest of Samos town.*

Samos had been a democratic state, but in 535 BC the town now called Pythagorio (formerly Tigani, or "frying pan") fell to the tyrant Polycrates (540–22 BC), who used his fleet of 100 ships to make profitable raids around the Aegean, until he was caught by the Persians and crucified in 522 BC. His rule produced what Herodotus described as "three of the greatest building and engineering feats in the Greek world." One is the Heraion (☞ *below*), west of Pythagorio, the largest temple ever built in Greece and one of the Seven Wonders of the Ancient World. Another is the ancient mole protecting the harbor on the southeast coast, on which the present 1,400-ft jetty rests. The third is the Efpalinio tunnel, built to guarantee that water flowing from mountain streams would be available even to besieged Samians.

An underground aqueduct, the **To Efpalinio Hydragogeio,** or Efpalinio tunnel, was finished in 524 BC with primitive tools and without measuring instruments. Efpalinos of Megara, a hydraulics engineer, set perhaps a thousand slaves into two teams, one digging on each side of Mt. Kastri. Fifteen years later, they met in the middle with just a tiny difference in the elevation between the two halves. The tunnel was used during the Middle Ages as a hideout from pirate raids. More than a mile of (long gone) ceramic water pipe once filled the space. Today the tunnel is exclusively a tourist site, and though some spaces are tight and slippery, you can walk the first 1,000 ft; it's fenced, thankfully. Although it is electrically lighted, you might want to bring a flashlight to note the chisel marks of human effort on the walls. ✉ *Just north of town,* ☎ *0273/61400.* 🎫 *500 dr./€1.47.* ☉ *Tues.–Sun. 9–2.*

Among acres of excavations, little else remains from the **Archaia Polis,** or ancient city (✉ Bordering small harbor and hill) except a few pieces of the **Polycrates wall** and the **ancient theater** a few hundred yards above the tunnel.

Pythagorio's quiet cobblestone streets are lined with mansions and filled with fragrant orange blossoms. At one corner sits a crumbling **Kastro fortress** (✉ East corner), probably on top of the ruins of the acropolis. Revolutionary hero Lycourgos Logothetis built this 19th-century edifice; his statue is in the **courtyard** of the church built to honor the victory, next door. He held back the Turks on Transfiguration Day, and a sign on the church announces in Greek: CHRIST SAVED SAMOS 6 AUGUST, 1824. At night the villagers light votive candles in the church cemetery, a moving sight with the ghostly silhouette of the fortress and the moonlit sea in the background.

The small **Archaiologiko Mouseio Pythagorio Museum** contains local finds, including headless statues, grave markers with epigrams to the dead, and portraits of Roman emperors. ✉ *Platia Pythagora, in municipal building,* ☎ *0273/61400.* 🎫 *Free.* ☉ *Tues.–Sun. approximately 9–2.*

Pythagorio remains a picturesque little port, with red-tiled roof houses and a curving harbor filled with fishing boats. To the west of town are remains of **Romaika Loutra,** or Roman Baths, their doorways still standing (☎ 0273/61400); they're open Tuesday–Saturday 11–2. A bit west of that are the remains of the ancient Aegean harbor, long ago bustling with the mighty naval fleets of samains, ships with five tiers of oarsmen. That harbor is now a silted-in lake and the ships a mere memory.

Dining and Lodging

$ ✗ **Maritsa.** This simple fish taverna, on a quiet, tree-lined side street, opened in 1992 and quickly established a regular Pythagorio clientele. In the garden courtyard, you can try grilled flying fish (!), red mullet, octopus, and squid garnished with garlicky skordalia (a thick lemony sauce with pureed potatoes, vinegar, and parsley). The usual appetizers include a sharp *tzatziki* (tangy lemon-yogurt dip) and a large horiatiki salad, piled high with tomatoes, olives, and feta cheese. ⊠ *Last street on right off Lykourgou Logotheti as you descend to harbor,* ☎ *0273/61957. No credit cards.*

$$$$ 🏨 **Doryssa Bay Hotel and Village.** Overlooking Glyfada Lake, the
★ body of water by the Aegean that was the site of the ancient naval port, this pseudo-village has pastel houses (containing housekeeping apartments) with a small church, a square, kafeneion, and shops. The hotel is modern and is centered on a large pool. Half-board is mandatory, but the food at the hotel's Taverna Asterias is unusually good—sample it at Tuesday's pricey Greek night, which entails lavish spreads and traditional dancers. ⊠ *Outside Pythagorio on main road to Chora, 83103,* ☎ *0273/61360,* ℻ *0273/61463. 172 rooms, 125 bungalows, 5 suites. 3 restaurants, 2 bars, pool, tennis court, beach, boating, fishing, waterskiing. AE, DC, MC, V. Closed Nov.–Mar.* 🐾

$$$ 🏨 **Hydrele Beach and Village.** On one of the longest and most beautiful beaches in Samos, this hotel behind a gate and lush garden is built in local style. Most of the rooms in the Village come with cooking facilities and are ideal for families. Rooms have balconies overlooking the huge, meandering pool, with the sea and brown hills beyond. There is a wide array of water sports available. ⊠ *Pototaki, a 15-min walk from Pythagorio, 83103,* ☎ *0273/61702 or 0273/61541,* ℻ *0273/61602. 130 rooms. Restaurant, 2 bars, kitchenettes, 2 swimming pools, baby-sitting, car rental. No credit cards. Nov.–Apr.*

Outdoor Activities and Sports

SAILING

On Samos, **Pythagorio, Karlovassi, Ormos Marathokambou,** and **Samos town** have fuel, water, and repair services.

Sun Yachting (⊠ 9 Dosmani St., Athens, ☎ 01/983–7312) in Athens specializes in charter rentals to Samos; you can pick up the boat in Piraeus or Pythagorio for one- and two-week rentals.

TENNIS

Near Pythagorio the **Doryssa Bay** (⊠ Outside Pythagorio on main road to Chora, ☎ 0273/61360), **Apollon** (⊠ Outside Pythagorio on main road to Chora, ☎ 0273/61683), and **Princessa** hotels (⊠ Outside Pythagorio on main road to Chora, ☎ 0273/61698) have courts to rent.

WATER SPORTS

On Samos many beaches have windsurfing rentals, including **Heraion, Karlovassi, Mykali, Potokaki, Tsamadou,** and **Votsalakia.**

Heraion

★ ㉛ *8 km (5 mi) southwest of Samos town, 6½ km (4 mi) southwest of Pythagorio.*

The early Samians worshiped Hera, believing she was born here near the stream Imbrassos and that there she also lay with Zeus. Several temples were built on the site, the last by Polycrates, who rebuilt the To Hraio, or **Temple of Heraion,** enlarging it and lining it with two rows of columns, 133 in all. The huge temple, four times larger than the Parthenon, and the largest Greek temple ever conceived, was damaged by fire in 525 BC and never completed, owing to Polycrates' untimely death. In the intervening years, masons recycled the stones to create other buildings, including a basilica (foundations remain at the site) to another highly worshiped woman, the Virgin Mary. Today, we can only imagine the Heraion's massive glory; of its forest of columns only one remains standing amid acres of marble remnants in marshy ground thick with poppies.

At the semiannual celebrations to honor Hera, the faithful approached from the sea along the **Sacred Way**, which is still visible at the site's northeast corner. Nearby are replicas of a 6th-century BC sculpture depicting an aristocratic family, whose chiseled signature reads "Genelaos made me." The originals and the world's largest *kouros* (statue of nude male youth), also found here, are in the Samos archaeological museum (☞ *below*). ⊠ *Near Imvisos River,* ☎ *0273/95277.* ☒ *800 dr./2.35.* ⊘ *Tues.–Sun. 8:30–3.*

Mytilini

③② *12 km (7½ mi) west of Samos town, 9 km (5½ mi) north of Heraion.*

Mytilini, an inland village with a pretty market square, has a **Paleontologiko Mouseio,** or paleontological museum, exhibiting local animal fossils dating back 15 million years. The prize exhibit, among the bones of ancient hippos, rhinos, and evolving three-toed horses, is a 13-million-year-old fossilized horse brain. ⊠ *City Hall,* ☎ *0273/52055.* ☒ *500 dr./€1.47.* ⊘ *Apr.–Oct., weekdays 9–2.*

Dining

$ ✕ **Dionyssos.** When you tire of eating on Pythagorio's waterfront, where food is often overpriced and monotonous, take a taxi to Mytilini and this taverna (there's no sign: just say the name to the first Greeks you'll encounter—pronounce it Dee-u-*neye*-sis—and chances are they will accompany you there) for inexpensive, well-cooked chops; *kotopoulo* krasato (chicken in wine); lemon chicken; and the seldom-seen chicken breast on a spit. The good appetizers go well with the chilled barrel retsina, which may prepare you for the random Gypsy vendor who parks his van next to your table and pulls out stereo speakers to foist upon you. ⊠ *Mytilini Sq. (Platia Kalymniou),* ☎ *0273/51820. No credit cards.*

Music

Clubs throughout Greece are named after everybody's favorite lusty Greek, and here on the road to Samos town is **Zorba's,** for bouzouki music (bring your own plates if, inspired by the movie, you want to smash any).

Pirgos

③③ *30 km (18½ mi) west of Samos town, 14 km (8¾ mi) west of Mytilini.*

This area produces distinctive honey, with a hint of herbs the Samian bees buzz around. The landscape here still shows the charred signs of a 1990 fire that destroyed acres of pine forest. Hilltop **Timiou Stavrou monastery,** 14 km (8½ mi) northeast of Pirgos, is considered Samos's most important monastery and is worth a stop to enjoy the icons, carved wooden iconostasis, and the bishop's throne.

Shopping

CERAMICS

Aesthetic ceramics are a specialty in the villages of **Koumaradei** and **Mauratzei.** The most popular item is the "Pythagoras" cup, which leaks when it's more than half full. It was invented by Pythagoras to ensure that his students didn't imbibe during lessons.

Platanos

③④ *27 (16¾ mi) west of Samos town, 11 km (7 mi) northwest of Pirgos.*

Mt. Kerkis, the second-highest peak in the Aegean (after Sao on Samothraki), hangs in the distance, and the island's undeveloped west coast plummets below as you follow the curve around the western side of the island. Platanos is a typical hillside village, where, except for during "Greek nights" staged by travel agencies in summer, very little changes from year to year.

Marathokambos

40 km (25 mi) west of Samos town, 8 km (5 mi) west of Platanos.

The village of Marathokambos stretches like an amphitheater across the lower flanks of Mt. Kerkis. In the afternoons, when the haze clears, the view down to the Bay of Marathokambos and the southern beaches is dazzling, with the island of Patmos looming on the horizon. Nearby caves are fun for spelunkers to explore.

Ormos Marathokambou

㉟ *40 km (25 mi) west of Samos town, 5 km (3 mi) south of Marathokambos.*

Ormos Marathokambou, on the bay, still has a small caïque-building industry, and these boats make daily trips to Fourni with its one fishing village and empty beaches, and the islet of Samiopoula. A few tavernas serve Samian wine, and strollers enjoy the quay, which is closed to traffic. But the port's unique attraction is at its western end: a lone traffic light.

Beaches

㊱ Ormos Marathokambou has a narrow pebble beach favored by windsurfers, but Samos's longest beach, **Votsalakia** (✉ 2 km [1 mi] west of Ormos Marathokambou), is a pine-shaded strip of sand backed by a growing, low-rise family resort. Several tavernas serve up informal food and drink. Mt. Kerkis looms dramatically above it all. Scant crowds and lots of rays reign at **Psili Ammos** beach, 15 km (9¼ mi) southwest of Votsalakia.

Outdoor Activities and Sports

HIKING

From Votsalakia beach (☞ *above*) you can climb **Mt. Kerkis** on a path that runs past a convent and, once above the tree line, embrace some grand views. The round-trip, including rest stops, will take most of the day. If you want to drive part of the way, a paved road goes past villages west of the summit. You can hike to caves that once housed religious hermits (and now, who knows?). Two isolated monasteries are also in the area.

Karlovassi

㊲ *33 km (20½ mi) northwest of Samos Town, 16 km (10 mi) north of Ormos Marathokambou.*

Karlovassi, Samos's second-largest harbor, is a good base for exploring the western beaches. It seems grim until you take a closer look at its neighborhoods. The area called Paleo spreads across a ravine above the harbor area of Limani; it is surprisingly pretty. Above it is a hilltop church, visible from the sea. Below the main square, richly decorated churches and elaborate neoclassical mansions, padlocked and slightly dilapidated, hint of a time when Karlovassi was a center of leather production. Note the empty tanneries as you drive through the coastal suburbs toward the ferry port and Potami.

OFF THE BEATEN PATH **MIKRO SEITANI AND MEGALO SEITANI –** Beach lovers can easily travel from Karlovassi, first by bus and then on foot, to two delightfully secluded coves: Mikro Seitani (pebble) and Megalo Seitani (sand). No food stands are around, and often no people, so bring your own picnic. From the port, walk or take the bus west to tree-rimmed Potami beach (☞ *below*), where the asphalt ends. After about 10 minutes you'll come to a dirt path that veers right. Ignore it. Two minutes later, turn off at the second path going right, marked by a stone pile. The trail is steep, and it's marked with blue and white paint dots all the way to the cove. After a small farm, it winds through olive trees, giving eyefuls of the turquoise sea below. After another 15 minutes, another path bears left, but continue straight, and some 40 minutes out of Potami you'll come upon the limpid cove of Mikro Seitani. If you can manage to tear yourself away, continue on, along a path that has good views of Mt. Kerkis and, in spring, winds through masses of wildflowers; after about 30 minutes you'll see a path going up to the left; continue straight and you will reach Megalo Seitani in another 15 minutes. Seitani Bay on this north coast is a marine preserve for the monk seal, an endangered mammal also found off Alonnisos, in the Sporades islands.

Beaches

Along the north coast near Karlovassi are some of the island's best beaches. Two kilometers (1 mile) west of Karlovassi is **Potami,** a wide pebble-and-sand beach (✉ About 45 minutes by foot on the coast road from Limani, or an hour's drive on the scenic road from Paleo). It has shady bushes under which people camp, pine trees overhead, and interesting rock formations. Hidden in a reedy area halfway along the beach is a small **white house** where a local family serves lunch amid greenery and under the scrutiny of the family donkey. A short walk inland is an isolated medieval settlement just waiting to be explored, with a Byzantine castle and an 11th-century church, the island's oldest.

Dining and Lodging

$$ ✕ **Steve's.** The owner has lived in South Africa, but the cuisine is all Samos, and his restaurant has earned a reputation for some of the best food on the island. Generous portions of standard Greek fare such as *fasolakia freska* (snap peas or green beans) and *pastitsio* (pasta layered with beef) are executed impeccably. The splendid homemade cheesecake will make you tap your shoes. ✉ *Karlovassi Harbor quay, easternmost establishment on harbor,* ☎ *0273/33434. MC. Closed Dec.–Mar.*

$ ✕ **Psarades.** It's worth a detour to find this family-run taverna, where occasional kittens may nip at your heels, but good, inexpensive fish is served on a terrace overlooking the waves. In spring or autumn there are trays of fresh saddled bream and grouper, and you can also order *fassolada* (bean stew), *yiouvarlakia* (rice-and-meat balls in white sauce), and pungent tzatziki and skordalia dips. ✉ *About 100 yards east of Ayios Dimitrios you'll come to a sign for the taverna; turn left down paved driveway and continue to end, Ayios Nikolaos, 5 km (3 mi) outside Karlovassi,* ☎ *0273/32489. No credit cards.*

$$$ ▨ **Samena Bay.** Without a doubt the best hotel in Karlovassi, the Samena Bay is convenient to the ferry. The hotel is spacious, with framed embroideries adding a homey touch in the reception and bar area; guest rooms have white lacquer furniture, the suites, bamboo. The polite young staff is fluent in several languages. A breakfast buffet is served on the veranda, and you can usually arrange for other meals, too. Potami beach is a 15-minute walk away. ✉ *Main road, near harbor, Karlovassi 83200,* ☎ *0273/30811 through 0273/30815,* ℻ *0273/30816. 75 rooms. Restaurant, bar, pool, sauna, playground. MC, V. Closed Nov.–Apr.*

$$ ▨ **Merope.** Though not much to look at, this four-story '70s hotel strives for high standards at reasonable rates. Each floor has a lounge; the sim-

ple rooms have the usual pine furniture and balconies, with fantastic views above the second floor. A local bus runs to Potami beach; otherwise lounge by the pool or stroll down the street to see some of Karlovassi's fine old tobacco warehouses, some of them deserted. If you get hungry, the kitchen always has some well-prepared magirefta on hand. ⊠ *Main road in Pefkakia area, by the post office, Karlovassi 83200,* ☎ *0273/32650 or 0273/32651,* ℻ *0273/32652. 80 rooms. Bar, pool. No credit cards. Closed Nov.–Mar.*

Manolates

㊳ *15 km (9⅓ mi) northwest of Samos town, 5 km (3 mi) east of Ayios Konstandinos through steep vineyards up Mt. Ambelos.*

The delightful village of Manolates is surrounded by forest. Squares are lined with balconied stone houses with tile roofs, and cats prowl narrow streets whitewashed with floral designs. Most hikers set out from here to gawk at coastal panoramas or to watch for birds. Steep vineyards on these lower slopes of Mt. Ambelos offer wide-ranging views and produce wines in white and rosé. But it is the dark, sweet moskhato grape about which Lord Byron wrote, "Dash down yon cup of Samian wine."

$-$$ ✕ **Filia.** Even though it's set on a balcony perched high over the tiered
★ vineyards of Samos, Filia has a view that is but an added attraction. The food in this traditional, stone taverna is what it's all about—indeed, this taverna has been listed among the best in Greece (in a country where food is revered that's no small achievement). The revithokeftedes are succulent and crispy and the *pikantiko sukoti* (spicy liver) infused with wine are just some of the culinary masterpieces that emerge from Argyro Zafeiri's accolade-covered kitchen. ⊠ *Manolates, at the edge of the village on the dirt road that leads to Vourliotes,* ☎ *0273/94678. No credit cards. No dinner Nov.–Mar..*

Kokkari

㊴ *27 km (16¾ mi) southeast of Karlovassi, 9 km (5½ mi) northeast of Manolates.*

Beyond the popular beaches of Tsabou, Tsamadou, and Lemonakia, the spectacular stretch of coast road with olive groves and vineyards ends suitably in the fishing village of Kokkari, one of the most appealing spots on the island. Until 1980, there was not much here except for a few dozen houses between two headlands, and tracts of onion fields, which gave the town its name. Though now there are a score of hotels, and many German tourists, you can still traipse along the rocky, windswept beach and spy fishermen mending trawling nets on the paved quay. Cross the spit to the eastern side of the headland and watch the moon rise over the lights of Vathi in the next bay.

Beaches
Acclaimed **coves of the north coast** are the partly nudist **Tsamadou, Lemonakia,** and **Tsabou;** all are just a few minutes from one another, and they're to be avoided when the *meltemi* (northern winds) blow, unless you're a professional windsurfer.

Dining and Lodging
$$ ✕ **Avgo tou Kokkora.** The name comes from the Greek tale of a woman who invited her son-in-law to dinner, promising such variety that there'd even be an *avgo tou kokkora* (rooster's egg). That is still the key here: besides fresh fish and the usuals, the seaside restaurant offers *kokkoras* (rooster), *flambé bastounia tou sef* (a fried ham-and-cheese appetizer), and *glosses tis petheras* ("mother-in-law's tongue,"

made from beef tongue). It stays open until 3 AM. If this won't do, head
for the adjacent Porto Picolo for Italian fare or Barino for a nightcap
(same management). ✉ *Kokkari promenade,* ☎ *0273/92113. DC,
MC, V. Closed Nov.–Apr.*

$$ ✕ **Kariatida.** Here you teeter on the water's edge, and the waiters can
always squeeze in another table. The fresh-fish menu features sea
bream and various incarnations of shrimp and swordfish. House spe-
cialties also include rabbit stew and pikilia. The wine list is long and
well chosen. ✉ *Kokkari promenade,* ☎ *0273/92103. MC, V. Closed
Nov.–Apr.*

$$ ⊞ **Galini.** Reached only by steps and with no cars passing nearby,
Galini—meaning tranquillity—is aptly quiet. The large marble-adorned
rooms face the town or the sea. You won't pay dearly for comfort at
this hotel (nice added touch: each floor has a refrigerator), and the Kanatas
family are friendly hosts, as you'll find out when they serve up breakfast in either the garden or the dining room. ✉ *Panayotis Moshous,
83100,* ☎ *0273/92331, 0273/92365, or 0273/28039. 9 rooms. Breakfast room, lobby lounge. No credit cards. Closed Nov.–Apr.*

$$ ⊞ **Olympia Beach/Olympic Village.** At this bright-white hotel with tra-
ditional marble and wood interiors, you can stroll into Kokkari for a
movie yet avoid the bustle. The immaculate rooms are spare but have
balconies overlooking the sea and are decorated with flowery Samian
ceramics. The same owners run the nearby Olympic Village, whose apart-
ments, including bedroom, living room, two baths, and a kitchen, are
ideal for families. You can walk to Tsamadou cove, favored for its shal-
low water, pine trees, and secluded setting. ✉ *Northwest Beach Rd.,
near Kokkari, 83100,* ☎ *0273/92420 or 0273/92353,* ℻ *0273/92457.
Olympia Beach: 22 rooms; Olympic Village: 12 apartments. Restau-
rant, bar. No credit cards. Closed Nov.–Apr.*

En Route After Kokkari you pass through Malagari, the winery where farmers
hawk their harvested grapes every September, hoping for a knockout
vintage.

Samos Town

④⓪ *33 km (20½ mi) southeast of Karlovassi, 6 km (4 mi) southeast of
Kokkari.*

On the northeast coast at the head of the island's deepest bay is the
capital, Samos town, also known as Vathi. Red-tiled roofs swirled in
a semicircle seem to reach toward the top of red-earth hills. In the morn-
ing at the sheltered harbor, fishermen are still grappling with their nets,
spreading them to dry in the sun, and in the early afternoon everything
shuts down. Tourism does not alter this centuries-old schedule.

The stepped streets ascend from the **shopping thoroughfare,** which me-
★ anders from the port to the city park next to the **Archaiolologiko Mou-
seio,** or archaeological museum, the town's most important sight. The
museum's older wing has a collection of pottery and cast-bronze grif-
fin heads (the symbol of Samos). Samian sculptures from past millen-
nia were considered among the best in Greece, and examples here show
why. An exceptional collection of tributary gifts from ancient cities far
and wide, including bronzes and ivory miniatures, affirms the impor-
tance of the shrine to Hera. The newest wing holds the impressive **kouros
from Heraion,** a votive offering to the goddess and the largest freestanding
sculpture surviving from ancient Greece, dating from 580 BC. It stands
alone in the room, massive, with an inscrutable smile, the enigma of
ancient Samos. It's so large (16 ½ ft tall) that the wing had to be re-
built specifically to house it. ✉ *Platia Dimarhiou,* ☎ *0273/27469.* 🖭
800 dr./€2.35. ☉ *Tues.–Sun. 8:30–3.*

④ In the quaint 17th-century village **Ano Vathi** (✉ Beyond museum, to the right), wood-and-plaster houses with pastel facades and red-tile roofs are jammed together, their balconies protruding into cobbled paths so narrow that the water channel takes up most of the space. From here you have a view of the gulf.

OFF THE BEATEN PATH — From Samos town (and Pythagorio) you can easily ferry to Turkey. Once there, it's a short drive from the Kuşadası Kud on the Turkish coast, where the boats dock, to Ephesus, one of the great archaeological sites and a major city of the ancient world. (Note that the Temple of Artemis in Ephesus is a copy of the Temple of Hera, destroyed in Heraion, so you can see it in Turkey, sort of.) A guided round-trip full-day tour costs about 25,000 dr./€73.74. Many travel agencies run this popular trip, which can be lengthened and customized. You leave your passport with the agency and it is returned when you come back from Turkey.

Beaches

④ One of the island's best beaches is sand **Psili Ammos** (✉ Southeast of Samos town near Mesokambos). Closer to Samos town is **Mykali beach** (✉ On coast east of Samos town), with a stunning view of Turkey and Mykali peak. From here you might fantasize about swimming the straits to Turkey, about 2 km (1 mi) across the sea.

Dining and Lodging

$$ ✕ **Apanemia.** The name of this ouzerie on the shore of Vathy bay means "the lee spot," and it's rather ambitious on choppy days, though the garden seating is pleasant. The Athenian proprietor-chef brings years of experience to the panoply of dishes—familiar Western favorites such as Stroganoff and cannelloni as well as Greek specialties. Among the latter choose *kopanisti* (spicy cheese puree), *pastourmas* (pastrami), and mussels saganaki or ahnista (steamed in wine). ✉ *Themistokleous Sofouli 26, Vathy,* ☎ *0273/28147. No credit cards. Closed Nov.–Apr. No lunch.*

$$ ✕ **La Calma.** Everybody always seems to be having a good time here. Maybe it's the setting, on a waterfront terrace, or maybe it's the large selection, from grilled fresh fish to traditional meat dishes. For dessert, go for the caramel custard or a glass of sweet Samian moskhato. ✉ *Kefalopoulou 5, Vathi,* ☎ *0273/22654. No credit cards. Closed Nov.–Apr.*

$$ ✕ **The Steps.** Climb the steps and enter a courtyard draped with ivy and flowers in an atmosphere of candlelight, crisp white linen, and soft music. One of the chef's specialties is the mixed plate, which gives you a chance to try the souvlaki, lamb, village sausage, and meatball. Lamb is roasted on a spit, sliced, and served with gravy. The Krissakis family also serve *exohiko,* or swordfish grilled with lemon-oil sauce, and sole breaded like schnitzel. To reach the Steps, turn left off the Samos waterfront, then left between the Dionyssos and Souda restaurants. ✉ *Near Samos Harbor,* ☎ *0273/28649. No credit cards. Closed Nov.–Apr. No lunch.*

$$ ▥ **Galaxy.** Off the harbor in a quiet neighborhood, this greenery-fringed hotel is a cheerful respite from the waterfront. Once in the courtyard, you see the pool shimmering and hear laughter from the bar area. The simply furnished rooms all have balconies overlooking the pool, the baby palm–sprouted lawn, or the adjacent grove. ✉ *Angeou 1, behind the Fourth Primary School, Samos 83100,* ☎ *0273/22265 or 0273/22266,* ℻ *0273/27679. 42 rooms. Bar, pool. No credit cards. Closed Nov.–Feb.*

$$ ▥ **Paradise.** Simple but elegant, this hotel is a cut above the rest, with cushy details: marble, dark wood, and bird-of-paradise flower arrangements. Avoid the six front rooms; others overlook the garden and the orchards of Perivoli district, so you're treated to evening birdsong. This hotel is convenient to the bus station and within walking distance of the harbor. ✉ *Kanari 21, Samos 83100,* ☎ *0273/23911 through 0273/23913,* ℻ *0273/28754. 50 rooms. Snack bar, pool. MC, V. Closed Nov.–Mar.*

Nightlife

The port area, as on most of the Greek islands, is the surest bet for clubs and action. If you seek smaller places, check out the adjoining streets, or ask if there's a strip, as bars tend to congregate, just as patrons do. Since the scene changes rapidly, it's always best to ask the locals.

THE NORTHERN ISLANDS A TO Z

Arriving and Departing

By Boat

If you can't get on a flight (☞ *below*), there's always the extensive **ferry network,** offering the consolation that you'll travel for a third of the airfare. Car ferries vary a bit, but most offer clean and comfortable overnight service between destinations. Newer ones offer buffet and sit-down meals, entertainment, and the carpeted, brass, and glass glitz of a small cruise ship. The Greek National Tourist Organization (GNTO or EOT) office in Athens distributes weekly ferry schedules. For last-minute departure times, call the **Athens port authority** (☎ 01/451–1311).

CHIOS

Boats arrive daily from Piraeus. The **Chios port authority** (☎ 0271/44433) can be of assistance.

LESBOS

There are at least four boats per week from Piraeus and three per week from Thessaloniki. The **port authority** (☎ 0251/47888) is in Mytilini.

SAMOS

Ferries arrive four to nine times per week from Athens, stopping at Paros and Naxos; and most of the year two or three ferries weekly serve Pythagorio from Kos and Patmos. Ferries and hydrofoils to Kuşadası the Turkish coast leave from Vathi. Samos has **port authority offices** in Vathi (☎ 0273/27318), Karlovassi (☎ 0273/32343), and Pythagorio (☎ 0273/61225).

By Plane

Even if they have the time, most people avoid the 10- to 12-hour ferry ride from Athens and start their island-hopping trip by air. Most flights are one hour or less. **Olympic Airways** (☎ 01/926–9111) has at least a dozen flights a week from Athens to each of the islands in summer. Watch out for overbooking problems; if you have a reservation, you should be entitled to a free flight if you get bumped.

LESBOS

Olympic Airways offices are in Mytilini (✉ 44 Kavetsou, ☎ 0251/28660) and at the airport (☎ 0251/61490). The **airport** (☎ 0251/61212) is 7 km (4½ mi) from Mytilini.

CHIOS

Olympic Airways has offices in the port town of Chios (✉ Prokymeia midport, ☎ 0271/20359) and at the airport (☎ 0271/23998). The **airport** is 4½ km (3 mi) from town (☎ 0271/24515 for airport information).

Olympic Airways offices are in Vathi (✉ Kanari 5, ☎ 0273/27237), in Pythagorio (✉ Logothetou 90, ☎ 0273/61300), and at the airport (☎ 0273/61219). The busiest **airport** (☎ 0273/61219 flight information) is here, 17 km (10½ mi) from Vathi. More than 40 international charters arrive every week in midsummer.

Getting Around

By Boat and Hydrofoil

Hydrofoil service via Flying Dolphin is available for travel among the local islands only; it is more expensive but quicker than ferry travel. Even in low season there are several connections weekly among Samos, Chios, and Lesbos. In summer, scheduling is usually more frequent.

By Bus

LESBOS

Lesbos's **KTEL bus system** (✉ Platia Konstantinopoleos, ☎ 0251/28873) is relatively expensive and infrequent, though there are several buses a day from Mytilini to Molyvos via Kalloni, and you can also get to Mandamados, Agiassos Plomari, Eressos, and Sigri.

CHIOS

Buses leave the town of Chios several times per day for Mesta and Pirgi, and three leave daily for Volissos. For information call the **KTEL station** (✉ Vlatarias 13, ☎ 0271/27507).

SAMOS

Samos has excellent **KTEL bus service** (✉ Ioannou Lekati and Kanari, near Olympic Airways office, ☎ 0273/27262), with frequent trips between Pythagorio, Samos town, Kokkari, and Karlovassi. Buses also travel at least twice daily to Ireon, Pirgos, Marathokambos, and Votsalakia beach.

By Car and Moped

A car is handiest on Lesbos and Chios, the bigger islands. Mopeds are the ideal way to see Samos. You won't have any trouble finding rentals.

By Plane

Other than two weekly flights between Lesbos and Chios, there are no direct flights between these northern islands; it's best to count on going by ferry or hydrofoil.

Guided Tours

LESBOS

Aeolic Cruises, with branches in Mytilini (✉ Prokimea, ☎ 0251/23960 or 0251/23266, FAX 0251/43694) and Plomari (✉ Ayios Isidoros, ☎ 0251/32009), offers a variety of island tours. In Molyvos, **Panatella Tours** (✉ Possidonion at town entrance, ☎ 0253/71520, 0253/71643, or 0253/71644, FAX 0253/71680) has two tours that take in villages, monasteries, and other sights.

CHIOS

Ionia Touristiki (✉ Rodokanaki 17, ☎ 0271/41047 or 0271/22034, FAX 0271/41122) organizes excursions to the mastikhohoria and other sights (one is a four-wheel-drive tour).

SAMOS

Most of the branches of **Samina** (Main office: ✉ Themistokleous Sofouli 67, Vathi, ☎ 0273/28841; 0273/28842 to find closest branch) run an island tour, a one-day trip to Patmos, and a picnic cruise.

Contacts and Resources

Emergencies
Police (☎ 100). **Ambulance** (☎ 166). **Fire** (☎ 199).

Visitor Information

LESBOS

Information offices are in Eressos (✉ Main square, ☎ 0253/53214), Molyvos (✉ Possidonios near bus stop, ☎ 0253/71347), Mytilini (✉ Harbor, ☎ 0251/28199; ✉ Airport, ☎ 0251/61279), and Plomari (✉ Harbor, ☎ 0252/32535). **Tourist police** (✉ Harbor, Mytilini, ☎ 0251/22776). The **Women's Agricultural Tourist Collective** (✉ Petra, ☎ 0253/41238) finds rooms with farming families.

CHIOS

Greek National Tourist Organization (EOT; ✉ 18 Kanari, Chios, ☎ 0271/44389 or 0271/20324). **Tourist police** (✉ 37 Neoriou, Chios, ☎ 0271/44344 or 0271/44427). The **Women's Agricultural Tourist Collective** (✉ Main square, Pirgi, ☎ 0271/72496) finds rooms with local families, as will **Mesta's tourist information office** (✉ Main square, ☎ 0271/76319).

SAMOS

EOT: Vathi (✉ Ikostipemptis Martiou 4, ☎ 0273/28530), Pythagorio (✉ Logothetou, 1 block up waterfront, ☎ 0273/61100), Kokkari (✉ Across from OTE, ☎ 0273/62274). **Tourist police** (✉ Vathi harbor, ☎ 0273/81000).

7 CORFU

Temperate, multihued Corfu—of emerald
mountains; turquoise waters lapping
rocky coves; ocher and pink buildings;
shimmering silver olive leaves; puffed red,
yellow, and orange parasails; scarlet
roses, bougainvillea, and lavender wisteria
and jacaranda spread over cottages—
could have inspired impressionism. The
island has a history equally as colorful,
reflecting the commingling of Corinthians,
Romans, Goths, Normans, Venetians,
French, Russians, and British. First stop, of
course, is Corfu town—looking for all the
world like a stage set for a Verdi opera.

By Lea Lane

Updated by
Melia Tatakis

T HE IONIAN ISLANDS ARE ALL LUSH AND LOVELY, but Kerkyra, or
Corfu, is the greenest and, quite possibly, the prettiest of all Greek
islands. Homer's "well-watered gardens" and "beautiful and rich
land" were Odysseus's last stop on his journey home. Corfu is also said
to be the inspiration for Prospero's island in Shakespeare's *The Tempest*. This northernmost of the major Ionian islands has, through the
centuries, inspired other artists, as well as conquerors, royalty, and, of
course, tourists. Today more than a million visitors a year—mainly English—enjoy and, in summer, crowd its evocative capital city. As a result, it is increasingly filled with stylish restaurants and resorts—but
also package resorts and clogged roadways, blighting areas of its
beauty. Still, the entire island has gracefully absorbed its many layers
of history and combines neoclassical villas and ecosensitive resorts, horse-
drawn carriages and Jaguars—simplicity and sophistication—in an alluring mix.

Corfu lies strategically in the northern Ionian Sea at the entrance to
the Adriatic, off the western edge of Greece. The lush, mountainous
landscape seems more classic European than Greek, and indeed, this
flower-filled island is only 72 km (45 mi) from Italy, and 1 km (⅔ mi)
or so from Albania; some geologists believe it is the top of a submerged
mountain range that broke off from the mainland. It is moderated by
westerly winds, scored with fertile valleys, and punctuated by enormous, gnarled olive trees, planted over the course of 400 years by the
Venetians. Figs, oranges, and grapes grow abundantly in the clear light
and mild climate, and sunny beaches, traditional villages, and cosmopolitan atmosphere remain a potent mix here.

The Ionian islands' proximity to Europe and their sheltered position
on the East–West trade routes made them prosperous; both their wealth
and strategic position assured them a lively history of conquest and
counter-conquest. The classical remains have suffered from this history and also from earthquakes; architecture from the centuries of Venetian, French, and British rule is most evident, leaving the towns with
a pleasant combination of contrasting design elements.

In classical times, Corinth colonized the northern islands, but Corfu,
growing powerful, revolted and allied itself with Athens, a fateful
move that triggered the Peloponnesian War. Subjection followed: to the
tyrants of Syracuse, the kings of Epirus and of Macedonia, and, in the
2nd century BC, to Rome. After the Byzantine Empire shattered, the
islands fended for themselves against sporadic Germanic and Saracen
invasions, and from the 11th to the 14th centuries were ruled by Nor-
man and Angevin kings. Then came the Venetians, who protected
Corfu from Turkish occupation and provided a 411-year period of peace
for commercial development and the flowering of arts and letters.
Venice also made Italian the official language, for a while, at least.
Napoléon Bonaparte took the islands, which he called "the key to the
Adriatic," after the fall of Venice. "The greatest misfortune which
could befall me is the loss of Corfu," he wrote to Talleyrand, his foreign minister. Unfortunately for Bonaparte, he lost it within two years
to a Russo-Turkish fleet; although, as the island was never occupied
by the Turks, local culture continued to thrive here during the hated
Turkish occupation of the rest of Greece.

For a short time the French regained and fortified Corfu from the Russians, and their occupation especially influenced the island's educational
system, architecture, and cuisine. Theirs was a Greek-run republic—
the first for modern Greece—which whetted local appetites for the in-

dependence that arrived later in the 19th century. But in 1814 the islands came under British protection; roads, schools, and hospitals were constructed, and commercialism developed. Corfu was ruled by a series of eccentric Lord High Commissioners, beginning with the much-hated Sir Thomas Maitland, and then by Sir Frederick Adam, who married a Corfiot lady with a heavy mustache. Nationalism finally prevailed, and the islands were ceded to Greece in 1864.

Corfu is the most developed of the Ionians, with a population of about 100,000. The island's northeast section has been heavily built up, although stony, inland farming villages seem undisturbed by civilizations that have come and gone, or even by today's events. Although it was bombed when the Italians and Nazis occupied it during World War II, the town of Corfu remains one of the loveliest in all of Greece and is a haven for travelers who return year after year. Corfu has also attracted, and become home to, a great many artists, writers, patrons of the arts, poets, and musicians. Most notable, perhaps, is the celebrated Greek poet Dionysios Solomos (1798–1857) who, though originally from Zakynthos, made Corfu his home and while in residence penned his poem, *Hymn to Freedom*; set to music by another prominent Corfiot, Nikolaos Mantzaros (1795–1872), it became Greece's National Anthem. Among Corfu's more modern celebrities are the Durrell brothers: Lawrence, who wrote *Prospero's Cell*—one of the most beloved of tributes to Corfu—and Gerald, whose fond memories of growing up in Corfu inspired his delightful *My Family and Other Animals*. Corfu's scholastic history, in fact, extends back to Lord Guilford, founder of the Ionian Academy, who endowed Corfu with its university in 1823—the first university in modern Greece and a truly liberal enclave, which encouraged both its students and professors to get into the classical spirit by donning the chiton and chlamys. Indeed, when you look at Corfu in toto, it's hard to believe that any island so small could generate a history so large; every nook and cranny tells a story, every street meanders to a myth. Corfu today is a vivid tapestry of cultures; a sophisticated weave, where charm, history, and natural beauty blend together to delight the traveler. Desirability, of course, comes at a price: Corfu is expensive.

Pleasures and Pastimes

Boating

Calm waters in the coves and bays make boating a popular pastime. Sailors can moor boats at the new ports in Corfu town, at Gouvia Marina on the east coast, and at Paleokastritsa on the west coast. Motorboats and sailboats can be rented at the Old Port in Corfu town, in Paleokastritsa, Kondokali, and Kassiopi, and on the northeast coast. To charter a yacht or sailboat without a crew, you'll need a proficiency certificate from a certified yacht club. Corfu has customs and health authorities, passport control, supply facilities, and exchange services, and it is one of the few official entry-exit ports in Greece; from here you can sail throughout the islands.

Dining

The food, atmosphere, and prices at some Corfu town restaurants are as European as they are Greek, although inexpensive tavernas and typical Greek cuisine predominate throughout the island. As elsewhere in Greece, the demand for fresh fish often exceeds the supply. Be aware that lobster and seafood are often priced by the kilo, and injudicious ordering can easily produce an expensive meal in a moderate restaurant. To be sure, ask the price before ordering a dish, even if the waiter recommends it.

Greeks have been successfully storing grape juice in barrels for thousands of years, producing fine and interesting wines. Two great Greek whites are Hadjimichalis or Strofilia—but consistency can be a problem, especially with Corfu's Theotoki wines and other labels. Unfortunately, *hima* (barrel wine) isn't readily available in Corfu, as there are too few vineyards and too many tourists. Occasionally, restaurants serve barrel house wine with meals, and sometimes sell it by the bottle to go; try it—you'll rarely be disappointed. Bottled water can be bought everywhere, and you'll want to order it because Corfu's tap water is *not* one of its pleasures.

Corfiot specialties are served at most restaurants and tavernas. Those worth a try are *sofrito* (veal cooked in a sauce of vinegar, parsley, and plenty of garlic) served with rice or potatoes; *pastitsada* (a derivation of the Italian dish *spezzatino*—layers of beef and pasta [always called "macaronia" in Greece] cooked in a rich and spicy tomato sauce and topped off with béchamel sauce); *bourdetto* (firm-fleshed fish stewed in tomato sauce with lots of hot red pepper); and *bianco* (whole fish stewed with potatoes, herbs, black pepper, and lemon juice).

If service has been satisfactory, it is customary to leave a tip of about 10% of the bill, since a service charge is included in the prices.

CATEGORY	COST*
$$$$	over 12,000 dr. (€35.39)
$$$	9,000 dr.–12,000 dr. (€26.54–€35.39)
$$	5,000 dr.–9,000 dr. (€14.74–€26.54)
$	under 5,000 dr. (€14.74)

*for a three-course meal, including modest service charge and tax but excluding drinks

Lodging

Corfu has accommodations to satisfy every taste and budget, from in-town bed-and-breakfasts in renovated Venetian mansions to sleek resorts with children's camps and spas. If you're after peace and quiet, you can find it; but disco, drink, and crowds are readily available, too. Expect air-conditioning only in the $$$ or $$$$ categories. Larger accommodations have historically catered to groups, but the explosion of tourism in recent years has led to prepaid, low-priced package tours; these masses can get rowdy and overwhelm otherwise pleasant surroundings. You'll recognize the haunts of these beer-guzzling revelers, mainly in towns along the southeast coast.

Bargain hunters should go to the Greek National Tourist Organization (GNTO or EOT), which has a list of basic accommodations that are usually clean, comfortable, and inexpensive (☞ Visitor Information *in* Corfu A to Z, *below*). Rates can be negotiable, but a double room should cost around 8,000 dr./€23.59–12,000 dr./€35.39; Continental breakfast is often included, but you should ask. Telephones and radios are standard on the island, but hair dryers are not. Televisions are a rarity; it's noted below which places have them.

CATEGORY	COST*
$$$$	over 40,000 dr. (€117)
$$$	20,000 dr.–40,000 dr. (€58.99–€117)
$$	12,000 dr.–20,000 dr. (€35.39–€58.99)
$	under 12,000 dr. (€35.39)

*All prices are for standard double rooms, usually including Continental breakfast but excluding tax.

✍ *following the text of a review is your signal that the property has a Web site, where you will find details and, usually, images; for a link, visit www.fodors.com/urls.*

Shopping

Prices are high here, but you can still find some bargains. Olive-wood bowls and carvings, hand embroidery, jewelry, silver, local wine and liqueurs, and dried herbs are a few of them. For the most picturesque picks, head to the shops that line the narrow streets of the Old Venetian Quarter in Corfu town.

Water Sports

Fishing is unrestricted in Corfu's clear coastal waters. For a special pleasure, join local fishermen, who often will take groups out if you negotiate a fair deal. Sand and pebble beaches and coves edge the island, but the west coast has the widest sand beaches for sunning and swimming. Snorkeling and diving are best in the many rocky inlets and grottos on the northwest coast, and Paleokastritsa, Ermones, and Ipsos have diving schools where you can take lessons and rent equipment. The winds on the west coast are best for windsurfing, although the water on the east coast is calmer. Sailboards are available, and pedalos and rowboats can be rented at many beaches. Waterskiing, water polo, parasailing, jet-skiing, and other water-related activities sponsored by resorts are easily available.

Exploring Corfu

Corfu, about 64½ km (40 mi) long and up to 29 km (18 mi) wide with 201 km (125 mi) of sparkling, indented coastline, is small enough to cover completely in a few days. Roads vary from gently winding to spiraling, but they're generally well marked. The focus is Corfu town, but historic attractions are nearby, while valley farming villages are spread inland, and a series of coastal villages and towns are separated by mountains, coves, or beaches. Within a couple of turns the landscape can vary from flatland to rocky outcrop to mountains, but the green landscape and clear blue sea are constant.

Numbers in the text correspond to numbers in the margin and on the Corfu Town and Corfu maps.

Great Itineraries

Corfu must often be explored in a day by people off a cruise ship or ferry on a tour of the Greek islands. Two days allows enough time to visit Corfu town's nearby environs and most famous sites. For those with four days, time can be spent exploring the island's other historic sites and natural attractions along both coasts. And those with six days will get a closer look at the museums, churches, and forts, and some time to relax, perhaps even with a day trip to Albania.

IF YOU HAVE 2 DAYS

On the morning of the first day meander along the narrow, cobbled lanes of ☒ **Corfu town** ①–⑲, have a bite at one of the cafés along the Liston, and then take in the view at the rooftop café of the Cavalieri hotel. If you can be torn away from the historic sector, spend the afternoon just south of Corfu town at the acropolis at nearby **Analipsis** ㉑, the ruins of the **Temple of Artemis** ㉒, and **Kanoni** ㉓, where you can see the most famous vista on Corfu—**Pontikonisi** ㉔, which includes Mouse Island. On the second morning drive to **Gastouri** ㉕ and the Achilleion, the 19th-century palace built for Empress Elizabeth of Austria. Then follow the inland road north from Corfu town to reach the beautiful northwest-coast resort area of ☒ **Paleokastritsa** ㉖. You can pedal-boat into the grottoes, snorkel, dive, or relax on the beach. If you choose, return to Corfu town area for an overnight stay.

Because Corfu is small, if you're driving, you can return to the same accommodations each night. Spend the first day the same way as in the two-day itinerary—but now you can relax, with more time to see Corfu town, before and after visiting other sites. On day two, start again at the Achilleion in **Gastouri** ㉕. In the afternoon, get to the beach resorts of **Ermones** ㉘ and/or ⚄ **Glyfada** ㉚. From ⚄ **Corfu town** ①–⑲, you hug the coast for a few miles with the mountains of Epirus a backdrop on your right; pass the bay at Gouvia, turn inland on Route 24, and explore the small farms in the fertile Ropa plain. On the third day go to ⚄ **Paleokastritsa** ㉖, and also see the ruins of Angelokastro in the mountains in **Lakones** ㉗. On the fourth day, take the coast road from Corfu town northeast around the bay, through a string of highly developed resort towns such as ⚄ **Dassia, Ipsos, Pirgi,** and **Nissaki,** set among olive groves, beaches, hotels, and restaurants. The pretty coastal road now leads north to the most mountainous part of the island, to **Kouloura** ㉛, historic **Kassiopi** ㉝, and the northern beaches of **Roda** ㉞ and **Sidari** ㉟.

Follow the four-day itinerary above. ⚄ **Corfu town** ①–⑲ is worth a second or third visit to shop, sightsee, visit museums, and sit in the courtyards and absorb the pace of Corfian life. From **Kanoni** ㉓, you can take a boat trip to **Pontikonisi** ㉔. Those who don't mind tourist-filled towns can go farther south on the island, or head north to hike around **Mt. Pantokrator.** You might return to ⚄ **Glyfada** ㉚, where the beaches are the best on the island, or to ⚄ **Paleokastritsa** ㉖. Adventurers will take a day trip to Albania, only about 2 km (1 mi) away from the northern part of the island. Or just spend the extra days relaxing in the Corfian sun, or on one of the other Ionian islands—or even in Albania.

When to Tour

The best time to enjoy Corfu is April through June, and September through October, when the weather is at its finest, crowds are smallest, and sites, dining, and lodging are up and running. This period is considered off-season, so drive a bargain; prices can be considerably lower than during the peak months of July and August. Unlike on most of the Greek isles, winter months in Corfu can be rainy and cool, and although summers are not quite as hot as some of the more southern islands, overcrowding and humidity can make things uncomfortable.

Festivals are held throughout the year, especially around the Greek Orthodox holidays. Worth noting are Carnival, with a parade on the last Sunday before Lent; and Holy Week, including Easter Sunday, and the breaking of crockery on Holy Saturday. Bands accompany the processions carrying the remains of St. Spyridon, Corfu's patron saint, held four times a year: Palm Sunday, Holy Saturday, August 11, and the first Sunday in November. The Corfu Arts Festival is in September.

Visiting attractions and participating in activities early or late in the day will help you to avoid heat and long lines (remember "only mad dogs and Englishmen go out in the noonday sun"). Be sure to check on times and schedules before setting out, and watch out for the midafternoon closings. Greeks eat lunch and dinner quite late by American standards, so if you don't mind being unfashionable you can lunch at noon and dine at seven without having to battle for tables, saving precious time for seeing the sights or lazing around.

CORFU TOWN

16 km (10 mi) east of Glyfada, 26 km (16 mi) east of Paleokastritsa.

This lovely capital and cultural, historical, and recreational center is just off the middle of the island's east coast. All ships and planes lead to Corfu town, on a narrow strip of land hugged by the Ionian Sea. Though beguilingly Greek, much of Corfu's old town displays the architectural styles of many of its conquerors—molto of Italy's Venice, a soupçon of France, and more than a tad of England.

A Good Walk

This walk can take half a day or more, depending on how long you wander in the medieval section, and how far south you go along the bay. It encompasses the highlights of Corfu town and offers views beyond, and if you linger a bit here and there, observe daily life, and let yourself feel the slightly languid pace, you can get a real taste of the history and beauty of this famous town. If you arrive from mainland Greece by ferry, you will dock at the **Old Port** ① on the north side of town, just to the left of the **New Fortress** ②, with its British citadel within. Just off the New Fortress Square is the **Museum of Sea Shells** ③, a short but charming stop to see what's under the Ionian Sea.

A five-minute walk from the museum has you crossing Tenedoy and continuing around the area of Velissariou, one of Corfu town's main streets, and the western edge of the historical center. Here is the former **Jewish Quarter** ④, with its old synagogue. From Velissariou, go southeast toward Voulgareos, turn left on Theotoki, and go left about 10 minutes to Theotoki Square (there are several Theotokis, with different first letters). Ahead is the ornate, marble, 17th-century **Town Hall** ⑤. Note the elaborate Venetian design, popular throughout the town. Adjacent is the neoclassical **Catholic Church of Ayios Iakovos** ⑥, the Cathedral of San Giacomo. Go north on Theotoki to Filarmonikis, four blocks to the **Orthodox Cathedral** ⑦. This whole area, known as the medieval **Campiello** ⑧, is filled with narrow winding streets filled with artisans' shops, restaurants, and pretty squares. Head north to the waterfront to explore the fascinating **Byzantine Museum** ⑨, then backtrack to the cathedral area.

From the cathedral, look up to see the nearby red bell tower of the **Church of St. Spyridon** ⑩, dedicated to the island's patron saint. The church is filled with silver treasures. If you keep the tower in sight you can wander as you wish without getting lost around this fascinating section. From the Church of St. Spyridon, continue northeast six blocks or so toward the water, enjoying the historic area as you go, and stopping whenever. At the north end of Kapodistriou is the historic **Corfu Reading Society** ⑪, with its grand outside staircase. From here go south two blocks to Ayios Ekaterinis. Just east is the colonnaded **Palace of St. Michael and St. George** ⑫. You are now at the north end of the **Esplanade** ⑬. You can stop at the arcaded Liston to shop or sit at a café and have a bite. Sunday cricket matches are played near here, and activity is always going on. Relax awhile, and then cross over the bridge to the **Old Fortress** ⑭ on the northeastern tip of Corfu town. In the southern section of the fort is the **Garrison Church of St. George** ⑮, with views of Albania.

On the walk back to the Esplanade along the central path is the **Statue of Count Schulenburg** ⑯, hero of the siege of 1716. The southern half of the Esplanade has a Victorian bandstand, Ionic Rotunda, and statue of Ioannis Kapodistrias, a Corfu resident and the first president of modern Greece. If you have the time and enjoy walking, go south along

Corfu Town

Leoforos Dimokratias along the water, about 10 minutes—longer if you stroll, which you may tend to do, enjoying the breeze. Just past the Corfu Palace hotel and the gardens of the Garitsa neighborhood on the right is the **Archaeological Museum** ⑰. The walk farther south along Garitsa Bay is pleasant, about 10 minutes to the **Tomb of Menekrates** ⑱, two blocks west on Menekratous. At the south end of Garitsa Bay, the suburb of Anemomilos (windmill) is crowned by the ruins of the Paleopolis church and the **Church of Ayios Iason and Ayios Sosipater** ⑲.

Sights to See

⑰ **Archaeological Museum.** This showcase exhibits finds from ongoing excavations. Note the Gorgon from the 56-ft-long pediment of the 6th-century BC Temple of Artemis (☞ *below*), from the ancient capital—one of the best-preserved pieces of archaic sculpture in Greece. This small museum is located just past the Corfu Palace hotel. ⊠ *South of Esplanade along Leoforos Dimokratias,* ☎ *0661/30680.* ☞ *800 dr./€2.35* ⊘ *Daily 8:30–3.*

⑨ **Byzantine Museum.** The church of **Panagia Antivouniotissa**, which dates from the 16th century and gets its name from the hill on which it was built, houses an outstanding collection of Byzantine religious art. About 90 icons, from the 13th to the 17th centuries, are on display inside this spectacularly ornate church. Keep an eye out for works by the celebrated "iconographers"—that is, icon painters—Tzanes and Damaskinos, who are perhaps the best-known figures of the Cretan style of icon painting. ⊠ *Arseniou Mourayio,* ☎ *0661/38313.* ☞ *Free.* ⊘ *Tues.–Sat. 8:30–3, Sun. 9:30–2:30.*

⑧ **Campiello.** Narrow, winding streets and steep stairways make up the Campiello, the large, traffic-free medieval area of the town. Balconied Venetian buildings are mixed among multistory, neoclassical 19th-century ones built by the British, with laundry often hanging between them. Small cobbled squares centered with wells, high-belfried churches, and alleyways that lead nowhere and back, with artisans' shops along the way, add to an utterly lovely urban space. ⊠ *West of Esplanade, between the 2 forts.*

⑥ **Catholic Church of Ayios Iakovos.** Built in 1588 and consecrated 50 years later, this elegant cathedral was erected to provide a grand place of worship for Corfu town's Catholic occupiers. If you use the Italian name, San Giacomo, locals will know it. Bombed by the Nazis in 1943, the cathedral's neoclassical facade of pediments, friezes, and columns was practically destroyed, but the bell tower remained intact. ⊠ *Next to town hall.*

⑲ **Church of Ayios Iason and Ayios Sosipater.** The suburb of Anemomilos is crowned by the ruins of the Paleopolis church and this 11th-century church. It is named after two of St. Paul's disciples, St. Jason and St. Sossipater, who brought Christianity to the island in the first century. The frescoes are faded, but its icons are beautiful, and the exterior, set in unspoiled greenery, is dramatic. This is one of only two Byzantine churches on the island; the other is in the northern coastal village of Ayios Markos. ⊠ *At south end of Garitsa Bay.*

⑩ **Church of St. Spyridon.** Built in 1596, this church is the tallest on the island, thanks to its distinctive red-domed bell tower. The patron saint's internal remains—smuggled here after the fall of Constantinople and contained in a silver reliquary—are carried in procession four times a year, along with his mummified body, which can be seen through a glass panel; his slippered feet are actually exposed so that the faithful can kiss them. The saint was not a Corfian but originally a shepherd from Cyprus, who became a bishop before his death in AD 350. His miracles are said to have saved the island four times: once from famine, twice from the plague, and once from the hated Turks. During World War II, a bomb fell on this holiest place on the island but didn't explode. Maybe these events explain why it seems every other man on Corfu is named Spiros. ⊠ *In center of old town,* ☎ *0661/41350.* ☜ *Free.*

⑪ **Corfu Reading Society.** The oldest cultural institution in modern Greece, the Corfu Reading Society was founded in 1836 and is filled with archives of the Ionian islands. Modeled after the Reading Society of Geneva, it is one of the loveliest buildings in Corfu and has a stunning exterior staircase leading up to a loggia. ⊠ *Kapodistriou,* ☎ *0661/39528.* ☉ *Daily 9–1, Thurs.–Fri. 5–8.*

⑬ **The Esplanade.** Central to the life of the town, this huge, open parade ground on the land side of the canal is, many say, the most beautiful *spianada* (esplanade) in Greece. It is bordered on the west by a street lined with seven- and eight-storied Venetian and English Georgian houses, and arcades, called the **Liston** (modeled on the Parisian Rue de Rivoli, by the French architect Mathieu de Lesseps, under Napoléon's short occupation of Corfu). The name Liston refers to a list that the Venetians kept of lucky upper-class townspeople who were allowed to walk and linger here. Today, happily, its beauty can be enjoyed by all. Cafés spill out onto the passing scene, and Corfiot celebrations, games, and trysts occur in the sun and shadows. Sunday cricket matches, a holdover from British rule, are played on the northern half of the Esplanade, which was once a Venetian firing range. On the southern half of the Esplanade are an ornate **Victorian bandstand**; a graffiti-covered **Ionic Rotunda,** built in honor of Sir Thomas Maitland, the not-much-loved first British Lord High Commissioner, appointed in 1814 when the island became a protectorate of Britain; and a **statue of Ioannis Kapodistrias,** a Corfu resident and the first president of modern Greece. He was also unfortunately, in 1831, the first Greek president to be assassinated. ⊠ *Between Old Fortress and old town.*

⑮ **Garrison Church of St. George.** Landmarked by its distinctive Doric portico, this church was built in the mid-19th century. In summer there's folk dancing, and in August sound-and-light shows relate the Old Fortress's history. The views from here, east to the Albanian coast and west over the town, are splendid. ⊠ *In middle of Old Fortress.* ☜ *Free.* ☉ *Daily 8–7.*

④ **Jewish Quarter.** This twist of streets was the home to 5,000 Jews from the 1600s until 1940. The community was decimated, sent to Auschwitz by the occupying Nazis. Fewer than 100 Jews survived. At the southern edge of the ghetto, a 300-year-old **synagogue** with an interior in Sephardic style still proudly stands. ⊠ *South of cathedral, 4th Parados, off Velissariou, 2 blocks from new fort.*

③ **Museum of Sea Shells.** A deep-sea collection considered the best in Europe is the treasure here, including shells, sponges, corals, sharks' jaws, snakes, and mysterious pickled creatures from throughout the world. ⊠ *Old Port on Solomou St. just off New Fortress Sq.* ☜ *500 dr./€1.47* ☉ *Daily 10–7.*

② **New Fortress.** Built in 1577–78 by the Venetians three decades later than the "older" fortress, to strengthen defenses, the New Fortress was expanded by the French and the British to protect Corfu town from a possible Turkish invasion. The fort was a Greek naval base until 1992, when it was opened to the public. A classic **British citadel** stands at its heart. You can now wander through the maze of tunnels, moats, and fortifications, and the moat (dry now!) is the site of the town's marketplace. Note the best time to come here is early morning or late afternoon, out of the noonday sun. The restoration work for the 1994 EU Summit Conference did much to improve the facilities and added an exhibition center as well as a much-needed café-bar. ⊠ *Solomou St., on promontory northwest of old fortress and medieval town,* ☎ *0661/27477.* ◩ *800 dr./€2.35* ⊙ *Apr.–Oct., daily 9–9.*

⓮ Old Fortress. Originally, Corfu's population lived within the walls of the Old Fortress, or Citadel. Separated from the rest of the town by a moat once spanned by a movable wooden bridge, the fort is on the promontory mentioned by Thucydides. Its two heights, or *korypha* (bosom), gave the island its Western name. This striking landmark on the edge of the sea was built by the Venetians in 1546 on the site of a Byzantine castle. Most of the fortifications were blown up by the British when they left, but it's interesting to wander through the parts that remain. ⊠ *On northeastern point of Corfu town peninsula.* ☎ *0661/48310.* ◩ *800 dr./€2.35* ⊙ *Daily 8–6.*

❶ Old Port. If you arrive from Igoumenitsa or Patras, on mainland Greece, your ferry will dock at the Old Port, on the north side of town, near the New Fortress.

❼ Orthodox Cathedral. This small, icon-filled cathedral was built in 1577. It is dedicated to St. Theodora, the island's second saint, whose headless body was brought to Corfu at the same time as St. Spyridon's remains. It now lies in a silver coffin by the altar; look for the shining gold icons, as well. Steps lead down to the harbor. ⊠ *In southwest of medieval quarter, east of St. Spyridon,* ☎ *0661/39409.*

⓬ Palace of St. Michael and St. George. This elegant, colonnaded 19th-century Regency structure was built as a residence for the Lord High Commissioner and headquarters for the order of St. Michael and St. George. The oldest official building in Greece, it was abandoned after the British left in 1864, and aptly renovated about a hundred years later by the British ambassador to Greece. The State Rooms were the setting for an EU summit meeting in June 1994. The palace is also home to the **Museum of Asiatic Art,** a notable collection of Asian porcelains and Sino-Japanese art as well as bronzes and Byzantine relics (but these are due to be moved sometime in the future to another venue). In 1995 the **Municipal Art Gallery** was added to the treasures of the palace. The work on display is mainly from the 19th and 20th centuries, and much of it is by Corfiot artists. Before entering the gallery, catch your breath and stop at the Art Café and bar settled in a shady courtyard here. ⊠ *At north end of Esplanade,* ☎ *0661/23124; 0661/48690 Municipal Art Gallery.* ◩ *Palace 500 dr./€1.47, Art Gallery 300 dr./€.88, Museum of Asiatic Art 300 dr./€.88* ⊙ *Tues.–Sat. 8:30–3, Sun. 9:30–2:30.*

⓰ Statue of Count Schulenburg. This monument to the Austrian mercenary immortalizes the hero of the siege of 1716, which was the Turks' last (and failed) attempt to conquer Corfu. ⊠ *Along central path of Esplanade.*

⓲ The Tomb of Menekrates. Part of an ancient necropolis, the funerary items from this site are now exhibited in the Archaeological Museum (☞ *above*). ⊠ *South around Garitsa Bay, to right of obelisk dedicated to Sir Howard Douglas.*

❺ Town Hall. The ornate marble, 17th-century Town Hall was built as a Venetian loggia and converted in 1720 into Greece's first modern theater—a far cry from the classic amphitheater pioneered in Epidaurus. A second story was added by the British before it became a grand town hall early in the 20th century. ⊠ *Theotoki Sq.,* ☎ *0661/40401.* ◩ *Free.* ⊙ *Weekdays 9–1.*

Dining and Lodging

$$$$ ✕ **Albatross and Panorama Restaurants.** Both of these expensive restaurants in the Corfu Palace hotel (☞ *below*) have Swiss chefs and stylish service. The Albatross's terrace overlooks the pool, Garitsa Bay, and the gardens, and the Saturday night barbecue and buffet is a Corfu tradition; book well in advance. The Panorama is more luxurious but remains Corfu-comfortable. At both, local specialties are particularly good, and the international cuisine is exceptional. If you can't afford staying here, eating here will give you a taste of the very good life. ⊠ *Leoforos Democratias 2, Corfu Palace hotel,* ☎ *0661/39485. Reservations essential. AE, DC, MC, V.*

$$$ ✕ **Aegli.** Right on the Liston, Aegli serves more than 100 different dishes, both local and international; the swordfish with red-pepper sauce is a treat. Tables in front, with comfortable armchairs and spotless tablecloths, overlook the nonstop parade on the promenade. For a more private meal, choose one of the 40 or so tables with white pine chairs inside, under the wood ceiling. The late-night cafeteria area serves beer, light snacks, sweets, and ice creams in more flavors than Baskin-Robbins. ⊠ *23 Kapodistriou St., Liston,* ☎ *0661/31949. AE, DC, MC, V. Closed Dec.–Feb.*

$$$ ✕ **The Four Seasons.** This is a small bistro, with a quaint mix of French and Greek food. Tables are laid on the small balcony overlooking the Cantouni tou Bizo. Owner and chef Giorgos Petrakis returned to Kerkyra after many years of training in France, as you'll see if you order the zucchini au gratin with smoked salmon or the succulent lamb chops with parsley and garlic. You'll even find showpiece dishes such as *canard à l'orange* and stuffed calamari. Too bad the wine list leaves something to be desired. No matter: the blessing here is good food, without too much strain on the wallet. ⊠ *Maniarizi and Arlioti 16,* ☎ *0661/34388. Reservations essential. No credit cards. Closed for lunch and Sun.*

$$$ ✕ **Spiros and Vassilis.** Just 9 km (6 mi) outside of Corfu in the less touristic area of Agios Ioanni and set in the farmland belonging to the Ploumeris family, this seemingly timeless and excellent restaurant is well worth the trek. Tables are set in a stylish veranda; the cuisine is traditionally French, with steak drizzled with the infamously delicious Café de Paris sauce, along with frogs' legs and snails, big winners on the menu. Adding to the pleasure are an extensive wine list and truly efficient, discreet service. ⊠ *Agios Ioannis,* ☎ *0661/52552 or 0661/52438. AE, D, MC, V. No lunch.*

$$$ ✕ **Venetian Well.** On the most charming little square in the old town, with tables around a 17th-century well, this romantic restaurant—its staff tiptoes around lingering lovers—is as delicious as the food. The dining rooms in the handsome Venetian building are painted classic Greek blue, one with a satirical fresco painted by the owner's ex-wife. Greek and international specialties are served to operatic music. Creative entrées might include duck with kumquats or wild boar. ⊠ *Across from Church of the Panayia, Kremasti Sq.,* ☎ *0661/44761. Reservations essential. MC, V. Closed for lunch and Sun.*

$$ ✕ **Fish Taverna Roula.** This is the place for bream, snapper, sardines, and whatever is fresh that day; you can even come early in the morning—and should during high season—to choose from the catch. When the fish runs out, Roula stops serving. Sit on the balcony under the enormous, ancient olive tree, and watch the boats on the bay. Follow the signs to the Kondokali Bay hotel (☞ *below*) and continue on, keeping your eyes open for the sign to Roula's. ⊠ *Kondokali,* ☎ *0661/91832. Reservations essential. AE, V.*

$$ ✕ **Rex Restaurant.** "We have air-conditioning," the waiter says, pointing up to a huge fan turning languidly, at this friendly Greek taverna set within a 19th-century town house. Try the local specialties such as *sti-*

fado (meat stewed with sweet onions, white wine, garlic, cinnamon, and spices) or the *lachano dolmades* (cabbage leaves stuffed with seasoned ground meat and rice). The *stamna* (lamb baked with potatoes, rice, beans, and cheese) is delicious. Outside tables are perfect for people-watching. ⊠ *Kapodistriou 66, just west of Liston,* ☎ *0661/39649. AE, MC, V.*

$-$$ ✕ **Gerekos.** One of Corfu's most famous seafood tavernas, Gerekos is located 6 km (4 mi) from Corfu town in the village of Kondokali. Fresh seafood is always a treat here: try the bianco *me ladi* (cooked in olive oil, garlic, and pepper) or the bourdetto. Opt for a table on the lovely balcony set under the shade of a vine tree. ⊠ *Kondokali,* ☎ *0661/ 91281. Reservations essential for lunch. AE, V.*

$ ✕ **O Yiannis.** South of town, this popular restaurant is unpretentious and full of locals. It's also cheap: you'll be hard-pressed to tally up 5,000 dr./€14.74 on the barrel wine and wide variety of imaginative dishes, which you can check out in the kitchen. Try the stifado, the pork with Brussels sprouts, or the dolmades. For the bold, there's also *hordi* (intestines baked with a flavorful sauce). Order an ample supply of starters and *hima* (wine), and eat in good company, while checking out the ancient photos of Corfu's old-timers. ⊠ *Sophia Kremona and Iassonos-Sossipatrou 30, Anemomilos,* ☎ *0661/31066. Reservations not accepted. No credit cards. Closed Sun.*

$$$$ 🏨 **Corfu Imperial.** On a 14-acre peninsula jutting into Komeno Bay in an upscale residential area, 10 km (6 mi) north of town, this deluxe resort complex run by top Greek chain Grecotel has luxury rooms, bungalows, and villas that focus on comfortable elegance, with balconies and sea views. The seven suites, all different, have large living rooms and bathrooms with Jacuzzis, while the Presidential Suite offers a dining room and a dramatic view across the Adriatic coast to the shores of Albania. This is a "green" hotel, respectful of the environment. The extensive facilities are perfectly harmonious with the lush landscape of olive, palm, and cypress trees—the extensive and beautiful gardens here truly make this a "paradise on earth." ⊠ *Komeno Bay, 49100,* ☎ *0661/88400,* ☎ ℻ *0661/91481. 178 rooms, 7 suites, 120 bungalows, 4 villas. 2 Restaurants, snack bar, 3 bars, pool, beauty salon, 2 tennis courts, beach, waterskiing, boating, shops, baby-sitting, laundry service, conference rooms. AE, DC, MC, V. Closed Nov.–Apr.* ✍

$$$$ 🏨 **Corfu Palace.** Overlooking the bay, 100 yards from the center of town, this elegant hotel is one of the most beautiful in Greece, filled with old-world grandeur. The spacious rooms, furnished in Louis XIV and Empire style, have TVs and wide balconies with splendid views of gardens and water. The 1995 renovation and the decorating talents of Dominique Bennier added pizzazz and additional splendor. The marble bathrooms all have hair dryers and telephones, and attention has been paid to every detail. Guests can play tennis at the nearby Corfu Tennis Club and use the facilities of the Corfu Yacht Club (☞ Outdoor Activities and Sports, *below*). ⊠ *Leoforos Democratias 2, 49100,* ☎ *0661/39485, ℻ 0661/31749. 101 rooms, 11 suites. 2 restaurants, 2 bars, minibars, room service, outdoor saltwater pool, indoor saltwater pool, shops, baby sitting, meeting rooms, conference room. AE, DC, MC, V.* ✍

$$$ 🏨 **Cavalieri Hotel.** In this venerable, eight-story building near the ar-
★ cade of the Liston, get a room on the fourth or fifth floor with a number ending in 2, 3, or 4 for a breathtaking view of the Old Fort. The building is swank, yet graceful and chock-full of history—it was built in the 18th century and is a landmark of old Corfu. Have a drink at the usually empty, but delightful English-style wood-paneled bar. Best of all is the roof garden, which offers light meals and the most remarkable view in town. ⊠ *4 Kapodistriou, 49100,* ☎ *0661/39041, ℻ 0661/ 39283. 50 rooms. Restaurant, bar, minibars. AE, DC, MC, V.*

$$$ ⛶ **Kontokali Bay.** When you tire of exploring the streets and museums in town, this hotel about 6½ km (4 mi) north of town is a fine place to relax. The pastel guest rooms, with modern wood appointments, are cheerful and sunlit, with safes, minibars, and balconies facing the sea, the mountains, or the lake. There's a buffet and grill restaurant that serves Greek and Italian cuisine. ✉ *Kondokali Bay, 49100,* ☏ *0661/90500 through 0661/90509 or 0661/99000 through 0661/99002,* ℻ *0661/91901. 152 rooms, 82 bungalows. 3 restaurants, 2 bars, room service, pool, wading pool, 2 tennis courts, beach, dock, waterskiing, boating, dance club, children's program. AE, DC, MC, V. Closed Nov.–Mar.*

$$ ⛶ **Hotel Bella Venezia.** This two-story Venetian building in the center of town was operated as a hotel as early as the 1800s. Though it's in a lower classification—and price range—because it lacks views and a restaurant, its large lobby with a marble floor and wood-paneled ceiling and its huge garden make it quite pretty and grand. The rooms are small but tastefully furnished, and they have radios, telephones, and TVs. Breakfast is held on a patio. All in all, it's a good value for the money. It's just behind the Cavalieri Hotel (☞ *above*). ✉ *4 Zambelli, 49100,* ☏ *0661/20707 or 066/44290,* ℻ *0661/20708. 32 rooms. Lobby lounge, snack bar. AE, DC, MC, V.*

$ ⛶ **Hotel Konstantinoupoulis.** A hotel for more than 200 years, this can be most ambitiously called traditional. But rooms are reasonably clean and acceptable if you're on a budget. Long-distance phone calls can be made in the lobby, a rarity in low-cost hotels. It's opposite the dock for car ferries to the islands, with a great view of the old port. ✉ *Zavitsianou 11, Old Port, 49100,* ☏ *0661/48716.* ℻ *0661/48718. 31 rooms. Breakfast room. No credit cards.*

$ ⛶ **Ionian.** It's not glamorous but its ideal location makes up for its lack of stylistic grace. This budget hotel is comfortable and suitably located near the ferry boats and just a few minutes' walk from the Esplanade and center of the town. The front rooms can be a bit noisy (particularly in high season). ✉ *Xenofondos Strati 46, 49100,* ☏ *0661/39915,* ℻ *0661/44690. 80 rooms. No credit cards.*

Nightlife and the Arts

BAR

For sunset views with your ouzo and *mezedes* (appetizers), try the **Acteon Bar,** on the water just south of the Old Fort. For even better views, the rooftop bar at the Cavalieri Hotel (☞ Dining and Lodging, *above*) can't be bettered. **Bill's Bar** (✉ On the main drag of the Commercial Center) has a quiet scene, with a definite trend toward music from the '60s, slower dancing, and even a taste of blues.

DISCOS AND NIGHTCLUBS

Just past the Commercial Center, 3 km (2 mi) west of town is a string of **discos** that really don't start swinging until after midnight. They have names like **Sax, Slik, Electron, Bora Bora, Slaze, Astral, Rondo, Mobile Club, Interview, Hippodrome,** and **LA Boom,** and they throb with all the latest international sounds and styles, from heavy metal to rap, techno, and fusion. Incredibly loud sound systems are just what the young T-shirted crowd needs for dancing into the wee hours of the morning. A drink costs about 1,000 dr./€2.94, and most of the clubs charge 3,500 dr. to get in and for the first drink. Greek clubs come and go by the minute, so be sure to ask the concierge and locals for the current hot spots.

At **Ekati** (✉ Opposite the main junction) crowds are more sophisticated and older, but the volume of the live music is nevertheless high for the *skiladiko* (roughly, "dog party"). Chichi is the theme here, with excessive baubles and Paris collections; buy a whisky bottle for your table, carnations to throw at your favorite performer, and a plate or two to break if you're in the mood. Drinks cost 1,500 dr./€4.42 to 2,000 dr./€5.89. It's at the end of the disco strip.

FILM

Corfu town has an indoor cinema showing undubbed American flicks at the **Pallas** (✉ North of Platia San Rocco). Go to the **outdoor theater** (✉ Halfway down Marasli, seaside, on the right) on especially nice evenings.

MUSIC

Corfiots love music, from traditional bouzouki to classical. Corfu town has more than a dozen **small orchestras,** a **choir,** and a **chamber music group.** Sunday concerts are held at the bandstand on the Esplanade throughout the summer, and brass bands can often be heard throughout the town. For entertainment information in English, tune in to Radio Rama: 96.3 FM, Monday–Saturday 3–5.

Outdoor Activities and Sports

SAILING

The **Corfu Yacht Club** (✉ Corfu town, ☎ 0661/25759) offers sailing training courses.

TENNIS

The **Corfu Tennis Club** (✉ Between I. Romanou and Kalosgourou Sts., west of the Corfu Palace hotel), founded in 1896, is the oldest in Greece. You may rent courts and take lessons.

SOUTH OF CORFU TOWN

Just south of Corfu town, near the suburb of Kanoni, are several of Corfu's most unforgettable sights, including the lovely vista of Pontikonisi—famed throughout the world as Mouse Island—and Empress Elizabeth of Austria's Achilleion, an amazing extravaganza of a palace. The villages south of Benitses have become overrun with raucous package-tour groups and have lost much of their original charm. Unless you seek a hard-drinking, late-night crowd, and beaches chockablock with activities and tanning bodies, opt for other parts of the island.

Mon Repos

4 km (2½ mi) south of Corfu town.

20 Along the road to Kanoni is the **palace of Mon Repos** (✉ Near the public beach of Mon Repos), surrounded by gardens. It was built in 1824 by Sir Frederic Adam for his wife, and it was later the summer residence of the Lord High Commissioners. Prince Philip, Duke of Edinburgh, was born here. The villa, which belongs to the former King Constantine of Greece, was expropriated by the Greek government in 1990; the king has appealed. Though closed to the public, the extensive grounds are open from April to October. Opposite Mon Repos are ruins of Ayia Kerkyra, the 5th-century church of the Old City.

Analipsis

21 *4 km (2½ mi) south of Corfu town, just south of Mon Repos.*

The village of Analipsis was built on the site of an acropolis, and a path leads to a spring where the Venetians gathered drinking water for their ships.

En Route Along the road to Kanoni, you'll pass through gardens and parks to **22** the ruins of the archaic **Temple of Artemis** and past the **lagoon of Halikiopoulou** down to the tip of the peninsula.

Corfu

Avliotes

Sidari 35

Kavadades

Karoussades

Roda 34

Pelekito

Acharavi

Episkepsi

Mount
Pantokrator ▲

Kassiopi 33

Ayios
Stefanos

Makrades

Ano
Korakiana

Lakones 27 26

Skripero

Barbati

Kouloura 32

Kalami

Paleokastritsa

Liapades

Pirgi

Ipsos

Nissaki

24

Sgombou

Dassia

Gianades

Gouvia

Kondokali

Ermones 28 **Vatos**

29

Pelekas

Corfu Town
1 — 19

Ptihia

Myrtiotissa ■

31

Glyfada 30

Airport

Mon Repos 20

Analipsis 21

**Temple
of Artemis** 22

Kinopiastes

Perama

Kanoni 23

Pontikonisi 24

Sinarades

*Ayios Gordis
beach*

Gastouri

25

Achilleion ■

Pendati

Benitses

Strongili

Ayios Matheos

Moraitika

Mesonghi

Korissia

Hlomos

Boukari

*Ayios Georgios
beach*

Argirades

TO
IGOUMENITSA

Lefkimmi

Perivoli

Neohori

TO
PIRAEUS

Paleohori

Dragotina

Kavos

N

KEY

- - - Ferry

0   6 miles

0   9 km

Kanoni

㉓ *5½ km (3½ mi) south of Corfu town. 1½ km (1 mi) south of Analipsis.*

At Kanoni, the site of the ancient capital, you may behold Corfu's most picturesque view, which looks out over two lovely islets. A French cannon once stood in this hilly landscape, which is now built up and often noisy because of the nearby airport.

From Kanoni, against the backdrop of the green slopes of Mount Ayia Deka, is the serene view of two tiny islets: one, **Moni Viahernes,** is reached
㉔ by causeway. The other islet, **Pontikonisi,** famed throughout the world as Mouse Island, has a **white convent** and, beyond, tall cypresses guarding the **13th-century chapel.** Legend has it that the island is really Odysseus's ship, which Poseidon turned to stone here: the reason why Homer's much-traveled hero was shipwrecked on Phaeacia (Corfu) in the *Odyssey.* In summer you can take a little launch or pedal boat to visit it—or even swim there.

Lodging

$$$$ ⊞ **Corfu Holiday Palace.** Don't get this big and busy group-oriented hotel confused with its more elegant, almost-namesake, the Corfu Palace. A sleek and curving former Hilton, it has extensive facilities, including the island's only casino. Modern wood-paneled rooms offer panoramic views. The less-expensive "lake view" rooms in back look over the lagoon and the nearby airport. ⊠ *On beach at Kanoni, 49100,* ☎ *0661/36540,* FAX *0661/36551. 205 rooms, 14 suites, 37 bungalows. 2 restaurants, bar, snack bar, room service, 2 saltwater pools, sauna, 2 tennis courts, golf privileges, bowling, health club, beach, boating, casino, meeting rooms. AE, DC, MC, V.*

Gastouri

㉕ *19 km (11¾ mi) southwest of Corfu town, 23 km (14¼ mi) southwest of Kanoni.*

The village of Gastouri, still lovely despite the summer onrush of daytrippers, is the site of the palace **Achilleion,** in remarkably bad taste (Lawrence Durrell called it "a monstrous building"), but redeemed by lovely gardens stretching to the sea. Built in the late 19th century by the Italian architect Rafael Carita for Empress Elizabeth of Austria, it was a retreat for her to nurse her health and her heartbreak over husband Franz Josef's numerous affairs. Elizabeth named the palace after her favorite hero, Achilles, whom she identified with her son. After she was assassinated, Kaiser Wilhelm II bought it and lived here until the outbreak of World War I, after which he still used it as a summer residence. After the armistice, the Greek government received it as a spoil of war.

The interior contains a **pseudo-Byzantine chapel, a pseudo-Pompeian room,** and a **pseudo-Renaissance dining hall,** culminating in a vulgar fresco called *Achilles in His Chariot.* One of the more interesting furnishings, as bizarre as the rest of the building, is Kaiser Wilhelm II's saddle seat, used at his desk. On the terrace, which commands a superb view over Kanoni and the town, is an Ionic peristyle, with a number of statues, in various degrees of undress. The best is *The Dying Achilles.* In 1962 the palace was restored and leased as a gambling casino and was the setting for the casino scene in the James Bond film *For Your Eyes Only.* The casino has since moved to the Corfu Holiday Palace (☞ Kanoni, *above*). A **museum** on the ground floor of Achilleion contains mementos and portraits, and rooms are available for meetings. ⊠ *Past resort area of Perama on the Gastouri, Corfu highway,* ☎ *0661/ 56210.* ▣ *1,000 dr./€2.94* ⊙ *Summer 8–7, winter 9–4.*

Dining and Lodging

$$$$ ✕ **Taverna Tripas.** Surrounded by dusty wine bottles, hanging meats, and sundry stuffed birds and animals, you are in for an experience at this most famous restaurant on Corfu, 13 km (8 mi) up the mountains southwest of Corfu town. It has now become terribly tourist-ridden, though you might recognize important politicians or well-known artists. You'll get an impressive array of *mezedakia* (delicious tidbits), and do try the fine barrel retsina. Live music and traditional Greek dances add to the festivity. ⊠ *Kinopiastes,* ☎ *0661/56333. Reservations essential. No credit cards. No lunch.*

$$$$ ⊞ **San Stefano.** Close to the Achilleion Palace and 900 ft from the beach, this modern hotel commands a hill overlooking the water in 35 acres of garden. Rooms have balconies to savor the coastline vistas. Families will find lots to do here, with a children's program and nightly entertainment, and the facilities are extensive enough to host big-deal European conferences. ⊠ *Benitses 49084, 11 km (6½ mi) from Corfu town on the main road,* ☎ *0661/71113 through 0661/71117,* 𝔽𝔸𝕏 *0661/71124 or 0661/72272. 200 rooms, 20 suites, 39 bungalows. 2 restaurants, 3 bars, pool, 3 tennis courts, boating, waterskiing, children's program. AE, DC, MC, V. Closed Nov.–Mar.*

THE WEST COAST

The agricultural Ropa Valley divides the sandy beaches and freshwater lagoon of the lower west coast from the dramatic mountains of the northwest. Hairpin bends take you through orange and olive groves, over the mountainous spine of the island to the rugged bays and promontories of the northwest coast. Here the road descends to the sea, where two headlands, 130 ft high and covered with trees and boulders, form a pair of natural harbors. This is an especially fine area for outdoor recreation.

Paleokastritsa

㉖   *25 km (15½ mi) northwest of Corfu town, 21 km (13 mi) northwest of Kanoni.*

Identified by archaeologists as the site of Homer's city of the Phaeacians, this area of grottoes and cliffs has a big rock called Kolovri, resembling the mythological ship that brought Ulysses home. The natural beauty and water sports of Paleo, as Corfiots call it, have brought hotels, tavernas, bars, and shops to the hillsides above the bays, and the beaches swarm with hordes of people on day trips from Corfu town. But this spectacular spot of three large coves, rock formations, and turquoise waters is definitely worth a visit.

A **17th-century monastery** is set on the site of an earlier one, among terraced gardens overlooking the Ionian Sea. Its treasure is a 12th-century icon of the Virgin Mary, and there's a small **museum** with some other early icons. On the ceiling, note the Tree of Life motif. Be sure to visit the **inner courtyard** (go through the church), built on the edge of the cliff, dappled white, green, and black by the sunlight on the stonework, vine leaves, and habits of the hospitable monks. Under a roof of shading vines you look precipitously down to the placid green cove and the torn coastline stretching south. ⊠ *On northern headland.* ▦ *Free, but donation expected.* ☉ *Daily 7–1 and 3–8.*

㉗   The village of **Lakones** (⊠ 5 km [3 mi] northeast of Paleokastritsa) is on the steep mountain behind the monastery. Crested by the grim **ruins of Angelokastro,** it was built in the 13th century on an inaccessible pinnacle by a despot of Epirus during his brief rule over Corfu.

It sheltered Corfiots in 1571 from attack by Turkish wanna-be conquerors. Look for the chapel and caves, which served as sanctuaries for hermits. The road to this spot was reputedly built by British troops in part to reach Lady Adam's favorite picnic place, the Bella Vista terrace. Kaiser Wilhelm also came here to enjoy the magnificent view of Paleokastritsa's coves.

NEED A   Though it may be crowded, having a drink and savoring the view at the
BREAK?   **Bella Vista Café** (⊠ On a bluff) is worth the wait.

Dining and Lodging

$$ ✕ **Chez George.** Overlooking the rock of the bay in Paleokastritsa, where Homer's wine-dark sea touches forest-green mountains, the view here is one of those Greek keys that explain all. As for the food, the pork chops are delicious and the *horiatiko* (village salad) is a tasty mix of carrot and onion with the hackneyed tomato, cucumber, feta, and olive combo. Some relevant thoughts: order simply, don't buy the wine, and remember that moderate prices seldom go with gorgeous vistas. ⊠ *The rock, Paleokastritsa,* ☎ *0663/41233. AE, MC, V. Closed Nov.–Mar.*

$$$ ▥ **Akrotiri Beach Hotel.** Newly renovated and looking sparkling, this modern, five-story resort sits on a private little peninsula, and balconies in the stylish, well-equipped rooms overlook dreamy views of grottoes and turquoise water. This place is great for families, and for nature-lovers who desire the comforts of room service and minibars as well. ⊠ *Paleokastritsa 49083,* ☎ *0663/41237,* ℻ *0663/41277. 127 rooms. 2 restaurants, 2 bars, pool, tennis court, boating, snorkeling, mountain bikes, shops. AE, MC, V. Closed Nov.–Apr.*

$$ ▥ **Fundana Villas.** On a hilltop in the mountains west of Corfu town, surrounded by gardens and olive and orange groves, this special complex comprises 10 villas built in and around a 17th-century stone-and-mortar Venetian storehouse, with walls almost a yard thick. The common room–bar still contains the huge olive press and an old stone mill. You can really imagine life hundreds of years ago and at the same time enjoy modern baths and kitchens. It's unique, and an ideal place for families interested in biking, exploring, and discovering history. The villas are a short drive from the Paleokastritsa beaches; you will need your own transportation. ⊠ *Spyros Spathas, Box 167, 49083,* ☎ *0663/22532,* ℻ *0663/22453. 10 villas. Snack bar, 2 pools, tennis court, video games, playground. No credit cards. Closed Nov.–Mar.*

Outdoor Activities and Sports

DIVING
The clear water is wonderful for underwater adventure, but it can get crowded in the shallows. Diving lessons and equipment are available at the **Barracuda Club** (⊠ On the water in Paleokastritsa, ☎ 0663/41211).

Ermones

28 *16 km (10 mi) west of Corfu town, 6 km (4 mi) south of Paleokastritsa.*

South of Paleokastritsa, across the fertile Ropa Valley, is the resort of Ermones, with good, pebbly sand beaches, heavily wooded cliffs, water with plentiful fish, large hotels, and a backdrop of green mountains. The Ropa River flows into the Ionian Sea here.

Beach

The little sheltered **beach at Kondo Yialo** (⊠ Just south of Ermones) is especially beautiful.

Outdoor Activities and Sports
GOLF

The island's only golf course is here, at the **Corfu Golf Club** (⊠ Ermones, ☎ 0661/94220), linked to the beach by an elevator. Look forward to a par-72, 18-hole course, with water hazards, well-kept fairways, rentals, lessons, a pro shop, and a clubhouse with a restaurant and bar. It's open to the public, and reservations can be booked through hotels.

Vatos

㉙ *24 km (15 mi) west of Corfu town, 2 km (1 mi) west of Ermones.*

Vatos is an inland agricultural village, clinging to a hill and to the simplicity of the past. Its considerable charms can be discovered by sitting at one of the couple of tavernas with the locals and just observing details and everyday goings-on. Let your eyes roam and you might find balconies filled with pansies in terra-cotta pots, whitewashed cottages and rocky walls, farmers tilling fields in the cool of the evening, boys throwing olives into black nets, a skinny dog chasing an even skinnier cat, men playing cards and laughing, women all in black sitting on stoops, gossiping. This is the real world, far from the sophistication of Corfu town, but in its way just as special.

Glyfada

㉚ *16 km (10 mi) west of Corfu town, 6 km (4 mi) south of Ermones.*

The large, sandy Glyfada beach is packed with busloads of bathers and sun worshipers on day trips from Corfu town. The area is filled with hotels, condos, tavernas, and discos.

In the village of Sinarades on the west coast, there's a **folk art museum** (⊠ Sinarades, ☎ 0661/35673) exhibiting a private collection of local costumes, embroidery, furniture, and pottery. It's open Tuesday to Sunday 9:30 to 12:30.

Lodging

$$$ ☷ **Louis Grand Hotel Glyfada.** Two patios with Japanese gardens redeem this otherwise overdone, quasi-Asian setting. The guest rooms are basic, and air-conditioning operates at the manager's whim. Buffets spotlight Greek specialties; the bar is done in a Viennese theme, a nod to the hotel's Germanic package tours. There's a children's program and a game room. The social staff keeps things jumping in summer, running courtesy cars to town and the golf course. The hotel is at the biggest, sunniest beach on the island. ⊠ *Glyfada 49100,* ☎ *0661/94140 through 0661/94145,* 𝔽𝔸𝕏 *0661/94146. 242 rooms. 3 restaurants, 2 bars, pool, tennis court, boating, waterskiing, nightclub, children's programs. AE, D, MC, V. Closed Nov.–Mar.* ✎

Pelekas

㉛ *13 km (8 mi) west of Corfu town, 2 km (1 mi) north of Glyfada.*

Just inland from Glyfada is Pelekas, a hilltop village that overfills with tourists because of its much-touted lookout point called the **Kaiser's Throne,** where German kaiser Wilhelm II enjoyed the sunset when not relaxing at the Achilleion Palace. This rocky hilltop does deliver spectacular views of the entire island and sea beyond.

A 14th-century monastery on the west coast is the **Myrtiotissa** (⊠ Below Mt. Ayios Georgios), 3 km (2 mi) or a one-hour walk north of Pelekas, and a half-hour walk (2 km) south of Vatos.

Beaches

The long, sandy **beach at Pelekas** is well known and popular with nudists. The isolated **beach at Myrtiotissa,** between sheer cliffs, is noted for its good snorkeling and nude sunbathing. Backed by olive and cypress trees, this sandy stretch was called by Lawrence Durrell in *Prospero's Cell* (with debatable overenthusiasm) "perhaps the loveliest beach in the world." Alas, the statement has brought summer crowds.

Dining and Lodging

$$ ✕ **The Nornberg.** Everybody in the area knows this restaurant as Mihali's in Livadi Ropa, about a mountainous 13 km (8 mi) west of Corfu town. It's a *psistaria* (grill taverna), and it's one of the best. First savor fried eggplant, *tzatziki* (yogurt, chopped cucumber, and garlic), fresh salad, and feta. Mihali Moumouris bastes the best local meat—maybe *paidakia* (lamb chops) or pork chops—with lemon juice and local olive oil, sprinkles it with salt and fresh oregano, and grills it over charcoal. And don't forget to order some of his homemade retsina. ✉ *Livadi Ropa,* ☎ *0661/51473. No credit cards.*

$$$$ 🏨 **Pelekas Country Club.** The old family mansion of Nikos Vellinaties, nestled amidst 200 acres of olive and cypress trees, became the kernel for this idyllic holiday retreat. Seven impeccably furnished bungalows and four state-of-the-art suites provide exclusive hospitality—all accommodations vary in size, are decorated with antiques and family heirlooms from England and Russia, and have large verandas overlooking the gardens (we award the prizes to the Olive Press House and the François Mitterand Suite). The grounds have their own private stable; guests can bring their horses and combine relaxation with riding. Breakfast is the first treat of the day, complete with fresh-squeezed fruit juices and homemade jams. ✉ *On Kerkyra Pelekas road, 49100,* ☎ *0661/52239 or 0661/52917,* 𝔽𝔸𝕏 *0661/52919. 7 bungalows, 4 suites. Bar, pool, tennis court, horseback riding. No credit cards.* ✎

$$–$$$ 🏨 **Levant.** Built just under Kaiser Wilhelm II's favorite lookout point, this hotel has breathtaking views (and sunsets) over the Adriatic Sea and across silver-green olive groves. Styled in the neoclassical manner, the Levant retains a touch of the romance of the traditional Corfiot style, particularly the charming and comfortable guest rooms, which come with small balconies. Start off your day with a soul-warming breakfast served on the main terrace. ✉ *Pelekas, 49100,* ☎ *0661/94230 or 0661/94335,* 𝔽𝔸𝕏 *0661/94115. 25 rooms. Restaurant, bar, pool, conference room. MC, V.* ✎

NORTH OF CORFU TOWN

The main roads along the northeast coast just above Corfu town are crowded with hotels, gas stations, and tourist cafés and shops. But head inland a bit and you'll find more peaceful settings—dusty villages where olives, herbs, and home-brewed wine are the main products, with goats roaming the squares and chickens pecking at the roadsides. Steep Mt. Pantokrator (The Almighty), at 2,970 ft the highest peak on Corfu, forms the northeast lobe of the island. The northern coastal area is replete with pretty coves, and it has the longest sand beach in Corfu, curving around Roda to Archaravi.

Kouloura

㉜ *31 km (19¼ mi) northeast of Corfu town.*

This pretty harbor town is on a U-shape bay enclosed by cypress, eucalyptus, and palm trees and has a small shingle beach with close views of the Albanian coastline. This is the part of Corfu immortalized by the Durrell brothers—much of Gerald Durrell's writing of *Prospero's Cell* was done in a taverna called the **White House** (✉ In Kalami). Donkeys still plod the roads, cafés serve local wine, and life here on the lower slopes of Mt. Pantokrator holds its sweet charm, even when besieged by tourists in July and August.

Dining and Lodging

$$$ ✕ **Etrusco.** Just past the town of Dassia, turn inland and follow the signs
★ for Kato Korakiana—this small village is proud home of Etrusco, Corfu's best restaurant. Run by the Botrini family, opened in 1992, and set in a traditional Corfiot mansion (and away from all the crowds), it offers memorable dinners in a romantic courtyard. Chef Etrusco Botrini will delight you with fresh, homemade pasta dishes like farfalle pasta with porcini mushrooms and shrimp. The showstoppers include the medallions of fish cooked in Triple Sec and sesame seeds or the fillet of grouper with champagne and vegetables. For starters there is an extraordinary array of dried meats (most cured at home) and marinated fish—particularly delicious is the marinated salmon in aromatic oil and poppy seed. The wine list, though not extensive, has been compiled with care and love, not surprisingly. ✉ *Just outside village of Kato Korakiana,* ☎ *0661/93342. Reservations essential. D, MC, V. No lunch.*

$ ✕ **Karidia.** If you're out for simple, hearty Corfiot fare, you can't miss with the *katsikaki sti gastra* (lamb or kid goat cooked in clay pots) offered here. This is a place to come if you are tired of the rich and heavy sauces of typical Greek food; grilled meats are cooked with care over charcoal and are especially delicious accompanied by a refreshingly cold salad. ✉ *Dassia,* ☎ *0661/93432. AE, MC, V. Closed Nov.–Mar. No lunch.*

$$$ 🏨 **Corfu Chandris and Dassia Chandris Hotels.** This huge two-hotel complex is set in 25 acres of gardens, with private chalets and bungalows for groups. The public areas feature scads of marble; the modern guest rooms are comfortable and basic, with large sea-view balconies, radios, and telephones. These two hotels are 11 km (7 mi) north of Corfu town and about the same distance south of Kouloura in an overbuilt stretch of roadway. A renovation, which began in 1996 and was completed in 1998, gave this hotel an entirely new, contemporary, and modern look, with spacious rooms and comfortable lounge areas. The best choice of accommodations is the studio apartments with living rooms and small built-in kitchen areas. ✉ *Dassia 49100,* ☎ *0661/97100 through 0661/97104; 01/941–4824 Athens Chandris Hotel (Dec.–Feb.),* ℻ *0661/93458. 526 rooms. 2 restaurants, 6 bars, lobby lounge, room service, 2 pools, wading pool, hair salon, 3 tennis courts, golf privileges, beach, boating, parasailing, waterskiing, shops, playground, meeting rooms. AE, DC, MC, V. Closed Nov.–Mar.* 🐢

$$$ 🏨 **Daphnila Bay.** Yet another dazzling hotel of the Grecotel chain, the Daphnila Bay is ideally located in the midst of an olive grove and surrounded by verdant pines which sweep down to the edge of a beach. The 1999 renovations thoroughly modernized the building and grounds and added yet another attribute: the Elixir Thalasso Spa, an impressive health spa that specializes in thalassotherapy and aromatherapy. The public lounges are an elegant mix of sophisticated high-tech design with traditional elements. Guest rooms are large and brightly decorated with spacious balconies. Like all Grecotel hotels it is child friendly with an extensive array of activities for guests of all ages. ✉ *2 km (1½ mi) before Dassia, 49100,* ☎ *0661/91520,* ℻ *0661/91026. 126 rooms, 134 bungalows, 2 suites. 3 restaurants, bar, indoor pool, outdoor pool, spa, tennis court, health club, water sports, beach, babysitting. AE, D, MC, V. Closed Nov.–Mar.* 🐢

Kassiopi

③ *36 km (22½ mi) northeast of Corfu town, 7 km (4½ mi) north of Kouloura.*

Kassiopi, north around the mountain, occupies a promontory between two bays, where the wind blows hard during late summer. It was an important town during Roman times, with a shrine to Zeus that Nero and other emperors visited; Tiberius had a villa here. A **church** with a 17th-century icon and frescoes now occupies what was probably the site of Zeus's shrine, on the western side of the harbor.

During the Byzantine era this area rivaled Corfu town. But the town declined when Kassiopi's fortress, built by the Angevins, was destroyed by the Venetians. Now the fishing village has discovered the tourist trade and has become a busy resort; its harbor is lined with tavernas, shops, and bars catering to charter groups.

Dining and Lodging

$$ ✕ **Tria Adelphia.** A view of the pretty fishing harbor framed by a cypress-covered hill is a big bonus at this authentic restaurant, where the menu depends on the day's catch by fishermen (you can even watch them hauling in their nets from here). Grab an outdoor table; order a glass of local wine; stick to seafood, the Greek classics, or the owner's recommendations; and you won't go wrong. ⊠ *On the harbor,* ☎ *0663/ 91136. MC, V. Closed Nov.–Mar.*

$$ 🏨 **Apraos Bay Hotel.** On the northern tip of the island sits this small, Venetian-style hotel. Rooms are fresh and airy with light-filled balconies. It's 40 yards from a private beach, with a fantastic view of the sea and the Albanian coast: a perfect place to relax in a friendly atmosphere, far from noise. Though it's almost completely isolated, just 2 km (1 mi) away in the village of Kassiopi is all the action anyone could want; it's about 32 km (20 mi) from Corfu town. ⊠ *Apraos, 49100,* ☎ *0663/ 98004 or 0663/98137,* 𝔽𝔸𝕏 *0663/98331. 16 rooms. Restaurant, piano bar, beach. V. Closed Dec.–Feb.* ♨

Roda

③ *37 km (23 mi) north of Corfu town, 8 km (5 mi) northwest of Kassiopi.*

On the north coast, Roda, a growing resort community, has pebble beaches and plenty of tourists, and though some spots farther west are less crowded, the roads to them are not as passable. Its narrow beach, which adjoins the beach at tiny Archaravi, has especially calm and shallow waters and a campsite, so it's popular with local families. The **remains of a 5th-century Doric temple** have been found here.

Sidari

③ *36 km (22½ mi) north of Corfu town, 4 km (2½ mi) west of Roda.*

Sidari has archaeological remains dating back to 7000 BC but today is heavily touristed with families splashing in its calm waters. Just to the west, unique striated cliffs are constantly being eroded into tunnels and caves, notably the "tunnel of love." Think carefully: legend has it that if you take a boat through this narrow channel, you will be able to marry whoever was in your thoughts at the time. A competing legend says that couples swimming through it will stay together forever; perhaps that is why this area is less crowded than nearby swimming areas.

CORFU A TO Z

Arriving and Departing

By Boat

Passenger ships stop at Corfu about twice a week, April to October, but schedules change frequently, so always check ahead. **Minoan Lines** (⊠ Piraeus, ☎ 01/619–7842 through 01/619–7844) runs the *Festos,* which connects Corfu with Ancona, Igoumenitsa, Heraklion, and Piraeus. The *Ariadne* connects Corfu with Kusadasi (Turkey), Samos, Paros, Kephallonia, and Ancona.

Ferries from Igoumenitsa on the mainland leave every hour in summer and every two hours off-season, landing in Corfu town (two hours) and in Lefkimmi, at the southern tip of Corfu (45 minutes).

By Bus

KTEL Corfu buses (☎ 0661/39862) leave Athens (☎ 01/513–6185) three or four times a day. The trip, via Patras and the ferry from Igoumenitsa, takes about nine hours. The fare is approximately 8,400 dr./€24.77 each way.

By Car

The best route from Athens is the National Road via Corinth to the Rion–Antirion ferry, then to Igoumenitsa (472 km [274 mi]), where you take the ferry to Corfu. In winter, severe weather conditions often close the straits at Rion–Antirion, and the ferries from Igoumenitsa can also stop running. Call the **Touring Club of Greece** (☎ 104) for information.

By Plane

Olympic Airways (☎ 0661/38694, 0661/38695, 0661/49484, or 0661/49485) has three flights a day from Athens that land at Corfu's airport (⊠ Northwest of Kanoni, a few miles south of Corfu town). For a round-trip, the fare is 34,600 dr./€102.06 each way; the one-way fare is 17,300 dr./€51.

Getting Around

By Bus

Bus travel on Corfu is inexpensive, and the bus network covers the island. Buses tend to run fairly close to their schedules, and you can get timetables and information at the depots of the two bus companies and at many other places. Publications such as *Mythos Guide to Corfu,* the *Corfiot,* and the *Corfu Sun* all give good information.

The **Spilia** (⊠ Avramiou St., ☎ 0661/30627) bus company's terminal is at the New Port. Buses also run from the **San Rocco** (⊠ San Rocco Sq., ☎ 0661/31595) bus company's depot.

By Motorbike and Car

The gentle climate and rolling hills make Corfu ideal motorbike country, but you should drive very slowly until you feel comfortable. There is little or no system to Greek driving, and "depend on the other guy's brakes" best expounds the basic philosophy of many drivers. The road surfaces deteriorate as the tourist season progresses, and potholes abound. Helmets are rarely provided, and then only on request. Check the lights, brakes, and other mechanics before you accept a machine. Be warned and be careful.

By Taxi

Radio-controlled **taxis** (☎ 0661/33811) are available 24 hours a day, and rates, which are set by the government, are reasonable—when adhered to. Many drivers speak English and they know the island in a very special way. If you want to hire a cab and driver on an hourly or daily basis, you must negotiate the fee; ask for advice at your hotel's front desk. Always check the prices before you travel.

Contacts and Resources

Car and Motorbike Rental

A 50cc motorbike can be rented for about 4,000 dr./€11.79 a day (100cc for 6,000 dr./€17.69), but you can bargain, especially if you want it for two or more days. Rentals are available in even the most remote villages. In Corfu town, try **George's Bikes** (⊠ El. Venizelou 38, ☎ 0661/32727).

Car rental can be considerably more expensive, starting at about 10,000 dr./€29.49 a day for a Fiat 127 (100 km minimum) plus insurance, delivery, and so forth. A four-wheel-drive Jeep, with the extras, can run to 25,000 dr./€73.74 a day. In Corfu town you can try **Olympus Rent-a-Car** (⊠ 29 National Stadium, ☎ 0661/36147). Also in Corfu, try **Suncars, Ginargirou Brothers Ltd.** (⊠ 40 Alexandras, ☎ 0661/31565).

Emergencies

Police (⊠ Alexandras 19, ☎ 100).

Medical: hospital (⊠ Polychroniou Kostanda, ☎ 0661/88200).

Guided Tours

Many agencies run half-day tours of Old Corfu town, and tour buses go daily to all the sights on the island. Tickets and information are available at travel agencies all over town. **Vaba Travel** (⊠ Ethnikis Antistaseos, New Port, ☎ 0661/44455, FAX 0661/22174) is reliable.

The main tour operator to Albania is **Petrakis Shipping Company** (⊠ Eleftheriou Venizelou 9, next to the Old Port, ☎ 0661/31649). The cost is around 7,000 dr./€20.64, plus a small additional charge to cover port taxes and an entry permit to Albania.

Visitor Information

Greek National Tourist Organization (GNTO or EOT; ⊠ 15 Zavitsianou, ☎ 0661/37520, 0661/37638, or 0661/37630, FAX 0661/30298).

Tourist Police (⊠ Kapodistriou 1, ☎ 0661/30265).

8 NORTHERN PELOPONNESE

NAFPLION, PATRAS, AND OLYMPIA

The gods of ancient Greece blessed the
Northern Peloponnese with natural beauty
and the mysteries of forgotten civilizations.
The ruined city of Mycenae, with giant tombs
to the heroes of Homer's *Iliad,* stands sentinel
over the Argive plain, where warriors once
assembled en route to Troy. In the rolling hills
of Elis, Olympia plays host to the scattered
remains of the ancient Olympic Games. And
Nafplion, its ancient Greek, Venetian, and
Turkish edifices jutting into the Bay of Argos,
is, to the Greeks, the embodiment of beauty.

By Mark J.
Rose and Toula
Bogdanos

Updated by
B. Samantha
Stenzel

ANGING LIKE A LARGE LEAF from the stem of the Corinthian isthmus, the Peloponnese had also been called Morea in the Middle Ages, which means mulberry leaf—because of the proliferation of mulberry trees in the area, grown to feed the silk worms raised to make the gauzy fabric used in the delicate folk costumes, not because its shape looks like the actual mulberry leaf. This slight botanical variance is nothing compared to the astounding variety of imposing ruins, situated in equally varied and beautiful scenery—massive mountains covered with low evergreen oak and pines surround coastal valleys and loom above rocky shores and sandy beaches. Over the millennia this rugged terrain nourished kingdoms and empires and witnessed the birth of modern Greece. Traces of these lost realms—ruined Bronze Age citadels, Greek and Roman temples and theaters, and the fortresses and settlements of the Byzantines, Franks, Venetians, and Turks—attest to the richness of the land. No wonder visitors who spend less than a week here usually wind up asking themselves why they didn't allot more time to this fascinating area of Greece.

Named for Pelops, son of the mythical Tantalos, whose intolerantly tragic descendants dominate the half-legendary Mycenaean centuries, the Northern Peloponnese comprises the Argive peninsula, jutting into the Aegean, and runs westward past the isthmus and along the Gulf of Corinth to Patras and the Adriatic coast. It is divided into seven nomes: Argolis (east), Corinthia (northeast), Achaea (northwest), Elis (northwest), Messenia (southwest), Laconia (southeast), and Arcadia (north center). The oldest region is the fertile Argive plain (Argolis), the heart of Greece in the late Bronze Age and the home of the heroes of Homer's *Iliad*. A walk through the Lion Gate to Mycenae, the citadel of Agamemnon, brings the Homeric epic to life, and the massive walls of nearby Tiryns glorify the age of might. The thriving market town of Argos, the successor to Mycenae and Tiryns, engaged in a long rivalry with Sparta, generally gets the short end of the stick. Corinth, the economic superpower of the 7th and 6th centuries BC, dominated trade and established colonies abroad. Although eclipsed by Athens, Corinth earned a reputation for ostentatious wealth and loose living. Today, modern Corinth is a bustling, if unremarkable, regional center. Not far from Corinth is Epidauros, the sanctuary of Asklepios, god of healing, where in summer Greek dramas are re-created in the ancient theater, one of the finest and most complete to survive. The main site lies far to the west: Olympia, the sanctuary of Zeus and site of that famous contest the Peloponnese gave mankind, the Olympic games.

Four thousand years of history are more fully and comprehensively illustrated in the Peloponnese than nearly anywhere else in Europe. A gap of a hundred years in the stately cavalcade of temples, palaces, churches, Crusader castles, and mosques is a rare exception (and is generally due to catastrophic barbarian invasions). By the 13th century, the armies of the Fourth Crusade (in part egged on by Venice) had conquered the Peloponnese after capturing Constantinople in 1204. But the dominion of the Franks was brief, and Byzantine authority was restored under the Palaiologos dynasty. Soon after Constantinople fell in 1453, the Turks, taking advantage of an internal rivalry, crushed the Palaiologoi and helped themselves to the Peloponnese. In the following centuries the struggle between the Venetians and the Ottoman Turks was played out in Greece. The two states alternately dominated the Northern Peloponnese until the Ottomans ultimately prevailed; as Venetian power declined in the early 1700s. The Turkish mosques and fountains and the Venetian fortifications of Nafplion recall this epic struggle. The Peloponnese played a key role in the Greek War of Independence, and after the Turks withdrew in 1828, from 1829 to 1834, Nafplion was the capital of Greece (after which it was moved to Athens). An insurrection of the garrison at Nafplion helped to bring about the abdication of King Otto in 1862, while in 1874, Heinrich Schliemann, the enigmatic amateur archaeologist, began his excavations of Mycenae, which led to the discovery of the Acropolis and the Treasury of Atreus.

Besides this illustrious historical heritage, the Peloponnese is the heart of modern Greece, having the largest population and area of any the regions. Interestingly, a large portion of Greece's emigrants to the United States in the 20th century (12%–25% of the male population) have roots in the Peloponnese (their family names are often identified with an ending in *poulos,* meaning "son of"); almost all dreamed of returning back to their Greek villages when they had raised their families and had accumulated a sufficient *ekonomies* (nest egg) that would allow them to retire. Quite a number of them have done just that, so if you find yourself unable to convey what you need through a combination of phrase-book Greek and body language in one of the remote villages here, no doubt an elderly *Helleno-Americanos* (Greek-American) will be called upon to assist. Delightfully, this often leads to an invitation to join a group of locals at the corner *kafenion* (traditional coffeehouse) for an ouzo or barreled wine and some *mezedes* (appetizers). Time seems to have stood still in the smaller towns here. The joy of exploring this region comes as much from the languid afternoons and evenings of lively question-and-answer sessions (Greeks have an insatiable curiosity about everything, *especially* foreign guests), always broken up frequently by laughter from town jokesters, as it does from seeing the impressive ruins.

Patras, in Achaea on the far northwest of the Peloponnese, remains the largest city of the Peloponnese (it's the third largest in Greece) and has long been known for its wine and festive pre-Lent Carnival season. It's the modern hub of business and trade, and renewed municipal pride has spurred many structural improvements in recent years. Capitalizing on the increased interest in Olympia due to the 2004 Olympic Games to be held in Athens, the business community has launched a campaign to promote Patras as a destination in itself and a base for exploration of the western Peloponnese, rather than just a one-night stop for visitors who have arrived by train or ferry boat.

While modern concrete-block buildings now deface most of the larger Peloponnese towns, Nafplion has maintained its traditional architectural heritage, which is largely inspired by Venetian, Ottoman, and German neoclassical trends. Travelers also head to holiday resorts such as Porto Heli and Tolo in the east and Killini in the west, attracted by sand and sea. But knowing visitors venture to this region for far more than suntans. After all, the "cyclopean" walls at Tiryns, the Lion Gate and beehive tombs at Mycenae, the theater in Epidauros, and the world-famous sculptures at Olympia are just some of the once-in-a-lifetime wonders to be seen and relished here.

Pleasures and Pastimes

Beaches

The beaches along the western coast of the Peloponnese are considered to be some of the best in Greece and are generally less crowded than those in other areas. Excellent stretches near Kastro, under Chlemoutsi castle, include Katakolo and Spiantza. Closer to Patras is Kalo-gria, a 6-km (4-mi) stretch of sand bordered by pine forests. Along the Gulf of Corinth are some beaches with spectacular views of the opposite shore, but some are of pebbles rather than sand. Xylokastro, near Corinth, starts out pebbly, but farther from town becomes sandy. The popular areas are well equipped for water sports: pedal boats can be hired, and you can arrange windsurfing lessons at small "beach-bum" operations at many beaches, such as Tolo. In some resorts, such as Porto Heli, waterskiing and jet-skiing are popular diversions.

Dining

One of the simplest pleasures of Greece is enjoying a late dinner of traditional food with good Greek wine, preferably *varelisio* (from the barrel). In the small towns here, any restaurant that pretends to offer more than this should be viewed with suspicion. Dress is always casual and reservations unnecessary, although you might be asked to sit on the side and have a drink while you wait for a table, if you're dining with the majority at 10 PM or later. Keep freshness and the season in mind; if you order fish, follow the lead of the Greeks and have a look at it before it's cooked. The gills should be pink, on most fish the eyes should be clear and the scales firm and well attached. There's no reason to eat something that has been frozen, although that's a better alternative than eating fish or seafood that has been kept too long. Grape leaves are best early in the season, no later than early July, when they're young and tender. Otherwise they may be slightly tough, or the pickled version will be substituted. Do as the Greeks do: ask to visit the kitchen—any chef worth his salt will tell you what's good and what's left over from lunch and you can just point to what you want to order.

Greek vintners, faced with EU competition, are producing better wines than ever before. Look for red wines from the region around Nemea, between Corinth and Argos. Be sure to try Patras's sweet *mavro-daphne* (a heavy dessert wine, literally "black Daphne"), so called because after the death of Daphne, Baron von Clauss's object of desire, he took his darkest grapes and made the sweet wine in her honor. Another favorite in Patras is *dendoura,* a clove liqueur served after dinner as a digestive.

CATEGORY	COST*
$$$$	over 9,000 dr. (€26.54)
$$$	5,000 dr.–9,000 dr. (€14.74–€26.54)
$$	3,000 dr.–5,000 dr. (€8.84–€14.74)
$	under 3,000 dr. (€8.84)

for a three-course meal, including tax, service, and usually beer or a small carafe of wine

Hiking and Climbing

The mountainous terrain of the Northern Peloponnese is an ideal habitat for hikers and climbers. The **Greek Federation of Mountaineering Associations** in Athens operates several huts in the Peloponnese that are open to the public (☞ Contacts and Resources *in* Northern Peloponnese A to Z, *below*).

Lodging

Visitors accustomed to traveling in the United States and Europe should not expect to find such amenities as color televisions, much less VCRs, everywhere they go. Hotels in the $$$$ and $$$ categories have air-conditioning unless noted; it is only specified when it exists in hotels of $$ and $ rank. Breakfast is not included in the price unless noted.

CATEGORY	COST*
$$$$	over 45,000 dr. (€132)
$$$	25,000 dr.–45,000 dr. (€73.74–€132)
$$	15,000 dr.–25,000 dr. (€44.24–€73.74)
$	under 15,000 dr. (€44.24)

*All prices are for a standard double room in high season, including tax and service.

🐾 following the text of a review is your signal that the property has a Web site, where you will find details and, usually, images; for a link, visit www.fodors.com/urls.

Shopping

Olympia has many shops specializing in big-ticket gold jewelry—some very nice, some very gaudy. Nafplion has an excellent selection of stores selling high-quality gold jewelry, especially around Constitution Square and on Staikopoulou Street. Patras is the best bet for fashion, especially downtown around Korinthos and Maizonos streets. Look for folk crafts in the smaller villages—with a bit of poking around, you can find outstanding examples of strikingly colored old weavings, especially *tagaria* (shepherd's bags), which command a higher price than the newer versions. They make wonderful wall hangings. If you are traveling by car, be on the lookout for roadside stands selling the wonderful peaches and apricots—perfectly ripe and far superior to grocery-store fruit.

Exploring the Northern Peloponnese

The Northern Peloponnese comprises several distinct geographical areas: on the eastern side is the Argolid plain and the Corinthiad, where we find Mycenae, Tiryns, Epidauros, and Nafplion; and on the western side, the provinces of Achaea and Elis, home of ancient Olympia and the bustling port city of Patras. We describe each of these regions in separate sections, below.

Numbers in the text correspond to numbers in the margin and on the Northern Peloponnese, Nafplion, Tiryns, Mycenae, and Ancient Olympia maps.

Great Itineraries

The eastern and western portions of the Northern Peloponnese are easily divided into two separate three- to four-day itineraries; a thorough exploration of both requires about eight or nine days. Those with less time should consider investigating either the eastern or western half only; for travelers entering Greece from Italy, Patras and Olympia are a must, and for those entering Greece through Athens, Nafplion and the Argolid are only a short hop away.

IF YOU HAVE 2 OR 3 DAYS

The wealth of interesting sites on either side of the Northern Peloponnese will keep the intrepid occupied for at least three days, but if your schedule allows for only two, consider a day trip to lovely ⛯ **Nafplion** ⑤– ⑳ followed by a day spent exploring some of the highlights of the Argolid—**Mycenae** ㉜–㉝ and **Tiryns** ㉑, for example. A third day near Nafplion will allow a visit to the theater at **Epidauros** ② and perhaps the beaches at **Tolo** ④ or **Porto Heli** ③. For those entering Greece from Italy and with only a couple of days to spare, try spending a day in and around ⛯ **Patras** ㊵ followed by a day trip to ⛯ **Olympia** ㊷–㊾. An extra day on the western side of the Northern Peloponnese could be spent either enjoying a train ride along the picturesque **Vouraikos Gorge** ㊲ en route to **Kalavrita** ㊳ or clambering over the parapets of the Frankish **Chlemoutsi Castle** ㊶.

Northern Peloponnese

TO ATHENS

Elefsis

Thebes

Salamina

Megara
E94

Saronic
Gulf

Aegina

Methana

Poros

Galatas

Hydra

Perahora

Loutraki

Isthmia

Kenchreai **1**

70

Ligourio

Epidauros **2**

Trahia

ARGOLID

Didima

Ermioni

Kranidi

Porto Heli **3**

Corinth

Corinth
Canal

70

Assini

Drepano

Gulf
of
Argolis

Xylokastro

Corinth

35

Mycenae **23–33**

Tyrins

Tolo **4**

Kiato

Ancient Corinth **34**

E93

23

22

21

Argos

Lerna

Ayios
Andreas

Gulf of Corinth

36

Galatas

Ancient Nemea

Myloi

Nafplion **5–20**

Ilea

Aigeira

E65

Trikala

CORINTHIA

Tripolis

TO
MYSTRAS

Diakofto

33

ARCADIA

1963

E65

Zahlorou

Zahlorou **37**

Kalavrita **38**

Stemnitsa

76

Vouraïkos
Gorge

60

Lousios

Megalopolis

Egio

16

31

Dimitsana

Karytena

Rion

39

Antirion

Nafpaktos

Patras

40

Halandritsa

ACHAIA

33

Andritsena

Temple of Apollo
at Bassae

Gulf of Patras

33

33

Olympia **42–59**

76

E55

Messolongi

Kato Ahaïa

ELIS

74

E55

Lehena

Amalias

Pyrgos

Gastouni

Spianiza

Chlemoutsi
Castle **41**

Kastro

Katakolo

Loutra
Killinis

Ionian
Sea

TO
ITALY

KEY

- - - - Ferry
———— Rail Lines

N

0   20 miles
0   30 km

Six days will allow you to see most of the major sites of the Northern Peloponnese. Spend two or three days in ☑ **Nafplion** ⑤–⑳ and use it as a base to explore the Argolid. You can get to Nafplion by boat, train, or car, and it is possible to rent transportation from there. After you have explored nearby **Mycenae** ㉓–㉝, **Tiryns** ㉑, **Epidauros** ②, and **Argos** ㉒, spend a day in ☑ **Patras** ㊵, visiting **ancient Corinth** ㉟ on the way, or forested **Kalavrita** ㊳ if you need a rest from antiquities! A fifth and sixth day can be divided between Patras and ☑ **Olympia** ㊷–㊾. Remember that this trip can be easily reversed if you are coming from Italy and arriving in Patras.

Starting at the isthmus, journey south toward Nafplion, visiting **Isthmia** ①, Kenchreai, and **Epidauros** ② en route. Spend your second day in ☑ **Nafplion** ⑤–⑳, perhaps visiting the beaches at nearby ☑ **Tolo** ④ or ☑ **Porto Heli** ③, both of which can be used as alternative bases for exploring the Argolid. The five major sites north of Nafplion—**Tiryns** ㉑, **Argos** ㉒, **Mycenae** ㉓–㉝, **ancient Nemea** ㉞, and **ancient Corinth** ㉟— could easily occupy two or even three days, using Nafplion as a base for daily excursions. ☑ **Olympia** ㊷–㊾ beckons the Peloponnesian traveler sooner or later, but don't rush! There's plenty to see en route from the Argolid, including the beaches of **Xylokastro** ㊱, and the alluring beauty of the **Vouraikos Gorge** ㊲ near ☑ **Kalavrita** ㊳, a sight best experienced from the train that winds its way up the gorge. Kalavrita can be enjoyed as a side trip on the way to Patras, or as an overnight stay, followed by a quick hop to **Patras** ㊵, with fashionable shops, sophisticated cafés, and lots of energy. Stay in Patras for a couple of nights, exploring the city itself and the nearby sights, including the traditional village of Halandritsa, and the best-preserved Frankish castle in the Peloponnese, **Chlemoutsi Castle** ㊶. Finally, take a languid trip through the verdant province of Elis to awesome, ancient Olympia, where the Olympic Games were first held almost three millennia ago.

When to Tour

As in much of Greece, late spring provides optimum conditions for exploration—this is when hotels, restaurants, and sites have begun to extend their hours of operation but the hordes of travelers have not yet arrived. September and October are also excellent times to travel here because the weather is still warm but not oppressive, the sea is at its balmiest, and the throngs of tourists have gone home. In summer, morning and early evening activity will avoid the worst of the heat, which can be a formidable obstacle. Remember that on Mondays most state museums and sites are closed. On off-season Sundays, many are free.

ARGOLID AND CORINTHIAD

Isthmus, Epidauros, Nafplion, Tolo, Porto Heli, Tiryns, Argos, Mycenae, Nemea, Corinth

Most of the sites in this area are in the Argolid—Tiryns and Mycenae gaze over the plain of Argos, which dominates the Argolid, and nearby Epidauros hosts audiences from around the world who come to see drama performed in its classical theater. Argos lies in the center of the plain of the same name; behind the mountains that surround the plain on all sides (except the south) is the Corinthiad, a more hilly region, with ancient Corinth as its principal site.

Isthmus

75 km (46½ mi) southwest of Athens, 7 km (4½ mi) southeast of Corinth.

More of a pit stop than a town, Isthmus is where the Peloponnese begins. Were it not for this narrow neck of land less than 7 km (4½ mi) across, the waters of the Gulf of Corinth and the Saronic Gulf would meet and would make the Peloponnese an island; hence the name, which in fact, means "Pelops's island." The tragic myths and legends surrounding Pelops and his family provided the grist for poets and playwrights from Homer to Aeschylus and enshroud many of the region's sites to this day.

For the ancient Greeks the isthmus was strategically important for both trade and defense; Corinth, with harbors on either side of the isthmus, grew wealthy on the lucrative east–west trade. Ships en route from Italy and the Adriatic to the Aegean had to go clear around the Peloponnese, so in the 7th century BC a paved roadway called the Diolkos was constructed across the isthmus, over which ships were hauled using rollers. You can still see remnants near the bridge at the western end of the canal. Nero was the first to begin cutting a canal, supposedly striking the first blow, with a golden pickax, in AD 67, a task he then turned over to 6,000 Jewish prisoners. But the canal project died with Nero the following year, and the roadway was used until the 13th century. The modern canal, built 1882–93, was cut through 285 ft of rock to sea level. The impressive sight is a fleeting one if you are traveling by bus, so keep a sharp lookout.

① **Isthmia,** an ancient sanctuary dedicated to Poseidon, scarcely a mile from the canal, isn't much to look at today, largely because its buildings were dismantled for stone to repair the Isthmian wall and to build a large fortress. Better preserved, not surprisingly, are the remains of the fortress, called the **Hexamilion,** and of the **wall** (east of the sanctuary is a stretch that rises more than 20 ft). Ancient Isthmia was an important place, the site, from 580 BC, of the Isthmian Games, biennial athletic and musical competitions on a par with those at Nemea, Delphi, and Olympia. ⊠ *1 km (½ mi) west of isthmus,* ☎ *0741/37244.* ⊠ *500 dr./€1.47.* ⊙ *Daily 8–7 (winter 8–3).*

Dining

The chain of rest-stop restaurants at the isthmus itself are mostly antiseptic imitations of their American counterparts, and are mostly overpriced as well. If you have the time and want a real meal and swim, it's better to stop at **Perama** (⊠ ☎ *0741/49305*), just down from the isthmus. You can get a simple snack, such as souvlaki, or a complete meal by ordering the fried fish, pork chops, or roast chicken. It has a terrace with a view of the sea, and a five-minute walk brings you to a public beach.

Epidauros

② *41 km (25½ mi) east of Nafplion, 62 km (38½ mi) south of the isthmus. When heading south from the isthmus on Hwy. 70 you may find the names confusing. You first pass a sign for Nea Epidauros (don't take this); 6½ km (4 mi) later there's a turnoff marked for Palaio Epidauros (don't take this either). After this seaside village the road turns inland, and gradually the tall pines give way to scrubby vegetation. Keep going—the Epidauros you want is about 8 km (5 mi) farther, about 3 km (2 mi) southeast of Ligourio. If you are coming from another direction look for and follow the signs that say "Ancient Theatre of Epidauros" which dot the highways.*

★ The Sanctuary of Asklepios remains world renowned for one thing: the **Theater at Epidauros,** the best-preserved Greek theater anywhere because it was covered up sometime in antiquity and had to be dug out. Built in the 4th century BC with 14,000 seats, it was never remodeled in antiquity, and because it was rather remote, its stones were never quarried for secondary building use. Its extraordinary qualities were recognized even in the 2nd century AD. Pausanias of Lydia, an early traveler and geographer, wrote, "The Epidaurians have a theater in their sanctuary that seems to me particularly worth a visit. The Roman theaters have gone far beyond all the others in the world . . . but who can begin to rival Polykleitos for the beauty and composition of his architecture?"— or for the acoustics of his theater, which are so perfect that even from the last of the 55 tiers every word can be heard. Test this fact out during the **summer drama festival,** which, as Pausanias might say, is definitely "worth a visit." The quality of the theater, the setting, and the productions are outstanding, which cannot be said of any other festival in Greece. The rest of the site—the ancient shrine of the god of healing—does not match the standard set by the theater. The **temple of Asklepios** is not well preserved; some copies of its sculptures are in the **site museum,** but the originals are in the National Archaeological Museum in Athens. An exhibit of ancient medical implements is of interest, as are detailed models of the sanctuary and blueprints. The **reconstruction of the tholos,** a circular building possibly also by Polykleitos, is noteworthy. Currently a large-scale restoration is taking place that includes reconstruction of the **temple of Hygeia.** ⊠ *Epidauros,* ☎ *0753/22009.* ⊡ *1,500 dr./€4.42.* ⊙ *Daily 8–7 (winter 8–5).*

Dining and Lodging

$$ ✕ **Leonidas.** Rest your weary bones at this friendly taverna with a rear garden. Have some excellent grilled pork chops, stuffed vine leaves in egg-lemon sauce, or moussaka, followed by rich brandy and cinnamon-laced *revani* (semolina cake) or luscious *kataifi*(shredded wheat pastry) topped with *kaymaki*(clotted cream). In cold or wet weather, warm yourself before a blazing fire on the raised brick hearth. If you're going to a performance at the ancient theater, it's wise to call ahead and book a table. Many of the other audience members will do likewise and actors often frequent Leonidas as well—as the theater decorations and photographs of celebs, such as Melina Mercouri, attest. ⊠ *Epidauros main road,* ☎ *0753/22115.* V.

$ ⊞ **Hotel Koronis.** The Koronis is a clean but very basic older hotel, whose main advantage is that it is in the little village of Kigourio, a short three miles away from the site of Epidaurus. Only two newer rooms have baths inside; the others share them in the hall. Breakfast is not served but a café right across the street is open early in the morning. ⊠ *Asklipiou 82, on Nafplio-Epidauros road in Ligourio, Kigourio 21300,* ☎ *0753/22450,* ⠶ *0753/22267. 8 rooms, 2 with bath. No credit cards.*

The Arts

FESTIVAL

The **Festival of Ancient Drama** in the theater at Epidauros offers memorable performances from late July through August, Friday and Saturday only, at 9 PM. All productions are of ancient Greek drama in modern Greek, many presented by the national theater troupe. Actors are so expressive (or often wear ancient masks to signal the mood) that you can enjoy the performance even if you don't know a word of Greek. Plan to get to the site early (and either bring a picnic lunch or eat at the small snack stand) because watching the sunset behind the mountains and fields of olives and pines is an unforgettable sight. The Festival offers tickets a short time before performance days at either the theater or at the Athens Festival Box Office (⊠ Stadiou 4 arcade, ☎

01/322–1459 or ☎ 0753/22006 or 0752/22691; ☉ Thurs.–Sat. 9:30 AM–1 PM and 6–9 PM), which also offers a bus ticket/performance combination. Four or five buses run between Nafplion and the theater daily, returning to Nafplion after the play. Look for those that say THEATER or EPIDAUROS, not NEA EPIDAUROS or ARCHEA EPIDAUROS.

En Route   From Epidauros, head south toward the resort town of Porto Heli. After 16½ km (10 mi), just beyond the village of Trahia, the road divides. Follow the left fork as it swings east to the coast, with a beautiful view across the Saronic Gulf to Aegina. After 30 km (18½ mi), a left turn takes you to the volcanic peninsula known as Methana, only worth visiting if you want to go to its spa in the small port of the same name, which offers treatments for rheumatism and skin disorders in very smelly hot sulfurous water. Continuing past Methana on the main road brings you to Galatas, overlooking the island of Poros. The road sweeps around the end of the peninsula and runs west along the coast to Ermioni and the upmarket resort of Porto Hydra, opposite Hydra, then to the beach at Kosta, opposite Spetses, and finally to Porto Heli.

Porto Heli

❸   *81 km (50⅓ mi) southeast of Nafplion, 54 km (33½ mi) south of Epidauros.*

A booming summer resort, Porto Heli is well supplied with tavernas, restaurants, souvenir shops, and discos. If you're in search of traditional Greek culture, look elsewhere. On the south side of the bay are the submerged ruins of the ancient city of Halieis.

Beaches
The beach at **Kosta** (✉ In the south of the Argolid, south of Porto Heli) is more pleasant and less crowded than those at Porto Heli.

Dining and Lodging
$$–$$$ ✕ **Papadias.** In a town of undistinguished dining options, this taverna near the church in the older part of Porto Heli stands out. Dishes include such appetizers as shrimp or *midia saganaki* (mussels baked with cheese), rabbit *stifado* (a baked stew with meat, white wine, garlic, cinnamon, and spices) resplendent with onions, and grilled crayfish. The seafood is good, and in general fish is the high-water mark of Porto Heli cuisine. ✉ *Beach Rd.,* ☎ *0754/52342. MC, V.*

$$$ ⌂ **Porto Heli.** This lodging of the former Kymata Club, like the other resorts around the sheltered bay, offers more than just a room for the night: the nearby beach has a range of water sports, and buffet breakfast is included in the price. The reasonably large white-stucco rooms have phones, stone floors, and, as wall decorations, colorful Byzantine-style plates. ✉ *Beach Rd., 21300,* ☎ *0754/53490 through 0754/53494. 210 rooms, 8 suites. Restaurant, pool, wading pool, miniature golf, 2 tennis courts, windsurfing, playground. MC, V.*

$$ ⌂ **La Cité.** The buildings climbing the hillside behind the beach here resemble gigantic, white-stucco Lego blocks. Inside, wood-frame furniture fills the rooms, which, although clean and well kept, could be larger. They do have balconies overlooking the beautiful bay, and each comes with a fan. There are rental bicycles and mopeds at the beach opposite, just 65 ft away. Continental breakfast is included in the price. ✉ *Beach Rd., 21300,* ☎ *0754/51415, ℻ 0754/51265. 164 rooms. Restaurant, 3 bars, outdoor pool, miniature golf, 2 tennis courts, beach, water sports. AE, DC, MC, V. Closed Nov.–Mar.*

$ ⌂ **Rozos.** An alternative to the giant resorts, Rozos can be summed up in a few words: crafty on a budget. The rooms are clean and decorated with nautical photos. Some of the furniture in each room matches, and large ceiling fans, like salvaged propellers from B–29 bombers, ensure good air circulation. A saving grace for this establishment, if you deem one is needed, is the front terrace, shaded by grapevines, lemon trees, and olive trees. ✉ *Kosta 7, 21300,* ☎ ℻ *0754/ 51415. 23 rooms. Restaurant. MC, V.*

Nightlife

DISCOS

Disco Alosis and the lively **Banana Club** have enraptured multiseason visitors. **Pop Rebel** and **Karamus** bars have managed to stay in tourists' good graces for more than a summer.

Outdoor Activities and Sports

WATER SPORTS

Although its beach is not as good as others in the vicinity, Porto Heli's circular bay offers sheltered water for windsurfing, waterskiing, and other aquatic sports, and a safe harbor for sailboats. Waterskiing lessons are given at the **Porto Heli** hotel (✉ Beach Rd., ☎ 0754/51546; ☞ *above*).

Tolo

❹ *11 km (7 mi) southeast of Nafplion, 77 km (47¾ mi) northwest of Porto Heli.*

Tolo is a resort center close to Nafplion, a good base for exploring the northeastern Peloponnese, especially for young people who like nightlife and for those who want to be on the beach. There are boats to the islands of Hydra and Spetses, and a hydrofoil to Athens in the summer. Organized tours to Mycenae, Tiryns, and Olympia are readily available in the tourist season. Tolo has many fine beaches strung along the coast's crystalline waters, discos, and seafood tavernas supplied by the local fleet, but little in the way of traditional Greek culture—although note the Mycenean site of Asine (☞ *below*). Many of the larger hotels are block-booked by agencies in the summer or filled with Greeks from the Peloponnese, so book far in advance (try smaller hotels first). There is frequent bus service from Nafplion's KTEL station to Tolo.

Beaches

Just before Tolo, at the Bronze Age and classical site of Asine, the road takes a sharp turn to the fine **Kastraki Beach** (listed on signs as Paralia Asinis)—it has a number of small hotels, is less crowded than Tolo, and offers pedalos (rafts with foot pedals), canoes, and windsurfers for rent. If you make a beach excursion out here, also fit in a bit of history: ancient **Asine**, open Tuesday–Sunday 8–2:30 at no admission charge, set 1 km (½ mi) inland, was an important Mycenean city, although all that remains are an ancient wall and ramparts in the lower town and Geometric and Hellenistic traces on the acropolis. It lies on a small peninsula that forms the left arm of the Bay of Tolo and offers a multitude of wildflowers in the spring. At its very tip is an odd bit of military history: a shattered but still legible mosaic made by Italian soldiers during World War II and dedicated to Il Duce—Mussolini.

Dining and Lodging

$ ✕ **Akroyiali.** Matriarch Anastasia Moutzouris still cooks up good traditional Greek fare at this almost 40-year-old beach taverna. Appetizers include fried eggplant slices, tender broad beans, marinated octopus, and grilled squid. For a main course, there is fresh fish, as well as *soutzoukakia* (spicy meatballs Smyrna style), souvlaki, tomatoes and peppers stuffed with rice accented with wild *rigani* (oregano), and grilled chicken. The barrel wine (white and red) is light but potent; locals order it a kilo at a time. ✉ *Aktis 10,* ☎ *0752/59789. No credit cards. Closed Dec.*

$$ ⊞ **King Minos.** One of the town's newest—it opened in 1992—this hotel offers amenities usually found in more expensive establishments. Almost all the rose and light-green rooms with bamboo touches have color TVs, hair dryers, air-conditioning, and balconies; many have sea views. A beautiful outdoor pool looks out over the bay. Buffet breakfast is included in the price. The hotel is not on the shoreline but up the hill, above the main road. ⊠ *Miaouli 56, 21056,* ☎ *0752/59902,* FAX *0752/ 59968. 57 rooms. Restaurant, 2 bars, air-conditioning, pool. AE, MC, V. Closed Nov.–Feb.*

$$ ⊞ **Minoa.** Renovated last year, this pleasant hotel has a crisp, clean, new feel to it—rooms are relatively large, done in the signature blue-and-white scheme, and all feature radio, hair dryer, safe, and television. The hotel is near the end of the town, and though there is a beach in front, it's a little walk to the wide sandy beach for which Tolo is known. Happily, many rooms feature delightful sea views. Buffet breakfast is included in the price. ⊠ *Aktis 56, 21056,* ☎ *0752/59207,* FAX *0752/59707. 44 rooms. Bar, outdoor café, air-conditioning, in-room safes. AE, MC, V. Closed Nov.–Feb.*

$$ ⊞ **Tolo and Tolo II.** Dimitris Skalidis and family run a tight ship at these
★ hotels opposite each other on the town's main street. The staff is fluent in several languages and exceptionally helpful. Skalidis's wife Ioanna manages Tolo Apartments, 14 fully appointed and air-conditioned apartments off the main road. The hotel rooms are straightforward in decor and well kept—ask for one with a sea view, in which balconies hover directly over the sea below (far closer than would be allowed if built today). Rooms facing the main road can be noisy in the main season. Tolo has immediate access to the nicest part of the town beach, while guests can also use a pool at a nearby hotel. Buffet breakfast is included in the price. Greek nights are offered occasionally, featuring Greek folk dancing in which owners and many guests often participate. ⊠ *Bouboulinas 15, 21056,* ☎ *0752/59248 or 0752/59464,* FAX *0752/59689. 59 rooms. Restaurant, bar, air-conditioning. MC, V. Closed Nov.–Feb.*

Nafplion

★ *65 km (40½ mi) south of Corinth, 11 km (7 mi) northwest of Tolo.*

Oraia (beautiful) is the word Greeks use to describe Nafplion. They say the word with assurance and enthusiasm, wanting to appreciate Nafplion's beauty while convinced that it is self-evident and that you share their recognition of it. The town's old section, on a peninsula jutting into the Gulf of Argos, mixes Greek, Venetian, and Turkish architecture; narrow streets, often just broad flights of stone stairs, climb the slopes beneath the walls of Acronafplia; statues honoring heroes preside over tree-shaded plazas surrounded by neoclassical buildings; and the Palamidi fortress—an elegant display of Venetian might from the early 1700s—draped over the high cliff guards the town. The Greeks are indeed right: Nafplion is beautiful. It deserves at least a leisurely day of your undivided attention.

Little is known about ancient Nafplion, although Paleolithic remains and Neolithic pottery have been found in the vicinity. The town grew in importance in Byzantine times, and it was fought over by the Byzantines and the Frankish crusaders. It has been held by the Duke of Athens, the Venetians, and the Turks. In the War of Independence, the Greeks liberated the city, and it briefly became the capital. During World War II, German troops occupied Nafplion from April 1941 until September 1944. Today it is once again just a "provincial town," busy only in the tourist season and on weekends when Athenians arrive to get away from city pressures.

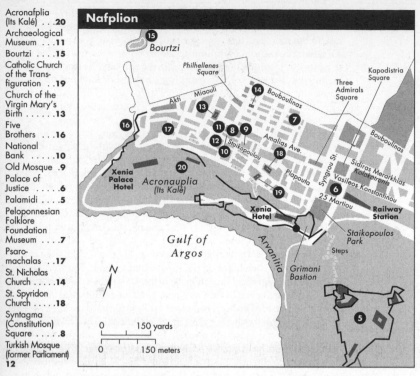

A Good Walk

Just wandering around Nafplion you'll quickly learn that this town is not merely picturesque, not merely beautifully situated, it's probably the prettiest in the Peloponnese and virtually seems to be designed for strolling. To get your bearings, you might start by climbing the hill of the **Palamidi**⑤, the elegant Venetian fortress that sits atop its 700-ft peak (take a taxi up the road or tackle the 800-step climb skyward)—an on-a-clear-day-you-can-see-forever view of the Nafplion peninsula and the surrounding Argive plain will be your reward. Once you explore the fort—incidentally, the name Palamidi is taken from the son of Poseidon, Palamedes, who, legend has it, invented dice, arithmetic, and some of the Greek alphabet—head back down to relax at the foot of the fort in a pleasant series of tree-shaded parks and platias, including Kolokotronis Park, Kapodistria Square, Staikopoulos Park, and Three Admiral Square. As you head north along Syngrou Street, another park awaits, replete with statues including one of the famed heroine Bouboulina. Turn the corner on which Bouboulina's pedestal sits and walk one block from the harbor along Sophoni Street to the award-winning **Peloponnesian Folklore Foundation Museum**⑦. Then walk south and turn right on Amalias or on Vasileos Konstantinou St. to reach **Syntagma (Constitution) Square**⑧, the center of the old town. The latter street is more picturesque, with older buildings; the more commercial Amalias is lined with butcher shops and grocery stores. Immediately to the left as you enter Syntagma from Vasileos Konstantinou Street is the **old mosque**⑨ (turned movie theater) that Henry Miller took as an example of Nafplion's crassness. Walking from the cinémosque along the south side of Syntagma, continue past the "Mycenaean"-style **National Bank**⑩, a fitting overture to your visit to the town's **Archaeological Museum**⑪, on the west side of Syntagma.

Westward you'll find the **Church of the Virgin Mary's Birth**⑬, an elaborate post-Byzantine structure. Continuing north, you come to quayside and Philhellenes Square and the church of **St. Nicholas**⑭. From St. Nicholas westward along the quayside (called Akti Miaouli) is an unbroken chain of restaurants, most just average, and, farther along, more-successful patisseries. It is pleasant in the afternoon for postcard writing, an iced coffee or ouzo, and conversation. Sparrows looking for handouts will flit around your feet; the air is warm and the sky blue; and Argos's high acropolis is clearly visible across the smooth sea. Back at the quay, you can embark on a boat trip out to the miniature fortress of the **Bourtzi**⑮ in the harbor. Walk along the waterfront promenade to the **Five Brothers**⑯ bastion, and then follow the winding Kostouros Street up to the parking lot below the Nafplia Palace hotel and explore **Psaromachalas**⑰, the picturesque fishermen's quarter. Return to the Five Brothers to continue the promenade around the peninsula or, instead, go through the tunnel that looks like a James Bond movie set from the parking lot, and take the elevator to the Nafplia Palace hotel and the top of the **Acronafplia**⑳ fortress. Repair to the Nafplia Palace hotel bar for a sundowner.

Timing

A full exploration of this lovely town takes an entire day; a quick tour, with some omissions, could be done in three hours. While the above itinerary will show you all the main sights, you can get a good sample of Nafplion's distinctive ambience by just following your nose through its winding streets and charming squares.

Sights to See

⑳ **Acronafplia.** Potamianou Street, actually a flight of stone steps, ascends from St. Spyridon Square toward this imposing hill, which the Turks once called Its Kalé. Until the Venetian occupation, it had two castles: a Frankish one on the eastern end and a Byzantine one on the west. The Venetians added the massive Castello del Torrione (or Toro for short) at the eastern end around 1480. If you have trouble locating the Toro, look under the Xenia Hotel, which was built on part of it. During the second Venetian occupation, the gates were strengthened and the huge Grimani bastion was added (1706) below the Toro. The Acronafplia is only accessible from the elevator on the west side, or by the road from the east side, near the Nafplia Palace hotel.

⑪ **Archaeological Museum.** This red stone building on the west side of Constitution Square was built in 1713 to serve as the storehouse for the Venetian fleet. To say that it is "well constructed" is an understatement; its arches and windows are remarkably well proportioned. It has housed the regional archaeological museum since 1930, and artifacts from such sites as Mycenae, Tiryns, Asine, and Dendra are exhibited here. Of special interest are a Mycenaean suit of armor, jewelry from Mycenaean tombs in the area, and 7th-century gorgon masks from Tiryns. ✉ *West side of Constitution Sq.,* ☎ *0752/27502.* 🎫 *500 dr./€1.47.* ⊙ *Tues.–Sun. 8:30–3.*

⑮ **Bourtzi.** If you like the view to distant Argos, the sight of the Bourtzi, Nafplion's pocket-size fortress, will captivate you. Built in 1471 by Antonio Gambello, one of those industrious Venetians, the Bourtzi (or Castelli) was at first a single tower, on a speck of land generously called St. Theodore's Island. Morosini is said to have massacred the Turkish garrison when he recaptured it for Venice in 1686. A tower and bastion were then added, giving it the shiplike appearance it has today. In 1822, after it was captured in the War of Independence, it was used to bombard the Turks defending the town. In the unsettled times after the revolution, the government retreated to the Bourtzi for a while; after 1865, it was the residence of the town executioners; and from 1930 until 1970 it was run as a hotel. During the day the Bourtzi is no longer menacing; a tree blooms bright red in its courtyard during spring. You can take a small boat out to it for spectacular views of the old part of Nafplion and the Palamidi. Illuminated by floodlights in summer, it is beautiful at dusk but becomes grimmer as darkness falls. Extending from the extreme end of the quay is a large breakwater, the west mole, built by the Turks as the anchor point for a large chain that could be drawn up between it and the Bourtzi, blocking the harbor completely. A **small café** operates on the Bourtzi, where you can take in the view and refuel. It can be reached via water taxi from the northeastern end of Akti Miaouli (700 dr./€2.06) and is open daily from 4 PM to 1 AM, May to September. ⊠ *In the harbor.*

⑲ **Catholic Church of the Transfiguration.** King Otho returned this Venetian-built church to Nafplion's Catholics. It is best known for the wooden arch erected inside the doorway in 1841, with the names carved on it of Philhellenes who died during the War of Independence (Lord Byron is number 10). Note also the evidence of its use as a mosque by the Turks: the mihrab (Muslim prayer recess) behind the altar and the amputated stub of a minaret. The church boasts a small museum and an underground crypt in which can be found a recent sculptural work commemorating the defeat of the Turks at the hands of the Greeks and Philhellenes. ⊠ *2 blocks south (uphill) from St. Spyridon.*

Church of Ayios Georgios. On Plapouta Street you'll find a square whose showpiece is the Church of Ayios Georgios, a Byzantine-era monument set at an angle, with five domes dating from the beginning of the 16th century and a Venetian arcade and campanile. Inside is the throne of King Otho. Around the square are several high-quality **neoclassical houses**—the one opposite the church is exceptional. Note the fine palmette centered above the door, the pilasters on the third floor with Corinthian capitals, the running Greek-key entablature, and the end tiles along the roofline. This house is matched perhaps by the one at the intersection of Plapouta and Tertsetou streets, whose window treatments are especially ornate. Nafplion has many other fine neoclassical buildings; keep your eyes open and don't forget to look up once in a while. ⊠ *2 blocks west of Syngrou on Plapouta.*

⑬ **Church of the Virgin Mary's Birth.** The church rises next to an **ancient olive tree**, where, according to tradition, St. Anastasios, a Nafpliote painter, was killed in 1655 by the Turks. Anastasios was supposedly engaged to a local girl, but he abandoned her because she was immoral. Becoming despondent as a result of spells cast over him by her relatives, he converted to Islam. Upon returning to his senses, he cried out, "I was a Christian, I am a Christian, and I shall die a Christian." A Turkish judge ordered that he be beheaded, but the mob, outraged by the insult to Islam, stabbed Anastasios to death. A local tradition holds that he was hanged on this olive tree and that it never again bore fruit. The church, a post-Byzantine three-aisle basilica, was the main Orthodox church during the Venetian occupation. It has an elaborate wooden reredos carved in 1870. ⊠ *West of Constitution Sq.*

⑯ **Five Brothers.** South of the Bourtzi is the bastion known as the Five Brothers, the only remaining part of the wall built around Nafplion in 1502. The name comes from the five guns placed here by the Venetians; there are five here today, all from around 1690 and all bearing the winged lion of St. Mark. ⊠ *Near promontory of the peninsula.*

NEED A BREAK?

A small taverna called the **Banieris** (⊠ Just south of Five Brothers) is a good place to sit with an ouzo and watch the sun set behind the mountains across the gulf. Keep an eye out for the arrival of the evening hydrofoil from Piraeus, as it comes up the gulf.

Kapodistria Square. Just west of Kolokotronis Park, this park is centered on a marble statue of the Corfiote diplomat and father of modern Greece. Standing statesmanlike, he's quite oblivious to the noise from the playground at his feet, the tavernas across the street, and the taxis and buses turning left onto Amalias Street. ⊠ *At Syngrou St. and Sidiras Merarkhias.*

Kolokotronis Park. The centerpiece of this park is a bronze equestrian statue surrounded by four small Venetian cannons, which commemorates the revolutionary hero.

Miniature triangular park. This contains, inevitably, a monument to **admiral Konstantinos Kanaris**, a revolutionary hero; across from its far end is the **bust of Laskarina Bouboulina.** Twice widowed by wealthy shipowners, she built her own frigate, the *Agamemnon.* Commanding it herself, along with three small ships captained by her sons, Bouboulina blockaded the beleaguered Turks by sea, cutting off their supplies. **Bouboulina's pedestal** sits on the corner. ⊠ *Syngrou, north of Three Admiral Sq.*

Nafplion Promenade. This promenade around the entire Nafplion peninsula, once a simple gravel pathway, is now paved with reddish flagstones and graced with an occasional ornate lamppost. Here and there a flight of steps goes down to the rocky shore below. (Be careful if you go swimming here, since the rocks are covered with sea urchins, which look like purple and black porcupines and whose quills can inflict a painful wound.) Just before you reach the very tip of the peninsula, marked by a ship's beacon, there is a little shrine at the foot of a path leading up toward the Acronafplia walls above. Little Virgin Mary, or **Ayia Panagitsa** (⊠ At end of promenade) hugs the cliff on a small terrace and is decorated with an array of icons. During the Turkish occupation it hid one of Greece's secret schools. Two other terraces, like garden sanctuaries, have a few rosebushes and the shade of olive and cedar trees. They are very restful places to sit and not much frequented. Along the south side of the peninsula, the promenade runs midway along the cliff—it's 100 ft up to Acronafplia, 50 ft down to the sea. All along there are magnificent views of the cliff on which the Palamidi sits and the slope below, known as the Arvanitia.

❿ National Bank. This structure displays an amusing union of Mycenaean and modern Greek architectural elements with concrete. (The Mycenaeans covered their tholos tombs with mounds of dirt; the bank's ungainly appearance may explain why.) Take a look at the **sculptures** (⊠ On the square next to National Bank) of a winged lion of St. Mark (which graced the main gate in the city's landward wall, long since demolished) and of Kalliope Papalexopoulou (a leader of the revolt against King Otho), whose house once stood in the vicinity. ⊠ *Just south of Constitution Sq.*

❾ Old mosque. Immediately to the left as you enter Constitution Square from Vasileos Konstantinou Street is this venerable mosque—once used as a school, a courthouse, and for municipal offices, its current incarnation is as a dingy movie theater. ⊠ *Constitution Sq.*

NEED A
BREAK?

Walking from the old mosque along the south side of Constitution Square, you pass a café and a store called **Odyssey** (⊠ Constitution Sq.), the best place in Nafplion for newspapers and books in English; the owners are very helpful if you need advice or directions. Once you have picked up an English-language newspaper or paperback, head over to the Stathmos (old train station) with a steam engine and vintage freight and passenger cars, which has been renovated and is now used

⏱ as a **Children's Museum** (✉ 25 Martiou, ☎ 0752/28947) with a playground and sandbox in front for the kids to play in. A secluded café, also called **Stathmos**, is set in the restored train station building to the south, where you can get a snack and drink and listen to both recorded and live Greek blues and pop.

❻ Palace of Justice. If Henry Miller loathed Nafplion for its lawyers and public buildings, you have to believe that he must have spent much of his time staring at the Palace of Justice, a neoclassical building (currently being restored) whose gracelessness is magnified by its large size. This monumentality makes it useful as a landmark, however, since the telephone company (OTE) office and pay phones are in the next building. Nearby, across Syngrou Street from the KTEL bus station, is a **square** with a statue honoring Nikitaras the Turk-Killer, who directed the siege of Nafplion. ✉ *Syngrou, 2 blocks down from Kapodistria Sq.*

★ **❺ Palamidi.** Seen from the old part of Nafplion, this fortress, set on its 700-ft peak, is elegant, with the red stone bastions and flights of steps that zigzag down the cliff face. A modern road lets you drive up the less precipitous eastern slope, but if you are in reasonable shape and it isn't too hot, try climbing the stairs. Most guidebooks will tell you there are 999 of them, but 892 is closer to the mark. From the top you can see the entire Argive plain and look across the gulf to Argos or down its length to the Aegean.

Built in 1711–14, the Palamidi comprises three forts and a series of freestanding and connecting defensive walls. Sculpted in gray stone, the lion of St. Mark looks outward from the gates. The Palamidi fell to the Turks in 1715 after only eight days, and if you climbed those stairs, you'll be able to feel the desperation of the fleeing defenders racing down them with the Turks in hot pursuit. After the war, the fortress was used as a prison, its inmates including the revolutionary war hero Kolokotronis; a sign indicates his cell. On summer nights the Palamidi is illuminated with floodlights, a beautiful sight from below. ✉ *Above town,* ☎ *0752/28036.* 🎟 *800 dr./€2.35.* ☉ *Weekdays 8:30–7 (8:30–3 in winter), weekends 8:30–2:30.*

NEED A BREAK?	For a respite, head to a pleasant series of tree-shaded **Staikopoulos platias** (✉ At foot of Palamidi). A tranquil café welcomes the weary, benches here are perfect for giving your less-than-bionic feet a time-out, while children will enjoy the playground, duck pond, and some small aviaries. At the west end of the park the Nafpliotes have reconstructed the Venetian Gateway that originally guarded the entrance to the Palamidi and commemorates the Venetian recapture of the city in 1487. Standing amidst the detritus of earlier Byzantine and classical ruins, the gateway invites contemplation on the passage of time.

❼ Peloponnesian Folklore Foundation Museum. An exemplary, small museum focusing on textiles, this won the European Community's 1981 Museum of the Year award for its displays. It has reopened after an extensive renovation and should be on your not-to-be-missed list. Exhibits change periodically and feature outstanding costumes, handicrafts, and household furniture from the museum's collection, many of them precious heirlooms which have been donated by leading Peloponnesian families. Its lovely gift shop has some fascinating books and handicrafts, such as weavings, kilims, and collector folk items such as *roka* (spindles) and wooden *koboloi* (worry beads). ✉ *Vas. Alexandrou 1, on block immediately north of Amalias, going up Sofroni,* ☎ *0752/28379.* 🎟 *1,000 dr./€2.94.* ☉ *Mar.–Jan., Wed.–Mon. 9–2:00.*

⑰ Psaromachalas. This is the fishermen's quarter, a small district of narrow, alleylike streets running between cramped little houses that huddle beneath the walls of Acronafplia. The old houses, painted in brownish yellow, green, and salmon, have had all sorts of additions and overhangs added. The walk is enjoyable, but it is a poor neighborhood, and it's easy to feel like a voyeur scrutinizing the private lives of the locals. The pretty, miniature whitewashed chapel of **Ayios Apostoli** (✉ Just off the parking lot of Psaromachalas) has six small springlets that trickle out of the side of Acronafplia. ✉ *Along Kostouros St.*

⑭ St. Nicholas Church. Built in 1713 for the use of sailors by Augustine Sagredo, the prefect of the Venetian fleet, this church has a facade and belfry that are recent additions. Inside, the church is furnished with a Venetian reredos and pulpit, and a chandelier from Odessa. ✉ *Off Philhellenes Sq.*

⑱ St. Spyridon Church. Just west of Ayios Georgios is this church, a one-aisle basilica with a dome (1702). It has a special place in Greek history, for it was at its doorway that the statesman Ioannis Kapodistrias was assassinated in 1831 by the Mavromichalis brothers from the Mani, the outcome of a long-running vendetta. The mark of the bullet can be seen next to the Venetian portal. On the south side of the square, opposite St. Spyridon, are two of the four Turkish fountains preserved in Nafplion. A third is a short distance east (away from St. Spyridon) on Kapodistria Street, at the steps that constitute the upper reaches of Tertsetou Street. ✉ *Terzaki, St. Spirdonas Sq., Papanikolaou St.*

⑧ Syntagma (Constitution) Square. This is the center of the old town and one of Greece's prettiest platias, distinguished by glistening multicolored, marble slab–paving bordered by neoclassical and Ottoman-style buildings. In summer, the restaurants and patisseries along the west and south sides of Constitution Square—a focal point of Nafpliote life—are boisterous with the shouts and laughter of children and filled with diners well into the evening. ✉ *Along Amalias and Vasileos Konstantinou Sts.*

⑫ Turkish mosque. Ironically now the *Vouleftiko* (Parliament), this mosque was where the Greek National Assembly held its first meetings. The mosque is well built of carefully dressed gray stones. Legend has it that the lintel stone from the Treasury of Atreus was used in the construction of its large square-domed prayer hall. The mosque recently served as a music school, and occasionally the sound of a Rossini overture played on a piano could be heard. Today it is undergoing restoration and is not open to the public. ✉ *Next to Archaeological Museum and behind National Bank.*

OFF THE BEATEN PATH	**AYIA MONI** – Before or after exploring Nafplion, drive out the Epidauros road and turn right after 1 km (½ mi) to visit the fine Byzantine convent and church of Ayia Moni, a place of Christian devotion with a pagan twist. It was built in 1149 by Leo, the Bishop of Argos and Nafplion, and an inscription on the west gate records his efforts in building it and hopefully expresses the possibility that the Virgin will reward him by absolving him of his sins. In the monastery garden is a fountain said to be the spring Kanathos, where Hera annually renewed her virginity. On the way back to town, be sure to stop and see the Bavarian Lion, a beast of more than life size carved from a rock outcrop in the Pronoia section, Nafplion's modern suburb. The sleeping lion, a memorial to the Bavarian troops who died of typhus while serving King Otho, is a sad symbol of mortality compared to the invincible Venetian lions on Nafplion's fortresses.

Beaches

In Nafplion, **Arvanitia Beach** (✉ on south side of town nestled between Acronauplia and the Palomides) is man-made of smooth rocks but nice for a plunge after a day of sightseeing. It has convenient changing cabins, shaded cabanas, a snack bar and ouzeri, as well as canoes for rent. If you want to make a day out of relaxing in the sun, you're better off heading for one of the beaches farther away from town. Close to Nafplion are **Kastraki** and **Plaka.** The closest is **Karathona,** favored by Greek families with children and picnic baskets and serviced by buses. **Tolo,** with its sandy beach and assortment of water sports, is a short bus ride from the main station or a reasonable taxi ride.

Dining and Lodging

With one or two exceptions you'll eat better for less at the tavernas on Staikopoulos Street or parallel Papanikolaou than at the ones along the waterfront or in Constitution Square. After dining have a dessert at **Galaxia** (✉ Constitution Sq.) or **Cafe Aktaion** (✉ Akti Miaouli 3) or one of the other *zacharoplasteia* (patisseries) on the harbor.

$$ ✕ **Paleo Archontiko.** This tiny taverna in an old stone mansion is wildly popular with locals (it's best to reserve on weekends and in high season). Tassos Koliopoulos and his wife Anya oversee the ever-changing menu, which highlights local specialties. Everything is fresh and appealing, but the beef stifado (beef casserole slow-cooked with fresh tomatoes and small onions) and *krassato* (rooster in wine sauce) are standouts. Koliopoulos often presents live Greek music, and much spontaneous dancing ensues. ✉ *Siokou and Ipsilantou Sts. (behind Commercial Bank, 1 block from Epidauros Hotel),* ☎ *0752/22449. No credit cards.*

$$ ✕ **Savouras.** Fresh seafood is served in this unpretentious nautical-theme taverna overlooking the bay; it is generally regarded as one of the best fish restaurants in the area, so don't let the modest interior fool you. Specialties are red mullet, pandora, and dorado. Good side dishes are the *melitzanosalata* (eggplant dip) and the fava with onions. ✉ *Bouboulinas 79,* ☎ *0752/27704. No credit cards.*

$–$$ ✕ **O Arapakos.** Settle in on the waterfront for excellent Greek cooking, starting with grilled octopus and moving on to specialties such as *yiouvetsi ton arapi* (beef with potatoes, tomatoes, carrots, and eggplants cooked in a ceramic dish) or *arnaki exohiko* (lamb stuffed with feta and potatoes). You can also have fresh fish, such as sea bream cooked over charcoal, or *bakaliaro skordalia* (dried cod, fried and served with a dollop of garlic sauce), all complemented by the light barrel retsina. To further entice you, there's usually some pan dessert such as *galaktobouriko* (a sinful custard pastry) or baklava. ✉ *Bouboulinas 81,* ☎ *0752/27675. V.*

$–$$ ✕ **Ta Fanaria.** This is one of the finest restaurants in Nafplion. Follow
★ this advice and enjoy: arrive late and sit at one of the tables in the narrow lane beside the restaurant, which is situated off a peaceful pedestrian way and covered by vine leaves. Look in the kitchen to see what looks best that night. It's known for its *ladera* (vegetables cooked in olive oil), but the charcoal-grilled lamb ribs, the *imam bayilda* (eggplant stuffed with onions), and the lamb baked with vegetables such as okra or green beans are equally delicious. ✉ *Staikopoulos 13,* ☎ *0752/27141. V.*

$ ✕ **Hellas.** This reliable restaurant is not Nafplion's finest, but it is probably the most inexpensive on Constitution Square. It's best to go here when you're simply too tired to venture farther and are looking for an inexpensive lunch and an opportunity to watch the comings and goings on the square. ✉ *Constitution Sq., opposite archaeological museum,* ☎ *0752/27278. V.*

$ ✕ **Kanakarakis.** Located on a quiet lane in the upper portion of the old town, Kanakarakis serves a variety of delicious mezedes appetizers such as *saganaki* (fried cheese), eggplant salad, and a choice of wonderful *pittas* (pies) filled with wild greens, chicken, pumpkin, and cheese. Main dishes include moist grilled chicken and lamb *souvla* ("on a spit"). Save room for desserts because the *kataifi* (shredded dough filled with chopped pistachio nuts) and *karidopita* (rich walnut cake) are luscious. ✉ *Vas. Olgas 18,* ☎ *0752/25371. No credit cards.*

$ ✕ **Karamalis.** Although it's on the waterfront, it's just far enough away from the tourist area to attract the locals but close enough to be within walking distance of everything "important." This simple taverna is an authentic treat, distinguished by courtly waiters who will patiently help you make your selections. At lunch it gets crowded with civil servants from the nearby courthouse who come for its tasty though limited number of *magirefta* (precooked dishes). The light fish soup makes a good starter, followed by *yiouvarlakia* (meat-rice balls), oven-baked potatoes, wild greens, and barrel retsina. Fresh fish is also available at very reasonable prices, and the pork and lamb chops are thick and flavorful. ✉ *Bouboulinas 1,* ☎ *0752/27668. No credit cards.*

$$$$ 🏨 **Candia House.** Nineteen kilometers (12 miles) south of Nafplion on
★ Kandia Beach, this beautifully decorated hotel is the creation of a Greek publisher, Hara Papadimitriou, who has flawlessly matched good taste with comfort. Fresh flowers, antiques, paintings by Greek artists, handcrafted mirrors, fireplaces—these are just a few of the embellishments in the suites. Each one is different in its decor, and their sizes range from palatial to truly enormous. The Presidential suite boasts glorious antique Greek furniture that has been in the family for generations. All have balconies, sitting rooms, televisions, and refrigerators, and buffet breakfast is included in the price. The hexagonal restaurant with large windows looking onto the sea specializes in healthy meals, and the hotel offers hydromassage and botanotherapy treatments. Hara's effusive and enthusiastic welcome is also complimentary. ✉ *Kandia-Irion, 21100,* ☎ *0752/94060 through 0752/94063,* 🖷 *0752/94480. 10 suites. Restaurant, pool, massage, exercise room. AE, DC, MC, V.*

$$$$ 🏨 **Nafplia Palace.** The view of the picturesque Bourtzi from the rooms in the Nafplia Palace is exceptional; it appears in Greek National Tourist Organization (GNTO or EOT) television advertisements, and the view is possible only because the hotel was built on the ruins of the Frankish fortification atop Acronafplia. Modern art adorns the lobby, the relatively spacious rooms have exposed stonework, and the marble bathrooms are, without qualification, among the best in Greece. Lighting in the rooms is dim, some of the furniture needs reupholstering, and half-board (included in the price) in the Anymoni Restaurant is mandatory. An elevator cut through the rock takes you to a tunnel leading straight into town, below. ✉ *Acronafplia, 21100,* ☎ *0752/28981 through 0752/28985,* 🖷 *0752/28783. 48 rooms, 3 suites. Restaurant, bar, pool, dance club. AE, MC, V.*

$$ 🏨 **Byron.** Definitely one of Nafplion's more popular hotels—particu-
★ larly with the younger crowd—this place has simply but tastefully decorated rooms, with Turkish carpets and the odd sloping ceiling. A light pink decor predominates, and a delightful outdoor patio set atop an old Turkish *hamam* (bath) compensates for the dark, bare breakfast room. Little touches make the difference here: welcoming staff, an atmosphere of intrepid adventure, and an absurd wooden phone at the front desk. Breakfast is an additional 1,800 dr./€5.30. Amenities such as telephones, televisions, air-conditioners, hair dryers, and minibars are available in all rooms. ✉ *Platonos 16, Platia Kapodistriou, near Agiou Spiridona, 21100,* ☎ *0752/22351,* 🖷 *0752/26338. 14 rooms, 4 studios. Breakfast room, air-conditioning, minibars. AE, MC, V.* ✪

$$ 🏨 **King Othon.** Completely renovated in 1999, King Othon has regained its former elegance, with its wrought-iron balustrade, decorative rosette ceilings, and restored antiques all creating a pleasing welcome. All rooms are air-conditioned with bathrooms and are newly decorated in a belle epoque style. Breakfast, which is included, is served in the lovely inner garden. The sitting areas are tastefully decorated and are quiet, despite the proximity to the heart of the old town. ⊠ *Farmakopoulou 4, 21100,* ☎ *0752/27585,* FAX *0752/27595. 11 rooms. Air-conditioning. V.*

$ 🏨 **Epidauros.** This hotel, a former merchant prince's home, is simple but delightful. The two buildings feature an assortment of room styles, all with pine decor. This was one of Nafplion's first three hotels. The owner brims with pride, but the staff can be a little indifferent. Rooms do not have telephones and breakfast is not served; however, Constitution Square is one block away and it has a number of cafés open early in the morning. One cautionary note: the hotel stands amid a number of night-clubs, whose proximity may delight you if you're into clubbing but may also keep you awake at night from all the noise—but on weeknights, the pedestrian way is usually very tranquil. ⊠ *Kokkinou 2, 21100,* ☎ FAX *0752/27541. 35 rooms, 25 with bath. Bar. No credit cards.*

Nightlife

BARS AND DISCOS

Paleo Lichnari (⊠ Bouboulinas 39), a restaurant-club along the eastern end of the waterfront, has live Greek *rembetika* (urban blues) and popular music every weekend and some weeknights during the summer; it's frequented by vacationing Greeks who usually arrive around midnight or later. Though Nafpliotes drive to Tolo for their evening revels, Nafplion enjoys (if that's the word) a strip of nightclubs and discos that prosper along the northwest coastal road to Argos, including **Perama.** Along the road to Tolo are more clubs, including **Club Memory** and **Zorba's.**

Shopping

Many stores in Nafplion have the reproductions of bronzes, frescoes, vase paintings, and an array of T-shirts for which your family, friends, and coworkers have been secretly hankering. In addition, a number of tasteful shops have a plentiful array of fine quality merchandise, including smart sportswear. The **Komboloi Museum,** in an old Nafpliote home (⊠ Staikopoulou 25, ☎ 0752/21618, 🎫 500 dr./€1.47), in addition to its fascinating museum of historic worry beads, has a shop on the ground floor, which sells antique and new worry beads and attractive beaded key chains. For antiques and woven goods, such as colorful *tagaria* (shepherds' shoulder bags), head toward the end of Vassilos Konstantinou Street near the bus station; several shops here also sell dried herbs and natural honey.

GIFTS AND JEWELRY

It's fun to poke around at **Ithaki** (⊠ 9 Farmaleopoulou, ☎ 0752/22816 or 0752/22091), which has hip jewelry, carved wooden handicrafts, and tasteful gift items. For good-looking jewelry of fine quality, there's **Camara** (⊠ Spiliadou 11 or Konstantinou 10, ☎ FAX 0752/24093).

Tiryns

★ ㉑ *5 km (3 mi) north of Nafplion.*

Partly obscured by citrus trees are the well-preserved ruins of the Mycenaean acropolis of Tiryns. Some tours skip the site in their mad dash to cover everything in a single day, but if you see this citadel, with its massive walls and its palace, before touring Mycenae, you can understand those rambling ruins more easily. Homer describes Tiryns as "the wall-girt city," while Pausanias gives the cyclopean walls his highest praise: "Now the Hellenes have a mania for admiring that which is foreign much more than that which is in their own land, and thus the most eminent writers have agreed to describe the Pyramids with the greatest minuteness, whilst they bestow not a word on the treasure-house of Minyas or the walls of Tiryns, which nevertheless are fully as deserving of admiration." Henry Miller was repelled by the place, as he records in *The Colossus of Maroussi:* "Tiryns is prehistoric in character. . . . Tiryns represents a relapse. . . . Tiryns smells of cruelty, barbarism, suspicion, isolation." Today the site seems harmless, home to a few lizards who timidly sun themselves on the Bronze Age stones and run for cover if you approach. Archaeological exploration of the site, which still continues, shows that the acropolis was occupied in Neolithic times.

The citadel makes use of a long, low outcrop, on which was set the circuit wall of gigantic limestone blocks (of the type called "cyclopean" because the ancients thought they could have been handled only by the giant cyclops—the largest block is estimated at more than 15 tons). Via the **cyclopean ramp** it was entered on the east side, through a gate leading to a narrow passage between the outer and inner walls. One could then turn right, toward the residential section in the **lower citadel** (now usually closed to the public) or to the left toward the **upper citadel** and **palace.** The heavy **main gate** and **second gate** blocked the passage to the palace and trapped attackers caught between the walls. After the second gate, the passage opens onto a rectangular **courtyard,** whose massive left-hand wall is pierced by a **gallery of small vaulted chambers,** or casemates, opening off a **long narrow corridor** roofed by a **corbeled arch.** (They were possibly once used to stable horses, and the walls have been worn smooth by the countless generations of sheep and goats who have sheltered there.) This is one of the famous galleries of Tiryns; another such gallery at the southernmost end of the acropolis also connects a series of five casemates with sloping roofs.

An elaborate entranceway leads west from the court to the upper citadel and palace, sited at the highest point of the acropolis. The complex included a colonnaded **court;** the great *megaron* (main hall) opened onto it and held the royal throne. Surviving fragments suggest that the floors and the walls were decorated, the walls with frescoes (now in the National Archaeological Museum of Athens) depicting a boar hunt, women riding in chariots, and a procession of women. Beyond the megaron, a large **court** overlooks the houses in the lower citadel; from here, a long **stairway** descends to a small **postern gate** in the west wall. At the excavated part of the lower acropolis a significant discovery was made; two parallel **tunnels,** roofed in the same way as the galleries on the east and south sides, start within the acropolis and extend under the walls, leading to **subterranean cisterns** that ensured a continuous water supply.

From the palace you can see how Tiryns dominated the flat, fertile land at the head of the Gulf of Argos. Schliemann, in his memoirs, waxed rhapsodic when recalling this scene: "The panorama which stretches on all sides from the top of the citadel of Tiryns is peculiarly splendid. As I gaze northward, southward, eastward, or westward, I ask myself involuntarily whether I have elsewhere seen aught so beautiful . . . and I confess that the prospect from the citadel of Tiryns far exceeds all of natural beauty which I have elsewhere seen." The view would have been different in the Late Bronze Age: the ancient shoreline was nearer to the citadel, and outside the walls there was an extensive settlement.

Profitis Ilias, the prominent hill to the east, was the site of the Tiryns cemetery. ⊠ *On low hill just past suburbs of Nafplion,* ☎ *0752/ 22657.* ⌑ *500 dr./€1.47.* ⊘ *Daily 8:30–7 (8:30–5, weekends 8:30–3 in winter).*

Argos

㉒ *12 km (7½ mi) northwest of Nafplion, 7 km (4½ mi) northwest of Tiryns.*

On the western edge of the Argive plain, amid citrus groves, is the city of Argos (population 21,000), the economic hub of the region. The fall of Mycenae and Tiryns at the close of the Late Bronze Age proved favorable for Argos. Under King Pheidon, Argos reached its greatest power in the 7th century BC, becoming the chief city in the Peloponnese. In the mid-5th century BC, it consolidated its hold on the Argive plain by eradicating Mycenae and Tiryns. But like Corinth, Argos was never powerful enough to set its own course, following in later years the leadership of Sparta, Athens, and the Macedonian kings. Twice in its history, women are said to have defended Argos: once in 494 BC when Telesilla the poetess (who may be mere legend) armed old men, boys, and women to hold the walls against the Spartans; and again in 272 BC when Pyrrhus, king of Epiros, who was taking the city street by street, was felled from above by an old woman armed with a tile. Remains of the classical city are scattered throughout the modern one, and along Tripoleos Street you can see in a small area the extensive **ruins** of the Roman bath, theater, *odeon*, and agora. ⊠ *Tripoleos St.* ⌑ *Free.* ⊘ *Tues.–Sun. 8:30–3.*

The Kastro is a Byzantine and Frankish structure incorporating remnants of classical walls, and it was later expanded by the Turks and Venetians. It's quite a hike to get to, but your reward will be an unsurpassed view of the Argolid plain. Nestle yourself into a ruined castle wall to guard against the fierce wind and ponder the mysteries of the long-lost Mycenean civilization. A small archaeological museum on the main platia, **Ayios Petros,** has well-displayed finds from Argos and nearby sites. ⊠ *Vasilissis Olgas,* ☎ *0751/68819.* ⌑ *500 dr./€1.47.* ⊘ *Daily 8:30–3.*

Shopping

MARKET

On Saturday mornings, the platia is transformed into a huge open **household-merchandise and produce market** (dwarfing that at Nafplion). It's more fun than yet another tourist shop, and you can often find good souvenirs, such as wooden stamps used to impress designs on bread loaves, at prices that haven't been inflated. Argos is also well known throughout Greece for its ouzo.

Mycenae

21 km (13 mi) north of Nafplion, 9 km (5½ mi) north of Argos.

The ancient citadel of Mycenae, which Homer describes as "rich in gold," stands on a low hill, wedged between sheer, lofty peaks but separated from them by two deep ravines. It is only 5 km (3 mi) from the Argos–Corinth highway to the gloomy, gray ruins, hardly distinguishable from the rock beneath; it's hard to believe that this kingdom was once so powerful that it ruled a large portion of the Mediterranean world at the apex of its power from 1500–1100 BC. This is one site that should only be seen after one has read a concise historical and mythological summary—only then will the setting come to life and the structures have significance. The major archaeological artifacts from the dig are in the National Archaeological Museum in Athens, so seeing these first

Mycenae

will also add to your appreciation of the site. Needless to say, the most famous object from this treasure trove is the so-called "Death Mask of Agamemnon," a golden mask that Schliemann found in the last grave he excavated. He was ecstatic and kissed it as he lifted it out, convinced this was the mask of the legendary king—but it is now known that this was impossible since it dates from an earlier period.

When you visit this site, make sure you are adequately protected from the sun by wearing long sleeves and a hat (there is no shade), carry a bottle of water, and wear sturdy walking shoes. The ground is uneven and often confusing to navigate; every week paramedics are called to carry out people who fell because they were not adequately geared for the climb or jumped from one level to another. If you have physical limitations, it's best to go only as far as the plateau by the Lion Gate and view the rest from there.

In their uncompromising severity, these ruins provide a fitting background to the horrors perpetrated by three generations of the hateful family of Atreus. The following saga seems more legend than history—but Heinrich Schliemann's belief in Homer was triumphantly vindicated when he discovered the royal town of Mycenae, which became infamous as Agamemnon's realm.

Mycenae was founded by Perseus, son of Zeus and Danae, and the Perseid dynasty provided many of its rulers. After the last of them, Eurystheus (famous for the labors he imposed on Herakles), the Mycenaeans chose Atreus, son of Pelops and Hippodamia, as their ruler. But Atreus hated his brother, Thyestes, so much that he offered Thyestes his own children to eat, thereby incurring the wrath of the gods. Thyestes pronounced a fearful curse on Atreus and his progeny; Atreus's heir, the renowned and energetic Agamemnon, was murdered on his return from the Trojan War by his wife, Clytemnestra, and her lover, Aegisthus

(Thyestes' surviving son). Orestes and his sister Electra, the children of Agamemnon, took revenge for this murder, and Orestes became king of Mycenae. During the rule of his son, Tisamenus, the descendants of Herakles returned and claimed their birthright by force, thus satisfying the wrath of the gods and the curse of Atreus.

In the 17th century BC, Mycenae began an extraordinary growth in wealth and power that was to influence all of the eastern Mediterranean. The Mycenaean civilization, at first heavily influenced by that of Minoan Crete, spread throughout Greece, and by 1350 BC the Mycenaean culture was predominant, not only on the mainland and in the Aegean but also on Crete. Clay tablets inscribed with Mycenaean Greek writing (called Linear B) have provided us with information about the society. At its height, it centered on palaces, from which kings or princes governed feudally, holding sway over various bakers, bronze workers, textile and perfumed oil manufacturers, masons, potters, and shepherds. And there were merchants, priests and priestesses, possibly a military leader, the nobility, and, perhaps, slaves. The dwellings of the elite were decorated with wall paintings depicting processions of ladies, hunting scenes, ox-hide shields, heraldic griffins, and such religious activities as priestesses bearing stalks of grain.

From the list of deities who received offerings, it seems that the Mycenaeans worshiped familiar classical deities, but the bizarre figurines found in a shrine at Mycenae (now in the Nafplion archaeological museum)—along with models of coiled snakes—are scarcely human, let alone godlike in the style of classical statuary. Mycenaeans usually buried their dead in chamber tombs cut into the sides of hills, but rulers and their families were interred more grandly, in shaft graves at first and later in immense tholos tombs—circular vaults, a hallmark of Mycenaean architecture, made by overlapping successive courses of stones, while reducing the diameter of the opening, until it was closed with a single stone on top. The tholos was built into a hillside, like a chamber tomb, entered by a long passage, or *dromos,* and covered with a mound of earth. Doors at the end of the dromos allowed the tomb to be opened and reused—not a bad feature, since the average life expectancy of a Mycenaean was about 36 years.

Massive fortification walls and gateways, also Mycenaean specialties, were necessary defenses in a culture whose economy of agriculture and trade was supplemented by occasional raiding and intercity warfare. The Mycenaeans had widespread trade contacts—their fine pottery has been found in Cyprus, southern Italy, Egypt, and the Levant. Wrecks of trading ships apparently headed toward Greece have yielded ox-hide-shape bronze ingots, aromatic resin, logs of ebony and ivory, and blue glass for jewelry. But the heyday of the Mycenaeans did not last. Drought, earthquake, invasion, and economic collapse have all been suggested individually and in combination for their fall. Around 1250 BC, arrangements were made to secretly secure the water supplies at Mycenae itself as well as at Tiryns and Athens. Coincidence? Sometime around 1200 many sites, but not all, seem to have suffered some destruction. An uprising, invasion, or earthquake? Recovery and rebuilding took place, but it is likely that the palaces were no longer used, and it is certain that a major shift in political and economic administration was under way. By 1100 BC, when there may have been another round of destruction, Greece was heading into a Dark Age. Writing became a lost art, connections beyond the Aegean were nearly severed, and many sites were abandoned. Whatever the cause, or causes, the lights eventually went out.

In 1841, soon after the establishment of the Greek state, excavations of the **ancient citadel** by the Archaeological Society uncovered the parts of the Lion Gate that lay below the surface, and in 1874, Schliemann began to dig. Today you'll enter the citadel from the northwest

★ ㉓ through the famous **Lion Gate.** The triangle above the lintel depicts in relief two lions, whose heads, probably of steatite, are now missing. They stand facing each other, their forepaws resting on a high pedestal representing an altar, above which stands a pillar ending in a uniquely shaped capital and abacus. Above the abacus are four sculptured discs, interpreted as representing the ends of beams that supported a roof. The **gate** was closed by a double wooden door sheathed in bronze. The two halves were secured by a wooden bar, which rested in cuttings in the jambs, still visible. The holes for the pivots on which it swung can still be seen in both sill and lintel.

㉔ Just inside on the right stands the **Granary,** so named for the many *pithoi* (clay storage vessels) that were found inside the building and held carbonized wheat grains. Between it and the Lion Gate a flight of steps used to lead to the top of the wall. Today you see a broad ramp leading steeply

㉕ up to the palace; the staircase is modern. Beyond the granary is the **Grave Circle A,** which contains six **royal shaft graves,** encircled by a row of upright **stone slabs** interrupted on its northern side by the entrance. Above each grave stood a vertical stone stele. The "grave goods" buried with the dead were an array of personal belongings including gold face masks, gold cups and jewelry, bronze swords with ivory hilts, and daggers with gold inlay, now in the National Archaeological Museum of Athens.

㉖ South of the Grave Circle lie the remains of the **House of the Warrior**
㉗ ㉘ Vase, the **Ramp House,** the **Cult center,** and others; farther south is the
㉙ **House of Tsountas** of Mycenae.

The palace complex covers the summit of the hill and occupies a series of **terraces;** one entered through a monumental gateway in the north-

㉚ west side and, proceeding to the right, beyond it, came to the **Great Courtyard** of the palace. The ground was originally covered by a plaster coating above which was a layer of painted and decorated stucco.

㉛ East of the Great Courtyard is the **Megaron** with a **porch, vestibule,** and the **throne room** itself, which had four columns supporting the roof (the bases are still visible) and a circular hearth in the center. Remains of an **archaic temple** and a **Hellenistic temple** can be seen north of the palace, and to the east on the right, on a lower level, are the **workshops** of the artists and craftsmen employed by the king. On the same

㉜ level, adjoining the workshops to the east, is the **House of the Columns,** with a row of columns surrounding its central court. The remaining section of the east wall consists of an addition made in around 1250 BC to ensure free communication from the citadel with the subterranean reservoir cut at the same time. ✉ *Site,* ☎ *0751/76585.* 🎫 *1,500 dr./€4.42 (includes admission to Treasury of Atreus;* ☞ *below).* ☉ *Weekdays 8:30–7 (8:30–5 in winter), weekends 8:30–3.*

On the hill of Panagitsa, on the left along the road that runs to the citadel, lies another Mycenaean settlement, with, close by, the most imposing

㉝ example of Mycenaean architecture, the **Treasury of Atreus.** Its construction is placed around 1250 BC, contemporary with the Lion Gate and after Grave Circle A was no longer used for burials. Like the other tholos tombs, it consists of a passageway built of huge squared stones, which leads into a domed chamber. The facade of the entrance had applied decoration, but only small fragments have been preserved. Traces of bronze nails suggest that similar decoration once existed inside. The tomb was found empty, already robbed in antiquity, but it must at one time have contained rich and valuable grave goods. Pausanias tells us that the ancients considered it the Tomb of Agamemnon, its other name. ⊠ *Across from ancient citadel.* 🎫 *Fee for citadel includes this site; hang on to your ticket.* ⊙ *Weekdays 8:30–7 (8:30–5 in winter).*

Dining

$ ✗ **Mykinaiko.** Two generations of the Tsiotakis family operate this true country inn, a little retreat in which you sit under a canopy on the front veranda, among flowering geraniums and bougainvillea and snoozing house cats, seemingly light years away from the violent past of the ancient civilization just down the road (and the traffic on the main road). Always ask what has been cooked up as a special that day—these can include fresh *lachanodolmades* (cabbage rolls) in a tart egg-lemon sauce, *patpoutsakia* (eggplant "shoes" filled with tomatoes and garlicky ground beef, topped with creamy béchamel), or a simple spaghetti embellished only with fresh tomato-meat sauce and topped with local *kefalograviera* cheese. Make sure to try the barrel wine from nearby Nemea, especially the potent dark red, known as the "Blood of Hercules" to the locals (after a few glasses, you may feel that you too could perform one of the Twelve Labors). ⊠ *Main road of village of Mycenae,* ☎ *0751/76724. AE, MC, V.*

Ancient Nemea

34 *18 km (11 mi) north of Mycenae.*

As the ancient storytellers once had it, *It was here that Herakles performed the first of the Twelve Labors set by the king of Argos in penance for killing his own children—he slew the ferocious Nemean lion living in a nearby cave.* Historians are interested in ancient Nemea as the site of a sanctuary of Zeus and the home of the biennial Nemean games, a Panhellenic competition like those at Isthmia, Delphi, and Olympia (today, there is a society dedicated to reviving the games and a modest competition was held here in 1996).

The main monuments at the site are the **temple of Zeus** (built about 330 BC to replace a 6th-century BC structure), the **stadium,** and an **early Christian basilica** of the 5th–6th centuries. Three columns of the temple still stand, and efforts have begun to re-erect two more. An extraordinary feature of the stadium, which dates to the last quarter of the 4th century BC, is its vaulted tunnel and entranceway. The evidence indicates that the use of the arch in building may have been brought back from India with Alexander, though arches were previously believed to be a Roman invention. A spacious **museum** displays finds from the site, including pieces of athletic gear, and coins of various city-states and rulers. Around Nemea, keep an eye out for roadside stands where local growers sell the famous red Nemean wine of this region. ⊠ *In upland valley,* ☎ *0746/22739.* 🎫 *500 dr./€1.47.* ⊙ *Tues.–Sun. 8–7, Mon. noon–7 (in winter Tues.–Sun. 8–3).*

En Route   As the road emerges from the hills onto the flatter terrain around Corinth, the massive rock of Acrocorinth peaks nearly 1,900 ft on the left. The ancient city sat at the foot of this imposing peak, its long walls reaching north to the harbor of Lechaion on the Gulf of Corinth.

Ancient Corinth

★ **35** *81 km (50½ mi) southwest of Athens, 35 km (21¾ mi) northeast of Nemea.*

West of the isthmus, the countryside opens up into a low-lying coastal plain around the head of the Gulf of Corinth. **Modern Corinth,** near the coast about 8 km (5 mi) north of the turnoff for the ancient town, is a regional center of some 23,000 inhabitants. Concrete pier-and-slab is the preferred architectural style, and the city seems to be under a seismic curse: periodic earthquakes knock the buildings down before they have time to develop any character. It was founded in 1858 after one of these quakes leveled the old village at the ancient site; another flattened the new town in 1928; and a third in 1981 destroyed many of its buildings. Most tourists avoid the town altogether, visiting the ruins of ancient Corinth and moving on. Visitors interested in folklore will certainly want to stop at the notable **Folk Museum,** located south of the town wharf. Exhibits include rare examples of 300 years of bridal and daily wear, old engravings, and dioramas. ⊠ *Town wharf,* 🕾 *500 dr./€1.47.* ⊘ *Tues.–Sun. 8:30–1:30.*

Ancient Corinth, at the base of the massive Acrocorinth peak (1,863 ft), was blessed: it governed the north–south land route over the isthmus and the east–west sea route. The fertile plain and hills around the city (where currants are grown, which are named for Corinth) are extensive, and the Acrocorinth afforded a virtually impregnable refuge. It had harbors at Lechaion on the Gulf of Corinth and at Kenchreai on the Saronic Gulf. In the 5th century BC, Corinth was a wealthy city with a reputation for luxury and vice, including a Temple of Aphrodite with more than 1,000 sacred prostitutes. These facts are emphasized too often today—amid all the titillation, the real story of Corinth is lost.

The city came to prominence in the 8th century BC, becoming a center of commerce and founding the colonies of Syracuse in Sicily and Kerkyra on Corfu. The 5th century BC saw the rise of Athens as the preeminent economic power in Greece, and Athenian "meddling" in the Gulf of Corinth and in relations between Corinth and her colonies helped bring about the Peloponnesian War. After the war, Corinth made common cause with Athens, Argos, and Boetia against Sparta, later remaining neutral as Thebes and then Macedonia rose to power.

In the second half of the 4th century BC, Corinth became active once more; in 344 BC the city sent an army to rescue Syracuse, which was threatened by local tyrants allied with the Carthaginians. Timoleon, the aristocrat who led the army, was in self-imposed exile after killing his own brother, who had plotted to become tyrant of Corinth. Corinthian opinion was divided as to whether Timoleon was the savior of the city or merely a fratricide, so no one objected to Timoleon's appointment to this dangerous mission (he wasn't present at the time). The Corinthian statesman Teleclides understood the challenge facing Timoleon perfectly, saying, "We shall decide that he slew a tyrant if he is successful; that he slew his brother if he fails." The tyrants were suppressed and Carthaginian armies expelled from Sicily; Timoleon, declared a hero, retired to a small farm outside Syracuse, where he died two years later.

Corinth was conquered by Philip II of Macedon in 338 BC, but it was named the meeting place of Philip's new Hellenic confederacy. After Philip was assassinated, Alexander immediately swooped down on Corinth to meet with the confederacy, to confirm his leadership, and to forestall any thoughts of rebellion.

After the death of Alexander, the climate continued to be profitable for trade, and Corinth flourished. When the Roman general Flamininus defeated Macedonia in 198–96 BC, Corinth became the chief city of the Achaean confederacy, and in fact the chief city of Greece. Eventually the confederacy took up arms against Rome, attacking with more impetuosity than brains or training, and was crushed. The Romans under Lucius Mummius marched to Corinth and defeated a second Greek army, and Pausanias says: ". . . Two days after the battle he took possession in force and burnt Corinth. Most of the people who were left there were murdered by the Romans, and Mummius auctioned the women and children." Corinth was razed and its wealth sent back to Rome, and for nearly 100 years the site was abandoned. In 44 BC, Julius Caesar refounded the city, and under Pax Romana Corinth prospered as never before; its population (about 90,000 in 400 BC) was recorded as 300,000 plus 450,000 slaves.

Corinth once again became a wealthy city equally devoted to business and pleasure. It was the capital of Roman Greece and was mostly populated by freedmen and Jews. The apostle Paul lived in Corinth for 18 months during this period (AD 51–52), working as a tent maker or leather worker, making converts where he could, and inevitably making many enemies as well. He preached to both pagans and Jews, causing the Jewish priests to drag him before the Roman proconsul, although he was acquitted.

The city received imperial patronage from Hadrian, who constructed an aqueduct from Lake Stymfalia to the city, and Herodes Atticus made improvements to its civic buildings. Corinth survived invasions but was devastated by earthquakes and began a long decline with further invasions and plague. After 1204, when Constantinople fell to the Fourth Crusade, Corinth was a prize sought by all, but it eventually surrendered to Geoffrey de Villehardouin (the subsequent Prince of Achaea) and Otho de la Roche (soon to be Duke of Athens). Corinth was captured by the Turks in 1458; the Knights of Malta won it in 1612; the Venetians took a turn from 1687 until 1715, when the Turks returned; and it finally came into Greek hands in 1822.

The ancient city was huge. Excavations, which have gone on since 1896, have exposed ruins at several locations: on the height of Acrocorinth and on the slopes below, the center of the Roman city, and northward toward the coast. Most of the buildings that have been excavated are from the Roman era; only a few from before the sack of Corinth in 146 BC were rehabilitated when the city was refounded.

The **Glauke Fountain** is just past the parking lot on the left. According to Pausanias, "Jason's second wife, Glauke (also known as Creusa), threw herself into the water to obtain relief from a poisoned dress sent to her by Medea." Beyond the fountain is the **museum,** which displays examples of the pottery decorated with friezes of panthers, sphinxes, bulls, and such, for which Corinth was famous; some fine mosaics from the Roman period; and a variety of marble and terra-cotta sculptures. The remains of a temple (Temple E) adjoin the museum, and steps lead from there left toward the **Temple of Apollo.**

Seven of the original 38 columns of the Temple of Apollo are still standing, and it is by far the most striking of Corinth's ancient buildings, as well as being one of the oldest stone temples in Greece (mid-6th century BC). Beyond the temple are the remains of the **North Market,** a colonnaded square once surrounded by many small shops. South of the Temple of Apollo is the main Forum of ancient Corinth. A row of shops bounds the Forum at the far western end. East of the market is a series of small temples, and beyond is the Forum's main plaza. A long line of shops runs lengthwise through the Forum, dividing it into an **upper (southern)** and **lower (northern) terrace,** in the center of which is the bema (large podium), perhaps the very one where the Roman proconsul Gallio refused to act on accusations against St. Paul.

The southern boundary of the Forum was the **South Stoa**, a 4th-century building, perhaps erected by Philip II to house delegates to his Hellenic confederacy. There were originally 33 shops across the front, and the back was altered in Roman times to accommodate such civic offices as the council hall, or *bouleterion,* in the center. The road to Kenchreai began next to the bouleterion and headed south. Farther along the South Stoa were the entrance to the **South Basilica** and, at the far end, the **Southeast Building,** which probably was the city archive.

In the lower Forum, below the Southeast Building, was the **Julian Basilica,** a former law court; under the steps leading into it were found two starting lines (an earlier and a later one) for the course of a footrace from the Greek city. Continuing to the northeast corner of the Forum, we approach the facade of the **Fountain of Peirene.** Water from a spring was gathered into four reservoirs before flowing out through the arcadelike facade into a drawing basin in front. Frescoes of swimming fish from a 2nd-century refurbishment can still be seen. The Lechaion road heads out of the Forum to the north. A colonnaded courtyard, called the **Peribolos of Apollo,** is directly to the east of the Lechaion Road and beyond it lies a **public latrine,** with toilets in place, and the remains of a **Roman-era bath,** probably the Baths of Eurykles described by Pausanias as Corinth's best known.

Along the west side of the Lechaion road is a large basilica entered from the Forum through the **Captives' Facade,** named for its sculptures of captive barbarians. West of the Captives' Facade the row of **Northwest Shops** completes the circuit.

Northwest of the parking lot is the **Odeon,** cut into a natural slope, which was built during the AD 1st century, but it burned down around 175. Around 225 it was renovated and used as an arena for combats between gladiators and wild beasts. Just north of the Odeon is the **Theater** (5th century BC), one of the few Greek buildings reused by the Romans, who filled in the original seats and set in new ones at a steeper angle. By the 3rd century they had adapted it for gladiatorial contests and finally for mock naval battles.

North of the Theater, just inside the city wall, are the **Fountain of Lerna** and the **Asklepieion,** the sanctuary of the god of healing with a small temple (4th century BC) set in a colonnaded courtyard and a series of dining rooms in a second courtyard. Terra-cotta votive offerings representing afflicted body parts (hands, legs, breasts, genitals, etc.) were found in the excavation of the Asklepieion, and many of them are displayed at the museum; similar votives of body parts can be purchased and blessed at some Orthodox churches in Greece today. A stone box for offerings, complete with copper coins, was found at the entrance to the sanctuary. Off the lower courtyard are the drawing basins of the Fountain of Lerna. ⊠ *5 km (3 mi) west of Corinth,* ☎ *0741/ 31207.* ▣ *1,200 dr./€3.53.* ☉ *Daily 8–7 (8–5 in winter).*

On the slope of Acrocorinth is the **Sanctuary of Demeter,** a small stoa (long, narrow portico) and a series of dining rooms with couches. The climb up to Acrocorinth is worth the effort for both the medieval fortifications and the view, one of the best in Greece. The entrance is on the west, guarded by a moat and outer gate, middle gate, and inner gate. Most of the fortifications are Byzantine, Frankish, Venetian, and Turkish—but the right-hand tower of the innermost of the three gates is apparently a 4th-century BC original. There is no access to the site; it can only be viewed. ⊠ *Below road to Acrocorinth and on its lower slopes.*

Xylokastro

🔟 *34 km (21 mi) west of Corinth.*

Xylokastro, a pleasant little town, is perfect if you want to soak your feet after trudging around Corinth. The road just west of town that climbs up Sithas Valley also climbs up to Ano Trikala, an alpine landscape where the peak (second highest in the Peloponnese) stays covered with snow into June.

Beaches
A wide, paved promenade along the shore, with a beautiful view of the mountains across the gulf, leads to a good if somewhat pebbly **beach** (⊠ Beyond the east end of town).

ACHAEA AND ELIS

Vouraikos Gorge, Kalavrita, Rion, Patras, Chlemoutsi, Olympia

Achaea's wooded mountains guard the mountain steadfasts of Arcadia to the south and mirror the forbidding mountains of central Greece on the other side of the Corinthian gulf. Those who venture into Achaea will inevitably find their way to Patras, a teeming port city, with all the flavor, color, and vices of port cities. Elis, farther to the south, is bucolic and peaceful. It is a land of rolling hills green with forests and vegetation, and it is not surprising that the Greeks chose this region as the place in which to hold the Olympic Games.

Vouraikos Gorge

🔟 *Diakofto, the coastal access point: 47 km (29¼ mi) west of Xylokastro; Kalavrita: 25 km (15½ mi) south of Diakofto.*

You don't have to be a train buff to enjoy the *Kalavrita Express,* an exhilarating narrow-gauge train ride starting at Diakofto. It heads up into the mountains through the Vouraikos Gorge, a fantastic landscape of towering pinnacles and precipitous rock walls. The diminutive train, a cabless diesel engine sandwiched between two small passenger cars, was built by the Italians between 1889 and 1896 to bring ore down from Kalavrita. It crawls upward, clinging to the rails in the steeper sections with a rack and pinion. To best appreciate the vista, get a first-class ticket so that you can sit in front by the engineer or in the last car. The train goes through 14 tunnels and bridges, rushing up and down wild mountainside terrain. The *Kalavrita Express* makes the round-trip from Diakofto six times daily. It takes about one hour, the first trip is at 6:48 AM, and the last returns at 5:51 PM. ☒ *Fare 1,000 dr./€2.94 round-trip, 1,500 dr./€4.42 first-class. Although the trip can be made from Athens (round-trip fare, Athens–Kalavrita: first-class 5,000 dr./€14.74, second-class 3,200 dr/€9.43), it is best enjoyed between Corinth and Patras.*

The trip is especially wondrous at daybreak on the first trip from Diakofto to Kalavrita—but if you want to take the early train, it is best to stay in the little town of Diakofto, a peaceful settlement that is nestled in a plain of citrus and olives groves with dramatic mountains as a background. The closest organized beach is **Akrata,** which is also a small town with a few hotels and a small crowded sandy strip.

After dinner, take a stroll on Diakofto's main street to have a look at the antique train car in front of the train station. Have a *gliko* (sweet) at one of the outdoor tables set in front of the cafés facing the train station. You'll get a glimpse of unembellished country life—nothing much happens, but daily events take on heightened significance, as you observe from the laid-back banter and expressive conversations among the mostly male crowd.

A road goes directly from Diakofto to Kalavrita; the spectacular 25-km (15½-mi) drive negotiates the east side of the gorge. A cab from Diakofto to Kalavrita costs about 7,500 dr./€22.12 round-trip.

Forty-five minutes into its trip, the *Kalavrita Express* train (☞ *above*) pauses at Zakhlorou, where you can hike up a steep path through evergreen oak, cypress, and fir to the monastery of **Mega Spileo** (altitude 3,117 ft). This hour-long trek along a rough donkey track offers superb views of the Vouraikos valley and distant villages on the opposite side. The occasional sound of bells carries on the wind from flocks of goats grazing on the steep slopes above. The monastery, founded in the 4th century and said to be the oldest in Greece, has been burnt down many times, most recently in 1934. It once had 450 monks and owned vast tracts of land in the Peloponnese, Constantinople (now Istanbul), and Macedonia, making it one of the very richest in Greece. It sits at the base of a huge (360-ft-high) curving cliff face and incorporates a large cavern (the monastery's name means "large cave"). You can tour the monastery to see a charred black wax and mastic icon of the Virgin, supposedly painted by St. Luke, found in the cave after a vision of the shepherdess Euphrosyne led some monks there in 362 AD. You will also see ornate vellum manuscripts of early gospels and the heads of the founding monks. ⊠ *Start hike on path in Zakhlorou.* ☉ *Daily 8–3. Women must wear long skirts and long sleeves; men must wear pants.*

Beyond Zakhlorou, the gorge widens into a steep-sided green alpine valley for the last 11 km (7 mi) to Kalavrita (☞ *below*), a small town of about 2,000 nestled below snowcapped Mt. Helmos.

Dining and Lodging

$ ✕ **Kostas.** This *psistaria* (grill house) is run by a hospitable Greek-Australian family. Their grilled chicken is the main attraction, but *horta* (boiled wild greens), huge *horiatiki* (village) salads with a nutty flavored feta cheese, and stuffed zucchini are other reasons to eat here. ⊠ *Main road coming into town opposite the National Bank, Diakofto,* ☎ *no phone. No credit cards.*

$–$$ ▥ **Chris Paul Hotel.** Located in Diakofto, built in 1981 in a lemon orchard, and run by two accommodating Greek-Australian brothers, Chris Paul has simple but attractive and well-maintained rooms. The hallways are whitewashed, and each floor has either blue, green, or brown as an accent color for matching curtains and bedspread. Each room has TV and a balcony; a small pool is in the garden, plus there is a congenial bar perfect for a cocktail before dinner. Breakfast is extra. ⊠ *Clearly signposted, in an orchard close to train station, Diakofto 25100,* ☎ *0691/41715,* ℻ *0691/42128. 24 rooms. Bar, air-conditioning, outdoor pool. DC, MC, V.*

$ ✕▥ **Romantzo Hotel.** This old wooden hotel set in Zakhlorou is aptly named—its location next to a most picturesque train station takes one back in time to a more graceful age. With its verdant hamlet watered by rushing streams, it's hard to imagine a more romantic setting than the one enjoyed by this hotel. The nine rooms are modest, but all have private bathrooms and balconies with views over the valley. Innkeeper Vassiliki Mitropoulou takes pride in her property and setting, as well as supervising the cooking at the hotel's reasonable restaurant across the way, which offers hearty country fare. It's a favorite getaway for adventurous Greek couples, who arrive on the *trenaki* (little train) and hike to the monastery. Book ahead, especially on weekends; breakfast is extra. The path to the monastery begins nearby. ⊠ *Next to railroad station platform, Zakhlorou 25001,* ☎ ℻ *0692/22758. 9 rooms. No credit cards.*

Kalavrita

③ *25 km (15½ mi) south of Diakofto.*

The mountain air here is refreshing, breezy, and cool at night, even in the middle of the summer, making Kalavrita a favorite retreat for people from Patras and Diakofto. The ruins of a **Frankish castle, the Church of the Dormition,** and a **small museum** are worth seeing, but Greeks remember Kalavrita as the site of the Nazis' most heinous war crime on Greek soil. On December 13, 1943, the occupying forces rounded up and executed the town's entire male population over the age of 15 (1,436), then locked women and children into the school and set it on fire. They escaped, but the Nazis later returned and burned the town to the ground. The clock on the church tower is stopped at 2:34 PM, marking the time of the execution. Off Konstantinou, signs will lead you to the **Martyr's Monument,** a white cross on a cypress-covered hill that stands as a poignant commemoration of the 1943 massacre.

Lodging

$$–$$$ 🏨 **Filoxenia.** This modern hotel caters largely to ski-season tours. All the rooms have balconies that look either to the gorge or the mountains of the Peloponnese. The decor appears to be a holdover from the '70s, but each room has a minibar and TV, and the friendliness of the staff allows you to overlook this minor flaw. Prices are much lower in the summer, which is low season. Breakfast is extra. ⊠ *Ethnikis Antistasios 10, Kalavrita 25001,* ☎ *0692/22290 or 0692/22493,* 𝔽𝔸𝕏 *0692/23009. 28 rooms. Restaurant, bar, minibars. AE, DC, MC, V.* ⊗

$$ 🏨 **Xenonas Fanara.** This complex of apartments was built in 1995 in the style of a country inn with spacious, rustic rooms that each feature all the amenities of home: a fully equipped kitchen, individual heat control, TV, lounge, and fireplace. A large home-style breakfast is included in the price. In winter, this is a favorite of the ski crowd, who have made the Mount Helmos Ski Centre a quickly expanding resort. ⊠ *Close to hospital for the elderly, Kalavrita 25001,* ☎ *0692/23665,* 𝔽𝔸𝕏 *0692/23667. 10 rooms. Restaurant. No credit cards.*

Outdoor Activities and Sports

Diaselo Avgou on Mt. Helmos has the **B. Leondopoulos Mountain Refuge** for hikers, with a capacity of 12 to 16. Contact the Kalavrita Alpine Club (⊠ Top end of 25 Maritiou [25th of March St.], ☎ 0692/22661), open weekdays from 7 to 3. The Athens travel agency **Trekking Hellas** runs a six-day "Mountains and Monasteries" hiking tour on Mts. Ziria and Helmos (☞ Contacts and Resources *in* Northern Peloponnese A to Z, *below*). The leading ski facility in the area is the **Mount Helmos Ski Centre** (☎ 0692/22661, 𝔽𝔸𝕏 0692/2241).

Rion

③ *5 km (3 mi) east of Patras, 49 km (30½ mi) west of Diakofto.*

Rion is distinguished by the **Castle of the Morea,** built by Sultan Bayazid II in 1499; it sits forlorn amid a field of oil storage tanks. Here the Turks made their last stand in 1828, holding out for three weeks against the Anglo-French forces. Along with the **Castle of Roumeli** on Antirion's shore opposite, it guarded the narrows leading into the Gulf of Corinth. A half-hourly car ferry connects Rion with Antirion, linking the Peloponnese with central and northwestern Greece. Plans for a titanic suspension bridge, proposed during the first Papandreou administration, are said to be in the works, with a completion date slated for 2004.

Beaches

Try **Agios Vassilios** (⊠ Near Rion), which received one of the highest cleanliness ratings from Perpa, Greece's ministry of the environment.

Patras

⑩ *135 km (84 mi) west of Corinth, 5 km (3 mi) west of Rion.*

Patras, the third-largest city in Greece, begins almost before Rion is passed. It is usually written off as a nondescript harbor town that one gets out of as quickly as possible, but locals are trying to change that first impression by promoting Patras as a destination in itself—the municipality has launched an extensive improvement plan, paving the harbor roads and creating pedestrian walks on inner-city shopping streets (sigh—not always in a tasteful manner). Patras was once called the "Little Paris of Greece" and in the 19th and early 20th centuries it was a gracious, elegant city with distinguished European-style buildings with stately arcades and ornate wrought-iron balconies. Unfortunately, a good portion of its historic buildings have been torn down or destroyed by earthquake.

Like all respectable Greek cities, it has an ancient history. Off its harbor in 429 BC Corinthian and Athenian ships fought inconclusively, and in 279 BC the city helped defeat an invasion of Celtic Galatians. Its acropolis was fortified under Justinian in the 6th century, and Patras withstood an attack by Slavs and Saracens in 805. Silk production, begun in the 7th century, brought renewed prosperity, but control passed successively to the Franks, the Venetians, and the Turks, until the War of Independence. Thomas Palaiologos, the last Byzantine to leave Patras before the Turks took over in 1458, carried an unusual prize with him—the skull of the apostle St. Andrew, which he gave to Pius II in exchange for an annuity. St. Andrew had been crucified in Patras and had been made the city's patron saint. In 1964 Pope Paul VI returned the head to Patras (perhaps thinking that Pius II had gotten his money's worth, or that it had been a while since Thomas last collected his annuity). Today it graces St. Andrew's Cathedral, seat of the Bishop of Patras.

The major western port for freighters carrying the all-important currants, and for passenger and car ferries sailing to Italy, thoroughly modern Patras has the international, outward-looking feel common to port cities. The waterfront is pleasant enough, though not overly interesting; you'll find lots of mediocre restaurants, a range of hotels (some of the older ones have crumbled and are closed), the bus and train stations, and numerous travel agents (caveat emptor for those near the docks). Back from the waterfront, the town gradually rises along arcaded streets, which provide welcome shade and rain protection. Of the series of large platias, tree-shaded Queen Olga Square is the nicest. Patras is built on a grid system and it is easy to find your way around. For a pleasant stroll before dinner, take Ayios Nikolaos Street upward through the city until it comes to the long flight of steps leading to the medieval Venetian castle overlooking the harbor. The narrow lanes on the side of Ayios Nikolaos are whitewashed and lined with absolutely charming village-style houses, many of which are being restored.

The **Archaeological Museum**'s small rooms are laden with Mycenaean through Roman period finds, many from the ancient Roman odeon in town, still in use for a summer festival. It is a pleasant surprise to find these antiquities in a city not known for them. ⊠ *Mezonos 42,* ☎ *061/275070.* ⊠ *Free.* ☉ *Tues.–Sun. 8–3.*

Platia Olga (⊠ 2 blocks uptown from Othonos Amalias, off Kolokotroni) is one of Patras's many popular squares—locals sip their ouzo and observe their fellow townspeople as they eat, drink, shop, and play in this quintessentially Greek meeting place. Other popular squares include **Platia 25 Martiou (25th of March Square)**, and **Platia Ypsila Alonia**.

In the evening the **Kastro** (✉ On the hill uptown, southeast of train station) overlooking Patras draws many Greek couples seeking privacy and a spectacular view, and visitors are well advised to follow suit: the sight of the shimmering ships negotiating the harbor stirs even the most travel-weary. A word of advice: going without a date can make you feel really out of place! You can have a taste of the famous Port-like Mavrodaphne wine in the dignified bar here, just a stone's throw from the huge purple grapes growing in the vineyard that are used to make the elixir; a shop is open so that you can buy some wine to take home with you.

A **Roman odeon** (✉ Southwest of the Kastro, off Platia 25 Martiou) remains in use in Patras, almost 2,000 years after it was first built. Today the productions of summer arts festivals are staged in the well-preserved theater, which was discovered in 1889 and heavily restored in 1960 (☞ Nightlife and the Arts, *below*).

NEED A   Some wineries are now open for tours and tastings; among them is
BREAK?   **Antonopoulos Winery** (✉ Tripolis, 19 km [11¾ mi] south of Patras),
              open daily 9–4, with shorter hours in summer. **Achaia Clauss** (✉ 9 km
              [5½ mi] east of Patras, ☎ 061/325051) operates tours daily 9–7:30
              and in winter 9–5. Call ahead for tours and tastings.

Beaches

The closest decent beach to Patras is **Kalogria** (✉ About 32 km [20 mi] west of Patras), a long sandy stretch backed by a pine forest and much favored by Greek families, so quite crowded on weekends. If you stay away from the large hotel complex at the north end of the beach, you can find estuaries which are great for bird watching. People swim in them as well, but you may feel like Hercules if you are joined by yard-long snakes, said to be harmless.

Dining and Lodging

Avoid most of the indifferent restaurants along much of Patras's waterfront. For lighter fare or after-dinner ice cream, coffee, and pastries, choose one of the cafés along upper Gerokostopoulou Street, which is closed to traffic, or go to the cafés in Platia Psila Alonia—a favorite watering hole of locals near the Kastro, which, as a bonus, offers a panoramic view of the harbor.

The streets leading through the Old Town up to the south end of the Kastro have many small *mezodopoleia*, which serve *mezze*, Greek-style tapas. These are frequented by locals, who wouldn't step foot in the overpriced foreign-style restaurants near the boat docks. Two of the most sympathetic are Mezodopoleo Mouries and Ouzerie Kastro, nestled in quaint houses with flower-bedecked verandas on Papadiamatopoulou Street, across from the Kastro entrance.

$–$$ ✗ **Apanemou.** This charming *mezodopoleio* (café serving appetizers) at the south end of the waterfront is convenient to the fishing harbor (from which the owner brings in his catch each day). The room has whitewashed walls, checked tablecloths, and nautical artifacts. Best bets are the crisp zucchini croquettes and the smokey *melitzanasalata* (eggplant spread). The *psarosoupa* (fish soup) is distinguished by its rich broth. Ask what fish or seafood is freshest that day—shrimp *saganaki* (in a casserole with tomatoes, cheese, and peppers) is just one stellar offering. ✉ *Posidonios 21, 9 km (5½ mi) north of Patras,* ☎ *061/994739. AE, DC, MC, V.*

$–$$ ✗ **To Konaki.** Nouli and Andonis Andrikopoulou take pride in offering local specialties in this homey inn set inland from the train station. *Hortopites* (pies filled with wild greens and feta) and *kolokokeftedes* (zucchini croquettes) are two of the most popular appetizers. Mouth-watering favorites include *bekri mezze* (the drunkard's appetizer, or marinated pork), *midhia saganaki* (mussels in a tomato, cheese, pepper casserole) and *arnaki tis gastras* (lamb slow-cooked in a clay pot). On Saturday night, a group occasionally plays traditional Greek music. During the summer months, this place closes and the family moves down the coast to a seaside restaurant, set under an arbor on the beach in the idyllic village of Kato Ararchovitika, just past Rio, 15 km. from Patras. ⊠ *Aratou and Karaiskai 44,* ☎ *061/275096. No credit cards. May–Aug.*

$ ✕ **Krini.** Patras still has a few venerable *oinopoleia,* or wine shops, once a staple of every neighborhood even in Athens, and this is one of the oldest. Set on the sloping streets heading up to the Kastro, it sells wine from barrels midafternoon to a loyal clientele (mostly moustachioed older men). Join them or follow an old Greek custom by bringing an empty wine or water bottle, sampling the wines, and then having it filled with the one that suits you (a great accompaniment for a picnic lunch). Taverna Krini is in the rustic village house to the left and is open in the evening, when it specializes in dishes made with wine, such as *soutzoukakia* (meatball sausages made with red wine) or rabbit braised with white wine and rosemary. ⊠ *Pandokratoros 57,* ☎ *no phone. No credit cards. Last 2 wks of Aug.*

$$$$ ▥ **Primorolia.** Primarolia is the Italian word for "the first pressing of the grapes" (in other words, the finest)—a fitting name for this unique little hotel, opened in 2000 on the waterfront across from the train station. Functioning as both art gallery and hotel, it is hung throughout with modern art by well-known Greek artists—even the inner courtyard is crowned with a dramatic hanging scupture suspended below the atrium skylights. Rooms have every possible comfort and are designed with dramatic fabrics and wallpapers to make the most of limited space in the smaller rooms of this old mansion. These have streetside views, while larger rooms have balconies with harbor views. A complete buffet breakfast is included. ⊠ *Othonos Amalias 33, 240740,* ☎ *061/624900,* FAX *061/240740. 11 rooms, 3 suites. mini-bars, hairdryers. AE, DC, MC, V. www.arthotel.gr.*

$$$ ▥ **Astir.** Near the Patras waterfront, the genteel Astir is easily the best
★ appointed large hotel in Patras, but discerning travelers will bemoan its shortage of character. It is, however, very convenient and has a professional, courteous staff. The lobby decor is nostalgic of the former glory days of Patras and has many restored antiques that exude a homey touch. The rooftop patio view over the quayside to the mountains on the other side of the gulf is a real winner. At night you can watch the brilliantly lighted ferries as they glide northwest toward Brindisi. The rooms are not overly spacious but are nice, some with TVs upon request, and there are plenty of public lounges. Continental breakfast is included in the price. ⊠ *Ayios Andreou 16, 26223,* ☎ *061/ 277502,* FAX *061/271644. 120 rooms. Restaurant, bar, pool, sauna, meeting rooms. AE, DC, MC, V.* ✎

$$ ▥ **Galaxia.** The Galaxia is dependable. Its wallpapered rooms are basic but have TVs and clean, gray-tile bathrooms with tubs, and some have balconies. Near, but not on, the waterfront, this hotel is on a pedestrian walkway and will allow you a good night's sleep without frills. It's conveniently located to walk to the Kastro and close to many trendy cafés frequented by students at the large branch of the university. Continental breakfast is included in the price. ⊠ *Ayios Nikolaos 9, 26221,* ☎ *061/275981 through 061/275983,* ☎ FAX *061/278815. 53 rooms. Air-conditioning. AE, DC, MC, V.*

$ ▥ **Adonis.** The Adonis has, for its class, very good, well-kept rooms,
★ and they all have TVs, a balcony, and views in those facing the gulf

and the Adriatic. On the down side, the bathrooms are closetlike, with showers of the curb-and-curtain variety. Adonis adjoins the bus terminal, and some rooms may be noisy during the day. Buffet breakfast is included in the price. ⊠ *Zaimi and Kapsali 9, 26221,* ☎ *061/ 224235, 061/224213, or 061/224257,* FAX *061/226971. 56 rooms. Bar, air-conditioning. AE, MC, V.*

Nightlife and the Arts

BARS AND CAFÉS

For nightlife, in general it's best to ask around when you arrive. On the northern side of 25th of March Square are the steps at the head of **Gerokostopoulou Street,** below the odeon. Closed to traffic along its upper reaches, this street has myriad cafés and music bars that make it a relaxing place to spend an evening. It is the place to be for the young and hip of Patras.

FESTIVALS

Patras holds a lively **summer arts festival** (⊠ Office: 104 Ayios Georgiou, ☎ 061/278206) with concerts and dance performances at the Roman odeon in the fortress. It usually runs from mid-June to early October. For more information, contact the **festival hot line** (☎ 061/ 279866) or the Patras EOT (☞ Visitor Information *in* Northern Peloponnese A to Z, *below*).

With a few successful vineyards in the area, Patras has also become the site of an annual **Wine Festival.** The festival aims at promoting Greek wines and usually runs during the first two weeks of September. Contact the organizers at ☎ 061/279866.

If you're lucky enough to be in Patras in late January to February, you're in for a treat: the **Carnival** (⊠ Office: 104 Agios Georgiou, ☎ 061/ 226063), which lasts for several weeks, is celebrated with masquerade balls, fireworks, and the Sunday Grand Parade competition for the best costume. Be warned, however: room rates can double or even triple during this time; tickets for seats (3,000 dr./€8.84) at the parade, which is held in front of the Municipal Theater at Platia Georgiou, are sold at the Carnival office.

NIGHTCLUBS

Worth a spin on the dance floor is the music club **Privé** (⊠ Germanou 55, ☎ 061/274912). **Utopia Music Hall** (⊠ Ayios Andreou 91, ☎ 061/ 222104) usually has a Greek bouzoukia variety program.

Outdoor Activities and Sports

HIKING AND CLIMBING

There is a hiking and climbing refuge at **Psarthi** on Mt. Panahaiko (capacity 50). Contact the **Patras Alpine Club** (⊠ Pantanassis 29, ☎ 061/273912) for information.

TENNIS

Patras Tennis Club (☎ 061/226028) is open to the public.

Shopping

Patras is a major city, and you'll find fashionable clothing, jewelry, and other products here. The best shops are on Riga Feraou, Maizonas, and Korinthou streets, near Platia Olga. However, unlike most other Greek cities, Patras also has shops that sell handmade and machine-made Greek icons, which make beautiful decorations. At night in the small narrow streets surrounding the Kastro, one can find Greek craftsmen burning the midnight oil in their workshops and stores painting images of saints on wood and stone.

Chlemoutsi Castle

④ *56 km (34¾ mi) west of Patras.*

At the foot of Chlemoutsi Castle, the **Kastro** (⊠ From Neokori 8 km [5 mi] along the Loutra Killinis) is the best-preserved Frankish monument in the Peloponnese. Geoffrey I de Villehardouin, who built it from 1220 to 1223, named it Clairmont. The Venetians called it Castel Tornese, perhaps on account of the Frankish *tournoi* (coins) minted in nearby Glarentza, stamped with the facade of St. Martin's Church in Tours. The Byzantine despot Constantine Palaiologos captured it in 1427 and used it as a base from which to attack Patras, the last Frankish stronghold. The castle has a huge irregular-hexagon keep, with vaulted galleries around an open court. After 1460 the Turks strengthened the gate and altered the galleries. It was captured by the Venetians in 1687, and shortly thereafter was ceded to the Turks. On the southwest side you can see a breach made by Ibrahim Pasha's cannon during the War of Independence. Basically untended, the castle is open for exploring at all hours.

Beaches

The coast south of Chlemoutsi Castle toward **Loutra Killinis** is a beach resort area, where its wide, sandy beach on the Adriatic is among the best in Greece. Farther south of the castle, near Gastouni and Pyrgos, are the fine beaches **Katakolo and Spiantza** (⊠ Off Hwy. 9).

Olympia

★ *112 km (69½ mi) south of Patras, 65 km (40½ mi) southeast of Chlemoutsi Castle.*

Ancient Olympia, the ancient Sanctuary of Zeus, is one of the most popular sites in Greece. Two hours is the minimum necessary to see the ruins and the fine museum, and three or four hours would be even better. Modern Olympia, of course, pales to its earlier namesake: the village is a one-street town (Praxitelous Kondilis Street, to be exact), consisting largely of hotels and tourist shops with a smattering of tavernas. It provides visitors to the ancient site with the services they need, and little else. For more of a stopover, soak up the surrounding pleasant hilly countryside, which is, for once in southern Greece, well watered and green.

Although the first Olympiad is thought to have been in 776 BC, bronze votive figures of the Geometric period (10th–8th centuries) reveal that the sanctuary was in use before that date. The festival took place every four years over a five-day period in the late summer during a sacred truce, observed by all Greek cities. Initially only native speakers of Greek (excepting slaves) could compete, but Romans were later admitted. Foreigners could watch, but married women, Greek or not, were barred from the sanctuary during the festival on pain of death. One woman caught watching was spared, however, since not only all her sons but her husband and father had won Olympic victories. The events included the footrace, boxing, chariot and horse racing, the pentathlon (combining running, jumping, wrestling, and both javelin and discus throwing), and the *pankration* (a no-holds-barred style of wrestling in which competitors could break their opponent's fingers and other body parts). By and large the Olympic festival was peaceful, though not without problems. The Spartans were banned in 420 BC for breaking the sacred truce; in 364 BC there was fighting in the Altis between the Eleans and the Pisans and Arcadians in front of the crowd who had come to watch the games; the Roman dictator Sulla carried off the treasure to finance his army and five years later held the games in Rome. The 211th

Ancient Olympia

festival was delayed for two years so that Nero could compete, and despite a fall from his chariot, he was awarded the victory.

The long decline of Olympia began after the reign of Hadrian. In AD 267, under threat of an invasion, many buildings were dismantled to construct a defensive wall; Christian decrees forbade the functioning of pagan sanctuaries and caused the demolition of the Altis. Earthquakes settled its fate, and flooding of the Alpheios and the Kladeos, together with landslides off the Kronion hill, buried the abandoned sanctuary.

Olympia's ruins are fairly compact, so it's easy to get a quick overview in an hour and then investigate specific buildings or head to the museum. The site is very pleasant, with plenty of trees providing shade. The ancient sanctuary occupies a compact, flat area at the base of the Kronion hill (on the north), where the Kladeos and Alpheios rivers join. It comprised the **sacred precinct**, or **Altis**, a large rectangular enclosure south of the Kronion, with **administrative buildings, baths, and workshops** on the west and south, and the **Stadium** and **Hippodrome** on the east. In 1829, a French expedition investigated the Temple of Zeus and brought a few metope fragments to the Louvre. The systematic excavation begun by the German Archaeological Institute in 1875 has continued intermittently to this day.

42 South of the entrance are the remains of a small **Roman bath** and the
43 **Gymnasion,** essentially a large open practice field surrounded by stoas.
44 The large complex opposite the Gymnasion was the **Prytaneion,** where the *prytaneis* (magistrates in charge of the games) feted the winners and where the Olympic flame burned on a sacred hearth. Just south is the gateway to the Altis, marked by two sets of four columns. Just
45 beyond is the **Philippeion,** a circular shrine started by Philip II and completed after his death by Alexander the Great.

ONE LAST TRAVEL TIP:

Pack an easy way to reach the world.

123 456 7891 2345
J.D. SMITH

Wherever you travel, the MCI WorldCom Card℠ is the easiest way to stay in touch. You can use it to call to and from more than 125 countries worldwide. And you can earn bonus miles every time you use your card. So go ahead, travel the world. MCI WorldCom℠ makes it even more rewarding. For additional access codes, visit **www.wcom.com/worldphone**.

MCI WORLDCOM.

EASY TO CALL WORLDWIDE

1. Just dial the WorldPhone® access number of the country you're calling from.

2. Dial or give the operator your MCI WorldCom Card number.

3. Dial or give the number you're calling.

Austria ◆	0800-200-235
Belgium ◆	0800-10012
Czech Republic ◆	00-42-000112
Denmark ◆	8001-0022
Estonia ★	800-800-1122
Finland ◆	08001-102-80
France ◆	0-800-99-0019
Germany	0800-888-8000
Greece ◆	00-800-1211
Hungary ◆	06▼-800-01411

Ireland	1-800-55-1001
Italy ◆	172-1022
Luxembourg	8002-0112
Netherlands ◆	0800-022-91-22
Norway ◆	800-19912
Poland ⁙	800-111-21-22
Portugal ⁙	800-800-123
Romania ⁙	01-800-1800
Russia ◆ ⁙	747-3322
Spain	900-99-0014
Sweden ◆	020-795-922
Switzerland ◆	0800-89-0222
Ukraine ⁙	8▼10-013
United Kingdom	0800-89-0222
Vatican City	172-1022

◆ Public phones may require deposit of coin or phone card for dial tone.   ★ Not available from public pay phones.
▼ Wait for second dial tone.   ⁙ Limited availability.

EARN FREQUENT FLIER MILES

Bureau de change

Cambio

外国為替

In this city, you can find money on almost any street.

NO-FEE FOREIGN EXCHANGE

The Chase Manhattan Bank has over 80 convenient
locations near New York City destinations such as:

      Times Square
      Rockefeller Center
      Empire State Building
      2 World Trade Center
      United Nations Plaza

Exchange any of 75 foreign currencies

◯ CHASE

THE RIGHT RELATIONSHIP IS EVERYTHING.®

Directly in front of the Philippeion is the large Doric temple of Hera, the **Heraion** (circa 600 BC). It is well preserved, especially considering that it is constructed from the local coarse, porous shell limestone. At first it had wooden columns, which were replaced as needed, so although they are all Doric, the capitals don't exactly match. Three of the columns have been set back up. A colossal head of a goddess, possibly from the statue of Hera, was found at the temple and is now in the site museum. Just south of the Heraion are the remains of a **6th-century** BC **pentagonal wall** built to enclose the **Pelopeion** (Shrine of Pelops), at the time an altar in a sacred grove. According to Pausanias, the **Altar of Olympian Zeus** was southeast of the temple of Hera, but no trace of it has been found. Some rocks mark its supposed location, the most sacred spot in the Altis, where daily blood sacrifices are said to have been made.

There is no doubt about the location of the **Nymphaion,** or Exedra, which brought water to Olympia from a spring to the east. A colonnade around the semicircular reservoir had statues of the family of Herodes Atticus and his imperial patrons. The 4th-century **Metroon,** at the bottom of the Nymphaion terrace, was originally dedicated to Cybele, Mother of the Gods, and was taken over by the Roman imperial cult. Nearby, at the bottom of the steps leading to the Treasuries and outside the entrance of the Stadium, were **16 bronze statues of Zeus,** called the Zanes, bought with money from fines levied against those caught cheating at the games. Bribery seems to have been the most common offense (steroids not being available). Olympia also provides the earliest case of the sports-parent syndrome: in the 192nd Olympiad, Damonikos of Elis, whose son Polyktor was to wrestle Sosander of Smyrna, bribed the latter's father in an attempt to buy the victory for his son.

On the terrace itself are the city-state **Treasuries,** which look like small temples and were used to store valuables, such as equipment used in rituals. Just off the northeast corner of the Altis is the **Stadium,** which at first ran along the terrace of the Treasuries and had no embankments for the spectators to sit on; embankments were added later but were never given seats, and 40,000–50,000 spectators could be accommodated. The starting and finishing lines are still in place, 600 Olympic ft apart.

The **House of Nero,** a 1st-century villa off the southeastern corner of the Altis, was hurriedly built for his visit. Nearby was found a lead water pipe marked NER. AUG. Beyond this villa, running parallel to the Stadium, was the **Hippodrome,** where horse and chariot races were held. It hasn't been excavated, and much has probably been eroded away by the Alpheios. Beyond the Altis's large southeastern gate, appended to its southern wall, is the **Bouleterion** and, just south of it, the **South Hall.** The Bouleuterion consisted of two rectangular halls on either side of a square building that housed the Altar of Zeus Horkios, where athletes and trainers swore to compete fairly.

In the southwestern corner of the Altis is the **Temple of Zeus.** Only a few column drums are in place, but the huge size of the temple platform is impressive. Designed by Libon, an Elean architect, it was built from about 470 to 456 BC. The magnificent **sculptures** from the pediments are on view in the museum at Olympia (☞ *below*). A gilded bronze statue of Nike (Victory) stood above the east pediment, matching a marble Nike (in the site museum) that stood on a pedestal in front of the temple. Both were the work of the sculptor Paionios. The cult statue inside the temple, made of gold and ivory, showed Zeus seated on a throne, holding a Nike in his open right hand and a scepter in his left. It was created in 430 BC by Pheidias, sculptor of the cult statue of Athena in the Parthenon, and was said to be seven times life size; it was one of the Seven Wonders of the Ancient World. It is said that Caligula wanted to move the statue to Rome and replace the head with one of his own, but the statue laughed out loud when his men approached it. It was removed to Constantinople and destroyed by fire in AD 475. Pausanias relates that behind the statue there was "a woolen curtain . . . decorated by Assyrian weavers and dyed with Phoenician crimson, dedicated by Antiochos." It is possible this was the veil of the Temple at Jerusalem (Antiochos IV Epiphanes forcibly converted the Temple to the worship of Zeus Olympias).

Just outside the gate at the southwestern corner of the Altis stood the ⑤⑦ **Leonidaion,** at first a guest house for important visitors and later a residence of the Roman governor of the province of Achaea. Immediately ⑤⑧ north of the Leonidaion was **Pheidias's workshop,** where the cult statue of Zeus was constructed in a large hall of the same size and orientation as the interior of the temple. Tools, clay molds, and Pheidias's own cup (in the museum) make the identification of this building certain. It was later used as a Byzantine church. North of the workshop ⑤⑨ is the **Palaestra,** built in the 3rd century BC, for athletic training. The rooms around the square field were used for bathing and cleansing with oil, for teaching, and for socializing. ✉ *½ km (¼ mi) outside of Olympia,* ☎ *0624/22517.* 🎫 *1,200 dr./€3.53.* ☉ *Weekdays 8–7, weekends 8:30–5.*

The **"new" museum at Olympia** (✉ Across from ancient Olympia), officially opened in 1982, has in its collections the sculptures from the Temple of Zeus and the Hermes of Praxiteles, discovered in the Temple of Hera in the place noted by Pausanias. The central gallery of the museum holds one of the greatest sculptural achievements of classical antiquity: the pedimental sculptures and metopes from the Temple of Zeus, depicting Herakles' Twelve Labors. The Hermes was buried under the fallen clay of the temple's upper walls and is one of the best-preserved classical statues. Unfortunately the famous Nike of Paionios is in the old museum, which is closed, so it can't be seen by visitors. There's also a notable terra-cotta group of Zeus and Ganymede; the head of the cult statue of Hera; sculptures of the family and imperial patrons of Herodes Atticus; and bronzes found at the site, including votive figurines, cauldrons, and armor. Of great historic interest are a helmet dedicated by Miltiades, the Athenian general who defeated the Persians at Marathon, and a cup owned by the sculptor Pheidias. ✉ *Southern end of main road,* ☎ *0624/22529.* 🎫 *1,200 dr./€3.53.* ☉ *Mon. noon–7, Tues.–Fri. 8–7, weekends 8:30–3.*

The **Museum of the Olympic Games** is just about the only tourist attraction in modern Olympia. Its impoverished collection is of some, if not great, interest. ✉ *Spiliopoulou St.,* ☎ *0624/22544.* 🎫 *500 dr./€1.47.* ☉ *Weekdays 8–3:30, weekends 1–4:30.*

Dining and Lodging

$ ✕ **Ambrosia.** Don't let the tour groups deter you; there's a reason why they flock here. You, too, should try the tasty dishes, such as rabbit or lamb *ladorigani* (with olive oil and dried crushed oregano), beef yiouvetsi (baked in a clay pot with orzolike pasta), *briam* (a baked dish of potatoes, squash, and eggplant), fresh green beans, pastitsio, tart *dolmades* (stuffed vegetables, grape leaves, or fruit) in the traditional avgolemono sauce, and savory grilled meats. Save room for some homemade galaktobouriko for dessert. ✉ *Near train station (no street numbers outside the center),* ☎ *0624/23414,* 📠 *0624/22439.* MC, V.

$ ✕ **Taverna Bacchus.** As in so much of Greece, the best restaurants are often in little villages outside the towns. Dimitris Zapantis's family-run taverna in the village of Miraka (just 3 km [2 mi] outside of

Olympia along the road to Lambia) is one such establishment and has been entertaining its guests for 20 years. Locals start to trickle in around 10:30, which is the standard dinnertime for Greeks (indeed it's a little early!). Try the delectable chicken with oregano and enjoy an evening in a quaint Greek village. ⊠ *Miraka Village,* ☎ *0624/22498. No credit cards. Closed Dec.–Feb.*

$ ✕ **Taverna Praxitelous.** This taverna serves an array of mouthwatering appetizers; to sample them all, order the *pikilia* (variety) plate, which includes zucchini fritters, *tirolates* (ham and cheese fingers), *tzatziki* (yogurt-garlic dip), eggplant dip, and moussaka. Besides grilled meats, the typical *magirefta* such as rabbit stifado and stuffed tomatoes go well with the barrel red or one of the local Achaea wines. In winter sit inside near the fireplace (the tables are always brightened with fresh flowers) and in summer sit out in the pedestrian zone. ⊠ *Spiliopoulou 7, near police station,* ☎ *0624/23570. V.*

$ ✕ **To Steki Tou Vangeli.** Just a block off the main drag, Vangelis and his wife Agapi run this peaceful corner taverna with a veranda. Ask for suggestions and the night's specials. Chicken *lemonata* (with lemon sauce) is a house specialty, and the moussaka, distinctly spiced with a fluffy béchamel, is reputed to be the best in the northern Peloponnese. Save room for sesame-based semolina-style halvah. ⊠ *Spiliopoulou 7, near police station,* ☎ *0624/23570. V.*

$$$$ ▥ **Olympia Palace.** The old Altis Hotel, in the heart of the modern town but within walking distance of ancient Olympia, was given a a complete facelift in 1999 and emerged as a classy beauty. Spacious lounges and restaurants are now decorated in rich rose and burgundy, and a cozy bar is convenient for a nightcap. The hotel has a small shopping center and exchange bureau. Public rooms and rest rooms are disabled accessible, as are the guest rooms, most of which look out over the fertile plains and mountains of Olympia, a lovely view that can also be savored from the roof garden. A buffet breakfast is included in the room rate. ⊠ *Praxitelous Kondili 2, 27065,* ☎ *0624/23101,* ℻ *0624/22525. 58 rooms, 6 suites. 2 restaurants, bar, pool, minibars, meeting facilities. AE, DC, MC, V. www.olympiapalace.gr.*

$$$ ▥ **Antonios.** This first-class hotel, set on a hill at town's edge, has fairly
★   spacious rooms with TVs and balconies. There's a swimming pool and barbecue patio, and the hotel operates the adjacent Touris Club, which has a restaurant, bar, disco, folk dance performances, and a pool. Buffet breakfast is included in the price. All rooms boast TV with a satellite connection to U.S. channels. The rather worn furniture in the public areas is scheduled for replacement sometime in the "near" future. ⊠ *Road to Krestena, 27065,* ☎ *0624/22348 or 0624/22349,* ℻ *0624/22112. 70 rooms. Restaurant, bar, pool. AE, MC, V.*

$$$ ▥ **Europa (Best Western).** One of Olympia's best, the Europa combines
★   white stucco, pine, and red tiles in a traditional style, then mixes in high ceilings and large windows. The rooms have large beds, *flokati* (sheep wool) rugs, marble bathrooms, and small terraces. Most face the pool. Buffet breakfast is included in the price. An excellent gift shop inside the hotel specializes in high-quality Greek icons and jewelry. Set just a few minutes away from ancient and modern Olympia, the Europa is surrounded by a small wood and offers a tranquil respite from the throngs of the tourist sites. ⊠ *Oikismou Drouba (off road to ancient Olympia), 27065,* ☎ *0624/22650 or 0624/22700,* ℻ *0624/23166. 42 rooms. Restaurant, pool, tennis court, shop. AE, DC, MC, V.*

$ ▥ **Pelops Hotel.** This friendly small hotel run by Suzanna and Theo Spiliopoulou is the best bargain in Olympia, considering the pleasant atmosphere and extras offered. Rooms are simple but comfortable and clean, and all have balconies, most with views of the nearby mountains. The Pelops is on a quiet side street and gets cool breezes from the mountains (air-conditioning is not necessary, even in July and August). The owners are a goldmine of information about Ancient Olympia and can help you with your itinerary for other locations in the Peloponnese since they also run a travel agency. They have a small restaurant as well (open only in high season), which, although quite modern, serves delicious Greek classics. Suzanna also organizes Greek nights at the Touris Club; guests can use the Touris Club pool. Breakfast is included in the room rate. ⊠ *Varela 2, 227065,* ☎ *0624/22543,* FAX *0624/22213. 26 rooms. MC, V.*

NORTHERN PELOPONNESE A TO Z

Arriving and Departing

By Bus
The regional **bus associations** (KTEL) provide frequent service at reasonable prices to Patras, Pyrgos (for Olympia), Corinth, Argos, Epidauros, Kranidi, Nafplion (for Mycenae), Sparta (for Mystras and Monemvassia), and Xylokastro. Some sample prices: Corinth (every 30 minutes, 1½ hours, 1,850 dr./€5.45), Patras (every 45 minutes, 3 hours, 3,650 dr./€10.76), Nafplion (hourly, 2½ hours, 2,450 dr./€7.22), Olympia (four buses daily, 5½ hours, 5,350 dr./€15.78), Tripolis (10 buses daily, 3½ hours, 3,000 dr./€8.84), Kalamata (12 buses daily, 4½ hours, 4,500 dr./€13.27) Epidauros (two to three buses daily, 2½ hours, 2,500 dr./€7.37). Buses leave from **Terminal A** (⊠ 100 Kifissou, ☎ 01/512–4910) on the outskirts of Athens (take Bus 51 at corner of Zinonos and Menandrou Sts. near Omonia Square). Pick up a bus schedule from the Athens EOT (☞ *below*) or call the following numbers for departure times or to reserve a seat: Corinth (☎ 01/512–9233); Sparta and Monemvassia, ☎ 01/512–4913; Patras (☎ 01/513–6185); Nafplion, Mycenae, and Epidauros, ☎ 01/513–4588.

By Car
It is best to take a bus to either Patras or Nafplion and rent a car there. The **toll highway,** known simply as *ethnikos odos* or National Road—which runs from Athens to the Isthmus of Corinth (84 km/52 mi, 1¼ hours) and on to Nafplion, Patras, and Olympia, is wide but heavily trafficked, especially during holiday periods. No speed limit is enforced, and the asphalt becomes very slippery when wet. The accident rate is alarmingly high. Others take the **car ferry** between Patras and Italy (Ancona, Bari, or Brindisi). Car ferries for Brindisi or the Ionian islands leave from Patras's main terminal on the port; for Bari and Ancona, the pier is about 1 km (½ mi) west. An alternative route from Athens to Patras is via Delphi and the Rion–Antirion ferry.

By Ferry and Hydrofoil
Minoan Flying Dolphin (⊠ Akti Miaouli 69, Piraeus, ☎ 01/419–9000) operates the Flying Dolphin hydrofoils (passengers only) from Zea Marina in Piraeus to ports on the east coast of the Peloponnese, sailing daily in summer to Porto Heli (1 hour 55 minutes, 3,375 dr./€9.95) and to Nafplion (3 hours, 4,040 dr./€11.91), and once or twice a day to Monemvassia (3 hours 10 minutes, 5,541 dr./€16.34). In winter, there is a much-reduced schedule, especially because hydrofoils leave port only in the calmest weather. You may take your car only on the slower-moving ferryboats, which leave Athens a few times weekly for Monemvassia (car: 9,887 dr./€29.16–12,866 dr./€37.95; passenger: 2,897 dr./€8.54) and Porto Heli (car: 8,986 dr./€26.50–10,397 dr./€30.66, passenger: 1,995 dr./€5.88). Call the **Piraeus Port Authority** (☎ 01/422–6000) or the Athens EOT (☞ *below*) for a ferry schedule.

Nafplion port authority (☎ 0752/27022) and **Patras port authority** (☎ 061/341002) can advise you about entry and exit in their ports for yachts. Patras's EOT (☞ *below*) is at the port. ·

By Plane

There is no plane service to the Northern Peloponnese.

By Train

Traveling by train is convenient for the Northern Peloponnese and is relatively inexpensive. Trains from Athens depart from the Peloponnissos station (✉ Sidirodromon); take Bus 057, which leaves every 10 minutes from Panepistimiou (fare 100 dr./€.29). There are five departures daily to Nemea–Mykines–Argos–Nafplion (3 to 5 hours to Nafplion, 1,950 dr./€5.75); 13 trains daily to Corinth (2 hours, 780 dr./€2.30; on the IC, the InterCity express, 1½ hours, 1,170 dr./€3.45); and eight daily to Patras (4½ hours, 2,370 dr./€6.99; IC 4 hours, 3,580 dr./€10.56). There is also a train line from Athens to Tripolis and Kalamata (7 hours, 2,200 dr./€6.48). Another line runs along the west coast connecting Kalamata with Patras (6 hours, 2,250 dr./€6.63). Going to Olympia by train isn't worth the trouble; the trip takes almost eight hours, with a change at Pyrgos. Note that continued rail service to the Peloponnese is in some doubt; the state-owned rail company recently recommended canceling all lines except to Patras because of aging equipment, but the government rejected the proposal. For schedule information call (☎ 01/513–1601 or 01/821–3882); some English is spoken.

Getting Around

By Bus

In addition to serving major centers, such as Nafplion, Argos, Corinth, and Patras, the coaches of the regional bus associations (KTEL) travel to virtually every village in the Northern Peloponnese. The bargain price and the extensive network make bus travel a viable alternative to renting a car, although frequency decreases off the beaten track. Schedules are posted at local KTEL stations, usually on the main square or main street.

By Car

The roads are good in the Northern Peloponnese, and driving can be the most enjoyable (if not the most economical) way of seeing the region. The **Greek Automobile Touring Club (ELPA)** has an office in Patras (✉ Patroon Athinon 18, ☎ 061/425411) and can assist with repairs and information. During the Epidauros Festival ELPA road-assistance vehicles patrol the roads around there.

By Train

Trains run from Athens to Corinth and then the route splits; you can go south to Argos and Nafplion or west along the coast to Patras and then south to Pyrgos and Kalamata. Alternatively you can go directly through the Peloponnese to Kalamata via Tripolis. On the western route the train stops at Kiato, Xylokastro, Diakofto, where a wonderful narrow-gauge branch line heads inland to Kalavrita, and Aigion, before arriving in Patras. In high summer the trains between Patras and Athens can be crowded with young people arriving from or leaving for Italy on ferries from Patras. Branch lines leave the main line at Kavasila for Killini and at Pyrgos for Olympia. If you know you are returning by train, buy a round-trip ticket (good for a month); there is a substantial discount.

The *Kalavrita Express* train makes the Diakofto–Kalavrita round-trip along the **Vouraikos Gorge** six times daily; the first trip is at 6:48 AM (leaving Diakofto), and the last returns at 5:51 PM. The fare is 1,000 dr./€2.94 round-trip. Although the trip can be made from Athens (round-trip fare, Athens–Kalavrita: first-class 4,000 dr./€11.79, second-class 2,800 dr./€8.25), it is best enjoyed between Corinth and Patras.

Contacts and Resources

Emergencies
Tourist Police: Patras (⊠ Patreos 53, ☎ 061/220902 or 061/220903); **Corinth** (⊠ Ermou 51, ☎ 0741/23282); **Nafplion** (⊠ 25 Martiou, ☎ 0752/28131); **Olympia** (⊠ Spiliopoulou 15, ☎ 0624/22550).

Guided Tours
Many companies offer bus tours from Athens to the major archaeological sites in the Northern Peloponnese, including half-board accommodations, guide, and entrance fees. **CHAT** (⊠ Stadiou 4, ☎ 01/322–2886) and **Key Tours** (⊠ Kallirois 4, ☎ 01/923–3166) organize a two-day tour to Corinth, Mycenae, and Epidauros (25,000 dr./€73.74) and a six-day tour to all major sites in the Peloponnese, with accommodations at the best available hotels (120,000 dr./€353). Many local travel agents offer whirlwind day trips to sites, especially Epidauros (usually including the performance and stops at some combination of Nafplion, Mycenae, and Corinth) and Olympia. These basic, no-frills tours are for those who don't expect a lot of hand-holding and have trouble planning in advance. They can be booked at travel agencies and at larger hotels.

If you are in Patras, either of the agencies listed above can arrange for a pickup for their tours at your hotel. Contact Manolopoulos Travel (⊠ Othonos Amalias 35, ☎ 061/223621, FAX 061/222246), which can make these arrangements for you. They can also offer tours within Patras and the surrounding areas.

Hiking and Climbing
For information on hiking and mountain climbing in the Northern Peloponnese, contact the **Greek Federation of Mountaineering Associations** in Athens (⊠ Milioni 8, Athens, ☎ 01/363–6617 or 01/364–5904), which operates several huts, open to the public; a detailed brochure is available at their offices.

Pharmacies
Pharmacies, clearly identified by red-cross signs, take turns staying open late. A listing is published in the local newspaper; it is best to check at your hotel to find out not only which pharmacy is open but how to get there.

Travel Agency
Trekking Hellas (⊠ Fillelinon 7, Athens 10557, ☎ 01/315–0853 or 01/325–0317).

Visitor Information
Greek National Tourist Organization (GNTO or EOT): **Athens** (⊠ Karageorgi Servias 2, ☎ 01/322–2545); **Nafplion** (⊠ 25th of March St., across from OTE, ☎ 0752/24444); **Olympia** (⊠ Praxitelous Kondili 75, ☎ no phone); and **Patros** (⊠ Harbor, Terminal 6, Glyfada, ☎ 061/430915, FAX 061/423866). **Local tourist police** (☞ *above*).

9 SOUTHERN PELOPONNESE

TRIPOLIS, KALAMATA, SPARTA, MYSTRAS, AND MONEMVASSIA

From its ebullient ports to its ghostly Byzantine ruins, from its olive groves to its dizzying gorges and languorous beaches, the southern half of the Peloponnese is a land of extremes, its scenery unsubtle, almost theatrical. Cement-laden towns like Tripolis, Sparta, and Kalamata are set amid startling natural beauty. Despite the waves of invaders—Franks, Venetians, and Turks—this land is considered the distillation of all that is Greek: indulged idiosyncrasy, intractable autonomy, appreciation of simple pleasures.

By Toula
Bogdanos

Updated by
Stephen
Brewer

A NCIENT RUINS AND MEDIEVAL MONUMENTS pervade the landscape here more than in any other region of Greece. Those who
penetrate the forbidding mountains of the Taygettus range in
the center of the Peloponnese discover not only the forgotten stone towns
of Arcadia—Stemnitsa, Dimitsana, and medieval Karitena—but also
the remote Temple of Apollo in Bassae. Farther south the sandy cape
of Messinia offers a low-key seaside retreat, while Messene with its mammoth fortifications conjures up images of ancient civilizations. The Mycenaean ruins of Nestor's Palace are almost a millennium older than ancient
Messene but only an hour away, as is Pylos, a white-washed village in
whose harbor was fought the famous 1827 sea battle that paved the
way to Greek independence.

Across the Taygettus lies Laconia, where the ancient Spartans practiced
their famously disciplined armies and where Byzantium's final flourish has left us the astonishingly well-preserved Mystras. Except for the
foundations of Artemis's sanctuary and some fragments of Apollo's
shrine at Amyclae, where hyacinths still bloom in spring from his lover
Hyacinthus's drops of blood, nothing remains of ancient Sparta—fitting tribute perhaps to what was the first totalitarian state. Boys were
taken from their parents at the age of seven and submitted to a training without parallel in history for ruthlessness; the kingdom's iron coinage
was not accepted outside Sparta's borders, creating a contempt for wealth
and luxury (and, in turn, rapacious kings and generals); Sparta's warrior caste subjugated the native Achaean inhabitants of the region. Today,
all that remains of this realm founded on martial superiority is dust.
As you move on, at the very tip of continental Europe dangles the Mani
peninsula, from the charming port of Gythion to the underground caves
of Pirgos Dirou and to villages studded with tower houses, vestiges of
the Mani's blood feuds and vendettas. Finally, on Laconia's southeast
peninsula sits the inhabited medieval city of Monemvassia, known as
Greece's Mont-Saint-Michel.

Pleasures and Pastimes

Dining

You won't find many fancy restaurants in the Southern Peloponnese,
but the countless local tavernas and *estiatoria* (restaurants) serve memorable Greek home cooking and a great variety of fresh fish. Villages
here in the south were the source of such international favorites as av-
golemono soup and lamb fricassee. Don't go by looks; a hole-in-the-
wall may serve the town's best meals, and what's available is what the
butcher, fisherman, and grocer sold that day, despite what's printed on
the menu. Local specialties to watch for: In the mountain villages near
Tripolis, order *stifado* (beef with pearl onions), *arni souvla* (lamb on
the spit), *kokoretsi* (entrails on the spit), and thick, creamy yogurt. In
Sparta, look for *bardouniotiko* (a local dish of chicken stuffed with
cheese, olives, and walnuts), and around Pylos, order fresh ocean fish
(priced by the kilo). In the rest of Laconia, try *loukaniko xoriatiko* (village sausage), and in the Mani, ask for ham. As for wines, the light
white from Mantinea is a favorite, and whenever possible, sample the
xima (barrel wines), which range from light, dry whites to heavy,
sleep-inducing reds. Casual dress is almost always acceptable, and unless noted, reservations are unnecessary or not accepted.

CATEGORY	COST*
$$$$	over 6,000 dr. (€17.69)
$$$	4,000 dr.–6,000 dr. (€11.79–€17.69)
$$	2,500 dr.–4,000 dr.(€7.34–€11.79)
$	under 2,500 dr. (€7.37)

*for a three-course meal, including tax, service, and usually beer or a small carafe of wine

Greek Dancing

Dance performances, accompanied by traditional music, are common in the region. You may well see the popular *kalamatianos* (a circular dance from Kalamata), or the *tsakonikos* (in which the dancers wheel tightly around each other and then swing into bizarre spirals), which resembles the sacred dance of Delos, first performed by Theseus to mime how he escaped from the Labyrinth; the *tsamikos,* from Roumeli in central Greece, is an exclusively male dance for showing off agility and derring-do.

Hiking

Throughout the Peloponnese there are many small trails or *kalderimi* (mule paths) to hike, as well as the international E4 European Rambler Trail, which starts in the Pyrenees, winds through Yugoslavia, and traverses Greece to Gythion. The southern half, from Delphi to Gythion, is considered less difficult than the northern section and can be walked most of the year; the best time is mid-May through early October. Pick up the southern section at Menalon Refuge, and continue through Vresthena, Sparta, Taygettus Refuge, and Panagia Yiatris monastery to Gythion. For more information, call the Tripolis Alpine Club, Sparta Alpine Club, or the Greek Federation of Mountaineering Associations; request a map from the Army's Geographical Service in Athens (☞ Contacts and Resources *in* Southern Peloponnese A to Z, *below for all*).

Lodging

Except for a few luxury complexes along the coast, most hotels are standard, with plain rooms, though the newer ones have more services and a bit more decorative flair—and, fortunately, are more likely to have air-conditioning. Bathrooms usually have showers instead of tubs. Wherever you stay in the warm months, come prepared with mosquito protection—most windows are screenless and the pests are ubiquitous.

It's important to reserve ahead if you plan to travel in the high season (July and August), especially in coastal hotels that cater to groups. It's often cheaper to book the larger hotels through a travel agent in the town or in Athens, and in most hotels you can negotiate a lower-than-official rate off-season. If the hotels are full, you can always find private rooms, though often without a private bath. Ask the tourist police or a local travel agency for assistance. Most hotels in the $$$ and $$$$ range feature air-conditioning; those in the $ and $$ categories do not, except where noted.

CATEGORY	COST*
$$$$	over 25,000 dr. (€73.74)
$$$	15,000 dr.–25,000 dr. (€44.24–€73.74)
$$	6,000 dr.–15,000 dr. (€17.69–€44.24)
$	under 6,000 dr. (€17.69)

*for a standard double room in high season, including tax and service

☙ following the text of a review is your signal that the property has a Web site, where you will find details and, usually, images; for a link, visit www.fodors.com/urls.

Water Sports

You can usually rent paddleboats and canoes on the beaches in front of major hotels; occasionally there are windsurfing and waterskiing instructors, though the rates are rather high. For example, waterskiing runs about 5,000 dr./€14.74 for 15 minutes.

Sailing in Greece isn't restricted to the Aegean Islands. Many people prefer to sail to the islands near Methoni, with stops at Sapientsa, Skiza, and Venetiko. When you rent a sailboat or charter a yacht, the agency will usually indicate where to find water and fuel. The local port authority and the Naval Association can advise you on mooring information (☞ Contacts and Resources *in* Southern Peloponnese A to Z, *below*). You can moor at Gythion, which has water and fuel; in Kalamata repair service and moorings are usually available; for sailing around the Messinian cape, the port authority at Pylos can be of help.

Exploring the Southern Peloponnese

Politically, the Southern Peloponnese is divided into regions established by the ancients—Messinia in the southwest, Laconia in the southeast, and Arcadia to the north. Massive mountain ranges sweep down the fingers of the peninsula; the beaches are some of the finest and least developed in Greece. The area is considered somewhat isolated from the rest of Greece, especially politically, but its people are great respecters of *filoxenia* (hospitality). For the traveler, the regions are best divided into four: Arcadia, Messinia, Laconia, and a fourth, the Mani, part of which is administered by Messinia, and the other part by Laconia. We describe each of these regions in its own section, below.

Numbers in the text correspond to numbers in the margin and on the Southern Peloponnese map.

Great Itineraries

Though it may be less accessible than other parts of Greece, this part of the Peloponnese holds forth for the visitor a less hectic pace, and fewer crowds. The best moments come to those who stray beyond the familiar, who take time to have a coffee in the square of a village on Mt. Taygettus, a picnic at the ruins of Bassae, or a sunset swim beneath the brooding towers of a Maniote fishing hamlet. A short visit forces the traveler to make some difficult choices: any of the four areas covered in this chapter can be explored in a few days, but in that time you will want to explore no more than *one* region. Arcadia is the most accessible region from Athens, and Messinia and Laconia are nearby. The Mani at the tip of the Taygettus mountain range awaits those wise enough to plan an extended stay in this outpost of Greece and Europe.

IF YOU HAVE 3 DAYS

Travelers who spend three days in the Southern Peloponnese would best be served with a quick visit to 🖼 **Tripolis** ①, from where you can visit the Arcadian mountain village of **Andritsena** ⑤ and the **Temple of Apollo at Bassae** ⑥. These can be explored in one day. On the second day, either head south to 🖼 **Sparta** ⑳ and **Mystras** ㉑, or go southwest, over the forbidding Taygettus mountains through 🖼 **Kalamata** ⑦ to the nearby ruins of **ancient Messene** ⑧. On the third day cross the famous and exquisitely beautiful Langada Pass, going east to Sparta if you're coming from Kalamata, or west to Kalamata if you're leaving Sparta.

IF YOU HAVE 6 DAYS

Begin by exploring Arcadia, passing through 🖼 **Tripolis** ① to the surrounding mountain villages of **Stemnitsa** ②, **Dimitsana** ③, **Karitena** ④, and **Andritsena** ⑤, and the **Temple of Apollo at Bassae** ⑥. After two days make your way across the Taygettus to Messinia's major center,

Southern Peloponnese

Mirtóön Sea

Mediterranean Sea

Ionian Sea

Gulf of Argolis

Gulf of Laconia

Gulf of Messinia

20 miles
30 km

ARGOLID

ARCADIA

LACONIA

MESSINIA

MANI

MT. PARNON

MT. TAYGETTUS

Methana
Poros
Hydra Town
Galatas
Ermioni
Hydra
Fanari
Kranidion
Spetses Town
Porto Heli
Spetses
Leonidion
Kiparissi
Geraka
Monemvassia 23
Neapolis
Elafonisos
Kythera
Tiryns 70
Nauplion
Argos
Lerna
Astros
Ayios Petros
Geraki
Gythion 19
Tripolis 1
Sternitsa 2
Dimitsana 3
Karitena 4
▲ Mt. Lykaeon
Andritsena 5
Temple of Apollo at Bassae 6
Megalopoli
Alphios R.
Nedhas R.
Kopanaki
Kyparissia
Filitra
Gargaliani
Nestor's Palace
Chora 9
Pylos 11
Sfakteria
Methoni 12
10
Meligalas
Petalidi
Koroni
Ancient Messene 8
Kalamata 7
Sparta 20
Amykles 22
Eurotas R.
Mystras 21
Vathia 18
Pirgos Dirou Caves 17
Areopolis 16
Itilo and Neo Itilo 14
Kardamyli 13
Limeni 15
Pamisos R.

E65
74
E65
39
39
1
76
E65
E55
9
6
39
39
86
86
9

KYTHERA
Ayios Pelagia
Potamos
Kythera Town

🖫 **Kalamata** ⑦, and from there to the ancient Mycenaean **Nestor's Palace** ⑩ and the port town of 🖫 **Pylos** ⑪, for its archaeological museum, castles, and a beautiful bay. Finally, venture into the Mani and see **Kardamyli** ⑬; **Areopolis** ⑯, the sun-baked gateway to the Inner Mani; and the gloomy **Pirgos Dirou Caves** ⑰. If the Mani fills you with foreboding, or if you haven't seen your fill of fine Byzantine ruins, cross the Langada Pass from Kalamata to 🖫 **Sparta** ⑳ where you can stomp about the Laconian Plain, seeing the last jewel in the Byzantine crown, **Mystras** ㉑, followed by a day's sojourn to the colorful Laconian port of **Gythion** ⑲.

When to Tour

Snow renders many of the mountain regions inaccessible in the winter, while temperatures can soar to uncomfortable reaches in many regions, especially the Mani, in summer. May, September, and October are especially comfortable months here, with pleasant temperatures (it's warm enough to swim) and little rain. Whenever you visit, remember that the Southern Peloponnese is not as popular a travel destination as the Northern Peloponnese, which means that services and resources are proportionally limited: be prepared to find a reduced selection of hotels and restaurants. As with the rest of Greece, on Mondays most state museums and sites are closed. On Sundays many have free admission.

ARCADIA

Tripolis, Stemnitsa, Dimitsana, Karitena, Andritsena, Bassae

Arcadia was named after Arcas, whom Zeus fathered with Callisto. According to one version of the legend, Callisto's father chopped Arcas into bite-size pieces and served him to Zeus for dinner. Zeus managed to give his son new life as a bear, but in a fit of ingratitude, Arcas eventually had his wicked way with his mother. That's when Zeus decided to turn both mother and son into the constellations Ursa Major and Minor, the Big and Little Dipper.

No conqueror ever really dominated the Arcadians. Even when Tripolis was the Turks' administrative center, the mountain villagers lived much as they pleased, maintaining secret schools to preserve the rudiments of Greek language and religion, and harassing the Turks in roaming bands. In recent years, locals have abandoned their pastoral life to look for work in Athens; Arcadia now has no more people than Corinthia, a region half its size.

Tripolis

❶ *150 km (93¼ mi) southwest of Athens, 70 km (43½ mi) southwest of Corinth.*

Regardless of the direction from which you approach the southern half of the Peloponnese, history suggests you're sure to at least pass through Tripolis. In the days of the Ottoman Empire, this crossroads was the capital of the Turkish Pasha of the Peloponnese, and during the War of Independence it was the first target of Greek revolutionaries. They captured it in 1821 after a six-month siege, but the town went back and forth between the warring sides until 1827, when Ibrahim Pasha's retreating troops burned it to the ground. Tripolis is a dreary town; one of its few redeeming features is Platia Areos, one of the largest and most beautiful *platias* (central squares) in Greece—definitely the place to while away the time if marooned in Tripolis. The best thing about

Tripolis is the mountain scenery, with attendant hillside villages, that surrounds it; you will soon understand why this regions is nicknamed the Switzerland of Greece.

If you do have some extra time, visit Tripolis's small **archaeological museum** to see the artifacts from the nearby sites of Mantinea, Tegea, and elsewhere. There are some excellent inscriptions dating from the Achaean League as well as some beautiful early Christian funerary stele. ✉ *Euaggelistrias 8,* ☎ *071/242148.* 🎫 *500 dr./€1.47.* ☉ *Tues.–Sun. 8:30–3.*

Catch an authentic Greek experience by visiting one of the **kafenions** on Platia Agiou Vasiliou. Here Greek men smoke, play cards, and talk politics; women may feel a little uncomfortable but will be treated with great respect if they enter. You can also grab a quick and juicy (and very inexpensive) souvlaki at **E Gonia** in a corner of the platia (*gonia* means "corner" in Greek).

Dining and Lodging

$$$ ✕ **Petit Trianon.** Locals no longer scowl at the gold statues and min-
★ iobelisks: they've discovered the decent prices and great cooking. Special dishes include *argitiko* (beef with pearl onions slow-cooked in a ceramic dish) and bacon-wrapped filet mignon with mouthwatering potatoes. Beware: many appetizers and desserts are perilously heavenly. French and German wines are well matched. ✉ *Platia Areos 24,* ☎ *071/237413,* 🆕 *071/241615. DC, MC, V.*

$$ ✕ **Café Kallisto.** Sit under the large white umbrellas of this café and order an exotic fruit tea, raisin crepes soaked in Grand Marnier, baklava, or the chef's special cake. Or savor drinks with a plate of *pikilia* (appetizers) such as meats, smoked trout, shrimp, olives, and cheese. The rosy pink interior with Hollywood prints is cozy, and a large evil-eye charm over the bar will protect you from jealous admirers. ✉ *Platia Areos 5,* ☎ *071/237019. No credit cards.*

$$ ✕ **Touristiko Periptero.** Pine trees and birdsong surround this refuge, nestled in a park—replete with a peacock and pheasant aviary—just outside of town. Try the wild chicory salad, chicken *rollo* (stuffed with ham, bacon, and cheese), *sofrito* (beef with parsley and garlic), or just a coffee. In a small hut nearby, **To Xayiati,** drinks only are served. ✉ *Off Ethniki Antistasis in Agios Georgios township, look for small parking lot on the right, amid the pines,* ☎ *071/238433 or 071/222971. No credit cards.*

$$ 🏨 **Arcadia.** Tripolis's hotels aren't as distinguished as its restaurants. This six-story green cement box with ordinary rooms is the town's most comfortable and convenient; saving graces are the high ceilings, heavy dark furniture, and the roof garden. ✉ *Kolokotroni Sq. 1, 22100,* ☎ *071/225551 through 071/225553,* 🆕 *071/222464. 45 rooms. Restaurant, bar. No credit cards.*

$ 🏨 **Menelaon.** When it opened in 1939, the Menelaon was the grandest hotel in town. It served as a hospital after the war, and thus began its denouement, although in 1960 King Constantine and his queen spent the night. It's no longer plush, but it's a good choice; spacious, clean rooms have balconies overlooking the main square. Rooms vary quite a bit; ask to see a selection. ✉ *Platia Areos, 22100,* ☎ *071/232740. 36 rooms. Restaurant, air-conditioning. No credit cards.*

Outdoor Activities and Sports

HIKING AND CLIMBING

The **Ostrakina Refuge** (✉ On Mt. Menalon, ☎ 0796/22227), northwest of Tripolis, houses 26 hikers and climbers, with a kitchen, oil- and wood-burning stoves, tank water, and indoor toilets.

On Mt. Parnon at Arnomoussa, southeast of Tripolis, the **George Pierce Refuge** has accommodations for 40 people, a kitchen, oil stoves, spring water, a fireplace, and indoor toilets.

SKIING

Mt. Menalon ski center (☎ 071/22227) at Oropedio Ostrakina (4,310 ft) has five downhill runs and three tows; food and overnight accommodations are available. The center is 30 km (18½ mi) from Tripolis, with the last 3 km (2 mi) a dirt road. For information, call the Tripolis Alpine Club (☞ Contacts and Resources *in* Southern Peloponnese A to Z, *below*).

Stemnitsa

❷ *43 km (26¾ mi) northwest of Tripolis.*

The town, also called Ipsous, is wondrously perched 3,444 ft above sea level amid a forest of fir and chestnut trees. For centuries it was one of the Balkans' best-known metalworking centers, and today a minuscule school is still staffed by local artisans. From the north side of town, a well-marked path leads through the mountains to the isolated monastery of **Moni Agiou Ioannitou,** with a little chapel covered in frescoes.

The unusual **folklore museum** devotes one floor to mock workshops for indigenous crafts such as candle making and bell casting; the other two floors house re-created traditional rooms and a haphazard collection of costumes, weapons, icons, and plates. ⊠ *Off main road,* ☎ *0795/ 81252.* ☑ *Free.* ۞ *Weekdays 4–6, Wed. and Thurs. 11–1, Sat. 11–1, and 4–6; Sun. 11–1.*

Lodging

$ ⊞ **Trikoloneion.** This simple but welcoming stone hotel is the only accommodation of note in Stemnitsa. A wood decor dominates in an attempt to evoke the traditional Arcadian style. When the mountain air is cool and the sky begins to darken, the warm well-lighted interior provides an enchanting refuge. As this is the only hotel in town it can get full on occasion, particularly if it has been booked by a tour. ⊠ *On main road, 22024,* ☎ *0795/81297,* ℻ *0795/81483. 20 rooms. Restaurant, bar, lounge. No credit cards.*

Dimitsana

❸ *50 km (31 mi) northwest of Tripolis, 10 km (6 mi) north of Stemnitsa.*

Dimitsana affords stunning views of the Arcadian mountains, and the best way to enjoy the delightful surroundings is to leave your car at the entrance to town and stroll the maze of narrow cobbled lanes. Archaeologists found ruins of a cyclopean wall (irregular stones without mortar) and classical buildings near the town that belonged to the acropolis of Teuthis, the ancient city.

The **town library** displays manuscripts, rare books, and memorabilia from the Greek revolutionary period, when Dimitsana was a center for revolutionary activity against the Turks. Also explore the site of a **gunpowder mill** and the monk Hatzi Agapios's **School of Greek Letters,** which educated leaders such as Germanos, the bishop of Patras. ⊠ *Main square,* ☎ *0775/31219.* ☑ *Free.* ۞ *Weekdays 8–2, Sat. 8– noon. Closed Nov.–Mar.*

Karitena

❹ *54 km (33½ mi) west of Tripolis, 26 km (16 mi) south of Dimitsana.*

Karitena, a picturesque medieval village of stone houses topped by a Frankish castle, is depicted on the back of the 5,000 dr./€14.74 bill. Now inhabited by fewer than 300 people, Karitena had a population of 20,000 during the Middle Ages. For a stunning view of the gorge and the town, walk over to the multiarched Frankish bridge that spans the Alpheios.

When the Franks took over from the Byzantines in 1209, they gave the town to Hugo de la Bruyères, who built the **Frankish castle** in 1245, then bequeathed it to his son Geoffrey, the only well-liked Frankish overlord—and praised in *The Chronicle of Morea* for his chivalry. The castle was known as the Toledo of Greece because of its strategic position at the mouth of the Alpheios Gorge. Later, during the Revolution, the hero Theodore Kolokotronis again made use of its location, repairing the fortifications and building a house and a church within the walls as his base, out of reach of Ibrahim Pasha.

The 11th-century **Ayios Nikolaos** church has vivid and generally well-preserved frescoes, though some of the faces were scratched out during the Ottoman Empire. Ask in the square for the caretaker, who has the keys. ⊠ *Below the town square.*

En Route As you continue west toward Andritsena in the prefecture of Elis, you have views down into the gorge, and the road skirts narrow passes guarded by castles, known during the Middle Ages as the *Escorta.*

Andritsena

⑤ *83 km (51½ mi) west of Tripolis, 29 km (18 mi) southwest of Karitena.*

Andritsena is a pleasant little hillside collection of stone houses and today enjoys a claim to fame for its collection of 15th-century Venetian and Vatican first editions and documents relating to the War of Independence. A new **library** has been completed recently. ⊠ *On main road, 100 yards after the square,* ☎ *0626/22242.* 🎫 *Free.* ☉ *Weekdays 8:30–3.*

Lodging
$$ 🏨 **Theoxenia Hotel.** While the only hotel for miles around is more geared to modern comfort than to quaint atmosphere, rooms are large and well furnished and offer delightful vistas of mountains and woods from their balconies. The hotel serves lunch and dinner in the summer, but you are better off at one of the eateries surrounding the main square. ⊠ *On main road on edge of village as you enter from Karitena, 27061,* ☎ *0626/31518,* 🅵🅰🆇 *0626/22219. 40 rooms. Restaurant, breakfast room. No credit cards. Jan.–Feb.*

Temple of Apollo at Bassae

★ **⑥** *97 km (60¼ mi) southwest of Tripolis, 14 km (8½ mi) south of Andritsena.*

The Temple of Apollo Epikourios at Bassae, splendidly isolated amid craggy, uncompromising scenery, is elegant and spare, and untouched by vandalism or commercialism—although, now, it is sadly "protected" by a make-shift canopy. Pausanias believed this temple was designed by Iktinos, the Parthenon's architect. Although this theory has recently been disputed, it is one of the best-preserved classical temples in Greece, superseded in its state of preservation only by the Hephaistion in Athens. The residents of nearby Phygalia built it atop an older temple in 420 BC to thank Apollo for delivering them from an epidemic; *epikourious* means "helper." Made of local limestone, the temple has some unusual details: exceptional length compared to its width; a north–south orientation rather than the usual east–west (probably because of the slope of the ground); and Ionic half-columns linked to the walls by flying buttresses. Here, too, are the first known Corinthian columns sporting the characteristic acanthus leaves—only the base remains now—and the earliest example of interior sculptured friezes illustrating the battles between the Greeks and Amazons and the Centaurs and Lapiths. The friezes now hang in the British Museum.

Take the time to climb to the **summit** northwest of the temple for a view overlooking the Nedhas River, Mt. Lykaeon, and, on a clear day, the Ionian Sea. Despite its setting, the temple has lost some of its impact, veiled as it is by a canopy to protect it from acid rain. ⊠ *14 km (8½ mi) south of Andritsena,* ☎ *0626/22254.* 🎫 *500 dr./€1.47* ⊙ *Daily 8:30–3.*

MESSINIA
Kalamata, Pylos

Euripides called this region "a land of fair fruitage and watered by innumerable streams . . . neither very wintry in the blasts of winter, nor yet made too hot by the chariot of Hellos." Long, relatively cool summers and mild winters may be Messinia's blessing, but nature was no ally in 1986 when an earthquake registering 6.2 on the Richter scale razed its capital, Kalamata, which has been hastily rebuilt with an eye to efficiency rather than charm.

Kalamata

❼ *91 km (56½ mi) southwest of Tripolis.*

Though not Greece's finest city, Kalamata does have a pleasant mixture of sights and seaside restaurants. The city is built atop ancient Pharai, described by Homer as subject to the kingdom of Agamemnon. In the 8th century BC, Pharai was annexed as a province of Laconia, and like most other towns in the area, was not independent again until the Battle of Leuctra ended Spartan domination, prompting the Theban general Epaminondas to erect the great fortifications of Messene.

The small, well-organized **archaeological museum** exhibits local stone tools, proto-Geometric and Geometric pottery, and a 1st-century AD Roman mosaic floor depicting Dionysos with a panther and a satyr. ⊠ *Benaki mansion, Benaki and Papazoglou Sts., near Platia 25 Martiou (25th of March Sq.),* ☎ *0721/26209.* 🎫 *Free.* ⊙ *Tues.–Sat. 8–2:30, Sun. 8:30–3.*

In the early 13th century William de Champlitte divided the Peloponnese into 12 baronies, bestowing Kalamata on Geoffrey de Villehardouin, who built a winter **Kastro** (⊠ at the end of Ipapandis). Through the centuries, the castle was bitterly fought over by Franks, Slavs, and Byzantines, and today it's difficult to tell what of the remains is original. From 25th of March Square, walk up Ipapandis Street past the church, take the first left at the castle gates, which are always open, and climb the small hill; the views of the town, coast, and the Messinian plain are lovely.

The oldest church in Kalamata is the 13th-century **Ayii Apostoli** (Holy Apostles), a small Byzantine church dedicated to the Virgin of Kalamata (of the good eye), from whom the town may get its name. Restored after its devastation in 1986, it is one of Greece's curious double churches with two naves—one for the Roman Catholics and one for the Orthodox—that resulted from 13th- and 14th-century ecumenical efforts. The Revolution was formally declared here on March 23, 1821, when Kolokotronis captured Kalamata from the Turks. Your best chance of finding the church open is to visit in the late afternoon (5–7). ✉ *25th of March Sq.*

Beaches

🐾 West of Kalamata at Petalidi is the beginning of a long chain of sandy **beaches** that are ideal for children because of the shallow water. Closer to town are **Verga** (✉ To the east) and the more crowded **Bouka** (✉ 7 km [4½ mi] to the west); both have showers and changing rooms.

Dining and Lodging

$$ ✕ **Selitsa.** Take in all of Kalamata and the Gulf of Messinia from the
★ tables at this hillside taverna. Wood, rock, and running water set the stage for hearty meats such as *katsiki tou fournou* (roasted goat) and roasted lamb. For a light snack, enjoy the special *paximadia* (rusks served with oregano and oil) while quaffing a glass of barrel white. Next door is a small castle, which in summer is a drinks-only bistro. ✉ *Take main road out of Kalamata to Almiro; signs indicate where to turn for Selitsa village,* ☎ *0721/41331 or 0721/41020. No credit cards.*

$ ✕ **Kaloutas.** At this waterfront restaurant, watch the men laying out their nets to dry while you enjoy copious helpings of well-cooked Greek food: tender beef *kokkinisto* (stew) and *arni lemonato* (lamb cooked in a light lemon sauce). Mr. Kaloutas prides himself on his selection and, if he's not too busy, he takes requests. He also prepares large breakfasts with croissants, eggs, orange juice, and drip coffee instead of the drearily ubiquitous *nes* (boiled Nescafé). ✉ *Navarinou 93,* ☎ *0721/29097. No credit cards.*

$ ✕ **Meltemi.** If you can't make it to this rustic taverna on the day they're serving a whole roast pig, you can still be smitten with the fresh fish, the *tsoutsoukakia* (rolls of spicy sausage), the *imam* (a Turkish version of moussaka), or the *exohiko* (grilled lamb). Standbys are pizza, pork chops, and the local retsina. Outdoor seating is on the harbor. ✉ *Navarinou 25,* ☎ *0721/21260. No credit cards.*

$$$ 🏨 **Pharae Hotel.** This A-class hotel in downtown Kalamata is *the*
★ place to stay for those who can swing it. The lobby is handsome, with tasteful green furniture and marble floors. The restaurant patio overlooks the sea, as will a rooftop patio that is being built. Rooms are modern and immaculate, with all the amenities you would expect, such as TVs. ✉ *Navarinou and Riga Fereou, 24100,* ☎ *0721/94421 through 0721/94424,* 🗏 *0721/93969. 75 rooms, 1 suite. Restaurant, breakfast room, sauna, meeting room. AE, MC, V.*

$$ 🏨 **Haikos.** This modest beach hotel is a less expensive alternative to Kalamata's grand establishments, and it's meticulously run by the Haikos brothers. The cool blue bedrooms have ocean views, showers, and comfy sofas; a pebble-and-sand beach is just a few steps away. ✉ *Navarinou 115, 24100,* ☎ *0721/82886 or 0721/82888,* 🗏 *0721/ 23800. 112 rooms. No credit cards.*

Festivals

The annual **Independence Day celebration** is held on or around March 25, the national holiday date. Stick around for the festivities—dancing, local bands, and a spirited parade. Contact the Greek National Tourist Organization (GNTO or EOT) for information (☞ Visitor Information *in* Southern Peloponnese A to Z, *below*). In summer Kalamata holds a **theater festival**; contact the **festival office** (☎ 0721/ 29909) for further information.

Shopping

LOCAL SPECIALTIES

Kalamata is famous for its *pastelli* (sesame seed and honey candy), figs, fleshy black olives, olive oil, and the silk scarves handmade by nuns from the convent of the Virgin Ypapanti in the cathedral square.

Ancient Messene

 75 km (46½ mi) southwest of Tripolis, 31 km (19¼ mi) north of Kalamata.

The ruins of ancient Messene near Mavromati are set on the slopes of majestic Mt. Ithomi (also known as Voulkanos). Epaminondas built Messene in 370–69 BC to provide a citadel, further undermining Sparta's authority. The Messenians had battled Sparta in two Messenian Wars (743–24 BC and 650–20 BC). Even after they were defeated and reduced to helots the Messenians seized the opportunity of a severe earthquake in 464 BC to wall themselves up in the stronghold of Ithome, so that Sparta had to beg Athens to help them recapture the acropolis.

Its most striking ruin is the city's **circuit wall,** a feat of defensive architecture. Four gates remain; the best preserved is the north or **Arcadian Gate,** a double set of gates separated by a round courtyard. On the slabs of ancient paving stone below the arch, grooves worn by ancient chariot wheels are still visible. The heart of the walled city is now occupied by the village of **Mavromati,** but excavations have uncovered the most important public buildings, including a **theater,** whose seats have now been restored; the **Synedrion,** a **meeting hall** for representatives of independent Messene; the **Sebasteion,** dedicated to worship of a Roman emperor; the **sanctuary to the god Asklepios;** and a **temple to Artemis Orthia.** Outside the walls lie a **stadium** and a **cemetery.** The guard at the site usually has the key to the village's **small museum** if you want to examine the finds. ✉ *From modern town of Messene, turn north at intersection of road to Mavromati; from village, you must walk the last 2 km (1 mi),* ☎ *0724/51257.* 🎫 *500 dr./€1.47.* ◷ *Daily 8:30–1.*

Chora

❾ *48 km (29¾ mi) west of Kalamata, 64 km (39¾ mi) west of ancient Messene.*

Stop in at Chora's **archaeological museum** to see golden cups and jewelry from the Mycenaean period; fragments of frescoes from nearby Nestor's Palace, including a warrior in a boar's-tusk helmet described by Homer; and plaster casts of the Linear B tablets—the originals are in the National Archaeological Museum in Athens. ✉ *Marinatou St. off town square,* ☎ *0763/31358.* 🎫 *500 dr./€1.47.* ◷ *Tues.–Sun. 8:30–3.*

❿ **Nestor's Palace** belonged to the king of Pylos, commander, according to Homer, of the fleet of "ninety black ships" in the Trojan War. Nestor founded the town around 1300 BC—only Mycenae was larger—but the palace was burned a century later. It was here, the *Iliad* tells us, that Telemachus came to ask for news of his father, Odysseus, from Nestor, who welcomed the young man to a feast at the palace. Most of the palace rooms are clearly marked, but it's a good idea to buy the guidebook, available at the site, prepared by the University of Cincinnati, whose archaeologists excavated the site; the illustrations will help you imagine the palace in its original condition. Archaeologists believe the complex, excavated in 1952, was similar to those found in Crete and Mycenae, except that it was unfortified, an indication that surrounding towns had sworn strict allegiance to and depended economically on Pylos. In the **main building,** a simple **entrance gate** is flanked by a **guard chamber** and two **archives,** where 1,250 palm leaf–shape tablets were discovered on the first day of excavation. The tablets—records of taxes, armament expenses, and debts in Linear B script—were the first such unearthed on the Greek mainland, thus linking the

Mycenaean and Minoan (Crete) civilizations, because the writing (like that in Knossos) was definitely Greek.

The entrance gate opens into a spacious **courtyard** with a balcony where spectators could watch the royal ceremonies. To the left are a **storeroom** that yielded thousands of tall-stemmed vases and a **waiting room** with built-in benches. Beyond the courtyard a **porch of the royal apartments** and a **vestibule** open onto a richly decorated **throne room.** In the middle of the room is a ceremonial **hearth** surrounded by four wooden columns (only the stone bases remain) that probably supported a shaft. Now completely destroyed, the throne once stood in the center of the wall to the right. Each **frescoed wall** depicted a different subject, such as a griffin (possibly the royal emblem) or a minstrel strumming his lyre. Even the columns and the wooden ceiling were painted. Along the southern edge of the throne room were seven **storerooms** for oil, which together with the one on the floor immediately above fueled the fire that destroyed the palace.

Off a corridor to the right of the entrance are a **bathroom,** where the oldest known bathtub stands, along with jars used for collecting bathwater. Next to it are the **Queen's apartments:** in the largest room a hearth is adorned with a painted flame, the walls with hunting scenes of lions and panthers. Other rooms in the complex include the **throne room** from an earlier palace, a **shrine, workshops,** and a **conduit** that brought water from a nearby spring. Several **beehive tombs** were also found outside the palace. ⊠ *On the highway 4 km (2½ mi) south of Chora,* ☎ *0763/31437.* 🎟 *500 dr./€1.47.* ⊙ *Tues.–Sat. 8:30–3, Sun. 9:30–2:30.*

Pylos

⑪ *52 km (32¼ mi) southwest of Kalamata, 22 km (13½ mi) south of Chora.*

With its bougainvillea-swathed, pristine white houses fanning up Mt. Saint Nicholas, Pylos will remind you of an island town. It was built according to a plan drawn by French engineers stationed here from 1828 to 1833 with General Maison's entourage and was the site of a major naval battle in the War of Independence. Ibrahim Pasha had chosen Sfakteria, the islet that virtually blocks Pylos Bay, from which to launch his attack on the mainland. For two years Greek forces flailed under Turkish firepower until, in 1827, Britain, Russia, and France came in to support the Greek insurgents. They sent a fleet to persuade Turkey to sign a treaty, were accidentally fired upon, and found themselves retaliating. At the end of the battle, the allies had sunk 53 of 89 ships of the Turko-Egyptian fleet without a single loss among their 27 war vessels. The Sultan was forced to renegotiate, which paved the way for Greek independence. A column rising between a Turkish and a Venetian cannon in the town's main square, Platia Trion Navarchon (Three Admirals Square), commemorates the leaders of the fleets.

For a closer look of the bay, take an hour-long boat tour to the various monuments on **Sfakteria,** sunken Turkish ships, and the neighboring rock of **Tsichli-Baba,** which has a vast, much-photographed natural arch, nicknamed Tripito, a former pirate hideout with 144 steps. It's said that if a pregnant woman sails under this arch, she will have a boy. Boat rentals can cost up to 8,000 dr./€23.59 (less expensive if you go with a group). They can also take you to the weed-infested 13th-century **Paleokastro,** one of the two fortresses guarding the channels on either side of Sfakteria, and make a stop also at **Nestor's cave.** Look for the many signs on the waterfront advertising captains' services. ⊠ *West of Pylos Port.*

For views of Pylos, the bay, and the Kamares Roman aqueduct, the **Neokastro,** the newer fortress that dominates the town, is unbeatable. It was built by the Turks in 1573 to control the southern—at that time, the only—entrance to the bay (an artificial embankment had drastically reduced the depth of the northern channel). Neokastro's well-preserved walls enclose a **church of the Transfiguration,** originally a mosque; cannons; and two anchors from the battle. The southwest wall, which could be attacked by sea, was especially strong. The highest point of the castle is guarded by a hexagonal fort flanked by towers. Until recently the fort was a prison, but unlike most Greek penitentiaries, which are fairly open, this was more secure, apparently to squelch feuds with the Mani prison, whose inmates were notoriously bellicose. ⊠ *Road to Methoni,* ☎ *0723/22897.* 🕮 *800 dr./€2.35.* ☉ *Daily 8–7.*

The small **archaeological museum** of Pylos has a collection of Hellenistic pottery, Roman bronze statues, engravings, battle memorabilia, gold pots, jewelry, and other objects of the Mycenaean period. ⊠ *Methonis 8,* ☎ *0723/22448.* 🕮 *500 dr./€1.47.* ☉ *Tues.–Sun. 8:30–3.*

Dining and Lodging

$$ ✕ **To Diethnes.** This rather nondescript restaurant serves solid Greek food. Especially good are the *briam* (a delicate mixture of potatoes and artichokes), *moschari psito* (roasted beef), and the squid. Look forward to an aromatic red barrel wine and a wide choice of Greek wines. Off-season, just the basics are served. ⊠ *Waterfront, next to police station,* ☎ *0723/22772. No credit cards.*

$ ✕ **Ta Pente Aderfia.** Blessed with perhaps the town's best sunset view, this unpretentious restaurant specializes in grilled meats, popular Greek *magirefta* (precooked dishes served at room temperature), and fresh seafood. Order the special dish called *navomaxia* (a seared fillet of beef) served in wine sauce; *psari macaronada* (an unusual combination of fish and pasta), which has to be ordered a day ahead; and the large mussels. After dinner, try the succulent local grapes or oranges. All in all, a meal here is a real treat. ⊠ *Waterfront,* ☎ *0723/22564. No credit cards.*

$$$ 🏨 **Karalis Beach.** This modern hotel is set on a piney bluff and clings to rocks just above the sea—in fact, the rooms and their balconies seem to hang directly over the water; the fetching setting can be appreciated as well from a flowery roof terrace that doubles as a breakfast room in good weather. This place would be a near-perfect option if only the management would undertake a much-needed renovation and replace the dull and worn furnishings. Contact the Karalis (☞ *below*) for reservations. ⊠ *Paralia, 24001,* ☎ *0723/23021 or 0723/23022. 14 rooms. Bar. MC, V. Closed Nov.–Mar.*

$$ 🏨 **Karalis.** Probably the best value in Pylos, the Karalis has well-appointed rooms, with comfortable light-pink decor and TVs, and most face the sea and have large, delightfully furnished balconies. Recent renovations include the addition of a spacious, high-ceiling restaurant. The owners also run the Karalis Beach (☞ *above*), and inquiries about that hotel should be made here as well. ⊠ *26 Kalamatis St., 24001,* ☎ *0723/22960 or 0723/22980. 35 rooms. Restaurant, bar, air-conditioning. MC, V.*

Methoni

⑫ *98 km (61 mi) southwest of Kalamata, 14 km (8½ mi) south of Pylos.*

Methoni, a resort at a cape south of Pylos, is so delightful it was one of the seven towns Agamemnon offered Achilles to appease him after his beloved Briseis was carried off. According to Homer, Pedasos, as it was called, was "rich in vines," and tradition says that the town got its modern name because *onoi* (donkeys) carrying the town's wine became *methoun* (intoxicated) from the aroma.

Methoni's principal attraction is its **Kastro**. After the Second Messenian War, the victorious Spartans gave Methoni to the Nauplians, who had been exiled from their homeland for their Spartan alliance. With its fine natural harbor, the town was an important stop on trade routes between Europe and the East during the Middle Ages. The Venetians took control of Methoni in 1209, building the impressive Kastro along the shoreline. A stone bridge leads over the dry moat to this imposing, well-kept citadel; various coats of arms mark the walls, including those of Genoa and Venice's Lion of St. Mark. A second bridge joins the fortified town with the **Bourtzi**, an octagonal tower built on an islet during the Turkish occupation (after 1500). ⊠ *By the coast*, ☎ *0731/25363*. ▨ *Free*. ☉ *Daily, winter 8:30–3; summer 8:30–9.*

Dining and Lodging

$$ ✕ **Louis's** (formerly Kali Kardia). Even though the owner's son Ilias
★ (Louis) has taken the reins, this place still serves the four-star food it has been renowned for since opening in 1950. In a neoclassical house, the restaurant's interior delights with checked tablecloths, lush plants, and family portraits. The swordfish, moschari psito flambé, and excellent desserts such as *ravani* (farina, almonds, and a heavy cognac-orange syrup) are all worthy of attention. Breakfast is also served. ⊠ *Main street of town center, across from Post Office*, ☎ *0723/31260. MC, V.*

$$ ✕ **Nikos's.** "The only time this kitchen closes is if I'm sick," says Nikos Vile, who insists on cooking everything from *mamboulas* (a moussaka made with tomatoes) to *maridakia* (lightly fried whitebait) each day. He also makes wonderful *fassolia* (beans) and *garides saganaki* (shrimp and cheese in a lemony red sauce). Or you may sip an aperitif at the bar or hide out in the secluded courtyard. ⊠ *Miali road, just off beach below fortress*, ☎ *0723/31282. No credit cards.*

$ ✕ **Rex.** Right on the beach, surrounded by large shady pines, Rex serves delicious food: hearty *dolmades* (stuffed vine leaves), pungent *tzatziki* (garlic-yogurt-cucumber dip), fresh fish such as sea bream, and for dessert, local grapes, honeydew melons, and fragrant peaches. A nearby playground entertains kids. ⊠ *On beach below fortress*, ☎ *0723/ 31239. No credit cards. Closed Nov.–Mar.*

$$$ ▥ **Ulysses.** From the shady, well-manicured side garden to fresh-cut flowers and traditional furnishings in the rooms, all aspects extend a welcome at this hotel. A room bonus is individual cooling and heating units. The breakfast spread includes 22 items, such as fresh orange juice, omelets, and yogurt with honey. The hotel also charters yachts; for every week's hotel stay, guests receive a free day of yacht use. ⊠ *Paralia, 24006*, ☎ *0723/31600. 12 rooms. Restaurant, bar. MC.*

$$ ▥ **Amalia.** Built in 1990, this modest hotel on a hill just outside of town has basic rooms at very reasonable prices. All rooms have huge verandas that face the sea or town, both close by. The lush garden is the pride of the Kalligas family. ⊠ *Coastal road to Finikoundas, 24006*, ☎ *0723/31129 or 0723/31139*, ☎ *0723/31195. 34 rooms. Restaurant, bar. MC, V. Closed Nov.–Apr.*

Festival

On *Kathari Deftera* (Clean Monday), just before Lent, Methoni holds a mock Koutroulis village wedding at the town platia, a riotous annual performance, in which both the bride and groom are played by men.

MANI

Kardamyli, Itilo, Limeni, Areopolis, Vathia, Gythion

You now enter the Mani, which, on its western side, stretches from Kardamyli to Cape Tenaro, the mythical entrance to the underworld, and on its eastern side from Cape Tenaro up to Gythion. The western half is the Messinian Mani, while the eastern half is the Laconian Mani. Isolated and invincible, this was the land of bandits and blood feuds. The Dorians never reached this far south, Roman occupation was perfunctory, and Christianity was not established here until the 9th century. Neither the Venetians nor the Turks could quell the constant rebellions.

The Maniotes were thought to be descended from the ancient Spartans and to have been expelled from northern Laconia by invading Slavs in the 7th century. An aristocracy arose—the Nyklians—whose clans began building defensive tower houses (the oldest dates to the 15th century) and fighting for precious land in this barren landscape. The object in battle was to annihilate the enemy's tower house, as well as its entire male population. Feuds could last for years, with the women—who were safe from attack—bringing in supplies. Mani women were famous throughout Greece for their singing of the *moirologhi* (laments), like the ancient choruses in a Greek tragedy.

A truce had to be called in long-lasting feuds during the harvest, but a feud only ended with the complete destruction of a family or its surrender, called *psychiko* (a thing of the soul), in which losers filed out of their tower house one by one, kissing the hand of the enemy clan's parents. The victor then decided under what conditions the humbled family could remain in the village. When King Otho tried to tame this incorrigible bunch in 1833, his soldiers were ambushed, stripped naked, and held for ransom. Today, few people still live in the Mani. If you have the good luck to share a shot of fiery raki with a Maniote, you may notice a Cretan influence in his dress—older men still wear the baggy breeches, black headbands, and decorated jackets wrapped with heavy belts.

Kardamyli

⑬ *122 km (75¾ mi) southwest of Tripolis, 31 km (19¼ mi) southeast of Kalamata.*

Kardamyli is the gateway to the Mani on the Messinian side. It is considered part of the outer Mani, an area less bleak and stark than the inner Mani that begins at Areopolis. Here the foothills of Mt. Taygettus are still verdant and the sun is more forgiving. The quiet town has become a tourist destination for the more discerning traveler attracted to its remoteness and stark beauty, and it is particularly popular with the English. Kardamyli's most famous resident is Patrick Leigh-Fermor, an Anglo-Irish writer who has written extensively on Greece and on the Mani in particular.

Kardamyli is dotted with small clusters of **tower houses** that are being restored; some are occupied, but it is possible for the public to stroll through the paths that cut through the enclave. ⊠ *Northwest of modern town.*

Dining and Lodging

$$ ✕⊡ **Lela's Taverna Pension.** Mrs. Lela is famous here for her cooking
★ (the secret is probably in the fragrant homemade olive oil and the exceedingly fresh tomatoes and herbs). On the shady, seaside terrace of

this oleander-covered stone building you can enjoy chicken with rose-mary, the light moussaka, and the fish soup. Carefully chosen wines from throughout Greece are excellent accompaniments. Three commodious rooms and two suites above the taverna provide some of the nicest accommodation in the region, with soothing sea views and handsome furnishings that include traditional fabrics and prints of indigenous flowers. ⊠ *Seaside, above a rocky beach near old soap factory,* ☎ ℻ *0721/73541. 3 rooms, 2 suites. Restaurant. No credit cards.*

Itilo and Neo Itilo

⑭ *68 km (42¼ mi) southwest of Kalamata, 37 km (23 mi) south of Kardamyli.*

Itilo and Neo Itilo are, respectively, the upper and lower parts of the same town. Neo Itilo is plunk on the curve of an enormous bay with a white pebble beach ideal for swimming; its uphill counterpart, Itilo, is nestled in a ravine amid slender cypresses. Formerly the capital of the Mani, verdant Itilo looks better from afar, with its red-tile roofs and bright blue window frames; up close, the houses are falling apart, neglected by a dwindling population. From the 16th to the 18th centuries, the harbor was infamous as a base for piracy and slave trading (Maniotes trading Turks to Venetians and vice versa, depending on who was in power).

Outraged by the piracy and hoping to control the pass to the north, the Turks built the nearby and deserted **Castle of Kelefa** (⊠ Across gorge from Itilo). You may walk or drive to Kelefa on a road that turns off to the right 4 km (2½ mi) before the Limeni junction.

Beach
Neo Itilo sits on a beautiful large bay with a **white pebble beach.** Enjoy a swim as you watch the fishermen fixing their nets, checking their ship hulls, and chattering among themselves amid the din of their portable radios.

Lodging
$$–$$$ 🏨 **Limeni Village.** Limeni Village is a handsome new resort that is perched on the edge of a cliff overlooking Limeni Bay and provides the most luxurious retreat in the region. More than a dozen stone towers make up the "village," each with two rooms, except for two suites, which have towers to themselves. All rooms come with balconies and overlook the sea. ⊠ *Seaside, on the road between Limeni and Areopolis, 23062,* ☎ *0733/51111 or 0733/51112,* ℻ *0733/51182. 33 rooms, 2 suites. Restaurant, air-conditioning, pool. No credit cards.*

Limeni

⑮ *70 km (43½ mi) southwest of Athens, 2 km (1 mi) south of Itilo and Neo Itilo.*

In Limeni the **restored tower** of Revolution hero Petrobey Mavromichaelis now guards little more than a string of cottages with their backs to the sea and a main street crammed with tiny shops. You may be mesmerized by the coastal scenery, but keep an eye out for donkeys, sheep, and flocks of goats that may suddenly trot into the road.

Areopolis

⑯ *74 km (46 mi) southwest of Kalamata, 4 km (2½ mi) south of Limeni.*

In Areopolis the typical Maniote tower houses began to appear in earnest, spooky sentinels in the harsh landscape. The town was renamed after the god of war Ares, because of its role in the Revolution: Mavromichaelis initiated the local uprising against the Turks here (his statue stands in the square). Areopolis now enjoys protection as a historical monument by the government, but although the town seems medieval, most of the tower houses were built in the early 1800s; the Taxiarchis (Archangels) church, though it looks like it has 12th-century reliefs over the doors, was actually built in 1798. It's easy to slip vicariously into a time warp as you meander down Kapetan Matapan Street through the fields to the sea or along the dark cobblestone lanes past the tower houses with their enclosed courtyards and low-arched gateways.

Lodging

$$$ 🏨 **Londas Guest House.** The diverse influences of Hans and Jacobis, Swiss
★   and Greek, respectively, have created a lovely little hotel in a restored tower house with only four rooms and two terraces. The white and blue decor is sparsely chic and soothing, and Jacobis—whose culinary skills have been touted in newspapers as far away as Paris—cooks upon request in the small dining room. ✉ *Near Archangels church, 23062,* ☎ *0733/51360,* 🖷 *0733/51012. 4 rooms, 2 with bath. No credit cards.*

$$ 🏨 **Kapetanakos Tower.** Twenty years ago the Greek government converted this traditional stone tower dating from 1826 into a simple but atmospheric hotel. The hotel is now in private hands, and offers unique and austere accommodation in white-washed rooms, several with sleeping lofts, and provides such amenities as an excellent breakfast and a pretty garden. ✉ *Near Archangels church at edge of town, 23062,* ☎ *0733/51233,* 🖷 *0733/51401. 8 rooms. No credit cards.*

Pirgos Dirou Caves

⑰   *84 km (52¼ mi) southwest of Kalamata, 10 km (6 mi) south of Areopolis.*

Carved out of the limestone by the slow-moving underground river Vlychada on its way to the sea, the **Alepotripia** and **Glyfada** caves were places of worship in Paleolithic and Neolithic times and hiding places millennia later for Resistance fighters during World War II. Alepotripia is closed for excavation, but visitors can see Glyfada's fantastical grottoes, with luminous pink, white, yellow, and red stalagmites and stalactites. The cave is believed to be at least 70 km (43 mi) long, with more than 2,800 waterways, perhaps extending as far as Sparta. In the **Great Ocean room,** the flowing water is nearly 100 ft deep. Visitors can take a half-hour guided boat tour for 2 km (1 mi) through nine large **chambers** full of surreal "buildings" and mythical beasts, with names such as Dragon's Lair, Cathedral, and Hanging Beds of the Water Sprites. The close quarters in the passageways are not for the claustrophobic, and even in summer the caves are chilly. During the high season, you may wait up to two hours for a boat, so plan to arrive early. Next to the caves are a small bathing beach, snack bar, taverna, and small **archaeological museum** (✉ Methonis 8), which houses the Neolithic finds from the caves. ✉ *Along southern coast, 5 km (3 mi) west of Areopolis–Vathia Rd.,* ☎ *0733/52222 or 0733/52223.* 🎫 *3,500 dr./€10.32.* ⊙ *Daily 8–2:45 in winter; 8–5 in summer.*

Vathia

⑱   *107 km (66½ mi) southwest of Kalamata, 33 km (20 ½ mi) south of Areopolis.*

Vathia's two- and three-story stone towers, clustered around the hilltop, have small windows and tiny openings over the doors through which boiling oil was poured on the unwelcome. Vathia is worth a visit sim-

ply because of the density of the tower houses and the pervasive feel
★ ing of emptiness. It is nearly a ghost town. Oddly enough, the **tower
houses** are now guest houses, restored by the government to entice visitors to the village.

Lodging

$$$ 🏨 **Tsitsiris Castle.** This 200-year-old fortified manor house is about 15
★   km (9 mi) north of Vathia, in a tiny hamlet of mostly ruined tower houses.
The main house contains handsome public rooms that include a stone
floored lounge and restaurant, and the guest rooms, attractively ap-
pointed with traditional furnishings and fabrics, occupy a low wing
built around a garden. A roof terrace and flowery courtyard are pleas-
ant retreats in which to catch an evening breeze. From Stavri you
make a memorable trek of about one hour to the Castle of Mina, built
by the Franks in 1248 into the rock face at the end of a long promon-
tory surrounded by crashing surf. ⊠ *Stavri 23062,* ☎ *0733/56297. 20
rooms. Restaurant, lounge. No credit cards.*

$$ 🏨 **Faros.** In contrast to the stark inland Mani villages, Gerolimenas,
★   about 10 km (6 mi) north of Vathia, has the feel of an island port with
its position at the end of a long natural harbor. This waterside house
provides delightful and bright studios, all with modest cooking facilities and terraces that hang over the water. ⊠ *Gerolimenas 23071,* ☎
0733/54271. 8 rooms. Air-conditioning, kitchenettes. No credit cards.

En Route   On the way to Areopolis, about 54 km (33½ mi) from Gythion, you'll
pass the fine sandy beach of Mavrovouni and the castle of Passava. It's
challenging to get to the top, albeit with no regular path, but the view
takes in two bays. Originally constructed in 1254 by French baron Jean
de Neuilly, the castle was rebuilt by the Turks in the 18th century.

Gythion

⑲   *46 km (28½ mi) south of Sparta, 79 km (49 mi) north of Vathia.*

Gythion, at the foot of the Mt. Taygettus range, is a welcome sight.
Graceful 19th-century pastel houses march up the steep hillside, and
along the harbor, fruit-laden donkeys sidestep the peanut vendors and
gypsies hawking strings of garlic. Laconia's main port, the town is the
Laconian gateway to the Mani peninsula. It claims Hercules and Apollo
as its founders, and survives today by exporting olives, oil, rice, and
citrus fruits.

Gythion has a few rather insignificant ruins, including a well-preserved **Roman theater** (⊠ Archaio Theatrou St.) with stone seats intact. Some remains of the ancient town (Laryssion) are visible on **Mt.
Koumaros** (⊠ 2 km [1 mi] along the road), a settlement that in Roman
times exported the murex shell for dyeing imperial togas purple.

It is on the tiny islet of **Marathonissi** (⊠ Just east of Gythion), once
called Kranae, that Paris and Helen (wife of Menelaos) consummated
their love affair after escaping Sparta, provoking the Trojan War described in the *Iliad*. A causeway now joins Marathonissi to Gythion.
Recently, the EOT restored a castle-house on the islet as an ethnological museum. The **Pyrgos Tzannetaki Tower** currently displays an exhibition on Mani traditional villages, which appears likely to remain
in the tower indefinitely. ⊠ *Marathonissi,* ☎ *0733/22676.* 🎫 *About
500 dr./€1.47.* ☼ *Daily 9–noon and 5–9.*

NEED A   Take a late-afternoon break for grilled octopus and ouzo; Gythion is the
BREAK?   octopus capital of Greece. The best place is **Nautilia** (⊠ Southern end of
waterfront, across from pier); look for the octopi dangling in the doorway.

Beaches

Near Gythion the best beaches (almost all are stony) are south on the coast between Mavrovouni and Skoutari; avoid the slightly littered public beach off the town waterfront.

Dining and Lodging

$$ ✕ **Poulikakos.** Word of mouth has made this small place a favorite for such traditional dishes as broiled stuffed peppers and *kotopoulo* (chicken) kokkinisto. Highlights are *soupies* (fresh cuttlefish) and octopus marinated in vinegar—excellent with ouzo. And sample the local barrel red if you're planning a beachside nap anyway. Heartwarming desserts, such as *rizogalo* (rice pudding with cinnamon), and a super breakfast are also served. ⊠ *Platia Limani (harbor square),* ☎ *0733/ 22792. No credit cards.*

$ ✕ **Sinantisi.** Since its opening, this grill hasn't been closed for a day. The freshest seasonal local produce—artichokes in spring, squash and eggplant in summer, wild greens in winter—construct the *casserolas* (casserole-style dishes). You may also order fresh fish, appetizers such as tzatziki and *taramosalata* (pink fish-roe dip), and homemade sweets such as clove-scented baklava. ⊠ *On square in Mavrovouni village, about 2 km (1 mi) outside town,* ☎ *0733/22256. MC, V. No lunch.*

$$$ 🏨 **Lakonis.** For romance, choose these white bungalows set like an am-
★   phitheater on a cliff 3 km (2 mi) out of town. Brilliant red and pink flowers dot the landscape, and the beach below is so popular the hotel drained the Olympic-size pool in defeat. Nestle up to the bar and fireplace at the lofty circular restaurant, enjoying the vistas through the plate-glass windows; in summer, the informal beach restaurant is great for lunch. ⊠ *Skalas 3, 23200,* ☎ *0733/22666 or 0733/22667,* ℻ *0733/ 23668. 100 rooms, 80 with bath. Restaurant, bar. No credit cards. Closed Nov.–Mar.*

$$ 🏨 **Aktaion.** This hotel is a pleasure. All rooms are squeaky clean and
★   modern, with subdued colors, seafaring balconies, and TVs. Lovely prints depict Maniote life. ⊠ *39 Vassileos Pavlou, 23200,* ☎ *0733/23500 or 0733/23501,* ℻ *0733/22294. 22 rooms. Breakfast room, air-conditioning. No credit cards.*

Outdoor Activities and Sports

SWIMMING

Gythion is best for daydreaming on the waterfront or swimming off the rocks of Marathonissi.

LACONIA

Sparta, Mystras, Monemvassia

The Laconian Plain is surrounded on three sides by mountains and on one side by the sea. Perhaps it was the fear that enemies could descend those mountains at any time that drove the Spartans to make Laconia their training ground, where they developed the finest fighting force in ancient Greece. A mighty power that controlled three-fifths of the Peloponnese, Sparta contributed to the Greek victory in the second Persian War (5th century BC). Ultimately, its aggressiveness and its jealousy of Athens brought about the Peloponnesian War, which drained its resources but left it victorious. The Greek world found Sparta to be an even harsher master than Athens, and this fact may have led to its losses in the Boeotian and Corinthian wars, at the Battle of Leuctra, and in 222–21 BC at the hands of the Achaean League, who liberated all areas Sparta had conquered. A second period of prosperity under the Romans ended with the barbarian invasions in the 3rd century, and Sparta declined rapidly.

Laconia can also claim two important medieval sites: Mystras and Monemvassia. Jewels in the Byzantine crown, the former is an intellectual and political center, the latter a sea fortress meant to ward off invaders from the east.

Sparta

㉟ *60 km (37¼ mi) south of Tripolis, 60 km (37¼ mi) east of Kalamata.*

For those who have read about ancient Sparta, the bellicose city-state that once dominated the Greek world, the modern city is a disappointment—it is all too spartan in its dreary angularity, unrelieved by the broad Eurotas River, which is screened by pleasant orchards. Given the area's earthquakes and the Spartans' no-frills approach—living more like an army camp than a city-state—no elaborate ruins remain, a fact that so disconcerted Otto, Greece's first king, that in 1835 he ordered the modern city built on the ancient site.

The Spartans' relentless militarism set them apart from other Greeks. They were expected to emerge victorious from a battle or not at all, and for most of its existence Sparta was without a wall, because according to Lykourgos, its leader, who wrote Sparta's constitution, "chests, not walls, make a city." From the 9th to the 4th centuries BC, Spartans trained for a life of war. From the age of seven, boys in the reigning warrior class submitted to a strict regimen, eating mostly herbs, roots, and the famous black broth. Rich foods were thought to stunt growth. Forbidden to work, they trained for combat and practiced stealing, an acceptable skill unless one was caught. One legend describes a Spartan youth who let a concealed fox chew out his bowels rather than reveal his theft. Girls also trained rigorously in the belief they would bear healthier offspring; for the same reason, newlyweds were forbidden to make love frequently.

At the **Temple of Artemis Orthia** (⊠ Just outside of town on Tripolis Rd., down the path to the Eurotas River), the young Spartan men underwent *krypteia* (initiations) that entailed severe public floggings. The altar had to be splashed with blood before the goddess was satisfied. Traces of two such altars are among sparse vestiges of the 6th-century BC temple. The larger ruins are the remains of a grandstand built in the 3rd century AD by the Romans, who revived the flogging tradition as a public spectacle.

Ancient Sparta's **acropolis** (⊠ At north end of town) is now part archaeological site, part park. Locals can be seen here strolling, along with many young couples stealing a romantic moment amid the fallen limestone and shady trees. The ruins include a theater, a stadium, and a sanctuary to Athena.

Stop a moment and contemplate the stern **Statue of Leonidas** (⊠ At end of Konstantinou St.). During the Second Persian War, with 30,000 Persians advancing on his army of 8,000, Leonidas, ordered to surrender his weapons, jeered, "Come and get them." For two days he held off the enemy, until a traitor named Efialtes (the word has since come to mean "nightmare" in Greek) showed the Persians a way to attack from the rear. Leonidas ordered all but 300 Spartans and 700 Thespians to withdraw, and when forced to retreat to a wooded knoll, he is said to have commented, "So much the better, we will fight in the shade," before his entire troop was slaughtered.

Enjoy an hour in the city's **archaeological museum,** tucked into a cool park. Its eclectic collection reflects Laconia's turbulent history: Neolithic pottery; jewels and tools excavated from the Alepotripia cave; Mycenaean tomb finds; bright 4th- and 5th-century Roman mosaics; and objects from Sparta, including an expressive clay woman's head, a Parian marble statue of Leonidas (490 BC), prizes given to the Spartan youths, and ritual dance masks. Most characteristic of Spartan art are the bas-reliefs with deities and heroes; note the one depicting a seated couple bearing gifts and framed by a snake (540 BC). ⊠ *Ayios Nikonos between Dafnou and Evangelistria,* ☎ *0731/28575.* ⊡ *500 dr./€1/47.* ◑ *Tues.–Sat. 8:30–3, Sun. 8:30–12:30.*

NEED A
BREAK?

If you should find yourself waiting for a bus out of Sparta at dinnertime, cross the street to **Parthenon** (⊠ Vrasidou 106, ☎ 0731/23767) for the best gyro you may ever eat. The meat, which has a local reputation for being a cut above, is served in pita with just the right amount of chew and generous doses of onion, tomato, and tzatziki sauce.

Dining and Lodging

$$ ✗ **Diethnes.** Local vernacular claims this is one of Sparta's best restaurants. You'll be wowed by classic specialties that, here, translate into a special fish dish made with garlic, parsley, wine, oil, and rusks; bardouniotiko made with onions, *sfela* (a hard Kalamatan cheese), and red sauce; and occasionally delicacies such as sheep's heads cooked on a spit and kokoretsi. The summer courtyard rounds out a perfect meal. ⊠ *Paleologou 105,* ☎ *0731/28636. No credit cards.*

$$ ✗ **Stelakos.** Just outside of Sparta in the quaint village of Parori, this spot has been delighting locals and visitors with its excellent chicken dishes, which are its specialty. After enjoying the charming and rustic pleasures of this place, take a stroll outside for an unimpeded view of the Taygettus mountain range. ⊠ *Parori, 5 km (3 mi) south of Sparta on the road to Mystras,* ☎ *0731/83346. No credit cards. Closed Sun.*

$ ✗ **Semiramis.** This underground restaurant, with fluorescent lighting
★ and a linoleum floor, is no visual treat, but the simple Greek dishes are perfectly cooked. In spring, try the *anginares antidia* (wild artichokes with red sauce) and in summer, the stuffed squash. The barrel wine is fragrant but deceivingly light. For dessert try the rich sheep yogurt with honey before you stagger outdoors. ⊠ *Paleologou 48,* ☎ *0731/26640. No credit cards. No lunch alternate Sun.*

$$$ 🛏 **Lida.** This hotel is pricey for its category, but it provides flawless service. The owner's wife is an interior designer, as is evident in the rooms and in the lobby with antique treadles, stones from flour mills and olive presses, and lithographs of Greek revolutionary heroes. Ask for a room above the third floor for views of Mt. Taygettus. ⊠ *Ananiou and Atreidon, 23100,* ☎ *0731/23601 or 0731/23602,* FAX *0731/24493. 40 rooms. Restaurant, bar. AE, MC, V. Closed mid-Nov.–Feb.*

$$ 🛏 **Hotel Maniatis.** It's hard to believe this hotel is so reasonably priced.
★ Though the color scheme is unfortunately reminiscent of the garish 1980s, it is unusually well run, with attention to detail. Ask for a room with a view, and, if you need a bathtub, a corner room. All the rooms were renovated in 1997 and have a fairly classy sleek decor (which contrasts sharply with the lobby)—the dark, rounded furniture provides a welcome break from the rectangular pine which is the usual favorite of Greek hoteliers. Rooms now come with TVs, air-conditioning, and wall-to-wall carpeting. The hotel's Dias restaurant is elegant, with specialties such as *arni araxobitiko* (lamb with onions, cheese, red sauce, and walnuts) and *bourekakia* pastries. ⊠ *Paleologou 72, 23100,* ☎ *0731/22665,* FAX *0731/29994. 80 rooms. Restaurant, bar, lobby lounge, air-conditioning. MC, V.*

Mystras

★ ㉑ *64 km (39¾ mi) southwest of Tripolis, 4 km (2½ mi) west of Sparta.*

At ethereal Mystras, with its abandoned gold and stone palaces, churches, and monasteries lining serpentine paths, the scent of herbs and wildflowers permeates the air, goat bells tinkle yonder, and the silvery olive trees glisten with the slightest breeze. An intellectual and cultural center where philosophers like Chrysoloras, "the sage of Byzantium," held forth on the good and the beautiful, it seems an appropriate place for the last hurrah of the Byzantine emperors in the 14th century.

In 1249 William de Villehardouin built the castle in Mystras in an attempt to control Laconia and establish Frankish supremacy over the Peloponnese. He held court here with his beautiful Greek wife, Anna Comnena, surrounded by knights of Champagne, Burgundy, and Flanders, but in 1259 he was defeated by the Byzantines. As the Byzantines built a palace and numerous churches (whose frescoes exemplified several periods of painting), the town gradually grew down the slope.

At first the seat of the Byzantine governor, Mystras later became the capital of the Despotate of Morea. It was the despots who made Mystras a cultural phenomenon, and it was the despots—specifically Emperor Constantine's brother Demetrios Palaiologos—who surrendered the city to the Turks in 1460, signaling the beginning of the end. For a while the town survived because of its silk industry, but after repeated pillaging and burning by bands of Albanians, by Russians, and by Ibrahim Pasha's Egyptian troops, the inhabitants gave up and moved to modern Sparta.

In spring Mystras is resplendent with wildflowers and butterflies, but it can be oppressively hot in summer, so get an early start. Bring water and sturdy shoes for the slippery rocks and the occasional snake.

Among the most important buildings in the lower town (Kato Chora) is **Ayios Demetrios,** the *mitropolis* (cathedral) founded in 1291. Set in its floor is a stone with the two-headed Byzantine eagle marking the spot where Constantine XII, the last emperor of Byzantium, was consecrated. The cathedral's brilliant frescoes include a vivid depiction of the *Virgin and Child* on the central apse and a wall painting in the narthex of the *Second Coming,* its two red-and-turquoise winged angels sorrowful as they open the records of Good and Evil. One wing of the church houses a **museum** that holds fragments of Byzantine sculptures, including an eagle seizing its prey (11th century), later Byzantine icons, jewels, decorative metalwork, and coins. ⊠ *Lower town.* 🕾 *1,500 dr./€4.42 covers all Mystras sites.* ☉ *Daily winter 8:30–3; summer 8–7.*

In the **Vrontokion monastery** are **Ayios Theodoros** (AD 1295), the oldest church in Mystras, and the 14th-century **Church of Panagia Odegetria,** or **Afendiko,** which is decorated with remarkable murals. These include, in the narthex, scenes of the miracles of Christ: *The Healing of the Blind Man, The Samaritan at the Well,* and *The Marriage of Cana.* The fluidity of the brush strokes, the subtle but complicated coloring, and the resonant expressions suggest the work of extremely skilled hands. ⊠ *Lower town, along path to the right.* 🕾 *1,200 dr./€3.53 covers all Mystras sites.* ☉ *Daily winter 8:30–3; summer 8–7.*

The **Pantanassa monastery** is a visual feast of intricate tiling, rosette-festooned loops mimicking frosting on a wedding cake, and myriad arches. It is the only inhabited building in Mystras; the hospitable nuns still produce embroidery for sale. Step out onto the east portico for a view of the Eurotas River valley below. ⊠ *Lower town.* ▣ *1,200 dr./€3.53 covers all Mystras sites.* ⊙ *Daily winter 8:30–3; summer 8–7.*

Every inch of the tiny **Perivleptos monastery,** meaning "attracting attention from all sides," is covered with exceptional 14th-century illustrations from the New Testament, including *The Birth of the Virgin*—in a lush palette of reds, yellows, and oranges—*The Dormition of the Virgin* above the entrance (with Christ holding his mother's soul represented as a baby), and immediately to the left of the entrance, the famous fresco of the *Divine Liturgy.* ⊠ *Lower town, in the southernmost corner.* ▣ *1,200 dr./€3.53 covers all Mystras sites.* ⊙ *Daily winter 8:30–3; summer 8–7.*

In the upper town (Ano Chora), where most aristocrats lived, stands a rare Byzantine civic building, the **Palace of Despots,** home of the last emperor. The older, northeastern wing contains a guardroom, a kitchen, and the residence. The three-story northwest wing contains an immense reception hall on its top floor, lighted by eight Gothic windows and heated by eight huge chimneys; the throne probably stood in the shallow alcove that's in the center of a wall.

In the palace's **Ayia Sofia chapel,** the Italian wives of emperors Constantine and Theodore Palaiologos are buried. Note the polychromatic marble floor and the frescoes that were preserved for years under whitewash, applied by the Turks when they transformed this into a mosque. Climb to the **castle** and look down into the gullies of Mt. Taygettus, where it's said the Spartans, who hated weakness, hurled their malformed babies. ⊠ *Ano Chora,* ☎ *0731/93377.* ▣ *1,200 dr./€3.53 covers all Mystras sites.* ⊙ *Daily winter 8:30–3; summer 8–7.*

Outdoor Activities and Sports

HIKING AND CLIMBING

The Athens travel agency **Trekking Hellas** (☞ Contacts and Resources *in* Southern Peloponnese A to Z, *below*) arranges weekend hiking trips to Mystras and a six-day walk through the Taygettus foothills, with visits to the Mani and Mystras.

A mountain refuge, with a capacity of 24, is set up at **Varvara-Dereki** on Mt. Taygettus. It has a kitchen, an oil stove, a tank, spring water, and outdoor toilets. Contact the Sparta Alpine Club (☞ Contacts and Resources *in* Southern Peloponnese A to Z, *below*).

Shopping

EMBROIDERY

In Mystras the nuns at **Pantanassa** (⊠ Lower town) monastery still make and sell their delicate embroidery.

Amykles

㉒   *67 km (41½ mi) south of Tripolis, 7 km (4½ mi) south of Mystras.*

Achaean rulers made Amykles their capital, which was inhabited from the early Bronze Age on, and eventually one of Sparta's settlements.

The **Temple of Apollo** (⊠ On the knoll) once housed a colossal statue of the god, which was engraved on coins of that period. Only a few traces of Amykles' **acropolis wall** (⊠ On the knoll) remain, but the site is an excellent picnic spot. A **tholos** (Mycenaean beehive tomb; ⊠ On a knoll at Vapheio) yielded important gold and silver artifacts, including two famous hammered gold cups depicting wild bulls savagely trampling a hunter, then peacefully grazing. The cups are now in Athens's National Archaeological Museum.

Monemvassia

★ ㉓   *96 km (59½ mi) southeast of Sparta, 89 km (55¼ mi) southeast of Amykles.*

The Byzantine town of Monemvassia clings to the side of the 1,148-ft rock that seems to blast out of the sea; in AD 375, it was separated from the mainland by an earthquake. Like Gibraltar, Monemvassia once controlled the sea lines from western Europe to the Levant. The name *moni emvasia* (single entrance) refers to the narrow passage to this walled community. If you come from Athens by ferry or hydrofoil, you'll get the most spectacular view; if you walk or take a taxi down the causeway from the adjoining town of Gefira, the rock looks uninhabited until you suddenly see castellated walls with an opening only wide enough for one person.

The town was first inhabited in the 6th century AD, when Laconians sought refuge after Arab and Slav raids. During its golden age in the 1400s under the Byzantines, Monemvassia was home to families made wealthy by their inland estates and the export of malmsey wine, a sweet variety of Madeira praised by Shakespeare. When the area fell to the Turks, Monemvassia ended up under the Pope's control and then came under sway of the Venetians, who built the citadel and most of the fortifications.

Well-to-do Greeks once again live on the rock in houses they have restored as vacation homes. Summer weekends are crowded, but off-season Monemvassia is nearly deserted. Empty houses are lined up along steep streets only wide enough for two people abreast, and remnants of another age—escutcheons, marble thrones, Byzantine icons—evoke the sense that time has stopped. It's worth a splurge to stay overnight here.

Christos Elkomenos (Christ in Chains; ✉ Platia Tzamiou, along the main street) is reputed as the largest medieval church in southern Greece. The carved peacocks are symbolic of the Byzantine era; the detached bell tower—like those of Italian cathedrals—is a sign of Venetian rebuilding in the 17th century.

The 10th-century **Agios Pavlos** (✉ Across from Platia Tzamiou), though converted into a mosque, was allowed to function as a church under the Ottoman occupation, an unusual indulgence.

For solitude and a dizzying view, pass through the upper town's wooden entrance gates, complete with the original iron reinforcement. Up the hill is a rare example of a domed octagonal church, **Agia Sofia** (✉ At top of the mountain), founded in the 13th century by Emperor Andronicus II and patterned after Dafni monastery in Athens. Follow the path to the highest point on the rock for a breathtaking view of the coast.

Dining and Lodging

$$ ✕ **Marianthi.** You'll feel like you're dropping into someone's home at dinner here: family photos of stern, mustachioed ancestors hang on the walls along with local memorabilia, someone's aunt is doing the cooking, and the service is just as homey. Order the wild mountain greens, any of the fish—especially the fresh red mullet—the addictive potato salad (you may have to order two plates), and the marinated octopus sprinkled with oregano. ✉ *Old town,* ☎ *0732/61371. No credit cards.*

$$ ✕ **To Kanoni.** After you roll out of bed, wander over to the Kanoni, which serves breakfast on a terrace overlooking the square's *kanoni* (cannon). Choose from omelets, ham and eggs, bacon, or thick, creamy

yogurt and honey. Inside you'll find red-and-white checked tablecloths, 19th-century prints of Greece, and a glorious sea view, accompanied by calming wave music. If you miss breakfast, you can always order a burger or beef *yiouvetsi* (meat baked in a clay pot with orzolike pasta). ⊠ *Old town,* ☎ *0732/61387. No credit cards.*

$$ 🏨 **Byzantinon.** The Byzantinon is housed in an old building, with a
★ few additional accommodations in other buildings in the old town. All the rooms are shaped differently, with beautiful decorations: a carved marble tile depicting a scale set in the floor; a Greek costume sketch adorning an alcove; sailors' lanterns for illumination. The best is Suite 1, a perfect hideout with an antique radio, marble bath, balcony, hidden kitchen, and large, cozy bed. ⊠ *Old town, 23070,* ☎ *0732/61351,* FAX *0732/61562. 25 rooms. MC, V.*

$$ 🏨 **Malvasia.** This hotel occupies several houses around the old town,
★ and rooms are tucked into nooks and crannies under cane-and-wood or vaulted brick ceilings. Each is decorated with bright patchwork rugs, embroidered tapestries, antique marble, and dark antique wood furniture. Many rooms have sea views, and some have fireplaces; suites are also available. ⊠ *Old town, 23070,* ☎ *0732/61323,* FAX *0732/61722. 32 rooms. Bar, breakfast room. AE, MC, V.*

$$ 🏨 **Ta Kellia.** Built in an old monastery (*kellia* means "cells"), this establishment is now run, albeit a little haphazardly, by the EOT. Though it's not glamorous like the competition, the rough-hewn rooms are a good alternative. Only a few rooms on the second floor have ocean views, and they can get quite hot in summer. ⊠ *Old town, on lower square opposite Church of Panagia Chrissafitissa, 23070,* ☎ *0732/ 61520. 11 rooms. Breakfast room. No credit cards.*

$ ⛺ **Kapsis Paradise.** This simple site is arranged on terraces above a pebble beach, a paradise for beach-lovers. It's open year-round. ⊠ *Above beach, 4 km (2½ mi) south of Monemvassia,* ☎ *0732/61123. 20 RV and tent sites. Grocery, common kitchen.*

OFF THE
BEATEN PATH

Island of Elafonisi – If you follow the Laconic peninsula south from Monemvassia south toward Neapolis, after about 35 km (21 mi) you will come to the village of Viglafia, where car ferries depart about every half hour (400 dr./€1.17) for the 15-minute crossing to the island of Elafonisi. This is where Greeks retreat for a fish lunch in the delightful little port town, then spend the afternoon on miles-long sandy strands that may well be the best, and least discovered, beaches in all of Greece. There are a number of small hotels on the island if you're tempted to linger.

SOUTHERN PELOPONNESE A TO Z

Arriving and Departing

By Boat

In both winter and summer the costly **Flying Dolphin hydrofoils** (☎ 01/452–7107) make the trip to Monemvassia several times a week. They leave from Piraeus's Marina Zea Harbor for Leonidion, Monemvassia, and Neapolis.

In the Peloponnese, call the local **port authority** for the latest information on boat travel: Gythion (☎ 0733/22262); Kalamata (☎ 0721/22218); Pylos (☎ 0721/23100 or 0732/61266); and Monemvassia (☎ 0721/ 23100 or 0732/61266).

By Bus

Buses leave Athens several times daily for Gythion, Kalamata, and Tripolis, and once a day for Andritsena, Monemvassia, and Pylos. For departure times, call the **KTEL station office** that handles your destination: Andritsena (☎ 01/513–4574); Gythion (☎ 01/512–4913); Kalamata (☎ 01/513–4293); Monemvassia (☎ 01/512–4913); Pylos (☎ 01/513–4293); Sparta (☎ 01/512–4913); and Tripolis (☎ 01/513–4575).

To get to the station at **Kifissou 100** on the outskirts of Athens, take Bus 051 (24 hours a day, every 10 minutes) from the corner of Vilara and Menandrou off Omonia square.

In the Peloponnese, you may buy tickets at the **local bus station:** Andritsena (✉ Main square, ☎ 0626/22239); Gythion (✉ Ebrikleous at north end of harbor, ☎ 0733/22228); Kalamata (✉ Artemidos 50, ☎ 0721/22851); Monemvassia (✉ Off main square, ☎ 0732/61432); Pylos (✉ Platia Trion Navarchon, ☎ 0723/22230); Sparta (✉ Vrasidou and Paleologou, ☎ 0731/26441); Tripolis (✉ Platia Kolokotronis, ☎ 071/224314).

By Car

Even if **highways** have assigned numbers, no Greek knows them by any other than their informal names, usually linked to their destination. For those traveling on the E-92 from Athens to Tripolis, the new section of the highway (the Corinth–Tripolis road) now cuts travel time in half, to little more than two hours. From Olympia in the northwest Peloponnese, you may take a smaller local road (number 74, the Pirgos–Tripolis road). Both approaches have mountainous stretches that occasionally close in winter because of snow, but conditions are otherwise good. An accurate road map is essential: the Greek Motoring Association (ELPA) publishes one of the most detailed map books on Greece, available in most Athens bookstores (4,000 dr./€11.79).

By Plane

Olympic Airways offers daily one-hour flights from Athens to Kalamata's airport, 10½ km (6½ mi) outside of town near Messinia. Call the Athens reservations line (☎ 01/966–6666) or Olympic Airways' office in Kalamata (✉ Sidirodromikou Stathmou 17, ☎ 0721/22376). For the latest flight information in Kalamata, contact the **airport** (☎ 0721/69442).

By Train

Train travel into the area is slower and much more limited than journeying by bus. Buy tickets before you leave; prices shoot up 50% when purchased on board. If traveling during a national holiday, when many Athenians head to the Peloponnese for their villages, it's worth paying the extra fee for first class to ensure a seat, especially in no-smoking compartments. Train food is dismal, so stock up if you're taking a long trip.

Trains (Lines 422, 424, 426, 428, and 436) run from Athens to Kalamata five times daily with stops in Corinth, Mycenae, and Tripolis, not to be confused with those traveling a second, longer route to Kalamata via Patras. Lines 421, 425, 427, 429, and 435 return from Kalamata to Athens. In Athens, the **Greek National Railway (OSE)** offices (✉ Fillelinon 17, ☎ 01/323–6747; or ✉ Sina 6, ☎ 01/362–4402) are the most convenient for visitors staying near Platia Syntagma (Constitution Square); otherwise purchase your ticket before departure at the **Peloponnese station** (✉ Peloponnesou 3, ☎ 01/513–1601). You can reach the station by catching Trolley 1 in front of Parliament above Syntagma Square (5 AM–midnight, every 10 minutes).

Kalamata station (✉ Sidirodromikou Stathmou, ☎ 0721/23904). **Tripolis station** (✉ Grigoris Lambraki at Xeniou Dios, ☎ 071/222402).

Getting Around

By Boat
The *Martha* runs five times weekly in winter and daily in summer between Gythion, Neapolis, and Kythera. Call ticket offices in Gythion (☎ 0733/22996).

En route from Piraeus, **Flying Dolphin hydrofoils** stop once or twice a week in winter, depending on the weather, and almost daily in summer at Monemvassia (☎ 0732/61219 or 0732/61419) and Neapolis (☎ 0734/22214). For departure information, you may also call the local port authority (☞ *above*).

By Bus
The network of bus routes lets you move easily about most of the towns mentioned, even to more remote sites such as the Pirgos Dirou caves, the Arcadian mountain villages, and Nestor's Palace museum in Chora. Keep in mind that there are fewer buses in winter and on weekends. For short distances, you may buy tickets on board; otherwise purchase them in advance at the station.

If you have trouble reaching a site—for example, there is no public transportation to ancient Messene—just take a taxi from a town's main square, which is always near the bus station. In rural areas, drivers may not switch on the meter if the destination has a fixed price, but make sure you agree on the cost before getting in—remember that it's the same price whether you're alone or in a company of four. It's the mileage that counts. When leaving town limits, the driver may switch his meter to the higher rate (Tarifa 2). Don't panic: this is perfectly legal, as is starting the meter at 200 dr./€.58. The price also goes up after midnight. If you think you've been had, don't hesitate to argue or threaten to report the driver to the police.

By Car
Especially off-season when buses don't run regularly, it's most rewarding to explore this region by car. In some areas—like the Mani peninsula—it's difficult to get around if you rely on public transportation. Rent a car in Athens or in any of the Peloponnese's bigger towns, such as Kalamata, Tripolis, Gythion, and Sparta, thus leaving the harrowing prospect of exiting Athens up to someone else.

By Train
Within the region, train travel is limited to the lines that run from Kalamata to Tripolis.

Contacts and Resources

Camping
There are several camping sites throughout the southern Peloponnese; contact the **EOT** (☞ *below*) for a free camping guide.

Car and Moped Rental Agencies
Gythion: **Motor Mani** (✉ On waterfront near causeway to Marathonissi, ☎ 0733/22853); Kalamata: **Maniatis** (✉ Iatropoulou 1, ☎ 0721/69166; ✉ 202 Faron, ☎ 0721/26025); Pylos: **Venus Rent-A-Car** (✉ Platia Trion Navarchon, ☎ 0723/22393); Sparta: **Kottaras Rent-A-Car** (✉ Menelaon 54, ☎ 0731/28966); Tripolis: **Stephany's Tours** (✉ Deligianni 23, ☎ 071/239577).

Emergencies
Police: Areopolis (☎ 0733/51209). Gythion (☎ 0733/22271 or 0733/22316). Kalamata (☎ 0721/23187). Methoni (☎ 0723/31203). Mon-

emvassia (☎ 0732/61210). Pylos (☎ 0723/22316). Sparta (☎ 0731/
28701 or 0731/26229). Tripolis (☎ 071/222411 or 071/222519).

Medical assistance: Areopolis (☎ 0733/51259 first aid; 0733/22315
hospital. Gythion (☎ 0733/22001 through 0733/22003 clinic). Kalamata (☎ 0721/23561 hospital; 0721/25555 first aid). Methoni (☎ 0723/
31456 clinic). Pylos (☎ 0723/22315 hospital). Sparta (☎ 0731/28671;
0731/28672 hospital). Tripolis (☎ 071/238542 hospital).

Guided Tours
Unlike in the Northern Peloponnese, the choice of **English-language
tours** in the south is limited. If an agency does venture into the region,
it's usually a detour through Tripolis and Sparta for a cursory visit to
Mystras, as part of a package to the Northern Peloponnese. Both **G.O.
Tours** (✉ Voulis 31, Athens, ☎ 01/322–5951 or 01/322–5955) and **CHAT**
(✉ Stadiou 4, Athens, ☎ 01/322–2886 or 01/323–0827) offer a five-
day combination called the Archaeological Tour for 81,000 dr./€239,
covering Corinth, Mycenae, Epidauros, Nafplion, Mystras, Olympia,
and Delphi. CHAT also offers a more extensive six-day Grand Tour
of the Peloponnese that adds Tiryns, a drive through Gythion to the
Pirgos Dirou caves, Kalamata, Methoni, Nestor's Palace and its museum at Chora, Bassae, and Patras for 150,000 dr./€442. If you can't
get to these tour companies, most travel agencies in Athens can book
the tour as well.

Hiking and Climbing
Army's Geographical Service (✉ Evelpidou 4, Athens, ☎ 01/884–2811).
Sparta Alpine Club (☎ 0731/24135). **Tripolis Alpine Club** (☎ 071/
232243).

Greek Federation of Mountaineering Associations (✉ Milioni 8, Athens,
☎ 01/363–6617 or 01/364–5904).

Road Assistance
The **Automobile Touring Club of Greece** (ELPA) provides assistance for
light repairs around the clock (☎ 104 anywhere in the country). There
are also ELPA main offices in Kalamata (✉ New Entrance, ☎ 0721/
93366) and Tripolis (✉ Vassileos Pavlou 3, ☎ 071/224101).

Sailing
Naval Association (☎ 0721/23860). **Port authority** (☞ *above*).

Skiing
Mt. Menalon ski center (✉ Oropedio Ostrakina, ☎ 071/22227); call
the Tripolis Alpine Club (☞ *above*).

Travel Agency
Trekking Hellas (✉ Fillelinon 7, Athens 10557, ☎ 01/315–0853 or 01/
325–0317).

Visitor Information
Greek National Tourist Organization (GNTO or EOT) Kalamata (✉ Marina, ☎ 0721/23187); Sparta (✉ Platia Vassileos Georgios in the town
hall, ☎ 0731/26517); Tripolis (✉ Ethnikis Antistaseos 43, ☎ 071/
231844). **Tourist police** often speak English and help you find accommodations: Gythion (☎ 0733/22236); Kalamata (☎ 0721/23187);
Sparta (☎ 0731/28701).

10 THE CYCLADES

ANDROS, TINOS, MYKONOS, DELOS, NAXOS, PAROS, AND SANTORINI

The magical words "Greek island" conjure up beguiling images. If you long for sun and sea, blazing bare rock and mountains, olive trees and vineyards, white peasant architecture and ancient ruins, fresh fish and fruity oils, the Cyclades are isles of quintessential plenty, the ultimate Mediterranean archipelago. "The islands with their drinkable blue volcanoes," wrote Odysseus Elytis, winner of the Nobel Prize for poetry, musing on Santorini. That Homer—who loved these islands—is buried here is unverifiable but spiritually true.

By Melissa
Dailey

Updated by
Jeffrey Carson

THE SIX MAJOR STARS IN THIS CONSTELLATION of islands in the central Aegean Sea, Andros, Tinos, Mykonos, Naxos, Paros, and Santorini, are the archetype of the islands of Greece. Here, it always seems—at least in summer—Zeus's sky is faultlessly azure, Poseidon's sea warm, and Dionysus's nightlife swinging (especially in Mykonos's discos). The prevailing wind is the northern *vorias*; called *meltemi* in summer, it cools the always sunny weather. In a magnificent fusion of sunlight, stone, and sparkling aqua sea, the Cyclades offer both culture and hedonism: ancient sites, Byzantine castles and museums, lively nightlife, shopping, dining, and beaches plain and fancy.

These arid, mountainous islands are the peaks of a deep, submerged plateau, and their composition is rocky, with few trees. They are volcanic in origin, and Santorini (Thera), southernmost of the group, actually sits on the rim of an ancient drowned volcano that exploded about 1600 BC. The dead texture of its rock is a great contrast to the living, warm limestone of most Greek islands. Santorini's geological colors— black, pink, brown, white, or pale green—are never beautiful; as you arrive by boat little shows above the cliff tops but a string of white villages—like teeth on the vast lower jaw of some monster. Still, the island was called Kállisti, "Loveliest," when it was first settled, and today, hordes of visitors find its mixture of vaulted cliff-side architecture, European elegance, and stunning sunsets all but irresistible.

Thankfully, a more idyllic rhythm of life can still be found on many of the other Cyclades (and, of course, in off-season Santorini). Well-to-do Andros, where ship-owning families once lived, retains an air of dignity, and its inhabitants go about their business largely indifferent to visitors. It's a good place for adults in search of history, fine museums, and quiet evenings. Tinos has stayed authentically Greek, since its heavy tourism is largely owing to its miracle-working icon and not to its beautiful villages. In the town of Mykonos, the whitewashed houses huddle together against the meltemi winds, and backpackers rub elbows with millionaires in the mazelike white-marble streets. The island's sophistication level is high, the beaches fine, the shopping varied and upscale, and it's the jumping-off place for a mandatory visit to tiny, deserted Delos. That windswept islet, birthplace of Apollo, still watched over by a row of marble lions, was once the religious and commercial center of the eastern Mediterranean.

Naxos, greenest of the Cyclades, makes cheese and wine, raises livestock, and produces potatoes, olives, and fruit. For centuries a Venetian stronghold, it has a shrinking, aristocratic Roman Catholic population, Venetian houses and fortifications, and Cycladic and Mycenaean sites. Paros, a hub of the ferry system, has reasonable prices and is a good base for trips to other islands. It's also good for lazing on long, white-sand beaches and for visiting fishing villages. Of course, throughout the Cyclades, there are countless classical sites, monasteries, churches, and villages to be explored. The best reason to visit them may be the beauty of the walk, the impressiveness of the location, and the hospitality you will likely find off the beaten track. Despite its depredations, the automobile has brought life back to Cycladic villages. Many shuttered houses are being authentically restored, and much traditional architecture can still be found in Ia on Santorini, Kardiani on Tinos, and Apeiranthos on Naxos—villages that are part of any deep experience of the islands. In the countryside, many of the sites and buildings are often or permanently closed, though the fencing around sites may have fallen, and monks and nuns may let you in if you are polite and nicely dressed. And the gods are still out there.

Pleasures and Pastimes

Beaches and Water Sports

The best sport in the islands is swimming, and the islands gleam with beaches, from long blond stretches of sand to tiny pebbly coves. Waterskiing, parasailing, scuba diving, and especially windsurfing have become ever more popular, though venues change from season to season. Anybody who invests in a mask, snorkel, and flippers has entry to intense, serene beauty.

Dining

Eating is a lively social activity in the Cyclades, and the friendliness of most taverna owners compensates for the lack of formal service. Unless you order intermittently, the food comes all at once. Reservations are not required unless otherwise noted, and casual dress is the rule.

Greek food, like English or indeed American, has a bad international reputation, and you can certainly find bad food in Greece. This is often a result of restaurants' trying to adapt to the tastes and wallets of the throngs of tourists. For example, when a tourist asks for less of the islands' culinary gem—fruity, expensive olive oil—in a dish, the essence is lost. Greece produces top-quality tomatoes, lamb chops, melons, olive oil, and farmer's cheese. When Greeks go out to eat, they expect good, simple food culled from these elements, as should you. A few things to watch out for: "fresh" fish on the menu when the weather has been stormy; store-bought eggplant salad; frozen potatoes. Pay attention, and you will dine with much pleasure.

Dishes are often wonderfully redolent of garlic and olive oil; as an alternative, order grilled seafood or meat—grilled octopus with ouzo is a treat. A typical island lunch is fresh fried calamari with a salad of tomatoes, peppers, onions, feta, and olives. Lamb on a skewer and *keft-edes* (spicy meatballs) are also favorites.

The volcanic soil of Santorini is hospitable to the grape, and Greeks love the Santorini wines. Greek wines have tripled in quality in the last decade. Santorini and Paros now proudly produce officially recognized "origin" wines, which are sought throughout Greece. Barrel or farmer's wine is common, and except in late summer when it starts to taste a bit off, it's often good. Try to be on Santorini on July 20 for the celebration of St. Elias's name-day, when a traditional pea-and-onion soup is served, followed by walnut and honey desserts and folk dancing.

Restaurant schedules on the Cyclades vary; some places close for lunch, most close for siesta, and all are open late.

CATEGORY	COST (ALL ISLANDS)*
$$$$	over 7,000 dr. (€20.64)
$$$	4,000 dr.–7,000 dr. (€11.79–€20.64)
$$	3,000 dr.–4,000 dr. (€8.84–€11.79)
$	under 3,000 dr. (€11.79)

per person for three-course meal, including tax, service, and beer or barrel wine

Hiking

The Cyclades are justly famous for their hiking, with the islands of Andros and Naxos being the largest and least explored. Ancient goat and donkey trails go everywhere—through fields, over mountains, along untrodden coasts. Rarely is the sea out of view, and almost never are you more than an hour's walk from a village. Since tourists tend to visit Greece for classical sites, for nightlife, and for the beach, walking is uncrowded even in July and August.

Lodging

Rooms in the islands have proliferated at a truly amazing rate. Although the simple room with oil lamp and Grandmother's furniture is a charming memory, tasteful modern accommodations with amenities are everywhere. Managers—and quality—change year by year, but overall the already high quality is rising.

Island accommodations range from run-down pensions or an extra bedroom in a private house to luxury hotels. It is customary to leave your passport with the proprietor when you check in (for Greek tax records—and to ensure payment). Unless you're traveling at the very height of the season (July 15–August 30), you're unlikely to need advance reservations; often the easiest—and most recommended—way to find something on the spot is to head for a tourist office and describe your needs and price range. Rates, which are regulated by the Greek National Tourist Organization (GNTO or EOT), vary tremendously from month to month: in shoulder season you can pay 2,000 dr./€5.89–3,000 dr./€8.84 less per room than you would in July or August. For budget travelers, room touts often meet the ferries with pictures advertising their properties: check the location. Alternatively, walk around town and ask where you can rent a cheap room, but take a good look first, and check the bathroom before you commit. If there are extra beds in the room, clarify in advance that the amount agreed on is for the entire room—owners occasionally try to put another person in the same room.

The best rooms and service (and noticeably higher prices) are on Mykonos and Santorini, where luxury out-of-town resort hotels are mushrooming—and our recommendations hardly represent the only choices. To experience the Cyclades properly, you should not go seeking technological amenities; make a room with a view your priority—preferably one with a balcony that overlooks the sea. Avoid hotels on main roads or near all-night discos. And an evening dip in a freshwater pool after swimming in the sea is a luxury.

Often only expensive hotels provide hot water 24 hours a day; in some hotels you must turn on a thermostat for a half hour to heat water for a shower (don't forget to turn it off). Signs tell you that water is in short supply in the Cyclades, reminding you to conserve it. Fresh water is often shipped from the mainland, and though the tap water is potable, you should not drink from fountains or springs. Most people drink bottled water, available everywhere. You should assume that hotels of $$$$ and $$$ rating will have air-conditioning; air-conditioning is noted when available at less-expensive establishments.

Hotels close from November through March unless otherwise noted. Some do not serve breakfast, and when they do, it sometimes costs extra—check when booking.

CATEGORY	COST (ALL ISLANDS)*
$$$$	over 39,000 dr. (€115)
$$$	22,000 dr.–39,000 dr. (€64.89–€115)
$$	13,000 dr.–22,000 dr. (€38.34–€64.89)
$	under 13,000 dr. (€38.34)

All prices are for a standard double room in high season, including taxes and service but excluding extra charges for breakfast.

✎ *following the text of a review is your signal that the property has a Web site, where you will find details and, usually, images; for a link, visit www.fodors.com/urls.*

Shopping

Mykonos, with Santorini taking a close second, is the best island in the Cyclades for shopping. You can buy anything from Greek folk items to Italian designer clothes, cowboy boots, and leather jackets from the United States. Although island prices are better than in the expensive shopping districts of Athens, there are many tourist traps in the resort towns, with high-pressure sales tactics and inflated prices for inferior goods. The Greeks have a word for naive American shoppers—*Americanaki.* It's a good sign if the owner of a shop selling traditional crafts or art lives on the island and is not a hotshot Athenian over for the summer to make a quick buck.

Each island has a unique pottery style that reflects its individuality. Santorini potters like the bright shades of the setting sun, though the best pottery islands are Paros and especially Siphnos. Island specialties are icons hand-painted after Byzantine originals; weavings and embroideries; local wines; and gold worked in ancient and Byzantine designs.

Don't be surprised when the stores close between 2 and 5:30 in the afternoon and reopen in the evenings; even on the chic islands everybody takes a siesta.

Traditional Festivals

Ano Aprovato, a village south of Batsi on Andros, holds a *paneyiri* (festival) on August 15, for the Dormition of the Virgin Mary, with feasting and dancing along with the religious rites.

In Chora on Tinos the icon is paraded with much pomp on Annunciation Day, March 25, and especially Dormition Day, August 15. As it is carried on poles over the heads of the faithful, including thousands of bedecked gypsies who make Tinos seem a gigantic glittering encampment, cures are effected, and religious emotion runs high. On July 23, in honor of St. Pelagia, the icon is paraded from Kechrovouni Nunnery, and afterward the festivities continue long into the night, with music and fireworks.

Naxos town celebrates the Dionysia festival during the first week of August, with concerts, costumed folk dancers, and free food and wine in the square. At other times, feast days are honored with a paneyiri. For example, during Carnival, preceding Lent, "bell wearers" take to the streets in Apeiranthos and Filoti, running from house to house, making as much noise as possible with strings of bells tied around their waists. They're a disconcerting sight in their hooded cloaks, with scarves concealing their faces, as they ritually escort a man dressed as a woman from house to house to collect eggs. In Apeiranthos, villagers square off in rhyming-verse contests: on the last Sunday of Lent, the *paliomaskari,* their faces blackened, challenge each other in improvising *kotsakia* (satirical couplets). At the May Day Festival in Koronos, wildflower garlands are made, and there's lively dancing. On July 14, Ayios Nikodemos Day is celebrated in Chora with a procession of the patron saint's icon through town, but the Dormition of the Virgin on August 15 is, after Easter and Christmas, the festival most widely celebrated, especially in Sangri, Filoti (August 4), and Apeiranthos.

On Paros each year on August 23, Naousa celebrates the heroic naval battle against the Turks, with children dressed in native costume, great feasts, and traditional dancing. The day ends with 100 boats illuminated by torches converging on the harbor.

Exploring the Cyclades

Numbers in the text correspond to numbers in the margin and on the Cyclades, Mykonos Town, Delos, Naxos, and Santorini maps.

Great Itineraries

There is no bad itinerary for the Cyclades. The islands differ remarkably, and are all beautiful. It is possible to "see" any island in a day, for they are small and the "must-see" sights are few—Delos, Santorini's caldera, the Minoan site at Akrotiri, and Paros's Church of a Hundred Doors. So planning a trip depends on your sense of inclusiveness, your restlessness, your energy, *and* your ability to accommodate changing boat schedules.

IF YOU HAVE 2 OR 3 DAYS

For a three-day trip that promises shopping, nightlife, a serious summer beach scene, classical Greece, and traditional Greece, go directly to ▣ **Mykonos** ①–⑩, the next morning visit **Delos** ⑪–㉛, and in the afternoon go to ▣ **Tinos** for its landscape, villages, and church.

IF YOU HAVE 5 DAYS

If you want to see the two most popular islands in five days you can visit ▣ **Mykonos** ①–⑩ (and **Delos** ⑪–㉛) and ▣ **Santorini** ㊻–㊾, with its volcanic bay, ancient site, and Greece's most-photographed village.

IF YOU HAVE 8 DAYS

If you want some hiking, Byzantine churches, and relaxation between Mykonos and Santorini, visit **Naxos** and **Paros** for an overfilled eight days. And if you have two weeks really to see the Cyclades, start the four-day itinerary in elegant, nontouristy ▣ **Andros**; then go to ▣ **Tinos**, ▣ **Mykonos** ①–⑩, and **Delos** ⑪–㉛; then ▣ **Naxos** ㉜–㊺, ▣ **Paros**, and ▣ **Santorini** ㊻–㊾. You may continue on to explore the other Cycladic islands—they are endless.

When to Tour

Most people come to Greece in the summer, especially August, when Greece is crowded and less personal, and the penetrating sun bleaches hot afternoons. Walkers, nature lovers, and devotees of classical and Byzantine Greece would do better to come in the spring and fall, both being cooler and less tourist-riddled. Spring's islands burst with thousands of varieties of wildflowers, and sprightly crimson poppies dapple stern marble blocks, but the sea is cold. Autumn's days are short but the sea remains alluringly swimmable. This is when zesty olives are gathered, bulging grapes are pressed, and verdant fields plowed.

ANDROS

The northernmost and second largest of the Cycladic islands, Andros is about 32 km by 16 km (nearly 20 mi by 10 mi), and its rugged, mountainous geography is best seen by foot, bike, or car. The highest peak, Mt. Kouvari, reaches 3,260 ft. A network of springs gives birth to streams, which whirl down from the mountaintops, feeding lush valleys; unlike the other Cyclades, Andros is green with pines, sycamores, mulberries, and oaks. In ancient times it was called Hydroussa, or "Well-Watered." The springs, streams, and falls have a cooling effect that, together with summer's northerlies (meltemia), ameliorate the Aegean heat. Spring's southerlies bring heat and many birds.

Foreign tourism is in an early stage on Andros, and most of the islanders are indifferent to it. Perhaps the reason for this snobbishness is that Andros has been a wealthy island since silk production began in the 12th century; today, Andros thrives on Greeks who own villas and bring their own cars on their two-hour journeys from Athens. The well-known Goulandris shipping family from Andros has founded two museums of modern art and the archaeological museum in Andros town, the best in the Aegean. Though Andros is an island for the cultured, low tourism means low prices for restaurants and hotels, especially compared to Mykonos or Santorini.

Across the entire landscape of Andros you will notice an interesting system of stone walls that marks the boundaries between the fields of different owners. In a building style unique to Andros, the walls are interrupted at regular intervals, and each gap is filled with a large, flat, upright slab. This saves stone and labor and allows herders to move the large slab for the passage of animals. Another common feature (also seen on Mykonos and especially Tinos) is the dovecotes: square towers whose pigeonholes form decorative geometric designs. The Venetians introduced them in the 13th century. Though many fell into disuse, when hard times struck the islands in this century, local farmers started breeding the pigeons and selling them abroad as a delicacy. Today only a few dovecotes are still maintained.

Gavrio

75 km (46½ mi) east of Rafina Port, 35 km (21¾ mi) northeast of Andros town.

Though recently spruced up, Gavrio, on the northwest coast, is Andros's dull little port town. The roads north and west lead to unspoiled beaches (Felos, for example), magnificent agricultural land, and historic landmarks (the ruined Byzantine church at Vitali and the Hellenistic tower at Ayios Petros). Although there are some accommodations here, most people go south to Batsi, the island's only resort, or to Andros town, on the opposite side of the island.

Batsi

27 km (16¾ mi) northwest of Andros town.

Originally a small fishing village, Batsi has developed only over the last 10 years, and as a new resort town, many of the businesses have a friendly, nonhustling quality. On the hillside, a few lovely houses from a century ago look down to the promenade along the sea, where Athenian and foreign visitors stroll, patronizing the new restaurants and bars. Many people stay here because the social life is a bit more lively than in Andros town and because of the beach, where windsurfing equipment and paddleboats can be rented.

Beach
Batsi beach is sandy, accessible, and protected from the north wind. Just to the south are **Dellavoya beach** and **Ayia Marina beach,** both with tavernas and rooms. To the north, **Ayios Petros** is also lovely.

Dining and Lodging
$$ ✕ **Balcony of the Aegean.** Ask an Andriot what his favorite restaurant
★ is, and he will inevitably name this one. Located in Ano Aprovato (6 km [4 mi] up from Batsi; follow Greek signs), it has a spectacular sunset view and lovingly traditional food. Upon your arrival Socrates and Stella Kolitsas usually offer a raki (like grappa). Sip it with *dra,* a spread made from fresh butter, or with unaged *kopanisti,* a sharp soft cheese. Stella is especially proud of her *fortalia* (homemade sausage omelet), and Socrates his finely toned meats, since he is a butcher who raises it all himself. With everything homemade or homegrown, this is what Greek food is supposed to taste like—even the yogurt with black cherry sauce

is made here. The Kolitsases are open for dinner all year and for lunch in season. ⊠ *Ano Aprovato,* ☎ *0282/41020. No credit cards.*

$$ ✕ **Stamatis.** Pity this high-class taverna has no sea view, but the food—
★ traditional Greek, since 1965—is better than at many other spots and the place is open year-round. Outside, green chairs and tables are crammed into the gleaming white alleys. The air-conditioned interior is homey and rustic; the walls display hunting relics (dinner's harbinger?). Stamatis's son Yannis will invite you to have a look at the wonderful dishes in the kitchen. If the sea is too rough for a fresh fish haul, try the fresh stuffed roasted chicken or the tender lamb chops with a special Andros stuffing; on Wednesdays, the special house lamb is prepared. The good barrel wine is their own. For dessert, splurge on the light crème caramel. ⊠ *One street up from the main quay,* ☎ *0282/41283. MC, V.*

$$$–$$$$ 🏨 **Epaminondas.** Looking something like a cross between a dovecote
★ and a monastery, the exterior of this quiet complex—all terra-cotta and white plaster—climbs Batsi's northern hillside, about 15 minutes by foot from the town center. If you have children, or even if you don't, this is the place, as duplexes or triplexes vary in size, with space for two to six people. The cool, spacious interiors are tasteful and relaxing, with marble floors and traditionally embroidered curtains. Most rooms have kitchenettes, and all have phones and huge verandas overlooking Batsi Bay. The hotel's deep freshwater pool is lighted all night. ⊠ *On road to lower Batsi, on left, 84503,* ☎ *0282/41682 or 0282/41177,* 🖷 *0282/41681. 23 apartments. Kitchenettes, pool. V.* 🐢

$$ 🏨 **Heide Apartments.** These comfortable, new, quiet apartments (two to six persons) in a residential area—white cubes on a green hillside— are 200 yards behind Batsi beach, it's a two-minute walk to the beach. All have terraces, some with sea views, and island furnishings. Close pool access can be arranged. Perfect for families, it's open all year. ⊠ *Up from Batsi beach, 84503,* ☎ *0282/41252,* 🖷 *0282/41608. 7 apartments. Kitchenettes, air-conditioning. V.*

Nightlife

NIGHTCLUBS

Beware: evenings at the **Titanium** (⊠ On perimeter road of Batsi) nightclub can extend into the wee hours. It has Greek dancing to live music in summer. There are several music bars on the Batsi waterfront where the young congregate: follow your ears.

Outdoor Activities and Sports

WATER SPORTS

Windsurfing equipment and pedal boats can be rented by the hour at Batsi beach. More adventurous travelers might want to try waterskiing or parasailing, tethered behind a motorboat (but the town hopes to limit these activities, as they bother swimmers).

Palaiopolis

18½ km (11½ mi) southwest of Andros town, 9 km (5½ mi) south of Batsi.

Unfortunately, most of Palaiopolis, the ancient capital of Andros, lies beneath the sea, destroyed in the 4th century BC either by an earthquake or a landslide. The town today is a quiet but gorgeous village that stretches down the slope of Mt. Kouvari to the shore. The road cuts through the **upper town,** where you'll find a café and an excellent roadside taverna. From the taverna you can look up to the hill and see the site of an **ancient acropolis,** 984 ft above the sea, now occupied by a small **Orthodox chapel;** some **waterfalls** are located a short climb up. In 1832 a farmer turned up the famous **statue of Hermes** in this area, which is now on display in the archaeological museum in Andros town (☞ *below*). Opposite the café, 1,039 steps lead down through the **lower village,** in the shade of flowering vines and trees heavy with lemons. Scattered near the **beach** are marble remnants of early buildings and statues. Though it has not been systematically excavated, archaeologists did enough digging around here in 1956 to conjecture that the bits and pieces are remains from the ancient agora.

NEED A BREAK?	Stop in **Menites** (⊠ ½ km [¼ mi] off main road, halfway between the fork in the road and Andros town) to see the sacred springs and have a glass of local wine and a bite to eat at the **shaded taverna**; it serves whole rooster—an Andriot specialty. Mineral spring water tumbles from a series of lion-head spouts along a stone wall, and hidden by greenery in the background is **Panayia tis Koumulous,** an Orthodox church supposedly built on the site of a temple to Dionysos. According to legend, these are the very springs whose water turned to wine each year on the god's feast day.

Andros Town

27 km (16¾ mi) south of Batsi.

Andros town (Chora) has been the capital of the island since the Venetian occupation in the 13th century. The city is built on a long, narrow peninsula, at the end of which is a **small island** with the remains of a **Venetian castle** built about 1220.

Take a leisurely stroll down the center's **marble promenade** (⊠ Main St.), past the impressive 13th-century **Palatiani Church** and the interesting **gift shops** that sell the local pottery. Handsome 19th-century stone mansions line the streets, and over their doors are carved galleons, indicating that the original owners were shipowners or sea captains. The town is deliberately kept traditional, and its tidy appearance and the distinction of its neoclassical houses bear witness to its long-standing prosperity.

The main street leads to **Kairis Square** (⊠ At tip of peninsula), where in the center stands a bust of **Theophilos Kairis,** a local hero. Born in Andros town in 1784, Kairis was educated in Paris, and returned to Andros in 1821 to become one of the leaders in the War of Independence. A philosopher, scholar, and social reformer, he toured Europe to raise money for an orphanage and school, which he founded in 1835. The school became famous in Greece, and enrollment eventually rose to 600, but the Orthodox church closed it down and tried Kairis as a heretic for his individualistic religious beliefs. He died in a Syros prison in 1852.

The **Museum of Modern Art** is the first of the three museums on Andros funded by the Goulandris Foundation. It stages exhibitions of international and Greek artists of the 20th century. ⊠ *Andros town,* ☎ *0282/22650.* ☞ *700 dr./€2.06 (free Sun.).* ۞ *Sat.–Mon. 10–2.*

The **Museum of Sculpture** displays rotating exhibitions by Greece's best modern artists and a permanent collection of the works of sculptor Michael Tombros (1889–1974), whose parents were born on Andros. ⊠ *Andros town,* ☎ *0282/22444.* ☞ *Free.* ۞ *Sat.–Mon. 10–2.*

The pride of Andros's **Archaeological Museum** is the life-size marble statue of Hermes discovered in Palaiopolis and thought to be a copy of a Praxiteles. The collections range from the Mycenaean through Roman eras. Upstairs is an extensive display on Zagora, the earliest known settlement in Andros, a town built during the Geometric period on the southwest coast, on a promontory 529 ft above sea level, surrounded by jagged cliffs. It was the main settlement from 900 BC to 700 BC, before the rise of Palaiopolis. The site is not open, but the museum provides a model. ⊠ *Kairis Sq.,* ☎ FAX *0282/23664.* ⌦ *500 dr./€1.47* ☉ *Tues.–Sun. 8:30–2:30.*

The Arts

Check the art museums for lectures, recitals, and opening nights.

Beaches

Nimborio Beach (⊠ About 300 ft from the Andros town center) is on the edge of Andros town. About a mile north of Andros town is **Yialia beach** (⊠ Stenies) with a taverna.

Dining and Lodging

$ ✕ **Parea.** This shaded taverna perched high above a windswept beach is a fine place to lunch on fortalia (the island's oven-baked version of an omelet, packed with potatoes, cheese, sausage or bacon, a handful of broad beans, and herbs). Other favorites are veal in lemon sauce, and *kannelonia* (cannelloni) stuffed with mincemeat. For dessert go to one of the cafés next door for homemade fruit ices. ⊠ *Kairis Sq., Andros town,* ☎ *0282/23721. V.*

$$$ ᵀ⁺ **Hotel Stagira.** Andros's newest hotel (the pool is not quite in) is peaceful, welcoming, attractive, and quiet. The lobby, contrasting Aegean white with dark wood, leads onto a terrace with a Italianate view of the cypresses of Livadia valley framing the sea. The suites, similarly designed, have balconies or gardens and full kitchens. Some suites have two baths. ⊠ *Dexameni (turn left just after Paradise hotel; after 10 yards turn up the hill on the right), Andros 84500,* ☎ *0282/23525 or 0282/24502. 30 rooms. Bar, kitchenettes. AE, DC, MC, V.*

$$ ᵀ⁺ **Hotel Egli.** Sometimes a simple cheap hotel is all you want. This one, in a 100-year-old building and serving as a hotel since 1955, is right in the center of town and open all winter. Some rooms feature balconies and refrigerators and all have fans. ⊠ *Andros town, 84500,* ☎ *0282/ 22303 or 0282/22525,* FAX *0282/22159. 15 rooms, 7 with bath. Bar, breakfast room, refrigerators. No credit cards.*

$$ ᵀ⁺ **Hotel Pighi Sariza.** This peaceful hotel is in a green mountain village near the Sariza mineral springs (be sure to buy a bottle) and is wonderful for a break from the summer heat. From here you can hike the many mountain trails nearby, view waterfalls, and—sigh—hear nightingales. Half the comfortable rooms have sea views and half have (just as good) mountain views. The spacious restaurant has an international menu. Nature lovers will appreciate the fact that the hotel is open year-round. ⊠ *Apikia Rd., 5 km (3 mi) north of Andros town, 84500,* ☎ *0282/23799,* FAX *0282/22476. 42 rooms. Restaurant, air-conditioning (some rooms), minibars, pool, sauna, recreation room. AE, DC, MC, V.*

Outdoor Activities and Sports

BOATING

The **Andros Naval Club** (⊠ Nimborio port, just north of Andros town) offers rowing and sailing.

HIKING

The mountainous geography and lush greenery make Andros a pleasant island for hiking, especially around Andros town and near Messaria (south), Apikia (west), and Stenies (north). The 5-km (3-mi) hike from the little village of Lamira to Andros town is popular. Andros Travel in Batsi organizes many hiking trips.

Shopping

GIFT SHOPS

Nearly unique, Andros's **main street** hasn't changed much in 50 years. A number of gift shops sell local pottery, embroidery, ship's models, and other handmade objects. Two of them are **Lasia** (⊠ Main street, ☎ 0282/25095), which features mementos of Andros's great shipping days, and **Paraporti** (⊠ Kairis Sq., ☎ 0282/23777), which features pottery.

SWEETS

Andros is noted for candies and sweetmeats, and there are several shops in Andros town that maintain the tradition. Perhaps the best, and most old-fashioned, is **Konstantinos Laskaris** (⊠ Main street, ☎ 0282/22305), where bitter almond taffy, rose petals in syrup, and *kaltsounia* (walnut-honey sweetmeat) are among the once common, now exotic, things for sale.

TINOS

Perhaps the least-visited of the major Cyclades, Tinos (or, as archaeologists spell it, Tenos) is among the most beautiful and most fascinating. The third largest of the Cyclades after Naxos and Andros, with an area of 195 square km (121 square mi), it is home to nearly 10,000 people, many of whom still live the traditional life of farmers or craftsmen. Its long mountainous spine, rearing amid Andros, Mykonos, and Siros, makes it seem forbidding, and in a way it is. It is not popular among tourists for several reasons: the main village, Tinos town (Chora), lacks charm; the beaches are mediocre; there is no airport; and the prevailing north winds are the Aegean's fiercest (passing mariners used to sacrifice a calf to Poseidon—ancient Tinos's chief deity—in hopes of avoiding shipwreck). For Greeks, a visit to Tinos is essential: its great Church of the Evangelistria is the Greek Lourdes, a holy place of pilgrimage and miraculous cures; 799 other churches adorn the countryside. Encroaching development here is to accommodate those in search of their religious elixir and not, as on the other islands, the beach-and-bar crowd.

Tinos is renowned for its 1,300 dovecotes which, unlike those on Mykonos or Andros, are mostly well maintained; in fact, new ones are being built. Two stories high, with intricate stonework, carved-dove finials, and thin schist slabs arranged in intricate patterns resembling traditional stitchery, the dovecotes have been much written about—and are much visited by doves.

Tinos is dotted with possibly the loveliest villages in the Cyclades, which, for some welcome reason, are not being abandoned. The dark arcades of Arnados, the vine-shaded sea views of Isternia and Kardiani, the Venetian architecture of Loutra, the gleaming marble squares of Pirgos: these, finally, are what make Tinos unique. A map, available at kiosks or rental agencies, will make touring these villages by car or bike somewhat less confusing, as there are nearly 50 of them.

Tinos Town

55 km (34 mi) southeast of Andros's port.

Civilization on Tinos is a millennium older than **Tinos town,** or Chora, founded in the 5th century BC. On weekends and during festivals, Chora is thronged with Greeks attending church and with restaurants and hotels catering to them. As the well-known story goes, in 1822, a year after the War of Independence began (Tinos was the first of the islands to join in), the Virgin sent the nun Pelagia a dream about a buried icon of the Annunciation. On January 30, 1823, such an icon was unearthed amid the foundations of a Byzantine church, and it started to heal people immediately.

The Tiniots, hardly unaware of the icon's potential, immediately built the splendid **Panayia Evangelistria,** or Annunciate Virgin, on the site, using the most costly marble from Tinos, Paros, and Delos. The church's **marble courtyards** (note the green-veined Tiniot stone) are paved with pebble mosaics and surrounded by offices, chapels, a health station, and **seven museums.** Inside the **upper three-aisle church** dozens of beeswax candles and precious votives—don't miss the golden orange tree near the door donated by a blind man who was granted sight—dazzle the eye. You must often wait in line to see the little icon, which is encrusted with jewels, donated as thanks for cures. To beseech the icon's aid, a sick person sends a young female relative and a mother brings her sick infant. As the pilgrim descends from the boat, she falls to her knees, with traffic indifferently whizzing about her, and crawls painfully up the main street—1 km (½ mi)—to the church. In the church's courtyards, she and her family camp for several days, praying to the magical icon for a cure, which sometimes comes. This procedure is very similar to the ancient one observed in Tinos's temple of Poseidon. The **lower church,** called the Evresis, celebrates the finding of the icon; in one room a baptismal font is filled with silver and gold votives. The chapel to the left commemorates the torpedoing by the Italians, on Dormition Day, 1940, of the Greek ship *Helle*; in the early stages of the war, the roused Greeks amazingly overpowered the Italians. ⊠ *Chora, at end of Megalohari,* ☎ *0283/22256.* ⊠ *Free.* ☉ *Daily 8:30–3.*

On the main street, near the church, is the small **Archaeological Museum;** its collection includes a sundial by Andronicus of Cyrrhus, who in the 1st century BC also designed Athens's Tower of the Winds. Here, too, are Tinos's famous huge, red storage vases, from the 8th century BC. ⊠ *Megalohari,* ☎ *0283/22670.* ⊠ *500 dr./€1.47* ☉ *Tues.–Fri. 8–2.*

One and a half kilometers (¾ mile) from Chora you'll see a copse of pines shading a small parking lot, from which a path leads down to Stavros (Holy Cross) chapel; right on the water is the unmarked **Markos Velalopoulos's Ouzeri** (⊠ Under church, ☎ 0283/23276), which serves *strophia* (raki), ouzo, and traditional snacks such as fried cheese or figs with sesame. This is Tinos's most romantic spot to watch the sunset. It is also good for swimming. Note that the sunken breakwater along the coastal road in Stavros Harbor is ancient.

....

OFF THE
BEATEN PATH

MOUNTAIN VILLAGES ABOVE CHORA – At night the lights of the hill villages surrounding Tinos's highest mountain, Mt. Tsiknias—2,200 ft high and the ancient home of Boreas (the wind god)—glitter over Chora like fireworks. By day they are worth visiting. Take the good road that runs through Dio Horia and Monastiri, ascending and twisting around switchbacks, passing fertile fields and a few of Tinos's most fanciful old dovecotes. After 9 km (5½ mi) you reach **Kechrovouni,** or just Monastiri, which is a veritable city of nuns, founded in the 10th century. One cell contains the head of St. Pelagia in a wooden chest; another is a small icon museum. Though a nunnery, Kechrovouni is a lively place, since many of the church's pilgrims come here by bus. Out front, a nun sells huge garlic heads and braids to be used as charms against misfortune; the Greeks call these "California garlic." One kilometer (½ mile) farther on, Tinos's telecommunications towers spike the sky, marking the entrance to **Arnados,** a strange village 1,600 ft up, overlooking Chora. Most of the streets here are vaulted, and thus cool and shady, if a bit claustrophobic; no medieval pirate ever penetrated this warren. In one alley is the **Ecclesiastical Museum,** which displays icons from local churches. Another 1½ km (¾ mi) farther on are the **Dio Horia** (Two Villages), with a marble fountain house, unusual in Tinos. The spreading plane tree in front of it, according to the marble plaque, was planted in 1885. Now the road starts winding down again, to reach **Triandaros,**

which has a good restaurant; many of the pretty houses in this misty place are owned by Germans. Yannis Kyparinis, who made the three-story bell tower in Dio Horia, has his workshop and showroom here.

Beaches

There is a series of beaches between Chora and Kionia (and beyond, for walkers). **Stavros** is the most romantic. **Ayios Yannis** (⊠ Near Porto) is long, sandy, and peaceful. **Pachia Ammos** (⊠ Past Porto, reached by a dirt road) is undeveloped and sparkling.

Dining and Lodging

$$$ ✕ **Xynari.** Thodoros and Nikos Mitardos keep a careful eye, from the homemade bread to the homemade spoon sweets, on Tinos's fanciest restaurant. In the second and third floors of a 19th-century house surrounded by neoclassical buildings, the main room is a warm cream with deep green accents and much wood. Among the many appetizers, try spicy cheese salad or stuffed potatoes with béchamel. Good entrées include eggplants stuffed with veal and cheese, and grilled local meats. The balcony is perfect for observing the promenade in the evening. ⊠ *Evangelistria 13,* ☎ *0283/23655 through 0283/23657. AE, MC, V.*

$$ ✕ **Alonia.** In a terraced hotel (☞ *below*) with magnificent views of fields
★ and sea, you can savor home-style meals prepared by the owners. To begin, try homemade onion focaccia (which they call bread), eggplant-olive salad, or marinated raw fish fillets (recipe: debone fish, salt well, drain 30 hours, rinse well, marinate in lemon juice two hours). Home-spun entrées may be chicken breasts stuffed with bacon, cheese, and herbs; beef in cream sauce with mushrooms; and beef stew with wine and onions—the menu changes. The barrel wine is excellent. ⊠ *2 km (1 mi) from Chora toward Porto (Ayios Ioannis), Alonia Hotel,* ☎ *0283/23541 through 0283/23543,* ℻ *0283/23544. MC, V.*

$$ ✕ **Metaxi Mas.** On a trellised lane by the harbor, Euripides and Marigo Tatsionas's elegant restaurant turns out to be no more expensive than a taverna. The name means "between us." The decor is traditional—warm ocher walls, wooden furniture, mirrors—the soft music is Greek, and the service is friendly. From starters to desserts, the food is homemade, but with a haute-Athenian flair. For starters try salad metaxi mas, deep-fried sun-dried tomatoes, or hot eggplant slices wrapped around cheese, mint, and green pepper. For a main dish the lamb (or kid) casserole is especially succulent. With a fireplace in winter and an air-conditioner for summer, this place is open year-round. ⊠ *Kontogiorgi alley,* ☎ *0285/29545. MC, V.*

$$$ ☷ **Porto Tango.** This ambitiously up-to-date, popular resort-hotel strives for the best in decor and service. Greece's late prime minister, Andreas Papandreou, stayed here during his last visit to Tinos. Modular Cycladic architecture lends privacy; the lobby, where an art exhibition is usually on display, has a wooden ceiling, marble floors, and Tiniot furnishings, both modern and antique. Rooms are simple, white, and private, with wood furniture and TVs. *Cement road up hill, Porto 84200,* ☎ *0283/24411 through 0283/24415,* ℻ *0283/24416. 62 rooms. Restaurant, bar, pool, sauna, exercise room. AE, MC, V.*

$$ ☷ **Akti Aegeou.** The family that runs this little resort must know they are lucky to own such a valuable piece of property. Akti Aegeou, or "Aegean Coast," is right on the fine, uncrowded beach at Porto. All airy rooms come with balconies, marble floors, traditional rag rugs, and personal amenities, including minibus service. The restaurant, specializing in fresh fish, is very good. It must take a lot of water to keep the lawns so green under the blazing Aegean summer sun. ⊠ *Beach of Ayios Ioannis, Porto 84200,* ☎ *0283/24248,* ℻ *0283/23523. 5 rooms, 6 apartments. Restaurant, bar, kitchenettes, pool. No credit cards.*

$$ \quad \star \quad $$ **Alonia Hotel.** This hotel is not exciting, aesthetically interesting, in town, or near the beach (1 km mi] away). It is, however, Tinos's very best. Comfortable, family-run, and quietly efficient, it is for you if you dislike snazzy resorts and want to be out of hectic Chora. The fairly large rooms all have dazzling views (rooms overlooking the pool are best), telephones, and bathrooms *with* bathtubs. Tinos's largest freshwater pool is surrounded by lawns, trees, and gardens—not baking cement. And the superb restaurant is often frequented by Tiniots. An hourly minibus makes the run to Chora; the hotel is open in winter for groups. ⊠ *2 km (1 mi) from Chora toward Porto (Ayios Ioannis), 84200,* ☎ *0283/23541 through 0283/23543,* ☒ *0283/23544. 34 rooms, 4 suites. Restaurant, bar, café, air-conditioning, pool. MC, V.*

Nightlife

Tinos has fewer **bars** and **discos** than the other big islands, but there is plenty of late-night bar action just behind the waterfront on the way to the new dock; **Syvilla,** on the street behind the fish market next to the Archeio Bar, is especially popular.

Outdoor Activities and Sports

Of all the major islands, Tinos is the least developed for sports. The strong winds discourage water sports, and their concessions come and go.

Shopping

FARMERS AND FLEA MARKETS

Tinos is a rich farming island, and every day but Sunday farmers from all the far-flung villages fill the **square** (⊠ Between new and old docks) with vegetables, herbs, and flowers. In the next square closer to town, the local pelican (a rival to Mykonos's) can often be found cadging snacks from the **fish market.**

Tinos produces a lot of milk. A short way up from the harbor, on the right, is the little store of the **Enosis,** or Farmer's Cooperative (⊠ Megalohari, up from harbor, ☎ 0283/23289), which sells milk, butter, and a variety of cheeses, including very sharp kopanisti, perfect with ouzo.

Evangelistria, the street parallel to the church, is closed to traffic and is a kind of **religious flea market,** lined with shops hawking immense candles, chunks of incense, tacky souvenirs, tin votives, and sweets. There are several good jewelers' shops on the market street where, as always on Tinos, the religious note is supreme.

JEWELRY

The selection at **Ostria** (⊠ Evangelistria, ☎ 0283/23893) is especially good; in addition to delicate silver jewelry, it sells silver icon covers, silver plate, and 22-karat gold. **Anna Maria** (⊠ Chora waterfront, on patio of Avra hotel, ☎ 0283/23456) sells traditional Greek silver jewelry amid much culture.

WEAVINGS

The 100-year-old weaving school, or **Biotechniki Scholi** (⊠ Evangelistria, three-quarters of the way up from the sea), sells traditional weavings—aprons, towels, spreads—made by its students, local girls. The largest of its three high-ceiling, wooden-floored rooms is filled with looms and spindles.

Kionia

2½ km (1¼ mi) northwest of Tinos town.

The large, untended **Sanctuary of Poseidon** (⊠ Northwest of Tinos town) is also dedicated to the bearded sea god's sea-nymph consort, Amphitrite. The present remains are from the 4th century BC and later, though the sanctuary itself is much older. The sanctuary was a kind of hospital, where the ailing came to camp and solicit the god's help. The marble dolphins in the museum were discovered here. According to the Roman historian Pliny, Tinos was once infested with serpents (goddess symbols) and named Serpenttown (Ophiousa), until supermasculine Poseidon sent storks to clean them out. The sanctuary functioned well into Roman times.

Beaches

The Kiona road ends at a long sheltered **beach,** which is unfortunately being worn away by cars heading for the two pretty **coves** beyond, including the **Gastrion cave,** whose entrance bears Byzantine inscriptions.

Dining and Lodging

$$ × **Tsambia.** Abutting the sanctuary of Poseidon, this multilevel taverna prepares homemade traditional fare. For starters try a mélange of indigenous specialties: *louza* (smoked peppered pork roll coated and preserved in wax), local Tiniot cheeses, and homegrown vegetables. Fresh fish is available, depending on the weather. Tried-and-true are *stifado* (rabbit stew), the strictly local meat, and the outstanding codfish croquettes in garlic sauce. To get here, follow signs for TRADITIONAL GREEK RESTAURANT just before the Sanctuary of Poseidon. ⊠ *Cement road, Kionia,* ☎ *0283/23142. No credit cards.*

$$$ ⛻ **Tinos Beach.** Part of the government's all-too-successful sponsorship to promote tourism in the '70s, this is Tinos's most varied resort. In the large, cool lobby, featuring lots of wood and tiles, a pianist sometimes plays at night. Many rooms in this hotel, which is being slowly renovated, have splendid sea views, and there are suites and bungalows with marble floors that sleep four. ⊠ *Tinos beach, at end (3 km [2 mi]) of Kiona Rd., just past sanctuary to Poseidon, Kionia 84200,* ☎ *0283/ 22626 or 0283/22627,* FAX *0283/23153. 80 rooms, 3 suites, 3 bungalows. Restaurant, bar, café, 2 pools, 2 tennis courts, shops. MC, V.*

Outdoor Activities and Sports

HIKING

Ktikados village is a beautiful hour-long walk up into the panoramic mountains; 9th-century BC graves have been found in the settlement.

RACQUET SPORTS

Tennis and Ping-Pong are usually going on at **Tinos Beach Hotel** (⊠ Kionia, ☎ 0283/22626).

VOLLEYBALL

You can usually join—or organize—a pick-up game of volleyball at **Tinos Beach Hotel** (⊠ Kionia, ☎ 0283/22626).

Kardiani

21 km (13 mi) northwest of Tinos town.

The mountainside village of Kardiani is 4,000 years old; views here are spectacular and its elegant peasant architecture preserved.

Isternia

24 km (15 mi) northwest of Tinos town, 3 km (2 mi) north of Kardiani.

The village of Isternia (Cisterns) is verdant with lush gardens. Many of the marble plaques hung here over doorways—a specialty of Tinos—indicate the owner's profession, e.g., a sailing ship for a fisherman or sea captain. A long, paved road winds down to a little port, **Aghios Nikitas,** with a **beach** and two **fish tavernas;** a small boat ferries people to Chora in good weather.

Pirgos

32 km (20 mi) northwest of Tinos town, 8 km (5 mi) north of Isternia.

The village of Pirgos, second in importance to Chora, is inland from the little harbor of **Panormos.** Tinos is famous for its marble carving, and Pirgos, a prosperous town, is noted for its sculpture school (the town's highest building) and marble workshops, where craftsmen make fanlights, fountains, tomb monuments, small objects for tourists, plus whatever you wish to order. The village's **main square** is aptly crafted of all marble. In fact, the quarries for the green-veined marble are just north of here, reachable by car. The cemetery here is, appropriately, a showplace of marble sculpture.

The marble-working tradition of Tinos survives here from the 19th century and is going strong, as seen in the **Kardamites Museum,** which features the work of Pirgos's renowned sculptor, Iannoulis Chalepas. ⊠ *1 block from bus stop.* ☎ *300 dr./€.88.* ☉ *Daily 10–2.*

Beaches
The beaches next to Panormos are popular in summer.

Shopping
CARVINGS

A number of marble carvers are, appropriately, found in Pirgos. You may visit the shop of probably the best master carver, **Lambros Dia-mantopoulos** (⊠ Near main square, ☎ 0283/31365), who accepts commissions for work to be done throughout Greece. He makes and sells traditional designs to other carvers, who may bring a portable slab home to copy, and to visitors.

Panormos

35 km (21¼ mi) northwest of Tinos town, 3 km (2 mi) north of Pirgos.

Panormos, an unpretentious port, has several seafood restaurants and a good beach with a collapsed sea cave. More coves with secluded swimming are beyond, as is the islet of Panormos.

Dining
$$ ✕ Ayia Thalassa. This taverna is undoubtedly the best on the Panormos waterfront. The name means "Sacred Sea," and seafood is the specialty here; fresh fish is charged by weight. The caïques sell their gleaming catch right on the quay, attended by cats, gulls, and a quackery of ducks. The appetizers are good, too: try the chickpea salad. This spot may look unpretentious but it's popular—on August evenings reservations are a good idea. ⊠ *In the middle of the Panormos waterfront,* ☎ *0283/31364. AE, MC, V.*

MYKONOS AND DELOS

Put firmly on the map by Jackie O, Mykonos has become one of the most popular of the Aegean islands. Although the dry, rugged island is one of the smallest of the Cyclades—it's only 16 km (10 mi) long and 11 km (7 mi) wide—travelers from all over the world are drawn to its many stretches of sandy beach, its thatched windmills, and its picturesque port town of Mykonos. Happily, the islanders seem to have been able to fit cosmopolitan New Yorkers or Londoners gracefully into their way of life. You may see, for example, an old island woman leading a donkey laden with vegetables through the town's narrow streets, greeting the suntanned vacationers walking by. The truth is Mykoniots regard a good tourist season as a fisherman looks at a good day's catch;

Mykonos Town

for many, the money earned in July and August will support them for the rest of the year. Not long ago Mykoniots had to rely on what they could scratch out of the island's arid land for sustenance, and some remember suffering from starvation under Axis occupation during World War II. In the 1950s a few tourists began trickling into Mykonos on their way to see the ancient marvels on the nearby islet of Delos, the sacred isle.

For almost 1,000 years Delos was the religious and political center of the Aegean and host every four years to the Delian games, the region's greatest festival. The population of Delos actually reached 20,000 at the peak of its commercial period, and throughout antiquity Mykonos, eclipsed by its holy neighbor, depended on this proximity for income, as it partly does today. Visitors interested in antiquity should plan to spend a morning on Delos. Most travel offices in Mykonos town run guided tours that cost about 8,500 dr./€25.07, including boat transportation and entry fee. Alternatively, take one of the caïques that visit Delos daily from the port: the round-trip costs about 2,000 dr./€5.89, and entry to the site (with no guide) 1,500 dr./€4.42. They leave between 8:30 AM and 1 PM and return noon to 2 PM.

Mykonos Town

16 km (10 mi) southeast of Tinos town.

For some, Mykonos town remains the Saint-Tropez of the Greek islands. The setting is memorable, with its whitewashed streets, Little Venice, the Kato Myli ridge of windmills, Kastro—the town's medieval quarter—and its cubical two-story houses and churches with their red or blue doors and domes and wooden balconies, long celebrated as some of the best examples of classic Cycladic architecture. Pink oleander, scarlet hibiscus, and trailing green pepper trees form a contrast amid the dazzling whiteness—kept up by frequent renewal of whitewash. Any visitor who has the pleasure of getting lost in its narrow streets (made all the narrower by the many outdoor stone staircases, which maximized housing space in the crowded village) will appreciate the fact that its confusing layout was designed to foil attacking pirates. After Mykonos fell under Turkish rule in 1537, the Ottomans allowed the islanders to arm their vessels against pirates, which had a contradictory effect: many of them found that raiding other islands was more profitable than tilling arid land. At the height of Aegean piracy, Mykonos was the principal headquarters of the corsair fleets—the place where pirates met their fellows, found willing women, and filled out their crews. Eventually the illicit activity evolved into a legitimate and thriving trade network.

❶ A bust of Mando Mavroyennis, the island heroine, stands on a pedestal in the **main square.** In the 1821 War of Independence the Mykoniots, known for their seafaring skills, volunteered an armada of 24 ships, and in 1822, when the Ottomans later landed a force on the island, Mando and her soldiers forced them back to their ships. After independence, a scandalous love affair caused her to be exiled to Paros, where she died.

The best time to visit the **central harbor** is in the cool of the evening, when the islanders promenade along the **esplanade** to meet friends and visit the numerous cafés. By the open-air fish market, Petros the Pelican preens and cadges eats, disdaining a group of ducks. In the 1950s a group of migrating pelicans passed over Mykonos, leaving behind a single exhausted bird; Vassilis the fisherman nursed it back to health, and locals say that the pelican in the harbor is the original Petros, though there are two.

The main shopping street, **Matoyanni** (⊠ Perpendicular to harbor), is lined with jewelry stores, clothing boutiques, chic cafés, and candy shops. The **Public Art Gallery** (⊠ Matoyanni, ☎ 0289/27190) is also here, with exhibitions changing weekly.

NEED A BREAK? For homemade ice cream, stop at **Snowstorm** (⊠ In middle of shopping area, ☎ 0289/24995), which has been making its creamy product, in 40 flavors, for 17 years.

② The **archaeological museum** affords insight into the intriguing history of the Delos shrine. The museum houses Delian funerary sculptures discovered on the neighboring islet of Rhenea, many with scenes of mourning. The most significant work from Mykonos is a 7th-century BC *pithos* (storage jar), showing the Greeks in the Trojan horse and the sack of the city. ⊠ *Ayios Stefanos Rd., between boat dock and town,* ☎ *0289/22325.* ⚑ *500 dr./€1.47.* ☉ *Tues.–Sun. 8:30–2:30.*

③ The charming **Aegean Maritime Museum** contains a collection of model ships, navigational instruments, old maps, prints, coins, and nautical memorabilia. The backyard garden displays some old anchors and ship wheels and a reconstructed 1890 lighthouse, once lighted by oil. ⊠ *Enoplon Dynameon,* ☎ *0289/22700.* ⚑ *500 dr./€1.47.* ☉ *Daily 10:30–1 and 6:30–9.*

Take a peek into **Lena's House,** an accurate restoration of a middle-class Mykonos house from the last century. ⊠ *Enoplon Dynameon,* ☎ *0289/22591.* ⚑ *Free.* ☉ *Apr.–Oct., daily 7 PM–9 PM.*

Many of the early ship's captains built distinguished houses directly on the sea here, with wooden balconies overlooking the water. Today,
★ **④** this neighborhood, at the southwest end of the port, is called **Little Venice** (⊠ Mitropoleos Georgouli). A few of the old houses have been turned into stylish bars, which are quite romantic at twilight. Overlooking them
⑤ on the high hill are the famous **Mykonos windmills,** echoes of a time when wind power was used to grind the island's grain.

The **Mykonos Agricultural Museum** displays a 16th-century windmill, traditional outdoor oven, waterwheel, dovecote, and more. ⊠ *Petassos, at top of Mykonos town,* ☎ *0289/22591.* ⚑ *Free.* ☉ *June–Sept., daily 4–6 PM.*

⑥ The **folk museum,** housed in an 18th-century house, exhibits a bedroom furnished and decorated in the fashion of that period. On display are looms and lace-making devices, Cycladic costumes, old photographs, and Mykoniot musical instruments that are still played at festivals. ⊠ *South of boat dock,* ☎ *0289/22591 or 0289/22748.* ⚑ *Free.* ☉ *Mon.–Sat. 4–8, Sun. 5:30–8.*

Mykoniots claim that exactly 365 churches and chapels dot their landscape, one for each day of the year. The most famous of these is the
⑦ **Church of Paraportiani** (Postern Gate; ⊠ Ayion Anargyron, near folk museum). The sloping, whitewashed conglomeration of four chapels, mixing Byzantine and vernacular idioms, has been described as "a confectioner's dream gone mad," and its position on a promontory fac-
⑧ ing the sea sets off the unique architecture. The **Greek Orthodox Cathedral of Mykonos** (⊠ On square that meets both Ayion Anargyron and Odos Mitropolis) has a number of old icons of the post-
⑨ Byzantine period. Next to the Greek Orthodox Cathedral is the **Roman Catholic Cathedral** (⊠ On square that meets both Ayion Anargyron and Odos Mitropolis) from the Venetian period. The name and coat of arms of the Ghisi family, which took over Mykonos in 1207, are inscribed in the entrance hall.

Beaches

There is a beach for every taste in Mykonos. **Beaches near Mykonos town,** within walking distance, are **Tourlos** and **Ayios Ioannis. Ayios Stefanos,** about a 45-minute walk from Mykonos town, has a minigolf course, water sports, restaurants, and umbrellas and lounge chairs for rent. The **south coast**'s **Psarou,** protected from wind by hills and surrounded by restaurants, offers a wide selection of water sports and is often called the finest beach. Nearby **Plati Yialos,** popular among families, is also lined with restaurants and dotted with umbrellas for rent. **Paranga, Paradise, Super Paradise,** and **Elia** are famously nude; Super Paradise is mostly gay. All have tavernas on the beach. At the easternmost end of the south shores is **Kalafatis,** known for package tours, and between Elia and Kalafatis there's a remote beach at **Kato Livadhi,** which can be reached by road. The great indentation on the **north coast** of the island, called **Panormos Bay,** has unprotected sandy beaches, which can get windy.

Dining and Lodging

$$$$ ✕ **La Maison de Catherine.** This famous restaurant is hidden, but the
★   Greek and French cuisine and hospitality—Katerina is still in charge—
      are worth the search. The splendid air-conditioned interior mixes Cycladic arches and whitewash with a French feeling and a faded 16th-century tapestry from Constantinople. Candles and classical music set the tone for baby squid stuffed with rice and Greek mountain spices, or soufflé, puffed to perfection and loaded with cheese, mussels, and prawns. For entrées, try leg of lamb with mint sauce or pasta with lobster. The apple tart is divine. ⊠ *Ayios Gerasimos, Mykonos town,* ☎ *0289/22169,* FAX *0289/26946. Reservations essential. AE, DC, MC, V.*

$$$$ ✕ **La Taverne.** Haute cuisine, in a tasteful room overlooking Mykonos Bay on one side and a pool on the other, makes for elegant dining. Amid graceful surroundings—dark wood-beam ceilings and quiet tones of peach and wood—start with *kataifi* pastry stuffed with seafood in grape sauce or roasted vegetable salad with *haloumi* cheese. Fresh fish is a specialty; try grilled sea bass with mashed pumpkin in mint sauce. The lamb chops with yogurt mint sauce are succulent. Large portions make the best dessert, an invigorating cream of sweet *myzithra* cheese on a cinnamon pastry, unnecessary—but why not? The maître d', Emilianos Sgutas, loves to advise on quality Greek food and wines. If you like the cooking, tell the chef, Yannis Argyriou, and he'll part with a recipe. ⊠ *Hotel Cavo Tagoo, 15 mins by foot north of Mykonos town on sea road,* ☎ *0289/23692 through 0289/23694. Reservations essential. AE, DC, MC, V.*

$$$–$$$$ ✕ **Edem.** Prompt service and excellent food are well received at the cool white garden of Edem; some tables are also on a platform over the lighted pool. The extensive menu offers three lamb dishes; lamb wrapped in vine leaves with a wine sauce is especially good. Fresh fish and lobster are specialties. For appetizers, winners include the baked potatoes stuffed with spiced meat and cheese or the Edem shrimp cooked in a garlic, olive oil, and tomato sauce. The *panna cotta* with fruit sauce makes for a satisfying conclusion. ⊠ *At an alley end off Matogianni (follow signs) behind the Panachra church,* ☎ *0289/22855 or 0289/ 23355. AE, DC, MC, V.*

$$ ✕ **Maria's Garden Restaurant.** Dine at this 30-year-old restaurant for lively atmosphere—sometimes with live music and dancing by Maria and family—for the zest of Greek living in a lovely candlelit garden. Octopus in wine, great cheese pies, and the fillet of beef with cheese and fresh vegetables will all keep you in the mood. So will the apple tart with ice cream and walnuts. ⊠ *30 Kaloyera,* ☎ *0289/27565. AE, D, V.*

$$ ✕ **Sesame Kitchen.** Dimitri and Violetta's little alley restaurant has a regular clientele that comes here for the fresh-daily seafood and the stir-fried regional vegetables. From the large assortment of starters, the *saganaki* (fried goat cheese with caramelized onions) will get you going. Then move on to the mixed seafood platter and seafood paella, both of which will quickly explain this kitchen's popularity. The lemon pie sends you away happy, but rarer fine Greek wines will keep you happy while there. ✉ *Three Wells district,* ☎ *0289/24710. AE, MC, V.*

$ ✕ **Kounelas.** This is the long-established fresh-fish taverna where many fishermen themselves eat, for no frills and solid food. The menu depends on the weather—low winds: lots of fish. ✉ *Just off the port near Delos boats,* ☎ *No phone. No credit cards.*

$$$$ 🏨 **Cavo Tagoo.** This hotel seems to emerge from its cliff-side backdrop
★   and reach out to the sea 150 ft below. A first-prize winner for its environmentally sensitive architecture in a competition sponsored by the Greek environmental ministry, this medley of white cubical suites features roof-level sunset terraces and an alluring saltwater pool. The reception area, restaurant, and guest rooms all have marble floors, dark beamed ceilings, and wood furniture. It's a 15-minute walk to town. ✉ *Follow coast road, north of the port, Mykonos town, 84600,* ☎ *0289/23692 through 0289/23695,* FAX *0289/24923. 68 rooms, 5 suites. Restaurant, bar, saltwater pool. AE, MC, V.* ☙

$$$$ 🏨 **Kivotos Clubhotel.** Spyros Michopoulos's deluxe hotel is architec-
★   turally ambitious, in a richly decorative island style, with statues in niches and stone-mosaic work, and unexpected little courtyards with bright flowers. The rooms, most with sea views, display local crafts. A hotel minibus runs into town, about 3 km (2 mi) away, and to the airport. ✉ *Ornos Bay, 2 km (1 mi) from Mykonos town, 84600,* ☎ *0289/25795 or 0289/25796,* FAX *0289/22844. 37 rooms, 6 suites. 2 restaurants, bar, 2 pools, hot tub, sauna, massage, exercise room, beach. AE, DC, MC, V.* ☙

$$$–$$$$ 🏨 **Petinos.** This casual resort community of four hotels on Plati Yialos beach is comfortable, convenient, and friendly, a favorite among extended vacationers and families. The wind-protected crowded beach, dotted with umbrellas and lounge chairs, is noisy with water sports, snack bars, and restaurants; a boat goes to five other beaches. In the seaside taverna, which comes to life two nights a week with Greek music and dancing, pink tablecloths and flower arrangements brighten the painted wooden tables. Fresh fish is good, or try the salad bar for 1,000 dr./€2.94. Make reservations on weekends. Frequent port and airport buses (4 km [2½ mi]) stop by the hotel. **Petinos Beach Hotel,** the most popular hotel, is yards away from the beach and has a saltwater pool. **Petinos Hotel,** a short walk up the street, has less-expensive, smaller rooms, with showers instead of bathtubs, and studios with kitchenettes upstairs. The elegant and pricier new **Palladium,** 500 yards up the road and so serenely quiet, is all cool colors and green marble. Farther down, the cheaper **Nissaki** completes the complex; top-floor rooms with a balcony are best. All the hotels have the standard wood beds with multicolor spreads, desks, and chairs. ✉ *Plati Yialos Beach, 2 km (1 mi) from Mykonos town, 84600,* ☎ *0289/22913 or 0289/23903,* FAX *0289/23680. 130 rooms. Restaurant, bar, snack bar, 2 pools, hot tub, exercise room, laundry service. AE, MC, V.* ☙

$$ 🏨 **Hotel Jason.** Of the inexpensive, unpretentious, and practical hotels springing up all over Mykonos, this one is particularly well cared for. Although it's set on a main route, it's a pleasant retreat with a pool and a heaping dose of quietude. ✉ *2 km (1 mi) from Hora, 1,300 yards from Plati Yialos beach, Plati Yiaolos 84600,* ☎ *0289/23481,* FAX *0289/24929. 15 rooms, 8 studios. Air-conditioning, freshwater pool. V.*

$$ 🖼 **Myconian Inn.** One of the inexpensive, unpretentious, and practi-
cal hotels right in town is the Myconian Inn. The small rooms are taste-
fully furnished in island style and have TVs and balconies overlooking
the port. ⊠ *Edge of town, Petassos 84600,* ☎ *0289/22663 or 0289/*
23420, FAX *0289/27269. 13 rooms. Air-conditioning, refrigerators. No*
credit cards.

Nightlife and the Arts

When the sun sets, Mykonos becomes an insomniac's paradise. Whether
it's bouzouki music, breakbeat, or transvestite techno, Mykonos's
nightlife beats to an obsessive rhythm until undetermined hours—lit-
tle wonder Europe's gilded youth comes here *just* to enjoy the night
scene. After midnight, they often head to the techno bars along the Par-
adise and Super Paradise beaches. Some of Little Venice's nightclubs
become gay in more than one sense of the word, while in the Kastro,
convivial bars welcome all for tequila-*sambukas* during sunset. What
is "the" place of the moment? The scene is ever-changing—so you'll
need to track the buzz once you arrive.

BARS AND DISCOS

Little Venice is a good place to begin an evening, and Damianos Gri-
paris's **Galeraki** (⊠ Little Venice, ☎ 0289/27118) is one of the best
cocktail bars in town; it's so close to the water you may get wet when
a boat passes. Upstairs in the old mansion (Delos's first archaeologists
lived here), you'll find an art gallery—a handy sanctum for drinks on
windy nights. **Montparnasse** (⊠ Little Venice, ☎ 0289/23719) has
Toulouse-Lautrec posters and a superb sunset view, with live music;
cabaret and musicals are featured. Leave your habit and robes behind
when you go to **Thalami** (⊠ Near Paraportiani Church, ☎ 0289/
23291), a small underground bar with Greek dancing in a cozy night-
club setting. As the night goes on you feel the heightened energy level,
which continues to build as dawn approaches. Kostas Karatzas's long-
standing **Kastro Bar** (⊠ Just behind Paraportiani, ☎ 0289/23072), with
heavy beamed ceilings and island furnishings, creates an intimate en-
vironment for enjoying the evening sunset over the bay; classical music
sets the tone. And at the famous gay **Pierro's** (⊠ Matoyanni), you can
find late-night wild dancing to American and European rock. In sum-
mer, Greeks dance all night at **Zorbas,** on the sea below the famous
windmills which are set above Little Venetia.

PERFORMING ARTS

The **Anemo Theatre** (⊠ Steno Roharis, ☎ 0289/23944) is a nonprofit
open-air center for the performing arts set in a unique olive garden in
the center of town, where, between July and September, distinguished
international artists present an eclectic array of concerts, performances,
and seminars.

Outdoor Activities and Sports

DIVING

For exciting diving and certification, try **Lucky Scuba Divers** (⊠
Mykonos town, ☎ 0289/22813) or **Psarou Diving Center** (⊠ Mykonos
town, ☎ 0289/24808).

HORSEBACK RIDING

Equestrians will find a horseback-riding program—for the novice or
expert—at the huge and luxurious **Aphrodite Beach Hotel** (⊠ Kalafati
Beach, ☎ 0289/71367), which includes beach access.

TENNIS

The **Kochyli Hotels** (⊠ On hill above Mykonos town, ☎ 0289/22929
or 0289/22107) has tennis courts. **Aphrodite Beach Hotel** (⊠ Kalafati
Beach, ☎ 0289/71367, FAX 0289/71525) also has courts.

Aphrodite Beach Hotel (✉ Kalafati Beach, ☎ 0289/71367, FAX 0289/71525) has water sports. The windy **northern beaches on Ornos Bay** are best; you can rent surfboards and take lessons. There's windsurfing and waterskiing at **Ayios Stefanos, Plati Yialos,** and **Ornos.** The program at **Surfing Club Anna** (✉ Agia Anna, ☎ 028971205) is well organized.

Shopping

FASHION

Yiannis **Galatis** (✉ Platia Manto, opposite LALAoUNIS, ☎ 0289/22255) has outfitted such famous women as Elizabeth Taylor, Ingrid Bergman, and Jackie Onassis. He will probably greet you personally and show you some of his coats and costumes, hostess gowns, and long dresses. He also has men's clothes. **Jella's** (✉ Nikiou 3, ☎ 0289/24153), a tiny boutique filled with custom-made silk, cotton, and wool knits that drape with special elegance, is next to the noted La Maison de Catherine restaurant and is just one of the fine shops found in these environs.

FINE AND DECORATIVE ART

Soula Papadakou's **Venetia** carries authentic copies of traditional handmade embroideries in clothing, tablecloths, curtains, and such, all in white; the women who work for her come from all over Greece, including a nunnery in Ioannina (✉ Ag. Anargiron St. 16, Little Venice, ☎ 0289/24464). In **Nikoletta** (✉ Little Venice, ☎ 0289/27503), Mykonos's last traditional weaving shop, Nikoletta Xidakis sells her skirts, shawls, and bedspreads made of local wool.

JEWELRY

Ilias LALAoUNIS (✉ 14 Polykandrioti, near taxis, ☎ 0289/22444, FAX 0289/24409) is known internationally for jewelry based on classic ancient designs, especially Greek; the shop is as elegant as a museum. The **Gold Store** (✉ On waterfront, ☎ 0289/22397, FAX 0289/24308), Mykonos's oldest jewelry shop (1959), is run by grandson Christos Iliopoulos, a gemologist.

SWEETS

Since 1950, Efthemios and family have been making traditional almond biscuits and almond milk (mix with five parts ice water) at **Efthemios** (✉ Florou Zouganeli 4, ☎ 0289/22281).

Ano Mera

8 km (5 mi) east of Mykonos town.

⑩ Monastery buffs should head to Ano Mera, a village in the central part of the island, where the **Monastery of the Panayia Tourliani,** founded in 1580 and dedicated to the protectress of Mykonos, stands in the central square. Its massive baroque iconostasis (altar screen), made in 1775 by Florentine artists, has small icons carefully placed amid the wooden structure's painted green, red, and gold-leaf flowers. At the top are carved figures of the apostles and large icons depicting New Testament scenes. The hanging incense holders with silver molded dragons holding red eggs in their mouths show an eastern influence. In the hall of the monastery, an interesting **museum** displays embroideries, liturgical vestments, and wood carvings. ✉ *On central square,* ☎ *0289/71249.* ⊙ *By appointment only; call in advance.*

Delos

25-minute caïque ride southwest from Mykonos.

Why did Delos, an islet with virtually no natural resources, become the religious and political center of the Aegean? One answer is that Delos,

Delos

- **18** Palaestras
- **21** Stadium
- **20** Gymnasium
- **22** Synagogue built by Phoenician Jews
- **17** Sacred Lake
- **19** Avenue of the Lions
- **23** Tourist Pavilion
- **24** Archaeological Museum
- **14** Sanctuary of Apollo
- **15** House of the Naxians
- **13** Propylaea
- **25** Sanctuary of Dionysos
- **16** Sanctuary of the Bulls
- *Harbor*
- **11** Agora of the Competialists
- **12** Sacred Way
- **30** Sanctuary of the Syrian Gods
- **26** Ancient Theatre
- **29** House of the Trident
- **28** House of the Masks
- **27** House of the Dolphins
- **31** Mount Kynthos

N

0   200 yards

0   200 meters

shielded on three sides by other islands, provided the safest anchorage for vessels sailing between the mainland and the shores of Asia. The saga begins back in the times of myth:

Zeus fell in love with gentle Leto, the Titaness, who became pregnant. When Hera discovered this infidelity, she forbade Mother Earth to give Leto refuge and ordered the Python to pursue her. Finally Poseidon, taking pity on her, anchored the floating island of Delos with four diamond columns to give her a place to rest. She gave birth first to the virgin huntress Artemis on Rhenea and then, clasping a sacred palm on a slope of Delos's Mt. Kynthos, to Apollo, god of music and light.

By 1000 BC the Ionians, who inhabited the Cyclades, had made Delos their religious capital. Homeric Hymn 3 tells of the cult of Apollo in the 7th century BC. A difficult period began for the Delians when Athens rose to power and assumed Ionian leadership. In 543 BC an oracle at Delphi conveniently decreed that the Athenians purify the island by removing all the graves to Rhenea, a dictate designed to alienate the Delians from their past.

After the defeat of the Persians in 478 BC, the Athenians organized the Delian League, with its treasury and headquarters at Delos (in 454 BC the funds were transferred to the Acropolis in Athens). Delos had its most prosperous period in the late Hellenistic and Roman times, when it was declared a free port and quickly became the financial center of the Mediterranean, the focal point of trade, and a slave market, where 10,000 persons were said to be sold every day. Foreigners from as far as Rome, Syria, and Egypt lived in this cosmopolitan port, in complete tolerance of one another's religious beliefs, and each group built its various shrines. But in 88 BC Mithridates, the king of Pontus, in a revolt against Roman rule, ordered an attack on the unfortified island. The entire population of 20,000 was killed or sold into slavery. Delos never fully recovered, and later Roman attempts to revive the island failed because of pirate raids. After 70 BC the island was gradually abandoned.

In 1872, the French School of Archaeology began excavating on Delos— a massive project, considering that much of the island's 4 square km (1½ square mi) is covered in ruins. Their work continues today.

⑪ On the left from the harbor is the **Agora of the Competialists** (circa 150 BC), members of Roman guilds, mostly freedmen and slaves from Sicily who worked for Italian traders. They worshiped the *Lares Competales,* the Roman "crossroads" gods; in Greek they were known as Hermaistai, after the god Hermes, protector of merchants and the **⑫** crossroads. The **Sacred Way,** east of the Agora, was the route, during the holy Delian festival, of the procession to the sanctuary of Apollo.

⑬ The **Propylaea,** at the end of the Sacred Way, were once a monumental white marble gateway with three portals framed by four Doric **⑭** columns. Beyond the Propylaea is the **Sanctuary of Apollo;** though little remains today, when the Propylaea were built in the mid-2nd century BC, the sanctuary was crowded with altars, statues, and temples—three of them to Apollo. Just inside the sanctuary and to the **⑮** right is the **House of the Naxians,** a 7th- to 6th-century BC structure with a central colonnade. Dedications to Apollo were stored in this shrine. Outside the north wall a massive rectangular **pedestal** once supported a colossal statue of Apollo (one of the hands is in Delos's archaeological museum, and a piece of a foot is in the British Museum). Near the pedestal a bronze palm tree was erected in 417 BC by the Athenians to commemorate the palm tree under which Leto gave birth. According to Plutarch, the palm tree toppled in a storm and brought the statue of Apollo down with it.

16 Southeast of the Sanctuary of Apollo are the ruins of the **Sanctuary of the Bulls,** an extremely long and narrow structure built, it is thought, to display a trireme, an ancient boat with three banks of oars, dedicated to Apollo by a Hellenistic leader thankful for a naval victory. Maritime symbols were found in the decorative relief of the main halls, and the head and shoulders of a pair of bulls were part of the design of an interior entrance. A short distance north of the Sanctuary of the Bulls

17 is an oval indentation in the earth where the **Sacred Lake** once sparkled. It is surrounded by a stone wall that reveals the original periphery. According to islanders, the lake was fed by the River Inopos from its source high on Mt. Kynthos until 1925, when the water stopped flowing and

18 the lake dried up. Along the shores are two ancient **palaestras,** buildings for the practice of exercise and debate.

★**19** One of most evocative sights of Delos is the 164-ft-long **Avenue of the Lions.** The originals have just gone into the museum; replicas are planned. The five Naxian marble beasts crouch on their haunches, their forelegs stiffly upright, vigilant guardians of the Sacred Lake. They are the survivors of a line of at least nine lions, erected in the second half of the 7th century BC by the Naxians. One was removed in the 17th century and now guards the Arsenal of Venice. Northeast of the palaes-

20 tras is the **gymnasium,** a square courtyard nearly 131 ft long on each

21 side. The long, narrow structure farther northeast is the **stadium,** the site of the athletic events of the Delian Games. East of the stadium site,

22 by the seashore, are the remains of a **synagogue built by Phoenician Jews** in the 2nd century BC.

23 A road south from the gymnasium leads to the **tourist pavilion,** which

24 has a meager restaurant and bar. The **Archaeological Museum** is also on the road south of the gymnasium; it contains most of the antiquities found in excavations on the island: monumental statues of young men and women, steles, reliefs, masks, and ancient jewelry. The museum, recently redone, keeps the same hours as the site.

25 Immediately to the right of the museum is a small **Sanctuary of Dionysos,** erected about 300 BC; outside it is one of the more boggling sights of ancient Greece: several monuments dedicated to Apollo by the winners of the choral competitions of the Delian festivals, each decorated with a huge phallus, emblematic of the orgiastic rites that took place during the Dionysian festivals. Around the base of one of them is carved a lighthearted representation of a bride being carried to her new husband's home. A marble phallic bird, symbol of the body's immortality, also adorns this corner of the sanctuary.

26 Beyond the path that leads to the southern part of the island is the **ancient theater,** built in the early 3rd century BC in the elegant residential quarter inhabited by Roman bankers and Egyptian and Phoenician merchants. Their one- and two-story **houses** were typically built around a central courtyard, sometimes with columns on all sides, and their floors were covered with decorative mosaics, which channeled rainwater into cisterns below. The colorful mosaics show fantastical natural themes: panthers, birds, and dolphins; the best preserved can be seen

27 28 29 in the **House of the Dolphins,** the **House of the Masks,** and the **House of the Trident.** A dirt path leads east to the base of Mt. Kynthos, where

30 there are remains from many **Middle Eastern shrines,** including the **Sanctuary of the Syrian Gods,** built in 100 BC. A flight of steps goes up 368

31 ft to the summit of **Mt. Kynthos** (after which all Cynthias are named), on whose slope Apollo was born. ✉ *Delos island and historic site, take a caïque from Mykonos town,* ☎ *0289/22259.* 🎫 *1,500 dr./€4.42* ⊙ *Apr.–Oct., Tues.–Sun. 8:30–3.*

NAXOS

"Great sweetness and tranquillity" is how Nikos Kazantzakis, premier novelist of Greece, described Naxos, and indeed a tour of the island leaves you with an impression of abundance, prosperity, and serenity. The greenest, most fertile of the Cyclades, Naxos, with its many potato fields, its livestock and its thriving cheese industry, and its fruit and olive groves framed by the pyramid of Mt. Zas (3,295 ft, the Cyclades' highest), is practically self-sufficient. Inhabited for 6,000 years, the island offers today's visitor memorable landscapes—abrupt ravines, hidden valleys, long sandy beaches—and towns that vary from a Cretan mountain stronghold to the seaside capital, strongly evoking its Venetian past.

Naxos Town

32 *Seven hours by ferry from Piraeus; 35 km (21¾ mi) east of Paros town.*

As your ferry chugs into the harbor, you see before you the white houses of Naxos town (Chora) on a hill crowned by the one remaining tower of the Venetian castle, reminding us that Naxos was once the beautiful capital of the Venetian semi-independent Duchy of the Archipelago. The tiny church of **Our Lady of Myrtle** (⊠ Perched on a sea rock off the waterfront) watches over the local sailors, who built it for divine protection.

While the capital town is primarily beloved for its Venetian elegance and picturesque blind alleys, Naxos's most famous landmark is ancient: the **Portara** (⊠ At harbor's far edge), a massive doorway that leads to nowhere. The Portara stands on the islet of **Palatia**, which was once a hill (since antiquity the Mediterranean has risen quite a bit) and in the 3rd millennium BC was the acropolis for a nearby Cycladic settlement. The Portara, an entrance to an unfinished Temple of Apollo that faces exactly toward Delos, Apollo's birthplace, was begun about 530 BC by the tyrant Lygdamis, who said he would make Naxos's buildings the highest and most glorious in Greece. He was overthrown in 506 BC, and the temple was never completed; by the 5th and 6th centuries AD it had been converted into a church; and under Venetian and Turkish rule it was slowly dismembered, so the marble could be used to build the castle. The gate, built with four blocks of marble, each 16 ft long and weighing 20 tons, was so large it couldn't be demolished, so it remains today, along with the temple floor. Palatia itself has come to be associated with the tragic myth of Ariadne, princess of Crete.

Ariadne, daughter of Crete's King Minos, helped Theseus thread the labyrinth of Knossos and slay the monstrous Minotaur. In exchange, he promised to marry her. Sailing for Athens, the couple stopped in Naxos, where Theseus abandoned her. Jilted Ariadne's curse made Theseus forget to change the ship's sails from black to white, and so his grieving father Aegeus, believing his son dead, plunged into the Aegean. Seeing her tears, smitten Dionysos descended in a leopard-drawn chariot to marry her, and set her bridal wreath, the Corona Borealis, in the sky, an eternal token of his love.

The myth inspired one of Titian's best-known paintings, as well as Strauss's opera *Ariadne auf Naxos*.

Old town (⊠ Along the quay, left at first big square) possesses a bewildering maze of twisting cobblestone streets, arched porticoes, and towering doorways, where you're plunged into cool darkness and then

Naxos

TO
MYKONOS

0   6 miles

0   9 km

KEY

--- Ferry

*Aegean
Sea*

N

Ayia

Apollonas

43

Ormos Abram 44

Koronida/
Komiaki

Paxia Ammos

Lionas

TO
PIRAEUS

Galini

Engares

Koronos

42

33 **Grotta**

32

Kourounochori

**Naxos
Town**

Ayios
Thaleleos

Stavros tis Keramotis
Church

Miloi

45

Flerio

Moni

38

Galanado

**Pano
Castle**

37

41

Apeiranthos

**Agia
Anna**

**Bellonia
Tower**

34

Potamia

Chalki

Moutsouna

35

39

**Ayios
Mamas**

36

Filoti

Sangri

Mikri Vigla

Kastraki

Mount Zas

**Psili
Ammos**

**Cheimarros
Pirgos**

40

Dyrgaki

Panormos

Koufonisi

**Askiti
Cave**

*Kato
Koufonisi*

suddenly into pockets of dazzling sunshine. The old town is divided into the lower section, **Bourgos,** where the Greeks lived during Venetian times, and the upper part, called **Kastro** (castle), still inhabited by the Venetian Catholic nobility.

You won't miss the gates of the **castle** (⊠ Kastro). The south gate is called the **Paraporti** (side gate), but it's more interesting to enter through the northern gate, or **Trani** (strong), via Apollonos Street. Note the vertical incision in the gate's marble column—it is the Venetian yard against which drapers measured the bolts of cloth they brought to the noblewomen. Step through the Trani into the citadel and enter another age, where sedate Venetian houses still stand around silent courtyards, their exteriors emblazoned with coats of arms and bedecked with flowers, the only sign of present-day occupants the drying clothes fluttering occasionally from a balcony. The **Venetian Museum,** in the 800-year-old Dellarocca-Barozzi house, lets you, at last, into one of the historic Venetian residences; admission is by guided tour only. The house's idyllic garden, built into the Kastro wall, provides a regular venue in season for a concert series, from classical to jazz to island music. ⊠ *At Kastro north gate,* ☎ *No phone.* 🎫 *1,500 dr./€4.42.*

The entire citadel was built in 1207 by Marco Sanudo, a Venetian who, three years after the fall of Constantinople, landed on Naxos as part of the Fourth Crusade. For two months he laid siege to the Byzantine castle at t'Apilarou and upon its downfall made Naxos the headquarters of his duchy. He divided the island into estates and distributed them to his officers, who built the *pirgi* (tower houses) that still dot the countryside. When in 1210 Venice refused to grant him independent status, Sanudo switched allegiance to the Latin emperor in Constantinople, becoming Duke of the Archipelago. Under the Byzantines, "archipelago" had meant "chief sea," but after Sanudo and his successors, it came to mean "group of islands," i.e., the Cyclades. For three centuries Naxos was held by Venetian families, who resisted pirate attacks, introduced Roman Catholicism, and later rebuilt the castle in its present form. In 1564 Naxos came under Turkish rule, but even then, the Venetians still ran the island, while the Turks only collected taxes. The rust-color **Glezos tower** was home to the last dukes; it displays the coat of arms: a pen and sword crossed under a crown.

The **cathedral** (⊠ At the Kastro's center) was built by Sanudo in the 13th century and restored by Catholic families in the 16th and 17th centuries. The marble floor is paved with tombstones bearing the coats of arms of the noble families. Venetian wealth is evident in the many gold and silver icon frames. The icons reflect a mix of Byzantine and Western influences: the one of the Virgin Mary is unusual because it shows a Byzantine Virgin and Child in the presence of a bishop, a cathedral benefactor. Another 17th-century icon shows the Virgin of the Rosary surrounded by members of the Sommaripa family, whose house is nearby.

The **convent and school of the Ursulines** (⊠ A few steps beyond cathedral) was begun in 1739. In a 1713 document, a general of the Jesuits, Francis Tarillon, mentions that the proposed girl's school should be simple; grandeur would expose it to the Turks' covetousness. Over the years, extensions were added, and the Greek state has now bought the building for cultural purposes. Wealthier Naxian women still recall the good education the Ursulines provided.

Today the convent and school of the Ursulines houses the **Naxos Archaeological Museum,** best known for its Cycladic and Mycenaean finds. During the early Cycladic period (3200 BC–2000 BC), there were settlements along Naxos's east coast and just outside Naxos town at Grotta. The finds are from these settlements and graveyards scattered around the island. Many of the vessels exhibited are from the early Cycladic I period, hand-built of coarse-grained clay, sometimes decorated with a herringbone pattern. Though the museum has too many items in its glass cases for a short visit, you should try not to miss the white marble Cycladic statuettes, which range from the early "violin" shapes to the more detailed female forms with their tilted flat heads, folded arms, and legs slightly bent at the knees. The male forms are simpler and often appear to be seated. The most common theory is that the female statuettes were both fertility and grave goddesses, and the males servant figures. ⊠ *Kastro,* ☎ *0285/22725.* ☑ *500 dr./€1.47, free Sun.* ☉ *Tues.–Sun. 8:30–3.*

The **French School of Commerce** is marked by an escutcheon bearing a fleur-de-lis surrounded by the collar of the Order of the Holy Spirit. The school was run in turn by Jesuits, Lazarists, and Salesians. Under the last it enjoyed its most distinguished period (1891–1927); the Cretan writer Nikos Kazantzakis attended the school for two years. Its library, archives, and opulent furnishings were destroyed during the German-Italian occupation, but it's easy to imagine rows of schoolboys running to class as you enter its vast, cool halls.

The **Greek Orthodox cathedral** (⊠ Bourgos) was built in 1789 on the site of a church called Zoodochos Pigis (Life-giving Source). The cathedral was built from the materials of ancient temples: the solid granite pillars are said to be from the ruins of Delos. Amid the gold and the carved wood, there is a vividly colored iconostasis painted by a well-known iconographer of the Cretan school, Dimitrios Valvis, and the Gospel Book is believed to be a gift from Catherine the Great of Russia.

The **Ancient Town of Naxos** was located directly on the square in front of the Greek Orthodox cathedral (☞ *above*). You'll note that several of the churches set on this square, like the cathedral itself, hint at Naxos' venerable history as they are made of ancient materials. In fact, this square was, in succession, the seat of a flourishing Mycenaean town (1300–1050 BC), a classical agora (when it was a 167-ft by 156-ft square closed on three sides by Doric stoas, so that it looked like the letter "G"; a shorter fourth stoa bordered the east side, leaving room at each end for an entrance), a Roman town, and early Christian church complex. Although much of the site has been refilled, under the square a new **museum** (open Tuesday–Sunday, 8:00–2:30 PM; free) gives you a well-marked sampling of the foundations. City, cemetery, tumulus, hero shrine: no wonder the early Christians built here. For more of ancient Naxos, explore the nearby precinct of Grotta (☞ *below*).

Beaches

The southeast coast of Naxos, facing Paros and the sunset, offers the Cyclades' longest stretches of fine beaches. In order, heading south: **Ayios Georgios** is now part of town and very developed; **Ayios Prokopios** has a small leeward harbor and lagoons with waterfowl; **Ayia Anna,** very crowded, has a small harbor with connections to Paros; **Plaka,** ringed by sand dunes and bamboo groves, is about 8 km (5 mi) south of town and only now developing; **Mikri Vigla** is sandy and edged by cedar trees; **Kastraki** has white marble sand; **Pyrgaki** is the least developed, with idyllic crystalline water. All these have tavernas and rooms.

Dining and Lodging

$$$ ✕ **The Old Inn.** Dieter von Ranizewski, a trained chef and instructor
  ★   of chefs from Berlin, has built his "dream place," and it is one of the Cyclades' very best restaurants. In a courtyard under a chinaberry tree,

with rough whitewashed walls and bits of ancient marble, two of the old church's interior sides open into the wine cellar and gallery; on the fourth side, with beams and wood paneling, is a fireplace, handy for the winter months. The menu is extensive. For starters you might try smoked ham, jellied pork, or liver pâté—all homemade. For entrées, Berlin liver with apples and onions, and the fresh trout with almonds and parsleyed potatoes are especially good. For dessert the homemade red forest-berry jelly with vanilla cream beckons voluptuously. Kids love both the small playground and the children's menu. ✉ *Naxos town, up car road around the town, 2 alleys in on right from waterfront,* ☎ *0285/26093,* FAX *0289/23325. AE, V.*

$$ ✕ **Apolafsis.** Lefteris Keramideas's second-floor restaurant offers a balcony with a great view of the harbor and sunset. It features live music (always in summer; often in winter), a large assortment of appetizers (try spinach or zucchini tart), local barrel wine, and fresh fish. The pork slices in wine sauce is good, too, to say nothing of *klephtiko* (kid with peas and carrots). For 30 years, there's been a "Greek night" of music and dancing in progress here. ✉ *Naxos town waterfront, 2nd floor* ☎ *0285/22178. No credit cards.*

$$ ✕ **Gorgona.** Bearded Dimitris and Koula Kapris's beachfront taverna is popular both with sunworshipers on Ayia Anna beach and locals from Chora, who come here winter and summer to get away, and sometimes to dance until the late hours, often to live music. The menu is extensive and fresh daily—the fresh fish comes from the caïques that pull up at the dock right in front every morning. Two good appetizers are *kakavia* (fish stew) and shrimp saganaki (with cooked cheese), while octopus in red wine is a fine entrée. The barrel wine is their own. They also have studio apartments for rent and a sunset roof garden. ✉ *Ayia Anna near dock,* ☎ *0285/41007. No credit cards.*

$ ✕ **Meltemi.** Mihalis Mathiassos's restaurant is typically Greek, with fluorescent lighting and plastic-wrap tablecloths, but it is by the sea and set among vines. It's known locally as the place to go for inexpensive Greek staples such as souvlaki, lamb *exohiko* (cooked in paper with vegetables), barbecued fish, and pans of *gigantes* (giant white beans in olive oil) and *tsoutsoukakia* (meat patties made from spicy sausage). *Kaloyero* (eggplant with ham and béchamel) is a bit more unusual. The crème caramel is heavenly. The waiters are fast and efficient, even when the place is packed. ✉ *Chora waterfront, at other end of dock,* ☎ *0285/ 22654. No credit cards.*

$$$ 🏨 **Apollon.** In addition to being comfortable, attractive, and quiet (it's ★ a converted marble workshop), this new hotel is convenient to everything in town. Even better, it offers parking facilities, a rarity within rural town precincts. The lobby blends wood, warm marble, deep greens, and many plants. The rooms are simple and have balconies; bathrooms are small. The outside, of ocher plaster and stone, is adorned with a feast of marble decoration. ✉ *Behind Orthodox cathedral, car entrance on road out of town), Fontana, Chora 84300,* ☎ *0285/ 22468,* FAX *0285/26802. 12 rooms, 1 suite. Breakfast room, kitchenettes. AE, MC, V.*

$$$ 🏨 **Chateau Zevgoli.** If you stay in Chora, try to stay here. Each room ★ in Despina Kitini's fairy-tale pension, in a comfortable Venetian house, is distinct. The living room is filled with dark antique furniture, gilded mirrors, old family photographs, and locally woven curtains and tablecloths. One of the nicest bedrooms has a private bougainvillea-covered courtyard and pillows handmade by Despina's great-grandmother; the honeymoon suite has a canopy bed, a spacious balcony, and a view of the Portara. Rooms can sometimes be had off-season for half price. Despina—who, as one of the leading tourist honchos of the island, runs her own information center—also has roomy studios, called Pension

Irene, in Chora's old town. ⊠ *Chora old town (follow signs stenciled on walls), 84300,* ☎ *0285/22993 or 0285/26143,* FAX *0285/25200. 10 rooms. Breakfast room. AE, MC, V.* ✍

$$$ 🏨 **Galaxy.** As you approach this hotel from a distance, it seems to shimmer—all whitewash and marble. Its three buildings rather resemble grand pueblos, except that they have wide stone arches; wooden doors in shades of green, purple, and turquoise; and balconies with grillwork depicting swans. Archways also span the large rooms, which have beamed ceilings and trim orange accessories, plus plants, kitchenettes, and dining areas. Most rooms have ocean views (the beach is a minute away); all have balconies. Though mostly shadeless, the carefully tended grounds are a pleasure, with yellow roses and a fountain. ⊠ *Ayios Georgios Beach, 84300,* ☎ *0285/22422 or 0285/22423,* FAX *0285/22889. 54 rooms. Snack bar, kitchenettes, pool, playground. AE, V.*

$$$ 🏨 **Lianos Village.** Yannis Lianos, a Naxian, has just built an attractive resort that resembles the Cycladic-village style he grew up with. A 10-minute walk from Ayios Prokopios beach, it has island furnishings, very private rooms with magnificent sea views across the lagoons and straits to Paros, immaculate and unobtrusive service, and heavenly quiet. A restaurant is nearby. ⊠ *Ayios Prokopios beach, 84300,* ☎ *0285/26366 or 0285/23865,* FAX *0285/26362. 42 rooms. Café, refrigerators, pool. MC, V.* ✍

$$$ 🏨 **Orkos Village Hotel.** When Norwegian doctor Kaare Oftedal first saw Orkos beach years ago, he fell in love with the almost isolated strand ringed by sand dunes and cedars. Today he returns from Norway every April to open his small, popular hotel, whose guests seem perfectly content never to leave their idyllic surroundings to go to town. The hotel's white cubist bungalows that stagger down the hillside to the sea's edge are simply furnished and decorated (dried flowers and blue wooden shutters just about covers it). They all have sea views and verandas; most have an additional sitting area. The stones by the walkways have been gathered from Naxian beaches. Guests love to hang around the friendly stone bar, where the doctor's Naxian wife, Katerina, leads dances and serves up classic Greek meals, and to ramble downhill to the idyllic beach (a pool would be profane here). ⊠ *Orkos beach between Plaka and Mikri Vigla, 84300,* ☎ *0285/75321,* FAX *0285/75320. 28 apartments. Restaurant, bar, kitchenettes. No credit cards.*

$$ 🏨 **Iria Beach.** Maria Refene's hotel is right on the crowded beach and
★ echoes Chora's old town with its stucco arches, peaceful nooks and crannies, sunlit courtyard, and bright red and blue shutters. The reception area is quite luxurious, with huge glass doors, cool marble floor, and brass details. The owners have eschewed the usual Greek hotel furniture for unlacquered wood with a gray wash, and an interior color scheme of light blue, gray, and white for the spacious one- and two-room apartments. Guests enjoy hanging out in the shady beach-bar and restaurant. ⊠ *Ayia Anna, 84300,* ☎ *0285/42600,* FAX *0285/42603. 17 rooms, 7 apartments. Restaurant, bar, kitchenettes. MC, V.*

Nightlife

BARS

Nightlife in Naxos is quieter than it is on Santorini or Mykonos, but there are several popular bars at the south end of Chora. **Veggera** (⊠ Chora waterfront near Ayios Georgios Beach, ☎ 0285/23567) has a garden that offers a respite from the rap and rock music inside. Next door to Veggera, in a small white house, **Cream** (⊠ Chora waterfront, second floor) is for when you want loudness late; it has a spacious bar, happy-hour specials, strong drinks, all kinds of music from surf to blues, and a terrace overlooking the sea. Head for **Super Island** (⊠ Chora,

Grotta road) for a large soundproof space with Portara view, active till dawn.

ARTS EVENTS

The **Catholic Cultural Center** (⊠ Kastro, near church, ☎ 0285/24729), among other things, runs art exhibitions; watch for posters.

The **Venetian Museum** (⊠ At Kastro north gate, Chora), in the 800-year-old Dellarocca-Barozzi house, offers a summer concert series in its lovely garden; check posters around town for schedules.

Outdoor Activities and Sports

SAILING AND WATER SPORTS

To rent a catamaran, or learn windsurfing, contact **Flisvos** (⊠ Ayios Yorgios beach, ☎ 0285/24308). At **Ayios Prokopios** and **Ayia Anna** beaches the wind and water conditions are ideal for inexperienced windsurfers, and there are also waterskiing equipment rentals, and instruction for both sports. The Mikri Vigla hotel complex has a **windsurfing center** (⊠ South of Chora, ☎ 0285/75241 or 0285/75242), but experienced windsurfers prefer **Kastraki, Pyrgaki, Moutsouna,** and **Agiassos beaches,** where wind speeds can reach Beaufort 7.

Shopping

ANTIQUE COSTUMES AND JEWELRY

Vassilis Koutelieris, the deskman at the town's Archaeological Museum also owns, with his wife Kathy, **Loom** (⊠ In Old Market, off main square, third street on the right, ☎ 0285/25531), which specializes in "handwoven items of Old Greece" (as his card says), antique silver jewelry, and quality cotton clothes.

ANTIQUES

Eleni Dellarocca's shop, **Antico Veneziano** (⊠ In Kastro, just down from the museum, ☎ 0285/26206), is in the basement of her splendid Venetian house, built 800 years ago. The columns inside come from Naxos's ancient acropolis. In addition to antiques, she has handmade embroideries, porcelain and glass, mirrors, old chandeliers, and vintage photographs of Naxos. Chances are that Eleni (or her associate) will tell you the house's fascinating background.

BOOKS

At Eleftherios Primikirios's **Zoom** (⊠ Chora waterfront, ☎ 0285/23675 or 0285/23676), there's an excellent selection of English-language history and picture books about Naxos. Zoom also has another shop (⊠ On cemetery square, ☎ 0285/24357).

FOOD, WINE, AND LIQUEUR

A large selection of the famous *kitro* (citron liqueur) and preserves, as well as Naxos wines and thyme honey, packed in attractive gift baskets, can be found at **Promponas Wines and Liquors** (⊠ Chora waterfront, ☎ 0285/22258), which has been around since 1915. Free glasses of kitro are always offered.

JEWELRY

For a large selection of beautiful jewelry, try **Midas** (⊠ Old Town, up the main street behind Promponas on the Chora waterfront, ☎ 0285/24852); Midas also has a smaller store (⊠ On waterfront, ☎ 0285/26291). The owner, Fotis Margaritis, creates talismans in different settings that feature a "Naxos eye," which is the operculum, or door, of a seashell with a spiral design that fishermen bring him. The workshop of **Nassos Papakonstantinou** (⊠ Old Town, far left street of main square, ☎ FAX 0285/22607) sells one-of-a-kind pieces both sculptural and delicate. The shop is easy to find, although it is tiny and has no sign.

TRADITIONAL KNITS, JEWELS, AND LINENS

The embroidery and knitted items made by women in the mountain villages are known throughout Greece; they can occasionally be bought in a Chora tourist shop such as **Old Market Naxos** (✉ Old Town, ☎ 0285/24767) or from villagers hawking their wares in front of tourist sites. For a wide selection of old designs for jewelry, linens, household items, and so forth, try **Techni** (✉ Near entrance to Chora's old town, ☎ 0285/24767 or 0285/25673).

En Route   On your way to Bellonia, on the main road from Naxos town, you'll go southeast past Galanado and drive through the reed beds, cacti, and plains of the Livadi Valley.

Grotta

③③ *Just a few steps east of Naxos town.*

If you head to the sea from the square in front of Naxos' Orthodox cathedral, you can discern **underwater remains of Cycladic buildings** strewn along an area called Grotta. Here, in an area of about 130 ft, are a series of large worked stones, also the remains of the mole, plus a few steps that locals say go to a tunnel leading to the islet of Palatia; these remains are Cycladic (before 2000 BC).

Bellonia Tower

③④ *5 km (3 mi) south of Naxos town.*

The graceful **Bellonia tower** (Pirgos Bellonia) belonged to the area's ruling Venetian family, and like other fortified houses, it was built as a refuge from pirates and as part of the island's alarm system. The towers were located strategically throughout the island; if there was an attack, a large fire would be lighted on the nearest tower's roof, setting off a chain reaction from tower to tower and alerting the islanders. Bellonia's thick stone walls, its Lion of St. Mark emblem, and flat roofs with zigzag chimneys are typical of these pirgi. The unusual 13th-century **"double church"** of St. John (✉ In front of Bellonia tower) exemplifies Venetian tolerance. On the left side is the Catholic chapel, on the right the Orthodox church, separated only by a double arch. A family lives in the tower, and the church is often open. dFrom here, take a moment to gaze across the peaceful fields to Chora and imagine what the islanders must have felt when they saw pirate ships on the horizon.

Ayios Mamas

③⑤ *8 km (5 mi) south of Naxos town, 3 km (2 mi) south of Bellonia Tower.*

A kilometer (½ mile) past a valley with unsurpassed views is one of the island's oldest churches (9th century), Ayios Mamas. St. Mamas is the protector of shepherds and is regarded as a patron saint in Naxos, Cyprus, and Asia Minor. Built in the 8th century, the stone church was the island's cathedral under the Byzantines. Though it was converted into a Catholic church in 1207, it was neglected under the Venetians and is now falling apart. You can also get to it from the Potamia villages.

Sangri

③⑥ *11 km (7 mi) south of Naxos town, 3 km (2 mi) south of Ayios Mamas.*

Sangri is the center of an area with so many monuments and ruins spanning the archaic to the Venetian periods, it is sometimes called "little

Mystras." The name Sangri is a corruption of Sainte Croix, which is
what the French called the town's 16th-century monastery of **Timios
Stavros** (Holy Cross). The town is actually three small villages spread
across a plateau. During the Turkish occupation, the monastery served
as an illegal school, where children met secretly to learn the Greek language and culture. Above the town, you can make out the **ruins of t'Apilarou** (⊠ On Mt. Profitis Ilias), the castle Sanudo first attacked.

Temple of Demeter

Take the new, mostly asphalt road right before the entrance to Sangri
and travel about 5 km [3 mi] to reach the **Temple of Demeter,** a marble archaic temple, circa 530 BC, lovingly restored by German archaeologists during the last decade. Demeter was a grain goddess, and
it's not hard to see what she is doing in this beautiful spot.

Chalki

37 *17 km (10½ mi) southeast of Naxos town, 6 km (4 mi) northeast of
Sangri.*

You are now entering the heart of the lush Tragaia Valley, where in
spring the air is heavily scented with honeysuckle, roses, and lemon
blossoms, and many tiny Byzantine churches hide in the dense olive
groves.

Chalki is home to one of the most important of these Byzantine
churches: the white, red-roof **Panayia Protothrone** (First Enthroned Virgin). Restoration work has uncovered frescoes ranging from the 6th
through the 13th centuries, and the church has remained alive and functioning for 14 centuries. The oldest layers, in the apse, depict the Apostles. ⊠ *On main road.* ☉ *Mornings.*

Chalki itself is a pretty town, known for its neoclassical houses in shades
of pink, yellow, and gray, which are oddly juxtaposed with the plain
but stately 17th-century Venetian **Frangopoulos tower.** ⊠ *Main road,
next to Panayia Protothrone.* ☉ *Sometimes in the morning.*

Moni

38 *23 km (14¼ mi) east of Naxos town, 6 km (4 mi) north of Chalki.*

At Moni is one of the Balkans' most important churches, **Panayia
Drosiani,** which has faint, rare Byzantine frescoes from the 7th and 8th
centuries. Its name means Our Lady of Refreshment, because once during a severe drought, when all the churches took their icons down to
the sea to pray for rain, only the icon of this church got results. The
frescoes are visible in layers: To the right when you enter are the oldest—one shows St. George the Dragon Slayer astride his horse, along
with a small boy, an image one usually sees only in Cyprus and Crete.
According to legend, the saint saved the child, who had fallen into a
well, and there met and slew the giant dragon that had terrorized the
town. Opposite him is St. Dimitrios, shown killing barbarians. The
church is made up of three chapels—the middle one has a space for
the faithful to worship at the altar rather than in the nave, as became
common in later centuries. Next to that is a very small opening that
housed a secret school during the revolution. Walk to the back of the
church for a view of its odd configuration; the undulating curves are
reminiscent of a Gaudi building. It is open mornings and again after
siesta; in deserted winter, ring the bell if it is not open.

Filoti

㊴ *20 km (12½ mi) southeast of Naxos town, 6½ km (4¼ mi) south of Moni.*

Filoti, a peaceful village on the lower slopes of Mt. Zas, is the interior's largest. Nothing much seems to happen here, but if you're lucky, you may see a festive bridal procession. According to custom, the groom, accompanied by musicians, goes to the bride's house to collect her and her family, and then the party strolls through the village picking up well-wishers. A three-day festival celebrating the Dormition starts on August 14. In the center of town is another Venetian tower that belonged to the Barozzi and the main church with its fine marble iconostasis and carved bell tower.

Hiking

Filoti is better known as the starting place for several walks in the countryside, for example, the climb up to **Zas Cave,** where obsidian tools and pottery fragments have been found; lots of bats live inside. Mt. Zas, or Zeus, is one of the god's birthplaces; on the path to the summit lies a block of unworked marble that reads *Oros Dios Milosiou,* or "boundary of the temple of Zeus Melosios." (Melosios, it is thought, is a word that has to do with sheep.) The islanders say that under the Turks the cave was used as a chapel, and two stalagmites are called the Priest and the Priest's Wife, who are said to have been petrified by God to save them from arrest. It's best to ask directions for the start of the path (✉ Southeast of town off a small dirt track).

㊵ Farther away but easier to get to on a good road (or take a level 3½-hour walk with excellent views, to **Cheimarros Pirgos** (Tower of the Torrent), a cylindrical Hellenistic tower preserved up to 45 ft, with marble blocks perfectly aligned. The tower, which also served as a lookout post for pirates, is often celebrated in the island's poetry: "O, my heart is like a bower/And Cheimarros's lofty tower!" The road begins from the main road to Apeiranthos, just outside Filoti.

Apeiranthos

㊶ *32 km (20 mi) southeast of Naxos town, 12 km (7½ mi) northeast of Filoti.*

Apeiranthos is very picturesque, with fine views and marble-paved streets running between the Venetian Bardani and Zevgoli towers. As you walk through the arcades and alleys, notice the unusual chimneys—no two are alike. The elders sit in their doorsteps chatting, while packs of children shout "Hello, hello" at any passerby who looks foreign.

A very small **archaeological museum,** established by a local mathematician, Michael Bardanis, displays Cycladic finds from the east coast. The most important of the artifacts are unique gray marble plaques from the 3rd millennium BC with roughly hammered scenes of daily life: hunters and farmers and sailors going about their business. If it's closed, ask in the square for the guard. ✉ *Off main square.* 🎟 *Free.* ☉ *Daily 8:30–3.*

Koronos

㊷ *36 km (23⅓ mi) east of Naxos town, 4 km (2½ mi) north of Apeiranthos.*

The paved road from Apeiranthos, winding and narrow in places, passes through the lovely village of Koronos, which tumbles spectacularly down the green mountainside. On the right you come to the

Stavros tis Keramotis church, the only point from which you can see both the east and west coasts of Naxos.

Apollonas

43 *54 km (39 ½ mi) northeast of Naxos town, 12 km (7½ mi) north of Koronos via road from Komiaki.*

Apollonas is a small resort town on Naxos's northeast corner. Look for the steps leading to the unfinished 35-ft **kouros** (youthful male nude statue) of Apollonas, which lies in an ancient quarry. It's thought to represent Dionysos. Initially, the Greeks represented gods with small idols; later, they were seen as supermen and depicted by these giant, highly stylized statues. This early 6th-century kouros was probably abandoned because cracks developed in the marble while the work was in progress. It lies on its back, eroded by the winds, but still, somewhat eerily, in the shape of a bearded man. ⊠ *On main road past Apollonas, on the left.* ☏ *Free.*

Beaches

In the far northeast, **Apollonas** is a spread-out beach with small white marble pebbles. Much more rewarding are the **bays** of Abram, Ayias Mamas, Xilia Brisi, and Paxia Ammos, small sand beaches to the west that are seldom crowded. Most of these can be reached by bus.

Dining

$$$ ✕ **Venetiko.** In Apollonas the pickings are slim, but this is the best of the tavernas encircling the harbor—it's so close to the water you can feed the fish. Between frying potatoes and garnishing Greek salads, Voula and Dimitris can often be found sitting down to chat with customers. Vegetables, cheeses, and most meats are local, and you can see where the fish comes from. Other options include fresh (local) cockerel in wine sauce or fresh rabbit stew with onions, along with some pleasant barrel wine from the mountain village of Komiaki. ⊠ *Apollonas waterfront,* ☏ *0285/67108. No credit cards.*

Ayia

2½ km (1¼ mi) west of Apollonas.

The newly paved coast road from Apollonas to Naxos town passes, in a lush valley, the **Ayia tower,** once a lookout post for northwestern Naxos. At the nearby church, during the feast of the Dormition (August 15), women who had taken a vow to the Virgin used to attend the service after walking barefoot from Apollonas along the rough paths.

Beaches

44 The road from Apollonas to Chora runs along steep cliffs, traversing inlets and secluded beaches; the most accessible is **Ormos Abram,** 5 km (3 mi) from Apollonas, which has a pension and taverna and is pleasant when the north winds aren't blowing.

Flerio

45 *12 km (7½ mi) east of Naxos town.*

The island's second famous **kouros** is at Flerio, in the Melanes Valley; though smaller (26 ft), it is more detailed and lies in a beautiful private orchard; it has become one of Naxos's more popular sights. The silent kouros, like Ozymandias, is a reminder of a once-glorious age. Archaeologists think the 6th-century statue was abandoned because its leg broke (as you'll see). Also, when the tyrant Lygdamis came to power, he confiscated all the orders of the rich that were still in the quarries. When he couldn't find a way to dispose of some of the kouroi, he tried to sell them back to former owners. ✉ *On right just before small white shack; through small gate.* 🎫 *Free.* ☉ *May–Oct., daily 8–sunset.*

NEED A BREAK?	After seeing the kouros, relax in the **garden** (✉ On right before small white shack), among bougainvillea and lilac, and order the local family's homemade kitro preserves or a shot of citron liqueur.

PAROS

In the golden age, the great sculptor Praxiteles prized the Parian marble that came from the quarries here; in the 19th century, Paros was beloved by Byron. Today, Paros is favored by people for its lower prices, golden sandy beaches, and charming fishing villages. It may lack the chic of Mykonos and have fewer top-class hotels, but at the height of the season it often gets Mykonos's overflow. The island is large enough to accommodate the traveler in search of peace and quiet, yet the lovely port towns of Parikia, the capital, and Naousa also have an active nightlife. Parikia is a focal point of the ferry network, and many people stay here for a night or two while waiting for a connection. It's particularly good for bars and discos, though Naousa has a more chic island atmosphere.

Paros Town

35 km (21¾ mi) west of Naxos town, 10 km (6 mi) southwest of Naousa.

One of your first impressions of Paros town will be the many travel agencies dispensing information on the waterfront and a multitude of car and motorbike rental agencies nearby. If you walk east on the harbor road you will see a lineup of bars, fast-food restaurants, and coffee shops—some owned by Athenians who come to Paros to capitalize on tourism during the summer. Past them are the bus stop, fishing-boat dock, ancient graveyard, and post office; then the beaches start. The better restaurants and the shopping district are in the town, where it is easy to get lost in the maze of narrow, stone-paved streets that intersect with the streets of the quiet residential areas. Though the tourist culture has not blended in as smoothly as it has on Mykonos, and Paros has looked neglected in the past, much restoration work, especially in the areas around the great church and along the waterfront, has recently been undertaken.

The splendid square above the port, to the northwest, was built in 1996 to celebrate the church's 1,700th anniversary. From there you will see a white gate, the front of the former monastic quarters that surround the magnificent **Panayia Ekatontapyliani** (Hundred Doors) church, the earliest remaining Byzantine church in Greece. According to legend, 99 doors have been found in the church and the 100th will be discovered only after Constantinople is Greek again. Inside, the subdued light mixes with the dun, reddish, and green tufa. The columns are classical and their capitals Byzantine. At the corners of the dome are two fading Byzantine frescoes depicting six-winged seraphim. The 6th-century iconostasis (with ornate later additions) is divided into five frames by marble columns. One panel contains the recently restored 14th-century icon of the Virgin, with a silver covering from 1777. The Virgin is carried in procession on the church's crowded feast day, August 15, the Dormition. The adjacent **Baptistery**, also built from the 4th to the 6th centuries, has a marble font and bits of mosaic floor.

In 326, St. Helen—the mother of Emperor Constantine the Great—

took a ship for the Holy Land to find the True Cross. Stopping on Paros, she had a vision of success and vowed to build a church there. She founded it but died before it was built. Her son built the church in 328 as a wooden-roof basilica. Two centuries later Justinian the Great, who ruled the Byzantine Empire in 527–65, had it splendidly rebuilt with a dome. He appointed Isidorus, one of the two architects of Constantinople's famed Ayia Sophia, to design it; Isidorus decided to send an apprentice, Ignatius, to Paros. Folk legends say that, upon its completion, Isidorus arrived in Paros for an inspection and discovered the dome to be so magnificent that, consumed by jealousy, he pushed the young apprentice off the roof. Ignatius grasped his master's foot as he fell, and the two tumbled to their death together. Two folk sculptures near the toilets at the sanctuary's baroque left portal portray them as two fat men, one pulling his beard with remorse and the other holding his cracked head. The church **museum**, at right, contains fine post-Byzantine icons. ✉ *750 ft east of the dock*, ☎ *0284/21243.* ✇ *Free.* ☉ *Daily 8–1 and 4–9.*

The **Archaeological Museum** is another must-see sight on Paros. It contains a fragment of the famed Parian chronicle, which recorded cultural events in Greece from about 1500 BC until 260 BC (a larger section is in Oxford's Ashmolean Museum). It interests scholars that the historian inscribed detailed information about artists, poets, and playwrights, completely ignoring wars and shifts in government. Some primitive pieces from the Aegean's oldest settlement, Saliagos (an islet between Paros and Antiparos), are exhibited in the same room, on the left. In the large room to the right rests a marble slab depicting the poet Archilochus in a banquet scene, lying on a couch, his weapons nearby. The ancients ranked Archilochus, who invented iambic meter and wrote the first signed love lyric, second only to Homer. When he died in battle against the Naxians, his conqueror was cursed by the oracle of Apollo for putting to rest one of the faithful servants of the muse. Also there are a monumental Nike and three superb just-found pieces: a waist-down kouros, a gorgon, and a dancing-girl relief. ✉ *Behind Church of a Hundred Doors*, ☎ *0284/21231.* ✇ *500 dr./€1.47.* ☉ *Tues.–Sun. 8:30–2:30.*

Beaches

From Parikia, boats leave throughout the day for beaches across the bay: to sandy **Krios** and the quieter **Kaminia. Livadia,** a 5-minute walk, is very developed but has shade.

Dining and Lodging

$$$ ✕ **Porphyra.** For the most civilized dining on Paros, Porphyra is
★ unique in the islands because the owner, Yannis Gouroyannis, farms his own shellfish in Lesbos's pellucid waters; the fresh oysters, shell of Venus, clams, and cockles are Aegean-sweet. His wife, Roula, cooks; her mussels saganaki (with feta and tomatoes) is a great favorite. Fresh fish, fish salads, and local seasonal vegetables round out the menu. And where else can you taste sea-urchin salad or marinated ray? Every meal starts, gratis, with iced *souma* (Parian for raki) and an oyster and concludes with a homemade semolina sweet. The interior, popular in winter, is simple and authentic, while the outdoor tables border an ancient ruin. ✉ *Parikia (along waterfront toward post office)*, ☎ *0284/23410. AE, MC, V.*

$$ ✕ **Levantis.** Owner George Mavridis does his own cooking—always
★ a good sign. Though this spot looks like a garden taverna, and, amazingly, is priced like one, the food is sophisticated and eclectic, as George often returns from winter travels with exotic new recipes. To name just one example, his Laska is a piquant Thai soup with coconut, salmon,

and mussels. The eggplant rolls stuffed with mushrooms and topped with mozzarella are closer to home. Among his entrées, the roast lamb rolled in Parian herbs served on a salad of chickpeas, feta, and black olives or the baked perch marinated in olive oil, lemon, garlic, and Parian sage (George grows or gathers most of his herbs) are likely to be on the menu. To finish, opt for the chocolate cake with berries and a splash of cream—it should win a prize. ⊠ *Central market street, Parikia,* ☎ *0284/23613. AE, MC, V.*

$$$–$$$$ 🛏 **Pandrossos Hotel.** If you want a good night's sleep away from the pulse of Paros town but you don't want to give up shopping, nightlife, restaurants, and cafés, the Pandrossos—built on a hill with a splendid view overlooking Paros Bay—is the best choice. The lobby, restaurant, and terrace form one great expanse of marble, perfect for sunset watching—unless you're watching it from your room's sea-view balcony. If you eat at the excellent restaurant (you should), try a bottle of their own white wine. To get to this hotel's hill location, take the seaside road from Paros town. ⊠ *On the hill at the southwest edge of Parikia, 21009,* ☎ *0284/21394; 01/360–5611 in Athens,* 𝖥𝖠𝖷 *0284/23501. 24 rooms. Restaurant, bar, pool. AE, MC, V.*

Nightlife and the Arts

MUSIC AND BARS

Turn right along the waterfront from the port in Paros town to find the town's famous bars; then follow your ears. For a classier alternative, head for **Pebbles** (⊠ On the Kastro hill), which often has live jazz and overlooks the sunset. **Art Café** (⊠ Road off the waterfront's southern end, next to the big church, then follow sign, ☎ 0284/24389) schedules live jazz, classical, and Greek, summer and winter; it is also Parikia's best art gallery. As a bonus, the espresso is good.

At the far end of the Paralia is the laser-light-and-disco section of town, which you may want to avoid. In the younger bars, cheap alcohol, as everywhere in tourist Greece, is often added to the more colorful drinks. The Parian young go late to **Myrobolos** (⊠ Seaside, next to ancient cemetery, 2nd floor) for live music, a restaurant, wine bar, and roof garden.

ARTS EVENTS

The **Aegean Center for the Fine Arts** (⊠ At end of Market St., Paros town, ☎ 𝖥𝖠𝖷 0284/23287🖝) periodically stages readings and exhibitions of students' work. It is run by John Pack, an American photographer who lives on the island with his family. Since 1966 the center has offered courses (two three-month semesters) in writing, painting, and photography, among other disciplines; it even takes a study group to Tuscany.

The **Archilochos Cultural Society** (⊠ Near bus stop, ☎ 0284/23595) runs a film club in winter, and offers a varied program of concerts, exhibitions, and lectures throughout the year (for instance, the New York mezzo-soprano Barrett Cobb performs every June). Watch for posters.

Outdoor Activities and Sports

GYM

To stay in shape, Fotis Skiadas's well-appointed **Gymnasium** (⊠ Hotel Zanet, near Livadia beach, ☎ 0284/22233), for aerobics and bodybuilding, is air-conditioned and has a sauna.

HORSEBACK RIDING

For riding along the coast, **Time Riding Center** (⊠ Livadi, Paros town, ☎ 0284/23408) has fine animals; the cost is 5,500 dr./€16.22 for 1½ hours.

For organized mountain-bike tours (one includes Naxos) and rentals, there's **Hellas Bike Travel** (☎ 0284/52010, ⅁ 0284/51720).

WATER SPORTS

Many beaches offer water sports, especially windsurfing. Every summer the **F2 Windsurfing Center** (✉ New Golden Beach, at Philoxenia Hotel, near Marpissa, ☎ 0284/41878) hosts the **International Windsurfing World Cup.**

Shopping

JEWELRY

Vangelis Skaramangas and Yannis Xenos have been making their own delicate, precious jewelry at **Jewelry Workshop** (✉ Paros town, at the far end of Market St., ☎ 0284/21008) for 18 years.

LOCAL FOODS

Enosis (The Agricultural Cooperative's shop; ✉ Manto Mavroyennis Sq., at the front of Parikia under the police station, ☎ 0282/22181) sells homemade pasta, honey, cheeses, and especially Paros's renowned wines. The new varietal wine Monemvasia (officially rated "Appellation of High Quality Origin Paros)" is made from white monemvasia grapes, indigenous to Paros.

En Route Halfway from Paros town to Naousa, on the right, the 17th-century **Monastery of Longovarda** shines on its mountainside; these days only six monks are in residence there. The monastic community farms the local land and makes honey, wine, and olive oil. Only men, dressed in conservative clothing, are allowed inside, where there are post-Byzantine icons, 17th-century frescoes depicting the Twelve Feasts in the Life of Christ, and a library of rare books; it is usually open mornings. ☎ *0284/21202.*

Naousa

10 km (6 mi) northeast of Paros town.

Naousa, impossibly pretty, long ago discovered the benefits of tourism. Its outskirts are mushrooming with villas and hotels that exploit it further. Along the harbor, red and navy-blue boats knock gently against one another as fishermen repair their nets and foreigners relax in the *ouzeris* (casual bars)—Barbarossa being the traditional favorite—by the water's edge. Navies of the ancient Persians, flotillas from medieval Venice, and the imperial Russian fleet have anchored in this harbor. The half-submerged ruins of the Venetian fortifications still remain; they are a pretty sight when lighted up at night.

Beaches

A boat goes regularly to **Lageri** (✉ North of Naousa), a long, sandy beach with dunes, and to **Santa Maria** (✉ Northeastern shore of Paros), the windsurfers' beach. Another boats crosses the bay to **Kolimbithres** (✉ Directly across the bay from Naousa), noted for its rock formations, water sports, a choice of tavernas, and several luxury hotels, and to **Ayios Ioannis** (✉ Across from Naousa) for nude sunbathing.

Dining and Lodging

$$$ ✕ **Taverna Christos.** For more than 20 years Christos has been Naousa's
★   best restaurant; it still is. Its spacious garden and decor—the walls are an art gallery—are bright and fresh, with gracious service and dishes from all over Greece. Excellent first courses include a light leek pie. Among entrées, try small fillet steaks with sun-dried tomatoes, or Thracian chicken with sesame sauce. For dessert, the warm chocolate mousse cake is sinful. ✉ *Naousa, up hill from central square,* ☎ *0284/ 51442. AE, V. Closed Oct.–May.*

$$ ✕ **Papadakis.** A couple of years ago, Captain Yannis Papadakis gave
★ his fine taverna to his daughter and son-in law, and it has gotten even
better. Since it is right on the picturesque little harbor at Naousa a few
feet from the fishing boats, it is not surprising that the specialty is fresh
fish, weather permitting. The many appetizers include eggplant with
feta and tomatoes, and beet salad with yogurt and walnuts. The veg-
etable pies are good for any course. Very popular with tourists and lo-
cals who like the nearby creak of tied up caïques, it is crowded all year.
⊠ *Naousa, on the fishing boat harbor,* ☎ *0284/51047. AE, V.*

$$$$ 🏨 **Astir of Paros.** Across the bay from Naousa twinkle the lights of
this deluxe resort hotel, an elegant and expensive retreat, with green
lawns, tall palm trees, lush gardens, and an art gallery. Rooms are pretty
and spacious—perfect for romantic couples of taste—with antiques,
artwork, and views of the sparkling Naousa Bay. Its two Greek restau-
rants are excellent. ⊠ *Take Kolymbithres Rd. from Naousa, 84400,*
☎ *0284/51976 or 0284/51984,* 𝔽𝔸𝕏 *0284/51985. 50 rooms, 7 suites.*
*Restaurant, piano bar, refrigerators, pool, sauna, miniature golf, ten-
nis court, exercise room, windsurfing, waterskiing, baby-sitting, laun-
dry service. AE, DC, MC, V.* ✇

$$$ 🏨 **Sovronos Bungalows.** These bungalow apartments always seem to
be fully occupied. The friendly Sovronos family tends the lush garden,
and the comfortable apartments and Cycladic whitewashed courtyards are decorated with antiques and objects from the host's extensive travels. This is convenient and quiet, with easy access to Naousa's
lively shopping and nightlife. ⊠ *Behind big church, 1 block in from
Santa Maria Rd., Naousa 84400,* ☎ *0284/51211 or 0284/51409,* 𝔽𝔸𝕏
0284/52281. 19 apartments. Bar. No credit cards.

Nightlife and the Arts

BARS

Linardo's (⊠ Fishing harbor) is lively and is open into the wee hours.
Agosta (⊠ Fishing harbor) is a pretty spot.

DANCE

The group **Music–Dance "Naousa Paros"** (☎ 0284/52284, 𝔽𝔸𝕏 0284/
52114), formed in 1988 to preserve the traditional dances and music
of Paros, performs all summer long in Naousa in the costumes of the
16th century and has participated in dance competitions and festivals
throughout Europe. Keep an eye out for posters.

Outdoor Activities and Sports

WATER SPORTS

Santa Maria Surf Club (⊠ Santa Maria beach, about 4 km [2½ mi] north
of Naousa) is popular, with windsurfing, jet-skiing, waterskiing, and
diving. If you're traveling with children, **Aqua Paros Waterpark** (⊠
Kolymbithres, next to Porto Paros Hotel, ☎ 0284/53271, 𝔽𝔸𝕏 0284/
53264), with its 13 water slides big and small, will cool a hot afternoon. Admission is 3,000 dr./€8.84. **Eurodiver's Club** (⊠ Pounda, in
the Holiday Sun Hotel, ☎ 0284/92071) offers scuba lessons and takes
you to reefs, shipwrecks, and caves.

Shopping

LOCAL JEWELRY AND ART

Metaxas gallery (⊠ On second street from harbor toward main church
near Monastery of Saint Andreas, Naousa, ☎ 0284/52667) shows painting, photography, sculpture, and especially jewelry, all done by Paros
residents. One of the jewelers, Gregory Altamirano, creates his elegant
designs in his workshop (⊠ On second street from harbor toward main
church near Monastery of Saint Andreas), with a splendid view overlooking Naousa Bay.

Marathi

10 km (6 mi) east of Paros town.

During the classical period the island of Paros had an estimated 150,000 residents, many of them slaves who worked the ancient marble quarries in Marathi. The island grew rich from the export of this white, granular marble known among ancient architects and sculptors for its ability to absorb light. They called it *lychnites* ("won by lamplight").

Marked by a sign, **three caverns** (⊠ A short walk from the main road) are bored into the hillside, the largest of them 300 ft deep. The most recent quarrying done in these mines was in 1844, when a French company cut marble here for Napoléon's tomb.

Shopping
LOCAL CRAFTS

At **Studio Yria** (⊠ 1½ km [1 mi] east of Marathi, above the road to Kostos village, ☎ 0284/29007⊗) master potters Stelios and Monique Ghikas and other craftsmen can be seen at work. Marble carvers, metalsmiths, painters, and more all make for a true Renaissance workshop. Both the ceramic tableware and the works of art make use of Byzantine and Cycladic motifs in their designs; they have even made ceramic designs for the Prince of Wales. Easily accessible by bus, taxi, and rental car, the studio is open 8–8.

Lefkes

10 km (6 mi) southeast of Paros town, 6 km (4 mi) south of Marathi.

Rampant piracy in the 17th century forced thousands of people to move inland from the coastal regions; thus for many years the scenic village of Lefkes, built on a hillside in the protective mountains, was the island's capital. It remains the largest village in the interior and has maintained a peaceful, island feeling, with narrow streets fragrant of jasmine and honeysuckle. Farming is the major source of income, as you can tell from the well-kept stone walls and olive groves.

Two **17th-century churches** of interest are **Ayia Varvara** (St. Barbara) and **Ayios Sotiris** (Holy Savior). The big 1830 neo-Renaissance **Ayia Triada** (Holy Trinity) is the pride of the village.

Beaches
Piso Livadi (⊠ On road past Lefkes) was the ancient port for the marble quarries and today is a small resort town convenient to many beaches; the harbor, from where boats go to Naxos and Delos, is being expanded.

Lodging
\$\$\$ ▣ **Lefkes Village.** All island-style rooms in this elegant hotel have bal-
★ conies with magnificent views down the olive-tree valley and over the sea to Naxos. The lobby is tasteful and comfortably simple. The restaurant is noted for its traditional Greek food; the folk museum here is chockablock with interesting objects. ⊠ *Just east of Lefkes on the main road, 84400,* ☎ ℻ *0284/41827 or 0284/42398. 20 rooms. Restaurant, bar, refrigerators, pool. AE, DC, MC, V.*

Shopping
WEAVINGS

On the main upper street, near the park where families stroll in the evening, Nikoletta Haniotis's shop, **Anemi** (☎ 0284 41182), features handwoven weavings colored with natural dyes and local designs. Also for sale are fine iron pieces made by her father, Lefkes' blacksmith.

Petaloudes Park

4 km (2½ mi) south of Paros town.

A species of moth returns year after year to mate in Petaloudes (the Valley of the Butterflies), a lush oasis of greenery in the middle of this dry island. In May, June, and perhaps July, you can watch them as they lie dormant during the day, their chocolate-brown wings with yellow stripes still against the ivy leaves. In the evening they flutter upward to the cooler air, flashing the coral-red undersides of their wings as they rise. A notice at the entrance asks visitors not to disturb them by taking photographs or shaking the leaves. ⊠ *Petaloudes.* ☎ *500 dr./€1.47.* ◷ *Mid-May–mid-Sept., daily 9–8. Closed Oct.–mid-May.*

NEED A   Even when the butterflies are not there, it is pleasant to have coffee in
BREAK?   the small *kafenion* coffeehouse (⊠ Inside entrance to park) and enjoy
             the shade of the cypress, olive, chestnut, mulberry, and lemon trees.

On the summit of a hill just beyond the garden reigns a lopped **Venetian tower.** Its founder's name, Iakovos Alisafis, and the date, 1626, are inscribed on it.

En Route   A 15-minute walk or 2-minute drive back toward Paros town from the Valley of the Butterflies leads to the convent known as **Christos sto Dasos** (Christ in the Wood), from where there's a marvelous view of the Aegean. The convent contains the tomb of Saint Arsenios (1800–77), who was a schoolteacher, an abbot, and a prophet. He was also a rainmaker whose prayers were believed to have ended a long drought, saving Paros from starvation. The nuns are a bit leery of tourists. If you want to go in, be sure to wear long pants or skirt and a shirt that covers your shoulders, or the sisters will turn you away.

Outdoor Activities and Sports

TENNIS
You can rent courts at the **Holiday Sun Hotel** (⊠ Pounda, ☎ 0284/91284 or 0284/91285, FAX 0284/91288), which also has an exercise room and sauna.

SANTORINI

Undoubtedly the most extraordinary island in the Aegean, crescent-shaped Santorini remains a must for Cycladic visitors—even if they have to enjoy the sensational sunsets from Ia, the fascinating excavations, and the dazzling white towns with a million other travelers. Arriving by boat, you are met by one of the world's truly breathtaking sights, the **caldera:** a crescent of cliffs, striated in black, pink, brown, white, and pale green, rising 1,100 ft, with the white clusters of the towns of Fira and Ia perched along the top. The encircling cliffs are the ancient rim of a still-active volcano, and you are sailing east across its flooded caldera.

Santorini and its four neighboring islets are the fragmentary remains of a larger landmass that exploded about 1600 BC: the volcano's core blew sky high, and the sea rushed into the abyss to create the great bay, which measures 10 km by 7 km (6 mi by 4 mi) and is 1,292 ft deep. The other pieces of the rim, which broke off in later eruptions, are Thirassia, home to a few hundred people, and deserted little Aspronissi ("White Isle"). In the center of the bay, black and uninhabited, are two sometimes smoldering cones, the "Burnt Isles" of Palea Kameni and Nea Kameni, which appeared between 1573 and 1925. The ancients called Santorini's island group Strongyle ("Round") and

Kalliste ("Loveliest"); the island was named Thera, and it still officially is. Its medieval name of Santorini (a corruption of Sant' Irene) is more common.

There has been too much speculation about the identification of Santorini with the mythical Atlantis, mentioned in Egyptian papyri and by Plato (who says it's in the Atlantic), but myths are hard to pin down. This is not true of arguments about whether or not tidal waves from Santorini's cataclysmic explosion destroyed the Minoan civilization on Crete. The latest carbon-dating evidence clearly indicates that the Minoans outlasted the eruption by a couple of hundred years.

Since antiquity, Santorini has depended on rain collected in cisterns for drinking and irrigating—the well water is often brackish—and the serious shortage is alleviated by the importation of water. The fertile volcanic soil produces small, intense tomatoes with tough skins used for tomato paste; the famous Santorini fava beans, which have a light, fresh taste; barley; wheat; and white-skinned eggplants. The locals say that in Santorini there is more wine than water, and it may be true; Santorini produces more wine than any two other Cyclades. The volcanic soil, high daytime temperatures, and humidity at night produce 36 varieties of grape, and these unique growing conditions are ideal for the production of distinctive white wine now gaining international recognition. Farmers twist the vines into a basketlike shape, in which the grapes grow, protected from the wind. Finally it's important to note that unrestrained tourism has taken a heavy toll on Santorini. Some of the villages can now be described as "a street with 40 jewelry shops," many of the natives are completely burned-out by the end of the peak season (the best times to come here are shoulder periods, because summer weeks are sometimes swamped by Greek school groups on holiday), and, increasingly, business and the loud ringing of cash registers have disrupted the normal flow of Greek life here. Still and all, Santorini is so beautiful *nothing* can really ruin it.

Fira

46 *10 km (6 mi) west of the airport, 14 km (8½ mi) southeast of Ia.*

Tourism, the island's major industry, adds more than 1 million visitors per year to its population of 7,000. As a result, Fira, the capital, midway along the west coast of the east rim, is no longer just a picturesque village but a major tourist center, overflowing with discos, shops, and restaurants. Many of its employees, young travelers extending their summer vacations, hardly speak Greek.

The modern Greek Orthodox cathedral of **Panayia Ypapantis** (✉ Southern part of town) is a major landmark; the local priests, with somber faces, long beards, and black robes, look strangely out of place in summertime Fira. Along **Eikostis Pemptis Martiou** (25th of March St.; ✉ East of Panayia Ypapantis), you'll find inexpensive restaurants and accommodations. The blocked-off Ypapantis Street (✉ West of Panayia Ypapantis) leads to **Kato Fira** (Lower Fira), built into the cliff side overlooking the caldera, where prices are higher and the vista wonderful. For centuries the people of the island have been digging themselves rooms-with-a-view right in the cliff face—many bars and hotel rooms have actually been made out of caves—for posh atmosphere and constant temperature.

The **Museum of Prehistoric Thera,** in a spacious new building, opened in March 2000. It displays—for the first time—pots and frescoes from the famed Santorini excavations at Akrotiri (☞ *below*). Note the fresco fragments with the painted swallows (who flocked here because

Santorini

they loved the cliffs). The fossilized olive leaves from 60,000 BC prove the olive to be indigenous. ⊠ *Mitropoleos St. behind the big church,* ☎ *0286/23217.* ☐ *Free.* ⊙ *Tues.–Sun. 8:30–3.*

The **Archaeological Museum** displays pottery, statues, and grave artifacts found at excavations mostly from ancient Thera and Akrotiri, from the Minoan through the Byzantine periods. ⊠ *Stavrou and Nomikos Sts.,* ☎ *0286/22217.* ☐ *800 dr./€2.35.* ⊙ *Tues.–Sun. 8:30–3.*

OFF THE BEATEN PATH | **NEA KAMENI –** To peer into a live, sometimes smoldering volcano, join one of the popular excursions to Nea Kameni, the larger of the two Burnt Isles. After disembarking, you hike 430 ft to the top and walk around the edge of the crater, wondering if the volcano is ready for its fifth eruption during the last hundred years—after all, the last was in 1956. Tours (about 4,500 dr./€13.27) are scheduled regularly (☞ Contacts and Resources *in* The Cyclades A to Z, *below*).

Dining and Lodging

$$$ ✕ **Kukumavlos.** This fine restaurant has an elegant vaulted room and a 12-table patio overlooking the caldera. The cuisine is creative Mediterranean, prepared by Nikos Pouliasis, the owner. Nikos recommends starters such as kataifi of Greek white cheeses with mandarin sauce and blackberries, or chicken pie with pumpkin sauce. For main dishes, shrimp sautéed in retsina with celery, beet greens, and grilled *manouri* cheese, or pork fillet with grilled oyster mushrooms, truffle oil, coriander, and cress olive oil. His panna cotta made with yogurt and drizzled with honey and sour-cherry syrup is perfect. The menu is ever-changing, so expect other unheralded delights. ⊠ *Right below the Atlantis Hotel,* ☎ *02286/23807. AE, MC, V.*

$$$ ✕ **Selene.** Since 1986, this has probably been Santorini's best place for quiet, elegant dining. The spacious terrace edged with flowers has a splendid caldera view, and the food is splendid, too. The indoors is an old cliff house with traditional vaulted ceiling and dark wood furniture; the banquettes are the built-in benches intrinsic to traditional island houses. The menu is full of interesting dishes, such as mushrooms stuffed with crabmeat and cheese; a *brodero* with fish, squid, octopus, prawns, and fish in a clay pot; and squab stuffed with bulgur and apricots. For dessert, the custard with fig preserves and almonds is both rich and light. Reservations are a good idea. ⊠ *Cliff-side walkway 310 ft to the left of the Hotel Atlantis,* ☎ *0286/22449,* ℻ *0286/24395. AE, DC, MC, V.*

$$$ ✕ **Sphinx.** When Fira locals want more than a taverna, they come here. Owner George Psichas is his own chef, and every dish is evidence of his loving care (even the bread and pasta are homemade). The warm peach interior in a vaulted room opens onto several terraces with caldera views. For a starter, try the sliced braised veal with tuna-caper sauce, then follow that up with fresh grouper steak with vegetables and lemon butter sauce or the ostrich fillet with cabernet and red peppercorn sauce. A dessert of ice-cream profiteroles will leave you happy. Lunch is popular here, and reservations are the way to go during July and August. ⊠ *Cliff-side walkway in front of the big church,* ☎ *0286/ 23823. AE, MC, V.*

$$ ✕ **Nicholas.** This is Santorini's oldest taverna, where you'll find locals in winter. Island dishes are prepared well and served in a simple, attractive room. Try the local yellow lentils and, for a delicious entrée, the lamb fricassee with an egg-lemon sauce. ⊠ *2 streets in from cliff side on Erythrou Stavrou, Fira,* ☎ *no phone. No credit cards.*

$$$$ 🏨 **Aigialos Houses/Villas.** Aigialos (Seashore) is new (1995), but its
★ renovated buildings are old and provide the most comfortable and discreetly luxurious—as well as the most poetic—place to stay in Fira. The one-, two-, and three-bedroom houses, with marble floors and beautiful furniture, also have terraces or balconies overlooking the caldera—no need to venture out at sunset. There's satellite TV, maid service twice daily, impeccable 24-hour service, and fresh flowers. The restaurant serves its fine Mediterranean cuisine only to residents, and you can eat on your private terrace. ⊠ *South end of Ypapantis Walkway (left from Hotel Atlantis), Fira 84700,* ☎ *0286/25191 through 0286/25195,* ℻ *0286/22856. 16 villas. Restaurant, bar, refrigerators, pool, spa. AE, DC, MC, V.* ✺

$$$$ 🏨 **Hotel Aressana.** Though the Aressana lacks a view of the caldera, its own slant of sea view is effulgent in its own way. The large freshwater pool, spacious lobby with traditional furnishings and wood-paneled bar, excellent service, famous breakfast, and location in central Fira make it first rate. The Aressana specializes in traditional wedding receptions and charming bridal suites—so don't be surprised at how many Americans honeymoon here. ⊠ *South end of Ypapantis Walkway, Fira 84700,* ☎ *0286/23900 or 0286/23901,* ℻ *0286/23902. 42 rooms, 8 suites. Bar, pool. AE, DC, MC, V.* ✺

$$$ 🏨 **Panorama Hotel.** From the cliff side of Fira, this white hotel, on the cliff-side street with no steps, provides a breathtaking view of the caldera from every room, almost all with balconies. A travel desk in the reception area can book tours and rent cars. ⊠ *Ypapantis Walkway, Fira 84700,* ☎ *0286/22481,* ℻ *0286/23179. 23 rooms. Café, travel services. AE, DC, MC, V.*

$$ 🏨 **Delphini II.** Owner-manager Vassilis Rousseas says he has "prices for everyone." Delphini II has spacious apartments, all different in architecture and decor, which once were village homes. (Ask to see the one with the old stove.) ⊠ *Down hill in front of Atlantis Hotel, Fira 84700,* ☎ *0286/24370,* ☎ ℻ *0286/22780. 3 studios, 4 apartments. Kitchenettes, refrigerators, air-conditioning (some). V.*

$–$$ 🖫 **Delphini I.** Vassilis's (☞ *above*) other property, Delphini I, is less expensive and has no views. ⊠ *Near hospital, Fira 84700,* ☎ *0286/22371. 10 rooms. Refrigerators. No credit cards.*

Nightlife and the Arts

DANCING

Bar 33 (⊠ Fira, ☎ 0286/23065) has bouzouki music and a celebratory atmosphere. The **Koo Club** (⊠ Fira, ☎ 0286/22025) is Fira's most popular outdoor disco by far. **Ellenes** (⊠ Opposite Fira's Olympic Office) is for Greek dancing.

FESTIVAL

The **International Santorini Music Festival** (⊠ Estis Hall, ☎ 0286/ 22220) takes place in late August–early September. The performance schedule, including internationally known musicians, is announced during the summer and posted about town.

MUSIC

As the sun sets on the caldera, **Palia Kameni** (⊠ Fira, ☎ 0286/22430) is the place to go for well-selected jazz, classical, and passionate Greek music. Try a strawberry margarita or one of the other reasonably priced drinks. **Franco's Bar** (⊠ Fira, ☎ 0286/24428), much written up, plays classical music; it's flights down from the Ypapantis Walkway and has a caldera view.

Outdoor Activities and Sports

SAILING

The **Santorini Sailing Center** (⊠ Merovigli, ☎ 0286/23058 or 0286/ 23059) arranges charters and runs weekly two- to three-day sailing trips around the Cyclades for groups up to 10.

TENNIS

The **Santorini Tennis Club** (⊠ Santorini Tennis Club Hotel, Kartaradoes, ☎ 0286/22122) has two concrete courts where two can play in high season for 2,000 dr./€5.89 per hour; it's open April– October.

Shopping

JEWELRY

Kostas Antoniou Jewelry (⊠ Ayios Ioannou, ☎ 0286/22633) is well known: *Vogue* and *Marie Claire* have even featured some of Kostas's original pieces, many inspired by ancient Thera; some solid gold necklaces are magnificent enough to earn their own names, such as Earth's Engravings, Ritual, and Motionless Yielding. Kostas also carries a selection of Van Cleef & Arpels watches from Paris. Fortunately, he takes plastic. ⊠ *Opposite cable car,* ☎ 𝔽𝔸𝕏 *0286/22633. AE, MC, V.*

EMBROIDERY

Costas Dimitrokalis (⊠ Ayios Ioannou, ☎ 0286/22633) features locally made embroideries from Greek linen and Egyptian cotton, rugs, pillow cases in hand-crocheted wool with local designs, and more. Purchases can be mailed anywhere. ⊠ *One block in from cable car,* ☎ 𝔽𝔸𝕏 *0286/222–2957. AE, D, MC, V.*

Firostefani

Firostefani used to be a separate village, but now it is the elegant suburb north of Fira. The 10-minute walk between them, along the caldera, is one of Santorini's highlights. From Firostefani's single white cliffside street, walkways descend to traditional vaulted cave houses, which are fast becoming pensions. Though close to the action, Firostefani feels calm and quiet.

Dining and Lodging

$$$ ✕ **Vanilia.** Set in a windmill—built in 1872 and preserved by the gov-
★ ernment after the 1956 earthquake—Vanilia also encompasses pretty
terraces, providing a lovely setting for excellent food. You might start
with a tomato eggplant napoleon with lemon oil and Parmesan, or a
fresh spinach salad with smoked mussels topped with caramelized
onions and toasted almonds. An especially good entrée—there are
many—is braised octopus, grilled and served with potato gnocchi in a
sauce of sautéed Santorini tomatoes. The pistachio chocolate pancakes
with ice cream will make you want to linger at this friendly place. ✉
Main Sq., Firostefani, ☎ *0286/25631,* ℻ *0286/71800. AE, MC, V.*

$$$-$$$$ 🏨 **Tsitouras.** Tsitouras has no sign; guests here are met (at the airport or
★ harbor) and brought to these extraordinary apartments—sparkling white
cubes with volcanic stone trimmings built around an 18th-century man-
sion. Dimitris Tsitouras is a well-known art collector, and each room dis-
plays a different aspect of his collection—porcelain, sketches of Nureyev,
portraits (including a fetching beauty beloved by Lord Byron); even the
hotel's wreath-insignia is designed by Greece's most famous artist, Ghika.
Blissfully, there are no TVs to mar the perfection, soon to be further en-
hanced by the addition of a pool set on the elegant terrace overlooking
the caldera. ✉ *Firostefani cliff face, down from main street, same stairs
as Nomikos Villas, Firostefani, 84700,* ☎ *0286/23747,* ℻ *0286/23918.
7 apartments. Minibars, kitchenettes. AE, D, MC, V.*

Ia

★ ㊻ *80 km (50 mi) southeast of Paros town (with a ferry connection on
Ios), 14 km (8½ mi) northwest of Fira.*

At the tip of the northern horn of the island sits Ia (or Oia), Santorini's
second-largest town and the Aegean's most-photographed village.
More tasteful than Fira (for one thing, no establishment here is allowed
to play music that can be heard on the street), Ia's cubical white houses
stand out against the green, brown, and rust-color layers of rock,
earth, and solid volcanic ash that rise from the sea. Every summer
evening, travelers from all over the world congregate at the caldera's
rim—sitting on whitewashed fences, staircases, beneath the town's
windmill, on the old castle—each looking out to sea in anticipation of
the performance: the Ia sunset. The three-hour rim-edge walk from Ia
to Fira at this hour is unforgettable.

In the middle of the quiet caldera, the volcano smolders away eerily,
adding an air of suspense to an already awe-inspiring scene. Its most
recent eruption, in 1956, caused tremendous earthquakes (7.8 on the
Richter scale) that left 48 people dead (thankfully, most residents were
working outdoors at the time), hundreds injured, and toppled 2,000
houses. The island's west side—especially Ia, until then the largest town—
was hard hit, and many residents decided to emigrate to Athens, Aus-
tralia, and America. And although Fira, also damaged, rebuilt rapidly,
Ia proceeded slowly, sticking to the traditional architectural style. The
perfect example of that style is the restaurant 1800 (☞ *below*), a ren-
ovated ship captain's villa.

The **Naval Museum of Thera** is in an old mansion. It displays ships'
figureheads, seamen's chests, maritime equipment, models, and more.
✉ *Near telephone office,* ☎ *0286/71156.* 🎟 *500 dr./€1.47* ⊙ *Tues.–
Sun. 8:30–3.*

Beaches

There are no beautiful beaches close to Ia, but you can hike down Ia's
cliff side or catch a bus to the small sand beach of **Baxedes** (✉ Port
of Armoudhi).

Dining and Lodging

$$$ ✕ **1800.** Though the roof garden here has a caldera view, you'll want
★   to sit inside this magnificent building, an old captain's house, now lov-
ingly restored with original furnishings and colors (white, olive green,
and gray) by owner, architect, and restaurateur John Zagelidis. For
starters try Greek caviar accompanied by chilled raki; the roe, from
Missolonghi, is enriched with sour cream and flavored with olive
mousse. Also good are the fresh grilled vegetables with pesto sauce,
wrapped in Spanish ham. For an entrée, lamb cutlets baked in a spicy
sauce of honey, sesame, and mustard seeds are splendid, and so is the
fillet of veal with a cardamom sauce, served with wild mushrooms and
sweet potatoes. An elegant dessert is the parfait (the ice cream is made
with honey, not sugar) sprinkled with pollen flakes. The wine list is
extensive. Clearly, this captain lived graciously. ⊠ *Main St., central Ia,*
☎ *0286/71485,* ℻ *0286/71800. AE, DC, MC, V.* ✎

$$ ✕ **Kastro.** Spiros Dimitroulas's restaurant is primarily patronized for
★   its view of the famous Ia sunset, and at the magical hour it is always
filled. Happily, the food makes a fitting accompaniment. The menu
changes frequently, but he always has the grilled fruit with honey
sauce. Luncheon is popular. ⊠ *Near the Venetian castle, central Ia,* ☎
0286/71045. AE, V.

$$$–$$$$ ☷ **Atlantis Villas.** Most of these "villas" are actually built into caves
★   in Ia's cliff face, making this one of the most unusual and dramatic
places to stay in Greece. The caves, linked into a small complex by steep
walkways, are quiet, always cool, and furnished with traditional woven
rugs and curtains. They all have private balconies or patios fitted with
umbrellas, and a glorious view, 600 ft up, across the caldera. As you
watch the sunset, you'll make your next year's reservation. ⊠ *Ia cliff
face, just before main town, 84702,* ☎ *0286/71214 or 0286/71236,*
℻ *0286/71312. 17 apartments. Kitchenettes, refrigerators, saltwater
pool, laundry service. AE, MC, V.*

$$$–$$$$ ☷ **La Perla Villas.** These quintessential cliff-face villas are the domain
of Kiki Moutsatsos, whose considerable claim to fame is that she was
the private secretary to Aristotle and Jacqueline Onassis for many
years (expect her to hustle her bestselling memoirs when you arrive).
These villas are authentic cave houses, accessed by steep cliffside stair-
cases, and have white rooms, small bathrooms, terraces, and kitchenettes
(you'll appreciate the fact you can keep fresh food at hand, since much
of a Santorini day is spent relaxing on a terrace). Note that U.S. book-
ings (payment by personal check or money order only) are made
through Ivy International Ventures. ⊠ *Ia cliff face, just before main
town, 84702,* ☎ *0286/71510,* ℻ *0286/71865; For U.S. bookings:* ☎
415/885–6846, ℻ *415/346–5084. 7 apartments. Kitchenettes, refrig-
erators, laundry service. AE, MC, V.* ✎

$$$–$$$$ ☷ **Lampetia Villas.** This EOT Traditional Settlement, 800 ft up the cliff
from the sea, offers charm, comfort, and friendliness. The owner, Tom
Alafragis, has a charm all his own. Each of the eight accommodations—
all have private balconies with a view—is different in size and furnish-
ings. ⊠ *Nomikou St., Ia cliff face, down from main street, 84702,* ☎
℻ *0286/71237. 8 houses. Kitchenettes, refrigerators, pool. No credit cards.*

$$$–$$$$ ☷ **Oia's Sunset.** This modern hotel looks like a castle made from minia-
ture Cycladic chapels. The rooms, decorated in traditional style, all have
balconies. ⊠ *Near main square, Ia 84700,* ☎ *0268/71420 or 0268/71490,*
℻ *0286/71421. 8 rooms, 7 apartments. Pool. AE, MC, V.*

$$$–$$$$ ☷ **Perivolas.** *Condé Nast Traveler's* cover photograph of the pool here
makes it seem that a swimmer could float off the edge into the caldera's
blue bay 1,000 ft below. In fact, this amazing effect is nearly accurate.
The vaulted apartments, converted from old wineries, are sculpted into

the red cliffs and simply furnished with handmade wooden pieces and weavings. Each house has its own terrace. ✉ *Nomikou St., Ia cliff face, 15 mins by foot from the town center street, 84702,* ☎ *0286/71318,* FAX *0286/71309. 14 houses. Kitchenettes, pool. AE, MC, V.*

Nightlife

BARS

★ In Ia, sophistication and architectural splendor are the selling points of the **1800** bar and restaurant (☞ *above*). Those in search of a happy-hour beer go to **Zorba's** (✉ On the cliff side). A peaceful note: establishments here are forbidden loud music.

Shopping

Ia is the right place for finding locally crafted items. The inhabitants are sophisticated, and here you will find art galleries, "objets" shops, crafts shops, and icon stores.

ART

Art Gallery (✉ Main shopping street, ☎ 0286/71448) sells large, three-dimensional representations of Santorini architecture by Bella Ko-keenatou and Stavros Galanopoulos. Their lifelike depth invites the viewer to walk through a door or up a flight of stairs. They also carry fine silver. **Art Gallery Oia** (✉ Main shopping street, ☎ 0286/71463) is the place to find a watercolor to take home; painter Manolis Sivri-dakis captures the limpid light of Santorini with remarkable accuracy. Shipping can be provided.

"OBJETS"

Meteor (✉ Main shopping street, ☎ FAX 0286/71015) has a rich collection of objects and antiques culled from just about everywhere, from Greek houses to junk shops abroad. Kilims, ceramics, and jewelry all bespeak the owners' taste. Chara Kourti's **Loulaki** (Main shopping street, ☎ 0286/71856) is similar except that her taste is distinctive and the antiques, odd pieces, jewelry, and art she features make exploring her shop a pleasure. Alexandra Solomos's painted plates are a favorite.

Messaria

★ ④ *3 km (2 mi) south of Fira, 9 km (5½ mi) south of Ia.*

Messaria's **Archontiko Argyrou Museum,** set on the second floor of a splendid neoclassical house with painted walls and traditional furniture of the 19th century, is well worth a stop on the way to the Monastery of Profitis Ilias. The collection includes lovingly preserved 19th-century furnishings, including wall paintings, lace, and implements. Delightfully, you can now even opt for an overnight stay at this locale, part of which has been transformed into a hotel (☞ *below*). ✉ *Messaria,* ☎ *0286/31669,* FAX *0286/33064.* ⊡ *1,000 dr./€2.94.* ⊙ *Hourly guided tours 11–7.*

Lodging

$$$-$$$$ ▥ **Archontiko Argyrou Guest House.** In the middle of the village, this exquisitely restored wine-grower's Cycladic-style mansion from 1860 (still in the Argyros family) is a restful, traditional, and unusual place to stay. You may not want to leave the garden courtyard after breakfast. Even if you don't get the former wine-making room, ask to see it. Some of the rooms can handle up to six guests. All in all, the superlative renovation here earned this place an official government preservation order, and in fact, found a special fan in the beloved late cultural minister and actress, Melina Mercouri. ✉ *Messaria 84700,* ☎ *0286/31669,* FAX *0286/33064. 6 rooms. Kitchen. V.* ✿

Nightlife

MUSIC AND DANCING

You can see the best traditional Greek music and dancing at **Canava Roussos Winery** (✉ Mesagonia, ☎ 0286/31276 reservations), the oldest winery on the island, founded in 1838, where professional and local dancers in costume perform nightly 8–midnight.

Pyrgos

★ ㊾ *5½ km (3¼ mi) south of Fira, 2½ km (1¼ mi) south of Messaria.*

Stop in Pyrgos to see its medieval houses, stacked on top of one another and back to back for protection against pirates. And you can also see the crumbling walls of the old Venetian castle here.

The **Monastery of Profitis Ilias** is at the highest point on Santorini, which spans to 1,856 ft at the summit. From here you can see the surrounding islands and, on a clear day, the mountains of Crete, more than 100 km (66 mi) away. You may also be able to spot ancient Thira on the peak below Profitis Ilias (☞ Kamari, *below*). Unfortunately, radio towers and a NATO radar installation provide an ugly backdrop for the monastery's wonderful bell tower.

Founded in 1711 by two monks from Pyrgos, Profitis Ilias is cherished by islanders because here, in a secret school, the Greek language and culture were taught during the dark centuries of the Turkish occupation. A **museum** in the monastery contains a model of the secret school in a monk's cell, another model of a traditional carpentry and blacksmith shop, and a display of ecclesiastical items. The monastery's future is in doubt because there are so few monks left. ✉ *Pyrgos, at highest point on Santorini.* ☉ *No visiting hrs; try to find a caretaker early in morning.*

Megalochori

㊿ *9 km (5 mi) southwest of Fira, 4 km (2 mi) east of Pyrgos.*

Megalochori is a picturesque, half-abandoned town set. Many of the village's buildings were actually *canavas*, wine-making facilities. The tiny main square is still lively in the evening.

Lodging

$$$$ 🏨 **Vedema.** Santorini's most deluxe hotel is a world unto itself.
★ Vedema's buildings are designed around a beautiful 15th-century winery—so it is both sublimely new and authentic. Every luxury is provided and the service is impeccable. The old vaulted dining room is the prettiest on Santorini; the wine cellar, with its many valuable wines, is worth exploration and enjoyment (there are wine tastings nightly). The spacious suites, in pastel-hued town houses, all have marble bathrooms, island-style furnishings, and terraces. Vedema is not cheap, but you'll see what you're paying for, in spades. A shuttle service ferries you to other parts of the island. ✉ *Megalochori 84700,* ☎ *0286/81796 or 0286/81797,* ℻ *0286/81798. 35 residences, 7 suites. 2 restaurants, pool, fitness center, kitchenettes (some rooms), laundry service. AE, D, MC, V.* ✺

NEED A
BREAK?

Heading south to Akrotiri, stop at **Antoniou Winery** (✉ Megalochori, ☎ ℻ 0286/23557), and take a tour of the multilevel old facility—it's so beautiful local couples get married here. An oenologist leads a wine tasting with snacks, and a slide show describes local wine production; it costs 1,000 dr./€2.94. Many think Antoniou's white wines Santorini's best—and that's saying a lot.

Akrotiri

★ ⑤ *13 km (8 mi) south of Fira, 7 km (4½ mi) west of Pyrgos.*

★ If you visit only one archaeological site during your stay on Santorini, make sure it is **ancient Akrotiri,** near the tip of the southern horn of the island.

In the 1860s, in the course of quarrying volcanic ash for use in the Suez Canal, workmen discovered the remains of an ancient town. The town was frozen in time by ash from an eruption 3,600 years ago, long before Pompeii's disaster. In 1967 Spyridon Marinatos of the University of Athens began excavations, which occasionally continue. It is thought that the 40 buildings that have been uncovered are only one-thirtieth of the huge site and that excavating the rest will probably take a century. You enter from the south, pass the ticket booth, and walk 100 yards or so up a stone-paved street to a vast metal shed that protects two acres of the site from wind and sun. A path punctuated by explanatory signs in English leads through the ancient town.

Marinatos's team discovered great numbers of extremely fine and well-preserved frescoes depicting many aspects of Akrotiri life, most now displayed in the National Archaeological Museum in Athens; Santorini wants them back. Meanwhile, postcard-size pictures of them are posted outside the houses where they were found. The antelopes, monkeys, and wildcats they portray suggest trade with Egypt. One notable example, apparently representing a festival, shows two ports: the left village has ordinary people in skins and tunics, and a symbolic lion runs overhead; and the other, probably Akrotiri, more aristocratic, has in its center a fleet of sailing ships at sea, with playful dolphins swimming alongside.

Culturally an outpost of Minoan Crete, Akrotiri was settled as early as 3000 BC and reached its peak after 2000 BC, when it developed trade and agriculture and settled the present town. The inhabitants cultivated olive trees and grain, and their advanced architecture—three-story frescoed houses faced with fine masonry (some with balconies) and public buildings of sophisticated construction—is evidence of an elaborate lifestyle. Unlike at Pompeii, no human remains, gold, silver, or weapons were found here—probably tremors preceding the eruption warned the inhabitants to pack their valuables and flee. After the eruptions Santorini was uninhabited for about two centuries while the land cooled and plant and animal life regenerated. The site is accessible by public bus or guided tour. ⊠ *South of modern Akrotiri, near tip of southern horn,* ☎ *0286/81366.* ☞ *1,200 dr./€3.53.* ☉ *Tues.–Sun. 8:30–3.*

Beaches
Red Beach (⊠ On southwest shore just below Akrotiri; sign on road) is quiet with a taverna.

Kamari

★ ㊾ *6 km (4 mi) south of Fira, 6½ km (4¼ mi) east of Akrotiri.*

Archaeology buffs will want to visit the site of **ancient Thira.** There are relics of a Dorian city, with 9th-century BC tombs, an engraved phallus, Hellenistic houses, and traces of Byzantine fortifications and churches. At the sanctuary of Apollo, graffiti dating to the 8th century BC record the names of some of the boys who danced naked at the god's festival (Satie's famed musical compositions, *Gymnopedies,* reimagine these). To get there, hike up from Perissa or Kamari or take a taxi up **Mesa Vouna.** On the summit are the scattered ruins, excavated by a

German archaeology school around the turn of the 20th century; there's a fine view. ✉ *On a switchback up the mountain right before Kamari, 2,110 ft high,* ☎ *0286/31366.* 🎫 *1,200 dr./€3.53.* ☉ *Tues.– Sun. 8:30–3.*

Beaches

If you're a beach bum, it's better to stay at the long **black beaches** in **Kamari** or **Perissa** (Perissa's is volcanic sand, not rock). The black beaches are a natural treasure of Santorini and are consequently overdeveloped. Deck chairs and umbrellas can be rented at both beaches, and tavernas and refreshment stands abound.

Dining and Lodging

$$$–$$$$ ✕ **Camille Stéfani.** This fine restaurant, founded in 1977, in a garden
★ on the black beach of Kamari, serves superb international cuisine with the local stamp of approval (especially in winter). For an appetizer, you can't do better than the *poikilia* (variety of calamari, octopus, fried tomato balls, deep-fried eggplant, and zucchini). For an entrée, owner Ares especially recommends beef fillet with green peppercorns and Madeira. A variety of fresh fish is also usually available. For dessert, chocolate crepes with whipped cream are sure to satisfy. ✉ *At end of coast road,* ☎ ℻ *0286/31716. AE, DC, MC, V.*

$–$$ 🏨 **Hotel Astro.** Makarios Sigalas owns and manages the Astro, and his own friendly nature permeates it. Redone in marble, the hotel is looking spiffier than ever. It is a short walk to the black sandy beach and minutes away from the local nightlife. Rooms on the lower level have verandas; those on the second floor have balconies facing the mountains or the Aegean. After spending the day at the sea, it's great to take a dip in the freshwater pool in the evening. And it's not far from Camille Stéfani restaurant (☞ *above*), Kamari's best. ✉ *Central Kamari 84700,* ☎ *0286/31366,* ℻ *0286/31732. 42 rooms. Breakfast room, coffee shop, air-conditioning, pool. AE, MC, V.*

Nightlife

DISCO

In Kamari the younger set heads for the **Yellow Donkey** disco (✉ Promenade, ☎ 0286/31462) and the other bars along the beach promenade.

THE CYCLADES A TO Z

Arriving and Departing

By Boat

Most visitors use the island's extensive ferry network, which has been much improved in recent years. Watching the islands, the sparkling Aegean, and occasional dolphins from the deck will let you know where you are. Ferries sail from Piraeus (Port Authority, ☎ 01/451– 1311 or 01/415–1321) and from Rafina, 35 km (22 mi) northeast of Athens (Port Authority, ☎ 0294/22300). Leaving from Rafina cuts traveling time by an hour; buses leave for the one-hour trip from Rafina to Athens every 20 minutes 6 AM–10 PM. Traveling time from Piraeus to Mykonos is 5 hours; to Santorini, 8–11 hours. The new high-speed ferries are twice as expensive and twice as fast. Interisland catamarans and hydrofoils are fast, closed in, and dependent on weather.

Third-class boat tickets cost roughly one-quarter the airfare, and passengers are restricted to seats in the deck areas and often-crowded indoor seating areas. A first-class ticket, which sometimes buys a private cabin and better lounge, costs about half an airplane ticket. For information on interisland connections, contact the port authorities on the various islands (☞ *below*). High season is June through September; boats are less frequent in the off-season. Very advance schedules must be checked, as they change with the season, for major holidays, and for weather.

ANDROS

For Andros, you must take a ferry from Rafina (not Piraeus); they leave at least three times a day in summer, and the trip takes about two hours. From Andros (✉ Port Authority, ☎ 0282/22250) boats leave twice daily for Tinos and Mykonos. Boats leave three times weekly for Paros, Naxos, Ios, and Crete; they also leave once a week for Skiathos and Salonica. An excursion boat goes daily to Mykonos and Delos, returning in the late afternoon. Big boats dock at Gavrio and hydrofoils at Batsi.

TINOS

Tinos is served in summer by two boats a day from Piraeus and one from Rafina. There are daily connections with Andros, Syros, and Mykonos; several boats a week for Paros, Naxos, and Santorini; and regular boats to Crete, Folegandros, Ikaria, Ios, Milos, Siphnos, Sikinos, Skiathos, and Salonica. An excursion boat goes daily to nearby Delos, returning in the afternoon. The Port Authority in Chora gives information, but it's not more reliable than that given at the agencies clustered near the old harbor (☎ 0283/22348).

MYKONOS

In summer, there are two to three ferries daily to Mykonos from Piraeus and Rafina. From Mykonos (Port Authority: ✉ Harbor, above National Bank, ☎ 0294/22218) there are daily departures to Paros, Syros, Tinos, and Andros, and five to seven departures per week for Santorini, Naxos, Ios, and Crete. Boats go regularly to Amorgos, Folegandros, Ikaria, Ios, Milos, Samos, Siphnos, Sikinos, Skiathos, and Salonica. Check which dock they leave from.

NAXOS

In summer, ferries leave Piraeus for Naxos at least four times a day. (The trip takes about seven hours.) Boats go daily from Naxos (✉ Port Authority, ☎ 0285/22300) to Mykonos, Ios, Paros, Syros, Tinos, and Santorini. Boats go regularly to Amorgos, Anaphi, Astypalea, Folegandros, Milos, Siphnos, Sikinos, Skiathos, Salonica, and Crete. Boats from Naxos serve the Little Cyclades, Iraklia, Schinousa, Koufonisi, and Donousa.

PAROS

About four ferries leave Piraeus for Paros every day in summer. Paros (✉ Port Authority, ☎ 0284/21240) has daily ferry service to Santorini, Ios, Mykonos, Syros, and Naxos. There are also boats to Anaphi, Andros, Astypalea, Folegandros, Kimolos, Milos, Samos, Seriphos, Sikinos, Siphnos, Skiathos, Tinos, Salonica, and Crete. All boats to Antiparos leave from Pounda. Cruise boats leave daily from Parikia and Naousa for excursions to Delos and Mykonos.

SANTORINI

Santorini is served at least twice daily from Piraeus; from Santorini, ferries make frequent connections to the other islands—daily to Paros, Naxos, and Ios, and often Mykonos, Anaphi, Andros, Crete, Syros, Tinos, and Salonica. All ferries dock at Athinios port, where taxis and buses take passengers to Fira, Kamari, and Perissa Beach. Travelers bound for Ia take a bus to Fira and change there. Some boats stop first below Ia, from where small caïques transport passengers to waiting donkeys at the bottom of the cliff below the village. The port below Fira is used only by small steamers and cruise ships. Passengers disembarking here face a half-hour hike or they can take the cable car (or ride up on the traditional donkeys, but spare the poor things). The port police (☎ 0286/22239) can give information on ferry schedules.

By Plane

There are no airports on **Andros** or **Tinos.** Schedules change seasonally and are often revised.

MYKONOS

Some European countries now have charter flights to Mykonos. **Olympic Airways** (⌧ Mykonos, ☎ 01/966–6666) has seven flights daily to Mykonos (10 daily during peak tourist season); reservations are always a good idea. There are also summer flights between Mykonos and Heraklion (on Crete), and Rhodes. The Olympic Airways offices in Mykonos are at the port (☎ 0289/22490 or 0289/22495) and at the airport (4 km [2½ mi] southwest of Mykonos town, ☎ 0289/22327).

NAXOS

Olympic Airways has four flights daily between Athens and Naxos airport (⌧ A few miles outside Naxos town, ☎ 0285/23292). The airport is now expanding for international flights.

PAROS

Olympic Airways (⌧ Parikia, ☎ 0284/21900) has five daily flights to the **Paros airport** (⌧ Near Alyki village, 9 km [5½ mi] south of Parikia, ☎ 0284/91257) from Athens and up to seven a day in high season.

SANTORINI

Olympic Airways (⌧ Ayia Athanassiou, Fira, ☎ 0286/22493 or 0286/22793) flies six times daily to **Santorini airport** (⌧ Monolithos, on east coast, 8 km [5 mi] from Fira, ☎ 0286/31525) from Athens in peak season. In summer there are flights to Mykonos and Salonica about three times per week.

Getting Around

By Bus

ANDROS

About six buses a day from Andros town (⌧ To right of marble walkway, ☎ 0282/22316) go to and from the harbor, in conjunction with the ferry schedule; all buses stop in Batsi. Daily buses also go to and return from Stenies, Apikia, Strapouries, Pitrofos, and Korthi.

TINOS

Buses run several times daily from the quay of Chora to nearly all the many villages in Tinos (☎ 0283/22440), and in summer buses are added for beaches.

MYKONOS

In Mykonos town the Ayios Loukas station near the Olympic Airways office is for buses to Ornos, Ayios Ioannis, Plati Yialos, Psarou, the airport, and Kalamopodi. Another station near the archaeological museum is for Ayios Stefanos, Tourlos, Ano Mera, Elia, Kalafatis, and Kalo Livadi. For bus information, dial ☎ 0289/23360.

NAXOS

The bus system is reliable and fairly extensive. Daily buses go from Chora (⌧ Waterfront, ☎ 0285/22440) to Engares, Melanes, Sangri, Filoti, Apeiranthos, Koronida, and Apollonas. In summer there is added daily service to the beaches, including Ayia Anna, Pyrgaki, Ayiassos, Pachy Ammos, Ayios Mamas, and Abram. The bus office is near the dock.

From the Paros town bus station (✉ 3 mins away from the town, east of the dock, ☎ 0284/21133) there is service every hour to Naousa and less-frequent service to Alyki, Pounda, and to the beaches at Piso Livadhi, Chrissi Akti, and Drios. Schedules are posted.

SANTORINI

Buses leave from the main station in central Fira (✉ Deorgala) for Perissa and Kamari beaches, Ia, Pyrgos, and other villages. Schedules are posted.

By Caïque

On all islands, caïques leave from the main port for popular beaches and interisland trips. You can also hire a caïque (and haggle over the price, of course) for your tour of choice. For popular routes, captains have posted signs showing their destinations and departure times.

By Car, Motorbike, and Bicycle

To take cars on ferries you must make reservations. All the major islands have car- and bike-rental agencies at the ports and in the business districts. Car rentals cost about 15,000 dr./€44.24 per day, with unlimited mileage and third-party liability insurance. Full insurance costs about 2,000 dr./€5.89 a day more. Motorbikes and scooters start at 3,000 dr./€8.84 a day, including third-party liability coverage. Jeeps and dune buggies are also available in Santorini, Mykonos, Paros, Tinos, and Naxos. Choose a dealer that offers 24-hour service and a change of vehicle in case of a breakdown. Beware: too many travelers end up in Athenian hospitals owing to poor roads, slipshod maintenance, and excessive partying.

ANDROS

Though there is bus service on this large and mountainous island, it is much more convenient to travel by car. Cars can be rented at **Rent a Car Tasos** (✉ Near the ferry-boat quay Batsi opposite beach, ☎ 0282/ 71391, 0282/71040, 0282/41252, or 0282/41751). It's easiest to let Helena Prodromou of Andros Travel (✉ Near the ferry-boat quay Batsi opposite beach, ☎ 0282/71391, 0282/71040, 0282/41252, or 0282/ 41751, ℻ 0282/41608) arrange for your needs.

TINOS

Vidalis Rent-a-Car (✉ 16 Z. Alavanou, ☎ 0283/23400) and **Dimitris Rental** (✉ Alavanou, ☎ 0283/23585, ℻ 0283/22744), almost next door to each other, are reliable.

MYKONOS

No cars are permitted in town. As you descend into town from the boat, you'll see—set on the second story of a building—**Kosmos Rent-a-Car** (✉ Kaminaki, ☎ 0289/24013 and 0289/24980, ℻ 0289/24981), where Salvanos Nikiforos is helpful and efficient. There are many agencies near the windmill bus stop. Or let George Ghikas of Sunspots Travel (☞ *below*) do it for you.

NAXOS

Roads on Naxos are being asphalted one by one. Drive carefully, and you shouldn't have any problem. Car-rental outfits are concentrated in the Chora new town: try **Palladium** (✉ Chora new town, ☎ 0285/ 26200, ℻ 0285/26201) or **Rental Center** (✉ Chora, ☎ 0285/23395 or 0285/25584, ℻ 0285/23771). Or let Despina Kitini, of the Tourist Information Centre (☞ Guided Tours in Naxos *in* Contacts and Resources, *below*) do it for you.

PAROS

It is a good idea to rent a vehicle here, because the island is large; there are many beaches to choose from, and taxis are in demand. Among the many agencies near the port, George and Deirdre Skaramagas's **Iria Cars and Bikes** (⊠ Opposite the marina toward the post office, ☎ 0284/ 21232) knows what travelers want: reliability and convenience. There is a **Thrifty** car-rental desk in Polos Travel (⊠ By OTE office, ☎ 0284/ 21309) and at the airport.

SANTORINI

Extreme caution is advised on Santorini, the car- and bike-accident capital of the Cyclades; the narrow roads are extremely crowded with inexperienced (and often drunk) drivers. **Europcar** (☎ 0286/23742 Fira; 0286/33290 airport; 0286/71360 Ia) has offices in Fira, the airport, and Ia. **Budget** (☎ 0286/22900 Fira; 0286/33290 airport, ℻ 0286/ 22887) is a popular option.

By Taxi

ANDROS

Taxi stands (⊠ Off main street, near bus station in Andros town; ⊠ In Batsi at the small quayside square beneath the Dolphins restaurant; ☎ 0282/22171 for both locations).

TINOS

Taxis wait on the quay (⊠ Near central boat dock, ☎ 0283/22470).

MYKONOS

Taxi stand (☎ 0289/22400 or 0289/23700). Meters are not used; standard fares for each destination are posted on a notice bulletin board.

NAXOS

Taxi stand (⊠ Near the harbor, ☎ 0285/22444).

PAROS

Taxi stand (⊠ Across from windmill on the harbor, ☎ 0284/21500); in high season taxis are often busy.

SANTORINI

Taxi station (⊠ Near Fira's central square [25th of March St.], ☎ 0286/ 22555).

Contacts and Resources

Emergencies

ANDROS

Police (⊠ Gavrio ☎ 0282/71220; ⊠ Batsi, ☎ 0282/41204; ⊠ Andros town, ☎ 0282/22300). **Medical assistance** (⊠ Batsi, ☎ 0282/41326; ⊠ Gavrio, ☎ 0282/71210). **Health center** (⊠ Andros town, ☎ 0282/ 22222).

TINOS

Police (⊠ Chora, ☎ 0283/22255; ⊠ Pirgos, ☎ 0283/31371). **Medical assistance**: Health Center (⊠ East end of town, ☎ 0283/22210; ⊠ Isternia, ☎ 0283/31206).

MYKONOS

Police (☎ 0289/22235). **Medical assistance**: hospital (⊠ Mykonos town, ☎ 0289/23994) has 24-hour emergency service with pathologists, surgeons, pediatricians, dentists, and X-ray technicians; first aid (⊠ Ano Mera, ☎ 0289/71395).

NAXOS

Police (⊠ Chora, ☎ 0285/22100 or 0285/23280; ⊠ Filoti, ☎ 0285/ 31244). **Medical assistance**: health center (⊠ Just outside Chora, ☎

0285/23333 or 0285/23676) is open 24 hours a day; Medical Center of Naxos (✉ Quay, ☎ 0285/23234, FAX 0285/23576).

PAROS

Police (✉ Paros town, ☎ 0284/23333; ✉ Naousa, ☎ 0284/51202). **Medical Center:** Paros town health clinic (✉ Paros town, ☎ 0284/22500; ✉ Naousa, ☎ 0284/51216; ✉ Antiparos, ☎ 0284/61219).

SANTORINI

Police (✉ Fira, ☎ 0286/22649). **Medical assistance:** first aid (✉ Fira, ☎ 0286/22237; ✉ Ia, ☎ 0286/71227).

Guided Tours

ANDROS

Helena Prodromou's **Andros Travel** (✉ Batsi, ☎ 0282/412252 or 0282/41751, FAX 0282/441608) arranges coach tours and especially walking tours, from strolling to climbing. Helena, a British Cypriot, is friendly and very knowledgeable.

TINOS

Windmills Travel (✉ Above new dock, behind playground, ☎ FAX 0283/23398) runs daily guided coach tours of the island for 2,000 dr./€5.89, a variety of specialty tours by Jeep, and unguided Delos–Mykonos trips (4,000 dr./€11.79).

MYKONOS

Sunspots Travel (✉ Near airport bus stop, into town, on left, 2nd floor, ☎ 0289/24196, FAX 0289/23790) takes a group every morning for a day tour of Delos (7,500 dr./€22.12). It has half-day guided tours of the Mykonos beach towns, with a stop in Ano Mera for the Panagia Tourliani Monastery. **Windmills Travel** (✉ Fabrica, ☎ 0289/23877 or 0289/26555 through 0289/26557) runs excursions (about 6,500 dr./€19.17) to nearby Tinos, arranges private tours of Delos and Mykonos and off-road jeep trips, charters yachts, and, in fact, handles all tourist services.

NAXOS

The **Tourist Information Centre** (✉ Waterfront, ☎ 0285/22993, FAX 0285/25200), run by Despina Kitini of the Chateau Zevgoli (☞ Naxos *in* Exploring, *above*), offers round-the-island tours, and a weekly boat trip, Mykonos by Night, for 5,500 dr./€16.22 Despina can usually tell exactly what you want after a short discussion and then swiftly arrange it. **Zas Travel** (✉ Chora, ☎ 0285/23330 or 0285/23331, FAX 0285/23419; ✉ Ayios Prokopios, ☎ 0285/24780) runs two good one-day tours of the island sights with different itineraries, each costing about 4,000 dr./€11.79, and one-day trips to Delos and Mykonos (8,000 dr./€23.59), and Santorini (9,000 dr./26.54).

PAROS

A variety of trips by land and sea, such as around Antiparos, are arranged by Kostas Akalestos's **Paroikia Tours** (☎ 0284/22470 or 0284/22471, FAX 0284/22450). **Erkyna Travel** (✉ Naousa, on main square, ☎ 0284/22654 or 0284/22655; ✉ Parikia office ☎ 0284/53180, FAX 0284/22656) runs many excursions by boat, bus, and foot.

SANTORINI

Bellonias Tours (✉ Fira, ☎ 0286/22469 or 0286/23604; ✉ Kamari, ☎ 0286/31721) runs coach tours that include Akrotiri, ancient Thera, Ia, wine tastings, and churches; it also has daily boat trips to the volcano and Thirassia and arranges private tours. **Nomikos Travel** (☎ 0286/23660 or 0286/26644) has tours to the same sights, and to the island's wineries and the Monastery of Profitis Elias.

Visitor Information

ANDROS

Police station (✉ Gavrio, across from ferry dock, ☎ 0282/71220) lists available accommodations. Your best bet is to ask **Andros Travel** (✉ Batsi waterfront, opposite the beach, ☎ 0282/41252, ⻏ 0282/41608).

TINOS

For all tourist services (schedules, room bookings, tours, happenings), see friendly Sharon Turner, manager of **Windmills Travel** (✉ Above new dock behind playground, ☎ ⻏ 0283/23398); she's a gold mine of information—there's nothing she doesn't know about her adopted island.

MYKONOS

Tourist police (✉ Harbor, near departure point for Delos, ☎ 0289/22716). George Ghikas's **Sunspots Travel** (✉ Near airport bus stop, into town, on left, 2nd floor, ☎ 0289/24196, ⻏ 0289/23790) is super-efficient, with a multitude of services.

NAXOS

Despina Kitini's **Tourist Information Centre** (✉ Waterfront, ☎ 0285/24525, 0285/24358, or 0285/22993, ⻏ 0285/25200) has free booking service, bus and ferry schedules, international dialing, luggage storage, laundry service, and foreign exchange at bank rates. You can also book airline tickets and rent Kastro houses.

PAROS

For efficient and friendly service—tickets, villa rentals for families, apartments, and quality hotel reservations—try Kostas Akalestos's **Paroikia Tours** (✉ Market St., ☎ 0284/22470 or 0284/22471, ⻏ 0284/22450). Kostas, efficient and full of the Greek spirit, has many repeat customers. **Polos Tours** (✉ Next to the dockside OTE office, ☎ 0284/22092, ⻏ 02284/21983) is big, inclusive, and efficient. **Erkyna Travel** (✉ Naousa, on main square, ☎ 0284/22654 or 0284/22655, ⻏ 0284/22656) has a full range of services. They also have a Parikia office (☎ 0284/53180).

SANTORINI

Nomikos Travel (☎ 0286/23660 or 0286/22660, ⻏ 0286/23666), which has offices in Fira and Perissa, can handle most needs.

11 CRETE

To Greeks, Crete is the Megalonissi (Great Island), a hub of sophisticated ancient art and architecture, where rebellion was endemic for centuries—against Arab invaders, Venetian colonists, Ottoman pashas, and German occupiers in World War II. Mountains, split with deep gorges and honeycombed with caves, rise in sheer walls from the sea. Snowcapped peaks loom against sandy beaches, vineyards, and olive groves. As spectacular as the scenery is, it can't compare to Crete's treasure of all treasures: the Palace of Knossos—the incomparable monument of ancient Minoan culture and one of the cradles of civilization.

By Kerin Hope

Updated by
Stephen
Brewer

AROUND 1500 BC, WHILE THE REST OF EUROPE was still in the grip of primitive barbarity, one of the most brilliant and amazing civilizations the world was ever to know approached its final climax. The sophisticated elegance of King Minos's court on the island of Crete was an appropriate manifestation of imperial power patiently built up over centuries. In fact, the Minoans, prehistoric Cretans, had founded Europe's first urban culture as far back as the third millennium BC, and the island's rich legacy of art and architecture strongly influenced both mainland Greece and the Aegean islands in the Bronze Age. From around 1900 BC the Minoan palaces at Knossos (near present-day Heraklion), Mallia, Phaistos, and elsewhere were centers of political power, religious authority, and economic activity—all concentrated in one sprawling complex of buildings. Their administration seems to have had much in common with contemporary cultures in Egypt and Mesopotamia. What set the Minoans apart from the rest of the Bronze Age world was their art. It was lively and naturalistic, and they excelled in miniature techniques. dFrom the scenes illustrated on their frescoes, stone vases, seal-stones, and signet rings, it is possible to build a picture of a productive, well-regulated society. Yet new research suggests that prehistoric Crete was not a peaceful place; there may have been years of warfare before Knossos became the island's dominant power, in around 1600 BC. It is now thought that political upheaval, rather than the devastating volcanic eruption on the island of Santorini, triggered the violent downfall of the palace civilization around 1450 BC.

Vestiges of the Minoan civilization abound at Knossos, Phaistos, and many other archaeological sites around the island. In addition to enjoying miles of beaches, evocative ruins, and fascinating towns and cities, immersing oneself in the island's lifestyle can be an immense pleasure. Even in the large cities Cretans remain family oriented, rooted in tradition, and openly inviting to their visitors who want to experience the real Greece.

Pleasures and Pastimes

Bicycling

Crete is rewarding biking country. Though the rugged White Mountains of the west are for hardened addicts, there is plenty of pleasant riding in the gentler landscapes of eastern Crete on the agricultural plains near the south central coast. Bicycle rentals are available in most Cretan towns. Mountain bikes for cycling in the uplands are now easier to find, especially in Heraklion and Hania.

Bird-Watching

Bird-watchers have access to a huge variety of bird life, though most species are not indigenous. There is a bird sanctuary east of Heraklion at the Gouves estuary, which is a stopover for a large range of migratory birds. Mt. Iuktas, south of Heraklion, is the place to spot vultures.

Dining

Crete cannot claim to be a center of gastronomy, but ingredients are always fresh, and the family-run tavernas take pride in their cooking. The island produces top-quality fruit and vegetables—cherries from the Amari Valley in June, oranges from the groves around Hania in winter, tomatoes and cucumbers all year round, and, increasingly, avocados and bananas. The Cretans enjoy grilled meat, generally lamb and pork, but there is also plenty of fresh fish. Cretan *graviera* cheese is prized, along with *mizythra* (a creamy white variety). Cretan olive oil is famous throughout Greece, though it's heavier than other varieties. The island's wines are improving fast: look for Boutari Kritikos, a crisp white, and Minos Palace, a smooth red. Retsina is not part of the Cretan tradition, but it can be found in town restaurants.

In restaurants, *magirefta* (precooked dishes served at room temperature) are prepared in the morning and are best eaten at lunch. As a rule, it is hard to go hungry in Crete; in a village *kafenion* (traditional Greek coffeehouse), you can almost always order salad and an omelet or eggs fried with graviera cheese. Make sure you try the *tsikouthia* (also known as raki), the Cretan firewater, which is drunk at any hour, often accompanied by a dish of raisins, or walnuts drenched in honey. You will almost certainly eat better in a taverna or restaurant than at a hotel, where, unless you are staying at a first-class resort, the menu is usually of the bland "international" variety. Hotel desk clerks willingly recommend a choice of tavernas. Dress is invariably casual, though except in the most casual places shorts are not worn in the evening, and reservations are unnecessary unless noted. Credit cards are usually accepted only in more expensive restaurants.

CATEGORY	COST*
$$$$	over 8,000 dr. (€23.59)
$$$	5,000 dr.–8,000 dr. (€14.74–€23.59)
$$	3,000 dr.–5,000 dr. (€8.84–€14.74)
$	under 3,000 dr. (€8.84)

*per person for a three-course meal, including tax and service but excluding drinks

Lodging

Crete has luxury resort hotels with sports and entertainment facilities that compare with those anywhere in the Mediterranean. For a more authentic way to experience Crete, opt for the simple whitewashed, cement-floor rooms in mountain and seaside villages. Unfortunately, Crete also has many undistinguished, concrete-block hotels, mostly along the north coast, that defile the landscape and have little character. Some of Greece's finest hotels line the shores of Elounda Peninsula, just outside the town of Ayios Nikolaos. In the west especially, old houses, Venetian palaces, and 19th-century mansions are being sensitively restored as small hotels. Hania has several such hotels, and they are excellent.

Unless the months of closing are noted, all hotels are open year-round. Prices rise in July and come down again in mid-September, but even in high season you can often negotiate a discount at medium-price hotels if you are staying more than a night or two. Resort hotels sometimes require half-board (MAP); many will give substantial discounts at the beginning and end of the season. If you are staying in Hania or Heraklion in July or August, you may want to pay a little more for a room with air-conditioning. You should assume that hotels of $$$$ and $$$ rating will have air-conditioning; air-conditioning is noted when available at less-expensive establishments. Travel agencies, the local Greek National Tourist Organization (GNTO or EOT) offices, and the tourist police all will help you find accommodation at short notice. In villages, ask at the kafenion about rooms for rent. Standards of cleanliness are high in Crete, and service is almost always friendly.

CATEGORY	COST*
$$$$	over 25,000 dr. (€73.74)
$$$	14,000 dr.–25,000 dr. (€41.29–€73.74)
$$	9,000 dr.–14,000 dr. (€26.54–€41.29)
$	under 9,000 dr. (€26.54)

*All prices are for a standard double room including breakfast, service, and tax.

✍ following the text of a review is your signal that the property has a Web site, where you will find details and, usually, images; for a link, visit www.fodors.com/urls.

Nightlife and the Arts

An evening out in Crete can pleasantly be spent in a *kentron* (a taverna that features traditional Cretan music and dancing). The star performer is the *lyra* player, who can extract a surprisingly subtle sound from the small pear-shape instrument, held upright on the thigh and played with a bow. Cretan dances range from monotonous circling to astonishing displays of athletic agility, but much depends on the *kefi* (enthusiasm) of the participants. In winter, the kentron moves indoors and becomes a more typical bouzouki joint. Ask at your hotel where the best-known lyra players are performing. Throughout the warmer months, almost every town and village celebrates the feast of its patron saint with a *panayiria* (celebration), with food, drink, and traditional music and dancing usually lasting until dawn. If you are lucky, you may be invited to a *glendi* (local party), or even a traditional Cretan wedding, where the celebrations can last 24 hours.

Crete has few serious arts activities and events. Though the island attracts painters from all over Europe, they rarely exhibit locally. In Heraklion, Rethymnon, and, occasionally, Hania, however, local authorities sometimes organize concerts, theater, and folk dancing events during the summer. Athenian and even some foreign musical groups stage open-air performances in the Koules fort at Heraklion and the Fortessa at Rethymnon. Ask at the EOT offices for up-to-date booking information (☞ Visitor Information *in* Crete A to Z, *below*). In winter, both local and visiting choirs and chamber-music groups perform occasionally. The town hall will have information on times and bookings.

Shopping

Crete is a serendipitous place for the shopper. Little serious attempt has been made to adapt the island's traditional crafts to the demands of foreign customers, but by poking around the backstreets of Heraklion, Rethymnon, and Hania, you can find things both useful and exotic— and sometimes even beautiful. Crete was famous even in Minoan times for its weaving. You still occasionally come across the heavy scarlet-embroidered blankets and bedspreads that formed the basis of a traditional dowry chest. Woven wool rugs in plain geometric designs from the village of Axos on the slopes of Mt. Ida are attractive, as are heavy sweaters in natural oily wool. All the villages on the Lasithi plateau have shops selling embroidered linens, made in front of the stove during the long winter months. All over the island, local craftsmen produce attractive copies of Minoan jewelry in gold and silver, as well as some with original modern designs. A shepherd's kit, a striped woven haversack, and a staff are useful for the hiker. Boot makers in Heraklion and Hania will make you a pair of heavy Cretan leather knee boots to order. A Cretan knife, whether plain steel or with a decorated blade and handle, makes a handy kitchen or camping implement. In the village of Thrapsano, 20 km (12½ mi) southeast of Heraklion, at one of the potteries you can choose a new *pithos* (the tall Ali Baba–style jar used by the Minoans for storing wine and oil and still popular today, often as a flowerpot); have it air-freighted home.

Water Sports

Water-sports enthusiasts will find Windsurfers available for rent on any beach frequented by tourists. Scuba diving, snorkeling, dinghy sailing, and yachting are available at large resort hotels or can be arranged through local travel agencies. As is the case elsewhere in Greece, diving is strictly limited because of the presence of underwater antiquities; local tourist boards can provide details.

Exploring Crete

From the glossy beach resorts along the north coast—with the faint echoes of Minoan hedonism in their stunning settings—to the backpackers' haunts in the south, from frescoed Byzantine churches deep in the countryside to beaches reachable only by boat, there are destinations on Crete to suit every tourist's taste. English is spoken widely.

Crete is a long narrow island, and therefore as a matter of convenience most visitors tend to approach it in halves. Western Crete is especially rugged, with inland mountains and the equally craggy southern shoreline; some of the best beaches on the island are on the western coast, surrounding the town of Falasarna. Hania and Rethymnon, both lovely, mysterious old cities that trace their roots to the Arab and Venetian worlds, are here in the west. The east begins at Crete's largest town, Heraklion, and most important archaeological site, Knossos, and includes many of its most developed resorts. In both the east and the west of Crete, you'll find the most development on the north shore, while for the most part the southern coast remains blessedly unspoiled.

Numbers in the text correspond to numbers in the margin and on the Eastern Crete, Heraklion, Palace of Knossos, Palace of Mallia, Western Crete, and Palace of Phaistos maps.

Great Itineraries

Although Crete is a large island, in the north, at least, it is crossed by a good highway and serviced by a good bus system. Even on a one-day stopover you can see the greatest of the island's Minoan sights, though beware: you will be tempted to stay longer. A three-day tour allows you to taste the pleasures of Heraklion and the cities of western Crete, and seven days will allow time to see most of the major towns and sights on a circular tour of the island.

IF YOU HAVE 1 DAY

Many visitors stop off in Crete for only a day, often en route from Santorini to Rhodes. This stopover doesn't allow much time, but you can begin in 🔧 **Heraklion** ①–⑬ with a visit to the **archaeological museum** ⑬, with its stunning displays of Minoan culture, then move on to the island's largest and most well-preserved Minoan sight, the **Palace of Knossos** ⑭–㉔. In the afternoon, make the hour-long trip to the **Palace of Phaistos** ㊻, another great Minoan site overlooking the south coast, and before returning to Heraklion.

IF YOU HAVE 3 DAYS

🔧 **Heraklion** ①–⑬ is the best starting point for a visit to the island. Spend one day visiting that city, its archaeological museum, and the **Palace of Knossos** ⑭–㉔. From there, follow the north coast west to the city of **Rethymnon** ㊾, with its Venetian and Arab heritage, and later in the afternoon travel on to 🔧 **Hania** ㊿, one of the most beautiful cities in Greece and, with its gorgeous harbor and fascinating old town, a delightful place to spend an evening. En route back to Heraklion, drive south from Rethymnon to the Minoan **Palace of Phaistos** ㊻, returning for the night to Heraklion.

IF YOU HAVE 7 DAYS

A week allows time to see all of Crete, if not exactly at leisure, at least at an enjoyable pace. The place to begin is 🔧 **Heraklion** ①–⑬, where a stay of a day and a night allows enough time to see the city, the archaeological museum, and the **Palace of Knossos** ⑭–㉔. From there you can explore the island on a more or less circular tour. However, since there is no road directly across the south shore, you will return to the north shore frequently as you travel. As you head east from Heraklion, your first stop is the **Lasithi plateau** ㉕, where you'll get a taste of one of the most scenic corners of rural Crete. After lunch there, you'll want to return to the north shore and, after a stop (via the 20-year-old north coast road still labeled NEW ROAD) at the Minoan ruins at the **Palace of Mallia** ㉗, continue on to **Ayios Nikolaos** ㉘. The nearby peninsula, ⛯ **Elounda** ㉙, with its fine hotels and wonderful views of the Gulf of Mirabello, is an excellent place to stay. The next day head south to the Minoan city of **Gournia** ㉞, and continue on to **Ierapetra** ㊺. After lunch and maybe a swim, it's back up to the north coast to ⛯ **Siteia** ㊳. The next morning you'll want an early start to the beautiful beach at **Vai** ㊵. The afternoon is devoted to driving, all the way to ⛯ **Rethymnon** ㊴ on the western side of the island; however, the distance is only a little more than 200 km (120 mi), and the highway along the north coast is wide and well paved. After an evening in Rethymnon, preferably staying in the charming old town, make the short trip on to ⛯ **Hania** ㊾. You may want to spend two nights here, allowing time to see the city and to explore the area. You might, for instance, want to take a day trip to the **Samaria Gorge,** to the beaches in the far west, or to the rugged southern coast around Paleochora or Hora Sfakion. From Hania take the long route back to Heraklion, making a loop south at Rethymnon to visit the Minoan **Palace at Phaistos** ㊻, then turning back to the north coast.

When to Tour

The best times for visiting Crete are April and May, when every outcrop of rock is ablaze with brilliant wildflowers, or October, when the sea is still warm and the light golden but piercingly clear. In July and August the main Minoan sites and the coastal towns come close to overflowing. Such places as Mallia and Limin Hersonissos, hideously developed towns where bars and pizzerias fill up with heavy-drinking northern Europeans, should be avoided especially in summer and in any other season as well. Driving can be especially hazardous in July and August amid the profusion of buses, jeeps, and motorbikes, not to mention the impatient Cretan drivers.

EASTERN CRETE

Eastern Crete includes the towns and cities of Heraklion, Ayios Nikolaos, Siteia, and Ierapetra, as well as the archaeological sites of Knossos and Gournia. Of course, many natural wonders lie between these man-made places, including the palm-fringed beach at Vai and the stunning Elounda Peninsula.

Heraklion

175 km (108¾ mi) south of Piraeus, 78 km (48½ mi) east of Rethymnon, 69 km (43 mi) west of Ayios Nikolaos.

The narrow, crowded alleys and thick stone ramparts of Heraklion, Crete's largest city and the fourth-largest city in Greece, recall the days when soldiers and merchants clung to the safety of a fortified port. In Minoan times, this was a harbor for Knossos, the largest palace and effective power center of prehistoric Crete. But the Bronze Age remains were built over long ago, and now Heraklion, with more than 120,000 inhabitants, stretches far beyond even the Venetian walls. In any event, any student interested in Minoan civilization and the Palace of Knossos makes this city an obligatory stop because of its renowned archaeological museum.

Eastern Crete

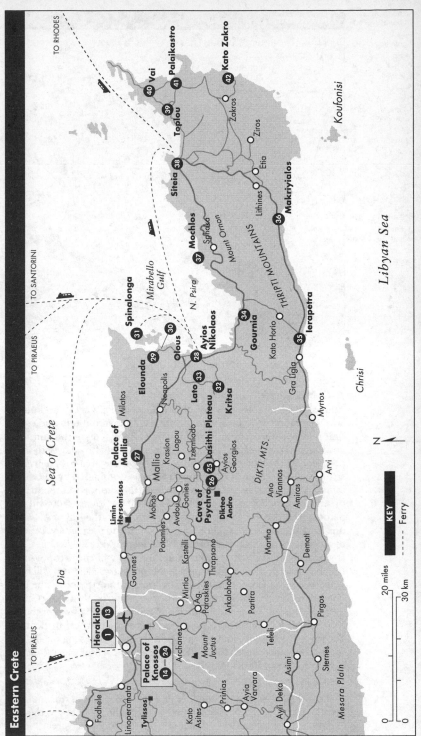

TO RHODES

Vai **40**
Palaikastro **41**
Kato Zakro **42**
Toplou
39
Zakros
Ziros
Etia
Siteia **38**
Mochlos
37
Sfaka
Mount Ornon
Lithines
Makriyialos **36**
N. Psira
THRIPTI MOUNTAINS
Libyan Sea

Mirabello Gulf
Spinalonga
31
30
29 Olous **28**
Elounda
Neapolis
Milatos
Ayios Nikolaos
Gournia **34**
Kato Horio
Ierapetra **35**
Gra Ligia
Myrtos
Arvi
Chrisi
Lato **33**
32 Kritsa
Lasithi Plateau
Izermiado
Logou
Krasion
Palace of Mallia **27**
Mallia
Limin Hersonissos
Mohos
Cave of Psychro **26** **25** Ayios Georgios
Dikteo Andro
Potamies
Avdou
Gonies
DIKTI MTS.
Ano Viannos
Amiras
Demati
Gournes
Miria
Kastelli
Thrapsano
Ag. Paraskies
Arkalohori
Martha
Pirgos
Sternes
Mesara Plain
TO PIRAEUS
Heraklion **1 — 13**
Palace of Knossos **14 — 24**
Archanes
Mount Juctus
Prinias
Ayia Varvara
Kalo Asites
Tefeli
Asimi
Ayii Deka
Fodhele
Linoperamata
Tylissos
Partira
TO SANTORINI
TO PIRAEUS
Sea of Crete
Dia

KEY
- - - - Ferry

20 miles
30 km

N

Heraklion

A Good Walk

You can nicely explore the compact old town in a walk of an hour or two, beginning at **Ta Leontaria** ① with its famous fountain and cathedral of **Ayios Markos** ②. As you follow Odos 1866 south from here, you will be in the heart of Heraklion's market—busy by day with shoppers, at night with residents who converge on the area for an evening stroll. The market ends in **Kornarou Square,** dominated by two fountains: one Turkish (which now actually is the site for a café) and the other Venetian. If you follow Vikela Street off the square, you will pass many of Heraklion's most famous churches: the cathedral of **Ayios Minas** ⑨, dedicated to Heraklion's patron saint, and the medieval church of the same name, then the church of **Ayia Aikaterina** ⑩, where El Greco is said to have studied. At Ayia Ekaterini you will come to Leoforos Kalokerinou, another major shopping thoroughfare; a left turn will bring you back to Ta Leontaria. If you now proceed north across the busy intersection, you will come to another remnant of Venetian occupation, the **Loggia** ③, then the church of **Ayios Titos** ④, named for the patron saint of Crete. You are now within sight of the fortifications known as the **Koules** ⑤ and the inner harbor. By following the old city walls, you will come to the famed **Archaeological Museum** ⑬ and the café-filled **Platia Eleftherias** ⑫.

Sights to See

★ ⑬ **Archaeological Museum.** Standing in a class of its own, this museum guards many of the Minoan treasures brought to light by the legendary excavations of the Palace of Knossos and other great monuments of Cretan culture. The civilization of 3,000 years is superbly illustrated by a unique collection of pottery and jewelry, including the famous seal-stones with Linear B script, which first attracted Sir Arthur Evans's attention. Yet it is the frescoes, restored fragments found in Knossos, that most catch the eye: delightfully sophisticated representations of broad-shouldered, slim-waisted youths, their large eyes fixed with an enigmatic expression on the Prince of the Lilies; ritual processions and scenes from the bullring, young men and maidens somersaulting over the back of a charging bull; and groups of bare-breasted court ladies, whose puffed sleeves and flounced skirts led a French archaeologist to exclaim in surprise, "des Parisiennes," a name still applied to this striking fresco.

The museum is best visited early in the morning before tourist buses start disgorging their passengers; happily, installation of air-conditioning has been recently completed, and all galleries are open. The Minoan collection compares to that in any of the great museums of western Europe. Even before the great palaces were built, around 1900 BC, the prehistoric Cretans excelled at metalworking and in carving stone vases, such as that seen in Gallery I in the box with a lid whose handle is in the shape of a lazing dog. They were also skilled at producing fine pottery, such as the eggshell-thin Kamares ware decorated in delicate abstract designs (in Gallery III), and miniature work such as the superbly crafted jewelry (in Galleries VI and VII) and the colored seal-stones (in Gallery III) that are carved with lively scenes of people and animals.

Though naturalism and an air of informality distinguish much Minoan art from that of contemporary Bronze Age cultures elsewhere in the eastern Mediterranean, you will also see a number of heavy, rococo set pieces, such as the fruit stand with a toothed rim and the punch bowl with appliquéd flowers (both in Gallery III). The Linear B script, inscribed on clay tablets (Gallery V), is now recognized as an early form of Greek, but the earlier Linear A script (Gallery V) and that of the Phaistos Disk (Gallery III) have yet to be deciphered. The Minoans' talents at modeling in stone, ivory, and a kind of glass paste known to archaeologists as faience peaked in the later palace period (1700 BC–1450 BC). A famous rhyton (vase for pouring libations) carved from dark serpentine in the shape of a bull's head has eyes made of red jasper and clear rock crystal with horns of gilded wood (Gallery IV). An ivory acrobat—perhaps a bull-leaper—and two bare-breasted faience goddesses in flounced skirts holding wriggling snakes (both Gallery IV) were among a group of treasures hidden beneath the floor of a storeroom at Knossos. Bull-leaping, whether religious rite or a favorite sport, inspired some memorable Minoan art. Three vases of serpentine (probably covered originally in gold leaf) from Ayia Triada (Gallery VII) are carved with scenes of Minoan life thought to be rendered by artists from Knossos: boxing matches, a harvest-home ceremony, and a Minoan official taking delivery of a consignment of hides. The most stunning rhyton of all, from Zakro, is made of rock crystal (Gallery VIII). Commodities were stored in the palaces: an elephant tusk and bronze ingots (Gallery VIII) were found at Zakro and Ayia Triada. Make sure to save some time and energy for the fresco galleries upstairs. Dating from the later palace period, they show both the Minoans' preoccupation with religious ritual and enjoyment of their island's natural beauties. ⊠ *Platia Eleftherias,* ☏ *081/226092.* ▩ *1,500 dr.€4.42.* ☉ *Apr.–mid-Oct., Mon. 12:30–7, Tues.–Sun. 8–7; mid-Oct.–Mar., daily 8–5.*

❿ **Ayia Aikaterina.** Nestled in the shadow of the Ayios Minas cathedral, this is one of Crete's most attractive small churches. Built in 1555, it is now a **museum of icons** by Cretan artists, who traveled to Venice to study with Italian Renaissance painters. Look for six icons (Nos. 2, 5, 8, 9, 12, and 15) by Michael Damaskinos, who worked in both Byzantine and Renaissance styles in the 16th century. ⊠ *Kyrillou Loukareos.* ▩ *500 dr./€1.47.* ☉ *Mon. and Wed–Sat. 9:30–1.*

2 Ayios Markos. This 13th-century church (now an exhibition center) is named for Venice's patron saint, but, with its modern portico and narrow interior, it bears little resemblance to its grand namesake in Venice. ⊠ *Eleftheriou Venizelou.*

9 Ayios Minas. This is a huge, lofty, but ultimately unprepossessing 19th-century cathedral. ⊠ *Kyrillou Loukareos, main road west from Platia Cornarou.*

4 Ayios Titos. As you head north toward the harbor, you'll pass this church, named for Crete's patron saint. A **chapel** to the left of the entrance contains the saint's skull, set in a silver-and-gilt reliquary. Ayios Titos is credited with converting the islanders to Christianity in the 1st century AD on the instructions of St. Paul. ⊠ *Set back from 25th of August St.*

7 Historical Museum of Crete. Once known as the Historical and Ethnological Museum, this is housed in an imposing mansion and contains a varied collection of early Christian and Byzantine sculptures in the basement and several rooms filled with Venetian and Ottoman stonework. Look out for a splendid **lion of St. Mark,** with an inscription that says in Latin I PROTECT THE KINGDOM OF CRETE, and some striking tombstones of Ottoman officials, topped with stone turbans. Left of the entrance is a room stuffed with memorabilia from Crete's bloody revolutionary past: weapons, portraits of mustachioed warrior chieftains, and the flag of the short-lived independent Cretan state set up in 1898. The 19th-century banner in front of the staircase sums up the spirit of Cretan rebellion against the Turks: ELEFTHERIA I THANATOS (Freedom or Death). Upstairs, look in on a room arranged as the study of Crete's most famous writer, Nikos Kazantzakis, the author of *Zorba the Greek* and an epic poem, *The Odyssey, a Modern Sequel.* The top floor contains a stunning collection of **Cretan textiles,** including the brilliant scarlet weavings typical of the island's traditional handwork, and another room arranged as a comfortable domestic interior of the early 1900s. ⊠ *Odos Kalokorinou, off western coast road near the Xenia Hotel,* ☎ *081/283219.* 🎫 *1,000 dr./€2.94.* ⊙ *Weekdays 9–5, Sat. 9–2.*

5 Koules. This Turkish-named miniature fortress dominates Heraklion's **inner harbor.** Fishing boats land their catch and yachts are now moored at what was once the city's Venetian port. To the right rise the tall vaulted tunnels of the arsenal; here, Venetian galleys were repaired and refitted, and timber, cheeses, and sweet malmsey wine were loaded for the three-week voyage to Venice. The Koules was built by the Venetians, and three stone lions of St. Mark, symbol of Venetian imperialism, decorate the exterior. The view from its battlements takes in both the outer harbor, where freighters and passenger ferries drop anchor, and the sprawling labyrinth of concrete apartment blocks that is modern Heraklion. To the south rises Mt. Iuktas and to the west, the pointed peak of Mt. Stromboli. ⊠ *Inner harbor, end of 25th of August St.,* ☎ *081/288484.* 🎫 *500 dr./€1.47.* ⊙ *Tues.–Sun. 8:30–3.*

3 Loggia. A gathering place for the island's Venetian nobility, this loggia was built in the early 17th century by Francesco Basilicata, an Italian architect. Recently restored to its original Palladian elegance, it adjoins the old Venetian Armory, now the City Hall. ⊠ *25th of August St.*

NEED A BREAK?

There are two ***bougatsa* shops** (⊠ Eleftheriou Venizelou), side by side, where you can stop for this envelope of flaky pastry stuffed with a sweet, creamy filling dusted with cinnamon and sugar, or with soft white cheese. A double portion served warm with Greek coffee is a nice change from a hotel breakfast, especially if you've just arrived off the ferry from Piraeus.

⑪ **Martinengo Bastion.** The largest of six bastions shaped like arrowheads jutting out from the well-preserved Venetian walls, the Martinengo was designed by Micheli Sanmicheli as one of the bastions built in the 16th century to keep out Barbary pirates and Turkish invaders. When the Turks finally overran Crete in 1648, the garrison at Heraklion held out for another 21 years in one of the longest sieges in European history. General Francesco Morosini finally surrendered the city to the Turkish Grand Vizier in September 1669. He was allowed to sail home to Venice with the city's archives and such precious relics as the skull of Ayios Titos—which was not returned until 1966. Literary pilgrims come to the Martinengo to visit the **burial place of Kazantzakis.** The grave is a plain stone slab marked by a weathered wooden cross. The inscription, from his writings, says: I FEAR NOTHING, I HOPE FOR NOTHING, I AM FREE. ⊠ *South of Kyrillou Loukareos on N. G. Mousourou.*

⑧ **Platia Cornarou.** This square is graced with a Venetian fountain and an elegant Turkish stone kiosk. Fruit and vegetable stalls alternate with butchers' displays of whole lambs and pigs' feet at the lively **open-air market** on Odos 1866. ⊠ *At top of Odos 1866, south of Ta Leontaria and across Kalokairinous.*

⑫ **Platia Eleftherias.** Sometimes called Treis Kamares, this is the city's biggest square. Daidalou, which follows the line of an early fortification wall, is now a pedestrian walkway lined with tavernas, boutiques, jewelers, and souvenir shops. ⊠ *At end of Daidalou St., one street east of Ta Leontaria, just south of Ayios Markos.*

⑥ **St. Peter's church.** Only a shell now remains of this medieval church, which was heavily damaged during World War II in the bombing before the German invasion in 1941. ⊠ *West of harbor along the seashore road.*

① **Ta Leontaria.** The centerpiece of Heraklion's town center—Eleftherious Venizelous Square, a triangular pedestrian zone filled with cafés—this stately marble Renaissance fountain, called "the Lions," remains a beloved town landmark. The square is named after the Cretan statesman who united the island with Greece in 1913. But for hundreds of years before then it had been the heart of the colony founded in the 13th century, when Venice bought Crete, and Heraklion became an important port of call on the trade routes to the Middle East. The city, and often the whole island, known then as Candia, was ruled by the Duke of Crete, a Venetian administrator. ⊠ *Eleftheriou Venizelou.*

Dining and Lodging

$$ ✕ **Kyriakos.** With its pink tablecloths and green chairs, this is no ordinary taverna. On the road to Knossos (☞ *below*), Kyriakos offers a handy and pleasant spot for a post- or pre-sightseeing meal with its wide range of well-prepared salads, grills, and fish dishes. Watch for seasonal Cretan specialties, such as snail stew in summer and *volvi* (baked iris bulbs in olive oil and vinegar) in spring. There is a good wine list, with Cretan and mainland wines. ⊠ *Leoforos Dimokratias 43,* ☎ *081/224649. AE, DC, V.*

$ ✕ **Terzakis.** This unassuming establishment is one of Heraklion's most popular *mezedopolio* (a *meze* joint), in which you choose half dozen or more dishes from a long list of fish, dips, and salads. Traditionally mezes are accompanied by ouzo, but beer or wine is equally acceptable. ⊠ *Loh. Marineli 17, behind Ayios Dimitrios church,* ☎ *081/221444. No credit cards. No dinner Sun.*

$ ✗ **Yacoumis.** This hole-in-the-wall is reputed to be the best of the small restaurants in the covered Meat Alley: follow the aroma of roasting meat and clouds of steam wafting out between the stalls. Sizzling chunks of spit-roasted lamb and pork are sold by weight, accompanied by salads of roughly sliced tomatoes and onions, drenched in thick Cretan olive oil. ⊠ *Meat alley, leading off market.* ☎ *No phone. No credit cards. Closed Sun.*

$$$ ▦ **Astoria Capsis.** Conveniently located opposite the Archaeological Museum in the liveliest area of the city, this recently refurbished hotel has delightful, modern-style rooms decorated in cool shades and furnished with sleek blond wood; it has a rooftop swimming pool, as well as a delightful poolside bar, and it is fully air-conditioned. ⊠ *Platia Eleftherias, 71201,* ☎ *081/229002,* FAX *081/229078. 120 rooms. Restaurant, bar, coffee shop, pool. AE, DC, MC, V.*

$$ ▦ **El Greco.** What is probably Heraklion's best moderately priced hotel is right in the center of town, just steps from the Ta Leontaria fountain. The rooms are simply but handsomely furnished, and all have balconies that overlook the street or a nicely planted interior garden. Since the word is out about what a bargain this is, it's best to reserve well in advance. ⊠ *1821 St. 4, 71202,* ☎ *081/281071,* FAX *081/281072. 90 rooms. DC, MC, V.*

$ ▦ **Daedalos.** On a pedestrian street in the city center, this small hotel is decidedly shabby but extremely friendly. The owner, Takis Stoumbidis, used to run an art gallery, and the rooms and corridors are lined with Cretan landscapes. The ground-floor bar is a local gathering place, where you may run into a distinguished archaeologist or folklorist downing a glass of tsikouthia. Be sure to ask for a room that does not face the street, which is loud with merrymakers into the wee hours. ⊠ *Daidalou 15, 71202,* ☎ *081/244812,* FAX *081/244391. 58 rooms. DC, MC, V.*

Outdoor Activities and Sports

BICYCLING

Bicycle rentals are available in all Cretan towns. Mountain bikes for cycling in the uplands are now easier to find. To rent a bike in Heraklion, ask at the **Creta Travel** (⊠ Epimenidou 20–22, ☎ 081/227002).

Shopping

BOOKSTORES

In Heraklion, you can find **English-language books** at **Kouvidis-Manouras** (⊠ Daidalou 6, ☎ 081/220135) or **Astrakianakis** (⊠ Eleftheriou Venizelou, ☎ 081/284248). **Newspapers and magazines** are available in Platia Venizelou.

Palace of Knossos

★ *180 km (111¾ mi) south of Piraeus, 5 km (3 mi) south of Heraklion.*

The palace of Knossos belonged to King Minos, who kept the Minotaur, a hybrid monster of man and bull, in an underground labyrinth.

Only the intuition of the great Hermann Schliemann, father of archaeology and discoverer of Troy, would have suspected that the huge mound hemmed in by low hills that once stood here covered one of the most amazing archaeological sites. Troy and Mycenae, Tiryns and Knossos—what a record of sensational finds, yet Turkish obstruction prevented Schliemann from exploring his last discovery. Cretan independence made it possible for Sir Arthur Evans to start excavations in 1899, and a forgotten and sublime civilization came again to light with the uncovering of the great Palace of Knossos. Its site had actually been occupied from Neolithic times, and the population spread to the sur-

Palace of Knossos

0   40 yards
0   40 meters

rounding land. Around 1900 BC, the hilltop was leveled and the first palace constructed; around 1700 BC, after an earthquake destroyed it, the later palace was built, surrounded by houses and other buildings. Around 1450 BC, another widespread disaster occurred, perhaps an invasion: palaces and country villas were razed by fire and abandoned, and though Knossos remained inhabited, the palace suffered some damage. But around 1380 BC the palace and its outlying buildings were destroyed by fire, and at the end of the Bronze Age, the site was abandoned. Still later, Knossos became a Greek city-state. Fine houses with mosaic floors and statuary have been excavated. Evidence of the Minoan civilization was unearthed in the early 1900s, when Crete had just achieved independence after centuries of foreign rule by Venice and then by the Ottoman Turks.

You enter the palace from the west, passing a **bust of Sir Arthur Evans,** the British archaeologist who excavated at Knossos on and off for more than 20 years after 1900. Opinions vary about his concrete restorations and copies of the **frescoes.** But without his reconstructions of the wonderfully theatrical great staircase and the throne room, it would be impossible to experience, even at second hand, the ambience of a Minoan palace, with its long pillared halls, narrow corridors, deep stairways and light wells, and curious reverse-tapering columns. But the restorations themselves are in need of renovation; some areas of the palace are now closed off. A path leads you around to the monumen- tal **south gateway;** the **west wing** encases lines of long, narrow storerooms where the true wealth of Knossos was kept in tall clay jars: oil, wine, grains, and honey. The **central court,** about 164 ft by 82 ft, lies before the cool, dark **throne room complex,** with its griffin fresco and tall, wavy-back gypsum throne. It is a spectacular sight to see the oldest throne in Europe, still standing on its original site.

⑱ The most spectacular piece of palace architecture is the **Grand Staircase,** on the east side of the court, leading to the domestic apartments. Four flights of shallow gypsum stairs survive, lighted by a deep light well. Here you get a sense of how noble Minoans lived; rooms were divided by sets of double doors, giving privacy and warmth when closed,
⑲ coolness and communication when open. The **Queen's Megaron** (apartment) is decorated with copies of the colorful Dolphin fresco and furnished with stone benches. Beside it is a bathroom, complete with a clay tub, and next door a toilet, whose drainage system permitted flushing into a channel flowing into the Kairatos stream far below. The east side
⑳ of the palace also contained **workshops.** Beside the staircase leading down
㉑ to the **east bastion** is a stone water channel made up of parabolic curves and settling basins: a Minoan storm drain. Northwest of the east bas-
㉒ tion is the **north entrance,** guarded by a relief fresco of a charging bull.
㉓ Beyond is the **theatrical area,** shaded by pines and overlooking a shal-
㉔ low flight of steps, which lead down to the **Royal Road.** This was perhaps the ceremonial entrance to the palace. In the end, a visit to the Palace of Knossos, resurrecting past splendor, can be one of the unforgettable experiences for all students of western civilization. ⊠ *Site,* ☎ *081/231940.* 🎟 *1,500 dr./€4.42.* ☉ *Summer, daily 8–7; winter, daily 8:30–3. Bus 2 leaves every 15 mins from Odos Evans, close to the market.* ☜

Lasithi Plateau

㉕ *52 km (32¼ mi) southeast of Heraklion, 47 km (29¼ mi) southeast of the Palace of Knossos.*

The Lasithi plateau, 2,800 ft high and the biggest of the upland plains of Crete, lies behind a wall of barren mountains. Covered with mechanical windmills pumping water for fields of potatoes and the apple and almond orchards that are a pale haze of blossom in early spring, the Lasithi plateau is remote and breathtakingly beautiful. It is ringed by small villages that in winter are sometimes cut off from the outside world by heavy snowfalls. It appears that the villagers spend these long winter months weaving and doing embroidery, and their handicrafts are for sale at shops in almost every village on the plateau.

㉖ The **Cave of Psychro** is an impressive, stalactite-studded cavern that was once a Minoan sanctuary. It's where Zeus, the king of the gods, was supposedly born, and it is well worth a visit. ⊠ *Descend slippery path near village of Psychro.* 🎟 *800 dr./€2.35.* ☉ *Daily 8–5.*

Dining

$ ✕ **Kronio.** The promise of a meal in this cozy, family-run establishment is alone worth the trip up to the plateau. A delicious array of meat and vegetable pies and homemade casseroles and lamb dishes emerges from the kitchen, and the charming young proprietors, Vassilis and Christine, will encourage you to linger over your wine and raki. ⊠ *Lasithi plateau,* ☎ *0844/22375. No credit cards. Closed Nov.–Mar.*

Mallia

37 km (23 mi) east of Heraklion.

In its effort to serve mass tourism, Mallia has also submerged whatever character it might once have had. Its sandy beach, overlooked by the brooding Lasithi mountains, is backed by a solid line of hotels and vacation apartments. Mallia itself may not be worth a visit, but the Mi-
㉗ noan **Palace of Mallia** on its outskirts definitely is. Like Knossos and Phaistos, it was built around 1900 BC, but it was less sophisticated both in architecture and decoration. The layout, however, is similar. Across the west court, along one of the paved raised walkways, is a double row

of **round granaries** sunk into the ground, which were almost certainly roofed. East of the granaries is the **south doorway,** from which to see the large, circular limestone table, or *kernos* (on which were placed offerings to a Minoan deity), with a large hollow at its center and 34 smaller ones around the edge. The **central court** has a shallow pit at its center, perhaps the location of an altar. To the west of the central court are the remains of an imposing **staircase** leading up to a second floor, and a terrace, most likely used for religious ceremonies; behind is a long corridor with **storerooms** to the side. In the north wing is a large **pillared hall,** part of a set of public rooms. The **domestic apartments** appear to have been in the northwest corner of the palace, entered through a narrow dogleg passage. They are connected by a smaller **northern court,** through which you can leave the palace by the **north entrance,** passing two giant pithoi. Much excavation has been done nearby, but only a few of the sites are open. ⊠ *3 km (2 mi) northeast of Mallia,* ☎ *0841/ 22462.* 🖃 *800 dr./€3.35.* ☉ *Tues.–Sun. 8:30–2:30.*

Ayios Nikolaos

★ ㉘ *69 km (43 mi) east of Heraklion, 32 km (20 mi) southeast of Mallia.*

Ayios Nikolaos, built just over a century ago by Cretans from the southwest of the island, is clustered around the **Gulf of Mirabello,** a dramatic composition of bare mountains, islets, and deep blue sea. Behind the crowded harbor lies a natural curiosity, tiny Lake Voulismeni, linked to the sea by a narrow channel. The **archaeological museum** at Ayios Nikolaos displays some unique finds, such as the *Goddess of Myrtos,* an early Minoan rhyton from a site on the southeast coast. The goddess is an appealing figure cradling a large jug in her spindly arms. There are also fine examples of late Minoan pottery in the naturalistic marine style, with lively octopus and shell designs. ⊠ *Odos Palaiologou,* ☎ *0841/24943.* 🖃 *800 dr./€2.35.* ☉ *Tues.–Sun. 8:30–3.*

Dining

$ ✕ **Itanos Restaurant.** This old-fashioned taverna, with a formal arrangement of palm trees at its center, is patronized by locals, as it offers much better value than the establishments on the seafront. The wine comes from a row of barrels in the kitchen. In summer you dine on a terrace with a view of the town's comings and goings in the square below. The *tsoutzoukakia* (oven-cooked meatballs) are tender and spicy, and vegetable dishes such as braised artichokes or green beans with tomato are full of flavor. ⊠ *Platia Iroon,* ☎ *0841/25340. No credit cards.*

Elounda

㉙ *80 km (49¾ mi) east of Heraklion, 11 km (7 mi) north of Ayios Nikolaos.*

A narrow corniche road with spectacular sea views runs north from Ayios Nikolaos around the Gulf of Mirabello to Elounda. This is not an area renowned for beaches, which tend to be narrow and pebbly, but the water is crystal clear and sheltered from the *meltemi* (the fierce north wind that blows in summer). Elounda village is becoming a full-scale resort, serving the dozens of villas and apartment hotels dotting the surrounding hillsides. You can escape the crowds in Elounda by

㉚ following signs for **Olous,** 3 km (2 mi) east of Elounda, an ancient city whose sunken remains are still visible beneath the sea as you cross a causeway to Spinalonga.

Dining and Lodging

$$ ✕ **Marilena.** If the scenery alone doesn't lure you out to the village of Elounda, this delightful family-run restaurant might. In good weather,

meals are served in the large rear garden, although you can also choose a table on a sidewalk terrace overlooking the harbor. The Gaitanos brothers serve an excellent selection of fresh grilled fish and a rich fish soup, and any meal should begin with a platter of assorted appetizers. ⊠ *Elounda Village,* ☎ FAX *0841/41322. MC, V.*

$$$$ 🏨 **Elounda Beach.** This is one of Greece's most renowned resort hotels, set in 40 acres of gardens looking across the Mirabello Gulf. It has inspired imitations on a half dozen other Aegean islands. The architecture reflects Cretan tradition: whitewashed walls, shady porches, and cool flagstone floors. You can have a room in the central block or a bungalow at the edge of the sea; 11 of the suites have their own swimming pool. The hotel has two sandy beaches and a wide range of beach and water sports, including scuba diving. ⊠ *Elounda 72053,* ☎ *0841/41412,* FAX *0841/41373. 250 rooms, 15 suites, 8 bungalows. Pool, sauna, Turkish bath, miniature golf, 2 tennis courts, windsurfing, boating, parasailing, waterskiing, cinema. AE, DC, MC, V. Closed Nov.–Mar.* 🍽

$$$$ 🏨 **Elounda Mare.** If you plan to stay in one luxurious hotel in Crete,
★ make it this extraordinary Relais & Château property on the Mirabello Gulf, one of the finest hotels in Greece. More than half of the rooms, all bathed in cool marble and stunningly decorated in traditional but luxurious Greek furnishings, are in villas set in their own gardens with private pools. The service is what you would expect from the best European hotel, yet the atmosphere is relaxed and welcoming. Verdant gardens line the shore above a sandy beach and terraced waterside lounging areas, a stone's throw from the large pool. Menus in three restaurants, all with outdoor dining, range from Greek to Continental cuisine. ⊠ *Elounda 72053,* ☎ *0841/41102 or 0841/41103,* FAX *0841/41307. 40 rooms, 55 bungalows. 3 restaurants, pool, sauna, Turkish bath, 9-hole golf course, 2 tennis courts, windsurfing, boating, waterskiing. AE, DC, MC, V. Closed Nov.–Mar.* 🍽

$ 🏨 **Akti Olous.** This friendly, unassuming hotel on the edge of the Mirabello Gulf is just a step away from a strip of sandy beach and a short swim from the sunken city of Olous—its remains are easy to spot while snorkeling. The rooftop bar, next to the swimming pool, has a stunning view across the gulf, especially at sunset, and there is a waterside taverna and beach. The rooms, decorated in a handsome, modern neoclassical style, all have balconies overlooking the sea. ⊠ *Elounda 72053,* ☎ *0841/41270,* FAX *0841/41425. 70 rooms. Bar, pool, beach. No credit cards. Closed Nov.–Mar.*

Spinalonga

㉛ *82 km (51 mi) east of Heraklion, 2 km (1 mi) east of Elounda.*

Spinalonga, a small, narrow island in the center of the Mirabello Gulf, is a fascinating if somewhat macabre place to visit. The Venetians built a huge, forbidding fortress here in the 17th century, and in the early 1900s the island became a leper colony. To reach it you must take an excursion boat from Ayios Nikolaos. Ask at the harbor; there are two or three trips every day in summer, some including a midday beach barbecue and a swim on a deserted islet. As you cruise past the islet of Ayioi Pantes, look for the *agrimi* (the Cretan wild goat), with its impressive curling horns. The islet is a reserve for about 200 of this protected species.

Kritsa

㉜ *80 km (50 mi) east of Heraklion, 20 km (12½ mi) south of Elounda.*

The village of Kritsa, 9 km (5½ mi) west of Ayios Nikolaos, is renowned for its weaving tradition. If you visit only one Byzantine church in Crete, it should be the whitewashed Panayia Kera. It has an unusual shape, with three naves supported by heavy triangular buttresses. Built in the early years of Venetian occupation, it contains some of the liveliest and best-preserved medieval frescoes on the island, painted in the 13th century. ⊠ *On main road just before town, Kritsa.* ☎ *200 dr./€.58.* ⊘ *Sat.–Thurs. 9–3.*

㉝ One of the best views in Crete can be had at **Lato** (⊠ 1 km [½ mi] beyond Kritsa's church of Panayia Kera; follow the dirt track), an ancient city built in a dip between two rocky peaks. Make your way over the ancient masonry to the far end of the site: on a clear day, you can see the island of Santorini, about 135 km (84 mi) across the Cretan Sea.

Gournia

㉞ *98½ km (61 mi) southeast of Heraklion, 18½ km (11½ mi) east of Kritsa.*

The Minoan site of Gournia was excavated in 1904 by Harriet Boyd Hawes, the first woman archaeologist to work here, along with her team of Cretan workmen and a chaperon. Most of what you see dates from the later palace period, though Gournia had only a small mansion set among dozens of small houses. Finds indicated that it was a fishing and weaving community, destroyed around 1400 BC and never resettled. ⊠ *To right of main highway, on low hillside.* ☎ *500 dr./€1.47.* ⊘ *Tues.–Sun. 8–2:30.*

Ierapetra

㉟ *113½ (70¼ mi) southeast of Heraklion, about 15 km (9 mi) south of Gournia.*

From Gournia, a road branches to the right and crosses the narrowest part of the island to Ierapetra. The only major town on the south coast, Ierapetra is a flourishing agricultural center, its prosperity based on the plastic-covered greenhouses where early tomatoes and cucumbers are grown and exported all over Europe. The climate in this part of Crete is North African; you are nearer to Libya than to mainland Greece.

Beaches

Tourism is fast developing to the east of Ierapetra, where there are some ㊱ fine sandy beaches. At the village of **Makriyialos,** 28 km (17 mi) east of Ierapetra, you can take your pick; even in high summer you might have most of a cove to yourself.

Lodging

$$ 🏨 **Astron.** Opened in 1992, all rooms at this comfortable hotel have a terrific vantage point, with balconies, of a quiet stretch of the town's waterfront. The beach is just a minute away. The coffee shop looks onto a pleasant interior courtyard with a fountain. ⊠ *Mihail Kothri 56, 72200,* ☎ *0842/25114,* 🖷 *0842/25917. 66 rooms. Restaurant, coffee shop, snack bar, air-conditioning, minibars. V.*

Mochlos

㊲ *50 km (31 mi) east of Ayios Nikolaos, 35 km (21¾ mi) northeast of Ierapetra.*

If you feel like a swim, or a leisurely taverna meal, wind along the north-coast road between the base of the mountains and the sea to the island of Mochlos, separated from shore by a swimmable channel. On the island is a Minoan cemetery excavated early in this century, now being re-excavated by a team of American archaeologists. Mochlos is a good place for lazing in the hottest part of the day; there are several pleasant tavernas on the shore and, if you want to stay longer, rooms to rent.

Siteia

38 *73 km (45 mi) east of Ayios Nikolaos, 23 km (14¼ mi) east of Ierapetra.*

Like Ierapetra, Siteia is an unpretentious town where agriculture is at least as important as tourism: raisins and, increasingly, bananas are the main crops. Siteia's waterfront, lined with cafés and tavernas, is lively in summer. From Siteia you can take a plane to Rhodes or a ferry via the small islands of Kassos and Karpathos. A Venetian fort, the **Kazarma** (⊠ Follow road up from waterfront), overlooks Siteia from a height

★ on the west: it offers a spectacular view across the bay. Siteia's **archaeological museum** contains a unique find: a **Minoan ivory and gold statuette of a young man,** found at Palaikastro on the east coast. The figure dates from around 1500 BC and, though incomplete, is a masterpiece of Minoan carving. ⊠ *Museum: outskirts of town.* 🖃 *800 dr./€2.35.* ☉ *Tues.–Sun. 9–3.*

36 The fortified monastery of **Toplou** (to the east of Siteia) is set among barren hills where the sparse trees are twisted into strange shapes by the fierce north winds that sweep this region. Only a few monks live here now, though the monastery is slowly being renovated. Inside the tall loggia gate, built in the 16th century, the cells are arranged around a cobbled courtyard with a 14th-century church at its center. It contains a famous icon, composed of 61 scenes, each inspired by a phrase from the Orthodox liturgy. ⊠ *12½ km (8 mi) east of Siteia on the road for Palaikastro and Zakro.* 🖃 *800 dr./€2.35.* ☉ *Daily 9–1 and 2–6.*

Beaches
A long, sandy beach stretches to the east of the waterfront.

Lodging
$ 🏨 **Hotel El Greco.** This friendly establishment on a narrow street several blocks above the waterfront is perfectly comfortable and not without charm. Many of the simple rooms have balconies overlooking the old town and the sea, and the manager, Jankov Marjan, goes out of his way to help guests. ⊠ *G. Arkadiou, 72300,* ☎ 🖶 *0843/23133. 15 rooms. MC, V. Closed Nov.–Apr.*

Vai, Palaikastro, and Kato Zakro

Vai is 170 km (105½ mi) east of Heraklion, 27 km (16¾ mi) east of Siteia.

★ **40** The palm grove of the renowned beach at **Vai** (⊠ 7½ km [4½ mi] northeast of Toplou) existed in classical Greek times; it is unique in Europe. The sandy beach with nearby islets set in clear turquoise water is one of the most attractive in Crete, but in summer it is very crowded.

41 Follow a dirt track through olive groves to the sandy beach at **Palaikastro** (⊠ 9 km [5½ mi] south of Vai; follow sign for Marina Village). It is rarely crowded, and service is friendly at the waterside tavernas. The sprawling Minoan town, currently being excavated by British and American archaeologists, lies off to the right.

At Ano Zakro, 20 km (12 mi) south of Palaikastro village, a path leads down through a deep ravine past caves used for early Minoan burials
★ **42** to the Minoan palace site at **Kato Zakro** (⊠ Ask at one of the cafés for directions to the start of the path). The walk down takes about one

hour. You can also drive 9 km (5½ mi) down to the site by a circuitous but spectacular route. The village of Kato Zakro, on a fine beach, is a cluster of tavernas with a few rooms to rent. Kato Zakro's **Minoan palace,** smaller than those of Knossos, Phaistos, and Mallia, is surrounded by a terraced town with narrow cobbled streets, like Gournia. ⊠ *Ascend paved Minoan Rd. from harbor, through once-covered gateway, reaching northeast court down stepped ramp,* ☎ *0841/22462.* 🎫 *500 dr./€1.47.* ☉ *Tues.–Sun. 8–3.*

WESTERN CRETE

Western Crete, with soaring mountains, deep gorges, and rolling green lowlands planted with olives and oranges, is much less affected by the growth of mass tourism than is the rest of the island. There is a wealth of interesting byways to be explored. This region is rich in Minoan sites, Byzantine churches, Venetian monasteries, and friendly upland villages. There are some outstanding beaches on the west and south coasts. South and west of Heraklion lies the traditional agricultural heartland of Crete: long, narrow valleys where olive groves alternate with vineyards growing sultana grapes for export. The outstanding archaeological site is Phaistos, the great Minoan palace.

Mesara Plain and Gortyna

Gortyna is 45 km (28 mi) south of Heraklion.

After climbing through a vine- and olive-clad valley, the narrow road south from Heraklion to Gortyna swings toward the Mesara plain. The plain, filled with silver-gray olives interspersed with plastic greenhouses for growing early tomatoes and cucumbers, rises again to the craggy **Asterousia Mountains;** beyond them is the Libyan Sea. In summer especially, the temperature rises sharply as you descend. The village of **Ayia Varvara,** with the whitewashed church of Profitis Ilias built high on a rock, said to mark the center of Crete, lies some 32½ km (20½ mi) south of Heraklion.

The village of **Ayii Deka** (14 km [8 mi] south of Ayia Varvara) is home to the church of **Ayios Titos** (⊠ Follow signs from road), an early 6th-century Christian basilica, reputedly St. Titos's burial place.

Ayios Titos is at the entrance to the Greco-Roman city of **Gortyna,** a huge expanse of scattered ruins sliced through by the main road. At Gortyna, which was made a capital by the Romans in AD 67, sights include the **Odeion,** a small amphitheater where musical recitals were staged in the 1st century AD. In the brick building behind it, the **Gortyna Law Code** is displayed. Inscribed on a set of stone blocks, this is Europe's earliest code, dating from the first half of the 5th century BC. In 600 lines it details the laws concerning marriage, divorce, inheritance, adoption, assault and rape, and the status of slaves. From the ruins of Gortyna, a path climbs a few hundred feet uphill to the **acropolis of Gortyna** (⊠ Above Gortyna), which has a fine view across the plain. Italian archaeologists, who have dug here since the 1880s, recently completed a detailed topographical survey. A plan is posted at several points around the site, enabling you to find your way through the olives to several temples, a small theater, and the public baths. Although it was destroyed by Arab raiders in the 7th century and never rebuilt, Gortyna did provide most of the building material for the town of Ayii Deka. Fragments of ancient sculpture and inscriptions can still be seen in the 13th-century village church. 🎫 *1,000 dr./€2.94.* ☉ *Daily 8–6.*

Western Crete

Sea of Crete

Libyan Sea

TO PIRAEUS

TO GITHION

TO GAVDHOS

KEY

Ferry

20 miles

30 km

N

Rodopos Peninsula

Gramvousa Peninsula

Akrotiri Peninsula

WHITE MOUNTAINS

Mount Ida

Mesará Plain

Samaria Gorge

Souda Bay

Nidha Plateau

Stavros and Kalathas

Profitis Ilias

Hania

Souda Port

Vrisses

Georgioupolis

Rethymnon

Arkadi Monastery

Ayios Ioannis

Fodhele

Ayia Varvara

Ayii Deka

Gortyna

Phaistos

Vori

Ayia Triada

Kommos

Matala

Idaean Cave (Ideo Andro)

Sklavokampos

Kamares Cave

Tylissos

Polyrrenia

Hrisoskalitissas Monastery

Aptera

Falasarna
Platanos
Sfinario
Kambos
Kefali
Elos
Elafonisi
Palechora
Kandamos
Lissos
Souyia
Ayia Roumeli
Loutro
Hora Sfakion
Frangokastello
Plakias
Moni Preveli
Ayia Galini
Nithavris
Mount Kedros
Spili
Apostoli
Kournas
Vamos
Sternes
Airport
Platanias
Tavroniitis
Maleme
Nea Roumata
Omalos
Xyloskala
Kandamos
Marathokefala
Kastelli
Prasies
Margarites
Panormos
Perama
Axos
Anoyia
Fourfouras
Platanos
Zaros
Prinias
Linaperamata
Gonies
Mires
Kali Limenes

43
44
45
46
47
48
49
50
51
52
53
54
55
56
57
58
59
60

Phaistos

★ **46** *50 km (31 mi) south of Heraklion, 18 km (11 mi) west of Gortyna.*

Enjoying an incomparably more splendid setting than that of Knossos, Phaistos is the site of one of the greatest Minoan palaces. Today, the traveler heads to Mires, a flourishing market town, which lies some 5 km (3 mi) west of Gortyna. dFrom here, a road crosses the Geropotamos River and climbs a hill to the Minoan **palace of Phaistos.** Like Knossos and Mallia, it was built around 1900 BC and rebuilt after a disastrous earthquake around 1650 BC. It was burned and abandoned in the wave of destruction that swept across the island around 1450 BC. You enter down a flight of steps leading into the **west court,** and climb a **grand staircase.** From here you pass through the **Propylon porch** into a light well and descend a **narrow staircase** into the **central court.** Much of the southern and eastern sections of the palace have eroded away. But there are large pithoi still in place in the old **storerooms.** On the north side of the court the recesses of an **elaborate doorway** bear a rare survival: red paint in a diamond pattern on a white ground. A passage from the doorway leads to the **north court** and the **northern domestic apartments,** now roofed and fenced off. The **Phaistos Disk** was found in 1903 in a chest made of mud brick at the northeast edge of the site. East of the central court are the **palace workshops,** with a metalworking furnace fenced off in the east court. South of the workshops lies a set of **southern domestic apartments,** including a clay bath. They have a memorable view across the Mesara plain. ⊠ *From Gortyna, cross Geropotamos River and ascend hill,* ☎ *0892/42315.* ▦ *1,200 dr./€3.53.* ⊙ *Daily 8–7.*

Vori

47 *65 km (40½ mi) southwest of Heraklion, 5 km (3 mi) north of the palace of Phaistos.*

48 The site of **Ayia Triada** dates from the later palace period and was destroyed at the same time as Phaistos. It was once believed to have been a summer palace for the rulers of Phaistos but now is thought to have been a group of villas and warehouse areas. There's another magnificent view toward the Paximadia islets in the Mesara Gulf. Rooms in the L-shape complex of buildings were paneled with gypsum slabs and decorated with frescoes: two now in the Archaeological Museum in Heraklion show a woman in a garden and a cat hunting a pheasant. A road from the upper courtyard leads to the sea. ⊠ *Follow signs from main road,* ☎ *0892/91360.* ▦ *500 dr./€1.47.* ⊙ *Daily 8:30–3.*

Beaches

49 One of the best and least crowded beaches on the south coast lies just below the recently excavated Minoan harbor site of **Kommos** (⊠ 3 km [2 mi] south of main road from Mires to Matala, near village of Pitsidia).

Matala

50 *70 km (42 mi) southwest of Heraklion, 10 km (6 mi) south of Vori.*

Renowned in the 1960s as a stopover on the hippie trail across the eastern Mediterranean, Matala is today a pleasant, low-key beach resort. The 2nd-century AD Roman tombs cut in the cliff side (where the hippies lived) are now fenced off but continue to attract day-trippers on coach tours from Heraklion, for whom Matala is a stop on the Phaistos–Ayia Triada circuit. Once the crowds leave (usually by the early afternoon), the town beach is delightful, and there is another excellent strand, the so-called Red Beach, accessible only by a 20-minute walk across a rocky promontory.

$$$ 🏨 **Shivas Village Hotel.** Although most of the accommodations in this part of Crete consist of basic rooms to rent, this sparkling new hotel in the tiny farm village of Sivas, a few miles from the sea, is quite deluxe. The rooms and suites, all with kitchenettes, are enormous, and nicely outfitted with chic furnishings, terraces, and large shuttered doors and windows. In fact, the only drawback is the fact that the hotel is a bit out of character with the delightfully simple, rural surroundings. ⊠ *Sivas, 70200,* ☎ *0892/42734 or 0892/42750,* ℻ *0892/42732. 12 rooms, 12 suites. Kitchenettes, pool, sauna, Turkish bath, tennis court, exercise room. AE, DC, MC, V. Closed Nov.–Apr.* ⬡

Tylissos

24 km (15 mi) southwest of Heraklion, 65 km (40½ mi) from Phaistos.

The road to the Minoan site at Tylissos, via the Heraklion–Rethymnon road turning at the town of Gazi, just west of Heraklion, winds uphill through vineyards. The pine-shaded complex reveals three later **palace-period buildings**: workshops, living quarters, and storerooms. ⊠ *To left of road at the 14-km (9-mi) mark.* 🎫 *800 dr./€2.35.* ⊙ *Daily 8:30–3.*

Fodhele

🔵 *12 km (7½ mi) west of Heraklion, 10 km (6 mi) northwest of Tylissos.*

The straggling village of Fodhele is said to be the birthplace of Domenico Theotokopoulos, the 16th-century Cretan painter known as El Greco.

🔵 The monastery of **Ayios Ioannis** (⊠ 23 km [14 mi] west of Fodhele) is dedicated to John the Baptist. It is just above the highway, with a spectacular view from its terrace across the Cretan Sea. Inside is a historic small chapel, but there is rarely anyone around to let you in.

Arkadi Monastery

★ 🔵 *30 km (18½ mi) west of Heraklion, 18 km (11½ mi) from Fodhele.*

Running parallel to the coast highway, the old Heraklion–Hania road follows a gorge inland before emerging into the flat pastureland that is part of the holdings of the Arkadi Monastery. The monastery is a place of pilgrimage for Cretans and one of the most stunning pieces of Renaissance architecture on the island. Built in the 16th century, of honey-color local stone, it has an ornate facade decorated with Corinthian columns and an elegant belfry above. In 1866, the monastery was besieged during a major rebellion against the Turks, and Abbot Gabriel and several hundred rebels, together with their wives and children, refused to surrender. When the Turkish forces broke through the gate, the defenders set the gunpowder store afire, killing themselves together with hundreds of Turks. ⊠ *Just south of town of Perama.* 🎫 *300 dr./€.88.* ⊙ *Daily 8–5.*

Rethymnon

🔵 *78 km (48½ mi) west of Heraklion, 54 km (33½ mi) west of Arkadi Monastery.*

Rethymnon is Crete's third-largest town, after Heraklion and Hania. As the population (about 30,000) steadily increases, villagers move into new houses on the outskirts of town. The old Venetian quarter is being restored, and the port has been expanded, allowing Rethymnon to have its own ferry service to and from Piraeus. Unfortunately, a long strip of beach to the east of the old town has been tastelessly developed with large hotels and other resort facilities catering to tourists on package vacations, diminishing much of the charm that Rethymnon once had.

Thankfully, much of Rethymnon's remaining charm perseveres in the **old section** (⊠ Town center). Wandering through the narrow alleyways, you come across handsome carved-stone Renaissance doorways belonging to vanished mansions, fountains, archways, and wooden Turkish houses. One of the few surviving minarets in Greece is in the **Neratzes mosque** (⊠ Old town), now a concert hall, and you can climb its 120 steps for a panoramic view. Don't miss the carefully restored **Venetian loggia** (⊠ Near center of town on Arkadiou St.), the clubhouse of the local Rethymnon nobility. Rethymnon's small **Venetian harbor,** with its restored 13th-century lighthouse, comes to life in summer, with restaurant tables cluttering the quayside.

Rethymnon is dominated by the huge Venetian castle known as the **Fortessa.** High, well-preserved walls enclose a large empty space occupied by a few scattered buildings and filled with wildflowers in spring. Forced labor from the town and surrounding villages built the fortress from 1573 to 1583, but it never fulfilled its purpose of keeping out the Turks: Rethymnon surrendered after a three-week siege. ⊠ *At village's western end.* ⊗ *Daily 8–8.*

The **archaeological museum** is in what used to be Rethymnon's Turkish prison. Look for the collection of beautifully made bone tools from a Neolithic site at Yerani, west of Rethymnon. An unfinished statue of Aphrodite, the goddess of love, is interesting: the ancient chisel marks show clearly. ⊠ *Western end, next to entrance of Fortessa,* ☎ *0831/54668.* ▧ *500 dr./€1.47.* ⊗ *Tues.–Sun. 8:30–3.*

One of the town's most delightful attractions is the new **Historical and Folk Art Museum,** housed in a restored Venetian palazzo near the mosque. Rustic furnishings, tools, and costumes provide a charming and vivid picture of what life on Crete was like until well into this century. ⊠ *Vernadou 28,* ☎ *0831/29975.* ▧ *400 dr./€1.17.* ⊗ *Daily 9–1.*

Dining and Lodging

$$ ✕ **Cavo D'Oro.** This is the most stylish of the handful of fish restau-
★ rants around the tiny Venetian harbor, and one of the finest restaurants in Crete. Lobster and a wide range of innovative fresh fish dishes are always served. The high, wood-paneled dining room was once a medieval storeroom, and diners also sit on the old cobbled waterfront. ⊠ *Nearchou 42–43,* ☎ *0831/24446. DC, MC, V.*

$ ✕ **Castelvecchio George.** Just down from the Venetian Fortessa, this pleasant taverna just above the narrow streets of the old town catches a refreshing evening breeze in summer. George's specialties, among the traditional Greek and international dishes, are pepper steak and *stifado* (a rich stew made with lamb and sometimes with hare). George has also recently added four simple guest rooms to his establishment. ⊠ *Heimaras 29,* ☎ *0831/55163. No credit cards.*

$$$ ⊞ **Hotel Fortessa.** This newer hotel has many of the advantages of the
★ larger hotels that have sprung up farther out of town on Rethymnon's charmless beach strip, yet it is only steps from the Fortessa, the old town, and the beach. The tile-floored rooms, with handsome traditional furnishings, are built around a marble atrium and sunny courtyard; many have balconies. The nicest rooms face the street, which is closed to vehicular traffic during tourist season, and the fortress. ⊠ *Melisi-*

nou 16, 74100, ☎ 0831/23828 or 0831/55552, ⅢX 0831/54073. 54 rooms. Restaurant, snack bar, pool. AE, DC, MC, V.

$$$ 🔟 **Palazzo Rimondi.** This all-suites hotel was formed from combining
★ several 15th-century houses in the heart of the old quarter. All of the tasteful, stylish rooms have sitting and sleeping areas and kitchenettes; many retain such architectural details as vaulted or paneled ceilings, fireplaces, and latticed Venetian windows. A courtyard with a tiny swimming pool offers a nice retreat from the tourist clamor. ⌧ Xanthoudidou 21, 74100, ☎ 0831/51289, ⅢX 0831/51013. 21 rooms. Bar, kitchenettes, pool. AE, DC, MC, V.

$ 🔟 **Liberty.** This quiet, friendly, family-owned hotel opposite a park has a roof garden with an attractive view up to the hills overlooking the town. The rooms are small but comfortable. ⌧ Themis Moatsou 8, 74100, ☎ 0831/55851 through 0831/55853, ⅢX 0831/55850. 24 rooms. DC, MC, V.

Outdoor Activities and Sports

BICYCLING

For bicycle rentals in Rethymnon, ask at the **Grecotel Rithymna Beach** hotel (⌧ Rethymnon, ☎ 0831/71002 or 0831/29491).

TREKKING

The **Happy Walker** (⌧ Tombazi 56, Rethymnon, ☎ 0831/52920) arranges walking tours in the surrounding mountains.

Shopping

BOOKS AND NEWSPAPERS

Several souvenir stores on the waterfront sell English-language books and newspapers, as does the **International Press Bookshop** (⌧ Venizelou 26, Rethymnon).

Georgioupolis

55 99½ km (61½ mi) west of Heraklion, 21½ km (13½ mi) west of Rethymnon.

Georgioupolis was named for Prince George of Greece, the high commissioner of Crete from 1898 to 1906. Here, at the mouth of the Vrysanos River, where migrating birds gather, he built a shooting lodge, which is closed to the public. There are several good fish tavernas and many rooms to rent.

Vrisses

56 30 km (18½ mi) west of Rethymnon, 5 km (3 mi) west of Georgioupolis.

Vrisses is famous throughout Crete for its thick, creamy yogurt. Served in the cafés beneath the plane trees as you come into the village, it's best eaten with a large spoonful of honey on top.

Souda Bay and the Akrotiri Peninsula

71½ km (45 mi) west of Rethymnon, 20 km (12½ mi) northwest of Vrisses.

The road from Vrisses to Hania climbs across the Vamos peninsula and approaches Souda Bay. This deep inlet, considered the best harbor in the eastern Mediterranean, can shelter the entire U.S. Sixth Fleet. Taking photos is forbidden around Souda Bay, a regulation to be taken seriously: if you are caught doing so you may be charged with spying.

57 At the top of Souda bay is **Souda port,** where passenger ferries arrive from Piraeus dock.

Beaches

⑤⑧ There are good beaches at **Stavros** and **Kalathas** on the Akrotiri peninsula.

Hania

⑤⑨ *78 km (48½ mi) west of Rethymnon, 6½ km (4 mi) west of Souda.*

As you approach Hania—one of the most attractive towns in Greece—a long avenue lined with eucalyptus trees takes you to the outskirts, where signs lead you around the one-way system to the large, cross-shape covered market in the town center. Highlights include its well-
★ preserved **Venetian quarter** and harbor. It was here that the Greek flag was raised in 1913 to mark unification with Greece, and until 1971 Hania was the island's capital.

On Sundays, Hania's time-honored flag-raising ceremony is repeated at the **Firka,** the old Turkish prison, now the naval museum. ⊠ *Waterfront, at far west end of port,* ☎ *0821/91875.* ▨ *600 dr./€1.76.* ☺ *June–Sept., daily 10–4; Oct.–May, Tues.–Sun. 10–2.*

From Hania's market, work your way through a maze of narrow streets to the **waterfront,** which is a pedestrian zone in summer. Walk around Hania's **inner harbor,** where the fishing boats moor, and east past the **Venetian arsenals.** If you head around to the **old lighthouse,** you'll get a magnificent view of the town with the imposing White Mountains looming beyond. The **Janissaries mosque** (⊠ East side of harbor), now an information center, was built when the Turks captured the town in 1645 after a two-month siege. The **Kastelli hill** (⊠ Above harbor), where the Venetians first settled, remained the quarter of the local nobility, but it had been occupied much earlier; parts of what may be a Minoan palace have been excavated at its base. Both **Theotocopoulou and Zambeliou streets** (⊠ Behind inner harbor) lead you into the narrow alleyways with predominantly **Venetian and Turkish houses.** Look for an old **synagogue** (⊠ In Parodos Kondylaki, behind outer harbor), formerly the Venetian Church of St. Catherine and now a warehouse. The **archaeological museum** occupies the Venetian church of St. Francis. Finds on display come from all over western Crete: the painted Minoan clay coffins and elegant late Minoan pottery indicate that the region was as wealthy as the center of the island in the Bronze Age, though no palace has yet been located. ⊠ *Venetian Church of St. Francis, Chalidron St.,* ☎ *0821/90334.* ▨ *500 dr.€1.47.* ☺ *Tues.–Sun. 8:30–3:30.*

⑥⓪ **Profitis Ilias** (⊠ 4½ km [3 mi] east of Hania in the Halepa suburb), the burial place of Eleftheriou Venizelou, Crete's great statesman, is lined with fine neoclassical mansions dating to the turn of the 20th century, when Britain, France, Russia, and Italy were active in Cretan politics. A panoramic view from here takes in Hania and its surrounding villages, along with much of the northwest coast.

Dining and Lodging

An almost unbroken row of **tavernas** lines Hania's harbor in summer. Their menus are nearly identical and almost all offer grills and fresh fish at reasonable prices. Among those frequented by Haniots are **Apostolis** (⊠ Inner harbor) and **Karnagio** (⊠ Outer harbor), with tasty Cretan specialties.

$$ ✕ **Tamam.** An old Turkish bath has been converted to one of the finest, and most atmospheric, restaurants in Hania's old quarter. Specialties served up in the cavernous dining room include peppers with grilled feta cheese, eggplant stuffed with chicken, and other tempting dishes. ⊠ *Zambeliou 49,* ☎ *0821/96080. No credit cards.*

$$ ✕ **Well of the Turk.** Part of the adventure is finding this restaurant on a narrow alley near the minaret in the old Arab quarter, just behind the Venetian warehouses on the harbor; you will have to ask your way, but just about everyone in the neighborhood knows this place. The food ranges from simple Greek fare—a prerequisite is the wonderful appetizer platter, a meal in itself—to some Continental dishes, such as sautéed chicken in a wine sauce. ✉ *Kalinikou Sarpaki 1–3 Splantiza,* ☎ *0821/54547. No credit cards.*

$$$$ 🏨 **Casa Delfino.** This small hotel, set in the heart of the old town, oc-
  ★   cupies a Venetian Renaissance palace. In the 1880s, it was home to Pedro Delfino, an Italian merchant, and now it belongs to two of his descendants. The cool pastel rooms, four of which are housed in an adjoining building of the same era, are located behind graceful stone archways surrounding a courtyard paved in pebble mosaic; most have stylish modern furniture and are on two levels. ✉ *Theofanous 9, Palio Limani, 73100,* ☎ *0821/87400,* FAX *0821/96500. 4 rooms, 15 suites. Minibars. AE, DC, MC, V.*☜

$$$ 🏨 **Doma.** This enchanting hotel occupies a converted 19th-century man-
  ★   sion facing the sea, on the outskirts of town, and feels like a private house. As it turns out, it was once the Austrian consulate and later the British vice-consulate, then the childhood home of proprietor Rena Valyraki. With their simple, elegant, Cretan-style furnishings, the attractive bedrooms overlook the garden or the sea; set on enormous terraces, the rooftop suites are especially charming. The Doma is one of the best places in town to dine; one of the owners prepares a traditional dinner each evening, which nonguests also enjoy. Breakfast features breads to be slathered with homemade jams, and yogurt comes with a Turkish topping: a delicious mix of spices, quince preserves, and honey. ✉ *124 Eleftheriou Venizelou St., 73100,* ☎ *0821/51772 or 0821/51773,* FAX *0821/41578. 22 rooms, 3 suites. Restaurant. DC, MC, V. Closed Nov.–Mar.*

$$$ 🏨 **Villa Andromeda.** Yet another of Hania's charming hotels occu-
  ★   pies a seaside, neoclassical mansion that once housed the German high command during World War II (Rommel supposedly enjoyed the plunge pool). The premises now contain large, handsomely furnished suites that surround a luxuriant garden and swimming pool or face the sea. ✉ *150 Eleftheriou Venizelou St., 73100,* ☎ *0821/28300 or 0821/28301,* FAX *0821/28303. 8 suites. Bar, swimming pool. DC, MC, V.*

$ 🏨 **Porto de Colombo.** Occupying a renovated Venetian house, this pleasant hotel is full of architectural surprises: wooden ceilings, small deep-set windows, two-floor rooms with loft areas. Furnishings are traditional and comfortable. Weather permitting, breakfast is served on the narrow street out front. ✉ *Old town, Theofanous and Moshon Sts., 73100,* ☎ FAX *0821/70945. 10 rooms. MC, V.*

Outdoor Activities and Sports

BICYCLING

You may arrange bike rentals through **G&A Travel** (✉ Halidon 25, ☎ 0821/44965).

HIKING

Alpin Travel (✉ Bonaili 11) offers many hiking tours throughout western Crete. The **Greek Federation of Mountaineering Associations** operates refuges in the White Mountains (☎ 0821/24647) and on Mt. Ida (☎ 081/267110). For more details on trekking from Hania, ask at the EOT office (☞ Visitor Information *in* Crete A to Z, *below*).

Shopping

ANTIQUE BLANKETS AND RUGS

Exceptional finds may be had at **Top Hanas** (✉ Odos Anghelou, No. 3), which sells a fine selection of antique blankets and rugs, most of them made for dowries from homespun wool and natural dyes.

BOOKS AND NEWSPAPERS

One or two souvenir stores on the waterfront sell English-language books and newspapers.

GOURMET GOODS

Take a stroll through Hania's **covered market** (✉ Town center), where local merchants sell rounds of Cretan cheese, jars of golden honey, lengths of salami, salt fish, lentils, and other pulse from sacks.

JEWELERS AND CRAFTS

The silver jewelry and ceramics are especially striking at **Carmela** (✉ Odos Anghelou, No. 7), which represents contemporary jewelers and other craftspeople from Crete and throughout Greece.

En Route   To venture to the southern coast of Crete, backtrack east to Vrisses to the turnoff for a spectacular drive traversing the Askyphou plain, watched over by an Ottoman fort perched on a knob-shape hill, and then descending to the Libyan Sea along the **Nimbros gorge.**

CRETE A TO Z

Arriving and Departing

By Boat

Heraklion and Souda Bay (5 km [3 mi] east of Hania) are the island's main ports. Two Cretan shipping companies, **Anek** (✉ 25th of August St. 33, Heraklion, ☎ 081/222481) and **Minoan Lines** (✉ 25th of August St. 78, Heraklion, ☎ 081/7512356), have daily ferry service from Piraeus year-round. **Cretan Ferries-Rethymniaki** (✉ Arkadiou 250, Rethymnon, ☎ 0831/21518) has service from Piraeus to Rethymnon three or four times a week. The overnight crossing takes 10–12 hours. You can book a berth in a first- or second-class cabin or an aircraft-style seat. Make reservations for summer crossings through a travel agent several days in advance. At other times of the year, you can buy a ticket from a dockside agency in Piraeus an hour before the ship sails. There is a cafeteria in second and tourist classes and a dining room in first class. All ferries take cars: a discount may be available if you buy a round-trip ticket for the car. In summer, you should make your return-trip reservation several days in advance at the shipping company: both Anek and Minoan Lines have offices in all the main towns on the island. A one-way first-class fare (with accommodation) costs about 17,000 dr./€50.14, second-class about 13,000 dr./€38.34, and tourist class 8,000 dr./€23.59, with little or no discount for round-trips. Car fares are 16,000 dr./€47.19 to 20,500 dr./€60.47, one-way, depending on size. Other **ferry services** change from year to year, but there are weekly trips in summer from Piraeus to Siteia and to Kastelli Kissamou. A small ferry links Siteia with the Dodecanese islands of Kassos, Karpathos, and Rhodes, and both ferries and catamarans operate in summer between Santorini and Heraklion. There is also a weekly sail from Heraklion to Limassol in Cyprus, and to Haifa, Israel. Ferries sometimes sail to Kusadasi, Turkey, and Alexandria, Egypt. Travel agents can advise you on schedules.

By Plane

The principal arrival point on Crete is **Heraklion airport** (✉ Center of island, 5 km [3 mi] east of city, ☎ 081/229191), where up to 16 flights daily arrive from Athens, daily flights arrive from Rhodes and Thessaloniki, and two weekly flights arrive from Mykonos. Heraklion is also serviced directly by flights, many of them charters, from other European cities. There are several daily flights from Athens to **Hania airport** (⊠ Western Crete, 15 km [10 mi] east of town, ☎ 0821/58005). There are flights two or three times weekly to **Siteia airport** (⊠ Eastern Crete, 2 km [1 mi] west of the town, ☎ 0843/22270). Twice-weekly flights from Rhodes via Karpathos also land in Siteia.

A municipal **bus** outside Heraklion airport will take you to Platia Eleftherias (⊠ Town center), known locally as Treis Kamares. Tickets are sold from a kiosk next to the bus stop; the fare is 200 dr./€.58 From Hania and Siteia airports, Olympic Airways buses take you to the airline office in the town center. The fare is 400 dr./€1.17 from Hania airport and 150 dr./€.44 from Siteia airport. **Cabs** are lined up outside Heraklion and Hania airports; the fare into town is 1,500 dr./4.42 from Heraklion and 1,800 dr./€5.30 from Hania. Taxis usually turn up to meet flights into Siteia airport, but if there are none to be seen, ask the information desk to call one from town. The fare will be approximately 800 dr./€2.35

Getting Around

By Boat

To reach the island of **Spinalonga,** you must take an excursion boat from Ayios Nikolaos. Ask at the harbor; there are two or three trips every day in summer, some including a midday beach barbecue and a swim on a deserted islet.

In summer, a boat service around the **Samaria Gorge** operates along the southwest coast from Hora Sfakion to Loutro, Ayia Roumeli, Souyia, Lissos, and Paleochora, the main resort on the southwest coast.

For the boat timetable from **Paleochora to Ghavdos,** check with any travel agency in Paleochora or Sfakia, or try the **Paleochora Harbor Authority** (☎ 0823/41214) or **Sfakia Harbor Authority** (☎ 0825/ 91292).

By Bus

The **public bus companies (KTEL)** have regular, inexpensive service among the main towns. You can book seats in advance at whichever bus station is the terminus for the district of the island you're going to. The efficient village bus network operates similarly, from the bus station in each *komopolis,* or market town. In **Heraklion,** the bus station for western Crete (☎ 081/221765) is opposite the Historical Museum; the station for the south (☎ 081/245019) is just outside the Hania Gate to the right; and for the east (☎ 081/282637), the station is just east of the traffic circle at the end of Leoforos D. Bofor, close to the old harbor.

By Car

Roads on Crete are not congested but, apart from the north-coast highway, tend to be winding and narrow. Most are now asphalt, but dirt tracks between villages are still found in mountainous regions. Most road signs are in Greek and English. Gas stations are not plentiful outside the big towns, and road maps are not always reliable, especially in the south. Driving in the main towns can be nerve-racking, especially during the lunchtime rush hour. Drive defensively wherever you are, as Cretan drivers are aggressive and liable to ignore the rules of the road. In summer, tourists on motor scooters can be a hazard. Sheep and goats frequently stray onto the roads, with or without their shepherd or sheepdog. Night driving is not advisable.

With Children

There is practically no provision made on Crete for the specific amusement of children, but people take them everywhere, and Cretans will welcome yours. Just remember that there is a limit to most children's tolerance for ruins, which can be greatly extended by frequent administrations of ice cream and cold drinks, and many dunks in the sea, a pleasure in itself.

Contacts and Resources

Bicycling

Hania: **G&A Travel** (✉ Halidon 25, ☏ 0821/44965). Heraklion: **Creta Travel** (✉ Epimenidou 20–22, ☏ 081/227002). Rethymnon: **Grecotel Rithymna Beach hotel** (✉ Rethymnon 74100, ☏ 0831/71002 or 0831/29491).

Bird-Watching

For Gouves estuary, contact the Grecotel group, which runs the **Creta Sun Hotel** (☏ 0831/71602).

Boating

Local travel agencies, large resort hotels, municipal information offices, or the **Greek National Tourist Organization (GNTO or EOT)** (☞ *below*) can help with information and arrangements for renting Windsurfers, dinghies, and yachts.

Car Rentals

You can rent cars, jeeps, and motorbikes in all the island's towns, or you can arrange beforehand with a major agency in the United States or in Athens to pick up a car on arrival in Crete. **Avis** (☏ 081/225421) and **Hertz** (☏ 081/229702) have offices at Heraklion airport as well as in the city. A medium-size, four-door car costs about 15,000 dr./€44.24–30,000 dr./€88.49 a day with 100 km (63 mi) of free mileage (extra mileage costs about 50 dr. per 1 km [½ mi]), including insurance and taxes. Weekly prices are negotiable, but with unlimited mileage they start at about 60,000 dr./€176

Emergencies

Your hotel will call an **English-speaking doctor. Pharmacies** stay open late by turns, and a list of those open late is displayed in their windows.

Police: Ayios Nikolaos (☏ 0841/22251); Hania (☏ 0821/98888); Heraklion (☏ 081/246539); Ierapetra (☏ 0842/24200); Rethymnon (☏ 0831/22289); Siteia (☏ 0843/24200).

Hospitals: Ayios Nikolaos (☏ 0841/25221); Hania (☏ 0821/44421); Heraklion (☏ 081/269463); Rethymnon (☏ 0831/27814).

Guided Tours

Resort hotels and large travel agents organize guided tours by air-conditioned bus to the main Minoan sites; excursions to spectacular beaches such as Vai in the northeast and Elafonisi in the southwest; and trips to Santorini and to some islands such as Gaidouronisi, south of Ierapetra, and Spinalonga, a former leper colony off Ayios Nikolaos.

Heraklion: Creta Travel (✉ Epimenidou 20–22, Heraklion, ☏ 081/227002).

Hania: Canea Travel (✉ Tzanakaki 28, Hania, ☏ 0821/28817); **El Greco Tours** (✉ Theotocopoulou 63, Hania, ☏ 0821/21829); and **G&A Travel** (✉ Halidon 25, Hania, ☏ 0821/44965) organize hikes through the Samaria Gorge and other local excursions. For example, a tour of the Archaeological Museum in Heraklion and Knossos costs 10,500 dr./€30.97; a tour of Phaistos and Gortyna plus a swim at Matala costs 6,000 dr./€17.69; a trip to the Samaria Gorge costs about 7,300 dr./€21.53. Travel agents can arrange for personal guides, whose fees are negotiable.

Hiking

The **Greek Federation of Mountaineering Associations** operates refuges in the White Mountains (☎ 0821/44647) and on Mt. Ida (☎ 081/289440). For details on trekking from Hania, ask at the EOT (☞ *below*).

Post Offices and Telephones

Post offices are open weekdays 8–8. You can sometimes buy stamps at a kiosk. **Hania** (✉ Tzanakaki 3). **Heraklion** (✉ Platia Daskaloyianni). **Rethymnon** post office and OTE (✉ Koundourioti).

You can often make metered calls overseas from kiosks and kafenions, even in small villages. To avoid heavy surcharges imposed by hotels on long-distance calls, you can make them from offices of the Greek phone company, known as OTE. **OTE** office: **Hania** (✉ Tzanakaki 5); **Heraklion** (✉ El Greco Park); **Rethymnon** post office and OTE (✉ Koundourioti).

Visitor Information

The **Greek National Tourist Organization (GNTO or EOT)** Heraklion (✉ Xanthoudidou 1, ☎ 081/228225), Hania (✉ Odos Kriari 40, ☎ 0821/92943), and Rethymnon (✉ Sofokli Venizelou, ☎ 08831/29148) are open 8–2 and 3–8:30.

12 RHODES AND THE DODECANESE

KOS, SYMI, AND PATMOS

The Dodecanese (Twelve Islands), wrapped enticingly around the shores of Turkey and Asia Minor, are the easternmost holdings of Greece. Romans, Crusaders, Turks, and Venetians left their mark through a remarkable array of temples, castles, and fortresses in exotic towns of shady lanes and tall houses. In addition, what is likely to capture the visitor is the varied landscape—from the cypress-clad hillsides of Patmos to the craggy shoreline of Symi and lush fields of Kos—and the possibility of finding a way of life that, despite invasions of armies and sunseekers, remains essentially and delightfully Greek.

By Stephen
Brewer

Updated by
Stephen
Brewer

L YING AT THE EASTERN EDGE OF THE AEGEAN Sea bordering the west coast of Asia Minor is the southernmost group of Greek islands, the Dodecanese, sometimes known as the Southern Sporades. Of them, the largest by far is Rhodes, for many years one of the most popular vacation spots in the Mediterranean; best known of the others are Kos and Symi; while one other island, Patmos, remains a place of pilgrimage, as it was here that St. John the Divine wrote the Apocalypse. Here, at the top of a hill, is the Monastery of the Apocalypse, which enshrines the cave where St. John received the Revelation; the voice of God spoke through a threefold crack in the rock, and the saint dictated to his disciple Prochorus—a slope in the rock wall is shown as the desk where Prochorus wrote, and silver haloes are set on the stone that was the apostle's pillow.

The dozen islands, plus additional tiny members of the archipelago, have long shared a common history and fate. Their landscapes, however, are sharply contrasting. Patmos, Karpathos, Symi, and Kassos, for example, resemble in some ways the Cycladic islands: rugged hills and mountains are almost devoid of vegetation, with villages and towns clinging in picturesque disarray to craggy landscapes. Rhodes and Kos unfold in fertile splendor, creased with streams and dotted with large stretches of green; their major towns sit next to the sea on almost flat land, embracing exceptionally large and well-protected harbors facing the mainland of Asia Minor. Leros, perhaps the greenest, is seldom visited by foreigners; its splendid harbor is adorned with monumental examples of Italian fascist architecture constructed in the 1930s in expectation of a supremacy that never came. Kalymnos, home to what was once one of the major sponge-diving fleets of the Mediterranean, still shows traces of its former prosperity, and its native sons have done well by their island and their town, whose colorfully painted houses ornament the amphitheatrical harborside. At the very edge of the archipelago, connected only administratively, is Kastellorizo, a lonely outpost that has lost much of its population through emigration.

Pleasures and Pastimes

Beaches

On both the south and north coasts of Kos there are highly developed little resort towns with sandy beaches, equipped with showers, and umbrellas and sun beds for rent; the beach on the Gulf of Kefalos is a haven for those wishing to escape the tourist fray—broad, sandy, scenically magnificent, and for much if its length devoid of development, curving around an enchanting bay. In the morning, caïques make regular runs from Skala to the beaches of Patmos; some can be reached by car or bus, and many delightfully empty strands are the reward for a short trek on foot. Most of Patmos's beaches are coarse shingle, but there are sand-and-pebble strips with cafés and tavernas nearby. Twenty-seven of the beaches in Rhodes have been awarded EU Blue Flags for cleanliness and infrastructure; and another 15 have received the *Golden Starfish* for outstanding natural beauty and limited number of bathers. Rhodes town and the more sheltered east coast have exquisite stretches of fine-sand beaches, while the west side, which is subject to prevailing on-shore winds, can be choppy.

Dining

Although Dodecanese cooking doesn't differ greatly from that of the mainland, there are some restaurants with unique locations and imaginative preparations. Rhodes produces most of its own foodstuffs, so you can count on fresh fruit and vegetables and, of course, a variety of fish (as everywhere, very expensive). Kos, too, is a garden island with lush fields; fresh vegetables are easy for chefs to come by, and even simple salads can be delicious. Despite the fact that neither Patmos nor Symi, with their barren landscapes, has much homegrown produce, tavernas and restaurants on both serve some excellent fare. Always check the food on display in the kitchen, and ask about the specialty of the day. Dress on all the islands is casual and reservations are not necessary unless specified.

CATEGORY	COST*
$$$$	over 9,000 dr. (€26.54)
$$$	6,000 dr.–9,000 dr. (€17.69–€26.54)
$$	3,000 dr.–6,000 dr. (€8.84–€17.69)
$	under 3,000 dr. (€8.84)

per person for an appetizer, main course, and dessert, including service and tax but excluding drinks.

Lodging

Except for Athens, Rhodes probably has more hotels per capita than anywhere else in Greece. Almost all of them are resort or tourist hotels; a few of the more luxurious cater to conference and incentive business as well. Some of the most elaborate, at the edge of town, have sea views and easy access to the beaches, which are extremely crowded in high season. You may have difficulty finding a room in Rhodes; in high season, it is best to book through an agent. The hotels in Kos tend to be only a bit more modest in size and facilities, and fully equipped tourist accommodation is plentiful. On both Rhodes and Kos, however, travelers may find it challenging to find lodging that is refreshingly Greek rather than anonymously international in style; keep in mind, too, that both islands cater largely to package tours from northern Europe, so you may find yourself surrounded by non-Greek merrymakers who never budge from the beach. Symi offers a greater number of small hotels with charm, since the island has never encouraged the development of mammoth caravansaries. Many hotels in Rhodes and throughout the Dodecanese are closed from November through April. Hotels in only the $$$ and $$$$ categories are air-conditioned unless noted otherwise.

CATEGORY	COST*
$$$$	over 39,000 dr. (€115)
$$$	22,000 dr.–39,000 dr. (€64.89–€115)
$$	13,000 dr.–22,000 dr. (€38.34–€64.89)
$	under 13,000 dr. (€38.34)

All prices are for a standard double room in high season, excluding breakfast, unless indicated.

✎ *following the text of a review is your signal that the property has a Web site, where you will find details and, usually, images; for a link, visit www.fodors.com/urls.*

Shopping

Although Rhodes is no longer a duty-free port, some people still consider shopping to be one of its major attractions. Upscale shops sell furs and jewelry as well as more affordable trinkets. The styling of the jewelry can be extremely attractive, but the prices are no better than in Athens and are often even higher. In both Rhodes town and in Lindos, you can buy good copies of Lindos ware, a fine pottery with green and red floral designs. Patmos, an upscale tourist island that caters largely to prosperous Athenians, has some elegant boutiques selling jewelry and crafts, including antiques mainly from the island. In Chora, you'll find a wide selection of traditional ceramics, icons, and silver jewelry.

Exploring Rhodes and the Dodecanese

Of the Dodecanese, we highlight four: strategically located Rhodes has played by far the most important role in history; Kos comes in second, particularly in its vestiges of antiquity, when its famous Sanctuary of Asklepeios, a center of healing, drew people from all over the ancient world. Both islands are worth visiting for a couple of days each. Symi, easily accessible from Rhodes, is a virtual museum of 19th-century neoclassical architecture, and Patmos, where St. John wrote his Revelation, became a renowned monastic center during the Byzantine period and continues as a significant focal point of the Greek Orthodox faith. Symi offers qualities that in large part have been lost on overdeveloped Rhodes and Kos—peace, quiet, and a way of life that remains essentially Greek

Numbers in the text correspond to numbers in the margin and on the Rhodes and the Dodecanese map.

Great Itineraries

If you have at least two weeks, exploring the Dodecanese by boat makes for a marvelous holiday. Ferries and hydrofoils run frequently between the main islands. Boats to the less-visited islands are infrequent, however, especially in winter, and no boats sail if the weather is bad— so you have to allow time for getting stranded.

Even on a short visit, travelers can partake of the diverse pleasures of the Dodecanese by combining a visit to one of the busier islands with a retreat to a quieter place. You may want, for instance, to begin in Rhodes (which has excellent air connections to Athens), to visit the architectural wonders of Rhodes town and Lindos, then make the crossing to nearby, much quieter Symi, with its neoclassical architecture and striking, arid landscape. Then you'll want to visit nearby Patmos, a hilly landscape that is as mystical as its famous monastery.

IF YOU HAVE 3 DAYS

Confine your visit to 🖼 **Rhodes** ①–⑧, where you can spend a day walking through the fascinating old town and visiting the Grand Palace of the Masters and other sights. You will definitely want to make a day trip to the old city of **Lindos** ②, where you can also enjoy a fine beach, and stop in **Petaloudes** ⑦, the Valley of the Butterflies, en route back to Rhodes town.

IF YOU HAVE 5 DAYS

🖼 **Rhodes** ①–⑧ is the best place to begin a longer tour of the Dodecanese. You will want to spend a couple of days there, following your own version of the itinerary above adding at least two overnights in Symi, famed for its idyllic beauty, then on the final day take the hydrofoil to 🖼 **Patmos** to visit the famous monastery and Chora, the charming village that sprung up around its walls.

IF YOU HAVE 7 DAYS

Again after exploring 🖼 **Rhodes** ①–⑧ and 🖼 **Symi,** where you should spend at least one night to enjoy the island once the day-trippers have returned to Rhodes, you will want to take a hydrofoil or ferry to 🖼 **Kos,** and spend a couple of days exploring this island with its Greek and Roman excavations, Venetian and Turkish architecture, and beautiful landscape that along the coast is flat enough to provide perfect biking terrain. After touring the mosque and narrow streets of 🖼 **Kos town,** which is also a good place to stay, make the trip just out of town to the archaeological site of Asklepieion; then venture farther afield to other archaeological sites and the island's excellent beaches. From Kos, you can travel on to 🖼 **Patmos** by ferry or hydrofoil.

When to Tour

The best time to tour Rhodes and the Dodecanese is during high season, from about March or April to November, when all establishments are open and the weather is most agreeable.

RHODES

The island of Rhodes (1,400 square km [540 square mi]) is, after Crete, Evia, and Lesbos, the largest Greek island and, along with Sicily and Cyprus, one of the great islands of the Mediterranean. Rhodes is a country unto itself, and in the years before tourism, it was easily self-sufficient. It lies almost exactly halfway between Piraeus and Cyprus, 18 km (11 mi) off the coast of Asia Minor, and it was long considered a bridge between Europe and the East. Geologically similar to the Turkish mainland, it was probably once a part of it, separated by one of the frequent volcanic upheavals this volatile region has experienced.

Rhodes saw successive waves of settlement, culminating with the arrival of the Dorian Greeks from Argos and Laconia sometime early in the first millennium BC. They settled in Ialyssos, Lindos, and Kameiros and together with Dorians from Kos, and from Knidos and Halicarnassos in Asia Minor, formed a kind of loose confederation, later known as the Hexapolis (Six Cities). From the 8th to the 6th centuries BC the three Rhodian cities established settlements in Italy, France, Spain, and Egypt and actively traded with mainland Greece, exporting pottery, oil, wine, and figs. By the end of the 6th century BC, the flourishing independence, creativity, and expansion came to an abrupt halt when the Persians took over the island, later forcing Rhodians to provide ships and men for King Xerxes' attack on the mainland in 480 BC. The Persian failure resulted in their final expulsion from the mainland and the creation of a league of city-states under Athenian leadership. In 408 BC the inhabitants of the three cities established the united city of Rhodes, on the site of the modern town; much of the populace moved there, and the earlier towns eventually became mainly religious centers.

The new city grew and flourished, and its political organization was the model for the city of Alexandria in Egypt. At the end of the 4th century BC the Rhodians commissioned the sculptor Chares, from Lindos, to create the famous Colossus, a huge bronze statue of the sun god, Helios, one of the Seven Wonders of the Ancient World. The next two centuries were prosperous for Rhodes's economy, thanks to its superb location on trade routes. In 227 BC, when an earthquake razed the city, help poured in from all quarters of the eastern Mediterranean, attesting to the city's importance. After the calamity the Delphic oracle advised the Rhodians to let the great Colossus lie where it had been toppled. So it lay, for some eight centuries, until AD 654, when it was sold as scrap metal and carted off to Syria allegedly by a caravan of 900 camels. After that, we know nothing of its fate.

In 42 BC, Rhodes came under the hegemony of Rome, and through the years of the empire, it was fabled as one of the most beautiful of cities, with parks and gardens and the straight streets that had been laid out in the 4th century BC. The roads were lined with porticoes, houses, and gardens, and according to Pliny, who described the city in the 1st century AD, it possessed some 2,000 statues, at least 100 of them of colossal scale. The sculptural school flourished through the Hellenistic period, and one of its most famous exemplars—probably executed in the 1st century BC—was the *Laocöon*, showing the Trojan priest who warned the Trojans to beware of Greeks bearing gifts, and his sons, in their death struggles with a giant serpent, a work that Pliny reports having seen in Rome in the 1st century AD. Excavations in Rome in 1506 uncovered the statue, which stands in the Vatican today. The intellectual life of Rhodes was also dazzling, attracting students and visitors from around the Mediterranean; its schools of rhetoric and philosophy found great favor among young Romans.

Today, there is almost nothing left of the ancient glory of Rhodes. The city was ravaged by Arab invaders in AD 654 and again in 807, and only with the expulsion of the Arabs, and the reconquest of Crete by the Byzantine emperors, did the city begin to revive. Rhodes was a crucial stop on the road to the Holy Land during the Crusades. It came briefly under Venetian influence, then Byzantine, then Genoese, but in 1309, when the Knights of St. John took the city from its Genoese masters, its most glorious modern era began.

The Knights of St. John, an order of Hospitalers organized in Jerusalem to protect and care for Christian pilgrims, were grouped into "tongues" by country of origin. Each tongue's inn, its place of assembly, was under the orders of a bailiff; the bailiffs were ruled by an elected Grand Master. By the beginning of the 12th century the order had become military in nature, and after the fall of Acre in 1291, the Knights fled from Palestine, withdrawing first to Cyprus and then to Rhodes. In 1312, the Knights inherited the immense wealth of the Templars (another religious military order, which had just been outlawed by the Pope) and used it to fortify the city. But for all their power and the strength of their walls, the Knights could not hold back the Turks. By the 16th century they manned the last bastions against the Turks in the eastern Mediterranean, as one by one the towns and cities of Byzantium fell. In preparation for the attack they knew would come, the Knights continually enlarged the moats and reinforced the sea walls, building new towers, fortifying gates, and installing artillery of all sizes. In 1522, the Ottoman Turks, with 300 ships and 100,000 men under Süleyman the Magnificent, began what was to be the final siege, taking the city after six months. During the Turkish occupation, Rhodes became a possession of the Grand Admiral, who collected taxes but left the Rhodians to pursue a generally peaceful and prosperous existence. They continued to build ships and to trade with Greece, Constantinople (later Istanbul), Syria, and Egypt. The Greek mainland was liberated by the War of 1821, but Rhodes and the Dodecanese remained part of the Ottoman Empire until 1912, when the Italians took over. After World War II, the Dodecanese were formally united with Greece in 1947.

Rhodes Town

★ ❶ *250 km (155 mi) east of Piraeus.*

Early travelers described Rhodes as a town of two parts: a castle or high town (Collachium) and a lower city. Today Rhodes town is still a city of two parts, but now the divisions are the **old town,** which incorporates the high town and lower city, and the **new town,** the modern metropolis that spreads away from the walls that encircle the old town. Old town contains numerous Orthodox and Catholic churches (a great number of which have disappeared), Turkish structures, and fine houses, some of which follow the ancient orthogonal plan. All the public buildings are similar in style, creating a harmonious whole, which has been enhanced in recent years by careful reconstruction. Staircases are on the outside, either on the facade or in the court; the facades are elegantly constructed of well-cut limestone from Lindos. Windows and doors are often outlined with strongly profiled moldings and surmounted by arched casements.

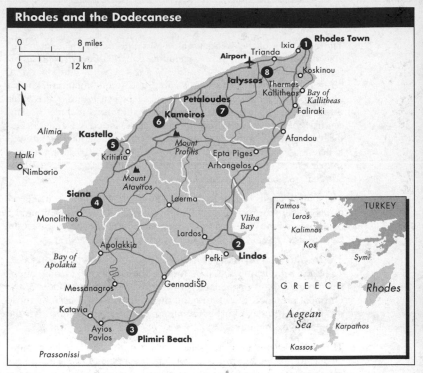

Rhodes and the Dodecanese

In the castle area, a city within a city, the Knights built most of their monuments. The **Palace of the Grand Masters,** at the highest spot of the medieval city, is the best place to begin a tour of Rhodes; here you can get oriented before wandering through the labyrinthine old town. Of great help is the permanent exhibition on the downstairs level, with extensive displays on the building, and maps and plans of the city. A large rectangular building with a broad central courtyard, the palace was so solidly built that it withstood unscathed the Turkish siege, but in 1856, an explosion of ammunition stored nearby in the cellars of the Church of St. John devastated the palace; the present buildings are Italian reconstructions. Note the Hellenistic and Roman mosaic floors throughout, which came from the Italian excavations in Kos. ✉ *Castle, old town,* ☎ *0241/23359.* 🎫 *1,200 dr./€3.53.* ⊘ *Tues.–Fri. 8:30–7 (8:30–3 in winter), weekends 8:30–3.*

The Knights of St. John were buried in the church that once stood at the site of the **Loggia of St. John** (✉ Old town, in front of court of Palace of the Grand Masters), which was also almost totally rebuilt by the Italians. From the Loggia, the **Street of the Knights** descends toward the **Commercial Port,** bordered on both sides by the **Inns of the Tongues,** where members supped and held their meetings.

The **Inn of France** (✉ About halfway down St. of the Knights from Loggia) was the largest of the Knights' gathering spots. The ground floor of this typically Rhodian building is occupied by vaulted utility areas opening onto the road; the first floor is reached by a stairway rising from the central courtyard. The facade is carved with flowers and heraldic patterns and bears an inscription that dates the building between 1492 and 1509.

The **Hospital** (✉ At end of St. of the Knights) was the largest of the Knights' public buildings. The imposing facade of this building, completed in 1489, opens into a courtyard, where cannonballs remain from the siege of 1522.

The main floor of the **Archaeological Museum** contains a collection of ancient pottery and sculpture, including two well-known representations of Aphrodite: the *Aphrodite of Rhodes,* who, while bathing, pushes aside her hair as if she's listening; and a standing figure, known as *Aphrodite Thalassia,* or "of the sea," as she was found in the water off the northern city beach. Other important works include the 6th-century *kouros* (statue of youthful male nude) found in Kameiros and the beautiful 5th-century BC funerary stele of Timarista bidding farewell to her mother, Crito. ⊠ *Platia Mouseou (Museum Sq.), reached by wide staircase from Hospital,* ☎ *0241/27657.* 🎟 *1,000 dr./€2.94.* ☉ *Tues.– Sat. 8:30–6 (8:30–3 in winter), Sun. 8:30–3.*

The soaring vaults of **Our Lady of the Bourg** (⊠ In ruins just inside remains of wall), the magnificent Gothic cathedral, are a startling reminder of Rhodes's Frankish past. The **Commercial Harbor** (⊠ Just past St. Catherine's Gate) is Rhodes's largest, close to the cathedral.

The **Mosque of Süleyman** (⊠ At top of Sokratous) was built soon after 1522 and rebuilt in 1808. The **Turkish Library** (⊠ Sokratous, opposite mosque) dates to the late 18th century. Striking reminders of the Ottoman presence, the library and the mosque are still used by those members of Rhodes's Turkish community who stayed behind after the population exchange of 1922.

The **walls** of Rhodes in themselves are one of the great medieval monuments in the Mediterranean. Wonderfully preserved (even before the extensive Italian reconstruction), they illustrate the engineering capabilities as well as the financial and human resources available to the Knights. Each stretch of the wall was called a "curtain," and its defense was the responsibility of a tongue. For 200 years the Knights strengthened the walls by thickening them, up to 40 ft in places, and curving them so as to deflect cannonballs. The moat between the inner and outer walls never contained water; it was a device to prevent invaders from constructing siege towers. Part of the road that runs along the top for the entire 4 km (2½ mi) is accessible through municipal guided tours. ⊠ *Old town,* ☎ *0241/21954.* 🎟 *800 dr./€2.35.* ☉ *Tours Tues. and Sat. 2:45 (arrive at least 15 mins early); departure from palace entrance.*

The medieval city of Rhodes is now completely surrounded by the **new city** (⊠ North of medieval walls, bordering small Mandraki Harbor); many of the city's official buildings are found here, their style heavily influenced by the Grand Masters' Palace and other medieval monuments and making abundant use of Lindos stone, crenellation, and Gothic architectural detail.

Rhodes's harbor is dominated by the **cathedral** (⊠ Harbor), modeled after the destroyed Church of St. John in the Collachium. The **Governor's Palace** (⊠ Harbor, next to cathedral) is constructed in an arcaded Venetian Gothic style. Other buildings in the vicinity include the **port authority** and **customs offices,** the **municipal buildings,** and a huge **open-air bazaar,** now faced by fancy confectionery shops. The **main shopping areas** of new Rhodes are just behind these buildings.

To the west of Rhodes town rises **Mt. Smith,** its slopes still dotted with villas and gardens that in the early part of this century made Rhodes look like a miniature Italian Riviera. Many of them, unfortunately, have been torn down to make way for modern apartment buildings. The **acropolis** contains the remains of many ancient buildings, including a heavily restored **theater,** a **stadium,** the three restored columns of the

Temple of Apollo Pythios, and scrappy remains of the **Temple of Athena Polias.** For a dramatic view, walk to the westernmost edge of Mt. Smith, which drops via a sharp and almost inaccessible cliff to the shore below, now lined with enormous hotels. ⊠ *At top of Mt. Smith,* ☎ *0241/21954.* 🎫 *Free.*

Beaches

Elli beach (⊠ New town) has fine sand, an easy slope, chairs and umbrellas for rent, showers, pedal boats, and Windsurfers. All of the coast around Rhodes town is developed, so you can reach some of the best beaches only through the hotels that occupy them.

Dining and Lodging

$$$ ✕ **Alexis.** Carrying on the tradition begun by his father in 1957, Yian-
★ nis Katsimprakis spares nothing to bring his loyal clientele the very best seafood, speaking passionately of eating fish as though it were a lost art. Don't bother with the menu; just look at the day's offerings, and if you're a neophyte, ask for suggestions. Whether it's beluga caviar, mussels in wine sauce and garlic, smoked eel, oysters, or sea urchins, you'll savor every bite. He even serves *porphyra* (murex), the mollusk yielding the famous purple dye for the Byzantine emperors. A side dish might be sautéed squash with local greens such as *vlita* (notchweed) and *glistrida* (purslane). Yiannis also offers bountiful menus for two, which include champagne. Eat your meal on the quiet, shady terrace, perhaps with the new local dry white, Rodos 2400 (in honor of the city's 2,400th anniversary), and don't miss the house salad and the dessert called *hilli* (baklava with ice cream). ⊠ *Sokratous 18, old town,* ☎ *0241/29347. AE, V. Closed Nov. No lunch Sun. in summer.*

$$$ ✕ **Ta Kioupia.** Set just outside Rhodes town in a group of humble farm
★ buildings, Ta Kioupia is anything but modest. The white-stucco rooms with exposed ceiling beams are elegant: antique farm tools are displayed, and there are linen tablecloths and napkins, fine china, and crystal. Regular customers get their own engraved plate and glass. Food is presented on large platters and you select what you fancy: pine-nut salad, *tiropita* (four-cheese pie), an eggplant dip that customers joke can't be beat, *bourekakia* (phyllo pastry stuffed with cheese and nuts), *korkorosouvlaki* (rooster kebab) . . . the list goes on—and the food is extraordinary in its variety and quality. ⊠ *Tris, about 7 km (4½ mi) west of Rhodes,* ☎ *0241/91824. AE, V. Closed Sun. Oct.–May. No lunch.*

$$ ✕ **Dinoris.** In a great hall built in 1530 as a stable for the Knights, Di-
★ noris has long specialized in fish. The food and service lure appreciative and demanding clients, from the mayor to hotel owners and visiting VIPs. Rusticity prevails, with embroidered tablecloths, brightly painted pottery, and thick, seemingly handwoven draperies on the windows. For appetizers, try the variety platter, which includes *psarokeftedakia* (fish balls made from a secret recipe) as well as mussels, shrimp, and lobster. Other special dishes are coquilles St. Jacques, grilled prawns, and the sea urchin salad. ⊠ *Museum Sq. 14a, old town,* ☎ *0241/35530. Reservations essential. AE, MC, V.*

$$ ✕ **Palia Istoria.** Never mind that this *mezedopolio* (meze joint) is a bit
★ out of the way in the new town. Gregarious former actor Haris Kerasiotis has created a visual treat in the space ensconced in an old house with high ceilings, beautiful floors, and genteel murals. Deciding among the entrées can be tantalizing—*ameletes piperaki* (testicles in pepper sauce), shrimp ouzo with orange juice, pork tenderloin in garlic and wine sauce. The flambéed banana dessert wrapped in phyllo, followed by the portlike Komantaria liqueur from Cyprus and an espresso, will complete this serendipitous meal. ⊠ *Odos Mitropoleos 108 (about 800 dr./€2.35 by taxi from old town),* ☎ *0241/32421. Reservations essential. MC, V. No lunch.*

$ ✕ **Kavo d'Oro.** This simple taverna is one of the few places in the old town where you can get a good, inexpensive roast chicken, veal, and lamb and grilled meat dishes. Especially good are the *papoutsakia* (eggplant "shoes" stuffed with mincemeat). The decor is taverna style: plain whitewashed walls, with the typical rush-seat, straight-back chairs, and a vine-shaded courtyard at the back for warm-weather dining. The same management runs a second taverna by the same name at Orfeous 40–42. ⊠ *Parodos Sokratous 41 (street behind Sokratous), old town,* ☎ *0241/36181. Reservations not accepted. V. Closed Nov.–Mar.*

$$$$ ▥ **Rodos Park.** Rhodes's most luxurious hotel is also one of its most
  ★   quiet retreats, with more staff than guests. The large, marble-floored guest rooms and suites have such amenities as Jacuzzis, satellite color TVs, minibars, and direct-dial phones; many have stunning views over the old town, which is just a few minutes' walk away. ⊠ *Odos Riga Ferous 12, Rhodes town 85100,* ☎ *0241/24612,* 𝔽𝔸𝕏 *0241/24613. 30 rooms, 30 suites. Restaurant, bar, minibars, sauna, steam room, exercise room. AE, DC, MC, V.* 🍽

$$$ ▥ **Grand Hotel Summer Palace.** A cut above other resort hotels in the area, the Grand is actually in Rhodes, near the beach, the old town, and the new town's nightlife scene. Though the hotel is not exceptional from the outside, once you enter the name makes sense: the atrium lobby is spacious, with giant plants and views onto the porticoed pool and garden. The best rooms are in the newer wing, with pink marble floors and pretty paintings of nymphs and goddesses. They feature subdued blue and rose furnishings, trompe l'oeil touches, alcoved bathtubs, and key cards that automatically turn on the lights. Breakfast is included. ⊠ *Akti Miaouli 1, new town, 85100,* ☎ *0241/26284; 01/291–7027 in Athens;* 𝔽𝔸𝕏 *0241/35589. 362 rooms, 18 suites. Restaurant, bar, 1 indoor pool, 2 pools, sauna, tennis court, exercise room, shops, casino, nightclub. AE, DC, MC, V.*

$$ ▥ **S. Nikolis Hotel.** One of the finest accommodations in the old town—and one of the most charming in Rhodes—occupies a restored house. The small but tidy rooms are enlivened by arches and other architectural details, and many have balconies overlooking a lovely garden. Breakfast is served on the roof terrace. Excellent service, including laundry, is caringly administered by Sotiris and Marianne Nikolis. ⊠ *Odos Ippodamou 61, old town, 85100,* ☎ *0241/34561,* 𝔽𝔸𝕏 *0241/32034. 10 rooms, 4 apartments. Breakfast room. AE, MC, V.* 🍽

$ ▥ **Pension Sofia.** The old town is full of rooms to rent, but budget-priced Sofia's, run by the same people that own Kavo d'Oro (☞ *above*), is bright, pleasant, and framed by trailing jasmine; each room has a little bath. ⊠ *Aristofanous 27, old town, 85100,* ☎ *0241/36181. 10 rooms. No credit cards. Closed Dec.–Mar.*

Nightlife and the Arts

BARS AND DISCOS

It's claimed that Rhodes has more bars and discos per person than New York, Berlin, or Paris—most are in the new town and resort areas such as Faliraki. They come and go, so it's best to check with your concierge or the free *Rodos News,* available at the Greek National Tourist Organization (GNTO or EOT) office (☞ Visitor Information *in* Rhodes and the Dodecanese A to Z, *below*).

CASINO

Rhodes's **casino** (⊠ In Grand Hotel Astir Palace, new town, ☎ 0241/28109) is open all year; you must show your passport to get in. The entry fee is 1,500 dr./€4.42, and it is open from 8 PM to 2 AM.

GREEK DANCE

With performances since 1971, the **Nelly Dimoglou Folk Dance Theatre** (⊠ Andronikou 7, behind Turkish baths, old town, ☎ 0241/20157) keeps alive the tradition of Greek dance, with strict adherence to authentic detail in costume and performance. From May until September it can be seen weekdays at 9:20 PM for 2,800 dr./€8.25. It also gives dance lessons.

SOUND-AND-LIGHT SHOW

From April through October the **Sound-and-Light Show** (⊠ Grounds of the Palace of the Grand Masters, ☎ 0241/21922) tells the story of the Turkish siege. English-language performances are Monday and Tuesday 8:15 PM; Wednesday, Friday, and Saturday 9:15 PM; and Thursday 10:15 PM. From mid-May to July performances start one hour later; the cost is 2,500 dr./€7.37.

Outdoor Activities and Sports

DIVING

The **Dive Med Center** (⊠ Dragoumi 5, new town, ☎ 0241/33654) offers a "resort dive" (11,000 dr./€32.44) for first-time divers and for those who don't have a certificate. Customized boats will take you to Thermes Kallitheas, the only place where you can dive on the island. After a 30-minute theory lesson and practice in shallow water, you'll descend to a moderate depth to explore the underwater world. The center also offers courses leading to PADI or NAUI certification. Keep in mind that even if you are certified, it is illegal to dive on your own in Greece. The center is open from May to October.

FISHING

No license is required for trolling or line fishing in Rhodes. The best fishing is reputed to be off Kameiros Skala, Kallithea, Lindos, and Gennadi. Sometimes the commercial fishing boats that moor opposite St. Catherine's Gate will take visiting anglers out on trips.

GOLF

There is an 18-hole golf course in the village of **Afandou** (⊠ about 20 km [12 mi] outside Rhodes town, ☎ 0241/51451). The course is open daily 8 to 8; a round costs 6,000 dr./€17.69 and a weekly pass worth seven rounds costs 32,000 dr. Prices are lower off-season. The Rodos Open takes place here in October.

SAILING

Information can be obtained on dinghy sailing and sculling from the **Rodos Yacht Club** (NOR; ⊠ Platia Kountouriotou 9, Rhodes new town, ☎ 0241/23287). To rent yachts, call the **Yacht Agency Rhodes Ltd.** (⊠ Amerikis 95, ☎ 0241/22927).

TENNIS

Several first-class and luxury hotels have courts, where equipment can be rented and where nonguests can usually play. The **Rhodes Tennis Club** in Elli (☎ 0241/25705) is open to nonmembers. Prices are 2,200 dr./€6.48 per hour for two people.

WATER SPORTS

The larger resort hotels offer windsurfing, waterskiing, and, in some cases, jet-skiing and parasailing. Windsurfing is best near Ixia and Ialyssos; waterskiing, on the sheltered east coast.

Shopping

BOUTIQUES

The **old city's shopping center** (⊠ Intersection at Sokratous) is lined with boutiques selling furs, jewelry, and other high-ticket items. In Rhodes town you can also buy good copies of **Lindos ware,** a fine pottery decorated with green and red floral motifs.

AROUND THE ISLAND

The island's east coast, particularly the stretch between Rhodes town and Lindos, is blessed with white sandy beaches and dotted with copses of trees, interspersed with fertile valleys full of figs and olives. Unfortunately, its beauty has meant that long stretches of this country are now given over to vast resort hotels and holiday villages. Even so, there are still some wonderfully untrammeled sections of beach to be found all around the island, and the town of Lindos alone warrants an excursion from Rhodes town.

Faliraki

16 km (10 mi) south of Rhodes town.

As you leave Rhodes town and travel south along the East Coast, you approach a strange sight: **Thermes Kallitheas** (✉ About 10 km [6 mi] south of Rhodes town; 6 km [4 mi] north of Faliraki), a group of buildings that looks as if it has been transplanted from Morocco. In fact, this is a spa built in 1929 by the Italians, now much neglected. The great physician Hippocrates of Kos extolled these mineral springs in the early 2nd century BC for alleviating liver, kidney, and rheumatic ailments.

Beaches

Faliraki Beach (✉ 6 km [4 mi] south of Thermes Kallitheas) is a splendid strip of sandy beach now ringed by hotels. At **Afandou Beach** (✉ About 7 km [4½ mi] past Faliraki), you'll see on the right small tavernas spread out under grape arbors in the brilliant sun. Before or after your meal, you can run across the road to the beach for a dip.

Dining

$$ ✕ **Epta Piges.** If you've had enough of Afandou Beach, take an easy, uphill walk through a pleasant ravine to a deeply shaded glen surrounding Epta Piges, or Seven Springs. Here an enterprising local shepherd began serving simple fare to visitors about 40 years ago, and his sideline turned into the busy taverna of today. He imported peacocks and turned them loose in the woods, where they pierce the silence with their scratchy shrieks and flaunt their bright plumage high up in the trees. If you arrive before mealtime, you can have a glass of freshly squeezed orange juice. ✉ *About 2 km (1 mi) from Afandou Beach via the footpath. No credit cards. Closed Oct.–Mar.*

Lindos

❷ *60 km (37 mi) southeast of Rhodes town, 30 km (18 mi) southwest of Faliraki.*

Lindos, cradled between two harbors, had a particular importance in antiquity. Before the existence of Rhodes, it was the island's principal maritime center. Perhaps the poverty of Lindos's land forced the Lindians to turn outward from their fine harbor for survival and led to their maritime success. Lindos possessed a revered sanctuary, consecrated to Athena, whose cult probably succeeded that of a pre-Hellenic divinity named Lindia, and the sanctuary was dedicated to Athena Lindia. By the 6th century BC, an impressive temple dominated the settlement, and after the foundation of Rhodes, the Lindians set up a *propylaia* (monumental entrance gate) on the model of Athens's. In the mid-4th century BC, the temple was destroyed by fire and almost immediately rebuilt, with a new wooden statue of the goddess covered by gold leaf, and with arms, head, and legs of marble or ivory. In the Hellenistic period, the Acropolis was further adorned with a great portico at the foot of the steps to the propylaia. Lindos prospered into Roman times, during the Middle Ages, and under the Knights of St. John. Only at the beginning of the 19th century did the age-old shipping activity cease. The population decreased radically, reviving only with the 20th-century influx of foreigners.

For about 1,000 dr./€2.94, donkeys can be hired for the 15-minute climb from the modern town to the **Acropolis.** The winding path leads past a gauntlet of Lindian women who spread out their lace and embroidery over the rocks like fresh laundry. The final approach ascends a steep flight of stairs, past a marvelous 5th-century BC **relief** of the prow of a Lindian ship, carved into the rock; and through the main gate of the **Crusader castle.**

The **entrance** to the Acropolis, almost all of it undergoing restoration, takes you through the **medieval castle,** with the Byzantine **chapel of St. John** on the next level above. On the **upper terraces** are the remains of the elaborate **porticoes** and **stoas,** initially restored by the Italians. As is the case with Sounion (☞ Chapter 2), the site and temple command an immense sweep of sea, making a powerful statement on behalf of the deity and city to which they belonged; the lofty white columns on the summit must have presented a magnificent picture. The main portico had 42 Doric columns, at the center of which an opening led to the staircase up to the **propylaia.** The temple at the very top is surprisingly modest, given the drama of the approach. There is no encircling colonnade; instead, as was common in the 4th century BC, both the front and the rear are flanked by four Doric columns, like the Temple of Athena Nike on the Acropolis of Athens (☞ Chapter 1). Numerous inscribed statue bases were found all over the summit, attesting in many cases to the work of Lindian sculptors, who were clearly second to none. ⊠ *Acropolis of Lindos,* ☎ *0244/31258.* ▦ *1,000 dr./€2.94.* ☉ *Tues.–Sun. 8:30–3.*

Lindos town (⊠ On land side of Acropolis) is remarkably well preserved, and many 15th-century houses are still in use. Everywhere are examples of the Crusader architecture you saw in Rhodes town: substantial houses of finely cut grayish Lindos limestone with inner courtyards containing stairs to the upper level. The facades are pierced by doors and windows crowned with stone arches, often elaborately carved in the characteristic rope patterns. Many floors are paved with the typical Rhodian black-and-white pebble mosaics. Intermixed with these Crusader buildings are other houses of almost Cycladic appearance: white geometric shapes pierced by plain square windows framed with blue shutters nestle in gardens filled with bougainvillea and hibiscus. Many of the owners of these homes offer rooms for rent; the **tourist office** (⊠ Platia Eleftherias, ☎ 0244/31227), open May through October, daily 9 to 10, can arrange rentals, but rooms are often booked well in advance by tour operators.

Like Rhodes town, Lindos town is enchanting off-season and almost unbearably crowded otherwise, since pilgrims make the trek from Rhodes daily. The main street is lined with shops selling clothes and trinkets of all types; the streets are medieval in their narrowness and twisting course, so the passage slows to a snail's pace. Lindos town can be reached only on foot from the parking lot.

The **Church of the Panayia** (⊠ Just off main platia) is a graceful building with a fine bell tower, now in perilous condition. The body of the church probably antedates the Knights, although the bell tower bears their arms with the dates 1484–90. The interior has frescoes painted in 1779 by Gregory of Symi.

Gennadi and the South Coast

80 km (50 mi) south of Rhodes town, 20 km (12½ mi) south of Lindos.

The area south of Lindos is less traveled than the rest of the island. The land is not as attractive as in the north, the sandy beaches are fewer, and the soil is less fertile, so there is much less development. The village of Gennadi offers some inexpensive pensions and rooms for rent, as well as tavernas.

Beach

❸ There's a detour to **Plimiri Beach** (✉ 10 km [6 mi] south of Gennadi), a good place for a swim to break the long drive. The ancient city of Kyrbe is believed to have stood in the hills behind the town until it was destroyed by a *plimiri* (flood); hence the name of the village.

En Route From Gennadi, turn inland on a road that leads west across the island, through a river valley dotted with curious hillocks, to the town of Apolakkia, where you bear right at the crossroads to begin your return trip north. The road to Siana climbs through spectacularly wooded hills.

Siana

❹ *60 km (37¼ mi) southwest of Rhodes town, 20 km (12 mi) northwest of Gennadi.*

The town of Siana perches above a vast, fertile valley and sits in the shadow of a rock outcropping crowned with the ruin of a castle.

Shopping

LOCAL SPECIALTIES

Siana is known for *souma* (a local liqueur distilled from grapes, resembling unflavored schnapps). Its renowned honey and walnuts can be obtained at **Tasia's Kafenion** (✉ Just past town church on the main road) or any of the other **cafés** at which hordes of tourist buses occasionally stop.

En Route Beyond Siana, the road continues on a high ridge through thick pine forests, which carpet the precipitous slopes dropping toward the sea. To the right looms the bare, stony massif of **Mt. Ataviros,** Rhodes's highest peak, at 3,986 ft.

Kritinia

35 km (21¾ mi) southwest of Rhodes town, 12 km (7½ mi) northeast from Siana.

❺ The **Kastello** (✉ South of Kritinia), a fortress built by the Knights in the late 15th century, is an impressive ruin, situated high above the sea with fine views in every direction.

Kameiros

❻ *25 km (15½ mi) south of Rhodes town, 17 km (10½ mi) northeast of Kritinia.*

The site of ancient Kameiros is one of the three ancient cities of Rhodes. The apparently unfortified ruins, excavated by the Italians in 1929, lie on a slope above the sea. Most of what is visible today dates to the classical period and later, including impressive remains of the early Hellenistic period. ✉ *Kameiros archaeological site,* ☎ *0241/41435.* 🎟 *500 dr./€1.47.* ☉ *Tues.–Fri. 8:30–4:45 (8:30–2:45 in winter), weekends 8:30–2:45.*

Petaloudes

❼ *22 km (13½ mi) from Kameiros, 20 km (12½ mi) from Rhodes town.*

Petaloudes, the Valley of the Butterflies, lives up to its name, especially in July and August. In summer the *kalimorpha quadripunctaria,* actually a moth species, cluster by the thousands around the low bushes of the pungent storax plant, which grows all over the area. Don't agitate the butterflies. Over the years, unfortunately, their number has diminished, partly owing to busloads of tourists clapping hands to see them fly up in dense clouds, startled by the slightest sound. Access to the valley is through a main road and admission booth. ⊠ *Petaloudes.* 🖃 *600 dr./€1.76.* ☉ *Butterfly season, May–Sept., 8–5.*

❽ Mt. Filerimos is capped by the site of **Ialyssos,** the third of the ancient Rhodian communities. There are some remains of an early Hellenistic Temple of Athena, as well as those of a Byzantine church. Because of its strategic position, Filerimos also was used by the Knights for a fortress, which stands above a monastery of Our Lady of Filerimos. ⊠ *Acropolis of Ialyssos; take turnoff, going on the coast road west from Petaloudes, at Trianda and head south for 5 km (3 mi),* ☎ *0241/ 92202.* 🖃 *800 dr./€2.35.* ☉ *Tues.–Fri. 8:30–5 (8:30–3 in winter), weekends 8:30–3.*

SYMI

The island of Symi, 11 km (7 mi) north of Rhodes, is an enchanting place, with its star attraction being Chorio, a 19th-century town of fine neoclassical mansions. The island has few beaches (and even some of those are accessible only by boat) and almost no flat land, so it is not attractive to developers. As a result, quiet Symi provides a peaceful retreat for travelers, who tend to fall in love with the island on first visit and return year after year.

Nireus, the ancient king of Symi, who sailed with three vessels to assist the Greeks at Troy, is mentioned in Homer. Symi was later part of the Dorian Hexapolis dominated by Rhodes, and it remained under Rhodian dominance throughout the Roman and Byzantine periods. The island has good natural harbors, and the nearby coast of Asia Minor provided plentiful timber for the Symiotes, who were fine shipbuilders, fearless seafarers and sponge divers, and rich and successful merchants. Under the Ottomans their harbor was proclaimed a free port and attracted the trade of the entire region. Witness to their prosperity are the fine neoclassical mansions that were fashionable elsewhere in Greece at the same time. The Symiotes' continuous travel and trade and their frequent contact with Europe led them to incorporate foreign elements in their furnishings, clothes, and cultural life. At first they lived in Chorio, high on the hillside above the port, and in the second half of the 19th century spread down to the seaside at Yialos. There were some 20,000 inhabitants at this acme, but under the Italian occupation at the end of the Italo-Turkish war in 1912, the island declined; the Symiotes lost their holdings in Asia Minor and were unable to convert their fleets to steam. Many emigrated to work elsewhere, and now there are just a few thousand inhabitants in Chorio and Yialos.

Yialos

11 km (7 mi) north of Rhodes, 452 km (281 mi) east of Piraeus.

As the boat from Rhodes to Symi rounds the last of many rocky barren spurs, the port of Yialos, at the back of a deep, narrow harbor, comes into view. The shoreside is lined with houses, and the ground floors of many of them have been converted to shops and restaurants with waterside terraces that provide the perfect locale in which to while away lazy hours; the esplanade at the head of the harbor, once the site of shipyards, is now full of pleasant outdoor tavernas and cafés. The **Church of Ayhios Ioannis** (⊠ Near center of Yialos village), built in 1838, incorporates in its walls fragments of ancient blocks from a temple that apparently stood on this site and is surrounded by a plaza paved in an intricate mosaic, fashioned from inlaid pebbles.

Dining and Lodging

$$ ✕ **Manos Fish Restaurant.** Many people think this outdoor, harborside eatery serves the best fish on Symi, and you will probably agree as you try the succulent mussels steamed in white wine, followed by a mixed grill of octopus, squid, prawns, and locally caught fish. Manos, an enterprising young man from Athens who married a local woman, is on hand to provide tips about what to see and do on his adopted island. ⊠ *Yialos harborfront, Symi,* ☎ *0241/72429. MC, V. Closed Nov.– Apr.*

$$ ✕ **Mylopetra.** This extraordinary restaurant is in the back streets of Yialos, just behind the church, and occupies an old flour mill, for which it is named. It is the creation of a German couple, Hans and Eva Sworoski, who painstakingly oversaw the delightful conversion and tend to the excellent cooking and gracious service. Dining is in the interior of the restored mill, where decorations include an ancient tomb embedded in glass beneath the floor, or on a candlelit terrace in front. The menu changes daily, though perpetual favorites include a wonderful lasagna with prawns and sea bream in a light mustard sauce. ⊠ *Yialos,* ☎ *0241/72333. MC, V. Closed Nov.–Apr.*

$ ✕ **Trawlers.** This pleasant taverna in Yialos does simple cooking better than most places on the island, and it is reasonably priced. Weather permitting, dining is also offered in a pretty square just a few steps from the port. ⊠ *Yialos,* ☎ *no phone. No credit cards.*

$$$ 🏨 **Aliki Hotel.** The most attractive hotel in Symi occupies an old mansion on the waterfront. Each of the rooms is different, but all are furnished with a tasteful mix of antiques and newer pieces. The best rooms, of course, are those that face the water, while two rooftop rooms share a tiled terrace. Breakfast is included, and in good weather is served on a waterside terrace that doubles as a bar in the evening. ⊠ *Yialos, 85600,* ☎ *0241/71665,* 𝔽𝔸𝕏 *0241/51655. 15 rooms. Bar. MC, V.*

$$ 🏨 **Dorian Studios.** You can cook your own meals in these small effi-
★ ciency apartments that climb a terraced hillside just above the waterfront in Yialos. Most have a miniature living and dining room and a cozy loft-style bedroom, both with dark wood furniture; the best accommodations face one of the several patios. ⊠ *Yialos 85600,* ☎ *0241/71181, 0241/71811, or 0241/71307. 2 rooms, 7 apartments. No credit cards. Closed Nov.–Mar.*

Chorio

1 km (½ mi) east of Yialos.

It's a 10-minute walk from the main harbor of Yialos up to Chorio, along a staircase of some 500 steps, known as **Kali Strata.** There is also a road that can be traveled in one of the island's few taxis or by bus (100 dr.), which makes an hourly circuit with stops at the harbor in Yialos, Chorio, and the little seaside community of Pedi. The Kali Strata is flanked by many elegant pastel stucco houses of neoclassical design, with fine, often classical stonework; lavish use of pediments; and intricate wrought-iron balconies. Just before the top of the stairs (where you'll come to a welcome little bar), a line of windmills crowns the hill of **Noulia.**

The collection at the **archaeological museum** displays Hellenistic and Roman sculptures and inscriptions as well as more recent carvings, icons, costumes, and handicrafts. ⊠ *Laikos Milos Sq., Chorio,* ☎ *0241/ 71114.* ☑ *Free.* ⊘ *Mon.–Sat. 8:30–2.*

Most of Chorio's many churches date to the 18th and 19th centuries, and many are ornamented with richly decorated iconostases and ornate bell towers. The **Kastro** (⊠ At the top of the town, Chorio's ancient Acropolis) incorporates fragments of Symi's history in its walls. The view from here takes in the village of Pedhi (a yachting center), as well as both Chorio and Yialos.

Dining and Lodging

$ ✕ **Georgio's Taverna.** Meals at this simple Chorio taverna, which is as popular with locals as it is with tourists, are served in a high-ceilinged, whitewashed dining room or on a terrace that is partially shaded by a grape arbor and affords wonderful views over the sea and surrounding hills. Fish is a specialty, and simply prepared *mezedes* (appetizers), such as roasted peppers topped with feta cheese and fried zucchini, can constitute a delicious meal in themselves. If you're lucky, one of the neighbors will stroll in with instrument in hand to provide an impromptu serenade. ⊠ *Chorio,* ☎ *0241/71665. No credit cards.*

$ 🏨 **Hotel Fiona.** This bright, new hotel, run by a family who recently
★ returned to Symi after years in Australia, is perched on the hillside in Chorio, affording splendid views over the island and sea. Just about all of the large rooms, with spotless white-tile floors and attractive blue-painted furnishings and pastel fabrics, have a sea-facing balcony. A full breakfast, with yogurt, homemade cakes, and marmalade, is served in the breezy, attractive lobby lounge. ⊠ *Chorio 85600,* ☎ 𝖥𝖠𝖷 *0241/72088. 14 rooms. Lobby lounge. No credit cards. Closed Nov.–Mar.*

$ 🏨 **Village Hotel.** On a small lane just off the main square of Chorio,
★ the Village Hotel is set in a traditional neoclassical mansion that has been enlarged and was nattily restored in 1992. The hotel has good views in all directions . . . and a steep climb home after you've had a morning coffee in the port. All the rooms open onto a balcony or terrace and surround an attractive garden. ⊠ *Symi 85600,* ☎ *0241/ 71800,* 𝖥𝖠𝖷 *0241/71802. 17 rooms. Breakfast room. No credit cards. Closed Nov.–Mar.*

Southern Area

Monastery is 7 km (4½ mi) south of Chorio.

The main reason to venture to the atypically green, pine-covered hills surrounding the little gulf of Panormitis is to visit the **Monastery of Taxiarchis Michael Panormitis,** Symi's patron saint, and also the protector of sailors. The entrance to the site is surmounted by an elaborate **bell tower,** of the multilevel wedding-cake variety already seen in Yialos and Chorio. In the **courtyard,** which is surrounded by a vaulted stoa, the floor is adorned with a black-and-white pebble mosaic. The **interior** of the church, entirely frescoed in the 18th century, contains a marvelously ornate wooden iconostasis, flanked by a heroic-size 18th-century representation of Michael, completely covered with silver. Note also the collection of votives, including ship models, gifts brought from all over, and a number of bottles with money in them, which, according to local lore, traveled to Symi on their own after having been thrown into the sea. Some rooms are available for lodging, and any trip to the monastery should be accompanied by a refreshing swim in the harbor. **Symi Tours** (⊠ In a distinctive stone house at the end of the harbor, Yialos, ☎ 0241/71307, 𝖥𝖠𝖷 0241/72292) offers excursions to the monastery that combines a truck trip over the most difficult terrain, a three-hour trek the rest of the way to the monastery, then a barbecue lunch and time for a swim, with return by boat. The company also arranges other boat trips and walking excursions around the island, as well as recommended lodgings on the island. ✉ *Symi's south side, at harbor,* ☎ *0241/71581.* 🎫 *Free.* ☉ *Daily.*

Beaches

Symi does have some excellent pebble beaches, though you may have to go to a little effort to reach them. The only beach near Yialos is a little strip beyond the harbor—just follow the road past the bell tower and the Aliki Hotel and you'll come to a seaside taverna that offers umbrellas and beach chairs. If you continue walking on the same road for about 3 km (2 mi) you'll come to the pine-shaded beach at **Niborios Bay,** where there is another taverna; swimming off the rocks along the way is excellent. From Pedhi, a little yacht harbor about 1 km (½ mi) beneath Chorio (a bus makes an hourly run from both Yialos and Chorio, 100 dr.), you can hire a boat (about 1,500 dr. a person) for an excursion to two of the island's best beaches: **Nanou Bay,** nestled beneath an imposing cliff, then on to **Marathounda Bay,** where you can enjoy a swim and a refreshing meal at a little taverna while your boatman waits.

KOS

The island of Kos, the third-largest in the Dodecanese, is certainly one of the most beautiful, with verdant fields and tree-clad mountains, surrounded by miles of sandy beach. Its highest peak, part of a small mountain range in the northeast, is less than 3,280 ft. All this beauty has not gone unnoticed, of course, and Kos undeniably suffers from the effects of mass tourism: its beaches are often crowded, most of its seaside towns have been recklessly overdeveloped, and the main town is noisy and busy between June and September.

In Mycenaean times and during the archaic period, the island prospered. In the 6th century BC it was conquered by the Persians but later joined the Delian League, supporting Athens against Sparta in the Peloponnesian War. Kos was invaded and destroyed by the Spartan fleet, ruled by Alexander and various of his successors, and has twice been devastated by earthquakes. Nevertheless the city and the economy flourished, as did the arts and sciences. The painter Apelles, the Michelangelo of his time, came from Kos, as did Hippocrates, father of modern medicine. Under the Roman Empire, the island's Asklepieion and its renowned healing center drew emperors and ordinary citizens alike. The Knights of St. John arrived in 1315 and ruled for the next two centuries, until they were replaced by the Ottomans. In 1912 the Italians took over, and in 1947 the island was united with Greece.

Kos Town

370 km (230 mi) east of Piraeus, 92 km (57 mi) north of Rhodes.

The modern town lies on a flat plain encircling a spacious harbor called Mandraki and is a pleasant assemblage of low-lying buildings and shady lanes. The fortress, which crowns its west side, where Hippocrates is supposed to have taught in the shade of a large plane tree, is a good place to begin your exploration of Kos town.

On one side of Platia Platanou, the little square named after the tree, stands the graceful Loggia (✉ Platia Platanou), actually a mosque, built in 1786.

The **Castle of the Knights,** built mostly in the 15th century and full of ancient blocks from its Greek and Roman predecessors, is a repository of fragments of ancient inscriptions, funerary monuments, and other sculptural material. A walk around the walls affords fine views over the town, whose flat skyline is pierced by a few remaining minarets and many palm trees. ⊠ *Over bridge from Platia Platanou,* ☎ *0242/ 28326.* 🎫 *500 dr./€1.47, free on Sun.* ⊙ *Tues.–Sun. 8:30–3.*

Excavations have uncovered the **Roman agora and harbor** (⊠ Over bridge from Platia Platanou, just behind Castle of the Knights), as well as portions of 4th-century BC and Hellenistic buildings. The **ruins,** which are not fenced, blend charmingly into the fabric of the modern city; it's a shortcut for people on their way to work, a place to sit and chat, an outdoor playroom for children. The ruins are now overgrown, and in spring they're covered with brightly colored flowers, which nicely frame the ancient gray-and-white marble blocks tumbled in every direction.

★ Kos town's **archaeological museum** contains extremely important examples of Hellenistic and Roman sculpture by Koan artists. Among the treasures are a group of sculptures from various Roman phases, all found in the House of the Europa Mosaic, and a remarkable series of Hellenistic draped female statues mainly from the Sanctuary of Demeter at Kyparissi and the Odeion. ⊠ *Platia Eleftherias, west of agora through gate leading to main square,* ☎ *0242/28326.* 🎫 *500 dr./€1.47, free on Sun.* ⊙ *Tues.–Sun. 8:30–3.*

The **West Excavations** (⊠ Just below ancient Acropolis) have uncovered a portion of one of the main Roman streets with many houses, including the **House of the Europa Mosaic.** Part of the **Roman baths** (⊠ Near main Roman street), it has been converted into a basilica. The **gymnasium,** distinguished by its partly reconstructed colonnade, and the so-called **Nymphaion,** a lavish public latrine that has been restored, are also of interest. These excavations are always open with free access.

Beaches

Kardamena (⊠ On south coast of Kos) and **Tingaki** (⊠ On north coast of Kos) are both highly developed little resort towns with sandy beaches, and showers, plus umbrellas and sun beds for rent. At **Mastichari** (⊠ On north coast, farther from Kos town), another resort, there's a wide sand beach, tavernas, rooms for rent, and a pier where boats sail on day trips to the uncrowded islet of Pserimos. The pebble beach at **Empros Thermes** (⊠ On north coast east of Kos town) has the added attraction of a bubbling, seaside hot springs. **Paradise Beach** (⊠ On southeast coast) has plenty of parking, and thus crowds, but the broad, sandy beach is magnificent and gives its name to a long stretch of sand that curves around the enchanting Gulf of Kefalos and, at its northern end, is undeveloped, almost deserted, and popular with nude bathers. If you must get wet but can't leave **Kos town,** try the **narrow pebbly strip** (⊠ Just south of main harbor).

Lodging

$$$ 🏨 **Ramira Beach.** This is one of the better resort hotels for family holidays, just outside Kos town. Most of the white and blue rooms, most with balconies and many situated in pleasant bungalows set amid gardens, have sea views. ⊠ *Psalidi Beach, Kos town 85300,* ☎ *0242/22891 through 0242/22894,* FAX *0241/28489. 268 rooms. Restaurant, bar, pool, 2 tennis courts. AE, DC, MC, V. Closed Nov.–Mar.*

$$ 🏨 **Titania Hotel.** This in-town hotel, right on the sea, delivers good quality at an easy price. Modern outside and in, its rooms are plain but comfortable. Because it's on the main road, the rooms may be noisy in high season, but offsetting this, you are within walking distance of town, and there's a little strip of beach right across the street. ⊠ *6b Vasileos Georgiou, Kos town 85300,* ☎ *0242/22556. 108 rooms. Bar,*

lobby lounge, beach. No credit cards. Closed Nov.–Apr.

Asklepieion

4 km (2½ mi) west of Kos town.

One of the great healing centers of antiquity is framed by a thick grove of cypress trees and laid out on several **broad terraces** connected by a monumental staircase. The lower terrace probably held the Asklepieian Festivals. On the middle terrace is an **Ionic temple,** once decorated with paintings by Apelles, including the renowned depiction of Aphrodite often written about in antiquity and eventually removed to Rome by the emperor Augustus. On the uppermost terrace is the **Doric Temple of Asklepieios,** once surrounded by colonnaded porticoes. ✉ *Asklepieion,* ☎ *0242/28763.* 🎫 *750 dr./€2.21, free on Sun.* ☉ *Daily 8:30–3.*

OFF THE BEATEN PATH	Leaving the main road southwest of Asklepieion (turnoff is at Zipari, 9 km [5½ mi] southwest of Kos town), you can explore an enchanting landscape of cypress and pine trees on a route that climbs to three lovely, whitewashed rural villages that cling to the craggy slopes of the island's central mountains: Asfendiou, Zia, and Lagoudi. The busiest of them is Zia, with an appealing smattering of churches; crafts shops selling local honey, weavings, and handmade soaps; and open-air tavernas where you can enjoy the views over the surrounding forests and fields toward the sea.

Dining

$$ ✗ **Taverna Ampavris.** The setting and the food are both delightful at
★   this charming, rustic taverna, just outside Kos town on a lane leading to the village of Platani. Meals are served in the courtyard of an old farmhouse, and the kitchen's emphasis is on local country food—including wonderful stews and grilled meats, accompanied by vegetables from nearby gardens. ✉ *Ampavris St., Platani, near Kos town,* ☎ *0242/ 25696. No credit cards.*

$ ✗ **Asklipios.** A memorable meal can be had at this little restaurant near
★   the Asklepieion, on the main square in the hamlet of Platani. Sit in the shade of an ancient laurel tree and try the exquisite selection of mezedes: home-prepared *dolmadakia* (stuffed vine leaves), bourekakia, *imam bayaldi* (baked eggplant). Even the boiled cauliflower is perfect. ✉ *Platani, near Kos town,* ☎ *0242/25264. No credit cards.*

Bay of Kamares

35 km (21¾ mi) southwest of Kos town, 10 km (6 mi) south of the Castle of Antimacheia.

Close to shore here is a little rock formation holding a **chapel to St. Nicholas,** and opposite are the ruins of a magnificent 5th-century **Christian basilica** (✉ On mainland, edge of public beach). The little beach community of Kamares is pleasant and much less frantic than the island's other seaside resorts, and perched on a summit above is the lovely old town of Kefalos, a pleasant place to wander just to enjoy its views and quintessential Greekness.

Dining and Lodging

$$ ✗ **Faros.** It's not too surprising that fish rules the menu at this seaside
★   taverna at the very end of the beach in Kamari, which is the beach town of Kefalos. In fact, some patrons arrive by dinghies from their yachts anchored just offshore. The friendly staff will take you into the kitchen

and show you the fresh catch of the day, then grill or bake it to your liking. ✉ *Kamari, Kefalos,* ☎ *0242/71240. MC, V.*

$ 🏨 **Hotel Eleni.** This new, family-run hotel is in the little community of the Kamari, just about the only seaside town on Kos not to have succumbed lock, stock, and barrel to tourism. Surrounded by gardens and fields, the Eleni is absolutely delightful; rooms are large and much better furnished and decorated than those in most hotels in this price range, and all have shuttered doors that opened to large terraces with views of the sea. ✉ *Kamari, Kefalos 85300,* ☎ *0242/71267. 32 rooms. Bar, breakfast room. MC, V.*

Beach

A chunk of the public beach (✉ Mainland) is now occupied by a Club Mediterranée, though the rest is given over to beach clubs renting umbrellas and chairs and offering activities that include waterskiing and jet-skiing; the northern stretch, though, is undeveloped, providing miles of deserted sand backed by pine forests and dunes.

Outdoor Activities and Sports

BICYCLING

The flat island of Kos, particularly the area around the town, is good for bicycle riding. Ride to the **Asklepieion** for a picnic, or visit the **Castle of Antimacheia.** Note: be aware of hazards such as cistern openings; very few have security fences around them. You can rent bicycles everywhere—in Kos town and at the more popular resorts. Try the many shops along Eleftheriou Venizelou Street in town. Renting a bike costs about 600 dr./€1.76 per day; scooter rentals begin at about 2,000 dr./€5.89.

OFF THE BEATEN PATH

Patmos – Rocky and barren, the small island of Patmos, set beyond the islands of Kalimnos and Leros northwest of Kos, is the site of the famed Monastery of St. John the Theologian. In AD 95, during the emperor Domitian's persecution of Christians, St. John was banished to Patmos, where he lived until his reprieve two years later. He writes that it was on Patmos that he "heard . . . a great voice, as of a trumpet," commanding him to write a book and "send it unto the seven churches." Skala, the island's main port, is the location now of almost all the hotels and restaurants. It's a popular port of call for cruise ships, and in summer, huge liners often loom over town, but there is not much to see in the town. Atop a hill due south of Skala, the village of Chora, clustered around the walls of the Monastery of St. John the Theologian, has become a preserve of international wealth; many of the houses, now exquisitely restored, are owned by Athenians. Though the short distance from Skala may make walking seem attractive, the heat and steep incline can make this a challenging mode of transport. A taxi ride is not expensive, about 2,000 dr./€5.89, and there is frequent bus service from Skala and other points on the island (240 dr./€.70).

According to tradition, St. John wrote the text of Revelation in the little cave, the Sacred Grotto, now built into the **Monastery of the Apocalypse** (2 km (1 mi) along the cobbled road from Skala heading to Chora). It is decorated with wall paintings of the 12th century and icons of the 16th. Its monastery, constructed in the 17th century from architectural fragments of earlier buildings, and further embellished in later years, also contains chapels to St. Artemios and St. Nicholas. Admission is free, and is usually open daily 8–noon and 4–6. Set along a cobbled road from Skala to Chora, the great **Monastery of St. John the Theologian** (☎ 0241/21954; monastery free, treasury 100 dr./€.29; open daily,

usually 8:30–noon and 4–6) is one of the finest extant examples of a
fortified medieval monastic complex. It became an intellectual center,
with a rich library and a tradition of teaching. The treasury contains a
wide range of relics, icons, silver, and vestments, most dating from
1600 to 1800.

RHODES/THE DODECANESE A TO Z

Arriving and Departing

By Boat

Of the several ferry lines serving the Dodecanese, the **Dane Sea Line**
(⊠ Akti Miaouli 33, Piraeus, ☎ 01/429–3240) and **G & A Ferries** (⊠
Etolikou 2, Piraeus, ☎ 01/419–9100) have the largest boats and the
most frequent service, both sailing daily out of Piraeus. Travel agencies throughout Athens and on all the islands represent these and other
lines serving the Dodecanese. The Athens–Dodecanese ferry schedule
changes seasonally, so call the **Piraeus Port Authority** (☎ 01/422–
6000), any Athens EOT (☎ 01/322–2545), or a travel agency before
booking.

If traveling to **Rhodes** by ferry, book one of the few ferries that goes
direct (like the *Rodos*); most stop first at Patmos, Leros, Kalymnos,
and Kos. Fares from Athens to Rhodes are about 6,500 dr./€19.17–
15,000 dr./€44.24 (the top range is for a bed in a two-berth cabin),
cars 14,000 dr./€41.29–17,500 dr./€51.62, not including taxes. Ferry
fares from Athens to **Patmos** are 5,000 dr./€14.74–8,200 dr./€24.18,
cars 13,500 dr./€39.82–17,500 dr./€51.62.

By Car

If you drive to Greece, you may take your car to the Dodecanese on
one of the large ferries that sails daily from Piraeus to Rhodes and less
frequently to the smaller islands.

By Plane

There are at least four flights per day to Rhodes from Athens, and extra
flights are added during high season. The flight, via **Olympic Airways**
(⊠ Ierou Lochou 9, Rhodes, ☎ 0241/24555; 01/966–6666 in Athens,
FAX 01/966–6111), takes less than an hour and costs 16,000 dr./€47.19
one-way. You can also fly to Rhodes from Heraklion four to five times
a week (45 minutes; 18,800 dr./€55.45) and from Thessaloniki usually twice weekly (75 minutes; 26,800 dr./€79). It is possible to fly directly to Rhodes from a number of European capitals, especially on
charters.

Rhodes airport (☎ 0241/92839) is about 20 minutes from Rhodes town,
and it's best to take a taxi (about 1,600 dr./€4.71). Though private
vehicles must have permits to enter the old town, a taxi may enter if
carrying luggage, no matter what a reluctant driver tells you. The
Olympic Airways office is in the new town (⊠ Odos Ierou Lochou 9,
☎ 0241/24555 or 0242/24571). In Kos, the **Olympic Airways office**
is in Kos town (⊠ 22 Vasileos Pavlou, ☎ 0242/28331 or 0242/28332),
and a bus runs between the office and the **Kos airport** (☎ 0242/51229),
about 45 minutes away, to meet the twice-daily flights from Athens.
The smaller islands of **Leros, Karpathos, Kassos,** and **Kastellorizo** also
have airports with less frequent service.

Getting Around

By Boat

There are frequent local boats, and in summer, hydrofoils connect the Dodecanese with one another. For information, contact any travel agency or local tourist office (☞ *below*).

By Bus

There is a good bus network on all the islands. Buses from Rhodes town leave from the **bus stop** (✉ Alexander Papagou, near Platia Rimini, ☎ 0241/27706) for points on the east side of the island, and from Averoff Street (✉ Beside new market, ☎ 0241/26300) for the west side.

By Car and Bicycle

On **Rhodes,** the roads are good, there are not many of them, and good maps are available. It is possible to tour the island in one day if you rent a car. Traffic is likely to be heavy only from Rhodes town to Lindos, and again as you near Kameiros. You can rent bicycles, including mountain bikes, as well as motor scooters, in Rhodes town from **Margaritis Rent a Moto** (✉ Kazouli 23, ☎ 0241/37420). In **Kos,** a car is advisable only if you are very pressed for time; most of what you want to see in Kos can by reached by bicycle or public transportation. Bicycle shops are plentiful. In **Patmos,** a car or motorbike makes it easy to tour the island, though most other sights and outlying restaurants are easily reached by bus or taxi and beaches can be reached either by bus or boat. There are no roads suitable for cars on **Symi,** where exploration is done on foot or by boat. The other Dodecanese islands are also best visited by public transportation.

By Plane

Olympic Airways (☞ *above*) runs five flights a week from Rhodes to Kos (30 minutes; 9,000 dr./€26.54) and other flights to the less-visited islands of Karpathos (8,800 dr./€25.95), Kassos (8,800 dr./€25.95), and Kastellorizo (7,000 dr./€20.64); the latter two are not served directly from Athens; air service is expected to begin operating soon from Athens, Kos, and Rhodes to the new airport on the island of Kalymnos. You can also hook up with the Cycladic islands by flying to Mykonos (weekly flight, 15,000 dr./€44.24) or Santorini (three times weekly, 15,000 dr./€44.24). Schedules are reduced in winter.

By Taxi

Taxis are available throughout the island of Rhodes, with ranks in most resorts—cars can be flagged down anywhere. The central rank is in Rhodes town (✉ Off Platia Rimini). If you call a radio taxi (☎ 0241/64712), the pickup charge is an extra 200 dr./€.58. Typical fares from Rhodes town are as follows: to Ixia, 600 dr./€1.76; to Ialyssos/Trianda, 900 dr./€2.65; to Faliraki, 1,600 dr./€4.71; and to Lindos, 5,000 dr./€14.74. Fares almost double between midnight and 6 AM.

Contacts and Resources

Car Rental

RHODES

Interrent-EuropCar (✉ 28th of October St. 18, ☎ 0241/21958; ✉ Airport, ☎ 0241/93105; ✉ Lindos, ☎ 0244/31132). **Roderent** (✉ A. Diakou 64, ☎ 0241/31831).

KOS

Helen's (✉ Hotel Ramira, Psaldi, ☎ 0242/28882, FAX 0242/21013).

Tassos (✉ Skala, ☎ 0247/31753, ⒻⒶⓍ 0247/32452).

Emergencies

As elsewhere in Greece, **pharmacies** in the Dodecanese post in their windows a list showing which locations are open 24 hours and on which days.

RHODES
Hospital (☎ 166 or 0241/22222). **Police** (✉ Ethelondon Dodekanissou 45, new town, ☎ 100 or 0241/23849). **Tourist police** (✉ On Museum Sq., old town, ☎ 0241/27423).

KOS
Police (☎ 0242/22100). **Tourist police** (☎ 0242/28277).

PATMOS
Hospital (☎ 0247/31211). **Police** (☎ 0247/31303).

SYMI
Police (☎ 0247/7111).

Guided Tours

A wide variety of local boat and land tours offered in Rhodes, Kos, Patmos, and Symi will take you to the usual sites (which you can probably reach by yourself anyway) and will give you a day picnicking on a remote beach, or even visiting the shores of Turkey.

RHODES
From April to October **Triton Holidays** (✉ Plastira 9, ☎ 0241/21690, ⒻⒶⓍ 0241/31625), for example, organizes a visit to Lindos by boat; a caïque leaves Mandraki Harbor in Rhodes in the morning, deposits you in Lindos for a day of sightseeing and beachgoing, and returns you to Rhodes in the evening (3,500 dr./€10.32–4,500 dr./€13.27). Triton also offers day cruises down the east coast of Rhodes (3,500 dr./€10.32), Symi (3,500 dr./€10.32), Kos (10,000 dr./€29.49), and Marmaris, Turkey (17,000 dr./€50.14), as well as a half-day inland hike (5,000 dr./€14.74); a half-day tour of Kameiros, Filerimos, and Petaloudes (5,000 dr./€14.74); and a scuba diving trip (9,000 dr./€26.54).

KOS
Aeolos Travel (✉ 8 Annetas Laoumzi, ☎ 0242/26203, ⒻⒶⓍ 0242/25948) organizes one-day cruises to other islands.

PATMOS
Apollon Travel (✉ Skala Harbor, ☎ 0247/31724, ⒻⒶⓍ 0247/31819). **Astoria Travel** (✉ Skala Harbor, ☎ 0247/31205 or 0247/31208, ⒻⒶⓍ 0247/31975).

SYMI
Symi Tours (✉ Symi Harbor, ☎ 0241/71307, ⒻⒶⓍ 0241/72292) will take you on a boat trip to the magical islet of Seklia (with a barbecue) for about 6,000 dr./€17.69, or on a round-the-island trip (by truck and boat, with an easy hike part of the way) for 6,000 dr./€17.69

Visitor Information

RHODES
The **Greek National Tourist Organization (GNTO or EOT)** (✉ Archbishop Makarios and Papagou, in the new city, close to the medieval walls, ☎ 0241/23655, 0241/23255, or 0241/27466) has brochures and bus schedules and is open weekdays 7:30–3.

The centrally located **Rhodes Municipal Tourism Office** on the east side of Platia Rimini near the bus station (☎ 0241/35945), open May–October, weekdays 8–7 and Saturday 8–6, is helpful with information and can exchange money for a 2% commission.

KOS
EOT (✉ Akti Miaouli, ☎ 0242/24460).

PATMOS
EOT (✉ Skala, near the ferry dock, ☎ 0247/31666).

13 BACKGROUND & ESSENTIALS

Portraits of Greece

Books and Videos

Chronology

Map of Greece

Map of Greek Ferries

Smart Travel Tips A to Z

Vocabulary

FROM ZEUS TO ZORBA

The wag who called Greece "a landscape and some old stones" left out one indispensable element: the Greeks. Maybe he wanted to ignore them. But this is impossible. You can't ignore 8 million electric eels even during siesta time when the battery runs down. Yet visitors to Greece, conditioned by museums, textbooks, and college Greek, are astonished to find that the country is populated at all. It is most unexpected to find real people here—like stumbling upon a cocktail party in a mausoleum. To add to the surprise, the Greeks don't have the "proper Greek look." Travelers who were nurtured on the truth and beauty of Keats' Grecian Urn find it surprising to see the natives roaring around in sport cars and talking about the latest nouvelle restaurant. Incongruous as it may seem, in fact, most Greeks have two arms and two legs attached to the torso in the normal places. The torso itself is not swathed in mother's best percale bedsheet, which would be unfashionable in Athens. But, in the end, although their countryside may be bleached and stony, the Greeks themselves—as the lucky visitor will soon learn—provide the vibrant color that has long since vanished from classic monuments once saturated with pigment, blue, gold, and vermilion, under the eye-searing Aegean sun.

Their spirit is a miracle. They are open, generous, and full of a frank probing curiosity about you, the foreigner. The Greeks do not have a word for standoffishness. Their approach is direct. American? British? Where are you staying? Are you married or single? How much do you make? Thus, with the subtlety of an atomic icebreaker, the Greeks get to know you, and you, perforce, get to know them. "Come back tomorrow night. We're always here at this time," is the gracious invitation that usually terminates the first meeting with your outgoing Greek hosts, usually a meeting set in a café, or *kafenion*—that living room–office–club–gambling casino that many Greeks call their real home. On repeat visits, you may be rewarded with native hospitality, the tenor of which recalls Nestor's orders to his servants in regard to departing Telemachus: "After him and force him to come back!" Many and touching are the tales of poverty-stricken villages which have slaughtered a kid or a lamb in honor of visiting tourists, thus conferring on them a truly Olympian status. In such villages there is always at least one English-speaking person for whom it is a matter of national pride and honor to welcome you and, perhaps, insist on lending you his only mule to scale a particular mountain, then offer a tasty dinner meal. This is the typically Greek, deeply moving hospitality which money cannot buy and for which, of course, no money could be offered in payment.

Chances are that your host—no doubt, luxuriantly moustached—will greet you as he counts the beads of what appears to be amber rosaries. They are *komboloia* or "worry beads," a legacy from the Turks, and Greeks click them on land, on the sea, in the air to ward off that insupportable silence which threatens to reign whenever conversation lags. Shepherds do it, cops do it, merchants in their shops do it. More aesthetic than thumb-twiddling, less expensive than smoking, this Queeg-like obsession indicates a tactile sensuousness, characteristic of a race which has produced the western world's greatest sculpture.

Although the Greeks are a practical and materialistic people, they know the secret of amusing themselves with little or no money. "They are," said an admiring French traveler, "the enchanters of themselves." The chief enchantments accessible to most tourists, since a language barrier usually keeps them from active participation in Greek political discussions, is singing and dancing. Occasionally at night in the narrow streets of the Plaka huddled at the foot of the Acropolis, you will hear the timeless strains of a lover's serenade, one of the flowing, melodic Ionian *cantades* which still have the power to ravish the ear and melt the heart of a dark-eyed beauty. The true place to discover the charm of Greek song and folk dancing is the taverna, an institution as old as Greece itself, mother of all the tavernas in the world. The entertainment, often featuring those extraordinary dances, the *zeimbekiko* performed by men, is sure to be vigorous, colorful, spontaneous, authentic. In the taverna you reach the apogee of Greek hospitality, Greek gaiety, Greek melancholy, Greek humanity.

When does Greece slow down? In Athens, it seems never. But head out to the countryside villages and you'll find another tradition as old as Homer himself, the siesta—the only time Greeks stop talking and really sleep it seems. Usually after lunch and until 4 PM, barmen drowse over their bars, waiters fall asleep in chairs, and all good Greeks drift off into slumber wherever they are, like the enchanted courtiers of Sleeping Beauty. Then, with a yawn, a sip of coffee, and a large glass of ice water, Greece goes back to the business of the day. But don't get us wrong—even some Athenians slow down for a siesta, and many enjoy another ritual as old as Aristotle—the *peripato,* or evening stroll.

"If you don't sing the praises of your house," says an old Greek proverb, "it will fall down on your head." Greece is an old house with a glorious history. It has survived four centuries of occupation by uninvited Turkish guests, a horrid tenancy by the Nazis, and the difficulties of being divided against itself, but the roof is miraculously intact and the legal tenants have a right to sing its praises. Don't be surprised if your taxi driver from the Athens airport does so—he only wants you to share his admiration for his country. He wants you to love it too. Remember, however, that you are in a taxi, not a chariot. You are not about to step into the Athens of Pericles. Although there are noble temples and ruins that evoke Homer, Sophocles, Plato, and the rest, today's Greeks are not just the cut-rate descendants of a noble people living in the ruined halls of their ancestors—modern Greece is a vital, living, enthralling, unforgettable nation.

SPLENDID STONES: A NOTE ON GREEK TEMPLES

Although today we are able to study the remains of a great variety of ancient Greek buildings, the mental picture formed at the sound of the words "Greek architecture" is likely to be that of a temple, and a Doric one at that. Though no city in classical times (500–355 BC) was deemed complete without its agora (or city-center), its defensible acropolis (*acro* = high; *polis* = city), its theater, gymnasium, and stadium, it was the temple of the city's patron god or goddess that was commonly given the dominant position and the greatest honor. The chief temple often stood at the highest point of the acropolis, the nucleus around which the city grew in safety, itself enclosed by fortification.

In Mycenaean Greece, 1,000 years before the classical period, the chief building of a citadel was the king's palace, as seen at Mycenae, Tiryns, and Pylos. In these palace complexes the central feature is the *megaron*—a large rectangular room with the long walls extended to form the sides of an open porch, the roof of which was supported by columns. A single large doorway gives access to the megaron. In the center is a large hearth, the focus of the room: around it, in a square plan, are four columns supporting the roof; in the right a raised platform for the royal throne. There are forecourts to these megara, and pillared gateways—copied from the Minoan palaces of Crete and replicated throughout Greek history. The Propylaea of the Acropolis at Athens (and of 20 other sites) derives from the Minoan gateway.

Clustered around the megaron and its forecourt are archive rooms, offices, oil-press rooms, workshops, potteries, shrines, corridors, armories, and storerooms for wine and oil and wheat—the whole forming an irregular complex of buildings quite unlike the precise, clear-cut arrangement that is later the hallmark of building in the classical period. This irregularity, characteristic of the Minoan palaces at Knossos, Mallia, and Phaistos on Crete, was one of the influences of that earlier and foreign culture on the Mycenaeans of the mainland.

But the megaron is Greek. The king's megaron, indeed a "great room," was essentially only the ordinary man's house built large; in some ordinary houses, as at Priene, the same megaron is found. And when the shrine ceased to be a mere house-chapel in a corner of the palace complex, as at Knossos, and the god was given a house of his own, his temple had the ground plan of that porched megaron. In its full development there is a porch, or maybe a room, also at the rear, and around it all runs a peristyle of columns. Thus the Greek temple is literally the god's house, intended not for the assembly of worshipers, but as a great room to contain the statue of the god.

The early temple builders found that sun-baked brick strengthened by horizontal and vertical timbers, if set on a stone footing, was a suitable material even for large buildings. This construction is seen at Knossos (circa 1900 BC) and at the Temple of Hera at Olympia 1,000 years later. The columns of the early temples were made of wood, and, later, when marble began to be used, constructional features appropriate to the use of timber were copied as decoration in the new material. It seems likely that the triglyph, the three-part stone slab set above the column and also above the space between columns in the Doric order, originates from a decorative wood slab that protected the beam ends of the ceiling from rain and rot—particularly when one looks at the six stone *guttae* always fixed below it, which seem to represent the six wood tre-nails, or pegs, that kept the slab in position. And the fluting of the Doric column is reminiscent of the grooves that the long strokes of the adze would make as the woodworker cut away the bark of a tree trunk before erecting it as the column.

If the origins of the Doric order are a matter of guesswork, this much is clear: that the Greeks used an elementary formula of vertical and horizontal lines of stone, so refined with skill and taste, with strict rules of proportion, that the total effect is one of balance, symmetry, and power. At the highest development, they added a series of optical corrections to ensure that the human eye, easily misled by the effect of light and shade in alternation, saw the whole as an apparent pattern of truly horizontal and vertical lines. In fact, with the application of these optical corrections, the entire building is made up of subtly curving or inclined surfaces. These refinements called for mathematical ability of a high order in the design and for extreme skill on the part of the masons.

In the Parthenon (5th century BC), the slight swell (*entasis*) and inward slant of the columns makes them seem straight-sided and vertical (which they are not); actual straightness would cause the eye to see them as waisted, and if vertical they would seem to be inclining outward. Also, without its slight upward curve, the steps of the platform (*stylobate*) would seem to sag under the line of standing columns. In short, the Greek mind took the simple idea of the upright and the crossbar, the child's building-block technique and, in developing it to its zenith in the Parthenon, produced a masterpiece that still informs us about those ingredients in a building that make for serenity combined with power, repose with majesty.

Marble was the perfect material for buildings in which sharp edges, clear-cut outline, precision, and the beauty of uncluttered wall surfaces were desired, so that each part, functional and decorative (the sculptured metopes and pediment), might do its work, and the horizontal members could lie without stress or mortar upon the supporting verticals.

The Doric order continued in use in Hellenistic (350–215 BC) and Roman times, but it is easy to distinguish Greek from Roman Dorica. The later architects dared a wider space, enough for three triglyphs, between columns; they used a base for their columns, whereas a Greek Doric column rests directly on the stylobate; they economized often by omitting the fluting in the lower part of a column (where damage most often occurred); and they reduced the size of the capital most meanly. All these Hellenistic and Roman "improvements" are seen in Delos.

The Ionic order came to mainland Greece almost certainly from Asia Minor and the islands, when the Doric order was well established both there and in the colonies of Magna Graecia (southern Italy). Ionic columns have bases; the flutes have no sharp edges to them but are separated by a substantial fillet; the columns are more tall and slender; the capitals with their beautiful spiral volutes decorative; the architrave has lost its alternating triglyphs and metopes and, in Greece proper, has a frieze of plain or sculptured stone, in Asia Minor a string of dentils to suggest the beam ends of the ceiling. If the feeling of the heavier, more austere Doric order can be described as masculine, then the Ionic is certainly feminine (and very lovely), especially suitable for such smaller buildings as the Erectheum and the Temple of Nike on the Acropolis of Athens.

The Corinthian order came later. Its first appearances were in the temple at Bassae (circa 430 BC) and in the circular building (*tholos*) at Epidauros (360 BC), where one of the perfectly preserved capitals can be seen in the museum. It is decorative and graceful, and one may contrast the simplicity of its sculptured acanthus leaves and their slender tendrils with the complications bestowed on the Corinthian capital by later Hellenistic and Roman architects, in their constant striving for magnificence.

The classical Greeks rarely departed from the straight line and the rectangular plan; only a few circular buildings have survived—for instance, the Tholos at Delphi, the "folly" of the family of Philip of Macedon at Olympia, a temple at Samothrace built by Queen Arsinoe, and in the Agora at Athens, the building where the executive of the day lived.

WHAT TO READ AND WATCH BEFORE YOU GO

Books

A. R. Burn's *The Pelican History of Greece* takes the reader from the Neolithic pioneers to the splendors of Athens to the last dark days when the philosophic schools were closed, capturing the culture of an amazing people. Extremely fluid, it is written for those who are not experts in classical literature. Just as erudite and enthusiastic is the *Oxford History of Greece and the Hellenistic World*, edited by John Boardman, Jasper Griffin, and Oswyn Murray, a comprehensive but never boring view of the ancient Greek world and its achievements. A late convert to classic Greece, Peter France will engage even the laziest reader in his *Greek as a Treat* (Penguin Books); theme by theme, with a sharp wit, he introduces readers to the greats—Homer, Pythagoras, Aeschylus, Socrates, and Plato—demonstrating how they still can enrich our 20th-century lives. C. M. Woodhouse's *Modern Greece: A Short History* (Faber and Faber) succinctly covers the ensuing development of Greece, from the fall of the Byzantine empire to the War of Independence and the monarchy to the ongoing struggle between the socialist PASOK party and the conservative New Democracy party. *The Greeks: The Land and People Since the War* (Penguin), by James Pettifer, takes readers behind the postcard imagery of lazy beaches and sun-kissed villages to modern Greece's contradictions as he examines the far-reaching effects of the country's recent troubled past, including civil war and dictatorship.

John Julius Norwich's three-volume *Byzantium* (available through Penguin) is a good introduction to the medieval Byzantine empire. Timothy Ware's *The Orthodox Church* introduces the Westerner to the religion of the Greek people, while Paul Hetherington's *Byzantine and Medieval Greece, Churches, Castles, and Art* provides a useful introduction to Byzantine and Frankish mainland Greece.

Unearthing Atlantis, by Charles Pellegrino, is a fascinating book about Santorini. The idyllic youth of naturalist Gerald Durrell on the island of Corfu is recalled in many of his books, such as *My Family and Other Animals,* which are written with an unpretentious, precise style in a slightly humorous vein and are underrated as works of literature. Henry Miller's *The Colossus of Maroussi,* an enjoyable seize-the-day-as-the-Greeks-do paean that veers from the profound to the superficial—sometimes verging on hysteria—is the product of a trip Miller took to Greece, during which he experienced an epiphany.

Greece's premier writer Nikos Kazantzakis captures the strengths and weaknesses and the color of traditional Greek culture in his wonderful *Zorba the Greek*; he also wrote the classics *Christ Recrucified* and *The Odyssey.* Other modern Greek fiction will immerse readers in the joys and woes of Greece today: Kedros Books has an excellent series, *Modern Greek Writers* (✉ Gennadiou 3, Athens 10678, ☎ 01/360–9712; distributed in the United Kingdom by Forest Books), which includes *Farewell Anatolia,* by Dido Sotiriou, chronicling the traumatic end of Greek life in Asia Minor, and *Fool's Gold* by Maro Douka, about an aristocratic young woman who becomes enamored of and then disillusioned with the resistance movement to the junta. Noted for his translations of Kazantzakis, the late Kimon Friar demonstrated exquisite taste in his superb translations of modern Greek verse, including works by C. P. Cavafy, and the Nobel Laureates George Seferis and Odysseus Elytis. Friar's *Modern Greek Poetry* is published by the Efstathiadis Group in Athens. Overseas readers may have less difficulty finding Edmund Keeley and Philip Sherrard's *Voices of Modern Greek Poetry* (Princeton University Press).

Some people like to go back to the classics while in Greece. Try either Robert Fitzgerald's or Richmond Lattimore's translations of the *Iliad* and *Odyssey* of Homer, done in verse, unlike the clumsy prose translations you probably read in school. Take the *Iliad* as a pacifist work exposing the uselessness of warfare; read the *Odyssey* keeping in mind the relationships between men and women as illustrated by Odysseus and Penelope, Circe, and Calypso. Lattimore also translated Greece's early lyric poets, Sappho and her lesser-known contemporaries, in a collection titled *Greek Lyric Poetry*. Aristophanes' play *The Wasps* is one of the funniest pieces of literature ever written. Although it isn't light reading, Thucydides' *Peloponnesian War* details the long struggle of Athens and Sparta, fought openly and through third parties, for and against democracy and autocracy. The events of the past 50 years and those of 2,500 years ago aren't so different.

Videos

A determination to live for the moment coupled with lingering fatalism still pervades Greek society. No film better captures this than Michael Cacoyannis's *Zorba the Greek* (1964; in English), starring the inimitable Anthony Quinn, Alan Bates, and Irene Pappas. Graced with the music of Mikis Theodorakis (the score won an Oscar even though Theodorakis's music was banned at the time in Greece), the film juxtaposes this zest for life with the harsh realities of traditional village society.

In perhaps the second-best-known film about Greece, Hellenic joie de vivre meets American pragmatism in *Never on Sunday* (1960; in English), directed by Jules Dassin. The late Melina Mercouri, a national icon, plays a Greek hooker, who in her simple but wise ways takes on the American who has come to reform her and teaches him that life isn't always about getting ahead.

The epic musical drama *Rembetiko* (1983; English subtitles), directed by Costas Ferris and awarded the Silver Bear in 1984, follows 40 years in the life of a rembetiko (Greek blues) singer, played by smoldering, throaty-voiced Sotiria Leonardou. The film, notable for its authenticity and the music's raw energy, spans the turbulent political history of Greece and the development of *rembetika* blues, which flourished from the 1920s until the '40s as 1.5 million Greeks were displaced from Asia Minor. They brought with them their haunting minor-key laments, as well as the Anatolian custom of smoking hashish; today rembetika is enjoying a resurgence with young Greeks.

Mediterraneo (1991; English subtitles) is a nostalgic, humorous depiction of life on a tiny, distant Greek island, occupied by Italian solders during World War II. The soldiers become inextricably involved with the island's vivid personalities—to the point that some refuse to leave when finally informed that the war has long been over. The movie, which won an Oscar for Best Foreign Film, features Vanna Barba, a popular Greek actress whose lusty yet stern gaze captivates the lead role.

One of Greece's leading directors, Theodoros Angelopoulos, has made several internationally acclaimed films, including *Journey to Kythera* (1984; English subtitles), which won for Best Screenplay in the 1984 Cannes festival. Considerably shorter than most of his films, it blends the mythical with the contemporary, detailing the life of a Greek civil war fighter who returns from the Soviet Union to reunite with his son in an adventure that leaves him and his wife on a raft bound for Kythera island. Manos Katrakis, considered one of Greece's finest stage actors, performs superbly (he died soon after), and the music and striking cinematography evoke Cavafy's famous poem, "Journey to Ithaki," familiar to all Greeks: "But do not hurry the voyage at all. It is better to let it last for long years; and even to anchor at the isle when you are old, rich with all that you have gained on the way."

A recent film that portrays life in Greece since tourism hit in the late '60s is *Shirley Valentine* (1989; in English). Set amid marvelous island scenes, the story is a cautionary tale about a bored British housewife who leaves her stultifying life to vacation in Greece. Here, she regains her iden-tity through a liberating romance with the local flirt (Tom Conti speaking abominable Greek). In England, apparently, an unusually high number of women signed up for Greek language lessons after viewing the film. Although a bit dated, since the "kamaki" (men who prey on foreign women) is no longer in full force given the increased independence of Greek women, the movie is full of humor, sharp dialogue, and dazzling shots of the Aegean.

GREECE AT A GLANCE

The Classical Era

499–79 BC Persian wars: Athens leads Greek states against Kings Darius and Xerxes. 490 BC: Battle of Marathon is a critical victory for Athens. 480 BC: Xerxes invades Greece; the Greek League, which includes Athens and Sparta, defeats him in a series of battles at Thermopylae, Salamis, and Plataea

478 77 BC Founding of Delian League of city-states under Athenian hegemony; it will evolve into an empire

ca. 475–00 BC Golden age of classical Greek culture, centered at Athens. Aeschylus (525–456 BC), Sophocles (ca. 496–06 BC), and Euripides (ca. 485–02 BC) form the great triumvirate of classical drama; the comedies of Aristophanes (ca. 450–385 BC) satirize contemporary mores. Socrates (469–399 BC) and his disciple Plato (ca. 429–347 BC) debate the fundamental questions of knowledge and meaning. Herodotus (ca. 484–20 BC) and Thucydides (471–02 BC) invent historical writing. The Acropolis epitomizes the harmony and precision of classical architecture and sculpture

462 BC Pericles (ca. 495–29 BC) rises to the leadership of Athens and leads the city to its cultural height

460–45 BC First Peloponnesian War between Athens and Sparta ends with the "Thirty Years' Peace" and recognition of the Athenian Empire. At the height of his power, Pericles rebuilds Athens

432 BC The Second, or Great, Peloponnesian War begins when Sparta declares war on Athens

429 BC A disastrous plague kills more than one-third of the Athenian population, including Pericles

415–13 BC Athens's disastrous invasion of Sicily reopens the war and sets the stage for its downfall

404 BC Athens falls to Sparta and its walls are dismantled, ending an era

398–60 BC Rule of Agesilaus at Sparta, whose aggressive policies lead to its ruin

394 BC Spartan fleet destroyed by Persians

386 BC Plato founds the Academy in Athens, a school of philosophy that trains statesmen

384 BC Birth of Aristotle, the greatest ancient philosopher and scientist (died 322 BC)

378 BC Second Athenian Confederation marks the resurgence of Athens

362 BC Death of Epaminondas at the battle of Mantinea ends Theban dominance, documented by Xenophon (ca. 434–355 BC)

355 BC Second Athenian Confederation collapses, leaving Greece in chaos

The Hellenistic Era

351 BC Demosthenes (384–32 BC) delivers the First Philippic, warning Athens of the dangers of Macedonian power

342 BC Aristotle becomes tutor to a young Macedonian prince named Alexander (356–23 BC)

338 BC Alexander's father, Philip of Macedon (382–36 BC) defeats the Greek forces at Chaeronea and establishes Macedonian hegemony

336 BC Philip is assassinated, leaving his empire to his son Alexander, soon to be known as "the Great." Aristotle founds his school, the Lyceum, at Athens

323 BC Having conquered the known world and opened it to Greek culture, Alexander dies of a fever in Babylon

ca. 330–200 BC Hellenistic culture blends Greek and other influences in a cosmopolitan style. Epicureanism, Stoicism, and Cynicism enter philosophy; Hellenistic sculpture blends emotion and realism. At the new city of Alexandria in Egypt, Greek science and mathematics flourish with Euclid (300 BC) and Archimedes (ca. 287–12 BC); Aristarchus (ca. 310–230 BC) asserts that the earth revolves around the sun

The Roman Era

215 BC The outbreak of the First Macedonian War signals Rome's rise in the Mediterranean

146 BC Rome annexes Greece and Macedonia as provinces. Roman culture becomes increasingly Hellenized

49–31 BC Greece is a battleground for control of Rome's empire: 48 BC: Julius Caesar defeats Pompey at Pharsalus; 42 BC: Caesar's heir Octavian defeats Brutus at Philippi; 31 BC: Octavian defeats Mark Antony at Actium and becomes, as Augustus, the first Roman Emperor

125 The guidebook of Pausanias makes Greece a favored tourist stop; the emperor Hadrian undertakes the renovation of ancient monuments

394 The emperor Theodosius declares Christianity the official religion of the Roman Empire and bans pagan cults, suppressing the Olympic Games and closing the oracle at Delphi

The Medieval Era

476 The fall of Rome leaves Greece open to waves of invaders, though it remains nominally under the hegemony of the Byzantine emperors at Constantinople

529 The Byzantine emperor Justinian closes Plato's Academy in Athens

1054 The Great Schism divides the Christian church into Greek and Roman orthodoxies

1204–61 Greece briefly reenters the sphere of western influence with the Latin capture of Constantinople in the Fourth Crusade

1453 The fall of Constantinople to the Ottoman Turks leads to nearly four centuries of Turkish rule

The Modern Era

1770 The Russian prince Orloff attempts but fails to establish a Greek principality

1814 The *Philike Hetairia*, a "friendly society" established by Greek merchants at Odessa (Russia), is instrumental in the growth of Greek nationalism

1821–29 The Greek War of Independence. 1821: The Greek Patriarch, Archbishop Germanos, declares Greek independence, and war with the Turks breaks out. Among those aiding Greece in her struggle is the English poet Lord Byron. 1826: A Greek defeat at Missolonghi stirs European sympathy. 1827: The Triple Alliance of Great Britain, France, and Russia intervene against the Turks and their Egyptian allies. 1829: The Turks are defeated and Greece is declared an independent state, guaranteed by the Triple Alliance

1832 Prince Otho of Bavaria is offered the Greek throne by the Triple Alliance

1834 King Otho chooses Athens as his capital

1844 Greece adopts a constitution that establishes a constitutional monarchy

1863 As a result of Otho's pro-Russian policies during the Crimean War, he is forced to abdicate and is replaced on the throne by Prince George of Denmark

1909–10 The Military League, a group of young army officers, leads a peaceful revolt and installs as prime minister Eleutherios Venizelos, who enacts a series of reforms

1912–13 Greece gains Macedonia, Epirus, and Crete as a result of the Balkan Wars

1917–18 Greece fights on the Allied side in World War I

1924 Greece is declared a republic

1935 Monarchy is restored; in the next year, King George II allows General Joannes Metaxas to establish a military dictatorship

1940 Italy invades Greece, leading to four years of Axis occupation

1946 Greece becomes a charter member of the United Nations

1946–49 Communist rebellion is defeated with U.S. help

1952 Women are given the right to vote

1963 George Seferis wins the Nobel Prize for Literature

1967 A military coup ousts King Constantine II

1974 In the wake of the Cyprus crisis, the military government collapses and the first elections in 10 years are held. Constantine Karamanlis is named prime minister. The republic is confirmed by popular vote

1980 Odysseus Elytis becomes the second Greek to win the Nobel Prize for Literature

1981 Greece joins the European Economic Community

1993 Andreas Papandreou returns to power

1994 Minister of Culture Melina Mercouri dies

1996 Former prime minister Andreas Papandreou dies; Costas Simitis becomes leader and wins a vote of confidence shortly after Papandreou's death, when he was elected to the position of PASOK party president, a position that Papandreou never relinquished

2001–02 Olympic fever continues to build for the 2004 Athens Games. Gaping construction sites line the extension of the subway, to be completed by 2001; other construction projects include an Olympic village at the base of Mount Parnitha, a sports complex near the Neo Faliro racetrack, an equestrian center in Tatoi, a sailing center in front of the present-day airport, and a rowing and canoeing basin near Marathon.

Black Sea

T U R K E Y

Istanbul

Xanthi

THRACE

Sea of
Marmara

Makri

Thassos

Samothrace

N

Limnos

0   50 miles
0   75 km

Lesbos

T U R K E Y

Aegean Sea

N
O
R
T
H
E
R
N

Chios

Izmir (Smyrna)

Andros   A E G E A N

I S L A N D S

Samos

Tinos   Ikaria

I
S
L
A
N
D
S

Siros   Mykonos
         Delos   Patmos

Paros   Leros
Sifnos   Naxos   Kalimnos
                                Kos
C Y C L A D E S   Amorgos   Bodrum
                                 Kos
                        Kos

Ios   Astypalea

Santorini   Anafi   Nissyros   Symi   Rhodes

D O D E C A N E S E   Tilos
                      Chalki

                      Rhodes

Sea of Crete   Rhodes

CRETE
Heraklion   Karpathos

        Ay.
        Nikolaos   Kassos
Ierapetra

Mediterranean Sea

Greek Ferries

Trikala
Tirnavos
Karditsa
Larissa
THESSALY
Lamia
Agios
Konstandinos
Itea
Orhomenós
Livadia
Thebes
Corinth
PELOPONNESE
Nafplion
Aegina
Methana
Ermioni
Poros
Spetses
Hydra
Piraeus
Lavrion
Volos
Skiathos
Skopelos
EVIA
Kymi
Halkida
Athens
Rafina
Marmari
Karystos
Kea
Kythnos
Ermoupolis
Siros
Serifos
Sifnos
Milos
Kimolos
Paros
Folegandros
Sikinos
Ios
Naxos
Naxos
Donoussa
Amorgos
Santorini
Anafi
Astypalea
Sea of Crete
Hania
Souda
Rethymnon
CRETE
Heraklion
Ayios
Nikolaos
Siteia
Kassos
Karpathos
Chalki
Rhodes
Rhodes
Symi
Tilos
Nissyros
Kos
Kalimnos
Bodrum
TURKEY
Leros
Patmos
Samos
Kuşadasi
Ikaria
Mykonos
Delos
Tinos
Andros
Psara
Chios
Izmir
(Smyrna)
Aegean Sea
Skyros
Alonissos
Thermaikos
Gulf
Polygyros
Stavros
Kalithea
Dafni
Kavala
Prinou
Thassos
Alexandroupoli
Samothrace
Mirina
Limnos
Troy
TURKEY
Lesbos
Mytilini
THRACE
Thessaloniki
Gulf of Corinth
Mediterranean Sea

N

0   50 miles
0   75 km

ESSENTIAL INFORMATION

Half the fun of traveling is looking forward to your trip—but when you look forward, don't just daydream. There are plans to be made, things to learn about, serious work to be done. The following information will give you helpful pointers on many of the questions that arise when planning your trip. In addition, the organizations listed in this section will supplement the information in this guide book. Note that much of the information in this section is Greece-wide; for specific details about the various topics covered below *within* the regions of Greece itself, also consult the A to Z sections at the end of each regional chapter in this book.

ADDRESSES

To make finding your way around as easy as possible, it's wise to learn to recognize letters in the Greek alphabet. Most areas, even Athens, have few signs in English. Sometimes there are several spelling variations in English for the same place: Agios or Ayios, Georgios or Yiorgos. Also, the English version may be quite different from the Greek, or even what locals use informally: Corfu is known as Kerkyra; island capitals are often just called Chora (town) no matter what their formal title; Vasilissis Sofias (Queen Sofia), a main Athens boulevard, now reads Eleftheriou Venizelou on maps since royalty was banned, but if you ask for that name, no one will know what you're talking about. A street may change names several times, and a city may have more than one street by the same name, so it's best to know the district you're headed for, or a major landmark nearby, especially if you're taking a taxi. Finally, there are odd- and even-numbered sides of the streets, but don't assume No. 124 is across from No. 125, which could be several blocks down the street.

AIR TRAVEL

BOOKING

Price is just one factor to consider when booking a flight: frequency of service and even a carrier's safety record are often just as important. Major airlines offer the greatest number of departures. Smaller airlines—including regional and no-frills airlines—usually have a limited number of flights daily. On the other hand, so-called low-cost airlines usually are cheaper, and their fares impose fewer restrictions, such as advance-purchase requirements. Safety-wise, low-cost carriers as a group have a good history—about equal to that of major carriers.

When you book **look for nonstop flights** and **remember that "direct" flights stop at least once.** Try to avoid connecting flights, which require a change of plane. Two airlines may jointly operate a connecting flight, so ask if your airline operates every segment—you may find that your preferred carrier flies you only part of the way, which means you may have to pick up your luggage between stops or walk to another terminal to continue your flight.

Ask your airline if it offers electronic ticketing, which eliminates all paperwork. There's no ticket to pick up or misplace. You go directly to the gate and give the agent your confirmation number. There's no worry about waiting on line at the airport while precious minutes tick by.

CARRIERS

When flying internationally, you must usually choose between a domestic carrier, the national flag carrier of the country you are visiting, and a foreign carrier from a third country. You may, for example, choose to fly Olympic Airways to Greece. National flag carriers have the greatest number of nonstops. Domestic carriers may have better connections to your home town and serve a greater number of gateway cities. Third-party carriers may have a price advantage.

Consider flying between destinations within Greece when faced with a drive of more than three hours or a six-hour-plus boat journey. Olympic Airways has dominated the domestic market, with flights to more than 30 cities and islands. Especially if you are traveling to a distant island such as Astypalia (23,400 dr./€69.02 for a one-hour flight, compared to 5,500 dr./€16.22 for a 12-hour boat trip), for example, fares are inexpensive considering the time saved and the miles covered. In the last five years, newcomers have captured some of Olympic's share by initially providing cheaper fares and sometimes better service, though Olympic still boasts the most flights. Alternative airlines include Aegean Air, Cronus Airlines, and Hellenic Star Airways (☞ Domestic Flights, *below*).

Although weather is usually not an obstacle when flying throughout Greece, high winds may preclude planes from landing on some islands. Delays in domestic departures are not uncommon, and Olympic seldom offers much information to waiting passengers about the cause of delay or new departure times. **Befriend a bilingual fellow passenger who can translate the announcements** and the crowd rumors about what happens next. Much improved communication is promised when Greece's leading airport hub in Athens moves to its ultramodern Spata facilities in spring 2001.

Olympic Airways, the state-owned Greek carrier, has in past years incurred criticism for its on-time record, indifferent service, and aging aircraft. In an attempt to improve the service, Speed Wing—a subsidiary of British Airways—was brought in to manage the airline, with an option to purchase up to 20% of the company; since British Airways is experiencing a financial crisis of its own, it declined to go ahead with the deal and the Greek government is now pursuing a privitization program. George Kessanis, U.S. Commercial and Marketing Manager, reports, "Olympic has purchased four modern A340-300 airbuses, which has helped to improve the on-time record by 73% in the last year." Travelers in 2000 were pleasantly surprised by the improvement in service, which included few cancelled flights (once a common occurance). Kessanis also noted that Olympic, which has mostly ex-military pilots, is rated among the top three carriers world-wide for safety. Olympic now strives to improve its mileage program and to develop several other gateway cities in the U.S.; the latter will be implemented after the purchase of other new aircraft.

➤ MAJOR AIRLINES: **Air Canada** (☎ 800/776–3000). **Delta** (☎ 800/241–4141). **Olympic Airways** (☎ 212/838–3600; 800/223–1226 outside New York). **United** (☎ 800/241–6522).

European national airlines that fly to Athens from the United States and Canada via their home country's major cities include the following: **Air France** (☎ 800/237–2747). **Alitalia** (☎ 800/223–5730). **Austrian Airlines** (☎ 800/843–0002). **British Airways** (☎ 800/247–9297). **Finnair** (☎ 800/950–5000). **Iberia Airlines** (☎ 800/772–4642). **KLM Royal Dutch Airlines** (☎ 800/777–5553). **LOT Polish Airlines** (☎ 212/869–1074). **Lufthansa** (☎ 800/645–3880). **Sabena Belgian World Airlines** (☎ 800/955–2000). **Swissair** (☎ 800/221–4750). **TAP Air Portugal** (☎ 800/221–7370). **Virgin Atlantic** (☎ 800/862–8621). Remember that these are connecting flights that include at least one stop and may require a change of planes.

➤ SMALLER AIRLINES: **Tower Air** (☎ 718/553–8500 or 800/348–6937).

➤ FROM THE U.K.: **Air UK** (☎ 0345/666777 or 01293/535353). **British Airways** (☎ 0181/897–4000; 0345/222–111 outside London). **Easy Jet** (☎ 01582/702900 or 0044/870–600000). **Olympic Airways** (☎ 0171/409–3400).

➤ DOMESTIC AIRLINES: **Olympic Airways** (main Athens ticket office at ✉ Fillelinon 15, near Syntagma Sq., ☎ 01/966–6666 for reservations; 01/936–3363 through 01/936–3366 for daily arrival and departure information, FAX 01/966–6111). Another convenient branch is in the Athens Hilton (✉ Vasilissis Sofias 46, ☎ 01/926–7445). **Aegean Air** (✉ Vouliagmenis 572, Argiroupoulis, Athens, ☎ 01/998–8300 for reservations, FAX 01/995–7598). **Cronus Airlines** (✉ Othonos 10, Syntagma Sq., Athens, ☎ 01/994–4444 for reservations, FAX 01/331–5505). **Hellenic Star Airways** (✉ Vouliagmenis 2, Athens, ☎ 01/961–1881, FAX 01/965–0373). **LTU International Airways** (✉ Nikodimou 2, Athens, ☎ 01/323–0541 through 01/323–0542, FAX 01/323–2952).

CHARTERS

Charters usually have the lowest fares but are the least dependable. Departures are infrequent and seldom on time, flights can be delayed for up to 48 hours or can be canceled for any reason up to 10 days before you're scheduled to leave. Itineraries and prices can change after you've booked your flight.

In the U.S., the Department of Transportation's Aviation Consumer Protection Division has jurisdiction over charters and provides a certain degree of protection. The DOT requires that money paid to charter operators be held in escrow, so if you can't pay with a credit card, **always make your check payable to a charter carrier's escrow account.** The name of the bank should be in the charter contract. If you have any problems with a charter operator, contact the DOT (☞ Airline Complaints, *below*). If you buy a charter package that includes both air and land arrangements, remember that the escrow requirement applies only to the air component.

CHECK-IN & BOARDING

You don't show identification for domestic flights but do need a passport for international flights. For domestic flights, arrive no later than one hour before; for flights to the rest of Europe arrive 90 minutes earlier, and for long-haul flights, especially on large carriers, it's a good idea to arrive two hours earlier (the added security measures add to check-in time). Remember that Greece may have a different Daylight Savings Time than your country, so at the end of October and April, stay alert. The best reason to come early is to avoid overbooking, common in summer, especially on charter flights. If you do get bumped, international carriers try to find an alternative route on another airline, but Olympic usually puts you on their next available flight, which might not be until the next day. (Under EU law, you are entitled to receive up to 150 Euros compensation for overbooking on flights under 3,500 km [2,100 mi] and up to 300 Euros for longer flights.) The dilemma: come early, beating the crowds and troubleshooting the inevitable problem, or come late, and avoid hours of sitting around when flights (especially domestic) are delayed. In the past, Olympic Airways staff and traffic controllers have gone on strike for several hours a day; keep attuned to the local news. Check-in is straightforward and easy at Greece's larger airports, but on small islands, it sometimes gets confusing since several airlines may use the same check-in counter, indicated solely by the occasional garbled announcements. Watch for any sudden movement en masse by the crowd.

If you have been wait-listed on an Olympic flight, remember that this list no longer applies on the day of departure. A new waiting list goes into effect at the airport two hours prior to take-off for domestic flights and three hours before international flights; you have to be there to get a place.

CONSOLIDATORS

Consolidators buy tickets for scheduled international flights at reduced rates from the airlines, then sell them at prices that beat the best fare available directly from the airlines, usually without restrictions. Sometimes you can even get your money back if you need to return the ticket. Carefully read the fine print detailing penalties for changes and cancellations, and **confirm your consolidator reservation with the airline.**

➤ CONSOLIDATORS: **Cheap Tickets** (☎ 800/377–1000). **Discount Airline Ticket Service** (☎ 800/576–1600). **Unitravel** (☎ 800/325–2222). **Up & Away Travel** (☎ 212/889–2345).

World Travel Network (☎ 800/409–6753).

CUTTING COSTS

The least-expensive airfares to Greece are priced for round-trip travel and usually must be purchased in advance. It's smart to **call a number of airlines, and when you are quoted a good price, book it on the spot**—the same fare may not be available the next day. Airlines generally allow you to change your return date for a fee. If you don't use your ticket, you can apply the cost toward the purchase of a new ticket, again for a small charge. However, most low-fare tickets are nonrefundable. To get the lowest airfare, **check different routings.** Compare prices of flights to and from different airports if your destination or home city has more than one gateway. Also price off-peak flights, which may be significantly less expensive.

Travel agents, especially those who specialize in finding the lowest fares (☞ Discounts & Deals, *below*), can be especially helpful when booking a plane ticket. When you're quoted a price, **ask your agent if the price is likely to get any lower.** Good agents know the seasonal fluctuations of airfares and can usually anticipate a sale or fare war. However, waiting can be risky: the fare could go *up* as seats become scarce, and you may wait so long that your preferred flight sells out. A wait-and-see strategy works best if your plans are flexible. If you must arrive and depart on certain dates, don't delay.

At the end of the tourist season in mid- to late October, you sometimes can find cheap seats to the rest of Europe, especially the U.K., Germany, and Scandinavia, on planes carrying package tours that aren't completely full. Ask your local travel agent about the possibilities.

Olympic Airways does not provide any discount passes, but they have begun a Frequent Flyer program called Icarus (☎ 01/926–7221), which eventually rewards members with free seats, cheaper car rental, and special services such as priority on waiting lists.

DOMESTIC FLIGHTS

The frequency of flights varies according to the time of year (with an increase between Greek Easter and November), and it is essential to book well in advance for summer or for festivals and holidays, especially on three-day weekends. Domestic flights are a good deal for many destinations. In summer 2000 the one-way Athens–Rhodes fare offered by Olympic was 26,700 dr./€78.76; to Corfu, 21,700 dr./€64; to Santorini, 25,500 dr./€75.22; and to Heraklion, 20,700 dr./€61.06 This includes the Spata tax (3,400 dr./€10) tacked onto every flight in order to fund construction of the new Athens airport. Unless the flight is part of an international journey, the baggage allowance is only 33 pounds (15 kilograms) per passenger.

Scheduled (i.e., noncharted) domestic air travel in Greece is provided predominantly by **Olympic Airways**, which operates out of Athens's West Terminal although this may change when the Spata airport opens. There is service from Athens to Alexandroupolis, Ioannina, Kastoria, Kavala, Kozani, Preveza, and Thessaloniki, all on the mainland; Kalamata in the Peloponnese; the Aegean islands: Astypalaia, Karpathos, Kassos, Kythira, Crete (Hania, Heraklion, and Sitia), Chios, Ikaria, Kos, Lesbos (listed as Mytilini in Greek), Limnos, Leros, Milos, Mykonos, Naxos, Paros, Rhodes, Samos, Skiathos, Syros, Skyros, Kastellorizo (only via Rhodes), and Santorini; Corfu (called Kerkyra in Greek), Kefalonia, and Zakynthos in the Ionian Sea. Flights also depart from Thessaloniki for Hania, Chios, Heraklion, Ioannina, Corfu, Limnos, Lesbos, Mykonos, Rhodes, Samos, and Santorini. You can also fly from Kozani to Kastoria on the mainland. Interisland flights, depending on the season, include the following: from Chios to Lesbos; from Karpathos to Kassos; from Santorini to Rhodes and Heraklion; from Rhodes to Karpathos, Kassos, Kastellorizo, and Mykonos, as well as Kos (summer only); between Kefalonia and Zakynthos (winter); and from Lesbos to Chios, Limnos, and Samos (winter).

For those traveling to Thessaloniki, a good alternative is **Cronus Airlines,** which has regular scheduled flights from Athens's East Terminal at cheaper prices than Olympic. It also flies from Athens to Heraklion and Hania in Crete and to Rhodes.

Other airlines flying within Greece include **Aegean Airlines,** which travels from Athens to Alexandroupolis, Hania, Heraklion, Ioannina, Kavala, Corfu, Lesbos, Rhodes, Santorini, and Thessaloniki. It also departs Thessaloniki for Heraklion, Rhodes, Santorini, and Lesbos. In summer, **LTU International Airways** operates several flights between points in Greece such as Rhodes and Kos or Athens and Samos. **Hellenic Star Airways** flies from Athens to Chios, Leros, Paros, and Syros. All fly out of the East Terminal.

ENJOYING THE FLIGHT

Flying overseas to Athens, especially in an economy seat, demands survival savvy. If you want special meals—kosher, vegetarian, low-fat, low-salt—order these when you book your ticket. Most in-Greece flights don't offer meals. On international trips, carry a snack and a small bottle of water because you may be delayed when switching flights en route and don't want to get stuck with $18 in zlotys when all you craved was a candy bar. Even better, have some small change in the foreign currency of the airports where you'll be stopping.

If you smoke, inquire about your airline's policy; you may need to wear a nicotine patch to make it through a long flight. More and more airlines, especially from the U.S., are banning smoking throughout the plane. Olympic Airways does not allow smoking on any flights within Greece, but these seldom last more than 45 minutes to an hour; they also ban smoking on flights to Cyprus and Israel. Many airlines traveling within the EU do not allow smoking on flights under two hours. Be aware that even if you stop en route, the airport usually provides few places where you can smoke other than the cafés or bars. Some U.S. airports like Los Angeles even forbid smoking outdoors except for designated areas.

Greeks are heavy smokers who light up everywhere, so it's the no-smoking areas that are few and far between in Greek airports. The airline may assign you a seat that's technically no-smoking but immediately behind the smoking section; **ask to sit at least two or three rows behind smokers.** Sometimes economy nonsmokers are positioned behind business class smokers; the curtain doesn't do much to contain the smell.

Too much free alcohol and salty airline food and you will end up dehydrated, so **eat lightly, imbibe sparingly, and drink as much noncarbonated water as possible** to avoid feeling like a slug upon arrival. To reduce swelling limbs, take off or loosen your shoes the minute you sit down (bring thick socks to pad around in), and try to keep your feet elevated. Get up and walk two hours or do simple seat aerobics; some airlines such as Lufthansa show tapes with suggested exercises. Unless you insist on a view, which most of the time you're too high up to enjoy anyway, **book an aisle seat.** It offers more leg room and lets you pop up without constantly disturbing others. Grab an available blanket when you first enter the plane, because compartments become chilly (travelers often leave Greece in flimsy clothing, a case of wishful thinking). Unless you are desperate to meet people, avoid sitting near the bathrooms; you will be jostled continuously by those waiting in line. Finally, the chatty stranger who is amusing for two hours may become annoying after you cross the second time zone. To ward off talkative neighbors, order a headset even if you aren't planning to listen to the music, or carry a fat paperback.

FLYING TIMES

Flying time to Athens is 3.5 hours from London, 18 hours from Sydney, 8 hours from New York, 10 hours from Chicago, and 14 hours from Los Angeles.

HOW TO COMPLAIN

If your baggage goes astray or your flight goes awry, complain right away. Most carriers require that you **file a claim immediately.**

➤ AIRLINE COMPLAINTS: U.S. Department of Transportation **Aviation Consumer Protection Division** (⊠ C-75, Room 4107, Washington, DC 20590, ☎ 202/366–2220, airconsumer@ost.dot.gov, www.dot.gov/airconsumer). **Federal Aviation Administration Consumer Hotline** (☎ 800/322–7873).

➤ COMPLAINTS AT ATHENS AIRPORT: **Civil Aviation Authority** (East Airport ☎ 01/969–4529 or 01/969–4820, West Airport 01/997–2816), 24-hour service. **Consumers' Protection Bureau** (⊠ East Airport, Departures Hall, 4th floor, Room 432, ☎ 01/969–4519).

RECONFIRMING

Even if an airline tells you it's unnecessary, you should reconfirm your outbound flight by phone 48 hours before departure. It's a good chance to discover if there are any changes (like your charter company went bankrupt or the airport is on strike). You do not need to reconfirm flights within Greece.

AIRPORTS

Although Athens is scheduled to start operating its new international airport at Spata in east Attica, it was unclear at press time (summer 2000), which airlines would move there immediately. Until then, Greece's major gateway is **Ellinikon Airport,** which has two terminals. The West Terminal serves **Olympic Airways** international and domestic flights only; the East Terminal is used by all other international carriers. At the East Terminal, between the arrivals and departures wings, there is a small, white building from which some charters such as Hapag-Lloyd leave. There is also a New Charters terminal, known as Terminal B, located just before the East Terminal on the former U.S. military base, which operates May through October. Ellinikon (the three letter code is ATH) is located between Alimos and Glyfada on the southwest coast of Attica 10 km (6 mi) from Athens center. Unless you mean to avoid Athens altogether or fly via your charter directly to the islands, the Athens airport is the most convenient, because it allows you to easily switch from international to domestic flights or go quickly to Greece's main harbor, Piraeus, about a 20-minute drive north.

➤ AIRPORT INFORMATION: **Ellinikon Airport** (☎ West Terminal, 01/936–3363 through 01/936–3366 for arrival and departure information; East Terminal, 01/969–4466 for arrivals and departures, or 01/969–4531 to page passengers or make announcements in waiting room; New Charters Terminal, 01/997–2686 or 01/997–2581. For lost baggage, domestic 01/936–2333, international 01/936–2120).

DUTY-FREE SHOPPING

The Ellinikon airport in Athens, as well as Thessaloniki and those island airports like Rhodes and Samos that receive international charters all have adequate duty-free shopping. Perfumes, cosmetics, and electronics are not worth buying; you can often find these for less money in your own country, especially if you live in the U.S. However, what *is* cheaper are cartons of cigarettes, alcohol (including Greek ouzo and Metaxa brandy), good-quality ceramics, and CDs of Greek music. In other words, only buy a product that you can't get in your own country, and if sold in Greece carries the usual 18% value-added tax.

TRANSFERS

In Athens express buses connect the three terminals, Syntagma Square, Omonia Square, and Piraeus. Express bus E93 travels between the three terminals every 40 minutes around the clock. Between the terminals and Athens center, express bus E91 runs about every half hour day and night. The trip takes about 30 minutes. You can catch the express buses at the bottom of Syntagma Square between Ermou and Mitropoleos or off Omonia Square at the intersection of Stadiou and Aiolou streets. From the airport terminals to Karaiskaki Square in Piraeus, the express bus E19 leaves every hour or so from 5 AM to midnight. The fare is 250 dr./€.73, 500 dr./€1.47 from 11:30 PM until 5:30 AM. The Greek National Tourist Organization (GNTO but known as EOT in Greece) dispenses schedules. You can also ride the regular city line (No. B2) from Syntagma Square to the West Terminal (Olympic flights) from about 4:30 AM to 11:50 PM every 15 minutes for most of the day; 120 dr./€.35 It's much faster just to queue at the taxi stands in front of each terminal: 1,200 dr./€3.53 between terminals, 2,200 dr./€6.48 to the city center, 2,800 dr./€8.25 to the main bus stations, 2,600 dr./€7.66 to the train station, 2,900 dr./€8.55 to Piraeus; the price goes up by about two-thirds between midnight and 5 AM. In Thessaloniki, municipal bus 078 picks up travelers about every 40 minutes until 11:15 PM (115 dr./€.33) for the 45-minute ride (90 minutes if there is traffic) into town; its final stop is the train station; the EOT office on Aristotelous Square can give you information. At other airports throughout Greece, especially on the islands, public transportation is either infrequent or nonexistent; ask your hotel to make arrangements or take a taxi, keeping in mind that rates are usually set to fixed destinations.

➤ LIMOUSINES: **Royal Prestige Limousine Service** (☎ 0944/305000 mobile phone, ☎ FAX 01/983–0378) provides limousine transfers from the airport to Athens hotels and vice versa if you call in advance; prices start at about 16,000 dr./€4.71 one-way to a central hotel.

BIKE TRAVEL

Not too many tourists or locals travel Greece by bike, although there are occasional tour groups that cycle across flatter islands (80% of Greece is mountainous). The pleasures are that you will meet the locals and go slowly enough to enjoy the quirky details that Greek life comprises. The downside is that roads are usually narrow and without bike lanes; Greek drivers don't have much experience with cyclists; spare parts may be hard to find away from major cities. The only place in Greece that has bike lanes, about 40 km (25 mi), is the island of Kos. The best places to bike are secondary roads on islands, where you will also find bike rentals from April through October, with prices starting from 2,000 dr./€5.89 a day for a mountain bike.

➤ BIKE MAPS: The best maps are the **Road Editions** (✉ Ippokratous 39, Athens 10680, ☎ 01/362–3242, ☎ FAX 01/361–4680) for each region in Greece, created in cooperation with the Hellenic Army Geographical Service and sold at the above address and most bookstores for 1,800 dr./€5.30 each.

➤ BIKE RENTALS: In Santorini **Motor Inn** (✉ Main road, 30 yards before promenade, Kamari 84300, ☎ FAX 0286/31165); in Naxos **Moto Naxos** (✉ Protodikiou Sq., Chora 84700, ☎ 0285/23420, FAX 0285/25707); in Samos **Giannis Rent-A-Bike** (✉ Themistokleous Sofouli 12, Pythagorio 83100, ☎ FAX 0273/23756); and in Kos **Ideal Rental, Efstratos Sernikos** (✉ Parodos Amerikis, Kos 85300, ☎ FAX 0242/22356).

BIKES IN FLIGHT

If your bike is within your baggage weight allowance, it's free if you check it on the plane; otherwise, there is a small fee. Ferries usually let you bring it on for free, though you may want to pay the 500 dr./€1.47 to store it in the bottom deck luggage room during the journey. Trains and buses require a little more negotiation to ensure the bike travels on the same vehicle with you.

BOAT & FERRY TRAVEL

Ships for the Ionian islands and I taly sail from ports on Greece's west coast, such as Patras and Igoumenitsa. Also on the west coast, the local ferry between Igoumenitsa and Corfu island runs many times daily in each direction. In Athens, ferries leave frequently from Piraeus, the main port 10 km (6 mi) south of downtown, for the Argo-Saronic islands, the Cyclades, the Dodecanese, and Crete. Shorter crossings to the Cyclades can be made from the other side of Attica; from Rafina to Andros, Tinos, and Mykonos; and from Lavrion to Kea and Kythnos. Some northern islands, like Thassos and Limnos, are more easily reached from Thessaloniki, and boats for the Sporades islands depart only from Agios Konstantinos and Volos on the northern mainland or Kimi on Evia island. **When choosing a ferry, determine how many stops you'll make and the**

estimated arrival time. Sometimes a ferry that leaves an hour later for your destination gets you there faster and not at 3 AM.

From Piraeus port, the quickest way to get into town, if you are traveling light, is to walk to the metro station and take an electric train to Omonia Square (150 dr./€.44) or Syntagma Square (250 dr./€.73, change at Omonia to the Ethniki Aminas line), a 30-minute trip. Alternatively, you can take a taxi, which may take longer owing to traffic and will cost around 2,200 dr./€6.48. Often, drivers wait until they fill their taxi with debarking passengers headed in the same direction, which could take 25 minutes, plus the extra time accommodating everyone's route. It's faster to walk to the main street and hail a passing cab.

To get to Attica's main port, Rafina, take a KTEL bus (☎ 01/821–0872), which leaves every half hour 5:30 AM to 9:30 PM from Aigyptou Square near Pedion Areos park in Athens. The fare is 500 dr./€1/47. The bus takes about an hour to get to Rafina; the port is slightly down the hill from the bus station.

Timetables change frequently, and boats may be delayed by weather conditions, especially when the northwestern winds called *meltemia* hit in August, so **stay flexible,** one advantage to not buying a ticket in advance. You can't make reservations, but you usually can get on a boat at the last minute. Still, it is better to buy your tickets two to three days ahead if you are traveling between July 15 and August 30, when most Greeks vacation, if you need a cabin, or if you're taking a car. **Don't travel by boat around August 15,** when most ferries are so crowded, the situation becomes comically desperate. If you don't join the crowd stampeding to the boat when it pulls in to the harbor, you will find yourself lying along the aisle corridors between the cabins—and feeling lucky you have any space at all. Reserve your return journey soon after you arrive.

Ticket prices don't vary because they're set by the government, and in most cases deck class (*triti thesi*) is good enough. Second-class entitles you to a cabin for a few thousand drachmas more, and better lounges, so it's worthwhile on packed boats. First-class tickets are almost as expensive as flying.

If the boat journey will be more than a few hours, take supplies, as food and refreshments on board are quite expensive, and the washrooms always seem to run out of toilet paper. Most of the shops aboard ferries sell Dramamine, as do the kiosks on the harbors.

If your ship's departure is delayed (with the exception of force majeure), you have the right to stay on board in the class indicated on your ticket or, in case of a prolonged delay, to cancel your ticket for a full refund. If you miss your ship, you forfeit your ticket; if you cancel in advance, you receive a 50% discount.

As for news on the boat and shipping scene, there's much. In preparation for the lifting of cabotage restrictions in 2003, Greece's largest shipping operators have ordered at least 20 new fast ferries from European and Asian shipyards; most will be delivered starting in 2001. Also, three high-speed catamarans have been ordered from Australia. The first, which was to begin crossing the Aegean in 2000, will halve travel time from Piraeus to Santorini. The aluminum twin-hull catamaran, lighter than Greece's regular ferries, can transport 1,050 passengers and 188 cars at speeds of 48 mi (42 knots) per hour, reducing the journey to just over three hours. Similar catamarans are used for the British Channel crossing. The end of cabotage restraints will increase competition in the Aegean and improve travelers' choices. Currently, the Greek merchant marine ministry issues licenses on a noncompetitive basis and sets fares and routes. When the market is liberalized, other EU ferry operators will be able to provide service between Greek ports. Already on the Adriatic crossing from Greece to Italy, used by more than one million travelers annually, competition is thriving after Italy, France, and Spain opened up routes to Greek ferries. The Adriatic crossing is also a main route for

Greek trucks loaded with exports to the European Union; truck traffic is expected to surge with the impending completion of the Egnatia highway, which will span northern Greece from the western port of Igoumenitsa to the Turkish border.

FARES & SCHEDULES

You can buy tickets from a travel agency representing the shipping line you need, from the local shipping agency office, or at makeshift stands in front of the boat before departure (if tickets are still available). Except when paying at a travel agency, where you might be able to use a credit card (this will be discouraged), you pay cash. For schedules, any travel agent can call the port to check information for you, although they may not be as helpful about a shipping line for which they don't sell tickets. On islands the local office of each shipping line posts a board with departure times, or you can contact the port authority (*limenarchio*), where some English is usually spoken. The Greek National Tourist Organization (EOT) distributes weekly lists and ticket prices for boats leaving Athens. The *Athens News* also lists daily departures from the capital. Or you can call for a recording (☎ 143, in Greek) of the day's domestic departures. At 1 PM, a new recording lists boats leaving the following morning.

➤ BOAT & FERRY INFORMATION: **Agios Konstantinos Port Authority** (☎ 0235/31759). **Kimi Port Authority** (☎ 0222/22606). **Igoumenitsa Port Authority** (☎ 0665/22240 or 0665/22235). **Lavrion Port Authority** (☎ 0292/25249 or 292/22188). **Patras Port Authority** (☎ 061/341002 or 061/341024). **Piraeus Port Authority** (☎ 01/451–1311 through 01/451–1319 or 01/451–1130). **Rafina Port Authority** (☎ 0294/22300). **Thessaloniki Port Authority** (☎ 031/531503 or 031/531504). **Volos Port Authority** (☎ 0421/28888).

INTERNATIONAL FERRIES

You can cross to Turkey from the northeastern Aegean islands, from Lesbos to Dikeli, from Chios to Cesme, and from Samos to Kuşadası. Note that British passport holders must have 10 pounds sterling with them to purchase a visa on landing in Turkey, Australian citizens need $20 (American dollars) and U.S. citizens need $45; New Zealanders don't need a visa. You can purchase the visa beforehand, paying drachmas, at the Turkish consulate in Athens.

There are frequent sails between Italy and Greece—at least seven a day in summer from Brindisi, two each from Bari and Ancona, four–five a week from Trieste, and daily to Venice; all go to Corfu and/or Igoumenitsa and Patras (three a week call at Kefalonia). Some of the shipping lines are Agoudimos Lines, Anek Lines, Hellenic Mediterranean Lines, Marlines, Minoan Lines, Strintzis Lines, and Ventouris Ferries.

Prices range widely, depending on when and how you travel, ship facilities, and the distance traveled. For Patras–Ancona in high season, passengers pay 17,000 dr./€50–23,000 dr./€67.84 for the deck; 67,000 dr.197–95,000 dr./€280 for a deluxe outside cabin, depending on the shipping line. Children 4–12 usually receive a 50% discount, and those under 4 pay a small fee (1,600 dr./€4.71) per passage if they don't occupy a berth or bed. To take your car from Patras to Ancona costs about 27,300 dr./€80.53 in high season (16,800 dr.€49.55 in low season), and to Brindisi, 15,900 dr./€47 (9,300 dr./€27.43 in low season), with a discount on the return.

A few years ago Superfast Ferries were introduced; although about one-third more expensive, they make the trip from Patras to Ancona in just 19 hours, or Bari in 15 hours, and from Igoumenitsa to Bari in 9 hours, faster than conventional ferries. Strintzis Lines also runs the new Blue Star Ferries, which travel from Patras to Ancona in 21 hours, to Brindisi in 9. The ferries are outfitted with several bars, a self-service restaurant, pool, two cinemas, casino, and shops. Blue Star offers family specials (two adults and two children in high season for 104,000 dr./€306 from Patras to Ancona) and super economy packages (up to five people and a car for 71,600 dr./€231 in high season, Patras to Ancona). **Book well in**

advance for summer and reconfirm shortly before sailing.

Blue Star Ferries offer a mini-cruise program from mid-September through June that takes passengers by bus from Athens to Patras and then by ferry to Venice, where passengers spend a day before returning to Greece; prices range from 49,000 dr./€144 to 80,000 dr./€235 per person.

➤ FERRY COMPANIES: **Agoudimos** (✉ Kapodistriou 2, Piraeus 18531, ☎ 01/413–3583 or 01/412–9649, FAX 01/422–0595) travels from Igoumenitsa to Brindisi via Corfu. In Igoumenitsa, the representative is Nikos P. Zois Shipping Agency (✉ Ethnikis Antistasseos 22, 46100, ☎ 0665/25682, FAX 0665/24960). **Anek** (✉ Amalias 54, Athens 10558, ☎ 01/323–3481 or 01/323–3819; 01/419–7430 for international reservations, FAX 01/323–4137). **Hellenic Mediterranean Lines** (✉ Loudovikou Sq. 4, Piraeus 18510, ☎ 01/422–5341, FAX 01/422–5317) travels Patras to Brindisi, with stops at the Ionian islands. **Marlines** (✉ Akti Poseidonos 38, Piraeus 18531, ☎ 01/422–4950 or 01/411–0777, FAX 01/411–7780) sails from Igoumenitsa to Bari. In Igoumenitsa (✉ Ethnikis Antistasseos 42, 46100, ☎ 0665/23301 or 0665/23911, FAX 0665/25428). **Minoan Lines** (✉ Vas. Konstantinou 2, Athens 11635, ☎ 01/751–2356, FAX 01/752–0540). **Strintzis Lines/Blue Star Ferries** (✉ Akti Poseidonos 26, Piraeus 18531, ☎ 01/422–5000 for international reservations, FAX 01/422–5265 or 01/422–5266). **Superfast Ferries** (✉ Amalias 30, Athens 10558, ☎ 01/331–3252, FAX 01/331–0369). In Patras (✉ Othonos-Amalias 12, 26223, ☎ 061/622500, FAX 061/623574). In Igoumenitsa (✉ Ag. Apostolon 147, Neo Limani, 46100, ☎ 0665/28150 or 0665/29200, FAX 0665/28156). **Ventouris Ferries** (✉ Nikodimou 5, Athens 10558, ☎ 01/324–0278, FAX 01/411–4915).

For those continuing beyond Greece through the Mediterranean, **Poseidon Lines** runs a twice-weekly car ferry in summer that leaves Piraeus and circuits Rhodes, Limassol in Cyprus, and Haifa in Israel (✉ Alkyonidon 32, Kavouri 16673, ☎ 01/965–8300,

FAX 01/965–8310). Another ferry that makes roughly the same journey (not Rhodes) is operated by **Salamis Lines** (✉ Filellinon 9, Piraeus 18536, ☎ 01/429–4325, FAX 01/452–8384).

➤ TURKISH CONSULATE: **Turkish Consulate** (✉ Vas. Pavlou 22, Palio Psychiko, Athens 15452, ☎ 01/671–4828, FAX 01/677–6430). Visa hours are 9–1.

HYDROFOIL

Hydrofoils, known as *delphinia* (dolphins), carry passengers from Zea Marina in Piraeus to the Saronic Gulf islands (Aegina, Hydra, Poros, and Spetses), Cycladic islands, and eastern Peloponnesian ports, including Hermioni, Kyparissi, Kythera, Leonidion, Methana, Monemvassia, Nafplion, Neapolis, and Porto Heli. In summer there is additional service, including from Palia Epidauros to Aegina and Piraeus. You can also take hydrofoils from Agios Konstantinos or Volos to the Sporades islands. These boats are somewhat pricey and the limited number of seats means you should reserve, but they cut travel time in half. However, they often cannot travel if the sea is choppy, and cancellations are common. Tickets can be purchased through authorized agents or one hour before departure. Book your return upon arrival if you are pressed for time. From Zea Marina, you can take a taxi to the city center (2,200 dr./€6.48) or trolley No. 20 (120 dr./€.35 to the Piraeus metro station, continuing by subway to Omonia or Syntagma squares (150 dr./€.44–250 dr./€.73).

➤ RESERVATIONS: To make reservations, absolutely necessary in summer, call the **Minoan Flying Dolphins** (✉ Akti Kondili and Aetolikou, Piraeus 18535, ☎ 01/419–9200 for reservations, FAX 01/413–5000).

BUS TRAVEL

Organized bus tours can be booked together with hotel reservations by your travel agent. Many tour operators have offices in and around Syntagma and Omonia squares in Athens. Bus tours often depart from Syntagma or adjacent streets. Refer to the Guided Tours section for each region for description of tours.

It is easy to get around Greece by bus, which travels to even the most far-flung villages (☞ Transportation, *below*). The price of public transportation in Greece has risen steeply in the last couple of years, but it is still cheaper than in other western European cities. Greece has an extensive, inexpensive, and reliable regional bus system (**KTEL**) made up of local operators. Each city has connections to towns and villages in its vicinity; visit the local KTEL office to check routes. Buses from Athens, however, travel throughout the country. The buses, which are punctual, span the range from slightly dilapidated and rattly to air-conditioned with comfy upholstered seats. There is just one class of ticket. Board early, because Greeks have a very loose attitude about assigned seating, and ownership is nine-tenths' possession. From Athens to Corinth costs 1,750 dr./€5.16 and takes about 90 minutes; to Nafplion, 2,650 dr./€7.81 2½ hours; to Patras, 3,900 dr./€11.50, 4 hours; and to Thessaloniki, 8,700 dr./€25.66, 7½ hours.

Although smoking is forbidden on KTEL buses, the driver stops every two hours or so at a roadside establishment; smokers can light up then. Drivers are exempt from the no-smoking rule; don't sit near the front seat if smoking bothers you.

In Athens, KTEL's **Terminal A** is the arrival and departure point for bus lines to northern Greece, including Thessaloniki, and to the Peloponnese destinations of Epidauros, Mycenae, Nafplion, and Corinth. **Terminal B** serves Evia, most of Thrace, and central Greece, including Delphi. To get into the city center, take Bus 051 from Terminal A (terminus at Zinonos and Menandrou off Omonia Square) or Bus 024 from Terminal B (downtown stop in front of the National Gardens on Amalias). Most KTEL buses to the east Attica coast—including those for Sounion, Marathon, and the ports of Lavrion and Rafina—leave from the **downtown KTEL terminal** near Pedion Areos park.

In Athens and Thessaloniki avoid riding city buses during rush hours. Buses and trolleys do not automatically stop at every station; you must hold out your hand to summon the vehicle you want. Upon boarding, validate your ticket in the canceling machines, at the front and back of buses (this goes for the trolleys and the subway train platforms, too). If you're too far from the machine and the bus is crowded, don't be shy: pass your ticket forward with the appropriate ingratiating gestures, and it will eventually return, properly punched. Keep your ticket until you reach your destination, as inspectors who occasionally board are strict about fining offenders. On intracity buses, an inspector also boards to check your ticket, so keep it handy.

CUTTING COSTS

If you are planning to take the bus, trolley, and metro several times in one day during your Athens stay, **buy a 24-hour ticket** for all the urban network (1,000 dr./€2.94). When assessing whether it's worth the money, remember that you must use a new ticket (120 dr./€.35–250 dr./€.73) or each leg of the journey for each method of transportation. A pass also saves you the hassle of validating your tickets numerous times. Students with ID qualify for half-off tickets. If you are staying several weeks in the capital, **buy a monthly pass,** available at the beginning of the month from downtown terminal kiosks and most metro stations (good value at 5,000 dr./€14.74 for unlimited bus and trolley travel; 10,000 dr./€29.49 if you also want to travel on the metro. You need a passport-sized photograph of yourself for the pass. You can reduce regional bus fares if you **purchase a round-trip KTEL ticket,** which saves you about 15%.

FARES & SCHEDULES

In large cities, you can buy individual tickets for urban buses at terminal booths, convenience stores, or at selected *periptera* (street kiosks). KTEL tickets must be purchased at the KTEL station. On islands, in smaller towns, and on the KTEL buses that leave from Aigyptou Square in Athens, you buy tickets from the driver's assistant once seated; try not to pay with anything more than a 1,000-dr./€2.94 bill to avoid commotion. Athens bus stops now have signs diagramming each route. It still helps if you can read some Greek, since most stops are only labeled in Greek. The Organization for Urban Public Transportation gives Athens route information, but the best source for non-Greek speakers is EOT, which distributes information on Athens and KTEL bus schedules, including prices for each destination and phone numbers for the regional ticket desks.

➤ ATHENS PUBLIC TRANSPORTATION: In Athens, the **Organization for Urban Public Transportation** (✉ Metsovou 15, Athens, ☎ 185) answers questions about bus routes from 7:30 to 3 and 7 PM to 9 PM weekdays. The office, just north of the National Archaeological Museum, also distributes maps (weekdays 7:30–3), although the more central EOT has helpful handouts on bus routes, timetables, and fares in English.

➤ REGIONAL BUS SERVICE: **Terminal A** (✉ Kifissou 100, ☎ 01/512–4910); EOT distributes phone lists for each destination. **Terminal B** (✉ Liossion 260, ☎ there is no phone number for the terminal; you must call each region's ticket counter for information; one popular destination is Delphi 01/831–7096). EOT has phone lists for each desk. **Downtown KTEL terminal** (✉ Aigyptou Sq. at the corner of Mavromateon and Leoforos Alexandras near Pedion Areos park, ☎ 01/821–3203 for Sounion, Rafina, and Lavrion; 01/ 821–0872 for Marathon).

PAYING

Throughout Greece, you must pay cash for local and regional bus tickets. For bus tours, a travel agency usually lets you pay by credit card or traveler's checks.

RESERVATIONS

For KTEL, you can make reservations for many destinations free by phone. Reservations are unnecessary on most routes, especially those with several round trips a day. Book your seat a few days in advance, however, if you are traveling on holiday weekends, especially if you are headed out of Athens. In fact, because reservations sometimes mysteriously disappear or get jumbled in the holiday exodus, it's best to go to the station and buy your ticket beforehand.

BUSINESS HOURS

Business hours don't vary that much from region to region, although there are exceptions such as the town of Raches in Ikaria, where stores *open* their doors at 9 PM. More establishments stay open longer hours in the major cities and tourist resorts, but for certain categories such as pharmacies, banks, and government offices, hours are standardized. Most businesses and shops close for several weeks in summer, usually from the end of July to mid-August. Many tourist establishments, including hotels, shut down on the islands and northern Greece from November until mid-spring. Restaurants, especially tavernas, often stay open on holidays; some close in summer or move to cooler locations (☞ Mealtimes, *below*). Christmas, New Year's, Orthodox Easter, and August 15 are the days everything shuts down, although, for example, bars work full force on Christmas Eve, since it's a very social occasion and not particularly family-oriented. Orthodox Easter changes dates every year, so check your calendar.

BANKS & OFFICES

Banks are normally open Monday–Thursday 8–2, Fridays 8–1:30. In Athens a central branch of the **National Bank of Greece** has extended hours for foreign exchange (✉ Karageorgi Servias 2, Syntagma Sq., ☎ 01/334–0011), open Monday through Thursday 8–2 and 3:30–6:30, Friday 3–6:30, Saturday 9–3, and Sunday 9–1. Hotels also cash traveler's checks on weekends, and the banks at both airport terminals have longer hours; some at the East Terminal are open all night. Most banks now have ATMs that accept cards on the Plus or Cirrus system.

Government offices are open from 8 to 2. For commercial offices, it depends on the business: a large advertising agency in Piraeus might be open 10–6, while a printing service in Exarchia might operate 11–2.

CHURCHES & MONASTERIES

Your guess is as good as the locals' as to when churches and monasteries are open to the public; in numerous cases monasteries are merely ruins, no longer functioning or looked after. In cities, opening hours are fairly standard, but in rural areas, visitors may need to find the caretaker to unlock the church doors; he or she usually lives nearby. In such cases it is customary to light a candle or buy a postcard in remuneration. The best time to find churches unlocked is during services, especially Sunday mornings; otherwise try from about 8 to noon and 5:30 to 7:30 on any day, unless where noted. The hours for monasteries are dependent upon their keepers, but they are generally more likely to be open in the morning to early afternoon; specific hours are noted.

GAS STATIONS

Most stations are open daily from 7 to 7, and several pump all night in the major cities and along the National Road. They do not close for lunch.

MUSEUMS & SIGHTS

The days and hours for museums and sites vary; they are usually open daily 8:30 to 3 except one weekday (usually Monday), although in summer, depending on personnel available that year, the hours are extended to as late as 7 PM; throughout the year arrive at least 30 minutes before closing time to ensure a ticket. Winter hours apply from about November through mid-April. Archaeological sites and museums remain closed on January 1, March 25, the morning of Orthodox Good Friday, Orthodox Easter, May 1, and December 25–26. Sunday visiting hours apply to museums on: Epiphany; Ash Monday, Good Saturday, Easter Monday, and Whitsunday (Orthodox dates, which change every year); August 15; and October 28. Museums close early (around 12:30) on January 2, the last Saturday of Carnival, Orthodox Good Thursday, Christmas Eve, and New Year's Eve. Throughout the guide, the hours of sights and attractions are denoted by the clock icon, ☉ . Admission to most museums and archaeological sites is free on Sunday November through March. Entrance is usually free every day for EU students, half off for students from other countries, and about a third off for senior citizens.

PHARMACIES

Pharmacies are open Monday, Wednesday, and Friday from about 8:30 to 3, and Tuesday, Thursday, and Friday from 8:30 to 2 and 5 until 8 or 8:30 in the afternoon. The pharmacy in Elliniko's West Terminal is open 8 AM to midnight, that in the East Terminal operates 24 hours. According to a rotation system, there is always at least one pharmacy open in any area; closed pharmacies post a list in their window of the nearest open establishment for Sundays and off-hours (☞ Pharmacies, *below,* in Emergencies).

SHOPS

Nominally shops may stay open from 9 AM to 9 PM in summer, though most stores close Monday, Wednesday, and Saturday around 3 or 4 PM. On Tuesday, Thursday, and Friday, they take an afternoon break between about 3 and 5. Most establishments close Sunday. In winter (November to mid-April) hours are slightly reduced, though the schedule changes annually. In tourist areas such as Mykonos, Santorini, and Athens's Plaka, shops extend their hours, sometimes until late into the night. Supermarkets are open weekdays 8 AM until about 8:30 PM, with reduced hours on Saturday.

If it's late in the evening and you need an aspirin, soft drink, cigarettes, newspaper, or a pen, look for the nearest open kiosk, called a *periptero,* which stands on street corners everywhere brimming with all kinds of necessities. Owners stagger their hours, and many towns have at least one kiosk that stays open until all hours, occasionally through the night.

CAMERAS & PHOTOGRAPHY

Greece is the perfect f-22 country, and the bright sunlight and endless color and variety of the landscape seem to cry aloud to be photographed or filmed. The best light, especially when photographing the sea or panoramas, appears late afternoon, when haze clears up and the landscape is bathed in a honeyed glow. (Your tan looks better, and unsightly bulges disappear, all part of the softening effect!) Use common sense when photographing locals; it's always better to elicit at least tacit approval; on the other hand, if you ask for permission, you may lose the shot. The people of the countryside, while friendly and hospitable, are sometimes camera-shy, and if you want them on film, it is better to play at candid photography than to try to set up a pose. Photography of, or near, military establishments is strictly forbidden (indicated by a sign with an X-ed out camera). In museums, flash photography is not allowed. It is considered extremely rude to photograph people other than those in your party at topless or nude beaches, where any camera is viewed with suspicion. Although you are obliged to photograph the Acropolis or whatever other ruin you're visiting, it will be your shots of the crystalline waters of some perfect beach that will make your friends ooh and aah every time.

➤ PHOTO HELP: **Kodak Information Center** (☎ 800/242–2424). *Kodak Guide to Shooting Great Travel Pictures,* available in bookstores or from Fodor's Travel Publications (☎ 800/533–6478; $18 plus $5.50 shipping).

EQUIPMENT PRECAUTIONS

Always **keep your film and tape out of the sun.** Carry an extra supply of batteries, and **be prepared to turn on your camera or camcorder** to prove to security personnel that the device is real. Always **ask for hand inspection of film,** which becomes clouded after repeated exposure to airport X-ray machines, and **keep videotapes away from metal detectors.**

In Greece, non EU-citizens should register laptop computers with customs on entry, then show the stamped passport page with the computer's serial number upon exit to prove they did not buy it in Greece. Although officials may never check you coming or going, it's good to follow procedure to avoid last-minute trouble on departure.

FILM & DEVELOPING

Film is widely available; the most common brands are Kodak, Agfa, and Fujifilm. A 24-exposure roll of Kodak Gold color print film, 100 ASA (works well in strong light) costs 1,400 dr./€4.12, 1,800 dr./€5.30 for 36 exposures. Prices are higher at tourist shops; Agfa is usually the cheapest choice. The Advantix system is available in large cities and major resorts (1,500 dr./€4.42 for 200 Ultra, 24 exposures). Disposable cameras are good in a pinch (2,500 dr./€7.37–3,000 dr./€8.84). You can find 24-hour film developing shops that provide satisfactory quality in all major towns and resort islands, but unless you're in a hurry, **develop your film at home,** where costs are bound to be lower: a 24-print color roll costs about 3,000 dr./€8.84 to process.

VIDEOS

VHS tapes are widely available at photo and electronic shops. A 60-minute tape starts at 1,100 dr./€3.24 Greece uses the SECAM system.

CAR RENTAL

Because driving in Greece can be harrowing, car rental prices are higher than in the U.S., and transporting a car by ferry hikes up the fare substantially, think twice before deciding on car rental. It's much easier to take public transportation or taxis, which are among the cheapest in Europe. The exception is large islands where the distance between towns is greater—and taxi fares higher—then you may want to rent a car or a moped for the day for concentrated bouts of sightseeing.

Official rates in Greece during high season (July through September) for an economy car such as an Opel Corsa or Hyundai Atos range from 8,300 dr./€24.48 a day (100 km minimum charge at 138 dr./€.40 per km) to 24,300 dr./€71.68 for three to six days (unlimited mileage). Smaller cars (Fiat Seicento, for example) rent for about 6,600 dr./€19.46 a day (113 dr./€.33 per km) in high season; four-wheel-drives (Suzuki Samurai 1.3) cost 17,900 dr./€52.80 a day (200 dr./€.58 per km). This does not include the 18% VAT (13% on Rhodes, Kos, Lesbos, Santorini, Chios, Thassos, Samos, Skiathos, Karpathos, Skopelos, Mykonos, Paros, and Naxos).

Luxury cars are available at some agencies. Europcar rents a BMW 520 Clima or a Rover 75 for 35,200 dr./€95.87 a day (350 dr./€1.03 per km) during low season, 40,250 dr./€118 (400 dr./€1.17 per km) in high season. Convertibles ("open" cars) and minibuses are also available. Probably the most difficult car to rent, unless you reserve from abroad, is an automatic. Off-season, rental agencies are often closed on islands and in less-populated areas.

➤ MAJOR AGENCIES: **Alamo** (☎ 800/ 522–9696; 020/8759–6200 in the U.K.). **Avis** (☎ 800/331–1084; 800/ 331–1084 in Canada; 02/9353–9000 in Australia; 09/525–1982 in New Zealand). **Budget** (☎ 800/527–0700; 0870/607–5000 in the U.K., through affiliate Europcar). **Dollar** (☎ 800/ 800–6000; 0124/622–0111 in the U.K., through affiliate Sixt Kenning; 02/9223–1444 in Australia). **Hertz** (☎ 800/654–3001; 800/263–0600 in Canada; 020/8897–2072 in the U.K.; 02/9669–2444 in Australia; 09/256– 8690 in New Zealand). **National Car Rental** (☎ 800/227–7368; 020/8680– 4800 in the U.K., where it is known as National Europe).

➤ ATHENS AIRPORT AGENCIES: At press time (summer 2000), the following companies had booths at the airport: **Alamo** (☎ 01/994–4257 East Terminal); **Avis** (☎ 01/981–4404 West Terminal, 01/995–3440 East Terminal); **Budget** (☎ 01/988–3792 West Terminal, 01/961–3634 East Terminal); **Eurocar** (☎ 01/982–9565 West Terminal, 01/961–3624 East Terminal); **Hertz** (☎ 01/981–3701 West Terminal, 01/961–3625 East Terminal); **Holiday Autos** (☎ 01/ 963–1923 East Terminal); **Lion Rental–SIXT Rent-A-Car** (☎ 01/ 984–8091 West Terminal, 01/994– 4163 East Terminal).

CUTTING COSTS

You can usually reduce prices by reserving a car before you leave through a major rental agency. Or **opt for a mid-sized Greek agency and bargain,** especially on when kilometers become free. These agencies provide good service, and prices are at the owner's discretion. It helps if you have shopped around and can dangle another agency's offer.

Do **look into wholesalers,** companies that do not own fleets but rent in bulk from those that do and often offer better rates than traditional car-rental operations. Payment must be made before you leave home.

➤ LOCAL AGENCIES: **Fantastico Rent-a-Car** (✉ Mihalakopoulou 62, Ilissia, ☎ 01/778–3771, FAX 01/778–4860). **Greece Rent-A-Car** (✉ Syngrou 7, City Center, Athens, ☎ 01/924–9802 or 01/924–9803, FAX 01/924–9804), which has monthly rates. Also in Athens: **Just Rent-A-Car** (✉ Syngrou 43, ☎ 01/923–9104, FAX 01/924– 7248). **Pappas Rent-A-Car** (✉ Amalias 44, Center, ☎ 01/322–0087 or 01/323–4772, FAX 01/322–6472). **Payless Traffic Car Rental** (✉ Syngrou 24 and Hatzichristou, Center, ☎ 01/923–8842, FAX 01/924–7969). The very helpful staff at **Swift Car Rental** (✉ Nikis 21, Center, ☎ 01/ 324–7855, 01/322–1623, or 01/324– 7875, FAX 01/325–0671) actually drive tourists bewildered by Athens traffic to the city limits.

➤ WHOLESALERS: **Auto Europe** (☎ 207/842–2000 or 800/223–5555, FAX 800/235–6321, www.autoeurope.com). **Europe by Car** (☎ 212/581–3040 or 800/223– 1516, FAX 212/246–1458, www. europebycar.com). **DER Travel Services** (✉ 9501 W. Devon Ave., Rosemont, IL 60018, ☎ 800/782–2424, FAX 800/282–7474 for information; 800/860–9944 for brochures, www. dertravel.com). **Kemwel Holiday Autos** (☎ 800/678–0678, FAX 914/ 825–3160, www.kemwel.com).

INSURANCE

When driving a rented car you are generally responsible for any damage to or loss of the vehicle. Before you rent see what coverage your personal auto-insurance policy and credit cards already provide.

Before you buy collision coverage, check your existing policies—you may already be covered. However, collision policies that car-rental companies sell for European rentals usually do not include stolen-vehicle coverage.

Rental agencies offer a full range of insurance: collision damage waiver costs about 3,800 dr./€11.20 to 5,800 dr./€17 a day, depending on the deduction; personal insurance 1,200 dr./€3.53; and theft 1,200 dr./€3.53 to 2,500 dr./€7.37, depending on the car, though some companies include this in the rate.

REQUIREMENTS & RESTRICTIONS

In Greece your own driver's license is not acceptable unless you are an EU citizen. For non-EU citizens, an International Driver's Permit is necessary; it's available from the American or Canadian automobile associations. To rent, you must have had your driver's license for one year and be at least 21 years old if you use a credit card (sometimes 23 if you pay cash), and for some of the car categories, you must be 25. You need the agency's permission to ferry the car or cross the border (Europcar does not allow across-the-border rentals).

SURCHARGES

Before you pick up a car in one city and leave it in another, **ask about drop-off charges or one-way service fees,** which can be substantial. Especially after hours, delivery can cost up to 7,000 dr./€20.64 Note, too, that some rental agencies charge extra if you return the car before the time specified in your contract. To avoid a refueling fee (1,500 dr./€4.42), **fill the tank just before you turn in the car,** but be aware that gas stations near the rental outlet may overcharge. Other surcharges include airport service charges (6% on the basic rate), additional driver (500 dr./€1.47 to 700 dr./€2.06 a day), and if needed, baby seats (700 dr./€2.06 to 900 dr./€2.65 daily) and luggage racks (1,000 dr./€2.95 to 1,200 dr./€3.53 daily).

CAR TRAVEL

In Athens, traffic is mind-boggling most of the time and parking, nonexistent; public transportation or taxis are a much better choice than driving. If you are traveling quite a bit by boat, taking along a car increases ticket costs substantially and limits your ease in hopping on any ferry. On islands, you can always rent a taxi or a car for the day if you want to see something distant. Intradestination flights are fairly cheap; and the Greek government is talking about letting private companies fix the roads and raise toll rates to cover expenses. So, the only real reason to drive is if it's your passion, you are a large party with many suitcases and many out-of-the-way places to see, or you need the freedom to change routes and make unexpected stops not permitted on public transportation.

Regular registration papers and insurance contracted in any EU country or a green card are required, in addition to a driver's license (EU or international). EU members can travel freely without paying any additional taxes. If you are a non-EU member, you may import your vehicle duty-free for six months, but if you must leave the country without the car, Customs "keeps" your car until your return; a Greek citizen must act as your guarantor. Cars with foreign plates are exempt from the alternate-day ban in Athens on driving in the center according to whether the license plate is odd or even. Rental cars, however, must follow the law. Full insurance, including coverage against collision with an uninsured motorist, is recommended. Accidents must be reported (something Greek motorists often fail to do) before the insurance companies consider claims. In case of an accident, try to get the other driver's details as soon as possible; hit-and-run is all too common in Greece.

The two main highways, both called Ethniki Odos (National Road), leave Athens going north and south. These highways, along with the secondary roads, cover most of the mainland, but on islands, some areas (beaches, for example) are only accessible via dirt or gravel paths. With the exception of a few flat areas like the Thessalian plain, you will average about 60 km (37 mi) an hour: expect some badly paved or disintegrating roads, stray flocks of goats, slowpoke farm vehicles, detours, curves, and near Athens and Thessaloniki, traffic jams. At the Athens city limits, signs in English mark the way to Syntagma and Omonia squares in the center.

When you exit Athens, signs are well marked for the highway, usually naming Lamia for the north and Corinth or Patras for the southwest.

AUTO CLUBS

Greece's Automobile Club, known as **ELPA**, operates a special phone line (☎ 174) for tourist information that works throughout the country, as well as several branch offices. If you don't belong to an auto club at home, you can join ELPA for 35,500 dr./€104, which gives you free emergency road service, though you must pay for spare parts. Membership lasts for a year and is good on discounts for emergency calls throughout the EU. **Visit your local auto association before you leave** for Greece; they can help you plan your trip and provide you with maps. They also can issue you an International Driver's License good for one year. Your local membership qualifies you for cheaper emergency service in Greece and abroad.

➤ IN GREECE: The **Automobile Touring Club of Greece** or ELPA (✉ Mesogeion 395, Agia Paraskevi, Athens 15343, ☎ 01/606–8800, FAX 01/606–8981). Other branches include Patras (✉ Patroon-Athinon 18, ☎ 061/425411, ☎ FAX 061/426416); Heraklion (✉ Knossou Ave. and G. Papandreou 46–50 and Knossou, ☎ 0181/289440); and Thessaloniki (✉ Vas. Olgas 230 and Aegeou, ☎ 031/426319 or 031/426386, FAX 031/411–0155).

➤ IN AUSTRALIA: **Australian Automobile Association** (AAA, ☎ 06/247–7311).

➤ IN CANADA: **Canadian Automobile Association** (CAA, ☎ 613/247–0117).

➤ IN NEW ZEALAND: **New Zealand Automobile Association** (☎ 09/377–4660).

➤ IN THE U.K.: **Automobile Association** (AA, ☎ 0990/500–600), **Royal Automobile Club** (RAC, ☎ 0990/722–722 for membership; 0345/121–345 for insurance).

➤ IN THE U.S.: **American Automobile Association** (☎ 800/564–6222).

EMERGENCY SERVICES

You must put out a triangular danger sign if you have a breakdown. Roving repair trucks, manned by skilled ELPA mechanics, patrol the major highways. They assist tourists with breakdowns for free if they belong to AAA or to ELPA; otherwise, there is a charge. An EOT initiative, in cooperation with ELPA, the tourist police, and Greek scouts, now provides an emergency telephone line for those who spot a dead or wounded animal on the National Road.

➤ ROAD EMERGENCY CONTACTS: **Automobile Touring Club of Greece** (☎ 104 for breakdowns; 171 for a dead or hurt animal or 01/323–5307, 01/323–5455, or 01/323–5465 if you are outside Athens).

GASOLINE

Gas pumps and service stations are everywhere, and lead-free gas is widely available. However, away from the main towns, especially at night, open gas stations can be very far apart (☞ Gas Stations, *above,* in Business Hours). **Don't let your gas supply drop to less than a quarter-tank when driving through rural areas.** Gas costs about 260 dr./€.76 to 270 dr./€.79 a liter for unleaded (ah-*mo*-lee-vdee), 280 dr./€.82 a liter for diesel (*dee*-zel). You aren't usually allowed to pump your own gas though you are expected to do everything else yourself. If you ask the attendant to give you extra service (check oil and water or clean the windows), leave a small tip. International chains (BP, Mobil) usually accept credit cards; Greek-owned stations (Elinoil, EKO) usually do not. Nobody *wants* to give you a receipt (a-*po*-dthee-ksee), but they must by law, so don't hesitate to ask.

FROM THE U.K.

Driving to Greece from Britain is now possible, though keep in mind that gas may be difficult to find in the former Yugoslavia, especially unleaded. Though it is expensive, you can take a car to Greece (and at the same time greatly reduce your driving and save gasoline and hotel costs) by using the Paris–Milan and Milan–Brindisi car sleeper and then a car ferry to Corfu, Igoumenitsa, or Patras.

IMPORTING YOUR CAR

Contact the **Greek Consulate** for a six-month duty-free license to import your car. When leaving Greece, you must get a customs stamp to take the car out of the country by contacting the **Directorate for the Supervision and Control of Cars, or DIPEA.** There are no extensions; you either must leave the country with the car and return again after six months, under a new six-month permit, or leave the car in Greece for six months (no one can drive it), and then start anew.

➤ CUSTOMS STAMPS: **Directorate for the Supervision and Control of Cars, or DIPEA** (✉ Amvrosiou Frantzi 14, Athens 11473, ☎ 01/922–7315, FAX 01/923–4720).

INSURANCE

In general, auto insurance is not as expensive as in other countries. You must have third-party car insurance to drive in Greece. If possible, get an insurance "green card" valid for Greece from your insurance company before arriving. You can also buy a policy with local companies; keep the papers in a plastic pocket on the inside right front windshield. To get more information, or to locate a local representative for your insurance company, call the **Hellenic Union of Insurance Firms/Motor Insurance Bureau.**

➤ INSURANCE BUREAU: **Hellenic Union of Insurance Firms/Motor Insurance Bureau** (✉ Xenofontos 10, Athens 10557, ☎ 01/323–6733, FAX 01/323–8370).

ROAD CONDITIONS

Driving defensively is the key to safety in Greece. Greece is one of the most hazardous European countries for motorists. In the city and on the highways, the streets are riddled with potholes, motorcyclists seem to come out of nowhere, often passing on the right, and cars may even go the wrong way down a one-way street. In the countryside and on islands, you must watch for livestock crossing the road, as well as tourists shakily learning the motorbikes they've recently rented.

The many motorcycles and scooters weaving through traffic and the aggressive attitude of fellow motorists can make driving in Greece's large cities unpleasant—and the life of a pedestrian actively dangerous; Greeks often run red lights or ignore stop signs on side streets, travel the wrong way on one-way roads, or round corners without stopping. It's a good idea at night at city intersections and any time on curvy country lanes to beep your horn to warn errant drivers. In cities, you will find pedestrians have no qualms about standing in the middle of a busy boulevard, waiting to dart between cars; make eye contact so you can both determine who's going to slow. Rush hour in the cities runs from 7 to 10 AM and 2:30 to 3:30 PM on weekdays, plus 8 to 9 PM on Tuesday, Thursday, and Friday. Saturday mornings means bumper-to-bumper traffic in shopping districts, and weekend nights guarantees crowding around nightlife hubs. In Athens, the only time you won't find traffic is very early morning and most of Sunday (unless you're foolish enough to go to a local beach at 4 PM in summer). If air pollution has reached dangerous levels in Athens, all cars are banned from the center. Finally, perhaps because they are untrained, drivers seldom pull over for wailing ambulances; the most they'll do is slow down and slightly move over in different directions—complete chaos.

In the countryside, off the National Road where tolls range from 250 dr./€.73 to 900 dr./€2.65, traffic is light, and driving is more enjoyable, but highway route numbers are largely nonexistent. The National Road is very slick when wet—avoid driving in rain and on the days preceding or following major holidays, when traffic is at its worst as urban dwellers leave for their villages. The highway is always under repair, night lighting is sometimes out, and the lane markings are often hard to fathom, so stay awake and follow all signs to slow down.

ROAD MAPS

On the road map distributed by EOT, the National Roads are yellow and labeled with European road numbers, although these are not used on the roads themselves. For Athens, the best street guide, frequently updated, is *Athina-Pirea-Proastia* (Athens-Piraeus-Suburbs), published by S. Kapranides and N. Fotis in conjunction with ELPA. The taxi driver's choice, it breaks down the capital into manageable sections and clearly depicts everything in each area from pedestrian zones and one-way streets to hotel and theater locations. Sold at large book stores for about 6,500 dr./€19.17, the book is sometimes peddled at major intersections by vendors. If you're driving around Greece, buy the company's country guide, *Ellas* (7,000 dr./€20.64) which includes regional maps, kilometer-by-kilometer close-ups of major routes, city center street maps, and archaeological site plans. Most islands sell decent road maps at tourist shops, usually published by a company called Toubi, for 500 dr./€1.47 to 1,000 dr./€2.94

RULES OF THE ROAD

International road signs are in use throughout Greece. You drive on the right, pass on the left, and yield right-of-way to all vehicles approaching from the right (except on posted main highways). Cars may not make a right turn on a red light. The speed limits are 120 kph (74 mph) on the National Road, 90 kph (54 mph) outside urban areas, and 50 kph (31 mph) in cities, unless lower limits are posted. There are very few traffic police on the highways to enforce speeding limits or any other rules. Often, no limits are posted, and even when they are, many Greeks don't obey them. In many city neighborhoods, alternate-side-of-the-street parking rules are in effect. Although it's illegal, sidewalk parking is common. Once in a blue moon, police walk city streets and dispense tickets for a few blocks as a warning. Although it's tempting as a visitor to ignore parking tickets, keep in mind that if you've surrendered your ID to the rental agency, you won't get it back until you clear up the matter. You can pay your tickets at the rental agency or local police station; fines start at 10,000 dr./€29.49 and can go as high as 50,000 dr./€147.49 It never hurts to

plead your case at the police station, especially if you have a reasonable argument. As a rule, police often give foreigners a break. However, they have become far stricter lately, regularly inspecting cars (which must have a fire extinguisher, emergency triangle, and first-aid kit) and introducing alcohol tests. The alcohol limit is 0.05, but police use their discretion when issuing citations, if you are not too far over the limit. If you are involved in an accident, don't drive away. If the police take you in (they can hold you for 24 hours), you have the right to call your local embassy or consulate for help getting a lawyer. The use of seat belts and helmets is compulsory, though Greeks tend to ignore these rules, or comply with them by "wearing" the helmet on their elbows.

CHILDREN IN GREECE

Greek parents, who dote on their children to the point of spoiling them, believe this is the natural order of things: you marry, have children, then shower them with attention. They will dote on your children, too, if you take them along. Couples traveling without children, on the other hand, are likely to be interrogated: How many do you have at home? When do you expect your first child? Despite this fondness for children, organized child-care services are scarce. You'll have to make arrangements for special activities and baby-sitting on an ad hoc basis.

Locals are quite tolerant of children in public places: you often see youngsters running around in tavernas between the tables and no one gives them a second glance until they step on the cat's tail. It's perfectly natural if your child is crying for other diners to try to cheer him up. About the only place you can't take kids is trendy nightclubs and upscale restaurants. Remember to bring a baby backpack for places where the stroller won't roll, such as archaeological sites. In terms of keeping your children happy, **don't overdo the ruins.** It's the sea that appeals to all ages. The Aegean is calm and warm, perfect for even the most timid child. You'll have a hard time coaxing your toddler out of the water and your teenager off the Jet

Ski. However, keep in mind that kids want to be with other kids, so forget that deserted beach. Perfect for couples with a newborn, it will drive your walking, talking child to vociferous boredom, and you won't be staying long. **Search out family beaches,** especially those with a café, where you can retire but still keep an eye on the brood. Whatever season you visit, your child will enjoy the local festivals with dancing, costumes, odd customs, and competitions: who wouldn't delight in seeing goatskin-clad masked men clanging their bells on Skyros or in flying a kite with hundreds of other kids on Clean Monday? Quick fixes for grouchy toddlers are the coin-operated rides (space ships, trains) in many main squares and the ubiquitous big freezer boxes full of ice cream and complete with a chart for your child to ponder, a key ingredient to successful travel. In Athens, children are intrigued by the Changing of the Guard (Evzones in skirts), the ducks at the National Gardens, the rinky-dink amusement parks called *luna park*. Most cities have scheduled activities for children from September through June, usually sponsored by the municipality, museums, and large stores. These events include story telling, art shows, costume parties at Carnival time, and a special puppet "Theater of the Shadows," which features the beloved but sly Karagiozis. Throughout this guide, sights and attractions of interest to children are identified with the duckie icon, ☺ .

The *Athens News* in its Friday edition details upcoming activities for children in the capital, but if you can read Greek, the weekly *Athinorama* devotes an entire section to kids; get the hotel staff to skim it for you. Both publications are available at newsstands throughout the country. In the rest of the country, it's best to ask at the municipal tourist office or a travel agency.

As a destination for children, Greece only falls short in the sense that you will have to be more aware of your child's physical safety: beaches and hotel pools rarely have lifeguards, archaeological sites may be perched on unfenced cliffs, playgrounds sometimes have ill-maintained structures, busy island roads may have no sidewalks. **If you're planning to rent bikes, bring the children's helmets.** Another concern: although Greek medical personnel will do their best to help you, if you are on a faraway island and your child has an accident or needs special equipment, there may be a delay in transporting him to the closest children's hospital. In general, such incidents are rare and Greece is quite safe for children.

Be sure to plan ahead and **involve your youngsters** as you outline your trip. When packing, include things to keep them busy en route. On sightseeing days try to schedule activities of special interest to your children. If you are renting a car don't forget to **arrange for a car seat** when you reserve.

➤ LOCAL INFORMATION: **Athens News** (✉ Christou Lada 3, Athens 10237, ☎ 01/333–3555, FAX 01/323–1384 http://athensnews.dolnet.gr). **Athinorama** (✉ Mesogeion 2–4, Athens Tower, Athens 11527, ☎ 01/745–0100, FAX 745–0211).

FLYING

Airlines provide in-flight bassinets for babies and free play packs with coloring books and trinkets to keep children busy. Best of all are planes in which each seat has its own TV, especially if it has a cartoon channel; this can make all the difference in the world on a trans-Atlantic trek. Otherwise, bring *many* on-board activities. On most international airlines, infants under 2 sit on your lap for free or for a small fee. However, know that in the slight chance of heavy turbulence or a crash landing, your infant is not as safe as if he were in a child-restraining device. You might want to bring a CRD on board (make sure it is safety approved and no wider than 16 inches so it fits the airline seat frame) and just pay for the extra seat; most airlines charge half of the adult fare. Children up to 12 years fly for 25% to 65% of the adult fare and are usually entitled to full baggage allowance.

As for intradestination flights, Olympic Airways says it provides bassinets for infants and baby food on every aircraft, as well as toys, but it is best to request such items when booking. One child under 2 accompanied by an adult and not occupying a separate seat usually pays only 10% of the adult fare. More than one infant under 2 and children from 2 up to, but not including, 12 pay 60% of the adult fare. Make special arrangements for unaccompanied children when booking.

FOOD

Hopefully, your child will be an adventurous eater, but usually toddlers and teenagers balk at strange cuisine. At restaurants, children often enjoy Greek snacks called *mezedes,* which come in small portions and include bite-size meatballs (*keftedakia*), various croquettes, sausage chunks, and cheese or minced meat pastries called *pites.* Even picky eaters will nibble on french fries (try to get the kids to taste the roast potatoes first) and spaghetti with red sauce or just cheese *makaronia,* available at all tavernas and restaurants. Cooks can also fry an egg for your child or make him an omelet, plain or filled with ham and cheese. If you need to appease your child's hunger momentarily, try a bakery, which sells savory pies, sweet rolls, and chocolate croissants. When it comes to grilled sandwiches, or *tost,* let your child pick out the stuffings; they are sold everywhere. The best sandwich chain, **Everest,** is fast, cheap, and clean and also offers ice cream and pastry. A popular Greek hamburger chain with a decent salad bar, **Goody's** provides all the usual fast food, as do the international chains of **McDonald's, Wendy's,** and **Pizza Hut,** found in larger cities. Finally, even the smallest town has at least one pizza parlor.

LODGING

Most hotels in Greece allow children under a certain age to stay in their parents' room at no extra charge, but others count them as extra adults; be sure to **ask about the cutoff age for children's discounts.** In off-season, you can often negotiate the price. Most hotels A-class and below have no special facilities (other than cots or roll-aways) for families, although a refrigerator in the room can make things easier and the hotel kitchen will accommodate parents who want

to warm formula or baby food. Luxe-category resorts usually boast a children's pool or playground, video arcade, billiard room or Ping-Pong tables, children's activity programs are offered, and baby seats and children's meals in the restaurants. They can also usually arrange baby-sitting. If your family is on a budget, **consider renting self-catering apartments,** if staying longer than a week. These include a kitchen with all necessary equipment, a small living area, and sometimes a separate bedroom. A supermarket and laundromat are often nearby. Best choice: those on the beach.

In Athens, the Athenaeum Inter-Continental lets one child up to 19 years stay in parents' rooms for free. The child gets an extra bed but unless it's an infant must pay for breakfast (from 5,000 dr./€14.74–6,000 dr./€17.69). Up to two children under 12 can stay free with parents in the city's Holiday Inn; both hotels can arrange baby-sitting. The Athens Hilton allows one child under 12 to stay free in parent's room, and they maintain lists of baby-sitters; rates are 2,000 dr./€5.89 an hour for up to two children and clients pay the sitter's taxi fare home at night. Grecotel Rhodos Imperial in Ixia, Rhodes, is quite family-oriented with children's meals in the restaurants and numerous activity programs for children aged 3 to 12. At Best Western hotels, in Athens, Olympia, Mykonos, Agios Konstantinos, and Arachova, children aged 2–12 stay at a 50% discount with parents; baby-sitting can be organized.

➤ BEST CHOICES: **Athenaeum Inter-Continental** (☎ 800/327–1177 reservations); **Holiday Inn** (☎ 800/327–1177 reservations); **Best Western** (☎ 800/528–1234 reservations); **Hilton** (☎ 800/445–8667 reservations); **Grecotel Rhodos Imperial** (✉ Ixia, Rhodes, ☎ 0241/75000, FAX 0241/76690).

SUPPLIES & EQUIPMENT

Disposable diapers (*panes, pah*-nes) can be purchased throughout Greece in supermarkets, convenience stores, and pharmacies. A package of 28 Pampers Baby Dries costs 1,860 dr./€5.48, the 34-pack of Pampers Premiums jumps to 3,790 dr./€11.17 Although baby formula (*vrefiko gala,* vref-i-*ko ga*-la) is available in big supermarkets, you will find a wider selection of good powder (*skoni, sko*-nee) formulas in the pharmacy for about 2,500/€7.37 to 3,900 dr./€11.50 for a box that will last about 10 days. American formula is not that common, and premixed formula is unavailable. Children older than five months in Greece drink evaporated milk (*evapore,* e-vah-po-*ray*) such as Noulac or Neslac, about 220 dr./€.64 for a small can. Fruit creams and such, called *crema,* are about 1,450 for a 700-gram box (Nutricia), and a jar of Nestlé's beef and vegetable is 354 dr./€1.04

TRANSPORTATION

Car seats are available at most rental agencies for a daily surcharge of 700 dr./€2.06–900 dr./€2.65 In Greece, car seats are not required, but that doesn't mean you shouldn't use one. By law, children under 10 are not allowed to sit in the front seat, although this is seldom enforced. School-age children receive a discount of at least 50% on city public transportation, KTEL buses, and trains. Neither bassinets nor special children's meals are available on trains.

COMPUTERS ON THE ROAD

Although major companies such as Toshiba, Canon, and Hewlett-Packard have representatives in Greece, computer parts, batteries, and adaptors are expensive in Greece and may not be in stock when you need them, so carry spares for your laptop. Most upscale hotels now have modem connections in the rooms, and many can rent you a laptop.

For those who want to access their e-mail, Internet cafés have sprung up throughout Greece. Athens, alone, has more than 35, most in the student area of Exarchia. Besides coffee, they offer a range of computer services and charge about 1,500 dr./€4.42 per hour.

➤ INTERNET CAFÉS: In Athens, **Mocafe** (✉ Marni 49 and Veranzerou, Exarchia, ☎ 01/522–7717, info@mocafe.gr); **Museum Internet Cafe** (✉ Patission 46, near National Archaeological Museum, ☎ 01/883–3418, www.museumcafe.gr, museum netcafe@yahoo.com); **Sofokleous. Com Internet Cafe** (✉ Stadiou 5, Syntagma, ☎ FAX 01/324–8105, www.sofokleous.com, sofos1@telehouse.gr or sofos1@ath.forthnet.gr), which includes faxing, printing, and photo-processing facilities.

CONSUMER PROTECTION

Whenever possible, **pay with a major credit card** so you can cancel payment or get reimbursed if there's a problem, provided that you can provide documentation. This is the best way to pay, whether you're buying travel arrangements before your trip or shopping at your destination. Disgruntled consumers may **lodge a complaint on the Consumers' Institute (INKA) hot line** about everything from overpricing to poor service in taxis, hotels, restaurants, and archaeological sites. According to INKA, most complaints filed by foreign tourists concern museums and archaeological sites, banking services, road signs, and travel agencies and are generally related to overpricing, especially at restaurants and nightclubs. INKA provides legal advice and support as well as a complaints and information service. **Learn your rights at the Citizens' Information Bureau** set up by the Hellenic Foreign Ministry. Here foreigners can lodge complaints and get suggestions for transactions with the state (always daunting) and information about their rights.

If you're doing business with a particular company for the first time, **contact your local Better Business Bureau and the attorney general's offices** in your own state and the company's home state, as well. Have any complaints been filed? Finally, if you're buying a package or tour, always **consider travel insurance** that includes default coverage (☞ Insurance, *below*).

➤ BBBs: **Council of Better Business Bureaus** (✉ 4200 Wilson Blvd., Suite 800, Arlington, VA 22203, ☎ 703/276–0100, FAX 703/525–8277, www.bbb.org).

➤ LOCAL RESOURCES: **Citizens' Information Bureau** (✉ Akademias 3,

Davaki Arcade, Athens, ☎ 01/368–2700, www.mfa.gr) weekdays 10–2. **Consumers' Institute (INKA)** (☎ 1721, hot-line), weekdays 8–4.

CRUISE TRAVEL AND YACHTING

CRUISE TRAVEL

Many travelers with limited time find traveling by boat an ideal way to see Greece's mainland ports and islands. It spares you the planning headaches of solitary island-hopping, when you can be stranded en route, waiting several days for the next ferry. The disadvantage: though cruise ships cover great distances at night, leaving days free for exploring, the usual stop in a port of call is often only a few hours, allowing for only a superficial visit. Often, an island's harbor is some distance from the main town, the more attractive, traditional villages, and the better beaches. Cruises are best for an overview that's useful for planning a return trip to the more appealing stops. Three-day cruises of the Greek islands, for instance, can be combined with a longer land tour. Among the major lines sailing to the most popular Greek islands, both Golden Sun Cruises and Royal Olympic Cruises offer three-day voyages mid-March through October that sail from Piraeus to Mykonos, Rhodes, Patmos, and Kuşadası in Turkey; their four-day cruises also stop in Heraklion, Crete, and Santorini. For the seven-day cruises, you can chose several combinations that add Delos, Hydra, Rethymnon, Amorgos, Kos, Itea (Delphi), and Corinth, as well as stops in Turkey, Italy, and Egypt. Minoan Lines has one-day cruises from Crete (Heraklion, Rethymnon, and Agios Nikolaos) to Santorini. For information on specific lines and ships that offer these sails, consult a travel agent.

➤ CRUISE LINES: **Golden Sun Cruises** (✉ Akti Miaouli 85, Piraeus 18538, ☎ 01/429–0650 through 01/429–0660 for reservations, FAX 01/420–0660). **Royal Olympic Cruises** (✉ One Rockefeller Plaza, New York, NY 10020, ☎ 212/397–6400); in Greece (✉ Akti Miaouli 87, Piraeus 18538, ☎ 01/459–7066 for reservations, FAX 01/429–0636). Both have

downtown Athens representatives. **Minoan Cruises** (✉ 25 Avgoustou 17, Heraklion, Crete 71202, ☎ 081/341701, FAX 081/341706).

Other major cruise lines that call in the Greek islands include **Club Med, Costa Cruise Lines, Crystal Cruises, Cunard Line, Holland America Line, Orient Lines, Princess Cruises, Radisson Seven Seas Cruises, Renaissance Cruises, Seabourn Cruise Line, Silversea Cruises, Star Clippers,** and **Windstar Cruises.** These cruises often call at ports outside Greece as well and may begin or end in Italy or Turkey. For more information and exact itineraries contact a cruise-only travel agency.

For a cruise of the islands aboard a small yacht, contact **Club Voyages** (✉ 43 Hooper Ave., Atlantic Highlands, NJ 07716, ☎ 908/291–8228) or **Zeus Tours and Yacht Cruises** (✉ 566 7th Ave., New York, NY 10018, ☎ 212/221–0006 or 800/447–5667). The refurbished 1931 *Sea Cloud* sailing yacht cruises the Greek islands and Turkey; contact the **Cruise Company of Greenwich** (✉ 31 Brookside Dr., Greenwich, CT 06830; ☎ 800/825–0862) for information. The Greek-based **Viking Star Cruises** (✉ Artemidos 1, Glyfada 16674, ☎ 01/898–0729 or 01/894–9279, FAX 01/894–0952; ✉ U.S. reservations: 4321 Lakemore Dr., Wilmington, NC 28405, ☎ 800/341–8020) offers a weeklong "Discovery" cruise on a 15-cabin yacht that lets you imagine traveling aboard your own vessel. The journey is relaxed, with just four hours of cruising a day, and leaves every Friday (April to October) for Tinos, Ios, Santorini, Paros, Naxos, Mykonos, and Delos. For information on sailing a private yacht through Greek waters, *see* Yachting, *below.*

YACHTING

Life aboard a private yacht or sailboat is quite different from a cruise ship. You can either hire one with a few of your own friends or else, through a travel agency, join a party of people. Once aboard, you can go from island to island, stopping to swim or fish wherever you please—if you don't happen to feel like going ashore one night to check out the nightlife, you can always stay on board and listen to the bouzouki wailing across the water from the tavernas dotting the little harbor where your boat has dropped anchor. Yacht-rental agencies and travel agents have boats of all sizes and at all prices—on condition that your budget is not too tight. Zea harbor in Piraeus offers the most modern mooring and wintering facilities. Among the remaining 90 or so yacht supply stations, Vouliagmeni, Rhodes, Patras, Syros, and Thessaloniki are among the largest.

Below we list two associations and a number of leading yachting outfitters. In order to avoid an endless exchange of letters with an agency, it is best to give the following information in your first letter when you inquire to reserve a yacht: desired dates and period of charter and voyage; the number of passengers; and the type of craft you desire—auxiliary sailing yacht, motor yacht, or caïque. For local agencies, *see* Sailing & Windsurfing, *below.* Two relevant organizations are **Hellenic Professional Yacht Owners Association** (✉ A8 Zea Marina, Piraeus 18536, ☎ 01/428–0465 or 01/452–6335, FAX 01/452–6335); and **Greek Yacht Brokers and Consultants Association** (✉ Filellinon 7, Athens 10557, ☎ 01/322–3221, FAX 01/322–3251). Two firms that organize highly sophisticated personalized yacht cruises and tours are **Club Voyages** (✉ 43 Hooper Ave., Atlantic Highlands, NJ 07716, ☎ 908/291–8228, FAX 908/291–4277) and **Hellenic Adventures** (✉ 4150 Harriet Ave. S, Minneapolis, MN 55409, ☎ 800/851–6349, FAX 612/827–2444).

Other yacht-chartering firms include the following: **Aegean Yachting Center** (✉ 17220 Newhope St., Fountain Valley, CA 92708, ☎ 800/736–5717, FAX 714/641–0303). **Alden Yacht Charters** (✉ 1909 Alden Landing, Portsmouth, RI 02871, ☎ 401/683–1782 or 800/662–2628, FAX 401/683–3668). **G.P.S.C. Charters Club** (✉ 600 St. Andrews Rd., Philadelphia, PA 19118, ☎ 215/247–3903, FAX 215/247–1505). **Grecian Charters** (862 Guy Lombardo Ave., Freeport,

NY 11520, ☎ 516/868–4050, FAX 516/868–4052). **Greek Island Charters, Inc.** (270 N. Canon Dr., Beverly Hills, CA 90210, ☎ 310/278–8427, FAX 310/275–9786). **Greek Islands Cruise Center** (✉ 4141 Heartside Dr., Wilmington, NC 24812, ☎ 910/341–3030, FAX 910/791–9400). **Huntley Yacht Vacations** (✉ 210 Preston Rd., Wernersville, PA 19565, ☎ 610/678–2628 or 800/322–9224, FAX 610/670–1767). **Lynn Jachney Charters** (✉ Box 302, Marblehead, MA 01945, ☎ 617/639–0787 or 800/223–2050, FAX 617/639–0216). **The Moorings** (19345 U.S. 19 N, 4th floor, Clearwater, FL 33764, ☎ 813/530–5424 or 800/535–7289, FAX 813/530–9747). **Ocean Voyages** (✉ 1709 Bridgeway, Sausalito, CA 94965, ☎ 415/332–4681 or 800/299–4444, FAX 415/332–7460). **SailAway Yacht Charters** (✉ 15605 S.W. 92nd Ave., Miami, FL 33157-1972, ☎ 305/253–7245 or 800/724–5292, FAX 305/251–4408). **Zeus Tours and Yacht Cruises** (✉ 566 7th Ave., New York, NY 10018, ☎ 800/447–5667).

CUSTOMS & DUTIES

When shopping, **keep receipts** for all purchases. Upon reentering the country, **be ready to show customs officials what you've bought.** If you feel a duty is incorrect or object to the way your clearance was handled, note the inspector's badge number and ask to see a supervisor. If the problem isn't resolved, write to the appropriate authorities, beginning with the port director at your point of entry.

IN GREECE

Passing through Greek customs is usually a painless procedure and certainly takes less time than retrieving your luggage. EU citizens can just walk through, and even non-EU citizens arriving from a European city should quickly pass down the green lane. Look like a tourist and you won't have a problem. But if you have flown direct from the U.S. or Australia and are carting many shiny new suitcases and lots of boxes that look like you've brought appliances for the relatives (whether they exist or not), you will be pulled over. In that case, it's better to politely bear the ordeal, which might just entail the opening of one bag. You are also more likely to be stopped if you're coming from a country that exports drugs.

You may bring into Greece duty-free: food and beverages up to 22 pounds (10 kilos); 200 cigarettes, 100 cigarillos, or 50 cigars; one liter of alcoholic spirits or two liters of wine; and gift articles up to a total of 51,000 dr./€150. For non-EU citizens, foreign bank notes amounting to more than $2,500 must be declared for reexport, but there are no restrictions on traveler's checks; you may export no more than 100,000 dr./€295 in Greek currency.

Only one per person of such expensive portable items as cameras, camcorders, computers, and the like is permitted into Greece. You should **register these with Greek Customs upon arrival** to avoid any problems when taking them out of the country again. Sports equipment, such as bicycles and skis, is also limited to one (pair) per person.

To bring in a dog or a cat, you need a health certificate issued by a veterinary authority and validated by the Greek consulate and the appropriate medical authority (in the U.S., the Department of Agriculture). It must state that your pet doesn't carry any infectious diseases and that it received a rabies inoculation not more than 12 months (for cats, six months) and no fewer than six days before arrival. Dogs must also have a veterinary certificate that indicates they have been wormed against echinococcus. For more information on Greek customs, check with your local Greek consulate.

IN AUSTRALIA

Australian residents who are 18 or older may bring home $A400 worth of souvenirs and gifts (including jewelry), 250 cigarettes or 250 grams of tobacco, and 1,125 ml of alcohol (including wine, beer, and spirits). Residents under 18 may bring back $A200 worth of goods. Prohibited items include meat products. Seeds, plants, and fruits need to be declared upon arrival.

➤ INFORMATION: **Australian Customs Service** (Regional Director, ✉ Box 8, Sydney, NSW 2001, Australia, ☎ 02/9213–2000, ℻ 02/9213–4000, www.customs.gov.au).

IN CANADA

Canadian residents who have been out of Canada for at least 7 days may bring home C$500 worth of goods duty-free. If you've been away less than 7 days but more than 48 hours, the duty-free allowance drops to C$200; if your trip lasts 24–48 hours, the allowance is C$50. You may not pool allowances with family members. Goods claimed under the C$500 exemption may follow you by mail; those claimed under the lesser exemptions must accompany you. Alcohol and tobacco products may be included in the 7-day and 48-hour exemptions but not in the 24-hour exemption. If you meet the age requirements of the province or territory through which you reenter Canada, you may bring in, duty-free, 1.14 liters (40 imperial ounces) of wine or liquor *or* 24 12-ounce cans or bottles of beer or ale. If you are 16 or older you may bring in, duty-free, 200 cigarettes and 50 cigars. Check ahead of time with Revenue Canada or the Department of Agriculture for policies regarding meat products, seeds, plants, and fruits.

You may send an unlimited number of gifts worth up to C$60 each duty-free to Canada. Label the package UNSOLICITED GIFT—VALUE UNDER $60. Alcohol and tobacco are excluded.

➤ INFORMATION: **Revenue Canada** (✉ 2265 St. Laurent Blvd. S, Ottawa, Ontario K1G 4K3, Canada, ☎ 613/993–0534; 800/461–9999 in Canada, ℻ 613/991–4126, www.ccra-adrc.gc.ca).

IN NEW ZEALAND

Homeward-bound residents 17 or older may bring back $700 worth of souvenirs and gifts. Your duty-free allowance also includes 4.5 liters of wine or beer; one 1,125-ml bottle of spirits; and either 200 cigarettes, 250 grams of tobacco, 50 cigars, or a combination of the three up to 250 grams. Prohibited items include meat products, seeds, plants, and fruits.

➤ INFORMATION: **New Zealand Customs** (Custom House, ✉ 50 Anzac Ave., Box 29, Auckland, New Zealand, ☎ 09/300–5399, FAX 09/359–6730, www.customs.govt.nz).

IN THE U.K.

If you are a U.K. resident and your journey was wholly within the European Union (EU), you won't have to pass through customs when you return to the United Kingdom. If you plan to bring back large quantities of alcohol or tobacco, check EU limits beforehand.

➤ INFORMATION: **HM Customs and Excise** (✉ Dorset House, Stamford St., Bromley, Kent BR1 1XX, U.K., ☎ 020/7202–4227, www.hmce.gov.uk).

IN THE U.S.

U.S. residents who have been out of the country for at least 48 hours (and who have not used the $400 allowance or any part of it in the past 30 days) may bring home $400 worth of foreign goods duty-free.

U.S. residents 21 and older may bring back 1 liter of alcohol duty-free. In addition, regardless of your age, you are allowed 200 cigarettes and 100 non-Cuban cigars. Antiques, which the U.S. Customs Service defines as objects more than 100 years old, enter duty-free, as do original works of art done entirely by hand, including paintings, drawings, and sculptures.

You may also mail or ship packages home duty-free: up to $200 worth of goods for personal use, with a limit of one parcel per addressee per day (except alcohol or tobacco products or perfume worth more than $5); label the package PERSONAL USE and attach a list of its contents and their retail value. Do not label the package UNSOLICITED GIFT or your duty-free exemption will drop to $100. Mailed items do not affect your duty-free allowance on your return.

➤ INFORMATION: **U.S. Customs Service** (✉ 1300 Pennsylvania Ave. NW, Washington, DC 20229, www.customs.gov; inquiries ☎ 202/354–1000; complaints c/o ✉ 1300 Pennsylvania Ave. NW, Room 5.4D, Washington, DC 20229; registration

of equipment c/o ✉ Resource Management, ☎ 202/354–1000).

DINING

The biggest mistake you can make is to think Greek cuisine is all about moussaka, pastitsio, and souvlaki. True, these are classic dishes, but you will be missing out if you don't try the staggering amount of regional specialties—from baked kid in a sealed oven in Metsovo to stuffed squash flowers or wild artichoke salad in Sparta to the fluffy *kaltsounia* pastries of Crete. In the cities, a new breed of restaurant has emerged: trendy eateries that combine the best of Mediterranean cooking with elements from other international cuisines. The chefs have dubbed this food "fusion." You can eat as well in Athens and Thessaloniki, as you can in Sydney, L.A., or London, and often at lower prices. In these posh eateries, of course, you don't get the full Greek experience—after all, this is the place where customers still visit the taverna kitchen to peek into the cauldrons or to fussily select *their* fish to be barbecued. Red mullet risotto on eggplant puree with a sprinkle of mastic is great, but nothing beats perfectly grilled octopus and a luscious homegrown tomato salad served at sundown with a sip of chilled ouzo on a rickety table, surrounded by shimmering waves.

Besides restaurants—fusion, Greek, international—Greece offers tavernas, informal places that serve classic Greek cooking, much of it cooked in advance in casseroles and served at room temperature, *magirefta*. Every neighborhood has at least one, and they range from the famous Taverna Nikolaos in Santorini, tucked into an alley, decorated with portraits of long-dead grandfathers and serving only three or four choices based on the market that day, to Vassilis Taverna near the U.S. embassy in Athens, where packed tables clamor for the almost 100 different specialties from Roumeli, Thrace, and Epirus. Another kind of eatery is the *ouzerie* or *mezedopolio,* somewhat like a tapas bar, where you sample appetizers. There are *psarotavernes,* fish tavernas, and *psistaries,* which offer grilled or spit-roasted meats called *tis oras,* or "of the hour."

Breakfast in Greece is pretty light. Hotels will ply you with a Nescafé-and-bread Continental breakfast, but you might try a "toast," a sort of dry grilled-cheese sandwich (a "mixed toast" if it has a paper-thin ham slice added), or a sesame-coated bread ring sold by street vendors in the cities. Local bakeries may offer fresh doughnuts in the morning. For lunch, heavyweight meat-and-potato dishes can be had, but you might prefer a real Greek salad (no lettuce, a slice of feta with a pinch of oregano, and ripe tomatoes) or souvlaki or grilled chicken from a taverna.

The hour or so before restaurants open for dinner is a pleasant time to have an ouzo or glass of wine and try Greek hors d'oeuvres, called *mezedes*. As the sun sets over the Aegean, seek out a seaside ouzeri. It's the perfect setting for conversation or postcard writing. Dinner is the main meal of the day, and there's plenty of food. Starters include *taramosalata* (a dip or spread made from fish roe) and *melitzanosalata* (made from smoked eggplant, lemon, oil, and garlic), along with the well-known yogurt, cucumber, and garlic *tzatziki*.

On menus all over Greece you'll run into three categories of staple entrée dishes: there's *magirefta* (food that has been cooked in the oven in advance and left in the pan all day, usually served at room temperature)—like moussaka, *pastitsio* (a baked dish of minced lamb and macaroni), or *gemista* (stuffed tomatoes or peppers, which usually has some ground lamb). Then there are *tis oras* ("of the hour"), with a subcategory called *sta karvouna*, or food that is cooked on the coals or grilled—like chops or steak. And last, there is fish, of all kinds, which is outstanding (look for gilt-head bream, or *tsipoura*).

The restaurants listed in this guide represent the best in each category at a variety of price ranges. They are indicated by a crossed knife-and-fork icon, ✕. Establishments denoted by the icon ✕▥ stand out for both their rooms and their meals. Although some prices have skyrocketed—a chicken pita sandwich at a chi-chi bar-restaurant, for example—dining in Greece, especially away from

Athens and resorts such as Mykonos, is less expensive than in other EU countries, with the exception of Portugal and Ireland. As a rule, if you see many Greek families eating somewhere, it's probably a safe bet in terms of the palate and the pocket.

MEALS & SPECIALTIES

Greeks don't really eat breakfast and few places serve that meal, unless it's a hotel dining room. You can pick up a cheese pie and rolls at a bakery or a sesame-coated bread ring called a *koulouri* sold by city vendors, order a grilled tost at a café, or dig in to a plate of yogurt with honey in a milk shop, a *galatopolio*. On islands in summer, cafés serve breakfast, from Continental to combinations that might include Spanish omelets and French coffee. Caffeine-junkies can get a cup of coffee practically anywhere, but decaf is only available in bigger hotels. Greeks eat their main meal at either lunch or dinner, so the offerings are the same. A typical dinner for a couple might be two to three appetizers, an entrée, a salad, and wine. If a Greek eats dessert at all, it will be fruit or a modest wedge of cake-like pastry. Only in fancier restaurants can diners order the mandarin torte with an espresso. Coffee and pastries are eaten in the afternoon, usually at a café or *zaharoplastio* (pastry shop). Diners can order as little or as much as they like, except at very expensive establishments. One option for those who want a lighter meal is the *mezedopolio*.

In most places, the menu is broken down into appetizers (*orektika*) and entrées (*kiria piata*), with additional headings for salads (this includes dips like tzatziki) and vegetable side plates. However, this doesn't mean there is any sense of a first or second "course" as in France. The food arrives all at the same time, or as it becomes ready (☞ Etiquette & Behavior, *below*).

MEALTIMES

Breakfast is available until 10 at hotels and until early afternoon in beach cafés. Lunch is between 1:30 and 3:30, and dinner is served from about 8:30 to midnight, later in the big cities and resort islands. Greeks dine around 10 or 11 PM. Unless otherwise noted, the restaurants listed in this guide are open daily for lunch and dinner.

PAYING

Credit cards are accepted in finer restaurants and some of the more upscale tavernas and fish tavernas. A credit card sign is usually posted in the window.

RESERVATIONS & DRESS

You don't need to make reservations except at the Athens and Thessaloniki restaurants that are "in" that season and at some fish tavernas on Sunday afternoons when families descend. Most informal establishments don't take reservations but will do their best to accommodate your party, jamming another table on the sidewalk if necessary. Dress is informal; no establishment requires a tie and jacket. Shorts, however, are just a little too casual for Greeks.

WINE, BEER & SPIRITS

Ouzo and brandy are the national aperitifs. Served in slim glasses and diluted with water or ice, which turns the liqueur milky white, ouzo is usually enjoyed on summer evenings and should be lingered over. Try a tiny sip undiluted first, and ask for mezedes, which might include anything from tomato slices, olive, and cheese to shrimp or sausage. In winter, people usually request brandy: Botrys and five- or seven-star Metaxa are good, and you might also like the *mavrodaphne* (a heavy dessert wine). Greek wine is relatively inexpensive. Restaurants and tavernas often sell locally produced *kokkino* (red) and *aspro* (white) table wine from the barrel; many of them, purchased by the quarter, half or full kilogram, are perfectly good. For bottled wines, look for Boutari or Tsantalis from Naoussa, Carras Estate from Chalkidiki, and red wines from Nemea in the Peloponnese. Enthusiasts should pick up a copy of Nikos Manessis's in-depth *Greek Wines* (Athens: Olive Press Publications, 2000; 10,500 dr./€30.97) for descriptions of regional vintages. The origins of retsina, considered Greece's *vin du pays,* are uncertain. According to ancient authors, resin was added to preserve the wine or to seal wine containers. Whatever the original intent, the results can be splendid, so give it a chance. You might try it chilled first, with souvlaki or grilled fish.

You can buy alcohol at convenience shops, supermarkets, and liquor stores called *caves.* Beer is also often available at kiosks and fast-food chains, even McDonalds. You can order wine and beer everywhere, at any time of day, and hard alcohol in restaurants, cafés, bars, and performance venues that have a hard liquor license (ouzo counts as wine). Most places serve drinks until 2:00 or 3:00 AM on weekdays, later on weekends. In most bars, if you order a straight drink, it's a generous portion, as much as a double. Keep in mind that if you want a martini (as in James Bond), you must order a martini cocktail; otherwise, you'll get Martini and Rossi liqueur.

DISABILITIES & ACCESSIBILITY

Many cruise ships are equipped to accommodate people with disabilities, but access to archaeological sites can present some difficulty, and most two-story museums do not have elevators. Bathrooms, especially in restaurants, may be down a steep flight of stairs in the basement, and the frequently high-curbed and auto-packed sidewalks are difficult to negotiate in larger towns. Call ahead to find out exactly what obstacles you might face and to enlist extra help from staff. Public transportation is generally crowded, and few special provisions are available. The easiest solution is to use taxis to get between different points, or hire a taxi for the day; most hotels can arrange this. You may encounter stares—until recently Greeks with disabilities were encouraged to stay at home—but people usually lend a helping hand, since this is a country where hospitality is a time-honored virtue. Athens has a few parking spaces to accommodate people with disabilities, but these are often illegally occupied by other drivers. Traveling with a companion or a group is advisable.

LODGING

Visitors will probably find it easier to manage in Greece's more modern resorts and hotels than in rented rooms. A frequent problem even then is the bathroom, which seldom has a tub but a narrow, step-in shower with a ledge. Sometimes cheaper accommodations have the shower attached to one of the bathroom walls—that way you can sit while bathing though the floor becomes wet and slippery. Think about requesting a spacious room near the elevator or on the ground floor. In better hotels, the rooms may be more manageable but the multilevel public areas might not be accessible. The **Hotel Inter-Continental** (☎ 800/327–1177) in Athens has seven rooms specifically adapted for travelers with disabilities (wider doors, handrails, storage space for wheelchair) and most public areas are accessible. The **Hilton** hotel (☎ 800/445–8667) in Athens has two rooms equipped with extrawide doors and accessible bathrooms, but some public areas, such as the pool, may be difficult to get to by wheelchair. The **Holiday Inn** (☎ 800/465—4329) in Athens has one single for guests in wheelchairs (handrails, less furniture).

RESERVATIONS

When discussing accessibility with an operator or reservations agent, **ask hard questions.** Are there any stairs, inside *or* out? Are there grab bars next to the toilet *and* in the shower/tub? How wide is the doorway to the room? To the bathroom? For the most extensive facilities meeting the latest legal specifications, **opt for newer accommodations.** If you're talking to staff at smaller hotels, remember that they usually don't have much experience with travelers with disabilities and might not volunteer the correct information. If you ask about stairs at the hotel entrance, they might tell you there aren't any, not considering the four little steps at the door as an obstacle—perhaps they've never even noticed them. **Make sure you book a hotel where a taxi can drive up to the entrance you will be using.**

SIGHTS & ATTRACTIONS

Because Greece's major attractions tend to be ancient ruins, and the government only recently has started building facilities with better access, it is hard for people in wheelchairs to negotiate several sights. For example, the Acropolis requires that you walk up many steep steps at the Propylaea. The bottom (and main) floor at the National Archaeological Museum is accessible but the Santorini frescoes are on the top floor, which means climbing a long flight of stairs, and there is no elevator. On the other hand, the charming district of Plaka, where you can see the Monument of Lysicrates, the Tower of the Winds, and the Roman Agora, is largely accessible, except for the upper reaches of Anafiotika at the top of staircases or steep lanes. Two of the capital's best museums, the Benaki and the Goulandris Cycladic, are fully accessible. Things are improving; at press time, the Delphi Museum was being renovated to improve access. It just depends—you can roll through the medieval streets of Monemvassia and the Old Town of Rhodes and see the Portara in Naxos at sunset, but you might have trouble climbing to Acrocorinth in Santorini or the Temple of Apollo in Delphi. Still, if you're really determined to see a particular sight, talk to the guards at the gate and see what they can suggest. Photographs prove that Cole Porter, the famous American songwriter who suffered from a leg affliction, was even carted around by attendants at various sites (for a fee) when he visited Greece in the 1950s.

TRANSPORTATION

Only some Athens buses have a mechanism that lowers to lift wheelchairs. If you can walk a few steps, you can use the buses and the trains. Drivers and conductors are usually patient, since they often deal with local senior citizens who need extra time to mount the steps. There are no bathrooms on the buses, and those on the trains are cramped. It's easier to rent a car and have a companion drive, or hire a taxi and driver for the day who can load and unload your wheelchair. Cars with hand controls are not available for rent. If you do find a handicap space, it's probably assigned to someone in the neighborhood (check for a license number on the sign). Especially in crowded Athens, Greeks leave their cars wherever they can, so park where it's most convenient for you, display your sign, and you probably won't have any problems. Airports are wheelchair-accessible but most domestic planes (Olympic) have a landing stair.

➤ COMPLAINTS: **Disability Rights Section** (✉ U.S. Department of Justice, Civil Rights Division, Box 66738, Washington, DC 20035-6738, ☎ 202/514–0301 or 800/514–0301; 202/514–0383 TTY; 800/514–0383 TTY, FAX 202/307–1198, www.usdoj. gov/crt/ada/adahom1.htm) for general complaints. **Aviation Consumer Protection Division** (☞ Air Travel, *above*) for airline-related problems. **Civil Rights Office** (✉ U.S. Department of Transportation, Departmental Office of Civil Rights, S-30, 400 7th St. SW, Room 10215, Washington, DC 20590, ☎ 202/366–4648, FAX 202/366–9371) for problems with surface transportation.

TRAVEL AGENCIES AND TOUR OPERATORS

As a whole, the travel industry has become more aware of the needs of travelers with disabilities. In the United States, the Americans with Disabilities Act requires that travel firms serve the needs of all travelers. Some agencies specialize in working with people with disabilities.

➤ TRAVELERS WITH MOBILITY PROBLEMS: **Access Adventures** (✉ 206 Chestnut Ridge Rd., Scottsville, NY 14624, ☎ 716/889–9096, dltravel@ prodigy.net), run by a former physical-rehabilitation counselor. **Care-Vacations** (✉ 5-5110 50th Ave., Leduc, Alberta T9E 6V4, Canada, ☎ 780/986–6404 or 877/478–7827, FAX 780/986–8332, www.carevacations. com), for group tours and cruise vacations. **Flying Wheels Travel** (✉ 143 W. Bridge St., Box 382, Owatonna, MN 55060, ☎ 507/451–5005 or 800/535–6790, FAX 507/451–1685, thq@ll.net, www.flyingwheels. com). **Hinsdale Travel Service** (✉ 201 E. Ogden Ave., Suite 100, Hinsdale, IL 60521, ☎ 630/325–1335, FAX 630/325–1342, hinsdaletravel@ hinsdaletravel.com).

Be a smart shopper and **compare all your options** before making decisions. A plane ticket bought with a promotional coupon from travel clubs, coupon books, and direct-mail offers may not be cheaper than the least expensive fare from a discount ticket agency. And always keep in mind that what you get is just as important as what you save. At this time, Greece has no multi-attraction passes.

DISCOUNT RESERVATIONS

To save money, **look into discount reservations services** with toll-free numbers, which use their buying power to get a better price on hotels, airline tickets, even car rentals. When booking a room, always **call the hotel's local toll-free number** (if one is available) rather than the central reservations number—you'll often get a better price. Always ask about special packages or corporate rates.

When shopping for the best deal on hotels and car rentals, **look for guaranteed exchange rates,** which protect you against a falling dollar. With your rate locked in, you won't pay more, even if the price goes up in the local currency.

You may get up to a 15% discount when you book a hotel through a Greek local travel agent rather than reserve directly with the hotel (the agent often has special rates), and prices may be lower than booking through your country's travel agent, who may take a heftier commission. Contact agencies by fax; many now have e-mail addresses, making comparison shopping even easier.

➤ AIRLINE TICKETS: ☎ 800/FLY–ASAP.

➤ HOTEL ROOMS: **Steigenberger Reservation Service** (☎ 800/223–5652, www.srs-worldhotels.com). **Travel Interlink** (☎ 800/888–5898, www.travelinterlink.com).

PACKAGE DEALS

Packages and guided tours can save you money, but don't confuse the two. When you buy a package, your travel remains independent, just as though you had planned and booked the trip yourself. Fly/drive packages, which combine airfare and car rental, are often a good deal. If you **buy a rail/drive pass,** you'll save on train tickets and car rentals. All Eurail- and Europass holders get a discount on Eurostar fares through the Channel Tunnel. Greek Flexipass options may include sightseeing, hotels, and plane tickets.

ECOTOURISM

Probably the most famous endangered species in Greece is the loggerhead turtle (caretta caretta) that nests on Zakynthos and Kefalonia beaches. During mating season, obey the sign directives, like no poking umbrellas in the sand in case you puncture an egg and no running around on the beach at night when the turtles mate (even a lighted cigarette will disturb their ritual). Throughout the rest of the country, treat the environment with respect. Don't pick wildflowers, stay on the paths rather than tromping through vegetation, pick up your garbage (no matter what some Greeks do), be extremely careful with campfires and cigarettes, especially on hot windy days, don't waste water. To limit the amount of laundry detergent passing into the streams and sea, hotel guests can avoid turning in all their towels daily if they aren't dirty—many ecology-conscious hotels now have signs to this effect. Remember that Greece has many bird and animal species threatened with extinction, mostly due to the reduction of forest and marshland, so treat them with all due respect.

ELECTRICITY

To use your U.S.-purchased electric-powered equipment, **bring a converter and adapter.** The electrical current in Greece is 220 volts, 50 cycles alternating current (AC); wall outlets take Continental-type plugs, with two round prongs.

If your appliances are dual-voltage, you'll need only an adapter. Don't use 110-volt outlets, marked FOR SHAVERS ONLY, for high-wattage appliances such as blow-dryers. Most laptops operate equally well on 110 and 220 volts and so require only an adapter, though remember that many outlets don't have surge protection.

EMBASSIES

➤ AUSTRALIA: **Australia** (✉ D. Soutsou 37, Athens, ☎ 01/645–0404).

➤ CANADA: **Canada** (✉ Gennadiou 4, Athens, ☎ 01/727–3400).

➤ NEW ZEALAND: **New Zealand (consulate;** ✉ Kifissias 268, Halandri, Athens, ☎ 01/687–4700 or 01/687–4701).

➤ UNITED KINGDOM: **United Kingdom** (✉ Ploutarchou 1, Athens, ☎ 01/723–6211 through 01/723–6219 or 01/727–2600).

➤ UNITED STATES: **United States** (✉ Vasilissis Sofias 91, Athens, ☎ 01/721–2951 through 01/721–2959).

EMERGENCIES

➤ CONTACTS: **Police** (☎ 100). Na**tional Ambulance Service (EKAV,** ☎ 166) (a taxi is often faster). **Fire** (☎ 199). **Forest Service** (in case of fire ☎ 191). **Coast Guard** (☎ 108). **Center for Battered Women in Athens** (☎ 01/523–5250 and 01/523–5318). The **Tourist Police** (✉ Dimitrakopoulou 77 Koukaki, Athens, ☎ 171 in Athens; 01/171 from outside Athens)—or contact the local tourist police in other regions (☞ Specific chapters for phone number)—can provide general information, help in emergencies, and mediate in disputes.

➤ POISON CENTER: **Poison center** (☎ 01/779–3777).

ENGLISH-LANGUAGE MEDIA

In all major towns and on islands in summer, there is at least one kiosk or bookstore selling international publications. The kiosks are usually close to the main square. Shops in larger hotels also carry English-language media. U.K. papers include the *Times, Daily Mail,* the *Independent,* and the *Guardian,* as well as most tabloids; U.S. papers include the *Wall Street Journal* and *USA Today.* The *New York Times* is not available, and Australian and Canadian papers are rare. On many islands, the papers are a day old because they have been shipped by ferry from Athens. Monday through Saturday the *International Herald Tribune* is available with a Greek news insert, and Tuesday through Sunday the local *Athens*

News can be bought at most stands in Athens and throughout Greece. The international versions of *Time* and *Newsweek* are easy to find, as are commercial magazines ranging from *Wallpaper* to *Playboy.* CNN International broadcasts in Greece, though it often suffers static; a good alternative is Euronews. BBC radio broadcasts on various stations throughout the country.

BOOKS

English-language books are easy to locate, but on a small island the selection may be limited to romance novels and spy thrillers, or dusty, second-hand volumes left behind in the lobby by hotel guests. You can purchase books at foreign-language bookstores, downtown kiosks, hotel shops, airports, flea markets, and jumble sales held by nonprofit organizations. Children's picture books are also sold at toy stores such as Jumbo. New books, even paperbacks, are at least one-third more expensive than the price in their country of origin, especially when the drachma is weak. An exception is English-language books printed in Greece, such as the Kedros translations of Greek novels, or history and museum guides; these are reasonably priced.

➤ BOOKSTORES: **I Folia tou Vivliou** or Booknest (✉ Panepistimiou 25–29 in arcade and on 1st floor, Athens, ☎ 01/322–9560), ample selection of British and American authors. **Compendium** (✉ Nikis 28 upstairs, Athens, ☎ 01/322–1248), travel books, books on Greece, and used books. **Eleftheroudakis** (✉ Nikis 4, Athens, ☎ 01/322–9388; ✉ Panepistimiou 17, Athens, ☎ 01/331–4180 through 01/331–4183), Greece's largest collection of Greek and English-language books, from psychology to macroeconomics. **Kauffman** (✉ Stadiou 28, Athens, ☎ 01/322–2160), limited selection of American fiction. **Pantelides** (✉ Amerikis 11, Athens, ☎ 01/362–3673).

NEWSPAPERS & MAGAZINES

The *Athens News* provides fairly neutral, good coverage of Greek events, a summary of the top international stories from the wires, financial information, and an arts section that reviews predominantly Athenian happenings. The paper offers good coverage on issues affecting foreign residents, including minority groups and migrant workers. It also prints useful information such as dates for pending bus strikes, ferry departure times, and addresses for all-night pharmacies and hospitals. The Friday and Sunday editions give visitors a closer look at Greek life with profiles of foreigners residing in Greece, travel and food articles, and letters to the editor. The paper falls under the umbrella of the Greek (rather liberal) paper *Ta Nea,* although it's unclear if this affects editorial content, since most articles are written by foreigners. A translated six-page version of the Greek (and rather conservative) paper *Kathemerini* appears as an insert in the *International Herald Tribune.* It also summarizes Greek and international news and includes more features and in-depth stories by Greek reporters, though these are harder to read because the translation ignores conventions of U.S./U.K. journalism: leads are long, quotes are unattributed, and sentences often are convoluted and passive. It has good arts and economics coverage. Local English-language magazines come and go and are mostly mediocre; at press time, the best of the lot, *Odyssey,* an upscale glossy written for the Greek diaspora, had not appeared on the stands for five months.

RADIO & TELEVISION

Athens has numerous radio stations, and even islands have at least one local station. Those playing foreign music include trendy KLIK (88.0), rave-oriented Geronimo Groovy (88.9), and mainstream pop Kiss (90.9). You can catch CNN Radio on the hour at Galaxy (92.0), which plays soft pop. Other foreign music stations include Status (world music, 92.7), Capital Gold (oldies but goodies, 96.5), Rock FM (96.8), the retro Radio Gold (105.0), and Era 3 (95.6), the only classical music on the dial.

Your television choices include the top four private stations—Mega, Antenna, Alpha, and Skai—and the better-quality government channels, ERT 1 and NET. Throughout the day the private stations carry many American and some British serials that are subtitled rather than dubbed. The best shows seem to appear after midnight. All stations run English-language soap operas in the afternoon. English-language documentaries are more likely to appear on the government stations. Antenna broadcasts their English-language version of local news plus the CBS Evening News. Unfortunately, the program begins at 6:20 AM.

ETIQUETTE & BEHAVIOR

Greeks are friendly and openly affectionate. It is not uncommon, for example, to see women strolling arm in arm, or men kissing and hugging each other. Displays of anger are also quite common. You may see a man at a traffic light get out to verbally harangue an offending driver behind him, or a customer berating a civil servant and vice versa, but these encounters rarely become physical. To the person who doesn't understand Greek, the loud, intense conversations may all sound angry—but they're not. When you meet someone for the first time, it is customary to shake hands, but with acquaintances, the usual is a two-cheek kiss hello and goodbye. One thing that may disconcert foreigners is that when you run into a Greek somewhere, they usually don't introduce the party they're with, even if you have a long verbal exchange. If you can't stand it anymore, just introduce yourself, or at least acknowledge the person with a smile.

Greeks tend to stand closer to people than North Americans and Northern Europeans, and they rely on gestures more when communicating. One gesture you should never use is the open palm, fingers slightly spread, shoved toward someone's face. The *moutza* is a serious insult. Another gesture you should remember, especially if trying to catch a taxi, is the "no" looks like "yes": a slight or exaggerated (depending on the sentiment) tipping back of the head, sometimes with the eyes closed and eyebrows raised. When you wave with your palm towards people, they may interpret it as "come here" instead of "goodbye"; and, Greeks often wave goodbye with the palm facing them, which looks like "come here" to English speakers.

In some areas it still doesn't do to overcompliment a baby or a child, thought to provoke others' jealousy and thus bring on the evil eye. You will often see Greeks mock spitting, saying "ftou-ftou-ftou" to ward off harm, as an American might knock on wood after a threatening thought. (At baptisms, the godparent mock spits three times to discourage Satan.) Although a woman who makes long eye contact with a man is interpreted as being interested in romance, in most cases, Greeks openly stare at anything that interests them, so don't be offended if you are the center of attention wherever you go.

When visiting a house for dinner, you can bring a small gift for the children—a foreign T-shirt, for example—or a box of pastries from the sweetshop. Greeks often eat out of communal serving plates, so it's considered normal in informal settings to spear your tomato out of the salad bowl, rather than securing an individual portion. Sometimes in tavernas you don't even get your own plate. Note that it is considered *tsigounia,* stinginess, to run separate tabs, especially because much of the meal is Chinese-style. Greeks either divide the bill equally among the party, no matter who ate what, or one person magnanimously treats (always accompanied by much protest from other diners). A good host insists that you eat or drink more, and only when you have refused a number of times, will you get a reprieve; be charmingly persistent in your "no." When you plan to meet someone, be aware that Greeks have a loose sense of time. They may be punctual if meeting you on a street corner to go to a movie, but if they say they'll come round your hotel at 7 PM, they may show up at 8 PM.

Namedays are more important than birthdays in Greece, and the person who does the celebrating holds open house. If invited, you should take sweets, flowers, spirits, or a more personal gift if you know them well. (It's common in business circles to send a telegram to associates and clients on their nameday.) You wish the reveler *chronia polla* (*hron*-ya po-*la*), or "many years."

Respect is shown toward elders; they are seldom addressed by their first name but called "Kiria" (Mrs./Ms.) and "Kirie" (Mr.) So-and-So. In country churches, and all monasteries and nunneries, shorts are not allowed for either sex, and women may not wear pants. Usually, there is a stack of frumpy skirts that both men and women can don to cover their legs. In very strict places—the Patmos monastery, for example—women cannot reveal bare shoulders or too much cleavage. It's a good idea to carry large scarves for such occasions.

Even if you make a mistake, it's unlikely Greeks will think you offensive. They're used to foreigners, don't expect you to know all the rules and will probably chalk up the impropriety to *your* culture's strange dictates.

➤ INFORMATION: To help you decipher the complexity of Greek culture, read the excellent, entertaining *Exploring the Greek Mosaic,* by Benjamin Broome (Yarmouth, Maine: Intercultural Press, 1996), which thoughtfully analyzes Greece's social landscape and provides valuable insights, especially for those who want to do business in Greece.

FOLK MUSIC AND DANCE

The dramatic ups and downs of Greek history and the five centuries of Turkish domination are clearly reflected in the wailing airs of popular folk music. Of national dances, to which this music is the accompaniment, there are two categories: one favored by the inhabitants of Athens, Piraeus, and the industrial suburbs, and the other, older and more traditional, by the provincial towns and villages. Of the former, the most popular is the *zeimbekiko,* of obvious Anatolian origin. A solo dance for men, it is performed with a panther-like grace and an air of mystical awe, the dancer, with eyes riveted to the floor, repeatedly bending down to run his hand piously across the ground. The music, played by bouzoukia, large mandolins, is nostalgic and weighted with melancholy. Other dances include the *chassapiko,* the butcher's dance, the *serviko,* probably of Slav origin, and the *tsiftetelli,* a sort of, believe it or not, belly dance

for men. The zeimbekiko remains the most popular of these. Bouzouki solos, which sound like frenzied cadenzas, demand a high standard of virtuosity. The burden of their sorrowful refrains invariably deals with death, exile, and the faithlessness of women.

The popular dances of the country are not only older, but more indigenous, and, like the folklore of the country, rooted in ancient mythology. The vase paintings of the classical age depict a variety of poses and movements which can be recognized in the traditional country dances. These include the Cretan *chaniotiko,* a circular dance originally performed by men preparing for battle; the *sousta,* danced by Achilles round the funeral pyre of Patroclus; and the Epriot dance of the *mirologhia,* a mixture of austerity, poetry, and almost unbearable anguish. The most popular, however, of all Greek dances are the *kalamatianos* and *tsamikos.* The former is performed in a circle, the male leader waving a handkerchief, swirling, bounding and lunging acrobatically. The latter, more martial in spirit, represents men going to battle, all to the sound of stamping, springing, and twisting cries of *oppa!* No matter which dance you may decide to jump up and perform in, remember that plate-smashing is now verboten in most places. In lieu of flying pottery, however, a more loving tribute is paid—many places have flower vendors, whose beautiful blooms are purchased to be thrown upon the dancers as they perform their dances.

GAY & LESBIAN TRAVEL

In Greece, homosexuality has been very much a part of life from antiquity to today. Indeed, many prominent figures of the country's cultural life (both past and present) are openly gay. Others, such as the late Minister of Culture, Melina Mercouri, have strongly supported gays. One should be aware, however, of the special mentality of the Greek male vis-à-vis homosexuality. Sociological reports indicate a large portion of the population is bisexual, though this does not indicate a conscious recognition of being gay. Greek society remains conservative regarding open declarations and displays of homosexuality by either sex, although homosexual relations for men over 17 have been legal for many decades in Greece. The nearest thing to a gay scene in the Western sense of the word exists in Athens, Thessaloniki, Mykonos, Rhodes, and Ios for men; for women, Athens and Eressos on Lesbos.

➤ LOCAL RESOURCES: *"To Kraximo"* and *"Greek Gay Guide"* (available from kiosks in Omonia Square in Athens and near the Thessaloniki train station) are both published by **Kraximo Publications** (✉ Box 4228, 10210 Athens). The weekly Greek-language entertainment magazines *Athinorama* and *Downtown,* available at all kiosks, also list Athens gay bars and dance clubs in their nightlife sections.

➤ GAY- & LESBIAN-FRIENDLY TRAVEL AGENCIES: **Different Roads Travel** (✉ 8383 Wilshire Blvd., Suite 902, Beverly Hills, CA 90211, ☎ 323/651–5557 or 800/429–8747, ℻ 323/651–3678, leigh@west.tzell.com). **Kennedy Travel** (✉ 314 Jericho Turnpike, Floral Park, NY 11001, ☎ 516/352–4888 or 800/237–7433, ℻ 516/354–8849, kennedytravel1@yahoo.com, www.kennedytravel.com). **Now Voyager** (✉ 4406 18th St., San Francisco, CA 94114, ☎ 415/626–1169 or 800/255–6951, ℻ 415/626–8626, www.nowvoyager.com). **Skylink Travel and Tour** (✉ 1006 Mendocino Ave., Santa Rosa, CA 95401, ☎ 707/546–9888 or 800/225–5759, ℻ 707/546–9891, skylinktvl@aol.com, www.skylinktravel.com), serving lesbian travelers.

HEALTH

Greece's strong summer sun and low humidity can lead to sunburn or sunstroke if you're not careful. A hat, long-sleeve shirt, and long pants or a sarong are essential for spending a day at the beach or visiting archaeological sites. Sunglasses, a hat, and sunblock are necessities, and insect repellent may keep the occasional horsefly and mosquito at bay. Drink plenty of water. Most beaches present few dangers, but keep a lookout for the occasional jellyfish and, in some

areas, sea urchins. Should you step on one, don't break off the embedded spines, which may lead to infection, but remove them with heated olive oil and a needle.

Food is seldom a problem, but the liberal amounts of olive oil used in Greek cooking may be indigestible for some. Tap water in Greece is fine, and bottled spring water is readily available.

For minor ailments, go to the local pharmacy first, where the licensed staff can make recommendations for over-the-counter drugs. Most pharmacies are closed in the evenings and on weekends, but each posts the name of the nearest pharmacy open off-hours. Newspapers, including the *Athens News,* also carry a listing of pharmacies open late. If you speak Greek, you can dial a recorded message listing the off-hours pharmacies (☎ 107 in Athens, 102 outside the capital). Most state hospitals and rural clinics won't charge you for tending to minor ailments, even if you're not an EU citizen; at most, you'll pay a minimal fee. In an emergency you can call an ambulance (☎ 166), but waving down a taxi is faster, since cars in big cities give way reluctantly to ambulances. Most hotels will call a doctor for you. In Athens, you can locate a doctor on call 2 PM–7 AM on Sunday and on holidays by dialing 105 (☎ 101 outside of Athens), but the message is in Greek. For a dentist, check with your hotel, embassy, or the tourist police.

DIVERS' ALERT

Do not fly within 24 hours after scuba diving.

OVER-THE-COUNTER REMEDIES

All kiosks carry aspirins (ah-spi-*ree*-nee), but other drugs are only available at the pharmacy (far-ma-*kee*-oh), though you often don't need a prescription. Condoms are available from kiosks, supermarkets, pharmacies, and sometimes vending machines in bar bathrooms or outside pharmacies. One aspirin substitute similar to Tylenol is Depon; other painkillers include Ponstan and Buscopan (good for menstrual cramps) and Salospir, which you can buy without prescription. Lomotil is widely available, and a good salve for sunburn is the inexpensive Bepanthol. The pharmacist will tell you what European medications equal yours and how to locate them. Many pharmacists also give shots and vaccinations. Pharmacies with a green cross sell homeopathic remedies. You will find a bigger selection of sunscreens at supermarkets and beauty stores such as Hondos Center or Beauty Shop. All tourist areas have at least one store selling sunscreen, but it will be expensive. There are no local brands but everything from Coppertone to Nivea is available.

PESTS & OTHER HAZARDS

In greener, wetter areas, mosquitoes may be a problem. You can burn coils (spee-*rahl*) to discourage them or buy plug-in devices that burn medicated tabs (pah-*steel*-ya). Hotels usually provide these. The only poisonous snakes in Greece are the adder and the sand viper, which are brown or red, with dark zigzags. The adder has a V or X behind its head, and the sand viper sports a small horn on its nose. When hiking, wear high tops and don't put your feet or hands in crevices without looking first. If bitten, try to slow the spread of the venom until a doctor comes. Lie still with the affected limb lower than the rest of your body. Apply a tourniquet, releasing it every few minutes, and cut the wound a bit in case the venom can bleed out. Do NOT suck on the bite. Whereas snakes like to lie in the sun, the scorpion (rare) likes cool, wet places, in wood piles, and under stones. Apply Benadryl or Phenergan to minor stings, but if you have nausea or fever, see a doctor at once.

HOLIDAYS

2001: January 1 (New Year's Day); January 6 (Epiphany); February 26 (Clean Monday, first day of Lent); March 25 (Feast of the Annunciation and Independence Day); April 13 (Good Friday); April 15 (Greek Easter Sunday); April 16 (Greek Easter Monday); May 1 (Labor Day); June 3 (Pentecost); August 15 (Assumption of the Holy Virgin); October 28 (Ochi Day); December 25–26 (Christmas

Day and Boxing Day). 2002: Dates are the same as above except March 18 (Clean Monday, first day of Lent); May 3 (Good Friday); May 5 (Greek Easter Sunday); May 6 (Greek Easter Monday); June 23 (Pentecost).

Only on Orthodox Easter and August 15 do you find that practically everything shuts down (☞ Business Hours, *above*). You will have a harder time getting a room at the last minute on Easter and August 15 (especially the latter), and traveling requires stamina and downright pushiness, if you want to survive on the ferries and the highways. On the other hand, the local rituals and rites associated with these two celebrations are interesting and occasionally moving (the Epitafion procession on Good Friday), allowing you a glimpse into customs that date to pagan times.

INSURANCE

Travel insurance is the best way to **protect yourself against financial loss.** The most useful plan is a comprehensive policy that includes coverage for trip cancellation and interruption, default, trip delay, and medical expenses (with a waiver for preexisting conditions).

Without insurance, you lose all or most of your money if you cancel your trip, regardless of the reason. Default insurance covers you if your tour operator, airline, or cruise line goes out of business. Trip-delay covers unforeseen expenses that you may incur due to bad weather or mechanical delays. It's important to compare the fine print regarding trip-delay coverage when comparing policies.

For overseas travel, one of the most important components of travel insurance is its medical coverage. Supplemental health insurance will pick up the cost of your medical bills should you get sick or injured while traveling. U.S. residents should note that Medicare generally does not cover health-care costs outside the United States, nor do many privately issued policies. Residents of the United Kingdom can buy an annual travel-insurance policy valid for most vacations taken during the year in which the coverage is purchased. If you are pregnant or have a preexisting condition, make sure you're covered. British citizens should buy extra medical coverage when traveling overseas, according to the Association of British Insurers. Australian travelers should buy travel insurance, including extra medical coverage, whenever they go abroad, according to the Insurance Council of Australia.

Always **buy travel insurance directly from the insurance company**; if you buy it from a cruise line, airline, or tour operator that goes out of business you probably will not be covered for the agency or operator's default, a major risk. Before you make any purchase, **review your existing health and home-owner's policies** to find out whether they cover expenses incurred while traveling.

➤ TRAVEL INSURERS: In the U.S.: **Access America** (✉ 6600 W. Broad St., Richmond, VA 23230, ☎ 804/285–3300 or 800/284–8300, FAX 804/673–1586, www.previewtravel.com), **Travel Guard International** (✉ 1145 Clark St., Stevens Point, WI 54481, ☎ 715/345–0505 or 800/826–1300, FAX 800/955–8785, www.noelgroup. com).

➤ INSURANCE INFORMATION: In the U.K.: **Association of British Insurers** (✉ 51–55 Gresham St., London EC2V 7HQ, U.K., ☎ 020/7600–3333, FAX 020/7696–8999, info@abi. org.uk, www.abi.org.uk). In Canada: **Voyager Insurance** (✉ 44 Peel Center Dr., Brampton, Ontario L6T 4M8, Canada, ☎ 905/791–8700, 800/668–4342 in Canada). In Australia: **Insurance Council of Australia** (☎ 03/9614–1077, FAX 03/9614–7924). In New Zealand: **Insurance Council of New Zealand** (✉ Box 474, Wellington, New Zealand, ☎ 04/472–5230, FAX 04/473–3011, www.icnz.org.nz).

LANGUAGE

Greek is the native language not only of Greece but also of Cyprus, parts of Chicago, and Astoria, New York. Though it's a byword for incomprehensible ("it was all Greek to me," says Casca in Shakespeare's *Julius Caesar*), much of the difficulty lies in its different alphabet. Not all the 24 Greek letters have precise English equivalents, and there is usually more

than one way to spell a Greek word in English. For instance, the letter delta sounds like the English letters "dh," and the sound of the letter gamma may be transliterated as a "g," "gh," or "y." Because of this the Greek for Holy Trinity might appear in English as Agia Triada, Aghia Triada, Ayia Triada, or even (if the initial aspiration and the "dh" are used) Hagia Triadha. It seems complicated, but don't let it throw you. With a little time spent learning the alphabet and some basic phrases, you can acquire enough Greek to navigate—i.e., exchange greetings, find a hotel room, and get from one town to another. Many Greeks know English but appreciate a two-way effort. Only in isolated mountain villages might you not find someone who speaks at least a few words; in most cities and tourist areas, all Greeks know at least one foreign language. Note that if you ask directions, you will often get numerous opinions and a slew of people involved, or at least the next table. It's best to use close-ended queries: "Is this the path to Galissas? Do I turn right at the stone church or left?" If you ask, "where is Galissas," a possible answer will be "down a ways to the left and then you turn right by the baker's house, his child lives in Chicago, where did you say you went to school?"

If you only have 15 minutes to learn Greek, memorize the following: *yiá sou* (hello/goodbye, informal for one person); *yiá sas* (hello/goodbye, formal for one person and used for a group); *miláte angliká?* (do you speak English?); *den katalavéno* (I don't understand); *parakaló* (please/you're welcome); *signómi* (excuse me); *efharistó* (thank you); *ne* (yes); *óhee* (no); *pósso?* (how much?); *pou eéne ee?* (where is?), . . . *ee twaléta?* (. . . the toilet?), . . . *to tahidromío?* (. . . the post office?), . . . *to stathmó?* (. . . the station?); *kali méra* (good morning), *kali spéra* (good evening), *kali níhta* (good night). Also *see* Greek Vocabulary at the back of this guide.

LANGUAGE-STUDY PROGRAMS

There are language-study courses in Athens, but these require more of a time commitment than your one- or two-week vacation. Such programs, usually combined with sightseeing, are best booked from your country; check with your local university. If you have the time, the professional Athens Centre offers an intensive one-month program for all levels in a lovely old Pangrati house where students often socialize in the peaceful courtyard. You might meet local diplomats, classics students, or businesswomen out to master this difficult language. The center also runs reasonably priced, one-month courses on the island of Spetses in July (about $800, including single-room accommodation). Both the Athens Centre and the Hellenic American Union offer longer courses as well, though the latter is geared more to Greeks learning English.

➤ PROGRAMS: **Athens Centre** (✉ Archimidou 48, Pangrati, Athens 11636, ☎ 01/701–2268, ᴲᴬˣ 01/701–8603). **Hellenic American Union** (✉ Massalias 22, Exarchia, Athens 10679, ☎ 01/362–4291, ᴲᴬˣ 01/362–2400).

LODGING

The array of accommodations ranges from luxury island resorts to traditional settlements that incorporate local architecture to inexpensive rented rooms peddled at the harbor. Family-run pensions and guest houses outside Athens and Thessaloniki are often charming and comfortable; they also let you get better acquainted with the locals. Self-catering apartments are available as well in most resort areas.

Although lodging is less expensive in Greece than in most of the EU and the U.S., the quality tends to be lower. The lodgings listed in this guide, denoted by a small house 🏠 were chosen because they were among the best in their category, location, and price range; establishments whose restaurants are also noteworthy are marked with an ✕🏠 icon. Often you can reduce the price by eliminating breakfast, by bargaining when it's off-season, or by going through a local travel agency for the larger hotels on major islands and in Athens and Thessaloniki. If you stay longer, the manager or owner will usually give

you a better daily rate. An 8.2% government tax and 2.4% municipality tax is added to all hotel bills, though usually the rate quoted includes the tax; be sure to ask. Many Greeks rent rooms in their houses, which can be less expensive and more homey than a hotel, but you might have to scout around a bit to find them, and it's a good idea to see them first before you commit. Accommodations may be hard to find in smaller resort towns during the winter and beginning of spring. Remember that the plumbing in rooms and most low-end hotels (and restaurants, shops, and other public places) is delicate enough to require that toilet paper and other detritus be put in the wastebasket and not flushed.

The lodgings we list are the cream of the crop in each price category. We always list the facilities that are available—but we don't specify whether they cost extra: when pricing accommodations, always ask what's included and what costs extra: the usual items that may cost extra to your basic hotel room rate are breakfast, parking facilities, and even air-conditioning at some hotels. Assume that hotels operate on the **European Plan** (EP, with no meals) unless we note that breakfast is included in the room rate. Also note that some resort hotels also offer half- and full-board arrangements; inquire when booking.

APARTMENT & VILLA RENTALS

If you want a home base that's roomy enough for a family and comes with cooking facilities, **consider a self-catering apartment or furnished rentals including villas.** These can save you money, especially if you're traveling with a large group of people. Home-exchange directories list rentals (often second homes owned by prospective house swappers), and some services search for a house or apartment for you (even a castle if that's your fancy) and handle the paperwork. Some send an illustrated catalog; others send photographs only of specific properties, sometimes at a charge. Up-front registration fees may apply. In Greece, luxury properties are limited and usually handled by international agents. For more modest villas, you can go through package holiday companies in your country. You could also check the *Athens News* classifieds under "Summer Holiday Rentals," which usually list seaside homes for long-term (weekly, monthly) rent. Self-catering apartments are found in almost every tourist area; ask the local tourist police for a list.

➤ INTERNATIONAL AGENTS: **Hideaways International** (⊠ 767 Islington St., Portsmouth, NH 03801, ☎ 603/430–4433 or 800/843–4433, 🕾 603/430–4444, info@hideaways.com, www.hideaways.com; membership $99).

Vacation Home Rentals Worldwide (⊠ 235 Kensington Ave., Norwood, NJ 07648, ☎ 201/767–9393 or 800/633–3284, 🕾 201/767–5510, vhrww@juno.com, www.vhrww.com).

CAMPING

There are numerous campgrounds, most privately owned, throughout Greece. One or more can usually be found close to popular archaeological sites and beach resorts—they aren't intended for those who want to explore the wilds of Greece. Their amenities range from basic to elaborate, and those operated by the EOT are cushier than most. You usually don't need an International Camping Carnet. There is no such thing as a typical campground. You might find landscaped, lanterned walkways between the tents and a restaurant, even a tennis court, or a barren stretch with nary a shrub for shade. Your fellow campers run the gamut from Scandinavian families of four to Greek teenage ravers juggling fire. In general, the atmosphere is loose and friendly, and camping can be especially pleasant if by a beach.

The EOT distributes information on available campgrounds with site listings; the tourist organization manages campgrounds in Athens (near Voula beach); in the Peloponnese at Killini; in Thrace at Fanari 31 km (18½ mi) from Komotini; in central Greece at Kamena Vourla; and in Macedonia at about nine sites, including Olympos, Bati beach in Kavala, and Thermaikos, 28 km (17 mi) from Thessaloniki. Many Greeks

prefer "freelance" camping, also available (though technically illegal), because the locations are better. These informal sites spring up annually, often around an island's nudist beaches. Usually there is some form of running water and a nearby taverna—ask around.

➤ INFORMATION: **Panhellenic Camping Association** (⊠ Solonos 102, Athens 10680, ☎ 🕾 01/362–1560).

HOME EXCHANGES

If you would like to exchange your home for someone else's, **join a home-exchange organization,** which will send you its updated listings of available exchanges for a year and will include your own listing in at least one of them. It's up to you to make specific arrangements.

➤ EXCHANGE CLUBS: **Intervac U.S.** (⊠ Box 590504, San Francisco, CA 94159, ☎ 800/756–4663, 🕾 415/435–7440, intervacus@aol.com, www.intervacus.com; $93 per year includes two catalogues).

HOSTELS

No matter what your age, you can **save on lodging costs by staying at hostels.** In some 5,000 locations in more than 70 countries around the world, Hostelling International (HI), the umbrella group for a number of national youth-hostel associations, offers single-sex, dorm-style beds and, at many hostels, rooms for couples and family accommodations. Membership in any HI national hostel association, open to travelers of all ages, allows you to stay in HI-affiliated hostels at member rates; one-year membership is about $25 for adults (C$26.75 in Canada, £9.30 in the U.K., $30 in Australia, and $30 in New Zealand); hostels run about $10–$25 per night. Members have priority if the hostel is full; they're also eligible for discounts around the world, even on rail and bus travel in some countries. Greek hostels run about $10 for a bed per night; some are quite loud and cater to a predominantly young crowd. Families with young children might do better to stay in a cheap hotel or rental room.

For the moment, hostels (whether officially recognized or not) are operating in Athens and Thessaloniki on the mainland; Nafplion, Patras and Olympia in the Peloponnese; Santorini; and Crete.

➤ ORGANIZATIONS: **Hostelling International—American Youth Hostels** (✉ 733 15th St. NW, Suite 840, Washington, DC 20005, ☎ 202/783–6161, FAX 202/783–6171, hiayhserv@ hiayh.org, www.hiayh.org). **Hostelling International—Canada** (✉ 400–205 Catherine St., Ottawa, Ontario K2P 1C3, Canada, ☎ 613/237–7884, FAX 613/237–7868, info@hostellingintl. ca, www.hostellingintl.ca). **Youth Hostel Association of England and Wales** (✉ Trevelyan House, 8 St. Stephen's Hill, St. Albans, Hertfordshire AL1 2DY, U.K., ☎ 0870/870–8808, FAX 01727/844126, customerservices@yha.org.uk, www.yha. org.uk). **Australian Youth Hostel Association** (✉ 10 Mallett St., Camperdown, NSW 2050, Australia, ☎ 02/9565–1699, FAX 02/9565–1325, www.yha.com.au). **Youth Hostels Association of New Zealand** (✉ Box 436, Christchurch, New Zealand, ☎ 03/379–9970, FAX 03/365–4476, info@yha.org.nz, www.yha.org.nz).

➤ IN GREECE: You can also contact the **Greek Youth Hostel Organization** (✉ Damareos 75, Pangrati, Athens 11633, ☎ 01/751–9530, FAX 01/751–0616), but because of some bureaucracy with the EOT, not all hostels fall under their jurisdiction. You can also try **Athens International Youth Hostel** (✉ Victoros Ougo [Victor Hugo] 16, Omonia, Athens 10438, ☎ 01/523–1095 or 01/523–4170, FAX 01/523–4015). The convenient **YWCA (XEN) in Athens** (✉ Amerikis 11, 10672, ☎ 01/362–4291 through 01/362–4293, FAX 01/362–2400) takes overnight guests, women only; visitors pay a 600-dr./€1.76 membership fee, good for one year.

HOTELS

The EOT authorizes the construction and classification of hotels throughout Greece. It classifies them into six categories: L (stands for De Luxe), and A–E, which govern the rates that can be charged, though don't expect hotels to have the same amenities as their U.S. and northern European counterparts. Ratings are based on considerations such as room size, hotel services, and amenities like furnishing of the room. Within each category, quality varies greatly, but prices don't. Still, you may come across an A-category hotel that charges less than a B-class, depending on facilities. The classifications can be misleading—a hotel rated C in one town might qualify as a B in another. For the categories L, A, and B, you can expect something along the lines of a chain motel in the U.S., although the room will probably be somewhat smaller. A room in a C hotel can be perfectly acceptable; with a D the bathroom may or may not be shared. Ask to see the room before checking in. You can sometimes find a bargain if a hotel has just renovated but has not yet been reclassified. A great hotel may never move up to a better category just because its lobby isn't the required size. The government is discussing switching to a star-rating system like several other European countries, hoping this standardization will encourage hotels to upgrade, as well as make things easier for travel agents.

Official prices are posted in each room, usually on the back of the door or inside the wardrobe. The room charge varies over the course of the year, peaking in the high season when breakfast or half board (at hotel complexes) may also be obligatory.

From mid-July to mid-August, it's harder to find hotels on the islands and near the beaches, just as it's more difficult to get a hotel near Peloponnese ski centers in winter and in Thessaloniki during the International Trade Fair in September. The rest of the time you can just walk in. A hotel may ask you for a deposit of up to 25% of the room rate. If you cancel your reservations at least 21 days in advance, you are entitled to a full refund of your deposit. If the room you booked is unavailable when you arrive, and you have proof of booking, the hotel must put you up in another hotel of at least the same category, in the same area, for the same length of time. If the hotel can't find you alternative lodging, it must reimburse you fully. Although a hotel is liable for damage to or theft of your valuables (unless it was your fault or the result of *force majeure,* it is only liable for up to 30,000 dr./€88.49 per customer, unless you can prove it assumed the safekeeping of your valuables. Just because these rights are guaranteed by the law doesn't mean you will automatically find compliance or a speedy resolution; contact tourist police if you have trouble.

EOT distributes lists of hotels for each region, although it does not make recommendations. Annual hotel directories are available at most English-language bookstores in Athens and Thessaloniki and at city kiosks in late spring. You can contact a hotel directly, go through a travel agent or write one month in advance for reservations to the Hellenic Chamber of Hotels.

Unless otherwise noted, in this guide, hotels in the first two price categories have air-conditioning, *climatismo,* and rooms in all price categories have ensuite baths, *banio.* Bathrooms mostly contain showers, though some older or more luxury hotels may have tubs. Beds are usually twins (*diklina*) pushed apart (*horista*) but you can push them together (*mazi*) yourself. If you want a double, ask for a *diplo.* Unless you're in a very good hotel, the mattresses are usually Full or Queen, and seldom orthopedic. The guide lists amenities that are available but doesn't always specify if there is a surcharge. **When pricing accommodations, always ask what costs extra** (TV, air-conditioning, private bathroom).

If you need a quiet room, get one with double-glazed windows and air-conditioning, away from the elevator and public areas, as high up as possible, and off the street. Check out the surroundings—is there a construction site nearby? A bar? Bus station? Airport? On Sundays and holy days, churches often broadcast the service over microphones in villages and small towns, and all ring their bells loudly. Even a braying donkey or crowing rooster can mar a bucolic setting at 5 AM. Sometimes older buildings are quieter due to their thicker walls, but if you're ultra sensitive, the only guarantee for a peaceful night's sleep is an effective set of ear plugs.

➤ RESERVING A ROOM: **Hellenic Chamber of Hotels** (✉ Stadiou 24, Athens 10564, ☎ 01/331–0022 through 01/331–0026, ℻ 01/322–5449, http://users.otenet.gr/àgrhotels). The Chamber also has a desk inside Athens's National Bank of Greece to help visitors find rooms (✉ Karageorgi Servias 2, ☎ 01/323–7193), open weekdays 8:30 to 2, Saturday 9 to 1.

➤ GUIDES: One of the most complete lodging guides is *Hellenic Traveling Pages* (✉ Info Publications, Pironos 51, Athens 16341, ☎ 01/994–0109 or 01/993–7551, ℻ 01/993–6564), a monthly publication available at most Greek bookstores; it also lists travel agencies, yacht brokers, bus, boat, and airplane schedules, and museum hours.

➤ TOLL-FREE NUMBERS: **Best Western** (☎ 800/528–1234, www.bestwestern.com). **Choice** (☎ 800/221–2222, www.hotelchoice.com). **Hilton** (☎ 800/445–8667, www.hilton.com). **Holiday Inn** (☎ 800/465–4329, www.basshotels.com). **Hyatt Hotels & Resorts** (☎ 800/233–1234, www.hyatt.com). **Inter-Continental** (☎ 800/327–0200, www.interconti.com). **Marriott** (☎ 800/228–9290, www.marriott.com). **Sheraton** (☎ 800/325–3535, www.starwood.com).

RENTAL ROOMS

Most areas have pensions—usually clean, bright, and recently built. On islands in summer, owners wait for tourists at the harbor, and signs in English throughout villages indicate rooms available. Around August 15, when it seems all Greeks go on vacation, even the most basic rooms are hard to locate, although you can query the tourist police or the municipal tourist office. In a pinch, owners may let you sleep on their roof for a small fee. On some islands the local rental room owners' association sets up an information booth. Few rooms are available in winter and early spring. Check the rooms first, for quality and location; if it's miles from town, you'll spend all your money on transportation. Also, **make sure you feel comfortable with the owners if**

they live on the premises; that inquisitive hostess feeding you warm goat milk may become prying, overly chatty, or the self-appointed guardian of your children's morals after a day or two.

TRADITIONAL SETTLEMENTS

In an effort to provide tourist accommodations in traditional settings, the EOT has begun a restoration program, converting older buildings that reflect the local architecture into guest houses. Some of the villages developed so far include Oia on Santorini; Vizitsa and Argalasti on Mt. Pelion; Mesta on Chios and nearby Psara island; Korischades in Evritania; Papingo in Epirus; Vathia in the Mani with its curious tower homes; and Monemvassia in the Southern Peloponnese.

Many of these settlements are detailed and photographed in an EOT handout, "Traditional Settlements," as well as in a guide called *Traditional Inns in Greece: Alternative Forms of Tourism,* in English, published by **Vertical Advertising.**

➤ RESERVATIONS & INFORMATION: For reservations call the **Greek Hotel and Cruise Reservation Center** (☎ 714/641–3502 or 800/736–5717, ℻ 714/641–0303). **Vertical Advertising** (✉ Katehaki 61A, Athens 11525, ☎ 01/691–2219, ℻ 01/649–6782).

MAIL & SHIPPING

Letters and postcards take about three to four days to reach the U.K., a week to 10 days for the U.S., about 10 days for Australia and New Zealand. That's airmail. It takes even longer during August when postal staff is reduced, and during Christmas and Easter holidays. And sometimes, your letter may never arrive at all, though that usually happens to post entering Greece. If what you're mailing is important, send it registered, which costs only about 600 dr./€1.76 in Greece. For a few hundred drachmas more, depending on the weight, you can also send your letter "express"; this earns you a red sticker and faster local delivery. However, avoid the post office's EMS Express Service. Although you pay about 5,000 dr./€14.74 for a letter and it arrives in the country of destination within two days, it takes another 24 to 48 hours for delivery. If sending a parcel, you must take it open to the post office for inspection. Bring brown butcher paper, tape, and string along, since the post office does not provide wrapping materials. Packages take even longer to arrive—"surface/air lift" means your parcel will need at least least two weeks to get to any destination.

COURIERS

Within Greece, there are many services that can get your items crosstown in a few hours or from a frontier island like Chios to the capital overnight. Costs depend on the distance covered and how fast you need your papers delivered. Rates start at about 1,500 dr./€4.42 for a simple intracity delivery. **ACS** has perhaps the best door-to-door delivery network.

➤ DOMESTIC DELIVERY: **ACS** (✉ Leoforos Alexandras 23, Athens 11525, ☎ 01/646–0604). **Kanga Services** (✉ Makrinitsas 3 and Panormou, Athens, ☎ 01/646–6400 customer service). **Speedex Courier** (✉ Skoufou 10, Athens, ☎ 01/324–3342 and 01/324–5407).

OVERNIGHT SERVICES

Overnight service to the U.S., U.K., Canada, Australia, and New Zealand is now available almost everywhere in Greece. Outside cities, you usually need to take the package to the office yourself, and the reliability of the services varies. One of the few truly "overnight" services is **DHL,** which is slightly more expensive than other companies but provides prompt door-to-door delivery and an extensive network. Overnight service from Athens to New York for documents up to 100 grams costs 7,850 dr./€23.

➤ MAJOR SERVICES: **DHL International Hellas** (✉ Fillelinon 28, near Plaka, Athens 11525, ☎ 01/989–0800 office; 01/989–0000 24-hr customer service, ℻ 01/984–1044; ✉ Alimou 44, Alimos (near the airport) 17455, ☎ 01/984–4702, ℻ 01/984–1044), both open weekdays 8 to 6, Saturday 9 to 2.

POSTAL RATES

At press time (summer 2000), airmail letters and postcards to destinations other than Europe and weighing up to 20 grams cost 200 dr./€.58, and 300 dr./€.88 for 50 grams (170 dr./€.50 and 270 dr./€.79, respectively, to other European countries, including the U.K.).

RECEIVING MAIL

Post offices are open weekdays 8–2, although in city centers they may stay open in the evenings and on weekends. The main post offices in Athens (⊠ Aiolou 100; Syntagma Sq. at Mitropoleos) are both open weekdays 7:30 AM–8 PM, Saturday 7:30–2, and Sunday 9–2. Throughout the country, mailboxes are yellow and sometimes divided into domestic and international containers; express boxes are red.

SHIPPING PARCELS

Mail service can be quite slow in Greece and not particularly reliable. **Send your important items registered.** To receive letters when you're traveling around, **have your mail addressed to "poste restante"** and sent to any post office in Greece (in Athens: ⊠ Aiolou 100, Athens 10200), where you can pick it up once you show your passport. Or have it mailed to American Express offices (⊠ Ermou 2, Athens 10563). The service is free for holders of American Express cards or traveler's checks. Other AmEx offices are located in Thessaloniki, Patras, Corfu, Rhodes, Santorini, Mykonos, Skiathos, and Heraklion in Crete.

MONEY MATTERS

Although costs have risen astronomically since Greece joined the EU, the country will seem reasonably priced to travelers from the U.S. and Great Britain. Popular tourist resorts (including some of the islands) and the larger cities are markedly more expensive than the countryside. Though the price of eating in a restaurant has increased over the past several years, it often remains a bargain. Hotels are generally moderately priced, and the extra cost of accommodations in a luxury hotel, compared to an average hotel, often seems unwarranted.

Transportation is a good deal in Greece. Bus and train tickets are inexpensive, though renting a car is costly; there are relatively cheap—and slow—ferries to the islands, and express boats and hydrofoils that cost more. If your time is limited, domestic flights are a fair trade-off in cost and time saved, compared with sea and land travel.

Some sample prices: admission to archaeological sites: 500 dr./€1.47–2,000 dr./€5.89; authentic Greek sponge: 2,200 dr./6.48; a cup of coffee in a central city café: 800 dr./€2.35–1,000 dr./€2.94 (Greek coffee is cheaper); beer: (500 ml) 450 dr./€1.32, in a bar 800 dr./€2.35–1,000 dr./€2.94; soft drink: (can) 150 dr./€.44, and in a café 600 dr./€1.76; spinach pie: 300 dr./€.88; souvlaki: 350 dr./€1.03; grilled cheese sandwich, *tost*: 800 dr./€2.35; taxi ride: about 2,200 dr./€6.48 from the airport to downtown Athens and 500 dr./€1.47 for a 2-km (1-mi) ride in the city center; local bus: 120 dr./€.35; foreign newspaper: 350 dr./€1.03-750 dr./€2.21. Admission, which is given in this guide for adults, is free to most museums and archaeological sites on Sunday from November through March. The rest of the year, prices range from 500 dr./€1.47 to 2,000 dr./€5.89; admission is substantially reduced for children, students, and senior citizens. For information on taxes, *see* Taxes, *below.*

ATMS

ATMs are widely available throughout the country. Virtually all banks, including the National Bank of Greece (known as Ethniki), have machines that dispense money to Cirrus or Plus card holders. You may find bank-sponsored ATMs at harbors and in airports as well. Other systems accepted include Visa, Master Card, American Express, Diner's Club, and Eurocard, but exchange and withdrawal rates vary, so shop around and check fees with your bank before leaving home. For use in Greece, your PIN must be only four digits long. The word for PIN is pronounced "peen" and ATMs are called *alpha taf mi,* after the letters, or just *to mixanima,* "the machine."

Machines usually let you complete the transaction in English, French, or German, and seldom create problems, except Sunday night, when they sometimes run out of cash. Also, for most machines, the minimum amount dispensed is 10,000 dr./€29.49. Sometimes an ATM may refuse to "read" your card. Don't panic, it's probably the machine. Try another bank.

CREDIT AND DEBIT CARDS

Should you use a credit card or a debit card when traveling? Both have benefits. A credit card allows you to delay payment and gives you certain rights as a consumer (☞ Consumer Protection, *above*). A debit card, also known as a check card, deducts funds directly from your checking account and helps you stay within your budget. When you want to rent a car, though, you may still need an old-fashioned credit card.

Both types of plastic get you cash advances at ATMs worldwide if your card is properly programmed with your personal identification number (PIN). Both offer excellent, wholesale exchange rates. And both protect you against unauthorized use if the card is lost or stolen. Your liability is limited to $50, as long as you report the card missing. However, shop owners often give you a lower price if you pay cash rather than credit, because they want to avoid the credit card bank fees. Note that the Discover card is not widely accepted in Greece.

Throughout this guide, the following abbreviations are used: **AE**, American Express; **D**, Discover; **DC**, Diners Club; **MC**, Master Card; and **V**, Visa.

➤ REPORTING LOST CARDS: To report lost or stolen credit cards, call the following toll-free numbers: **American Express** (☎ 800/327–2177); **Diners Club** (☎ 800/234–6377); **Discover Card** (☎ 800/347–2683); **Master Card** (☎ 800/307–7309); and **Visa** (☎ 800/847–2911).

➤ REPORTING LOST CARDS/GREECE: To report lost or stolen credit cards in Greece: **American Express** (☎ 01/324–4975 during office hours or 24 hrs; 00–800–44/122296 toll-free); **Visa** (☎ 00–800–11/638–0304, toll-

free). The local Citibank, which issues Diners Club and Master Card, can't cancel your cards but will pass on the message to the head offices of **Diners Club** (☎ 01/929–0130) and **Master Card** (☎ 01/929–0100.

CURRENCY

The drachma (dr.) is the Greek unit of currency. Bills are in denominations of 10,000, 5,000, 1,000, 500, 200, and 100 dr. Coins are 100, 50, 20, 10, and 5. As yet, you can't use euros to pay for much except electricity and telephone bills.

Up to January 1st, 2002, the Greek drachma (GRD) will remain the main unit of currency in Greece but after that date, the new single European Union (EU) currency, the euro, will take over. Until then, people will use the drachma in their day-to-day transactions and travelers will continue to exchange their money for its 10,000, 5000, 1000, 500, 200, and 100 banknotes; 100, 50, 20, 10, and 5 drachma coins. At press time (summer 2000), the exchange rate was about 402 drachmas to the U.S. dollar, 266 to the Canadian dollar, 585 to the pound sterling, 213 to the Australian dollar, 162 to the New Zealand dollar, and 431 to the Irish punt. As of 2000 the Euro (ECU) began to be quoted (taxi drivers were among the first to include euro prices on their rate cards); at press time, 1 ECU equaled about 339 Greek drachmas. Starting in 2001, all shops will be obliged to display their prices in drachmas and euros. For the euro denomination, the exchange rate was about 0.95 euros to the U.S dollar, 0.62 to the pound sterling, 1.40 to the Canadian dollar, 1.61 to the Australian dollar, 2.06 to the New Zealand dollar, and 0.78 to the Irish punt. These rates can and will vary.

At this point, most transactions not involving cash, such as bank transfers or paying public utility bills by check, may currently be transacted in euros. The Greek finance has announced that drachmas will remain in circulation for two months after the introduction of euro notes and coins but should be phased out by March 1, 2002.

Under the euro system, there are eight coins: 1 and 2 euros, plus 1, 2, 5, 10, 20, and 50 euro cent, or cents of the euro. Euros are pronounced "evros" in Greek; cents are known as "lepta." All coins have one side that has the value of the euro on it and the other side with each countries' own unique national symbol. Greece's range from images of triremes to a depiction of the mythological Europa being abducted by Zeus transformed as a bull. There are seven banknotes: 5, 10, 20, 50, 100, 200, and 500 euros. Banknotes are the same for all EU countries.

CURRENCY EXCHANGE

For the most favorable rates, **change money through banks.** Although fees charged for ATM transactions may be higher abroad than at home, Cirrus and Plus exchange rates are excellent, because they are based on wholesale rates offered only by major banks. You won't do as well at exchange booths in airports or rail and bus stations, in hotels, in restaurants, or in stores, although you may find their hours more convenient. Off Syntagma in Athens, the National Bank, General Bank, Credit Bank, Ionian Bank, Commercial Bank, and Macedonia-Thrace Bank all have automated machines that change your foreign currency into drachmas.

If you do use an exchange booth, good options are American Express and Eurochange. Watch daily fluctuations and shop around. Daily exchange rates are prominently displayed in banks and listed in the *Athens News*. In Athens, around Syntagma Square is the best place to look. Those that operate after business hours have lower rates and a higher commission. You can also change money at post offices—located in even the most remote parts of Greece; commissions are lower than banks, starting about 900 dr./€2.65 for amounts up to 100,000 dr./€294. To avoid lines at airport exchange booths, **get a bit of local currency before you leave home.** At press time (summer 2000), the average exchange rate was 352 dr. to the U.S. dollar, 241 dr. to the Canadian dollar, 556 dr. to the pound sterling, 215 dr. to the Australian dollar, and 170 dr. to the New Zealand dollar.

➤ EXCHANGE SERVICES: **International Currency Express** (☎ 888/278–6628 for orders, www.foreignmoney.com). **Thomas Cook Currency Services** (☎ 800/287–7362 for telephone orders and retail locations, www.us.thomascook.com).

➤ ATHENS EXCHANGE SERVICES: **American Express Travel Related Services** (✉ Ermou 2, Syntagma, ☎ 01/324–4975), open weekdays 8:30–4 and Saturday 8:30–1:30. **Eurochange** (✉ Karageorgi Servias 2, Syntagma, ☎ 01/331–2462), open 8 AM–11 PM daily; ✉ Fillelinon 22 and Kithadineon, near Plaka, ☎ 01/324–3997, open daily 8 AM–10 PM.

TRAVELER'S CHECKS

Traveler's checks are the best way to carry your money into Greece, keeping your funds safe until you change them into drachmas. As far as paying with checks, it depends on where you're headed. **It's important to remember that Greece is still a cash society, so plan accordingly.** If you're going to rural areas and small towns, go with cash; traveler's checks are best used in cities, though even in Athens most tavernas, for example, won't take them. Lost or stolen checks can usually be replaced within 24 hours. To ensure a speedy refund, buy your own traveler's checks—don't let someone else pay for them: irregularities like this can cause delays. The person who bought the checks should make the call to request a refund.

OUTDOORS & SPORTS

BICYCLING

Bicycling is no fun on crowded city streets but can be a pleasure on the islands and in the countryside. Resort areas usually have at least one bicycle rental shop but helmets are seldom provided. Greek drivers still aren't used to seeing cyclists on the road, which can make bicycling occasionally nerve-racking, especially on narrow, curvy mountain roads. Most adventure travel agencies, such as Trekking Hellas and F-Zein (☞ Hiking & Mountain Biking, *below*), offer mountain-biking tours, and depending on the difficulty level, these may be your best bet.

BIRD-WATCHING

The **Hellenic Ornithological Society** (✉ Em. Benaki 53, Athens, ☎ 𝔽𝔸𝕏 01/381–1271 or 01/330–1167) arranges two- and three-day trips to important bird habitats, such as the Dounavi Delta, the Vikos Gorge, and the Messolonghi wetlands.

GOLFING

Golfing in Greece is possible, but there aren't many 18-hole courses. Those with complete facilities include the **Glyfada Golf Course** (☎ 01/894–6820, 𝔽𝔸𝕏 01/894–3721) near Athens, **Golf Afandou** (☎ 0241/51256 or 0241/51451, 𝔽𝔸𝕏 0241/51255) on Rhodes, which combines a sea view with a course designed by world-famous David Harradine, **Porto Carras Golf and Country Club** (☎ 0375/71381, 𝔽𝔸𝕏 0375/71502) in Chalkidiki, and the **Corfu Golf Club** (☎ 𝔽𝔸𝕏 0661/94220) in the central part of the island near Ermones Beach. Golf courses are open year-round. Prices run about 6,000 per person per round on weekdays, more on weekends and less in summer. You should reserve.

HIKING & MOUNTAIN BIKING

The closest refuges near Athens, located on Mt. Parnitha, are Flambouri (☎ 01/246–4666), run by the **Alpine Club of Aharnon** (✉ Filadelfias 126, Aharnes, 13671, ☎ 01/246–1528, 𝔽𝔸𝕏 01/246–9777), and the Bafi refuge on the same mountain (01/246–9050), run by the **Alpine Club of Athens** (✉ Ermou 54 and Aiolou, 5th floor, Monastiraki, 10531, ☎ 01/321–2355, 𝔽𝔸𝕏 01/324–4789). The country offers plenty of rugged terrain for serious hiking and mountaineering. The **Hellenic Federation of Mountaineering Associations** (✉ Milioni 5, Kolonaki 10673, ☎ 01/364–5904, 𝔽𝔸𝕏 01/364–2687) can supply details on refuges, mountain paths, and contact numbers for local hiking clubs. Both clubs arrange hikes in Attica and throughout the mainland to places like Evritania and Arcadia, as well as adventure camps for children in summer.

Treks throughout Greece are organized by adventure travel agencies, which also offer kayaking, rafting, mountain-biking, and camping trips; try **Trekking Hellas,** in Athens (✉ Fillelinon 7, 3rd floor, Syntagma, 10557, ☎ 01/331–0323 through 01/331–0326, 𝔽𝔸𝕏 01/324–4548) and in Thessaloniki (✉ Tsimiski 71, 54622, ☎ 031/222128, 𝔽𝔸𝕏 031/222129); and **F-Zein** (✉ Syngrou 132, 5th floor, Athens 11741, ☎ 01/921–6285, 𝔽𝔸𝕏 01/922–9995). Walking day trips are usually 7,000 dr./€20.64–15,000 dr./€44.24, which includes a meal; weekends run about 20,000 dr./€59–35,000 dr./€103. Try to book at least a week in advance.

HORSEBACK RIDING

The helpful **Hellenic Equestrian Federation** (✉ Messinias 55, Goudi, Athens 15341, ☎ 01/748–6875 or 01/748–6876, 𝔽𝔸𝕏 01/778–1572) provides a list of riding clubs throughout the country. Hotels that offer horseback riding, often in cooperation with the local club or riding center, include Kanale's, Iria, Astir, and Poseidon on Paros island; Capsis Beach and Sofitel Palace in Crete; Aphrodite Beach and Apollonia Bay in Mykonos; B. W. Zante Park Hotel in Zakynthos; Montana and Anesis in Karpenissi; and Aphrodite's Inn outside of Kalavrita. The price is about 5,000 dr./€14.74 an hour per person.

RAFTING & KAYAKING

Alpin Club (✉ Mihalakopoulou 39, Ilisia, Athens 11528, ☎ 01/721–2773, ☎ 𝔽𝔸𝕏 01/729–5486) organizes trips, including transportation, guides, and equipment, to rivers throughout Greece; the price runs about 32,000 dr./€94.39 for a weekend. Trekking Hellas and F-Zein (☞ Hiking & Mountain Biking, *above*) also offer many white-water expeditions.

ROCK CLIMBING & MOUNTAINEERING

The **Alpine Club of Aharnon** (☞ Hiking & Mountain Biking, *above*) runs rock-climbing seminars throughout Greece, including the monastery-crowned pinnacles of Meteora, as does the equipment shop **Alpamayo Mountain Gear** (✉ Harilaou Trikoupi 6–10 in the Atrium shopping mall, Athens 10679, ☎ 01/362–7032, 𝔽𝔸𝕏 01/363–9215), which also has mountaineering and paragliding classes, and provides mountain guides if necessary.

SAILING & WINDSURFING

The **Hellenic Yachting Federation** (✉ Leoforos Poseidonos 51, Moschato, Athens 18344, ☎ 01/940–4825, FAX 01/940–4829) can provide lists of clubs with equipment and lessons available for both sailing and windsurfing. The best windsurfing beaches in Attica are Schinias, Varkiza, Vouliagmeni, Rafina, Loutsa, and Anavyssos, and in the rest of Greece: Ftelia in Mykonos; Prassonissi in Rhodes; Loutra Kaiafa in the Peloponnese; Mikri Vigla in Naxos; and New Golden Beach in Paros, the site of windsurfing world championships. Those who have a diploma for sailing on the open sea can legally rent a sailboat (without a captain, if two people on board are licensed); rentals range from about 30,000 dr./€88.49 to 210,000 dr./€619 a day, depending on the size and age of the boat and whether a skipper is included. Charter companies usually provide suggested sailing routes. Most have branch offices at designated marinas along each of these routes, and sometimes you can avoid Athens altogether by picking up your boat at these stations. Contact **Ghiolman Yachts** (✉ Fillelinon 7, Syntagma, Athens 10557, ☎ 01/322–8530 or 01/323–0330, FAX 01/322–3251). **Kyriacoulis Mediterranean Cruises** (✉ Leoforos Poseidonos 51, Palio Faliro, Athens 17562, ☎ 01/988–6187 through 01/988–6191, FAX 01/984–7296). They also run a sailing school, Offshore Escape (✉ Palamidiou 14, Alimos, Athens 17455, ☎ FAX 01/985–9780) with 8- and 10-week courses for beginners, as well as a refresher course for licensed sailors. **Sun Yachting** (✉ Leoforos Poseidonos 21, Kalamaki, Athens 17455, ☎ 01/983–7312, FAX 01/983–7528). **Vernicos Yachts** (✉ Leoforos Poseidonos 11, Alimos, Athens 17455, ☎ 01/985–0122 through 01/985–0128, FAX 01/985–0130).

SCUBA DIVING

Greece, according to the recent EU Blue Flag survey, has the cleanest beaches in Europe. With its numerous islands and long coastline, it offers tourists everything from glamorous trendy stretches such as Super Paradise in Mykonos, packed with Bodies Beautiful, to secluded coves like Mikro Seitani in Samos, reached only after an hour's hike. Greeks don't really go swimming until June, but the water is fine usually by May and stays warm through September or even mid-October.

In Athens **EOT outlets** (main info office, ✉ Amerikis 2, Athens, ☎ 01/331–0561 or 01/331–0562) can give you a list of their local beaches, which have snack bars and beach umbrellas, chairs, dressing rooms, and sports equipment for rent, and occasionally windsurfing and waterskiing lessons.

Scuba diving is heavily restricted to protect underwater artifacts. It is forbidden to dive at night or remove anything from the sea floor. Areas where limited diving is permitted include Corfu, Chalkidiki, Mykonos, and Rhodes. A travel agent can steer you to a supervised dive trip, or you can call the **Greek Diving Center** (✉ Vas. Pavlou 26, Kastella, Piraeus 18533, ☎ 01/412–1708, FAX 01/411–9207), which offers lessons up to the instructor's level, rents equipment, and organizes one- to two-day diving excursions on weekends. The **Aegean Dive Center** (✉ Pandoras 42 and Zamanou 53, Glyfada 16674, ☎ 01/894–5409, FAX 01/898–1120) provides equipment rental and service, diver training including first-aid courses, dive trips, and an air center. For those who want an introduction to the sport, **Scuba Diving Club of Vouliagmeni** (✉ Leoforos Poseidonos below Agnadi café-bar, 16671 Ormos Vouliagmeni, ☎ 01/896–4609, FAX 01/896–1914) runs a one-hour orientation for about 15,000 dr./€44.24 called Discover Scuba, where complete beginners can dive with an instructor. The center also provides regular diving courses, equipment, boat rentals with guides for expeditions, and water sports. A 12-day course, leading to the 1* diploma, costs 70,000 dr./€206. Call a day ahead to arrange matters. Remember that any school dispensing diplomas should be recognized by the Greek state.

SKIING & SNOWBOARDING

The **Alpine Club of Athens** (✉ Ermou 64 and Aiolou, 5th floor, Monastiraki, 10531, ☎ 01/321–2355, FAX 01/324–4789) organizes mountain skiing classes for experienced skiers and snowboarding lessons for kids on Parnassos as well.

Ski Center Parnassos (☎ 0234/22689 or 0234/22693 through 0234/22695, FAX 0234/22596) is one of the country's best resorts, about two hours (170 km [105 mi]) north of Athens, near the famous Oracle of Delphi. The more than 20 trails include downhill runs, cross-country, and slalom pistes. Off-piste skiing and ski de tour are permitted. Try to go midweek because the area is jammed on weekends with Athenians who also come for the nightlife in nearby Arachova. The second largest center is **Kalavrita Ski Center** (☎ 0692/22174 or 0692/22661) on Mt. Helmos in the Peloponnese, 214 km (133 mi) from Athens, 100 km (62 mi) from Patras. The center offers about 10 km (6 mi) of piste, and the slope north of the Styga lift is one of the best in Greece, with excellent snow conditions. The **Hellenic Skiing Federation** (✉ Karageorgi Servias 7, 8th floor, Syntagma, Athens 10563, ☎ 01/323–0182 or 01/323–4412, FAX 01/323–0142) only gives information about professional ski competitions, but EOT can give you addresses for ski centers and mountain refuges.

SPELUNKING

Tourists with troglodyte tendencies are welcome to subterranean Greece. So far about 7,500 karstic formations have been recorded and explored; about half of these are on Crete. Thirteen caves have tourist facilities and more are being developed. These include **Paiania** in Attica (☎ 01/664–2108), **Perama** in Ioannina (☎ 0651/81521), **Diros** in the Peloponnese (☎ 0733/52222), and **Petralona** in Halkidiki (☎ 0373/72270), where in 1960 a Neanderthal human skull was found, along with the bones of Pleistocene horses. Admission fees range from 400 dr./€1.17 to 1,200 dr./€3.53. Spelunkers in search of wild caves should contact the **Hellenic Speleological Society** (✉ Manzarou 8, Athens 10672, ☎ 01/361–7824, FAX 01/364–3476).

TENNIS

There are tennis clubs in most large cities and island resorts. Call the **Hellenic Tennis Federation** (✉ Ymittou 267, Pangrati, Athens 11636, ☎ 01/756–3170 through 01/756–3172, FAX 01/756–3173) for information on tennis clubs, from which you can rent courts by the hour (often included on EOT beaches), or check with your hotel concierge to help you find one that admits nonmembers.

PACKING

It's a good idea to itemize the contents of each bag and keep the list, in case you need to file an insurance claim. Be certain to put your home or business address on and inside each piece of luggage, including carry-on bags. It's also a good idea to mark your bags with a bright ribbon, since few Greek airports check passengers' baggage claim checks against luggage upon exit. Only larger airports, such as the East Terminal in Athens's Ellinikon, have free luggage carts; they are to the right of the baggage carrels. Baggage carts are limited at train stations, and nonexistent at bus stations.

Outside Athens, Greek dress tends to be middle of the road—you won't see patched jeans or extremely expensive suits, though locals tend to dress up for nightclubs and bouzoukia. In the summer bring lightweight, casual clothing and good walking shoes. A light sweater or jacket is a must for cool evenings, especially in the mountains. There's no need for rain gear in high summer, but don't forget sunglasses and a sun hat. Be prepared for cooler weather and some rain in spring and fall, and in winter, add a warm coat.

Casual attire is acceptable everywhere except in the most expensive restaurants in large cities, but you should dress conservatively when visiting churches or monasteries. It's not appropriate to show a lot of bare arm and leg; men wearing shorts must cover up as well, as must women in pants, in some stricter monasteries. Monasteries (e.g., in Meteora) and churches do not admit improperly dressed men or women, though they often provide some sort of draping at the entrance. Most beaches are top-less (and legally so), except those near the harbor or town center. The number of beaches where nude bathing is acceptable is slowly growing. Watch to see what others do, and err on the conservative side.

For dimly lighted icons in churches and moonless island walks, a small flashlight comes in handy, as does a jackknife with a corkscrew for picnicking, though they may show up on the airport security scanner and cause you to open your bag. It's a good idea to bring zip-closing plastic bags, mosquito repellent for more verdant areas, moist towelettes, a roll of transparent tape, and a pocket calculator, all indispensable. A pair of opera glasses can greatly enhance the appreciation of an archaeological site or give the tourist a better view of wall paintings in a church, for example.

In your carry-on luggage, **pack an extra pair of eyeglasses or contact lenses** and **enough of any medication you take** to last the entire trip. You may also ask your doctor to write a spare prescription using the drug's generic name, since brand names may vary from country to country. In luggage to be checked, **never pack prescription drugs or valuables.** To avoid customs delays, carry medications in their original packaging. And don't forget to carry with you the addresses of offices that handle refunds of lost traveler's checks.

CHECKING LUGGAGE

How many carry-on bags you can bring with you is up to the airline. Most allow two, but not always, so make sure that everything you carry aboard will fit under your seat or in the overhead bin, and get to the gate early. Note that if you have a seat at the back of the plane, you'll probably board first, while the overhead bins are still empty.

If you are flying internationally, note that baggage allowances may be determined not by piece but by weight—generally 88 pounds (40 kilograms) in first class, 66 pounds (30 kilograms) in business class, and 44 pounds (20 kilograms) in economy.

Airline liability for baggage is limited to $1,250 per person on flights within the United States. On international flights it amounts to $9.07 per pound or $20 per kilogram for checked baggage (roughly $640 per 70-pound bag) and $400 per passenger for unchecked baggage. You can buy additional coverage at check-in for about $10 per $1,000 of coverage, but it excludes a rather extensive list of items, shown on your airline ticket.

Before departure, **itemize your bags' contents** and their worth, and label the bags with your name, address, and phone number. (If you use your home address, cover it so potential thieves can't see it readily.) Inside each bag, **pack a copy of your itinerary.** At check-in, **make sure that each bag is correctly tagged** with the destination airport's three-letter code. If your bags arrive damaged or fail to arrive at all, file a written report with the airline before leaving the airport. Always ask if your luggage is going through to the final destination; sometimes, you have to pick up your bags and haul them through Customs depending on where your plane stops (i.e., returning from Athens, you might have to get your luggage at the baggage claim in Chicago and clear Customs because it's your first U.S. point of entry, then get back on the plane for L.A.).

PASSPORTS & VISAS

When traveling internationally, **carry your passport** even if you don't need one (it's always the best form of I.D.) and **make two photocopies of the data page** (one for someone at home and another for you, carried separately from your passport). If you lose your passport, promptly call the nearest embassy or consulate and the local police.

ENTERING GREECE

All U.S., Canadian, Australian, and New Zealand citizens, even infants, need only a valid passport to enter Greece for stays of up to 90 days. If you leave after 90 days and don't have a visa extension, you will be fined (about 30,000 dr.€88.49) by Greek airport officials, who are not flexible on this issue. Worse, you must provide *hartosima* (revenue stamps) for the documents, which you don't want to have to run around and find as your flight is boarding. U.K. citizens, like all EU nationals, need a passport but can stay indefinitely.

PASSPORT OFFICES

The best time to apply for a passport or to renew is during the fall and winter. Before any trip, be sure to check your passport's expiration date and, if necessary, renew it as soon as possible. (Some countries won't allow you to enter on a passport that's due to expire in six months or less, but this doesn't seem to be a problem in Greece.)

➤ AUSTRALIAN CITIZENS: **Australian Passport Office** (☎ 131–232, www.dfat.gov.au/passports).

➤ CANADIAN CITIZENS: **Passport Office** (☎ 819/994–3500; 800/567–6868 in Canada, www.dfait-maeci.gc.ca/passport).

➤ NEW ZEALAND CITIZENS: **New Zealand Passport Office** (☎ 04/494–0700, www.passports.govt.nz).

➤ U.K. CITIZENS: **London Passport Office** (☎ 0870/521–0410, www.ukpa.gov.uk) for fees and documentation requirements and to request an emergency passport.

➤ U.S. CITIZENS: **National Passport Information Center** (☎ 900/225–5674; calls are 35¢ per min for automated service, $1.05 per min for operator service; www.travel.state. gov/npicinfo.html).

REST ROOMS

In Greece, be prepared to find everything from a ceramic hole in the floor at a public school to gleaming Italian fixtures in a nightclub. Bathrooms are getting better and are downright luxurious in some nicer hotels, restaurants, and bars. But the standard of cleanliness and the state of repair varies tremendously, and there's no rhyme or reason to what you'll find. Out in the country, as a rule, the bathrooms tend to be worse, though you never know—some mom 'n' pop ouzeri might have immaculate facilities while those at the medical clinic are unspeakably grungy. The usually subterranean public toilets, such as those in parks and on main squares,

are dirty, so go to a restaurant, hotel, or bar. In bus and train stations, attendants hand you a few sheets of toilet paper; leave 100 dr./€.29 on their plate (☞ Tipping, *below*). You can walk into any large establishment, use their bathroom, and leave, especially if you are discreet. Always carry extra toilet paper, because many places don't provide any or it runs out early. Gas stations don't have rest rooms for the public, but on the highways there are restaurant-convenience stores where you can stop. You are expected to buy a snack or souvenir, but again, it's not necessary.

SAFETY

Greece is still one of the safest countries in Europe. Even Athens has a low crime rate, but the number of thefts, burglaries, and pickpocketing at train and bus stations has gone up substantially in the last five years, and Greeks are starting to install alarms and lock their doors at night. You still see people sitting at cafés with their handbag carelessly dangling over chairs, or women and elderly people walking home late at night. If you take the normal precautions of carrying your money in a security pouch, and if you avoid isolated places at night, you should have little problem. After hours, many ATMs require that you use your card to enter a locked glass vestibule; if the machine is unprotected, make sure it's well-lighted and leave immediately if someone suspicious starts lurking about. So far, ATM robberies are rare. If you feel unsure about the safety of an area, ask your hotel before setting out. For example, in the last few years, crime has gone up around Omonia Square in Athens, because of the large transient population that congregates there.

LOCAL SCAMS

Men in Athens around Syntagma Square should be careful of any stranger that tries to talk them into going to a local bar. Here, the unsuspecting foreigner will order drinks under the encouragement of hostesses hired by the establishment without realizing these cocktails are astronomically expensive. Hesitation in paying your whopping bill may result in uncomfortable encounters. Grab a policeman or call the tourist police (☎ 171).

WOMEN IN GREECE

In general, women traveling alone are safe in Greece, though Greek men will try to talk to them, especially if they look foreign. It's best to do as the Greek women do, and ignore the amorous overtures; responding will only be interpreted as a sign that you're interested. If you feel threatened, don't hesitate to shout; this will be enough to scare off most offenders. Greeks, especially in Athens, where people are out until all hours, will usually come to your aid. One way to avoid unwanted advances is to try to blend in with the Greeks: dress as they do (try carrying a plastic Greek supermarket bag), walk like you know where you're going, and don't openly carry a map or a foreign newspaper. If you are taking a taxi at night, the driver won't usually pick up a male passenger; if he does, he is obligated to ask your permission.

SENIOR-CITIZEN TRAVEL

Despite the dearth of facilities at hotels, museums, and archaeological sites for those with impaired movement, traveling in Greece can be quite pleasurable. Elders are treated with respect: most Greeks still take care of their parents at home, and crimes against the elderly are infrequent. Most people—even taxi drivers—go out of their way to make sure senior citizens receive good treatment.

To qualify for age-related discounts, **mention your senior-citizen status up front** when purchasing tickets— whether to enter a pay beach, see a movie, or visit an archaeological site. Greece does not have senior discounts for hotels or restaurants, but does for just about everything else, including admission fees and public transportation. When renting a car, **ask about promotional car-rental discounts,** which can be cheaper than senior-citizen rates.

➤ EDUCATIONAL PROGRAMS: **Elderhostel** (✉ 75 Federal St., 3rd floor, Boston, MA 02110, ☎ 877/426–8056, FAX 877/426–2166, www.elderhostel.org). **Interhostel** (✉ University of New Hampshire, 6 Garrison Ave., Durham, NH 03824, ☎ 603/862–1147 or 800/733–9753, FAX 603/862–1113, learn.dce@unh.edu, www.learn.unh.edu).

SHOPPING

Because of hefty VAT taxes, most items in Greece, especially electric appliances and clothing, cost more than in the U.S. and Canada, though Greece does have inexpensive shoes, furs, and leather goods. Good gift ideas are the natural Kalymnos sponges; flokati rugs made from long-haired goat wool; handicrafts such as embroidery, ceramics, and kilims; fisherman's caps and hand-knit sweaters; *koboloi* (worry beads) in plastic, wood, and onyx; and blue-and-white amulets that protect against *mati* (the evil eye). What is cheaper in Greece is silver and gold jewelry, often original and unusual pieces. In some stores, chains are sold by the gram. Always bargain in tourist shops and with street vendors (except for sponges—prices are set by the government), and always get a receipt from shops. In an attempt to diminish tax fraud, the government heavily fines buyers who walk out of a store without proof of purchase. Most stores do not give you a cash refund, but they may give you a credit slip; they are liable if the item you purchased is defective. Pay attention when buying bargain items, since stores rarely allow exchanges or grant refunds during sales. Traditional sale periods run for about a month in February and August, though shop owners have extended these periods recently to bolster flagging sales.

KEY DESTINATIONS

A delightful institution in Greece is the *laiki* (open-air market), which offers fresh produce at prices lower than in produce stores, as well as items sold by political and economic refugees, such as linen tablecloths (sold by the meter), caviar, and Russian lacquered dolls. Every town has a laiki, and big cities like Athens have several a day in different neighborhoods. In Athens, the main shopping areas are the Ermou pedestrian zone near Syntagma, entertaining on Saturday mornings, Patission street north of the National Archaeological Museum, and the ritzy Kolonaki district near the center. Plaka has mostly tourist shops, but their jewelers will go quite low on gold and silver prices. For icons, try the side streets around the Metropolitan Cathedral. In Thessaloniki, the longest shopping street is Tsimiski, and on the islands, shops are usually clustered off the main square and near the harbor.

WATCH OUT

Note that the export of antiquities from Greece is forbidden. If any such articles are found in a traveler's luggage, they will be confiscated and the individual will be liable for prosecution. You are required to have an export permit (not normally given if the piece is of any value) for antiques and Byzantine icons, but replicas can be bought fairly cheaply, although even these require a certificate stating they are copies.

SIGHTSEEING GUIDES

Many travel agencies or the national guides union can provide guides for individuals or groups, starting at about 28,000 dr./€82.59 including taxes for a four-hour tour of the Acropolis and its museum. Only hire guides licensed by EOT, which means they have successfully completed a two-year state program. The best guides are snatched up by travel agencies for their longer tours, so in general, those who freelance in high season at sights like the Acropolis and the National Archaeological Museum may be competent but are not of the same caliber. In any case, talk to the guide a bit to see how articulate they are in English. Do they have interesting details to bestow or just a bunch of measurements? Do they recite in a monotone or enthusiastically give you all the juicy details of Zeus's peccadillos? Trust your instincts and agree on the price and length of the tour beforehand.

➤ HIRING GUIDES: **Union of Official Guides** (✉ Apollonas 9A, Athens, ☎ 01/322–9705, ℻ 01/323–9200).

STUDENTS IN GREECE

For students, Greece is an inexpensive destination. Not only are museums and archaeological sites free for EU members and cheaper for non-EU students (you must have an ISIC card), but student and youth rates are offered on public transportation as well as domestic and EU flights. Many travel agencies catering to students are on Fillelinon and Nikis streets in Athens, off Syntagma Square.

Rented rooms and camping are the most inexpensive lodging—in summer, you can rent roof space if you've brought a sleeping bag. Take advantage of souvlaki stands (the filling fast food of Greece), local tavernas, and the open-air market; convenience stores in tourist areas are wildly overpriced. Finally, watch expenditures in bars—in most, an alcoholic drink costs at least 1,800 dr./€5.30.

TRAVEL AGENCIES

To save money, **look into deals available through student-oriented travel agencies.** To qualify you'll need a bona fide student I.D. card. Members of international student groups are also eligible.

➤ IN GREECE: A good agency to try, especially if you haven't managed to get your ISIC card and need a student pass for Greece, is **International Student and Youth Travel Service** (✉ Nikis 11, 1st floor, Athens 10557, ☎ 01/323–3767 or 01/322–1267, ℻ 01/322–1531); **USIT/ETOS Student and Youth Travel** (✉ Fillelinon 3, Athens 10557, ☎ 01/321–9811 through 01/321–9813, ℻ 01/322–5974) can help with the ISIC card and the International Youth Travel Card (IYTC).

➤ I.D.s & SERVICES: **Council Travel** (CIEE; ✉ 205 E. 42nd St., 14th floor, New York, NY 10017, ☎ 212/822–2700 or 888/268–6245, ℻ 212/822–2699, info@councilexchanges.org, www.councilexchanges.org) for mail orders only, in the U.S. **Travel Cuts** (✉ 187 College St., Toronto, Ontario M5T 1P7, Canada, ☎ 416/979–2406 or 800/667–2887 in Canada, www.travelcuts.com).

➤ STUDENT TOURS: **Contiki Holidays** (✉ 300 Plaza Alicante, Suite 900, Garden Grove, CA 92840, ☎ 714/740–0808 or 800/266–8454, ℻ 714/740–2034). **AESU Travel** (✉ 2 Hamill Rd., Suite 248, Baltimore,

MD 21210-1807, ☎ 410/323–4416
or 800/638–7640, ℻ 410/323–4498).

TAXES

Taxes are always included in the
stated price, unless otherwise noted.
The Greek airport tax (3,400 dr./€10
each way on all flights) is included in
your ticket, and the 10.6% hotel tax
rate is usually included in the quoted
price.

VALUE-ADDED TAX

Value-added tax, 4% for books and
about 18% for almost everything else,
called FPA (pronounced fee-pee-ah)
by Greeks, is included in the cost of
most consumer goods and services,
except groceries. If you are a citizen
of a non-EU country, you may get a
VAT refund on products worth
40,000 dr./€118 or more bought in
Greece from licensed stores that
usually display a Tax-Free Shopping
sticker in their window. Ask the shop
to complete a refund form called a
Tax-Free check for you, which you
show at Greek Customs, along with
the item to prove you are taking it out
of the country. If you're leaving
Greece late at night, the Customs
desk is immediately after the X-ray
machine in the East Terminal; just call
from the desk phone available and
someone will appear. Customs—at
the airport or port—will stamp the
paper, which you can then mail back
to the shop from the airport. You
should have arranged the method of
repayment with the shop; it can take
up to a year to see your money.

Global Refund is a VAT refund service
that makes getting your money back
hassle-free. The service is available
Europe-wide at 130,000 affiliated
stores. In participating stores, **ask for
the Global Refund refund form** (called
a Shopping Cheque). Have it stamped
like any customs form by customs
officials when you leave the European
Union (be ready to show customs
officials what you've bought). Then
take the form to one of the more than
700 Global Refund counters—conveniently located at every major airport
and border crossing—and your money
will be refunded on the spot in the
form of cash, check, or a refund to
your credit-card account (minus a
small percentage for processing).

➤ V.A.T. REFUNDS: **Global Refund**
(✉ 707 Summer St., Stamford, CT
06901, ☎ 800/566–9828, ℻ 203/
674–8709, taxfree@us.globalrefund.
com, www.globalrefund.com).

TAXIS

In Greece, as everywhere, unscrupulous taxi drivers try to take advantage
of out-of-towners, using such tricks as
rigged meters or tacking on a few
zeros to the metered price. All taxis
must display the rate card; it's usually
on the dashboard, though taxis
outside the big cities don't bother.
Rather than memorize all the allow-
able surcharges, you might ask your
hotel concierge or owner before
engaging a taxi what the fare to your
destination ought to be. You are more
likely to be overcharged in Athens
than elsewhere, especially when
traveling from the airport. It should
cost no more than 2,200/€6.48–
2,700 dr./€7.96 from the airport
(depending on the terminal and the
traffic) to the city center, 2,200 from
Piraeus port to the center. It does not
matter how many are in your party
(the driver isn't supposed to squeeze
in more than four); the metered price
remains the same. Make sure that the
driver turns on the meter to Tarifa 1,
unless it's between midnight and 5
AM, when the price goes up. Remember that the minimum is 500
dr./€1.47. An extra 300 dr./€.88 is
expected when taking a taxi to and
from the airport and 150 dr./€.44
from (but not to) ports and bus and
train stations. There is also a surcharge during holiday periods, about
120 dr./€.35. Each item of baggage is
likewise charged (50 dr./€.14), although drivers expect 100 dr./€.29. If
you suspect a driver is overcharging,
demand to be taken to the police
station; this usually brings them
around. Complaints about service or
overcharging should be directed to
the tourist police (☎ 171 in Athens);
at the Athens airport, contact the
Airport Traffic Police (☎ 01/969–
4214 or 01/964–7753). When calling
to complain, be sure to report the
driver's license number.

Taxi rates are inexpensive compared
to fares in most other European
countries, mainly because they operate
unofficially on the jitney system,

indicating willingness to pick up others by blinking their headlights or simply slowing down. Would-be passengers shout their destination as the driver cruises past. Don't be alarmed if your driver picks up other passengers (although protocol indicates he should ask your permission first). Drivers don't pick up anyone if you are a woman traveling alone at night. Each new party pays full fare for the distance he or she has traveled.

A taxi is free when his sign (ELEFT-HERO) is up or his light is on at night. Once he indicates he is free, the driver cannot refuse your destination, so get in the taxi before you give an address. He also must wait for you up to 15 minutes, if requested, although most drivers would be unhappy with such a demand. Drivers are familiar with the major hotels, but it's a good idea to know a landmark near your hotel and to have the address and phone written in Greek. If all else fails, the driver can call the hotel from his mobile phone or a kiosk.

On islands and in the countryside, the meter may often be on Tarifa 2 (outside city limits). Do not assume taxis will be waiting at smaller island airports when your flight lands; often, they have all been booked by arriving locals. If you get stuck, try to join a passenger going in your direction, or call your hotel to arrange transportation.

When you're taking an early morning flight, it's a good idea to reserve a radio taxi the night before (600 dr./€1.76–1,000 dr./€2.94 surcharge, 400 dr./€1.17 for immediate response). They are usually quite reliable and punctual; if you're not staying in a hotel, the local tourist police can give you some phone numbers for companies.

TELEPHONES

Greece's phone system is rapidly improving; many phones now are digital, which makes dialing a cinch compared to the old days when you had to try 10 times for one number. You can direct dial in most better hotels, but there is usually a huge surcharge, so either use your calling card or a card telephone in the lobby or on the street (☞ International

Calls and Local Calls, *below*). You can make calls from most large establishments (card or coin phones), kiosks, card phones, which are everywhere, and from the local office of the Greek telephone company, known as OTE (oh-*tay*).

Throughout this guide, establishments may include several phone numbers rather than a central switchboard. Until recently, getting a second phone line was an expensive and lengthy process (some areas had to wait up to 10 years), so owners may "rent" lines directly from other people. Also, they now use mobile phones, indicated by an area code that begins with 09. Less than a decade after the cellular phone came to Greece, the number of users has skyrocketed to 3.9 million (just 5.4 million own conventional phones). By the end of 2000, 50% of Greeks were expected to own a mobile phone (the European average is 37.8%).

Doing business over the phone in Greece can be extremely frustrating—the lines always seem to be busy, and English-speaking operators and clerks are few. You may also find people too busy to address your problem—the independent-minded Greeks are not very service-conscious. It is far better to develop a relationship with someone, for example a travel agent, to get information about train schedules and the like, or to go in person and ask for information face-to-face. Though OTE is updating its phone system, it may take you several attempts to get through when calling from an island or the countryside. Try dialing slowly, and if you get a wrong number, don't assume it's your mistake—the lines frequently get crossed. Don't discuss highly sensitive matters on the phone; party lines are still a social hazard in Greece.

AREA & COUNTRY CODES

The country code for Greece is 30. When dialing Greece from the U.S. or Canada, you would first dial 011, then 30 (011–30). From continental Europe or the U.K. you just dial 0030. Each region in Greece has several area codes (01 for Athens, 031 for Thessaloniki, 061 for Patras). When dialing from outside Greece, you drop the "0" in the area code;

within Greece you must include the
"0." So, for example, if you dial
Athens from New York, you direct
dial: 011-30-1-XXX-XXXX, but
from Thessaloniki, you would have to
dial 01-XXX-XXXX.

To call the U.S. or Canada from
Greece, you dial 001 as the country
code, and then the area code and
number (New York would be 001-
212-556-XXXX). The country code
for the U.K. is 0044, for Australia
0061, and for New Zealand 0064.

DIRECTORY & OPERATOR ASSISTANCE

For Greek directory information, dial
131; many of the operators speak
English. You usually must give the
surname of the shop or restaurant
proprietor to be able to get the phone
number; tourist police are more
helpful for tracking down the numbers of such establishments. For
operator-assisted calls and international directory information in English, dial the International Exchange
at ☎ 161. In most cases, there is a
three-minute minimum charge for
operator-assisted station-to-station
and person-to-person connections.

Pronunciations for the numbers in
Greek are: one (*eh*-na); two (*dthee*-
oh); three (*tree*-a); four (*tess*-ehr-a);
five (*pen*-de); six (*eh*-ksee); seven (ef-
ta); eight (och-*toh*); nine (eh-*nay*-ah);
ten (*dtheh*-ka).

LOCAL CALLS

Local numbers have seven digits in
Athens, six in Thessaloniki and
Patras, and five in the rest of the
country. At kiosks, you either use a
100 dr. coin in the machine or pay the
kiosk owner (about 20 dr./€.05 for a
short call). There are also a few coin
phones in bars and restaurants; wait
until your party answers, before you
drop in the coin. You can also make
local calls from card phones (☞
Public Phones, *below*). The dial ring
will be familiar to English speakers:
two beats, the second much longer
than the first. The price decreases
50% for local calls from Sunday 10
PM through Monday 8 AM.

LONG-DISTANCE SERVICES

AT&T, MCI, and Sprint international
access codes make calling the United

States relatively convenient, but you
may find the local access number
blocked in many hotel rooms. First
ask the hotel operator to connect you.
If the hotel operator balks, ask for an
international operator, or dial the
international operator yourself. One
way to improve your odds of getting
connected to your long-distance
carrier is to travel with more than one
company's calling card (a hotel may
block Sprint, for example, but not
MCI). If all else fails, call from a pay
phone in the hotel lobby. You can
also make international cards from
card telephones or metered kiosk
phones (☞ Public Phones, *below*).
For OTE lines, the price drops about
50% for long-distance calls daily
from 10 PM until 8 AM.

➤ LONG-DISTANCE CARRIERS: **AT&T**
(☎ 800/225–5288). **MCI** (☎ 800/
888–8000). **Sprint** (☎ 800/366–
2255).

➤ ACCESS CODES: **AT&T Direct**
(☎ 00/800–1311; 800/435–0812 for
other areas). **MCI WorldPhone**
(☎ 00/800–1211; 800/444–4141 for
other areas). **Sprint International
Access** (☎ 00/800–1411; 800/877–
4646 for other areas).

PUBLIC PHONES

OTE has card phones virtually everywhere, though some may not be in
working order. Phone cards with 100
units (1,000 dr./€2.94) or 500 units
(4,500 dr./€13.27) can be purchased
at kiosks, convenience stores, or the
local OTE office. If you want more
privacy—the card phones tend to be
on busy street corners and people
waiting to make their own calls may
try to hurry you—use a card phone in
a hotel lobby or OTE offices, though
these tend to have limited hours. You
can also use a kiosk phone. If you
don't get a dial tone at first, you
should ask the kiosk owner to set the
meter to zero (Boreéte na to
meetheneéste?). Try to avoid making
calls from your hotel, where the
surcharge can be quite hefty.

TIME

Greek time is Greenwich Mean Time
(GMT) plus 2 hours. To estimate the
time back home, subtract 7 hours
from the local time for New York and

Washington, 8 hours for Chicago, 9 for Denver, and 10 for Los Angeles. Londoners subtract 2 hours. Those living in Sydney or Melbourne, add 8 hours. Greek Daylight Savings Time starts on the last Sunday in March and ends the last Sunday in October, different from the U.S. for one week a year when you may need to add or subtract an extra hour. Stay alert—newspapers barely publicize the change.

TIPPING

How much to tip in Greece, especially at restaurants, is confusing. By law a service charge is figured into the price of a meal (menus sometimes list entrées with and without service, to let you know their net cost—not to imply you have a choice of how much to pay). However, it is customary to leave an 8%–10% tip if the service was satisfactory. During the Christmas and Greek Easter holiday periods, restaurants tack on an obligatory 18% holiday bonus to your bill for the waiters.

The appropriate tip for maid service at your hotel depends on the quality of the service, the length of your stay, and the quality of the hotel. A service charge is included in the price of the room, but you might consider in $$$–$$$$ hotels leaving an additional 200 dr./€.58 per night. Porters, found only at the more expensive hotels, should get 200 dr./€.58 per bag; room-service waiters merit 100 dr./€.29 per delivery. If a concierge has been very helpful, you can leave from 1,000 dr./€2.94 to 5,000 dr./€14.74. For rest-room attendants 100 dr./€.29 is appropriate. People dispensing programs at cinemas also get 100 dr./€.29. On cruises, cabin and dining-room stewards get about 600 dr./€1.76 a day; guides receive about the same. For taxis, round up the fare to the nearest 100 dr./€.29; during holidays, drivers legally receive a mandatory "gift"; the amount is posted in the cab during applicable days.

TOURS & PACKAGES

Because everything is prearranged on a prepackaged tour or independent vacation, you'll spend less time planning—and often get it all at a good price.

Operators that handle several hundred thousand travelers per year can use their purchasing power to give you a good price. Their high volume may also indicate financial stability. But some small companies provide more personalized service; because they tend to specialize, they may also be more knowledgeable about a given area.

BOOKING WITH AN AGENT

Travel agents are excellent resources. But it's a good idea to collect brochures from several agencies as some agents' suggestions may be influenced by relationships with tour and package firms that reward them for volume sales. If you have a special interest, **find an agent with expertise in that area**; ASTA (☞ Travel Agencies, *below*) has a database of specialists worldwide.

Make sure your travel agent knows the accommodations and other services of the place they're recommending. Ask about the hotel's location, room size, beds, and whether it has a pool, room service, or programs for children, if you care about these. Has your agent been there in person or sent others whom you can contact?

Do some homework on your own, too: local tourism boards can provide information about lesser-known and small-niche operators, some of which may sell only direct.

BUYER BEWARE

Each year consumers are stranded or lose their money when tour operators—even large ones with excellent reputations—go out of business. So **check out the operator.** Ask several travel agents about its reputation, and try to **book with a company that has a consumer-protection program.** (Look for information in the company's brochure.) In the United States, members of the National Tour Association and the United States Tour Operators Association are required to set aside funds to cover your payments and travel arrangements in the event that the company defaults. It's also a good idea to choose a company that participates in the American Society of Travel

Agents' Tour Operator Program (TOP); ASTA will act as mediator in any disputes between you and your tour operator.

Remember that the more your package or tour includes the better you can predict the ultimate cost of your vacation. Make sure you know exactly what is covered, and **beware of hidden costs.** Are taxes, tips, and transfers included? Entertainment and excursions? These can add up.

➤ TOUR-OPERATOR RECOMMENDATIONS: **American Society of Travel Agents** (☞ Travel Agencies, *below*). **National Tour Association** (NTA; ✉ 546 E. Main St., Lexington, KY 40508, ☎ 859/226–4444 or 800/ 682–8886, www.ntaonline.com). **United States Tour Operators Association** (USTOA; ✉ 342 Madison Ave., Suite 1522, New York, NY 10173, ☎ 212/599–6599 or 800/468–7862, FAX 212/599–6744, ustoa@aol.com, www.ustoa.com).

TRAIN TRAVEL

Fares are reasonable, and trains offer a good, though slow, alternative to long drives or bus rides. One of the most impressive stretches is the rack-and-pinion line between Kalavrita and Diakofto, which travels up a pine-crested gorge in the Peloponnese mountains. In fact, the leisurely Peloponnesian train is one of the more pleasant ways to see southern Greece. **IC express service** from Athens to Thessaloniki is fast and reliable. The IC costs 8,250 dr./€24.33 (4,100 dr./€12.09 for a regular train) but cuts the time by 70 minutes to about six hours. The Athens–Patras IC train (3.5 hours) costs 2,980 dr./€8.79 (compared to 1,580 dr./€4.66 and about 4 hours for a regular train). If you order your IC tickets no later than three days in advance, you can have them delivered to you in Athens by courier for a small fee (☎ 01/529–7313, ◷ Mon.– Sat. 8–2:30).

The main line running north from Athens divides into three lines at Thessaloniki, continuing on to Skopje and Belgrade; the Turkish border and Istanbul; and Sofia, Bucharest, and Budapest. The Peloponnese in the south is served by a narrow-gauge line dividing at Corinth into the Tripolis–Kalamata and Patras–Kalamata routes. Some sample fares: Athens–Corinth, 780 dr./€2.30, Athens–Nafplion, 1,400 dr.€4.12, Athens–Volos, 3,120 dr./€9.20. Any ticket issued on the train costs 50% more.

The Greek Railway Organization (OSE) has two stations in Athens, side by side, off Diliyianni Street west of Omonia Square. Trains from northern Greece and abroad use **Stathmos Larissis** (☎ 01/529–8837). Take Trolley 1 from the terminal to Omonia Square or the Metro to Omonia and Syntagma squares. Trains from the Peloponnese use **Stathmos Peloponnisou** (☎ 01/529–8735) next door. To Omonia and Syntagma squares, take Bus 057 or the Metro. Both stations have left-luggage service and snack bar. Since the phones at the stations are inevitably busy, it's best to call the general information switchboard for timetables and prices (☎ 01/529–7777); it's open daily 7 AM–9 PM. **OSE buses** for Albania, Bulgaria, and Turkey also leave from the Peloponnese station.

CLASSES

On any train, it is best during high season or for long distances to travel first class, with a reserved seat, as the difference between the first- and second-class coaches can be vast: the wagons are cleaner, the seats wider and plusher, and most important, the cars are emptier. Without a reservation, in second class you sometimes end up standing among the baggage. The assigned seating of first class (*proti thesi*) is a good idea in July and August, for example, when the Patras–Athens leg is packed with tourists arriving from Italy. First-class costs about 20% more than second-class (*thefteri thesi*).

➤ INFORMATION: Contact the **Greek Railway Organization** (OSE) at your local station, or visit their main offices in Athens (✉ Karolou St. 1 near Omonia Sq., ☎ 01/529–7006 or 01/529–7007; ✉ Sina St. 6, ☎ 01/ 529–8910; ✉ Filellinon St. 17 near Syntagma Sq., ☎ 01/323–6747). The best, most efficient contact is OSE's general information switchboard for timetables and prices (☎ 01/529–7777), open daily 7 AM–9 PM. You may also call 145 for a recorded departure timetable, in Greek, of trains within Greece; call 147 for information on trains to Europe.

CUTTING COSTS

To save money, **look into rail passes.** But be aware that if you don't plan to cover many miles you may come out ahead by buying individual tickets.

Greece is one of 17 countries in which you can **use Eurailpasses,** which provide unlimited first-class rail travel, in all of the participating countries, for the duration of the pass. If you plan to rack up the miles in several countries, get a standard pass. These are available for 15 days ($538), 21 days ($698), one month ($864), two months ($1,224), and three months ($1,512).

If Greece is your only destination in Europe, **consider purchasing a Greece Flexipass Rail 'n Fly.** For $202 you get three days of first-class rail travel within a one-month period and two selected Olympic Airways flights, with an option to buy more flights at reduced rates.

If you're planning to make the Athens–Thessaloniki trip several times, buy an **Intercity 6+1,** which gives you seven trips for the price of six ($163 first class), and a discount on the next card when you return the old one. You can combine this with a **Rail 'n Drive** package offered by Hertz (☞ Major Agencies in Car Rental, *above*). They will have a rental car waiting for you at any of the IC stations—Athens, Larissa, Thessaloniki, Volos—at lower prices.

The **Balkan Flexipass** covers first- and second-class train travel through Greece as well as Bulgaria, Romania, FYROM, Turkey, and Yugoslavia (including Serbia and Montenegro); there are passes for 5, 10, or 15 travel days in a one-month period for about $129, $224, and $269, respectively (first-class). Youths pay about 50% less, seniors over 60, 25% less. The pass is also good for some hotel and sightseeing discounts in Greece, Romania, and Yugoslavia.

In addition to standard Eurailpasses, **ask about special rail-pass plans.** Among these are the Eurail Youthpass (for those under age 26), the Eurail Saverpass (which gives a discount for two or more people traveling together), a Eurail Flexipass (which allows a certain number of travel days within a set period), the Euraildrive Pass and the Europass Drive (which combines travel by train and rental car). Whichever pass you choose, remember that you must **purchase your pass before you leave** for Europe.

Many travelers assume that rail passes guarantee them seats on the trains they wish to ride. Not so. You need to **book seats ahead even if you are using a rail pass;** seat reservations are required on some European trains, particularly high-speed trains, and are a good idea on trains that may be crowded—particularly in summer on popular routes. You also need a reservation if you purchase sleeping accommodations. On high-speed (IC) trains, you pay a surcharge.

➤ INFORMATION AND PASSES: **Rail Europe** (✉ 500 Mamaroneck Ave., Harrison, NY 10528, ☎ 914/682–5172 or 800/438–7245, FAX 800/432–1329; or ✉ 2087 Dundas E, Suite 106, Mississauga, Ontario L4X 1M2, ☎ 800/361–7245, FAX 905/602–4198). **DER Travel Services** (✉ 9501 W. Devon Ave., Rosemont, IL 60018, ☎ 800/782–2424, FAX 800/282–7474 for information; 800/860–9944 for brochures). **CIT Tours Corp.** (✉ 15 W. 44th St., 10th floor, New York, NY 10036, ☎ 212/730–2400; 800/248–7245 in the U.S.; 800/361–7799 in Canada).

FARES & SCHEDULES

You can get train schedules and fares from EOT and from Greek Railway offices (☞ Information, *above* in Train Travel). The **Thomas Cook European Timetable** is essential. It is available in U.S. from Forsyth Travel Library (✉ Box 2975, Shawnee Mission, KS 66201-1375, ☎ 800/307–7984) and in the United Kingdom from Thomas Cook, Timetable Publishing Office (✉ Box 36, Thorpe Wood, Peterborough, Cambridgeshire PE3 6SB).

FROM THE U.K.

There are two main routes to Greece by train from the United Kingdom: the overland route via Munich, Salzburg, Ljubljana, and Zagreb (about three days), or the more pleasant ride through Italy, then by ferry from Brindisi to Patras in the Peloponnese. In high summer, catch the train from London's Victoria Station to Dover for the crossing to Calais and the connecting service to Paris's Gare du Nord. dFrom there, transfer to the Gare de Lyon for the train that runs via Switzerland to Milan. Switch there and travel through to Brindisi Maritime station, where you connect with the ferry to Patras (about 17 hours), and arrive the following day. From Patras there is bus and train service to Athens (total time London–Athens, 2½ days). Given the numerous and inexpensive deals available from summer, and taking into account food costs, it might be cheaper to fly from London.

TRANSPORTATION AROUND
GREECE

Try to avoid driving in Greece. In big cities, it's easier and cheaper to take taxis, especially for couples or families. Urban public transportation is also a good alternative, inexpensive, frequent, and operating until at least midnight. To travel throughout Greece's mainland, rely on KTEL buses, which operate an extensive network to even the most remote villages. Trains have fewer stops, are slower (except for the ICs between Athens and Patras or Athens and Thessaloniki), but are slightly cheaper. To get to an island, the ferry is usually the best bet, if the journey is six hours or less. Those pressed for time can take the much more expensive hydrofoils to nearby islands or fly, usually with Olympic, which may mean delays and cancellations. However, a 45-minute flight to Santorini beats the arduous ferry trip (10 to 12 hours), especially in summer around August 15, when every cranny of the decks is jammed with vacationing Greeks. If you do take a long ferry trip, try to book a cabin. For most islands, it's liberating to rent a motorbike for long-distance sightseeing not tied to bus schedules, but be extremely cautious and drive defensively.

TRAVEL AGENCIES

A good travel agent puts your needs first. Look for an agency that has been in business at least five years, emphasizes customer service, and has someone on staff who specializes in your destination. In addition, **make sure the agency belongs to a professional trade organization.** The American Society of Travel Agents (ASTA), with 27,000 agents in some 170 countries, is the largest and most influential in the field. Operating under the motto "Integrity in Travel," it maintains and enforces a strict code of ethics and will step in to help mediate any agent-client disputes if necessary. ASTA also maintains a Web site that includes a directory of agents. (If a travel agency is also acting as your tour operator, *see* Buyer Beware *in* Tours & Packages, *above*.)

➤ LOCAL AGENT REFERRALS: American Society of Travel Agents (ASTA; ☎ 800/965–2782 24-hr hot line, FAX 703/684–8319, www.astanet.com). Association of British Travel Agents (✉ 68–71 Newman St., London W1P 4AH, U.K., ☎ 020/7637–2444, FAX 020/7637–0713, information@abta.co.uk, www.abtanet.com). Association of Canadian Travel Agents (✉ 1729 Bank St., Suite 201, Ottawa, Ontario K1V 7Z5, Canada, ☎ 613/237–3657, FAX 613/521–0805, acta.ntl@sympatico.ca). Australian Federation of Travel Agents (✉ Level 3, 309 Pitt St., Sydney 2000, Australia, ☎ 02/9264–3299, FAX 02/9264–1085, www.afta.com.au). Travel Agents' Association of New Zealand (✉ Box 1888, Wellington 10033, New Zealand, ☎ 04/499–0104, FAX 04/499–0827, taanz@tiasnet.co.nz).

VISITOR INFORMATION

Tourist police, stationed near the most popular tourist sites, can answer questions in English about transportation, steer you to an open pharmacy or doctor, and locate phone numbers of hotels, rooms, and restaurants. Also helpful are the **municipal tourism offices.** Finally, you can contact the **Greek National Tourist**

Organization (GNTO, but known as EOT in Greece), which has offices throughout the world.

➤ EOT IN GREECE: EOT main office, near Syntagma Square (✉ Amerikis 2, ☎ 01/331–0565, 01/331–0561, or 01/ 331–0562). There are also information booths at the Athens airport (✉ East Terminal [Arrivals], ☎ 01/961– 2722 or 01/969–4500), and the Zea Marina, near where the hydrofoils dock (✉ EOT Building, 1st floor, Zea Marina, ☎ 01/452–2591 or 01/452– 2586). In Thessaloniki, the EOT runs offices in the city center (✉ Mitropoleos 34 on Platia Aristotelous, ☎ 031/222935 or 031/271888) and the airport (☎ 031/471170). In Patras (✉ Filopimenos 26, ☎ 061/620353). To locate the EOT office nearest nearest your destination, check with your country's EOT representative.

➤ GREEK NATIONAL TOURIST ORGANI-ZATION: In the U.S. (✉ 645 5th Ave., New York, NY 10022, ☎ 212/421– 5777, FAX 212/826–6940; ✉ 611 W. 6th St., Suite 2198, Los Angeles, CA 90017, ☎ 213/626–6696, FAX 213/ 489–9744; ✉ 168 N. Michigan Ave., Suite 600, Chicago, IL 60601, ☎ 312/782–1084, FAX 312/782–1091). In Canada (✉ 1233 Rue de la Mon-tagne, Suite 101, Montréal, Québec H3G 1Z2, ☎ 514/871–1535, FAX 514/ 871–1498; ✉ 1300 Bay St., Toronto, Ontario M5R 3K8, ☎ 416/968– 2220, FAX 416/968–6533). In the U.K. (✉ 4 Conduit St., London W1R 0DJ, ☎ 0171/734–5997).

➤ U.S. GOVERNMENT ADVISORIES: **U.S. Department of State** (✉ Overseas Citizens Services Office, Room 4811 N.S., 2201 C St. NW, Washington, DC 20520, ☎ 202/647–5225 for interactive hot line; 301/946–4400 for computer bulletin board, FAX 202/ 647–3000 for interactive hot line); enclose a self-addressed, stamped, business-size envelope.

VOLUNTEER VACATIONS

The most common volunteer holiday in Greece involves people accompany-ing archaeological digs; these are usually arranged through the classics department of your local university. **WWF Greece** (✉ Filellinon 26, 4th floor, Syntagma, Athens 10558, ☎ 01/324–7586, FAX 01/324–7578)

sometimes has opportunities for volunteer fieldwork. Under the super-vision of **ARHELON, Organization for the Protection of Sea Turtles** (✉ Solomou 57, Athens, 10432, ☎ FAX 01/523–1342), volunteers on Zakynthos are trained and selected to help protect the caretta caretta. They patrol the beaches and tag turtles at night and observe and record nests during the day. Contact the organiza-tion early; the nesting-hatching season runs from May through October.

WEB SITES

Do check out the World Wide Web when you're planning your trip. You'll find everything from current weather forecasts to virtual tours of famous cities. Fodor's Web site, www.fodors.com, is a great place to start your online travels; just hook up to the Greece mini-guide section and click on "Links." When you see a 🕸 in this book, go to www.fodors.com/ urls for an up-to-date link to that destination's site.

WHEN TO GO

The best time to visit Greece is late spring and early fall. In May and June the days are warm, even hot, but dry, and the sea water has been warmed by the sun. The evenings, which seem endless, are pleasant enough to dine alfresco. For sightseeing, exploring the cities or countryside, or hitting the beach, this is the time. Greece is relatively tourist free in the spring, so if you don't like crowds, and the beach and swimming aren't high on your agenda, April and early May are a good time to tour the country. Carnavali, usually in February just before Lent, and Greek Easter, with its religious processions, lambs, and red eggs, are the highlights of the season.

September and October are a good alternative to spring and early sum-mer, especially in the bustling cities where bars, theaters, and other cul-tural institutions reopen. Throughout the rest of the country, things begin to shut down in November. Transporta-tion to the islands is limited in winter, and many hotels outside large cities are closed until the beginning of April. Unless you are going to Greece in pursuit of winter sports, try a different season.

CLIMATE

Greece enjoys a typical Mediterranean climate: hot, dry summers and cool, wet winters. Chilliness and rain begin in November, the start of Greece's deceptive winters. Any given day may not be very cold—except in the mountains, snow is uncommon in Athens and to the south. But the cold is persistent, and places are often not well-heated. Over the course of a few days you will feel chilled to the bone. Spring and fall are practically perfect, with warm days and balmy evenings. Toward the end of June and throughout July the temperatures climb, pushing the 100°F (38°C) mark. In the south a hot wind may blow across the Mediterranean from the coast of Africa. The air quality in Athens, which is surrounded on all sides by mountains (except in the direction of the harbor), can be unhealthy on especially hot days, and air-conditioning is far from ubiquitous. The situation is alleviated somewhat in August when millions leave the city and the brisk northwesterly *meltemia* start to blow, cooling the city and many of the islands to a comfortable temperature.

The average high and low temperatures for Athens and Heraklion (Crete) and average temperatures for Thessaloniki and Northern Greece are presented below. Note that although average temperatures in the north and the south may not be too dissimilar, the temperature on a given day can differ substantially.

➤ FORECASTS: **Weather Channel Connection** (☎ 900/932–8437), 95¢ per minute from a Touch-Tone phone.

Climate in Greece

ATHENS

Jan.	52F	13C	May	77F	25C	Sept.	84F	29C
	43	6		61	16		66	19
Feb.	57F	14C	June	86F	30C	Oct.	75F	24C
	45	7		68	20		59	15
Mar.	61F	16C	July	91F	33C	Nov.	66F	19C
	46	8		73	23		54	12
Apr.	68F	20C	Aug.	91F	33C	Dec.	59F	15C
	52	11		73	23		46	8

HERAKLION

Jan.	61F	16C	May	73F	23C	Sept.	81F	27C
	48	9		59	15		66	19
Feb.	61F	16C	June	81F	27C	Oct.	75F	24C
	48	9		66	19		63	17
Mar.	63F	17C	July	84F	29C	Nov.	70F	21C
	50	10		72	22		57	14
Apr.	68F	20C	Aug.	84F	29C	Dec.	64F	18C
	54	12		72	22		52	11

THESSALONIKI AND NORTHERN GREECE

Jan.	45F	8C	May	74F	24C	Sept.	80F	27C
Feb.	51F	11C	June	86F	30C	Oct.	69F	21C
Mar.	54F	13C	July	90F	32C	Nov.	58F	15C
Apr.	65F	19C	Aug.	90F	32C	Dec.	50F	10C

GREEK VOCABULARY

The phonetic spelling used in English differs somewhat from the internationalized form of Greek place names. There are no long and short vowels in Greek; the pronunciation never changes. Note, also, that the accent is a stress mark, showing where the stress is placed in pronunciation.

Basics

Do you speak English?	Miláte angliká?
Yes, no	Málista *or* Né, óchi
Impossible	Adínato
Good morning, Good day	Kaliméra
Good evening, Good night	Kalispéra, Kaliníchta
Goodbye	Yá sas
Mister, Madam, Miss	Kírie, kiría, despiní
Please	Parakaló
Excuse me	Me sinchórite *or* signómi
How are you?	Ti kánete *or* pós íste
How do you do (Pleased to meet you)	Chéro polí
I don't understand.	Dén katalavéno.
To your health!	Giá sas!
Thank you	Efcharistó

Numbers

one	éna
two	dío
three	tría
four	téssera
five	pénde
six	éxi
seven	eptá
eight	októ
nine	enéa
ten	déka
twenty	íkossi
thirty	triánda
forty	saránda
fifty	peнínda
sixty	exínda
seventy	evdomínda
eighty	ogdónda
ninety	enenínda
one hundred	ekató
two hundred	diakóssia
three hundred	triakóssia
one thousand	hília
two thousand	dió hiliádes
three thousand	trís hiliádes

Days of the Week

Monday	Deftéra
Tuesday	Tríti
Wednesday	Tetárti
Thursday	Pémpti
Friday	Paraskeví
Saturday	Sávato
Sunday	Kyriakí

Months

January	Ianouários
February	Fevrouários
March	Mártios
April	Aprílios
May	Maíos
June	Ióunios
July	Ióulios
August	Ávgoustos
September	Septémvrios
October	Októvrios
November	Noémvrios
December	Dekémvrios

Traveling

I am traveling by car . . . train . . . plane . . . boat.	Taxidévo mé aftokínito . . . me tréno . . . me aeropláno . . . me vapóri.
Taxi, to the station . . . harbor . . . airport	Taxí, stó stathmó . . . limáni . . . aerodrómio
Porter, take the luggage.	Akthofóre, pare aftá tá prámata.
Where is the filling station?	Pou íne tó vensinádiko?
When does the train leave for . . . ?	Tí óra thá fíyi to tréno ya . . . ?
Which is the train for . . . ?	Pío íne to tréno gía . . . ?
Which is the road to . . . ?	Piós íne o drómos giá . . . ?
A first-class ticket	Éna isitírio prótis táxis
Smoking is forbidden.	Apagorévete to kápnisma.
Where is the toilet?	Póu íne í toaléta?
Ladies, men	Ginekón, andrón
Where? When?	Póu? Póte?
Sleeping car, dining car	Wagonlí, wagonrestorán
Compartment	Vagóni
Entrance, exit	Íssodos, éxodos
Nothing to declare	Den écho típota na dilósso
I am coming for my vacation.	Érchome giá tis diakopés mou.
Nothing	Típota
Personal use	Prossopikí chríssi
How much?	Pósso?

I want to eat, to drink, to sleep.	Thélo na fáo, na pió, na kimithó.
Day, night	Méra, níchta
Morning, afternoon	Proí, mesiméri, *or* apóyevma
Straight ahead	Kat efthían
To the right, to the left	Dexiá, aristerá
Show me the way to . . . please.	Díxte mou to drómo . . . parakaló.
Where is . . . ?	Pou íne . . . ?

Shopping

I would like to buy	Tha íthela na agorásso
Show me, please.	Díxte mou, parakaló.
May I look around?	Boró na ríxo miá matyá?
How much is it?	Pósso káni? (*or* kostízi)
It is too expensive.	Íne polí akrivó.

At the Hotel

A good hotel	Éna kaló xenodochío
Have you a room?	Échete domátio?
Where can I find a furnished room?	Pou boró na vró epiploméno domátio?
A single room, double room	Éna monóklino, éna díklino
With bathroom	Me bánio
How much is it per day?	Pósso kostízi tin iméra?
A room overlooking the sea	Éna domátio prós ti thálassa
For one day, for two days	Giá miá méra, giá dió méres
For a week	Giá miá evdomáda
My name is. . . .	Onomázome. . . .
My passport	Tó diavatirió mou
What is the number of my room?	Piós íne o arithmós tou domatíou mou?
The key, please.	To klidí, parakaló.
Breakfast, lunch, supper	Proinó, messimergianó, vradinó
The bill, please.	To logariasmó, parakaló.
I am leaving tomorrow.	Févgo ávrio.

At the Restaurant

Waiter	Garsón
Where is the restaurant?	Pou íne to estiatório?
I would like to eat.	Tha íthela na fáo.
The menu, please.	To katálogo, parakaló.
Fixed-price menu	Menú
Serve me on the terrace.	Na mou servírete sti tarátza.
Where can I wash my hands?	Pou boró na plíno ta héria mou?

INDEX

FODOR'S GREECE

EDITOR: Robert I. C. Fisher

Editorial Contributors: Toula Bogdanos, Stephen Brewer, Jeffrey Carson, Lea Lane, B. Samantha Stenzel, Melia Tatakis

Editorial Production: Linda K. Schmidt

Maps: David Lindroth, *cartographer;* Rebecca Baer, *map editor*

Design: Fabrizio La Rocca, *creative director;* Guido Caroti, *art director;* Jolie Novak, *senior picture editor;* Melanie Marin, *photo editor*

Cover Design: Pentagram

Production/Manufacturing: Colleen Ziemba

SPECIAL SALES

Fodor's Travel Publications are available at special discounts for bulk purchases for sales promotions or premiums. Special editions, including personalized covers, excerpts of existing guides, and corporate imprints, can be created in large quantities for special needs. For more information, contact your local bookseller or write to Special Markets, Fodor's Travel Publications, 280 Park Avenue, New York, NY 10017. Inquiries from Canada should be directed to your local Canadian bookseller or sent to Random House of Canada, Ltd., Marketing Department, 2775 Matheson Boulevard East, Mississauga, Ontario L4W 4P7. Inquiries from the United Kingdom should be sent to Fodor's Travel Publications, 20 Vauxhall Bridge Road, London SW1V 2SA, England.

PRINTED IN THE UNITED STATES OF AMERICA

10 9 8 7 6 5 4 3 2 1

PHOTOGRAPHY

Stone: *Sylvain Grandadam, cover. (Santorini)*

Art Resource: *Nimatallah, 8I, 9K.*

Atlantis Villas, *30I.*

Kindra Clineff, *10A, 10C.*

Corbis, *2 top left, 3 top right, 27B. Jan Butchofsky-Houser, 12B. Chris Hellier, 13E. John Heseltine, 14A. Dave G. Houser, 15B, 25A. Andrea Jemolo, 32. Wolfgang Kaehler, 20A. Gianni Dagli Orti, 24C. Vanni Archive, 8G. Sandro Vannini, 13C. Patrick Ward, 23C.*

DIAF: *Jean-Paul Garcin, 15C. Camille Moirenc, 6A, 7D. Pratt-Pries, 28D. Rassias, 15A. Jacques Sierpinski, 20B. SIME, 11A, 11C, 18A, 19D, 19E. Giovanni Simeone, 16A, 16B, 16C, 17D, 21D. Daniel Thierry, 10B, 18C, 30H. Yvan Travert, 6C, 13D, 14B, 14C, 20C, 25C, 30F.*

Elounda Mare Hotel, Relais & Chateaux, *30J.*

Goulandris Foundation-Museum of Cycladic Art, *30D.*

Greek National Tourist Organization, *2 top right, 26A, 28C, 29E, 29F, 30A, 30C, 30E.*

Blaine Harrington III, *11B, 19F, 24B.*

The Image Bank: *Grant V. Faint, 7E, 8H. Andrea Pistolesi, 21E.*

Eliza Jackson, *7F.*

Liaison Agency: *Tim Crosby, 4-5. Saola, 25B.*

Steve Outram, *17E.*

PhotoDisc, *2 bottom right, 3 bottom left.*

PictureQuest: *Artville, 3 bottom right. PhotoSphere, 1, 30G.*

Christian Prager, *2 bottom left, 2 bottom center.*

Stendor SA, *30B.*

Stone: *Glen Allison, 12A. Bruce Forster, 9J, 23B. Sylvain Grandadam, 23D. George Grigoriou, 6B, 18B. Hugh Sitton, 22A. Chris Simpson, 3 top left. World View, 24A.*

Important Tip

Although all prices, opening times, and other details in this book are based on information supplied to us at press time, changes occur all the time in the travel world, and Fodor's cannot accept responsibility for facts that become outdated or for inadvertent errors or omissions. So **always confirm information when it matters,** especially if you're making a detour to visit a specific place.

ABOUT OUR WRITERS

Every trip is a significant trip. Acutely aware of that fact, we've pulled out all stops in preparing *Fodor's Greece*. To help you zero in on what to see in Greece, we've gathered some great color photos of the key sights in every region. To show you how to put it all together, we've created great itineraries and neighborhood walks. And to direct you to the places that are truly worth your time and money, we've rallied the team of endearingly picky know-it-alls we're pleased to call our writers. Having seen all corners of the regions they cover for us, they're real experts. If you knew them, you'd poll them for tips yourself.

Toula Bogdanos—updater of our Athens and Essential Information chapters—has savored many an island sunset over ouzo and octopus and can dance a mean tsifteli under duress. At this point, she considers one of her greatest accomplishments knowing how to hail an Athenian taxi during rush hour on a rainy day. She is the managing editor of the *Journal of Southeast European and Black Sea Studies* and teaches journalism at Campus Arts and Sciences.

For more than 25 years, native New Yorker **Jeffrey Carson** has lived on Paros, where he teaches and writes—when not swimming in the dazzling Mediterranean. Along with teaching, lecturing, and updating our chapter on the Cyclades, he has, most recently, edited *The Collected Poems of Odysseus Elytis*.

Stephen Brewer is a New York–based writer who travels to Crete and other Mediterranean shores for various national magazines and guidebooks. He's climbed many a terrying hairpin-bend on the roads between Knossos and Phaestos and has always wondered if the pained expressions of hardy travelers along these roads, fearing their last hour has struck, once inspired Domenikos Theotokopoulos, the famed El Greco, whose birthplace was Crete. He updated our chapters on the Southern Peloponnese, Crete, and Rhodes and the Dodecanese.

B. Samantha Stenzel succumbed to Greece's irresistible siren's song by emigrating there in 1979. She arrived from the United States with two bulging bags, a full range of many humorously incorrect Greek phrases, and no job. Along with writing the *Athenian* magazine's cinema column and contributing to publications such as *Variety,* she soon conveyed her passion for the best-known and least-known corners of Greece by shepherding friends and students around the country for some 14 years. The response was so positive, she set up her own touring company, Mediterranean Odysseys. Today, her custom-tailored architecture, food, and wine tours through regions of Greece make travelers purr. Updater of the chapters on Excursions from Athens, Epirus and Thessaly, Northern Greece, and Northern Peloponnese, she can be reached at Mediterranean Odysseys, 1943 West Berteau Ave., Chicago, Il., 60613, tel. and fax 773/472–2765, or via e-mail at Samodyssey@aol.com.

Based in Greece, **Melia Tatakis** is an anglophile living in a non-English speaking world. A Vassar girl—though some might not necessarily think so if they ever saw her attack a Greek squab stuffed with truffles and apricots—she grew up in London and went on to earn an M.A. in creative writing at Stanford after her days at Vassar. Along with contributing to such publications as *Odyssey,* she has charmingly updated our chapters on the Northern Sporades, the Northern Islands, and Corfu, and lives mostly on the Greek island of Andros with two fox terriers.

Don't Forget to Write

We love feedback—positive and negative—and follow up on all suggestions. So contact the Greece editor at editors@fodors.com or c/o Fodor's, 280 Park Avenue, New York, New York 10017. Have a wonderful trip!

Karen Cure

Karen Cure
Editorial Director